The Rise of Modern Chinese Thought

The Rise of Modern Chinese Thought

WANG HUI

Edited by MICHAEL GIBBS HILL

HARVARD UNIVERSITY PRESS
Cambridge, Massachusetts
London, England
2023

Printed in the United States of America

This volume comprises a selection of essays originally published in Chinese in *Xian dai Zhongguo si xiang de xing qi,* Volumes 1–2, SDX Joint Publishing Company, Beijing, 2004, 2008

Harvard University Press gratefully acknowledges the financial contribution of Tsinghua University to the production of this book.

First printing

Library of Congress Cataloging-in-Publication Data

Names: Wang, Hui, 1959– author. | Hill, Michael (Michael Gibbs), editor.
Title: The rise of modern Chinese thought / Hui Wang ; edited by Michael Gibbs Hill.
Other titles: Xian dai Zhongguo si xiang de xing qi. Shang juan. English
Description: Cambridge, Massachusetts ; London, England : Harvard University Press, 2023. | Translation of an abridged version of a work originally published in Chinese as Xian dai Zhongguo si xiang de xing qi in 2004. This translation focuses on Part One (volumes 1–2) of the original text. | Includes bibliographical references and index.
Identifiers: LCCN 2022044883 | ISBN 9780674046764 (hardcover)
Subjects: LCSH: Philosophy, Chinese—19th century. | Philosophy, Chinese—20th century. | Confucian education—China. | Confucianism—China. | China—Intellectual life. | China—Civilization.
Classification: LCC B5231 .W3413 2023 | DDC 181/.11—dc23/eng/20230211
LC record available at https://lccn.loc.gov/2022044883

Contents

Preface to the English Edition

WANG HUI

Translated by MICHAEL GIBBS HILL

The Rise of Modern Chinese Thought (*Xiandai Zhongguo sixiangde xingqi*), which is 1,700 pages long in Chinese, was first published in 2004, with a revised edition published in 2010 and reprinted in 2018 and 2020. In 2010, Academia Universa Press translated the introduction (*daolun*) of *Rise* into Italian and published it as a stand-alone book under the title *Impero o Stato-Nazione? La Modernità intellecttuale in Cina.* In 2011, Iwanami Shoten published a Japanese translation of the introduction and conclusion (*zonglun*) to the book under the title *Kindai Chūgoku shisō no seisei,* and in 2014, Harvard University Press published an English translation similar to the Italian text, also based on the introduction, under the title *China from Empire to Nation-State,* but dropped the question mark from the title of the Italian translation. Finally, a Korean translator has completed what will be the first full translation of the book into any language, and it is scheduled to be published in 2023.

Thanks to the continued efforts of Michael Gibbs Hill, an English version now finally appears in a more complete form. Given the length and complexity of the book, it made good sense for Harvard University Press to decide to publish an abridged translation. The original Chinese work is divided into two parts, each of which is divided into two volumes, thus comprising four volumes in total. The first volume of Part One, *Principle and Things* (*Li yu wu*), follows developments in the School of Principle (*lixue*), the School of Mind (*xinxue*), and the School of Unadorned Learning (*puxue*) to examine changes in Confucianism and its social and political conditions in the Song, Ming, and Qing dynasties. The second volume, *Empire and State* (*Diguo yu guojia*), focuses on Qing-dynasty scholarship on history and the classics, with an emphasis on the relationship between the New Text (*jinwen*) classical learning that emerged in the middle period of the Qing and the evolution of the dynasty's inner / outer relations and political forms. Therefore, although Part One is divided into two volumes, both trace the changes of Confucian learning and constitute a full schematic of interpretation.

The first volume of Part Two, *Universal Principle and Anti-Universal Principle* (*Gongli yu fangongli*), focuses on Yan Fu (1854–1921), Liang Qichao (1873–1929), and Zhang Taiyan (1868–1936), and examines the intellectual environment, knowledge formations, and sociopolitical changes roughly from the Hundred Days' Reform (1898) to the Xinhai Revolution (1911); the second volume of Part Two, *The Community of Scientific Discourse* (*Kexue huayu gongtongti*), extends this line of discussion to times of the First World War and the New Culture Movement. The key terms of this part of the study—Universal Principle (*gongli*), Anti-Universal Principle (*fangongli*), and the community of scientific discourse (*kexue huayu gongtongti*)—are all closely related to new forms of knowledge, especially the scientific worldview, and can no longer be described in the context of Confucianism and its changing forms. For these reasons, although the arguments in Part One and Part Two of the original book are coherent, there is a rupture between the objects of discussion and the central issues taken up in them. In fact, the two volumes of Part Two also serve as a prologue to the study of twentieth-century China that I have developed since then. To preserve the coherence of the original exposition, the translation—this book—focuses on the first and second volumes of Part One, preserving as much as possible the integrity of the Chinese text, except for, as appropriate, deletions of some sections and long quotations found in the original.

Since the publication of *The Rise of Modern Chinese Thought*, symposia have been held in Beijing, Shanghai, Tokyo, and elsewhere, and many reviews have been published in the media and in publications in China, Japan, the United States, and Europe. Discussions arising from the book have also stimulated me to reflect on the issues raised in it. During the long process of writing,

I asked myself: What is "modern"? What is "China"? What is "thought"? What is a "rise"? The "rise of modern Chinese thought" is not a general tracing of the origins of modern thought at the level of conceptual history. What, then, is a "rise"? One can explain it as the "production and reproduction" *(shengsheng)* portion of "production and reproduction are what constitute change" *(shengsheng zhi wei yi)*, which, according to the *Book of Changes* (*Yijing*), is a process full of change and growth. As a proposition, *Rise* addresses the prevailing paradigms in modern Chinese historical research and intellectual history: for example, the Kyoto school proposed the idea of the "Tang-Song transformation" and further argued that the Song dynasty was the beginning of the "modern age." If this is true, then was the Mongol Yuan dynasty an extension or disruption of this modern age? Another example is that, since the May Fourth Movement, scholars have come to accept the idea that the late Ming dynasty was a fount of early Enlightenment thought. If this is true, then should we understand Qing-dynasty thought as a reaction against the early Enlightenment, or as a renewal of it? How do we explain the relationship between this period and its ideas and modern China? To me, we should think less about absolute origins than about the repeated appearance across history of certain key elements and their changing meanings in different discursive contexts. In these continuous historical changes, different dynasties established legitimacy as Chinese dynasties in their own ways, a process that cannot be expressed in a linear historical narrative. Therefore, if the rise of Confucianism, and especially the School of Principle (*lixue*), involves a reflection on historical discontinuity and a desire to carry over tradition, then continuity must be considered in the context of discontinuity and considered from the perspective of historical agency. In terms of politics, we should seek to understand discontinuity in the context of a continuous process of the construction of legitimacy.

Since the publication of this book, Chinese-speaking academic circles have seen many discussions about empire, the tribute system, All-under-Heaven (*Tianxia*), civilizational states (*wenming guojia*), and Grand Unification (*da yitong*), which also echo and respond to discussions in Europe, America, and Japan. The reemergence of these concepts or categories stems from dissatisfaction with the nation-state paradigm, but in most cases this is again the result of looking at China and its historical changes through the prism of the nation-state. However, since the nineteenth century, categories such as empire and civilization have become entangled with the concept of nation-state and nationalist ideas, becoming racialized and one-sided. For example, the concept that emerged in Japan of "East Asia" and its Confucian civilizational sphere is a transnational and transcivilizational category, but this concept cannot contain the vast western and northern regions of China and their civilizational diversity. Therefore, this book does not propose to replace the concept of nation-state (*minzu guojia*) with that of empire or civilizational state, but rather to critique the empire/nation-state binary and to explore how a political culture centered on Confucian learning operates in a transsystemic society and changes in response to the conditions of the times.

What is transsystemic society (*kuatixi shehui*)? As they are spread out across a region, families, villages, and rural and urban communities often contain different social systems, whether in terms of ethnicity, religion, language, social customs, and so forth, to the extent that we can say that these systems are embedded in a society, a village, a family, or even a person. In the writing and compilation of history, using an ethnic group, a religion, or a linguistic community as the unit of narrative is a common phenomenon in the era of nationalism. However, if these communities, religions, and languages are intermingled in a region, a village, or a family, then this narrative approach may result in the diminishment, overstatement, or distortion of these complex relationships. For me, "transsystemic society" encompasses these unique historical phenomena that are often overlooked or simplified by modern knowledge, and thus offers the possibility of redescribing these phenomena.

This concept has several similarities to the idea of "plurality and unity" proposed by Fei Xiaotong (1910–2005) in 1988.[1] According to Fei:

> The Chinese people became a conscious national entity only during the past century, as a result of China's confrontation with the Western powers, but their formation into a single nation has been the result of a historical process of millennia. Here I will go back into the process of formation of the Chinese people's pluralistic yet unified configuration. The general situation was the simultaneous existence of a multitude of ethnic groups who were separated and independent of each other. During a long period of mutual contact many groups were mixed, aligned, or integrated, while others were divided and became extinct. In time

> the groups unified into one group which consisted of a number of subunits that kept emerging, vanishing, and reemerging, so that parts of some subunits became a part of others, yet each retained its individual characteristics. Together they formed a national entity which was at once pluralistic and unified. This may have been a process of creation common to all nations the world over; yet the Chinese people, as a nation, came into being through a process of their own. Three thousand years ago, a nucleus assembled in the middle reaches of the Yellow River and gradually melded together a number of national groups. Known as *Hua-Xia,* this nucleus attracted all groups around it, growing larger like a snowball. By the early fifth century, its domain enclosed the East Asian plain in the middle and lower reaches of the Yellow River and the Yangtze. These people were called Hans by other ethnic groups. The ethnic entity of the Hans grew steadily by their absorption of other groups. In the meantime, groups of Hans seeped into the habitats of other nationalities, where in time they became centers of liaison and assembly. These in turn formed a network which was the foundation for the Chinese people to be unified and to emerge as a single nation.[2]

This well-known discussion contains important insights, but it is a narrative limited to the territories of modern China that needs to be expanded and revised for today.

First, in its emphasis on the intermingling of Chinese societies and the internal diversity of the whole, "transsystemic society" overlaps in some places with the concept of plurality and unity but is not limited to the categories of nation or ethnicity. The transnational, transethnic, and transregional activities of modern capitalism are a force that governs various cultural and political elements through economic activities. The social divisions generated by economic inequality are commonly seen in the form of the polarization of classes and social ranks, polarization between regions, or polarization between the cities and countryside. In multiethnic regions, these divisions can result in distortions such as the making of ethnic groups into economic classes or making economic classes into ethnic groups, which in turn provides a breeding ground for different types of identity politics and separatism, triggering violent social conflict. Under the conditions of globalization, the prefix "trans-" (*kua*) has been overused, representing trends and orientations governed by economic activities that transcend traditional categories such as nation, state, and region. "Transsystemic society" is different in that the "trans-" in this concept centers on a series of forces found in culture, customs, politics, and ritual, and sees economic relations as only one type of interaction that is embedded in these complex social connections. Therefore, what the concept of transsystemic society provides is a mutually connected social and political form that arises through the interaction, transmission, and coexistence of different cultures, ethnic groups, and regions, which can provide a sense of commonality based on social solidarity that serves as a basis for a process of continuous socialization.

Second, classic nationalist discourse often sees the unification of political and cultural borders as a characteristic of the nation-state.[3] However, this classic discourse has forgotten to acknowledge the preconditions for this model. The vast majority of states in the contemporary world are transsystemic societies, and if one is to speak of the unification of political and cultural borders, the precondition for this must be that transsystemic societies and their definition of culture themselves have led to the unity of cultural and political borders: in transsystemic societies, culture is necessarily political, and its borders are necessarily ambiguous, often beyond the scope of the political. Kant said that the state is "a society of human beings over whom no one but itself has the right to rule and to dispose. Like the trunk of a tree, it has its own roots."[4] But Kant's concept of the state overlaps with the classical form of nation-state from his time. If we place Kant's argument into the context of Chinese history, we can say that the state as a society of human beings is a transsystemic political structure, and that only when its unification and transsystemic character overlap can we call this state "*a* society of human beings"—which comprises a number of mutually interpenetrating societies, linked in unique ways. Socialization in this society is a long-term process. The meaning of "a" or "one" society can only be understood in a transsystemic sense, not in an antisystemic or monolithic sense. The state as a society of human beings not only involves various elements of material culture, geography, religion, ritual, political structure, ethics and cosmology, and the imagination of the world, but also links the material cultures, geographies, religions, rituals, political structures, ethics and cosmologies, and the imagined worlds of different systems with one another. In this sense, transsystemic society is different not only from the various social narratives proposed from the perspective of the nation but also from the concept of a pluralistic or diverse (*duoyuan*) society. Compared to the concept of plurality, it weakens (but does not deny) aspects of the system that are originary or distinct (*yuan*) or unipolar (*yiji*), foregrounds the dynamics of movement between systems, and emphasizes the essential many (*duo*) of the one (*yi*). Systems do not exist in isolation from one another but are interpenetrating. They are therefore the main internal elements and driving force of the continuous motion of social networks. The basis for a transsystemic society is found in the interconnectedness of the world of everyday life, but it also relies on a continuously evolving political culture that integrates the elements of various systems within shifting organic connections, without denying the uniqueness and agency of these elements.[5]

As a transsystemic society, China is a continuously emerging transcivilizational civilization that internalizes and takes on the traces of the other while maintaining its own unique vitality. For these reasons, however, transsystemic society is interrelated with and mutually defined by transsocietal systems (*kuashehui tixi*). As with Kant's definition of "a society of human beings," since the early modern period, "society" and the "social" (*shehui*) have often been defined by states and their borders, but this concept has also been used in a broader way, combined with other terms such as territory, class, culture, or other units for defining the boundaries of a society. (In the Chinese context, this would be such combinations as Chinese society, Jiangnan society, middle-class society, peasant society, Confucian society, etc.) However, commonly used concepts such as the "acquaintance society" (*shuren shehui*) or the "imagined community" are both also in fact transsystemic societies, and the "systems" that make up their substance (such as language, ethnicity, religious beliefs, cosmology, customs, legal and institutional traditions, economic ties, etc.) are not confined to their state/society borders, but undergo another process of localization under other social conditions, thereby becoming intrinsic key elements of their respective "transsystemic societies." In China we see not only examples from earlier historical periods of the adaptation of both Buddhism and Islam to China but also examples in the modern period of the adaptation of various modes of thought, institutions, and social organization derived from the West, including Marxism, while the influence on other societies of Chinese cultural traditions and experiences in modern times has likewise undergone a process of intersection, intermingling, localization, and creative transformation. The events of 1968 in Europe, the Maoist movements in South Asia and Latin America, and the paths toward transformation in Vietnam and other countries that were shaped by China's reforms all need to be seen and explained within this perspective, rather than from the simple terms of one-way relationships of influencing and being influenced.

Plurality in unity is a global phenomenon, not just a Chinese one, and the concept is not sufficient to explain the question of what makes China China. If we move away from the continuous process of *becoming China* (*Zhongguohua*) and the many changes in the political culture that have so deeply influenced the process, then it becomes difficult to explain China's enduring vitality. This political culture, as it transformed across history, has continued to overcome the contradictions and conflicts of transsystemic societies and, as the nature of the political subject changed, to construct and reconstruct China's continuity. It is this unique historical phenomenon that has given rise to debates about the rupture and continuity of Chinese history and how to understand the plurality of "China" (*Zhongguo*) and its historical formation, the most recent of which involves a fierce debate about the "new Qing history" (and whether the new Qing history exists as a school of thought). In August 2010, six years after the first edition of *The Rise of Modern Chinese Thought* was published, the Institute of Qing History of Renmin University of China held an international symposium at the Fragrant Hills in Beijing on "Qing-Dynasty Politics and National Identity." The discussion of the New Qing History and its significance for understanding the process of becoming Han or Han-ification (*Hanhua*) and "foreignization" (*Huhua*) touched off a controversy that continues to this day and goes far beyond the influence of this line of scholarship in the United States.

On this issue, it is impossible to draw meaningful conclusions if we cannot go beyond the dualistic historical view of *becoming Han* (*Hanhua*) and *foreignization* (*Huhua*) and arrive at a new interpretation of *becoming China* (*Zhongguohua*) as a historical process. In Chinese, becoming China (*Zhongguohua*) and becoming Han (*Hanhua*) are different concepts. The former refers to the dynamic process of China's formation, in which different ethnic groups and cultures interact and connect with one another as part of this dynamic process and, from different orientations, advance China's continuous emergence and changing. Regardless of the historical period or what the political situation may have been, China has never been a purely Han state, and different ethnic groups, religions, and cultures all played a role in the formation of the civilization that we call China. This was and is a hybrid, multidirectional process. As for the latter, becoming Han or *Hanhua* is often understood and translated as "Sinicization" and used alongside the term "assimilation" to emphasize the assimilation of other ethnic groups and cultures by the Han as the primary nationality. In Chinese, concepts such as China or Middle Kingdom (*Zhongguo* 中国), Han 汉, and Hua 华 carry different meanings and values, but, under the influence of early modern European nationalist knowledge, the Western idea of China (*Zhongguo*) was so marked by ethnonationalism that whenever *Zhongguohua* (becoming China), which was not a hybrid concept, was translated into other languages, it was all too easily equated with *Hanhua* (becoming Han). As a result, in English or other Western languages, the concept of *Hanhua* is indistinguishable from and often translated as the concept of "Sinicization," to the point that the subtle yet meaningful differences between them disappear. Because "Sinicization" serves as a standard translation for *Hanhua,* the process of *Zhongguohua* is often understood as a process of the Han absorbing and assimilating other cultures, completely ignoring that, in the historical formation of China, different peoples and cultures have all served important functions, as well as the fact that the supreme rulers of dynasties such as the Yuan and Qing dynasties were not Han. To understand China as a transsystemic society, therefore, it is important to go beyond the conceptual framework of ethnonationalism. However, in the English-speaking world, what should be used to explain the term *Zhongguohua* if not the concept of Sinicization?

Modern China inherited the geographic scope and demographic composition of the Qing dynasty, and explanations of modern China cannot avoid the question of how to interpret the history of the Qing. Some historians have revisited the category of empire or the concept of All-under-Heaven, using perspectives on these diverse political communities to think through the limitations of the concept of the nation-state. The introduction of these categories into descriptions of modern history also implies that a system of unitary sovereign states and its accompanying normative relations of formal equality cannot provide a substantive description of state forms and international relations. In contrast to other imperial histories, a question worth asking about Chinese history is: Why did the so-called conquest dynasties established by the Mongols, Manchus, and others eventually integrate themselves into the Chinese dynastic lineage? What role did the political culture of Confucianism play in constructing the legitimacy of these new dynasties? In this process of legitimation, what was the relationship between Confucian political culture and other religions and cultures? Put another way, how should we understand the "continuity" of Chinese history that emerges amid such massive historical events and transitions?

The two opposing views on this question, both of which concentrate on the debate on *Hanhua* and foreignization, also demonstrate the profound influence of ethnonationalist knowledge on the study of modern Chinese history. For example, Chen Yinke (1890–1969) wrote in his "Manuscripts on the Political History of the Tang Dynasty" (*Tangdai zhengzhishi shulun gao*) that "in the Northern Dynasties era, culture was more important than bloodlines [for understanding] the distinction between Han and the Hu (Northern tribes). Any person who had been *Hanhua* was seen as Han, and any person who had been *Huhua* was Hu [i.e., foreign]. As for their bloodlines, little was said."[6] For these reasons, Chen Yinke emphasized culture rather than bloodlines or lineage in understanding the distinction between Han and Hu. In North America, this debate can be traced back to Ping-ti Ho's 1967 paper, "The Importance of the Ch'ing Period in Chinese History" in the *Journal of Asian Studies*, Evelyn Rawski's 1996 presidential address at the Association for Asian Studies conference entitled "Reenvisioning the Qing: The Significance of the Qing Period in Chinese History,"[7] and Ho's 1998 article "In Defense of Sinicization," a response to Rawski's paper.[8] In fact, discussions of Chinese pluralism have been around longer than these debates in the United States, with Chinese historians such as Chen Yinke, Gu Jiegang (1893–1980), Fu Sinian (1896–1950), and Yao Congwu (1894–1970), and Japanese scholars such as Shiratori Kurakichi (1865–1942) and Inaba Iwakichi (1876–1940) also addressing "foreign rule" (*yizu tongzhi*) in Chinese history.

This decades-long debate has recently resurfaced in a different way in the New Qing History in the United States: some American scholars of Qing history have argued that *Hanhua* was a dominant pattern in the narrative of Chinese history from the late Qing to the present, and they reject the notion of a single, unified China as a political entity that has existed since ancient times. They took up the "conquest dynasties" theory, which is based on distinct ethnic identities, that European, American, and Japanese scholars had proposed after World War II.[9] According to this theory, ethnic relations in dynasties such as the Northern Wei gradually moved toward acculturation and sameness, while conquest dynasties (the Liao, Jin, and Yuan dynasties, etc.) retained clear features of institutional pluralism: the conquerors sustained a certain rejection of Han culture, and thus the tendency toward acculturation or integration within the unified empire did not ultimately result in acculturation or commonality. In terms of historical narrative, the New Qing History distinguishes between two dynastic genealogies in Chinese history: first, the "conquest dynasties" established by northern peoples, such as the Northern Wei, Liao, Jin, Yuan, and Qing dynasties; and second, the "traditional Chinese imperial model" of the Song and Ming dynasties. They argue that the political system of the Qing dynasty was marked by the racialized nature of its reliance on the Eight Banners system. Nearly everyone acknowledges the plurality of the Qing dynasty, but scholars such as Ping-ti Ho emphasize that the formation of the Qing multiethnic state resulted from a continuous, unbroken process of *Hanhua*, thereby providing ground for understanding modern China in terms of continuity, while practitioners of the New Qing History view China as a constantly changing symbol or sign and argue that the Qing multiethnic empire was premised on its Manchu institutional and cultural identity, and thus put forward a historical narrative of rupture. Spatially, this view is also closely related to European knowledge of the East or Orient regarding the distinction between Inner China (so-called China Proper) and Outer China.

The formulation of *Hanhua* emerged from late Qing nationalist thought, which, in its interpretation of the phenomenon of the combination of different nationalities in Chinese history, concentrated complex and multifaceted processes in the idea of the "Han." The political connotation of this concept changes when we depart from the historical context of opposition to the Manchu dynasty. As is well known, the concept of "Han" originally was not a racial concept, but a cultural one. In his defense of Sinicization, Ping-ti Ho clearly states that "the truly correct Chinese term should be *Huahua* because the forces of Sinicization had begun to operate millennia before the Han dynasty came into being."[10] The concept of *Huahua* that he discusses here can be traced back to Chen Yuan's 1923 book *The Huahua of the Peoples of the Western Regions in the Yuan Dynasty* (*Yuan xiyuren Huahua kao*), which explains *Huahua* as follows: "As for the meaning of *Huahua*, it is what has been acquired over time and is unique to the people of Hua (*Huaren*)."[11] As for what is meant by "what has been acquired over time and is unique to the people of Hua," Chen Yuan also explains that this refers to qualities such as loyalty, filial piety, politics and governance, and valuing merit: "that which is bestowed by Heaven or what was originally common to all humans cannot be called *Huahua*." Although literature and art are acquired, even if people have been domesticated to China without seeing changes in their literature or artistic forms, they can only be called the arts of the people of the Western Regions (*Xiyu ren*). Therefore, *Huahua* is a cultural characteristic, and even if people have not been domesticated, their "heart-mind" (*xin*, expressed in ritual, habits, and literary and artistic expressions) can still be made Hua. In the wake of early modern nationalism and in the European framework of civilizational hierarchy, however, this category has undergone a process of racialization, just like the concepts of state (*guojia*) and civilization. Against this backdrop, the concept of China reflected by *Hanhua* weakened "China" (*Zhongguo*) and its related categories with respect to the historical changes it underwent and its internal plurality across history.

The influence of late-Qing nationalism and nationalist historiography is extensive, but this does not mean that the study of Chinese history after this period can be summarized as a historical narrative that emphasizes *Hanhua* in history, especially not with a one-sided emphasis on race within the concept of *Hanhua,* which would accord with European nationalist knowledge. In addition to the Chinese historians I have already mentioned such as Chen Yinke and Chen Yuan (1880–1971), numerous historians such as Gu Jiegang, Jian Bozan (1898–1968), Bai Shouyi (1909–2000), and Tan Qixiang (1911–1992) paid much attention to the history of China's different regions and nationalities within the state, and their histories of China were never the history of a single ethnic group. In the fields of anthropology and ethnology, many scholars, including Fei Xiaotong and Lin Yaohua (1910–2000), have also made great contributions to the study of Chinese history.

There are many aspects of *Huahua* and *Zhongguohua* that overlap, but the former emphasizes cultural integration and recognition in migration and interactions, while *Zhongguohua* also includes elements of institutional, legal, and political values. As early as 1907, Zhang Taiyan discussed China and related concepts in depth in his essay, "The Meaning of the Republic of China" (*Zhonghua minguo jie*). He examined the multiple meanings of the concept of China in terms of historical formation of the relationship between names (geographic, political, etc.) and reality, making a historical and political argument for the question of what China is through an etymological examination of several terms related to China, including *Xia*, *Hua*, and *Han*. His examination can be summarized as follows. *Hua* was originally the name of a state, not a race or ethnic group. *Xia* carried more of an ethnic or racial connotation, even as it derived its name from the Xia River. Originally, Xia was the name of a tribe, "not the name of a nation, and not the name of a state," and it was also used to refer to "the Xia states" or "the central domains" (*Zhu Xia*). The boundaries of these terms were gradually blurred across history, so that the terms *Han*, *Hua*, and *Xia* were "used as one name, drawing on the meanings of all three. The Han name was established as a tribe, but the meaning of the state was there. By establishing Han as the name of the race, the meaning of 'a state' is included, and the use of Hua as the name of the state also incorporates the racial sense of the word. These are the reasons for using the name *Zhonghua Minguo*—The Republic of China."[12] Although the historical concepts of Hua, Xia, and Han contained the meaning of ethnic, cultural, and political communities, the long and complex changes they underwent eventually led them to be drawn together in the emergence of modern China.

Unlike concepts such as *Hanhua* or *Huahua*, the concept of *Zhongguohua* highlights the significance of political culture. In 1938, Mao Zedong put forward the idea of the *Zhongguohua* of Marxism in "On the New Stage" (*Lun xin jieduan*), which can be regarded as a classic formulation of the problem of *Zhongguohua* in modern Chinese history. He said, "The concrete application of Marxism in China, making certain that in all its manifestations it is imbued with necessary Chinese characteristics, which is to say, using it according to China's particularities, becomes a problem that must be resolved by the whole Party without delay." Mao criticized "foreign-style Eight-Legged Essays" (*yang bagu*), "empty abstraction," and "dogmatism," and suggested "replacing them with a new and vital Chinese style and manner, pleasing to the eye and ear of the common Chinese people."[13] In other words, Mao's *Zhongguohua* was directed at the Communist Party itself and the movement it promoted, and it had no direct connection with *Hanhua* in the ethnic or racial sense. There are four reasons, then, for transposing *Zhongguohua* to explain the ruptures and continuities in Chinese history.

First, after their entry into the Central Plains, the northern peoples sought to establish their legitimacy on the genealogy of Chinese dynasties while maintaining their own national identity. This identification was active and the concept of *Hanhua*, which often connotes a passive process, is not sufficient to describe it. For example, the Jin, Yuan, and Manchu rulers all constructed their legitimacy as Chinese dynasties through a series of ritual, legal, and institutional arrangements and interpretations of classical learning; the connotation and denotation of the "China" that they constructed also underwent historical changes. Rather than oppose the concepts of rupture and continuity, *Zhongguohua* unites the two in a concept of China that recognizes change and plurality.

Second, the *Zhongguohua* of these dynasties was neither a single process of integration nor a one-way process of conquest; it involved a complex relationship of *recognition*. This relationship of recognition included both the recognition of dynastic orthodoxy through the integration in daily life of the peoples of the Central Plains with their neighbors and the recognition of these dynasties (especially the Qing dynasty) as Chinese dynasties by neighboring dynasties and European states through tribute relations or diplomatic relations. Recognition was not one-sided on any level. For example, the recognition of the Qing dynasty by the Han people and other ethnic groups was linked to their struggle for equality within the dynasty, which I define as a struggle for equality distinct from modern egalitarianism; the recognition of the Qing dynasty as China by neighboring dynasties was also accompanied by the Qing's conscious effort to position itself as a Chinese dynasty and to inherit Chinese dynasties' role in the world. According to Huang Xingtao's research, the use of the term "China" (*Zhongguo*) for the entire area ruled by the Qing dynasty had appeared in court documents by the time of the Shunzhi Emperor (r. 1644–1661); moreover, the Qing dynasty's interactions and treaty relations with the Westerners mostly referred to the parties as China (*Zhongguo*) and the West (*Xiyang*). The term China / *Zhongguo* is used more than 1,680 times between 1644 and 1911 in the *Veritable Records of the Qing* (*Da Qing lichao shilu*), and the term very rarely refers solely to Han territories, but instead mostly to the entire Qing dominion, as well as to ancient China.[14] When the dynasty referred to all of its territories as China or used the concept of China in diplomatic documents, it implied a process of internal and external *Zhongguohua* that took place on two different levels and in two different directions, a process that significantly involved the integration of geography, bloodlines, customs, habits, language, culture, and politics, but which cannot be equated with a mere *Hanhua* process.

Third, *Zhongguohua* was also based on migration, intermarriage, changes in customs, and adjustments to institutions that occurred within the dynasty, along with other social changes in daily life. All of these phenomena are common in world history, and in Chinese history, these changes and integrations also included localized instances of Islamization, Buddhification, Mongolization, Manchu-fication, and *Hanhua,* as well as processes of localization in different regions. In the process of dynastic state-building and long-term socialization, however, these elements and orientations were often mutually interpenetrated and intricately intertwined, culminating in a predominant direction toward *Zhongguohua* and forming a transsystemic society and becoming an intrinsic part of a constantly emerging Chinese civilization. The openness and inclusiveness of civilization are the product of a complex, multilateral history that can neither be equated with unilateral absorption and inclusion nor used to deny or exclude tension and struggle, and therefore has never aimed to eliminate diversity. From the perspective of dynastic evolution, a civilization that recognizes the diversity of religious, cultural, ethnic, and other identities is necessarily a political civilization. Therefore, in addition to the linking of bloodlines and integration in daily life, key questions for understanding China and its historical transformation, regardless of the era, concern what institutions and values can establish a strong and resilient political community and maintain its growth and development.

Fourth, it is for these reasons that *Zhongguohua* does not imply that China is monolithic. Whether it is a multiethnic unified dynasty or a multiethnic unified state, China's unity cannot be equated with a monocultural political entity; quite the opposite, unity or convergence takes incomparably rich diversity as its core elements or mechanisms. This is a transsystemic society, that is, a political entity that is transethnic, transreligious, translingual, and even transcivilizational, and its political unity is always premised on its transsystemicity (*kuatixi xing*). Transsystemicity means that the "one" contains the essence of the "many," and that "many" is the organic substance of the "one." Not only are ethnic groups, religions, and so forth transsystemic, but all social bodies such as villages, families, and individuals also possess characteristics of the transsystemic. Transsystemic societies are always closely related to transsocietal systems that link together different societies (whether in terms of region, religion, language, or other means), and their openness goes without saying. In this sense, concepts such as transsystemic society and transsocietal system offer a framework of understanding that is different from the concept of community based on any single identity, and even from categories such as the Confucian civilizational sphere or the cultural sphere of the Chinese written script (even though Confucianism and Chinese characters are the most cohesive parts of Chinese civilization). These concepts suggest a way of understanding China and its political culture as a dynamic relationship of heterogeneity and convergence.

One thread in this book is the observation of the questions described above from the perspective of the history of ideas, especially Confucianism and its transformations. From the perspective of comparative cultural history, the roles of Christianity and Confucianism in defining what is cultural Europe or cultural China are somewhat similar, but what are the differences? R. Bin Wong has offered this insight: "Christianity transcends the political boundaries of European states while Confucianism fuses the cultural and political into a single, though complex, compound. Were we to grant the premise that the fusion of politics and culture is a unique feature of modern nationalism, we would face the awkward dilemma of treating imperial Chinese state-making strategies as 'modern.'"[15] According to this account, Christianity defined cultural Europe but had no way to unify culture and politics, and by the age of nationalism, cultural and political boundaries were integrated under the framework of the nation-state. In contrast, China is a complex but single compound predicated on Confucian civilization. This description provides a kind of "civilization-state" form that is distinct from the nation-state. In a certain sense, it is both the historical form of China and the future form envisioned by Europe.

However, the key question that cannot be avoided here is how to understand "Confucianism." Is it a political culture that can be reconciled with other ideas and values (and thus capable of being defined from other perspectives), or is it a relatively homogeneous value system? Because concepts such as Confucian culture, and even Chinese civilization, tend to become homogenized in our everyday use—such as when we juxtapose Chinese civilization with Christian civilization and Islamic civilization, in effect defining

Chinese civilization as a relatively purely Confucian civilization—the question arises of how to interpret non-Confucian cultural systems in Chinese society. This was especially true in the Qing dynasty from the eighteenth century onward. The Qing dynasty's grand unification was centered on Confucian culture but was not established on the basis of a homogeneous or single culture, religion, or even civilization. On the contrary, the Qing dynasty was a transcultural, transreligious, and transcivilizational transsystemic society—it both contained multiple systems and formed a flexible, resilient society. For the Central Plains, Mongolia, Tibet, Muslim-majority areas, or southwestern frontier regions, the emperor was not only the ruler according to their internal standards, with a multiple and unified identity as emperor of China as well as a Mongolian khan, a Manchu patriarch, and a Tibetan reincarnation of Manjushri; the emperor was also what Marshall Sahlins called a "stranger-king."[16] In the end, the emperor was not just the ruler of a region; the transsystemic nature of his identity was the source of legitimacy for the entire empire. For these reasons, when we discuss the synthesis and unification of cultural and political boundaries in Chinese history, we need to redefine "culture" (*wenhua*) or "civilization" (*wenming*)—not in terms of religion, language, or ethnicity, or other single key elements, but as a transsystemic society that is a compound of everyday life, customs, beliefs, values, rituals, symbols, and political systems. In this sense, it is not Confucian thought alone but rather a political culture that can integrate Confucian traditions, Tibetan Buddhism, Islamic culture, and other *systems* to achieve a certain unity between cultural and political boundaries, thus continuously expanding the connotation and denotation of the concept of China. The political culture of the Qing dynasty resulted from the operations of interactions between multiple cultures. From this perspective, it was transsystemic society and its defining of culture itself that led to the unification of cultural and political boundaries—in a transsystemic society, culture is necessarily political.

Confucian culture could not articulate sufficiently the unification of the political and cultural domains under the Qing dynasty, but when it came to bringing together the rich threads of Chinese society, there is no doubt about the dominant role that Confucian culture played in dynastic politics. For Confucian thinkers, politics is the act and process of ritual, and its ideal function is to create a common world that is also harmonious in its diversity. If

Confucian thought was dominant in the Qing dynasty, it was precisely because Confucian thought possesses a deeper political nature, and is adept at serving as a go-between or intermediary, weaving other systems into a flexible, resilient network, without denying the uniqueness of these systems. Confucian society does not require Tibet, Mongolia, or other regions to regulate their social relations according to Confucian ethical-political principles and ritual systems. In the frontier territories, especially minority areas, the dynasty did not impose its own political and legal systems on local relationships, but rather followed what was customary and appropriate, which is to say the dynasty reconciled the relationship between the unified dynasty and local order according to specific situations and social changes. The dynasty used the Confucian view of All-under-Heaven to explain tribute relations but also left open the possibility of flexible interpretations of this relationship by other communities. The balance struck by Qing imperial power between Tibetan Buddhism and Confucian thought is a case in point. If the Qing emperor could be seen by Tibetan society as the reincarnation of Manjushri, then there must also have existed within Tibetan society a political culture that defined internal and external relations in a flexible way. (Even if this political culture appeared in the form of religious beliefs or local customs and rituals, it was also necessarily political in that it had to manage the relations between different communities and provide corresponding institutional forms.) In fact, tributary and vassal relationships were not homogeneous and always varied according to the characteristics of the participants. For these reasons, the political nature of Confucian thought manifests in its sustained definition—sometimes strict and sometimes flexible—of its own boundaries. According to this scenario, the distinction between Yi (foreigner) and Xia (Chinese), between inner / inside and outer / outside, is both strict and relative, and Confucian thinkers and political figures of different eras not only have proposed a series of interpretations grounded in different classics and their interpretative traditions, but also have transformed these interpretations into institutional and ritual practices. Of course, this is only an ideal description; across actual historical events, relations between the center and the local continued to change, with interpenetration, domination, exclusion, and struggle also occurring throughout the course of history (e.g., wars, conversion of the frontier to regular provinces or *gaitu guiliu*). Whether they are ritual systems or mechanisms of coercion, they are always related to the problem of domination. But from another point of view, one of the subjects of historical research is precisely the difference between different forms of domination.

If the relationship between cultural borders and political borders is placed not in the domain of "China" but in the domain of the Asian region, the assertion that "Confucianism fuses the cultural and political into a single, though complex, compound" must confront the challenge of how to define the boundaries of the political. We can look at this issue from two different directions. First, Japan, the Korean Peninsula, the Ryukyu Islands, Vietnam, and other places were all within the so-called Confucian cultural sphere and the cultural sphere of the Chinese script, but they did not, as a result, form a "single, though complex, compound." When Meiji- and Showa-era Japan tried to use the ideas of "same writing, same race" (*tongwen tongzhong*, J. *dōbun dōshu*) and the creation of a "co-prosperity sphere" as the basis for their expansion plans for a Greater East Asia, they met with fierce resistance from various countries and peoples in the region. Second, in contrast to the Ryukyu Islands, the Korean Peninsula, and Vietnam, which were heavily influenced by Confucian culture and the Chinese script, organic parts of Chinese dynasties such as Tibet, Mongolia, and Muslim-majority areas (and the modern states that followed them) were not within the cultural spheres of Confucianism and Chinese characters. Neither Chinese loyalists to the emperor nor the revolutionaries were fundamentally divided in their efforts to find unity in China, but in the era of nationalism, Mongolia, Tibet, and Muslim-majority areas generated problems of unity and division, and faced the challenge in different linguistic contexts of the ethnicization of social issues. Throughout the twentieth century, many different political claims were made, and the disagreements between them were related to the problem of how to interpret the "transsystemic" character of "China" and create a corresponding political-legal system.

From a regional perspective, the role of Confucianism in East Asia resembles the role of Christianity in Europe, in that its definition of aspects of culture in the region does not overlap with political boundaries. Although the Confucian civilizational sphere tended toward convergence in some ways, it did not strongly pursue the unification of culture and politics, but rather used other means to connect the different dynasties as a "transsocietal system," the most distinctive sign of which was the constitution of center-periphery relations into the so-called tributary-vassal network. This set of relationships may explain why East Asia was almost never characterized by the religious wars of varying magnitude that recurred in European history. Thanks to the efforts of Japanese scholars such as Takeshi Hamashita, the tribute system has received widespread scholarly attention as an Asian regional model that is different from the European nation-state system. In the field of cultural history, some scholars have also gone on to link the tribute trade with concepts such as the Confucian cultural sphere and the cultural sphere of the Chinese script. Many of these studies offer a picture of a Confucian tribute system based on "East Asia" as a regional unit, following maritime tribute and migration routes that extended from Northeast Asia to Southeast Asia. However, the tribute system did not particularly overlap with Confucianism, Chinese script culture, or similar religious faiths. It was also used in Central Asia and the Himalayas. Tibet, Nepal, Bhutan, Sikkim, Ladakh, and Burma had not only tribute-vassal relations of varying types with the central dynasties, but also intersecting and complex vassal and tributary relations with each other. Since neither "transsystemic societies" nor "transsocietal systems" have cultural homogeneity as their sole basis for existence, the linkages and interpenetration between them are natural.

"Transsystemic societies" and "transsocietal systems" are not static structures but dynamic processes. Any way of understanding historical categories such as "region," China, and Asia that departs from historical changes, historical power relations, and human activities is meaningless. In the dramatic shifts of the twentieth century, the forces shaping the region, China, and Asia have become global; the nation-state has become the dominant model; wars, revolutions, trade, capitalist economics, and social mobility have produced new social relations and state forms; and the transsystemic character and internal differences of societies have been markedly reduced. For these reasons, to interpret the complex relations between contemporary China and the Asian region, it is necessary to consider the enormous role of the twentieth century in reshaping China's sovereignty, its people, and its regional relations. Even so, however, in terms of intra- or interregional relations, concepts such as "transsystemic society" or "transsocietal system" can provide a unique perspective for observing, understanding, and reflecting on historical relations—after a long period of revolution and reform in

China, the "transsystematic" nature of Chinese society remains an important phenomenon.

In a complicated, multifaceted context, the question of how to interpret China also involves questions of how to interpret China's political culture. They include, for example: How should we interpret the multiple functions of Confucianism? How should we explain political concepts interpreted primarily from or through Confucianism? And how do these concepts relate to Western concepts that entered the Chinese linguistic context through translation from the nineteenth century onward? To answer these questions, *The Rise of Modern Chinese Thought* takes up three sets of ideas about political institutions. The first set is empire and nation-state, both products of early modern European thought that are often seen in binary opposition to one another. I take on this set of ideas because the study of Chinese history is dominated by two interrelated frameworks of understanding that are outgrowths of this empire / nation-state binary: one framework sees China as an empire (or civilization, or continent) that stands opposed to or forms a contrast to the modern Western nation-state; the other argues that an early nation-state structure built upon a system of centralized administration *(junxian zhi)* appeared long ago in Chinese history. My criticism of this binary does not call for us to abandon concepts of empire or nation-state. Instead, by integrating these narratives at another level, I try to reveal key aspects of Chinese history. The second set of concepts is centralized administration (*junxian*) and enfeoffment (*fengjian*) as they were understood in traditional China. When I discuss Confucianism from the Song to the Qing dynasties and specific questions of politics, I begin from the categories of centralized administration and enfeoffment because, unlike empire or nation-state, they were more commonly used by Confucian scholars and the gentry elite. My account of the establishment of the concept of Heavenly Principle during the Song dynasty, for example, emphasizes the debate among Confucian thinkers surrounding centralized administration and enfeoffment and the questions that were internal to this debate. The third set of concepts involves the ancient rites and music and their relationship to institutions (the term *zhi* in pre-Qin documents later developed into *zhidu,* or "institutions"). My discussion of the Song dynasty deals with the differentiation of rites and music from institutions but does not treat them as completely separate categories; rather, I place the differentiation of rites and music from institutions within the internal horizon or perspective of debates within Song-dynasty historiography and the School of the Way (*daoxue*) and thereby lead what on the surface appears to be an objective historical account to become a domain where judgments about history and values are made.

When we begin from this historical perspective that is rooted in Confucian learning to open up questions about the establishment of Heavenly Principle, the contrasts between enfeoffment and centralization, and other issues that have often been understood by contemporary historians in terms of economic history, the history of political institutions, cultural history, or the history of philosophy, we are then interpreting history from its internal perspective and horizon (*neizai shiye*). This internal perspective is produced in constant dialogue with contemporary times. Methodologically, this is neither using antiquity to interpret the modern, nor using antiquity to interpret antiquity, nor using the modern to interpret antiquity. Rather, through the dialogue between these historical viewpoints, we make this internal perspective into our own self-reflexive outlook and approach.

The writing of *The Rise of Modern Chinese Thought* began in the stifling and pessimistic atmosphere that followed 1989, a time quite different from today's China. As is the experience for many scholars, when you begin the process of research, history's richness and its internal logic guide your progress, such that the best method is to develop the broadest perspective and, while respecting that internal logic, to cut across history's labyrinth to offer a series of accounts that are connected to one another and still enlightening to people now. At the end of this preface, then, I also want to say that the impetus for my inquiry was and is rooted in a particular propensity of the times, and this inquiry and exploration are an attempt to cut across the ruptures of history.

Editor's Introduction

MICHAEL GIBBS HILL

Wang Hui's *The Rise of Modern Chinese Thought* (*Xiandai Zhongguo sixiangde xingqi*) was first published in 2004 and has since drawn considerable response and attention in multiple languages. The book was the subject of several long reviews and responses written in English well before anyone undertook a translation—a reception that is remarkable in the Anglo-American intellectual world, which is often slow to give attention to works published in foreign languages.[1] Harvard University Press published my translation of the general introduction (*daolun*) to the book under the title *China From Empire to Nation-State* in 2014, and the present book continues that effort by translating revised and abridged chapters from the first two volumes of the original four-volume work.[2] Those two volumes comprised seven chapters; here in English, they are now divided into eight chapters.

My view of Wang Hui's decision to focus this publication on the first two volumes, *Principle and Things* (*Li yu wu*) and *Empire and State* (*Diguo yu guojia*), is that *The Rise of Modern Chinese Thought* is an ongoing project, one that works, at times, in dialogue with its translations. Pieces of *The Rise of Modern Chinese Thought* were published in Chinese in many venues, including both journals and essay collections, before and after the appearance of the four-volume book. Essays and articles that later formed the core of the third and fourth volumes, *Universal Principle and Anti-Universal Principle*

(*Gongli yu fangongli*) and *The Community of Scientific Language* (*Kexue huayu gongtongti*), were published in the 1990s in journals such as *The Scholar* (*Xueren*) and *Chinese Social Sciences Quarterly* (*Zhongguo shehui kexue jikan*); some of those pieces then made their way into translation.[3] The first two volumes, *Principle and Things* and *Empire and State,* were written later, as Wang Hui worked through the larger project in the late 1990s and early 2000s. More importantly, Wang wrote the introduction (*daolun*) last.[4] Although the four-volume work that was published under the title *The Rise of Modern Chinese Thought* was definitive for its moment, it is not surprising to see its structure and arguments continue to evolve. Wang Hui argues in his preface that the two volumes translated here comprise a systematic critique of Chinese intellectual history from the Tang–Song period to the early twentieth century. Another English-language book, based on Wang's *Birth of the Century* (*Shijide dansheng*) and featuring revised versions of chapters that originally appeared in *The Rise of Modern Chinese Thought* on Yan Fu (1854–1921), Liang Qichao (1873–1929), and Zhang Taiyan (1869–1936), is currently in preparation.

Widely considered Wang Hui's magnum opus, *The Rise of Modern Chinese Thought* will astonish readers with the breadth of materials and problems from intellectual history that it covers. More importantly, it will challenge readers with its relentless search for new meanings in the classics and in the works of generations of interpreters and exegetes that have been handed down across the centuries—its insistence that we treat all of these works as living texts. The great contribution of this book is that it presents far more of Wang Hui's writings on thinkers and texts from middle-period and late-imperial China than have yet to appear in an English-language volume.[5] Here we see the full extent of Wang's ambition: the question of what is modern in Chinese thought begins with the establishment of the concept of "Heavenly Principle" in the writings of thinkers such as Cheng Hao (1032–1085), Cheng Yi (1033–1107), and Zhu Xi (1130–1200) and continues through many rounds of debate and creative return to the sources of antiquity, both in the evidential learning of Gu Yanwu (1613–1682), Dai Zhen (1724–1777), and Zhang Xuecheng (1738–1801), and in attempts to recover the "subtle words and profound meanings" (*weiyan dayi*) of the classics by Zhuang Cunyu (1719–1788), Gong Zizhen (1792–1841), Kang Youwei (1858–1927), and others. Many of the works quoted in this book, often at length, also appear in English translation for the first time, including key sections from Gu Yanwu's *Record of Daily Knowledge* (*Ri zhi lu*) as well as Gu's letters and essays, Zhuang Cunyu's *Rectification of Terms in the Spring and Autumn Annals* (*Chunqiu zhengci*), and Kang Youwei's *Confucius as Reformer* (*Kongzi gaizhi kao*). This shift in emphasis should expand our perspective on Wang's contributions to intellectual history and to the possibilities opened up by thinkers (whether or not they are associated with the so-called New Left) who have argued for some time that China needs to seek an alternative to the capitalist market economy and the liberal nation-state model.

As readers, we might begin by reflecting on the "propensity of the times" or *shishi*,[6] a term that Wang brings to the forefront in these volumes by asking: How do these texts, some of which would be roped off in the museum of traditional thought, speak to the current situation of not just China but the globe? How did Wang's inquiry into the internal perspective or horizon (*neizai shiye*) of middle-period Chinese thought respond to the propensity of the times of the 1990s and early 2000s? And now, two decades or more after they were first written, how might they speak to our times?

Wang's preface to the English edition addresses the propensity of the current moment by laying out his view of China as a transsystemic society (*kuatixi shehui*). After inheriting the borders, territories, and peoples of the Qing dynasty, first the Republic of China and then the People's Republic of China struggled to create and sustain the intellectual and institutional foundations for a multilingual, multiethnic, multireligious state. By returning to the Qing and earlier periods, Wang argues, it is possible to find some of the resources for the present day, however partial they might be, and to find an understanding of China that goes beyond the standards and models of nation-state and empire. Wang contends that the concept of "becoming China" (*Zhongguohua*), which he sees as distinct from the English term "Sinicization" and the Chinese terms *Hanhua* and *Huahua*, offers a way beyond some of the long-standing debates about the Qing dynasty concerning ethnicity, ethnic hierarchy, and acculturation. The essay also discusses Wang's motivations behind the study and the major questions he takes up throughout *The Rise of Modern Chinese Thought*.

Due to space limitations, we do not reproduce the seventy thousand words of the introduction (*daolun*) here, because they are already available in *China from Empire to Nation-State*. Although I strongly recommend that work for its responses to major thinkers such as Hegel, Marx, and Adam Smith and for its overview of the larger book, readers can also proceed directly to Wang's account of Song-dynasty thought. If *China from Empire to Nation-State* offers a critique of the modes of thought that show China to be irredeemably incompatible with the nation-state form and therefore with modernity itself, then the eight chapters in this book deliver on Wang's call to attend to the internal perspective of Chinese thought and to "liberate the object" of discussion from models that view Chinese history since the Song dynasty with an excessive focus on the transition to the modern nation-state.

Chapters 1 through 5, which make up *Principle and Things,* the first volume of the original, offer a history of the transformation of Confucian thought from the Song dynasty through the middle of the Qing dynasty. Chapters 1 and 2, "Heavenly Principle and the Propensity of the Times" and "Heavenly Principle and the Centralized State," examine the Song-dynasty School of Principle (*lixue,* translated elsewhere as Neo-Confucianism) and the School of the Way (*Daoxue*) and their role in the emergence of Heavenly Principle (*tianli*) and related concepts. Arguing against multiple accounts of the Song period, Wang musters evidence to show that the School of Principle and its focus on ancient institutions of governance and Heavenly Principle was not simply a conservative reaction to social, economic, and political trends of the Song, but rather a "paradoxical mode of thought" that used the appeals to times long past to critique the present and offer alternatives to changes in social relations. Wang emphasizes, contrary to many later critics, that Song Confucian thought was more than abstract metaphysics and moralizing. Song intellectuals' calls to revive the institutions of ancient times engaged directly with political and institutional issues of the present moment, particularly the growing power of both the market and the state and its system of centralized administration (*junxian*).

Chapter 3, "The Transformation of 'Things,'" moves through Song and Ming Neo-Confucianism to the eve of the Ming-Qing transition with further discussions of thinkers such as Cheng Hao, Cheng Yi, Zhu Xi, Lu Xiangshan (1139–1192), and Wang Yangming (1472–1529), Yan Yuan (1635–1704), and others. The persistent questioning of the relationship between abstract Principle (*li*) and actually existing things (*wu*) and affairs (*shi*) and the ability of humans to "investigate things and extend knowledge" (*gewu zhizhi*) led to moments of what Wang calls the "self-negation" of the Neo-Confucian

School of Principle (*lixue*). In each case, these realignments touched on social issues related to the tax system, the power of local families, and the power of the state to guide education and culture through the examination system. By focusing on the internal perspective of these debates, we see how the many calls to return to restore aspects of the Three Dynasties of Antiquity or the Qin and Han dynasties both functioned as a critique of contemporary political and institutional circumstances and continuously renewed the past as a resource for thought and political action.

Chapters 4 and 5, "Classics and History" parts 1 and 2, examine the transformation of knowledge production and scholarly practices in the Qing dynasty. Two Ming loyalist figures, Huang Zongxi (1610–1695) and Gu Yanwu (1613–1682), take center stage in Chapter 4, as Wang shows how their work shifted the emphasis away from Heavenly Principle and, through detailed inquiries into phonology and ancient historical institutions, sought an intellectual basis for resisting the consolidation of the Qing dynasty's authority in the late seventeenth century. In Chapter 5, Wang rejects the opposition between evidential learning (*kaozheng* or *kaoju*) and moral philosophy or "expositions on principles and meanings" (*yili*) that is often taken for granted in scholarship on Qing-dynasty intellectual and literary history. Wang insists, for example, that Dai Zhen's criticism of the excesses of Song thought did not preclude a commitment to moral philosophy and the questions it raised about rapid changes in economy, society, and politics in the mid-eighteenth century.

Chapters 6, 7, and 8, which make up the volume *Empire and State*, examine how thinkers and officials from the Yuan dynasty through the end of the Qing sought to construct legitimacy for Chinese dynasties, whether for minority rule under the Mongols or the Manchus, or for China as one struggling state among many in the system of nation-states from the nineteenth and early twentieth centuries. These chapters are very relevant for ongoing debates about whether Chinese thought from before the twentieth century can serve as a resource for understanding the PRC's relations with other states and its management of its peripheries and frontiers. This section is considerably enriched by recent translations of the three extant commentaries of the *Spring and Autumn Annals* (*Chunqiu*), the Gongyang, Guliang, and Zuo commentaries, all of which have come into print in English since 2010.[7]

In these later chapters, Wang argues that thinkers as different as Dai Zhen, Wei Yuan, and Kang Youwei continue to engage in moral philosophy or *yili;* in other words, even the work of those that seem far afield from the Song thinkers who are closely associated with this type of inquiry carries deep moral and political significance that resonates—often in new ways—with the classics. Chapter 6 studies how scholars understood writings such as the Gongyang commentary to the *Spring and Autumn Annals* in relation to their own situation of minority rule. Early studies of the Gongyang commentary and related texts from the Yuan dynasty, Wang argues, resonate with the New Text scholarship of the Qing dynasty, which used the Gongyang commentary and other ancient writings to establish a moral basis for minority rule by the Manchu court. Chapter 7 looks closely at texts such as Wei Yuan's *Gazetteer of the Maritime States* (*Haiguo tuzhi*), a work that translated and compiled large amounts of historical and geographical information on countries around the world, to show that Wei's work was not simply a turn outward to the West or the world—as it is often portrayed—but a sophisticated attempt to reconfigure long-standing ideas about inner and outer (*nei/wai*) in Chinese thought to account for the Qing dynasty's place in the world of the myriad states (*wanguo*). The final chapter argues that Kang Youwei's writings presented a new Confucian universalism that recast Confucius himself as a reformed, uncrowned king whose ideas were relevant far beyond the border of the Qing empire or the Republic of China. Even as he hoped to make Confucius a "doctrine for all" (*wanshi fa*), however, Kang struggled with the same problems of diversity and unity within the Qing and the Republic of China that occupied so many of the thinkers who came before him.

Eleven scholars completed translations of the various chapters. Some of the translators regularly consulted with one another regarding terminology and difficult passages in the text. I reviewed each chapter and worked with the translators to ensure consistency in the translation of key terminology, book titles, and similar information. We were keen to make sure that choices on terminology accorded with other published translations of Wang Hui's work, especially *China from Empire to Nation-State* and *The Politics of Imagining Asia*, and to adjust or correct earlier translations as needed. Wang Hui also graciously responded to questions and queries on each chapter.

The breadth of materials cited in the book, as well as the volume of long quotations from classical Chinese, creates a special challenge for the translators. Where possible, the translators have borrowed or referred to existing translations in English of major texts (e.g., *The Analects* of Confucius, the *Mencius*, etc.), and each translator chose editions that suited their specific needs. Wang Hui also cites many secondary sources translated from other languages into Chinese, and for works originally written in English, the translators refer to those English versions if appropriate and if those editions were available.

Translations of key terms will shift according to context. In theory, these shifts seem natural when the discussion ranges across the centuries, but they can also confuse the reader; therefore, major changes are indicated by the translators. For example, the term *lixue* is rendered in the earlier chapters as the School of Principle (in relation to *xinxue* or the School of Mind) and more generally in later chapters as Neo-Confucianism. In Chapter 6, which examines closely the evidential learning (*kaozheng xue*) of Dai Zhen and Zhang Xuecheng, the term is given mostly in romanization as *lixue*, because *li* (Principle or pattern) received special scrutiny from scholars of evidential learning. In another case, the translators of Chapter 7 elected to give the terms Yi (foreigner or barbarian) and Xia (Chinese) in untranslated romanization and provide a note that explains their choice.

Harvard University Press began discussions about bringing out a translation of *Xiandai Zhongguo sixiangde xingqi* almost immediately after it was first published in Chinese. The challenges of translating such an expansive study, however, are legion, which explains in part why this book is appearing nine years after *China from Empire to Nation-State.* Since no single person could take on the entire project—an epic task—I assembled a team of scholar-translators to translate individual chapters. Much of this work, especially the revisions of the translators' first drafts, was completed under the difficult conditions of the coronavirus pandemic. I am extremely grateful to the translators and have been humbled by their erudition, their persistence, and their good humor. I also thank my two research assistants, Zhengyuan Ling and Kaiming Chen, who helped me and the translators with tracking down sources and citations. The Interlibrary Loan Department at William & Mary's Swem Library obtained books from across North

America for me when travel to larger research collections was impossible. My colleagues in William & Mary's Department of Modern Languages & Literatures, who study and understand the value of translation as scholarship and intellectual labor, always offered their support and encouragement. Finally, I thank my editors at Harvard University Press: Lindsay Waters, who championed this project from the beginning, and Joseph Pomp, who guided it to conclusion.

CHAPTER 1

Heavenly Principle and the Propensity of the Times

Translated by JESSE FIELD

> The myriad things follow the movements of the Way of Heaven; the myriad peoples are transformed by the cultivation of sagely virtue.
>
> —ZHOU DUNYI, *Penetrating the Text of the Book of Changes (Tong shu)*

I. Heavenly Principle and the Evolution of Confucian Methods of Moral Evaluation

1. The School of Principle (*lixue*) and Early Modernity

Between the 1920s and the 1940s, first Naitō Konan and then Miyazaki Ichisada introduced several important propositions regarding the Tang-to-Song transition, capitalism during the Song dynasty, and East Asian early modernity. Since then, despite constant controversy, revision, and improvement, one Kyoto School proposition has garnered universal acclaim: there is a basic difference between the Tang and Song, and the Song dynasty deserves a special status in history. As Naitō Konan writes, "There are marked differences in the cultural quality of the Tang and the Song: the Tang Dynasty was the end of the Middle Ages, while the Song Dynasty was the beginning of early modernity, with a transitional period in between, the end of the Tang through the Five Dynasties."[1] Summarizing expositions on the special status of the Song dynasty, we list the following facets: first, although the Song dynasty had unified All-under-Heaven with martial strength, it saw unprecedented strengthening of the connections between political control and commerce, or economic control. The Song dynasty was "the first unified dynasty in which the commercial system served as the foundation of centralized state power. The accomplishments of this economically centralized state ensured that its basic structure would be utterly unassailable by later dynasties."[2] Two decisive elements leading to the formation of commercial power were transformations to the systems of transportation and to the economy. Canal and river transport spurred long-distance trade; and population movement, increased urbanization, new forms of social relations, and new specialization in labor all supplied the foundations for a new society. Important changes occurred in the land system, the tax system, and the currency system, spurring the transition from a barter to a currency economy. Moreover, the institutional replacement of the "grain, labor, cloth" model (*zu-yong-diao*) with the Two-Tax Policy (*liangshui fa*) brought great change to the ways people were tied to the land. It was in the midst of these transformations that Miyazaki observed a "clear tendency toward capitalism," and he went on to call the period a mark of a new age, different from those centered on the Yellow River or inland areas, and instead centered on canal and river transport.[3] Second, along with economic transformation came the decline of the aristocratic social structure and the culture centered on the "Nine-Rank" system of government. Replacing this was a maturing system of centralized administration (*junxian*, "commanderies and counties"), centralized government, and a bureaucracy, into which rose the gentry-bureaucrat class to take positions, thanks to the institutionalization of the examination system. This rise of this gentry-bureaucrat class greatly influenced Chinese culture from the Song forward, as it would form the basis of a political culture quite different from that of the Han and Tang empires. Third, owing to the Five Dynasties division and the later formation of linked states confronted with the *minzu*, or nation, as their dominant body, the Song and later Chinese dynasties had a greater sense of national community, a sense of identity that produced "signs of apposite and mutually reinforcing sense of self-consciousness and consciousness of national ideology."[4] Unlike the cultural identity of the multinational empires of the Han and Tang, Song-dynasty society exhibited protonationalism (bringing together state (*guojia*) and nation / ethnicity (*minzu*), along with a new ideology of exclusion, in cultural terms). Fourth, in response to the conditions described above, the School of Principle (*lixue*) began to replace the Ancient Text schools of the Han and Tang dynasties, establishing a combination of "state and people ideology" (*guomin zhuyi*) with egalitarianism (as opposed to aristocracy) and secularism. Such aspects of a new Confucian worldview constituted signs of "recent modernity" or "early modernity" in intellectual historical terms, argued Miyazaki. In his words:

> The Song dynasty took a socioeconomic leap, with increasing urbanization, and spread of knowledge comparable to the European Renaissance, to which it should be seen as a parallel and equally valuable development. The early stage of the Chinese Renaissance, especially, was notable for its development of a unique book-printing technology. . . . In the world of medieval thought, the three teachings of Confucianism, Buddhism and Daoism are representative, and of these, Buddhism had the widest influence. . . . Sometimes Buddhist activity in the secular world was excessive, with expanding temple lands, hiding away able young men, disturbing social order, and influencing government finance. For these reasons, it was sanctioned by ruling powers, and then suppressed. But most of the ruling powers at this time had a Daoist behind their strategizing. . . . Beginning with the Tang and Song, and following the rise of the examination system, Confucian scholars established a world of social networks centered on the exams, beginning a movement toward governing and guiding the general population through Confucian teachings. The result was a Confucian attack on Buddhism, an early sign of which was the remonstrance of the great Han Yu against the emperor venerating a "bone of the Buddha."[5]

In his eyes, Song thought was a secular "religion" produced by the evolving social relations described above. And precisely for this reason, a work centered on the rise of Chinese modern thought cannot but begin from a new understanding of Song-dynasty thought.

Modern Confucian researchers use early modern European philosophy and history as reference points for interpreting the significance of some of the features of Song Learning of the Way or *Daoxue* (especially the School of Principle of Zhu Xi and the Cheng brothers). In the philosophical frameworks of Hu Shi's pragmatism, Feng Youlan's new realism, and Mou Zongsan's Kantian approach, the basic principles of Confucianism are organized not only into the European philosophical categories of ontology and epistemology, but also into such European historical categories as an inward turn, rationalization, and secularization. In the Enlightenment currents, European thought of the eighteenth and nineteenth centuries passed through rationalist and individualist transitions, the core of which were views such as secularism that opposed religious despotism and calls for self-determination that opposed absolute political despotism. For this reason, the concepts modern scholars of Confucianism use—like the inward turn, rationalization, and daily life and its ethics—are all categories formed with reference to early modern European metaphysics, individualist values (the internalized moral view that takes the self as the center), urban social culture, and empiricist scientific views. They presuppose the rebellion of secularized individuals and rationality against religious authority and absolute monarchy. Joseph Needham clearly believed that "the opposition of Neo-Confucianism to Buddhism was in substance a scientific view striking back at an ascetic faith that refused the world."[6] His tone carries almost the same aggression and mockery that figures in the approach that the May Fourth New Culture Movement took toward Neo-Confucianism. Even if Chinese scholars rarely use the concepts "recent modernity" or "early modernity," the concepts described above imply some differences in Song-era thought and the character of the "Middle Ages." In fact, rationalization narratives of the Song and Ming School of Principle, and Kyoto school narratives of Song society in the European categories of "capitalism" (market economy), "state and people ideology" (*guomin zhuyi;* i.e., nationalism), long-distance trade (division of labor), and urbanization (social movement), all echo one another and are narratives of Chinese and East Asian modernity constructed with reference to historical imaginaries of European modernity.[7]

Ever since the late Qing, we have seen two completely different methods for understanding the formation and meaning of a worldview based on Heavenly Principle (*tianli*), both of which are deeply rooted in modern values. In the interpretive framework of the May Fourth New Culture Movement, the worldview of Heavenly Principle was an ideology altogether reactionary (preserving imperial rights), medieval (taking as the basis for its political system patriarchal institutions and the teaching of the rites), and leading China to lose its shot at being modern (opposing science and opposing markets). Quite in opposition, the Kyoto school and the modern new Confucian learning, working from different considerations, took the emergence of Song learning as a marker of early modernity in the cultural spheres of China and East Asia, establishing the presence in it of tendencies at once nationalist (*minzuzhuyi*, indicating *guomin zhuyi*, an ideology of state and people), egalitarian (opposing aristocracy), individualist and secular (opposing religion), and supportive of the separation of powers. These utterly opposing evaluations both take their measure from the moral genealogy of the European Age of Enlightenment—especially views on subjectivity and immanence.[8] For example, Mou Zongsan, interpreting the claim of Mencius, "Seek and you shall obtain it, neglect and you shall lose it. It is the seeking that helps to obtain, and the seeking is internal to the self," defines the "self" of Mencius within the category of individual nature, and so sees Confucianism, an ideology that never strayed far from politics, as a "counterpolitical" or "antipolitical" declaration of individual independence:

> To make Confucian learning not entangled in politics, not to follow the vicissitudes of the age, and only to take the completion of individual human virtue as the gateway to human enlightenment, allowing it to preserve eternal and independent meaning. . . . This "learning of the inner sage" is also called the "teaching of perfected virtue (*cheng de*)." The highest goal of "perfected virtue" is sagehood, is being a person of humaneness, is being a great person. Its true meaning is to obtain boundless and perfect meaning out of limited, individual human lives.[9]

To pull Confucianism away from government and the specific era or age is also to pull the essentials of perfected virtue—sagehood, humaneness, and the great man—away from their historical conditions. From the inner logic of the School of Principle, the possibility of this interpretation is owed to the fact that many conclusions of the school were established in an expository framework related to Heavenly Principle, from which moral-political conclusions are developed according to methods for knowing the order of the universe and its internal original nature, with the post-Mencius school being the most important source for this line of thinking. However, to encompass the political nature of Confucian propositions within a framework of cosmology and ontology is insufficient to establish an "antipolitical" or "nonpolitical" original nature; quite the contrary, cosmology and ontology and other "nonpolitical" expository forms per se are in fact imbued with political nature, from which it follows that "nonpolitical" expository forms require placement in a network of political contexts to be understood. If individual moral perfection is pulled away from the specifically classified cardinal human relationships, becoming proof of "eternally independent meaning," to what degree can this category be understood as the thought of Confucius and Mencius? To what degree is it, instead, an affirmation of the early modern values represented by the New Culture Movement? Without the context of early modern Europe's secular subjectivity and ideas of immanence that called for casting off religious relations, aristocratic government, and absolute monarchy, we would have a hard time understanding Mou Zongsan's analysis of Mencius. With regard to a historical analogy, if we take clan ethical relations as an authoritarian restriction external to humans themselves, then the School of Principle is simply "medieval." If we take the philosophy of Heavenly Nature as the rise of views on immanence (the self) and the School of Principle's promotion of ancestor worship as opposing the social conditions of absolute monarchy (or the formation of Chinese-style "civil society"), and take the school's mandate for "investigating things and extending knowledge" (*gewu zhi zhi*) as the source of empiricist scientific method, then the School of Principle can be said to contain yet another trait of "early modernity." The above oppositions by no means exceed the basic framework of the narrative of the emergence of modernity.

Within the framework of an ideology attempting to restore ancient values, the Confucianism of the Song Dynasty used two classical ideas to strike back at the new norms and new systems of its time. One of these was the new classical view of Heavenly Principle (*tianli*), which was generated combining views regarding Heaven (*tian*), the Way (*dao*), and the Way of Heaven (*tiandao*). Another was the kingly Way, along with the rites and music of the Three Dynasties of Antiquity (of the Xia, the Shang, and the Zhou). The former was a banner to hold high; the latter, a latent measure. We can summarize the basic stance of the School of Principle in this way: it opposed the techniques of politics (imperial power and bureaucratic government under the conditions of centralized administration) with Heavenly Way/Heavenly Principle, opposed market movements with a recovery of the patriarchal clan system, opposed trade and tax law with the "well-field" system (*jingtian*), opposed the examination system with a school system, opposed the official ranking system (*gongming*) with the ideal of perfected virtue (*chengde*), and opposed foreign cultures (Buddhism) and historical changes with the restoration of antiquity. In the narrative of the May Fourth New Culture Movement and the Marxists, the tendencies of the School of Principle observed above were seen as ideologies of aristocracy, restoration of antiquity, and "reaction." If the aforementioned are encompassed within the key elements of Song society—centralized political authority, market economy, long-distance trade, so-called nationalism or "protonationalism," and individualism—if these can be summed up as "early modernity," then the political and social significance of Confucian intellectual currents centered on Heavenly Principle can be presented in broad outline as a critical theory responding to these elements of "early modernity."

However, the critical nature of the School of Principle was established under a premise that accepted the rationality of historical evolution, from which it followed that these historical relations were prerequisite to the structural elements—such as Principle (*li*), *qi*, Mind (*xin*), Nature (*xing*), and so on. Heavenly Principle itself indicated the propensity of the times (*shishi*). In this respect, the establishment of the Heavenly Principle concept was intended to seek certainty and a preexisting foundation during a period when the propensity of the times was changing. It was also intended to help the basic principles of the old Confucian schools adapt to the constantly shifting circumstances. For this reason, rather than say the School of Principle stood outside the aforementioned social relations and cultural tendencies to offer critique, it is better to say its attitude, both critical of the times and in favor of restoring ancient practices, formed a paradoxical method of thought.

For example, members of the School of the Way opposed conventional Confucian "political arts" with their own *Daoxue* notions of enfeoffments, but they acknowledged and accepted imperial authoritarianism and central administration; they sought to suppress profit seeking with righteousness and desire with Principle, but they also acknowledged that profit and desire possessed a certain degree of legitimacy; they opposed reforms of the land and taxation systems with their notions of patriarchal household allotment, but they also acknowledged and accepted the rationality of reforms. They opposed the examinations system for producing scholar-officials by upholding the ideal of ancient schools, but they also acknowledged the necessity of the decline of the aristocratic system. They took patriarchal clans and feudal lordships as moral ideals, but they also instituted the practice of perfecting virtue (*chengde*) as a practice of self-cultivation for individuals. They decried the "two invading teachings" (Buddhism and Daoism) but their own theoretical forms (cosmology, ontology, and the discourse of Mind-Nature, *xinxinglun*) were deeply influenced by both teachings, so much so that later generations would criticize them as "Confucians on the outside and Buddhists on the inside" (*yang ru yin shi*). Even if the aforementioned transformations to Song society could be placed, reluctantly, within our concept of "early modernity" (or "near modern"), still, the main tendency of the School of Principle could only considered at best an intellectual framework for a certain kind of "modernity in opposition to early modernity." Miyazaki Ichisada's determination to fuse the notion of nationalism and central administration with the School of Principle is at the very least an oversimplification of the situation.

The paradoxical stance of the Heavenly Principle worldview can be summarized in this way: First, the Heavenly Principle concept and its methods criticized new developments in Song society by calling for a return to the ancient ways. But these very criticisms took form in the midst of the transformations, and hence these critics often based their theory on transformed historical meanings. Second, the intellectual genealogy that centered on Heavenly Principle was by no means a philosophical system with only abstract metaphysics. It also developed social-political theories, and thus the historical meanings of this ideology and worldview were not stable. Precisely for these reasons, the notions and propositions of the School of Principle become a "common space": rulers work on systematizing it and bureaucratizing it; the scholar-official class tries to purify itself and renew its critical nature; and rebels turn to Heavenly Principle to legitimize their opposition. Thus the controversy and debates surrounding Heavenly Principle form the reality of Song and later intellectual history. In the end, the genealogy of thought with Heavenly Principle as its center incorporated many political-moral debates, which shows that the establishment of Heavenly Principle marks a transition in Confucian moral-political evaluation methods.

Terms such as "near modern" (*jin shi*) and "early modern" (*zaoqi xiandai*) bring obvious indications of historical teleology. And yet, we might as well temporarily skirt these controversies to focus on an understanding of the form and historical significance of the School of Principle. The Song School of the Way eliminated the mistakes of the two teachings (Buddhism and Daoism), turned away from the specialized studies within Han Confucianism, and so recovered the true face of Confucianism, the Ru learning (*Ru xue*); these results within a Confucian movement established Confucian cosmology, Mind-Nature theory, and epistemology, all centered on Heavenly Principle. The concept of Heavenly Principle was made from the combination of Heaven and Principle: Heaven expressed the highest position of Principle and the root of ontology. Principle implied that the myriad things of the universe were the basis of the cosmology. Heaven (*tian*) and Principle (*li*), combined into one word, *tianli* (Heavenly Principle), replaced categories such as Heaven (*tian*), God-Emperor (*di*), the Way (*dao*), and the Way of Heaven (*tiandao*) that had once held the highest status in traditional cosmologies, theories of the Mandate of Heaven, and theories of morality, and thereby organized the various categories and concepts of Confucianism in a way that placed Heavenly Principle at the center. Relying on the basis of the concept of Heavenly Principle, Confucians were able to use a form internal to the real world and yet opposed to the real world to illuminate their place in the world, even as they placed their imagination of an ideal world within the framework of Principle. Viewed in light of later conjecture, Cheng Yi (1033–1107) and Cheng Hao (1032–1085), who had come up with the notion, and Zhu Xi, who had turned it into a universal system, had a special status different from other School of the Way masters, including the Northern Song pioneers of the School of the Way. A. C. Graham writes, "The Cheng brothers thought that Heaven, Mandate, and Dao were no more than different names for Principle. This way, they conjectured a natural law transformed into rational principle based on an analogy with human society."[10] Heaven, Mandate, and the Way carry the traces of Way of Heaven theory (laws of nature [*ziran*]), while Principle represents a turn toward rationality.[11] Among modern new Confucian studies, the notion of an "inward turn" or "rationalization" is produced precisely in answer to this historical understanding. The "inward turn" so called is generally used to describe the rebuttal of School of the Way thought to the ideology of an absolute Heaven. What are called "rationalization" or "laws of rationality" are generally used to describe how the concept of Principle transformed the basis of moral judgment from the Will of Heaven to the rational nature of humanity; and they turned, as well, from external ritual systems toward immanence, and from ways of describing cosmologies to ways of describing original nature (*benxing*).

However, this "rationalization" notion was constructed within the scope of the secular / religious opposition. If the "inward turn" of Song learning means constructing "a rational model," how do we then understand Miyazaki's designation of Song learning as "secular religion," or propositions regarding the "religious nature of Confucianism"?[12] As we further describe the features of Song Confucianism, we must acknowledge that placing rationalization and the inward turn into opposing categories of secular and religious may lead us into some difficulties. First, in the debates with Buddhism and Daoism, Confucianism used affirmations of daily life and ethics to undercut the social motivation and ethics of Buddhism, but whether in the late Tang or in the Northern Song, the context of these controversies was always deeply political in nature. Second, in the category of Confucianism, affirmation of the real world could hardly be said to be nonreligious or secularized, which leads to even more difficulty in applying the binary categories of secular and religious to define the aforementioned controversies. Faced with Buddhist hermeticism, Confucianism affirmed daily life, and precisely this feature made modern scholars believe that Song learning had worked as European Enlightenment philosophy had, by criticizing religious or cloistered life. In European discourse, the category of "daily life" stands opposite to the category of Christian life, which implies that nonreligious secular life developed along with the near-modern markets and market society. But daily life in Confucianism referred to a category of ritual (*li*), much as the vinaya rules (*lü*) category set down norms for daily life in Buddhism. Principle and ritual complement each other, with Principle being the original substance of ritual, as well as the basis for people to reference in ritual conduct (practice, or practical steps). In the Tang and Song eras, when Buddhism flourished, the worshipful respect for Confucian ritual never ceased. Third, School of Principle scholars defined ritual practice with reference to Principle outside of ritual, believing that the rituals as they were actually practiced, in their very system itself had lost internal value (and become mere empty forms). So they tried to connect ritual back to Principle, and so recover the sacredness and value of ritual and ritual practice. In this respect, the School of Principle's affirmation of daily life also affirmed the sacredness of ritual. From the viewpoint of Confucian learning, what daily life presented was not some random or chance structure or process, but rather a structure and process directly corresponding with the original substance of ritual. And from this could be observed direct correspondence in structure and course with the original substance of Heaven. Thus, rather than call the establishment of Heavenly Principle a form of secularization, we should say that ritual practice and daily life practice alike were made sacred again. With daily practice (ritual and regulatory practice) having devolved into empty, casual, and random forms, the School of the Way demanded they be restored to substance with sincerity and reverence.[13] In certain respects, the School of Principle was simply advancing moral sayings to help people once again exhibit sincerity and respect.

As Confucianism evolved, it constantly rang a note of anxiety, with concern for the collapse, decline, and formalization of the system of rites and music, of customs and folkways, and of language and rhetoric. Confucius saw ritual propriety as humaneness (*yi ren shi li*). He tried, in the context of the collapse of the rites and music, to use the category of "humaneness" (*ren*) to bestow ritual with substance once again (with humaneness as the core of the rites and music, and if we take the rites and music as exemplifying Heaven, it follows that humaneness is the original substance of Heaven, and hence was the original substance of humanity). The Song Confucians replaced ritual with Principle, and used this category of Principle to supply anew internal norms for the practice of institutions / rites and music in a context where institutions had separated from rites and music (with Principle or Mind exemplifying Heaven and so the original substance of humanity). Qing Confucians would replace Principle with ritual, in an effort to use the category of ritual to stave off the disintegration of the ritual system caused by the conversion of ritual into Principle and Mind. To the Confucians, rites and music, rituals, institutions, Heavenly Principle, Mind, and Nature all exemplified Heaven, or the existing form of Heaven, from which it followed that Heaven and the sacred were by no means external to the existence of human daily life. In this respect, the Confucian categories of humaneness, Principle, Mind, and Nature were intended to counter the formalization and emptying out of institutions, rites and music, ceremonies, and daily life. And thus it follows that to claim these concepts were products of the trend toward rationalization is not as correct as to say that all are reactions against rationalization—they are antirational rational trends. If we still hope to understand the School of Principle's affirmation of daily life with regard to ritual within the categories of secularization and rationalization, then we must offer completely new understandings of these two notions.

2. The Establishment of the School of Principle and the Transformation of Confucianism

Before we open our discussion on the historical significance of the Heavenly Principle worldview, we must be able to give satisfactory answers to the following questions: First, does the establishment of the Heavenly Principle worldview mark a major transformation or rupture in Confucian moral-political evaluations? Second, how can we understand this transformation or rupture amid the important differences among the moral-political evaluation methods of the School of Principle, Pre-Qin Confucianism, and classical studies (*jingxue*) during the Han and Tang? Third, what social and political conditions did the Heavenly Principle worldview succeed in establishing? According to evidence discovered by historiographers, the term "School of Principle" (*lixue*) arose relatively late, as can be seen from the Yuan-dynasty compilers of the *History of the Song Dynasty* (*Song shu*) describing it using the term "School of the Way tradition" (*Daoxue chuan*). Song-dynasty scholars had used the term "School of Principle," but with entirely different meaning, as when Zhu Xi, Lu Jiuyuan (Lu Xiangshan), and Huang Zhen had used the term to refer to that branch of "moral philosophy" or "expositions on meanings and principles" (*yili*) related to evidentiary research and hermeneutics.[14] The volume *Categorized Pieces on the School of Principle* (*Lixue lei bian*) by Zhang Jiushao (Zhang Meihe, 1314–1396) at the end of the Yuan dynasty is seen as the first to introduce the concept of School of Principle, but the idea of Learning of the Mind (*xinxue*) had not yet arisen to oppose Principle, which means this School of Principle is unrelated to the later one. During the Ming dynasty, after the text known as *Diagram of Mind Learning* (*Xin xue tu*) by Chen Zhensheng (1411–1474) (also known by the honorifics Shengfu and Meifu, later self-styled Buyi, a native of Zhenhaiwei, Fujian), the "School of Mind" concept began to gain currency, but Master Chen's learning paid respects to the Cheng brothers and to Zhu Xi, and his notion of "School of Mind" had no internal connections to that of Lu Xiangshan before him, nor of Wang Yangming after.[15] The "School of Mind" was brought to completion in certain propositions of Wang Yangming that extended the thought of Lu Xiangshan, but its establishment still depended on opposition to the School of Principle of Zhu Xi and the Cheng brothers.[16] Modern New Confucianism sees the School of Principle as a system of metaphysics, and for this reason differentiates it from all preceding schools of Confucian philosophy; the oppositions New Confucianism makes between studies of Principle (*lixue*) versus classical learning (*jingxue*), and moral philosophy (*yili*) versus evidential learning (*kaozheng*), are clear signs of this process. How, then, can we include methods of thought that undertook "moral philosophy" (*yili*) through annotation, evidentiary study, and exegetical studies? And on what basis can we distinguish between the various types of moral philosophy? The Cheng brothers and Zhu Xi not only undertook classical studies on a large scale, but also made detailed designs and studies in the fields of daily life, including clan rituals, and rules and ethics. Their attitude toward the classics was not so much philosophical as it was interpretative and hermeneutic. This is why there are scholars who place the Song and Ming School of Principle within the category of classical studies (*jingxue*), and also periodize the historical evolution of the Song and Ming intellectual context into four mutually intersecting stages. In this respect, no matter how we divide "the study of principles of ideas" from specialized evidentiary studies, or distinguish between metaphysics and specific practice, we still cannot do justice to the innovative place of the School of Principle in Chinese thought.

Zhu Xi gives us an outline of the major threads formed in the School of Principle in his *Origins of the School of Zhou Dunyi, the Two Chengs and Their Disciples* (*Yi duo yuanyuan lu*). He continues to mine the larger project of the School of Principle already founded by Zhou Dunyi and pioneered by the five masters of the Northern Song, with the two Cheng brothers as his immediate generational masters, all the while also mentioning many other participants in this movement. This thread is Zhu Xi's genealogy outlining the path of influence, and it certainly cannot indicate the multiple and important origins of the School of Principle.[17] As Peter Bol demonstrates:

> It is clear that the *tao-t'ung* thesis of transmission from Chou [Zhou Dunyi] to the Ch'engs [Cheng Hao and Cheng Yi] is neither historically

> tenable, as Quan Zuwang noted, nor philosophically plausible. Indeed, careful analysis of the so-called *Tao-hsüeh* masters of the eleventh century has demonstrated that they lacked a shared philosophical system.[18]

There were many discrepancies and disagreements within the School of the Way, from which we may say that the consistency of the "School of the Way" and the statement that it was determined by a single philosophical system are not as true as saying it was determined by relations with its antitheses (such as the School of the Way versus the School of Mind, the School of Principle versus classical studies, the *Daoxue* [the School of the Way] versus *Wenxue* [the Learning of Patterning], and the school of moral philosophy versus the "school of practical learning" [*zhiyong zhi xue*]). Zhu Xi's line of descent and its historical changes appeared in the context of all this change, so if we limit ourselves to excavating the philosophical system supplied by the School of the Way, we seem unable even to grasp the true significance of the School of the Way genealogy constructed by Zhu Xi.

However, the system of interpretations of Heavenly Principle by Zhu Xi and the Cheng brothers indicates the emergence of a particular form of Confucianism. Not only are later developments in Confucianism almost all internal to the School of Principle, or else in dialogue with it; any other intellectual currents establishing new modes of thought would also have to manage a relationship with the School of Principle worldview. For example, during the Song and Yuan transition, the ideas, works, and specific practices people attended to within the School of the Way formed a very influential and famous movement, establishing a mode of discussion from which it came about that even those opposed to the School of the Way accepted that it existed and was important. What, then, were the basic features and stances of the School of the Way in the minds of its opponents? We may also consider the development of Qing thought. The thought and aims of Gu Yanwu, Huang Zongxi, Dai Zhen, Zhang Xuecheng, and even Kang Youwei and Liang Qichao all took the School of Principle, including its issues and ideological commitments, as their starting point. In these discussions, it was not the fine details within the formation of the School of Principle in Tang and Song learning but rather the great history of thought that had gradually formed and established itself during the Song, Yuan, Ming, and Qing eras, and the political conditions of these, that formed the object of later thinkers' consideration, conversation, and debate. Believing that School of the Way scholars shared a "philosophical system" was one thing; quite another was the conjecture that the School of the Way or School of Principle utterly lacked coherent ideological stances. Those refusing to acknowledge any such stances also refused to even use the terms "School of the Way" or "School of Principle." In this respect, to carry out a general inspection of the stances of the School of Principle means neither to repeat the interpretation of the School of the Way for modern philosophy, nor to set out the main features of the School of Principle within some teleological framework. Instead, it is the work of genealogy: to connect the production of ideological features with the historical conditions of the dialogue among the Confucian scholars embedded in those historical conditions, and thereby to grasp, within this dialogue and debate, the course of the construction of ideology, its historical conditions, and its self-disintegration.

The establishment of the genealogy of the School of the Way and the School of Principle marks a key transformation of moral-political evaluation methods in Confucianism. The establishment of the School of Principle involved transformations to all areas of Confucian learning, so why do I here single out moral evaluation methods as the main locus of transformation of the major features of the stances of the School of Principle? First, Confucian learning starts off centered on morality, with an epistemology linking government, economy, culture, and nature in one basic framework of rites and music, a moral-political narrative centered on renewing the connection between Heaven and humanity. The ultimate end of Confucianism was to return to moral evaluation, from which understanding it follows that to understand transformations to Confucianism, one must observe whether and how its moral evaluation methods changed. Second, moral evaluation in Confucianism extends into political, economic, cosmological, and other fields of social life, which means that it is not to be confused with modern categories of moral evaluation. In the categories of Confucianism, morality had strong and specific relationships with systems of ritual, institutions, and customs, from which it follows that any methods for understanding the transformations of moral evaluation methods must share a close connection to transformations in the systems of ritual, institutions, and customs. Third, among Confucian ideological stances, the School of Principle especially emphasized the internal aspect of the evaluative process, a feature that came from the establishment in the School of Principle of an ideological stance that placed Principle or Heavenly Principle as the highest standard, thus breaking free from the evaluation methods of Han and Tang Confucianism. For this reason, merely describing the entanglement of the categories of Nature (*xing*), Mind (*xin*), Principle (*li*), and *qi* is not sufficient to understand the historical significance of the School of Principle. It would be more substantial to ask: Why did these categories of Confucian moral evaluation rise to their core positions? As key categories of the School of the Way, what were their relations with the political arts, rites and music, institutions, and daily life? In other words, if the School of Principle marks the transformation of the very categories of moral-political evaluation, then in what form did the School of Principle engage in moral, political, and other social studies? What were the motivations and historical conditions that spurred the transformation?

First and foremost, the School of Principle's modes of discussing morality and politics were set within an overarching understanding of order whose origins are found in the concept of Heaven that forms the center of pre-Qin thought. Feng Youlan described the Chinese character *tian,* "Heaven," as covering five different areas:

(1) A material or physical *tian* or sky, that is, the *tian* often spoken of in opposition to earth, as in the common phrase which refers to the physical universe as "Heaven and Earth."
(2) A ruling or presiding *tian,* that is, one such as is meant in the phrase "Imperial Heaven Supreme Emperor" (*Huang tian shang di*), in which anthropomorphic *tian* and *di* are signified.
(3) A fatalistic *tian,* equivalent to the concept of Fate (*ming*), a term applied to all those events in human life over which man himself has no control. This is the *tian* Mencius refers to when he says: "As to the accomplishment of a great deed, that is with *tian*" (*Mencius,* Ib, 14).
(4) A naturalistic *tian,* that is, one equivalent to the English word "Nature." This is the sort of *tian* described in the "On Heaven" chapter in the *Xunzi* (chapter 17).
(5) An ethical *tian,* that is, one having a moral principle and which is the highest primordial principle of the universe. This is the sort of *tian* which the Doctrine of the Mean (*Zhong yong*) refers to in its opening sentence when it says: "What *tian* confers (on man) is called his nature."[19]

This outline is in large part correct, but the distinctions of the five layers of meaning are too close to the modern understanding. For example, it is not accurate to describe the Heaven within the dual categories of Heaven and Earth as "material heaven." In the "Treatise on Astronomy" (*Tiangong shu*) chapter of the *Records of the Grand Historian* (*Shiji*), it is stated that,

> Since the first beginnings of the people, what generation of rulers has not recorded the days and months and the stars and constellations? When we come to the five legendary masters and the Three Dynasties of Antiquity, we see that they grew ever more enlightened on these matters. Those on the inside wore cap and belt, while those outside were the Yi and Di barbarians. The central states (*zhong guo*) were divided into twelve provinces. Looking up, they observed the Signs in Heaven looking down, they modeled those categories on Earth. Heaven has sun and moon, thus Earth has yin and yang. Heaven has five planets, thus Earth has five phases. As Heaven has the arrays of constellations, so Earth has its provinces and regions. The three illuminations are the essence of yin and yang; *qi* is rooted in Earth. So the Sage combines them and puts them in order.[20]

The *Zuo Commentary to the Spring and Autumn Annals* (*Zuozhuan*), at Duke Zhao year twenty-four, says further: "*Li* (propriety), the superior and inferior record, is the weft and warp of Heaven and Earth," and, "Zichan said, 'Now as for *li* (propriety), it is the warp of Heaven, the righteousness of Earth, and the conduct of the people. Heaven and Earth have their ways and the people in turn model their principles on these.'"[21] The symmetrical relation of Heaven with Earth not only is a relation with such material phenomena as the patterns of Heaven and principles of Earth, but moreover also bears mutual interrelation with the Five Emperors of Antiquity and the ritual system of the Three Dynasties of Antiquity, which is quite different from the modern concept of "material substance" or "materiality" (*wuzhi*). The movements of yin-yang and the five phases are also the movements of ritual propriety (*li*), which in turn are the movements of Nature (*ziran*). Thus, in this universe, there are no distinctions between the Heaven of Nature or the Heaven of values, or Natural things and things with value. In fact, pre-Qin discourse has no pure concept of Nature (*ziran*). Nature is simply the original state of the world, and in this category, it is hard to understand any such things as "things with value." Among the five meanings of Heaven given above, the School of Principle's idea of order observed mainly the ruling or presiding sense collected in texts like the *Book of Odes* (*Shi*), the *Book of Documents* (*Shu*), the *Zuo Commentary on the Spring and Autumn Annals* (*Zuozhuan*), the *Discourses of the States* (*Guoyu*), and the *Analects* (*Lunyu*), especially those involved in Han-dynasty theories of Heaven and human, as well as the conception of Heaven as a deity with human traits (this current links up with the network of arguments regarding Heaven-human relations among the later Tang figures Han Yu, Liu Zongyuan, and Liu Yuxi). And this order making internal restrictions on the meaning of Heaven (but not external restrictions) was the highest internal source for morality.

By unifying Heaven and Principle, the School of Principle created a cohesive system of order that put at its center the categories of Principle, *qi*, Mind, and Nature. According to this new view of order, on the one hand, the Way of Heaven and Heavenly Principle formed the original body of the universe, the norms of the myriad things, and the origin of morality. On the other hand, both were also internal to phenomena, and even our own bodies. Thus the central responsibility of the School of Principle was to show Heavenly Principle in our daily lives, along with what methods could bring Heaven into unity with Principle. Because Heaven represents an internal order, "Principle" becomes a category of the utmost importance to manifest this internal order. Because Heaven is internal to our bodies, following Heaven's commands is directly related to adhering to our internal natural demands. Because Heaven was an internal nature, what was needed were methods to approach this internal nature. Because the order Heaven manifests is internal and of original substance, not external or phenomenal, there thus exists a very close relation between Heaven and the order of reality (the world of *qi* and of phenomena), so much so that people can always resort to Heaven to express resistance, criticism, or affirmation of the order of reality.

For these reasons, this entire body of thought has no ultimate reality beyond that of Heavenly Principle. It is a system of thought in which Heaven, the Way, Mind, and Nature are all seen as aspects of Principle. Taking as their premise the establishment of the Heavenly Principle worldview, Confucians placed internal to this view of order their critical methods for morality, knowledge, politics, and other social issues of all kinds: rites and music, institutions, historical achievements, and the words of the Former Kings were all important, but only insofar as they manifested the universal and yet internal Principle or Heavenly Principle; the moment rites and music, institutions, historical achievements, or knowledge depart from Principle, they fade, one and all, into unsubstantial forms or valueless facts. In this respect, it is not rites and music, institutions, historical achievements, nor the words of the Former Kings that serve as the source and final standard for moral evaluation, but rather Principle or Heavenly Principle. Thus rites and music, institutions, historical achievements, and the words of the Former Kings, along with the evaluation and interpretation of moral status, must be placed within the framework of Heavenly Principle. What the School of Principle supplied was a perspective connected to the order of the universe and the world, a basic framework for understanding the universe and the world of human life, a method of moral-political evaluation based on internal order: that is to say, a worldview that understands the world from Heavenly Principle as a basic or ontological category.

Unlike the Way of Heaven theory that emphasizes description of the movements of the universe, the Heavenly Principle worldview seeks to reveal the universe (including the human self) by internal principles, and so quits itself of the method of using natural processes to reveal the Will of Heaven (*tianyi*). Because of the special nature of the internalization of "Principle," its descriptive power is produced in a dualist framework: Principle and *qi;* Principle and things (*wu*); Nature that is anterior to Heaven and material nature; moral knowledge and knowledge via perception, and so forth. If Principle, Nature, and Mind are complementary categories, then *qi,* Things (*wu*), and Substance (*qizhi*) are actualizing categories, and the universe is formed from these two layers. Principle is manifest in the myriad things, but remains invariant with respect to the myriad things' superiority or inferiority, or good or evil. Thus a tense relation forms between Principle and reality (the world of *qi*): Principle is in the myriad things, and the myriad things take Principle as the original substance and purpose. The School of Principle took as its major task to discover and interpret what it was that separates Principle from *qi,* and then to proceed to achieve its ultimate frontier of unity of Heaven and human, unity of Principle and ritual propriety, and unity of governance and the Way. To elucidate the dualism of Principle and *qi,* Cheng Yi and Zhu Xi drew on controversies long present within Confucianism, and all of the theories generated among later generations of Confucians, from

Mind-based monism, to *qi*-based monism, to new theories of ritual propriety, can all be seen as efforts to conquer the difficulties for theorizing morality and politics brought by the dualism of Principle and *qi*.

Next, when we observe the Heavenly Principle worldview in the context of a transforming Confucian moral evaluation, we discover a marked difference between the School of Principle and the earlier Ru learning of Confucius: the Ru learning of Confucius took ritual, "the rites and music" (*liyue*), as its core, placing both shamans and the kingly Way within the category of rites and music, and thus understood rites and music as the "root" of Heaven, and of moral-political judgment. But the Song and Ming School of Principle takes Heavenly Principle, Mind, and Nature as its core, reconstructing the old system of rites and music according to "Principle"; that is to say, by understanding Principle as Heaven. To the School of Principle, moral evaluations are produced within an order that is universal and yet internal. This order is called "internal" because it cannot be equated to the existing rituals, institutions, or laws, but rather emerges only in subjective cognition and embodied awareness, as well as in unity with Principle. It is called "universal" because it is by no means external to the processes themselves of ritual, institutions, and daily life; it must go through study of the classics, practice of ritual, and management of daily affairs and so obtain "true" knowledge of ritual, institutions, customs, and events. In this framework, a tension or difference forms between moral evaluation and regulatory evaluation, which is that regulatory and ritual practices cannot, in and of themselves, guarantee moral perfection. But it is not a suspicion or refutation of regulatory and ritual practices so much as a reconstruction of the sageness of regulatory and ritual practice—to newly connect ritual, institutions, and daily practice to Heaven through the category of Principle. Zhang Zai wrote, "The imperial court has always taken the learning of the Way (*daoxue*) and political techniques as two [distinct] matters, which has really been troublesome since ancient times."[22] He speaks here of the major concern of the School of the Way scholar, which is the split between politics and the learning of the Way. The immense effort devoted to the Way of Heaven and Heavenly Principle was to reconstruct a new pattern by which government could be united with the Way. What opened up these differences between the Song and Ming School of Principle and the Confucian schools of pre-Qin Ru learning and Han and

Tang classical studies were the differences between these methods of moral evaluation.

In this respect, the School of Principle engages in discussions of rites and music, of institutions, and of morality using "philosophical" or "metaphysical" methods. This judgment is premised on the following two judgments: First, in the discursive field of Confucianism, the School of Principle, studies of the classics (*jingxue*), conventional Confucianism (*shixue*), and historical studies each have their ideological stance, but they all in the end still answer a basic Confucian question: how can we reestablish moral standards in the midst of historical change? (The propositions that "the School of Principle is no more than classical studies" or "the Six Classics are all history" make these assumptions: the first proposition believes that only through the methods of classical studies can School of Principle questions be answered. The second proposition holds that historical studies is the only path back to the way of the Former Kings. But in the end, they both must answer the basic question of what is morality or what is legitimate.) Second, differences in Confucian epistemological stances reflect differences in the origins, measures, and norms of moral evaluation. For example, which should we follow, after all, as the highest source of moral evaluation: the Principle of Heaven, or the political institutions of the Former Kings? The Way of the Cosmos, or the words of the Sages? Internal Nature (*ziran*), or utilitarian relationships? If we speak of Confucius as having reconstructed the Way of Heaven and rites and music as a coherent moral evaluation system patterned after the Former Kings, in the context of the collapse of the ritual system (the parting of the Way from political techniques), then the School of Principle, on the basis of Heavenly Principle, tried to "investigate" the correct principles of morality, ancient and modern, and to reconstruct a moral evaluation system. In this respect, arguments about morality must be premised on theories of rites and music, of institutions, or of the Way of Heaven.

Third, intimately related to these transformations of moral evaluation methods, the School of Principle turns the central issue away from rites / music and institutions and toward methods to attain knowledge. If a dependable foundation of morality could be found in knowledge, embodied awareness, and practice of the highest order or the highest substance, and this highest order or substance existed in the world of *qi*, then the School of Principle and the program it supplies for knowledge, experience, and practice form the most appropriate theory of morality. For this reason, even though School of Principle thinkers attended to institutions and rites and music as much as Confucius, as well as other specific normative questions, problems of cognition and understanding took up the central position for debate in the School of Principle. Diverse inquiries on the issues regarding "investigating things and extending knowledge" (*gewu zhi zhi*) and "investigating things to fully explain Principle" (*gewu qiongli*) became key points of divergence within the School of Principle (including the School of Mind). In his genealogy of Song and Ming Confucianism, Mou Zongsan looked past the customary boundaries between the School of Principle and the School of Mind, taking up the difference in methods for attaining knowledge as the basis for placing the latter in the category of School of Principle.[23]

This shows that the fragmentation of Ming-dynasty Confucianism from Song-dynasty Confucianism developed along an axis of how to argue for, arrive at, and practice the universal original nature or order. The differences between the categories of Nature-body (*xingti*), Mind-body (*xinti*), and Principle are produced by different ways of understanding universal order. With the establishment of the School of the Way's cosmology and the concept of Heavenly Principle, any rationalizing exposition had to be premised upon the Heavenly Way and Heavenly Principle, which meant that explaining Heavenly Way, Heavenly Principle, and the order behind these terms at once became prerequisite to expositions on morality, politics, economics, and society. In this respect, from the Northern Song onward, the basic questions, epistemological categories, internal differences, and ideological stances of Confucianism must all be understood in relation with the School of the Way and the School of Principle. When, in recent times, the Western scientific view of the universe, with its methods and epistemological categories, entered China, the resistance it faced came first and foremost from the School of Principle worldview.

The method by which Heavenly Principle governs both universal order and the origins of morality begins from the Cheng brothers and culminates with Zhu Xi. But the placement of theories of Nature and Mind and morality into the framework of cosmology and ontology is, however, the universal pursuit of all the School of the Way Confucians. In Cheng Yi's age, the concept of Heavenly Principle was just one of many competing views of Nature (*xing*), but from this time on, the concept of Heavenly Principle gradually replaced the concept of the Way of Heaven and took up the core portion of the School of Principle's moral evaluation methods. The most perfect moral substance and moral order manifested by Heavenly Principle gradually was understood to be the primary cause for all events. It is worth pointing out that the appearance of causation as an issue in moral evaluation marks the disjunction between the processes of moral judgment and ritual, thereby also marking the larger transformation in Confucian moral evaluation methods. The key significance of building moral judgment systems with the Heavenly Principle concept at their core lies in the following: As with traditional Confucianism, the School of Principle believes that each kind of thing or event can only form the state it ought to be in, which is to say its moral state, when it aligns with the order of Heaven. But what the School of Principle emphasizes is that this order exists in the midst of the phenomenal world, but is not equal to the phenomenal world. Thus the basic method to realize this moral substance or moral order is to fully develop our capacity for cognition or embodied awareness, to present and to confirm this order and substance and self-nature internal to world and self and yet not equivalent to world and self, and thereby to achieve unity of the world and self. Song Confucianism's continued concern about the split between the School of the Way and politics originated in this fundamental judgment: politics itself had turned its back on the values explored in the School of the Way. Therefore, the unification of the School of the Way and politics required an aspect of internal realization. The practice of ritual had long turned its back on the central value within the School of the Way, which meant that moral practice also needed an aspect of internal realization. "Internal" here refers not to the meaning of internal and external relations between people and things, but rather to the universal internal, the internal potentiality within all people and things, which requires a process of self-realization (meaning to sublate, or abandon, the external nature of the self). In this respect, moral states are those states in which an internal effort is made to throw off limitations of the self. Instead of moral practice following external norms, it was following internal Nature (*ziran*), and this Nature was the order or original substance of the universe itself.

In sum, the School of Principle tries to establish a connection between universal order and ritual order based on original substance (and neither direct, nor oppositional). The Heavenly Principle concept results, within ethical philosophy, in a reconstruction of relations between cosmology and moral argumentation. This pursuit of unity of methods of moral argumentation is premised on a certain distancing and tension between moral argumentation and the system of regulations and institutions (each in its place). Acting as a universal and internal but not necessarily actual (or apparent) category, Heavenly Principle must go through a process of cognition, embodied awareness, and practice before it can be made to show itself. Thus the relation between moral actualization and subject must be made apparent by means of the view that "Principle lies within affairs" (*li zai shi zhong*). Principle is something that awaits realization and exists in the process of practice. This new method of moral argumentation is established on the basic premise that institutions have already been divided away from the ritual world of the Sage-Kings, and so the norms of institutions cannot manifest the Will of Heaven. The Will of Heaven is the foundation for moral practice. If institutions and their norms cannot manifest the Will of Heaven, then the Will of Heaven must be the basis for critiquing institutions. This idea about the separation between institutions and rites and music is important for understanding differences between the methods of moral argumentation of Northern Song School of the Way thinkers and the Pre-Qin and Han and Tang Confucians. For this reason, we can observe a dual phenomenon from the expositions of the School of Principle: On the one hand, thinkers of the School of Principle never ceased to investigate the relations of ritual order, but on the other hand, they also believed that the embodied awareness of the Way of Heaven could not be simply equal to regulatory practice.

Allow me to summarize the several points made above. The establishment of the Heavenly Principle worldview marks a transformation in Confucian methods for moral-political evaluation: according to this moral evaluation method, morality and government must align with natural, spontaneous propensity (*ziran zhi shi*), an order that arises of itself in the myriad things and in ourselves. Heaven or Heavenly Principle unifies natural propensity and internal basic nature within one category. Thus, a basic feature of Song learning is to take the universe, Nature (*ziran*), and human affairs as a system mixed into the world of Heavenly Principle. The Heavenly Principle worldview on the one hand refuses to use the existing institutions and order as the standard for evaluating morality and politics, while on the other hand it also refuses use of the method of Heaven and human in corresponding categories to understand the relation between Heaven's order and the order of Human affairs as a direct, oppositional relation. Thus the Heaven which was seen in the Han-dynasty cosmology as the highest spirit (*shen*) is transformed into an original substance immanent in ourselves and the world, awaiting self-actualization. What, then, is the relation between this method of moral evaluation and the social and political changes we mentioned at the opening of this chapter? To answer this question, we must undertake a comparative analysis of the normative features of the School of Principle, pre-Qin Confucianism, and Han-dynasty thought, so that we may deepen our understanding of the School of Principle's method of moral evaluation.

II. The Communal State of Ritual and Methods of Moral Evaluation

1. Understanding Ritual Propriety as Humaneness and the Issue of "Rationalization"

Much as the moral system of the School of Principle has been interpreted as "rationalization" (*lixing hua*), so another tradition of modern Confucian studies subsumes both the Duke of Zhou's formalization of ritual and Confucius's own dictum to "transmit and not create" (*shu er bu zuo*) within a process of rationalization of the shamanic tradition.[24] Fu Sinian writes, "The moral views of Confucianism are purely the rational development of a society that worshipped ancestors."[25] What he calls a "rational development" refers to the transformation of Zhou "virtue" (*de*) from the primitive rituals of shamans into the conduct, rituals, and regulations of the ruler. In this respect, "Confucius's theory of interstate politics [that is, political thought regarding relations between kingdoms of feudal lords—author's note], is no more than the Way of hegemons, utterly different from what Mencius called the Kingly Way. Its ideal figures were Duke Xuan of Qi, and Guan Zhong. . . . Confucius's theory of domestic politics was naturally an ideology intended "to strengthen states and community altars, and families and households."[26] Fu Sinian evades entirely the relation of Heaven and human contained within the royal regulations, and draws a veritable equals sign between Confucius's thought and the institutions of the Zhou dynasty. This narrative was established on the understanding that Confucius "transmitted, and did not create": Confucius's theory objectively recorded the basic contents of the Zhou institutions, namely the hegemon's Way of interstate politics and the autocratic Way of domestic government, both of which are products of the rationalization of relations under primitive patriarchy (*zongfa*). Here, the passage from shamanic ritual to royal regulations has been taken as categorically as the passage, in European history, from religious rule to secular rule (rule by kings of states), with Confucius's theory of ritual "traced from the royal regulations" naturally defined as symbolic of the "secularization" and "rationalization" of Chinese culture. In contrast to Fu Sinian, Li Zehou sees it not as an ideology of kingly power "to strengthen states and community altars, and families and households," but rather as "internal desires and self-determined consciousness that now took as an imprimatur 'the humane' (*ren*) where before it had been the 'divine' (*shen*)," which is to say a tendency away from the "patriarchal and the mysterious" and toward the individual (of "self," and "desires within the mind") and toward the secular (affirming the desiring "person").[27] But these two different historical narratives may both be subsumed within the category of "rationalization."

From the formation of the Zhou-dynasty and Confucian tradition to the establishment of the Song-dynasty School of Principle, "rationalization" becomes an ever-present historical perspective. Its basic premise is that Chinese thought or culture is "nonreligious," and that Confucian moral judgment from the beginning attended to humans and the world they live in. Confucius is believed to be the first person to turn Chinese thought away from Nature, the divine, and sages, and instead toward humanity itself, with proof of this in his famous concept of "humaneness" (*ren*). But what were the assumptions on which this distinction of human from Nature, of human from things divine and sagely, was constructed? The emphasis of Confucian learning on the daily life of humanity is a clear fact, but just as discussed above, the key here is how to determine how the relations were defined between terms such as "daily life" or "daily norms of the human situation," and the "person" with their "internally self-determining consciousness of desires." In Confucian discourse, there is close connection between the "daily norms of the human situation" and the "ritual propriety" (*li*) affirmed so many times by Confucius. Ritual propriety develops from primitive rites and sacrifices for military campaigns, and its ideas about the human condition and the natural world did not stand in opposition to other notions of deities and divine spirits:

> Confucius said, "Now regarding the rites, the former kings by these inherited the Way of Heaven, and so govern the conditions of humanity. And so to lose them is death, and to keep them is life. . . . So it is that ritual propriety is rooted in Heaven, intermixed with Earth, and finds precedent among divine spirits. It extends to funeral practices, sacrifices, archery, chariot-driving, capping ceremonies, weddings, court audiences, and diplomatic missions. So it was that the sages observed ritual propriety, and so it is that state and family under Heaven are rectified in obtaining it.[28]

In this respect, daily life comprises ritual practices within daily life, including funeral practices, sacrifices, archery, chariot-driving, capping ceremonies, weddings, court audiences, and diplomatic missions, which are ritual life per se. The concept of "humanity" is similar.

According to the Confucian account of the Three Dynasties of Antiquity, and especially of the feudalism of the Zhou dynasty, early Confucian moral evaluation methods can be subsumed within a cohesive and continuous system, within which Nature, institutions, rites and music, morality, and even to a certain extent laws and norms all become difficult to distinguish clearly. As moral presences, the concept of humanity and the concept of ritual are consistent, because away from the category of ritual, there is no basis for human existence. As it says in the "Meaning of the Capping Ceremony" (*Guan yi*) chapter of the *Book of Rites* (*Li ji*):

> Generally, what makes humanity human is ritual meaning. Ritual meaning begins in correcting bodily appearance, getting in order the countenance, and making fluent the sounds of speech. Only with correct bodily appearance, orderly countenance, and fluent speech is ritual meaning prepared. Only when ruler and subject are of correct relation, father and son are aligned as kin, and elders and youth are in harmony is ritual meaning

> established. So it is that only with the capping ceremony is the costume prepared, and only with costume prepared is the bodily appearance corrected, and the countenance put in order, and the sounds of speech made fluent. So it is said that, "The capping ceremony is the beginning of ritual propriety." This was why the ancients and sage kings placed so much weight on the capping ceremony.[29]

And we also have:

> Treating him as a grown man, they would charge him with the ritual responsibilities thereof. And the charging of the ritual responsibilities of the grown man would be to charge him with the ritual practices of son, younger brother, subject, and junior. Charging these four ritual responsibilities to be practiced among humanity, is it not the case that ritual propriety is a weighty matter?[30]

The mark of adulthood was establishment within the ritual order. Commentator Lü Dalin adds here, "The term 'grown man' (*cheng ren*) here does not refer to one whose limbs have changed from those of a child, but to one whose knowledge of the human relationships is sufficient. Taking kin as kin, nobles as nobles, elders as elders, and not forgetting the order of things, is what we mean by 'sufficient.'"[31] Mou Zongsan believed that the rituals of adulthood as described in the *Book of Rites* were merely formal rules, or what Xunzi called the "utmost regulations of the kings." But it is rather only when "the superior man (*junzi*) self-consciously practices human relations to complete his virtue," that he knows what is termed "utmost ethical relations of the sages."[32] But as above, it is difficult to distinguish the utmost ritual propriety of kings and the utmost ethical relations of the sages. They are both practices with bases in divisions of position or ritual regulations. The proposition "He is a superior man" not only contains the evaluative judgment "He should act like this," but also contains the sense that he is self-consciously practicing the moral principles of the superior man.

The continued connection between pre-Qin Confucian moral judgment and the context of specific regulations (regulations or relations) formed the internal structure of moral exposition. In this respect, whether it be the category of humanity itself, or "human internal desires and self-determining consciousness," is determined from a specific relation to ritual, from which between "human internal desires" and "'divines' granting divine commands" there exist no such opposed positions as secular and religious, nor any "rationalization" process produced by such an opposition. Within the categories of Confucian thought, the "rationalization" narrative that proceeds from divine to human in the sense of the European Enlightenment in fact possesses no true explanatory power, and the category of "rationalization" is better seen as the self-verification of modern thought. The approach that placed the Zhou regulations and Confucius's elicitation of Confucian learning within the framework of rationalization was the product of the combination of the major conclusions of Qing-dynasty classical studies with the narrative of rationalization found in Western social theory.

In the course of criticizing Song scholarship, Qing Confucianism gradually formed a view different from that of Mencius, namely that Confucianism originated in the Zhou-dynasty rituals themselves. King Wen and the Duke of Zhou held the pride of place as exemplars, while Confucius was merely a "compiler." The key thing here was how to understand the relation between the formation of the Zhou-dynasty institutions and the propositions that Confucius "transmitted and did not create" and "understood ritual propriety as humaneness." Confucius recorded and summarized an outline of Zhou-dynasty rituals and institutions, using the method of "transmitting the kingly relations" to rebuild the rituals to completeness, and further through the fuller application of the categories of the Way (*dao*) and virtue (*de*), sincerity (*cheng*) and reverence (*jing*), humaneness (*ren*) and ritual propriety (*li*), the superior man (*junzi*) and the inferior man (*xiaoren*) to reestablish and reconnect the relation of Heaven and human, interpreting the significance of rituals and institutions in innovative ways. These innovations supplied dynamism and flexibility to later generations of Confucian learning. And yet we cannot simply put an equals sign between King Wen of the Zhou, the royal regulations (as sublation or rationalization of shamanic tradition), and the process whereby Confucius seeks the submission of the subject to the course of practice of the royal regulations and King Wen of the Zhou (referring in the main here to the quality endowed to the gradually forming terms "rites and music," "royal regulations," and "Heaven"), thus taking two things as subsumed along one path into the category of "rationalization." The learning of Confucius was a critique of the aforementioned rationalization, which was caused by the formalization and hollowing out of the rites and music and destruction of norms; this critique included concerns that the development of the royal regulations was leading to a cutting off of the connection between Heaven and human. Over the course of the decline of the Zhou institutions, Confucius tried to elucidate the norms of the Zhou institutions, along with their sacred internal source. He tried, by keeping "humaneness" as the center, to elucidate the moral qualities and convictions that could restore the connection between Heaven and human: virtue, sincerity, reverence, humaneness, righteousness. In the moral world of Confucius, only with these moral virtues, feelings, and convictions could rites and music truly become ritual propriety.

For these reasons, the two propositions "The rites and music are Heaven" and "Understand ritual propriety as humaneness" both express Confucius's effort to recover, on the basis of the Zhou ritual, regulations of the basic value of unity of Heaven and human and the basic state of affairs and emotive states (*qing*) interconnected with Principle (*li*) during the age when there was communication between Heaven and human. Both propositions illustrate the connection between ritual regulations and shamanic culture. Within the category of Zhou ritual regulations, the Heaven-human connection did not require the wild trance of the early shamans in their practices; what was now appealed to was the Heaven-human connection within daily ritual practice. This also formed the basic difference between Confucius's theory of ritual propriety learning and early shamanic ritual. However, there was no decisive break of Western Zhou ritual regulations from shamanic rituals, and the relation between Confucian learning and the essence of shamanic ritual is by no means this simple. Zhou-dynasty royal regulations used patriarchy, royal regulations, and ritual forms as the path connecting Heaven and human; however, from the myth of the prehistoric king who "cut off Heaven's connection to Earth" recorded in the "Marquis of Lü on Punishments" (*Lü xing*) chapter of the *Documents of Zhou* (*Zhou shu*), as well as the interpretation by Guan Shefu of this myth recorded in the "Discourses of Chu" (*Chu yu*) chapter of the *Discourses of the States,* we see that, during the age of the superior kings, the human connection to Heaven was hardly unobstructed. In early societies "the people and the gods had separate enterprises, respected each other without getting involved, so that the gods would come down and give them good life, the people used things for sacrifices, disasters never came, and all was sufficient and not hidden away." Shamans used their power to make the divine descend to connect human and Heaven; but after this "the people and gods struggled, things were not produced sufficiently, and so the people made sacrifices, the masters of which were the shamans."[33] The legendary emperor Zhuan Xu "then ordered Zhong to be 'Corrector of the South,' in command of Heaven and so responsible for the divinities, while Li was to be 'Corrector of the Fire,' in command of Earth and so responsible for the people. This was the cutting off of the connection between Heaven and Earth." In interpreting this passage, Xu Xusheng, Yang Xiangkui, and Zhang Guangzhi all emphasize that early shamans were professionals in causing the gods to descend to Earth, to provide service to the people; and in later generations, the gateway of Heaven and Earth was held in the hands of Zhong and Li, sent by the superior ruler, so that Heaven and Earth were gradually no longer connected. This "disconnect" mainly applied to the people, because the emperor monopolized the position of the shaman, and so still had special access from Earth to Heaven.[34]

In this sense, even as the royal regulations could connect Heaven with human, they also held the potential to obstruct communication between Heaven and human. In the age when Confucius lived, the ritual regulations of the Zhou dynasty were facing this crisis. The rupture of Heaven-human connection in ritual regulations can be seen in the formalization and hollowing out of rituals, making rituals that once contained the Will of Heaven (*tianyi*) into meaningless rules and regulations. If people only considered ritual to be no more than the jade and silk ritual implements, or the bells and drums used for ritual music, then the ritual system would no longer be what it once was. Confucius for this reason lamented, "'Ritual propriety,' they say. 'Ritual propriety,' they say! Is it no more than jades and silk? 'Music,' they say. 'Music,' they say. Is it no more than bells and drums?"[35] When rites and music lose their meaning, there remains little to distinguish the authentic from the fake. It is just this situation that Book 3 of the *Analects* laments, both that "the rituals are not observed in full," and, further down, that "serving the ruler with full observance of ritual is taken by the people as flattery."[36] "Confucius said with a sigh, 'If a human be inhumane, what then of ritual propriety? If a human be inhumane, what then of music?'"[37] It was setting out from precisely this state of separation of rites and music (institutions formed naturally by human conduct according to ritual propriety with moral content) from institutions (externalized ritual forms not possessing substantial content) that Confucius came to suggest that "humaneness" should signify "ritual propriety." The result is that the concept of "humaneness" tries to manage the problem of authenticity in the conditions of ritual propriety being hollowed out and formalized. If authentic ritual propriety was able to manifest the will of Heaven, then the core of "understanding ritual propriety as humaneness" was to use humans to connect Heaven to human and so recover the sacredness of ritual propriety. Here, rites and music and institutions are referred to separately, with "rites and music" meaning the ritual relations that could manifest Heaven's will or possess moral significance, while "institutions" refers to the rules and structures that had lost their internal connection with Heaven. Rites and music as conceived by Confucius and Mencius were not separated into ritual propriety and institutions, but the result of the collapse of rituals was the separation of ritual from institutions: rites and music would no longer be ritual propriety, and institutions would no longer possess any moral significance.

The problem of the authenticity of rites and music is an important idea underlying Confucius's moral-political theory. Does not the above citation distinguish between authentic ritual and formal ritual?[38] The maxim "Transmit and do not create" emphasizes the rigor of institutions themselves. It was a reaction made in response to the decline of ritual. The recommendation to "understand ritual propriety as humaneness" attends to the authenticity of the course of ritual; it attends on the course of ritual practice and its internal state in itself. These two recommendations are ultimately implemented within what Confucius expects from the superior man: apprehension that enables respect for Heaven and its Mandate, acceptance of great responsibility down from Heaven into his person, the restoration of ancient forms that would preserve the rituals of the Former Kings, and the masterful spirit to achieve ritual propriety, bringing it into the present by enlarging upon the ancient. In the course of "conduct and service," he recovers the unity of rites and music and institutions, and through subjective practice and moral quality he endows the ritual forms that daily decline and are formalized with rich, substantial meaning. From the perspective of recovering ritual regulations, this process touches on specific political views and regulatory practice. From the angle of completed virtue, this regulatory practice is also a course of moral conduct. In this respect, the unification of rites and music and institutions does not refer to combining formalized rites and music with rationalized institutions, but rather refers to manifesting within the course of ritual and regulatory practice the state of unity between Heaven and human, unity between government and the Way, and embodiment of the Way in the ritual implements. Formalized ritual cannot be seen as authentic ritual, and formalized institutions also cannot be made into institutions with true significance as institutions of rites and music.

For these reasons, we cannot use "rationalization" to understand either Confucius's call to "transmit and do not create" or to "understand ritual propriety as humaneness." "Transmit and do not create" was said not in order to objectively realize the ritual system of the first kings, but rather in order to implement strict ritual norms for practice. "Understand ritual propriety as humaneness" did not replace rigor in rituals with immanence, but was an internal stimulus calling forth stricter adherence to ritual under the conditions in which ritual was disintegrating, or formalizing. As we said above, owing to the formalization of ritual propriety, Confucius was faced with two different kinds of ritual propriety, with the first being a perfect, ideal propriety, one that could manifest the Will of Heaven and connect Heaven with human, also known as the "authentic" propriety; the second was a ritual propriety in which form and substance had separated from each other, also known as the "fake" ritual propriety. With respect to the first, humaneness and ritual propriety were completely unified, and with respect to the second, humaneness and ritual propriety were disconnected. To "understand ritual propriety as humaneness" means to place one's hopes in the sincerity (*cheng*) and reverence (*jing*) of the subject and attempt to transform the spiritual attitude of dedicating oneself to Heaven (as seen in primitive shamanic activities' reverence and awe before Heaven and impulse to become one with Heaven) into the ritual practice of the "loving person" (*ai ren*), and thereby to reestablish a connection between Heaven and human and to rebuild the fullness and sacredness of rites and music. For these reasons, quite in contrast to so-called "rationalization" or "disenchantment," the important categories of Confucius's "humaneness theory"—such as "virtue" (*de*), "sincerity" (*cheng*), "reverence" (*jing*), and "faith" (*xin*)—all originate in the tradition of shaman-ruler sacrificial government of affairs. We can see Confucius's efforts as a form of "reenchantment." The rise of virtue came earliest, which will be elucidated below. Here, we examine the case of "reverence" (*jing*). The early Zhou decrees had many instances of the character *jing*, "reverence," as in the "Counsels of Gaoyao" (*Gao yao mo*) from the *Book of Documents* (*Shu*): "Heaven hears and sees as our people hear and see; Heaven brightly approves and displays its terrors as our people brightly approve and would awe—such connection is there between the upper and lower [worlds]. How reverent ought the masters of territories to be!"[39] In the "Summary of the Sacrifices" (*Ji tong*) chapter of the *Book of Rites,* we have: "Such sincerity and faith were what is called doing their utmost; and such doing of their utmost was what is called reverence. When they had reverently done their utmost, they could serve the spiritual Intelligences—such was the way of sacrificing."[40] The first example discusses the reverence of serving Heaven, of serving the people, and of the ruler, highlighting the connection of the royal regulations with Heaven. The second example discusses the Way of sacrifices, proving that the categories of sincerity, faith, reverence, and doing the utmost originate in sacrificial ritual and practice. Both prove that the concept of "reverence" (*jing*) is closely related to the emotions of fear, awe, and veneration within early shamanic practices. Confucius's "understanding of ritual propriety as humaneness" meant to use the cognition and practice of "humaneness" to recover the harmonious state of sacrificial rituals, which, although they did not refer back to mysterious experience, still actively showed reverence toward Heaven.

In this respect, we can say, first, that "human consciousness of self-determination" can be defined as the determination and faith to devote self to ritual practice, and so has no relation to the modern trend toward secularism; second, it is not "fragmenting, formalization, and rationalization," but resistance against these, a self-conscious seeking of the fearful reverence itself, that makes Confucius advocate for "humaneness" and "reverence."[41] The preservation of ritual is produced by the feeling of fearful reverence, which cannot be subsumed within the trend toward "rationalization," or else we could not explain how the Confucius who "transmitted and did not create" did not understand ritual propriety as ritual propriety, but as humaneness. Third, this feeling of fearful reverence does not present itself as the mad fervors of the shamanic process, but as the internal sacredness of the ritual process, which means we may subsume it under a trend toward "antirationalizing rationalization," thus to explain how this course of "antirationalization" depended on the "regulation of rites and music" (*zhi li zuo yue*) during the early Zhou (a rationalization process).

In terms of what has been described above, "Understand ritual propriety as humaneness" also cannot be taken to mean the transfer of external ritual to human immanence. Confucius explained this saying, "The day you subdue self and restore ritual propriety, All-under-Heaven will ascribe humaneness to you." "Humaneness" is a state achieved by "subduing self and restoring ritual propriety," and is also the ultimate motive pushing people to "subdue themselves and restore ritual propriety." When the sacredness of ritual is built anew, All-under-Heaven returns to humaneness and All-under-Heaven returns to ritual, meaning they are completely unified. What is referred to here as the sacredness of ritual does not refer to the sacredness of the external form of ritual, but rather the sacredness filled with ritual spirit when human practice is humane. There is no tension and opposition between the sacred and the quotidian. For this reason, the "theory of humaneness" (*ren xue*) is not a refutation of rites and music and institutions and their forms of moral evaluation, but rather is a second affirmation of the forms of moral evaluation of the ritual community. However, this reaffirmation especially highlights the internal spiritual condition of ritual practice. "Understand ritual propriety as humaneness" makes the category of ritual central: the rigor, austerity, and nobility of ritual are the necessary conditions of "humaneness," but "humaneness" also is the basic premise for the rigor, austerity, and nobility of ritual. The concepts of "humaneness" and the "self" in early modernity are quite remote from each other. Confucius did not speak about "novelty, or power, or chaos, or the gods," and rarely spoke of the Way of Heaven, believing that respect for Heaven could only appear with ritual regulations. This is premised on the close relation between Zhou ritual regulations and their basic values with shamans who revered Heaven and performed rituals to Earth; otherwise there would be no basis for ritual propriety to be Heaven.

According to the narrative in Book 10 of the *Analects,* Confucius was extremely knowledgeable on all the formal rituals. From food and drink, to housing, birth, death, marriage, and funerals, all have their norms and rules—even walking is regulated by ritual.[42] Was this fearful reverence toward great men, or the words of the sages, and preservation of rites a "rationalizing" sentiment, or was it a state of fearful reverence for Heaven and Earth?

Late-Qing (1899) studies of the oracle bone and tortoise shell inscriptions prove that the unity of ancestor worship and worship of the Shangdi deity (and Heaven) was a feature of the Shang and Zhou and even earlier ancient societies and their faith systems.[43] Shangdi helps humans with prosperous harvests and victory in war, but he also is by no means a deity over particular nations. The ancestors of the ruler were the symbols of the national collective, and they could speak to Shangdi. The ruler himself communicated with the ancestors through sacrificial activities, which meant he could gain knowledge of Shangdi's intentions through sacrifice. In the sacrificial activities and beliefs of the Shang and Zhou, the differences and distances between Shangdi, Heaven, and the ancestors were extremely limited.[44]

"These three categories of divine beings clearly existed simultaneously. For this reason, any argument that these divine beings evolved—that is to say, nature deities evolved into ancestor spirits, and then evolved once more into Shangdi—are difficult to substantiate."[45] Without this premise, we could hardly understand the statement in the "Meaning of the Sacrifices" (*Ji yi*) chapter of the *Book of Rites:* "When King Wen did sacrifices, he served the dead as if he were serving the living."[46] Nor the statement by Confucius that, "Not having served humans, how can you serve ghosts?"[47] These surely manifest the unified relation of Shangdi and the ancestors. Precisely owing to the unified relation of Shangdi and the ancestors was Confucius able to transform the feeling of apprehension toward Heaven into the internal spark toward reverence—ritual is the course of practice and the ceremonial form of both ancestor worship and Shangdi worship in one.

2. Zhou-Dynasty Ritual, Regulations, and Unity of Government and the Way

In this respect, to understand ritual propriety as humaneness is at once to express that moral practice is a systemic process. The expositions surrounding the commands to "transmit and not create" and "inherit the royal regulations from the ancestors" express the rigor of the ritual regulations, and the necessity of strict adherence to ritual. Portions of the *Analects* that directly record the royal regulations are limited, but Confucius took the Six Classics to be doctrine, a fact that can help people understand the regulatory significance of what Confucius referred to as "To transmit and not create." Regarding the authenticity and date of composition of the *Book of Rites* (*Li ji*), there are different opinions, but one thing is certain: the various rituals and regulations recorded within it can at least partially serve as a basis for understanding the regulatory or ritual nature of Confucius's learning. To advance the forthcoming argument, we should briefly summarize the all-encompassing "Way of the Zhou" (*Zhou dao*), especially its core regulations and institutions. At the core of the "Way of Zhou" were regulations for enfeoffments, the well-fields, and schools, passed down from the ancient age of the Sage-Kings, with additional developments, while the categories of ancestor worship, ruler rituals, hierarchy, and such values as final piety (*xiao*), awe (*ti*), loyalty (*zhong*), and faith (*xin*), along with ritual warfare, all had a basis in the system of patriarchal enfeoffment. Were we to leave behind the significance of ancestor worship and patriarchal enfeoffment, we would have no way to explain the various forms of ritual.

It is far from certain who first established the Zhou enfeoffments. Based on excavations of Longshan culture, archaeologists discovered that Taosi in Xiangfen County, Shanxi Province, and Chengzi, in Zhucheng County, Shandong Province are both distributed with groups of buried remains, and within each grouping there are large, medium, and small gravesites. Zhang Guangzhi deduced, "This grouping of gravesites clearly belonged to a kin-based clan, and within the group, differences in level represented different statuses of clan members." For this reason, "Not only was a patriarchal system in place by the Shang dynasty, it can even be deduced to have existed during the Longshan era."[48] The problem here is that the Zhou-era patriarchal system developed into a dynastic political structure, from which it developed into a system of enfeoffment, but the above archeological discovery cannot actually prove that the Shang era had already expanded the patriarchal system into a king-based system divided into enfeoffments. What is certain is that if Longshan culture already had a patriarchal system, then the view that shamanic culture is entirely distinct from ritual culture has hardly any footing at all.

The so-called patriarchal feudalism or patriarchal system of enfeoffments (*zongfa fengjian*) followed the principle that, "When a son other than [the eldest] became the ancestor [of a branch of the same line], his successor was its patriarch (*zong*), and he who followed him [in the line] was its smaller patriarch (*xiao zong*)." Through the investiture ceremony, the Zhou Son of

Heaven took land and people outside the kingly domain and enfeoffed them to the Zhou King's noneldest child who would not ascend to the throne, and so established the states of the feudal lords.[49] The noneldest son who accepted enfeoffment was also the ancestor of the feudal state, for he still passed down his aristocratic title to the eldest son of his principal wife.

The relation of the Zhou patriarch with the fiefdoms, namely that of the Son of Heaven with enfeoffed lords, was also the relation of an eldest son with other sons. Within the governments of each of the states, there were also patriarchal clans based on blood relations. The "Achievements of the Ru" (*Ru xiao*) chapter of the *Xunzi* says that the Duke of Zhou "put together All-under-Heaven, establishing seventy-one states, with Ji clansmen alone taking up fifty-three positions."[50] These were all the descendants of the ancestors of kings Wen and Wu, and the Dukes of Zhou. During the early Zhou, enfeoffments included some feudal lords of different surnames, the majority of whom were descendants of the small states also related to the Zhou house (as with descendants of Shennong, the Yellow Emperor, Yao, Shun, and Yu) or else relatives of the Zhou house. In the main, however, the principle held to enfeoffment of feudal lords of the same surname according to the patriarchal system. For this reason, the patriarchal principle preserved the basic order of the blood-based clan relations, even as it formed a universal principle for the Zhou dynasty. In the language of the Western Zhou, the "central states" (*zhong guo*) were a political-patriarchal community centered on a particular region and based on universal principles, comprising the Zhou king and the various fiefdoms of his male relatives.

The patriarchal system of enfeoffments was not only a political system, but also an economic and military one. In the *Zuo Commentary to the Spring and Autumn Annals* (*Zuo zhuan*), the entry for year 12 of Duke Xi records, "Thus the Duke of Zhou, grieved by the want of harmony during the past, enfeoffed and raised up his relatives, so that the new frontiers acted as buffer states for the Zhou."[51] This clearly shows that enfeoffment served to annex frontiers to screen the house of Zhou.[52] The specific content of enfeoffment was the conferring of peoples and frontier land, but "during the feudal age, the division and government of frontiers was never subject to systematic and unified institutions, and was also not consistent over the longer term."[53] Land distribution systems after enfeoffment also exhibit differences. For example, the house of Zhou awarded the lands of Shu and Yu to the remaining peoples of the Xia, "they who held to the nine names of the patriarchs," lands close to those of the Rong and the Han, with customs quite different from those of the "central states." The royal house demanded that "they be enlightened with the government of the Xia, with the frontier under the laws of the Rong," which amounted to using land systems different from the Zhou in frontier areas. But within the "central states," land systems and feudal systems were implemented simultaneously. The Zhou overseers demanded that the rulers of Lu and Wei treat the survivors of the Shang by the policy of "enlightening all by means of the Shang government, but on the frontiers applying the laws of the Zhou."[54] This supplied the basis for later Confucians to transform the category of the "central states" into a ritual category (which is to say, ritual or cultural transformation could bring other nations and tribes into the category of "central states").[55] As for the theory of the well-field, the major sources are the *Mencius* and the *Zhou Officials (Zhou guan,* another name for the *Rites of Zhou*), as well as supplemental information found in such Han-dynasty documents as the "The Royal Regulations" (*Wang zhi*), the *Gongyang Commentary to the Spring and Autumn Annals* (*Gongyang zhuan*), the *Guliang Commentary to the Spring and Autumn Annals* (*Guliang zhuan*), *Han Ying's Commentary on the Book of Odes* (*Han shi wai zhuan*), and the *Mao Commentary on the Book of Odes* (*Mao shi zhuan*). According to the exposition on the well-field in Book 3a of the *Mencius,* we can affirm, in the main, that the well-field was a specific economic and military apparatus of the enfeoffment system.

First, the well-field system was a product of the enfeoffments, and also an economic institution that supported the enfeoffments. Second, the well-field system laid out methods for production and labor and the form of taxation, leading also to the regulation of basic social organizations. Third, the well-fields were also a military system, with soldier and farmer as one. Dividing enfeoffments and setting up well-fields served both expansionary and border-protecting functions, stabilizing the military situation of the frontiers between "the central states" and the Yi and Di barbarians. In this respect, the well-field was a system that combined economy, military, and government into one. All aspects of the system bore intimate relation to the patriarchal partitioning of enfeoffments, from the structure of how fields were divided by ditches into public and private, to the one-in-ten taxation system and the ranks of the official positions to manage land, to using the well-fields as bases to form troop deployments and public works projects. Since the principles of the patriarchal system for partitioning enfeoffments extended into the political and economic spheres, we may understand the entire political body as having expanded along the lines of the kinship principle. For example, in acting as a military system for the Zhou court to control its frontiers, the well-field system followed the principle of patriarchal partition of enfeoffments and the old standards of ritual propriety regarding inner and outer, Yi (barbarian) and Xia (Chinese). We can place the well-field institution within the moral genealogy of the community.

As one of the institutions of the Three Dynasties of Antiquity repeatedly discussed by later Confucians, schools were the bonds tying together the transmission of the rites. As the *Book of Rites* puts it, in the "Different Teachings of the Different Kings" (*Jing jie*) chapter:

> Confucius said, "When you enter any state you can know its teachings. If they show themselves men who are mild and gentle, sincere and good, they have been taught from the *Book of Odes.* If they have a wide comprehension, and know what is remote and old, they have been taught from the *Book of Documents.* If they be large-hearted and generous, plain and honest, they have been taught from the *Book of Music.* If they be pure and still, refined and subtle, they have been taught from the *Book of Changes.* If they be courteous and modest, grave and respectful, they have been taught from the *Book of Rites and Ceremonies.* If they suitably adapt their language to the things of which they speak, they have been taught from the *Spring and Autumn Annals.* Hence the failing that may arise in connection with the study of the *Odes* is a stupid simplicity; that in connection with the *History* is duplicity; that in connection with *Music* is extravagance; that in connection with the *Changes* is corruption; that in connection with the practice of *Rites and Ceremonies* is fussiness; and that in connection with the *Spring and Autumn Annals* is insubordination."[56]

If we enter a state we and thereby learn about its teachings, then the institutions of rites and music are premised materially on the "state" (as the conditions of institutions): "The ancient kings established states and ruled over the people, making teaching their top priority."[57] Ancient education was a suite of regulations and rituals in combination, which is to say it was an organic part of the royal regulations. Ancient schools were divided into elementary and secondary, manifesting a protocol that went from teaching the person to transmitting the Way to professing knowledge.[58] "In the teaching of the ancients, households had *shu* (private schools), *dang* had *xiang* (government-run local schools), *shu* had *xu*, and the states had *xue* (colleges)." According to the commentary of Kong Yingda on Zheng Xuan we can learn that according to the rites of Zhou, within every hundred *li*, twenty-five families comprised a *lü*, sharing one neighborhood lane, with a gate at the head of the lane, and a private school by each gate. When the people were at home, they came and went, morning and night, and would be taught in the schoolyards. Hence it was that "households had private schools." Five hundred families comprised a *dang*, and within each *dang* was established a school of one order higher than that in the *lü*, and these were the *xiang*. In the sentence "*shu* had *xu*," *shu* was a variant for *sui*. According to the rites of Zhou, *sui* were units of 12,500 households, and a school was established within these of one order magnitude higher than those in the *dang*, and these were the *xu*. By "states" is meant the capitals of the son of Heaven and the feudal states. "The son of Heaven established four big schools, and feudal lords when established went to the schools of the kings."[59] Regarding the *xiang*, the *xu*, and what was studied in them, we still await further explanation. These concepts were interrelated, forming a hierarchical order within the system of enfeoffments. The contents and sequence of what was studied under this system formed the ritual system, and the ritual system itself was the course through which one "became a person" (*cheng ren*):

> Every year some entered the college, and every second year there was a comparative examination. In the first year it was seen whether they could read the texts intelligently, and what was the meaning of each; in the third year, whether they were reverently attentive to their work, and what companionship was most pleasant to them; in the fifth year, how they extended their studies and sought the company of their teachers; in the seventh year, how they could discuss the subjects of their studies and select their friends. They were now said to have made some small attainments. In the ninth year, when they knew the different classes of subjects and had gained a general intelligence, were firmly established and would

> not fall back, they were said to have made grand attainments. After this the training was sufficient to transform the people, and to change their manners and customs. Those who lived near at hand submitted with delight, and those who were far off thought of it with longing desire. This was the Way of the Great Learning.[60]

"Study" had the central duty to cultivate "the person." And by "person" was meant attending to knowledge of the rites. According to the description in the "Record of Studies" (*Xue ji*) chapter of the *Book of Rites,* the time, contents, and form of "study" should follow a systematic ritual order, which meant that "study" itself manifested the divisions of ritual and regulatory premises, and any specific knowledge and training were all connected to this cohesive goal.

Within the framework of ritual discourse, the regulatory apparatus was also a moral relation, and so it follows that enfeoffment, the well-field, and the school were also moral systems premised on regulations. Ancient and Zhou-dynasty documents make much use of the character for virtue (*de*) with the Way (*dao*), with conduct (*xing*), and with punishments (*xing*). These show that "virtue" was an internal moral quality, a norm closely related to the communal rituals and institutions, all of which originate in the Way of Heaven (*tiandao*) itself. *The Ancient Lost Text That Comes after Copy A of the Laozi* (*Mawangdui Laozi jiaben hou Shi shu*) states, "Goodness is the Way of humans. Virtue is the Way of Heaven." It also has the lines, "The goodness of the superior man: he begins in having it; without it, he is ended. The virtue of the superior man: he begins in having it; without it, he is ended." And also: "There must be virtue, and only after will there be a state for it; to have a state for it means that All-under-Heaven goes with humaneness and righteousness."[61] Jao Tsung-I comments on these lines, saying:

> Virtue is the Way of Heaven. Hence one can leave the body and focus with the mind, seeking not with form. Nature (*ziran*) is the movement and flow of the Way of Heaven, suspended everywhere between Heaven and Earth. Such were the pronouncements of Zisi on the eternal laws of the five virtues. . . . That which is called goodness, and that which is called virtue . . . one is the Way of humans, and the other the Way of Heaven. Heaven and human complement each other.[62]

As the ruler puts All-under-Heaven in order, completion of virtue is connected with the regulations. The ancient notions of virtue and punishments imply that the ruler inherits the will of Heaven to distribute rewards and punishments. During the Shang dynasty, "virtue" was synonymous with "reward." In the "Announcement to the Prince of Kang" (*Kang gao*), there is the line "I make this declaration to you about virtue in the use of punishments," which already contains the concept of punishments.[63] The ancients' view of Heaven included a sense of Heaven as judge, from which would later come the categories of punishment and law. Wang Guowei wrote of the connection between Zhou morality and institutions: "Zhou institutions and rituals are the mechanisms of morality, the combination of four things: proper respect for what was respectable, taking as kin one's kin, taking as worthy the worthy, and the roles of men and women. This was known as the morality and ethics of the people (*minyi*). Anything that didn't come from these was not of the morality and ethics of the people."[64] The system of patriarchal enfeoffments and the genealogies of politics, economics, and culture derived from it determined a high degree of unity among Nature (*ziran*), morality, and institutions. What the hierarchal view on moral evaluation of the Western Zhou realizes are the principles of patriarchal enfeoffments and their ritual and institutional relationships derived from them.

3. The Communal State of Ritual and the Maxim "Transmit, Do Not Create" as Moral-Political Theory

If the rites and music and institutions are unified, then moral judgment is an objective premise for the regulations of the institutions of the communal state (*gongtongti de zhidu*), which means moral judgment is related to social and political ranking. "Ranking" is a principle within political institutions, and also the basis for moral judgment. This is the product of combining the system of status based on blood and affinal relation with the ranks, privileges, and duties of the feudal political system.[65] In the moral theory of Confucius, humaneness and ritual propriety cannot be explained in isolation from each other. There is no morality but the substance of the social structure, and there is no separation of morality from events, meaning, and thinking. Owing to morality and the social structure (the order of ritual regulations) being the same thing, questions of evaluation are questions of social reality, and hence the most essential path to maintain this commonality is, namely, "rectification of names." The five relations of master and subject, father and son, husband and wife, older and younger brother, and friends were the "Way received of Heaven" in Confucian theory. Of the five, the relations of husband wife, father and son, and master and subject were the most essential, comprising what the ancients called "the six positions" or "the six duties." Sageliness, wisdom, humaneness, righteousness, loyalty, and fidelity were the corresponding "six virtues"—from these, people defined their positions and moral demands based on their positions and responsibilities.[66]

Within the discourse of ritual, such notions as ruler, subject, father, son, husband, wife, friend (*you*), and ally (*peng*) are both functional and practical (moral), which means they could never stray far from definitions based on evaluative concepts, as with "enlightened ruler," "loyal minister," "loving father," and "filial son." In this moral theory, we can find nothing like the opposition, in early modern thought, of what is and what ought to be, or of fact and value. Logically, unless there were major changes to the context behind concepts like ruler, subject, father, and son, then what is and what ought to be could never form contradictory propositions. These are not universal logical propositions, but rather specific historical ones—when institutions become separate from moral judgment and transform into facts without moral meaning, what is and what ought to be come into conflict. Owing to the existing connections between rites and music and institutions, it follows that all studies of rites and music and morality are at once explorations of issues related to institutions. In a world of discourse in which monarchic absolutism grew stronger by the day, punishments were becoming separated a step further from ritual propriety. Those Confucians who were later considered to be Legalists took ritual propriety as the law, and to such an extent that the followers of Confucius and Mencius tended to see the punishments as external and compulsory norms with no relation to human moral practice. In this respect, the fragmentation of punishments and the disintegration of rites and music were two sides of the same coin. Within the patriarchal enfeoffment system, rites and music and institutions were unified to a high degree, leaving no way for ritual and punishments to be two different systems, much less opposed ones. Moral judgment had to be premised on ritual regulations in order to be in accord with the Will of Heaven. Confucius took the Six Classics as doctrine, precisely for building common values in institutions of rites and music and their practice, and to show the basis of the connections among ritual, institutions, and morality, which was tantamount to saying that the theory of rites and music was the same as the theory of institutions and politics. The Qing historian Zhang Xuecheng wrote:

> Although later generations cannot see the Former Kings, when they grasp the ritual implements that they can preserve, they think of the Way that cannot be seen. Hence that we memorialize on the teachings of government of the Former Kings and the institutions of the ministers, in order to show others, and do not of ourselves make theories, which might cause us to leave the ritual implements to speak of the Way. Confucius himself said that the reason he wrote the *Spring and Autumn Annals*, was that "What I might lodge into empty words is not nearly as good as seeing with depth and clarity records of the events of the past." Thus, the orthodox doctrines and institutions, besides being of use for human relations in daily life, have an even more salient narrative, which has already been made clear.[67]

If moral theory is equivalent to narrating and laying out government, educational institutions, and the daily activities of people, then morality must take its objective basis for behavioral norms from the common system of regulations, ritual, and customs.

With respect to the above exposition, "to transmit and not to create" was a political theory implemented under the name of the institutions of the Former Kings, while "understanding ritual propriety as humaneness" was an effort to find the motivation and path to ideal government, one that Confucius subsumed within a human moral quality, internal and with the special feature of loving others. However, this "humaneness" that takes as its special feature "loving others" is not an abstract or purely individual emotion or moral quality, but rather, the expansion of a political principle, namely the kinship principle on which patriarchal feudalism was based. Just as shamanic ritual depended on the course of ritual conduct, so in the world of ritual propriety, any departure from "conduct and affairs" used to express the Will of Heaven would be unable to truly connect Heaven with humanity, and any form of "conduct and affairs" that departed from ritual propriety could not even be considered of the category of "conduct and affairs." Thus, "Transmit and do not create," and "Pass down the royal regulations of the ancestors," should be seen as admonishments to follow rigorously ritual propriety. Mencius said, "Heaven does not speak, but reveals itself in conduct and in affairs."[68] "Conduct and affairs" are the way to show the will of Heaven, but not purely individual conduct. On the one hand, "conduct and affairs" are no more than the course of implementing institutions of rites and music, from which it follows that individual moral perfection (*cheng de*) is regulatory-political conduct. On the other hand, regulatory and political conduct must have an internal connection with conduct and affairs to form the course of moral reality, from which it follows that any regulatory-political systems that are separate from the impulse, urge, and signs of moral perfection cannot form the necessary conditions for moral reality. The former demands purity of ritual; the latter, inner sincerity. This classical moral view supplied two historical premises to Confucius and his immediate followers: first, to further engage with the classical institutions in the mode of "transmit and not create," emphasizing the unity of moral conduct and the ritual institutions (*liyue zhidu*); and second, to interpret the substantial meaning of moral behavior in the mode of "understanding ritual propriety as humaneness," emphasizing that no form of ritual lacking internal motivation or substantial meaning could be seen as "true" ritual.

Were it the case that contradictions within moral philosophy between what is and what ought to be, between fact and value, produced the fragmentation of ritual and regulations or laws, then it would be natural to ask: Didn't Confucius live in an age when rites and music were in decline? And why, given this historical context, did Confucius begin his moral philosophy precisely with the unification of what is and what ought to be? In 1926, Gu Jiegang asked the question this way:

> From the perspective of the *Analects,* Confucius is only the transmitter of old culture, and not the creator of a new era. But from the Qin and Han onward, it was indeed a new era. How did Confucius become the central figure of it? In the view of materialist history, Confucian thought was a product of feudal society. But it was feudal society no longer after the Qin and Han dynasties. Why were his theories dominant for so long, then? Another aspect of this question is: Shang Yang, King Wuling of Zhao, and Li Si were all founders of new ages; why, then, after creating

> the new age, did they "become the target of arrows, censured by all of that age"?[69]

The real question here is, How should we evaluate Confucius's relation to rebuilding Western Zhou ethical reality and the above-described evolution of regulations?

First and foremost, unity of ritual and institutions, of institutions and morality (also known as the "the government of the Three Dynasties"), was the method by which Confucius observed the age he was in, and its crisis. That Confucius based his entire moral theory on the classical form of Western Zhou ritual and institutions signifies two major points: first, total opposition to the severe fragmentation of ritual and institutions (including punishments) and institutions from morality; and second, a call, in the spirit of "reverence" and "ritual propriety," to recover the ritual communal state (*gongtongti*) centered on the royal regulations. In other words, the very proposition that virtue should be in unity with social position faced off against an era in which virtue and position had splintered off from each other. "One may have position, but without virtue, and thus not dare to perform ritual in it; one might have virtue, but without position, one also dare not perform ritual for it."[70] "Transmit and do not create" provides the ritual basis for what above was described as "not daring" (*bu gan*), but "not daring" here can be seen as the expression of a restriction, namely a warning against all behavior that transcends position. In this respect, the complete unity of ritual, institutions, and moral judgment is an ethical construction produced by Confucius in his time, a pursuit of unity from within a state of rupture. The critical force of Confucian learning lies in the close relation between the construction of a theory of restoring antiquity and the real and present institutions. Owing to this theoretical construction, the crisis of legitimacy of the real and present institutions was interpreted as a fissure between institutions and ritual.

Second, the concept of rankings was by no means sufficient to encompass the ethical thought of Confucius. In the *Analects,* the *junzi* (superior man) and *shi* (scholar-official) figures, imbued with the ancient conduct of virtue, are the true inheritors of the new moral institutions (in the form of restored antiquity) during an age of great historical change. The *shi* were early on warriors, knights, and only after the Spring and Autumn period and the Warring States era, and a period of intense transformation, did they become *wen shi,* cultured scholar-officials. During the Warring States era, the *shi* rank already had the status of a level of employment, along with peasant, worker, and merchant forming the "four ranks of the people," which shows that the transformations of the Spring and Autumn era and following were structural, and cannot be equated with the Zhou-era phenomena of the decline of the aristocracy as dynasties gave way to one another. Amongst these transformations, the commoner class rising to the level of scholar-official appropriated the opportunity and right to interpret and establish moral norms, and scholar-officials who had descended to that level from the aristocracy, or others nostalgic for institutions of rites and music from the past, also gained opportunities to extend the ritual order of the feudal era.

In Book 13 of the *Analects,* we have the following:

> Zi Gong asked, saying, "What qualities must a man possess to entitle him to be called a scholar-official? The Master said, "He who in his conduct of himself maintains a sense of shame, and when sent to any quarter will not disgrace his prince's commission, deserves to be called a scholar-official." Zi Gong pursued, "I venture to ask who may be placed in the next lower rank?" And he was told, "He whom the circle of his relatives pronounce to be filial, whom his fellow villagers and neighbors pronounce to be fraternal." Again the disciple asked, "I venture to ask about the class still next in order." The Master said, "They are determined to be sincere in what they say, and to carry out what they do. They are obstinate little men. Yet perhaps they may make the next class." Zi Gong finally inquired, "Of what sort are those of the present day, who engage in government?" The Master said "Pooh! they are so many pecks and hampers, not worth being taken into account."[71]

Those in position were not even worth being considered, because position was utterly divided from virtue. The *shi* could rise up and emerge, because he possessed the internal courage and virtuous conduct ("in his conduct maintaining a sense of shame") to build the connection between ritual order and morality. If we take the rituals stipulated by patriarchal enfeoffment regulations as an absolute measure, we have no way to understand how condescending this view is taking of the ranking system. We can deduce from this that Confucius is not holding to the form of ritual, but rather restores what makes ritual propriety what it is via the "conduct and affairs" of the scholar-official, from which he proceeds to achieve the complete unity of form and content in ritual. There is a close connection between Confucius's theory and the growth of the scholar-official class.

Precisely for this reason, Confucius's concept of humaneness is in no sense a transcending of ritual propriety. He wants to theorize ritual propriety within the category of humaneness, with the goal being to make even more apparent the reliance of moral practice based on ritual on "process," on the states of the practitioner of ritual (sincerity, reverence, awe, faith, and love of humanity), and on the spiritual impulse. Book 1 of the *Analects* has the line, "Filial piety and fraternal submission: these are the root of humaneness."[72] And the "Questions of Duke Ai" (*Ai Gong wen*) chapter of the *Book of Rites* has, "The humane human does not overstep things; the filial son does not overstep things." Zhang Taiyan explains this line by saying, "So the Master said, the speech of the superior man does not overstep proper rhetoric, *ci*. In his movements does not overstep the rules. This is called having normative dimensions which cannot be crossed. In the *Book of Changes,* it says, 'Words possess things, while conduct has rules.' 'Investigating things' means to parse out the normative degrees."[73] Rhetoric (*ci*), rules (*ze*), and things (*wu*) all refer to a certain legal or moral standard or norm, and refer to certain specific relations, factually indicating or normatively indicating complete unity: to measure the degree of the humane human or the filial son is to see that their words and conduct can naturally accord with these standards and norms.

Also see Book 12 of the *Analects:*

> Yan Yuan asked about humaneness. The Master said, "To subdue one's self and return to ritual propriety, is perfect virtue. If a man can for one day subdue himself and return to propriety, All-under-Heaven will ascribe humaneness to him. . . ." Yan Yuan said, "I beg to ask the steps of that process." The Master replied, "Look not at what is contrary to ritual propriety; listen not to what is contrary to ritual propriety; speak not what is contrary to ritual propriety; make no movement which is contrary to ritual propriety.[74]

What these negative imperative sentences express here are not admonishments about external threats, but that a fearfully reverent heart that makes it so; thus "returning to ritual propriety" and "returning to humaneness" are both predominantly decided by inner moral quality, courage, and cultivation. "Zizhang asked Confucius about perfect virtue. Confucius said, 'To be able to practice five things everywhere under Heaven constitutes perfect virtue.' He begged to ask what they were, and was told, 'Gravity, generosity of soul, sincerity, earnestness, and kindness.'"[75]

When we link together the humaneness of Confucius and the historical category of superior man, or scholar-official, we can discover that a structural characteristic of Confucius's thought is similarly paradoxical—by using a "religious" attitude to recover classical sacredness and instill the spirit of sacrifice into the person of the scholar-official who is the product of the collapse of the classical institutions, Confucius's criticism of heterogeneity in the institutions of rites and music must necessarily also contain something of this heterogeneity. In this respect, to explain Confucius's historical stance purely as the restoration of antiquity and the power of aristocracy overlooks the sensitivity to historical change and moral appropriation, and to see Confucius as the compiler and completer of the rationalization of institutions of rites and music also fails to explain how Confucius's thought stubbornly rejects and critiques this evolutionary process.

4. The Heavenly Principle Worldview and the Zisi-Mencius School

Confucius understood ritual as exemplifying Heaven (*tian*), and so the disintegration of the institutions of rites and music could be interpreted as the darkening of Heaven, or a rupture in the relationship between Heaven and human. If recovering the rites and music depended on the practice of humaneness and knowledge of Heaven associated with the superior man or the scholar-official, then there must be something in the person of the superior man or scholar-official that connects to the Way of Heaven (*tiandao*). The efforts of Song Confucianism to return to the Way of Confucius and Mencius are especially focused on the Zisi-Mencius school, and their elucidations of Nature (*xing*) and the Way of Heaven proceed just from this logic. What we refer to as the return to the Way of Confucius and Mencius was actually a new interpretation of Confucius's thought by the Zisi-Mencius school.[76] Through raising the status of the Four Books and opening up areas of complex connection between the thought of Confucius and the Six Classics, they proceeded to weaken the internal relations between Confucius's methods of moral judgment and the ritual regulations. During the Northern Song, Li Gou criticized School of the Way intellectual currents from his position vis-à-vis the achievements of classical studies, indicating features of the new Confucianism from a special direction:

> Today's scholars . . . proclaim Mencius without the Six Classics, loving the kingly Way while forgetting the Son of Heaven. I think we could go on without Mencius, but not without the Six Classics. We could get along without the kingly Way, but not without the Son of Heaven. Thus I have written these *Discourses on the Norms* (*Chang yu*) to rectify the meaning of master and subject, to illuminate the way of Confucius, and to prevent chaos and catastrophe from affecting later generations.[77]

"Mencius without the Six Classics" highlights how the School of the Way emphasizes Nature (*xing*) and the Way of Heaven, but places less emphasis on the institutions of the Former Kings. "Loving the kingly Way and forgetting the Son of Heaven" explains how the School of the Way observes the value of enfeoffment (division of power in government) and its lack of engagement with the absolute imperial authority of the centralized administration system. Mencius inherits from Confucius the idea of taking the "humane government" of Yao and Shun as the moral-political ideal. But the most important concept in Mencian thought is something Confucius rarely spoke of: "Nature" (*xing*) or "human nature" (*ren xing*). It is not the ancient legal codes recorded in the classic documents, but rather human nature—upon which the institutions of rites and music depended—that form the essence of Mencian humane government. "Mencius discoursed on the goodness of human nature, words attributed to Yao and Shun."[78] But when we compare, we can see he admired Confucius even more, the reason being that in Confucius humane learning contained moral courage and internal moral quality, which the ancient system transmitted in the classics could hardly express. The superior man or scholar-official that Mencius admired was the person who "moved about, teaching on behalf of Heaven," that person for whom it was that "fulfilling the Way of Heaven by the sage is the Mandate of Heaven. But as for the nature in himself, the superior man does not call this the Mandate of Heaven."[79] This clearly represents the problem within moral practice of restoring the shamanic tradition to connect Heaven and human. In this respect, in contrast to how Confucius interpreted humaneness between ritual and humaneness, Mencius connects humaneness directly to Heaven. Mencius said, "The Three Dynasties of Antiquity obtained All-under-Heaven by means of humaneness, and lost them again by not having humaneness. So it goes the success or failure, survival or destruction of the states."[80] In Mencius's system of thought, humaneness, righteousness, ritual propriety, and wisdom all accrue to the "nature of the superior man," or else are "rooted in the mind."[81] "To preserve one's mind, and cultivate one's nature, is the way to serve Heaven. When neither a premature death nor long life causes a man any double-mindedness, but he waits in the cultivation of his personal character for whatever issue; this is the way in which he establishes his Heaven-ordained being."[82] Following this line of thought, the Zisi-Mencius school can link the discussions on ritual to those on human nature, from which we may go a step further in the internalization of Heaven or ritual. Thus Mencius can say, "Humaneness, righteousness, ritual propriety, and wisdom are not infused into us from without. We are certainly furnished with them."[83]

Although Mencius and the *Doctrine of the Mean* both emerge from the school of Confucius, there is already a key difference between their interpretations and the forms of Western Zhou ritual that Confucius had presented as the basis of morality. Ascribing the inner strength of humanity directly to ontology or the Way of Heaven and not to institutions of rites and music also meant rejecting Confucius's ideas about adhering to Western Zhou ritual forms. After all, Confucius had seldom discussed the relation between Heaven and humans. Xu Fuguan, in discussing the status of the *Doctrine of the Mean,* writes, "Confucian thought is centered on morality. And the *Doctrine of the Mean* instructs in the immanent and yet transcendent personal character (*xingge*) of morality which then establishes a basis for morality," with his phrasing here, "immanent and yet transcendent," reflecting the intent of the *Doctrine of the Mean.*[84] The Zisi-Mencius School clearly strengthened the connection between the Mandate of Heaven and Shangdi and the immanence and subjectivity of Confucius's concept of "humaneness."

Song Confucians highly esteemed the "mean" (*zhong*) in the *Doctrine of the Mean,* with its reference to "a personal spiritual-emotional state that absolutely refuses all external forces of disturbance," with the origins of the self's internal force thought to derive from "an ontological state."[85] It is worth noting here that from the Qing dynasty onward, the cosmological or Mandate of Heaven discourses of Confucianism were seen as "non-Confucian elements" that had gotten mixed in with the Confucian elements, to the point that even the provenance of the *Doctrine of the Mean* within the Confucian canon came under suspicion, though recent archaeological discoveries (especially the discovery of the Guodian Chu slips) prove that the *Doctrine of the Mean* certainly came from Zisi, and the *Great Learning* (*Da xue*), too, may have some connection to Zengzi, from which it follows that there was a sound basis for the Song Confucian canon (especially the arrangement of the Four Books).[86] From the *Doctrine of the Mean*'s opening line, "What Heaven mandates is called nature; what guides nature is called the Way; what cultivates the Way are called the doctrines," we can discover a rare example of densely religious color in the teachings of Confucius (though in fact there is no connection to the concept or category of religion; this is only a metaphor); we can go so far as to find from another place direct connections among the understanding of the Mandate of Heaven, human nature, and the implementation of some rituals and sacrifices. The *Doctrine of the Mean* speaks of sincerity (*cheng*), saying, "Sincerity is the way of Heaven. The attainment of sincerity is the way of men. He who possesses sincerity is he who, without an effort, hits what is right, and apprehends, without the exercise of thought; he is the sage who naturally and easily embodies the right way. He who attains to sincerity is he who chooses what is good, and firmly holds it fast."[87]

Here, "sincere" is not only a state of a humanity, but also a state of the Way of Heaven, from which it follows that this description of "sincerity" must develop in the form of cosmology:

> Thus ultimate sincerity is without ceasing. Not ceasing, it lasts long. Lasting long, it makes itself evident. Making itself evident, it reaches far. Reaching far, it becomes large and substantial. Large and substantial, it becomes high and brilliant. Large and substantial; this is how it contains all things. High and brilliant; this is how it overspreads all things. Reaching far and continuing long; this is how it perfects all things. So large and substantial, the individual possessing it is the co-equal of Earth. So high and brilliant, it makes him the co-equal of Heaven. So far-reaching and long-continuing, it makes him infinite. Such being its nature, without

> any display, it becomes manifested; without any movement, it produces changes; and without any effort, it accomplishes its ends.[88]

This method of discussing "sincerity" within the framework of cosmology left a deep impression in Zhou Dunyi's *Penetrating the Book of Changes*, as when he writes, "How grand is the world! The material beginning of the myriad things is the origin of sincerity."[89] He also has, "With fine sincerity comes enlightenment, with responsive divinity comes subtlety, and with multiplication of the infinitudes comes profundity."[90] This linking of the internal state of "sincerity" and the existential state of Heaven has its origins in how shamanic culture connects Heaven and human. If we go deeper into Confucius's call for inner spirit in ritual, one that would understand ritual propriety as humaneness and the impulse of the superior man toward self-sacrifice, we can find without difficulty that the cosmological or ontological method of the Zisi-Mencius school originates in the disintegration of institutions and as a reaction against the formalization of rites and music, from which we can conclude that their effort to circumvent forms of rigor regarding ritual and instead appeal directly to such original categories as the Mandate of Heaven, Nature, and the Way also has as its goal recovering the sacredness of ritual.

Song and Ming Confucians saw "Heavenly Principle" as the special nature of the myriad things, the wellspring of morality, and the standard of praxis, and on this basis they combined the three areas of moral practice, ritual relations, and metaphysics. This is the most important area of difference between the School of Principle and Confucius's school of "ritual propriety." Regarding the political significance of the School of Principle, I will say more below, but here let us first say something about their tendency to claim that "Mencius was correct, and not the Six Classics." Following the logic of the Zisi-Mencius school that went from ritual to humaneness, humaneness to Nature (*xing*), Nature to Mind, and Mind to Heaven, Song Confucians placed Heaven, the Way of Heaven, and Heavenly Principle at the center of moral practice. Instead of thinking of this trend toward an "inward turn" within the category of "rationalization," it would be more useful to see it as a new effort to connect Heaven and human in a time when the institutions of rites and music were disintegrating. In this respect, this is an internal "religious attitude": moral evaluation would no longer happen within its relation to institutions of rites and music, but instead within the relation of moral behavior with Heaven. We can do worse than to compare Zhu Xi and Wang Yangming on humaneness with the humaneness of Confucius to elucidate this principle. In "On Humaneness" (*Ren shuo*), Zhu Xi wrote, "'The mind of Heaven and Earth is to produce things.' In the production of man and things, they receive the mind of Heaven and Earth as their mind. Therefore, with reference to the character of the mind, although it embraces and penetrates all and leaves nothing to be desired, nevertheless, one word will cover all of it, namely, *ren* (humaneness)."[91] In the framework of the Heavenly Principle worldview, he understands the "self" of "subdue self to restore ritual propriety" (*ke ji fu li,* in *Analects,* Book 12) as "the private desires of the self," and he understands "ritual propriety" as "the patterning of Heavenly Principle."[92] From this, we may say that the formerly close relations among humaneness, righteousness, ritual propriety, wisdom, loyalty, and indignation with the institutions of the Former Kings had loosened. Wang Yangming, in *Instructions for Practical Living* (*Chuan xi lu*) volume 1, section 9, entry 3, explains Principle as humaneness:

> Humaneness is the principle of unceasing production and reproduction. Although it is prevalent and extensive and there is no place where it does not exist, nevertheless there is an order in its operation and growth. That is why it is unceasing in production and reproduction. . . . Mozi's universal love makes no distinction in human relations and regards one's own father, son, elder brother, or younger brother as being the same as a passer-by. That means that Mozi's universal love has no starting point. It does not sprout. We therefore know that it has no root and that it is not a process of unceasing production and reproduction. How can it be called humaneness? Filial piety and brotherly respect are the root of humanity. This means that the principle of humaneness grows from within.[93]

The interpretation above elides the dependence of Confucius's humaneness on the ritual forms, and strengthens the sense within the theory of humaneness that it contains the mysterious embodied experience of the connection between Heaven and human.

Because out of the discourse of ritual came the category of "Nature" (both universal and internal), the inner meaning of moral self-consciousness underwent an important transformation. Cheng Yi wrote, "Principle is Nature. And is the Mandate. The three have never been different. To plumb Principle is to fully understand Nature. And to fully understand Nature is to know the Mandate of Heaven. The Mandate of Heaven resembles the Way of Heaven in that the latter is what we speak of in practice, while when we speak of Mandate, that which makes Mandate is called 'Creator.'"[94] In contrast to Confucius's practice of ranking, Cheng Yi invites people to "dwell in the Mandate of righteousness." He interprets the hexagram 63, "incomplete" (*wei ji*), in the *Book of Changes,* as follows: "To abide in the ultimate of incompleteness means not to take the rank of the completeness, for there is no principle of completeness, but to please Heaven and follow the Mandate, nothing more . . . for the entirely sincere to be placed within the Mandate of righteousness and please itself, is unassailable."[95] Zhu Xi's explanation is very similar: "To say that father and son desire their kinship, or that ruler and subject desire their righteousness, means that they are this way of themselves, not that they wait on desires. Father and son of themselves associate in kinship, and ruler and subject of themselves associate in righteous duty."[96] "Of themselves associate" means that the ritual meaning of ruler and subject, and of father and son, is produced in an internal substance. In this excerpt, the practice of father and son, and ruler and subject, is the externalization of the internal quality of Nature. Clearly, the Song School of the Way brought basic questions of Confucianism into the framework of cosmology and ontology, with the goal of returning to the moral evaluation methods of pre-Qin Confucianism, in which moral evaluation is related to universal order.

But, though similarly attending to the relation of moral judgment with universal order, humaneness and ritual propriety in Confucius were more specific than the "Heavenly Principle" of Song learning. In the age of the Sage-Kings Yao and Shun that he imagined, the institutions of rites and music themselves were the action of Heaven and the Will of Heaven, with no moral origins existing beyond ritual. A person's morality corresponded directly with his role in the ritual order, which meant there was no way to evaluate morality separately from its ranks within the ritual order. That David Hall and Roger Ames understood the philosophy of Confucius as encompassed within "event ontology" and not a "reality ontology" was reasonable, for within the categories of ritual discourse, understanding human events did not require the assistance of "substance," "property," or "feature."[97] But

Confucius never attended to such questions as of the opposition of event and substance or "thing in itself" (*benti*). In his world, "events" were not stand-alone, but occurred within the ritual order. Without a premise within the ritual order, events could not form the "substance" of moral judgment; they could not even become "events." For these reasons, in the moral discourse of Confucius, moral judgment does not need a cosmological or ontological framework, because ritual theory itself contained classical views of Nature (*ziran*). Song Confucians constructed a relation of moral judgment and order that was not unified with ritual or royal regulations but rather took as intermediates Heavenly Principle and the Way of Heaven. This means that what we find this strong effort to return to Confucius and Mencius is in itself actually a sign of huge transformation in Confucian moral judgment. Serving as universal moral ideas, the categories of Heavenly Principle and conscience (*liangzhi*) were different from the categories of ruler and subject, father and son, brother and brother, or friend and friend. And they were also different from the categories of the superior man and the scholar-official, in that having cast off social framework and moral specificity, they could supply moral practice with an impulse that was transcendent and at the same time internal.

Why didn't Song Confucianism directly use the pre-Qin ritual discourse form to rebuild a genealogy of morals, instead of seeking the possibility of unity through establishing Heavenly Principle and associated concepts? The method of moral evaluation in Song learning was connected to that of Confucius's learning, even in the midst of differences. For Confucius, the collapse of the ritual order had touched off an effort to build an internal relation between the ranking order and morality. Through a description of the superior man as the moral model, practicing humaneness and knowing Heaven, a moral world in which moral conduct and ritual order are in complete union is built anew. Confucius did not build his moral origins with individuals or selves. Quite the contrary, individuals and selves can only recover and build the impulse and subject of the Western Zhou forms of ritual, which meant that individuals and selves were none other than the superior man or scholar-official who could manifest the unity of rank and virtue of ritual through their individual efforts. This scholar-official or superior man must devote himself to "conduct and affairs" with the utmost reverence for Heaven. Song learning was produced in an age when the system of centralized administration was becoming mature, so it refused categorically the moral rationality of this system, thereby also rejecting moral evaluations that linked moral evaluation methods directly with regulatory form.

Following Confucius's understanding of ritual propriety as humaneness, Mencius's ideas on Nature and the Way of Heaven, and the logic of the Mandate of Heaven and the mean in the *Doctrine of the Mean,* Song learning placed the moral evaluation problem into the category of Heavenly Principle, trying to go through the subjective practice of investigating things to fathom Principle (*ge wu qiong li*), thus causing people to recover Heavenly Principle and original nature (*benxing*) by going through differentiated regular evaluation systems. For this reason, even though the practice of "investigating things and extending knowledge" (*ge wu zhi zhi*) regularly applies forms of knowledge, Principle, and reflection, it still has the same quality as a shaman casting himself into the course of ritual practice of connecting Heaven and human.

Wang Yangming writes,

> The Master said, "The word 'ritual propriety' refers to the same thing as the word 'Principle.' [Those aspects of] Principle that are manifested and can be seen are called 'culture.' [Those aspects of] culture that are hidden and cannot be seen are called 'Principle.' This involves only one thing. Restraining oneself with ritual is simply to want 'this mind' to remain pure Heavenly Principle. If one wants this mind to remain pure Heavenly Principle, one must apply effort wherever Principle is manifested."[98]

Naturally there are differences between using the mind to "apply effort wherever Principle is manifested" and the shaman's use of bodily motion, dance, and sacrifices to Heaven with entrancements of the spirit, but there is a consistency to their starting points: in states of sincerity and reverence, with the subject cast into an immanent or ritual process, a connection is made between Heaven and human. In this respect, Wang Yangming's interpretation is not bad: "The word [or character] for ritual property (*li*) is the word [or character] for Principle (*li*)." If we say that Confucius faced the decline of enfeoffments, well-fields, schools, and associated institutions of rites and music with his understanding of ritual propriety as humaneness, and his pledge to transmit and not create, what then is the historical significance of the abstract category of Heavenly Principle in Song thought, along with its method of moral-political evaluation?

III. The Combined Han-Tang System and Moral Ideals

1. "Religious" or "Scientific"? Of Shamanic Techniques or Royal Regulations?

Buddhism and Daoism, the specialized scholarship of the Han and the Tang dynasties, and the utilitarian Confucianism that focused on the study of regulations: these three formed the major opponents that the School of Principle tried to surpass, refute, and criticize in the process of legitimizing itself. The critique of Han and Tang classical studies began during the Late Tang, with the new studies of Heaven and human, including new interpretations of the Heavenly Way (*tiandao*), Nature, and the human world undertaken by Han Yu, Liu Zongyuan, Liu Yuxi, and Li Ao. This intellectual current reaches deep into the School of Principle during both the Song and the Ming dynasties. Han Yu's statement that "with Mencius's death, the transmission of the Dao was cut off" was tantamount to denying the legitimacy of classical studies since the Han dynasty, with the implication that only by skipping past Han and Tang classical studies completely, and reconnecting with the Ru learning of Confucius and Mencius, could one transmit the Dao. In the moral theory that the Song Confucians took, one clear tactic was to claim that the art of governing from the Three Dynasties of Antiquity served as a reproach to the policies of the Han and the Tang dynasties, using the Dao in Confucius and Mencius as a critique of classical studies, and thereby clarifying distinctions between theories of morality drawn from the rites and music of the Three Dynasties of Antiquity and the ethics of the Han and Tang regulations. Within the discourse of Song Confucianism, this opposition of the Han and Tang regulations against the rites and music of the Three Dynasties of Antiquity had implications for government (opposing centralized administration with enfeoffment), land appropriation (opposing the Two-Tax Law with the well-field system), education (opposing school system development with exams), and even the military. In the pre-Qin framework, the regulations are one with the rites and music, from which it follows that if the methods of evaluating morality had not changed, the differences between

Han-dynasty regulations and the rites and music of the Three Dynasties of Antiquity would never have been produced. In this respect, the critique begins with historical views of the separation of institutions from the rites and rituals of the ancients. Thus, the question remains: why did Song-dynasty Confucians believe that the regulations and classical studies alike of the Han and Tang had betrayed the moral standards of the communal state (*gongtongti*) of the rites and music? And finally, what role did this historical view have for the formation of the School of Principle?

From the time the Han dynasty succeeded the Qin dynasty, the central concerns of political theory became how to balance the centralized administration of the Qin with the tradition of enfeoffment, the central government with the aristocracy, and also the old "central states" with the "uncivilized" (*Yi Di*) areas gained by imperial expansion. This was a major reason why the *Spring and Autumn Annals* (*Chunqiu*) and the *Rites of Zhou* (*Zhou li*) both had such essential positions during the Han dynasty, with the former able to provide legal, regulatory, and moral interpretations within the larger categories of historical change, and the latter able to advance the legality and appropriateness of regulatory principles within a cosmological context. Han-dynasty Confucianism understood Heavenly Way nature (*tian dao ziran*) through the five-phases theory of Zou Yan, the yin-yang theory of *Master Lü's Spring and Autumn Annals* (*Lüshi chunqiu*), and Han-era scientific knowledge. Later, it would also interpret the basic framework and concepts of the *Spring and Autumn Annals* and the *Rites of Zhou* with the principles of Heaven-human response and Heaven-human correlation, based on the categories of yin and yang, the five phases, and the four seasons.[99] In his work *Masters of Techniques and Confucians during the Qin and Han Dynasties* (*Qin Han fangshi yu rusheng*), the scholar Gu Jiegang claimed that Han political theory extended from yin-and-yang theory in three major areas: the Five Virtues theory of Zou Yan, the mostly similar "Three Unities" theory, and the "Bright Hall" (*mingtang*) rituals stipulated in the "monthly ordinance" chapters of the twelve-almanacs part of the *Master Lü's Spring and Autumn Annals,* which sufficiently shows the internal relations of Han political theory and the yin-yang and five-phases theories.[100] From the annotated bibliography section (*wenyi zhi*) of the *History of the Han Dynasty* we can learn the basic method by which Han Confucianism built up the more ancient tradition of the "shamans and scribes" (*wu shi*) by linking together the numerical methods of prognostication found in the *hetu* and *luoshu* diagrams associated with the *Book of Changes,* along with the eight trigrams of that text, as well as the historical narratives then extant, to develop political ideas appropriate to the condition of the world as it was then. In contrast with the old school of Confucius, at its heart, Han Confucianism turned toward exploring the responsive relation between Heaven and human affairs and regulations, and away from the human ritual practice per se. If we take the pursuit of humaneness as an internal moral good in Confucius and Mencius as a kind of "religious attitude" (here using the term "religious" only metaphorically), then the Han Confucian understanding of Heaven was closer to a kind of "scientific attitude," an attempt to establish principles and laws by comprehending the connections between Heaven and human. In this respect, although Han Confucianism learning was so often criticized for being "religious superstition" or "mysticism," in fact it possessed a certain "scientific" quality.

With Heaven, the universe, and Nature all occupying such a prominent place in Han-dynasty thought, should we, in the end, consider their theories of Nature "science"? Or rather an ideology based on religious mysteries? Does what is employed here have more the quality of shamanistic technique, or of the kingly Way? To answer this question, we must begin from the relation of shamanistic technique to the kingly Way. The institutions of rites and music of the Shang and Zhou dynasties manifested historical relations between clan communities, which incorporate clan and tribal culture, including shamanism, and states (*guojia*), with national laws and rituals developed from rituals and beliefs within clan-based societies. From shamans to kings, from clans to nations, from communal states built on bloodline frameworks to nation-states built from bloodline ties, this expansion of regulations was from the beginning related to the system of rites and music. Historical and anthropological studies of the Shang and Zhou eras often describe Shang and Zhou regulations as evolving from a tradition of "shaman and ruler in one," which means that viewed from the prehistoric ages, the kingly Way and systems of faith were merely two sides of the same coin. In the system of rites to Heaven, it was taken for granted that the King was a shamanic figure with a connection to Heaven.[101] On the oracle bone inscriptions, "shaman" (*wu*) and "dance" (*wu*) both derive from the same character, "a thaumaturgic shaman holding plumes, feathers, or other ritual objects in his, or her, hands": "Dancing has always been a particularly important element in shamanic rites, but ventriloquy appears to have been used also, as well as juggling and tricks whereby the shaman releases himself from bonds."[102] The techniques of the shaman were related to those of medicine, including the use of medicines and even poison, as well as the arts of calling forth rain, from which we can observe that the shaman is seen as connecting the human body with the universe and the Mandate of Heaven. The transitional era from tribes and clans to early states is marked with unity of ruler and shaman: as the intermediary between human and divine, the shaman-ruler might enter a state of madness or other abnormality to connect with the gods and spirits (*shen*). There is a close connection between changes and standardizations in the community of the rites (*gongtongti*) leading to early states, and changes within the shamanic arts, a process whereby the shamans (*wu*) and the scribes (*shi*) implementing the ritual system of the early tradition gradually evolved into two separate spheres of political state culture.

The process of rituals by shamans, with their music and dance, to ritual by scribes (*shi*) has to do with the category of signs and numbers (*shu*). According to the records of divinations on Shang and Zhou oracle bones, there are two layers of significance to divinations using the tortoise shell inscriptions or the yarrow stalks: firstly, they use performative prediction and calculation to replace the embodied ritual activity of the shaman, connecting Heaven and human and predicting whether events will be auspicious or inauspicious, good fortune or disaster, continuity or ceasing; and secondly, these divinations probe the signs of Heaven (*tian xiang*) to record events and predictions regarding the king, and so became the origins of *shi* as history.[103] That signs and numbers could become history derived from the fact that the numbers manifested the relation between Heaven and the laws and regulations, with both as a record for human events. As the "Quli" section of the *Book of Rites* records, "Divination by the tortoise shell is called *pu;* by the stalks, *shi.* The two were the methods by which the ancient sage kings made the people believe in seasons and days, revere spiritual beings, stand in awe of their laws and orders; the methods, also, by which they made them determine their perplexities and settle their misgivings. Hence it is said, 'If you doubt, and consult the stalks, you need not think that you do wrong. If the day be clearly indicated, boldly do what you desire to do.'"[104] And in the "Single Victim at the Border Sacrifices" (*Jiaotesheng*) section, we find:

> That which is most important in ceremonies is to understand the idea intended in them. While the idea is missed, the number of things and observances in them may be correctly exhibited, as that is the business of the officers of prayer and the scribes. Hence that may all be exhibited, but it is difficult to know the idea. The knowledge of that idea, and the reverent maintenance of it was the way by which the sons of Heaven secured the good government of the kingdom.[105]

Here, the "officers of prayer" and the "scribes" transmit only the form of the numbers, but do not interpret the essence of the numbers. Sun Xidan's commentary here reads, "The numbers of the ceremonies, are seen at the ends of events; the meaning of the ceremony is transmitted into the essence of its nature."[106] Thus the numbers are not sufficient to form the Mandate of Heaven (*tian ming*) in and of themselves, but require a system of regulations, rites and music, and human sentiments. In the "Zhongni at Home at Ease" (*Zhongni yanju*) section of the *Book of Rites,* it says, "The Master said, 'The regulations are in the rites; and the embellishments of them are also so; but the carrying them into practice depends on the men.'"[107] In the same section, we have, "The Master said, 'Ceremonial usages are Principle (*li*); music is the definite limitation [of harmony, *jie*]. The superior man makes no movement without [a ground of] reason, and does nothing without its definite limitation.'"[108] If the divinations by stalks and tortoise shells embody, in the form of numbers and signs, the formalization or rationalization of shamanic culture, then the Confucians emphasize human conduct and affairs, as we see in the reference back to no movement without reason or Principle, no action without definite limitation, and management of and attention to human sentiments. The signs and numerals were closely connected with the royal regulations, while Confucianism placed more emphasis on specific ritual practice.

Zhang Xuecheng's thesis that "all of the Six Classics are histories," with its claim to read the *Book of Changes* as "history," is an even more concrete argument for the historical connections among numerical signs and symbols, the regulations of the first kings, and the rites and ritual activities in early texts. The "Teachings of the *Book of Changes*" chapter of his *Comprehensive Meaning of Literature and History* (*Wenshi tongyi*) argues that "the political model" of the *Book of Changes* "gives it the same integrity (*yi*) as historical material."[109] In his view, the *Book of Changes* is a book of divinations, but also a "history" in which conclusions are drawn by means of signs and numbers. Gong Zizhen, deeply influenced by Zhang Xuecheng, went on to assert:

> The greatest office of the Zhou dynasty was that of *shi*—the scribe and historian. But for the scribe, there are no words. But for the scribe, there is no writing. But for the scribe, there is no judgment of men. The Zhou existed when the scribe existed, and the Zhou was lost when the scribe was lost. . . . Thus, of the Six Classics, the *Book of Changes* is the patriarch of them all. The *Book of Changes* is the historian's record of divination; the *Book of Documents* is the historian's record of speeches; the *Spring and Autumn Annals* are the historian's record of events and actions; the "Airs" are the historian's record on bamboo and silk of [songs] collected from among the people, which were turned over to the ministers of music. The "Odes" are the selections from the scholar-officials. The rites are the rules and regulations of an age . . . cappings and weddings, funerals and sacrifices, and all the rituals regulating the system of the scholar-officials, all are signs and numbers. Thus I have never believed one could set aside the signs and numbers and still speak of integrity.[110]

The distinction that formed between scribe and shaman was that the scribe should use divination, based on a grasp of numbers and signs, and so surpass shamans, with their reliance on shamanic dances. The further rationalization of institutions of rites and music was concretely manifest in the forms of the numbers and signs.

2. Yin-Yang–Five-Elements Theory and the Normalization of a Unitary Monolithic Imperial Political Constitution

Gong Zizhen's comment that "I have never believed one could set aside the signs and numbers and still speak of integrity" describes well the Han-dynasty methodology for combining signs and numbers, history and the "great integrity," or *da yi*. If Confucius had been proposing "Understand humaneness as ritual propriety" to be the spiritual fulfillment of the kingly Way, then the Han Confucians sought legitimacy by making the divinations by tortoise shell (*pu*) and by stalks (*shi*) into a vision of Heaven and human in grand unity. Here we may take as an example the *Luxuriant Dew of the Spring and Autumn Annals* (*Chunqiu fanlu*) by Dong Zhongshu (179–104 BCE). Dong Zhongshu linked the learning of the yin-yang and the five phases with Ru learning, or Confucian thought, with two important contributions in his work *Luxuriant Dew of the Spring and Autumn Annals*: first, interpreting the moral-political principles of the *Spring and Autumn Annals* by the standards of the Gongyang commentary; and second, adding new interpretations to these moral-political principles of the *Spring and Autumn Annals* driven by the cosmology of yin-yang, the five phases, the four seasons, and portents and disasters, which had come from the *Master Lü's Spring and Autumn Annals* (*Lüshi chunqiu*) and Zou Yan. These two combined form a totally comprehensive and interlinked cosmological system. The book comes in seventeen facsicles (*juan*) with the received edition (*tongxingben*) of today having eighty-three chapters (*pian,* of which chapters 39, 40, and 54 no longer exist), divided into two parts: the first seventeen chapters, which use the Gongyang commentary to interpret the *Spring and Autumn Annals,* deducing the ideal moral-political model; and chapters 18–82, which apply cosmological models based on yin-yang, the five phases, the four seasons, and portents and disasters to demonstrate how moral-political practice and principles could operate in accord with universal nature. The second part further divides into two major sections, one mostly focusing on yin-yang and the four seasons, and the other on the five phases. Heaven and Earth, and yin and yang, manifest mutual response by means of a cosmic hierarchal relation of resonance; ruler and subject are the responsive pair within this hierarchical order. The five phases are the natural categories of the cosmos, from the division of labor in the human world (including the organization of officialdom) to human relationship norms (such as loyalty and filial piety). The four seasons indicate patterns of space, time, and order; humaneness, righteousness, loyalty, and virtue are described as the four virtues; and the universe and history are understood within structural transformation as naturally evolving toward goals. In order to strengthen Heaven's hold on the absolute and highest position, Dong Zhongshu gave descriptions of certain rituals and sacrifices (particularly the "Suburban Sacrifice," or *jiaosi*), in which the ruler would gain connection to the Will of Heaven (*tianyi*).[111] According to this understanding, the rituals within the sacrifices are paths to connect and communicate with Heaven, as well as methods indicating the utmost authority and status of the emperor. To take yin-yang, the five phases, and the four seasons as natural processes, along with political, economic, and social relations, is to accept as a premise that there are interaction and exchange between Heaven and the human world, which are the principles of mutual responsiveness of Heaven and humanity *(tianren xianggan)* and of Heaven and human in complementary categories. From chapter 57 of the text, "Things of the Same Kind Activate One Another," for example, we can conclude the following:

First and foremost, Dong Zhongshu's theory of mutual responsiveness of Heaven and humanity (*tianren ganying*) is entirely shamanic, or magical (*wushu*) in nature. According to James Frazer's description of "Contagious Magic":

> If we analyze the principles of thought on which magic is based, they will probably be found to resolve themselves into two: first, that like produces like, or that an effect resembles its cause; and, second, that things which have once been in contact with each other continue to act on each other at a distance after the physical contact has been severed. The former principle may be called the Law of Similarity, the latter the Law of Contact or Contagion. . . . Regarded as a system of natural law, that is, as a statement of the rules which determine the sequence of events throughout the world, it may be called Theoretical Magic: regarded as a set of precepts which human beings observe in order to compass their ends, it may be called Practical Magic.[112]

Second, Dong Zhongshu's theory is also "scientific" in nature. He elucidates "the laws of nature as a single system" with examples from resonance in music and the rise of the ancient Sage-Kings, bringing a "scientific" perspective to the notion that Heaven and human are connected. Joseph Needham sees Dong Zhongshu's use of acoustic resonance as a demonstration experiment of the signs of the five categories to be a manifestation of scientific thought:

> To those who could know nothing of sound-waves it must have been very convincing, and it proved his point that things in the universe which belonged to the same classes (e.g., east, wood, green, wind, wheat) resonated with, or energized, each other. This was not mere primitive undif-

> ferentiatedness, in which anything could affect anything else; it was part of a very closely knit universe in which only things of certain classes would affect other things of the same class.[113]

Needham explains the special character of Chinese thought in terms of a "philosophy of the organism," but in doing so he does not identify the internal relation between acoustic demonstration and institutions of rites and music. He lacks clear insight into the relation between the perfection of music, the perfection of virtue (*de*), and the state and All-under-Heaven that was drawn on above in the Old Text *Book of Documents* (*Yishu*). The *Record of Music* (*Yueji*) says, "The rites distinguish hierarchical levels; music takes harmony as its main theme." Does this not transcend "primitive undifferentiatedness"? And can it not serve to encompass the diversity and distinctiveness of the rites and rituals? Here, there exists an organic and analogical relation among the shamanic or magical view of mutual response of Heaven and human, the "scientific exposition" of Heaven and human in mutual categories, and institutions of rites and music, from which it follows that the Will of Heaven (*tianyi*) can present itself simultaneously from these three states.

Third, as a premise to the organic system told above, Dong Zhongshu comes up with the concept of "objects mutually seeking by category" (*wu yi lei xiang zhao*) for the purpose of using signs and portents that supplied the conditions for the emergence of the ancient Sage-Kings: "Activating each other without form is often referred to as 'spontaneously so' (*ziran*). In reality, it is not that they do so spontaneously but that something causes them to be so. There is definitely something concrete that stimulates them, but what stimulates them has no [visible] form."[114] Thus, there are connections among natural phenomena, the Will of Heaven (*tianyi*), and the Mandate of Heaven (*tianming*), so it follows that inspecting natural phenomena is one way to comprehend the Will or Mandate of Heaven.

If we may say that Confucius's maxim "transmit and do not create" equates the kingly Way of the rites and music with Heaven, while his advice to "understand humaneness as propriety" places these regulations into the practice of the reverent subject, then we can see that Dong Zhongshu's theory of the mutual responsiveness of Heaven and human pushes the sacredness of the institutions of rites and music one step further in their transformation into scientific understandings of natural phenomena, as well as the context of shamanic or magical experience in its highest possible intention. For Confucius, shamanic heritage manifests mainly in the practice of the rites, as well as the moral fiber internal to the person, while for Dong Zhongshu, shamanic heritage is found in the formalized and more scientific elucidation of Heaven in the tradition of divination.[115] But it was precisely these "more scientific" elucidations that made later people see many of these ideas as "religious mysticism." As Frazer writes, "Magic is a spurious system of natural law as well as a fallacious guide of conduct; it is a false science as well as an abortive art."[116] But isn't it the case that, given the incomplete grasp on the universe and Nature by humanity, that all knowledge of Nature can be considered "a spurious system of natural law"? Just consider for instance the transformations of Confucian moral-political judgment: Dong Zhongshu clearly favored tighter links between moral-political judgment and knowledge of Nature, so he tried hardest to show the moral-political principles behind naturalistic descriptions of Heaven. In this respect, the methods of Han Confucian thought were both scientific and mystical, shamanic and magical even as they were also a "kingly Way" (*wangzhi*). The dichotomy of science and mysticism and of shamanic arts and the kingly Way alike were the products of more modern determinations.

Henri Hubert and Marcel Mauss have a strong argument that goes like this: "Magic has nourished science, and the earliest scientists were magicians. . . . Magic issues by a thousand fissures from the mystical life, from which it draws its strength, in order to mingle with the life of the laity and to serve them. It tends to the concrete, while religion tends to the abstract. It works in the same sense as techniques, industry, medicine, chemistry and so on. Magic was essentially an art of *doing* things."[117] Han-dynasty astronomy and calendrical calculation, and agricultural studies, medical studies, and chemistry (experiments by wizards, or *fangshi,* seeking elixirs of immortality had transformed knowledge regarding the material qualities and laws of reactions regarding mercury, lead, and sulfur) had all seen rapid development, except for the needs of agricultural development, but whether or not there is any connection in this with the expansion of travel and transport in the Han dynasty (as with Zhang Qian penetrating into the far West) has yet to be shown. The study of the stars and constellations was closely connected to the determination of the agricultural seasons, and the Han dynasty had a rich understanding of heavenly bodies. Of the three theories of cosmology, the school of Xuan Ye is now lost, and the canopy Heaven (*gai tian*) theory, described in the *Mathematical Classic of the Zhou Gnomon* (*Zhou bisuanjing*), was already popular during the reign of Emperor Wu of the Western Han, while the more scientific celestial sphere (*hun tian*) theory achieved outstanding results later in the Han dynasty. During the reign of Emperor Wu, Luo Xiahong, She Xing, Deng Ping, and Sima Qian all revised the Zhuan Xu calendar and composed the Taichu calendar, which began calendars with the first lunar month and used the twenty-four solar terms so useful for agriculture. They also added intercalary months, to correct for the discrepancy between lunar calendars and the solar year, transforming a situation described as "on the first and last days of the lunar month, the moon appears one quarter increasing, one quarter decreasing, full or empty." Luo Xiahong and Geng Shouchang designed the armillary sphere, which served as a basis for the improved spheres designed by Zhang Heng in the Eastern Han, as well as other improvements in observing the heavenly bodies.[118] The "Heavenly Offices" chapter of the *Records of the Grand Historian*, as well as the astronomical section of the *History of the Han Dynasty*, records in detail the names and positions of the twenty-eight heavenly mansions (*su*) into which the celestial sphere was divided. Han people deduced from the movements of the stars and constellations the twenty-four divisions of the year, the names and order of which are still in general use.

With the development of astronomy also came new discoveries in mathematics. The *Mathematical Classic of the Zhou Gnomon* records using pole marks measuring the sun's shadow to find the height of the sun above the Earth, which led to the discovery of the Pythagorean theorem. Although the text *Nine Records on the Calculating Arts* (*Jiu zhang suan shu*) took shape during the Eastern Han, in the reign of Emperor He, the ideas must have been formed, revised, and supplemented in a process that dates much earlier. Among these are the many "arts of doing things," mathematical concepts and methods of calculation intended to help in the lives of the common people, as with surveying the fields, measuring the land, proportional distribution, calculating the volumes of barns, and tax apportionments. Corresponding with developments in astronomy and calendrical calculation, Han agricultural science had already become a specialized field of knowledge, with the bibliography chapter of the *History of the Han* recording nine works on agriculture. Among these was Cui Shi's *Monthly Observances for the Four*

Ranks of People (*Si min yue ling*), which took shape in the latter part of the Eastern Han, although by the Western Han, the "monthly observances" (*yue ling*) of the *Master Lü's Spring and Autumn Annals,* compiled by the former Qin prime minister Lü Buwei, was already exerting influence on Dong Zhongshu and other Confucians.[119]

Three parts comprise *Master Lü's Spring and Autumn Annals:* almanacs *(ji),* surveys (*lan*), and discussions (*lun*), the most noteworthy aspects of which are the symbolic meanings regarding the connection of Heaven and human found in the text's layout. The almanacs comprise twelve fascicles (*juan*), corresponding to the twelve months of the year, with each fascicle divided into five chapters (*pian*), which comes to a total of sixty, matching the total number of heavenly Stems and earthly Branches, the sexagenary cycle of the years. In the almanacs, each set of three fascicles corresponds to one of the four seasons, and each season has a central theme, as with spring: cultivating life; summer: music and education; fall: war; and winter: death. The first chapter of each fascicle is borrowed from the "monthly observances" chapter of the *Lost Book of Zhou* (*Yi Zhou shu*), discussing what is to be done at each moment during the year, the better to ensure the smooth operation of the state; the succeeding four chapters each in turn explore the ideas and behaviors proper to that season. The surveys are divided into eight fascicles, and each fascicle has eight chapters, so the total comes to sixty-four, which matches exactly with the eight trigrams and sixty-four hexagrams of the *Book of Changes.* The discussions contain six fascicles, each with six chapters, the last four of which discuss agriculture, while the first thirty-two take as their central theme the conduct of the just and humane ruler. Just what the six fascicles and thirty-six chapters of the discussions correspond to is not known, but given the structure of the whole, some correspondence seems likely.[120] In the preface to the twelve almanacs, besides having four seasons for the twelve months, there is also, most importantly, a movement of the two *qi,* yin and yang, within the four seasons, as well as a correspondence between the five phases and the four seasons. Spring is strong in wood, summer is strong in fire, fall is strong in gold, winter is strong in water, and in the final part of the summer season, the sixth month, there is an added section reading, "Earth goes at the very center, along the fifth and sixth of the heavenly stems, in the position of the Yellow Emperor and the earth god," in this way reconciling the five phases with the four seasons.[121] This yin-yang–five-phases

Heaven is an intermediary between human pattern and natural order, not a deity or god as patterned after a human, but nevertheless something with a will, that rewards and punishes.

Starting from here, we may gain a new understanding of Dong Zhongshu's theory of the mutual response of Heaven and human. Why did he think Confucian ritual needed to be combined with scientific discoveries, be these the yin-yang and five-phases theories of the *Master Lü's Spring and Autumn Annals* and Zou Yan, or the Han-dynasty work on the astronomy of the celestial sphere rotation and on agriculture and the four seasons? Why did numerology enjoy such an apparent rise in status within Confucian learning, so much so that it nearly eclipsed the traditions of divination? (Use of the five phases to interpret the direction of a state originated among the yin-yang masters, corresponding to Confucian concepts such as we see from Zi Chan's dictum, "The rites following Heaven is the Way of Heaven." And these yin-yang masters can be said to derive from the divination tradition.) Why did Dong Zhongshu see the *Spring and Autumn Annals* as only achieving its full significance when understood as receiving the natural law of Heaven?

Consider first the structure of the exposition regarding Heaven-human correspondences in the *Luxuriant Dew of the Spring and Autumn Annals* in connection with the *Master Lü's Spring and Autumn Annals.* According to the structure as presented in the *Master Lü's Spring and Autumn Annals,* the regulations of the government of the Sage-Kings were thoroughly connected to the laws of Heaven, with the Sage-King appointed by Heaven, and required conduct matching the intentions of Heaven, from which it follows that political order and conduct must adapt to the times. Heaven, along with the yin-yang, five phases, and four seasons manifesting the Will of Heaven (*tianyi*), forms the basis for the legitimacy of the government of the Sage-Kings and the standards of conduct. The *Luxuriant Dew of the Spring and Autumn Annals* applies this logic to interpretations of historical cases in the *Spring and Autumn Annals,* with the rule that the order and Will of Heaven must not be broken, thus supplying the basis for imperial authoritarianism. Dong Zhongshu's goal, in combining the Gongyang commentary with yin-yang–five-phases theory, was to legitimize unified rule with theories of Heaven as the framework. He likely yoked the Will of Heaven to the *Spring and Autumn Annals* because Heaven is the supreme measure of the cosmological system. Understanding the *Spring and Autumn Annals* as the laws established by Confucius for later kings implies that Confucius was none other than a "new king" (*xin wang*) himself; and establishing the *Spring and Autumn Annals* to serve as laws for the Han required a new hermeneutics aimed at revealing the deepest meaning of the text. The Gongyang commentary applies the concept of *quan bian,* or changes of power, which the *Luxuriant Dew of the Spring and Autumn Annals* applies to the fullest, because only by incorporating changes of power can Dong Zhongshu interpret the *Spring and Autumn Annals* so that the ritual order of the enfeoffment system could apply to the political and legal institutions of the unified and centralized administration system.[122]

The Han dynasty established an imperial authoritarian state, but one "at the borders of Chu and Han, once the six feudal states were established."[123] The aristocracy of the enfeoffment system was still extant, and thus the Han empire can be considered a mixed-mode political system with elements of centralized government and enfeoffments, but in which central government in the form of the centralized administration became dominant. When the Han instituted the centralized government and enfeoffment systems side by side, deep tension existed between powers vested in centralized administration and the more divided powers of the feudal lords. The early Han was once divided among eight feudal kings, which were later destroyed; later still the Han was once again divided into enfeoffments after the manner of the Zhou dynasty, with enfeoffments going to members of the imperial house, which led yet again to fierce conflict between the central imperial authority and the feudal lords and kings. Emperors Wen and Jing accepted the proposals of Jia Yi and Zhao Cuo to weaken the powers of the feudal lords. And in Emperor Wu's time, things went even further, with it announced that he would institute a new law, enfeoffing his own children and other relatives into the *wang* states, leading to disintegration of feudal states.[124] Chapter 10, "The Essentials of Covenants and Meetings" of the *Luxuriant Dew of the Spring and Autumn Annals,* summarizes the main idea of the *Spring and Autumn Annals:*

> The terminology of [the humane ruler] expresses [sorrow for the misfortunes of the world]. Thus we may say [the *Spring and Autumn Annals*]
>
> Establishes principles to illuminate the distinction between lofty and humble;

> Strengthens the trunk and weakens the branches to illuminate duties great and small;
> Differentiates conduct that appears deceptively similar to illuminate the righteous principles of rectifying the age;
> Selects various people with the intention of assigning to them praise or blame, to rectify those who stray from correct ritual practice.[125]

The phrases "strengthens the trunks" and "weakens the branches" refer to the power of the emperor and the complete dependence of the feudal lords on this power, distinguishing lofty from humble, great from small, and all as a matter of absolute order. Dong Zhongshu's views in this regard transformed the relations of the jobs of Son of Heaven, feudal lords, and the great ministers in the *Spring and Autumn Annals,* creating a concept of "grand unity" (*da yitong*) severed from feudal relations.[126]

The argument in the *Luxuriant Dew of the Spring and Autumn Annals* is that Confucius received a mandate to change the institutions by basing them on yin and yang, the five phases, and the five virtues of the Three Sequences (*san tong*) cycle, from red to white to black and back again, which must all be understood in the context of this historical transformation with its new theory of "Grand Unity" (*da yitong*). The absolute nature of Heaven found its complement in imperial absolutism.[127] Fu Sinian has summed it up: "Under the Western Zhou, enfeoffment was a means of founding a state and setting up rule over the people, so it was a special form of social organization. The enfeoffment of the Western Han split up the commanderies and counties, so what was here termed enfeoffment (*fengjian*) was only so in a geographic sense."[128] In the eyes of the Confucians, the differences between the feudalism of Western Zhou and that of the new Han dynasty could be summed up as a division between the rites and music and institutions, with rites and music embodying the values of feudalism, while institutions embodied the view centered on imperial power. Under the new central administration, the relation between government and the rites and music was ended, meaning that the rites and music were no longer a condition for the legitimacy of the political body.

In addition to imperial authoritarianism, the idea of grand unity touched on expansion of imperial domains. As the Han expanded past its former borders, relations with the outside world reached unprecedented levels. Internal and external relations became one of the important measures of the self-understanding of the empire. Empire expanded the pre-Qin scope of China as the "central states" (*zhong guo*), with the idea of grand unity coming up against the idea that the Chinese (*Xia*) faced off against the "barbarians" or foreigners (*Yi*). It was also because of these conditions that it became necessary to change the feudal rites and rituals as described in the *Spring and Autumn Annals.* Dong Zhongshu's argument opposing Chinese and barbarian wrought enormous change on the studies expressed on these issues in the *Spring and Autumn Annals* and its Gongyang commentary. Chapter 3, "Bamboo Grove," of the *Luxuriant Dew of the Spring and Autumn Annals* begins:

> The usual terminology of the *Spring and Autumn* grants that the Central States participate in proper ritual, but not the Yi and Di peoples. Why, on the contrary, is this reversed when it comes to the battle of Bi? The answer is: The *Spring and Autumn Annals* does not employ consistent terminology but rather shifts according to alteration. Now if Jin changes and acts like the Yi and Di peoples, or conversely, if Chu changes and acts like a noble man, then it shifts its terminology to reflect these facts. When King Zhuang of Chu retreated from Zheng, he exhibited an inner beauty that was truly admirable. The man of Jin did not understand his goodness and wanted to attack him. What he wanted to rescue [i.e., Zheng] had already been spared, and yet he still wanted to provoke [Chu] into battle. This was to disparage the good-heartedness [of King Zhuang] and to slight his intention to spare the people [of Zheng]. This is why the *Spring and Autumn Annals* degrades [the Jin general] and does not grant that he was equal to the worthy who engaged in proper ritual.[129]

The distinction between Yi, or barbarians, and Xia, or Chinese, is one of the core propositions of the *Spring and Autumn Annals* and the Gongyang commentary, but under the conditions of the expansion of the empire, it was clearly considered an issue of utmost importance to revise the distinction of barbarians and Chinese, adapting them to the new relations of internal and external. Between Dong Zhongshu's relativized theory of the rites and the new Han natural studies—especially the geographical theory (*yudi lun*) of Zou Yan—we can find that yin-yang and five-phases theory begin to encompass a theory of external and internal. In the *Records of the Grand Historian*

(Shi ji), section 74 is titled "Biographies of Mencius and Xun Qing," but Zou Yan and his theory take an important position:

> Zou Yan saw that the rulers were becoming increasingly dissolute and extravagant, unable to rectify themselves and then spread their virtue among the common people. . . . Thereupon he delved deep into the interplay of the yin and the yang and wrote more than a hundred thousand words about their strange transmutations. . . . Using wild and magniloquent language he went on from a study of some minor object to extend his deductions to infinity. Going back from contemporary times to the Yellow Emperor and the common origin of all teachings, he covered the rise and fall of different ages, the good and bad omens, and the various institutions, tracing these to the remote past before Earth and Heaven were created, and to the mysterious and unknown origin of things. He began by tabulating the famous mountains, mighty rivers and valleys of China, its birds and beasts, products of water and land and precious objects, going on from these to things hidden from men's eyes beyond the Four Seas. He claimed that since the separation of Heaven and Earth all things must change according to the specific laws of the Five Elements and show definite manifestations. He maintained that what Confucians called the "Central States" were only one of eighty-one regions of the world. The Middle Kingdom, known as the Red Divine Land, comprised the nine "continents" of which Great Yu spoke, but these were not real continents. Outside the Middle Kingdom there were nine regions as large as the Red Divine Land, and these were the true Nine Continents. These were each surrounded by "small seas" separating the people and beasts on one from those on others and formed one region which made up one continent. There were nine such continents, surrounded by a "great ocean" at the boundary of Earth and Heaven. Zou Yan's theories were all of this sort. Yet these were the premises for his conclusions about humanity, justice, frugality, and the relationships between ruler and ruled, high and low, and kinsmen. Princes and nobles were impressed and influenced by their first acquaintance with his teachings.[130]

Zou Yan perceived how the ritual order had fallen into disarray, and he turned instead toward observations of the cosmos and Nature, applying this new method of theorizing on Nature in relation to politics and government in China in the context of its history and geography. His exposition on the nine continents, large and small, supplied to ritual and government alike a basis in Nature and with a concept of the central states (*Zhongguo*) that nevertheless did not put these at the center of the world. In concert with Zou Yan and his new theory of the earth that divided the earth into continents and defined the central states, Dong Zhongshu revised the traditional model in the *Spring and Autumn Annals* and the Gongyang commentary, introducing a new and more relative exposition of Chinese versus barbarians under the guidance of the concept of Grand Unity.[131]

The third part of the Grand Unity theory was a system of complementarity between the natural categories of Heaven and the official ranks of the bureaucracy. Han-dynasty Grand Unity was closely related to the central administration system: in contrast to the system of enfeoffment based on networks of bloodline relations, centralized administration relied on a model of governance erected in tandem by imperial authority and formalized bureaucratic government institutions. The Qin had annihilated the six warring states to form a unity, the aristocracy of the six states became civilians, and the enfeoffments, well-field systems, and schools of the Zhou government all collapsed in the wake of this. Under these conditions, moral theories that were melded together from the rites and music based on patriarchal clans and bloodline relations required fundamental revision; and the unified, imperial bureaucratic administration system based on functionalism, and not on personal moral qualities, became the object of concern and exposition by Han Confucians. What remained in use of the rites-and-music system no longer retained the significance it had had during the Zhou era. In a context where institutions were separating from rites and music, if the functional system of the bureaucracy and laws was seen as a genealogy of morality, then it had to seek a source of legitimacy and rationality outside its own system. The internal connection between an absolute Heaven and the regulations or laws arose from a moral quandary. Dong Zhongshu had relied on the *Spring and Autumn Annals* to compose the 232 cases of the *Spring and Autumn Annals Determining Cases* (*Chunqiu jueyu*), which had been based on the subtle words of sages as well as the Will of Heaven; this was an advancement of pre-Qin legalist systems for imperially unified government.[132] To endow Han regulations with moral ideals and ideas of a moral standard, Dong Zhongshu used the signs and numbers to connect Heaven with official ranks, as he writes in chapter 24, "Regulations on Officialdom Reflect Heaven":

> The king regulates the offices. With the three dukes, nine ministers, twenty-seven great officers, and eighty-one senior functionaries, a total of 120, his hierarchy of officials is complete. I have heard that the standards adopted by the sage-kings were modeled on the great warp of Heaven, which completes each season with three months and each year with four [seasonal] revolutions, so the regulations of the offices are as they are. This is the standard. That three men constitute the first selection [of officials] is a standard derived from the fact that three months constitute one season. That four such selections are made, and no more, is a standard derived from the fact that with the four seasons, [the year] is brought to its conclusion. The three dukes are the means by which the king supports himself. With three [months], Heaven completes [each season]; with three [dukes], the king supports himself. When he establishes the number [three], that brings things to completion as his foundation, and four times repeats it, then the ruler can be free from error. . . . For this reason, the Son of Heaven assisted himself with the three dukes;
>
> > [each of] the three dukes assisted himself with nine ministers;
> > [each of] the [nine] ministers assisted himself with three great officers;
> > [each of] the [twenty-seven] great officers assisted himself with three senior functionaries.
>
> There is [a multiple] of three men in [each] selection, repeated four times. [Thus] from the "Way of Three" is derived the government of the world. So also Heaven's four repetitions are derived from the three [months] that make up each season, thus ending and beginning the yearly cycle. There is one yang but three [months in each] spring; does this not accord with there being three [months in each] season? Heaven repeats this four times so that its numerical pattern is identical.
>
> > Heaven has its four seasons, and [each] season comprises three months;
> > the king has his four [rounds of] selections, and [each] selection comprises [a multiple of] three officials. . . .

> They distinguished them according to their permutations and thereby created the four selections [for office]. Each selection established three officials, just as Heaven distinguishes the permutations of the year and thereby creates the four seasons, in each of which there are three [monthly] divisions.[133]

By "four selections for office" is intended the selections of dukes, ministers, great officers, and officials. "With three [months], Heaven completes [each season]; with three [dukes], the king supports himself. When he establishes the number [three], that brings things to completion as his foundation," means to take three as a fundamental number, followed by repeating it four times, which is to say that the three dukes are one of those threes, while the nine ministers are another, the twenty-seven great officers are the third, and the eighty-one senior functionaries are the fourth, three for each of the twenty-seven. Four repetitions, namely four accumulations of threes. All of these numbers on the official ranks are interrelated by the principle of the transformations of the four seasons, meaning that number is intermediary, and the legitimacy of the officialdom is traced back to the movements of Heaven. In chapter 28, "Ranking States," from the *Luxuriant Dew of the Spring and Autumn Annals,* he attached more to the numbers of three for the dukes and nine for the ministers, saying, "The departments of the Son of Heaven were divided into right and left, with five grades totaling 360 men, in imitation of the number of days in Heaven's yearly cycle," emphasizing the number 360.[134] Three hundred and sixty corresponds to the degrees of the celestial sphere, and so it is a heavenly sign (*tianxiang*).

In the mixed relations of unification and enfeoffment, enfeoffment became ancillary to unified imperial institutions, and thus the rites and music were also not entirely separated from institutions. For example, regarding the heavy criminal punishments of Qin and Han times, Dong Zhongshu advocated "establishing the Academy to teach the state, erecting government schools (*xiangxu*) to transform the cities, soak the people with benevolence, mold the people with friendship, temper the people with the rites, then even if punishments are light the people will not dare do wrong. If you make efforts to educate them, then customs and habits will improve."[135] This combined the unity of central administration and the "learning" of the rites and music of Three Dynasties of Antiquity. In another example, Dong Zhongshu praised the well-field system from the Three Dynasties of Antiquity and criticized the Qin for "using the methods of Shang Yang, altering the imperial institutions, doing away with the well-field system, and allowing people to buy and sell land. The rich bought up great connecting tracts of ground, and the poor were left without enough land to stick the point of an awl into." He continued, "In the past, the tax on the people did not exceed one part in ten, a demand easy to supply. Corvée labor would not exceed three days, which they easily found sufficient resources for." In his time, however, "Taxes on fields and population and profits from salt and iron increased to twenty times those of old. Those who worked the land of the rich had to give half their crops in rent." These developments were the origin of the corruption, depravity, cruelty of the wealthy, and the misery and desperation that turned to the banditry of the poor. He referred to the structure of the well-field not to call for a return to that system but rather to promote the spirit of adapting to power changes (*quan bian*):

> Although it would be difficult to restore at once the ancient well-field system, it is proper that the present usage be brought somewhat closer to the old ways. Ownership of land should be limited so that those who do not have enough may be relieved and the road to unlimited encroachment blocked. The rights of salt and iron should revert to the people. Slavery and the right to execute servants on one's own authority should be abolished. Poll taxes and other levies should be reduced and labor services lightened so that the people will be less pressed. Only then can they be well-governed.[136]

The cosmology of the *Luxuriant Dew of the Spring and Autumn Annals* supplies at once moral-political legal principles and also an epistemology suited to understanding these principles. The new sacredness with which the relation between Heaven and human was described clearly changed the form and structure of the theory of rites and music from Zhou times, yielding a new trend in moral-political philosophy. Chapter 29, "Standards of Humaneness and Righteousness," outlines Dong Zhongshu's basic principles of the moral-political ideals, centered as they were on humaneness and righteousness:

> For this reason, the *Spring and Autumn* creates standards of humaneness and righteousness. The standard of humaneness lies in loving others, not in loving the self. The standard of righteousness lies in correcting the self, not in correcting others. If we do not correct ourselves, even if we are capable of correcting others, [the *Spring and Autumn*] will not grant that this is righteousness. If others are not the recipients of our love, even though we are replete with self-love, [the *Spring and Autumn*] will not grant that this is humaneness. . . . Thus
>
> the love of the king extends to the four tribes;
> the love of the hegemon extends to the Lords of the Land;
> the love of the secure [ruler] extends to those within his territory;
> the love of the imperiled [ruler] extends to his dependents and aides;
> and the love of the [ruler] bereft [of his state] extends only to his person.
>
> Although one who is isolated might achieve the position of Son of Heaven or Lord of the Land, he will not be able to employ a single person from among the officials or the common people. This being the case, even if no one destroys him, he will self-destruct. . . . Thus I say: Humaneness means loving others; it does not consist of loving the self. This is the standard. . . .
>
> Righteousness does not refer to rectifying others but to rectifying the self. When there are chaotic times and depraved rulers, everyone aspires to rectify others. Yet how can this be called "righteousness"? . . . Thus I say: Righteousness lies in rectifying the self; it does not lie in rectifying others. This is the standard. . . . The Noble Man sought out the distinction between humaneness and righteousness to bring order to the interactions between others and the self. Only then could the Noble Man distinguish between the internal and the external and determine compliance and deviance. For this reason, the Noble Man brought order to the internal by reverting to proper principles to rectify the self, relying on propriety to encourage good fortune. He brought order to the exter-

nal by extending his compassion to ever-widening circles of activity, relying on generous regulations to embrace the multitudes.[137]

Dong Zhongshu's examination of moral ideals here is close to Confucius's understanding of morality, but the difference is this: within the framework of the rites and music, Confucius saw the rites as a complete set of interrelated regulations among themselves, and this set formed the basic scope of moral-political conduct, but within Dong Zhongshu's framework of the mutual responsiveness of Heaven and human, regulatory relations must obey the assignments of the Will of Heaven and the Mandate of Heaven to obtain legitimacy. The former finds internal relation with Heaven (the rites and music as Heaven), while the latter matches with Heaven via the heavenly signs and numbers, meaning that the Will of Heaven has become something observable. Sacrifices and other rituals are paths to observing the Will of Heaven. And so, the principles exposited by Dong Zhongshu are completely different from the patriarchal Sage-King institution of Confucius. He tried to reconstruct regulations and rites and rituals based on transformed historical relations and to endow under the name of Heaven the legitimacy of these regulations and rites and rituals. Guided by this central concern, the Confucian principles "transmit and do not create" and "understanding ritual propriety as humaneness" would no longer serve as appropriate theoretical methods.

3. The Heavenly Signs and Numbers and Official Ranks

The method of using the alignment of heavenly signs and numbers (*xiangshu*) to lay out the connections between the official ranks and the universe itself was later thought to have achieved a more systematic articulation in the *Rites of Zhou,* with the "Old Text" version later being the more revered. The links between Heaven and the formalized system of laws and regulations were preceded by the collapse of the moral-political genealogy of the communal state (*gongtongti*) characterized by the rites and music: to distinguish themselves from the rites, the regulations and laws required external sources of legitimacy. Han-dynasty learning distinguished between "Old" and "New Texts," but in its discussions of the kingly Way (*wang zhi*) it found yet another network of inheritance. When the Eastern Han was first established, the consolidating government reissued the law first promulgated during the reign of Emperor Wu of the Western Han, *Against Forming Parties and Cliques* (*A dang fu yi zhi fa*), which limited the powers of the feudal lords and kings. This law came with a series of regulations, including proscriptions against the feudal lords and kings holding rituals proper to the Son of Heaven, and rules that feudal lords and kings should apply Han regulations for employing petty clerks (*li*). Feudal lords and kings had to pay tribute to the Han at specified periods. They could not send forth troops if they were not in possession of the tiger tally (*hufu*). Feudal lords and kings were not allowed to independently forge metal and mine salt, nor were they permitted to marry into the families of the emperor's wives.[138] In this respect, Heaven in Eastern Han thought, with its absolute and distributing natures, still influenced relations among the Son of Heaven, the feudal lords, and the bureaucracy, or "hundred officials" (*bai guan*). *Zhou Officialdom* (*Zhou guan*) was the original title of the text *Rites of Zhou,* which was referred to using the older title in both the "Tributes to Heaven and Earth" (*Feng chan shu*) chapter of the *Records of the Grand Historian* and the *History of the Han Dynasty,* in the bibliography chapter, where it was called the *Classic of Zhou Officialdom* (*Zhou guan jing*), in six sections (*pian*), which shows that the work was already a classic by Han times. According to tradition, the *Rites of Zhou* was thought to have been produced during the mid-second century BCE, but the text was only known in Han times; it contains ideas from Liu Yin and Wang Mang,[139] as we can see from the effort by this Liu Yin (46–23 BCE) to establish an official post involving academic study of the *Rites of Zhou.*[140]

The dominant feature of the *Rites of Zhou* is its system for organizing the ranks of officials by means of numerology, forming a system intended to express political ideals. As described above, numerology's crucial role in the rites traces back to the divination methods of the Yin (Shang) dynasty, further developed among the yin-yang masters. As Han-dynasty theories of Nature came to sudden prominence, numerology represented a way to understand Nature and experience and observe the Will of Heaven and the human world. We might well call this a quasiscientific method of understanding. The *Rites of Zhou* uses the numbers associated with the years and months, matched against the categories of yin-yang, the five phases, and the four seasons, to build a complete system of official ranks. One thing worth our attention is that during the reign of Emperor Cheng, Liu Xin created the *Santong* calendar, based on the *Taichu* calendar, standardizing the year to 365.25 days, and one lunar month to 29.53 days, which are close to today's durations, and the most accurate calendric system in the world at the time. Liu's interpretations of the numerology of the *Rites of Zhou* relate to the numbers associated with the celestial sphere (*zhoutian*). At the center of the *Rites of Zhou* is the structure and organization of the official rankings of the Zhou dynasty, in six sections: The Office of Heaven, with authority over administration and general affairs of state; the Office of Earth, in charge of policies in the state and at its borders, as well as education; the Office of Spring, in charge of state rituals, including sacrifices; the Office of Summer, in charge of political affairs, which is to say, military affairs; the Office of Autumn, in charge of criminal punishments; and the Office of Winter, in charge of industry and crafts, as well as inspecting public works and record keeping. Each Office led a set of 60 further offices ranked below it, for a total of 360 offices, thus matching the four seasons and Heaven and Earth to the degrees of the celestial sphere, and so completing a system of correspondence of Heaven and human. Zheng Xuan comments of the first office, "The post is set up by heavenly signs. *Zhong* means 'great,' and *zai* means 'official.' Heaven is the unifying principle of all the myriad things, and the Son of Heaven establishes the Great Official to be in charge of ordering the affairs of state, managing the full set of the offices, and leaving none unfilled. He is not called a supervisor (*si*), but an official (*zai*) generally in charge of the amassed officials (*guan*), and not posted to take charge of the affairs of one single office."[141] According to these words, the official rankings are established by Heaven, and by not calling the Office of Heaven by the title *si*, we see that Heaven dictates strict hierarchical order, with the set of offices being organized by "affairs."

The operation of the political body required this separation of labor into the ranks of the officials, even back during the age of ritual society, but using the system of official ranks to express social ideals was a new development.[142] In the tradition of shamans and scribes, righteousness (*yi*) was expressed through number and sign, and the *Rites of Zhou* linked these to the official ranks, so that the ranks themselves expressed righteousness. There is a formal resemblance between these ideals expressed by ranks and the kingly Way as transmitted by Confucius, namely that both lodged moral ideals into rules and regulations. But in the old category of rites and music theory, royal regulations were united with institutions of rites and music, yielding a system that could serve as an objective basis for moral judgment, while in a political system based on centralized authority, the ranks of the officials were formal job functions in a system separate from the rites and music. Thus the ranks of the officials did not in themselves have any significance for moral judgment. Recovering the tradition of shaman / scribe through heavenly signs endowed the ranks of the officials with moral rationality. The process of constructing moral ideals was premised on the separation of the rites and music from institutions.

What the relation between Heaven and its signs and symbols demonstrates is not imperial power per se, but rather the mixed centralized administration and feudal political system with imperial power at its center. In the central government, this system took as its basis the three dukes and the nine ministers, with the rank of Counselor in Chief (*chengxiang*) the most central in the administration. In its understructure, the smallest units of the system were the township (*xian*), the village (*xiang*), the postal district (*ting*), and the neighborhood (*li*).[143] Each level of political organization resembled the central government, with a combined system comprising administration, law enforcement, military affairs, and finance and economics. Because there could be only one power center, local government often tended to separate from the central government, from which grew tensions between the collective and its parts. Governments under centralized administration depended on laws and regulations from decrees, commands, and policies issued from the imperial court. Under these conditions, administration and law systems became a functional structure around which the feudatories accreting under centralized administrative rule lost the power and significance granted during the Zhou dynasty. We see, then, that the separated enfeoffments of the Shang and Zhou dynasties, with their recognition of clan rights and powers, were useless for the conditions of central national politics, and so to continue the moral-political principles of rites and music could not supply legitimacy to the central administration system centered on imperial power. It was in this situation that Han Confucians appealed to the idea of divinely granted authority to provide legitimacy for the ideology of centralized imperial power. And thus, the Han-dynasty theory of mutual response of Heaven and human became the theoretical basis for the legitimacy of the unified political community (*gongtongti*) centered on imperial power.

However, use of such dense and rigorous symbolic relations to interpret the system of official ranks also expresses rigor within the official ranks per se, meaning that *ruling power is limited.* Within regulations by central authority, formalized laws and political ranks were by no means autonomous, for the following main reasons: first, the emperor had the final authority; second, the laws and regulations were incomplete or else there were laws without basis; and third, some decisions were made arbitrarily.[144] During the reign of Emperor Wu, the "inner court" (*zhongchao*) was formed out of the offices of the Generals in Chief (*dajiangjun*), Palace Attendants (*shizhong*), and Imperial Secretaries (*shangshu*), with added duties over affairs of minor officers (*xian ling*), arbitration (*ping*), acting officials (*shi*), and record-keeping secretaries (*lu shangshu*), while the office of the Counselor in Chief (*chengxiang*), being part of the "outer court" (*waichao*), saw its powers weakened. During the reign of the Han Guangwu Emperor, it was said, "Despite setting up the triumvirate of the three Excellencies, affairs were seen to by the throne itself."[145] This other inner-court structure was by then more influential than the three dukes. Under these conditions, building up the connection between official ranks and the Will of Heaven by means of numerology, thus strengthening the sacred nature of the official ranks system, clearly also meant to honor the system and limit changes to the official ranks and meddling with administration processes. The Western Han–dynasty policies that promulgated stronger imperial powers and central authority brought with them many economic and political implications, such as allowing merchants to purchase official positions and encouraging landlords to operate simultaneously as merchants. These arrangements created a unified force of officials, merchants, and landlords, with many household bankruptcies among peasant families caused by annexation of their lands. In this context, Wang Mang teamed up with the patriarchal clan gentry to recover the regulations of the Three Dynasties of Antiquity and rebuild patriarchal aristocracy; this was the so-called New Administration (*xin zheng*, 9–23 CE). The New Administration revised the divisions and organizational system of the administration, recovering the five noble titles of duke, lord, earl, viscount, and baron; reestablishing the well-field system; and, in the field of merchant enterprise reinstating the policy of "artisans' and merchants' industry and commerce feed the officials," implementing the five-*jun* and the six-*guan* tax system. The New Administration used the *Rites of Zhou*, with its heavenly signs structure, much as in the previously described governments. Between the *Luxuriant Dew of the Spring and Autumn Annals*, which was later made a classic of the New Text school, and the *Rites of Zhou*, a classic of the Old Text school, we can see similarities in their forms of exposition, one of the reasons for which is that they both try to make certain limited demands on the operation of imperial power, by the assignment of the relation of Heaven and its signs and numbers, and through the strict interpretation of the regulations themselves.

4. Transformation of Cosmology; Imperial Right as Center Ideology; and the Political Constitution Based on an Ideology of Separation of Powers

The formation of the Northern Song School of the Way bears a historical relation to late Tang Confucian discussions of Heaven and human, which in turn look back to Heaven-human response theory in Han-dynasty politics and Confucianism. Han Yu (768–824), Liu Zongyuan (733–819), and Liu Yuxi (772–842) criticized the widespread attention given in Tang-dynasty politics to Buddhism, to producing auspicious signs and phenomena, and to the commentaries found in Kong Yingda's *Correct Meanings of the Five Classics* (*Wu jing zheng yi*) and similar works. The critiques directed at Han-dynasty classical learning were actually an extension of this larger trend. In refuting the Heaven-human response theory, the text most deserving of attention is the essay "On the Seasonal Commands" (*Shiling lun*) by Liu Zongyuan, which supplied sharp and direct criticism of the yin-yang and five-phases theories that had flourished ever since the Han dynasty:

> I see that the theories propounded in the "Monthly Observances" carelessly matched everything with the Five Events [i.e., humanity, righteousness, propriety, wisdom, and trustworthiness] and the Five Elements, and wanted governmental measures to be carried out [according to this system]. Did this not stray too far away from the Way of the sages? Now, among all matters of political administration, there are those that can be done according to the seasons, and those which cannot so be done. It was for this reason that the first month of the lunar new year, the boundary markers of the enfeoffments were erected along the frontier, the roads were smoothed over, the soil was examined carefully for what plants should be put in, and without assembling the masses. In the third lunar month of the spring it is beneficial to put up the dams and dikes, to clear out the irrigation canals, to cease hunting in the field, to prepare

> the equipment for sericulture, and to breed cows and horses, while the hundred artisans need not worry over the seasons. Now, then, in the summer, if the earth is not turned over in work, there is nothing to hand out to the masses. So we must push the farmers and urge on the people. In the mid-summer, administer to the brindled horses, and gather medicinal herbs. As the season passes summer, run the waters and cut the hay, fertilize fields, work the good soil and border soil. No military business is done. As autumn comes on, gather up the thatch and wicker. At mid-autumn, urge the people to plant the wheat, and as the season passes autumn, all the hundred artisans rest. The people go indoors, and all have clothes and coats. . . . As winter comes on, they clear out their stoves and rebuild their city walls. These things are determined by the seasons. It is what we might call "timing with reverence for humanity." Besides, there are the suburban temples and the hundred sacrifices, which are left to us by the ancient extant classics, and these must not be abandoned. As for those who made sincere implementation of the government of the ancients, only during spring would they distribute virtues or observances, bestow rewards or dignities, care for the young, visit prisoners, give to the poor, or pay ritual respect to great worthies. Only in the summer would they pay respects to martyrs and heroes, select worthies and great ones, raise the statuses, activate the lords to give out emoluments or deal with minor crimes, and resolve small offenses, act especially frugally, and pacify the multitude of officials. Only in the autumn did they set up generals or array their armies, employ the most useful, punish the violent and recalcitrant, illumine who was good and who bad, and revise the laws and regulations. . . . Only in the winter did they honor those who died for great causes, take pity on orphans and widows, report on cliques and parties, ease market custom, bring in itinerant merchants, survey the districts, rectify bad habits, dismiss officials who would not serve, and get rid of useless implements. So much here relates back to government! It was certainly not necessary to conduct these according to the season.[146]

This essay demolished the relation between government and political administration and the Mandate of Heaven, from which it follows that it left more ground for the development and transformation of human affairs in themselves.

Why was it that although they both defended a political ideology centered on imperial authority, Dong Zhongshu needed to resort to theories of mutual response of Heaven and human, while Liu Zongyuan on the other hand sought to sever the relations between politics, laws, and morality and yin-yang, the five phases, the four seasons, and signs and portents? In the first place, in Dong Zhongshu's theory, imperial power represented the feudal lords, the aristocracy, and officialdom; to connect imperial power directly with Heaven was to respond to a still-influential feudal system. But the imperial authoritarianism of Liu Zongyuan was, on the other hand, an expression of the collapse, just then in progress, of the aristocratic system. At the beginning of the Tang dynasty, there had been a struggle between enfeoffment and the system of centralized administration, the result of which had been the formation of certain power centers dominated by the counties and commanderies, while others were dominated by feudal kingdoms (*houguo*). After the middle period of the reign of Gaozong, owing to the decline of central political control over military authorities, the Nanya guard became something with only ritual significance, while the court depended entirely on the Beiya army for protection of the imperial capital. Adapting to the military situation, the Tang court set up regulation officers (*jiedushi*); the end of the militia system (*fubing*) led directly to rapid growth in the influence of the martial regulation officers. After the An Lushan Rebellion was put down, the court had no choice but to accept the generals and officials who had done the most to bring peace, leading to the spread of a provincial governor system led by military governors and regulation officers. With the three garrison posts of Hebei each controlling its own territory and refusing to pay taxes to the central government, and with military governors willing to defy the court, the Tang dynasty gradually declined. Liu Zongyuan's critique of the Heaven-human mutual response theory occurs in this context, as he tried to turn away from arguments about the Mandate of Heaven and focus instead on the causes of historical developments.

In his essay "On Enfeoffment" (*Fengjian lun*), Liu Zongyuan traces a concept of propensity (*shi*), understanding the enfeoffment and centralized administration systems as the results of historical evolution, from which he took it that no particular political regulations were absolutely rational. In his view, the political form that saw "strong rulers, and governing through punishments" was the result of human struggles during earlier stages of history, when the feudal lords had been produced by competition. Struggle between tribes and among feudal lords led to the emergence of "regional aristocratic lords (*fangbo*), and martial generals over linked and extended armies (*lianshuai*)." Centralized administration was a product of a long historical process. Liu Zongyuan thus created a historical philosophy centered on political form, arguing in the main that centralized power possessed both historical and moral rationality:

> This, then, established the various nobles, and the strife between them was still greater. They took one of great virtue and obeyed his commands so as to bring peace to their fiefs. This established the *fangbo* and *lianshuai,* which brought strife on an even larger scale, and virtue which was proportionally greater. The *fangbo* and *lianshuai* in turn accepted and obeyed [the victor] in order to bring peace to their people. When this happened, all under Heaven was united. . . . From emperor to local official, their virtue among the people was such that when they died their heirs were chosen as successors. In view of all this, enfeoffment was not something intended by the sages, but a matter of propensity. . . . The feudal system [is something that] even in highest antiquity the sage-kings Yao, Shun, Yu, Tang, Wen, and Wu could not do away with. Not that they did not want to do away with it, but the propsensity [of the era] prevented them from doing so.[147]

As a hereditary aristocracy, the feudal system easily led to separatism and war, and also obstructed the use of talented officials to their full potential, while central administration could possess a more productive hierarchy, with the most talented on top and the unworthy remaining inferior. "Propensity" here was not the Mandate of Heaven, but internal to the tendency and impulse of historical movement. Tracing "propensity," Liu Zongyuan believed that the replacement of the enfeoffment system by the central administration system was a natural and rational historical course.

That Liu Zongyuan wanted to disrupt the idea of Heaven and human being in direct contact, besides the fact that Tang political interpretations of disasters and portents had long become corrupt and useless, stemmed from another factor as well, which was that the Tang political structure was thick with enfeoffments, often tracing back to rituals first affirmed in the *Rites of*

Zhou. And as we wrote above, the *Rites of Zhou* featured links of Heaven with human through numerology. In this context, to assail Zhou feudalism was also at once to reject the Heaven-human framework that had ensured the perpetuation of enfeoffments during the Han dynasty. However, resorting to social relations within the category of "propensity" to supply rationality inevitably led to two nearly insurmountable difficulties. First, "propensity" was unstable, which meant that social frameworks produced by propensity were also constantly threatened and dissolved by ever-changing propensity. And second, using protection of the hierarchy of superior and inferior officials as one major reason to assert the superiority of central administration is a functionalist politics. In sum, abandoning the theory of Heaven-human response once again highlighted the fact that functionalist political systems sorely lacked a moral basis.

Han Yu's more moderate views on the Heaven-human connection reflect the separation, explained above, between political system and moral rationality. In his essay "On the Origins of Humanity" (*Yuan ren*), Han Yu elucidated the three terms Way of Heaven (*tiandao*), Way of Earth (*didao*), and Way of Humanity (*rendao*) by means of the terms "beyond form" (*xing'er shang*), "beneath form" (*xing'er xia*), and "mandated between the two" (*ming yu liang jian*) to distinguish the way of Heaven from that of human.[148] For Han Yu, it was clear that social order and ritual alike had their origins in human creativity. However, he still believed in the Mandate of Heaven: "For the historian-scribes, if there weren't human disasters, then there were Heavenly punishments, so how could they possibly take things lightly, without fear?"[149] And, "The fates of the three masters hang upon Heaven. . . . Thus I report their fate to Heaven to understand it."[150]

His language on the three varieties of human nature (*xing*) also falls within the structure of his views on the Mandate of Heaven: "The birth of Houyi, giving his mother no pain, led to him being precocious and even wise in his early years. And King Wen's mother never felt any pain with King Wen in her, but when he was born, he immediately began learning without any instruction or encouragement at all, giving his teachers no trouble."[151] Setting forth views on the Mandate of Heaven, Han Yu's genealogy of Confucian orthodoxy (*daotong*) and his effort to build up a theory of Confucian orthodoxy in themselves can be said to be the results of the "Mandate of Heaven": "He who has created order knows why his teachings are tossed aside. [For this reason] he castigates all things strange and dangerous and promotes instead the way of imperial perfection, repressing ornament and overstylization in favor of loyalty and substance. How great is the Mandate of Heaven, how profound the Creator. Such be the workings of the Way!"[152] If Confucian orthodoxy requires the guardianship of the Mandate of Heaven, then how could moral philosophy abandon the influence of Han-dynasty theories of Heaven and human?

Zhou Dunyi, Shao Yong, Zhang Zai, Cheng Yi, and Zhu Xi of the Southern Song, in establishing their own cosmological theories, all to one degree or another preserved some impressions of Han-dynasty Heaven-human theory, facing the same issues in this regard as Han Yu before them. As central figures building up the Way of Heaven theories for the Northern Song, Zhou Dunyi, Shao Yong, and Zhang Zai differed in argument and concepts, but shared the vision of a holistic order, with ways of deriving moral values from cosmology. Zhou Dunyi (1017–1073) has been called the major forerunner of the Song Daoxue Confucian schools. His "Explanation of the Diagram of the Supreme Ultimate" (*Taiji tu shuo*) and *Penetrating the* Book of Changes (*Tong shu*) establish a dual-featured system, combining metaphysics and cosmology with interpretations of the *Book of Changes*. The first text describes the human world with appeals to the proposition "from Ultimate Non-Being comes the Supreme Ultimate," while the second works from the Way of Heaven to the mind of morality (*daode xin*), expanding on the latter to speak of ritual, and so lays the way to develop a theory of ritual, yielding a Northern Song School of the Way with links between the Way of Heaven, metaphysics, morality, and ritual. The "Explanation of the Diagram of the Supreme Ultimate" classifies Ultimate Non-Being, Supreme Ultimate, yin and yang, and the five phases together in the layer of Heaven. The five phases and the myriad things are the second layer, while the human world is the third. Sages and worthies are in the fourth layer. Using the Ways of Heaven, Earth, and Man to exposit the layers builds a view of the universe unifying Heaven and human. This cosmo-ontology supplies people with a diagram of a dynamic universe in which the Ultimate Non-Being and Supreme Ultimate are involved, as are yin and yang and the five phases, which refer back to the Ways of Heaven, Earth, and Man, yielding a holistic order. With this interpretation based on the *Book of Changes*, Zhou Dunyi develops a diagrammatic description of the universe that shows clear influence from previous studies of the *Book of Changes* by Daoist philosophers, religious Daoists, and yin-yang masters.[153] Heaven gives life to the myriad things by means of *yang*, and completes the myriad things by means of *yin*. Life is humaneness (*ren*); completeness is righteousness. Thus the sages above use humanity to incubate the myriad things and rectify the myriad peoples by means of righteousness. The myriad things follow the operation of the Way of Heaven. The peoples of the world are transformed by the virtue of the sages.[154] On this theory of the universe, humaneness and righteousness follow from the order of the universe, and serve as the foundation for the virtue of the sage.

Shao Yong (1011–1077), an expert on numerology, used signs and numbers with great facility to explain the development of the universe and history. He was concerned with historical events that were an expression of the universe with a holistic order, but hidden beneath myriad signs. In his *Outer Chapters on Observing Things* (*Guan wu wai pian*), he wrote: "Circular are the stars: here commences the numbering of the calendrical record. Square is the earth: here begin the land surveys and the well-field system. Now, the circle is the sign of the Yellow River Chart (*hetu*), and the square is the sign of the Luo River Writing (*luoshu*). Thence it was that Fu Xi and King Wen created the *Book of Changes,* while King Yu and Jizi wrote the Great Plan (*Hong fan,* in the *Book of Documents*)."[155] Zhu Xi later appended the comment, "The circle refers to the stars. Where it says, 'the circle is the sign of the Yellow River Diagram (*hetu*),' this refers to the lack of four corners, because it is round in shape."[156] "The Yellow River Diagram does not have four sides," he adds, "so it is more round than the Luo River Writing square." "The square is the earth, like the diagram of the Luo River Writing, the magic square and the great plan, used to survey the land and mark out the fields for taxation." Similarly, he linked universe, continents, and fields by number, believing that the well-field system was "similar to the nine-part magic square of the Luo River Writing."[157] This shows that the theories of Shao Yong and Zhu Xi both retained many elements of Han-dynasty cosmology. The relations between Shao Yong's *Book of the Supreme Principles Governing the World* (*Huang ji jing shi shu*) and Chen Tuan's *Diagram of the Anterior to Heaven* (*Xiantian tu*) have inspired many studies and discussions over the ages; worth mentioning is that the *Diagram of the Anterior to Heaven* argues for patterns of eight trigrams and sixty-four hexagrams, connecting Heaven and human with numerology, yet also locating all of these as a single body within the mind (*xin*). We can compare Shao Yong's numerology with that of the *Rites of Zhou* and the *Luxuriant Dew of the Spring and Autumn Annals* of Dong Zhongshu to find clear differences. Where Dong Zhongshu builds complementary correspondences comprehensively with the political system, Master Shao's numerology does not have strict complementarity with political systems. Shao Yong wrote:

> According to the *Book of Changes,* to plumb Principle and Nature, is to arrive at our destiny (*ming*). This is why what is called Principle is the Principle behind all things; what we call Nature (*xing*) is the Nature from Heaven; and what we call destiny (*ming*) is located with Principle (*li*) and Nature. What locates destiny among Principle and Nature is the Way (*Dao*)—it's that or nothing at all! It means knowing that the Way is the root of Heaven and Earth, while Heaven and Earth are the root of the myriad things. To observe the myriad things by means of Heaven and Earth is thus to take the myriad things as a thing; to observe Heaven and Earth by means of the Way is thus to take Heaven and Earth also as of the myriad things.[158]

A major trait of Shao Yong's "Anterior to Heaven Learning" (*Xiantian xue*) was to see the mind (*xin*) as the origin of the myriad things, which not only directly connects Way with Mind, but also places universal order within the category of Mind. In this sense, order is first and foremost closely related to the internal perspective of observing and representing this order. Only by returning to Mind can one obtain knowledge of the substance of the universe, because Mind is the wellspring of the universe. "Heaven is born in the Way; Earth is completed in the Way; things are formed in the Way; humanity conducts itself according to the Way."[159] "Heaven divided yields Earth. Earth divided yields the myriad things. But the Way cannot be divided. In the end, the myriad things return to Earth, Earth returns to Heaven, and Heaven returns to the Way."[160] Heaven, Earth, humanity, and the myriad things are all divisible, but the Way is "one," an absolute, indivisible order, the original substance and wellspring. The absolute and objective nature of the Way stems from the fact of the return to mind, which people tend to think of as subjective. "Anterior to Heaven Learning is a way of the mind. Consequently all diagrams begin from the mind; the myriad transformations and events begin life in the mind."[161] If the universe and myriad things begin life in the mind, and the universe diagram "begins from the mind," then universal order is given life and completed internally, and this internal process forms an order that is indivisible, uninfluenced by the myriad things or their context, and most objective. Given this objective, internal order, Shao Yong raises two further propositions: "The Way is the Supreme Ultimate," and "Mind is the Supreme Ultimate." Thus, the "Supreme Ultimate" unifies Mind and the Way.[162] The Way, the Supreme Ultimate, and the order of the universe are thus understood as patterns obtained and discovered internal to the mind.

"Mind" (*xin*) in Shao Yong is unrelated to the uniqueness of the individual person's subjectivity or passions, for it does not follow from "myriad things as Mind" that the final material of the universe is Mind. "Mind is the Supreme Ultimate" (*xin wei taiji*) and "Myriad things are Mind" (*wanwu wei xin*) indicate that the myriad things of the universe are based on an internal order, from which it follows they can only be inspected through the internal gaze of natural order. Perhaps we can conclude that this is an existing order or existing vision. Cheng Hao gave a critique of this, writing:

> The learning of Shao Yong derives meaning from the Pattern, discussing the Images and Numbers [of the *Book of Changes*]. It discusses how the Pattern of the world must emanate from "the Four," to infer the specifics of the Pattern. [Shao Yong] says, "When I apprehend the Great, the myriad affairs proceed from myself, and none fail to be fixed." However, there is not necessarily any technique to [Shao Yong's method].[163]

Here the Way, the Supreme Ultimate, Mind, and Principle are linked with one another, and Mind is not subjective or internal to our bodies or closely associated with the "mind" that ever pulses with passion and cognition, but rather is a kind of order or original body (*benti*) that manifests when Mind and matter are united. Shao Yong's learning possesses a quality that seems paradoxical but is actually cogent, which is that it is deeply colored by determinism, but on the other hand it also emphasizes the subject and the subject's cognitive ability. These aspects combine in the description of universal order, in which Shao Yong determines that the Way, the Supreme Ultimate, Mind, and the One (*yi*) all exhibit oneness such that human understanding is not limited to individual experience but must take on vantage points transcendent of humanity. Hence his call "not to comprehend things in terms of self, but to comprehend things as things." "To comprehend things as things" (*wu wu*) means to observe matter as possessing natural order, the principle of All-under-Heaven, from which it follows that this perspective is objective.[164] The concept of "vision and perspective of internal natural order" can also reveal the deeper meaning behind Shao Yong's call to "comprehend things as things." Here, "vision of internal natural order" has an important difference from what we know today as the self with its own internal depth, for the two represent completely different views of order and methodologies for understanding order; but on a rhetorical level, these two different views both tend to turn inward.

The "Guan learning" (*Guan xue*) of Zhang Zai (1020–1077) grounds itself in "respecting ritual, valuing virtue, pleasing Heaven and making peace with the Mandate, taking the *Book of Changes* as the line of descent, the *Doctrine of the Mean* as the dominant body, using the methods of Confucius and Mencius, deleting the strange and the fabricated, and distinguishing god from ghost."[165] In this respect, he has the deepest connection with pre-Qin rites-and-music theory. But on Zhang Zai's theory, the rites and music are now folded into the new cosmology and visions of natural order.

Zhang's "Western Inscription" (*Xi ming*) argues that the myriad things are one body, and Principle is one divided into many characteristics, first and foremost taking that the myriad things, Heaven, and Earth form one body with humanity, which is then taken to be the root of all of them. The maxim "All humanity is my kin; and all things related with me" crisply encapsulates Zhang Zai's theory.[166] In *Correcting Youthful Ignorance* (*Zheng meng*), he describes the gestalt of myriad generations, completions, and transformations as the "great harmony" (*taihe*), but unwilling to stop there, he advances an idea of the original substance of the universe, which he labels the "great vacuity" (*taixu*). "The great vacuity has no form, but is the original substance of *qi*. That it coalesces and separates is the external form of transformation, and nothing more. Utmost stillness and without feeling is the origin of Nature (*xing*); being with knowledge and awareness is merely the objective sense of the exchange of things and nothing more."[167] Such is the cosmology scholars have ascribed to Zhang Zai as a monism based on *qi*, or ontology based on *qi*, which expresses itself in a dialectical structure whereby *taixu* (great vacuity) coalesces into matter and separates again into *qi*. The ontology of *qi* bursts asunder the cosmology of philosophical Daoism, with its ontology of "nonaction" (*wuwei*), and so was thought to be "the highest achievement of natural science of its time, aligned with the schools of the *Book of Changes,* and thoroughly refuting the theories behind Buddhism and Daoism, superficial and contradictory as they were, and replacing them with a plainly materialist and dialectical ontology of *qi*."[168] With its acknowledgment that *wu,* matter, and *qi* are both external and material, Zhang Zai's theory was useful for those advocating greater understanding of natural processes. Under his influence, Guan learning "was primarily about practical application, with crossing through vacuity as the mechanism," and so tended toward a practical understanding of "the Way" (*dao*).[169] Li Fu and Li Yeming, for example, affirmed the concepts of "principle of Nature" and "numbers of Nature," and even went so far as to see Heaven as matter in motion, which far exceeds the scope of the learning of Zhou Dunyi or Shao Yong.[170]

Qi-based ontology led people to understand the basic substance and origins of the universe as emerging within the world, thus drawing a clear line of distinction from the more transcendent and hermetic Buddhism and Taoism. *Qi*-based ontology and investigations of Nature can be seen as the logical conclusions of Northern Song learning, because once the pursuit of moral principle was combined with the model of cosmology, there was a demand for an epistemology of the natural order, the form of which epistemology would be an arrangement by descending layers, the highest of which was the Way of Heaven (*tiandao*).[171] Whatever the particular features of Zhang Zai's theory, its basic feature was a vision of universal order informed by *qi* ontology, so we should not exaggerate differences between it and the theories of the Supreme Ultimate or the Anterior to Heaven by Zhou Dunyi and Shao Yong, respectively. Zhou, Shao, and Zhang all tried to construct cosmological ontologies in order to place morality and ethics and theories of Mind and Nature, from which would follow basic methods of thinking in which Heaven, the Way, Nature (*xing*), and Mind (*xin*) all accord in a common logical structure. The central intention of Zhang Zai's learning was not to deal with questions of natural philosophy, but rather as Wang Fuzhi puts it, "to place ritual at the root,"[172] from which it follows that the *qi* ontology should provide the warrant for "right mind" (*zheng xin*) and life living out its nature to the utmost (*jin xing*).[173] In other words, "to place ritual at the root" in Zhang Zai learning meant extending the natural order out into ethical principles for daily practice. Hence the internal logical structure of the seventeen chapters of the *Correcting Youthful Ignorance:* beginning with chapter 1 on "great harmony" (*taihe*), in which all things were one, and on to chapters 2 through 5 on Heaven, Earth, and humans over the course of *qi* transformations. Then, eleven more chapters fashioning theories of human nature, knowledge, morality, and government, all centered on the Way of humanity (*rendao*), followed by the final chapter combining the Way of humanity with the Way of Heaven, reiterating an ontology premised on "the myriad things are one" and "Heaven and human are one in *qi*." The dual nature of Heaven and Earth, and the nature of *qi* as a substance, would be topics that long occupied the Song and Ming School of Principle, but without the substantial order contained in the concept of the "great vacuity," such a dualist approach would lack a theoretical basis.[174] In this respect, Zhang Zai's *qi* ontology supplied a holistic theory of internal order.

My rough outline and comparison of Han- and Song-dynasty theories of Heaven can show the significance of the establishment of a "worldview of Heavenly Principle" (*tianli shijie guan*) for intellectual history. First, the School of the Way inherited and continued many elements of Han-dynasty cosmology, such as the methods of connecting the signs and numbers to the Way of Heaven (*tiandao*) and human events, as well as the extension of discussions regarding the Yellow River and Luo River diagrams, and also the "scientific turn" that extended from cosmology. But in the midst of these extensions and continuations, we can also discover deep differences and distinctions: School of the Way cosmology was formed between practical and metaphysical studies related to cosmology, with the ideas from metaphysics taking ever more central positions. Following this direction of the Northern Song School of the Way, the Cheng brothers and Zhu Xi developed theories of the myriad things of the universe being of one principle, of Principle being one but differing in characteristics, of things each having their principle, each having their position. They stated demands for understanding things from within moral theory. Within the framework of the Northern Song School of Principle (*lixue*), "things" (*wu*) meant external events and things, and also human conduct. To the question, "In investigating things, are the things external, or are they internal to natural endowment?" Cheng Yi answered by saying, "It does not matter. All before our eyes are material things, and all things possess Principle (*li*). As with fire's having heat, water's having coolness, and even extending to ruler and subject, father and son, all possess Principle."[175] This conjecture that all things have Principle demands progress in understanding concrete events and things, but not as according to numerology; rather, "things" here have become more internalized.[176] Clearly, in the metaphysical world of Heavenly Principle, the correspondence of Heaven and human is no longer as specific as in the Han-dynasty theory, as the absolute nature of Heaven is gradually replaced by a view of Principle as order.

Second, following the orientation of the early period of the School of the Way, the Cheng brothers introduced Heavenly Principle, or simply Principle, as a category. Principle preserves the correspondence of Heaven and human, but abandons the naturalist turn, pushing more toward Heaven as a metaphysical category. "Heaven is Principle," wrote Cheng Hao. "The term 'divine' (*shen*) expresses the mystery of the myriad things. The term 'emperors' (*di*) names what controls events and affairs."[177] Here, the Mandate of Heaven concept is preserved, but the differences between Heaven, divine, and the emperors (*di*) are made clear. And this all became a premise to the Song Confucian transformation of the Mandate of Heaven into Nature and Principle; Nature and Principle formed the Principle of Nature, the relations of which lacked the oppositional dimension of Han-dynasty views.[178]

And so, third, Principle or Heavenly Principle is not an absolute top-down command, but rather an original substance awaiting manifestation, immanent in the universe, the myriad things, and humanity itself, and thus it follows that Heavenly Principle follows our internal natures. From the proposition that the Supreme Ultimate has no boundary, to the proposition that all things have their principles, the concept of Heavenly Principle becomes a strong challenge to cosmologies with a single center. Within this theory, the material order of the real world is in tension with Principle, or Heavenly Principle, and therefore following Principle, or Heavenly Principle, is internal moral conduct, and a basis for maintaining self-mastery within the material order.[179] From this, in order to resolve the so-called contradiction of is and ought, of fact and value, Song Confucians established a cosmological binary of Principle (*li*) / *qi* and an epistemological binary of Principle (*li*) / things (*wu*). They also established, within their theory of original nature (*benxing*), a dichotomy between the nature of Heaven and Earth and the nature of substance (*qizhi*), as well as, within their theory of morality, a dichotomy between Principle (*li*) and desire (*yu*). Under this dual structure with Principle and *qi*, the model that connected Heaven and human via numerology was no longer effective.

Fourth, the epistemology of investigating things to fully understand Principle was a precondition for self-cultivation and self-actualization, as well as the channel leading to the ideal communal state (*gongtongti*):

> Fully extending knowledge means investigating things, and is called the root, which means the beginning. Putting the state and All-under-Heaven in order is called the branch, the end.
>
> Putting the state and All-under-Heaven in order requires the rooting of many selves. There has never been anyone who could bring order to All-under-Heaven without rectifying the self. The term "to investigate" (*ge*) means "to fully grasp" (*qiong*); the term "things" (*wu*) means "Principle" (*li*). So it is like saying: it's just about fully grasping Principle. If Principle is fully grasped, then it will be sufficient to reach full understanding. If Principle is not fully grasped then full understanding cannot be reached.[180]

The government of the state and All-under-Heaven relies on the self-cultivation and wise practice of the scholar-officials (*shi*); this transformation signifies that the direct relation between Confucian learning and the government of the ancient Sage-Kings has loosened. In the School of Principle there developed a new form of scholar-official, one who tried hard to maintain the tense relationship between the imperial political system and moral judgment.

* * *

In sum, from Han-dynasty cosmology to the establishment of the Northern Song Way of Heaven was a transition, with the center of focus no longer on the correspondence of Heaven and human, but rather on the internal moral qualities of humans, and their conduct. The evolution of the Way of Heaven theory into the Heavenly Principle worldview, or "theory of original nature" (*benxing lun*), was yet another transition, with deep transformations to Confucian philosophies of moral and logical practice occurring from here forward. This transformation can be summarized as follows: cosmology took an inward turn, and moral and political practice went from following the mastery or commands of Heaven to following internal nature, and the understanding of the relationship between human and the world went from building relations of numerology to those specific and concrete understandings of events and things. With respect to these two ideas, we can see the similar moral-political stances of the Song and Ming School of Principle and the Way of Confucius and Mencius.

CHAPTER 2

Heavenly Principle and the Centralized State

Translated by JESSE FIELD *and* MATTHEW A. HALE

> During the Three Dynasties of Antiquity and earlier times, order came from unity, with the rites and music reaching all under Heaven. Since the Three Dynasties, order has come from two [the rites and music, and the bureaucracy], with the rites and music becoming but empty names.
>
> —*The New History of the Tang (Xin Tang shu)* 11: Treatise on Rites and Music

I. Establishing the Concept of Heavenly Principle

1. The Evolution of "Principle"

The emergence of the concept of "Heavenly Principle" (*tianli*) in the Song dynasty was an event of profound historical significance. During the period between the Han and Song dynasties, as both Buddhism and Daoism rose to prominence, the differentiation between "Principle(s)" or "pattern" (*li*) and "rites" or "ritual" (also pronounced "*li*") demonstrated the influence of these currents upon Confucianism.[1] The Chan school of Buddhism emphasized the inability of words to express the highest principles, but it also acknowledged that "language can be used to illuminate the purpose" of such principles.[2] If principles depended upon words to be established, then it became an essential task to divide principles into categories on a lexical basis. For the Song and Ming Confucians, however, principle took on a distinctly secular orientation, so the broader historical dynamics behind the establishment of the

Heavenly Principle worldview cannot be grasped within the categories of cosmology, ontology, or theories of human nature alone. Before we can summarize the Song Confucian conception of Principle, then, it is first necessary to trace how "Principle" (*li*) transformed from a marginal category into one possessing major political significance.

In Confucian documents dating from the early Zhou until the Spring and Autumn period, the character *li* 理 was used only to distinguish between territories and to name certain official positions (such as judges).[3] Xu Shen's explanation in the *Shuowen* dictionary (*Discussing Writings and Explicating Characters*) states: "*Li* 理 means to carve jade, combining *yu* 玉 [the character for "jade" as a semantic component] with the sound of *li* 里 [a different character serving as a phonetic component]," as in: "[When Cang Jie, the scribe of the Yellow Emperor, observed the tracks left by birds and beasts, he] understood that patterns (*li*) of distinctions (*fen*) could be differentiated from each other. [Thus he began to invent writing.]"[4] In pre-Qin texts, the use of *li* to indicate the Will of Heaven or the principle of "the myriad things" began with the *Zhuangzi.* Its chapter titled "Constrained in Will" (*Ke yi*) stated: "He discards knowledge and purpose, following along with the *li* of Heaven."[5] For Zhuangzi, the *li* of Heaven flowed through everything in the universe, transcending everyday phenomena such as life and death; motion and stillness; calamity and good fortune; things, people, and spirits; pondering and scheming; sleeping and waking—"knowledge and purpose" of these phenomena causing an obstruction to the adherence to *li* that must, therefore, be discarded. Similarly, the chapter titled "Knowledge Wandered North" (*Zhi bei you*) stated:

> Heaven and earth have their great beauties but do not speak of them; the four seasons have their clear-marked regularity but do not discuss it; the ten thousand things have their principles (*li*) of growth but do not expound on them. The sage seeks out the beauties of Heaven and earth and masters the principles of the ten thousand things. Thus it is that the Perfect Man does not act, the Great Sage does not move—they have perceived the Way of Heaven and earth, we may say.[6]

Here *li* was a sort of universalist principle, rather than knowledge of any specific thing.

Zhuangzi linked "Heaven's Will" (*tianyi*) to a natural concept of Heaven and, in that sense, legitimated "the principle(s) of the people" (*min zhi li*). The chapter titled "The World" (*Tianxia*) stated:

> [T]o keep a constant eye on administrative affairs, give first thought to food and clothing, keep in mind the need to produce and grow, to shepherd and store away, to provide for the old and the weak, the orphan and the widow, so that all are properly nourished—these are the principles by which the people are ordered. [. . .] The *Book of Odes* describes the will; the *Book of Documents* describes events; the *Book of Rites* speaks of conduct; the *Record of Music* speaks of harmony; the *Book of Changes* describes the yin and yang; the *Spring and Autumn Annals* describes [distinctions among names (*mingfen*)].[7]

The concept "principles of the people" suggested that sovereigns could not simply rule according to their own will. As a natural order corresponding to Heaven's Will ("the principles of Heaven and Earth," "Heavenly Principle," or the patterns of nature), principles or "distinctions among names" meant that the world was composed of various forces, each possessing its own principles, so to conduct oneself according to unilateral power relations would be to contradict Heaven's Will.

Daoists were not the only thinkers who employed this method of creating an immanent linkage between the principle of what ought to be and the fundamental order of the universe. Such immanent association of principles, meant for humans to follow, with a natural order of the universe was not the exclusive domain of Daoism, but also took place in Legalism. The *Han Feizi* chapter on "Explicating Laozi" (*Jie Lao*) stated:

> The Way is that which makes the myriad things so, and that which fixes the myriad principles of things. These principles are the patterns of completed things, and the Way is the means by which all things are completed. Thus it is said: "The Way constitutes the ordering principles of the myriad things." Things have their ordering principles and cannot overlap with one another, so ordering principles are the determinants of things. Each of the myriad things in the world possesses a different ordering principle, and the Way to the very last fixes the ordering principles of things.[8]

The Way was the reason that the ten thousand things existed as they did, and the *li* were their formative principles, each of which differed according to the variation among those myriad things. The phrase "the *Spring and Autumn Annals* describes distinctions among names" referred to the order formed according to the Way's principles of distinctions (*fenli*) for each of these things. According to Xiong Shili, "Distinctions among names are always explained as referring to the distinction between upper and lower ranks. This is a far-fetched analogy based on imperial thinking rather than the intention of the *Spring and Autumn Annals.* Actually this term means to differentiate cases according to their corresponding principles, and to rectify names according to the principles behind the things to which they refer."[9] Distinctions among names were related to the order of ritual institutions: "the principles of things" referred to distinctions among names within the ritual order. Compare this passage with "The Achievements of the Scholars" (*Ru xiao*) in the *Xunzi:* "The *Book of Odes* recounts their will. The *Book of Documents* recounts their events. The *Book of Rites* recounts their conduct. The *Classic of Music* recounts their harmony. And the *Spring and Autumn Annals* recounts their subtlety (*wei*)." And again with "Seldom Seen" (*Gua Jian*) in the Han-dynasty *Fayan* by Yang Xiong: "As for the principles, there is no explanation better than that in the *Spring and Autumn Annals.*" Therefore, "distinctions among names" and "subtlety" both described the broader sense in the *Spring and Autumn Annals:* namely, a clear differentiation between right and wrong according to the concept of ritual institutions was used as a basis for governance, always involving relativistic concepts.

In the *Zhuangzi,* the universality and immanence of principles and the negation of specific knowledge provided evidence to support "nonaction" (*wuwei*), whereas in the Legalist classics, the same concept was used to argue for the transcendence of the direct power relations involved in monarchical rule and the will of the sovereign. The *Guanzi* emphasized "action according to inherent principles" (*yuan li er dong*), clearly showing the influence of Daoist teachings, but here "adherence to the principles" was not developed along the lines of nonaction. Guanzi wrote: "To enlighten the people so that they may examine their own natures, be certain that you yourself adhere to the principles. [. . .] It is because he follows the principles that the sovereign knows what is suitable for himself and what is suitable for the people."[10] And, "When the speech of the ruler conforms to the principles and accords with the sentiments of the people, the people will accept his instructions."[11] The sovereign must proceed from the principles, as well as from the "sentiments" (*qing*) of the people. If we can say that Zhuangzi synthesized the concepts of adherence to principles and a natural Heaven, then Legalism linked the restrictive aspect of Heaven to legal principles, with "adherence to principles" expressed not only as efforts to ascertain the will of the people, but also as the solemnity of the law. The *Guanzi*'s chapter on "Laws and Prohibitions" (*Fa jin*) stated:

> Since sovereigns could not judiciously establish their laws as the system for managing those below, it inevitably became general practice for the commoners to institute their own principles and follow their own interests. [. . .] If the sovereign is not consistent in establishing these rules of conduct, there are certain to be many of his subordinate officials who will turn their backs on the law and replace it with their own private principles.[12]

Law was a universal order that transcended the ruler's personal will and private affairs, guiding relations between lord and ministers, as well as between teacher and students—as illustrated by the precepts "follow the Way, not the sovereign"[13] and "follow the principles, not the teacher."[14] In an era when the system of clan law (*zongfa*) and decentralized enfeoffment (*fengjian*) was in crisis, relations of enfeoffment based upon kinship were no longer able to govern society effectively—this was the context in which relations based upon law stepped onto the stage. If the principles represented a legal system that transcended the absolute hierarchy of relations between teacher and student, or between sovereign and ministers, then law as institutionalized principles came to constitute a modality of Heaven's Will.

In the Warring States period, legal relations were still enveloped within the categories of ritual order, so "principles" and "rites" were interchangeable concepts. The *Guanzi*'s chapter "On Military Taxes" (*Sheng ma*) stated:

> The court sets the principles for righteous conduct (*yi*). Thus ranks and positions are bestowed in orderly fashion, so the people are not resentful and disorders do not arise. Only then can a principle be established for righteous conduct. Without proper order in the bestowal of ranks and

> positions, it would be impossible to govern. Now, it is not possible for all people of a state to have honored positions—if they did, production would fail and the state would suffer. However, if one were to eliminate honored positions entirely lest production fail and the state suffer, the people would not be able to establish principles for righteous conduct on their own.[15]

According to Gu Fang's research, the concept of "principles" evolved from the category of "rites." On the one hand, the former was used as a substitute for the latter under conditions where "the [Zhou system of] rites and music had collapsed" (*li beng yue huai*).[16] On the other hand, the principles were also contained within the category of ritual. In the *Xunzi,* for example, "the principles" were a component of "the rites."[17] However, the relationship between the two terms was not fixed: on some occasions they were equivalent to one another, but on others the one could be subordinate to the other, or could replace or subvert it. This relationship shows that the principles could achieve expression only on the basis of some specific order such as the system of rites and music.

The Han dynasty inherited from the Qin dynasty the institutions of a vast, politically centralized empire. In order to unite the nobles of the Six States and obtain political legitimacy from pre-Qin traditions, the founding rulers of the Han dynasty had no choice but to fuse the centralized bureaucracy with aristocratic institutions, reviving the enfeoffment system of clan law under imperial control. Han Confucian texts all explained the principles as involving "distinctions" (*fen*) or "separation" (*li*), strongly suggesting the dynasty's arrangement of fusing the Qin-style centralized administration of "commanderies and counties" (*junxian*) with the pre-Qin system of enfeoffment. Jia Yi's *New Writings* (*Xinshu*) stated: "Principles take the form of divisions."[18] Similarly, Zheng Xuan's commentary on the *Record of Music* (*Yueji*) stated: "principles are distinctions."[19] The *Virtuous Discussions from the White Tiger Pavilion* (*Baihutong delun*) noted: "Ritual and righteous conduct possess the principles of distinctions."[20] And again, the introduction to the *Shuowen* dictionary recounted: "[The Yellow Emperor's scribe] understood that *li* [patterns or principles] of distinctions could be differentiated from each other."[21] The "principles of distinctions" concept continued uninterrupted all the way from the Han down to the Qing dynasty, seeking out some kind of autonomy for things and situations within universalist concepts of morality, while also providing an epistemological justification for decentralist political views (i.e., aristocratic or feudal ones). Throughout the Western and Eastern Han, this concept of "distinctions" remained limited to the categories of unified monarchy, a situation we can read as a way for the imperial system, merging centralized administration with enfeoffment, to be expressed within the system of Heaven's Way. Dong Zhongshu wrote that in the *Spring and Autumn Annals*, "Ethical standards, distinctions among names, and the ranking of events do not depart from their respective principles."[22] Also: "This is why in spring both [yin and yang] are in the south; in autumn both are in the north; yet they do not share [the same] circuit. In summer they intersect in the front; in winter they intersect in the rear, yet their *li* (pattern or principle) is not the same."[23] He linked the ritual system of order to the concept of the Five Phases (*wu xing*), folding the principles of things or matter (*shiwu zhi li*) into the framework of "the mutual responsiveness of Heaven and humanity" (*tian-ren*) that he constructed.

The late Han and Wei-Jin dynasties saw a major shift in the power relations between imperial authority and the aristocracy. The power of the Great Families (*shijia dazu*), comprising the imperial clan together with those staffing the bureaucracy, continued to expand, ultimately dissolving the empire's unity from within. Cao Pi (187?–226 CE), emperor of Cao Wei in the Three Kingdoms period, adopted his minister Chen Qun's proposal to establish the Nine-Rank System, appointing controllers in all the provinces and commanderies. Among the men serving as officials in the capital, locals with talent and virtue were selected to serve as controllers who would evaluate candidates for the civil service on a scale of nine ranks according to their virtue, talent, and familial status, on which basis the Ministry of Civil Service would recruit officials. The establishment of this system was not only an epoch-making event in the history of institutions for selecting officials, but was also key to the formation of a new aristocratic system. In contemporary discussions of whether names lived up to reality, "principles" became the standard for measuring people. Liu Shao was one Three Kingdoms–era thinker who became famous for living up to his name—including by the comments and suggestions he made about the system of granting official positions. In his *Treatise on Human Abilities* (*Renwu zhi*), chapter I ("Nine Proofs" [*Jiuzheng*]) states: "Now, the root of human abilities emerges from sentiment and nature. The principles of sentiments and nature are obscure and esoteric; observed by non-sages, they can hardly be fully understood!"[24] Similarly, in chapter IV ("Principles of Human Talent" [*Caili*]) we have:

> Principle comes in four categories, illumination comes in four classes. [. . .] Filling in voids and subtracting from overflows is the Principle of the Way. Rectifying affairs by means of law and government is the Principle of Affairs. Making the rites and teaching appropriate and adjusted is the Principle of Righteousness. The key motivating force of human sentiments is the Principle of Sentiment. The differences in the Four Principles lie in ability, and it requires illumination to organize them. Illumination proceeds according to substance. For this reason, substance aligns with Principle, and illumination comes only with alignment. Illumination is sufficient to make visible Principle; Principle is sufficient to make the master. It is for this reason that one whose substance and nature are even and mild, yet whose thoughts are obscure and esoteric, and who comprehends fully Nature, is the master of the Principle of the Way. One in whom substance and nature are at peace, and who can discuss rites and teachings, and who distinguishes one's rights and one's wrongs, is a master of the Principle of Righteousness. One in whom substance and nature have their motivating forces explained, and who can push their sentiments to the intents they wish for, and who can adjust to the transformations, is a master of the Principle of Sentiment.[25]

The Heavenly Principle was that of Heaven's Way, administrative principles (*shili*) were those concerning state affairs, principles of righteousness (*yili*) were those involving cultural transformation through rites and music (*liyue jiaohua*), and principles of sentiment (*qingli*) were those related to human emotions, habits, and the will. The motivation for undertaking the categorization of principles was to evaluate people, that is, to translate principles into a set of virtues that could be used as a reference for classifying people according to different types. In this way, Liu Shao divided people into "four families," providing a basis for creating a taxonomy related to the objective world. In this sense, the taxonomy of principles derived not from epistemological demands, but from discussions in the late Han and Wei-Jin eras of the standards for evaluating people (i.e., moral standards). It was through this process of rebuilding moral pedigree and institutional relations that the concept of Principle began to link metaphysical moralism to the new social division of labor and its epistemology.

Guo Xiang's (c. 252–312 CE) commentary on the *Zhuangzi* reflected new trends in Wei-Jin *Xuanxue* metaphysics ("Dark Learning" or Neo-Daoism). Noritoshi Aramaki summarized Guo's approach to Principle as marking a humanistic turn—that is, a turn from the principles of pre-Qin monarchical politics to the philosophical ones of a culture where everything was centered on people, effecting a "great transformation" toward "practical philosophy."[26] However, this association of Principle with naturalistic concepts was not the unique invention of Guo, but rather an activation of pre-Qin ideas, especially Zhuangzi's conception of Principle. The important question is, Why did this notion of Principle as Nature or self-so-ness (*ziran*) acquire a status comparable to that of "the Way" in Guo's work? If Guo's Principle broke away from the principles of monarchical politics to become "the philosophical ones of a culture where everything was centered on people," then who were these people? Here, rather than using such categories as "humanistic culture" to describe Guo's conception of Principle, it would be better to shed some light on its political character.

Guo Xiang's notion of Principle emerged from the debates of *Xuanxue* metaphysics, which were closely related to the political conditions of the Wei and Jin dynasties. Wang Bi (226–249 CE) had written: "No thing ever behaves haphazardly but necessarily follows its own principle. To unite things, there is a fundamental regulator; to integrate them, there is a primordial generator. Therefore, things are complex but not chaotic, multitudinous but not confused."[27] He also proposed: "It is a fact that, if [someone] is unable to differentiate between names, it is impossible to talk with him about principles; and, if [someone] is unable to define names, it is impossible to discuss reality with him."[28] Wang claimed that the establishment of principles depended on the establishment of names, but ultimately names and principles would be united in the great "Way" that was without body, without name, reaching everywhere, and emanating from everywhere—and which was also the root or essence of the myriad things. His explanation of Principle was founded on his ontological concept of non-being or nothingness (*wu*), but nothingness itself did not have any substantial content. At the end of the paragraph preceding the quotation above, Wang provided a simple but layered historical explanation of the relationship between Principle and the imperial ranking system, summarizing both as part of a ritual-legal system unified under a monarchy.[29]

Guo Xiang's differences from Wang Bi centered on the relationship between being and nothingness. On the one hand, Guo persisted in maintaining Pei Wei's position that nothingness could not create being, in contrast with Wang's views.[30] On the other hand, Guo opened up a third category between being and nothingness—the concept of "autogeneration" (*zisheng*): "The world and the myriad things change day after day in a ceaseless process of unfolding in a way of their own; at any given moment, the sprout of change is budding but nobody really knows why. It is just a matter of spontaneity!"[31] Here spontaneity or "self-so-ness" (*zi ran er ran*) emphasized that each of the myriad things was itself foundational (*wan wu jie ben*), negating the idea of a single, ultimate source for their existence. In this sense, "autogeneration" expressed both the way that things transformed and the rootless (*wuben wugen*) character of that transformation. If autogeneration was indeed generated of its own accord, then nothingness could not become being, and being could not become nothingness, so that which did the creating was the creator itself. In his commentary on Zhuangzi's "Making All Things Equal" (*Qi wu lun*) Guo wrote: "Since non-existence is indeed non-existence, it cannot generate existence. But before existence is generated, neither can it generate anything either. So what is that which generates generation? Alone, things are simply generated of themselves."[32] Since things were self-generating, so too was "that by which they were so" (*suoyiran*): there was no absolute ruler governing the creation of things (*zaowuzhu*).[33] In the space between being and nothingness, then, Guo produced an ontology of "the generation of generation" (*shengsheng*).

For Guo, then, the principles were immanent within the myriad things; they were "that by which [the things] were so," in contrast with the idea shared by Wang Bi and Pei Wei that if the Way was not "being," then it was "nothingness." Guo used categories such as "obscure" or "indeterminate" (*ming*), "self-so-ness," and "inner necessity" to express the principles' characteristics, suggesting that they were the essence of autogeneration.[34] What was meant by "indeterminate"? In his commentary on the *Zhuangzi*'s "Free and Easy Wandering," Guo wrote: "Indeterminacy beyond life and death can be called 'limitlessness' (*wuji*)," and "Only those who grant things with indeterminacy and follow along with great changes can act without dependence and always remain unhindered."[35] On the one hand, the principles had "extremes" (*zhiji*) but on the other hand, they were "unhindered and limitless" (*changyu wuji*),[36] so the pursuit of these immanent, self-so principles could only adhere to a self-so method whose essence and substance were obscure. However, the principles were not necessarily "nonexistent" (*wu*). An extremely important concept in Guo's thought was that of the "traces" or "tracks" (*ji*)—a key medium for understanding the relationship between Principle and the ritual system. According to this concept, the Six Classics so revered by the scholars of the Han and Wei dynasties were nothing but traces left behind by early kings, and there was no direct relationship between those books and the Way of Heaven. In Guo's commentary on Zhuangzi's "The Turning of Heaven," he wrote: "That which left the traces (*suoyi jizhe*) was genuine nature (*zhenxing*). As for those who employed the genuine nature of things, their traces were the Six Classics. How much more so today, when people deal with things, should they do so according to those things' self-so-ness, treating the Six Classics as traces."[37] Or as his commentary on "Fit for Emperors and Kings" put it, "genuine nature" was "that which left the traces," that is, "the traces of nothingness" (*wuji*); the Six Classics and the Sage-Kings Yao and Shun could not themselves be equated to "that which left the traces," while "the *Book of Odes* and the *Book of Rites* were the old traces of former kings."[38] Therefore, rather than following the traces in search of the principles, it would be better to "grant things with indeterminacy and thereby become limitless," acting in tranquility without antagonism or dependence; rather than mechanically copying the ritual system of the ancients, it would be better to act according to the self-so-ness of the principles.[39]

Guo's discussion of the relationship between the traces and that which produced them clearly derived from Zhuangzi's naturalistic ideas about "governance through nonaction." In terms of political significance, the goal of separating the principles from the traces was to oppose "self-interested autocracy" by dissolving the absoluteness of the Six Classics and the ritual system, and by constructing a relative relationship between differentiated positions. The rites of the Six Classics, however, were the self-so-ness of Heavenly Principle: if we proceeded according to them, we would naturally conform to the order of the top-down relationship between sovereign and ministers, and of the inner-outer relationship between hands and feet—so why must we cling to the words of the sages? Guo's elevation of the concept of Principle here was not meant to be a complete negation of the Way's unified order, but, by merging ontology and epistemology, a means to treat Nature and ritual order as a relationship of indeterminate unity.

Although this way of fusing ontology with epistemology found its origins in the early Neo-Confucian "School of the Way" (*Daoxue*), it was in fact a harbinger of the coming "School of Principle" (*Lixue*). We could encapsulate Guo Xiang's conception of Principle as a call, yearning, and evidence to support a kind of order without the power of absolute domination, or order without one-sided domination. Tian Yuqing described aristocratic *menfa* politics as a synarchy of imperial power and the *shi* gentry clans, in which "the emperor rules without personal involvement (*chuigong*), while the gentry assumes power"—a "metamorphosis of ancient Chinese imperial politics under distinct conditions." Although "from a macroscopic vantage point, for nearly three centuries during the Eastern Jin and Southern dynasties, the main current of the political system was imperial rather than aristocratic," the latter *menfa* forces may have been on par with or even more powerful than the emperor during certain periods.[40] Therefore, instead of saying that Guo's conception of Principle reflected a shift from the principles of kings to those of the people, it might be more accurate to say it reflected a balance of power between the emperor and the gentry under conditions of synarchy.

Maybe the worldview Guo constructed of "things generating themselves independently" had no direct relation to the Song Confucians' concept of "one principle divided into myriad forms" (*li yi fen shu*), but both contained a tendency toward decentralized synarchy, even as their historical content was exceedingly different. The concept of Principle refused to acknowledge the ultimate existence of any entity external to itself, including the senses of "rule" or divided rule. In this singularly hidden respect, we can see the difference between Wei-Jin *Xuanxue* metaphysics and the Buddhist approach to interpreting Principle through the lenses of Dharma, Buddha-nature, and "profound awakening to the mysterious principles" (*xuan wu miao li*), alongside the deeper consistency between *Xuanxue* metaphysics and Tang-Song Confucianism with regard to their understandings of this concept. The concept of "principles in things" rescinds the absolutely dominant status of imperial power and "the sage" in the Han-dynasty worldview, providing a basis for establishing a political order of balanced relations between the emperor and the aristocracy. According to an archaic view of order, the center of moral evaluation was relationships based upon ritual order, which were necessary to maintain even if only nominally or formally. These were the political conditions for the rise in status of Principle as a concept: it negated the substantial content of relationships based on ritual order while preserving their formal content. Through this we can see historical relations defined by the interaction between centralized administration and enfeoffment, centralized power and decentralized local power, bureaucratic politics and aristocratic politics. Guo Xiang's ontology of self-so "generation of generation" and his political perspective of governance through nonaction still preserved the top-down relation between sovereign and ministers, therefore, because aristocratic political forms were not forms of self-rule without imperial power, but instead forms of imperial compromise that had emerged from the forms of decentralized power.

Wei-Jin *Xuanxue* (dark learning) established Principle's metaphysical quality, providing theoretical resources for later application of this concept by Buddhist philosophy.[41] After the Wei-Jin period, Buddhism gradually rose to prominence and the trend of using Buddha-nature, Dharma-nature, and "emptiness" (*kongwu*) to interpret Principle continued unabated among luminaries such as Zhi Daolin (314–366 CE), Zhu Daosheng (360–434), Sengzhao (384–414), and Xie Lingyun (385–433). For example, Zhi Daolin regarded Principle as "the nothingness that remains," equivalent to the phrase "the traces that remain" used by Guo Xiang and Xiang Xiu. Sengzhao understood Principle as "not being not nothingness, neither being nor nothingness, neither not-being nor not-nothingness"—surpassing Guo Xiang's "neither being nor nothingness" in sophistication, but consistent in theoretical direction.[42] Up until the Sui and Tang dynasties, Buddhist schools such as Tiantai, Sanlun (East Asian Mādhyamaka), Huayan, Faxiang (East Asian Yogācāra), and Chan described Principle as "true emptiness" or "empty nothingness," interpreting it as Dharma-nature, thusness, or "mysterious awakening" (*miaowu*) and, in exceedingly complex ways, used constructions such as double negatives to express the concept's ontological character as "neither root nor beginning," but also "neither not-root nor not-beginning." From the vantage point of the subsequent development of the School of the Way (*Daoxue*) and the School of Principle (*Lixue*), not only were the ontology and cosmology of Song Neo-Confucian philosophy deeply inspired by *Xuanxue* metaphysics and Buddhism; their way of defining Heavenly Principle was also significantly influenced by them. Liu Zongyuan carried on the Daoist legacy of self-so nonaction, advocating in politics "to achieve victory without aggression, following the principle of nonaction."[43] In the political context of the Tang dynasty, however, Liu's call to "take the sages' doctrine of 'The Great Mean' (*dazhong*) as the principle"[44] gave the impression that his naturalistic phrasing actually referred to governance through words—that his Principle meant to rule the state through "the unified authority of the classic texts."[45] Liu rejected the feudalism of the aristocratic clans and the frontier garrison towns, believing that enfeoffment had emerged from the propensity of the times (*shishi*) rather than the will of the sages. The focus of his "governance through words" had shifted from the principles described by Guo Xiang to the revival of the orthodox Great Mean, which could be regarded as a justification for the centralization of power. In this sense, Liu's negation of "mysterious awakening to the profound principles" (*ming wu xuan li*) derived from an antinomy between his "principle of the Great Mean" and those of *Xuanxue* metaphysics. It was not until the Song-dynasty emergence of the School of Principle that the concept of Principle as universal yet immanent, rejecting the existence of any ultimate substance, could once again radiate forth enormous energy under new sociopolitical conditions. Elevating a unitary Heavenly Principle to the highest position, and emphasizing its characteristics of immanence and differentiation into myriad concrete forms, scholars of the Song and Ming constructed a form of thought that was distinct from all those preceding it.

2. The Establishment of Heavenly Principle

While Song Confucian descriptions of the "Way of Heaven" retained certain elements of Han-dynasty cosmology, their conceptions of Principle constituted an important breakthrough in methods of moral evaluation. Zhou Dunyi, Shao Yong, and Zhang Zai each proposed or adopted concepts of Principle, but categories such as "Supreme Ultimate" (*taiji*) used by Zhou and Shao or "Supreme Void" (*taixu*) used by Zhang held more central positions in their systems of thought. It was the brothers Cheng Hao (1032–1086) and Cheng Yi (1033–1108) who truly laid the foundation for this concept within the framework of the dualism of "Principle" versus *qi* (energy)—as opposed to Zhang Zai's monism of *qi* or Shao Yong's monism of "mind" (*xin*). The Cheng brothers asserted that the myriad things ultimately stemmed from a single principle, and that "Heaven," "Mandate" (*ming*), "Nature" (*xing*), and "the Way" were just different names for this principle. They thus took the natural laws that had been conceived in Han thought through the analogy of human society and converted them into "laws of rationality."[46] This was where the real rupture between Han and Song thought began to unfold. Modern New Confucian scholarship has attempted to draw a strict delineation between the thought of the two Cheng brothers. Setting aside technical matters such as uncertainty about which of the brothers made certain statements recorded in their *Surviving Works* (*Er Cheng yi ji*), the crux of the matter centers on how to explain the category of Principle. These painstaking efforts at delineation, and especially the particular praise bestowed upon Cheng Hao, reflect a basic presupposition of modern New Confucianism: that there was an unbridgeable chasm between the moral principles recognized by all the School of the Way scholars, on the one hand, and the naturalistic orientation of the "Way of Heaven" perspective, on the other, and that, therefore, the cosmology of the Northern Song School of the Way was facing an "is-ought problem"—like that described by David Hume and Immanuel Kant in their theories of morality and knowledge. The precise meaning of this presupposition is: (a) if the goal of morality and ethics is to cultivate, rectify, and develop human virtue, then it could not be deduced from the description of the existing conditions of the world and humanity; and (b) any efforts to seek out moral laws according to a trajectory based on knowledge alone would be doomed to fail. Feng Youlan's *History of Chinese Philosophy* made a detailed analysis of this, and other works, such as Mou Zongsan's *Substance of Mind and Substance of Human Nature* (*Xinti yu xingti*) and *From Lu Xiangshan to Liu Jishan* (*Cong Lu Xiangshang dao Liu Jishan*), and Lao Siguang's *New History of Chinese Philosophy* (*Xinbian Zhongguo zhexue shi*), pushed this approach to the extreme. Although each of them took different things from the School of the Way, all attempted to explain its structure through the contradiction between "is" and "ought"—treating Zhu Xi's Principle and Lu Xiangshan's (i.e., Lu Jiuyuan's) "Mind," and the problems derived therefrom, as different ways of escaping this contradiction inherent within the cosmology of the School of the Way. The importance of the Cheng brothers lay in their use of Principle as a category to link up the naturalism of the Way of Heaven perspective with the rational foundation of moral praxis. If we can say that Cheng Hao's thought still retained the naturalist orientation of the School of the Way's ontology, then Cheng Yi's Principle-*qi* dualism constituted an epistemic breakthrough, providing a framework for a mature moral rationalism. To put this on a political level, the concept of Principle dissolved the direct correspondence between sovereignty and Heaven or the Supreme Ultimate, placing a concept of internal orderliness (*tiaoli*) and a postulate that "each thing has its own principle" or "the one principle is divided into myriad forms" at the center of the cosmos and the world.

Cheng Hao describes Principle within the categories of cosmology, treating it as a natural propensity:

> If it were true that myriad things all had only one Heavenly Principle, how would we relate to it? As it is written, "When there is crime, Heaven's retribution is the five punishments and five employments of such. Heaven's Mandate allows for the virtuous, with five ceremonial habiliments to organize the five." This is all so because of Heavenly Principle. At what time did humanity ever have anything to do with it? If they did, then it would have been private intentions.[47]

This passage is close in meaning to other sections indicated as having been authored by "Mingdao" (i.e., Cheng Hao).[48] To unfold the explication of Principle within the framework of cosmology meant to take the monism of Principle and *qi* as the precondition for the category of Principle. If Principle was the origin of morality, then the only appropriate orientation of moral praxis would be to obey its natural propensity.[49] This orientation of "not saying that Principle existed independently outside of things" was extremely close to the cosmological monism of Zhou, Shao, and Zhang, including with regard to the difficulties that came along with such a framework. These difficulties can be summarized as follows: If the movement of the myriad things takes place with the guidance of Heaven's Way, or if it is its expression, then how can we explain those events that run contrary to the Way? How can we explain the possibilities of "evil," moral life, and value judgments? Since the "Way of Heaven" concept possessed strong cosmological traits, its description could be understood as an account of the actual world.

Inquiry into the Origin of Humanity (*Yuan ren lun*) by the Tang Buddhist philosopher Guifeng Zongmi (780–841)—later canonized by Song Confucianism—once asked pointedly that if the myriad things all derived from "the Great Way," then why did it also give birth to tyrants, such as Jie and Zhou, and people who were as vicious as tigers or wolves; why did it let such a sage as Yan Hui die prematurely; and why did infants have the feelings of love and hatred? It was in this sense that arguments about the Way of Heaven could contain the contradiction between the description of facts and the description of values (as well as the aforementioned contradiction between "is" and "ought").[50] In other words, if the Way of Heaven was the origin of the myriad things and existed within their activities, then it could not provide a definitive value judgment or the basis for "goodness"; if the Way of Heaven was the origin of value and "goodness," then it could not be a cosmic reality (*yuzhou shiyou*). From this perspective, although Cheng Hao had first elevated his conception of the Principle to an unprecedented position, it still failed to resolve the aforementioned contradiction involving the Way of Heaven cosmology.

Cheng Yi's writings on Principle differed to such an extent that modern Confucians canonized him as "the greatest Confucian thinker in two millennia."[51] First, Cheng Yi tried to clearly differentiate between the categories of Principle and *qi*, or concrete things, with *qi* as substance (*zhi*) and Principle as form (*shi*)—concrete things as physical or "formed" (*xing er xia*), and Principle as metaphysical or "formless" (*xing er shang*). Cheng Yi's writings on Principle are extensive and cannot be quoted in detail, but the selections below are all representative of his views:

> As for that which is "still and not moving, yet communicates upon perception," all are supplied this by Heavenly Principle, and no original elements lack this. It is not preserved thanks to Yao, nor is it lost thanks to Jie. Father and son, ruler and subject, are everlasting norms that do not change. How could they ever have been moved? Hence not moving, and so they are said to be still. But though unmoving, yet they communicate upon perception. Reception here does not come from externals.[52]

> All things have Principle, such as fire which has heat, and water which has cold. . . . [53]

> Things and self are of one principle. To illuminate ability in that is to understand this, uniting the Way of inner and outer. To call it great, is that its height and breadth are as of Heaven and Earth. To call it small, is that the reason even a single thing is so, which scholars will all take as the coming together of Principle. Scholars should all understand this.[54]

In this Principle/*qi* dualism, Principle was akin to those "images and numbers" (*xiangshu*) abstracted from concrete things in *Book of Changes* numerology, both controlling the existence of the universe and indicating what the myriad things ought to do. In contrast with that Han-dynasty model of divination, Principle's relationship with concrete things was not one of contraposition, as with the relationship between images and numbers. Principle was eternal, neither existing and fluctuating in response to human knowledge and ignorance, nor rising and falling in response to the presence or absence of corresponding instances in the universe, nor waxing and waning in response to changes in things or situations. The reason Principle could unite Confucian categories such as Heaven, the Way, Mandate, and Nature (*xing*) is that it could combine the following, apparently contradictory relationships: On the one hand, there was only one Principle under Heaven, taken as a standard extending out to all the Four Seas, but on the other hand, each of the myriad things had its own principle, being that which each thing ought to do. On the one hand, the myriad things' principle was in our minds, and we could grasp the Heavenly Principle upon "sincere self-examination" (*fan shen er cheng*), but on the other hand, each thing had its own principle that did not change according to subjective fancies, and that people could grasp only through concrete cognition and praxis.[55]

Secondly, due to this sharp distinction between Principle and *qi*, a question that Confucianism had to address was how to deduce the causal and normative Principle from the myriad things (i.e., the category of *qi*). This deduction process, however, differed from that of Han-dynasty *Book of Changes* numerology by attending closely to the specificity of things and the subjectivity of cognition:

> The investigation of things and the thorough search into Principle does not mean that one should search into all the things in the world. The way

> is to probe one thing to the depths and then to reason about other things by analogy. Take for instance the question of filial piety: the [correct] way is to find out what makes the quality of filial piety. In the search for laws, if one tries on one thing without result, one can try another. Some may want to do what is easy first, some may want to do the difficult first, depending on one's capacity. It is like a thousand tracks and ten thousand paths all leading to the same country. All that one needs is to find one of them. The reason why it is possible to make a thorough search is because of the fact that it is the same principle that permeates all things. A thing or an event may be small, yet the same principle is there.[56]

The Principle comprised the nature or self-so-ness of the universe, so to follow the Heavenly Principle was to follow Nature. The natural principles were that by which the myriad things were such as they are, so to follow Nature was not the same as simply to follow the myriad things, but was rather to investigate their principles. Since the principles of the myriad things were "set up within the self," a fathoming thereof was closely intertwined with the sincere and reverent work of self-cultivation. Moreover, since each of the myriad things had its own principle, the fathoming of principles could not be achieved in isolation from the cognitive procedure of "the investigation of things." In both respects, natural principles were converted into principles of rationality, with profound consequences for the subsequent development and transformation of Confucianism. Cheng Yi's conception of Principle combined universality (the myriad principles are all one) and diversity (the differentiation of the single Heavenly Principle into the myriad principles of things), immanence (the reasons things are so, the rules they ought to follow, the deduction of principles from the investigation of things) and substantiality (there is nothing under Heaven without a principle), constructing a new "order of things."

The contrasting views of Zhu Xi (1130–1200) and Lu Jiuyuan (1139–1193) will be analyzed systematically in the following section, but here their features are outlined briefly with regard to the historical significance of the "Heavenly Principle" worldview. Zhu has been called the great master who synthesized the various strands of the School of the Way, creating a metaphysical system centered on the Heavenly Principle that took Zhou Dunyi's "Explanation of the Diagram of the Supreme Ultimate" (*Taijitu shuo*) as its backbone and combined what Shao Yong had written about numerology, what Zhang Zai had written about *qi*, and what the Cheng brothers had written about the differences between the "formless" and the "formed," and between Principle and *qi*, finally elucidating his own account of categories such as "Principle" and "*qi*," "the Supreme Ultimate" and "the Limitless" (*wuji*), "Nature" (*xing*) and "sentiment" (*qing*), "the investigation of things" and "the comprehension of Principle." Lu Jiuyuan's scholarship centers on "first establishing the most important things," emphasizing that the Way was "our mind," but this mind in turn was Principle. He wrote, "The ten thousand signs are forested in a single square inch; they fill the mind and extend outwards, filling up the universe, with no part differing from this principle."[57] Zhu and Lu disagreed insofar as, for Zhu, the principles were to be found in Nature (*xing*), whereas for Lu, they were to be found in the mind; and Zhu called for "the investigation of things," whereas Lu called for "the investigation of this particular thing" (*ge ci wu*). For both, however, cosmology and morality were centered on the principles and a corresponding view of order. Their contrasting notions of where the principles were located both belonged to the same categories of the School of Principle, the differences between them being premised on an affirmation of the same basic cosmological order of Principle. Zhu's proposition that "Nature is Principle" carried on the tradition established by Cheng Yi, built on the premise of Principle-*qi* dualism, according to which phenomenological things—including the mind—comprised a world that was contingent and in constant flux, wherein Principle functioned as an eternally existing order that was immanent to that world, simultaneously plural and singular. Lu's thinking was closer to that of Shao Yong and especially Cheng Hao, equating "the universe" with "our mind" and writing:

> This principle infuses the universe; there is nothing external to what we call the Way; beyond all things, there is no Way. If we abandon this and have instead calculation, tendencies, scale and measures, forms and traces, commercial enterprise, and achievements—if any such affair not be done in according with the Way, then it is corrupt; then it is desire for profit. To speak of it is evil speech; to witness it is evil witnessing..[58]

Therefore, Lu's proposition that "the mind is Principle" was built on the premise of a monism where the mind and "things" (*wu*), or phenomena in the world, were one.

The establishment of the Heavenly Principle concept meant that ethics-morality had to take a transcendental Principle as its basis and standard. This was the case for both Zhu Xi and Lu Jiuyuan: it was not any specific institution, ritual system, or ethics, but an abstract and ubiquitous Principle that constituted the source and highest standard of morality. All that existed had to pass the test of Principle. It was this concept that enabled the Song School of the Way to break from the orthodoxy that had been established by late Tang Confucianism. This may be supplemented here by comparing how Han Yu and Liu Zongyuan wrote about "the Way." Han Yu's conception of the Way was directly expressed in his statement that

> its texts are the *Odes*, the *Documents*, the *Changes*, and the *Spring and Autumn Annals*. Its methods are the rites, music, chastisement, and government. Its classes of people are scholars, peasants, craftsmen, and merchants. Its social relationships are ruler and minister, father and son, teacher and pupil, guest and host, older and younger brother, husband and wife. Its dress is hemp and silk; its dwellings are houses; its foods are rice and grains, fruits and vegetables, fish and meat.[59]

Setting out from the *Classic of Filial Piety*'s line that "[the ancients] had perfect virtue (*de*) and the essential Way," Han Yu mobilized the Way as the Confucian ethical order validated by orthodox pedigree. Liu Zongyuan set out from the cosmology of the *Ten Wings* (*Shiyi*, Confucian commentaries on the *Book of Changes*), in which "one yin and one yang comprise the Way," to build a logical structure with the Way as its central category—a conception no less influential on the Song School of the Way than that of Han Yu, concerning its contribution to theoretical form.[60] Liu wrote:

> Things are merely the standards of the Way. Conserve things by following the standards, and so the Way is preserved. To neglect [things and their standards] is to lose the Way. The way the Sage could ascertain weave and warp, and name things, can never be separate from the Way. . . . Thus from the Son of Heaven to the commoner, whoever holds

> to his portion of the path, and does not lose the Way, is an extremum of harmony.[61]

Taking "things" as the "standard of the Way" expressed that the existence of the Way depended upon "preserving the thing by its standard," and upon each "holding to his portion of the path," with "things" comprising the direct standard for evaluation. Here, although the Way was already being unfolded within a cosmological framework, its precondition and standard of measurement still consisted of material entities such as the Three Bonds and Five Virtues, ritual, and institutions.

The School of Principle emphasized the specific context and ritual of moral praxis, but in its logical structure, Principle was an immanent, transcendental, and eternal entity without any material thing as its standard or precondition. In this sense, it was not concrete things, administrative institutions, or ethical practices that provided standards for evaluating Principle or endowing it with moral significance, but rather Principle that constituted the standard and basis for things, regulations, institutions, ritual, and ethical practice, endowing these material entities with meaning. The value of the Six Classics lay in their embodiment of the Heavenly Principle. For Zhu Xi, the principles were given to people and things by Heaven, forming the basis by which the myriad things were so.[62] Each thing had its own principle, but the existence or nonexistence of things (the forms of ritual, institutions, states, moral practice, etc.) within time and space could not determine the principles' condition. Herein lay the essential meaning of the "Principle-*qi* dualism." This is why the category of "effort" (*gongfu*) played such an important role in Zhu Xi's theoretical system, since effort was the only way to connect the "is" (*shiran*) with the "ought" (*yingran*):

> However, the sages and worthies of ancient times had at their root only one essential and unitary achievement (*gongfu*), which is why they were able to hold on to it and were not thoroughly good at everything they did. Later the so-called heroes did not have this achievement, but appeared and disappeared in the field of profit and pleasure. [. . .] Whether they hit their marks or not, the later aphorism that held "The Three Dynasties of Antiquity did all to the utmost, but the Han and Tang do not," refers to this.[63]

Here, the standard for measurement consisted not of the rites and music of the Three Dynasties of Antiquity or the institutions of the Han and Tang, but the degree to which something was "extended to the utmost" (*jin*), that is, matched with or embodied the principles.

Lu Jiuyuan fused the universe with "our mind" (*wuxin*), attempting through this monism of the mind to resolve the inherent tension between Principle and the material world created by Principle-*qi* dualism. Lu's conception of "mind," however, was not a material one, but rather meant the principles filling up the universe itself. Lu's disciple Yang Jian (1140–1226) wrote, "Heaven and Earth are my Heaven and Earth. The transformations are my transformations. They are not other things. [. . .] 'The three hundred rituals and the three thousand protocols' are not external to my mind. Hence it is said, 'The virtue of Nature combines the inner and outer of the Way. Hence it changes over time.' This says that it adapts of itself, not that it seeks to adapt."[64] Principles filled the universe, and the universe was our mind, so the mind was Principle, with this monism of the mind reducing Principle to the mind itself through their immanence. Zhu Xi and Lu Jiuyuan both valued ritual and institutions, with the Three Bonds and the Five Virtues as their basic content, but in the context of their writings, the Three Bonds and Five Virtues were equivalent not to any material ritual or institution, but rather to an immanent and natural order. In this sense, the basic yardstick for moral judgment still consisted of Principle: the value and significance of rites and music, institutions, or ethical practice hinged upon whether they embodied or matched up with the eternal and immanent Principle.

The method of moral evaluation embodied by the School of the Way's cosmology was both a sublation of those methods advocated by pre-Qin "rites-and-music" theory and Han-Tang studies of the classics (the latter's commentary form postulating a primeval order that was material, authoritative, and theologically teleological, regarding adherence to this order as a precondition for moral rationality and political legitimacy) and a transformation of late-Tang Confucianism. If a person's moral perspective must be extended from a cosmic or essential order, then how to understand or approach this order became a central question in the theory of morality. Those who conceived of the order and meaning of the universe on the surface of things alone, and who understood the universe as cold facts or abstract imperatives with no connection to our inherent nature (or immanent order), could not be regarded as people who understood the cosmic order, because the cosmic order or the process of Heaven itself was an order or process that could and should be corroborated or affirmed within ourselves. On the basis of this assessment, a question that the theory of morality must attend to is, According to what method (epistemological, empirical, practical, etc.) must which kind of information be received from the myriad things of the cosmos? Following this logic, the Northern Song School of the Way's inquiry into the origins of humanity, the myriad things, and morality must be linked to a theory of knowledge or cognition. Moral anxiety over the unity of Heavenly Principle was ultimately converted into cognitive practice concerning how to understand, know, grasp, and arrive at the Heavenly Principle. Was Principle Nature or mind? Should we "investigate things" or "investigate the mind"? Should we throw ourselves into the real world through praxis or return to our original mind through quietude? Almost all the cosmological, ontological, methodological, and mind-Nature theory (*xinxinglun*) disagreements, differentiations, and divisions within the School of the Way were related to these questions.

II. The Centralized State and the Separation of Institutions from the Rites and Music

1. The Vision of the Three Dynasties of Antiquity and the Separation of Institutions from Ritual

In the process of the confirmation of the worldview of Heavenly Principle in its own terms, we can see several salient tendencies: First, the Heavenly Principle worldview was promulgated with the stated intention of recovering ancient Confucian learning, and especially the Way of Confucius and Mencius. However, Song Confucianism was not prepared to restore in its entirety the moral evaluation methods of the rites and music, nor was it prepared to apply the political ideals of the Three Dynasties of Antiquity to contemporary practice. Second, the Heavenly Principle worldview developed a system of moral evaluation within a relation of Heaven to human, but it declined to place the relation of Heaven and human within the framework of Heaven-human response theory. It also declined to see the relation of institutions and Heaven as one of mysterious resonance of signs and numbers, from which it followed to further decline to understand the existing institutions and norms of conduct as those aligned with the Will of Heaven within a naturalistic and deterministic cosmology. Third, the Heavenly Principle worldview developed as a course of study and self-cultivation, erecting a direct bridge between the Way of Heaven and the moral practice of the *shi,* or scholar-official, from which it followed that moral practice would once again be put into a state of tension with "institutions."

From the above three tendencies, we may make the following conclusions. First, the Heavenly Principle worldview, in taking as its goal the restoration of pre-Qin ritual institutions, also declined to make practical rituals and institutions an objective foundation for moral evaluation. This state of affairs could only be established on the judgment about the propensity of the times: from the Han and the Tang dynasties onward, institutions were divided from ritual, and vice versa, and could not supply an objective foundation for moral evaluation, from which it follows that premises for moral evaluation had to be built outside the discourse of institutions. Second, the Heavenly Principle worldview was established alongside the view that the propensity of the times changed. Its stance for restoring the Three Dynasties of Antiquity and reconstructing the unity of ritual and institutions would in the end be located within the process of understanding, being aware of, and practicing Heavenly Principle. For this reason, its rebuttal in moral terms of the Heavenly Mandate view of the Han and Tang was by no means a return to the rites and music of the pre-Qin period, but a reconstruction of the Heaven-human relation that formed a moral system adapted to the changes of those times. Third, the Heavenly Principle worldview takes as a moral ideal the unity of ritual and institutions, but this moral ideal must be implemented within the moral practice of scholar-officials. Of the features so far outlined, those related to the consciousness of the propensity of the times toward the divisions occurring between ritual and institutions formed the central questions—if there had not been a consciousness of and perspective on the divide, there would have been no question of restoring pre-Qin Confucianism and institutions, and it would not have been necessary to reconstruct a relation of Heaven and human according to the category of Heavenly Principle.

The division of ritual from institutions is a historical narrative that proceeds from the unique outlook of Confucianism. For this reason, one unavoidable question is: In whose historical consciousness is this historical perspective actually produced? Confucius's method of "transmit and not create" describes the institutions of the Sage-Kings as a state of ritual and institution in complete unity (or unity in political terms), but this narrative itself, as well as its expectations for the *junzi,* or superior person, implies that the relation of ritual to institutions (especially the formalization, hollowing out, and disintegration of ritual) had formed the internal perspective of those Confucians self-appointed as scholar-officials, observing the age they found themselves in. As explained above, the belief that the moral responsibility-taking of "the scholar-officials (*shi*) must be great and courageous" comes from the judgment that the propensity of the times is one of the "collapse of rites and music." It was because they were in an age during which enfeoffment class relations were dissolving that people and great talents could extend themselves and emerge out of the class of the common people and take responsibility for affairs. "The collapse of rites and music" was thus the very condition that produced the scholar-official class, and it was the moral viewpoint from which these scholar-officials described the separation of institutions from ritual.

The evolution of using ritual and morality to oppose institutions was one part of the historical heritage of pre-Qin Confucianism, as for example the unity of the well-field system with peasant military service. The goal of the land tax (*tian fu*) was to give the feudal lords a supply of troops. However, during the Warring States era, this institution gradually evolved into separate provisional accounts (taxes).[65] Thus the partisans of ritual in the Lu state saw the development of laws and taxes as an invasion against traditional ritual. During the Warring States era, each state came to be centered on its ruling power, and promoted a transition to laws and institutions with the goal of advancing production power and increasing military might. The division of Legalism away from Confucianism is the ideological reflection of this process. The above currents finally resulted in the establishment of the centralized administration of the Qin and Han era, and the political ideology centered on imperial rule, with its associated legal institutions, military institutions, and economic institutions. Within this new system, even though imperial power preserved the contents of "clan law" (*zongfa*), and even though the Han dynasty would go on to establish first the *yi xing,* or cross-surname enfeoffments, and then the *tong xing,* or same-surname enfeoffments, the rituals, institutions, and culture of enfeoffments were now subsumed as an accessory to centralized authoritarian government. Under these conditions, the division of ritual from institutions meant, in substance, the course of replacement of the Zhou-dynasty enfeoffments system by the centralized and authoritarian system. The ceremonial order of the five protocols (*wu li*) during Qin and Han times mostly began to develop in response to the rise of imperial power to the utmost heights, and the concomitant whittling down of Yin-Zhou ceremonial order. It came with fundamental differences from the so-called ritual of the Three Dynasties of Antiquity. Whether the system be one of imperial power, or of ritual, or of a bureaucratic system with institutions for supervision and inspection of a centralized administration; or whether it be military institutions based on a king's court, or economic institutions and personnel systems, all were different from the Zhou enfeoffment system and its principles. Seen from the perspective of Confucianism, the transition or transfer from enfeoffments to centralized administration could be ascribed precisely to the proposition that institutions had been divided from ritual.

The clear division produced between ritual and institutions, along with the building up of a moral view outside of institutions, was itself an effort that can be seen as one of the strategies of the School of the Way Neo-Confucians in their struggle with Wang Anshi and Confucian officialdom. Wang Anshi (1021–1086), Li Gou (1009–1059), and Chen Liang (1143–1194) of the Song dynasty all placed high emphasis on the functions of government, with their thought centered on the resolution of political problems. Helped by the new division, as well as the establishment of School of the Way concepts, they tried to form a transcendent morality as a point of commanding elevation over institutions. But here we must remember: as a historical perspective, the division of ritual from institutions had formed a universal perspective for the Song Confucian inspection of history during the Northern Song. With biographies, treatises, and tables by Ouyang Xiu (1007–1072), who also emphasized the functions of government and institutions, the *New History of the Tang Dynasty* (*Xin Tang shu*) states, in its "Treatise on Rites and Music":

> During the Three Dynasties of Antiquity and earlier times, order came from unity, with the rites and music reaching All-under-Heaven. Since the Three Dynasties, order has come from two, with the rites and music becoming but empty names.

> In ancient times . . . when it came to any matter of the people, all emerged from ritual. It was based on these that they taught the people to be filial and good, to be friendly and fraternal, to be loyal and trustworthy, and to be humane and righteous, evincing a norm that did not stray, whether in place of residence, or action, or clothing, or in food and drink—because all they did, dawn to dusk, involved observing the norms. This is the order out of unity of which we speak. And that the rites and music should reach All-under-Heaven, caused All-under-Heaven to implement it wherever they were and practice it, making it into the custom without even knowing what it was that moved to the good and distanced itself from wrong.
>
> And then the Three Dynasties of Antiquity were lost, and the misfortune of the Qin led to the transformation of the ancients. Those who afterward possessed all under Heaven all employed the Qin in the names and ranks of the Son of Heaven and all the officials, in the institutions of the country, and in the palace sedans and costume and implements. Among these, there might be a ruler who desired order, whose thoughts turned to reform, but he would not be able in the end to exceed or restore the Three Dynasties of Antiquity, but would draw on the customs of his times, and so make additions and subtractions. In the main he would have to be satisfied with a crude and simplistic approach, and nothing more. Among their daily duties, the most pressing involved government reports, law cases, and provision of the military. They said, "This is government. It is the means by which order is brought to the people." When it came to the rites and music of the Three Dynasties, they simply registered the names of the ritual objects, then archived them among the bureaus and agencies, only bringing them out to the court for certain occasions, like the suburban sacrifices and sacrifices to the ancestors. And they said, "This is ritual. It is the means by which the people are taught." This is what is meant by order coming from two [the rites and music, and the bureaucracy], but with the rites and music only empty names.[66]

Ouyang Xiu's description expresses how, during the Northern Song era, the division of ritual from institutions to describe ancient history, to weigh the Three Dynasties of Antiquity against the later Han, Sui, and Tang dynasties, and to describe the practical state of morality and politics at the time, had become a deeply influential historical, moral, and political view. The statement that "the rites and music" were "empty names" shows that ritual existed still, but had become formalized; not only was it entirely separate from substantial institutions in government, economy, or military affairs, but ritual was unable to influence the conduct or custom of commoners.

The *Comprehensive Mirror for Aid in Government* (*Zizhi tongjian*) by Sima Guang (1019–1086) supplies another example. The opening of that volume, "Annals of Zhou" (*Zhou ji*), full of respect and reverence for ritual and the king, and describing the chaos brought to good government by the feudal lords from the perspective of the breakdown of ritual order, says:

> We have heard that among the offices of the Son of Heaven, none is greater than ritual, and among rituals, none is greater than the divisions, and among divisions, none is greater than the name. What is it that we call ritual? It is the Law (*ji gang*). What is it we call the divisions? It is ruler and subject. And it is in dukes and marquesses, and grand and high ministers, also. . . . Thus we say that of the offices of the Son of Heaven, none is greater than ritual.[67]

Thus it is that Sima Guang, holding that ritual "distinguishes noble from base, arranges in order kin and strangers, outlines groups and things, and regulates the common affairs," narrates the historical changes of the Zhou era within dichotomies of "ritual" (*li*) versus "political savvy" (*zhili*), "virtue" (*de*) versus "talent" (*cai*), "sage" (*shengren*) versus "the benighted" (*yuren*), and "superior person" (*junzi*) versus "inferior person" (*xiaoren*). Addressing the triple partition of the Jin state, Sima Guang writes:

> The house of Zhou was weak, and the three Jin clans were flourishing in strength. Though the house of Zhou wanted not to acknowledge them, how could it not do just that? . . . Nowadays the request is made of the Son of Heaven and the Son of Heaven permits it. It is now that the mandate of the Son of Heaven is made unto the feudal lords. Who is there who can send forces to stop them? Thus were the three Jin included among the feudal lords. This was not a matter of the three Jin having ruined ritual, but rather that the Son of Heaven ruined them himself.

> Alas! The rite of ruler and subject is in ruins now. And the Son of Heaven vies with his ministers, the feudal lords who have succeeded the sages find their altars to hearth and grain destroyed, and the people's livelihoods lost. Is it not a disaster?[68]

And in a passage further down from there, he also says,

> Your servant says, the death of Zhi Yao [Xun Yao, also known as Zhibo] is an example of virtue losing out to talent. Now talent is different from virtue, though the vulgar of this world cannot distinguish them, but call both worthies. This is the reason men are selected and used wrongly. . . . And it is for this reason that some with talent and virtue used entirely up are called "sages." People in whom talent and virtue are both lost entirely are known as "benighted people." If they are more virtuous than talented they are called the *junzi,* or "superior person," and those with more talent than virtue are called "inferior people."[69]

This dialectic developed from Confucius's own "collapse of rites and music" narrative, and by no means clearly applies the dialectic of ritual and institutions. However, in the *Comprehensive Mirror for Aid in Government,* the upheaval of the Warring States is precisely the historical basis for the Qin unification. Ritual, centered on "virtue" and "the superior person," incubates the later social forces centered on "political savvy" and "the inferior man," with the differences of the two produced from the differences between the ritual of the Three Dynasties of Antiquity and the moral-political evaluation standards of later institutions. For this reason, Sima Guang's method of historical evaluation bears internal similarity to the methods of moral evaluation found in the Northern Song School of the Way.

Producing division in the relation between ritual and institutions before and after the Three Dynasties of Antiquity shows the Song Confucian attitude of admiration for the old institutions of the sages and kings, and the attitude of dividing enfeoffments and of centralized administration; but when it comes specifically to the evaluation of the Tang institutions, this division also holds specific historical meaning. Qian Mu (1895–1990), reviewing Chen Yinke's (1890–1969) work *On the Origins of the Institutions of the Sui and Tang Dynasties* (*Sui Tang zhidu yuanyuan lue lungao*), made much of the differences between the imperial sacrifices at Mount Tai (*fengchan*), the Suburban Sacrifices (*jiaosi*), the rankings of carts and costumes (*yufu*), and the ceremonies, with the bureaucracy, land tax system, and military system, with one of the bases for this being Ouyang Xiu on the evolution of ritual before and after the Three Dynasties of Antiquity. Qian Mu wrote that Chen

> closely examines the rituals, carts and costumes, and ceremonies at the start of the Tang Dynasty, which in the main are inherited from the Southern dynasties. However, ritual and institutions had been separate from the Qin and Han onward. In the histories and documents, the bureaucracy, the land tax system, and the military were all considered "institutions," whereas the sacrifices to Mount Tai, the Suburban Sacrifices, and the carts and costumes were all considered "ritual." In the "Treatise on Rites and Music" section of the *New History of the Tang*, this distinction is clear. Sui and Tang institutions were aligned with those of the Northern dynasties. Master Chen combines them without distinction, and speaks only of the ritual which was transmitted from the southern dynasties, overlooking the institutions of the North, but the distinction is necessary.[70]

Here, Qian Mu considered the bureaucracy, land taxation, and military entirely to be classified as institutions, and so of no relation to ritual, which clearly separates these "institutions" from ritual. This view is certainly inconsistent with the description given above of the unity of ritual and institution under the Zhou-era patriarchal clan enfeoffment system, but is instead closely related to the evolution of the relationship of north and south following the end of the Han dynasty.

Turning back to Chen Yinke, while northern institutions have definite differences from southern institutions, they can also be considered "in combination without distinction." Take the Tang garrison militia (*fubing*) system, for example: It "was, in its early stage, a Xianbei system that in the main distinguished peasant from soldier, served as a system for distinguishing chiefs (*buqiu*), as well as for a special aristocracy; in its later stage, it was a Chinese military system that in the main combined soldier with peasant, put all under the jurisdiction of the ruler, with a relatively equal class of commoners (*pingmin*). The dividing line from early and late stages was the Sui dynasty."[71] The Military Commissioners (*fanzhen*) of the Tang Dynasty (such as the followers of Xue Song and Tian Chengsi) "may have been ethnically Han, but in reality they were frontier generals (*fanjiang*), whose armies, regardless of ethnicity, were actually the same as barbarian tribes." For precisely this reason, he criticized Ouyang Xiu's discussion of the Five Dynasties for "limiting itself to the scope of heavenly nature, human relational norms, bonds of friendship, and ritual protocols, with no sense of the Five Dynasties system of *yi'er*, or adopted children, as for example the *yi'er* generals of the Tang, which in fact emerged from the customs of the barbarian tribes. They likely had the same origin as the *fanjiang*, frontier generals, in the Tang Dynasty. If we speak of these things from moral views and not using historical documents, there would seem to be fewer distinctions."[72] Clearly he places the Tang *fubing* military system within the northern traditions.[73] Take also the example of ritual and law, where northern institutions and southern rituals again exhibit parts of interpenetration.

> In ancient China, law and ritual were closely related. It was the Sima clan who used the larger organization of Ru learning (*Ru xue da zu*) to create the house of Jin at the end of the Eastern Han and so unify China. The criminal code so established particularly bears Confucian character. The very [code] that the Southern Dynasties continued to follow and pass down, the Northern Wei readopted upon reform of its laws, as they passed through many hands, changing along the way, through the Northern Qi, the Sui, and eventually the Tang. This is in fact an unchanging orthodoxy of Chinese criminal law.[74]

The Xiaowen Emperor (of the Northern Wei, r. 471–499) reformed institutions with clear reference to the *Rites of Zhou*, and moreover used institutional reform to advance the mixing of northern Chinese ethnicities with southern culture.

The differences between institutions and ritual which Ouyang Xiu describes are an expression of Song-dynasty orthodoxy. Union of ritual and institution is a Confucian moral ideal, but discussions of this issue within the category of northern and southern relations show the more specific historical relations related to division of ritual from institutions, among which is the split between north and south which had been forming since the end of the Eastern Han dynasty. The pattern of "northern and southern histories of China" is a product of history, which appeared only with the rise of the Yangtze River delta region in Chinese political life. Fu Sinian has written, "It was only during the age of Sun Bin (d. 316 BCE) and Wu Qi (ca. 440–ca. 361 BCE) that the Yangtze River valley began to have independent political organizations. Before and during the Three Dynasties of Antiquity, political progress had gone from tribes to empires, but the original areas were the basins of the Yellow, Ji, and Huai Rivers. In this larger region, the geographic forms were divided between east and west, and were not delimited by north and south."[75] During the fourth century of the common era, peoples from more remote areas, like the Xiongnu, the Jie, the Xianbei, the Di, and the Qiang, all entered the north, leading to the situation referred to as "the five barbarians attacking the Chinese" (*wu hu luan hua*). During the three centuries after the fall of Emperor Yongjia of the Western Jin (r. 307–312), these peoples from beyond occupied half the North, with extremely intense conflicts among different nations and ethnicities. In the context of North-South conflict, it became extremely important that ritual serve as a marker of political legitimacy. The reforms of Emperor Xiaowen were in the main reforms of rituals, the core of which entailed "referring back to the ancient ways, and modelling the system on the ancient institutions," as well as "equaling the greatness of the Yin and the Zhou eras," which meant ritualizing the political system according to the basis laid out in the *Rites of Zhou*. The ritual institutions of the northern court since the reforms of the Xiaowen Emperor can be summed up, in larger part, under the headings of sacrifices at patriarchal clan temples, funeral practices, determination of clan names by marriage, and respect for the elders.[76] The equal-field reforms implemented by the Xiaowen Emperor in the ninth year of Taihe (485 CE) were also a product of the same currents. During the three centuries of the Eastern Jin, the Song, the Qi, the Liang, and the Chen in the South, having all throughout supported the Han Son of Heaven, the aristocracy, high officials, and most influential families of the North all moved to the South, where imperial power declined and the elite families came to control government; these latter manifested their own influence in institutions, ritual, learning, and culture. This situation showed strong indications of enfeoffment, and formed an important contrast to the northern institutions that emphasized central rulership. The ritual culture of the South in this age was produced and disseminated through a historical process of war, migration, and ethnic conflict. What is referred to as the North-South conflict inevitably contains some elements of ethnic conflict, and it became an intensification of the struggle for cultural orthodoxy.[77] The perspective of the orthodox doctrines of Confucian learning is expressed as a view of ritual and institutions from the perspective of North and South that includes northern culture within the category of "institutions," which is tantamount to not admitting that northern institutions possess the moral substance of ritual. In the perspective of the Song Confucians, the above transformations to economic and political institutions cannot be simply seen as a history of institutional transformations, but must also be seen as a history of the division of ritual from institutions, which is to say a history in which institutions broke away from ritual and no longer could serve as the basis for moral legitimacy.

Song Confucians' use of this method to evaluate the relationship between Han and Tang institutions and morality clearly has a more practical motivation, because the institutions of the early Song were an extension of the institutions of the Han and the Tang. In their view, the Two-Tax System, the examination system, consolidation of imperial power, and bureaucratic government, which had been implemented gradually since the Tang and expanded during the Song, had taken the place of the most important contents of the ritual institutions of the Three Dynasties of Antiquity, namely enfeoffments, the well-field system, and schools. If the Three Dynasties of Antiquity and the rule of Sage-Kings Tang and Yu could be called manifestations of moral principle, then the governments of the Han and Tang were instead institutional measures with no connection to morality. If the rites and music could be said to contain the ranking concept that supplied moral meaning, then institutions possessed independent meaning, which means they were unable to supply a universal basis for morality. In other words, rather than call the division of institutions from ritual an objective historical narrative, it would be better to call it a conclusion made by Song Confucians about the various transformations to society and ethics since the Qin and Han. They used the perspective of the division of ritual from institutions to judge the state of institutions and morality in their age, and to embed various topics in politics, economics, and society into an ethical narrative. Even Ye Shi (1156–1223), a critic of the School of the Way, similarly built his framework for evaluating history on the contrast between the ritual of the Three Dynasties of

Antiquity and the laws of the Han and Tang. This is sufficient to show that "division of ritual and institutions" had become a universal proposition among Song Confucians: The Han and the Tang "took power and military strength as the Way to rule, with penal code and commerce as their political body. Emperor Wenxuan of the Han and Emperor Taizong of the Tang are known as enlightened rulers, but in fact they were few steps short of Jie and Zhou." To the political forms of the Han and Tang, he compared the rule by virtue of Tang Yao, Yu Shun, and the Three Dynasties of Antiquity: "Tang, Yu, and the Three Dynasties kept all in accord, inner and outer. Consequently the Way preserved itself without need for minds to labor. Those who take up the Way now, take up duties from within in order to govern without. Consequently, the norms are not matched."[78] For this reason, the historical view concerning division of ritual from institutions contained two different directions for interpretation: Should the basis for moral judgment be sought outside of existing institutions and their policies (including reform-oriented institutions and policies)? Or to build a moral outlook out of the perfection of institutions themselves? In the political debates of the Song dynasty, the School of the Way masters chose the former—this choice touches on various issues in the debates of schools within Song learning, as for example the debate that extends from the Northern to the Southern Song over the issue of *wangba*, or hegemonic rule. Sima Guang and Li Gou set out with affirmative attitudes toward imperial power, while Shao Yong and Cheng Yi championed, from various angles, the political ideal of government by nonaction and Nature (*wuwei ziran*), and the kingly Way (*wang dao*) based on moral intentions.[79]

The historical-moral view of "separation of institutions from ritual" was closely associated with transformations in the structure of society during the Tang and Song; the scholar-official (*shi*), the subject of this historical-moral view, was itself a product of the transformations. The markers that constitute the Tang and Song transformations are first, the decline of aristocratic government and the appearance of autocracy; second, the withering away of the old hereditary clan organization and the appearance of a new form of clan institutions featuring memorial halls (*citang*), genealogies (*jiapu*), and the common clan lands (*zutian*); third, the decline of the aristocratic selections system and unprecedented expansion of government by bureaucratic officials; and fourth, the collapse of imperial government with multiple centers, over multiple ethnicities (*minzu*), and the formation of a mature centralized administration, alongside an intense nation-group consciousness produced by the history of the "Five Dynasties and Ten Kingdoms" and sustained conflicts between ethnicities.

Within the Confucian perspective of "division of ritual from institutions," these four markers can be considered one part of the longer struggle between enfeoffment and central administration. Viewed from the angle of class structure, the above transformations were already nascent by the late Tang, and especially during the Five Dynasties and Ten Kingdoms. Signs of them can be seen in the way the Tang social structure, characterized by great families, the military aristocracy, house slaves, abject lower classes, corvée laborers, and maidservants, transformed into the Song social structure, with its officials-cum-landlords and hired farmers, the poor of the village, informal and contracted artisans, hired labor, and hired servants. In this period, a transitional role is played by the continuation of the *yiguanhu* class (the Song official class) along with the development of the *xingshihu* (or local official and elite class), with one of the spheres of this development being the deep transformation of the social category of *shi* or scholar-official. Peter Bol includes this development as part of the historical transition from the great families marking the Tang dynasty to the Northern Song marked by scholar-official clans, and to the Southern Song with its cultured society and local elites.[80] Just as the disintegration of the patriarchal clan enfeoffment system during the age of Confucius made way for the *shi* to emerge in all their talent from out of the common class and take on new pride and responsibility, so the disintegration of the Tang aristocratic system and its relation to ritual and ceremony supplied the on-ramp by which the new *shi* took to the historical stage. And just as Confucius reconstructed the ritual government of the Sage-Kings with his gaze on the "collapse of rites and music," the Song Confucians understood the various problems and crises they observed in society from the moral-historical perspective of "division of ritual from institutions," and so got involved in contemporary social problems through reconstructing the basic problems of Confucian thought, and settled by their own accord their position in history.

From a political perspective, the "division of ritual and institutions" viewpoint is a product of the historical transition from enfeoffment to centralized administration. It sees the institutions of centralized administration as separate from ritual and, therefore, as opposed to the system of enfeoffments in the Three Dynasties of Antiquity, which were imbued with moral meaning. However, even though Song Confucians generally took up a stance of "restoring the ancient" (*fugu*), they still admitted the historical appropriateness of having centralized administration supersede enfeoffments. Thus it was not a question of simply restoring enfeoffments, but rather how to reconstruct the spirit of enfeoffment and its ritual conditions under centralized administration, which became the chief concern of the School of Principle. Some of them took up scholar-official posts via the imperial examinations, and so directly participated in the practice of politics, combining morality and politics in their role as *shi*. Others rebuilt clan and regional pedigree into a basis for the local gentry's political power, establishing moral roots in new forms of clan relations. Still others took as their mainstay School of the Way practice, distancing themselves from politics and challenging institutional practices, using their self-determination as *shi* to build the foundation for a new moral center. The theory and practice of the Song School of the Way reflect the *shi* class's understanding of, interpretation of, and debate over the basic problems of their times. But we cannot vulgarly take the School of Principle as a theory with *shi* at its center. The School of Principle includes broad thinking on society and politics. It takes the Heavenly Principle as its center, "the extension of knowledge through the investigation of the things" (*ge wu zhi zhi*) and the cultivation of self and mind as its methods of learning, and moral practice as its main contents. Its main social and political contents were restoring clans, building ancestral memorial halls (*citang*), deliberating on land politics, debating the imperial examinations, distinguishing Chinese from barbarian, and promoting local autonomous government. In the end, it became a broad central discourse for arguments on metaphysics, politics, and society.

2. The Vision of "Enfeoffments": Clan Law, Clans, and Community Compacts

During the centuries between the Eastern Han and the end of the Tang dynasty, the generational clan system was in practice a combination of the tenant farming economy and the gentry elite system and exhibited close relation to the enfeoffment rituals in its apportionment of power in politics.

Under the system of elite families, or *menfa,* of the Wei and Jin dynasties, clan heads not only had large amounts of land and property, but also grouped extended family members and even peasants and commoners with different surnames in their households, in which they were tenants or peasant households without national household registration. In wartime, the elite family system had a propensity to develop into a unified soldier-and-peasant system, turning tenants and peasant households into clan units (*zongbu*), clan divisions (*zongwu*), and clan troops (*zongbing*), or other military divisions, with the clan heads as the "clan marshals." The Tang inherited the clan inheritance system from the Wei-Jin period, but the militarized situation that had once nurtured the clan inheritance system was gradually disappearing.[81] Following the disintegration of the equal-field system and the collapse of the aristocratic system, later Tang governments had no choice but to establish new government agencies to take responsibility for taxes, corvée labor, and social management, and the elite class of society would no longer simply comprise aristocrats, but now would also include landlords, merchants, professional soldiers, and all manner of experts.

The Five Dynasties were an age of complete breakdown in the aristocratic system, with knowledge about pedigree and lineage thrown into disarray. Li Tao (1115–1184) wrote, "During the disorder at end of the Tang and during the Five Dynasties, the old aristocrats of the capital mostly left their old homes, with some titles and ranks lost, their rightful heirs uncertain."[82] Qian Daxin (1728–1804) described the relation of the patriarchal clan system after the Five Dynasties to that of times from the Wei and Jin down to the Tang by writing, "The records of the heirs were not kept up and so the patriarchal clan system was left in ruins. From the Wei and Jin to the Tang, the high officials and ranking nobles of the court all had their pedigrees recorded in the official histories. Some were of the same surname but from different regions, while others were from different regions but shared surnames. All were fit into their place, and everything had its beginning and its full recording. Since the Five Dynasties, these records of pedigree have been lost."[83] Among the nine ranks of the officials of the Tang court, all descendants of officials of rank five and above enjoyed status as officials (pending selection by the Board of Civil Office). The records show that the 369 Grand Secretaries all came from just 98 elite clans, with the other official ranks largely similar. But of 72 Grand Secretaries of the Northern Song, only two passed the title down, and these were the Lü and Han families, with the former supplying three generations of Grand Secretaries, and the latter, two; furthermore, both families were poor clans, and neither were clans with accumulated pedigree. Under these circumstances, descendants of degraded clans who saw the study of their pedigrees as lifelines were already seen as worthless, like old shoes (*bi xi*). Ethical and moral principles needed to be liberated from the form of social organization from earlier times. As Zheng Qiao of the Southern Song (1104–1162) writes,

> From the Sui and the Tang and times previous, the officials had their records of identity and rank, and the families had their pedigrees. The selection and examination of officials was required to follow the record, and the marriages of the families were required to align with pedigree. For generations, they also had offices for genealogy records, which were overseen by directors and clerks, and which employed Confucians with erudite knowledge of past to present, who thoroughly comprehended the study of genealogy and pedigree. All of the hundred clans of officials had complete records, so that when a person took office, the office would confirm all the details, and then store these in the Confidential Archive (*mige*), with a supplementary copy place in the Census Section (*zuo hu*). If there were excessive amounts of secret correspondence, these were to be grouped together with the official documents; if they could not be put with the official documents, then their status as secret correspondence was disputed. This more ancient system kept control over all under Heaven and so ensured "long-lasting respect for the aristocracy, and different status for the mean and the great." People placed high esteem on the study of genealogy because of the documents in their own family archive of genealogies. From the time of the Five Dynasties onward, neither do they check the pedigree of scholar-officials, nor do they check clan merit and distinction for marriages; therefore, the documents were scattered and lost, and the study of them was not transmitted.[84]

The great families of the Northern Song were by no means descendants of the Tang aristocracy. The majority of them depended on the examinations for their scholar-official careers, and they had gained high status indeed. Under the new social conditions, the rulers of the Song court and the School of the Way scholars both tried to reconstruct the patriarchal clan system and family pedigrees, albeit with different goals, to establish long-lasting advantage for the landlord ranks, and to supply a theoretical basis for the new division of central and local government. Precisely for this reason, the issue of enfeoffments under centralized administration form centered on the issue of the evolution of the patriarchal and clan institutions.

The Song rulers and gentry elite tried to reconstruct the moral-political communal body via the idea of "respect to clan and patriarchy" from the *Book of Rites,* the specific methods of which included building memorial halls (*citang*), marking off clan fields, and maintaining written genealogies.[85] What was called centralized and divided governments were the views of the court and the gentry. The Song-dynasty absolutist authoritarian political form was produced by the separatist powers of the late-Tang military commissioners. Its administrative, military, and economic institutions were all targeted at canceling the aristocracy and preventing separatist powers. The collapse of the royal tenant (*zhuangtian*) system was of benefit to incorporating the country's farming tenants into a national household tax registry (*guojia huji*), forming an agricultural management system centered on individual families and making universal the tenancy relationship. The relative freedom of this production-and-employment relation opened the door to social mobility, and prior relations of social organization faced the danger of disintegration. For this reason, the court encouraged all to "respect clan and kin," with the goal being to form administrative, taxation, and military service systems that supported centralized power based on the landlord system as the foundation of society. From the perspective of the gentry landlord class, forming a base-level local autonomous government on the basis of the landlord system using the forms of clan law (*zongfa*) and Community Compacts (*xiangyue*) was the only path toward forming a political structure with imperial power and clan patriarchy governing together under the transforming historical conditions.

It was in precisely this context that the School of the Way masters threw themselves intensely into the work of recovering the patriarchal laws and reconstructing genealogies. "Patriarchal clan laws" (*zongfa*) referred to the clan regulations of the Western Zhou, and the study of pedigree (*pudie*) referred to the clan regulations of the hereditary houses of the Wei, Jin, Sui, and Tang eras. They hoped to use these patriarchal clan laws and pedigrees to bring peaceful ends to grudges and feuds, and to evenly distribute the wealth, with each person getting their share. As Zhang Zai says,

> The ways of the patriarchs were lost, but later generations had the genealogies, so some heritage was preserved. Then the genealogies were also lost, and no families knew where they came from. In families of less than even a hundred years, the bones and flesh lack union; even the closest kin are thin in affection.
>
> The ways of the patriarchs not set up, the court would have no hereditary ministers. [. . .] If the patriarchy could be set up, then each person would know where they came from, and the court would be much benefited by it. [. . .] Today those who have obtained wealth and nobility suddenly can only make plans for thirty or forty years. They construct a residence in a single area, which touches on all that they have. Then they die, and all their children divide and tear it apart. Before long it is totally squandered, and then that family will exist no longer. If we can't preserve such families, how much less can we preserve the country!
>
> If the high officials each protect their families, then how are not loyalty and righteousness not established? With loyalty and righteousness established, will not the court have more stable roots?[86]

Cheng Yi advocated building strict family order and clan rules, in complete accord with the logic of *The Great Learning*'s call to "organize the family and so put the state in order." He wrote, "If the law of the patriarch is broken, then the people do not know their own origins, and the problem spreads across the country. Sometimes people no longer know each other long before their clans go extinct."[87] And, "If the patriarchal clan law is in place, then the people know to respect the ancestors and put weight on the roots. If people place weight on the roots, then the power of the court respects itself."[88]

Taking up the ideas of Zhang Zai and Cheng Yi, Zhu Xi of the Southern Song compiled works on family rituals, the *Regulations of Families, Old and New* (*Gu jin jia ji li*) and the *Regulations of Families* (*Jia li*), and gave detailed designs for the memorial halls to be among the living quarters of the clans. Through sacrifice to the ancestors and establishing clan fields and patriarchs (*zongzi*), Zhu Xi recovered, on the basis of the landlord system during an age of central administration, the feudal spirit and symbolic importance of patriarchal clan enfeoffment during the early period.[89]

In one of his essays on family rituals, Zhu Xi clearly distinguishes ritual from issues of enfeoffment, and so brings issues of ritual into the political framework of centralized administration:

> Alas! Ritual propriety was lost long ago. The scholar-officials do not take their studies to heart when they are young, so they cannot carry them out with their families when they are grown. They cannot carry them out with their families when they are grown, so there is no way they can deliberate at court when they are present. Sent forth to the commanderies and counties [provincial and local government offices of the centralized administration], they retire without having taught anything to the villages and towns. This they pass down to their sons and grandsons, with none knowing how little they practiced of their own true professions.[90]

The advocacy for and service to the practice of Community Compacts undertaken by Zhu Xi and Wang Yangming can be seen as an expansion of this practice of patriarchy and clan: they attempted to use the gentry landlord system as the basis to create a form of local self-rule that aligned with the system of centralized administration under which they were already working. Because it adapted to authoritarian centralized administration and achieved long-term development after the Song, the "early modern (*jindai*) clan institutions" characterized by memorial halls, genealogies, and clan fields became the universal form of social organization during the Song, Yuan, Ming, and Qing dynasties. However, precisely because the effort to recover the patriarchal clan system was a new social practice under the conditions of the centralized administration, there was no way for this new practice to simply "return" to Western Zhou forms of patriarchy and enfeoffment. Under these conditions, the question of how to adapt to the transformed historical conditions and absorb the essence of the enfeoffments system became an issue that required consideration, understanding, experience, and practice. The Heavenly Principle worldview and its program for achieving ultimate knowledge provided people with a basis and method for combining earlier Confucian teachings with the conditions created by historical change, and thereby provided the basis for restoring the patriarchal clan system under centralized administration. Zhu Xi wrote, "There is but one principle in the universe, by the obtaining of which Heaven is Heaven, by the obtaining of which Earth is Earth, and all that lives among Heaven and Earth also is granted its nature by obtaining this principle. The three foundational principles (*gang*) comprise its span; the five constants comprise its law (*ji*). I believe it is the flowing of this Principle; it is present everywhere."[91] The order of Principle was not a vertical one directed from above to below, but rather established itself according to the level of mutually complementing relations of what is natural (*ziran*) and what ought to be (*yingran*). This is an expansive ethical framework. While Zhu Xi's ethical theory bore close relation to his effort to rebuild the patriarchal clan system, bloodlines, and local clans, the connection between his moral views and practical politics was still to a large degree dependent on balanced relations between the imperial state and the principles of clan law, Community Compacts, and private schools.

However, this balanced relation was never stable. First and foremost, the moral doctrines of the School of the Way scholars bore some connection to the "Community Compacts" practice they advocated, but the relation between the political reforms since the Tang and Song and the Community Compacts system was all the while going through changes. Zhu Xi, in his essay on land distribution, "Debating the Opening of Paths and Ridges" (*Kai qianmo bian*), affirms the Two-Tax System of Yang Yan and the way the land laws suppressed the consolidation of landholdings, but he believed that this top-down legalizing institution no longer had moral significance. His call for the recovery of the system of the Three Dynasties of Antiquity was by no means a simple call to restore an ancient system, but rather a consideration of practical problems of the time: by placing the landlord gentry at the center, via "Community Compacts" and clan laws, he hoped to reconstruct a social foundation in which the moral, economic, and political were all unified with one another. In the context of recovering the patriarchal clan system and rituals and ceremonies, Zhu Xi personally supplemented and corrected the *The Lü Family Community Compact, with Additions and Deletions* (*Zengsun Lü shi xiangyue*), describing the Community Compacts set up by the Lü brothers of the Northern Song for their home region of Lantian, in Shaanxi Province. He wrote in detail of designs and for clan rituals, ceremonies, and rules of etiquette, and argued for the necessity of clan fields, as well as expansion of sacrifices to ancestors to include local worthies.[92]

In this schema for Community Compacts there existed an element of criticism of the Song dynasty's centralized administration based on imperial power. "Community Compacts" were foundational social relations organized around bloodlines, geographic origins, and people's sentiments and feelings, rather than the legal order implemented from above by imperial power via officialdom. Hiroaki Terada, in his chapter "The Nature of Compacts (*Yue*) in the Legal Order of the Ming and Qing," gave this summary:

> What are called "Community Compacts" derive from terms like "village compacts and regulations" (*xiangli zhiyue*) and "criminal regulations" (*fanyue*), showing that they define the obligatory norms and regulations by which members [of a community] supervise each other in ethics and support each other in daily life, within a specific scope. In light of the three main forms of membership legitimacy—"consent to be regulated," "fellow follower of the regulations," and "formulating regulations"—the Community Compacts also made reference to specific modes of organizations such as executive leadership, the membership list, and distinction between members and nonmembers. Examining these two aspects together, we can say that the substantial body of the Community Compacts was created by a cohesion of a group or organization within certain rules and of people consenting to respect the rules.[93]

Whether it was the military-style "regulations" of the Warring States and Qin and Han eras, or the Community Compacts of the Song dynasty and after, "compacts" are all socially existing general ideologies that make various efforts to form or achieve general rules of behavior.[94] "Compacts" have this difference from statutory laws: the criminal laws are enforced within the broader scope of the state, with practice dependent on formalized and institutionalized systems of power, while "compacts" have special and sentimental features formed from civil intercourse, with a course of practice dependent upon regional or kinship-based communal relations.

Zhu Xi's conjecture was that local communities should be able to mediate between state intervention and family interests, and the autonomy of the Community Compacts could therefore be found in shared governmental authority. From the late Tang and the Five Dynasties to the Song dynasty, the land ownership system had gone from the equal-field system toward a system of private land ownership, and in the area of tax systems, the *zu-yong-diao* system (paid in grain, corvée, and textiles) had taken a turn toward the Two-Tax System. This transformation can be summarized with the statement that "with the transformations of the allotment object, i.e., the change of allotment by authorities from single individuals to allotment to household production units, control over the peasants by the Song court rulers was realized through a system organized by household production unit." This is to say, "Based on how much land they occupied, the peasants were bound to the production units, which was made into a class; rural villages were then governed by this class."[95] The Song-dynasty bureaucracy (the *guanhu*, official households) had mostly been produced through the examinations; the main body of the official households came from wealthy regional clans (*xingshihu*, influential households) who had not originally been scholar-official families. They enjoyed many kinds of privileges, the main one of which was to avoid corvée labor. According to studies by Yoshiyuki Sudō, what are referred to as the largest landholdings of the Song dynasty actually developed out of the landholdings of influential households and official households. "During the Northern Song, in both northern China and in the southern Yangtze River valley alike, private landholdings increased, and from the end of the Northern Song down through the end of the Southern Song, the largest landholdings in the southern Yangtze River valley developed greatly. Moreover, the landholders on the large land plots operated major farm estates (*zhuangyuan*)."[96] The formation of the new-style official taxation bureaus would of course have been disliked by those members of the Northern Song School of Principle who put so much weight on pedigree and rank.

The implication of self-rule within the Community Compact had been produced during the course of transformations of the equal-field system toward a private-property system, and from the *zu-yong-diao* system to the Two-Tax System, from which it followed that the core problem was to determine what principles should be used to draw up the new social and economic institutions (especially that of landlords); self-rule did not come from refuting imperial authority. During the Southern Song, when Zhu Xi was alive, the schema for Community Compacts contained two important social elements. On the one hand, the Community Compacts system was a social system premised on the collapse of the great hereditary clan system; it was closely connected with the centralized administration system based on imperial power. On the other hand, the social scheme of Community Compacts was in tension with the political, economic, and cultural systems centered on imperial power since the Tang and Song. In addition to the conflict with moral evaluation already mentioned, this tension is also manifest in what comprised the basic organization of local rules and allotment of land, as well as how to evaluate the social rank of the landlord gentry class. Zhu Xi and the other members of the School of Principle all praised the gentry landlord system and opposed the organization of agricultural society according to the imperial-bureaucratic system. They tried to establish a local community order using the principle of "government by virtue," through the form of "Community Compacts" and the clan institutions. Thus there was a clash of interests in the top-down view of order.

The patriarchal clan system thus contained some appeal to egalitarianism, as well as an ethics of hierarchy. The conflict between the landlord system and the state political form centered on imperial power was not a relation without its periodic changes. For example, the significance of family temples and ancestral memorial halls transformed along with the evolution of the era. Some of the conflict of these institutions with imperial power and its political system began to ease, and the two sides even came to cooperate, creating the conditions for the social basis of a new hierarchical order.[97] Before the Northern Song, family temples were the special privilege of only the aristocratic official clans, with commoners (including small- and medium-sized landlord gentry) generally making sacrifices in the main halls. Zhang Zai began referring to these main halls used by commoners to conduct sacrificial offerings as temples (*miao*): "All family halls are like what are known as temples, just as the Son of Heaven receives in the hall of grand monthly ceremonies (*zheng yue zhi dian*), yet people cannot live in these halls, for they are for sacrifice, prognostication, and ceremonies of capping and marriage and the like."[98] Cheng Yi was "the first in history to formally not distinguish between the establishment of family temples among aristocracy or commoners. And he moreover was someone who made specific suggestions about the plans and layouts of family temples."[99] He wrote, "For putting the minds of the people into harmony, nothing is better than the clan temple. . . . Nothing is better for settling human minds and bringing back the Way that was dispersed."[100] He demanded that the scholar-official family select a quiet plot of land outside the main residence to build the family temple.[101] Zhu Xi took up the use of the term "memorial hall" (*citang*), which had been for sacrifices to noteworthy local scholar-officials, using this term where the Cheng brothers and Zhang Zai had spoken of family temples. They were to be for the family to sacrifice to its ancestors and to serve as a clan gathering center. He also suggested setting up sacrificial fields to guarantee the practice of sacrifice and drawing on clan members to come up with ideas for the material side. He advocated that "the superior man should, in building his quarters, first set up the memorial hall (*citang*) to the east of the main hall (*zhengqin*), with four altar-niches to make offerings to the spirits of the ancestors."[102] And he went on to set out a clan system with various abstruse and detailed notes on the memorial halls, the clan fields, sacrifices, family rules, clan heads, and family ceremonies. After this, the main halls in the homes of scholar-officials and commoners alike began gradually to decline and be replaced by the memorial halls.[103] Ellen Neskar's work has shown that the imperial court was an important factor in the rise and fall of memorial hall construction. During the Song dynasty, local memorial halls were neither part of the academic world nor special privileges of the court. In fact, the best place to make offerings to Song-dynasty local worthies would have been the local government school (*guanxue*). In the late Southern Song, when the School of the Way was taken up as the court orthodoxy, construction of independent memorial halls immediately began to decline, and court officials obtained more direct jurisdiction over memorial halls for local worthies. This trend affirmed that the court held the initiative in these matters and was the first step in central government taking control over memorial halls.[104]

Discussions about the relation between community compacts and imperial rule supply specific context for us to renew our understanding of the relation between the Cheng-Zhu School of Principle and the School of Mind of the Ming dynasty. In Zhu Xi's new editions of the *Family Regulations, Family Regulations (Old and New)*, and *What Children Should Know* (*Tong meng xu zhi*), he vigorously advocated for clan ritual and ancestral temples, and his method of moral argumentation seemed to indicate his return to the discourse of pre-Qin Confucian ritual institutions. However, when the Cheng brothers and Zhu Xi came to understand Heavenly Principle as the highest of concepts, they had already strayed far from the method of moral argumentation based objectively on institutions and affairs. Thus it was their effort to recover ritual that transformed how moral evaluation worked in ritual. Song Confucianism emphasized grave memorials and clan temples, believing them to be virtuous practices. They supplied the medium. But at bottom, grave memorials and clan temples and such practices were not the basis and wellspring of our moral natures; rather, Heavenly Principle was. The orthodoxy of Song learning emphasized human issues and issues in moral nature, placing pursuits related to moral nature within the scope of Heavenly Principle. In this respect, the School of Principle and the School of Mind show no difference at all. Their true difference lies in this: the School of Mind took moral practice at a remove from external cognition and logical operations, from which it evinces deeper tension between conscience (*liangzhi*) and reality.

Although one single principle runs through both the Heavenly Principle view of Zhu Xi and his theory of a ritual system, there exists a contradiction within his theoretical logic: On the one hand, when he sought the basis for morality in the logical relation between Heavenly Principle and the discourse of "extending knowledge through the investigation of things," Zhu Xi had already strayed far from moral demonstrations of the theory of rituals and regulations, and in so doing had supplied the basis for the evolution of the School of Mind. On the other hand, Zhu Xi's view of Heavenly Principle had to be implemented in specific clan ritual law and ritual ceremonial practices, from which it followed that the abstract and transcendent nature of Principle would constantly be intertwining with the specific and external nature of the ritual system. The development of the School of Principle and of the School of Mind were in fact extremely similar in terms of the consequences they had, namely the disintegration of the effective dialogic relation between subjective experience and the objective world, and so in the end they left no objective basis to supply moral evaluation.

There is a historical connection between the rise of Wang Yangming thought and the development of local regulations. Yuzo Mizoguchi believed that, in the late Ming, the concepts of "public" (*gong*) and "Heavenly Principle" were merely the outer surface of the advocacy for a theory of authoritarianism allowing wealthy families greater political and economic privileges, with much political and economic content contained in their affirmations of "the private" (*si*) and "desire" (*yu*).[105] When the School of the Way and especially Zhu Xi thought became court orthodoxy, even those who would sustain Zhu Xi's ideals could no longer simply repeat what Zhu Xi had done, such as building up moral norms by reconstructing old graves and temples and admiring sages of the distant past. Quite the contrary, only by breaking with these traditional methods could one reach the moral goal of "rectified mind and sincere intentions" (*zheng xin cheng yi*). This has great significance for our understanding of Wang Yangming thought and how it developed in the late Ming, because the concepts such as "no self" (*wuren wuji*) and "the heart of the newborn babe" (*chizi zhi xin*) and the freewheeling spirit contained in this line of thinking amounted to a rejection of the overly elaborate and orthodox ritual order. In a certain sense, it was just this reaction against Zhu Xi thought that restored the egalitarian and critical thrust of the early period of Song learning. During the Ming and Qing eras, the landlord system and the patriarchal clan system featuring the memorial hall and clan heads became more and more a lower-level social institution that corresponded to the upper-level political system. The political power and demands of the landlord gentry were, along with the local rules system, absorbed into the track of the court political systems. "The state has its laws; the people have their local rules and regulations." This aphorism implied a dual social structure: one level was a system of statutory laws in which the people's crimes were punished by the bureaucracy acting as an official body for the political power that originated in the emperor. The other level was the "economic living space that formed under the assignment of an imperial 'one ruler for the myriad people' style of unitary apportionment and simultaneously formed by the various social relations of the people in all their interactions and mediated by their agreements."[106] The gentry landlord class played an important role between these two.

During the succession of the Ming to the Qing, this special historical relationship was already well established, and it was no longer possible to make an analysis using terms such as officials and civilians, or state and society, in a mode of two opposed poles. Hiroaki Terada explains this idea in two main areas. First, in terms of the implementation of the "local rules," what looked on the surface like agreements mutually defined were actually commands carrying authoritative strength issued forth from one side against the other residents, from which people could distinguish the hybrid state of the two agreement types, "commands (restrictions) issued from above" and "agreements based on mutual consent." Second, under established imperial order, agreements among commoners no longer possessed the significance of political alliances between authoritative subjects as during the Spring and Autumn and Warring States periods. For this reason, from the Ming onward, when the ethical norms centered on Community Compacts were replaced by the "Six Maxims of the Ming Hongwu Emperor" (*Taizu liu yu*) and the "Sacred Edicts" (*Sheng yu*) of Qing Emperors Kangxi and Yongzheng, Community Compacts also gradually combined with the Community Self-Defense (*baojia*) system, and the so-called "system of Community Compacts and Community Self-Defense" became mainstream. Community Compacts during the Qing dynasty became a system of national rules under the supervision of local officials, as for example the "taxation by employment" (*tan ding ru mu*) system implemented by the Yongzheng court, which was implemented by the gentry and the bureaucracy in tandem. Under these conditions, "Community Compacts" had already become a phenomenon crossing the two fields of the bureaucracy and the commoners, which is difficult indeed to explain with the assumptions of Zhu Xi.[107] This is because, within this historical context, the "Community Compacts" advocated in Zhu Xi thought and its ethics became the theoretical basis for clan law, yet we can hardly discover here any opposition between moral evaluation and institutional evaluation. When the teaching of the Confucian ethical code (*lijiao,* or ritual teaching) had become the ideology holding together the subordinate social order and the superior political system, then ritual and institutions, long divided and in conflict, once again gained unity. This unity of course could not be produced with the Three Dynasties' "government by virtue" as imagined by the Song and Ming Confucians, because the realization of the Confucian ethical code could not change the fact that it had been externalized. Only when we understand this historical context can we understand why the School of Principle from the Ming dynasty onward contained a tendency to oppose the Confucian ethical code (as for example Li Zhi's deep animosity toward Community Compacts, especially their restrictive elements, and Dai Zhen's severe criticism that "Heavenly Principle could kill" [*tian li sha ren*]). Internal tension between "Community Compacts" and the state institutions had now become a cooperative relationship. Not only had the critical nature Community Compacts once possessed transformed into patriarchal dogma, but also they also worked in close association with the Confucian ethical code.

What modern Chinese thought criticizes and opposes is not just the theory of Zhu Xi, but is (in the main) the dogmas of patriarchy and their institutional foundations that formed under the influence of Zhu Xi thought. For this reason, criticism of Zhu Xi thought signifies the formation of a new social order and its legitimacy. The May Fourth New Culture Movement was an anti-imperialist and republican movement that propagated in the discursive field of an imperial system that had already collapsed. The direct targets of the movement were thus no longer the imperial system per se, but rather the imperial social foundations and ideological mind-sets, the social order and moral foundation dominated by the gentry landlords. Ethically, it demanded liberation of the individual from the ethical and political relations of patriarchy, clan, and even community, and organization of individual subjectivities amid modern national laws. This individual would be a national citizen, as well as a private subject under the law. Modern positivism, with atomism at its core, understood humans as atomistic social bodies, and would, in the name of the individual, advance the deconstruction and criticism of patriarchal clans, family clans, and communities based on geography and kinship, from which they would construct an ideology whose basic tendency and framework would use individualism and scientism (*kexue zhuyi*).

3. Visions of the Well-Field System: Land Tenure, Tax Law, and Moral Evaluation in the Commercialization Process

The dissolution of the aristocratic system was not a sudden or isolated event: the transformation of land tenure and tax law in the Tang and Song dynasties was one aspect of this dissolution. Starting in the Northern (Tuoba) Wei, changes in land tenure followed a basic direction of changing the situation where great landlord families with high social status or official ranking had been able to hide the extent of their landholdings, and of developing new tax collection methods based on the equal-field system. This system was first implemented in the ninth year of the Taihe Period of the Xiaowen Emperor (485 CE), the term "equal-field" (*juntian*) imitating the style used in the tradition of land tenure systems since the "well-field system" in the Three Dynasties of Antiquity. It was characterized by the combination of land grants with land restrictions into one system, and by the creation of landed property relations where state ownership existed alongside private ownership. In this sense, the equal-field system, presented as an adaptation from the Zhou dynasty, represented the transition from traditional to privatized land tenure, and its eventual relaxation was precisely an outcome of the conflict between the two forms of land tenure that coexisted within this system. The Tang dynasty's "equal-field decree" (*juntianling*) and the *zu-yong-diao* taxes (paid in grain, corvée, and textiles) were premised on the equal-field system, promulgated in the seventh year of the Wude Period (624).[108] The equal-field decree distributed land according to gender, age, rank in the bureaucracy or nobility, and so forth; abolished the granting of state land (*shoutian*) on the basis of the number of one's slaves (*nubi*), retainers (*buqu*), and oxen; and prohibited the excessive occupation of farmland in areas that were land poor and densely populated (*xiaxiang*), allowing officials to receive grants of "inheritable land" (*yongyetian*) and "reward land" (*xuntian*) only in areas with sufficient farmland available for the population (*kuanxiang*). By the middle years of the Tang dynasty, land grabs were becoming more severe by the day, unwanted population migration was increasing, and the economic relations between equal-field peasants and small-scale landlords with economic advantages, which had been protected by the equal-field order, were being destroyed.[109] The dissolution of the equal-field system was the outcome of land grabs and the establishment of private ownership over land.

The transformation of land tenure relations was reflected in the tax system as the dissolution of the *zu-yong-diao* system, because as the population fled, it became difficult to sustain those centralized taxes based on human labor. Under conditions where land, population, and taxes were being severely encroached upon by local powers, the Tang court had no choice but to adjust the property tax system and implement the "Two-Tax Policy" (*liangshuifa*). During the Dali Period of the Daizong Emperor (766–779), the Tang state's tax income was already gradually becoming centered on household taxes (*hushui*) and land taxes (*dishui*). In year one of the Jianzhong Period of the Dezong Emperor (780), Chancellor Yang Yan formulated the Two-Tax Policy, whose main content included the following: the central government would determine the amount of tax revenue to be collected on the basis of its budgeted expenses, and each locale would collect taxes from its population according to the amount specified by the central government; both "native households" (*tuzhuhu*) and "guest households" (*kejuhu*) would be registered as residents of each prefecture and county, and then ranked according to their workforce (*dingzhuang*) and property; taxes would be collected twice a year, in the sixth and eleventh months (of the Chinese lunisolar calendar); *zu-yong-diao* and other forms of corvée would be abolished; the Two Taxes would be collected according to the ranking of each household, and grain according to the field; field tax would be based on the amount of land under cultivation in the fourteenth year of the Dali Period, collected according to average yields; and merchants were to pay one-thirtieth of their income in the place where they did business.[110]

The implementation of the Two-Tax Policy not only required the great noble families to pay tribute, but also tried through this to take over those "guest households" they had been concealing, thus transforming the traditional system of "calculating taxes per capita," or "based on workforce." Since the Two-Tax Policy took each household's amount of property as the standard for collecting taxes, the scope was expanded so that the burden of payments and corvée would no longer be concentrated on the shoulders of poor peasants.[111] Also, since taxes were determined according to the amount of property one owned, the implementation of the Two-Tax Policy indirectly defined land as private property, and since it allowed people to substitute cloth for corvée in paying the Two Taxes, it also institutionally abolished corvée, so labor would no longer be a fixture of landed property. As private property in land and the personal rights of peasants became clearly defined in law through the tax system, the relationship entangled with land rights between the central imperial authorities and the local bastions of landlord power—a relationship that had formed under the equal-field system of land allotments—became weaker, with each side becoming agents with their own independent interests.[112] This was the foundation of market relations and commercial culture, as well as the institutional and policy preconditions for the further concentration of landholdings. In *Policy Questions for the Jinshi Examination, First Series* (*Jinshi cewen yidao*), Li Ao (772?–841) criticized the fact that, after the Two-Tax Policy, "the common people's land was seized by the powerful, who took more than a third for themselves,"[113] completely confirming the statement that "the rich seized tens of thousands of *mu* of land, leaving the poor without a place to live."[114] Li Ao was regarded as a pioneer of the School of the Way, but hardly anyone has undertaken an analysis of the relationship between his writings on Heavenly Principle and his *Revising the Tax Law* and *Policy Questions for the Jinshi Examination*.

According to Miyazaki Ichisada's research, the original intention of the Two-Tax Policy was to use copper coins for tax collection, but due to the absolute shortage of coins, later the government was forced to accept the substitution of grain or cloth of equal value—a practice known as *shena*.[115] After the Song had pacified the southern states, it collected the lead and iron coins from the various states of the Five Dynasties and forged new copper coins, distributing them among the population and using them to set standards for the state price system as well as for the crime of bribery.[116] This unprecedented economy of copper currency clearly pushed forward the commercialization and marketization of social life. At the same time the South was being incorporated into the copper economy, the continued circulation of silver there influenced the North in turn: the coexistence of an official price system (including bribery) calculated in copper money alongside a system of silver currency still used for commerce outside of official channels, comprising an era in which "the policy of expanding the northern currency system and forcing it on the South was successful."[117] This expansion of the currency system shows that long-distance trade was already becoming an important economic form during this period, in which respect the ease of transportation provided by the Grand Canal was a major factor, because the commercial activities that moved along the canal worked together with the policy reforms of tax law and the equal-field system to strongly push forward the population movements that accompanied commerce.[118] In sum, the development of trade, the expansion of cities, the increase of the population's size and mobility, and the strain on land resources exacerbated by the Song dynasty's military weakness—together, all these factors inevitably gave rise to new social relations and contradictions.

The Two-Tax Policy provided conditions for freer market relations, but it also opened a path toward the concentration of land and the polarization of social classes. As the monetary economy developed, the material economy was bound to be deeply affected.[119] When the policy was first launched, one roll of tax-cloth would sell for 3,200–3,330 *wen* (copper cash coins), but by the tenth year of the Zhenyuan Period (794), the price had fallen to 1,500–1,600.[120] According to the *History of the Song Dynasty's* "Record of Food and Goods" (*Shi huo zhi*), the establishment of the Two-Tax Policy led to "powerful officials and rich families seizing farmland without limit, annexing [land], and [practicing] fraud, [to the point that it] became customary."[121] The

"Food and Goods" section of another work, the *Compiled Institutional History of the Song Dynasty* (*Song huiyao jigao*), described the contradictions caused because "the registrations and tax records of the households were not in order for use, and the local clerks were all secretly collecting taxes for themselves. Many families fled, bankrupt, squatters risked planting on taxable land, and households were lost to fraud. Taxes and tributes were thus heavy or light in unfair fashion, as were corvée labor and penal labor service."[122] Since the Two-Tax Policy was a product of the failure of the equal-field system, whose concept had in turn derived from the pre-Qin period, it was easy for the Confucians to criticize the equal-field system within a framework of Three Dynasties of Antiquity governance and Han-Tang law. Li Gou (1009–1059), an expert on the *Book of Changes* and the *Rites of Zhou* as well as a strident critic of the School of the Way, published political works such as "On the Equalization of Land" (*Ping tu shu*), "Policy for Enriching the State, Strengthening the Army, and Pacifying the People" (*Fuguo qiangbing anmin ce*), "The *Rites of Zhou* Bring About Peace" (*Zhouli zhi taiping lun*), and "Deep Thoughts" (*Qian shu*), whose key ideas were "the equalization of land," "the equalization of corvée" (*junyi*), "the stabilization of prices" (*pingzhun*), and "the equalization of purchases" (*pingdi*)—most importantly the first, "the equalization of land" (i.e., the equal-field system). Regarding the situation where "the laws were not established, the land and fields were not equal, the wealthy daily grew wealthier and the poor were daily exploited, and even when the harvest was good, there was not enough grain to eat," Li advocated "equalizing the land"[123] according to principles derived from the well-field system: "I now know that the method of the well-field is the key to sustaining the people's livelihood. Once the well-field is established, then the fields will be equal. Once the fields are equal, then the planters will get food. When they get enough to eat, the silk producers can get clothes. Without plowing and sericulture, few will avoid famine and cold."[124]

The Song School of the Way scholars' appeal to clan law and the well-field system were historically connected to the formation of new market relations, the development of land buying and concentration, the significant expansion of imperial power, the implementation of a draconian legal system, and the displacement of people from their homes. These scholars regarded enfeoffment, the well-field system, and schools as critical, oppositional institutions and concepts—that is, as critical responses to the expansion of imperial authority and laws, the development of commercial culture, the contradiction between land and population, and the rise of social mobility. In the chapter on the *Rites of Zhou* in Zhang Zai's *Assembled Principles in the Study of the Classics*, Zhang condemned the increasingly widespread use of the death penalty and the development of markets, writing that the former was leading paradoxically to "a situation where presumptuous people nowadays frequently take their own deaths lightly," while the latter meant "that management of markets is a matter for market officials only, and not one for kingly government."[125] If we put such critical views together with Zhang's call to revive the well-field system, we can observe something about social change more generally: increasingly widespread use of the death penalty was closely related to the increase of displacement, population movements, and the collapse of clan institutions. It was precisely in this new context that a melody of nostalgia for the well-field system and clan institutions could be detected in Neo-Confucian works, echoing Mencius: "Neither at the occasion of a death nor of a change of a residence should people leave the village. When those in a village who hold land in the same well-field befriend one another in their comings and goings, assist one another in their protection and defense, and sustain one another through illness and distress, the hundred surnames will live together in affection and harmony."[126]

Zhang Zai's "Western Inscription" (*Xi ming*) used Heaven and Earth to encompass the state, the familial ethics of filial piety, and benevolence (*ren'ai*) as norms for the behavior of the sovereign and the state, and the well-field system and clan law as objective foundations for state ethics. Beyond the logical structure of his Heavenly Way worldview, we can observe a set of efforts at social experimentation according to Zhou-dynasty clan law and the well-field system. He wrote:

> If those who govern All-under-Heaven do not begin with the well-field system, there will never be equality. The Way of Zhou was simply to equalize. . . . The well-field system could be put into effect with the greatest of ease, but when the court gives a single command, it can do so without punishing any person. I believe that then no landlords would take the land of the people, and the people would serve with pleasure. When more have fields, it makes them able to hold on to wealth. If any high minister held lands of a thousand *qing* [an area equivalent to one hundred *mu*], one

> would just enfeoff them with a state (*guo*) of fifty *li,* and this would be more than what they held. Others were given official positions in accordance with how much land they held, which prevents losses among the original rent- and tax-seekers. Any arts of government must begin here.[127]

Since the well-field system was closely related to clan law and enfeoffment, Zhang Zai also linked these institutions together within a new historical context. When he returned to his hometown of Hengqu at the age of fifty-one, Zhang divided his time between writing and arranging fields in experiments with the well-field system, a small-scale experiment in land tenure that attempted to revive the ancient institutions of clan law. In his piece "Clan Law," he described in detail the significance for property rights, also demonstrating that clan sacrifice was a special economic institution: when the eldest sons of the lords participated in a sacrifice, it was necessary for them to donate labor services to the clan, while those who did not participate had to pay tribute.[128] That was an economic form that differed from both the Two-Tax Policy and the commercial economy linked to population movement. For the School of the Way scholars, these economic activities themselves involved moral significance—that was the essence of the ancient institutions. Clan law was an important foundation of the ancient system of rites, and a condition for social maintenance. The unrest in relations between the scholar-gentry and commoners during the Warring States period derived from the transformation of class divisions that had resulted from the decline of clan law, when it was said "the big clans were no longer big, and the small clans had risen up" and "the system of rites and music had collapsed"—a process similar to the Tang-Song dissolution of aristocratic institutions and their own ritual system. Therefore, the basic impetus for rebuilding clan law was to rejuvenate the system of rites, not only as a purely moral process of cultivation, but also as an economic and political one.[129] Echoing Zhang Zai, Hu Hong (1105–1155) regarded the equal-field system as a precondition for reviving ancient institutions such as enfeoffment and the well-field system, placing these institutions within the School of the Way categories of Heavenly Principle versus human desires, public versus private, and so forth:

> The equal fields are the priority of government. If field and village are not equitable, then the people will not reap the benefits, though rulers

be humane. The well-field system was the essential method of the sages for equal fields.[130]

Once the well-field laws are implemented, then the wise can be picked out from the benighted. In the field of learning, there will be no incompetent scholars, and in the fields, there will be no incompetent peasants. Human talent will be encouraged at its source and idle hands will be few. The ruler leads the high ministers, high ministers lead senior scholar-officials, senior scholar-officials lead ordinary scholar-officials, scholar-officials lead the peasants, the artisans, and the merchants, with everyone getting a share in the system, in equality and without any in poverty. If everyone gets land, then it will be preserved through the generations. There will be no cheating and stealing in trade and exchange. With no cheating and stealing in trade and exchange, there will be no court cases on fights. With no court cases on fights, the people are at peace and punishments are spared. With punishments spared and the people being at peace, the rites and music are cultivated, harmony is achieved.[131]

Enfeoffments—these are the main methods and great basis for kings to align with Heavenly Principle, capture the people's hearts, and bring public order to All-under-Heaven. Eschewing enfeoffments is the evil and treacherous path of the hegemons and warlords to let loose human desires, turn against the Great Way, and make all into private selfishness.[132]

It is worth noting that Hu Hong's writings on the well-field and enfeoffment systems were closely related to his critique of the centralized system of administration, which was in turn linked to the "distinction between barbarian and Chinese" (*Yi-Xia zhi bian*) within relations of enfeoffment. By doing so he closely connected land tenure with rituals, military affairs, and internal-external relations. On the one hand he wrote, "The centralized administration was put in place only by abandoning government by enfeoffment. And the system of inheritance was lost when centralized administration was put in place."[133] But on the other hand he asserted, "It was the governing of the noble fiefdoms that enabled government of the kingly domain. A kingly domain at peace and strong, with the many fiefdoms closely attached, is what protects and guards China (*Zhong-Xia*) and stands against the barbarians (*si Yi*). . . . Since the Qin, with centralized administration, the central plains were frequently plagued with problems at the borders. It's tragic!"[134] According to Xiao Gongquan, "Hu Hong implies that the blame for the great southern migration lay with the Song-dynasty centralized government, which is in keeping with the later thesis of Wang Fuzhi, that 'the Qin was left solitary, the Song, abject' (*gu Qin lou Song*)."[135]

In the Southern Song, Zhu Xi's attitude continued along these lines. In "Debating the Opening of Paths and Ridges," Zhu made a profound analysis of the consequences of the collapse of the land grant (*fenfeng shoutian*) system: "The open paths and lands [the land system of Shang Yang] cut up the fields of the people, with also many secret landholders using private privilege, so that tax revenue did not reach the public system." He believed that land tenure reforms such as Shang Yang's "Opening Paths and Ridges" (i.e., the privatization of land in the protoimperial Qin state, 361–338 BCE) and Yang Yan's Two-Tax Policy, although beneficial in mitigating the abuses related to the destruction of the well-field and land-grant systems, also lost the profound moral significance of the institutions of the ancient sages:

> [The ancients worked] to completely open the paths, and so rid all limits, and to allow the combination of purchase and sale of land, to make the most of human effort. To open up waste lands, and make them all into marked land for farming . . . to make the most from the land. It was to ensure the people had fields and thus permanent livelihood that would never again be taken away from them or given to others, and thereby to bring an end to the ills caused by interference [from outsiders], cheating, and corruption. To make all land into fields, and make all fields put out tax revenue, enabled the discovery of the tax-dodging of private holders. This strategy was just like Yang Yan's annoyance at the problem of floating labor, with the subsequent repeal of the *zu-yong* system and replacement with the Two-Tax System. It's my opinion that although the short-term injury is removed, the nuanced intentions of a millennium of sagely wisdom passed down are hereby lost altogether.[136]

How was Zhu Xi able to conclude from the reform of land tenure that "the nuanced intentions of a millennium of sagely wisdom" would be lost? Such a conclusion would be impossible without the Confucian perspective of "the separation of institutions from the rites and music." Therefore, the Song Confucians' economic and political views can be properly understood only within the context of the transformation of methods of moral judgment.

Traditional patriarchal clan regulations were centered on the clan heads (*zongzi*) and established on land tenure relations defined according to kinship. From a perspective where the Son of Heaven granted land according to clan law, this institution could be regarded as a derivative of a state administration system that rewarded its subjects with land grants. The institutions of clan law were based on the granting of hereditary state salaries, itself based on "salary fields" (*lutian*), that is, land. Without salary fields there could be no hereditary salaries, and without hereditary salaries there could be no clan law. This sort of clan ethics and its method of allocating land and labor required compatibility between emotions and laws, and the valuation of righteousness over self-interest, conditions that were bound to oppose the use of legal formulas for the delineation of land ownership relations in an excessively definitive manner. From a historical vantage point, the struggle between the well-field system and the "opening of paths and ridges" could be summarized as a contradiction between enfeoffment and centralized administration. We can see this in the *History of the Han*'s "Record on Food and Goods" (*Shi huo zhi*), which recorded that the Shang Yang reforms implemented during the reign of Duke Xiao of Qin "destroyed the well-field system and opened paths and ridges." Long before Zhu Xi, during the Han dynasty Chao Cuo and Dong Zhongshu had already written similar critiques, stating that "the destruction of the well-field system and the opening of paths and ridges" had led to land grabs, division between rich and poor, merchants annexing the land of peasants, and the displacement of peasants. It is only within this long-term relationship between Confucianism and institutional reform that we can understand Zhu Xi's views on institutional innovations such as the Two-Tax Policy, why he invested so much passion in Community Compacts and clan ethics, and why he refused to base his conception of Heavenly Principle on existing institutions, even as he took clan ethics as its main content.

From Li Ao in the late Tang dynasty, to Zhang Zai in the Northern Song, and on to Zhu Xi in the Southern Song, we can see two intertwined threads: while criticizing the various institutions and their consequences since the Han and Tang dynasties, these scholars also constructed a new moral genealogy centered on the Way of Heaven and the Heavenly Principle. A question that naturally arises is: In using the governance of the Three Dynasties to oppose the Han-Tang policies, why did the School of the Way scholars not use the rites and music as a basic framework for moral-political evaluation, but instead created a new method of moral-political evaluation within the framework of the Way of Heaven or inherent nature (*benxinglun*) centered on the Way of Heaven or Heavenly Principle? Here, historical change and consciousness consistent with this change—that is, consciousness of "the propensity of the times" (*shishi*)—played an important role. The School of the Way scholars used the governance of the Three Dynasties to criticize existing institutions and their social consequences, but did not believe that the revival of old institutions such as the well-field system could solve those problems—they were still affirming the power structure that was seen under centralized administration. Zhu Xi wrote:

> Enfeoffment and well-fields are the institutions of the Sage-Kings, the methods which brought all under Heaven to serve the common good (*gong Tianxia*). How could we not find this to be so! But nowadays I am afraid they are difficult to implement. Even if we set up enforcement to make them work, it might well only lead to more corruption and problems. Better to take care of this beforehand than have to turn around, when it would be hard to clean up.[137]

Regarding Cheng Hao's conception of the well-field system, Zhu commented: "Master Cheng said many times in his younger days that we must have the well fields and enfeoffments, but in his later years he also said that they would be hard to implement. . . . I think that as his experience of the world increased, he saw that such enterprise was not practicable."[138]

The preceding discussion brings us to a few basic conclusions: First, Zhu Xi endorsed the trend of suppressing land grabs and their consequences, but believed that the new institutional innovations involved long-term moral costs. Second, Zhu's affirmation of the moral significance of ancient institutions did not amount to a call for reviving the aristocratic system, because the Community Compacts based on the rural landlord system that he emphasized had emerged precisely from the dissolution of that system. Third, Zhu's critique of existing institutions was founded on the postulate that those institutions could not provide an objective basis for moral judgment. Therefore, returning to the Way of Confucius and Mencius did not mean that the rites and music they had described could be used as a blueprint for actual politics, but that the starting point and objective premise for moral practice and judgment had to be reconceptualized. "Principle" (*li*) comprised an order, a yardstick, and an essence that existed within things, and the affirmation of Principle could not be simplified into an affirmation of those things themselves, nor into a negation of them. Regarding Zhu's complex attitude toward institutions of land tenure, tax policy, and commercial culture, combining historical affirmation with moral critique, a typical expression can be seen in his "distinction between Principles and desire" (*li-yu zhi bian*). The twelfth *juan* of the *Classified Sayings of Master Zhu* reads: "All the myriad words of the sages teach is for persons to illuminate Heavenly Principle and destroy human desire," but *juan* 13 responds: "Between drinking and eating, which is Heavenly Principle and which is human desire?" Thus it is said, "Food and drink are Heavenly Principle; to seek delicious flavors is human desire."[139] Therefore, the key to determining whether a certain desire should be gotten rid of, or whether it was a reasonable one that should be preserved, was to first determine whether the situation or condition was appropriate, and Heavenly Principle was the yardstick for measuring whether the situation was appropriate.

4. Visions of "Schools": The Examination System, Employment of Officials, and Moral Evaluation

By reconstructing an ethics based on blood relations and local community, the Song-Ming School of Principle renounced the institutional discourse that had developed since the Han dynasty and, unlike the Classical Studies school (*jingxue*) of the Han dynasty, was not directly subordinate to imperial power and imperial politics. The transcendent characteristics of the Heavenly Way emerged from Confucians' historical judgment that ritual had separated from institutions, which meant that the establishment of the Heavenly Way and Heavenly Principle implied a turn toward negation—namely that it would no longer be effective to argue for the rationality of morality by way of the relation of ritual to morality, and of function to moral integrity. For this reason, moral judgment must appeal to Heavenly Principle or one's own body and mind, rather than resorting to actual institutions and achievements. To Song Confucians, the institutional reforms of the Han and Tang onward had created a separation of institutions and knowledge having to do with associations from other discourses (e.g., rules, ceremonies, and goals). The imperial examination system, the Two-Tax System, and the paired Grand Councilor system (*shuang chengxiang*) were only functional institutional designs, with no inherent moral meaning as in the institutions of the Three Dynasties, which meant these later institutions were now separated off from their original discourse fields. In the face of the unprecedented development of the examination system and other political institutions, Song Confucians separated institutional evaluation and moral evaluation, but tried to reconstruct a unified relation between "order" (also called "order of Principle") and moral evaluation, which meant one order would be in critical conflict with another. They devoted much of their efforts to the development of Community Compacts, clan law, and private schools, promoting the methods and spirit of "extending knowledge through the investigation of things," and not only to argue for the necessity of ritual order, but also to supply a moral basis to the community linked by blood relations, region, and human sentiment, as well as on a practical level. Wang Anshi, who devoted much energy to institutional reform, lamented that "in the past, the Way and virtue (*dao de*) were held in common by all the people. Thus when the scholar-officials (*shi*) took their principles from the ways the ancients preserved themselves, there were no heterodox theories. Today every school has a different moral system, different people have different senses of virtue, and the scholar who would maintain high virtue, is also affected by the influence of vulgar custom. Unable to conduct affairs as of old, would it not be better to put a stop to these heterodox theories?"[140] In the eyes of the Confucians, be it the promotion of the Six Classics by Emperor Wu of the Han, or the way Han Emperor Guangwu continued studying even in the midst of battle, or the way Emperor Xiaowen of Wei wanted to reform the customs of the Rong barbarians, or the flowery language of the decrees issued by Emperor Taizong of the Tang, "All these examples were merely extravagant shows that put too much emphasis on outward appearance, and really not cases in which propriety was incessantly at work in the hearts of men."[141]

After the Sui dynasty, the selection system for officials (*xuanjuzhi*) first begun by Emperor Wen of the Han dynasty, and continued for eight hundred years, was replaced by the civil examination system, thus replacing a standard for selecting talent based mainly on virtuous behavior with a standard for selecting talent based on knowledge. During the later Tang, and especially during the Northern Song, the examination system and its significance underwent important changes. It became not only the path for selection of officials, but also the standard by which to inspect the character and ability of scholar-officials. In this respect, what examination reform changed was not the system of education and selection of officials, but rather the base assumptions of moral evaluation. The scholar-official class in this way replaced the aristocratic class to become the central class of society. Of interest is that as the Song Confucians wished for the government of the Three Dynasties, questions about educational institutions took up a central position. In his *Critical History of Institutions* (*Wen xian tong kao*), Ma Duanlin (1254–1323) recorded the development of decrees and institutions from ancient times to the Ningzong reign of the Song dynasty (1194–1224), summarizing many of the views of Song Confucians. In his section 42 on "schools," we find him elaborating on the words of Lü Zuqian (1137–1181):

> The political system of the first kings, despite decay since the Qin and Han, preserves other things like the system of rites and music; through its shadow we can see its form. Following along the branches and leaves, one can seek the roots. Only the schools seem to have utterly turned their backs on the ancient kings, and cannot be recovered. . . . Just consider the example of the government schools. Emperor Shun commanded Kui to be Manager of Music to teach his sons. During Zhou times, the Musician in Chief held the methods for the Royal College . . . why was it that the director of teaching was the Musician in Chief? It must have been his ample self-restraint, which could activate into rhythm and movement, and so enter deeply into men's hearts. . . . As for those who do not follow the teachings, we must keep them at a distance, and look down on them until the end. . . . Schools were, for the most part, not overseen by appointed officials during the times of Tang and Yu and the Three Dynasties and earlier, but after the Qin and Han dynasties, there were officials supervising and overseeing. To see why one can hardly examine the learning of later eras, it is enough to look at Tang, Yu, and the Three Dynasties.[142]

In Lü Zuqian's view, the rituals of the Three Dynasties are entirely different from the institutions of Qin, Han, and later times, especially when it came to the system of schools. Even if later ages had laws and examinations, these merely propped each other up institutionally, and completely lost the Way and Principle that had entered deeply into the human mind. The above passage develops the dichotomy between the "education" of the Three Dynasties and the "government" of the Qin and Han, and between the former's "meaning of Principle" and the latter's "literary ornament." According to Lü, only the Southern and Northern Dynasties, with their elements of enfeoffment, could make manifest the essentials of the Three Dynasties schools. In their characteristic view that institutions had separated from ritual, the Song Confucians demanded a new examination of the institutional evaluation standards, and they believed that the reforms of the Tang and Song (especially the establishment of the Nine-Rank household system, the examination system, and the Two-Tax System) produced a series of institutions not matching with ritual and not appropriate for advancing moral argument, from which it followed that to reestablish basic standards for moral-political evaluation was the logical result of the historical perspective regarding "the separation of institutions from ritual."

Learning from the collapse of autocratic military rule during the Five Dynasties, and the collapse of the elite-scholar aristocracy system, the Song dynasty established an unprecedented system of civil offices and a complex suite of imperial exams. Based on data collected by Zhang Xiqing, during the Song dynasty, an average of 361 men per year entered the scholar-official class via the examinations, a number five times greater than that of the Tang dynasty, thirty times greater than during the Yuan dynasty, four times greater than during the Ming dynasty, and almost three and a half times greater than during the Qing dynasty. From high ministers, to servants of the emperor, to frontier generals, tax and grain officials, and provincial magistrates, all were scholar-officials who had passed the examinations.[143] By abolishing the recommendation custom (*gongjian*), establishing the palace examination system, and reducing the systematic privilege of the aristocracy (*bietoushi*) or restricting family members from taking the exams together—and instituting such measures as the "locked hall," sealing names on examination papers, and the use of transcription copies—the Song examination system supplied institutional conditions for equal competition among the landlord class and the upper ranks of the peasants. As a large batch of well-known officials emerged from the examinations, the social status of the scholar-official class saw an unprecedented rise. From generous salaries to lighter punishments, from number of positions available to space allowed for comment and suggestions, "The advantages conferred by the Song court on the scholar-officials were unparalleled."[144]

The examinations of the early Song were inherited from the Tang dynasty, but the exam types were fewer, with the main Song exams (*gongjuke*) being the presented scholar (*jinshi*), the "various field" examinations (*zhuke*), military examinations (*wuju*), and the apprentice examinations (*tongzi*). The *jinshi* remained primary. Cai Xiang was a scholar who passed the *jinshi* during the reign of Emperor Renzong and rose to the State Finance Commission (*sansi*) in the court of Yingzong; he described the examinations and selection officials this way: "Selecting officials is about choosing scholars. Among those scholars who are chosen nowadays, those admitted through the various field examinations (*zhuke*) are erudite and with strong memories; those who become presented scholars can all write regulated poems and poetic expositions, with good style; and those who took the classics examination (*mingjing*) can recite from the histories and the classics and are good at formulating the paired propositions [of the examination essay]. Officials who come up the ranks from good postings to high minister positions mostly are of these three types."[145] Closely related to the rise in the social status of the scholar class, many officials who gained status from the *jinshi* examinations, which emphasized literary essays and poetic exposition, were not only some of the most famous and worthy ministers, but were also cultural figures of Confucian background. The various examinations all had their differences, with subjects that could include the Nine Classics, the Five Classics, the Three Histories, the Three Books of Ritual, the Three Commentaries, detailed research on single texts (*xuejiu*), the *Ritual Codes* (*Kai yuan li*), and the Law Examination (*mingfa*), though the common content was hard memorization of Han and Tang commentaries. The Tang orthodox tradition of classical studies, expounded in *The True Meaning of the Five Classics* (*Wujing zhengyi*), still retained great influence during the early Song. According to records in the "Veneration of Confucian Scholarship" (*Chong ru xue*) chapter in the *Essence of Politics* (*Zhenguan zhengyao*), when the *The True Meaning of the Five Classics* was first ordered for compilation by decree of Tang Emperor Taizong in the fourth year of the Zhenguan reign period, the fact that it applied a method of commentaries was a result of the fact that, as the Confucian teachers said, "There are many schools of Confucian learning; the chapters and lines are numerous and complex."[146] Tang Taizong tasked Kong Yingda (574–648) and various other Confucians with establishing the correct version of the classics using ancient editions, and employing the commentarial method of classical studies to unify the various schools since the Han dynasty. According to the "Treatise on Examinations" (*Xuan ju zhi*) in the *New History of the Tang*, the Tang-dynasty selection of scholar-officials by the classics examination (*mingjing*) clearly affirmed the status of the various classics: "Of all, the *Book of Rites* and the Zuo commentary on the *Spring and Autumn Annals* (*Chunqiu Zuozhuan*) were the great classics, while the *Book of Odes*, the *Rites of Zhou*, and the *Book of Changes* were intermediate classics, and the *Wings to the Book of Changes*, the *Book of Documents*, and the Gongyang and Guliang commentaries to the *Spring and Autumn Annals* were the minor classics."[147] And the classics (*mingjing*) and presented scholar (*jinshi*) examinations must also "be conducted according to the *Six Statutes* (*Liu dian*), with all taking three sessions."[148] Orthodox classical studies and the examination system together built a Confucian bureaucratic system. In this context, the currents in critical thought of orthodox classical studies in the examinations built up an important line connecting the Confucianisms of the Tang through the Song. From the *Detailed Conditions Established for Examinations* (*Xiang ding gong ju tiao zhi*) promulgated during the Qingli New Policies period to the New Policies of Wang Anshi, discussions surrounding reform of the examination system often focused on changing the dogmatic and unyielding orthodoxy of the Six Classics in favor of full expression in moral philosophy or expositions on meanings and principles (*yili*).

In this context, during the Northern Song a sharp opposition between the study of "moral philosophy" (*yili*) and the study of "focused topics" (*zhuanzhu*) emerged. Here, moral philosophy refers mainly to the study of Han and Tang commentaries on the classics, which covered a broader scope than the School of the Way. The latter was also a form of moral philosophy, one whose rise was closely connected to the currents of criticism of the examination system and its contents. However, there were deep tensions within the study of moral philosophy. From the stark opposition of the fields of knowledge of Li

Gou and Wang Anshi against the School of the Way, extending down to the intense debates between Chen Liang and Zhu Xi during the Southern Song, disagreements within the study of fields of knowledge formed even sharper and longer-sustained contradictions than the tensions between fields of knowledge study and commentarial study. Li Gou, taking the *Rites of Zhou* as the central text, understood ritual as the legal system of the ancients, and so discussed political forms and land management systems and tax systems within the framework of ritual, using the form of institutional discourse to dismiss the School of the Way as just so much empty talk.[149] Wang Anshi (1021–1086) similarly placed a high degree of emphasis on the *Rites of Zhou,* which had first been listed among the classics during the Han dynasty. After being appointed to the post of Grand Secretary in the third year of the Xining reign period, 1071, Wang immediately instituted the New Policies: the following year, the examination system would be reformed, and during the sixth year, in 1073, a new Bureau for the Meaning of Classics was set up, to revise three classics: the *Book of Odes,* the *Book of Documents,* and the *Rites of Zhou.* During the eighth year, the *New Commentaries on the Three Classics* (*San jing xinyi*) was promulgated in the Academy, or Xueguan, with the announcement, "Previous Confucian commentaries will all be discarded and no longer used."[150] Of the three prefaces to the *New Commentaries on the Three Classics,* Wang Anshi himself is said to have penned the preface to the *On the Meaning of the Rites of Zhou* (*Zhou li yi*). The preface to this text reads:

> Literati have been blinded by commonplace learning for a long time. The sage above has been concerned about this and has used the learning and methods of the Classics (*jing shu*) to create [this book]. He has further assembled Ru ministers to explicate its points for distribution to the schools. Your minister [Wang] Anshi has been responsible for the *Offices of Zhou.*

> When the Way is present in the affairs of government, noble and lowly have their proper place, last and first have their proper order, many and few have their proper number, and slow and fast have their proper time [i.e., ranks, priorities, amounts, and timing are all appropriate to the tasks at hand]. Their institution and deployment depend on policy, but pro-

> moting and putting them into practice depends on the person. No time was better than that of the Duke of Zhou for having people capable of filling the offices and officials capable of putting policy into effect. And of texts that can be found in the written record no document is more complete than the *Offices of Zhou* for policies that can be applied in later ages.[151]

Li Gou and Wang Anshi both took as their path the classical studies of the Han dynasty, with explication of the meaning and Principle of the classics as the blueprint for court reforms. To a very large degree, the criticism of Han and Tang classical studies by the Northern Song School of the Way was accompanied by stark opposition to the new classical studies and its theory of reform. We can in large measure summarize the disagreement as follows: supporters of the new classical studies suspected that the content of the examinations had no usefulness for administering the state, while the School of the Way's suspicion was that the system of selecting officials by examinations would fail to supply a foundation for moral-political evaluation.

We might consider the case of Wang Anshi's reforms and their relation to the School of the Way. Among Northern Song Confucians, it was commonplace to criticize the faults of the examination system from the perspective of the intents of the ancient kings. Wang Anshi would later be criticized by the School of Principle members for promoting his New Policies, but there was no basic difference between the School of Principle and Wang Anshi in how they all modeled themselves on the ancient kings. In the fourth year of Jiayou (1059), Wang Anshi went to the capital in Bianliang (Kaifeng) to take up the position of Assistant Manager of the Bureau of General Accounts (*duzhi panguan*). It was in this position that he presented the Renzong Emperor with his "Ten Thousand Word Memorial," which criticized the fact that "many of today's laws do not accord with the government of the ancient kings," demanding that they institute reforms based on the intentions of the ancient kings. When it came to discussion of the examination system, he gave a thoroughgoing denunciation of policies enacted during the Northern Song, including promotions given to the "Worthy and Upright" (*xianliang fangzheng*), "Extraordinary Talents" (*maocai yideng*),[152] Metropolitan Graduate exams, classics exams, the Single Classic examination (*xuejiu*), and the Law Examination (*mingfa*), and he especially opposed the method whereby some entered the government via inheritance from their fathers' families. He also came up with the method whereby appointments could be made after recommendation and selection by candidates' fellow villagers, or court investigation of their virtue, actions, talent, and speech. Wang Anshi was not alone in these opinions, as his political opponents, Sima Guang, Lü Gongzhu (1018–1089), Han Wei (1017–1098), Cheng Hao, and Sun Jue (1028–1090), all advocated dispensing with poetic exposition and focusing instead on the "meanings of the classics" (*jingyi*). Behind their critical views, we can clearly see a line of thinking that would set the Sui and Tang examinations in opposition to the schools of the Three Dynasties. In his "Ten Thousand Word Memorial," Wang Anshi wrote, "In ancient times, the Son of Heaven and the feudal lords, from the state to the village, all had their schools, with broad instructional officials established by strict selection. Court rituals and punishments were all based in learning. What scholar-officials observed and practiced were the intents of the former kings, who governed All-under-Heaven with their model words and virtuous behavior. These talents still can be employed for all states under Heaven." But the new system for selecting officials placed emphasis only on erudition, strong memory, and literary style. "On the grand scale, they are not fit to put the whole state into order, while on the smaller scale, they are not fit for service to the state."[153] In a memorial of the first year of the Xining reign period, Cheng Hao wrote, "People today all hold their private opinions, and each school entertains unorthodox doctrines, causing divergences in training in the classics, with no way to unify them. This is the reason the Way is not applied and the people are not enlightened."[154] Lü Gongzhu's opinion was not far from this: "The teaching in schools is what makes for unity of Way and of Virtue, aligning customs. Today if people teach themselves, then they will study heterodox doctrines, and then have heterodox practices."[155]

The above-described skepticism toward institutions was often placed in the opposing relation between the examination system and the ancient ritual tradition (especially its school system), which is to say that these skeptics believed the corruption and incompetence of the institutions arose from their abandonment of the traditional ritual system, from which it followed that reestablishing the unified relation of ritual and institutions became the basic path through which these Confucians addressed contemporary problems. In the opening of his "Plea for Changes to the Examinations" (*Qi gai ketiao zhi*), Wang Anshi wrote, "The selection of scholar-officials in ancient times was always based in schools, consequently the Way and Virtue were unified above, and the practices and customs were accomplished below, with sufficient talents contributing to the world." The Three Dynasties school system Wang Anshi hoped to restore was not merely a matter of literary ornamentation, for as he also wrote: "Now I want to restore the old system. I wish to correct the defects, but I unfortunately find the solutions coming to me only gradually."[156] It is apparent that his new examination system was only the first step in restoring the ancient system. Wang Anshi's reforms concerned the content of the exams, removing sections on poetic exposition and recitation of the commentarial classics, while also touching on institutional reforms (such as the restructuring of the National Academy [*Taixue*] into Inner, Outer, and Upper divisions at court, as well as establishing local schools on the regional level). There was a turn toward using testing the scholar-officials on the meaning of classics, and on policy questions. In a related entry of the New Policies, the *jinshi* would cease testing poetic exposition, filling in gaps in texts (*tiejing*), and short-answer questions (*moyi*), and begin testing on the meanings of the classics and policy discussions. One text would be selected from the *Book of Odes* (*Shijing*), the *Book of Documents* (*Shangshu*), the *Rites of Zhou* (*Zhouyi*), or the *Book of Rites* (*Liji*) to be the base classic (*benjing*), with the *Analects* (*Lunyu*) and the *Mengzi* serving as auxiliary classics (*jianjing*). Because the New Policies stipulated that "one need not fully utilize the commentaries to comprehend the meaning [of the classics] and Principle fully," the conditions were thus supplied for the decline of the commentarial studies and the rise of moral philosophy (*yili*). Exactly in this context, Wang Anshi led the compilation of the *New Commentaries on the Three Classics* (*San jing xinyi*), completing the New Policies reforms with the goal of restoring the Three Dynasties.[157]

The reforms of the New Policies reflected the gradual transfer of the center of value, at the time of the Tang transition to the Song, from literary learning to ethics. The removal of poetry and poetic expositions and new emphasis on policy discussions indicated the increasing focus of the bureaucratic selection system on capability, function, and institutions, instead of teaching and cultivation, morality, or ritual. The conflict between the School of the Way and the new classical studies thus happened in this context of institutional reform. Wang Anshi had not followed Han-dynasty

Confucian conventions, which took the *Spring and Autumn Annals* as a classic for study and testing in general examinations. What Wang emphasized instead was the *Rites of Zhou,* a text about institutions, which shows how Wang Anshi emphasized the holistic and structural, rather than historical-temporal, relations between classics and institutions. In 1071, he ordered that all new scholars applying for office through familial connection (*zou pu chu shi*) and those awaiting such placements must pass the *quanshi* examinations on judgments of cases, or else other examinations on judging cases of the penal codes, and then be sorted into their official positions according to their test grades. In 1073, this rule was expanded: "All *jinshi* candidates and candidates of other examinations who are of the same class, as well as examiners and examinations supervisors," must get past the relevant examination types in order to apply for office. In 1075, all the best candidates from that year's *jinshi* would also have to take exams on the legal principles and case verdicts.[158] The admiration for the *Offices of Zhou* was closely related to institutional reforms. Why would Wang Anshi have valued the works on bureaucracy once used by Wang Mang and that Liu Xin had once used as blueprints for restoring the ancient ways? In the assessment of Pi Xirui (1850–1908):

> Wang Anshi's reforms were not based on the *Rites of Zhou,* but from special factors having to with trade and markets. The real reason was that Song people were ashamed of speaking of wealth and power, so they just had to draw on the Duke of Zhou and so clamp down any dissent. Later men who said that Wang Anshi had sent All-under-Heaven into disorder using the *Rites of Zhou* had also been deceived by Wang Anshi. Wang Anshi once said, "To follow the ways of the old kings is only to follow their intentions, nothing more." These words really say it all. So we know that when he says he is "following," he did not mean copying the Zhou in all affairs.[159]

Wang Anshi's assessment of institutional failings fell on the issue of the separation of institutions from ritual, but what he undertook were still reforms that were institutional in nature. In Wang Anshi's eyes, the ideal system exhibited in the form of the official rankings system in the *Offices of Zhou* supplied a mode for unifying completely both institutional and moral evaluation, such that it could supply a moral argument in order to adapt to the new policy with new political, economic, and social relations. Very salient here is that the new moral philosophy that Wang Anshi promoted had direct political motives. The compilation of the *New Commentaries on the Three Classics* made manifest the Song court's intention to unify the explanations of the classics in order to implement the New Policy.[160] Although Wang Anshi's starting point was the separation of the Han and Tang institutions from the Three Dynasties ritual, still his renewal of institutions and promotion of moral philosophy (*yili*) did not in fact attend to any internal relation of institution and morality, but rather replaced Confucian ritual discourse with institutional practice, from which to a certain degree it made Confucian ritual discourse fall into the same track as Legalist institutional discourse.

Wang Anshi's method was to transform the content of education, strengthening the unity of high officials and the bureaucracy (employed nationally), but under the conditions of the new institutions, it was difficult to implement institutions and policies modeled on the ideal of the Three Dynasties. When Wang Anshi used his own powers to push for the New Policies, the main things that he could do were also to adjust the names and subjects of the examinations.[161] Even more severe a difficulty was that the reform policy did not achieve the results predicted, but instead brought new problems. On the one hand, the application of meanings-of-the-classics methods dragged teacher-student relations (private, corruptible sentiments) into the examination halls; it was under these conditions that the great literary inquisition of the Imperial University (*Taixue zhi yu*) occurred, during the second year of Yuanfeng (1079). On the other hand, even Wang Anshi's dispensing with the *mingjing* and *zhuke* examinations, and application of the meanings-of-the-classics method with the *jinshi* examinations, could not guarantee parity between the scholars of the North and of the South, each with their own traditions. Reconstructing institutions through the innovations of the New Policies, and unifying ideology and knowledge, did not bring about unity of ritual and institutions.

Precisely in facing how the discourse of merit manifested with the New Policies, along with the various ways that the process of implementation of the New Policies turned out differently than was intended, we discover in the new Confucian learning many writings that make use of Three Dynasties ritual to oppose the methods of the Han and Tang. Essays such as three of those in the sixth volume of the Cheng brothers' *Collected Writings*—"Proposed

Reforms to the Education System" (*Lun gai xuezhi shi mu*), "Back to the Ministry of Rites to Check the Records" (*Hui libu qu wen zhuang*), and "On the Examinations Held by the Bureau of Rites" (*Lun libu kan xiang zhuang*)—examine in detail the corrupt features of the system, such as "showing off for profit" and "love of competition," and tried to restore the "ritual propriety of the government-run school" and to enlist the "moral scholars under Heaven" to protect the integrity of ritual.[162] The influence of this argument was widespread and far-reaching, not limited to the Northern Song era. There are similar writings in the *Collected Works of Master Lu Xiangshan*, as for example the essays in *juan* 31, "Questioning the Examinations" (*Wen zhi ke*) and "Questions about Taxation, Military Rankings, and Officialdom During the Tang" (*Wen Tang qu min, zhi bing, jian guan*), which address how the institutions from Tang times onward, including the examination system, the equal-field system, the *zu-diao* system, the *fubing* military system, and the various ranks of the officials, have gradually gone bad or fostered corruption, suggesting in the end that "to restore the laws of the Three Dynasties is the work of a single month; within three years it will lead to success."[163] Opposing exam preparation for its own sake with "seeking the Way" became a major element within the School of the Way.[164]

Here, problems in new and old institutions supplied the very best reason to separate morality from institutions—for those who were unable to pass the exams to become scholar-officials, reestablishing a moral standard to affirm their pursuit was a natural choice. In those changed historical circumstances, calling for a return to the model of the Three Dynasties could be a forceful method of criticism, but rarely did people truly believe that the institutions of the Three Dynasties could become a realistic plan or standard. If advocates for the New Policies prided themselves on these policies' utility for the state, then skeptics would have to establish a new source of morality, and even if it did manifest the moral ideals of the Three Dynasties, it would not take the institutions of the Three Dynasties as a specific plan for reform. The Heavenly Principle worldview was the product of this historical fissure: on the one hand, it recovered the internal relation of moral evaluation and order, and on the other hand, it did not locate this unified moral evaluation method directly in the relations of institutions, and so placed itself on the margins of the institutions centered on imperial power. Here, the expression of the essence of the Three Dynasties was abstracted into internal substances—its methods of expression were "Principle," "Nature," and "Mind." And the path to mastery over this internal order was no longer classical studies, with its rigid copying and commentary, but rather investigation of things or investigation of mind so as to attain knowledge. Only by plumbing Principle and investigating things could one grasp the essence of morality, and only persons who could plumb Principle and investigate things—and not those certified by the evaluation of institutions—could obtain the legitimacy of morality. This unique method of moral argumentation led the School of the Way not only to differ from the New Learning's institutional theory, but also to differ from the form of classical studies on which this institutional theory relied: The core of classical studies and its exegetics had been to seek connections between ancient ritual and institutions of their time, with an expectation for the restoration of ancient institutions, while most thinkers of the School of the Way no longer saw the contents of the classics as applicable to ritual in their time. They gave more attention and consideration to the thought or spirit of the classics, and thereby produced a revivalist mode of thought that nonetheless rejected Han-Tang ideology and calls to restore antiquity. As the School of the Way developed over the course of the Northern and Southern Song, the Four Books gradually superseded the Five Classics, which is consonant with the attitude among Song Confucians that to focus on meanings of the classics (*jingyi*) was more important than attention to evidentiary studies (*kaozheng*).

The conflict between the School of Principle and the New Learning was certainly closely related to the struggle between the old and new cliques, and for this reason, many scholars have seen the School of Principle as an ideology for the great elite families. But struggles among the cliques occurred after the implementation of the "green shoots" policy (*qingmiaofa*) that had no relation to the examination reforms. Although many members of the School of Principle stood in opposition to the New Policies, what they represented was the public opinion of the landlord-scholar-official class, or the political appeals of the local elite *shi*, or scholar class, which by no means completely opposed the New Policies. Setting out from just such practical political problems, Zhu Xi said approvingly that Wang Anshi's reforms "were reforms that accorded with the times" and that "the New Policies of the Xining era were the result of the trends of the times."[165] There are in his works a great many pieces on statecraft (*jingshi*). His debates with Chen Liang on righteousness and profit for hegemons were also a distant echo of the disagreements between Wang Anshi and the School of the Way thinkers, one with implied questions about how to evaluate the connection of the Han and Tang institutions (especially local bureaucrats) to the Way. Of crucial importance here was that to criticize existing institutions for not being in accord with the Three Dynasties policies and laws did not mean that one must restore the institutions of the Three Dynasties, but rather that "the natural propensity of Principle" (*ziran zhi lishi*) should be the basis to build new institutional forms, and thereby to bridge the gap between institution and ritual. For this reason, the question lies not in whether to emphasize practical affairs, but in determining the basis for establishing moral-political evaluative premises. The School of Principle gave expression to the transformations in methods of ethical judgment that were produced along with institutional reform. The innovations of the New Policies in fact followed the historical changes since the late Tang, and the New Policies' push for institutional reforms changed the traditional relation of ritual to institution, and so also changed the methods of moral judgment: the reforms put the basis of moral judgment on the institutional and the functional levels, thereby generating conflict with the Confucian ritual theory favored by the School of the Way. Zhu Xi acknowledged that policy reform "was unavoidable given the propensity of the times" (*shi bu rong yi*), but he also emphasized that policy reforms in and of themselves were not matched with "the Three Dynasties institutions."[166] But he did not call for a simple return to the old institutions of the Three Dynasties as a way to seek unity of institutions and ritual, but rather for using moral cultivation as the basis for learning and living: "between reading history and responding to phenomena, [one should] seek where their Principle is, and nothing more."[167]

It was just this moral discourse centered on "Principle" that formed the true disagreements over Wang Anshi's theory of king versus tyrant (*wangba*) and Chen Liang's (1143–1194) school of political achievement (*shigong*). Wang Anshi's "kings versus tyrant" theory posited unity between morality and political accomplishments, whereas the School of the Way scholars tended to see morality as separate from political accomplishments, because in their view morality originated in "Principle," a category interior to the myriad things and yet not equal to the myriad things, and so having nothing to do with kings or tyrants or the political institutions per se. Zhu Xi criticized the

Eastern Zhejiang school's version of such theories for covering up Heavenly Principle in history, while the only way to thoroughly comprehend Heavenly Principle was to turn toward the self and plumb Principle: "Eastern Zhejiang scholars generally study the learning of heroes . . . and avoid entirely reflection and introspection. What is needed is to begin all affairs from Principle in the mind, to set up the right countenance and so proceed, so that all affairs have a Way and Principle. The least act not so done leads to the lack of Way and Principle."[168] In an atmosphere where it was common to use the Emperors Tang and Yu and the example of the Three Dynasties of Antiquity to criticize the institutional reforms of the Han dynasty, Tang dynasty, and later times, the core problem brought out by the School of the Way was that the New Policies were functional institutions, not rituals with moral significance. In the context of institutions not of themselves supplying moral resources, the pursuit of morality became even more intense, thereby making Song Confucians face twin problems: on the one hand, moral evaluation had no recourse but to appeal to forces transcending existing institutions; and on the other hand, the Heaven that Han and Tang cosmology proposed as transcending existing institutions was also part of the physical institutions per se, so Song Confucians had to discover resources for moral argument outside of this cosmology that was included in political discourse. This was the basic premise behind the establishment of the concepts of the Heavenly Way worldview and Heavenly Principle: Heavenly Principle and the Heavenly Way were absolute truths that transcended and yet were also internal to the myriad things of the universe. The function of understanding and the internal turn of moral judgment were products of the historical judgment that institutions had separated from morality.

In moral terms, rather than say the thinkers of the School of the Way were closer to the teachings of Confucius, it is better to say that Wang Anshi bore a closer resemblance to the Zhou-dynasty tradition, since he saw morality and institutions as entirely unified. But why was Wang Anshi seen as someone who had turned his back on the essence of Confucian thought? It was because in the eyes of Confucians, the so-called connection between institutions and ritual reflected the historical evolution from enfeoffment to the system of centralized administration. Their theory of institutions took the imperial power-centered system of centralized administration as legitimate, while School of the Way scholars took ritual views of the patriarchal clan system and enfeoffments as the basis for moral-political judgment. Here, the propensity of the times had become an element internal to Heavenly Principle. This was the political core of Confucian orthodoxy and views on history. Zhu Xi's criticisms that the institutions in place since the Han and Tang didn't accord with "the laws of the Three Dynasties of Antiquity" can only be understood when placed in this context. It is even more accurate to say that the conflict between the School of Principle and the New School cannot be ascribed to the problems of Nature and Way and political administration, but rather ought to be understood as a conflict between two different methods of moral evaluation. Hidden behind these methods of moral evaluation are differences over the moral stations they ascribe to imperial power and its political institutions. In this respect, the oppositions between "is" and "ought," and "fact" and "value," in Song and later Confucian theory were products of historically evolving moral-political judgment, namely the separation of institutions from ritual.

In Zhu Xi's world, the practices of extending knowledge through the investigation of things, Community Compacts, and rituals and ceremonies implied a conflict with the bureaucracy, while in Ming and Qing times, Zhu Xi learning had become the internal essence of government school regulations. This phenomenon shows that, as with the evolution of Community Compacts, the relation of the School of Principle with the examination system is an important vantage point from which to view the relation of the School of Principle to social institutions. Part of the context for the development of the School of Principle in the Song dynasty was the development of private schools (*si xue*), and the relation between these private schools and public schools (*guan xue*) was not as clear as people imagine. Early private schools emerged when the Han fashion of studying the classics held sway. In many cases they were the results of the Han government's demand that future officials should study the Five Classics. Gathering to give lessons required economic subsidy, and the scholar clans produced in the Nine-Rank System created just the conditions for development and creation of private schools. However, according to research by Li Hongqi, during the Wei and Jin periods, private and public schools exhibited little difference in content. During Sui and Tang times, the examination system took on new importance, the aristocracy disintegrated, and private lessons on a large scale became impossible. What replaced these was the formation of the academy (*shuyuan*) system, influenced by Buddhist temple training. In the early local education systems of the Song dynasty, there were no examples of schools established by the bureaucracy. It was only during the reign periods of the Zhenzong and Renzong emperors (early to mid-eleventh century) that some local officials began to establish schools and endow public funds for their support. These schools received copies of the Confucian classics published by the government, and accepted government-appointed "school lands" (*xuetian*), with a schoolhouse and construction of a Confucian temple.[169] "The provision of school lands by the government had special significance, because this practice later became a permanent feature of Chinese local education, with local education afterwards endowing itself and remaining self-sufficient, with most of the funds paid out from rent and tribute on school lands." During the periods of the Wang Anshi New Policies and Cai Jing's (1047–1126) time in office, reformers went so far as to demand that the selection of officials be united with the local education, making for the saying that "all scholars under Heaven were selected from the highest examinees of the schools." Under these conditions, it became a general norm that the officials implementing the imperial examinations came from the local areas' government schools, so that "the goal of local official schools became mixed up and unclear."[170] This situation persisted until the rise of the new school system at the end of the Qing dynasty.

The above context supplies an explanation for the relation between the School of Principle, especially Zhu Xi thought, and government schools. Zhu Xi's Community Compacts not only were a design for political autonomy in villages; they were also tools for mass education, because they could take on the function of advancing students to the community schools by first putting them through local schools, as with the local lecture system within the academies that Zhu Xi enthusiastically endorsed and supported. The popularity of local schools and community schools in later periods had an influence that was not less than that of the academies. One of the functions of academy education was to ameliorate the tense relation of state authoritarianism with the moral cultivation of the common people. When the examinations were announced in the second year of the Renzong Emperor of the Yuan dynasty (1313), its entries featured an initial testing with two questions on problems in "illuminating the classics (*mingjing*), with questions taken from the Four Books, employing as standard the text of Zhu Xi. After this, the Four Classics and the works of Zhu Xi would replace the Five Classics of the Han and Tang as the standard study texts for later exams.[171] During the reign of Ming Taizu (r. 1368–1398), there was very strict regulation of materials used for interpreting the classics, and the examinations adopted the standards of the Eight-Legged Essay, which shaped the various types of examinations. During the second year of Hongwu (1369), Zhu Yuanzhang called for establishing schools at all levels as a means to "put the state in order by putting education first, and making schools the root of education," with schools and village schools at the prefectural, provincial, and county levels.[172] When the Yongle Emperor (r. 1402–1424) compiled the *Complete Four Books* (*Si shu daquan*), the *Complete Five Classics* (*Wu jing daquan*), and the *Complete Collection on Nature and Principle* (*Xing li daquan*), the official status of Zhu Xi thought was further solidified, which was to last until the end of the Qing dynasty. Because the School of Principle was incorporated into the very system of the examination and selection of officials that it had once opposed, the tensions between these respective systems of thought and institutional theories completely disappeared. During the Ming and Qing, the court would often go through the School of Principle and civilian education agencies—schools, clan organizations, and even trade associations (*hanghui*)—to push for ideological unification. During the reign of Emperor Kangxi of the Qing, the emperor placed great weight on Zhu Xi thought and evidential studies of the classics alike, in an effort to unite moral and political orthodoxy. This was never predicted by early School of Principle thinkers, but their intellectual premises certainly predisposed these results.

In sum, in one respect, the Northern Song School of the Way and Zhu Xi thought both had a critical attitude toward the examination system and its standards of evaluation, but when Zhu Xi thought became the standard readings for the imperial examinations, its effectiveness as opposition to the "political achievements" (*shigong*) school and its institutional supports disintegrated. In another respect, because the Community Compact and the ethics of clan law were forming together into a basic social structure that was becoming ever more compatible with elite political institutions, the landlord-gentry system Zhu Xi attended to no longer functioned to criticize the unified, top-down political system of imperial power. If we say that the emergence of the School of Principle was to a certain degree to be understood as the process by which Heavenly Principle and the Heavenly Way separated from institutional evaluation systems, then the relation between the method of moral evaluation of the School of Principle and institutional evaluation became, along with Zhu Xi thought, changed across history as they became model texts for the examinations. Under the guidance of the School of Principle, ritual teachings and the imperial system depended on each other to become important social features of Ming and Qing times. It is only in this context that we can understand how Wang Yangming thought criticized and superseded certain elements of Zhu Xi thought, and moreover we can understand why the thinkers of the May Fourth Movement considered Zhu Xi thought and the extension of knowledge through the investigation of things as ethical theories of the patriarchal clan system. For this reason, if they wished to preserve the critical heritage possessed by Zhu Xi thought, later Confucian scholars would have to consider problems with even sharper, anti-Zhu Xi, methods, so that they could draw a clear distinction between themselves and official learning (*guanxue*). This transformation would lead to important changes in the arrangement of the concepts of the broader categories of Principle, Mind, Nature, things, and the extension of knowledge through the investigation of things.

The "investigation of Mind" (*ge xin*) doctrines of the School of Mind assailed all external designs of progress and material with internal moral practice, and opposed the dualism of Principle and *qi* with the monism of Mind, thus establishing the ontological status of Mind. The School of Mind carried in its values a tendency to deny the physical reality of "things" (*wu*), but rather than calling this a tendency to oppose knowledge, it would be better to call it a "knowledge tendency" that opposed the examination system after the Southern Song. Zhu Xi was extremely erudite, with a keen interest in the natural studies (*ziran zhi xue*) of the Song dynasty. His theory of extending knowledge through the investigation of things set up a concept of "thing" that also unintentionally supplied the starting point for theories for scholars of things and Nature (*bowu xuezhe*). The late Southern Song and the early Yuan was a golden age for natural studies (especially astronomy and mathematics). In this scholarly atmosphere, it was certainly natural that Zhu Xi's theory of extending knowledge through the investigation of things was aligned with natural studies. For example, the concept of "thing" in works passed down from the Song era like the *Resonance Between the Categories of Things* (*Wu lei xiang gan zhi*) and the *Simple Discussions on the Investigation of Things* (*Ge wu cu tan*) clearly also referred to things in the natural world. And the medical text *Supplementary Treatise on Knowledge from Practice* (*Gezhi yu lun*), by Zhu Zhenheng (1281–1358), a representative figure of one of the four great schools of medical learning of the Jin and Yuan dynasties, and a fifth-generation descendent of Zhu Xi, made direct use of Zhu Xi's concept of investigating things (*gezhi*) in the field of medicine. These examples suggested that there were many possible links between extending knowledge through the investigation of things and natural studies. Mainstream Ming-dynasty thought refused to use an orientation toward cognition to discuss moral problems, which has up to now been seen as an obstacle to the development of natural studies. But based on the research of Benjamin Elman, after the Southern Song and the Yuan, "natural studies" (*ziran zhi xue*) was one of the parts of "erudite studies" (*boxue*) that every official needed to have, so its status was rather higher, and it even obtained the support of the emperor. In addition, the dividing line between the universality of classical studies and the specialized features of factual or practical studies (*shixue*), did not by any means become a problem. But astronomical and calendrical studies in the three-level examinations were required contents for the policy questions and so were absorbed into the examination system."[173] After Zhu Xi, "natural studies" became required content for the exams, along with Zhu Xi thought. In this respect, "natural studies" was not like ordinary knowledge of nature, but rather a systematized body of knowledge. For this reason, just as there were two different types of School of Principle, so there were two different forms of natural studies, namely the study and understanding by people of Nature and the natural studies that served as special content for the examinations. Ming-dynasty scholars advanced sharp criticisms of the examinations and Zhu Xi thought, which also influenced their view of natural studies, but these views were criticisms of natural studies as a systematized body of knowledge. Even though Wang Yangming learning and its evolution became the important contents of Ming history of thought, still, Zhu Xi thought was solidified in its position as official ideology. Besides the system of selection through the Eight-Legged Essay, the official imperial textbook in seventy *juan*, *Complete Collection on Nature and Principle* (*Xing li daquan*), compiled to order by Hu Guang (1370–1418), shows that in this respect, the School of Principle as such was now the *imperial* School of Principle, and not the School of

Principle of the scholar-elite. The orientation of the School of Mind could neither explain how it came to represent the dominant ideology of the Ming nor show that natural studies was in decline.

The gradual decline in status that "natural studies" experienced in the examinations and in policy questions was more a matter of the influence of Qing-dynasty evidentiary studies than it was a result of the Song and Ming School of Principle.[174] The salient feature of Ming-dynasty examinations was the successful adaptation of Confucianism with "natural studies," and it was only after 1680 that this feature was gradually lost. This research refutes the assessment, once taken for granted, that Song and Ming Confucianism could not be reconciled with science, and that Qing-dynasty evidentiary studies were the harbingers of modern science. Viewed from the internal logic of the Ming-dynasty School of Mind, its attention on the internal world strengthened the immanence and absolute nature of "Mind," thereby making it possible to separate out knowledge about nature and society from the category of moral theory. Worth attending to here is that the establishment of epistemology in early modern Europe depended on the establishment of subjectivity. There is a historical connection between the early modern ethics that emphasizes moral self-regulation and early modern epistemology that emphasizes engaging in understanding of the objective world. This logic perhaps can help in understanding the connection between the School of Mind and natural studies. For example, Song Lian was the Director General in charge of compiling the history of the Yuan dynasty during the Hongwu reign of the Ming dynasty. He was deeply learned in the study of institutions, classics, and cultural artifacts, with a pedigree believed to make him a transmitter of Zhu Xi thought. But after he repeatedly studied and analyzed the principles of Heaven and Human (*Tian ren zhi li*), he nonetheless based his learning deeply in an idea of "I" or "the self" (*wo*). "The world seeks sages among humans and seeks the Way of the sages in the Classics. These are far [from us]. That I could become a sage—my words could become classics—is not to be thought of." "All affairs under Heaven, small and large, simple and complex, some leading to loss and others to profit, some similar and some different, are hard to bring into unity. The superior person grasps them deep within those few inches of his heart, clearly, and seeing nothing else."[175] He was an erudite scholar of Zhu Xi learning who was seen as a "harbinger of the later School of Mind."[176]

In this respect, it was precisely the critique of Zhu Xi learning that was leveled by Wang Yangming and his followers that extended and even revived the critical force that Zhu Xi learning once wielded, which means that Wang Yangming learning cannot simply be seen as purely opposing Zhu Xi thought. It was within these special historical relations that Ming-dynasty thought engaged in dialogue with Zhu Xi thought, restructuring modes of thought and working to discover the roots of the classics. The School of Mind did not change the practical contents of conscience (*liangzhi*) and Heavenly Principle. It sought all along in theory for the path by which Mind could turn to the practice of social morality. For this reason, we might say it was inevitable that the practice of "investigation of the mind" (*gexin*) would involve aspects of "statecraft" (*jingshi*), and the effort to seek the original substance (*benti*) also cannot be simplified as a refutation of knowledge regarding the outside world.

The emphasis on inner nature or immanence (*neizaixing*) in the School of Mind was in conflict with the existing order, but in its theoretical logic, it rid itself of the binary contradictions produced by internal and external, and mind and material. Zhu Xi's investigation of things denied that the existing order was directly aligned with Heavenly Principle, demanding that each person in their specific practice of investigating things seek evidence of Heavenly Principle. This not only contains new vitality for knowledge, but also contains an element of criticism within reality. Namely, the process of fully understanding Principle by investigating things assumes a conjunction between fact and value, from which it follows in the end to deny that the process of understanding is built on a separation of fact from value. However, the process of making Zhu Xi thought into orthodoxy combined Confucian doctrines in this theory with the existing order, and so dispelled its critical nature. Eliminating the introspective element of the process of "extending knowledge through the investigation of things" could only produce one result: to make "things" absolute and thereby affirm the legitimacy of the existing order. For this reason, if one wishes to restore the element of criticism in Zhu Xi thought, one must rid this theory of its worship of fact and recover the subjective nature of arriving at knowledge. Precisely in this respect, the rise of the School of Mind could not be seen as a denial of the School of Principle, and was better seen as a deepening and extension of the internal logic of Principle.[177] Here, "Principle" became the internal motivation driving the transformation of the School of Principle, because "Principle" refuses to see itself as a reification of the existing order. But "Principle" also is not a transcendent view beyond experience, but rather an internal element of the course of experience. The rise and fall and intermixing of the School of Principle and the School of Mind during Ming and Qing times to a great degree arise from a need to refuse to make Principle reified, transcendental, or externalized, and yet not to deny Principle in itself. The School of Principle believed that the "original body" (*benti*) was the original body of moral practice, that time and effort were the time and effort of moral practice, and that there was no "natural body" (*xingti*), nor any Heavenly Principle, external to moral practice. For this reason, extending knowledge through the investigation of things was not simply taking a thing and plumbing its principle, but rather a return to its original Mind (*ben xin*). This was the basic meaning of "Mind is Principle" (*xin ji li*). To oppose the tendency in official Zhu Xi thought to make "things" (*wu*) absolute, the conclusion developed by the School of Mind was to make "Mind" (*xin*) an absolute. This turn at the level of the concept of "things" produced an important result, which was to dispel the reality of "things" and to understand them as "this thing" (*ciwu*), that is, "Mind."

5. Visions of "Inner and Outer": The North-South Problem, the Distinction between Barbarian and Chinese, and the Concept of Orthodoxy

In Song Confucianism, the separation of institutions from the rites and music was expressed as a distinction between the existing institutions and the ideal order, with the ideal order being directly expressed as a revivalist (*fugu*) conception of orthodoxy (*zhengtong*). This conception of orthodoxy not only provided Confucians with a specific set of categories for distinguishing between the two (what were institutions, and what were rites and music?), but also established a standard of judgment for observing institutions. Why did the difference between institutions and the rites and music require an appeal to an ideology of orthodoxy?

First, Song Neo-Confucian conceptions of orthodoxy, cosmology, and their "intellectualism" (*zhishi zhuyi*) were products of the cultural atmosphere of "synthesizing the Three Teachings" (Confucianism, Buddhism, and Daoism) since the Sui and Tang dynasties, in which Buddhism actually occupied the dominant position. Following the decline and fall of the Tang dynasty, the chaos and social dislocation of the Five Dynasties, and the long period of conflicts with northern peoples after the establishment of the Song dynasty, Song thought aimed to unite the Three Teachings around Confucianism, to supersede the Han-Tang philology centered on textual exegesis, and to synthesize into one body the inclination toward orthodox revivalism with efforts to research genuine knowledge. Precisely in their struggle with Buddhism, Daoism, and the Han-Tang studies of the classics, School of Principle Neo-Confucians placed "Heaven" within a cosmological and metaphysical framework, establishing a worldview that affirmed the world, turning it into a basic category that would come to dominate cosmology, conceptions of Nature, theories of human nature, and ideas of personal cultivation. This approach had ancient roots.[178] Regarding the relationship between the School of Principle, on the one hand, and Buddhism and Daoism, on the other, we must take note of the following two issues: First, the concepts of the School of Principle were not a simple reiteration of these intellectual resources, but quite the contrary—while drawing on these resources, the School of Principle also resisted and filtered them. According to Wang Fuzhi, "Zhuangzi and Laozi spoke of emptiness and nothingness, of the absence of form; the Buddha spoke of nirvana, of the absence of usefulness. But the true vacuity spoken of by the Buddha finds even more application in the return to formlessness."[179] In order for the Song Neo-Confucians to strike an effective blow against the Buddha and Laozi, it was necessary on the levels of cosmology and ontology to destroy "nothingness" (*wu*) and establish "being" (*you*) and to replace "emptiness" (*xu*) with "substance" (*shi*), forging a worldview with an orthodox genealogy that would oppose Buddhism and Daoism systematically while affirming the actual world of the senses. Second, the School of Principle's rejection and critique of Buddhism and Daoism did not stop at the purely conceptual level—we can also observe an intense struggle in the transformation of ritual and customs at the level of everyday life. Buddhist withdrawal from the world not only used the abstract level of philosophy to fight against the clan law centered on filial piety, but also penetrated into the sphere of household rites such as funerals, constituting a serious threat to traditional ritual of the family; so the refutation of Buddhism was not an abstract debate over theory. In the late Tang, Li Ao wrote "Against Buddhist Fasting Rituals" (*Qu Fozhai lun*), criticizing Buddhism for having "transformed Chinese culture with its barbarian ways," singling out Yang Chui's "Funerary Rites" (*Sang yi*), which contained descriptions of Buddhist rites such as "the seven-week fasts, on these days sending clothing for the deceased to temples in order to extend the pursuit of wealth and fortune."[180] Prior to the Song dynasty, Confucians and court officials rarely concerned themselves with the familial and religious practices of commoners, but as the Song Neo-Confucians developed and renewed their ethical theory, they discovered that it would be necessary to carry out struggle against many quotidian customs. According to Patricia Ebrey's research, these new customs included the transformation of wedding practices (including dowry) and rites associated with graveyards and ancestor worship (such as cremation, the use of painted images in ancestor worship, and the role of Buddhist monks in funerals). In the Song dynasty, graves had become the most important site of ancestor worship—the place where people made offerings, and where relatives from the same clan gathered during the Spring Festival. The Song Confucians were well aware that such uses of the graveyard had no textual basis in the classics, but they attempted to link these new customs to the Confucian concept of "filial piety." Zhu Xi's *Family Rituals* (*Jia li*) and Cheng Yi's earlier remarks demonstrate this approach. However, other Buddhist customs, such as cremation, could not be absorbed so easily by Confucianism. Popular from the tenth through the fourteenth century, cremation not only differed markedly from traditional Confucian rites, but its concept of "releasing souls so they can cross over to the other side" (*chaodu*) contradicted the secular values of Confucianism. Sima Guang, Cheng Yi, and Zhu Xi all expressed profound astonishment at the popularity of cremation rites, calling it a "savage" (*yeman*) custom.[181] The many discussions of clan law and ancestral temples in the Northern Song School of the Way may be regarded as a direct response to such customs, in some senses. The ritualism of the School of Principle was inherently linked to its cosmology and its theories of Mind and Nature (*xinxinglun*)—a linkage that is also visible in the relationship between Buddhist philosophy and its own rites and customs.

In response to the influence of Buddhism on ritual practices, the School of the Way Neo-Confucians reexamined the teachings of the early Confucians and the ancient rites, and the distinction between "barbarian" (*Yi*) and "Chinese" (*Xia*) played an important role in the process of establishing an orthodox current. Han Yu's "Origin of the Way" (*Yuan Dao*) paid homage to

Mencius, prominently cited *The Great Learning,* and promoted the concept of "the Way"; it also used the Way of Confucius to strongly refute Buddhist and Daoist ideas and thus provide a historical thread for the later emergence of Neo-Confucianism in the Song dynasty. Han Yu's account of the Way ultimately concludes with the tracing or construction of orthodoxy, rather than a philosophical examination of the concept of the Way itself. The idea of a single clear-cut thread of orthodoxy had a direct political significance, namely the use thereof to reject the legitimacy of Buddhism and Daoism, and to reestablish the Confucian rites and institutions. Precisely for this reason, Han Yu's critique of Buddhism unfolded within the categories of distinction between "barbarian" and "Chinese." In the history of Buddhism's eastward dissemination, we can find multiple incidents where the Confucian distinction between barbarian and Chinese was employed against Buddhism. During the Western Jin, for example, Wang Fu's *Classic on Laozi's Conversion of the Barbarians* (*Laozi hua Hu jing*) used old rumors to disparage Buddhism; in the Eastern Jin, Cai Mo wrote that "Buddhism is a barbarian custom, not a product of the classics";[182] and during the Southern Dynasties period, Gu Huan honored Daoism while dismissing Buddhism by writing that "Buddhism is a method of extirpating evil," whereas "Daoism is an art of promoting goodness," the former being a barbarian custom and the latter belonging to Chinese orthodoxy.[183] Han Yu's method of argumentation clearly continued along these lines: "Buddhism is a barbarian teaching that began entering China in the Later Han period, not present in earlier times. [. . .] The Buddha was a barbarian unfamiliar with Chinese language, with clothing of different designs. His sayings did not speak after the manner of the first kings, and his apparel was not like that of the first kings. He knew not the rightness of the ruler and subject, or the bond of father and son."[184] He also wrote:

> Nowadays we raise the ways of the barbarian above the teachings of the first kings—how much time do we have before we become barbarians. . . . This Way, what Way is it? I say: that which I call the Way, is not what has been called the Way of Laozi and of Buddha. Yao transmitted it to Shun, Shun transmitted it to Yu, Yu transmitted it to Tang, Tang transmitted it to Wen, Wu, and the Duke of Zhou; Wen, Wu, and the Duke of Zhou transmitted it to Confucius; Confucius transmitted it to Mencius. Since his death, none have transmitted it to others.[185]

In this sense, orthodoxy was closely intertwined with the sociopolitical motive of differentiating the barbarian from the Chinese. Li Ao's *Treatise on Restoring Nature* (*Fu xing shu*) cited the *Doctrine of the Mean*, treated the rites and music as a way to exercise one's nature to the utmost, and elucidated the concept of "extending knowledge through the investigation of things" in *The Great Learning*, but like Han Yu he also traced back "the Way" as a unilinear pedigree, describing himself as a successor of Mencius. Feng Youlan later argued that this notion of orthodoxy was inspired by the Chan School of Buddhism's account of its own genealogy, in which the Buddha's spirit or mind had been passed down through generations of patriarchs in a continuous line to the school's founders Hongren and Huineng: Han Yu, Li Ao, and the Song Neo-Confucians described a similar genealogy for the passing down of Confucius's spirit and teachings (*xinfa*).[186] In this sense, affirming the relationship between the *Doctrine of the Mean* and the Zisi-Mencius school was not a sufficient basis for establishing the orthodox pedigree of the Song-Ming School of Principle—it also required the exclusion of other currents.

Second, the exclusion of Buddhism and Daoism, within the orthodox framework of differentiation between barbarian and Chinese, echoed the historical conflicts between North and South during the Tang and Song dynasties. From the beginning, the Northern Song had faced pressures from northern and western ethnic groups and was unable to reclaim the Sixteen Prefectures. With the Khitans to the north (the state of Liao), the Tanguts to the west (the Western Xia), and the Tibetans and Muslims to the west of the Yellow River, war and peace with the northwestern ethnic minorities had become crucial circumstances of life in Northern Song society, and even the Dali Kingdom in the Southwest constituted a challenge to Song rule. In 1115 the Jurchens established the state of Jin, which conquered Liao in 1125 and overthrew the Northern Song in 1127, thus beginning the long standoff between the Southern Song clinging to its rump state in the South and the Jin dynasty occupying the North. Henceforth the Southern Song would not escape the threat to the North until the united Mongol state arose and conquered the Jin in 1234—swallowing up the Southern Song in turn in 1279. From the fourth century's Disaster of Yongjia and the Jin court's relocation to the South until the twelfth century's Jingkang Incident and the Song court's flight to the South, Chinese history had undergone two eras of North-South conflict, from which the scholar-gentry (*shidafu*) class developed an intense sense of the distinction between barbarian and Chinese. In Song scholarship on the classics, besides those staples the *Book of Changes* and the *Book of Rites,* the *Spring and Autumn Annals* became especially popular, with 128 Northern Song works on that classic listed in the "Bibliography of Arts and Letters" (*Yiwen zhi*) of the *History of the Song* (*Song shi*). The "three teachers of the early Song" (Jie Shi, 1005–1045; Hu Yuan, 993–1059; and Sun Fu, 992–1057), who have been called the pioneers of the School of the Way, and other famous Confucians who came after them, such as Ouyang Xiu, Sun Jue, and Su Zhe (1039–1112), all wrote about the *Annals,* with Hu An'guo (1074–1138) being a particularly representative figure in Song scholarship on the book. In the School of the Way, Cheng Yi wrote "Commentary on the *Spring and Autumn Annals*" (*Chunqiu zhuan*), Zhang Zai wrote "Discussing the *Spring and Autumn Annals*" (*Chunqiu shuo*), and Yang Shi wrote a work by the same title. During the Southern Song, Zhu Xi did not write any one text specifically about the book, but his *Summary of the Comprehensive Mirror for Aid in Government* (*Zizhi tongjian gangmu*) was actually similar to the *Annals.* His disciple Li Fangzi commented on the *Summary:* "Its meanings are correct, its methods rigorous. Its style is direct but with deep import. It casts the bends and bumps of history and brings them together into the pure essence of one principle."[187] In this work, there was an inherent connection between "uniting the principles" (*hui gui yi li*) and the orthodox distinction between Chinese and barbarian—as Zhu Xi wrote in "Punitive Expedition" (*Taofa*):

> In any orthodoxy, opposition from below is called "revolt." If there is a plan to revolt but it is not initiated, it is called "intention to revolt." When the soldiers attack the palace it is called "raising troops in revolt." . . . When the central states (*Zhongguo*) have a ruler, the barbarians are called "invading marauders" (*rukou*). . . . When they have no ruler, then it is called "invading the borders" (*rubian*). . . . In any orthodoxy, the high officials' use of troops to quell rebellion is called a punitive expedition, or "suppressing revolt." When they attack barbarians, and not their own subjects, it is called "suppression" (*fa*), "attack" (*gong*) or "strike" (*ji*).[188]

In his "Sealed Document Requested by the Emperor in the Year of Renwu [1162]" (*Renwu zhao ying feng shi*), Zhu Xi writes, "All states require a fixed strategy. And the strategy of today is nothing more than cultivating government to cast out the barbarians."[189] The core of the Song dynasty's scholarship on the *Spring and Autumn Annals* was the idea of "revering the sovereign and casting out the barbarian" (*zun wang rang Yi*)—"revering the sovereign" as an adaptation to the development of centralized politics, and "casting out the barbarian" as a response to the intense ethnic conflicts that defined the Northern and Southern Song periods. Hu An'guo's "Commentary on the *Spring and Autumn Annals*" continued the tradition of scholarship begun with Sun Fu and Cheng Yi, using this formula: "revere the sovereign, cast out the barbarian," as a central thread for the explication of phrases such as "grand unification" (*da yitong*), "the rectification of ethics" (*zheng ren lun*), "compassion for the people and consolidation of the roots" (*xu min gu ben*), "extension of the sovereign's [power] and restriction of the ministers" (*shen jun yi chen*), "putting traitors and usurpers to death" (*zhu luan zei*), "strictly guarding the distinction between barbarian and Chinese" (*yan Yi-Xia zhi fang*), and issues of revenge—thus constructing a complete system of scholarship on the *Spring and Autumn Annals*.[190] This was the intellectual context within which the School of the Way became intertwined with the rejection of Buddhism and Daoism and the concept of "revering the sovereign and casting out the barbarian."

However, in discussing the distinction between barbarian and Chinese, School of the Way scholars still focused on how to constitute virtuous governance and distinguish between evil and righteousness, so with regard to external struggles they often placed the relation between barbarian and Chinese within the context of internal affairs. This differed from the clearly spatial demarcation between "*Zhongguo*" (China or "the central states") and "the barbarian hordes" (*yidi*) emphasized by the more utilitarian Confucians. Chen Liang stated,

> Your humble subject believes that only the Central States are formed of the true substance (*qi*) of Heaven and Earth, the place Heaven's Mandate favors, the place with the mind of humanity, the place where the cloth and cap and rites and music are honored, the place a hundred generations of emperors and kings inherited. How could the evil *qi* of the barbarians corrupt this place! Should it corrupt this place, then the cap and cloth and rites and music of the Central States could be brought away to

> distant lands. Although it would seem on the surface that the Mandate of Heaven and the mind of humanity still have a base, could it possibly be so for long without harm?"[191]

In this antagonistic relation between "the central states" (*Zhongguo*) and "the barbarian hordes," the Southern Song's "Central States problem" consisted especially of the empire's spatial reduction to a rump state, so relations between the Chinese and the barbarian became directly expressed as an inner-outer relation on the spatial level. This idea of treating as absolute the relation between barbarian and Chinese on the spatial level also influenced Chen Liang's emphasis on the continuity between the Three Dynasties and the Han-Tang institutions on the temporal level, with the goal of maintaining a positive attitude toward the latter. The School of the Way scholars' mode of argumentation differed by contrasting the Three Dynasties' rites and music from the Han-Tang institutions, using the revival of the former as a basis for criticizing the latter. The moral-ethical and ritual relationship between barbarian and Chinese was not just a question of inner and outer, but also involved an evaluation of the institutions of the descendants of "the Central States" (*Zhongguo*), namely: relations between barbarian and Chinese existed not only between inner and outer, but also within "the Central States." For example, the Tang-Song reforms of land tenure and tax law were closely connected to the social contradictions caused by the consolidation of landholdings, and to the protracted struggle between imperial authorities and aristocrats over population and taxes, with the new institutions often deriving from the North. The School of the Way scholars criticized the Han-Tang institutions for violating the Three Dynasties' principles of enfeoffment, the well-field system, and schools, arguing that the new institutions were merely utilitarian arrangements lacking in moral significance. If we connect this critique to the distinction between the southern rites and music and the northern institutions, we can clearly observe the orthodoxy centered on North-South relations inherent within this mode of critique. In other words, the concept of orthodoxy must be understood not only in the struggles of North-South relations, ethnic identity, and cultural power, but also in the relationship between the tradition of rites and music and the reform of institutions. On this level, the North-South problem was not only one of ethnic conflict or internal-external relations between Chinese and barbarian, but already one of how to evaluate the rationality and legitimacy of social institutions.

There was a profound tension between the School of Principle's tradition, centered on the Heavenly Principle, and the existing institutions, including their system of evaluation. This was because the School of Principle Confucians adopted the intellectual method of restoring the practice of genealogical recordkeeping, reconstructing the rites, and seeking to learn from the Three Dynasties, expressing the significance of using the orthodoxy of rites and music to critique external and exogenous institutions. Chen Yinke's research in the twentieth century on the institutions of the Sui and Tang dynasties was an observation of the formation process of multiethnic centralized states, noting that in those dynasties, "The artifacts and institutions were broadly disseminated, crossing the deserts to the north, south to Jiaozhi, east to Japan, west to the farthest reaches of Central Asia. And that there were so few monographs tracing the origins of these flows is a shameful lack in our national studies." Chen traced those institutions back to three main sources: the Wei-Qi, the Liang-Chen, and the Wei-Zhou periods.[192] In the opening of his *Manuscript on Tang Political History,* Chen quoted the *Classified Sayings of Master Zhu* (*Zhuzi yulei*), *juan* 116: "The Tang originated from the barbarians, so incidents of promiscuity among the women should not be taken as utterly surprising."[193] This he used to explain the relationship between Tang customs and northern ethnic groups, while also revealing the mutual interaction between the Song Confucian view of moral integrity and the southward spread of those groups, and how the ideology of distinction between barbarian and Chinese transformed into a conservative ethics. The Han-Wei–period custom of widow chastity was related to the differentiation between Han people and the Xianbei, but since chastity became associated with traditional virtue, this Southern Dynasties custom was embraced by the Song Confucians. According to Jennifer Holmgren's research, there was a very high rate of remarriage among widows during the Song dynasty, with the custom of widow chastity not achieving prominence until the Ming and Qing, and, moreover, the vigorous promotion, encouragement, and rewarding of chastity as a traditional virtue on the part of the Song government and the School of the Way Neo-Confucians was directly related to the differentiation between barbarian and Chinese customs.[194] The custom of footbinding began among upper-class courtesans in the late Tang, becoming more popular in the Song dynasty. Patricia Ebrey argued that this reflected Song culture's glorification of refined fashions among the scholar-gentry, as the era's genteel form of masculinity required the construction of a more delicate female counterpart.[195]

Song society's more mature system of centralized administration was intertwined with the era's ethnic relations, long-distance trade, and military conflicts. Its bureaucratic system, land tenure system, and imperial exams all followed on those inherited from earlier dynasties (with some moderate reforms) and showed significant influence from northern institutional cultures. The School of the Way scholars criticized these institutions for various reasons. One effective means for questioning the rationality or legitimacy of these institutions was to appeal to orthodoxy, using the rites and music to challenge the authority of Han-Tang institutions and, within this comparison, to imply that the latter themselves were merely barbarian inventions that had violated the tradition of the Three Dynasties. Taking land tenure as an example, the Southern Dynasties' system of "official fields" (*gongtian*), "allotted fields" (*zhantian*), and "taxable fields" (*ketian*) carried on the Han-dynasty tradition of official fields and "scion fields" (*tuntian*), so it could be said that there was an internal continuity from the Han through the Wei and Jin down to the Southern Dynasties. The subsequent Northern Dynasties period differed considerably in that its "equal-field" law, although based on the old system of official, scion, and taxable fields, was formally a system of public land tenure—in contrast with the large-scale privatization of land during the Han dynasty. After northern ethnic groups came to power and this public system was implemented, it became the basic premise of land tenure from the Sui and Tang dynasties onward. On the foundation of official fields, scion fields, and taxable fields, the Tang continued and developed this Northern Song equal-field system. This was a system first practiced by northern nomadic pastoralists and then propagated in other regions. Before the Xiaowen Emperor had established the equal-field system, the Tuoba Wei had already begun to calculate the population and redistribute land, as the "Record of Food and Goods" (*Shi huo zhi*) in the *Book of Wei* recounts: "And in the subjugation of the central mountains, they separated out the officers and civilians and the other people in their walks of life, and workers and artisans of more than ten thousand families filled the capital, each with their plow oxen and fields allotted according to population."[196] Similar accounts are recorded in other regional annals of the Tuoba Wei, such as those for the Taizu, Taizong, and Gongdi emperors. It is worth noting that at first, all tenant farmers (*dianke*) of the government were Han people, with the Xianbei tribes administered separately in an ethnic differentiation that gradually disappeared only in the Sui and Tang dynasties. To a certain degree, the Six Garrisons Uprising later in the Tuoba Wei period resulted from discontent with reforms to institutions such as the equal-field system among those Xianbei nobles who were being reduced to a servile status.[197] Clearly, this system of land tenure and its corresponding methods of taxation came hand in hand with the development of the bureaucratic administrative organization of a centralized state, whose central government attempted to use this system to make a mobile population settle down and work as tenants or serfs of the government. Ideologically, however, this institutional innovation required Mencius's description of the ancient well-field system and the *Rites of Zhou*'s own equal-field system in order to prove its legitimacy. Yang Yan's (Tang dynasty) reform introducing the Law of the Two Taxes similarly involved struggles between the central government and aristocracy over population and taxes, so Song Confucians discussed its drawbacks within the framework of the Three Dynasties' well-field system and the Han-Tang system of land tenure, continuing the process outlined above. In this kind of historical context, some of the historical tasks that the School of the Way assigned to itself were the establishment of "Heavenly Principle" as a yardstick, the use of different historical systems for undertaking prudent evaluation, and renewal of the spirit of enfeoffment under conditions of centralized administration.

Heavenly Principle and its related themes provided intellectual resources for constructing a sort of moral community: the revivalist orientation, especially retracing the origins and trajectory of Confucian orthodoxy itself, provided this moral community with a historical basis for distinguishing itself from other social groups. The scholar-gentry's moral assumption of duty for All-under-Heaven could, under certain conditions, become a sense of responsibility for the historical fate of this moral community. It was precisely according to this logic that the School of Principle could become a resource for a quasinationalism. However, within the School of Principle's own logic itself, this shift was still mainly centered on a sort of moralistic orientation (as in the cultivation of "humane governance" or "virtuous governance")—in contrast with what have been called "utilitarian Confucians," who elevated military activities and strategies to a central position for resolving crises. These two different orientations toward reality took root in two different ways of distinguishing between barbarian and Chinese.

III. Heavenly Principle and "The Natural Propensity of Principle"

Although the epistemological framework of "the separation of institutions from the rites and music" possessed a strong inclination toward revivalism and orthodoxy, the Song Confucians' admiration of the Three Dynasties was premised on an acknowledgment of historical change. The Heavenly Principle concept itself involved an understanding of "the propensity of the times" (*shishi*), being both a rejection and an embrace of that propensity: the affairs of the times were also "the natural propensity of Principle" (*ziran zhi lishi*). If the concept of Heavenly Principle could achieve full development, it would completely match up with the best thought of the "rites-and-music" institutions because both concerned the question of how to evaluate what kind of action should be considered appropriate or good according to the natural propensity of Principle. This was the political character of the Heavenly Principle, but this character could also be read as its natural essence. The salient features of the Song-dynasty social system consisted of a centralized form of government, formalized institutions for selecting officials through the examination system, relatively liberal relations of taxes and commerce, developed long-distance trade and monetary policy, complete dissolution of the hereditary aristocratic system, establishment of a landlord system, and a significant rise in status of the scholar-gentry (*shi*) in social life. The School of the Way criticized this system's loss of the pre-Qin spirit of the rites and music, but did not call for a complete restoration of the Three Dynasties institutions, instead attempting to revive the spirit of enfeoffment within the context of the centralized administrative state. The category of "Principle" provided a basis for assessing and seeking out appropriate institutions, norms, and rituals. The tense relationship between the Heavenly Principle and the centralized state, and the connection to the Three Dynasties rites and music that was envisioned within this worldview, both made it impossible for Song thought centered on the Heavenly Principle to simply fall into a framework of an ideology based on state and people (*guomin zhuyi*)—although its critique of the centralized state itself implied an affirmation of such a state's historical rationality.

In this sense, the Heavenly Principle worldview involved an open-minded attitude toward historical change, with the propensity of the times itself being an inherent element of that worldview. In his debate with Chen Liang, Zhu Xi criticized Chen for reducing the Three Dynasties to the level of the Han-Tang era by rejecting the distinction between those periods, leading Zhu to posit an absolute demarcation between ancient times and subsequent history.[198] This famous Southern Song war of words strengthened such an impression of an absolute demarcation between those two eras for many readers. Of more importance to Zhu, however, was the inherent quality of people. In his view, Heavenly Principle and human desire need not be sought out in the traces of the ways of the great kings, but rather can be sought within our minds, between righteousness and profit, what is wicked and what is correct. This method of judgment itself contains an affirmation of the changing propensity of the times. Zhu Xi wrote, "Would the Master [Confucius] gain leadership over the country, then he would have added and subtracted from the methods of the Four Dynasties of Antiquity to make a way that could go unchanged for a hundred kingships, and not be only from the Zhou."[199] And again:

> Now on the transformations from the ancient to the present: when extremes are reached, there must be an opposite reaction, just as day gives way to night and vice versa, which is all a matter of Principle, and not the doings of human effort. When it comes to our inheritance from the Three Dynasties, there are elements that we can bring down without changing, and other factors that were injurious and should not be made permanent fixtures. Only a sage can ascertain wherein Principle lies and enact changes accordingly, and it is in this way that the bonds and laws of human life are passed down a hundred generations without corruption.[200]

The "Principle" in "ascertaining wherein Principle lies and enacting changes accordingly" became a confirmation of the rationality contained within historical change. The School of the Way scholars' admiration of the Three Dynasties, therefore, did not directly propose using that era's institutions as an objective basis for moral judgment, but instead reconceptualized Heavenly Principle as the source of morality, because the latter could provide insights into the trends of historical change and engender the will to act in accordance with those trends.

Juan 139 of the *Classified Sayings of Master Zhu* records Zhu Xi's response to Chen Zhongwei's question about Liu Zongyuan's account of enfeoffment, which uses categories such as "the natural propensity of Principle" to provide legitimacy for the historical replacement of enfeoffment with centralized government:

> [Liu Zongyuan, in "On Enfeoffment"] was quite correct in saying that "enfeoffment was not something intended by the sages, but a matter of propensity." But later in his writings there are points of prejudice, and later people who argued over these were also excessive. [. . .] Enfeoffment existed from ancient times. Only the sages enfeoffed their realms because of the natural propensity of Principle; in it, we see the civil heart of the sage. As with Zhou enfeoffing Kang Shu and other such cases, it is because this political system dates from very early times. Because they had strength and had virtue and close relatives, those that could be enfeoffed were enfeoffed. It was not because of the sages that they were enfeoffed. If it is as Liu Zongyuan wrote, that the sages wished to swallow up the states but could not do so, then they must not have had any other method than enfeoffment! You all do not know that what is called propensity is the natural propensity of Principle, not the inevitability of propensity.[201]

It was neither enfeoffment nor centralized government that was "natural," but the historical process whereby enfeoffment had replaced earlier institutions, only to be replaced by centralized administration in turn. This use of "the natural propensity of Principle" (or "what is not allowed by propensity") to describe the sages' intentions and the establishment of enfeoffment was equivalent to bringing historical change itself into the argumentation about moral rationality. If the Qin defeat of the Six Kingdoms and the replacement of enfeoffment by centralized administration both worked according to the natural propensity of Principle, then those Song Confucians who admired the Three Dynasties could not use that era's enfeoffment system itself as a basis for moral judgment or political imagination.[202] "Qin tried to learn from the mistakes of the enfeoffment system to change to centralized administration. Even so, their patriarchal clans all became weak and crippled together. Then came the Han dynasty, which enfeoffed clans of like surname into large states, and all of these exceeded their authority."[203] Precisely from this perspective, Zhu Xi affirmed that the New Policies were also "unavoidable, because of propensity." What he criticized was only that reforms themselves "did not of themselves take the moderate path."[204]

From these two sentences by Zhu Xi about the Xining Reforms, we can deduce the following: First, the reforms were necessary and could not be denounced on the basis of the old conventions of Three Dynasties enfeoffment. Second, the statement that "the reforms did not of themselves take the moderate path" expressed that the reforms themselves could not embody the value of history or moral evaluation. What was needed was a natural principle as a standard for judgment, which was immanent within historical change but which could not be equated to specific changes. The concept of "natural" implied a distinction from the unnatural. That which could help people decrease or increase changes under Heaven, or differentiate between the natural and the unnatural, was Principle, as in "All of Heaven and Earth and the myriad things have only one Principle." And also, "Even if mountains, rivers, and the earth were all to fall away, still Principle would be only here."[205] Regarding the relationship between the scholar-gentry (*shishen*), the aristocracy, and imperial power, the moral system embodied by Principle was closely linked to the scholar-gentry class under the institutions of centralized administration and the historical trends it represented.

On the one hand, the concepts of the "Way of Heaven" and "Heavenly Principle" directly marked the separation between moral argumentation and institutions, while on the other hand, their goal was to restore the rites and music. Admiration and reaffirmation of the ritual system was both an opposition to the "institutions" that were becoming ever more divorced from the rites and music, and an argument for the necessity of Community Compacts and the ritual system, with the goal of redeveloping ethical relationships based on kinship and bonds of place. School of the Way Neo-Confucians were concerned with the relationship between moral and institutional evaluation, advocating that the rites and music of the Three Dynasties be made into into an internal yardstick and method for moral practice. This practice was not a simple revivalism, but the obtainment of correct, appropriate knowledge of the principles of things through "the investigation of things," thereby achieving unity with the principles. This method of argumentation, which used the Three Dynasties governance to oppose Han-Tang institutions, showed that the School of the Way scholars were representatives not of the great noble families left over from the Han and Tang dynasties, but rather of the emerging class of commoner landlords. In this sense, their yearning for clan law and genealogy was not a revival of the aristocratic system but an effort to form a new social order: the School of the Way was a theory of morality based on clans, community compacts, and a more perfect dynastic system, in the context of a centralized government, with the Heavenly Principle or Way of Heaven as its transcendental principle. As with Confucius, the moral order emphasized by School of the Way scholars was the result of human practice, but for Confucius, the sages' ritual system comprised the ideal order itself, whereas for the Song Neo-Confucians, research on the Three Dynasties' rites and music was a means toward arriving at the Heavenly Principle or Principles. The tension within Confucius's ethics lay between the Three Dynasties system he idealized and the existing order, whereas the tension within the Heavenly Principle worldview lay between the actual order and the Principles that both transcended and were immanent to the myriad things.

Now that this explanation has been completed, let us return to the more philosophically significant proposition: the establishment of Heavenly Principle. If, as Zhu Xi claimed, even an empire's collapse could not affect the eternal existence of Principle, then Principle was a pure sphere of "existence" (*cunzai*) separate from the world of things. In this sense, the Heavenly Principle concept transformed the Heavenly Way worldview of Han-dynasty cosmology into a sort of immanent law, sharply delineating between "what is" and "what ought to be" in moral evaluation. But was this proposition in the theory of morality a universal law or the product of historical relationships?

In the European Enlightenment of the eighteenth century, "the incommensurability of isness and oughtness" became a universal law of early modern European ethics that remains a central issue troubling Western political theory, ethics, and metaphysics. In his commentary on the conflict between fact and value in European ethics, Alasdair MacIntyre wrote:

> This change of character, resulting from the disappearance of any connection between the precepts of morality and the facts of human nature, already appears in the writings of the eighteenth-century moral philosophers themselves. For although each of the writers . . . attempted in his positive arguments to base morality on human nature, each in his negative arguments moved toward a more and more unrestricted version of the claim that no valid argument can move from entirely factual premises to any moral or evaluative conclusion. . . .[206]

He linked this early modern ethical principle to the decline of the aristocratic system, asserting that only "when the classical tradition in its integrity has been substantially rejected that moral arguments change their character so that they fall within the scope of some version of the 'No "ought" conclusion from "is" premises' principle." And it was only when "man" came to be regarded as an independent entity "prior to and apart from all roles that 'man' ceases to be a functional concept."[207] In this sense, the conflict between isness and oughtness, or the paradox of fact and value, was a cultural product of individualism in early modern Europe. Long before that time, however, a similar logic was playing out in the Song-dynasty formulation of the Heavenly Principle worldview, as I have attempted to demonstrate above.

To separate moral argumentation from institutional norms is not a philosophical issue so much as it is a historical one. Pre-Qin Confucian argumentation about morality had always expressed a concept of humanity involving an inherent essence and goals ("humaneness," "the human mind"), but this essence and these goals were not abstract, but rather the objective value embodied in the system of rites and music. We could say that a person without this sort of essence and goals, or who could not find his or her own objective position within the system of rites and music, could hardly be called a human. In this sense, humans (*ren*) and humaneness (*ren*) were basically identical. Setting out from this horizon established by Confucius, the School of the Way scholars then explained their era's moral crisis as a separation of institutions from the rites and music, attacking the latter's reduction to a mere formality, the divergence of political institutions and their laws from Community Compacts and their kinship ethics, and the departure of top-down bureaucratic administrative institutions centered on imperial power from the feudal rule over society based on Community Compacts and the scholar-gentry class. They tried to reflect upon historical relationships, resolve the contradiction between institutions and the rites and music, and achieve unity with the Heavenly Principle through individual moral practice.

In the world of the Song Confucians, "the separation of institutions from the rites and music" became a moral-historical horizon for observing history and contemporary reality—less a matter of historical facts as one of historical imagination and understanding. By contrasting the governance of the Three Dynasties with the law of the Han and Tang dynasties, they revealed the contradiction between evaluation based on existing institutions, on the one hand, and moral evaluation, on the other. In this sense, the establishment of the Heavenly Principle worldview was closely related to specific historical conditions and motivations: to transcend the Mandate of Heaven concept of royal divine right centered on imperial absolutism, to transcend the ritual system centered on hierarchical ethics and the system of great aristocratic families, to transcend the system of institutional evaluation under conditions of centralized administration, and to seek out and argue for a new model of ethics and politics premised on a holistic order of one Principle with many manifestations.

The Northern Song School of the Way, therefore, cast off the framework of ritual system theory to discuss questions of morality not because it had discovered the universal ethical principle of the antinomy between isness and oughtness, but because of the following pair of historical conditions: First, the separation of institutions from the rites and music, especially the development of the bureaucracy and imperial examination system, had transformed people's relationship with institutions within the system of rites and music such that the social identities and roles provided by the institutions could no longer offer an objective foundation for moral evaluation or ritual conditions for understanding oneself. Second, the "new classes" (commoner landlords and scholar-gentry) had rejected the traditional aristocratic system and its moral legitimacy, but a theoretical basis was needed to provide morality for the new system of landlords and clan law, and it had become urgent to create a means of moral evaluation beyond the traditional ritual system and the Mandate of Heaven worldview. In pre-Qin Confucianism, the rites and music had represented ethical-political principles or norms, whereas the School of the Way was based on the method of "extending sincerity" (*zhicheng*) by "understanding the mind and observing one's nature" (*ming xin jian xing*). In the Heavenly Principle worldview, the ultimate fountainhead of the human Way (*ren dao*) was not one's position within the existing order, but one's connection to the Heavenly Principle, so the means for developing an immanent moral practice became an important preoccupation of the School of Principle Neo-Confucians. Since Principle was both immanent and transcendent, the things of the empirical world and its order were not necessarily in accordance with their essence or nature, so the worlds of "things" and "Principles" were distinguished from one another. Due to this distinction between things (or *qi*) and Principles, the epistemology of "investigating things and fathoming Principle" became a central concern of the School of Principle, giving rise to long-lasting debates within this current. In the categories of the School of Principle, epistemological questions carried over from questions of moral-political evaluation, and the latter, in turn, were closely related to the issue of immanence. In this sense, Song-Ming Neo-Confucianism was a "Learning of Nature and Principle" (*xing li zhi xue*), having already changed from an ethics of conventions and institutions into a metaphysics, a psychology, and an epistemology of the moral-political sphere. However, behind this "Learning of Nature and Principle" there was always a revivalist historical perspective on "the separation of institutions from the rites and music." Between this perspective and actually existing politics there was a strong interaction, so efforts to rebuild ritual, political, and economic relations to serve as objective premises for moral judgment became another aspect of the "Learning of Nature and Principle."

If discussions of morality based on the differentiation between what is and what ought to be marked the origin of modern ethics, then Heavenly Principle was a radical critique of the social basis and historical conditions of this differentiation. However, it was precisely this critical theory itself that postulated a dualism of Principle and energy, in turn setting up the overcoming of this dualistic division as a central task for later Confucian moral-political investigations. In this sense, the Heavenly Principle worldview, based on this revivalist historical horizon of the separation between institutions and the rites and music, was itself precisely what provided the theoretical discourse for distinguishing between what is and what ought to be. Now we can explore this issue by turning our attention to the division between "Principle" and "things" within the epistemology of the School of Principle.

CHAPTER 3

The Transformation of "Things"

Translated by MARK MCCONAGHY

> That which is called the extension of knowledge by investigating things refers to a desire to extend one's knowledge by engaging with things, fathoming their Principle.
>
> —ZHU XI, *Commentary on The Great Learning*

I. The Transformation in the Concept of "Things"

Following the establishment of Heavenly Principle, the classical theory of the universe underwent a profound transformation, at whose center was the separation of Principle (*li*) and *qi;* from Cheng Hao, Cheng Yi, and Zhu Xi onward, the points of repeated debate within Confucianism became centered around the previously secondary concept of "the investigation of things" (*gewu*) rather than such concepts as Principle, the *Dao,* and the Great Ultimate. An entire series of changes within Confucianism, including the separation of the Neo-Confucian School of Principle (*lixue*) from the School of Mind (*xinxue*), and the different orientation of Song-dynasty learning from Qing-dynasty learning, as well as other more subtle changes, were almost all related to different understandings of this central topic. Why is this so?

Within the system of thought defined by a worldview centered on the Way of Heaven and Heavenly Principle, a new concept emerged out of the division between Principle and *qi:* a notion of factual "things" (*wu*). It was because of this division that a new theme emerged, which was investigating things and extending knowledge (*gewu zhizhi*). Of course, "things" as well as "investigating things and extending knowledge" were not entirely new terms. However, within the development of Song thought, they acquired meanings that differed from what they had signified in the past. In logical terms, the transformation in the understanding of "things" was a result of a transformation in an understanding of the concept of *qi*, which itself represented a particular theory of the universe, while this transformation in the understanding of *qi* was a result of the establishment of the notion of Principle. In classical Chinese thought, the concept of *qi* was related to the concepts of yin and yang, all being geographical terms, though not purely so. In the "Arts of Numbers" (*Shu shu*) section of the "Treatise on Literature" (*Yiwen zhi*) portion of the *History of the Former Han*, it is written: "Forms and *qi* are interrelated: while there are things with form without a corresponding *qi*, as well as those with *qi* without corresponding form, these are subtle and particular instances."[1] Within the ancient unitary understanding of the universe, Heaven and Earth and the system of rites and music were an integrated whole; you could not divide these into two different fields. In the "Treatise on Astronomy" (*Tianguan shu*) section in the *Records of the Grand Historian* (*Shiji*), it is written: "Heaven has its days and months, Earth has its yin and yang."[2]

The Grand Scribe saw Heaven and Earth isomorphically, with the constellations above and terrestrial prefectures below aligned, and as such he placed cosmology, geography, political systems, and rites together under the auspices of the vital *qi*. In another section of the work, Sima Qian also invested the cosmos and the Earth with a sense of historical transformation, placing the transformations that occurred from earliest times down to the Qin and Han periods—including the relations between China and foreign countries, Huaxia and the four barbarians—within the context of the transformations of the forms and energies of yin and yang. Jao Tsung-I (1917–2018) consulted the oracle bones and the bronze inscriptions, cross-referencing and corroborating them with the *Discourses of the States* and the *Zuo Commentary to the Spring and Autumn Annals* (*Zuozhuan*), in order to explain that the various earthly and cosmic phenomena associated with "forms and energies" of yin and yang in fact were all related to the question of "moral rites" (*de li*). As Jao put it, "During the era of the *Spring and Autumn Annals* moral rites became a specialized term, with the concept of rites also invested with new cosmological meaning, the term coming to have a position of similar importance to the term *wen* (文) from the early Zhou period."[3] Three things constituted the highest goals of moral rites: 1) the morality of Heaven (that is, benevolence); 2) human morality (that is, moral rectification); and 3) earthly morality (that is, utility). From the perspective of benevolence, moral rectification, and utility, the six critical elements (water, fire, gold, wood, earth, grain) were all within the domain of moral rites. Within this discourse, there did not exist yet a binary relationship between form / *qi* and morality / rites—such a binary mode of configuring relations would be posited during the Song period, seen most prominently in how thinkers during that later time thought in binary terms of the relations between Principle and *qi*.

In the imagination and practice of Confucianism during the pre-Qin period, the order of rites and music had Heaven at its center as well as its foundation, and as such the system of rites and music was itself a manifestation of Heaven's Will. In a context in which factual judgment (as manifested through the relationship between *qi* / forms) and value judgments (moral rites) were unified, it is very difficult to find a conceptualization of "things" as a question of pure and independent facticity. Within the conceptual domain of rites and music, "things" were classified according to type, being the manifestation of the natural and intrinsic order. For example, in the "Offices of Summer" (*Xia guan*) section of the *Rites of Zhou*, within the discussion of the official position known as *Xiaoren* (the official in charge of managing the emperor's horse stable), it is written: "There are six types of horses, stallions are one, military horses are another, horses that pull the golden chariots are another, horses that pull the vermillion chariot are another, horses used in hunting are another, and short horses are another." Zheng Xuan notes: "This is called interrelation according to type."[4] In the *Zuozhuan* we find: "Officials of varied rank move like things." In Gu Yanwu's *Du* commentary on the *Zuozhuan* it is said: "Things are like types . . . officials of varied rank all act in conformity to their thing-like typifications, they do not act indiscriminately."[5] In Kong Yingda's *Zhengyi* commentary on the *Zuozhuan* and *Spring and Autumn Annals* it is stated: "It is said that typification is like the figures drawn on banners and flags. The myriad of officials differ from high to low, and as such they each establish their different images."[6] Here, natural and systemic classifications are completely uniform, and as such, natural judgment and systemic judgment are also completely uniform. This view of Nature is the precondition for the functionality and meaning of the system of rites and music. In the "Grand Officer of Music" (*Da si yue*) portion of the "Offices of Spring" (*Chun guan*) section of the *Rites of Zhou* we find: "Rites and music are used to accord with the transformations of Heaven and Earth and the production of numerous things. They [enable] engagement with the ghosts and spirits, the harmonization of the myriad things, the extension of numerous things."[7]

On the one hand, rites and music can make the myriad things enter into harmonious relations with one another, and as such, "things" or the "plurality of things" are not independent, objective facts, but in fact are "things" that belong to a set of relations, a system, an order, a norm; on the other hand, that rites and music have such capacities is itself preconditioned on the notion that they are grounded in a theory of the universe in which the human and the spiritual are interlinked. In the *Zhongyong* section of the *Book of Rites,* we find: "Sincerity is the end and beginning of things." Zheng Xuan notes: "Things here means the myriad things."[8] In the "Record on Music" section of the *Book of Rites* we find: "[Music] emerges from the human mind-heart's ability to be moved by things." Kong Yingda notes: "'Things' here means the exterior world."[9] Sincerity here is the essential nature of the universe and the end and the beginning of all things. It is also the essential nature and beginning and end of rites and music. As such, "the capacity of the human heart-mind to be moved by things" can become the direct source of music.[10] If the order of music and ritual is also the order of the universe, then the "things" represented by the "myriad things" are also a normative function of rites. The notion that "officials of varied rank all act in conformity to their thing-like typifications" can be said to be the best explanation of this particular judgment. In the "Offices of Earth" section of the *Rites of Zhou* we find: "Use the three things of the village to teach the multitude of the people, and students of virtue will emerge."[11] Here, the "three things" mean the Six Virtues ("knowledge" [*zhi*], "benevolence" [*ren*], "sageliness" [*sheng*], "righteousness" [*yi*], "loyalty" [*zhong*], "peacefulness" [*he*]), the Six Behaviors ("filiality" [*xiao*], "friendship" [*you*], "harmoniousness" [*mu*], "marriage" [*hun*], "service" [*ren*], "aid" [*xu*]), and the Six Arts ("rites" [*li*], "music" [*yue*], "archery" [*she*], "chariots" [*yu*], "writing" [*shu*], "mathematics" [*shu*]). As such, the notion of "things" is irrevocably related to an entire set of categories grounded in the norms of the system of rites. Owing to the fact that "things" and "sincerity" are uniform, and that "sincerity" is the essence of

Nature, then "things" are in fact the manifestation of this natural order; additionally, owing to the fact that rites and music give direct expression to this natural order (with rites and music serving Heaven), as such, the "things" that make manifest this natural order are also the norms of music and rites and institutions.[12] In this sense, "things" have a normative meaning. Zhang Zai's learning was able to, within a framework that understood *qi* in unitary terms, pursue "establishing rites as foundation" as the goal for the School of the Way (*Daoxue*), a goal that stemmed from the association between this extremely ancient view of the universe and "moral rites."

However, because the relationship between things and Nature was decided by the state of things, there existed variables within the relationship; that is, we can differentiate "things" into two categories in accordance with the concept of Nature: natural things and unnatural things. Within the context of Zhou-period thought, in which rites and music were conducted for Heaven, Zhuangzi believed that benevolence, righteousness, and rites were all natural states. However, he insisted that the source of a false benevolence, one that betrayed Nature, was found if one had the will to "exert oneself toward benevolence," if one "sought fame in righteousness," or if one "conducted rites." As such, for Zhuangzi rites and music manifested through practice were unable to express Heaven's Will. This judgment can be viewed from two different levels: first, benevolence, righteousness, and rites are all natural things, and as such, natural things are isomorphic with benevolence, righteousness, and rites; second, the moment that human elements destroy the natural order, then benevolence, righteousness, and rites become unnatural "things," which is to say they no longer possess moral meaning (the inherent nature of the universe). In this way, Zhuangzi here constructs an opposition between natural and unnatural benevolence, righteousness, and rites. He further states: "'To lose morality and afterwards be moral, to lose morality and afterwards be benevolent, to lose benevolence and afterwards be righteous, to lose righteousness and afterwards practice rites. Rites comes to mean the decadence of a *Dao* in chaos' . . . today it is already all being-for-things, is it not ever so difficult to return to our roots!"[13] The result of everything "being-for-things" is that things lose the position they should have in the natural order, and as such, the "things" of "being-for-things" no longer have a natural existence. Here, what is natural refers to a state of benevolence, righteousness, and rites, while what is unnatural refers to a state in which one seemingly manifests these three virtues but in fact does not actually do so, being in a state of nonbenevolence, nonrighteousness, and nonconformity to rites. According to this logic, the category of "Nature" is intimately connected to the concept of a propositional order *that ought to be,* while the "unnatural" represents that chaotic breakdown of such an order, a sense of facticity that is absent a propositional, essential, and natural sense of meaning. We could perhaps to the end of the above parallel sentences attach the following saying: "The loss of rites is followed by the emergence of things." That is to say, when benevolence, righteousness, and rites are ripped apart from inherent Nature they transform into "things" absent moral meaning and value. Here, to be against benevolence, righteousness, and rites is tantamount to being against Nature, and to be against "things" in their natural sense is to rend oneself from the propositional state of Nature, the Nature that should be, and to finally be "things" only in the factual sense.

Although Zhuangzi's perspective has been relegated (by others) to the realm of Daoism, the relations he describes between the natural Way of Heaven, the order of rites and music, and the transformation of things are in fact the harbingers of the School of Principle. One of the major breakthroughs of the School of Principle was to link closely together the question of becoming moral with the question of cognition and its processes. It was precisely from this interrelationship that one of the most controversial questions within the moral discourse of the School of Principle was formed, that is, the question of the relationship between morality and cognition. The so-called paradox between fact and value, between what is and what ought to be, emerges from this interlinking of moral discourse and cognitive questions. Owing to the fact that moral judgment became severed from the theory of rites and music, and to the fact that the process of judgment became differentiated from objective declarations regarding rites, what resulted was that the previous unity between what ought to be and what is, between statements of value and statements of fact, transformed into oppositions, so that there was no longer a necessary relationship between statements of fact (for example the objective judgments provided by institutions and systems) and moral judgments (assessments of individual moral condition). From the perspective of cognition, the so-called statement of fact that is entirely severed from value judgments must presuppose a concept of "things" grounded in the factual, that is to say, a category that has no relationship to norms, value, and judgments. This is a category that is absolutely distinct from the concept of "things" inherent within the classical system of rites and music. Within the system of the School of Principle, the concept of "things" grounded in facticity finds its origin in the deformation of the order of rites: once the system of rites and music no longer exemplifies Heaven's Will (i.e., Heavenly Principle, inherent Nature), such a system no longer possesses the ability to offer moral judgment, and as such, the system of rites and music as well as the norms and forms it established drift away from structures of judgment, becoming categories of fact that do not possess moral meaning or values. In his "Letter on Calming Nature" (*Ding xing shu*), Cheng Hao wrote: "It is the common state of the Heaven and Earth to universalize its heart-mind across the myriad of things, as if there was no heart-mind; it is the common state of the virtuous person to submit their feelings to the myriad things, as if they had no feelings. As such, when it comes to the learning of the sage, nothing is better than being quiet, open, and magnanimous, to submit to things when they come."[14] Here, Cheng Hao interprets "benevolence" to be one with things, and is very close to Zhuangzi's own perspective. This is quite far from Confucius's placing of benevolence only within the realm of human intention and affairs. After Cheng Hao, Cheng Yi, and Zhu Xi, the notion of investigating things and extending knowledge was placed at the center of moral practice, amply demonstrating that moral practice could no longer be understood separately from the experience and recognition of, as well as integration with, "things."

In this sense, Confucianism's changing conceptualization of "things" was grounded within this transformation in modes of moral judgment. Within Confucius's theory of rites and music, moral judgment was established on the basis of the "differentiation of [social] positions," while the notion of moral judgment inherent within Song Confucianism's vision of Heavenly Principle required that such a principle itself offer an objective basis (for moral judgment). Song Confucianism linked closely together the theory of rites and music and the theory of human nature found in the *Analects* and the *Mencius* with the theory of the universe as well as that of the epistemology found in the *Doctrine of the Mean* and *The Great Learning*. As such, the concept of "things" from Confucius and Mencius, which was understood to be embedded within the norms of ceremony and propriety, steadily transformed into being a notion of "things" understood within the framework of Heavenly

Principle, in which "things" themselves became an object of knowledge and practice. Within the theory of rites and music offered by Confucius, rites, music, institutions, norms, and behavior all developed within Heaven's internal order, and as such these elements represented an order that ought to be. However, within the conceptualization of a world-vision grounded in Heavenly Principle, there is a wide chasm between Heavenly Principle and actually existing rites, music, norms, behaviors, and institutions. These latter (actually existing) elements do not embody an order that ought to be, nor can they be said to equate to a principle that ought to be. As such, they come to be "things" grounded within a binary relation between things and Principle. The division between Principle and *qi,* Principle and things, signifies the estrangement of moral judgment from factual judgment, and also signifies the tremendous importance that the cognitive practice of searching for Principle through an engagement with things comes to have within processes of moral judgment. Here, one can provide a brief example. In the *Book of Odes* it is written: "Heaven produced this teeming people, / And for each thing there is a norm, / The rules maintained by the people are appreciated as moral excellence."[15] The "things" that are spoken of here are similar to the "three things" found in the *Rites of Zhou,* and as such possess the same meaning as "norms"; all come to express a particular system, set of behaviors, and standards: put differently, one can say that things are the norms of rites and music. In his interpretation of the above passage, Cheng Hao states: "As such, to have things is by necessity to have norms, these are the rules maintained by the common people; as such there is an appreciation of moral excellence. The myriad things all possess Principle, and to be in accordance with norms is easy, to run counter to norms is difficult. All things follow their Principle, why should one struggle against one's very own power?"[16] To claim that to have things by necessity entails having norms is not the same as suggesting that things are themselves norms. Cheng Hao interprets "things" to mean the myriad of things, and discusses the former concept within the framework of "the myriad of things all possess Principle." As such, moral excellence does not mean following norms associated with things, but means rather following the *Principle internal to things.* In the former position, "things" are simply the moral values decided by (the social or political) system, while for the latter position, "things" represent a factual category that contains Heavenly Principle but is differentiated from it. Cheng Hao's interpretation bears the deep markings of a perspective grounded in the Way of Heaven, which differentiates itself from the binary relation between Principle and *qi* propounded by Cheng Yi and Zhu Xi. Yet the formulation of "following Principle" put forth by Cheng Hao has already removed "things" from the system of rites and music, becoming a notion of "things" conceptualized within the framework of the myriad things of the universe.

Differing interpretations regarding "things" exemplified a transformation in moral understanding that saw moral understanding moving away from being grounded in a theory of rites and music toward being grounded in a theory regarding the universe as well as one regarding inherent Nature. In the example from the *Book of Odes* quoted above, moral judgment was a structure that contained three factors: people, the ritual propriety (things, norms) positioned between people, and the Heaven or Supreme Being that is a constitutive force for both people and rites and music. Serving as a moral system, the characteristics of this structure are as follows: people are born from Heaven, Heaven's Will is directly manifested as "things" and "norms," and as such, the means by which people follow Heaven's Will is to submit to the "things" and "norms" that exemplify Heaven's determination, orders, and regulations. In contrast with this, within the framework of Song thought, "things" are no longer norms of the system of ceremony and rites, nor are they the goal of human behavior as decided by such a system. Instead, things belong to the universe or Nature, and exist waiting to be understood. Within this transformation, "things" understood in factual terms become a crucial category, as does the category of the human now understood as the interpreter and user of things (rather than the human understood simply as a general follower of ceremony and rites). This is the process by which Confucianism extricates itself from the moral framework of rites and music. Zhu Xi wrote:

> QUESTION: Even tigers and wolves understand the mutual affection that exists between sons and fathers, even bees and flies understand the righteousness that exists between ministers and monarchs, wild dogs and otters do not forget their essence and understand the debts of gratitude, while waterfowls understand the need to maintain respectfully differentiated but warm affections [like those between men and women]. While things are often slanted, gaining only a small amount

of the positive essence that *qi* has naturally imbued them with, they have within their bodies, from head to foot, a principle that is just right. In the beginning people possessed and cherished this pure, complete, beautiful principle, imbued to them by the cosmos, yet this endowment of *qi* has been assaulted by material desire, turning people foolish. As such, people cannot be like the tigers, wolves, bees, flies, dogs, otters, and waterfowls, who by understanding a small truth can open themselves up to the entire horizon of meaning, why is this so?

ZHU XI'S REPLY: Things [animals, objects, etc., outside of the perceiving human subject] can only understand one element of essential truth, and stop there; they do not continue their explorations. But humans seek to understand, in however slight a way, the meaning of all the myriad of things, and can become inundated, without direction, and as such easily become foolish.

QUESTION: Do even dead things like withered trees have an essence imbued in them by the creative movements of Heaven?

ZHU XI'S REPLY: Yes. When they come into existence they have a principle that is just right. As such, Cheng Yi said that "All-under-Heaven there are no things without an inherent Nature."

RESPONSE: As long as there are things, there is Principle. Heaven does not in the beginning produce the form of a writing brush, it is within a process of development that humans take rabbit's hair and use it to form a writing brush, and as such, the principle of the writing brush exists.

ANOTHER QUESTION: How do you differentiate benevolence and righteousness when it comes to the brush?

REPLY: In such small matters there is no need to differentiate between benevolence and righteousness.[17]

Humans, things, as well as the things produced by humans all have Principle. The precondition for such a judgment is the notion that "All-under-Heaven there are no things without an inherent Nature." In accordance with the understanding that "inherent Nature is Principle," another way of expressing the notion that "All-under-Heaven, there are no things without an inherent Nature" is the notion that "All-under-Heaven there are no things without Principle." However, when Principle is differentiated, the proposition that things each have their own principle cannot be equated with the proposition that things *are* Principle; in fact it is just the opposite, the notion that things all have their own principle precisely expresses the difference between things and Principle.

Within the transformation that occurred in Confucianism's moral discourse, if there was no questioning of the framework of rites and music / institutions, then "things" could not transform into being a factual category; if one could not presuppose that behind things lay an entire order (Heavenly Principle or inherent Nature), then the concept of things imbedded in the Song-dynasty category of "investigating things and extending knowledge" could not emerge. Though a similar proposition was already imbedded in the discourse of other Confucians, the theme of "investigating things and extending knowledge" is still the defining characteristic of the Neo-Confucian thought of Cheng Hao, Cheng Yi, and Zhu Xi. For example, Shao Yong in his *Book of the Supreme Principles Governing the World* (*Huang ji jing shi shu*, juan 11–12) repeatedly raises the notions that "Heaven and Earth are the myriad of things" and "humans are also things, the sage is also human," as he sought to understand the position and value of humans from within the category of "things." His notion of subjectivity included the concept of "knowing."[18] However, the notion of "knowing" raised here is not a process of recognition and research that unfolds within the interrelationship between the subjective and the objective. It is instead a form of reflection, the notion of "reflecting back upon" that Shao Yong raises. This is a concept that does not seek to establish as a condition of its operation an oppositional relationship between people and the myriad of things (that is, so-called epistemological relations), nor does it seek to establish as its precondition a form of reflection grounded in "employing the self to observe the self" (that is, the self-consciousness found in modern thought and its extensions). Rather, what "reflecting back upon" demands is "employing things to observe things," a notion that, similar to Cheng Hao, Cheng Yi, and Zhu Xi's notion of seeking Principle through the investigation of things, takes as its goal the attainment of a so-called "comprehensive objectivity."[19] However, there are different preconditions for Shao Yong's and Cheng / Zhu's positions: the latter clearly presupposes the object and subject of "investigation" and "seeking," while the former never explains the difference between things and Principle. As such, "employing things to observe things" demands that one use the point of view of things in order to look upon things, and does not touch upon the differentiation between "things" and "the inherent Nature of things."

The contradiction within modern European moral theory between *what is* and *ought to be* emerged from a twofold division: first, taking as its precondition the notion of order offered by mechanism and empiricism, the category of the factual was severed from a theory of values, becoming a distinct field in its own right; second, taking as its precondition the concept of immanence (*neizaixing*) imbedded within the notion of the self, the category of morality was severed from a theory of institutions, coming itself to form a transcendent field. Within the context of Neo-Confucianism, these two conditions at best only partially existed: the concept of Heavenly Principle and its related theory of order understood fact and value to be internally linked together, and as such, the process by which one came to understand morality was not thoroughly severed from a theory of the institution of rites, though the latter could now gain expression only in an internalized form. Categories of "things" such as Heaven, Earth, humans, and so forth, ultimately were subordinate to "Heaven" or "Principle," terms that denoted an internal, inherent Nature or a correct order. In a worldview that took as its center the notion of Heavenly Principle, even though the sense of actuality associated with the category of "things" increased tremendously, they were never completely severed from moral value—within this new concept of things, moral value became an internal category awaiting realization. "Heaven," "the Way of Heaven," and "Heavenly Principle" were understood as the essence of the universe and the world. They could not be made manifest via a depiction of the existing universe or actual social systems, but rather lay inherent within the existing universe or actual social system. Within Zhu Xi's worldview, things and individuals all had their own divisible and particular natures, rationales, or "Supreme Ultimates," and it was precisely such natures, rationales, or "Supreme Ultimates" that provided the condition of possibility for the division of "things" into different categories. If the unity of things and their differentiable natures presupposed an order of the universe that was harmonious and supremely virtuous, then one can say that this notion of "things" was still quite distant from the notion of fact that emerged from under the domination of a mechanistic view of the natural world. As such, from a historical perspective, the central question of Song-

Ming Neo-Confucianism was not formed through a contradiction between what is and what ought to be, but rather through the transformation that occurred in the theory of morality, moving as it did from one grounded in a worldview centered on rites and music to one centered around the notion of Heavenly Principle.

The transformation in moral discourse outlined above necessarily had to influence Song Confucians' perspectives regarding intellectual methodology: their knowledge practices included techniques for studying the classics such as textual compilation and correction, evidential learning, and the creation of commentaries and subcommentaries. However, they could not use such methods to strengthen definitions: the study of the classics took as its guiding aim the recovery of ancient laws and institutions and their specific delineations, while the School of Principle's methodology was defined by the attempt to gain an understanding of Heavenly Principle via knowledge regarding the essential nature of the myriad things and the self, set within a specific understanding of the order of the universe and its interrelationships. Though Heavenly Principle had to be grasped via an understanding of the "Principle of things," such a concept was not equivalent to things in and of themselves (including the formalized system of rites and music). The transformation from evidential learning and textual commentary to the investigation of things, the investigation of heart-mind, and the seeking of Principle was not simply a question of a transformation in methodology. Rather, it was *the result* of a transformation in modes of moral evaluation. Mou Zongsan, working from a standpoint that focused on the question of Heavenly Principle and the study of inner Nature / Principle, has termed the question of the Confucian ethical code "external" (*waibude*), and in doing so has clearly explained how Song-Ming Neo-Confucianism already severed the question of one's individual moral state from the institutional relations of rites and music, linking it directly instead with the question of Heavenly Principle or Heavenly Nature.[20]

The transformation in the concept of "things" played a crucial role in determining the meaning of "the investigation of things and the extension of knowledge." I have in Chapter 2 already demonstrated that the changes experienced in the system of social identification during Tang-Song times had a certain reciprocal relationship with the transformation then occurring in methods of moral argumentation. That is to say, owing to the fact that new features of the social system (for example the civil service examinations, the system of land management, and the bureaucracy) did not necessarily ensure the moral fitness of members within the system, the system itself could no longer serve as the objective basis for moral judgment. For example, a person who had obtained a high bureaucratic position through success in the civil service examinations was not necessarily a moral person. Within such a situation, moral argumentation was in a certain sense an expression of negation toward the social system itself. Yet this negation was not expressed in terms of a simple critique of the system itself. Rather, operating within the framework of Heavenly Principle, it took the form of an attempt to reconstruct unified relationships between norms and facticity, ethics and institutions. The severing of moral judgment from social institutions found its origins in transformations within those institutions themselves. Operating within the framework of Heavenly Principle and the Heavenly Way, the reconstruction of a basis for morality was in fact an attempt to reconstruct the relationship between moral judgment and the social order. However, this order was not the actually existing social order of the day made up of actually existing things, but rather a notion of order formed by the inherent Natures of such things. In short, owing to transformations in the social context of moral argumentation, moral conclusions could no longer be reasonably demonstrated, as they were before. This is the origin of Zhu Xi's "investigating things and extending knowledge."

Morality no longer took as its objective basis the norms imbedded in the system of rites (family status, social position, rank and title), but rather took as its objective basis the Way of Heaven or the metaphysical presuppositions of Heavenly Principle. Such a transformation resulted in the concepts of the Way of Heaven and Heavenly Principle coming to possess a unique position within Confucian thought: moral exposition would no longer take place between morality and social institutions, but rather within the interrelationship between humans and the Way of Heaven or Heavenly Principle. Logically speaking, the collapse of the concepts of Heavenly Way and Heavenly Principle had two sources: first, if these concepts once again come to have a close relationship with an actually existing system, then Heavenly Principle would lose its sense of transcendence; second, if exposition and comprehension of Heavenly Principle had to resort to a concept of "facticity" that was hollowed out of any notion of value, then moral exposition could not avoid falling into the contradiction between what is and what ought to be. The essentially metaphysical nature of Heavenly Principle was such that it could not resort to actual moral and political practice as a means of offering a common or objective standard, nor could it be demonstrated by empirical or experiential methods: the objectivity of Heavenly Principle could be argued only via the particular relations that existed between humans and Heaven. As such, the basic challenge facing the School of Principle was as follows: on the one hand, its transcendence of the form of moral exposition grounded in the institutions of rites and music (as well as status differentiation) was not so much a negation of such institutions, but rather a demand made regarding the unity of such institutions with their own internal nature; within the systematization of the School of Principle (i.e., its process of establishing its own orthodoxy), would the School of Principle's critique of institutions of rites and music trend toward a critique of the School of Principle itself? On the other hand, the School of Principle unceasingly resorted to the concepts of Principle, Nature, *qi*, and things in order to enact a critique of the ossified discourse regarding institutions of rites, placing "the investigation of things and extension of knowledge" at the center of moral exposition. Would this practice of "investigating things" in the end sever itself from the field of moral values and become a purely cognitive process, leading to the collapse of the entire endeavor of the School of Principle? Here, what must be stated is that the fatal attack that the modern scientific worldview launched on the School of Principle and Neo-Confucianism was premised on the notion of "facticity" and "materiality" provided by atomism, with both of these concepts being products of the thorough "demystification" of the traditional concepts of "things." Ironically, the most popular translation for the concept of modern science was originally the "investigation of things" (*gezhi*).

II. The Things and the Knowledge of "Investigating Things and Extending Knowledge"

Cheng Hao and Cheng Yi's interpretation of "things" abided by the notion that affairs and Principle were uniform, and that what was manifest and hidden emerged from one source. They emphasized that one could examine Principle through phenomena, rejecting the notion that one could look at the essential nature of things or Heavenly Principle as an exteriorized standard. They believed that the "Principles" of "objects" and "things" were internal to them, and as such, "things" or "objects" could not in and of themselves be directly equated with norms in and of themselves. The concepts of "the principle of things" or "the Nature of things" raised the necessity and possibility of cognition. If things each had their own principles, then understanding the notion of "investigating things and seeking principles" could not depart from "things" and the particular conditions in which they were imbedded. Additionally, the goal of "investigating things and seeking principles" did not take "things" as its aim, but rather the recovery of "the principle of things."

The importance of the concept of "things" and the notion of "investigating things and extending knowledge" emerged around Song Confucians' repeated debates regarding how to interpret *The Great Learning.* That work was originally a part of the *Xiaozai* version of the *Book of Rites* (*Xiaozai Li ji*), but during the Song period it began to be published independently. Han Yu's "On the Origin of the Way" (*Yuan dao*) and Li Ao's *Treatise on Restoring Nature* (*Fu xing shu*) both relied heavily upon *The Great Learning* as a text that expounded on the meanings and principles (*yili,* or moral philosophy) of Confucianism, and offered a tool for differentiating between Confucianism and Buddhism. Sima Guang of the Northern Song also used the notion of "investigating things" as a means of providing a new explanation regarding the origins of moral decline.[21] However, it was not until the Cheng brothers used the notion of "entering the gate of morality" and "differentiations within forms of learning" as a means of explaining the meaning of *The Great Learning* that the text's central place within Neo-Confucianism was confirmed. They worked to arrange the different parts of the work, revising it toward producing a definitive edition, repeatedly engaging in such editorial work so that *The Great Learning* could be used by Zhu Xi and later Confucians. In doing so, they blazed a path for the reevaluation of the meaning of the work. Zhu Xi said: "Cheng Yi claimed: '*The Great Learning* is a surviving work of Confucius; with this work beginners can enter the gate of morality.' Today we can see how when the ancients classified learning they all relied on this particular work, with the *Analects* and the *Mencius* being secondary. Scholars had to conduct their studies through this work *The Great Learning,* and in this way scholarship was strengthened."[22] For Zhu Xi, *The Great Learning* was based on the methods of instruction of the Three Dynasties of Antiquity the Xia, Shang, and Zhou, and its utility was to work through the order of rites and music in order to preserve the innate nature of benevolence, righteousness, rites, and wisdom. As Zhu Xi put it: "What was taught [in the schools] were the experiences and moral lessons of the rulers themselves, and what was required to study was all within the bounds of ethical principles and rules of common people in their everyday lives. Because of this, there was not a single person at that time who did not study in this fashion." The classifications of learning were grounded in the order of rites and music, and as such, it was only when conformity to such an order steadily deepened that "all would know the innateness of their distinct nature, and the appropriateness of their rank, and all could strive to the utmost, giving full play to their abilities. [Such a condition] was found in the flourishing ancient times, where prosperous governance emerged from above, and below was found an exquisite common virtue. It is not a state that can be reached by successive eras!"[23] Through its discourse regarding the "classifications of learning," *The Great Learning* linked together the body, the family, the state, and All-under-Heaven, and the initial foundation of this discourse was directly related to the theory of the system of rites. However, Zhu Xi maintained that the rites and music of the Three Dynasties were already completely lost, and as such, there was a need to create a different path, seeking and examining Heavenly Principle or inherent Nature through the investigation of things. It was only in this way that one could recover the spirit of rites and music. As a result, he clearly took the notion of "investigating things and extending knowledge" and made it independent of the *Book of Rites,* linking it with the notion of "seeking Principle in order to give full play to Nature" that could be found in the *Commentary on the Changes* (*Yi zhuan*), turning this into an important methodological concept for the School of Principle.[24] Within the three guiding principles and eight measures that he outlined in his introduction to his *Interlinear Commentary on The Great Learning* (*Da xue zhangju*), the investigation of things and the extension of knowledge have a prominent place within the classifications of learning.

Many aspects of Zhu Xi's teachings are internally related to one another, but their core is the process and procedures by which one seeks and attains Heavenly Principle, which is understood as the basis of existence. As outlined in his *Interlinear Commentary on The Great Learning,* Zhu Xi's conceptualization of "things" and his conceptualization of "knowledge" did not thoroughly depart from the concepts of moral behavior and moral knowledge of Confucian ethics, and as such it is very difficult to use the differentiation between what is and what ought to be as the basis for describing these two concepts. However, the theory of investigating things and extending knowledge did indeed include the notion of recognizing things. Zhu Xi did not like to discuss concepts such as "the roots of malady" (*bing gen*), "grounding origin" (*ben yuan*), or "the comprehensive structure of the heart-mind" (*xinti zhi quanti*). He felt that it was only through specific explorations regarding things that Heavenly Principle could be grasped. If one were to compare Zhu Xi to Confucius, the importance of "things" within Zhu Xi's thought becomes easy to see. Confucius said: "At fifty I understood the Mandate of Heaven." Zhu Xi's commentary on this passage states: "This means that the flow of the Heavenly Way is invested in all things, and this is the reason why things are just so."[25] Qian Mu evaluated this exchange in the following way:

> "Mandate" means the Way of Heaven, and one can say that this is what Confucius means here. However, [Zhu Xi's] claim that [the Mandate of Heaven] is invested in things is seemingly quite different than Confucius's position. Mencius spoke of inherent Nature, but only spoke of it in terms of human nature, the doctrine of the mean, and the Nature of things. . . . Today, Zhu Xi speaks of the reason things are just so, and the investiture of the Mandate within things, that is to say being internal to things, in and of themselves, and not outside of them. That is to say [that for Zhu Xi] there is no [exteriorized] mandate to speak of.[26]

This is a most correct observation. When Zhu Xi theorized knowledge and action, the process of first obtaining knowledge and then acting later, the reason was that behavior was grounded in the order of rites, and as such, "Following the decline of the Zhou dynasty, the virtuous sages did not act, the affairs of schools were not reformed, teaching was brutally deformed, and customs descended into decadence."[27] If one could not start from "the investigation of things and the extension of knowledge," how was one to find the basis for "action"? This question can be looked upon as the foundation of the theory of the investigation of things and extension of knowledge.

In terms of Zhu Xi's concept of the investigation of things, his final conclusion on the matter can be found in his "Supplemental Discussion on the Investigation of Things" in his *Interlinear Commentary on The Great Learning:*

> That which is called the extension of knowledge by investigating things refers to a desire to extend one's knowledge by engaging with things, fathoming their Principle. There is not a single human soul that does not possess knowledge, while there is not a single thing under Heaven that does not possess Principle. Yet if one does not fathom Principle one's knowledge will remain undeveloped. So *The Great Learning*'s initial teaching is that scholars must engage with all things under Heaven, and it is precisely because one knows that all things possess Principle that one seeks to understand them more deeply, seeking to push that knowledge to the utmost extent. There comes a point when, upon diligently exerting oneself for a great period of time, one will suddenly see things in a clear light, and one will be able to distinguish within the multitude of things the coarse and the fine, the inner and the outer, and the comprehensive structure and grand purpose of one's heart-mind will no longer be unclear. This is called investigating things; this is called the extension of knowledge.[28]

Comprehensively speaking, Zhu Xi's theory of the investigation of things and the extension of knowledge includes the following points: First, the "investigation of things and the extension of knowledge" was the organic part of Zhu Xi's Neo-Confucian system. The problem that it sought to solve was the question of how does "Principle" return to itself. "Principle" was understood as the grounding source of the universe and the noumenon of morality and ethics in their highest forms; it worked through *qi* to produce the myriad of things. The so-called return of "Principle" to itself was a question of how Principle was to move through the myriad of things of the world to once again return back to its own body. Yet this return was only a logical process; it was not one that could be understood by the notion of something outer returning to something inner. For according to the notion that inherent Nature is Principle, inherent Nature did not have an inner or outer, nor did Principle; there was nothing All-under-Heaven without inherent Nature, just as there was nothing All-under-Heaven without Principle. As such, though the investigation of things and the extension of knowledge in its most direct form was the process by which human beings would come to know the "Principle" of various objects, and the various forms by which such a process of recognition would take, within the structure of the School of Principle this was in fact only the process by which "Principle" in its noumenal form returned to itself. In this sense, "investigation of things and the extension of knowledge" was the critical link that enabled "Principle" to become one with itself.

Second, the relationship described above between Principle and things offers the process of recognition as an a priori result, while also defining this process as itself a form of moral practice. Here, morality is not pure, like modern society's rationalized moral field, for between the ethical codes of human relations and the arrangement of the multitude of things there is no division between what is and what ought to be. The essential meaning of the phrase "inherent Nature is Principle" is the notion that Heaven is Principle, and humanity is inherent Nature. At the end of the *Interlinear Commentary on The Great Learning,* Zhu Xi emphasized that his commentary work regarding the investigation of things "was the benevolence of illustrious virtue," ultimately understanding the extension of knowledge as a moral state represented by the phrase "the comprehensive structure and grand purpose of one's heart-mind will no longer be unclear."[29] As such he indicated that the extension of knowledge was not only a path of learning; even more it was the most basic method by which to rectify heart-mind, nurture sincerity, understand illustrious virtue, and rest in a maximal kindness. Here, Zhu Xi has departed from the notion of "morality" of the Western Zhou period, which was tied closely with the system of rites, and has interpreted "morality" as a kind of internalized state that is constructed within a cosmological framework. In Zhu Xi's own words:

> When it comes to those who speak about investigating things, the matters that the gentleman from Henan spoke of [i.e., Cheng Yi]—that is "the reading of books, the discussion of moral philosophy, or discussing the ancients so as to distinguish between whether they are true and false, or engaging with things and determining whether they are proper or not"—all of these are instances of the investigation of things.[30]

> To study but not to seek Heavenly Principle, not to clarify human ethics, not to speak the words of the sages, not to understand the causes of

> the affairs of the world, and then to put our mind-heart hastily among the grass and the tree, among the tool and the implement, what kind of learning is this?[31]

Investigating things and extending knowledge is not just a recognition of the myriad things of the universe; it is also a subjective moral practice ("a cultivation of the heart-mind"), a mode of reflection regarding inner nature.[32] However, the moral practice that the theory of investigating things and extending knowledge presupposes differs from that advocated by Lu Jiuyuan, which sought to take the sense of love, mourning, and reverence one had regarding one's own family clan and extend it to encompass the entire universe. "Zhu Xi focused on all of the contradictions of the clan, the village, the nation, and the world, and developed his ideas so as to solve these contradictions, producing his teachings regarding examining Principle."[33]

Third, what was called "investigating things" included three dimensions: "approaching things" (*jiwu*), "examining Principle" (*qiong li*), and "reaching the utmost point" (*zhi ji*). The "examination of Principle" lay at the center of these gradations of learning. Zhu Xi believed that Principle and *qi* were essential elements of both the universe and humanity. If Principle was a kind of internal essence and order, then *qi* was the materiality through which the physical world was constructed as well as human sense perception (emotion, feeling, desire, etc.). Zhu Xi developed the notion of "singular Principle and its differential expressions" from the Cheng brothers, believing that the myriad of things under Heaven all expressed a general Principle as well as their own differentiations of it ("Principle under Heaven has myriad differentiations"). These "differentiations" did not refer merely to the synchronic relations of things, but also to their historical changes as well as their plurality: "[When one] does not comprehend a thing, one fails to grasp its principle." The knowledge that the human mind possessed naturally was of course not equal to the knowledge one had after having examined Principle: "if one does not examine Principle, one's knowledge will not be developed to its utmost." If one does not undergo the real work of approaching things, examining their principles, and finally of reaching the utmost point of knowledge, one will not have the true knowledge that penetrates deeply to the marrow of things. Precisely because this is so, Zhu Xi put tremendous emphasis on a "variegated program" by which "today one investigates one thing, tomorrow one investigates another, accumulating much through study, coming to contentedly possess an integrated understanding."[34] Zhu Xi would further remark that "regarding the theory of things, while Cheng Yi said there is nothing before my eyes that are not 'things,' however in examining each of them, one must have an order in which there is an earlier and a later, a sense of what is more critical and less critical. Does one rashly think that one can gain immediate enlightenment by hastily putting one's heart-mind among the grass and trees, among the tools and implements?"[35] In terms of knowledge, he put a tremendous emphasis on the notion that if one wanted to understand the "singular Principle," one had to accumulate experiential knowledge. When it came to ethics, one had to take specific, particular norms and elevate them into being general moral principles. As such, though the final goal of "examining Principle" was to understand Heavenly Principle, this process broadly involved the inherent natures of specific things as well as their patterns. Within the "gradations of learning," the notion of "approaching things" was an absolutely essential part of the examination of things and extension of knowledge.

Fourth, if we think about the concepts "approaching things and examining Principle" and "singular Principle and its differential expressions" in an integrated manner, then the meaning of "the investigation of things" comes to lie in understanding the particular "Principle" of specific things. The notion of "suddenly seeing things in a clear light" not only points to the integration of the mind-heart's knowledge with the Principle of things, but also provides insight into the unified relationship that exists between the differential expressions of Principle inherent to things and Principle in its noumenal self. The School of Principle's method of knowing is not one that seeks to understand the position of various things within a universal order via processes of clear classification; however, it does recognize the differential expressions of inherent Nature and the sudden enlightenment one can attain regarding them. As such, the School of Principle must by necessity include an understanding of the order of the world and the relations that exist between the various things within it. This being the case, on the one hand Zhu Xi's concept of things is of a Nature "differentially expressed": this is captured by the notion that "when differentiations are seen to be ever more diverse, the Principle one witnesses is ever greater."[36] On the other hand, his notion of Nature is one that exists in a state of qualitative differentiation, a nonorderly, disharmonious, nonpeaceful, nonuniform order in which things each express their individual "Principle" or "Nature." This is the process by which Principle becomes integrated with itself through its expression via the differentiated natures of the myriad of things. The theory of the investigation of things and its process-based method of knowing cannot be denied; it demands that one employ research into the classification of things in order to define the general order of the universe, Nature, and society. With regards to this point, the investigation of things is not altogether different from the concept of science, which itself is grounded in the creation of a genealogy of knowledge based upon the classification of things.[37]

According to the above analysis, the theory of investigating things and the extension of knowledge is a methodology that seeks to promote an order that ought to be. The critical position that this theory occupies within Zhu Xi's learning is itself replete with significance. First, it indicates that the objective basis for moral evaluation is not the actually existing order (which one must recognize has already been formalized to a considerable degree), but rather the original principle of existence of the universe. Second, it indicates that such an existential principle cannot be pursued outside of the actually existing world occupied by human beings themselves. In fact, it is just the opposite: "Principle" can only be made manifest through the world of "things" and "humans." The proposition of "engaging with things and examining Principle" entails that Heavenly Principle is a "Nature" or "arrangement" that is internal to "things," one that "is suited to be just so." The relationship between "Principle" and "things" did not develop the kind of absolute division and opposition between the self and the exterior world that is presupposed in the very concept of the self. For example, speaking of the relationship between affairs and things, Zhu Xi proposed the notion that "before there was this affair, first there was this Principle" and "before there was Heaven and Earth, there was after all only Principle." Yet at the same time he clearly indicated that the relationship that he was discussing between affairs and Principle was a logical relationship that should be understood in existential terms, and was not referring to the actual relations that existed between Principle and affairs.[38] The Cheng brothers believed that things were affairs, and that the difference between affairs and Principle was not so great for the two to have no relationship with one another. In fact it was just the opposite: between affairs and Principle there existed an internal consistency.[39] In this sense, the process of "conforming to Principle" was not the transcendence of "things" in and of themselves, but rather a return to the Nature of "things" in and of themselves, a Nature that was "suited to be just so." As a new mode of moral cognition, the theory of the investigation of things and the extension of knowledge insisted that an examination into moral principles should be conducted through (and not according to) the examination of specific things. Within this process, the Cheng brothers and Zhu Xi proposed a series of subtle concepts—for example their notions of "restraint" (*zhi*), "extension" (*jin*), "just so" (*hedang*), and so forth—as a means of redefining the system of rites and music and its divisions. The precise meaning of these concepts was that relations between minister and monarch, father and son, husband and wife, and friends were only moral if they were grounded in a state of "restraint," "extension," and being "just so."

On the one hand, these concepts bore witness to the fact that the actually existing relations within the order of rites were not genuine (or natural) rites-based relations; on the other hand, only the relations between minister and monarch, father and son, husband and wife, and friends that were in a proper state were genuinely moral relations. This was the Neo-Confucian recovery of a means of moral exposition regarding the system of rites and music, a recovery that took place within the framework of Heavenly Principle. From within such a recovery we can sense to some degree an echo of Confucius's efforts to interpret rites in terms of benevolence: if the monarch could not "restrain" himself toward benevolence, and the minister could not "restrain himself" toward respect, then they could not bear the righteous responsibility of the minister-monarch relation, nor should they carry the titles of minister and monarch. The core of Zhu Xi's theory of the investigation of things and the extension of knowledge was not in things in and of themselves, nor was it in the heart-mind in and of itself, but rather it was the process of "investigation" by which things and the heart-mind were comprehensively integrated. This process offered a path one had to follow if one wanted to make manifest moral and ethical standards. The dual nature of Zhu Xi's learning was first expressed in its making "Principle" or "the examination of Principle" its goal. This "Principle" could become the basis for the actually existing order of things, but it could also become an element one could use to negate the actually existing order. Within Zhu Xi's worldview, "inherent Nature" and "Principle" were expressed as the order of things being appropriately "just so" rather than an actually existing state.[40] The concepts of "point of restraint" (*zhiyu*), "the time for restraint" (*dangzhi*), "limit point" (*jinchu*), and so forth, are all exceptionally important within Zhu Xi's thought; these are not simply the goals of the investigation of things, but also indicate the state by which the myriad of things conforms to Heavenly Principle.[41] Here, what becomes the central vocabulary of the investigation of things and extension of knowledge are not particular affairs (for example, the relationships between minister and monarch, father and son, husband and wife, and friends), but rather notions such as "suitably just so," "limit point," "base" (*di*), and "restraint." To use a perhaps not entirely appropriate metaphor, the ultimate goal of Zhu Xi's explorations did not lie with actually existing things, but rather in the state of existence itself. Yet these concepts for expressing such an existential condition place Heavenly Principle within a dynamic process, and as such clearly indicate that existence (Principle) cannot be severed from the evaluation of the things of existence (affairs). The understanding that investigating things and extending knowledge has with regard to the pluralism of things and their specific contexts is constructed on this understanding of the relations between Principle / affairs as well as Principle / things.

For Neo-Confucianism after Zhu Xi, *The Great Learning* and its theory of investigating things and extending knowledge became not simply the central topic of the philosophical school, but the major focus of its moral argumentation as well. Interpretations of investigating things and extending knowledge contained presuppositions regarding both the principle of existence and the Way of Ultimate Virtue (*zhishan zhi dao*), while also arguing that one could reach the pathway of Heavenly Principle through the examination of various "facts"; if moral evaluation did not originate in the practices of "rites," but rather in the understanding of Heavenly Principle, then the question of how one should recognize, arrive at, and integrate oneself with Heavenly Principle became the central question of Neo-Confucianism. Owing to this, "From Song times onward, it was nearly true that if a thinker offered a general philosophical platform, what followed was a discourse on the investigation of things."[42] The *Analects,* the *Mencius,* the *Doctrine of the Mean,* the *Commentary on the Changes,* and *The Great Learning* were appointed by Song Confucians as representative works of the Confucian tradition's teachings regarding inner sageliness. In particular, after Cheng Yi, and especially after Zhu Xi, expounded upon *The Great Learning*, the work came to be promoted as the preeminent text of the Four Books, becoming the critical link that enabled the demonstration of the new Confucianism's system.[43] The Cheng brothers and Zhu Xi's theory of the investigation of things and extension of knowledge opened up a means of seeking and demonstrating morality via a cognitive channel, and this cognitive channel was the most important characteristic of the mode of moral evaluation inherent to the notion of Heavenly Principle.

If we take the establishment of a viewpoint centered on Heavenly Principle as symbolizing this transformation in Confucianism's mode of moral evaluation, then how do we understand the School of Principle's persistent research into, recovery of, and practice of "rites"? For example, Zhu Xi's *Explaining and Transmitting the Classic of Rites* (*Yili jing chuan tongjie*) sought to clarify such different kinds of rites as those of the family, of the village, of learning, of the state, and of the dynasty, while also taking the communities of the clan, the village, the culture, and the state as a basis for analyzing the ancient system of rites. Clearly, rites were still very much at the center of the School of Principle's concerns. How did this enthusiasm for the concept of rites differ from Confucius's teaching regarding rites? Just like Confucius, Zhu Xi believed that the system of rites and music had collapsed long ago, and that such a system was the precondition for the relations between ceremony and morality. However, where he differed from Confucius was that the latter interpreted the system of rites and music (as well as its ethical relations) in terms of "understanding ritual propriety as humaneness" (*yi ren shi li*) as well as the concept of "to transmit but not to create" (*shu er bu zuo*), whereas Zhu Xi believed that rites could now only exist as a metaphysical essence ("Principle"), and as such, efforts to recover rites and music could only be successful if they were carried out via the exposition of Heavenly Principle or the sequential program entailed within "the recovery of inherent Nature" (*fu xing*). According to the logic of "inherent Nature is Principle" (*xing ji li*), "benevolence, justice, rites, and wisdom were all internal qualities that had not yet arrived at full expression"[44]: such things were not exterior restrictions, but rather "inherent" qualities. "Principle" both transcended and yet constrained specific rites. Put differently, specific rites took (by necessity) "Principle" as their basis. Why was an internalized or generalized Principle necessary to constrain "rites"? For rites and music themselves had already been exteriorized, as had an understanding of rites itself. For example, in the *New History of the Tang* we find that "rites and music are empty names"; they have no ability to reveal the real relations that exist between rites and music. Precisely because of this, School of Principle thinkers demanded that it was only from within the order of the universe (Heavenly Principle) that an expression of moral order could be worked out. As such, the investigation of things and extension of knowledge was a means of recognizing the order of the universe, a practice pertaining to such an order, becoming the only pathway for connecting specific ethical codes with Heavenly Principle. Instead of saying the divergences in interpretation that Song and Ming Confucians had regarding *The Great Learning* originated in their unceasing rearrangements and reinterpretations of the work, it would be more accurate to say they emerged out of the specific nature of the concept of "Heavenly Principle" as well as the expositional procedures presupposed by it. The notion of "things" imbedded in facticity would come to launch an assault on the discursive framework of the system of rites / morality, subsequently elevating status of the subject who perceives and understands "things."

III. "Inherent Nature is Principle" and the Nature of Things

Zhu Xi emphasized existence rather than actually existing things, and his major reason for doing so has already been outlined above. This mode of discourse, which separates existence from the actually existing things, finds its direct origins in Confucianism's internal understanding of the "actuality" of rites and music. Song society was situated in an historical era defined by transformation. Neo-Confucians believed that this was an era of tremendous moral crisis, in which the patriarchal clan system and the learning associated with the recording of clan genealogies had been severely damaged. For these thinkers, the actually existing world and its order could not provide a moral foundation. Such a foundation could only be found in the recognition people had of Heavenly Principle and the practices they performed in relation to it. The theory of cultivation associated with "investigating things and extending knowledge" demanded that people work within the order of rites to transcend their own sense of reality, doing so through a series of specific practices and a commitment to self-reflection. In doing so, they would obtain the goal of becoming integrated with their own essence. The transformation in the notion of "things" can only be understood when it is placed in the context of these changes occurring within this particular moral system.

The concept of Heavenly Principle included hierarchical visions of order and morality; however, the relationship between this moral consciousness and the actually existing political order, which took the emperor at its center, was far from stable. The separation that had occurred from Han and Tang times onward between rites and music and actually existing social institutions (and the particular sense of imagination engendered by such a division, which included reflections on the Three Dynasties of Antiquity), and in particular the changes that occurred within the Song political system, transformed the once-unified relations that existed between the system of rites and music and moral judgment. Within this context, the attempt by Song and Ming School of Principle thinkers to overcome the unified relations that existed between institutions / morality, that is to say their attempt to reconstruct a mode of moral evaluation by centering Heavenly Principle, was in essence the reconstruction of a moral genealogy outside of institutional evaluations. As such, the relationship that this vision of Heavenly Principle had with actual politics, as well as the institutional practices associated with such politics, was defined by an internal tension. Generally speaking, what School of Principle thinkers hoped for was a moral rule or kingly Way in which the power of the emperor and the power of the common people was balanced, a social order that could accommodate values from the system of enfeoffment within the system of centralized administration. The order of the common people was understood to have the scholar-gentry and landowning class at its center, and where village self-governance (*xiangcun zizhi*) was linked together by a Community Compact (*xiangyue*).[45]

One of the most difficult questions that both the theory of the universe that developed during the Han dynasty and the notion of the Heavenly Way that developed during the Northern Song period had to reckon with was how to understand the relationship that existed between ethics and the myriad things of the universe. That is, if "things" was no longer a normative category, but was only a factual category, then how were statements regarding "things" to provide a sense of the moral regulations that we were supposed to follow? The notion of Heavenly Principle, the theory of the binary between

Principle and *qi*, as well as the idea that "inherent Nature is Principle," were all meant to overcome this difficulty. Cheng Yi wrote: "Inherent Nature is Principle. So-called Principle is inherent Nature."[46] "Inherent Nature" and "Principle" were to be understood as universal categories (a universal Nature, a universal principle) set in opposition to the real hierarchical world, which is to say that they did not differentiate between the old and the young, men and women, or between differences in rank or class: as Cheng Yi put it, "From Yao and Shun to common people, Principle is uniform."[47] Nor did such concepts differentiate between Heaven, Earth, humans, and things: "In terms of Heaven it is known as a command, in terms of righteousness it is known as Principle, in terms of people it is known as inherent Nature, and in terms of the body it is known as heart-mind, in fact it is all one."[48] The two interrelated implications of such a proposition are: by differentiating between the real world and the world of Heavenly Principle, morality and ethics are depicted as a transcendent world, one that is completely independent of our positions, attitudes, preferences, and emotions, that is to say our actual existence (the world of "*qi*"). But here "transcendent" and "independent" do not mean a complete separation, for "Principle" is also internal to us and the world in which we subsist. As such, the only path one can follow to reach the world as it should be is a practice of self-cultivation, which is a comprehensive process through which one can gain a sense of illumination and apprehension regarding Heavenly Principle. The proposition "inherent Nature is Principle" replaces the pre-Qin notion of "recovering rites" with the notion of "recovering inherent Nature." In doing so, it reconstructs a kind of teleology of human nature. The concept of "inherent Nature" developed by the Cheng brothers and Zhu Xi took the notions of one's own Nature, human nature, and the Nature of things and linked them together, doing so within a cosmic framework defined by the notion of Heavenly Principle. As such, they differed from Mencius, who only spoke of human nature. Using Cheng Hao's own words: "The sagely person is fond of things; the sagely person is angered by things. The anger and fondness of the sagely person does not reside in their heart-mind, but rather in things themselves."[49] The notion of "heart-mind" invoked here is not an abstract essence, but rather is the heart-mind that is vexed by practical scheming; the notion of "things" invoked here is not experiential things, but rather the Nature of "things" or the essence of "things." The dichotomy between heart-mind / things demonstrates the objective and transcendental nature of "Heavenly Principle." People and things are both within the realm of inherent Nature, and as such, the nature or essence of "things" can become the goal of human nature. In this sense, the proposition that "inherent Nature is Principle" emphasizes the internal and a priori Nature of "Heaven" or "Principle," sublating the transcendent, fatalistic, and cosmological qualities inherent within the concept of the Way of Heaven. As Zhu Xi put it: "For example this fan is an object, it has the sense of being an individual fan. That fans are made like this, that they are used just so, this is a metaphysical principle. . . . with regard to instruments in the physical world [lit. "instruments in the realm below formal abstraction," *xing er xia zhi qi zhong*], each has its own sensibility, this is in fact the metaphysical Way."[50] Via this distinction between the metaphysical and the physical, the relations between things and Principle are clarified. As a kind of natural order, Principle is a notion of order that is internal to things, one that is "just so."

The proposition that "inherent Nature is Principle" also includes another dimension: that "inherent Nature" can be divided between a universal nature and a particular nature. According to Cheng Hao, inherent Nature is *Dao* (the universal essence of the universe), while it is also *qi* (Nature manifest by all the myriad of things), and it can also be understood in particularized terms (that is, each of the myriad of things has its own particular inherent Nature).[51] The proposition that "inherent Nature is *qi*" came from Zhang Zai. To a certain extent this notion provides an interpretation of the structure of the world, analyzing why the universe took *Dao* and inherent Nature as its preconditions, and why such a universe could also produce evil phenomena.[52] For if the myriad of things each has an inherent Nature specific to the categorization of each, then Heavenly Principle could possibly include "differentiations of Principle." Cheng Hao stated: "The principles of the myriad of things of Heaven and Earth do not exist in isolation, they must have correspondences."[53] He also said: "When the sagely person devotes himself to the good of all, his heart-mind extends itself toward the principle of the myriad of things in Heaven and Earth, in each of their differentiations."[54] Cheng Hao's statement that "the principles of the myriad of things of Heaven and Earth do not exist in isolation, they must have correspondences" suggests that things exist in an order in which they each correspond to each other, while the notion that each has its "differentiations" illuminates the interrelation between moral realization and the notion of differentiation. This notion of "differentiation" is different than the notion of differentiation imbedded in the order of rites, for it demands that the myriad of things of Heaven and Earth exist in a natural order that "is just so," and that they all take their respective positions within this order in a manner that "is just so," meaning that "things" return to their own "internal Natures." As such, on the one hand Cheng Yi believed that "all things under Heaven could be illuminated by Principle," while on the other hand he also said that "if there are things then there are also norms, a single thing has to have a single Principle,"[55] advocating that one examine to the greatest extent the principles of all things under Heaven, accumulating knowledge so as to grasp Heavenly Principle. As such, the discussion moved from differentiation with regard to inherent Nature to differentiation with regard to Principle itself. Not only did the proposition that one should study Principle so as to give full play to inherent Nature emerge vividly; the hierarchical nature of the order of "Principle" was also made manifest on a metaphysical level. These are the new formal implications suggested by the notion of the study of the differentiations of "Principle"; it is also the theoretical precondition for Zhu Xi's "investigating things and extending knowledge."

If we say that the perspective that places the Heavenly Way at the center of its understanding is unable, within its own moral expositions, to clearly separate the real world from the Heavenly Way, then the notion of Heavenly Principle, particularly its proposition that "inherent Nature is Principle," realizes this separation. The blueprint of the universe inherent within the notion of "Heavenly Principle" is not a purely vertical system, moving from on high and descending downwards. Rather, it is an order within which things are weaved together each according to their own principle. Within Zhu Xi's discourse, "Heaven," "Principle," and "inherent Nature" possess close, unbreakable, and integrated relations, and the question of which has priority among them at most is a question of the narrative logic one employs to present their relations.

Zhu Xi said: "Inherent Nature is Principle, Heaven employs yin and yang and the five elements to produce the myriad of things, *qi* becomes form, and Principle follows, like a command." It seems as if "inherent Nature" / "Principle" really does possess its own will, like rulers who are able to issue commands. Yet before the term "command" here there is the word *ji*, which means "just like" or "as if." The passage is not saying that these categories are truly like God himself, in possession of personality and will. So immediately after "like a command" Zhu Xi says: "Because with the birth of every person each obtains the principle that is bestowed on them, which is taken as a vibrant morality grounded in adherence to the five cardinal virtues; this is called inherent Nature."[56] He also said: "When the five elements emerged, each possessed their own inherent Nature . . . there is not a single thing that does not contain within itself the entirety of the Supreme Ultimate . . . inherent Nature is the entirety of the Supreme Ultimate,"[57] and "Inherent Nature is simply Principle, as it is endowed within humans, it is thus called inherent Nature."[58] Following this logic, Heavenly Principle (the Supreme Ultimate) is the source and basis for the myriad things in the universe, and the myriad things (which are produced from *qi*) and human beings also possess Heavenly Principle within themselves. As such, in Qian Mu's gloss on Zhu Xi's words, "Principle is the structure of Heaven, while commands are the exercise of Principle. This entails that not only is there no emperor serving as master, there is furthermore no Heaven which exists. There is only singular Principle which is thereupon called Heaven."[59] If Heavenly Principle is a subject that is both domineering and creative, then why does Zhu Xi place "investigating things and extending knowledge" in such an important position?

According to the understanding that Song Confucians had, within the culture of rites and music that defined the pre-Qin era, moral evaluation was absolutely consistent with the position that people held within the order of rites, and there did not exist the question of the division between so-called fact and value, what is and what ought to be. However, within the context of the institutions of administration, the selections of officials, and the governance of land that were becoming steadily more developed over time, Zhu Xi and other School of Principle thinkers felt that there was no way to carry out moral evaluation through the ethical relations that actually existed between humans or through the structure of social institutions itself. The notions they put forward such as "illustrious virtue" (*mingde*) and "illustrious orders" (*ming ming*) were aimed precisely at addressing a condition in which they felt people's virtue was marred by material desire. The goal of "investigating things and extending knowledge" was to work through a specific process in order to clarify the intimacy that should exist between father and son, the righteousness that should exist between minister and monarch, the differentiations that should exist between husband and wife, the order that should exist between elderly and youth, and the trust that should exist between friends. The intimacy, righteousness, differentiation, order, and trust invoked here differed from the relations found in actually existing institutions or the order of rites and music. Rather, they were connected to relations that Zhu Xi often expounded on, defined by such concepts as "the limit point," "the base," "restraint," and "just so." This was an order that was yet to be realized, and that existed in tension with the actually existing social order. As such, though benevolence, righteousness, rites, and wisdom were inherent to illustrious virtue, they required "investigating things" in order to be made manifest. Actually existing monarchs and ministers could not represent the benevolence that a monarch should have, or the sense of respect that a minister should have. As such, the relations between minister and monarch that were "just so" not only formed an idealized order; they were also a critical standard against which the currently existing relations between monarch and minister could be evaluated. This was the social import of Zhu Xi's binary theory of Principle and *qi*.

IV. This Thing (*ciwu*) and Things (*wu*)

During the entirety of the Ming-dynasty period, thinkers directed their efforts mainly toward attacking, critiquing, and extricating themselves from the binary of Principle / *qi* that the Cheng brothers and Zhu Xi had created. Working in two different directions, one around the notion of heart-mind and the other that of things (*qi*), they sought a unitary theory regarding heart-mind and a unitary theory regarding *qi*, doing so as a means of bridging the rift created by the separation of Principle and *qi*. From the fourteenth to the sixteenth centuries, a unitary theory of heart-mind came to be the paradigm of thought with the greatest capacity to attract interest, and as such there came to emerge the opposition, conflict, and mutual imbrication between the study of Principle and the study of heart-mind. However, the division between the School of Principle and the School of Mind did not emerge out of a natural process of evolution; the intellectual debates and divisions of Zhu Xi's era already provided a foundation for later developments. During the Southern Song period, Zhu Xi's notion of Principle (which included the concepts of "the limit point," "the base," "restraint," and "just so") and Lu Xiangshan's (1139–1193) notion of heart-mind (which included the notions of "this object" [*ci wu*] and "this knowledge" [*ci zhi*]) both presupposed the notion of Heavenly Principle, and both existed in a certain tension with actual social conditions; as a contemporary of Zhu Xi's, Lu clearly took a unitary theory of heart-mind as the starting point for his vision of the world, doing so as a means of resisting Zhu Xi's binary theory and its correlated methods of knowledge. Within the world of his thought, Heavenly Principle does not simply exist in itself; it also manifests itself, with the myriad of things of the world and the existential order they exist within being manifestations of Principle. As such, Heavenly Principle was not an object that was merely awaiting observation, understanding, and study, but rather was the unfolding of heart-mind itself. Lu advocated notions such as "first establish its grandeur" (*xian li qi da*) and beginning directly from a "rectified heart" (*zhengxin*); and he sought to carry out the principles of the universe through the practicing of rites established in the ancient works. His notion of heart-mind cannot be understood as an "internal" heart-mind (akin to the notion of heart-mind that is presupposed by the modern conception of the self), but rather is a vast field that includes the entire world. Lu professed that "heart-mind is Principle," and as such, his notions of "first establish its grandeur" and "the rectified heart" touched upon the question of universal order—that is to say, the question of "Principle." However, the establishment of the study of heart-mind did not come about via advocating for a vision of order that was different than one grounded in Principle, but rather through the development of a discursive and rhetorical mode that could enable the notion of inherent Nature to include and account for the myriad of things of the universe, and thereby to overcome the binarial theory of Principle and *qi* advocated by the Cheng brothers and Zhu Xi.

A variety of Lu Xiangshan's social views were very close to those of the Cheng brothers and Zhu Xi. However, their methods of critique and their starting points differed. For example, in relation to the system of civil service examinations and its various corruptions, Lu engaged in withering critique, asserting that the "custom of the civil service examination" was evidence of a social condition in which "this *Dao* is incorrect" and "this *Dao* is unenlightened." This position differed very little from the Cheng brothers and Zhu Xi's own stance regarding the civil service examination. As such, when the notions of "heart-mind is Principle" and "inherent Nature is Principle" are placed within the context of the critique of the mode of evaluation embodied within the civil service examination, the areas of mutual accord between these thinkers far outstrip those areas of divergence. However, Lu used the rhetoric of "immanence" as an entry point into these questions, and as such, his discursive perspective was already different from Zhu Xi's "inherent Nature is Principle." From Lu's perspective, though within the system of civil service examinations Song Confucians revered the *Book of Odes*, the *Book of Documents*, the *Analects*, and the *Mencius*, they would eventually all become "documents of the civil service examination," and as such, he resolutely rejected the study of the classics as a path for extending knowledge regarding benevolence and righteousness. "Internal" here connoted the rejection of the placement of the category of "knowledge" within an epistemic order. Lu expressed impressive foresight regarding the historical fate of Zhu Xi's learning. Lu lamented the decline of the Way of the Zhou, and in turn placed his hopes for "rectified Principle" in the realm of the "human heart-mind" rather than in any external social system or canonical body of works. This is a different kind of logic of thought. However, understood as an effort to reinvest rites, the social system, and knowledge with a kind of sagely meaning (and here, sageliness is not opposed to a sense of the quotidian), the notion of Heavenly Principle elucidated by the Cheng brothers and Zhu Xi shares common cause with Lu's notion of the genuine heart-mind.

Could Lu Xiangshan's teachings avoid the fate of Zhu Xi's teachings? In his "Letter to Li Zai" (*Yu Li Zai*), Lu wrote:

> As Principle is grounded in the human heart, Mencius called it inherent (*gu you*). "Transformation" (*yi*) as spoken of in the *Book of Changes* is a question of the ease around which one can gain knowledge of the changes, and the simplicity with which one can study them. In the beginning, it was not some abstruse, difficult task to practice. However, as we began to speak of "those who have lost rectitude," learning became a question of studying "correct teachings," and the goal of learning became a question of overcoming selfish desire; only then could one say that Principle was in the human heart. However, if one has not yet discovered the true heart-mind, then the heart-mind will not have correct guidance, and the Principle of the human heart will remain unclear, so that

> if one in this condition speaks of a "heart at peace," one does not know what one is making peaceful. In *The Great Learning* is it said: "Before rectifying one's heart-mind, one most rectify honestly one's intentions. Before rectifying honestly one's intentions, one must deeply study one's own sense of knowledge, and to study one's own sense of knowledge one must study deeply the reasons for the existence of all things." In that you have studied deeply things, you will naturally have knowledge. In that you have knowledge, your intentions will naturally become rectified. In that your intentions are rectified, your heart-mind will naturally become rectified. This process is completely natural, it is not something that can be forced. From the Duke of Zhou onward, the path for studying rectified Nature has not been followed; after Mencius's teachings were drowned out, the correct path has been unclear. Today, all scholars under Heaven have become mired in study for the civil service examinations. Look at their words, always citing the *Book of Odes,* the *Book of Documents,* the *Analects,* the *Mencius.* In reality, they simply take these works as being nothing but documents for the exams.[60]

Lu Xiangshan sought to distinguish between the heart-mind's rectitude and evil, and was uninterested in the external things of the world. This is completely in line with Zhu Xi's use of the terms "the limit point" and "just so" as a means of interpreting the principle of things. However, Zhu Xi analyzed heart-mind and inherent Nature, the human heart and the heart of the *Dao* in dualistic terms, advocating that "heart-mind unites emotive Nature," and that through strenuous study and cultivation Heavenly Principle could be grasped, while Lu's notion of heart-mind is a singular one in which Principle and mind are united. What he emphasized is the following of a Heavenly Principle internal to one's heart-mind, rather than the trivial work of the investigation of things. His notion of the heart-mind is not one defined by emotional disposition, but rather the heart-mind of the ancient sages. Through the notion of "heart-mind is Principle," he sought to make manifest an internal but also objective order. Internal, because this method rejects the external order, demanding that people scrutinize their own inner hearts; objective, because this method suggests that to follow the inner heart necessarily means a transcending of the self and a subsequent discovery of a mode of vision, a perspective, in which heart-mind and Principle are united.

Here, what is most important is not an essential differentiation of heart-mind and Nature, but rather the differentiation between heart-mind understood as a category of expression related more thoroughly to interiority and Nature understood as a category of expression related more thoroughly to objectivity. This differentiation implies an opposition between a unitary notion of heart-mind and a dualistic understanding of Principle and *qi*. This language of internalization presupposes an internal path through which Heavenly Principle can be reached, and as such no longer has to exhibit an epistemological practice that rests within the oppositional relations between Principle / *qi* and heart-mind / things. In the "Note Regarding Education in Wuling District" (*Wuling xian xueji*), Lu Xiangshan interprets "investigating things and extending knowledge" in the following way:

> What is called "investigating things and extending knowledge" means investigating *this* thing, which means extending one's knowledge about this one particular thing. In attending to all things one makes manifest one's illustrious virtue under Heaven. The thorough inquiry regarding Principle spoken of in the *Book of Changes* means thoroughly understanding the Principle inherent within *this* heart-mind, and in this way understanding fully the inherent, pure goodness of the inner nature gifted to humans by the Heavenly cosmos. Mencius's [notion of] expressing the heart-mind to its fullest means to express *this* heart-mind, to experience the "inherent heart-mind" that one possesses, giving it full play toward its greatest possible limit. In this way one can know the inherent Nature of people and the design of the Heavenly cosmos.[61]

"This thing" means this heart-mind and this Principle, that is to say cardinal human relations and innate moral conscience (*liang zhi*). As such, "knowledge of this thing" and "the extension of this knowledge" take as their precondition that "heart-mind is Principle." That the "investigation of things and the extension of knowledge" requires a direct and genuine heart-mind is because knowledge is understood as "*this* knowledge," things are understood as "*this* thing"; neither of them is exterior to human moral practice. Lu Xiangshan's notion of "this thing" eliminates the exteriorized, objective dimension of "all things and all matters" (*shishi wuwu*) that is embodied in Zhu Xi's notion of "things." It also eliminates the binary opposition between inner and outer that can easily be generated from the categories of heart-mind/things. When the "investigation of things and the extension of knowledge" transforms itself into "this thing," this proposition unifies cognition and inner reflection, two becoming one. Taking this as a precondition, the endless duplication of variegations of learning until they become hopelessly fragmented becomes unnecessary.

Lu Xiangshan takes the investigation of things and interprets it as being the investigation of the heart-mind, rejecting the externalized dimensions of the extension of knowledge. However, another dimension of his project is precisely to emphasize the intermediary procedures of the social order such as ritual ceremonies and specific institutions. Ceremonies and institutions are the intermediary forms that practice takes as it develops. Though Lu takes "the extension of heart-mind" to be the only mode through which one can arrive at Heavenly Principle, within the context of moral practice he also emphasizes greatly the importance of ceremonies marking coming of age, marriage, burial, and ancestor worship; protocols surrounding rites; and the political and educational systems. In comparison to the cognitive practice developed by the Cheng brothers and Zhu Xi in relation to Principle and *qi*, Lu's method is much closer to that of shamanistic tradition. The notion that "heart-mind is Principle" entails including the myriad things of the universe within the category of the heart-mind, and taking the vision of order imbedded within the category of the heart-mind as a means of suturing the division between values and materiality generated out of the divergence of the systems of rites and music. As such, what is made manifest through ceremonies and social systems is a structure of practice, an intermediary that unifies on an internal level the heart-mind with the structures of the life-world, an effort similar to that of Confucius's when he sought to use the notion of benevolence to interpret rites, unifying subjective experience with the order of rites. In emphasizing intermediary elements such as ceremonies and protocols regarding rites, Lu's learning came to resemble European religion's own reliance on ceremonial conduct; however, it differed in that the ceremonial nature of religion looked down upon the secular world, relegating the meaning and value of life to God or an entity that was above everyday life. For Lu, ceremonies, systems, order, and the practice of self-cultivation were themselves parts of real life, an internal element of domestic life and ceremonial protocols, a means of returning to a natural moral path that was within us, a gateway that would enable a return to the Will of Heaven, the Mandate of Heaven, and Heavenly Principle. Within the world of Confucianism, the division between the sagely and the secular was unnecessary, which can be summed up by the notions of "the sagely for the secular" or "the secular for the sagely." Within this discourse, the concept of "fully expressing the heart-mind" was not the same as the European notion of religious belief. Here, what was crucial was that actually existing institutions—for example, that of the civil service examination—had already become external norms that existed in tension with internal order, that is to say the natural order, and that a barrier had already become erected between the "heart-mind" (along with the Heavenly Principle presupposed by it) and ceremonies, protocols of rites, and politics and education. As such, the necessary path that the unification of heart-mind with things had to follow was the reconstruction of ceremonies, the protocols of rites, and politics and learning in accordance with the universal spirit of Heavenly Principle.

As such, what the tension or conflict that existed between the category of heart-mind and the externalized system truly entailed was the rift between an internalized notion of ceremonial protocols, the laws of rites, and social system and the actual existing version of such things, which represented a material reality that had become severed from values, spirit, or an internalized order. If one says that Zhu Xi's "investigating things and extending knowledge" emphasized the observation of the exterior world, then one can say that Lu put a greater degree of emphasis on ceremonial norms for living that existed outside of the system of state laws and regulations. In Lu's world, "behavior" that originally emanated from heart-mind was not simply purely internal, for it existed within a given system of ethical human relations; it was a practice in which the heart-mind and things were unified. However, this set of ethical human relations was not the equivalent to the system of rites and music established within the state structure of centralized administration (*junxian zhi*). Within the ethical human relations that Lu articulated, the division between the external and the internal was meaningless; an internalized language did not produce a kind of internalized moral theory. Lu's notion of the "heart-mind" cannot be understood in simplified terms as indicating "internality," and the ceremonies and institutions that he discussed can also not be simplified as representing mere "externality"—after the fall of the Way of Zhou, it was necessary to go through a practice of "rectifying Principle" and "rectifying learning" in order to take the ceremonies, laws of rites, and institutions that resided internally in the "heart-mind" and extend them into everyday life. As such, Lu's learning of the heart-mind presupposed an opposition between two different conceptions of the institutions of rites and protocols: the formalized institution of rites and music and the institution of rites and music embodying values from the system of enfeoffment. In this sense, Lu's "heart-mind" was not a rejection of the institution of rites and music and its related method of evaluation; his doctrine of practice contained within it an understanding of the unified relations that should exist between "the true heart-mind" and the norms of rites and ceremonies. In terms of its elimination of the division between inner and outer, his doctrine of practice was closer to pre-Qin-dynasty Confucianism's methods of moral evaluation. However, it differed in that the latter did not use the rhetoric of "heart-mind" as a dominant category to replace the notion of rites and music, which themselves were understood in pre-Qin Confucianism as capable of manifesting the Will of Heaven.

Lu Xiangshan's teachings have been seen as the origin and harbinger of the School of Mind of the Ming dynasty. The catchphrases "Lu-Wang Learning of the Mind" and "Lu-Wang Neo-Confucianism" (*Lu-Wang xinxue*), which directly associate Lu Xiangshan with Wang Yangming, are well-known examples of this consensus. However, the notion of "origin" or "harbinger" cannot explain everything, and a more comprehensive understanding of the development of Wang Yangming's learning requires a different genealogy. Wang Shouren (courtesy name Bo'an, also known as Yangming, hailing from Yuyao in Zhejiang Province, 1471–1529) upheld Lu's notion that "heart-mind is Principle"; however, he had a more complicated understanding of such a concept.

From the time of the Yuan dynasty until that of the Ming, Zhu Xi's teachings came to occupy a position of orthodoxy within the civil service examinations. While many different themes of Ming-dynasty "heart-mind" learning can be traced back to Lu's elucidations regarding the notion of heart-mind itself, the rise of this current of thought is deeply related to the movement that Ming-dynasty literati launched to critique Zhu Xi's learning, which had come to occupy an orthodox place within the civil service examination system. Wang Yangming's teachings were developed in opposition to Zhu Xi's teachings; however, the relations between these two schools of thought cannot simply be summarized through the use of such negative concepts as critique and resistance. There was an internal dialogue that existed between Wang Yangming's emphasis on "heart-mind" and Zhu Xi's theory of "the investigation of things and extension of knowledge": they each presupposed the universally benevolent order of Heavenly Principle, and they each concerned themselves with the basic question of whether one could come to obtain knowledge of Heavenly Principle. Where they differed was regarding the means and methods that were to be employed to realize this goal.

The famed moment of realization at Longchang emerged from Wang Yangming's new understanding of the investigation of things.[62] He suddenly realized that all one has to do is to take the word "things" from the notion of "the investigation of things" and understand it as the things within the heart-mind, and all difficulties were resolved. Within his "Reply to Gu Dongqiao" found in *Instructions for Practical Living,* we find this famous passage:

> What the extension of knowledge and investigation of things means is to discover within all affairs and things my innate moral knowledge and extend it to its greatest possible extent. The innate moral knowledge found in my heart-mind is Heavenly Principle. When the Heavenly Principle that is my innate moral knowledge is extended through all things and affairs, it means all things and affairs obtain their principle. As such, the "extension of knowledge" [spoken of in *The Great Learning*] is the extension of innate moral knowledge, or conscience. The "investigation of things" [spoken of in the *Great Learning*] means that things and affairs each obtain their principle. In this way the heart-mind and Principle are unified.

The extension of knowledge and the investigation of things is not a process of "utilizing my heart-mind to seek Principle in the myriad of things and affairs, with 'heart-mind' and 'Principle' being understood differentially, as two" (that is to say, recognizing things and affairs).[63] Rather, it is taking "the innate moral knowledge in my heart" and extending it outward toward the myriad of things and affairs. Here, Wang Yangming's notion of heart-mind moves from being "the heart-mind of people" to being "my heart-mind." Compared with Lu's notion of the ancient heart-mind of the sages, this notion of heart-mind emphasizes individual experience and subjectivity. Knowledge means innate moral knowledge, while "obtaining their principle" is making objective things conform not to their own specific, individualized laws, but rather to "the innate moral knowledge of Heavenly Principle." In this sense, the investigation of things is a moral practice designed to dispel evil and promote benevolence, and is not a means of coming close to exterior things through intuitive cognitive operations; for the Heavenly Principle of innate moral knowledge is not exterior to itself, it is conscience itself. The notion of the "innate moral knowledge of my heart-mind" emphasizes the close relations that exist between intuitive moral knowledge and individual practice; however, this relation does not suggest that intuitive moral knowledge and its extension is a practice outside of the realm of the social—in Wang Yangming's discourse, one cannot find the notion of the individual as an isolated atom. People are always enmeshed within relations, and themselves are relations, and as such, people can utilize their intuitive moral knowledge to construct an internal relation with the world.

Precisely because of this, the notion of "extending intuitive moral knowledge" becomes the source of the notion of "statecraft." Wang Yangming says: "The 'knowledge' of 'knowing Heaven' is like the 'knowledge' of 'knowing the prefectures' and 'knowing the counties.' To know a prefecture is to take all the affairs of that prefecture as one's own affairs, to know a county is to take all the affairs of that county as one's own affairs, it is to become one with Heaven."[64] If the "knowledge" of "knowing Heaven" is equivalent to the "knowledge" of "knowing prefectures" and "knowing counties," then heart-mind or intuitive moral knowledge cannot be understood as something internal. If the rejection of norms, values, or measures that are exterior to the space of everyday practice produces an impetus to positively affirm the practice of everyday life and its values, then, in order to challenge a sense of sagely authority that stands outside of norms and measures, everyday practice must be imbued with sageliness itself—everyday life becomes the sole space in which Heavenly Principle, this highest of all orders, becomes manifest. Here, dedication to a specific practice cannot be equated with a mere dedication to reaching a single individual goal, it is in fact just the opposite: what is demanded here is that a specific practice be carried out in accordance with the universal spirit of Heavenly Principle. One utilizes practice to reach a state of harmony with the order of the universe, an order that is embodied in the notion of Heavenly Principle.

Starting from the logic imbedded in School of Mind, Wang Yangming redefined the meaning of "statecraft." This is already different from Lu's understanding of the practice of rites and music, which he interprets in relation to the ceremonies of the Confucian clan system. With Lu, there is a wide chasm that exists between clan protocols and the political system, and it is from within this chasm that we discover the oppositions that leave such a profound imprint upon the intellectual world of Song Confucianism, including those between enfeoffment and centralized administration, between political institutions and rites / music. However, Wang Yangming extends the notion of "heart-mind" from Lu and Shao Yong's "innate heart-mind" (*ben xin*) toward the notion of "my heart-mind" (*wu xin*) while at the same time taking the concept of "statecraft" and linking it closely to bureaucratic responsibility within the system of centralized administration, which indicates how Wang Yangming already reconstructed the internal relations between individual and systemic practice. The monistic theory of the heart-mind offered by Lu took as its precondition the unity of the heart-mind with the practices of rites and music that existed outside of the system of centralized administration, while the monistic theory of heart-mind proposed by Wang Yangming took the system of centralized administration to be the institutional basis of practice itself—rites and music were already absorbed within the category of centralized administration.

Propelled by such logic, within Wang Yangming's thought we find the concept of the "things" of everyday life being placed within a series of conceptual chains, themselves forming a pathway for the manifestation, practice, and understanding of Heavenly Principle. Wang Yangming emphasized the need to steel oneself in the realm of human affairs, and he opposed efforts to extend knowledge by simply reading books to seek Principle. Indeed, he went further and rejected the procedures of the investigation of things as a cognitive method. As he put it:

> If you desire to extend your innate moral knowledge, is this not to speak vague and impractical talk, to pursue vigorously a truth that is empty and unreal? [No.] The extension of innate moral knowledge must be made manifest within the realm of affairs and things. As such, the extension of innate moral knowledge must be pursued through the investigation of things. Things mean various phenomena both big and small. When

> people begin to think there is a notion, an idea, that emerges, doing so in relation to a particular aspect, item, or phenomenon, the latter of which is what is called things. Investigation means rectification, to rectify that which is not in good order so as to return it to good order. To rectify that which is not good order is called dispelling evil. To return to good order is called promoting benevolence. This is called investigation.[65]

To train oneself to "investigate" in order to "rectify," that is to say, to use the Heavenly Principle of intuitive moral knowledge to rectify things or use the universal spirit imbedded in Heavenly Principle in order to carry out specific practices ("to steel oneself in the realm of human affairs"): what this proposition negates are the cognitive relations established between mind-heart and things. Within Wang's exposition on "rectifying things," the concept of "things" itself undergoes a critical transformation: understood as "affairs," the concept represents human activity; understood as "things," the concept is the place of meaning, or the place where meaning is made manifest, and as such, to "rectify things" means also to "rectify ideas." A basic characteristic of "affairs" is to imbricate the inner and the outer within a single relation, and as such, within the concept of "affairs," there is no way of understanding the division between the inner and outer.

If extending knowledge is the extension of a knowledge of my innate moral goodness toward all things and affairs, then, extending knowledge means carrying out specific practices in accordance with the universal spirit of Heavenly Will; if there are relations of direct interconnection between things and affairs and between heart-mind and meaning, then a binarial mode of dividing affairs from things and heart-mind from meaning appears as far too inflexible. Within the vision offered by the learning of heart-mind, "affairs" is not an objective category, one that can be understood via cognitive operations. Rather it is the extension of the activities of the subject. However, these activities are not random, but rather are related to institutional practices, and they can manifest Heavenly Principle. As such, Wang Yangming places "affairs" and "meaning" in close relation to one another:

> For meaning to be utilized, it must have its things, and things are affairs. If meaning is used in affairs regarding family, then affairs regarding family are one thing; if meaning is used in the governance of the people, then

> governance is one thing; if meaning is utilized in the reading of books, then the reading of books is one thing; if meaning is utilized in litigating a legal case, the litigation is a thing; there is not a single utilization of meaning that is not related to things. If there is meaning there are things. If there is no meaning then there are no things. Are things not the utilization of meaning?[66]

To take "things" and define them as "affairs" is to speak from the perspective of the moral practice of the subject; yet the "meaning" that is closely related to "affairs" is not equivalent to individual will, for "meaning" has an internal connection to the general will and order imbedded in the notion of "returning to rectitude" or "for benevolence." As such, the internal relations between the categories of meaning, things, and affairs produce an even more basic presupposition, that is, that the order of the world is constructed through the encompassing benevolence of Principle. As such, the notion that "all things and affairs obtain their principle" means that every singular thing one does must accord with the rectified Principle of "things," and that it is not necessary to pursue the dogmas of the classics in order to obtain moral cultivation. It is also to say that things and affairs are things and affairs because they are the manifestations of Heavenly Will, which is an order of supreme benevolence. The teachings of Zhu Xi and Wang Yangming both understood Heavenly Principle as an order of supreme benevolence. However, when Wang Yangming takes out the cognitive operations imbedded within Zhu Xi's teachings, which took as their goal a merging with Heavenly Principle as one, the importance of things and affairs in themselves lessens the teleological power of Heavenly Principle. The notion of "steeling oneself in the realm of human affairs" means focusing on what is immediately present, and this notion of immediacy takes as its precondition "things" within the system of rites and music. Mou Zongsan repeatedly argued that Wang Yangming's understanding of "things" transcended the notion of "affairs," and that Wang not only discussed "things" from the perspective of "the realm where meaning resides," but also discussed "things" from the perspective of our "sensory reaction to enlightened realization," and as such, Wang recognized that "things" had an existence-in-themselves.[67] In this sense, Wang Yangming's concept of "things" included two levels of meaning: "activity as things" (*xingwei wu*) and "the things of knowledge" (*zhishi wu*). However, looking at the passage quoted above, the "investigation of things" of the learning of heart-mind took as its core the notion of "carrying out in practice" and what it sought to destroy was precisely the binary method of separating the inner from the outer, the subjective from the objective. If one wants to continue to use the concept of "the things of knowledge" to define Yang Wangming's notion of things, then one must redefine knowledge itself. The method of dividing "activity as things" and "the things of knowledge" in a dualistic manner must be carefully defined.

Wang Yangming's discourse on "things" linked closely together the body, the heart-mind, meaning, and knowing; what he emphasized was that "things" and the body, heart-mind, meaning, and knowing were part of a comprehensive whole:

> The gentleman said: "You only must know that body, heart-mind, meaning, knowledge, and things are all one and the same." Jiuchuan asked in confusion: "Things are outside of us, how can they be the same as the body, heart-mind, meaning, and knowledge?" The gentleman said: "Ears, eyes, the mouth, the nose, and four limbs, this is the body; if your heart-mind is not at peace can you listen, hear, speak, and move? If the heart-mind seeks to see, listen, speak, and move, one cannot do so without ears, eyes, mouth, nose, and four limbs. As such, to be without heart-mind is to be without body, and to be without body is to be without heart-mind. However, when we speak of the area that can be filled up, we call it the body; when we speak of the area that governs, we call it the heart-mind; when we speak of the movement of heart-mind we call it meaning; when we speak of the brightness of meaning we call this knowledge; when we speak about what meaning relates to we call it things, this is all one. Meaning is not empty, it must have corresponding things and affairs; as such, when we seek sincerity of meaning, we in turn investigate the meaning manifested in a particular affair, dispelling human desire and returning to the realm of Heavenly Principle, and as such, our intuitive moral knowledge is manifested within this affair and extended without obstacle. This is the practice of sincerity.[68]

"Things" are first interpreted as "what meaning relates to"; that is to say, things are not the myriad of things under Heaven, but rather are the "things" of moral practice, and as such, things can never be discussed in a manner that disconnects them from the impetus behind moral practice and the process of moral practice itself. If "intuitive moral knowledge" is not reliant upon exterior things, and is not dependent on the words of sages or the habits of everyday life, then what is dispelled is the sense of actuality that defines "things" (in the sense of exterior objects, affairs, or moral knowledge). The concept of "intuitive moral knowledge" includes a rejection of the established order as well as established protocols of knowledge, and as such, its emphasis on immediacy has the effect of producing a certain liberation of thought.

The dispelling of the sense of actuality that defines things is done in order to place benevolence, which is understood as a grounding heart-mind, at the center of specific forms of practice, such as those involving familial relations, governance, book learning, litigation, and so forth. However, this is not to say that familial relations, governance, book learning, litigation, and so forth become the goals of practice. In this sense, though, the notion of "intuitive moral knowledge" rejects the binary division of things and Principle, and the process of the investigation of things derived from this division. It also opposes placing the specific natures of various things over and above the order represented by the concept of "Principle." Wang Yangming's working out, within the framework of a singular entity, the relations between body, heart-mind, meaning, knowledge, and things was done in order to overcome this dual error in Zhu Xi's thought. The concepts of "all things being one body" and the "unity of heart-mind and Principle" presupposed a specific method for classifying "affairs" and the emergence of related moral precepts. Thus the notion of "steeling oneself in the realm of affairs" presupposed a particular order. Wang Yangming's claim that "the 'knowledge' of Heaven is the same as the 'knowledge of prefectures' and the 'knowledge of counties,'" aside from emphasizing the fact that knowledge of the affairs of prefectures and counties is "all your own affairs" (that is to say, Principle resides within these affairs), also suggested that Heaven works through practices associated with specific, differentiated "affairs," and as such, the institutions of governance and bureaucratic rankings associated with "knowing prefectures" and "knowing counties" are included within the realm of moral practice itself.[69] Wang Yangming admired a social system in which structure and application are equally emphasized, and where learning and cultivation are integrated.

However, in terms of his understanding of society, he is not only quite distant from the notions of rites and music offered by Confucius and Mencius; he is also quite distant from the suspicions that Song Confucians had regarding the system of centralized administration.

Once there existed a division between things and essential moral precepts, at that point the development of scholarly methods and mechanisms became an absolute necessity. In this sense, the difference between Wang Yangming and Zhu Xi did not lie in whether or not they recognized knowledge ("learning" or *xue*), but rather in how they understood knowledge. In discussing the teachings of the sages, Wang Yangming summarized their overall meaning as "overcoming one's selfishness, dispelling one's ignorance, and recovering the unity of one's heart-mind with one's body." However, he did not reject the classification of specific "things" and the development of moral precepts:

> The essential point of the *Book of Documents* (*Shangshu*) is to introduce the teachings of the ancient rulers Yao, Shun, and Yu, particularly the notion that "human beings have a minute and singular heart-mind path (*dao xin*), through which they can follow the Confucian path of the Middle Way." In terms of its detailed manifestation, one finds it in Yao's commandment of Qi to become Minister of Education, where Qi outlined the five cardinal relations: "intimacy between fathers and sons, righteousness between monarch and ministers, differentiations between husband and wife, differentiated order between the elderly and the young, trust between friends." During the time of Yao and Shun and the Three Dynasties, teaching took only these principles at its core, and scholars studied only such precepts as learning. At that time, there were no discordant ideas between people, nor were there discordant customs promoted by different schools of thought. Those who could carry out these ideals naturally could be called sages, those who could carry them out after encouragement could be called virtuous, while those who betrayed them could be called unvirtuous, even if they were as brilliant as Dan Zhu.[70] If one descends among the village gates, wells, and fields, among the common peasants, workers, traders, and merchants, there is not a single one of them that does not have this learning, as they hope to further realize moral behavior.[71]

Wang Yangming here transitions from moral classification toward the social division of labor, emphasizing that every division of labor in society possesses within itself "learning." In this sense, moral practices do not need to take a form that is abstract or overtly specialized, for humanity's social activities and their subsequent division into discrete forms of labor encompass a kind of internally transcendent moral quality. Regardless of what occupation or status a person has, everyone can become a sage by "steeling oneself in the realm of human affairs": that is, by becoming moral. This logic presupposes, within the realm of the social differentiation of labor, an egalitarianism that takes as its starting point the goal of "realizing moral behavior as duty," which becomes an ethic enacted within everyday practice under the conditions of social differentiation. Wang Yangming places moral goals into a form of practice that is marked by the social differentiation of labor, and in doing so offers a moral basis for the conduct that occurs within different occupations—of course, what he is emphasizing is not a question of occupational ethics, but rather the notion of "knowledge and action being united" and the moralization of everyday life itself. Wang Yangming wrote: "Studying, questioning, thinking, doing, acting, as these are all a form of learning, there is no learning without doing."[72] A methodology of knowledge is unified with social practice as process, and in this way a theory of practice can be understood as a theory of knowledge.

Wang Yangming's model for his ideal society was a school that operated as if it were a human organism, where individuals according to their talents and bearing divided labor cooperatively, and where within each individual's specific practices one could realize a return to the ideal of a coherent unity. His goal in imagining such a model was to realize a common morality for All-under-Heaven, taking as the foundation for his thought the classification of specific affairs, with his pathway for bringing about his moral ideal being the unity of knowledge and action. In this sense, this school is a system by which labor is divided according to a universal method of division; it recognizes that individual talents vary in strength, but it refuses to recognize the distinctiveness of specific customs and habits, and it refuses to recognize different standards of good and evil that have emerged out of different historical conditions, for all differences in function are ultimately subordinated to a common organism. In this sense, Wang Yangming looks upon the goal of "learning" as the overcoming of historical, temporal, and cultural particularity in order to return to a common morality under Heaven. As he puts it:

> Within the school, the principal matter [to attend to] is the realization of one's morality, while differences in ability will exist, and there will be those who excel in rites and music, those who excel in the realm of politics, those who excel in the realm of education, and those who excel in questions of land, water, and agriculture. Because students will realize their moral natures, they will be able to more precisely richen their abilities inside the space of the school. When they utilize morality in their occupations, this will enable them to work for a lifetime in these occupations, and will not change occupations on a whim. Those whose utilize people [i.e., the emperor or officials] know that all people have the capacity to understand and give full play to their innate moral goodness, and that this can be used to make the realm peaceful for the common people. [When it comes to the utilization of people in specific occupations and roles], one should take talent as the sole measure, rather than looking at social status or wealth as the measure of what is good and bad, important and not. As for those who serve [i.e., ministers and subordinates], this too is a question of understanding and giving full play to their innate moral goodness, and they too know that this is done in order to make the realm peaceful for the common people. If one gets the opportunity to conduct a job that is exactly in accordance with one's abilities, even if one's entire life one is dealing with arduous matters, one will not feel tired, and will deal with even trivial things with a peacefulness of heart, and will not think one is lesser. At this moment, All-under-Heaven are calm and content, as they all look at themselves as one family. According to their talents, they are at ease in their roles as peasant, worker, trader, merchant, as each works diligently, assisting one another, helping nurture one another, and none of them possess a heart-mind that yearns with expectation or envy for something greater beyond themselves.

As such, the Learning of the Mind is pure and bright, realizing a moral benevolence that takes the myriad of things as a singular body. Because of this, [the subject of the Learning of the Mind] has a spirit that is open and flowing [with all things], its will interconnected [with all things], and

> there is no division between self and others, between objects and the self. For example in an individual person's body their eyes see, their ears hear, their hands hold, their feet move, all contributing toward the capacity of the body . . . the learning of the sageful person is in this way supremely clear and simple.[73]

The organizational methods and the cooperative division of labor of Wang Yangming's own "school" are today impossible to know; however, what can be said with certainty is that his imaginative plan for his school was imbued with a vision of society defined by self-governance, and was in complete conformity with the direction his practice took regarding the development of regulations and rules for local village administration. As such, from his vision for local village administration we can imaginatively extrapolate something of his vision for his school. In his famous work, "Nangan Community Compact," Wang Yangming posited that benevolence or wickedness within the customs of the people was due to accumulated customs and habits. The ignorance of village people was completely a result of the fact "that our form of governance had not followed the Way, and education has been improper." As such, he discussed the goals of establishing protocols for local village self-governance and for the coordination of village people in the following way: "mutual aid in sickness and death, mutual support in times of disaster, mutual exhortation toward benevolence, mutual admonishment against wickedness, the ending of conflict and the ceasing of litigation, the teaching of trust and harmony, and the diligent cultivation of an inherently good people, collectively producing customs grounded in benevolence and honesty."[74] Though local village governance sought to produce "customs grounded in benevolence and honesty" as its goal, yet its actual implementation required certain relations of order, responsibility, and power. For example a local chief was selected collectively, and village people had to attend meetings, where the chief would coordinate with the people of the locality in order to solve various local struggles and lawsuits among the people, with the local chief paying attention to the public will, and making known to the public who the morally false people among them were, and so forth. Huang Zongxi (1610–1695) was deeply influenced by Wang Yangming, and in his work *Waiting for the Dawn: A Plan for the Prince* we can find a similar sense of universal order. Within this order, ethical, political, and economic relations can be looked upon as the direct manifestation of Heavenly Principle within specific things and their relations. This was one of the grounding tenets of Confucian political discourse, which took the order of the universe, political relations, and ethical conduct and unified them within a universal framework, and this was precisely the manner in which Wang Yangming placed heart-mind, things, knowledge, actions, and institutions in interrelation with one another. If we take Wang Yangming's notion of heart-mind as well as his notion of knowledge, and link them with those elements that had institutional dimensions, such as his notion of local village governance, schools, "knowing prefectures and counties," and so forth, can we say that the relations between moral practice and institutions have appeared, however faintly, within the monistic framework of the heart-mind? Can we anticipate that this interconnection between Nature, heart-mind, and the institutions of rites and music, which had imbedded within itself a unified relationship between action and knowledge, would once again generate a scholarly movement toward the study of the classics grounded in the textual study of ancient systems?

V. Nothing, Something, and Statecraft

Among the followers of Wang Yangming, there were a multitude of perspectives regarding the concept of the investigation of things and the extension of knowledge. But regardless of whether scholars were on the left or right, the elimination of the sense of facticity inhering to "things" was a relatively recent development. The sense of reality inhering to "things" not only refers to the sense of reality of the objective world, but also refers to the authority of the various norms present in the classics. As such, this rejection of a sense of reality can also be understood as a rejection of a sense of exteriority, that is to say, a rejection of any mediating element that exists within moral practice and the process of cognition. If human behavior relies solely on an intuitive judgment of correct Principle at a given time and place, then the authority of exteriorized norms (including the inherited system of kinship, the dogmas of the classics) will come under suspicion. Nie Bao's (courtesy name Wenwei) notion of "returning to quiescence" (*gui ji*), Liu Wenmin's (courtesy name Yichong) notion of "taking tranquil emptiness as one's aim" (*yi xu wei zong*), Luo Hongxian's (courtesy name Dafu, 1504–1564) notion of "restraint and conservation" (*shou she bao ju*), Liu Bangcai's (courtesy name Jun Liang) notion of "understanding Nature and cultivating life" (*wu xing xiu ming*)—all such concepts express contempt for exteriorized knowledge, the myriad appearances of things, and the actively moving heart-mind, believing that inherent Nature is undeveloped Principle, and further advocating the centrality of silence and the absence of desire as an overarching aim, seeking to organize learning around the notion of "an intuitive [ontological] stillness" (*weifa yi ji*, that is, "utilizing an intuitive stillness to grasp phenomenological unfolding").

Within the context of critiquing the orthodoxy of Zhu Xi's learning, they emphasized that the originary heart-mind is precisely an intuitive moral sense. In doing so, they not only rejected the intellectual orientation that was internal to the School of Principle, but also opposed a theory of practice (*gongfu lilun*) grounded in the notion of being "tempered in the realm of worldly affairs." For example, Nie Bao said:

> Today you claim that "'investigating things' means extending your knowledge within the various things big and small that we can see every day, and in this way you can at any time and anywhere give play to your innate moral conscience, and all can flow completely in things, without any errors [i.e., without any overstepping of the mark]." If one applies this state of mind to affairs of governance, with all under the auspices of human artifice, where all day long one is in oppositional relations with things, can one avoid the possibility of things being yoked under your own control, forcing them to follow in submission?[75]

According to Nie Bao, intuitive moral sense is quiescent in its original state, and as such, it is only through a return to quiescence that one can perceive the tranquil body that has not yet emerged. Here, this doctrine of quietude includes two different dimensions: first, a "return to quiescence" means that "knowledge" and the exterior world are unrelated; and second, the precondition of taking a "return to quiescence" as a means of "extending intuitive moral sense" must be the notion that world order was constructed through a supreme benevolence.

Employing the notion of "return to quiescence" as a means of rejecting the exteriorized nature of cognition and moral practice is a move that bears deeply the traces of Buddhist thought, and in fact such a move can lead to rejecting the actually existing world itself. How then does one harmonize the contradiction between "returning to quiescence" and the affirmation of the existing world that is inherent to a Confucian position? Addressing such a question, Wang Ji (style name Longxi, 1498–1583), Chen Jiuchuan (courtesy name Wei Jun, 1494–1562), and Zou Shouyi (courtesy name Qianzhi, 1491–1562) all opposed Nie Bao's position, doing so via the invocation of three notions: the nonestrangement of the *Dao,* the fact that the *Dao* does not divide between action and stillness, and the unity of heart-mind and affairs. The positive result of this critique of the notion of the "return to quiescence" was that the affirmation of a life conforming to Heavenly Principle had to be sought within the space of everyday life. The majority of scholars working within the legacy left by Wang Yangming, with the exception of Luo Hongxian (courtesy name Dafu), criticized Nie Bao's position, and yet they all also rejected the notion that one could verify intuitive moral sense by resorting to operations of knowledge. As such, the division between Nie Bao and other followers of Wang Yangming was not grounded on the question of whether or not they recognized the reality of "things." Let us examine Wang Ji's explanation of the notion of investigating things and extending knowledge:

> The notion of the investigation of things within *The Great Learning* presents, through and through, a clear and real mode of practice [*gongfu*]; as such, it says, "Extend knowledge through the investigation of things." If, as you say, *The Great Learning* presents no notion of practice in association with the investigation of things, then *The Great Learning* becomes nothing but superfluous words, its teachers plagiarizers. If one takes the words of *The Great Learning* and seeks to understand them in relation to one's own heart-mind, then you will in reality have your answer. If one looks at matters this way, one too will understand Principle. For the inherent Nature of the subject is to serve as the ground upon which Principle coalesces. The heart-mind is the master which coalesces these many principles, with "meaning" being the expression of this mastery, and "knowledge" being the vehicle through which one realizes intuition, with "objects" corresponding to the consciousness of the subject and in doing so manifesting their utility. As such, it is said there is no principle under Heaven that is outside of inherent Nature: is it possible that there are things outside of inherent Nature?[76]

Wang Ji affirmed the notion of the investigation of things, grounding his position in Wang Yangming's notion of the "unity of body, mind-heart, meaning, knowing, and things." He interpreted "investigation" as investigating "the patterning of Nature" or "Heavenly norms," infusing his discourse with Daoist sensibilities, invoking Laozi and Zhuangzi's submission to the Heavenly norms of Nature.[77] There was no principle under Heaven outside of inherent Nature; as such there were also no things outside of inherent Nature; in that there were no things outside of inherent Nature, there was no "investigation of things" that simply took knowledge to be an innate moral sense. "'Things' means to understand the traces of the interactions of things": as such, to seek innate moral knowledge through things was not the same thing as what is commonly referred to as cognition. The notion that "the noumenal *Dao* (*ben ti*) is practice (*gongfu*)" rejected a theory of the latter concept that stated one could reach the noumenal *Dao* via practices that lay outside of the realm of the noumenal itself.

Naturally, the linking of the notions of "no-desire" / "nothingness" with statecraft was, in actuality, accomplished by integrating the rejection of the exteriorized nature of "things" with the affirmation of the exterior world. In doing so, a form of logic was offered that respected interiority and the will of the subject. From the Qing dynasty onward, the notion of statecraft was even more closely linked with that of practical study, being often invoked alongside the notion of "extending utility" from the phrase "absorbing deeply essential ideas, using them to extend utility" to be found in the *Xici* section of the *Book of Changes* (*Yijing*).[78] In 1825, Wei Yuan began to edit his *Collected Writings on Qing Statecraft* (*Huangchao jingshi wenbian*), criticizing "the speculative emptiness of Principle" and "talking loftily about heart-mind and inherent Nature," instead placing local administration, the suffering of the people, border defense, state budgets, farming and sericulture, governmental affairs, and so forth, at the center of the study of statecraft. The extension of utility within the realm of statecraft from this point onward became a movement to sustain the traditions of the Donglin Faction and to oppose Wang Yangming's teachings and their adherents.[79] However, the notion of statecraft not only emerged before the Opium War (and as such, it does not follow that it was a response to Western aggression), in fact it was itself one of Confucianism's foundational topics. It was a notion developed by both Neo-Confucian scholars and those of the practical studies school,[80] and indeed was a major focus of learning for adherents of Wang Yangming. The position that places statecraft and the study of the kingly Way (particularly the work of Wang Yangming's students and adherents) in opposition to one another is in fact a judgment that was made by the Donglin Faction and its later adherents, a judgment that was itself grounded in their own particular historical context.

From the perspective of the study of the heart-mind, the notion of statecraft is essential to the differentiation between Confucianism and Buddhism. Lu Xiangshan in his "Letter to Wang Shunbo" (*Yu Wang Shunbo*) states:

> I once attempted to distinguish Confucianism and Buddhism by using two characters: "righteousness" (*yi*) and "interest" (*li*). In speaking of public and private, in fact what is being discussed is the distinction between righteousness and interest. Confucians understand human beings as being situated between Earth and Heaven, in possession of the *qi* that suffuses Heaven and Earth. [Within this schema] humans are seen as being more vigorously prescient than the myriad of things, more important than the myriad of things, standing alongside of Heaven and Earth in a structure that can be called a three-part ultimate (*san ji*). Heaven has the Heavenly Way, Earth has the Earthly Way, humans have the humanly way. If humans don't exert themselves toward the human way, then they are unworthy of standing alongside Heaven and Earth. Humans have five organs, with each of the five organs possessing its own functions. As such, there is right and wrong and loss and gain, as well as teaching and learning. This is why its forms of learning have been established via the notions of righteousness and the public. Buddhists understand the relations between human life and Heaven and Earth as possessing birth and death, the cycles of rebirth, and terrible vexations, thinking all of this to be incredibly bitter, and search out for a means of avoiding it . . . as such, they ask, "What kind of major events are birth and death?" . . . This is why Buddhism's forms of learning have been established via the notions of interest and the private. Only when one concerns oneself with righteousness (*yi*) and the public (*gong*) is one in the realm of statecraft (*jingshi*); when one only concerns oneself with the private (*si*), with interest (*li*), one is discussing how to transcend the confines of this world. Though Confucians also pursue [an ontological state defined by] the

> soundless, the orderless, the formless, and the immaterial, they all put prominent emphasis on statecraft. Though Buddhists spend their utmost energy in preparing for their limitless future, going about teaching the laws of Buddha, determined to save the multitude of people, their major point of emphasis is on transcending this world of suffering.[81]

Lu's learning takes heart-mind as representing the entirety of the universe, and as such, his method of learning is to excise the points of obscurity from the heart-mind in order to restore it to its noumenal self. Unconsciously, following a natural course, this heart-mind can respond to the limitless multiplicity of things. The notion of statecraft as a means of differentiating Buddhism and Confucianism takes as its precondition the fact that we have already entered this world, and within this context discusses the concept of "nothingness." Wang Ji looked upon his concept of the "Four Nothings" as being consistent with the notion of statecraft, and in doing so inherited to some degree Lu's spirit, explaining that the starting point of statecraft is the notion of "nothingness." The logical precondition of "the investigation of things" is the notion of "knowledge" as a realizable form of practice, with the error of "closing one's door and meditating" being the fact that this particular mode of seeking the Way departs from the practice of statecraft, and as such, it is like seeking Principle from reading books: the true meaning of investigating things and extending knowledge is lost.

Put differently, only in emphasizing knowledge's capacity to be implemented in practice, and rejecting a path of solitude that revels in quietude and despises action, can the possibility emerge to link the practice of extending knowledge with the goals of statecraft, unifying the practice of "reflecting upon the self" with the secular nature of human life, linking the vision of order inherent in the notion of Principle with the specific conditions of human affairs. Precisely because of this, a negation of the actuality of things is a negation of any mediating or exteriorizing element within the process of extending knowledge. Yet this negation also possesses within itself an exteriorizing tendency toward guiding secular life and its internal "quiescent body."

In this sense, the revival of the promotion of the concept of "statecraft" was still rooted in Wang Yangming's notion of the unity of the myriad of things, as well as the unity of knowledge and practice. Wang Ji said:

> If you say that the investigation of things is a skill, how then does one discuss giving full play to the extension of knowledge? If one claims that the investigation of things is not a skill, how then does one discuss conducting the investigation of things? Things are the actual happenings of the state under Heaven, beginning from the sensations of our intuitive moral conscience. The extension of knowledge happens in relation to the investigation of things, such as when one states the desire to extend intuitive moral conscience, it is discussed as being extended within the context of the affairs of the state under Heaven. . . .
>
> The learning of the sages concerned itself with statecraft, originally being closely connected to the world . . . if one revels in quietude and despises action, if one has already stopped engaging with the world, how then is one able to restore statecraft and govern the world?[82]

Generally speaking, the School of Mind emphasized the noumenal *Dao,* the notion of the grounding heart-mind, and ignored the movement of *qi,* lacking thoroughgoing historical reflection on the question of transformations of historical eras, changes in social conditions, and systemic questions. However, in making such a judgment one must at the very least put forth two supplementary points. First, the kind of antihistorical reflection offered by the School of Mind utilized such concepts as "grounding heart-mind" (*benxin*), "the heart-mind of young children" (*tongxin*), "the heart-mind of the newborn child" (*chixin*), "grounding structure" (*benti*), "this thing" (*ci wu*), and "emptiness" (*xuwu*) to resist structures of authority that utilized historical conventions and classical dogmas as the basis for their laws and regulations, and in doing so produced a pointed critique within a particular social context. In this sense, a mode of thought that is antihistorical possesses its own historicity. Second, what the rejection of exteriority (such as that offered by Wang Ji in his emphasis on nothingness) expresses is the reconstruction of the internal link between morality and behavior. It is not done in order to reject altogether any and every actually existing system and their related practices.[83] In this sense, the tendency to return to the original heart-mind, the heart-mind of children, Nature, and nothingness does not entail the rejection of any systemic practice. As such, on the one hand, from Wang Yangming's own learning to that of his followers (particularly Li Zhi, 1527–1602), the notion that the Six Classics were all historical documents was extended without interruption—that is to say, utilizing a historical perspective to relativize the classics, and in doing so construct a critique of the orthodoxy of Zhu Xi learning; on the other hand, categories such as the original heart-mind, the heart-mind of children, and Nature take the basis of morality and separate it from actually existing hierarchical relations, offering a theoretical precondition for the fields of emotion and desire. In emphasizing that the pursuit of the *Dao* must be grounded in a purely natural condition, this discourse separated early Confucian dogmas, the system of rites and protocols, laws, and politics from the loftiest of categories, such as the *Dao,* Nature, and Principle.

Regardless of whether it is Nie Bao's notion of the "return to quiescence," or Wang Ji's notions of "no desire," "Nature," or "noumenal *Dao* is practice" (*gongfu*)," all of these ideas within certain limits serve as a rejection of ethical relations that had become dogmatic and hierarchical. Such thinkers worked from different directions to demand the restoration of the unified relations that should exist between morality and reality. The notion of "statecraft" is precisely established in relation to the understanding such thinkers had of the relations between morality and reality. However, just what exactly is actual reality? Understandings of this concept are of course varied. For Nie Bao, reality is the "quiescent body," while for Wang Ji, reality is Nature. For the latter, there exists a close, internal relation between the practice of statecraft and the notion of the return to Nature. This is because here Nature is posited in opposition to the actually existing order, demanding that such an order return to its own Nature. There perspectives are not uniform; however, they both raise Nature, inherent heart-mind, intuitive moral conscience, and desire to the level of true reality, pitting them against the actually existing order. In this sense, the resuturing of the unified relations that should exit between moral evaluation and Nature is not a return to the mode of Confucian evaluation offered by Confucius, with its focus on the man of virtue (*junzi*). This is because the latter demands, in conformity to the system of rites, the direct unification of a person's behavior and their social identity, their position within the relations of rites and protocols, even the way they walk, eat, and the clothes that they wear. It would be better to say that the critical force of the scholarship of those who followed in the wake of Wang Yangming emerges precisely from its rejection of this line of thinking.

It is precisely in relation to this point that the teachings of the Taizhou schoolmaster Wang Gen (courtesy name Ruzhi, commonly known as Mister

Xinzhai, 1483–1541) exhibit their uniqueness. He sought to use the *Classic of Filial Piety,* the *Analects,* and *The Great Learning* as model texts, restoring the moral ideal of the Confucian man of virtue within the realm of practice. Within the world of his thought, "peaceful and orderly governance" was not the privileged power of the emperor, but rather the product of the moral cultivation of every single person. If one can say that the conception of statecraft that Wang Ji had was based on his notion of "nothing," then Wang Gen's notion of statecraft possessed as its precondition the notion of "something":

> Things have roots and extensions (*benmo*), and, as such, we first investigate things and only then come to understand their roots. To know these roots, this is the extension of knowledge to its absolute. To extend knowledge to its absolute is at the same time to understand the limits of that knowledge. In *The Great Learning,* the section that discusses "from the emperor" can be said to embody an understanding of this ultimate extension, providing an explanation regarding the meaning of the investigation of things and the extension of knowledge. [Seen within this context], the body [the subject] and the state under Heaven are one thing. Every thing grounded in a specific condition has roots and subsequent extensions. Investigation means taking a measure. When one takes the measure of the root and its subsequent expression, one comes to understand that if the root is chaotic, there can be no way that its subsequent expressions can be orderly. This is the meaning of the investigation of things. When one investigates things, one comes to understand the roots of learning; to understand the roots of learning is to extend knowledge to its ultimate point. As such, one can say, as *The Great Learning* does, that "From the emperor to the common people, all take cultivation as the primary task." Cultivation means to establish the foundation of learning; to establish the foundation of learning is to find stability and ground for the body [the subject].[84]

The myriad things in the world are in fact one thing, and as such, there are no differences between them. Though they are the same thing they differ in their roots and extensions, and as such, the general meaning of "the investigation of things" is found in differentiating the roots and extensions of things. Wang Gen took the body as the roots, and took the state under Heaven as the extension, and as such, the categories of roots and extensions in his thought rejected the ethical imperative to place the realm under Heaven in a primary position. For Wang Gen, what was critical for statecraft was moral self-cultivation, and the key to moral self-cultivation lay in self-reflection. Wang Gen's notion of "investigation of things" circumvented the step of cognition. Wang Gen understood "investigation" as the "investigation" of "patterns," and in this way, the investigation of things meant imbuing things with a certain pattern:

> *QUESTION:* "What is the meaning of the character *ge* [to investigate]?"
>
> *REPLY:* "To investigate (*ge*) is like the *ge* of *geshi* (pattern, norm, law), it refers to "taking the measure" as discussed in *The Great Learning.* If I understand myself to be a carpenter's square, [a specific phenomenon such as] the state under Heaven is the square that is designed [using such a tool]. When the subject "takes the measure," he can come to understand that the squares and carpenter's squares of the world are perhaps out of order. Thus one seeks to correct the "carpenter's square" in one's heart-mind, and will not seek learning in the larger [out-of-order] "square." If the carpenter's square within the heart-mind is rectified, then the square that is designed [using that tool] will be rectified, and that square can be truly become a *ge* [pattern, norm, law]; as such, we speak of things being rectified through the operations of the heart-mind (*wuge*). To investigate means to utilize the capacity to take the measure within our heart-mind, which is what we call *ge*, to respond to all the specific phenomena around me [above and below, behind and in front, left and right], which I encounter as objectified things (*wu*) . . . the investigation of things means to understand the root of learning, it is a learning that can make the subject settled and calm. When the life of the subject is settled, one can make the life of the family orderly; when the life of the subject is settled, one can make the country peaceful, bringing orderly government to it; when the life of the subject is settled one can make All-under-Heaven calm, bringing peace to all.[85]

Wang Gen understood behavior in accordance with the ancient systems as representing the path to self-cultivation, attempting to restore the unified relations that exist between action, identity, and the system of rites within the processes of moral evaluation and moral realization. In terms of moral evaluation, Wang Gen is closer to the Confucian form of the virtuous man (*junzi*); this is to say that he does not turn inherent Nature and heart-mind into abstractions. For him, the ancient ideal was invested in ancient laws and institutions; if one wants to restore the ancient ideal one must restore ancient laws and institutions. If on the one hand one used the concepts of Nature as well as the childish heart to negate the ancient laws and institutions, while on the other hand wanting to restore Confucian morality, then these were certainly at cross-purposes to one another.

As such, Wang Gen's thought rests finally in the realm of "the study of music," the world of rites and music. He used the *Classic of Rites* (*Li jing*) as a model in order to manufacture a hat of five virtues, long gowns, and a great belt. He set off for his journeys in ancient clothing, while sitting holding a notational tablet; he also modeled Confucius's carriage used for travelling to neighboring states, creating a carriage whose wheels were wrapped in cattail, garnering the attention of people passing by on the roadways.[86] Wang Gen did not take into consideration historical changes, coming from a salt-producing family background to publicly advocate for a return to the ancient system of Confucian rites, and in doing so making apparent the ironic relations that existed between Confucian morality and the actually existing world. Wang Gen refused to understand moral practice from the perspective of historical transformation and developments in the social system. Instead, he sought to understand in isolation the relations between the practice of moral self-cultivation and the ancient social system. In doing so, he went against ongoing efforts to reconstruct the order of rites via an understanding of moral practice as being imbedded in the changing social circumstances of the time.

The movement to revise Wang Yangming's teachings was not simply the result of discord over moral philosophy; it was also the product of a bitter political struggle. As it developed its own moral principles and reputation, the Donglin Faction looked upon the tail end of post-Wang Yangming scholarship in an extremely negative manner.[87] The left wing of the Wang Yangming-aligned scholars shared with the Donglin Faction an interest in statecraft, but the former's status was rather marginal (with some of these scholars being common urbanites), and they mainly used antipolitical means to express their politics. The latter group held a Confucian-gentry viewpoint, engaging directly in political struggle. As such, while these two groups both held statecraft as their goal, their sociopolitical orientations were different. The practical learning associated with the statecraft of the Donglin Faction emphasized the Confucian ethical code, moral integrity and righteousness, and the promotion of the investigation of things, seeking to return to Zhu Xi via Wang Yangming's teachings. The turning point in thought during the time of the Ming-Qing transition was concealed precisely here: first, the reconnection of "benevolence" to "righteousness, propriety, wisdom, and faithfulness," restoring the solemnity of the system of rites and music;[88] second, the restoration of the importance of knowledge based on what one has seen and heard, and the embodying of that knowledge in practice. In this way they opposed theoretically indulging in empty talk regarding moral conscience, returning to the well-trod path of the investigation of things.[89] As such, the reestablishment of the internal link between extending knowledge and the investigation of things became an unavoidable task:

> For those who speak now of intuitive moral conscience, when they outline the major points of the extension of knowledge, they no longer link them to the investigation of things, and as such, their teachings have the effect of being clever but utterly abstruse, [with their discussions] lingering in the realm of emotional cognition, rather than discussing the norms of nature ruled by Heavenly norms. They thus arrive somewhere very, very far away from the encompassing benevolence discussed in *The Great Learning*. When we talk about the meaning of the investigation of things, it is an extension toward the utmost benevolence, taking the utmost benevolence as our principal aim, rather than taking consciousness as our principal aim. As such, the sentence "the extension of knowledge through the investigation of things" found in *The Great Learning* provides us with a means distinguishing Confucianism from Buddhism.[90]

The return to quiescence, as well as emptiness, is not the nature ruled by Heavenly norms. Supreme benevolence resides in the practice of the investigation of things. Here, to reassert the actuality of things is indeed a transformative moment.

The divergences and transformations in opinion that scholars of the School of Mind had regarding the notions of the heart-mind / things and

Principle / *qi* were closely related to their political stances. In terms of the political system at the superstructural level, scholars associated with Wang Yangming advocated the reform and replenishment of the scholastic system—a breaking through of the restrictions imposed on learning by familial status and personal privilege—and emphasized the practice of statecraft and, in doing so, offered resources and talent for the renewal of a failed politics. In terms of their thinking regarding schools, they advocated restoring one aspect of the order of rites, and in this sense their position continued the critique of the civil service examination system launched by Song-dynasty Confucian scholars. In terms of the social system at the base of society, Yangming scholars emphasized the design and development of the Community Self-Defense (*baojia*) and Community Compact (*xiangyue*) systems. They believed that the social relations that existed around networks of kinship and village governance could not be implemented simply via the institutions of the central state. As such, they attempted to form a grassroots social system that took kinship, blood relations, geographic relations, and emotional ties as its key nodes of cohesion—all of which required the practice of Confucian ethics in order to be maintained.

The practice of heart-mind learning offered a moral basis for this kind of social system, as well as a method for carrying it out. As such, the notion of an intuitive moral conscience had to be implemented in specific practices around benevolence, righteousness, propriety, and wisdom. Within the left wing of the Wang Yangming school, the question of individual self-determination was articulated via the notions of returning to silence, Nature, and the childish heart, which were all seen as a part of moral practice. Their object of critique (and what they sought to avoid) was not simply the civil service examination and bureaucratic institutions, but also included the social system (and related moral practices) at the grass roots of society that took local Community Compact governance and clan relations as its core organizational components. Li Zhi (courtesy name Zhuowu, 1527–1602) advocated the notion of the childish heart, clearly separating the category of Nature from such notions as "regulations of the self" and "a system of morality and rites combined with governance of laws and punishments." For him, the investigation of things was the absence of things, and though the extension of knowledge created the absence of knowledge, he understood "no knowledge and no artifice as Confucius's teaching."[91] This rejection of moral philosophy was an affirmation of immanent nature (such as desire, emotion, etc.). The affirmation of desire is a kind of confirmation of immanence; that is to say, the nature that is within us is entirely proper, and as such, all dogmas of learning, systemic penalizations, and formalized conventions of kinship can be critiqued.

This argument uses the concept of desire to redefine Nature. The logic here is: if Nature is understood to be a kind of final source, submitting to it can be looked upon as submitting to an external rule or worshipping of external norm. This kind of logic can lead in two diametrically different directions: on one hand, raising desire up to being a kind of Nature that we should worship can perhaps lead to the destruction of all exterior norms, leading to a state in which we have no self-discipline whatsoever, indulging completely in our desires. In this way, submission to desire can become a compulsive force internal to our own bodies; on the other hand, the affirmation of desire in itself entails the creation of conditions by which desire can be realized, and as such, desire becomes the motive force for practical reflection over questions of finance, the military, the governance of foodways, taxation, and so forth. Seen from this perspective, an affirmation of immanent nature, desire, emotion, and everyday life becomes precisely the motive force for the study of statecraft.

However, when statecraft is interpreted in this fashion, the logic of the study of the heart-mind begins to break away from the category of Heavenly Principle. If Community Compact governance and the system of kinship offered the institutional preconditions for the moral practice associated with Wang Yangming's teachings (as well as its notion of Heavenly Principle), then the critique that post-Wang Yangming learning made of social and ethical relations at the grass roots of society necessitated a break from the mode of interconnected social ethics described above. In this sense, the origin of the crisis in the study of heart-mind lay in the rupture between the field of learning and its institutional basis; in terms internal to Confucianism as a system of knowledge, the origin of the crisis in the study of heart-mind lay in a sense of suspicion regarding the notion of Heavenly Principle presupposed by heart-mind learning, and the natural, interconnecting relations it was supposed to have to its particular model of ethics. As such, if one wanted to make the study of heart-mind return to its "proper path," one had to reestablish the internal connection that existed between heart-mind learning and institutional practice, and in doing so incorporate new ethical rules into the supremely benevolent order of Heavenly Principle that is presupposed by the School of Principle or the study of heart-mind. Here, the core question is not to make moral judgment yield to institutional judgment, but rather it is to rethink the reform and reconstitution of institutional judgment via a form of thought that places moral evaluation at its center, and in doing so make this a system that accords with morality, one that that is indelibly connected to the notion of order imbedded within the School of Principle. For Wang Yangming and his followers, the moral order is not a functionalist installation (or system); rather it is an order that accords with Heavenly Principle, and as such, it cannot be expounded on by resorting to the actually existing social system. This logic presupposes the arrival of a new theory of institutions and the end of the School of Mind.

VI. A New Theory of Institutions, and the End of the World of Things and the School of Principle

1. The Transformation in the School of Mind and the Emergence of a New Theory of Institutions

Reestablishing moral regulations and their corresponding institutional relations entailed establishing the central position of *qi* in this theory. After the emergence of the theory of a unitary *qi* (Zhang Zai), the theory of a binary relation between *qi* and Principle (Cheng-Zhu), and a theory of a unitary notion of heart-mind (Lu-Wang), there emerged a unitary theory of Principle and *qi*, one that sought to integrate all of the above tendencies. The key link in the transformation in Wang Yangming's learning was the reaffirmation of the tangibility of "things," and it was precisely this point that made the relations between Wang Yangming's learning and Zhu Xi's learning ambiguous. In reality, the reaffirmation of the tangibility of "things" was not only not the discovery of Qing learning; it was in fact not even the original idea of late-Ming teachings regarding *qi*. Indeed, one could almost say that at the same moment as Yangming learning was criticizing the orthodoxy of Zhu Xi's learning, the teachings on *qi* of Luo Qinshun (courtesy name Yunsheng, 1465–1547) and Wang Tingxiang (courtesy name Ziheng, 1476–1544) had already overturned the relations between *qi* and Principle posited by Zhu Xi's teachings, seeing *qi* as the root of existence. The critical force of Yangming learning lay in its negation of the tangibility of "things," joining Heavenly Principle and heart-mind directly together; in contrast, Luo and Wang insisted upon the tangibility and effectiveness of "things," seeking to provide a basis for "Principle" in objective terms, to the point of believing that the truthfulness or falseness of moral philosophy had to be proved on the basis of evidence collected from the classics, foretelling the critical transformation in Confucianism that would take place in the late Ming and early Qing (among Ming scholars Gu Yanwu particularly respected Luo).[92] They insisted upon the tangibility of "things" (and thus the objectivity of Heavenly Principle), believing that the notions posited by Wang Yangming of "training in investigation in order to rectify, training in things in order to develop thought" were baseless, for this kind of reasoning would make the discourse of *The Great Learning* tautological.

Liu Zongzhou (courtesy name Qidong, 1578–1645) formed the rearguard of late-Ming intellectual thought. He believed that between Heaven and Earth all was heart-mind, the Way, and *qi*, negating the notion that first there was Principle and then there was *qi*, affirming the notion that "*qi* was Principle," and affirming that Principle, *qi*, heart-mind, and Nature were uniform.[93] Operating under the presumption that Principle and *qi* were uniform, Liu replaced Wang Ji's notion of "something and nothing" with the notion of "the relations between roots and extensions, the fundamental and the secondary." Within the relationship between the fundamental and the secondary, statecraft was not the goal of moral exposition; rather it was the result of extending knowledge sincerely. Just like Wang Gen, within Liu's notion that "things have roots and extensions," the categories of *Tianxia*, state, family, the body, heart-mind, and meaning were all considered "things." Within these six categories, Liu emphasized that "meaning" was fundamental, while the others were secondary. Why was "meaning" fundamental? Within his discourse, "meaning" was not as described in *The Great Learning*, subordinate to heart-mind, but rather it was the principle of the universe itself, it was "where heart-mind resided" or the "ruler of heart-mind." If the heart-mind of people and the heart-mind of the Way were one heart-mind, if *qi* and Principle were of a singular nature, and if heart-mind, Nature, and practice were also unified, then was the "meaning" that acted as "the ruler of heart-mind" not itself the most fundamental of things? Taking meaning as essential did not negate outward-bearing practice, nor was it simply to say that, when it came to the question of practice, statecraft and sincerity were internally related, but rather it was to say that "meaning" was the grounding principle of the universe. During his middle years Liu Zhongzhou spoke of a learning grounded in "solitary circumspection," while in his later years he shifted and discussed "sincerity as essence." However, his teachings regarding circumspection in solitude, which asserted that "aside from solitude there is no other noumenal *Dao,* aside from circumspection there is no other practice," did not conflict fundamentally with his discourse on "sincerity."[94]

Within the framework of a unitary theory of Principle and *qi,* on the one hand investigating things and the extension of knowledge encompassed the practice of statecraft as directed toward the outside world, while on the other hand this sense of exteriority was not theorized as the mere recognition of exterior things. The learning of "solitary circumspection" returned to a practice of investigating things in which one was "tempered in the realm of worldly affairs." Why, in the process of "investigating the six things," could "sincerity" as a subjective activity of the heart-mind transform itself into the practice of statecraft?

In the first volume of *Liu Zongzhou's Teachings* (*Zi Liuzi xueyan*), heart-mind is explained in the following manner:

> On the basis of this singular heart-mind, one can naturally respond to specific circumstances, for example by using the carpenter's square to make things square, by using the compass to draw a circle, by using the horizontal wooden block to make [furniture] level, to use a rope to make things taut . . . these four can be developed into a Way for responding to the things under Heaven as encountered by the subject in the world. Because the heart-mind has these four vital capacities of flow and movement, we have the capacity for engagement and interaction with Heaven, we also have the capacity to wind and course our way through Earth. If one sees this from the perspective of endless flow and movement, we can call these [four capacities] the four *qi;* if one sees this from a perspective in which one is grounded in the world but does not lose a sense of [moral] direction, one can call this the four directions. Seen from the perspective of inexhaustible creation, innumerable types emerge; from turbid

> chaos to the establishment of civilization, there is a constancy that can be followed, what we can call the five constants [benevolence, righteousness, ritual, wisdom, and sincerity]; to constantly renovate and reform but to not betray these principles, we call this the three traditions [the historical laws and institutions of the Xia, Shang, and Zhou dynasties]; the world of human relations was well governed and paradigmatic texts were handed down, [which related to us] the five rituals, six forms of music, eight campaigns, and nine battles. To know of the flow of yin and yang one studies the *Book of Changes,* to know of political institutions one studies the *Book of Documents,* to know of the nature of emotion one studies the *Book of Odes,* to understand punishments and rewards one studies the *Spring and Autumn Annals,* to know of ceremony and propriety one studies the *Book of Rites,* to know when to engage and when to withdraw, one examines the writings of Huang-Lao Daoism. The unified heart-mind is dispersed into the myriad of things, with the myriad of things returning back to it.[95]

Here, Liu Zongzhou not only takes the category of "heart-mind" and expands it to become the myriad of things; he also returns the interconnected order of the myriad of things back into the category of "the Six Classics." In doing so, he not only responds to Wang Yangming's proposition that "the Six Classics are none other than the correct path of my heart-mind"; he also provides a foundation for practice that is grounded in the study of the classics.[96]

Huang Zongxi followed Liu Zongzhou, believing that "Suffused between Heaven and Earth is but one *qi*,"[97] demanding to return to the deciding role that "meaning" played, offering a basis for (as well as a restraining force in regard to) individual behavior as well as judgments relating to what was true and false. In his introduction to *Studies in Ming-Dynasty Confucianism* Huang wrote: "Suffused between Heaven and Earth is heart-mind, changing in ways unfathomable, there cannot but be a myriad of forms. Heart-mind is without a grounding structure (*benti*), what one's practice strives to arrive at is precisely the grounding structure of heart-mind. As such, he who seeks Principle is seeking precisely these myriad permutations of the heart-mind. He is not seeking the myriad permutations of things."[98]

The notions that "suffusing Heaven and Earth is heart-mind" and "suffusing Heaven and Earth is *qi*" seem to be oppositional, but in fact are mutually supportive and constitutive, because 1) they both take as their precondition a unitary mode of thought; and 2) the heart-mind of Liu Zongzhou and Huang Zongxi is not heart-mind of a singular self, but encompasses the entirety of all that is between Heaven and Earth, and as such, *qi* and heart-mind have no fundamental distinction between them. This is a revision of Wang Yangming's teachings rather than an outright rejection of them. Nor is it a simple return to Zhu Xi's teachings. It is best thought of as a dual form of critique, on the one hand directed toward Zhu Xi orthodoxy, on the other directed toward the later-era Wang Yangming school, reconstructing a Neo-Confucian (*lixue*) worldview in the process. Huang Zongxi does not discuss Nature and heart-mind in the abstract, but rather from specific circumstances seeks out the truth and order of the world, emphasizing that every single person can through specific practice achieve an understanding of the myriad of things and affairs.

However, the categories of heart-mind and things cannot, in and of themselves, prove the correctness of specific positions taken in relation to questions of knowledge and practice. If there is not a theory regarding political-economic institutions, it is very difficult for Confucians to offer an objective basis for knowing and doing. Within the severe social conditions of the late Ming and early Qing, when "Heaven collapsed and Earth was ripped apart," questions of politics and identity became intimately entangled, and a moral stance of blamelessness and circumspection was insufficient to respond to a complex reality. Liu Zongzhou used the tangibility of things and the necessity of practice to reinterpret the meaning of the unity of knowing and doing, linking the order of the myriad of things with the system of the Six Classics, and in doing so suggesting that the objective basis of moral evaluation could take the Six Classics as a standard. The reemergence of the study of the classics and histories was not simply a response to the demands of actual politics; it was also a means of resolving a long-held source of confusion within Confucianism: how to properly manage the relationship between personal moral practice and the machinations of statecraft. From the reestablishment of the unified relationship between practice and Nature in the wake of Wang Yangming's teachings, to the reestablishment of the unified relationship between ritual and behavior of Wang Ji, to the reestablishment of the unified relationship between morality and practical statecraft of late-Ming and early-Qing Confucians, the forms and basis of moral practice underwent important transformations; however, the goal of pursuing moral practice and its preconditions was always consistent.

For new directions to emerge and gain confirmation one had to wait until Huang Zongxi (1610–1695) developed his new theory of institutions and Gu Yanwu developed his teachings regarding the classics and histories. Huang and Gu's work was not a simple call to return to the Six Classics, but rather was the reestablishment of a theory of practice that had, as part of its internal structure, the question of society's political institutions, and took as its base the order of rites and music and its transformations. This theory looked upon moral practice as a series of social, political, and economic behaviors, and in doing so changed the mode of thought that the School of Principle employed, which was one that had set out from the question of the Nature and heart-mind, seeking to become sagely internally and kingly externally. Within the historical context of the late Ming and early Qing, knowledge regarding society, politics, and economics gained a new standing and value in Confucian learning. Owing to the fact that Song-Ming learning regarding Nature and heart-mind took as its central categories Heavenly Principle, inherent Nature, and the innate heart-mind, a split emerged in the relation between moral practice and other social practices, forming a long-standing source of anxiety within the School of Principle and the School of Mind: what center, and what method, was one to use to reconstruct the internal connection between moral evaluation and institutional practice? In this sense, instead of saying that Huang Zongxi's new institutional theory was an innovation or invention within the development of Confucianism, it is more appropriate to say that it was the return of Confucianism's form of moral evaluation to itself. It demanded that the highest of moral values be invested in the life of humanity and its institutional conditions, rather than insisting upon abstract Heavenly Principle or innate heart-mind. Precisely because of the transformations in Confucianism described above, "the return to the Six Classics" became the general outlook of Confucians of this time period, with textual research regarding names, things, and institutions being understood as the correct path of learning. The School of Principle and the School of Mind became subject to unprecedented suspicion and attack during the first generation of the Qing dynasty.

Huang Zongxi's teachings regarding the classics and histories were not simply a theory of moral practice, but rather formed a social theory in its own right, with the order of rites once again forming the internal structure of Confucian thought. During the Ming-Qing transition, he at once had to make a thoroughgoing analysis of the political crisis that had beset the Ming, while at the same time utilizing the retrospective search for cultural orthodoxy as a means of resisting the rule of a foreign people. In a certain sense, Huang's teachings regarding the classics and histories were an explanation of the historicity of the existential foundations of a particular social collective; or they could be termed an affirmation of the cultural foundations of a particular social collective. As such, the new theory of institutions was a form of social thought that took as its center a particular social collective and its traditions. Its understanding of individual moral practice was founded upon the various factors that made up a social community (collective qua collective), such as historical laws and institutions, cultural artifacts, language, and the social system. Within this Confucian mode, if one does not have an understanding of these formative elements of society, then it is impossible to discuss the question of moral practice. There was no doubt that the reconstruction of individual practice and social behavior in the mode of the Three Dynasties of Antiquity was to ground moral practice within the relations between culture and social institutions. When the question of practice transformed into being the question of the construction of society, then the form by which such social construction would take place also became a critical question of practice, which touched upon issues of culture, institutions, and orthodoxy. Within the early-Qing context, defined as it was by rule by a foreign people, the political implications of this transformation in Confucianism were clear.

As such, in Huang Zongxi's *Waiting for the Dawn: A Plan for the Prince,* the ideal of the Three Dynasties of Antiquity, which had up that point been a latent implication within Song-Ming Neo-Confucianism, could finally transform itself into a definitive analytical framework. This analytical transformation is incredibly important, for it represented Huang Zongxi's recognition that the study of the heart-mind, which focused on the question of individual moral practice, was incapable of establishing broader institutional conditions, while also having no ability to provide the institutional preconditions for moral practice, and as such had no way of offering a systemic analysis of a collective qua collective. Huang took the School of Principle's emphasis on *qi* and things and transformed it into a comprehensive mode of thought regarding the social system: serving as the material form in which tradition appeared, the system of past virtuous monarchs was at once the measure for critiquing corrupt government, while also being the basis for imagining a new society. Huang's theory represented the construction of a cultural tradition and its corresponding institutional forms. Within the condition of foreign rule, his theory provided members of society with resources for understanding their identity. What Huang's new institutional theory explored was not a pure system, but rather a new system of rites and music. It not only established the basis for moral criticism via its narrative on social structure; it could also take such a narrative regarding social structure and turn it into a narrative regarding moral behavior. Huang's new institutional theory reestablished the unified relations between social structure and moral practice; however, the precondition for this unity was that this social structure was not the currently existing one.

From the perspective of theoretical form, Huang's new theory in fact established internal, mutually constitutive relations between a number of specialized institutions, producing what was clearly a composite model that combined the system of enfeoffment (*fengjian zhi*) with the system of centralized administration (*junxian zhi*). Within this model, we are unable to confirm that any single institution or relation—be it political relations, economic relations, or moral relations—is the deciding factor within the system, for they are an integrated whole. There are thirteen chapters within *Waiting for the Dawn,* covering various aspects of the traditional system such as the monarch, officials, ministers, laws, schools, the awarding of degrees, urban construction, counties, the field system, the military system, finances, petty officials, and eunuchs. Huang Zongxi's discussion was not only grounded in the imaginary of the Three Dynasties of Antiquity inherent within the Confucian tradition, but also employed Mencius's basic principle of "the people are to be valued, not the monarch" as well as the social ideal of "All-under-Heaven is for all" that appears in the "Conveyance of Ritual" section of the *Book of Rites.* Huang did not set out asking questions from within the confines of the doctrines of the Cheng-Zhu or Lu-Wang schools. Rather, he excavated from within their thinking the traces of the early Confucian system, taking this as the basis for his own theory, establishing a new common ideal. There are some similarities between Huang's work and the "school" system described by Wang Yangming in his "Reply to

Gu Dongqiao" as well as the specific measures discussed in Wang Yangming's "Community Compact of Nangan" (*Nangan xiangyue*): all such works operate within a particular notion of life-practice to organize an understanding of society's internal division of labor, social order, social tasks, and power relations. Huang Zongxi's "On the Prince" (*Yuan jun,* found in *Waiting for the Dawn*) takes "the Commons of All-under-Heaven" (*Tianxia zhi dagong*) as its standard, affirming the interests of people All-under-Heaven, and critiquing the great selfishness of monarchs who take the position that "all power under Heaven comes from me."[99] In "On Ministership" (*Yuan chen*), Huang demands that ministers work on behalf of All-under-Heaven, rather than work "on behalf of one single name."[100] The standard of judgment here is not what is typically called political institutions, but rather is the notion of "duty" for monarchs and ministers that is established by the ideal of the Three Dynasties of Antiquity, which is that monarchs and ministers must complete their "duty," and the basis for measuring whether one's "duty" is just or not is the interests of the people. Huang Zongxi emphasized the legitimate nature of "the private"; however, this notion of the private was established in relation to the legitimacy of each person's own "duty." The concept of "duty" encompasses an understanding of institutions; it does not resort to the notions of Heavenly Principle, Nature, and heart-mind as a standard for morally judging monarch and officials, as the Song-Ming Confucians did. Rather, the notion of "duty" used institutional practices as the objective basis for moral judgment. Within the moral context constructed by Huang Zongxi, the meaning of institutions is closer to rites and music, and as such, its form of moral evaluation is relatively close to Confucius's understanding of rites and music. Because of this, the notion of institution spoken of here is not one that emerges out of a split with rites and music, but rather is an institution of rites and music that includes within it a sense of moral potential and moral goals. Because this kind of moral foundation exists, a monarch that is inadequate to his "duty" must be overturned, a minister that is inadequate to his "duty" must be recalled, and only a sense of the "private" that is in accordance with "duty" can be given protection. The notion of "duty" here is established on the basis of the division of labor, but it is also generated within, and is responsive to, a social order that takes the interests of the people All-under-Heaven as its goal. Moral evaluation resides in the specific functions of the various "divisions of duty," and as such, a form of research that concerns itself with the specific divisions of labor in society is entirely in conformance with a theory of the social that concerns itself with moral foundations. In this sense, this transformation in Confucianism's theory of morality engendered an entirely new understanding of the social division of labor and social structure.

What is unique about Huang Zongxi's new theory of institutions was that it looked upon the institutions of Three Dynasties of Antiquity as a complete social system, and on this basis provided a new interpretation of it. Furthermore, it sought to directly apply this ancient system in the contemporary age. As such, the Three Dynasties of Antiquity emerged not simply as an imaginative and critical source; it was also the principle upon which the current system could be improved, providing the enabling elements for a society to be constructed. For example, in the context of a discussion of the concept of "appointing ministers," Huang Zongxi proposed a cabinet system; in the context of a discussion of the notion of a "Ministry for Political Affairs," Huang researched the internal structure of administrative organs of power; in the context of discussions regarding "schools," Huang explained the absolute necessity of legislation and oversight; in discussing the "military system," Huang explained the necessity for a system of conscription, and so forth. All of this requires a "legal" spirit. In his chapter on "original law" (*Yuan fa*), he stated:

> Until the end of the Three Dynasties of Antiquity there was Law. Since the Three Dynasties there has been no Law. Why do I say this? Because the Two Emperors and Three Kings knew that all-under-Heaven could not do without sustenance and therefore gave them fields to cultivate. They knew that All-under-Heaven could not go without clothes and therefore gave them land on which to grow mulberry and hemp. They knew also that All-under-Heaven could not go untaught, so they set up schools, established the marriage to guard against promiscuity, and instituted military service to guard against disorders. This constituted Law until the end of the Three Dynasties. It was never laid down solely for the benefit of the ruler himself . . . among the major changes from the past to the present are one complete upheaval, which came with the Qin dynasty, and another with the Yuan dynasty. Following these two upheavals nothing at all survived of the sympathetic, benevolent, and constructive

> government of the early sage-kings. So, unless we take a long-range view and look deep into the matter, tracing back through each of these changes until the original order is restored with its well-field system, enfeoffment system, school, and military service systems, then even though some minor changes are made, there will never be an end to the misery of the common people. Should it be said that "There is only governance by men, not governance by law," my reply is that only if there is governance by law can there be governance by men.[101]

The difference between the law of the Three Dynasties of Antiquity and the "law without the rule of law" that came afterwards is found not in whether there exists the systemic form of the law and its complicated procedures, but rather in what the goal of the law is as well as the results that are derived from the balances that are put in place in accordance with this goal. For example, the difference between the schools that were present during the Three Dynasties of Antiquity and the imperial colleges, academies, and civil service examinations that came afterwards lay in the fact that the former took as its goal the Commons of All-under-Heaven, and in conformity with that goal encouraged every person to cultivate their talents, while the latter institutions were grounded in simply the power of the court, being completely unable to "publicly exclaim their sense of truth and falsehood within the schools."[102] The goal of Huang Zongxi's demand to restore the well-field system was to eliminate privilege in the land and taxation systems: "After land has been invested with wells, the people will flourish."[103] That excessive taxation was the cause of the banditry of the Ming period was a consensus among scholarly circles during the Qing dynasty. "As seen in the *Collected Writings of Zhang Taiyue* (*Zhang Taiyue ji*), taxation during earlier periods of the Ming accounted for only 2.3 million taels, by the Wanli years it was four million, by the Chongzhen reign it was eight million."[104] In his "Third Treatise on the Field System" (*Tian zhi san*), Huang Zongxi restates Zhu Xi's critique of the adjusted system of rents and of Yang Yan's Two-Tax Law (as outlined in Zhu Xi's "Debating the Opening of Paths and Ridges" [*Kai qianmo bian*]), while also providing a thoroughgoing critique of the laws on punishment of the Ming period. What is worth noting here is still the method of critique he employs, which compares the Three Dynasties of Antiquity with what came afterwards: "The ancients employed the well-field system to nourish the people, the people's fields were the sovereign's fields. From the Qin onward, people possessed their own fields, and the sovereign could not nourish the people, but rather made the people nourish themselves, and instituted a land tax, with a ratio of thirty to one, which was not necessarily a lighter burden than in the ancient period."[105]

Within the category of Confucianism, the institutional theory that called for the restoration of ancient forms cannot be understood as merely an economic or political doctrine. The studies of politics and economics are fields that take as their core the functions of institutions, while the institutional theory offered by Confucianism is first and foremost a moral theory. Huang Zongxi's new theory of institutions at every turn touches upon questions of interests; it is not constrained by a narrow morality. However, the moral foundations of the system of rites and music already encompassed relations of interest, and as such, to discuss the question of interests does not negate its moral import. What the new theory of institutions seeks to establish is the precondition for moral judgment, doing so on the basis of objective institutions, and as such integrates moral criticism and relations of utility. Seeing that the majority of Song-Ming thinkers rarely occupied themselves with the institutions discussed in the classics and placed singular emphasis on moral philosophy, Huang Zongxi attempted to use his framework of a new theory of institutions to reconstruct the internal relationships between scholarship on the classics and history (*jing shi*), moral philosophy, and institutions. When moral evaluation and the principles of moral rule were established under the conditions of institutional practice, there was no need to resort to an abstract Heavenly Principle. Under the call to return to ancient institutions, the relationship between morality and institutions gained a new lease on life. This is the particular meaning of *Waiting for the Dawn: A Plan for the Prince*. Though Huang Zongxi still respected some essential ideas and values of both the School of Principle and the School of Mind (such as circumspection and blamelessness, sincerity, and the unity of knowing and doing), as a theoretical form, the School of Principle reached its end (*zhongjie*) with Huang Zongxi, for it was precisely within his theoretical explorations that the foundational tenets of the School of Principle—its view of the universe, its theory regarding Nature and heart-mind, and its ontology—ultimately gave way to his new theory of institutions, which was capable of constructing the organic relations between morality and institutions, moral philosophy, and textual scholarship. The objectivity of moral judgment was thus once again established. The term "end" here also at the same time suggests a completion, for Song-Ming Confucians used their admiration for the Three Dynasties of Antiquity as a means of criticizing the contemporary age: the general goal of their view of the universe and their understanding of Nature and heart-mind was to pursue the unified relations between what was and what ought to be. However, their view of the universe and their understanding of heart-mind produced a drive to transcend institutions, one that was internal to these very concepts themselves, and that led to a severe rupture between moral evaluation and institutional evaluation. As such, the Song-Ming School of Principle had to use a form of self-negation in order to achieve the unity of what is and what ought to be.

In this sense, what the new theory of the institutions reestablished was not simply the unified relations between moral evaluation and systemic evaluation, but also a new theoretical form for Confucianism itself. Within this new theoretical form, the basic call of the School of Principle to restore the past ultimately achieved completion. In other words, "the end" did not mean a simple negation of the School of Principle. Precisely the opposite, "the end" represented the attainment of the School of Principle's internal goal. Within this new scholastic mode, "rites" and "things" occupied the central place, becoming the goal of the study of the classics and the study of the histories.

2. The World of Things and its Social Division of Labor

The new theory of institutions was not a passive social theory; it includes a sense of exploration regarding institutional practices. Yan Yuan (courtesy name Hunran, 1635–1704) reaffirmed the moral goals of the institutions of the Three Dynasties of Antiquity, and in doing so not only revealed the emptiness of the teachings of the Cheng brothers, Zhu Xi, Lu Jiuyuan, and Wang Yangming, but also asserted that Qing-dynasty evidential learning (*kaozheng*) and its methods were a false form of Confucianism. For Yan Yuan, the extensive developments that evidential learning underwent were accompanied by the loss of its original goal, ultimately falling into a condition in which evidential learning was done for the sake of evidential learning alone. Yan Yuan would go on to forcefully negate not just the learning of the Cheng brothers, Zhu Xi, Lu Jiuyuan, and Wang Yangming, but also Buddhism and

Daoism, as well as so-called Han learning (*Hanxue*), using the methods of statecraft of the Three Dynasties of Antiquity and the institutions outlined in *The Great Learning* as his standard.[106]

There are many works that analyze the emphasis on concrete practice that is found in the thought of Yan Yuan and his pupil Li Gong, yet there as of yet have been no works that have clearly identified that their notion of practice takes as its precondition Huang Zongxi's new theory of institutions. Yan Yuan's work "On the Kingly Way" (*Wang dao lun,* later known by the name "On the Preservation of Governance" or *Cun zhi bian*) very clearly takes the Three Dynasties of Antiquity as its guide, including in its discussions the well-field system, the system of enfeoffment, schools, the ancient "rural and local selection" system for promoting officials, the government bequeathment of fields to the people, and battle tactics.[107] His "On the Preservation of Teachings" (*Cun xue bian*) directly pursues the sagely learning of Confucius and his pupils, taking the notions of rites, music, soldiers, farming, heart-mind, meaning, body, and world as the categories of proper study.[108]

Within the applied learning of Yan Yuan and his world of things, the establishment of the new theory of institutions was directly related to the end of the School of Principle. Just like Huang Zongxi, Yan Yuan placed at the center of his political thought the Three Dynasties' well-field system, schools, and the system of enfeoffment. However, when he spoke of such things he did not think of them simply as institutions, but rather as the central content of the ancient notions of rites and music. As such, for Yan Yuan the first step in returning to the Three Dynasties of Antiquity was to reconstruct rites and music. The Yan Yuan school's notion of practice was intimately related to its understanding of the social division of labor. Yan Yuan believed that the world as it had developed over two thousand years was one defined by *wen* / writing / culture (that is, a world in which the rhetorical forms of texts were aesthetically elegant but rhetorically vacant, defined by vacant writings, dogmatic writings for moral instruction, Eight-Legged Essays, Chan Buddhism, and moral hypocrisy).

He believed that these various forms of *wen* / writing / culture could not provide an objective moral basis for behavior and its functions within a context defined by a clear social division of labor. Beginning from this point, he gained inspiration from the Three Dynasties' notions of the well-field system, the system of enfeoffment, and schooling, demanding a return to the world of "things"—this notion of "things" was not an objective factual reality that existed in the universe, but rather the so-called "six elements," "three affairs," "three things," and "four doctrines."[109] As such, this was a notion of applied learning that honored the system of rites and music, one that was implemented thoroughly in one's own actions. In this sense, practice was not a behavior that was carried out rashly by simply relying upon an intuitive moral conscience, but rather was conducted within a specific institutional form, utilizing the model of the Three Dynasties of Antiquity to richen and develop one's own era, promoting the prosperity, equality, desires, and division of labor of All-under-Heaven. Yan Yuan understood the "Six Bureaus" of Yao and Shun as well as the "Six Arts" of the Duke of Zhou and Confucius as social principles for the technical division of labor, and as such made the social division of labor, the classification of knowledge, and practice the basis of his system. Precisely because of this, he summarized his notion of practice as "a learned and habitual governance."

A society defined by the division of labor is not one that simply takes as its central point of emphasis notions of functionality and efficiency. Rather, the moral ideal that is constructed in the process of building the system and its divisions of labor represents a return to Confucius's own moral ideal, that of the "Confucian Person of Cultivation" (*Junzi Ru*). The ancient Confucian notion of the division of duty is directly developed here into a technical and professional division of labor:

> Confucians study in order to excel in the responsibilities of the various occupations that exist underneath the roles of monarch and ministers, [while the importance of each occupation differs, they all] can be made to ensure that the people each have a livelihood that can became their own individual mandate; this is a learning that studies thoroughly and harnesses the movements of *qi* as a question of the vitality of life. Just like the era of Yao and Shun, there was no one that did not praise the five ministers [Yu, Ji, Qi, Gao Yao, Bo Yi], the sixteen virtuous officials, Siyu, and the Qunmu [an ancient term for officials who ruled over the people in the nine divisions, later used to refer to local officials in general] . . . all of them embodied the learning of the encompassing human, the Confucian person of cultivation. While there were minor official roles such as subordinate ministers within the *Sikong* [one of the nine ancient

> official bureaucratic branches, responsible for the management of wood and water], subordinate ministers under *Houji* [an ancient titular name for ministers of agriculture], and deputies under the chieftains in the nine regions, all remained consistent with the three major tasks of governance outlined above and they followed the learning of the encompassing human, the Confucian person of cultivation. In the dynasties of Xia, Shang, and Zhou, all praised the legendary Bo Yi, Mi, Reng, Yi, Lai, Fu Yue, and the ten officials of talent that served the emperor, they all followed the learning of the encompassing human, the Confucian person of cultivation; though they were ministers, vice ministers, subordinate officials, they were all in accordance with the three principles of governance, and they all followed the learning of the encompassing human, the Confucian person of cultivation. Of the pupils of Confucius, there was not a single one that did not praise Yan, Zeng, and the seventy worthies; they all followed the learning of the encompassing human, the Confucian person of cultivation. Though there were two thousand nine hundred and twenty-eight pupils, they all practiced a unified morality, a unified set of behavior, a unified set of techniques, the learning of the encompassing human, the Confucian person of cultivation. The place of Confucianism was the cultivation and application of benevolent behaviors and customs. . . . The outward expression of Confucianism was governance . . . if one left this path . . . even if one recollated the Four Books and Five Classics, without missing a single character, and the entire set of books emerged, it would not be Confucianism . . . once this proposition is clear, one can return to the study of the three affairs and three things of Confucianism, and all those who are a menace to Confucianism will by their own accord cease their activities.[110]

The encompassing human, as well as the person of cultivation, integrates the functions of human moral behavior, divisions in social rank, and the social division of labor. The precondition for this integration is the transformation of society into a world of things in which every person could give full expression to their talents. Yan Yuan believed deeply that "the ground of one's source" was not in the court, but rather in the academies of learning. The notion of the academy of learning,[111] which is established in distinction to the court, is not some mere school as a place of education, but rather is the world of things in itself. Because the world of things is a world grounded in the division of labor, as such, ethical relations are established to a certain degree upon utilitarian relations. This world affirms the qualities, emotions, desires, and labor of people, and it rejects the School of Mind, whether in the form of its inner doctrine (Daoism and Buddhism) or its outer doctrine (Confucianism), as well as religious doctrines that insist on renouncing the world and hiding away from it. If one says that people such as Li Zhi used rebellion to express their affirmation of desire, then one can say that Yan Yuan returned desire, emotion, customs, and other social elements to the world of things.[112] The world of things is at the same time the world of human emotion, the principle of the division of labor is one part of the world of things; knowledge, technique, and emotions are not objective fields, but rather elements internal to the universe and humanity, in constant creation and dynamic, unceasing unfolding.

The notions of the encompassing human, of the person of cultivation, and of the social division of labor are linked together, with moral practice transforming itself toward the differing classification of knowledge. This is manifested explicitly in Yan Yuan's notion of education and its principle of different branches and fields. In his *Records of the Zhangnan Academy* (*Zhangnan shuyuan ji*), the opposition between the world of *wen* / writing / culture and the world of things is expressed in an opposition between two forms of knowledge and their differing courses. This is the opposition between the "Studio for the Study of Principle / "Studio for Terms for the Civil Service Exam" and the "Hall for Study and Lecture." The "Hall for Study and Lecture" was divided into four sections: "matters of *wen* / culture," with teachings regarding rites, music, books, mathematics, cosmology, and geography; "martial preparations," with teachings regarding the Yellow Emperor, Jiang Ziya, and works of military strategy such as the *Sunzi* and *Wuzi,* touching on such martial questions as attack and defense, fortifications, land and sea operations, aerial attack and defense, and so forth; "the classics and histories," with teachings regarding the thirteen classics, official histories, imperial mandates, memorials to the emperor, poetry, and belles lettres; and "arts and techniques," including water management, fire management, engineering, divination techniques from the *Book of Changes,* and so forth; while the "Studio for the Study of Principle" / "Studio for Terms for the Civil Service Exam" (which were established within the doors of the academy) taught meditation and the Eight-Legged Essay of the civil service exams. From the perspective of the School of Principle, what the "Hall for Study and Lecture" represented was a kind of technical capacity, a technical worldview, while from the perspective of the person of cultivation, this worldview that emphasized technique, technical capacity, and the division of knowledge came from the moral governance of the Three Dynasties of Antiquity. As such, the worldview that emphasized the division of labor was developed on the basis of ethical relations.

From Huang Zongxi to Yan Yuan, the basis of the new theory of institutions was a world in which a "collective" (*qun*) appeared, one that did so through the auspices of rites and music. Within this world, notions of the "personal" as well of "human emotions and complex affairs" were affirmed, but the precondition of this affirmation was not the atomistic concept of the individual, but rather the Commons of All-under-Heaven. This latter concept takes as its precondition the affirmation of the personal under Heaven, while such a personal dimension takes the Commons of All-under-Heaven as its ultimate goal. Liang Qichao and Hu Shi understood Yan Yuan as a Qing-dynasty intellectual who advocated utilitarianism and opposed the School of Principle. However, Yan Yuan was adamant about defending Confucian orthodoxy, and in his personal behavior he held fast to norms of ritual and propriety. The origins of his learning can be traced to the Wang Yangming school as well as the Southern Song Yongjia school.[113] Whether or not his critiques of the School of Principle and the School of Mind can be defined as a total rejection and resistance to Neo-Confucianism is a question that requires sustained research to answer. The reasons for this are that 1) Yan Yuan's criticism of the Cheng-Zhu and Lu-Wang schools was made on the basis of a worldview that asserted the need to revitalize ancient ways. His call to return to the system of rites and music of pre-Qin times was a call internal to the School of Principle and School of Mind. In this sense, while "the world of things" was a rejection of Neo-Confucianism, it was also a call to reaffirm Confucianism's orthodox path by following the internal logic of Neo-Confucianism. 2) His call to "investigate by hand every beast of prey" was absolutely not founded on the empiricism of atomistic thought, but rather was established on his understanding of ancient forms of music and ritual within Confucianism, and as such contained within it a rich sense of moral import.

Yan Yuan's thought is defined by a kind of ancient restorationism that is responsive to the contemporary world, reality, and life itself. He defined his notion of the investigation of things in the following manner: "As such, I define things as consisting of three dimensions, and I define investigation as the investigation by hand of every beast of prey."[114] The key to understanding his notion of "the investigation by hand of all beasts of prey" is understanding the meaning of his notion of "things": it is not here the myriad things and elements within the natural world, but rather the "things" of the three dimensions, these three being the "Six Morals," the "Six Forms of Behavior," and the "Six Arts." The "investigation by hand of all beasts of prey" is a rejection of abstract musings and speculations regarding Heavenly Principle and intuitive moral goodness; it is a call to revitalize the Six Arts of Confucian learning. This revitalization is one that takes place not in the realm of imagined relations, but rather in a reality defined by "human emotions and complex affairs." Things possess tangibility. This is the unity of knowing and doing that is internal to rites and music, internal to the world of things.

From the Song onward, an imagination regarding the Three Dynasties of Antiquity was a basic discourse internal to all the various branches of Confucian learning, serving as the motive force for change and innovation within Confucianism itself. The transformations in the social system that took place following the Han and Tang dynasties forced Neo-Confucians to carve out a new path. Their efforts to return to the ideal of the Three Dynasties of Antiquity could only be expressed through the categories of Heavenly Principle, Nature, and heart-mind. The crucial characteristic of the new theory of institutions of Huang Zongxi and Yan Yuan was not its pursuit and admiration of the Three Dynasties of Antiquity, nor was it a drive to reestablish the unified relations between what is and what ought to be, for these modes of thought were consistent characteristics of Song-Ming Neo-Confucianism. The defining characteristic of the thought of Huang Zongxi and Yan Yuan was that they managed to richen institutional forms by amplifying them with the content of the age, taking the rule by ritual of the Three Dynasties of Antiquity and moving it from the inner realm of Neo-Confucian learning to the outer realm, from the darkened background to the bright foreground, from a scattered and sparse form of criticism regarding institutions to composing the very structure of the new theory of institutions itself. In doing so they completed the task that Neo-Confucianism had up to that point failed to complete.

When one looks back upon the long history of debate and change that took place within Neo-Confucianism from this perspective, we discover that Neo-Confucianism's self-negation was far more radical than its criticism of the contemporary era it found itself in; every innovation within itself was done via the mockery and rejection of the efforts that came before it. Theories of the heart-mind and Nature critiqued the contemporary system and its cultural relations by utilizing the notions of Heavenly Principle, Nature, the heart-mind, and the dynamic forms through which their unceasing changes were expressed, searching for the foundation of moral practice. Yet the result of such a search was unceasing transformations and changes to itself as a philosophical discourse. Huang Zongxi and Yan Yuan utilized different methods to turn the imagination of the Three Dynasties of Antiquity into a form of institutional relations, and in doing so they discovered that the world of the Three Dynasties was not in fact what people often imagined—an ancient world of antiquity—but in fact it was the contemporary world, with its repressions, its human emotions, and complex affairs. Within their efforts to reconstruct the institutions of rites and music, they combine a ferocious call to restore the past with a deep concern regarding the present. As such, their restorationism never expressed itself in a sentimental, anachronistic mantra of condolence for the world of the Three Dynasties and Six Classics. Rather, they took the Three Dynasties and Six Classics to be a repressed, but never completely eliminated, spirit and set of universal values, which were realized within the practices of rites and music as well as institutions. Precisely because of this, the Three Dynasties and Six Classics not only stood for an ideal world, but also provided a perspective through which the contemporary world could be grasped, a contemporary world defined by human emotion and complex affairs. Within this new historical space, at the moment that the system of the Three Dynasties and the teachings of the Six Classics were propelled toward the foreground, providing dynamic sustenance for real-world practice, suspicion of the system of the Three Dynasties and the learning of the Six Classics could not but emerge. This historical movement that expressed suspicion regarding antiquity emerged out of the practical needs of the study of antiquity.

CHAPTER 4

Classics and History (1)

Translated by MINGHUI HU

> A sense of shame should guide one's moral practice, and scholarly erudition is revealed in cultural scope.
>
> The shortcomings of the system of enfeoffment are concentrated at the bottom of society, whereas the weaknesses of the system of centralized administration are concentrated at the top of society.
>
> —GU YANWU

I. A New Theory of Rites and Music and the Establishment of Classical Studies

1. The World of Ritual (*li*) and Culture (*wen*)

The new theory of institutions restored the intrinsic relationship between moral evaluation and institutions, but this restoration did not simply regard institutions and the relationships they regulated as the basis for moral evaluation. Rather, it integrated institutions themselves within the scope of morality. That is, within the framework of Confucian learning, it restored consistency between institutions and rites and music. Accordingly, what Gu Yanwu (courtesy name Ningren, aka Mr. Tinglin, from Kunshan, Jiangsu, 1613–1682) and Huang Zongxi were concerned about was: What kind of institutions contain the essence of morality, and so can be applied to the goals of statecraft? As the methods of *kaozheng* (evidential learning), etymology, and historical research flourished in the Qing dynasty, Gu and Huang's initial intention was to understand the model of the Three Dynasties of Antiquity's statecraft better. From Gu Yanwu's classical studies to Huang Zongxi's theory of institutions, there existed an inherent continuity. They both put the concrete matters of the new theory of institutions, such as regulations, institutional rules, cultures, and customs, at the core of their thinking: "They intended to bring order to chaos and clean the dirt out of the system; they wanted to use antiquity as exemplars to promote Chinese civilization, open up extensive learning for posterity, and to await the unified rule of future kings."[1] In the context of the history of thought, this new theory of institutions criticized the late Ming dynasty's transcendental moralism by reconstructing the ancient system of rites and music. Jiang Fan's book *Interpretative Comments on the Records of the Genealogy of Han Learning* (*Hanxue shicheng ji*) drew sharp lines between Han and Song learning. It began with Yan Ruoqu (1636–1704) and Hu Wei (1633–1714) as the beginning of the lineage, arguing that Huang Zongxi and Gu Yanwu were not the trendsetters and champions of Han learning because they also accommodated Song learning; for this reason they are listed only in the appendix of Jiang Fan's book. However, in a dialogue between Gu and a guest in the eighth *juan* of his book, Jiang unintentionally revealed the pivotal positions of Gu and Huang: "Since Huang rose to shake up their ruin and disorder and Gu followed suit, many scholars realized how critical it was to study the ancient classics and their implications."[2] "To await the unified rule of future kings" meant that they completely rejected the legitimacy of the Qing dynasty and that their critique of the collapse of the Ming dynasty was based upon a critical reconstruction of Song and Ming orthodoxies. "To study the classics and their implications" meant that they placed their hopes for the political future in the utopia of rites and music depicted in the Six Classics.

After the Qing soldiers entered China and brutally slaughtered innocents in Yangzhou, Jiading, and elsewhere, the ethnic and hierarchical distinction between bannermen in the banner armies and the rest of the population had become the main feature of social formations in Qing China. Against this backdrop, Huang Zongxi and Gu Yanwu carried out an arduous struggle as Ming loyalists against the conquest dynasty. Their thought and scholarship were preoccupied with the distinction between the Chinese and barbarians, orthodoxy and heterodoxy, expressed in Confucian language as "discerning the Chinese from the barbarians" (*Yi Xia zhi bian*). However, the ethnic consciousness of "discerning the Chinese from the barbarians" cannot fully characterize Gu Yanwu and Huang Zongxi's thinking. There are two factors worth considering: First, their anti-Qing struggle was parallel to their profound reflection on the Ming dynasty's collapse. Second, the Manchu conquest of China and Qing empire-building were processes with multiple and sophisticated components. For example, the Chinese turncoats' decision to join forces with the Manchu conquest of China and the Southwest, the Ming dynasty's own internal mismanagement, and the peasant uprising against the Ming state all contributed to the rapid destruction of the Ming dynasty. Therefore, we cannot simplify Gu and Huang's intellectual formation regarding the Ming implosion and the Manchu conquest of China as merely "ethnic consciousness" or "discerning the Chinese from the barbarians." The late Ming dynasty's social crisis provided a possibility for a comprehensive and systematic analysis of political, economic, and cultural relationships in Chinese society, and it gave Confucian scholars a chance to abandon the ideological style that had gradually been formed since the Song dynasty. Gu Yanwu, Huang Zongxi, Wang Fuzhi (1619–1692), and others transformed moral impulses into a comprehensive investigation of statecraft, exploring the meaning of morality in a theory of institutions or ritualist framework, which they set up as a foil against their existing institutions. As mentioned earlier, Song and Ming scholars also discussed institutional issues such as the Community Compact, patriarchal clan law, land systems, tax law, and so forth. However, the central part of Song and Ming Confucianism was to use Heaven as a source of morality, and therefore these thinkers' institutional criticism was unable to build a new and systematic theory of institutions. The academic efforts by the Qing scholars were precisely the opposite of those of the Song and Ming scholars: Qing scholars examined moral issues within the framework of a new theory of institutions and a ritualist standpoint, and they used this examination as the basis of a critique of institutions. In their thinking, theories of Heavenly Principle and of transcendental Mind and Nature that prevailed in the Song and Ming dynasties gradually retreated to a position of secondary importance.

During the nationalist tide in the late Qing (1870–1910), anti-Qing or anti-Manchu slogans became a critical factor in mobilizing revolutionaries, and views redefining the Manchu as a foreign people and a foreign dynasty prevailed. Rather than simplify the new nationalist distinction between Chinese and barbarian as a natural outcome of the Confucian tradition, this phenomenon should be seen as a response to Western nationalism. In this intellectual circumstance, historical research on Gu Yanwu's thought has focused on his "national" or "ethnic" consciousness but has somewhat ignored the more complicated aspects of his intellectual formation. For instance, in Zhang Taiyan's (1869–1936) extensive explorations of statecraft learning centered on institutions, he reveals a latent nationalism in the teachings of Confucius, in institutions and cultural artifacts, and in classical and historical studies:

> Therefore, I think that nationalism (*minzuzhuyi*) is like the act of planting and harvesting in the field. It is necessary to water the field with the historical figures, institutional details, geographical settings, and social customs in our historical records. Then our crop [of nationalism] will flourish. For those who only know the importance of "ism" but are unaware of the loveliness of our nation, I am afraid their field is going to become barren. The teaching of Confucius was based upon historical studies. Those who follow Confucius should set aside Confucian teachings that help them with examination and bureaucratic success and frequently revisit only the esteemed and irreplaceable accomplishments of former rulers. Before the *Spring and Autumn Annals,* there existed the Six Classics, which were Confucius's historical studies. After the *Spring and Autumn Annals,* there existed the *Records of the Grand Historian* (*Shi ji*), *History of the Former Han* (*Han shu*), and many official histories and biographies, which were also historical studies that followed Confucius [and his methods].[3]

Zhang Taiyan's interpretation focuses on the idea of "nation" (*minzu*) in the classical and historical studies of the early Qing dynasty. He did not further pursue why the concept of "nation" had to be invested in Confucian doctrines, studies of institutions, regulations and cultural artifacts, and historical studies. For Gu Yanwu, however, classical and historical studies had to include a systematic reflection on the relationships among politics, economics, and culture. Such a new theory of institutions both bolstered Chinese identity and encompassed a more general institutional approach in terms of reflection and critical thinking.

Early Qing-dynasty classical studies and scholarship were not limited to ethnic consciousness or to classical and historical studies in themselves. Gu Yanwu had turned the racial consciousness and anti-Manchu resistance movement into a pivotal moment of critical reflection, distinguishing the issue of "preserving the state" (*bao guo*) from the concept of "All-under-Heaven" (*Tianxia*). Gu had recast the reconstruction of the political and moral order as the new fundamental goal and transcended the horizon of merely restoring the Ming dynasty and opposing alien rule. He explored historical figures, institutions, geography, and customs in history in an exceedingly rigorous way. However, we should not consider Gu's research as merely a regular empirical study, because Gu imparted a universal and normative value and meaning to his empirical research in a distinctive way. This is the key to understanding Gu's statecraft learning. Before further delving into many of Gu Yanwu's ideas and theoretical propositions, it is indispensable to clarify the concept of *Tianxia* (All-under-Heaven) and the concepts of "state" (*guo*) and "emperor" (*jun*) in his writings.[4] Gu Yanwu said:

> There are two dire situations: The state perishes, and *Tianxia* perishes. How do we tell the difference? The answer goes like this: If the dynasty changes its surname and reign title, then we know the state has perished. When evil blocks humanity and righteousness and causes beasts to devour humans, and when people starve and eat each other's flesh, then we know that *Tianxia* has perished. . . . Therefore, to protect *Tianxia* is more urgent than protecting the state. Those who should protect the state are the emperor, his advisors, and those who work for them. Everyone should be responsible for safeguarding *Tianxia*. Even the individual members of the lowest status in the society should shoulder such a responsibility.[5]

The difference between *Tianxia* and the state is not based on geographical scope, nor is it based on a political structure. These two concepts indicate two different social formations: On the one hand, "the state" has its society maintained by a political system (such as a state dominated by one family name, a dynasty). On the other hand, *Tianxia* indicates that society is built upon the condition of a universal virtue (that transcends the domination of one family name). *Tianxia* has a community of rites and music, which is coherent through the institutional practices that preserve the internal relationship between Heaven and humans.

The distinction between *Tianxia* and "the state" is established on the distinction between rites and music and the monarchical system. The concept of *Tianxia* attempts to restore Heaven and humanity's internal relationship through ritual and musical practice, and it was precisely this connection that gradually disappeared during the transition from ritual and musical practice to the monarchical system. Under the condition "when evil blocks humanity and righteousness and causes beasts to devour humans, and when people starve and eat each other's flesh," even if the "state" (the political system centered on kingship) still exists, it is no longer a human community with moral consistency if we consider the situation from the perspective of rites and music; the difference between *Tianxia* and the state stems from an ancient concept of Heavenly Mandate: The ancients communicated with the heavens through rituals such as sacrifices, and the clan chiefs were the wizards who controlled the shamanic rituals. With the emergence of the early state, the role of the shamanic intermediary who communicated the relationship between Heaven and human gradually changed from a wizard, a sorcerer (clan leader), to a king (*junwang*) who governed the country with institutions and rituals. Therefore, a king's role must be based on the practice of rites and music (to communicate with Heaven) and listening to the people, because the rites and music and popular support are the secular manifestations of a Heavenly Mandate. What is called "making rituals and composing music" (*zhi li zuo yue*) is the ritualization of Heaven or the relationship between Heaven and the people; what is called unification of governance and *Dao* is how institutions, order, and social relationships can all manifest moral meaning (i.e., the Heavenly Mandate); and what is called the community (*gongtongti*) of rites and music is where political practice is part of moral practice, and moral practice is part of the system of rites and music. Suppose the king can't really communicate with the heavens but only relies on power, institutional (legal) structure, and functional relations to maintain his own rule. In that case, this society must be a political community lacking moral consistency; that is, the external relationship is the mechanism that keeps society together.

In this sense, the concept of *Tianxia* is not a rejection of the political community but a yearning for a form of community that unifies governance and

Dao. When the dynasty collapses and the rituals are still there, then *Tianxia* will not succumb. When the dynasty collapses and the rituals die with it, then *Tianxia* will be lost. The condition of rule by virtue refers to a political system that could still be a vessel of moral meaning and value and guide people's daily practice. In the historical circumstance of resisting foreign aggression, when scholars insisted on the difference between "*Tianxia*" and "the state," they were making a moral point. The state's politics must follow ceremonial virtue; any deviation from the path of true virtue would result in the debasement of humanity and righteousness, and, consequently, *Tianxia* would be lost. A discussion of severe political and social crisis that is premised on the distinction between *Tianxia* and the state seeks to supply normative guidance for the literati in thought and practice. It is a call on scholars to transcend their servitude to the emperor and to go beyond protecting the state. They should be committed to maintaining the moral practice of rituals in their daily life and hope to build "China" into a community of rites and music.

There has been much discussion about the relationship between *kaozheng* and statecraft scholarship. I will not comment on the literature here. My question instead goes as follows: For Gu Yanwu and his followers, why did the fundamental mode of moral argumentation shift from the moral practice of self-cultivation to the "intellectual" exercise of investigating words and their pronunciation to unveil the evolution of ancient institutions? Why did the premise of moral argumentation change from Heavenly Principle to institutions and customs? What is the relationship between Gu Yanwu's *Tianxia* and his scholarly approach? Gu's ideas about rites and music unify the external system with the individual's behavior, internalizing the exterior design and the harmonious operation between human emotions, desires, moral needs, and ritual systems. Gu attempts to reconstruct the intrinsic relationship between institutions and morality within a framework of a theory of rites and music. Duan Yucai (1735–1815) later said:

> The immensity of the ancient design lay in scrutinizing the principles of people and things between Heaven and Earth. The ancients had found the nature and essence of people and things, their beginnings and ends. They made clear the classes and categories of all things, and they promoted each institutional design's benefits and prevented its shortcomings. It is why antiquity could be stable and set exemplars for ten thousand generations.[6]

Duan is well known for his *kaozheng* research, but his interest in statecraft and politics was negligible. He believed the fundamental approach of Confucianism was to use *kaozheng* methods "to scrutinize and encompass the principles of people and things between Heaven and Earth." To some ears, Duan may have sounded a bit defensive of *kaozheng* methods. He nonetheless inherited Gu's scholarly agenda and revealed the premise of his classical studies. The premise was to understand the fine points and essence of the classical texts ("grand classics and grand methods") through *kaozheng* and etymology, and to use these fine points of classical texts to turn the world from a deviant path back to the right road.

Like Huang Zongxi, Gu Yanwu believed that the *Dao* of statecraft was part of institutional practice. However, both the *Dao* of statecraft and institutional practice need to be carefully defined: the so-called *Dao* of statecraft did not include politics, economics, or military affairs unrelated to one's moral action, and so-called institutional practice was not to follow the existing regulations blindly without considering the specific context or circumstance. In the context of a new theory of institutions and classical studies, political, economic, military, and individual moral practices were all interwoven into ritual relations and their changes. Gu Yanwu's *kaozheng* learning and the internal connection between illuminating the *Dao* and statecraft were expressed through his investigations of the ritual system and its evolution. For Gu, institutions and regulations were not a rigid dogma or a simplistic functional design. They constituted a norm and order in daily life and historical practice. They also constituted a ritual system that could only be fully presented and guide life's value through concrete individual actions.

Gu Yanwu's classical learning covers all aspects of rites and music, institutions, laws, customs, traditions, characters, language, nature, and so forth. However, they are not a messy hodgepodge. Instead, they together illustrate a world of "ritual" (*li*) and "culture" (*wen*). In his writings, "ritual" and "culture" have an intertextual relationship. It is the key to understanding Gu's motto: "A sense of shame should guide one's moral practice, and scholarly erudition is revealed in cultural scope" (*xing ji you chi, bo xue yu wen*). Gu Yanwu said:

> The gentleman learns broadly to accomplish a cultured status. From his personal life through his family and to the state and the world, the gentleman acts within the confines of degrees and numbers and expresses

> himself with a good countenance and voice. Everything he does is culture. If one acts with constraints and knows one's place in the hierarchy, then one behaves according to ritual. . . . The Commentary [to the *Book of Changes*] says: The human cultural pattern [as opposed to the celestial pattern] is how the bright spots of culture are arranged. We should observe the human cultural pattern and use it to teach everyone under Heaven. Therefore, after King Wen died, the culture was no longer here! But culture is [King Wen's] posthumous legacy of modeling Heaven and Earth. Various disciples who are learning the Six Classics would result in different comprehension levels.[7]

The word *wen* 文 refers not only to written characters or literary writing but also to unspoken rules manifested in individual behaviors and institutions. The concept of *wen* as "culture" has a historical connection with the etiquette of the Zhou dynasty (the so-called *Zhou wen*). However, Gu Yanwu emphasized the immanence of *wen* and meant something similar to what Confucius had meant by "understanding ritual as humaneness" (*yi ren shi li*): "If one makes it, then it will be in right measure. If one expresses it, then it will be manifested in a good countenance and voice. Aren't these just culture?" Culture will exist in one's every move when interiorized as such. When Quan Zuwang (1705–1755), memorializing Gu Yanwu, wrote that "the gentleman must learn rituals," the rituals (*li*) he referred to are not a narrow sense of etiquette but a natural / external order spontaneously normalizing our lives. Therefore, "Various disciples who are learning the Six Classics would result in different comprehension levels" represents a situation that would frequently occur. Still, the case to "observe the human cultural pattern and use it to teach everyone under Heaven" seems to be closer to Gu's idea of culture. Gu Yanwu said:

> *Wen* (literature / culture) is indispensable to Heaven and Earth because it is there to clarify the *Dao*, record political affairs, investigate the hidden troubles in society, and celebrate our people's good nature. If one may compose a piece of literature to do the above, it will benefit everyone under Heaven and in the future. For each additional piece of literature like this, there will be additional benefit. If a piece of literature only depicts the monstrous, the coercive, the chaotic, and the supernatural, in-

cluding nonsense, plagiarism, and flattery, it will harm ourselves and others. If there is one less piece of literature like this, there will be one less harm caused.[8]

The main point in this quote is not only that the text is the vehicle of the *Dao*, but also how the text could be the kind of vehicle that carries the *Dao* in harmony with the natural pattern of the world. Without this premise, the number of texts is irrelevant. Dai Zhen (1724–1777) once used "pattern" (*tiao li*) to gloss "*li*" (principles):

> Ritual is the pattern of Heaven and Earth. When we address the pattern's utmost case, we would not be able to exhaust the detail of the Heavenly pattern without truly knowing Heaven. The readings of astronomical instruments, patterns, measures, and numbers are nothing but how the sages see Heaven's pattern. They set the instrument and model of numbers and degrees as a Doctrine for All (*wanshi fa*). The design of the rituals is to govern the nature of everything under Heaven. Sometimes it trims the excessive, and sometimes it makes up the deficient. The design is to show what is adequate.[9]

Dai Zhen's explanation is quite similar to Gu Yanwu's. The minor difference lies in the following: Dai Zhen's concept of "pattern" is closely related to the category of "spontaneous" (*ziran*). It has more or less a hint of abstraction and transcendence. Gu Yanwu, on the other hand, combines the concepts of "literature / culture" and "ritual," encompassing all institutions of rites and music and the social order.

For this reason, Gu Yanwu extended "the investigation of words and their sounds" (*kao wen*) to all the norms and practices of daily life: He studies the Six Classics and all ancient philosophers' texts, not only the social customs all over China but also their foreign counterparts.[10] He does not limit himself to the Six Classics, but extends his investigation from the Six Classics outward, even citing "foreign customs" or "barbarian customs" to give sharp insight and to critique China's overwrought and trivial ceremonies and fashions that prize appearance over substance. According to Gu, such an approach will eventually lead to the intellectual liberation he seeks. Why is this so? The Six Classics are the records of the Three Dynasties of Antiquity. As time went by, the system of enfeoffment turned into the system of centralized administration, and the system of centralized administration turned into an empire. If one is fixated on antiquity, then one would not only be unable to accomplish the goal of statecraft, but also be incapable of identifying the "state" that one wants to craft. His advocacy of "scholarly erudition revealed in cultural scope" is premised on this unique and evolving ritual order. It was not a requirement for scholars, but an expectation for "gentlemen."

Therefore, Gu's fundamental precept for engaging in learning, "A sense of shame should guide one's moral practice, and scholarly erudition is revealed in cultural scope," is closely related to this ritual order and cannot be discussed in isolation from it. Why does "a sense of shame should guide one's moral practice" need to be supplemented by "scholarly erudition is revealed in cultural scope"? People's daily life includes all kinds of different things, and the scope of rites and music and the theory of institutions is vast. Without the efforts of "scholarly erudition revealed in cultural scope," there is no way to know when you should be ashamed, or to talk about an actual "sense of shame to guide one's moral practice." Then, why is "scholarly erudition" mainly reflected in textual and classical research? It is because the ancient system of rites and music had long been in decline, and only Confucian learning and classical texts could be of help in "bringing order to chaos, changing habits and social customs, taming and extending the practice of governance, and leaving aside useless matters."[11] Here, the most critical matter is: the measurement of moral action cannot merely come from the Mind and human nature. Ethical practice should be premised on the specific system of rites and music and measured against the specific historical circumstances. In comparison with Wang Yangming's discussion on culture and rituals, breadth and brevity of learning, Gu Yanwu's theory is precisely the reverse of Wang Yangming's. Wang Yangming said:

> The Teacher said, "The word *li* [meaning propriety, ceremonies], means the same as *li* [Principle]. When principles become manifested and can be seen, we call them patterns [*wen,* meaning literature], and when patterns are hidden and abstruse and cannot be seen, we call them *li* [Principle]. They are the same thing. Restraining oneself with rules of propriety means that this mind must become completely identified

> with Heavenly Principle. In order to become completely identified with Heavenly Principle, one must direct one's effort to wherever Principle is manifested. For example, if Principle is manifested in the serving of one's parents, one should preserve it in the very act of serving one's parents. If Principle is manifested in serving one's ruler, one should learn to preserve it in the very act of serving one's ruler. If Principle is manifested in one's living in riches or poverty or humble or noble station, one should learn to preserve it in these situations. And if Principle is manifested in one's being in difficulty and danger or being in the midst of barbarous tribes, one should learn to preserve it in these situations. And one should do the same whether working or resting, speaking or silent. No matter where Principle may be manifested, one should learn right then and there to preserve it. This is what is meant by extensive study of literature. This is the work of restraining oneself with the rules of propriety. To study literature extensively means to be refined in one's mind, and to restrain oneself with the rules of propriety means to have singleness in one's mind."[12]

However, for Gu Yanwu, if you cannot extend your learning to become intelligent enough about all plausible political circumstances, you will not be qualified to speak or comment on the moral principles that govern your political actions. As quoted at the beginning of this chapter, Gu repeated his motto many times on multiple occasions and argued that one must "reveal scholarly erudition in cultural scope" sufficiently before one could speak of "the sense of shame guiding one's moral practice." The reason is simple. How can we know the basis of "the sense of shame" if we do not survey and understand the political circumstances in which we are supposed to act? Without the "the sense of shame" as the purpose, "revealing scholarly erudition in cultural scope" will become meaningless. In this sense, Huang and Gu's scholarship is both a new theory of institutions and a new theory of rites and music. Classical studies and historiography are the expressions of their new theory of rites and music. In its critique of the Neo-Confucian School of Principle (*lixue*) and especially the School of Mind (*xinxue*), the new theory of rites and music has a robust institutional orientation because Gu, Huang, and others believe that Neo-Confucianism and its main categories obscure the intrinsic relationship between moral practice and institutions / rites and music. Gu Yanwu's focus is not only on the family and state but also on daily behavior, the evolution of social customs, and differences in astronomy, geography, and the natural environment. In this respect, Gu's idea of the community of rites and music differs in important ways from the idea of "schools" put forward by Wang Yangming and even from Huang Zongxi's model for society and its views on rights, obligations, laws, institutions, and the division of labor.

In short, Gu Yanwu does not merely discuss the design of institutions. He regards the change of social customs as the key to the problem, because in his understanding, *Tianxia* is a community of rites and music, not a structural or functional system based on a framework of a political institution or a legal system; nor is it formed from the community of a common will. The thirtieth *juan* of Gu's *Record of Daily Knowledge* (*Ri zhi lu*) is an encyclopedic account of social customs. The author discusses social customs from the end of the Zhou dynasty, the Former and Later Han dynasties, the Song dynasty, and the later dynasties, and refers to marriage, agricultural fields, human talents, morality, superstition, property, political criticism, and so on. Consequently, Gu incorporates historical information about institutions and cultures into the categories of social customs, conventions, and so on: "When you witness the world, you understand that the key to order and chaos under Heaven lies in in the customs of the people, and therefore to change people's mindset and to rectify customs, you must rely on indispensable education and legal discipline."[13] This vividly shows his understanding of ritual and culture that encompasses every aspect of cultural and political order.

Gu Yanwu opposes the speculative style of the Song and Ming scholars. He believes that Heaven, *Dao,* human nature, Mind, and heart are all present in rites and music, institutions, and customs, and that they all exist in people's daily practice. Because of this, *kaozheng* and etymological research must go deep into all areas of life, not just the Six Classics. In his famous "A Letter Discussing Learning with a Friend," Gu said: "For more than a hundred years scholars have often spoken of human Mind and Nature, but they have no way to explain it. Confucius rarely discussed destiny and benevolence; Zigong [Confucius's disciple] never heard of human nature and the Way of Heaven; Confucius's disciples wrote *Commentary on the Book of Changes* to illustrate the principles of human nature and destiny, but they never spoke to anyone about it."[14] What he sought was to practice the culture of the Six Arts, to investigate the institutions of the hundred kings, to encompass contemporary affairs, and to rediscover the great principles of Confucius's discussions of learning and governance, as the solid learning of cultivating oneself and governing others.[15] All of this is demonstrated in his *Record of Daily Knowledge* and *Five Books on Phonology* (*Yinxue wushu*).

2. Classical Studies, *Kaozheng* Methodology, and the Return to the Concept of *Wu* (Things)

Gu Yanwu argued that Neo-Confucian methodology could not accomplish the goal of statecraft:

> The Mind (*xin*) does not need to be transmitted. What prevails between Heaven and Earth, links past and present, and never differs is Principle. Principle is lodged in my mind and verified in things. The Mind is that by which this Principle is governed, and by which truth and falsity are distinguished and understood. It is what evaluates the worthiness of human character, the success or failure of undertakings, and the order or chaos of the world. It is that by which a sage is able to examine and distinguish with regard to its own precarious subtlety and refined unity, and to transmit the way of holding fast to the mean, making sure that there is no matter that does not accord with Principle, and that there is no partiality of overstepping or of falling short. Chan Buddhist learning regards Principle as an obstacle and relies only on the Mind, passing on its seal with no reliance on words. The learning of the sages extends from a single Mind to applications in the family, in the state, and in All-under-Heaven, and in all respects is the operation of Ultimate Principle.[16]

The Mind, reason, things, and learning are closely linked, and the idea of the mind as an isolated, absolute existence cannot supply a basis for moral judgment or for statecraft. This point is the foundation upon which Gu Yanwu transitioned from Song- and Ming-dynasty moral philosophy or expositions on meanings and principle (*yili*) to his theory of institutions or theory of rites and music: in his view, Mind, human nature, *Dao,* and principles are coupled with the ever-changing rites and music, institutions, and customs in history.

Gu Yanwu did not entirely deny Neo-Confucianism, and fell in line with what Fang Yizhi called "embedding Neo-Confucianism in classical studies." In so doing, they incorporated Neo-Confucianism into the categories of classical studies. To transform Neo-Confucianism into the study of classics and history was, in essence, a move to cope with the relationship between the universal and absolute Heavenly Principle and historical change. The crucial link in between is the conceptualization of "classics." Is a classic an embodiment of general principles, or is it a specific understanding of principles in a particular historical circumstance? The pursuit of understanding the classics eventually led to an understanding of Principle: Are general principles something permanent that will never change, or do they exist only in specific historical and linguistic circumstances? Suppose that a general principle exists only in one particular historical context, which is today within one particular relationship between rites and music and institutions. In this case, how do we grasp such a principle? If a principle is closely related to a particular social relationship, and the adequate expression of the social relationship is ritual, what is the relationship between rituals and principles? The fundamental significance of classical studies lies in scrutinizing classical texts to retrieve the meanings of ancient systems and customs, to outline the refined implications of the historical change of the ancient systems and customs, and finally to discuss how general Heavenly Principle can come into effect within the categories of ritual and musical relationships. Gu was following an approach that was similar to Huang Zongxi's new theory of institutions.

The new theory of institutions, driven by concerns about statecraft, restores the pre-Qin theory of rites and music. Despite their apparent difference, the new theory of institutions does not entirely leave behind the theoretical goals of Neo-Confucianism. If we do not understand the relationship between Huang Zongxi's new theory of institutions (or new theory of rites and music) and Neo-Confucianism, and if we do not understand Gu Yanwu's core study of ancient texts in the pursuit of the true meaning of the institutions and rites and music, then we also would not understand the rise of the *kaozheng* method and its relationship with Neo-Confucianism. Under these conditions, while institutions were alienated from the rites and music, the Neo-Confucians in the Song dynasty could not rely on institutions as the external and objective standards for their moral argumentation and turned to the theory of the Way of Heaven, human nature, and Mind as the starting point of moral evaluation. In the climate of opinion favoring the knowledge of statecraft in the late Ming and early Qing years, Huang Zongxi and Gu Yanwu abandoned the theory of the Way of Heaven, human nature, and Mind. They tried to restore the unity between rites and music and followed an institutional approach to reconstructing the intrinsic relationship between moral evaluation and the theory of institutions, and their theoretical path began to change to a new institutionalism (or the transformation of classical studies). It is this transformation that brought a unique opportunity to move toward a historical orientation within classical studies: Suppose the classics were not a direct expression of the sages' understanding of Heavenly Principle but a record of the system of ancient rites and music and its moral evaluation. In that case, the ancient system's history is bound to be a critical approach to understanding "Heavenly Principle." Because of this, whether it was Huang Zongxi explicating the theory of institutions or Gu Yanwu exploring ancient politics and society, they no longer put the study of human Mind and Nature in the center, nor did they regard abstract Heavenly Principle as the highest source of morality. In the framework of the new theory of institutions and the new theory of rites and music, moral choice must be the product of social relationships (institutions, rites and music, customs) and depends on how each individual confronts specific ritual and ceremonial circumstances. Therefore, any abandonment of the study of classics, history, and customs, and the construction of a moral system based on speculation, is a departure from the goal of the new theory of rites and music.

Gu Yanwu's statement, "The study of Principle (*lixue*) is the study of classics (*jingxue*)," is a high-level summary of the relationship between Neo-Confucianism, the new theory of institutions, and *kaozheng* methodology. Gu used *kaozheng* methods to unify moral philosophy and institutions as an internally correlated and coherent object of study. We couldn't fully understand his writings without appreciating the structure of his theory of rites and music. In his "Letter to Shi Yushan," Gu wrote:

> The transmission of the study of Principle (*lixue*) is naturally what each gentleman should cultivate by himself. I humbly consider that scholars in the Song dynasty coined the phrase "study of Principle." During ancient times, the study of Principle was the study of classics. And it would

> usually take them decades to master classical studies. Therefore, it is said: "When a gentleman studies the *Spring and Autumn Annals,* he would have no choice but devote himself entirely to the task." Today's so-called "School of Principle" is Chan Buddhist learning. They do not consult the Five Classics, but merely base their studies on records of discussions between eminent scholars and their disciples. The text of such discussions is more manageable than some examination essays. [But some scholars would reply by saying:] "Is the *Analects* not a record of discussions between Confucius and his disciples?" Precisely! We will not cover the fundamentals if we avoid the *Analects* and study the discussions of later scholars instead.[17]

Why is it the case that "when a gentleman studies the *Spring and Autumn Annals,* he would have no choice but devote himself entirely to the task?" It is not only because the scope of classical learning is vast, and there is no true mastery without such devotion. It is also because the *Spring and Autumn Annals* contains the essence of rites and music, and "devotion" also implies devotion to a specific relationship of rites and music.

It is only in this sense that Gu Yanwu can say "what is called the study of Principle in ancient times is classical learning," which is an accurate interpretation of how Confucius used the Six Classics for pedagogical purposes: the *Six Classics* recorded the etiquette, institutions, actions, and character of the former kings, and reason and righteousness could only be obtained through understanding and restoring the etiquette, institutions, actions, and character of the former kings. Gu made an excellent comment to this point in "Confucius's Words on Human Nature and the Way of Heaven," a passage in *Record of Daily Knowledge:*

> In the Master's "outward manifestations of conduct," nothing is greater than the *Spring and Autumn Annals.* The meaning of the *Spring and Autumn Annals* is that "to venerate the Heavenly King," "to punish the barbarians," and "to put to death rebellious ministers and villainous sons" are all aspects of Nature and the *Dao* of Heaven. Therefore, Mr. Hu took the *Spring and Autumn Annals* to be literature stemming from the Sage's decreed nature [and accepted Zigong's statement]: "If you, Master, do not speak, what shall we, your disciples, record?"[18]

Human nature and Heavenly Mandate are achieved in political practice. This passage not only reveals the inner connection between moral practice and the rites and music but also shifts the discourse away from intuitive moral knowledge (*liangzhi*) as the basis of political practice. The difference between the methodologies of Neo-Confucian learning as the "study of Principle" and of classical studies is extremely clear, and so scholars regard Neo-Confucianism and classicism as two forms of knowledge. Some even go so far as to argue that Gu's statement that "the study of Principle is the study of classics" means "not that the study of Principle is equivalent to classical learning but that the study of Principle is part of classical learning."[19] This is a significant misunderstanding of Gu Yanwu's statement.

In this regard, we should also consider Quan Zuwang's statement, "The study of classics (*jingxue*) is the study of Principle (*lixue*)."[20] The relationship between the study of classics and that of Principle is identical, not hierarchical. From Gu Yanwu's point of view, there is never such a thing called the study of Principle that could transcend the study of classics. Gu did not suggest that the study of Principle is part of the study of classics. Instead, he meant that every component of classical studies should aim to accomplish Neo-Confucianism's transcendental goals. If there are no concrete details of classical studies, then there would be no intrinsic goal in studying Principle. The inherent goal is Confucian rituals. "From one body to the state and everyone under Heaven, all should be the objects of learning. From [social relationships] such as prince and ministers, father and son, siblings and friends, to [social actions] such as coming and going, visiting and welcoming, giving and receiving, all are affairs bounded by shame."[21] The investigation of historical institutions, cultures, customs, and social changes is precisely the undertaking of Neo-Confucianism as the study of Principle. It is concerned with the external mechanism that governs individual actions and the action and motivation of social actions such as coming and going, visiting and welcoming, giving and receiving. In this sense, there is no study of Principle outside classical studies, and there are no classical studies and *kaozheng* methodology outside the study of Principle. The interchangeable relationship between the concept of *li* (Principle) and the concept of ritual (*li*) has reemerged here.[22] Huang Zongxi's new theory of institutions is a non-Neo-Confucian form of the study of Principle (*feilixue de lixue xingshi*). Is Gu Yanwu's scholarship also not so? For him, the Neo-Confucian study of Principle should not be part of classical studies. It *is* classical studies.

Gu Yanwu criticized late-Ming scholarship for abandoning broad learning and only seeking the way of moral coherence, ignoring poverty and exhaustion within the empire and discussing all day long the "subtle and precarious" task of achieving a "refined unity" of the mind. Gu found such scholarship disgusting and appalling.[23] He disliked Lu Jiuyuan scholarship, which he said meant "establishing your own doctrine to reject anyone else in the past thousand and five hundred years."[24] On such issues as whether Zhu Xi reached a new philosophical position later in life that contradicted his earlier views, Gu's rebuttal of Lu Jiuyuan and Wang Yangming clearly showed a positive appraisal of Zhu Xi. For this reason, some intellectual historians would classify Gu Yanwu as a Zhu Xi scholar, as opposed to a Wang Yangming scholar.[25] For instance, Zhang Xuecheng and Gong Zizhen considered Gu Yanwu as the fifth-generation Zhu Xi scholar. The initiator of such a genealogy was Zhang Xuecheng—mainly written in the second inner chapter dubbed "Zhu Xi / Lu Xiangshan" of his *Comprehensive Meaning of Literature and History* (*Wenshi tongyi*). As early as the Qianlong-Jiaqing era (1735–1820), Zhang Xuecheng criticized the factional and vulgar views promoted by Qing scholars, suggesting that "those who criticized Zhu Xi were the true successors of Zhi Xi's scholarship after several generations." Zhang then mentioned both Gu Yanwu and Huang Zongxi as exemplars to illustrate that there were both Cheng-Zhu and Lu-Wang genealogies in the Qing dynasty.[26]

There is undoubtedly a connection between the Han and Song learning, as evidenced by the statement, "The study of Principle is the study of classics."[27] But if we only examine connections between some aspects of Gu Yanwu's thought and those of his predecessors, then why are we not saying that Gu inherited Wang Yangming's idea of practice? (Wang also understood moral practice as social actions such as coming and going, visiting and welcoming, giving and receiving.) Why do we not say that Gu's classical studies can be traced to the study of the Mind by Wang Yangming? In making such judgments, the key is to identify some of the more subtle but significant differences: Is the significance of the question of knowledge in the Heavenly Principle worldview the same as its significance in relation to the categories of rites and music? Is the meaning of practice within the category of intuitive moral knowledge (*liangzhi*) the same as that in the relationship of ritual, music, and social customs? The premise behind the establishment of this form of classical learning was to view ritual as an objective existence for moral evaluation and moral practice. It is difficult to meld it together in purpose or method with either Zhu Xi scholarship, which promulgates Heavenly Principle, or with Wang Yangming scholarship, which highlights intuitive moral knowledge. Zhu Xi attaches great importance to the Four Books, and Gu Yanwu highlights the Five Classics. Zhu Xi's purpose was to investigate things and extend knowledge to understand Heavenly Principle. Gu Yanwu, on the contrary, searched to drill down into the meanings of the classical texts with *kaozheng* methodology. The discrepancy was not merely a methodological difference between *kaozheng* and moral philosophy (*yili*), but rather a difference in how they framed *wu* (things) in their epistemologies.

As mentioned earlier, without understanding the concept of *Tianxia*, it is impossible to understand the profound meaning in Gu Yanwu's investigation of the classics and history: This is how the gentry-literati maintained dignity during the total loss of institutional support from Ming to Qing. Most scholars ignored this circumstance during the late Qing. For example, Liang Qichao believed that Gu Yanwu was second to none in setting the direction of Qing scholarship. Such an evaluation could not be any higher. But Liang's historical judgment focused primarily on the intellectual transformation from Ming to Qing: Liang used Gu Yanwu's criticism of the School of the Mind (e.g., Wang Yangming, etc.) and the School of Principle (e.g., Zhu Xi, etc.) as the standard, and assigned Sun Xiafeng, Huang Lizhou, and Li Yiqu to the label "residual scholarship of the late Ming." Liang also used Gu Yanwu's classical methodology as a yardstick to justify a negative assessment of Wang Fuzhi and Zhu Shunshui, who had opposed Ming scholarship.[28] Classical studies and the *kaozheng* method emphasized searching as widely as possible for evidence and logical reasoning based on proof to reach the ultimate comprehension of classical texts. Liang Qichao and Hu Shi discovered what they thought were scientific methods in this approach, but they also complained that the *kaozheng* method only examined ancient texts, not a wide range of natural knowledge, thus failing to develop actual scientific research. When they applied this scientific perspective to Gu Yanwu's unique contribution, Liang and Hu could not explain the significance of the regulations and institutions, ritual, music, and social customs. They also replaced Gu's core values with their utilitarianism and pragmatism. Since Gu Yanwu lived in an entirely different political and moral world from Liang Qichao and Hu Shi, however, no matter how much Liang and Hu wanted to praise Gu's "scientific method" and his opposition to Neo-Confucianism (Hu Shi considered Gu as the first anti-Neo-Confucian thinker of the preceding three hundred years), they ignored a fundamental fact: although these Qing scholars took one another as a model for their anti-Neo-Confucian stances, their opposition itself was a particular expression of Confucian discourse. The modern perspective based upon the scientific method's vantage point cannot account for the starting point of classical studies and *kaozheng* methodology: as the object of the classical studies and *kaozheng* methods, "things" (*wu*) are neither "this thing" (*ciwu*) studied by the School of Mind (*xinxue*, i.e., Wang Yangming scholarship), nor the "myriad things of the universe" (*yuzhou wanwu*) investigated to attain Heavenly Principle by the School of Principle (the "things" in "the investigation of things and extension of knowledge" of Zhu Xi scholarship). Things (*wu*) as the object of the classical studies and *kaozheng* methods can neither be simplified as a matter of fact nor be understood in the epistemological categories of modern positivism. Instead, classical studies and the new theory of institutions attempted to overcome precisely the conceptualization of *wu* as a matter of fact, namely, the myriad things in the Neo-Confucian framework of investigating things and extending knowledge (*gewu zhizhi*) or in the myriad things derived from modern scientific methodology.

Whether it is Huang Zongxi's new theory of institutions or Gu Yanwu's classical studies and *kaozheng* methods, "*wu*" (things) have normative and regulatory implications because they only exist in the ritual order. The normative significance of *wu* needs to be compatible with the categories of "ritual" and "culture," which are established in the theory of rites and music or new theory of institutions or must be based on these theories in order to be established. In this sense, the *wu* in the Cheng-Zhu Neo-Confucian framework is closer to what we mean by "things" in modern science. Here we may compare Gu Yanwu's explanation of the line from the *Book of Odes* (*Shi jing*) that reads, "Heaven produced this teeming people, / And for each thing there is a norm," with Cheng Yi's understanding of the "myriad things" (*wan wu*) that is described in Chapter 3. Gu Yanwu wrote in *Record of Daily Knowledge:*

> The *Book of Odes* says: "Heaven produced this teeming people, / And for each thing there is a norm (*you wu you ze*)." *Mencius* [said]: "[The legendary emperor] Shun reckons mundane *wu* (things) and investigates human morality." In the past, the visit made by King Wen, Master Ji's visits to Chen, the inquiries from Master Zeng and Ziyou, and the response from Confucius, all these are *wu*. Therefore [quoting *Mencius*], "Every *wu* should be ready in me." Only a gentleman could empathically feel all the *wu* under Heaven. Therefore, the *Book of Changes* says: "A gentleman should always speak with *wu* in his content and act with perseverance," [and the] *Book of Rites* (*Li ji*) says: "A humane gentleman would not exceed the *wu* in his action; a filial son would not exceed the *wu*, either."[29]

Wu is not a matter of fact or things in "the myriad things" but a premise and norm of moral actions. It is the classical and natural sense of ten thousand *wu* (under Heaven), directly connected to the concepts of "culture" and "ritual." The Qing classical scholars universally recognized the *wu* as such and rejected "the investigation of things" (*ge wu*) in Cheng-Zhu Neo-Confucianism. It was also a restoration of the "three *wu*" or "three things of the village" from pre-Qin antiquity.[30] Wan Sitong (1638–1702) explained it with clarity:

> The later scholars do not know that the *wu* in *The Great Learning* refers to three *wu*. Some thought it meant the fathoming of principles, the rectification of occurrences, resistance to external seductions, communication between the self and others, etc. Despite their refined analyses of the passage, controversies persisted, and the correct gloss of the word *wu* in *The Great Learning* remained unsettled. . . . The idea of *wu* was part of the regular curriculum in ancient schools, learned regularly by the beginners. The later scholars searched for its meaning in the vast arena of vague ideas and never got it right. Others who determined to understand it could not find the right path forward because they did not know that the word "*wu*" refers to three *wu*.[31]

If "*wu*" indeed means three *wu*, then the transformation of the idea of "*wu*" would inevitably lead to the implication of the extension of knowledge. Gu Yanwu said:

> The extension of knowledge means knowing the limits of knowledge. Where does knowing stop? . . . As a prince, it stops at humanity; as a minister, it stops at reverence; as a son, it stops at filial piety; as a father, it stops at kind affection; as a fellow statesman, it stops at trustworthiness. When knowing stops, then the extension of knowledge is known. The prince, ministers, father, son, and social interaction with a statesman, as well as three hundred rituals and three hundred dignified manners, all these are called "*wu*." . . . If you think the investigation of things (*wu*) as merely to know the names of birds, animals, plants, and trees, then you are pursuing a trivial purpose. Those who know would know everything. It is the most urgent task.[32]

Only by restoring the concept of "*wu*" to the normative system of rites and music, humanity, and the classical category of the natural order (which means the unification of "is" and "ought" in the same category) will the practice of seeking knowledge not be separated from moral practice. The ultimate purpose of knowledge is to know where knowledge stops. This "limit" is not any concrete normative structure but only a manifestation of the structure itself. The limit can therefore be understood as proof that such a concrete normative structure exists.

As with the concepts of "ritual" and "culture," the idea of "*wu*" (things) must be understood in its broadest sense: "*Wu*" (things) exist in the world of "rituals" and "culture." They live in all rituals, norms, and order of the world. The world of "things" is a world of the natural order, and the world of the natural order is a world of ritual and culture. It is difficult to understand this internal transformation without the background of the new theory of institutions or the new theory of rites and music. Therefore, at first glance, *kaozheng* methods first of all work to restore the sanctity of the Sage-Kings' institutions through the study of classical texts. This sanctity was derived not so much from the institution itself as from the harmony and consistency between people and *wu* in antiquity (rituals, music, institutions, social customs, etc.). In this sense, unlike those positivists who deconstructed the

West's theological worldview, the *kaozheng* scholars, with their emphasis on evidence and method, did not liberate the world from the sanctity of tradition and transform it into a pile of cold facts that had now become untethered from value. Quite the opposite, *kaozheng* scholars wanted to establish the sanctity or moral essence of the universe, thereby achieving the valuation of real affairs and events (*wu*) or the substantiation and materialization of values. The reconstruction of the concept of "*wu*" can therefore be to overcome the dualism of *li* (principles) versus *qi* (material forces or energy)—the Neo-Confucian dichotomy that requires constant clarification in history.

The restoration of the concept of "*wu*" and Gu Yanwu's understanding of practice support each other: There is no particular kind of moral practice, but only the mundane practice of daily life, that is, daily practice under specific norms, institutions, and social customs. Gu does not avoid all kinds of detailed analyses to criticize Neo-Confucians' idea of the coherent Way. His goal was precisely to present this institutional or ritual practice through detailed studies of their historical conditions. However, as mentioned above, the ultimate purpose of knowledge is not a particular ritual, social norm, or behavior, but a specific circumstance in which people would show the limits of their action in a given ritual, social norm, and thinking. Such a "limit" is only reflected in the dynamic process. The process is similar to when the wizard performed a sacrificial ritual to Heaven in ancient China to reveal Heavenly Will or Mandate. Therefore, Gu Yanwu's investigation of the ancient pronunciation of words and texts was not merely to pursue knowledge for knowledge's sake. Instead, he insisted on the significance of "loving antiquity and studying it diligently, accumulating knowledge to see [the true picture]" and did not exclude the Neo-Confucian emphasis on "comprehensive synthesis" or "unification and penetration":

> "I love antiquity and study it diligently and accumulate knowledge to see [the true picture]." It is how Confucius described himself. . . . Is it not the case that all paths lead to the same destination, namely, the principles of *Tianxia?* A great man's learning should illustrate the fundamentals and the details. For instance, some literati could not see the whole picture with comprehensive synthesis, and other high and bright gentlemen could only speak of virtue instead of learning. They both missed the true intentions of the sage![33]

Why must we include the Neo-Confucian emphasis on "comprehensive synthesis" or "unification and penetration?" *Wu* (things), as normative categories, are not inflexible dogma but will evolve with the changing times and social customs, so knowledge practices must be situated in history. "History" is a changing circumstance, not a presupposed destiny (such as teleology in some modern Western historical writings), which emphasizes the intrinsic relationship among human activities and the evolution of social customs, habits, and institutions. Therefore, the Neo-Confucian "comprehensive synthesis" is a balancing act of concrete events, real people, and moral philosophy in changing circumstances that helps us to grasp, adhere to, and act on correct moral philosophy. In the worldview of classical and historical studies, there is no ethical practice without knowing, no ethical practice without a cognitive process of right and wrong in ritual, music, social customs, and changing historical circumstances. Gu's statement that "the sense of shame should guide one's moral practice, and scholarly erudition is revealed in cultural scope" is precisely to the point here.

Phonology was the core of the Qing-dynasty *kaozheng* methods, and Gu Yanwu used it to approach statecraft scholarship. We might ask: How did Gu link the investigation of the ancient pronunciation of words to the system of rites and music? Why is it the case that "reading the Nine Classics begins with examining their written characters, and examining written characters begins with knowing their sounds. This is also true of the writings of the masters of the hundred schools"? Is this a simple methodological point or is there a hidden and ulterior motive?[34] Before discussing Gu's views, let us briefly discuss the relationship between phonology and the theory of rites and music. According to Confucius, the Zhou dynasty's rituals began to decline when its music became obscure. The Zheng and Wei states also made disturbing and disorderly music. As a result, the period "when ritual collapsed and music degenerated" refers to the historical moment in which the system of rites and music had declined into chaos. The *Record of Music* (*Yueji*) in the *Book of Rites* (*Li ji*) correlates five musical scales (*gong, shang, jue, zheng, yu*) to the five ritual orders (prince, minister, commoners, events, *wu* [things]). It suggests that "if no one undermines the five ritual orders, then we will not hear cacophony."[35] "Therefore, the former Sage-Kings invented rites and music not to satisfy the desires of mouth, stomach, eyes, and ears but to teach the commoners what to love and what to revile. The purpose was to turn humanity to the right path."[36] The investigation of ancient sound is to search for the system of rites and music's original intention, namely, the correct sounds representing the system of rites and music's purpose. According to Sima Qian's *Records of the Grand Historian:*

> During Confucius's times, the Zhou House declined, and rites and music were abrogated. The *Book of Odes* and the *Book of Documents* were missing. Confucius traced the rituals of Three Dynasties, prefaced the *Book of Documents* and its *Commentaries,* which chronicled events from Tang and Yu's times to the Qin abuse. Confucius said: "I can comment on Xia rituals, but for a small Qi state in the Xia dynasty, I will not be able to comment because there are not enough records. I can comment on Shang rituals, but for a small Song state in the Shang dynasty, I will not be able to comment because there are not enough records. If there were enough records, then I would be able to verify them." Confucius observed that Shang inherited and modified the Xia ritual system. Confucius said: "Then we will know the continuation and modification of the ritual system after one hundred generations. One is culture, and the other is simplicity. The Zhou dynasty inherited and modified from both predecessors, and its culture thrived. I will follow Zhou." Therefore, the *Commentary of the Book of Documents* (*Shu zhuan*) and the *Book of Rites* began with Confucius. Confucius told a high minister of the Lu state: "We can undoubtedly know music. When [the musical instruments] start, the music proceeds in a harmonious manner; as the music continues, [all the musical instruments sound] pure, clearly distinguished from, and yet supporting one another. It completes [the performance]." Confucius continued: "I returned from Wei to Lu, and the music is rectified. The Ya and Song music all went to the right places." In ancient times, there were more than three thousand odes. Confucius eliminated those heavy ones and selected those conforming to the ritual and righteousness. . . . And he settled with 305 songs and matched lyrics with melodies, so they all sounded like the ancient music of Shaowu and Yasong. Now the rites and music could be passed on and annotated, ready to serve the kingly Way and complete the Six Arts."[37]

Confucius made music for all 305 songs in the *Book of Odes*, so the rites and music could be "passed on and annotated." The sound had a direct bearing on music. The ancient music, which had the highest status, communicated with Heaven and man, harmonized inner and outer, and coordinated the high and low of the political hierarchy. Music also worked with the rituals, criminal punishments, and politics as four main pillars of the "kingly Way."[38] The purpose of the investigation of the ancient sound is to rectify the system of rites and music.

The ancient sound was closely related to the diversity of regions, customs, and local preferences. The variation of sound indicates differences across regions, social customs, institutions, and local priorities, and the evolutionary changes from sound to word pronunciation and then to music. In the end, the *Book of Odes* would integrate all varieties of local sounds into a harmonic system. The *Book of Odes* collected folks songs from each different state, and Confucius matched their lyrics with melodies so they could be compatible with the system of rites and music, resulting in a process of the rectification of music. "Music is the same, but rituals are different in each locality. When they were the same, they loved each other. When they were different, they respected each other. . . . When ritual and righteousness are established, the noble and the plebeian became equal. When music and culture are unified, then the high and low were in harmony."[39] Such were the internal connections between the rites and music and the royal regulations (*wang zhi*). It was understood as ways to adapt to local conditions, or what is called following the popular and following the good. These sayings show the diversity within the system of the rites and music in ancient China. They also show how the system of rites and music could incorporate diversity and difference. In this sense, making rituals and composing music means to allow ritual to distinguish local differences and to let music promote unity and harmony. The goal was to reach a society in which "music is perfected and there is no resentment, ritual is perfected and there is no contention, . . . matching affections between fathers and sons, clarifying precedence between elders and the young, so that everyone is respectful within the four seas."[40]

However, what is "correct" music? According to Sima Qian's prompts, music of the Lu state (*Lu yue*), the elegant, legendary, and ancient Shao and Wu music (*Shao Wu*), and the state and sacrificial music (*Ya song*) in the *Book of Odes* were the exemplars of correct music. They were the correct music not because they came from a particular place or because of the location of their performance, such as in the court and a sacrificial ritual, but because this music was correct by itself. Although it was concretely implemented in the music of the Lu state, in the elegant, legendary, and ancient Shao and Wu music, and in the state and sacrificial music in the *Book of Odes,* the correct music itself is not equivalent to any specific music. Its "correctness" refers to the natural state of music—because the natural order of Heaven is the order of rites and music itself. One must implement the natural state of the correct music into a specific expression embedded in the diverse forms of ritual and musical relationships. According to the *Record of Music,* a part of the *Book of Rites* (*Li ji*): "In all cases, the arising of Music (*yin*) is born in the minds of men. The movement of men's minds is made so by things (*wu*). They are touched off by things and move, thus they take shape in [human] sound (*sheng*). Sounds respond to each other, and thus give birth to change. Change forms a pattern called Music (*yin*). The Music is brought close and found enjoyable, and reaches the point of shields and axes, feathers and pennants, and this is called Music (*yue*)."[41] Music comes from sound and melody, which in turn arise from "the mind moved by *wu*" and are expressed by making sounds. The *wu* here are not external things, but rather the *wu* defined within the classical natural categories (i.e., in the world of culture and rituals or in Heaven itself). Otherwise, how could the ancients have claimed, "Ritual, music, criminal punishments, and political administration are the four main pillars, by which the people's minds are united people and the way of governance emerges"?[42] Sound was the initial element of music and a response to the *wu*. The combination of different scales led to melodies, which became music with additional sounds performed by musical instruments.

Therefore, the investigation of music was inseparable from specific sounds and music, and it is necessary to distinguish music from a wide variety of sounds. The criterion is music's correctness, which could transcend regional differences and other variations and yet be realized in regionality and variation (as in *Lu yin, Shao wu,* and *Ya song*). Accordingly, the investigation of a word or a sound implies a political and moral proposition, which, on the one hand, investigates diversity versus unity, rites and music versus institutions, enfeoffment (*fengjian*) versus centralized administration (*junxian*), and multiplicity versus integration. Another aspect of this inquiry, on the other hand, involves a search for the highest and most abstract form of rites and music (i.e., ritual and music that exist together with Heaven). The former studies the royal regulations, and the latter examines the political and aesthetic justification of the royal regulations.

Let us understand the relationship between Qing scholars' *kaozheng* method and the Neo-Confucian "comprehensive synthesis" in the system of rites and music by analyzing Gu Yanwu's *Five Books on Phonology* and observing how the idea of "*wu*" changed in the course of his investigations. First of all, Gu Yanwu described himself: "Ever since I turned fifty, I determined to study the classics and history earnestly and developed a deep understanding of them." He discovered the true meaning of system of rites and music, social customs, and institutions by investigating words and their pronunciation. He did so to "connect to the long-lost tradition of the *Three Hundred Songs* [i.e., the *Book of Odes*]."[43] Gu's work was a criticism of Song and Ming academic styles and an appraisal of historical change since the Qin and Han dynasties. Gu Yanwu inherited the outstanding work *An Investigation of Ancient Sounds in Mao Poetry* (*Mao shi gu yin kao*) by Chen Di, and his accomplishments went far beyond that of his predecessors and gave music a new significance in the system of rites and music. In the preface of *Five Books on Phonology,* Gu said:

> The *Book of Rites* says, "When sounds (*sheng*) form patterns (*wen*), these are called 'harmonic tones' (*yin*)." When there is a patterned text (*wen*), then rhymes (*yin*) exist. When rhymes are arranged together, it is poetry. After poetry is formed, then it is set to music. These all come from Heaven and are not man-made. In the Three Dynasties of high antiquity [Xia, Shang, and Zhou], texts were all based on the Six Classics, and people were all educated in their local community schools. Their natures were trained and transformed to be moderate and harmonious, and when they expressed themselves in [rhyming] sounds (*yin*), these never failed to accord with righteousness."[44]

From sound to text, from text to voice, from voice to poetry, from poetry to music.[45] Although in this process, humans act and make sound, text, voice, poetry, and music, fundamentally the process was not entirely up to the individual, neither did it depend on any others' help. It was a natural (and spontaneous) process, and thus it is said that music "comes from Heaven and cannot be a human creation." The sound had to become a text to form voice. From voice to poetry, the investigation of ancient sound cannot proceed without words in a text. The Six Classics reveal patterns and relationships between sound, voice, and text, which were produced according to the Six Principles of character formation in communities and schools, namely, a specific relationship within the ritual system. In such an idealized relationship, voice and music "never deviated from correctness." Here correctness is rooted not in music but in the relationship between rites and music. Precisely because of this insight, Gu Yanwu considered the examination of ancient sound as the primary methodology to study the system of rites and music in ancient China. The study of ancient sound must begin with ancient texts because we can only reconstruct the ancient sound and voice from ancient texts. Without the texts, there is no way to study the ancient sounds.

In addition, Gu Yanwu built his theory of music upon a model of historical evolution: On the one hand, the relationship between sound and text underwent a process of being disseminated, mixed with something else, and changed. From ancient times to Qin and Han and from Qin and Han to the Tang dynasty, the radical alteration of word pronunciation and the classical texts' relative stability constituted the most significant challenges in classical studies. Later scholars often did not know about this, and they used their contemporary pronunciation of words to interpret the ancient texts, thus losing the critical meanings and important points in the ancient texts. On the other hand, however, these scholars' mistakes often provide clues to trace how they misidentified the pronunciation of words in the classical texts and can be used as indirect evidence to recover the ancient sounds. What is called "investigation of the ancient texts to know the ancient sounds" is a journey through a historical labyrinth. And the "historical labyrinth" implies that retrieving the "correct sound and voice" (*zheng yin*) is a historical process in itself. There is no way to study ancient sounds without historical investigation. Gu said:

> The 305 poems of the *Odes* are a guide to the rhymes of classical antiquity.
>
> By the Wei (220–265) and Jin (265–420) dynasties and thereafter, antiquity was ever more remote, and [examples of] nonclassical verse (*ci*) and rhymed prose (*fu*) were ever more abundant. Later, rhymes

[originally called *yin,* referring to the integral sound of a full monosyllabic word] became called by the name *yun* [referring only to the final segment of a fragmented sound]. By the time of Zhou Yong in the Six Dynasties Song (420–479) period and Shen Yue in the Liang period (502–557), charts systematically distinguishing the four tones had been constructed. But from the Qin (221–210 BCE) and Han (206 BCE–220 CE) dynasties, writing had gradually turned away from ancient models, and in the Eastern Jin (318–420) dynasty [this trend] became increasingly extreme. So, when Shen Yue made his charts, he was not able to base them on the *Odes* [from high antiquity], or to make supplementary references to *[Li] Sao* (*Encountering Sorrow*) and the Masters [of the Warring States period], in order to compile an imperishable classic. Rather, Shen Yue based his tone charts only on the rhymes used in the rhymed prose of various writers since the time of Ban [Gu] and Zhang [Heng, both of the Eastern Han dynasty], and in the [pentasyllabic] poetry of various writers since Cao [Zhi] and Liu [Cheng, both of the Jian'an era (196–219) in the late Eastern Han]. Shen Yue wrote a definitive work on this subject, with the result that modern rhymes circulated while ancient rhymes fell into disuse; this was the first major transformation in the history of rhymes. Coming down into the Tang (618–906) period, composition of poetry and rhymed prose was used to select civil officials, and the uniform standard for their rhymes was the [set of 206 rhyme groups in] Lu Fayan's *Countertomic Rhymes* (*Qieyun;* completed in 601, in the Sui dynasty). Although there were [various] commentaries concerned with use of single or multiple [rhyme groups to classify certain characters], still the division of rhyme groups remained unchanged. At the time of the [Northern] Song reign period Jingyou (1034–1037) there were some slight changes. Then, during the late years of [Southern Song] Emperor Li Zong (r. 1225–1264), Liu Yuan, a native of Pingshui district, for the first time merged the 206 rhyme groups into 107 groups. In the Yuan dynasty (1279–1368) Huang Gongshao's work *Assembled Rhymes* (*Yun hui*) followed this [example], which has been continued to the present. Thus, the Song rhymes were circulated and the Tang rhymes fell into disuse; this was the second major transformation in the history of rhymes. As each age became more distant [from antiquity], the transmission [of ancient models] became ever more corrupted. The demise of this Way occurred more

> than two thousand years ago now. I have immersed my mind [in this subject] for [many] years, but only after obtaining a copy of [the 1101 CE redaction of *Qieyun,* known as] *Expanded Rhymes* (*Guang yun*) did I comprehend its essential principles and understand its applications. On this basis, I used the Tang-dynasty writers [represented in *Guang yun*] to correct the errors of the Song-dynasty writers, and used the ancient classics to correct the errors of Shen Yue and the Tang writers. As for the rhymes of high antiquity, their division in groups is now put in order; this is a matter of the most profound significance and cannot be left unclarified. So I set forth the changes of ancient and modern rhymes, probed the reasons for their differences, and composed *Treatise on Rhymes* (*Yin lun*) in three chapters, to examine and rectify the most ancient rhymes. I annotated the 305 poems [of the *Odes*] and wrote *The Original Rhymes of the "Odes"* (*Shi ben yin*) in ten chapters. I annotated [the *Book of*] *Changes (Yijing)* and wrote *The Rhymes of "Changes" (Yi yin)* in three chapters. I clarified Shen Yue's errors of classification, and one by one used the ancient rhymes to correct them, so I wrote *Corrections to "Tang Rhymes" (Tang yun zheng)* in twenty chapters. I comprised ancient rhymes in ten groups, and wrote *Table of Ancient Rhymes (Gu yin biao)* in two chapters. From this time, the text of the Six Classics can be read [accurately aloud]. As for the other writings of the various [Eastern Zhou dynasty] Masters, they may vary more or less, but not by very much. [As Confucius said,] "That Heaven has not allowed this culture to be entirely lost" [indicates that] a new sage will surely arise who can cause modern speech to be restored to the pure ancient model.[46]

The *Book of Odes* was a guide to the rhymes and pronunciations of classical antiquity. But the Qin and Han eras' sounds and voices had gradually deviated from ancient times and in Wei-Jin times had descended to rhetoric and rhymes. The later scholars learned to write poetry from the standards of Wei-Jin times. As a result, the ancient sounds perished, and the contemporary rhyming prevailed.

The Tang dynasty's imperial examination system adopted Lu Fayan's rhyming book *Countertomic Rhymes* (*Qieyun*) as the standard. The next shift took place during the Song and Yuan dynasties, leading to the Tang rhyme system's decline, and the Song-dynasty rhyme system became popular. Gu

Yanwu argued: because ancient sound was corrupted or lost over time, the ancient *Dao* had been lost for more than two thousand years. From this perspective on epochal change, Gu Yanwu established a methodological principle that used Tang sources to modify the mistakes made in the Song times and used the ancient classics to correct Shen Yue's and other Tang scholars' mistakes. As a result, he could slowly and gradually recover the structure of the ancient sounds. In particular, Gu mentioned the correlation between the phonological and institutional changes; for instance, the Tang dynasty used poetry as selection criteria in the examination system. So, the investigation of texts, sounds, and voices cannot be detached from social mobility, institutional change, and evolution of social customs. In the circumstances where the correct sounds and voices were lost, the classical texts had been tampered with, and the truth was no longer attainable, "the Three Dynasties of Antiquity and the Six Classics were no longer comprehensible to scholars of later generations, and, because of their lack of understanding they often altered the classical texts according to their contemporary pronunciations." Consequently, the problem of alterations in classical texts arose.[47] Therefore, the *kaozheng* methodology to restore and authenticate the classical texts became a key to understanding the Six Classics and an approach to illuminating the *Dao* comprehensively. Wei Yuan (1794–1857) said:

> Since the clarification of the debates on the Four Beginnings [of the *Book of Odes*], the actual reason why the Duke of Zhou made the system of rites and music is now available. Once one can understand rites and music, then one can read the state and sacrificial music in the *Book of Odes.* When the traces of [the kingly Way] disappeared, and the [meaning of] the *Book of Odes* was lost, Confucius composed the *Spring and Autumn Annals* to take over the *Book of Odes'* function. Once we understand the *Spring and Autumn Annals,* we should be able to read the "Airs of the States" (*Guo feng*) chapter in the *Book of Odes.* . . . The system of rites and music is to govern and create peace and prevent chaos. It moves from simplicity to culture. The *Spring and Autumn Annals* is to turn chaos to order. It moves from decorative multiplicity to simplicity. The *Dao* [of the *Book of Odes*] is for the leaders on top to understand rites

> and music and for the commoners below to understand the *Spring and Autumn Annals.* And then the ancient sages' mind that concerns the future under Heaven will not cease.[48]

These dualities—culture versus simplicity, rites and music versus *The Spring and Autumn Annals*—constitute how a Confucian scholar conceives an ideal political world. Although this passage comes from a Gongyang Confucian scholar, Wei Yuan, it also conforms to the Qing-dynasty evidential scholars' basic views.[49] The purpose of the investigation of ancient sound was to illustrate the *Book of Odes* and reveal the social customs, ritual, and music through the classical texts. It was to restore the true meaning of the ancient system and use it as the basis for statecraft. In this sense, the *wu* (things) in the investigation of things were no longer the natural objects (including sound) but rather the civilizing role of ritual and music in the ancient world. And the ritual, music, and the civilizing work of the ancient world (culture) were, naturally, entirely compatible with the way of Heaven.

Phonology reflects an archaeological vision of classical learning; it was not merely a method of studying the *Book of Odes.* In addition to the relationship between sound and text, the relationship between speech and writing is also an essential issue in the study of classics. Kang Youwei's argument that "Confucius established literary composition" indicates the belief that, in ancient times, speech (sound) was the most important thing for the sake of communication, and words (writing) were secondary because speech was closer to "nature." From the perspective of Confucian classical studies, we cannot help but ask a question: Since speech (sound) is disseminated in the form of writing, what is the inherent difference between speech and writing? The *Analects* say: "Pi Chen drafts the [diplomatic] documents." The Zuo commentary has: "Zichan masters elegant words, and the princes benefit accordingly"; it also tells us that "Confucius said: "Speech will not go very far without ornament (*wen*)."[50] From the viewpoint of communication, then, speech depends on writing. In ancient texts, in addition to written correspondence and war declarations, face-to-face conversations—such as political discussions among princes and officials, solicited questions from enemies and rivals, socialization among friends, and questions from teachers and disciples—were all recorded in writing. We should not ignore the difference between speech and writing, given that speech could not be preserved and disseminated without being worded. Kang Youwei once had an excellent remark on this:

> The Six Classics were written discourses, and even the *Analects* are records of conversations (*yulu*). Zhuangzi said: "Debaters will not be pleased if they cannot argue." He also said: "The speaker sounds like a debater." So, when the political philosophers [who lobbied for a living], such as Yi, Qin, and Chen Zhen, tried to persuade their masters, it was all by means of speech. Zou Yan's discourses on Heaven, and Zou Shi's intricate restatement of them, which more than a thousand people discussed in Jixia, were all speech. In their famous expositions, Hui Shi and Gongsun Long, . . . used speech to make their arguments. When Song Xian and Mo Di traveled from state to state persuading people, they relied on speech. If today we examine their rhetorical style, all this can be verified.[51]

In this sense, the records of ancient philosophers were all written down from spoken discourse or from conversations. In converting speech into written forms, those ancient philosophers added many modifications and changes in the writing process to adapt to various relationships and needs. We cannot understand the Sage-Kings based on the writing itself—the relationships between speech, sound, ritual, and music are more direct. The most concealed parts of the writing process are the relationships between speech, sound, and the system of rites and music. For example, the texts in the *Book of Rites from the Older Dai* (*Dadai liji*) and *The Discourses of the States* (*Guoyu*) are sophisticated and modified by later generations. And yet, the patter of their concise style still retains the characteristics of speech. Therefore, the way to understand the meaning of the classical texts is to eliminate the various literary decorations of later generations and go directly to knowing the ancient sounds. The *Book of Odes* is a collection of poems from different states, and its rhymes, vocabulary, and music reflect the characteristics of the customs of multiple states. If readers do not know the ancient sounds and only understand writing, then they will not understand the ancient customs described in the *Book of Odes* or why Confucius edited out so many poems, which revealed Confucius's true intentions in rectifying music.

From the perspective of written records, the Three Dynasties' texts include "fixed substance" (*ding ti*) and "fixed names" (*ding ming*) determined by rites and music. The fixed name refers to the hierarchy of status defined in the scope of rites and music, and speech's "fixed substance" refers to the formation of a fixed language according to specific ritual rules, such as prayers, coronations, meetings, congratulations, making alliances, and so on. These documents had particular formats and rhetoric. Without changing a word, the exact formulaic wording could spread far and wide. One could trace such formulaic genres to the rituals of ancient shamanic sacrifices. These styles of speech still exist today (such as in some epistles). Later scholars often mistakenly regarded them as merely literary styles and did not understand that they were closely related to the ancients' rituals, music, tones, and dances. For example, in the *Book of Filial Piety* (*Xiao jing*) we have: "Zengzi avoids the seat and said: 'I am not smart, how can I figure it out?'" The "Duke Ai Asked" chapter in the *Book of Rites* reads: "I am not firm, how can I hear this?" The *Record of Music* has: "[He] is a cheap laborer, how could he possibly be able to ask what is appropriate? I recite what I heard, and my friend, you are trapping yourself." These examples sum up the specific, fixed style of resignation and humility found in antiquity.[52]

The style of resignation and humility was adjusted due to changes in specific situations, but the basic format has not changed, so the fixed substances themselves retain the connotations of "sound," "tone," and "music." Because the status of ancient speech is very high, special knowledge is necessary to accord with its standards. In the *Book of Documents* we have: "Spoken style values concise substance." Confucius said: "If you don't study the *Book of Odes*, you won't be able to speak adequately." In other words, like fixed names, the fixed substance of speech is not a human-made "substance" (*ti*) but one based on rites and music. It is precisely because of this that we can understand Kang Youwei's explanation:

> The ancients are serious about their words, rituals are used to determine their substance, music is used to harmonize their spirits (*qi*); men of broad learning depend on [this arrangement] to explain their ideas, while men of specialized knowledge use them to refine their learning. The practice is the same among scholars, so when applied to ordinary people, it

> will not vary much. When culture and customs are the same under Heaven, there is no danger of separation [between different people], no useless learning, its appearance and rhetoric, its culture is apparent, and its substance is clearly sufficient. Their words are for proclamation. If those above and below communicate with each other, then governance will be successful.[53]

In this sense, "fixed substance" and "fixed names" embody the style and name of rites and music, that is, the "cultural" aspect of how "scholarly erudition is revealed in cultural scope."

In ancient times dialects and habits varied by region, and the precondition for communication with words is that they should express themselves in a specific fixed substance and name. Otherwise, dialogue, persuasion, and communication are impossible. Substance (*ti*) and name (*ming*) are not only based on rites and music but also produced from the practice of rites and music, so the so-called fixed substance and fixed name do not exclude the diversity of expressions (in sounds, voices, and written words).

As mentioned earlier, Gu Yanwu aims to return to rites and music, and the investigation of words and their sounds constitutes the primary approach for the return. Due to historical change, the essence of rites and music was no longer self-evident, and it had to be revealed in a specific way. In this sense, the investigation of words and their sounds lies in understanding the relationship between the true meaning of rites and music and historical changes. For example, from the perspective of changes in speech and writing, how can we define the "correctness" of speech? With the establishment of fixed names in speech, scholar-officials discussed and studied with each other day and night, competing to be the most elegant, and a distinction between high and low tastes appeared. Confucius said: "Speech without ornamentation (*wen*) won't travel far." Then he said: "Crafting words establishes the sincerity [of the speaker]." Zengzi said: "Speak words with *qi;* then we may quickly staying away from vulgarity." Here "ornament," "crafting," and "staying away from vulgarity" all denote high taste, but for Confucius, only "establishing the sincerity [of the speaker]" is authentic high taste. Later generations thought that words seen in ancient texts such as *hu, zhe, yi,* and *yan* were auxiliary words used in speech, but in fact, these words had been rhetorically processed and become different from the actual tone of the spoken language because the latter was considered too "vulgar." In this sense, the development of rhetoric often conceals the fixed name, fixed substance, and "sound and voice" of rites and music, and the distinction between elegance and vulgarity may be apparent, but cannot constitute the standard of "correctness." Confucius's statement that "crafting words establishes the sincerity [of the speaker]" highlights the meaning and role of "sincerity" in the process of constructing the relationship between rites and music. Such an emphasis is entirely consistent with his "understanding ritual (*li*) as humaneness (*ren*)."

In this sense, we can understand why Gu Yanwu tried to eliminate the chaos caused by later generations' focus on formal style and rhyme and tried to investigate the inner motivation of the ancients' search for correct sound. Gu Yanwu said:

> Thus the *Rites of Zhou (Zhouli)* says that the royal court's chief ceremonial officer "in the ninth year convenes the musicians and scribes [from the various feudal states], instructs them in [correct] written and spoken forms [of words], and determines [normative] sounds and tones." This is a means by which to integrate moral standards and reconcile social customs, and one dare not neglect it. For this reason, although the 305 poems of the *Book of Odes* (*Shijing*) . . . [had originated in] a broad area of fifteen feudal states and over more than a millennium's time, still their rhymes were undifferentiated. [In the *Book of Documents* (*Shangshu; Shujing*) there are] the *Song* by the sage-ruler Shun and its *Continuation* by his minister Gaoyao, as well as the Viscount of Ji's *Statement* [of royal perfection]; [in the *Book of Changes* (*Yijing*) there are] the appended *Judgments* by King Wen and the Duke of Zhou. [The rhymes in all these] are entirely like [the rhymes in the *Book of Odes*]. Thus, the 305 poems of the *Odes* are a guide to the rhymes of classical antiquity.[54]

As mentioned above, the distinction between high and low taste is based on a particular political premise. Gu Yanwu believed neither in the Qin and Han dynasties' sounds and voices nor in those of the Wei and Jin dynasties, nor could he trust the Tang and Song dynasties' rhymes. The sounds and voices of the Qin and Han dynasties are relatively unified, while those of the Wei and Jin dynasties have changed a lot, but none of them constitutes the standard of "correctness." Gu Yanwu tried to restore the Zhou dynasty's voice and music, collected in the *Book of Odes*. Confucius matched them with melodies and edited them into the system of rites and music.

We can explain the possible implications of this phonology from two perspectives: division and unity. Since the Spring and Autumn period, the lords had become independent from the Son of Heaven; during the Warring States period, the Seven Kingdoms contended for hegemony; the hundred schools competed with one another, and geographical differences became politicized. The linguistic condition was one of "differing sounds in speech and differing forms in written characters." At this time, there were mounting calls to end the chaos and restore order. "Division" obviously did not mean "order" or "correctness" (*zheng*). Confucius focused on speech, but he attached great importance to the "rectification of names" (*zheng ming*). He aimed at addressing the collapse of rites and music in the Spring and Autumn period by theorizing the world under Heaven with the categories of rites and music again. What he asked for was what Xunzi had called "following the Shang [dynasty] in names for punishments, following the Zhou in names for official titles, and following their rituals in names for cultural forms. In applying various names to the myriad things, [the later kings] followed the set customs and generally agreed usage of the various Xia states."[55] Due to the collapse of the system of rites and music, "correctness" could not refer to the actual conditions of speech and writing. It had to mean the potentiality of language to embody rites and music (the world of culture, pattern, or *wen*) in the future. From the perspective of unity, "rectification" (*zheng*), "rectification of names," "rectification of sound" (*zheng yin*), or "rectifying and restoring order" (*bo luan fan zheng*) could not be readily equated to imposing a uniform standard of language and music by political means, because what Gu Yanwu meant by "rectification" could only be understood to exist in the institutional settings of "culture" (*wen*) and "ritual" (*li*). We must understand correctness in the domain of rites and music: in the realm of music, harmony reigns supreme, while in the realm of rituals, determining difference is the key. For example, after the Qin and Han dynasties, the variety of speech had disappeared, and the imperial regime unified the written scripts; literature thrived, and institutions proliferated, and words and prose became more technical and arcane. The political "unity" not only did not constitute the cultural condition of "rectification," but on the contrary, it produced differences between genres:

for example, the differences between the various types of poetry, such as rhapsodies (*fu*) and lyrics (*ci*); between rhymed and unrhymed prose; between official correspondence and private letters; between common folk writings and scholarly writings; and between officials' writings and the writings of the literati. Such institutional differences of genres produced a completely different circumstance from the ideal realm of ritual diversity and musical harmony. It signaled a historical rupture and internal disconnect from the past. In this sense, the Qin dynasty's demand that all writing should be in the same script did not make that writing correct or rectified. Gu Yanwu's theory of institutions of rites and music implies that "correct music" and "rectified names" themselves can encompass the diversity of sounds, languages, customs, and habits. If the "correctness" of correct music is placed at the center, then correctness in the cultural system and the political system will be integrated into one body, thus conflating the systems of centralized administration (*junxian*) and enfeoffment (*fengjian*). The following passage from Kang Youwei shows how his political understanding of the unified system of centralized administration related to phonology. He equates "correct sound and voice" (*zheng yin*) with unified spoken Mandarin and names the "uneven evenness" (*buqi zhi qi*) as a law that governs all others. His view is the opposite of Gu Yanwu's phonological theory:

> The later Confucian scholars passed on their learning by standardizing the nomenclature. Therefore, we know that books on dialects and local systems do not help govern the state. The way for the ruler to manage unevenness [*buqi,* diversity and differences] is to make it even [i.e., uniform], determine words to express ideas, and implement oral teaching so that the world will be even and unified. When one travels to every corner in China, one will understand and be understood. The so-called "sound and correct voice" nowadays is what we mean by the spoken Mandarin (*guanhua*). If everyone under Heaven learns to talk in the correct voice, then dialects will disappear, and everyone will understand one other.[56]

Based upon the different comprehensions of "sound and voice" and "dialect," we can see the profound difference between Gu Yanwu's and Kang Youwei's politics and their theories of rites and music: Gu's "correctness" in the theory of rites and music can tolerate and even encourage all kinds of diverse material that is regional, customary, or based in daily life; it attempts to understand diversity from the perspective of "correctness" (*zheng*). At the same time, Kang Youwei's "correctness" is a theory of institutions designed to abolish what is regional, customary, or based in daily life. It aimed to promote maximum uniformity. In Gu Yanwu's view, rites and music are a natural and spontaneous order. The word *wen* (culture) refers to the symbolic system that embodied the universal order and the system of rites and music's refined culture. Without this meaning, it is impossible to say, "When one expresses oneself in voice and music, it is always compatible with correctness." Therefore, the purpose of the investigation of words and their sounds and voices is to understand those fixed substances and names contained in ancient scriptures, which included the Sage-Kings' politics and culture and also reflected the purpose for which Confucius edited the *Book of Odes* and the *Book of Documents* and formalized the rites and music. In this sense, the investigation of words and their sounds and voices had become a necessary part of the intellectual agenda for statecraft.

3. Classical Studies, the Three Dynasties of Antiquity, and Social Thought

Many scholars have conducted detailed and innovative research on Gu Yanwu's social thought, but most of them only discuss Gu's "political thinking" or "theory of institutions." However, in such a framework, how do we explain his concept of "things" (*wu*), "rituals," and "texts"? How to explain the relationship between morality and his specific strategy of statecraft? His book *Record of Daily Knowledge* has three parts: The first part is about classical studies, the second part is about the *Dao* of governing, and the third part is about broadening the scope of knowledge. On nearly every page of his detailed analytical process, painstaking efforts, and *kaozheng* methods, Gu reveals his intention to apply classical studies to statecraft and practical affairs. His disciples praised him, saying: "[Our teacher] has synthesized one hundred masters in the past thousand years, conducted a detailed investigation of their insights and mistakes, made a concise assessment, and penned them in this book. [The content of the book includes] imperial regulations, state institutions, and social and folk customs. It covers all fundamentals from the beginning to the end with remarkable insights. We may use the book to correct our times' mistakes, and we may also use the book to save the world. Mr. Gu's work is truly an exemplar of a Confucian polymath."[57] Huang Rucheng, the author of *Collected Commentaries on Record of Daily Knowledge,* saw the intrinsic relationship between its *kaozheng* methods and the ritual system:

> Mr. Gu's comments on the classics and history employ subtle words with profound meanings; his method was sound and his politics were good. He urged us to get to the bottom of the rites, music, morality, and punishments and to understand the evolution from substance to culture and from misfortune to prosperity. Mr. Gu has cross-referenced and examined principles and synthesized the key points of issues regarding the following: land, tax laws, official positions and selection, monetary policies, market and measurement, hydraulic engineering, river works, transportation along the grand canals, regulations of salt and iron monopolies, human talents, the army and military logistics, and so on. Mr. Gu could thoroughly understand these family and state institutions and identify their rise and fall and their benefits and shortcomings. He then generously spells out the *Dao* of [natural] transformations and of the evolution of [human-made] systems.[58]

Gu Yanwu's scholarship was to promote the goals of "getting to the bottom of the rites, music, morality, and punishments, and of understanding the evolution from substance to culture and from the depth of misfortune to the beginning of prosperity." As a result, we should understand his analysis of the historical changes of politics, the economy, military affairs, and morality in terms of the theory of rites and music, which was also the key to his motto: "The sense of shame should guide one's moral practice, and scholarly erudition is revealed in cultural scope." Moral practices are no longer merely moral acts but rather everyday practices in life. No moral practice could go beyond managing land, tax laws, official positions and selection, monetary policies, markets and measurements, the grand canals, regulations of salt and iron monopolies, human talents, the army and military logistics, and the political system. Likewise, no grand plan of statecraft could go beyond practices of daily life. Gu Yanwu examined all rituals, institutions, cultural artifacts, regulations, social customs, and their evolution in the framework of "ritual" and "culture." He disclosed a substantive explanation of how society could form and move in a specific direction. His method itself could be an important hint for us: Modern social theorists have been searching for a possibility of a substantive theory of society, but their endeavors, including their discovery of the historicity of social theory, could never allow them to accomplish such a goal. Social theories are always trapped in a normative structure of theoretical reasoning.

Gu Yanwu discusses various political and social issues within the categories of the Confucian classics, and this theoretical form cannot be simply regarded as camouflage for restoring antiquity. Without the form of the Confucian classics, one cannot understand why theories and discussions of monarchy, the land system, remonstrance and debate, centralized administration (*junxian*), the selection of officials, issues related to entry-level examination candidates, the analysis of finance and food supply, and so on, can be understood as categories of ritual or culture. The *kaozheng* analysis of concrete political, economic, and social problems is not a study of general facts but a discussion of *wu* (things) as norms, rituals, and etiquette. The transformation of the theoretical framework is a consequence of a change in worldview. We will not understand the real meaning of the transformation of Gu's worldview if his theoretical transformation is merely regarded as a "camouflage." If we do not raise questions in this way, we will not understand Gu Yanwu's overall theoretical conception and the internal reasons behind the transformation of his theoretical framework. In this sense, we need to ask: When he analyzes the specific problems of politics, the economy, the military, scholarship, the environment, social customs, human sufferings, costs and benefits, human relations, and so on, was there an internal structure?

Gu Yanwu used the *kaozheng* method to analyze a wide variety of affairs item by item, and his works do not seem to be systematic at first glance. Many Qing scholars have used ideas in Gu's *Record of Daily Knowledge* by conveniently putting these ideas in the categories of economy, politics, and education, just like using a reference book. Still, at the same time, it made them forget that Gu's ideas were all joined together in a complete and extensive system. For example, Ruan Yuan said that "the scholars who praised Gu Yanwu thought that his [writings on] statecraft were better than his [studies of] classics and history." Such a statement presumes a division between the classics and history on the one hand and statecraft on the other. It does not highlight the interconnectedness between Gu's studies of statecraft and of classics and history. Scholars in modern times have even gone beyond this level of relationship and asserted that Gu Yanwu, like a public legal scholar, "had plans on all issues of public law, matters of state organization, systems of administration, the exercise of public power, and agencies of public opinion 'to draw from the ancients as a resource for the present.' . . . His interpretation of the monarch was also equivalent to modern scholars' ideas of voiding the monarch's power. He advocated that the people should have public rights."[59] Gu Yanwu was indeed a social thinker, but we must place his social thought in the ritual system's structure to fully understand it. Otherwise, he would not belong to his times, and he would not have been considered a great Confucian. We will call Gu Yanwu's scholarship a new theory of institutions and call Huang Zongxi's scholarship classical studies or a new theory of rites and music.

Let us start with the similarities and differences between Gu Yanwu and Huang Zongxi. After reading Huang Zongxi's *Waiting for the Dawn: A Plan for the Prince* (*Mingyi daifang lu*), Gu wrote a letter to Huang, expressing his admiration and at the same time saying that 60 or 70 percent of his research was similar to the content of Huang's book. If we read *Record of Daily Knowledge* and his other works closely, then we will discover that all entries focus on the purpose of "rediscovering the errors of a hundred kings and slowly returning to the prosperity of the Three Dynasties of Antiquity." Such fine-grained *kaozheng* research cannot conceal the internal ritual system's structure: The basic principle of the Three Dynasties ritual system is to consider the actual issues and internal structure of institutional reform.[60] In other words, just as in *Waiting for the Dawn*, the ritual systems of the Three Dynasties—especially the well-field (*jingtian*) system of land ownership, enfeoffment (*fengjian*), and official schools—constitute the internal structure of Gu Yanwu's scholarship.[61] To understand his scholarship, we must grasp his discussion on the land ownership and tax system, centralized administration versus enfeoffment, officials' selection, and the system of official ranks. For example, Gu Yanwu advocated scholarly remonstrance (*qingyi*), opposed the civil examination system, and supported selection of the worthy and able. Gu's opposition to the examination system was similar to how Northern Song Confucians appropriated the Three Dynasties system against the imperial civil examinations: "The system of recruiting scholars and recommending them is similar to the selection of local worthies in ancient times."[62] He quoted Sima Guang on a few official selection standards and repeatedly stated that "the enlightened ruler works hard to seek talents, but he employs others with ease." He also said: "It rings true about what Zixia told Fang Chi, saying: [the legendary Sage-King] Shun had the world, and he appointed Gao [minister] Yao from among the people, and consequently, the less humane candidates dispersed. Tang had the world, and he chose Yi Yin from among the people, and consequently, the less humane candidates dispersed."[63]

However, compared to Huang Zongxi's new theory of institutions, Gu Yanwu pays more attention to the origin and evolution of institutions, social customs, and academic styles. His item-by-item *kaozheng* research method contains an understanding of the relationship between moral practice and specific situations, rather than merely linking practice with institutions. If Huang Zongxi's new theory of institutions shows an apparent idealism, focusing on the internal structure and mechanisms of society, then Gu Yanwu pays more attention to the evolution of customs and institutions. His propositions on the land system and tax law, centralized administration and enfeoffment, and officialdom are all permeated with a dialectic of change and permanence, which is by no means an inflexible imitation of the ancient institutions. This dialectic of "change" does not deny the meanings of the ancient institutions designed by the Sage-Kings, but it requires that the Sage-Kings' institutions be regarded as ones that adapt to changes of the times, and the dialectic is the opposite of dogma. For example, in "On Examination Candidates" (*Shengyuan lun*) and "On Examination Candidate Quotas" (*Shengyuan shu'e*), Gu harshly criticized the examination candidates trained in the imperial schools. He listed four significant drawbacks of the current civil service examination system: it caused disorder in the local government, impoverished the people by leading them to invest money in expensive education, caused scholars to form factions, and failed in selecting true talents. He argued: "Abolish [the role of] examination candidates, and the bureaucracy will become free of corruption; abolish examination candidates, and fewer commoners will fall into poverty; abolish examination candidates, and factional groups in the bureaucracy will be eliminated; abolish the examination candidates, and useful talents will come forth."[64] But Gu did not immediately call for abolishing the civil examination system. Instead, he searched for new remedies: Rebuilding the official recommendations system would open up another career path for examination candidates. Establishing "family protection" official posts outside the examination system would allow examination candidates to purchase seats. Reforming the imperial examination system would limit and reduce the quota of examination candidates and encourage substantial scholarship by reducing the number of unqualified candidates. We see here that, regarding the evolution of institutions, Gu opposed simply "borrowing from the past":

> If one considers taking today's place name as [less tasteful] because it is not ancient and borrows its ancient name; if one considers taking today's official title as [less tasteful] because it is not ancient and borrows its ancient name; and if one chooses ancient words to replace contemporary terms, these behaviors are precisely how the scholars cover up their conceit and superficiality. . . . The establishment of an official prefecture has a history. If one must call it by the name of the previous generations, how will we investigate its history and evolution? This is an unnecessary act that gets in the way for no good reason.[65]

Place names, official titles, and prefectures are continually changing, so sticking to the old forms does not amount to "Principle." It is more an obstacle for historical development itself. Observing changes over time is not a betrayal of the classical texts. Doesn't the *Spring and Autumn Annals* imply changes in current events? The Qing dynasty was a new and different empire from the Ming dynasty and its territory, official system, and political structure had very different configurations from the previous dynasties.[66] Putting this passage by Gu Yanwu in the early Qing dynasty's historical context, we can feel his tolerant attitude toward the new system, territory, and official positions. Here, notions about Gu's "nationalist ideology," and especially his Han nationalist thinking, cannot explain his understanding of these historical changes. Gu's passage implicitly expressed a dialogue with his contemporary political reality.

While Huang Zongxi paid attention to the function and value of institutions, Gu Yanwu, who aimed to verify ancient institutions' essence, paid more attention to the context of practice. Gu Yanwu opposed imperial examinations and advocated a different selection mechanism for officials. However, by examining his current circumstances, he still suggested "searching for an alternative method coexisting with the system of civil service examinations."[67] He attributed dynastic decline to the fact that "when the Minor Odes chapter [in the *Book of Odes*] was abolished, the central state was in decline. Social customs disintegrated, and chaos ensued." The statement may seem nostalgic, but Gu did not underestimate the effective practice of later generations. For example, in his entry from *Record of Daily Knowledge* on "The Customs of the Former and Later Han Dynasties," Gu praised the Later Han's politics of remonstrance. He believed that "the exquisite social customs in Later Han were unparalleled since the Three Dynasties."[68] Likewise, academic custom is part of social customs, and so it too is part of the historiography of "change." Regarding scholarship, Gu said: "Classical studies has its origins, and its changes from the Han dynasty to the Six Dynasties and through the Tang and Song dynasties must be meticulously examined one by one. Only then can it be compared to the works of contemporaneous scholars, and then we can know the similarities and differences."[69] If scholarship had its origins and evolution, why would the same not be true for institutions? "If our method does not change to adapt to current circumstances, then it will not aid us in the present. If one has arrived at the position that one has no choice but to adapt to the changing propensity [of the times], and one decides to hide the fact of such changes and pretend that nothing has changed, huge problems will arise."[70] For instance, in his essay "On Finance and Food Supply," Gu insisted that, "According to the Sage-Kings' institutions, the state must tax what the land can afford," but the specific taxation method in his times had gone beyond the scope of the ancient institutions. On the one hand, Gu Yanwu criticized cities and the currency system; on the other hand, he advocated a less restrictive economic policy and promoted private property. Some historians even claim that the vital point of Gu Yanwu's monetary policy was agricultural reproduction. Where can we detect traces of the ancient well-field system in his theory?

Gu Yanwu's views on centralized administration (*junxian*) versus enfeoffment (*fengjian*) are the most well known. Even as an admirer of the Three Dynasties of Antiquity, Gu favored centralized administration, but at the level of a theory of institutions, he was inclined toward a hybrid system. The concept of "central state" (*Zhongguo*, also the term for "China") is closely related to the distinction between inner and outer in the relationships of enfeoffment, and so the institutional formation of his times was itself a redefinition of "central state." Gu Yanwu's hybrid theory of enfeoffment and centralized administration did not arise from his imagination of an ideal system but from his sensitivity to the changes of the times and from his attention to China's traditions and social customs. His historical vision was extremely broad: from the Three Dynasties to the Qing dynasty, he studied domestic customs in detail and compared them with their foreign counterparts. He asserted in *juan* 29 of *Record of Daily Knowledge* that "from an examination of China's social customs and the histories of previous dynasties, we see that, in some instances, China was not as good as foreign states." By introducing foreign customs into the scope of classical studies, Gu Yanwu was clearly surpassing the tradition in Song studies of emphasizing the distinction between *Yi* (barbarian) and *Xia* (Chinese), thus substantially expanding how he envisioned "China." From the perspective of Confucian learning, the distinction between inner and outer was a prerequisite for establishing rites and music, and the difference between "cultured" (*wen*) and "uncivilized" (*ye*) was a prerequisite for establishing "China" as a political category. Therefore, acknowledging that "in some respects, China was not as good as foreign states" meant not only breaking the strict division between inner and outer but also shaking up the hard boundary between cultured and uncivilized. It was the forerunner of the "relativization of *Yi* and *Xia*" and of views that "there is no distinction between inner and outer" that arose in the mid-Qing period. Citing the *History of the Liao* (*Liao shi*), Gu praised the Khitan custom of "not migrating just because they saw shining and strange things." Citing the *History of the Jin* (*Jin shi*), Gu explained that the ancient Manchu customs of "sacrificing to Heaven and Earth, respecting relatives, respecting the elderly, receiving guests, believing in friends, and acting with courteous intentions and sincere words all arose spontaneously." Citing from *Records of Empirical Knowledge from the Shao Family* (*Shaoshi wenjian lu*), Gu noted approvingly that "the Muslim Uyghur customs are honest, the differences between ruler and minister are not that great, and therefore they are united in one mind, strong and invincible." Citing the *Records of the Grand Historian,* Gu noted that the Xiongnu (considered a barbaric and ferocious enemy by the Han dynasty) were sensitive to external affairs and had light punishments. The citations of foreign customs were a form of critique of the decadence of "Chinese" customs. They showed from another perspective that although the Qing dynasty's ritual system inherited a large number of Confucian traditions and Chinese customs, it also included the values and systems of other ethnic groups. Through the simplicity of Khitan customs, the spontaneity of the Manchurian etiquette, the relative equality and unity resulting from Muslim Uyghur customs, and the freedom and agility of the Xiongnu system, Gu Yanwu demonstrated a positive and nuanced view toward these social customs and institutions.[71]

The theory of institutions that imbues the idea of enfeoffment in centralized administration was a theory that took into account historical evolution and differences in local customs. This strong sense of change, along with attention to questions of territory, customs, and institutions, formed an internal connection that was not so much simple ethnonational thought, but rather an ideological response to a new imperial system that could not be contained within the idea of the Han nationality. The Manchus conquered Mongolia and China and established a large-scale multiethnic empire. The Qing dynasty confronted complicated internal and external ethnic relationships and governed the entire imperial territory by being aware of local customs and by continuously adjusting its policies in response to differences in ethnic groups, customs, political-legal traditions, and other areas in China proper, Mongolia, Tibet, and the southwestern regions. The Qing dynasty became an imperial system characterized by its centralized monarchy and by legal and institutional pluralism. The Qing empire implemented a system of centralized administration in China proper but diversified systems in the northwest and southwest borderlands with a distinctive flavor of enfeoffment. This political reality, in turn, had a significant impact on the central power structure. For example, the Court of Frontier Affairs (*Lifan yuan*) was a unique border-governing institution. The process of imperial expansion raised the necessity of practicing enfeoffment because of the need to govern border regions. The Eight Banners of Manchuria and Mongolia, the local headman system in the Southwest, and the policies of peaceful negotiation with border ethnic groups, in combination with a tributary system and reciprocity of gifting and exchanging favors, coexisted in the relationship between the imperial center and frontiers. The "foreign states" that Gu Yanwu examined in *Record of Daily Knowledge* possessed the power of autonomy within the dynastic system. They belonged to the Qing dynasty's political structure, but were governed through specific, local, and diverse political forms. Their ruling modality and vassal relationship to the imperial center were drastically different from the Confucian bureaucracy in Han-majority areas. The governing modalities of border regions were also different from each other. The word "enfeoffment" here describes a form of political autonomy in border regions and their relationship with the imperial center. As a Ming loyalist, Gu Yanwu did not explicitly express his views on the Qing empire and its domestic and foreign policies. However, he paid attention to historical changes and to the differences between domestic and foreign customs. He opposed the recycling of old institutions without adequate adaptation to historical circumstances. It is hard to imagine that Gu's advocacy for using Chinese ways to change barbarian peoples was entirely irrelevant to the changing historical conditions of his times.

The distinction, as mentioned earlier, between *Tianxia* and the state shows that Gu Yanwu was not a narrow-minded Confucian who saw ethnic identity as the only basis of his politics and culture. However, he could not identify himself with the existing political system—the Qing empire. Therefore, the concept of *Tianxia* and its implied order of rites and music constituted an opposition to the external political system imposed during his day. Gu Yanwu saw the shortcomings of centralized administration but did not approve of adopting the enfeoffment system. Instead, he believed that the spirit of enfeoffment should be imbued in the system of centralized administration to refine the ancient system in a unique, "hybrid" way. In so doing, Gu could connect the refined implications of ancient institutions and the current political reality of his times. He said:

> The abolition of enfeoffment did not happen in one day. If a sage had appeared, the system of enfeoffment would still have evolved into the system of centralized administration. Today the defects of centralized administration have reached the extreme. Even if a sage appears, the officials will continue their same routines one by one, which is precisely why the common people are getting poorer and why China is becoming weaker and more chaotic. . . .[72]
>
> If we understand why the system of enfeoffment became the system of centralized administration, then we will understand the problems of centralized administration, which will soon evolve to become something else. However, will it revert to enfeoffment? I would say no. If a sage appears and could imbue the idea of enfeoffment within centralized

> administration, then everyone under Heaven would prosper. . . . The shortcomings of the system of enfeoffment are concentrated at the bottom of society. In contrast, the weaknesses of the system of centralized administration are concentrated at the top of society.[73]

Gu Yanwu did not adopt the romantic view of enfeoffment that Neo-Confucians had. His attitude toward enfeoffment was one that concerned evolution and historical context. Judging by their functions in each political system, Gu Yanwu believed that enfeoffment and centralized administration both had their advantages and disadvantages. Only by understanding the historical circumstances and weighing the costs and benefits carefully could one devise an effective system. Therefore, it was necessary to create a highly autonomous but centralized political system that maintained the unity of monarchical power while preserving the autonomy of local power. This concept was theoretically close to Guo Xiang's "cogovernance" (*gong zhi*) between imperial power and large clans. However, their theories' specific content was not the same, because Gu Yanwu did not favor the aristocratic system. He understood local autonomy in the context of centralized administration and the gentry-landlord system, and he called for an antiaristocratic economic relationship. In an essay on "Retraction and Correction of Official Documents" (*fengbo*) from his *Record of Daily Knowledge*, Gu Yanwu held that if the emperor could refrain from dictating to the gentry in times of peace, then the gentry members would be able to bear the burden of protecting the emperor and *Tianxia* during times of chaos. His concept of a "hybrid system" was more or less close to a modern republican political system. At its core was a division of political power for maintaining cogovernance in the realm, which included allowing self-governance of counties and towns and relying on institutions like the Community Self-Defense (*baojia*) system.

The key to imbuing the spirit of enfeoffment in the bureaucratic state system was to take "protecting and preserving the people" as the political system's purpose. The sages' rule starts with "humanity" (*ren dao*) and includes aspects of change and constancy: institutions, regulations, and ritual must evolve in tandem with the changes among the "people," but the spirit of the ritual system established by the Three Dynasties of Antiquity should be permanent. What is called "protecting the people" is just such a fundamental spirit and principle that rites and music should embody as they adapt according to historical circumstances. Gu Yanwu said:

> When the sage faces south and rules *Tianxia,* he must begin with humanity. He will establish units of measurement, set standards for writing, select the first day in the imperial calendar, change the color of the ritual apparel [according to the five-phases theory], select a new reign title, discern the various ritual implements, and determine the hierarchy of symbolic garments. These are the ways in which he should accord with the transformations of the people. But there are also some ways in which he should not change. In affection for those who are close, in respecting those who should be respected, in observing the precedence of elders, and in maintaining the separation of men and women—in these ways he should not accord with popular changes. After the Spring and Autumn period, city-states merged into seven large states; the Qin conquered these seven states and drastically changed the former kings' rituals. However, the fundamentals by which relations of hierarchical precedence and of closeness and distance were determined, by which suspicions and doubts were resolved, and by which the true and the false were distinguished remained the same as in the Three Dynasties of Antiquity. . . . From the vantage point of the succession of generations of emperors, the Qin drastically changed the rules of propriety. However, the reasons why the Qin dynasty fell, and the Han dynasty rose, were not matters of prognosticating knowledge. There has never been a case when inhumanity could win *Tianxia,* and I can predict this outcome for the next hundred generations. No one can stop those who rule by protecting the people. I can also predict this outcome for the next hundred generations.[74]

What Gu meant by institutional evolution was the process by which institutions change in tandem with historical circumstances under the premise of "protecting the people." What, then, is meant by "protecting the people"? This can be explained from the two aspects of the people (*min*) and the ruler (*jun*). From the perspective of the people, "protecting the people" means protecting the "private interests of the *Tianxia*": "Everyone under Heaven favors his family and his children; it is normal to feel that way. To act as emperor is to act on behalf of the people's minds; it is different from when the emperor acts on his own behalf. . . . The sage, therefore, puts this into effect, using the private interests of *Tianxia* to accomplish the public interest of each person, so that *Tianxia* will be governed well."[75] In other words, Gu Yanwu believed that the hybrid system of mixing aspects of enfeoffment with the system of centralized administration embodied respect for the private interests of the "people," and that in this way, the legitimacy of the "public" was built on the self-interest of the "people." From the ruler's point of view, "protecting the people" required a division of power in the political organization:

> The Son of Heaven is the one who holds the power of *Tianxia*. What can he do with the power? *Tianxia's* power is delegated to the people of *Tianxia*, yet the power in the end belongs to the Son of Heaven. From metropolitan officials of the highest rank to local elites and minor officials, every one of them shares the Son of Heaven's power and takes care of his business. As a result, the Son of Heaven's power is increasingly more respected and elevated. If in a later age someone who is not skilled at governing comes forth and concentrates all power at the top, the vast breadth of administrative detail would be beyond one person's ability to control.[76]

Combining these two aspects is what it means to imbue enfeoffment in the bureaucratic system of centralized administration. It means to unite politically the patriarchal and patrilineal lineages with the Confucian bureaucracy's fundamental unit—the District Magistrate (*xianling*).[77] The former guarantees the local society's autonomy, while the latter gives imperial governance its political form. The denial of these two aspects opens the door to two kinds of political domination: aristocratic domination of local society by the feudal vassals, and monarchical autocracy. Political power is here understood as a power derived from the universal "masses" (*dazhong*).

Gu Yanwu, driven by an interest in statecraft and practical learning, applied *kaozheng* methods and classical studies to the practice and judgment of his times and thus could not avoid relativizing the significance of the classics to a considerable extent. Gu's classical studies and new theory of institutions resulted from the disenchantment of Neo-Confucianism. However, to accomplish the purpose of disenchanting Neo-Confucianism, Gu first had to make the classics sacrosanct. Within the scope of classical studies, the institutions of the Three Dynasties of Antiquity and historical names and things, regulations, institutions, and social customs became the sources of morality. Therefore, the *kaozheng* methods' mission was to investigate the utmost intent and significance of the Sage-Kings and to restore the internal and consistent relationship between moral practice and ritual, music, and customs. However, when Gu Yanwu offered solutions to contemporary practices in the language of classical studies, the classics' meaning was inevitably relativized. If we say that classical studies brought the Way of Heaven and Heavenly Principle into the concrete details of institutions and the system of rites and music, thereby leading to the disenchantment of the learning of Principle and Neo-Confucianism, then the practice of applying the classics to practice in the real world (as a kind of strategic response to the problems in the world) would also inevitably lead classical studies itself to face disenchantment.

II. The Transformation of Classical Studies

1. Classical Studies, *Kaozheng* Methods, and the Disenchantment of Classical Studies

Gu Yanwu's scholarship takes the theory of the ritual system as its internal structure. He uses *kaozheng* methods and the viewpoint of "change" (*bian*) as the primary method of observing classics and history. This methodological principle is a critique of Neo-Confucian views on moral philosophy (*yili*) and constitutes the basic premise of Han learning in the Qing dynasty. Dai Zhen said when summing up Hui Dong's (1697–1758) academic studies:

> People often say: "There is the classical learning of the Han Confucians and the classical learning of the Song Confucians; one emphasizes Han-style philology (*guxun*) and the other emphasizes Song-style empty discussion of principles and meanings (*liyi*)." This is something that I find very puzzling. As to what is called order and rightness, if one could set aside the classics and rely solely on what is deep in one's mind, allowing

> everyone to conjecture to reach their own conclusions, why would there be such a thing as learning from the classics? . . . If the philological exegesis is clear, then the ancient classics will be clear; when the ancient classics are clear, then the order and rightness of worthies and sages will be clear, and then what concords in my mind with them will also be illuminated. The order and rightness of worthies and sages is nothing other than what is lodged in the institutions and regulations of classical antiquity. Mr. Hui Dong studies the classical texts by following Han Confucian classicists' glossing to confirm and verify broadly the Three Dynasties' regulations and institutions. If we logically derive principles and meanings in this manner, then we will have an evidentiary basis [for our conclusions].[78]

Here, there is a clear continuity between Huang Zongxi and Gu Yanwu's presuppositions and Dai Zhen's views. They all emphasize the interdependence among moral philosophy, institutions, and the Six Classics. However, there are subtle differences under the appearance of this continuity. The new theory of institutions and Gu Yanwu's studies presupposed institutional contexts as the basis for moral practice. While Dai Zhen's point of view leaned strongly toward methodology, Dai had repeatedly demonstrated that *kaozheng* methods were indispensable in retrieving the principles and meanings from the classical texts, which embody the regulations and institutions in the Three Dynasties. Dai Zhen was a unique figure among scholars of the Qianlong (1735–1796) and Jiaqing (1796–1820) periods. He attached great importance to *kaozheng* methods and classical exegesis but thought that they were not sufficient on their own and emphasized the internal connection between classical principles and meanings and *kaozheng* methods. From Gu Yanwu and Huang Zongxi to Qianlong-Jiaqing scholarship, scholarly methods grew more and more sophisticated. Classical studies was becoming a domain of specialized knowledge, and the tension between knowledge and reality was gradually disappearing. What I want to explore is: Under what conditions did these changes in classical studies occur?

Past historians of scholarship have addressed this question in two ways. Liang Qichao represents an earlier view that regarded Qianlong-Jiaqing scholarship and its relationship with political reality as resulting from the literary inquisition in the Qing dynasty. Liang argued that Qing China's alien rule suppressed intellectual development. In an atmosphere of specialized learning, *kaozheng* methods had developed on a massive scale. Ying-shih Yu represents a later view that emphasizes that the shift in the intellectual development in the Ming and Qing dynasties cannot be merely explained away by external political pressure. According to Yu, there is an internal logic for this shift. I cannot analyze Yu's arguments one by one here, but I only want to point out the following: the era in which the *kaozheng* methods arose was not a simple one. For example, Yan Yuan and Li Zhi's scholarship emerged at the exact historical moment as Yan Ruoqu's debut. How can we account for the simultaneous occurrence of these opposing agendas and explain other complex intellectual phenomena simply in terms of external conditions? Before I further analyze the relationship between the political and economic conditions of the Qing dynasty and the emergence of classical studies, let me first raise the following questions regarding the methodology of classical studies: Is there a mutually deconstructive relationship between the internal structure of classical studies and its methods? Could *kaozheng* methods alter the fundamental premise for the establishment of classical studies? Will the investigation of things (*gewu*) in classical studies turn into some analysis of ancient facts and no longer have the meaning of moral practice and normative implications?

First of all, the internal structure of the classical studies advocated by Gu Yanwu was "ritual" (*li*) and "culture" (*wen*). These two concepts wove people, institutions, rituals, customs, and everything in the cosmos into a complex and changing network. Gu wanted to connect the Heavenly realm to the human domain through institutions of rites and music, and to establish moral goals of ritual practice in everyday life through the actual practices of society and its members. The purpose of investigating ancient texts to know ancient sounds was to offer objective conditions for moral practice, that is, to associate ethical practice closely with the world of "ritual" and "culture," rather than just discussing moral behavior and moral judgment from the perspective of subjectivity. In this sense, *wu* (things) were not a fact or object of classical studies but rather a domain of ethical norms, yet these norms were not an abstract dogma but depended on the world of "culture" and "ritual." Moral standards lay in customs, rituals, and knowledge, but they lay outside in a practical world of dominant institutions. "Culture" and "rituals" were in the world itself, but at the same time, they were a kind of normative order.

Therefore, "scholarly erudition is revealed in cultural scope" was not only a knowledge practice but also an ethical practice, because this practice was built on a complete rejection of the legitimacy of the actual political order.

However, *kaozheng* methods must presuppose a final and actual existence, which led to their objectivity and rigorous evidential arguments. Regardless of the purpose of classical studies, in *kaozheng* research, the *wu* (things) in a ritual system and social customs must be regarded as an actual existence or objective fact. Therefore, the concept of "things" had evolved in *kaozheng* scholars' hands from Gu Yanwu's normative meanings to objective facts. In this sense, tensions and contradictions developed between the goal of statecraft, maintaining fidelity to the ritual system's internal structure, and investigation of ancient texts to understand ancient sounds. Liang Qichao once compared evidential scholars' works, such as Yan Ruoqu's *Yan Ruoqu's Notation Book* (*Qianqiu zhaji*), Wang Yinzhi's *An Etymology of the Classics and Commentaries* (*Jingzhuan shi ci*) and *Statement and Hearsay of the Meanings of the Classics* (*Jingyi shu wen*), and Chen Li's *Records of Studying Notes in the Eastern School* (*Dong shu dushu ji*), with Gu Yanwu's research. Liang believed that the works listed above were not comparable with Gu's masterpiece *Record of Daily Knowledge.* His criterion was that the various entries of Gu's *Record of Daily Knowledge* were interconnected, and that the interconnectedness was indeed meaningful, while the evidential works listed above mainly were notation books made up of notes taken down about primary sources or undigested facts.[79] Liang's comparison was relatively crude, however, because the difference between Qianlong-Jiaqing scholars and Gu Yanwu was not in their *kaozheng* methods' precision and interconnectedness. For many Qianlong-Jiaqing scholars, classical studies no longer had the moral impulse of what Gu Yanwu called the study of Principle (*lixue*). Although the objects of their classical studies were still the Three Dynasties of Antiquity (as in the Wu school) or the regulations and institutions in the classical system (as in the Wan school), these scholars' *kaozheng* methods assumed that the meaning of these objects—*wu* (things)—had fundamentally changed.[80] They were not "things" in the sense in which Gu Yanwu and Huang Zongxi had framed them, but concrete and objective facts—even if these facts existed in the context of rituals, rules, and norms. In the eyes of evidential scholars and historians, the ritual principles, norms, and various Confucian teachings were "facts" that appeared in specific historical situations rather than a set of universal values. We can understand the distinction between "things" and "facts" by focusing on primary theoretical motivations, yet it is impossible to draw this conclusion from the perspective of general methodology. According to the above analysis, this notion of *wu* (thing) as a matter of fact is embedded both in the *kaozheng* research method and in the fundamental frameworks of Huang Zongxi and Gu Yanwu. Here we see that the *kaozheng* research method itself acted to deconstruct the internal structure of the theory of rites and music or the new theory of institutions.

Second, Gu Yanwu applied the meaning of ancient classics to the practice of statecraft, and, as a type of "Neo-Confucianism" or study of Principle, his classical studies could barely avoid the flair of "strategic response" (*duice*) examination essays. The historiography of "change" was driven by a search for practical application for learning, and it also implied the ruining of any idea of the sanctity of the ancient Sage-Kings' institutions. For Gu, "change" included two points of view. On the one hand, history had shifted, and the true meaning of the Sage-Kings' institutions had gradually become submerged. Statecraft scholarship must therefore overcome layers of obstacles in the past to discover the true meaning of these institutions. On the other hand, the true meaning of the Sage-Kings' institutions was not permanent or invariable. It existed in specific historical customs and evolution. Therefore, statecraft scholarship cannot be contented with the recovery of the classics' ancient meaning; it must also observe the development of customs in the historical process. The former was the source of Confucian classics, and the latter was the source of history. In this sense, we cannot easily distinguish classical from historical studies. Classical studies took a nostalgic approach to reveal why political decline took place and suggested the correct political direction in history. In contrast, history used a forward-looking way of confronting the present and the future to eliminate the absolute authority of the Sage-Kings' institutions and of Confucian dogmatism. This methodological emphasis on practical effectiveness was bound to change the apparent purpose of classical studies, which had been to investigate the true meaning of classical texts and the subtlety of canonical institutions. In the end, it would lead to the relativization of both the classics and institutions.

In short, both the *kaozheng* method of textual research and the historical view of change implicitly led to the possibility of the disenchantment of the classics. From a theoretical perspective, the process of disenchantment refers to how classical studies transformed from a new theory of rites and music (Gu Yanwu's framework) to historical studies of facts (*kaozheng* scholars' framework). When Huang Zongxi's disciple, Wan Sitong, discussed historical method, he bluntly claimed "the veritable records [of the imperial court] are the fundamental model [for writing history]":

> The veritable records are a matter of recording what happened and what was said without additions or embellishments. By following the person's family through generations and examining the circumstances, investigating their words and verifying them impartially, I would be able to understand about 80 to 90 percent of this person's history. . . . Whenever I encounter something complicated or unclear in the veritable records, I check other books to confirm it. When I find mistakes and abuses in other books, I use the veritable records to edit them. Although I dare not say that the veritable records are entirely reliable, they rarely bend right and wrong for the readers![81]

The power of the veritable records comes from their empirical method of "direct recording of events." In contrast, "following the person's family through generations and examining the circumstances" originates from the historiography of "change" to restore the Sage-Kings' institutions by applying them to the contemporary world. The result of *kaozheng* methods, then, is to return the ancient to the ancient. Zhang Xuecheng even found a theoretical basis for this kind of "veritable record." He said:

> Three Dynasties scholarship knew of history but not the classics; everything [they wrote] concerned human affairs. Later scholars valued the classics, because they are the history of the Three Dynasties. When recent scholars have commented on the classics, however, they seem concerned with matters other than human affairs, particularly in what is called discussion of moral philosophy (*yili*). When the scholars of Eastern Zhejiang discuss human nature and destiny it is through their study of history, and this is why they are outstanding.[82]

The significance of the Three Dynasties is still there. But the Three Dynasties have already become the object of historiography. Zhang's view of "change" is more radical than that of Gu Yanwu: it is a bit similar to the Legalists' historical view that "the Five Emperors do not overlap. The Three Dynasties do not follow each other, each governs by its own rule. And circumstances change over time."[83] Zhang Taiyan later concluded:

> From the Duke of Zhou and Confucius to the present, there have been thousands of sacrifices, and politics and customs have changed repeatedly; how can all the methods and rules be workable in the present? Therefore, those who study the classics do so to preserve antiquity, not to apply the ancient models to the present. The forefathers' handwritten notes are passed on to their descendants. Although some are stained and inferior, later generations should value them as precious. But it would be wrong to say they are perfect.[84]

Gu's original goal was to use the notion of change to break apart dogmatism about the classics. However, what Zhang Taiyan saw was the constraints the Sage-Kings' dogma placed on modern people, while Gu Yanwu was concerned that, if there were no such canonical system, then there would be nothing to rely on in moral practice. We cannot help asking: How can one resolve the dilemma of moral evaluation when the Three Dynasties model becomes only the object of history and no longer has a normative value? In the late Qing period, Zhang Taiyan advocated establishing religion to solve ethical problems as a Confucian classicist. From Gu's perspective, it is almost unimaginable: Do we need to install a new special field (religion) outside of Confucian classics, rituals, music, and criminal punishments to manage, coordinate, and maintain our morality? Outside the discursive context of Confucianism, the phenomenon of Zhang's resorting to religion is itself a result of the disenchantment of classical studies—classical studies can no longer be an objective basis for morality, so the establishment of religion was put on the agenda as an appeal to morality. From the beginning to the end of the Qing dynasty, even for the Confucian classicists, the relationship between the Sage-Kings' system and moral evaluation underwent a fundamental change, and the intricate relationship between classics and history, classics and principles, and complex interactions of different academic schools played a significant role in this fundamental change.

2. The Unity of Governance and the Way and the Predicament of Classical Studies

There was a methodological basis for the transformation of classical studies, but this transformation was also inseparable from political conditions, especially scholars' reactions to these political conditions. Huang and Gu used the new theory of institutions or the new theory of rites and music against the moral argumentation of Neo-Confucianism, attempting to restore the inherent relationship between ethical practice and institutions of rites and music. Taking the ritual system as the internal structure of academic scholarship could lead toward two diametrically opposite results: first, under the premise of negating the current institutional reality, it could provide a basis for moral practice and moral evaluation; second, under the premise of affirming the current institutional reality, institutions themselves could be regarded as a moral system, so that the consistent and identical relationship between moral evaluation and institutions could provide an argument for current political legitimacy. Of course, there could also be a third result, which would be to affirm and deny the current system simultaneously. Such a result would lead to entanglement in academic struggle between the theory of ritual and institutions and opposition to such theory. In other words, the critical premise of the new theory of institutions or the new theory of rites and music was its tension with the existing political reality. Once this tension disappeared or eased, the new theory of institutions or the new theory of rites and music would turn into an argument in defense of the current political reality. "Disappearance or alleviation of tension" here has two meanings: (1) alleviation of the tension between scholars of classics and the political reality they faced, or (2) reform of the current political system to include the new theory of institutions or the new theory of rites and music, thus dissolving the basis for their critique. Let us see if this possibility existed.

The Qing dynasty, as a Manchu conquest regime, was also a multiethnic empire. This empire had the apparent characteristics of Manchu rule, but at the same time, it combined the empire's authoritarian control with cultural tolerance and institutional flexibility. To maintain its rule, the Qing government rebuilt the Confucian orthodoxy, using culture instead of race as the legal basis for its rule. It was a multiethnic imperial system under the control of a minority ethnic group, and thus was different from the quasi-nation-state system of centralized administration found in the Song and Ming dynasties. In the late Qing period, reformers working within the system used cultural identity to fight against ethnic nationalism. Some of their arguments were grounded in the features of the Qing empire, as mentioned above. As a conquest dynasty, the Qing dynasty had to legitimize itself as a "Chinese" dynasty, and to do this, it had to restructure its historical relationship with China institutionally and culturally. Emperor Kangxi made the most significant contribution in this regard. He abolished Manchu laws, took up and continued Ming-dynasty institutions, restored the civil service examinations, used classical Chinese, learned from reflections of Ming scholar-officials regarding the fall of the Ming dynasty, and promoted land reform and other institutional reform. Under Confucianism's guidance, the emperor regarded the unity of political legitimacy and Confucian orthodoxy as his political ideal and guide for ruling the state. When Kangxi first ascended to the throne, Xiong Cilu (1635–1709), Reader-in-Waiting of the Office of Advancement of Literature (*Hongwen yuan*), submitted a memorial and asked the emperor to examine the Six Classics, review the records of the past dynasties, incorporate them in his body and mind, and use them as the foundation of policy design and governance. Kangxi agreed and approved the recommendation. The emperor said that "the emperor's learning should prioritize the illumination of Principle, the investigation of things and extension of knowledge. All these should be ready for consultation and discussion." He especially hoped that moral philosophy could be confirmed in the essence of classics and history.[85] He expanded the Confucian temple rites and rituals. He said in his comment on the Four Books: "The legitimacy of *Dao* is right here, and political legitimacy is also right here," and he was determined to integrate civil governance with military skills in a single mode of rule.[86] Kangxi held a grand banquet to celebrate the classics in November of 1670. In 1673, he changed the Imperial Academy lecturers' schedule from every other day to every day. While implementing effective economic and political reforms, in 1678, Kangxi enacted a special examination dubbed Erudite Literatus (*Boxue hongci*) to recruit scholars from throughout the realm. Kangxi elevated Zhu Xi to the imperial hall of worship, and Cheng-Zhu Neo-Confucianism reached its zenith at this moment. The emperor ordered the compilation of *The Official History of the Ming Dynasty* (*Ming shi*), thus confirming the Qing's political legitimacy as the successor of the Ming. In this project, many Ming loyalists collaborated with the Qing empire. It was a successful cultural policy.

The revival of Zhu Xi's paradigm during the Kangxi era echoed the scholar-officials' reflections on scholarly thought on Wang Yangming since the end of the Ming dynasty. Xiong Cilu, Li Guangdi (1642–1718), Zhang Boxing (1652–1725), Yu Chenglong (1638–1700), Lu Longqi (1630–1693), Yang Mingshi (1661–1736), Zhu Shi (1665–1736), and others who held official positions, and Lu Shiyi (1611–1672), Zhang Luxiang (1611–1674), Lü Liuliang (1629–1683), and others outside the Qing bureaucracy, differed slightly in their intellectual tendencies and political commitments depending on their relation to the Qing dynasty. However, it is clear that Zhu Xi's paradigm dominated the scholarship of the Qing dynasty. A key point of consensus was their rejection of Ming Confucians' empty discussion of the human mind and their emphasis on statecraft and practical learning as the goal of Neo-Confucianism.[87] Xiong Cilu held discussions with Kangxi on governance, benevolent policies, and ways to relieve people's malaise. Li Guangdi was not only a learned Neo-Confucian scholar but an active participant in politics. For example, when the Fujian navy admiral Shi Lang (1621–1696) conquered Penghu and incorporated Taiwan into Qing territory in the twenty-second year of Kangxi's reign (1683), it was Li Guangdi who had suggested both Shi Lang's appointment and the capture of Taiwan. Li Fu (1675–1750) was a well-known minister who spoke truth to power, and he admired Kangxi very much. He even said in a eulogy for the Kangxi Emperor that he had "reached the highest meritorious virtue at the level of the legendary emperors in China's antiquity." Such views also came from the mouths of famous officials such as Wei Xiangshu (1617–1687) and Chen Tingjing (1639–1712). Huang Zongxi was an anti-Qing Confucian, but in his later years (1686), he lamented that "no one among the ancient and modern Confucians has experienced more honor and glory than the scholars today; [According to Mencius], a Sage-King will come every five hundred years, and famous ministers will appear to assist him. We are now witnessing it."[88] Along with the promotion of Zhu Xi's paradigm, "The ministers promoted substantial and practical learning. They praised scholars who could command the techniques of classical learning" during the Kangxi and Qianlong emperors' reigns[89]—successively compiling *The Complete Collection of Illustrations and Writings from the Earliest to Current Times* (*Gujin tushu jicheng*) and *The Complete Collection of the Four Treasuries* (*Siku quanshu*). These measures originated from Kangxi's understanding of the study of classics and history. The emperor said: "The way to govern the realm under Heaven is in the classics, and history tells us how to govern the affairs under Heaven." And, "Classics are to explain the *Dao*, and history is for examining current issues. If we adopt the internal and external lessons from classical and historical studies, the [Qing's] future prosperity can be expected."[90]

Both Kangxi and Qianlong authored several pieces on classical studies, and Li Guangdi mostly ghostwrote Kangxi's works. Li Guangdi promoted Zhu Xi over Wang Yangming and wrote more than fifty works on human nature (*xing*) and Principle (*li*). As a writer on behalf of the Kangxi Emperor, Li regarded the unity of political legitimacy and the legitimacy of *Dao* as the criterion for commenting on governance and policies. More than one scholar has quoted the following passage:

> I observe the relationship between political legitimacy and the legitimacy of *Dao* [in history]; they were unified in antiquity but split into two in later ages. Mencius tracked the beginning of Yao and Shun to King Wen as a period of five hundred years. At the end of this period, the unity of the legitimacy of *Dao* and political legitimacy was resumed. The following five hundred years started from Confucius and lasted to the Jianwu reign [of the Later Han dynasty]. It was another five hundred years from Jianwu to the Zhenguan reign [in the Tang dynasty], and another five hundred years from Zhenguan to the Southern Song dynasty. In the Later Han dynasty, social custom had risen [to the Sage-Kings' level of] *Dao;* during Zhenguan's reign, Tang governance was nearly as effective as King Cheng and King Kang at the beginning of the Zhou dynasty. . . . Confucius's life coincided with the time when the Zhou House moved to the east [i.e., the time when the system of rites and music collapsed], and Zhu Xi's life overlapped with the time when the Song capital moved to Hangzhou in the South. Heaven endowed them with the *Dao,* but they were born into the wrong times. This was why the *Dao* and political

> legitimacy diverged. From Zhu Xi's time to Your Majesty, another five hundred years have passed. It is time to anticipate a new Sage-King who will practice the learning of the sages and worthies. Heaven will restore and usher in a unique moment of Yao and Shun, and political legitimacy and the legitimacy of *Dao* will again be unified![91]

Li Guangdi used the prediction that "political legitimacy and the legitimacy of *Dao* will again be unified" to provide a moral argument for Qing politics, which repeated Kangxi's views.[92] His argument was precisely the argument provided by classical studies: using the Three Dynasties of Antiquity as a model, he regarded moral judgment and ethical practice as a process entirely unified with political institutions. Li saw the distinction between *Dao* and governance as a historical distinction. His view critically inherited the early Qing scholars' critique of Neo-Confucianism: The problem with Neo-Confucianism (particularly Zhu Xi learning) lay in the separation of moral judgments and political institutions, and this separation itself was nothing but a specific historical outcome. Therefore, the restoration of unity in the context of classical studies between moral judgment, moral practice, and political institutions provided legitimacy for Qing-dynasty politics.

The fact that Li Guangdi used classical studies to provide political legitimacy for the Qing dynasty forces us to reexamine the relationship between Qing-dynasty politics and the classical studies of Gu Yanwu and Huang Zongxi. As I have mentioned above, the new theory of institutions and theory of rites and music included an ethnic consciousness that opposed foreign rule, and Huang and Gu's call to restore the ancient political models and their relationship to moral evaluation was based on a rejection of contemporary politics. However, with the consolidation and legitimation of the Qing dynasty's rule, the relationship between the literati and the political system changed accordingly. Many of them were engaged in classical studies under the premise of participating in the current political system. Few people were so profoundly trusted by Emperor Kangxi as Li Guangdi, who had served as the Minister of War and Director of the Shuntian Examination District and was "an outstanding Confucian scholar serving as a famous minister" (in Jiang Fan's words). Nonetheless, during the Qing dynasty it was not uncommon for scholars to move between the official bureaucracy and private academies.[93] Setting aside its political implications, Kangxi's formulation of comprehending the classics to illuminate the *Dao* was nearly identical to classical studies' original intention. This cultural policy and continuations of it had an enormous impact on Qianlong- and Jiaqing-era scholars. They focused their energy on the authentication of classical texts and ritual institutions, and their efforts gradually dissolved the clear political agenda of classical studies on regulations and institutions found in the early days of the Qing dynasty.

In these circumstances, work on editing, *kaozheng,* and research eased the tension and opposition between the classics and the existing political system, resulting in work that was entirely different from the critical and practical character of Gu Yanwu and Huang Zongxi's studies. In the historical perspective of the May Fourth New Culture Movement, Dai Zhen was once regarded as a rebellious scholar. However, Dai never rejected participating in the Qing-dynasty imperial examinations or in the compilation of the classics and history in the Qing bureaucracy. In 1773, Dai Zhen became an editor of the *Four Treasuries* imperial library project. He helped edit the *Commentary on the Classic of Waterways* (*Shuijing zhu*), *Nine Chapters of Mathematical Arts* (*Jiuzhang suanshu*), *Mathematical Classics of Sea Islands* (*Haidao suanjing*), *Mathematical Classic of the Zhou Gnomon* (*Zhoubi suanjing*), *Mathematical Classic of Master Sun* (*Sunzi suanjing*), *Reckoning Mistakes in the Etiquette Ritual* (*Yili shiwu*), *Explanations of Palaces in the Etiquette Ritual* (*Yili shigong*), *Collective Explanations of the Etiquette Ritual* (*Yili jishi*), *The Older Dai Rituals* (*Dadai liji*), *Regional Dialects* (*Fangyan*), and so on. In his times, editing Confucian ritual classics had become the common pursuit of official and private scholars. For example, in 1753, Qin Huitian's (1702–1764) *Comprehensive Investigation of Five Rites* (*Wuli tongkao*) was published, which included the research results of Wang Mingsheng (1722–1798), Qian Daxin (1728–1804), and Dai Zhen (1724–1777). The compilation of *Comprehensive Rituals of the Great Qing* (*Da Qing tongli*) started in 1736 and was completed in 1756, and *The Regulations and Institutions of the Great Qing* (*Da Qing huidian*) was published in 1763. Many renowned classical scholars participated in these projects. Ruan Yuan, as a third-generation scholar of the Qianlong-Jiaqing school and a provincial governor, promoted Han learning and suppressed Song learning, yet evenhandedly affirmed the theories of both classical exegesis and of philosophical discussions of principles and morality. In the climate of *kaozheng* textual research, Ruan Yuan gave a profound historical analysis of Song learning's theories of human nature and the decree (*ming*);[94] he also praised Zhu Xi as a classical scholar, who used the unity of ritual and Principle in place of the unity of governance and *Dao*. Ruan's conclusion was surprisingly in line with Li Guangdi's promotion of Zhu Xi's paradigm: "Zhu Xi . . . speaking of ritual in his later years is especially tolerant of complicated details and difficulties. He had genuine insight into the way Principle is grounded in ritual. That by which rulers have governed *Tianxia* in ancient and in modern times is ritual. The Five Ethical Rules are all ritual, and that is why proper loyalty and proper filiality are also Principle."[95] Ruan Yuan affirmed that the Qing dynasty "esteemed the [views of] human nature and the Way in *Daoxue* [learning of the Way, Zhu Xi's paradigm], and used the [classical studies of] the Han Confucians to substantiate them." He regarded the integration of moral philosophy and ritual systems in academic studies as the basis for the Qing dynasty and its cultural policies. The unity of ritual and Principle, the unity of governance and *Dao*, and the unity of *Dao* and its vessels (*qi*), on the one hand, reflect the academic critique of Song learning; on the other hand, they also led to pioneering scholarship on the comparison of inscriptions on ancient bronze objects and ancient texts to explain the ritual systems (the unity of *Dao* and its vessels) in ancient history. Ruan Yuan said:

> Whatever is above form and shape is *Dao*, and whatever is below form and shape is an instrument or vessel (*qi*). The *Dao* of the Shang and Zhou dynasties still exists in the Nine Classics today, but few artifacts have survived to our time. Only some bronze bells and vessels are available for us to examine today. The ancient bronze bells and vessels have inscriptions, and the inscriptions are the ancients' writings. . . . They are as significant as those of the Nine Classics. . . . If an ancient sage saw what had survived in the inscriptions today, how do you know he would not have written them into the Classics? Those bells and vessels were repositories of the rituals. Therefore, Confucius said: "It is precisely ritual objects (*qi*) and names that cannot be granted to others."[96] When the Sage-Kings made ritual objects, they made standard units of measurement, selected the same system of writings, and established the [ritual] hierarchy. When [these ritual objects were] applied and used in the court rituals, then everyone could see the dignity of the Son of Heaven and the favor of the

> Heavenly Mandate. . . . The Sage-Kings used the ritual objects to tame the hearts of everyone under Heaven to respect the king and revere the ancestors and teach everyone under Heaven to learn culture broadly and to practice the rituals. Shang lasted six hundred years; Zhou lasted eight hundred years, during which time the *Dao* and ritual objects did not fall. . . . The Sage-Kings used people's talents, strength, ritual, and culture in the ritual objects, so ritual became clear, culture reached everyone, everyone's place was determined, and the king was respected. It was rare to have foolish, lazy, arrogant, or violent people around! . . . I said that to observe the *Dao* and ritual objects of the Three Dynasties and beyond, apart from the Nine Classics, where do you find them except in inscriptions of bronze bells and vessels![97]

Wang Guowei later built on Ruan Yuan's view. Most modern scholars see the continuity between them only in terms of their historical method of working between bronze and stone inscriptions and ancient texts from literature and history, paying no attention to the idea implied in this methodology that "the *Dao* and its vessels are inseparable" and "the ritual objects bear the rituals." For Ruan Yuan, the internal structure of the ritual system was the premise of his historical methods. His historiography here is the study of classics and history, which is an effort to support classical studies with historical methods. However, Wang Guowei's ultimate contribution was not to apply the classics to political affairs but to pave the way for modern historiography with sophisticated textual research. Take, for example, his research on Shang and Zhou bronzes, the rituals designed by the Duke of Zhou, and Shang-dynasty rituals: their meaning as a moral theory is so thin that people can only regard his textual research as pure historical research. In other words, one of the intellectual results of the "unity of governance and *Dao*" was the "disenchantment" of the classics or the transformation of classics toward modern historiography (specialized, objective, and empirical historical research), which at the time was mutually compatible with the "the unity of political legitimacy and the legitimacy of *Dao*."

The power of Gu Yanwu's renowned motto, "The study of Principle is the study of the classics," came from the unified framework in which moral philosophy (*yili*) was identical with the ritual system. However, it was precisely this framework itself that eventually destroyed the critical power of the approach. For Gu and Huang, the internal connection between ritual, music and institutions, the ritual system and Principle, and the legitimacy of *Dao* and political legitimacy was a source of their critical power. The subsequent development of classical studies did not change this internal connection methodologically, but it did alleviate the critical methodology's tension with the current political system. The question is: Was it not the case that the methodology behind Qianlong-Jiaqing scholars' critique of Song learning was already implied in Gu Yanwu and Huang Zongxi's scholarship? The concept of "the unity of political legitimacy and the legitimacy of *Dao*" in the Qing dynasty not only was the ideology of the ruler but also had its foundation among scholar-officials, because the rise of Qing thought was originally built on the critique of Neo-Confucianism and its genealogy of *Dao* in the Song and Ming dynasties. Compared with Neo-Confucianism's discursive relationship with classical studies in the seventeenth century, there was nothing special in Ruan Yuan's statement quoted in the previous paragraph. The slight difference was that he talked about loyalty and filial piety as a minister, while Kangxi regarded Neo-Confucianism (the study of Principle) and classical studies as the foundation of governance.[98] Investigating the unity of political legitimacy and the legitimacy of *Dao* was an internal theme of the Neo-Confucianism of the Song and Ming dynasties. However, this theme was "internal" because School of Principle and School of Mind Neo-Confucianists tried to use the concepts of Heavenly Principle, Mind, and human nature within each individual subjectivity and to establish them as a preexisting set of tensions with their political reality. When "the unity of political legitimacy and the legitimacy of *Dao*" became a demonstration of the current political reality's legitimacy, then if its critical spirit concerning politics was to be sustained, classical studies itself would have to change. Wang Fuzhi's *On Reading Comprehensive Mirror for Aid in Government* (*Du Tongjian lun*) contains many satirical critiques of the so-called "unity of political legitimacy and the legitimacy of *Dao*" in the Qing dynasty. Read today, it seems to be a prediction of the subsequent development of Qing classical studies. What I want to ask here is: In addition to the cultural policies of the Qing rulers, did the development of Qing politics itself provide a social foundation for a change in the relationship between classical studies and politics? The Kangxi era's achievements and the praise of Qing governance by literati of the time provide several examples of the relationship.

Some scholars conceded that the Qing dynasty (especially Kangxi) had successfully realized the unity of governance and *Dao,* and even believed that the Qing dynasty as a conquest dynasty "had taken over the social foundation upon which the Donglin Faction had been based," asserting that Huang Zongxi's new theory of institutions "was a standpoint within the institutions of the Qing dynasty."[99] What position, then, could the intellectual practice of Gu Yanwu and Huang Zongxi be identified as occupying in the political and economic practice of the Qing dynasty?

One of the political concepts that ran through both *Waiting for the Dawn: A Plan for the Prince* and *Record of Daily Knowledge* was to rebuild the ritual order based on the relationship between the gentry and patriarchal clan law. The rulers of the Qing dynasty indeed adopted it as an official policy. The reason was that the Qing was a conquest dynasty ruled by ethnic minorities, which meant that the Qing imposed a new aristocracy of Manchu princes and aristocrats on the existing social structure. In this context, the contradictions between imperial power and Han Chinese landlords and gentry members often gave way to conflicts with the Manchu aristocracy. At the end of the Ming dynasty, scholar-officials expected to rely on the relationship between the gentry and patriarchal clan law for local autonomy. Their demand for redistributing official land was closely related to their antimonarchist political views. Huang Zongxi used the dichotomy of "people's land" versus "imperial land" and regarded the private property of the imperial court (such as farms run by officials like a military colony) as excessive, and even concluded that the monarchy should be abandoned. Their writings "On Enfeoffment" (*Fengjian lun,* Huang Zongxi) and "On Centralized Administration" (*Junxian lun,* Gu Yanwu), and their discussion on land reform directly reflected the resistance of the landlord and gentry class to the expansion of the imperial power over land. They reflected the interests of landlords and self-employed peasants, as well as of urban industrial and commercial workers.

The separation of powers requested by the gentry class was not a new thing. However, its combination with an antimonarchy position resulted from the special political circumstances of the late Ming dynasty. Since the Han dynasty, the Chinese autocracy had organized agrarian society by the unit of rural villages, forming the village (*li*) system in the Han dynasty, the township and villages (*xiangli*) system in the Sui and Tang dynasties, the Community

Self-Defense (*baojia*) system in the Song dynasty, and the Community Self-Monitoring (*lijia*) system in the Ming dynasty. The main functions of these rural organizations were to collect taxes, maintain public order, and organize the corvée system for large-scale engineering projects. However, since the Song dynasty, the scholar-official class had especially respected the Community Compact (*xiangyue*) and the patriarchal clan systems. They tried to rebuild the system of rites and music to counter the excessive expansion of imperial power. Wang Yangming's Community Compact is the best illustration of this point. In the early Ming dynasty, the central government began implementing the Community Self-Monitoring system and the *Guanjin* system after a general household registration survey, compilation of "yellow books" (for corvée registration), and land surveys.[100] In the middle of the Ming dynasty, with the intensification of land annexation, the land occupied by emperors, nobles, and officials surpassed that of previous generations, and occupation of land by local gentry and bureaucrats was also significantly increasing. The following statistics can briefly show us the rapid changes in land mergers and household registration status: In the early Ming dynasty, the total amount of registered arable land in the country was more than 8.5 million hectares, while in the seventh year of the Tianshun reign (1463), there was only a little more than 4.29 million. In the fifteenth year of the Hongzhi reign (1502), the actual amount was only 4.22 million hectares, which was only half of that of the early Ming dynasty. At the beginning of the Ming dynasty, the number of registered households nationwide was more than sixteen million, which in the Yongle reign increased to twenty million. But by the fourth year of the Hongzhi reign (1491), there were only a little more than nine million registered households, less than half the number in the Yongle reign (1403–1424). The covert seizure of household registrations by landlords and the forced migration of landless peasants led to a crisis in the Community Self-Monitoring system during the Wanli reign (1573–1620). In 1578, Zhang Juzheng ordered a new survey of cultivated land and registered more than seven million hectares of land, and some estates and military settlements covertly held by powerful imperial relatives and military officials were liquidated.[101] In 1581, Zhang Juzheng began to implement the single-whip method of tax apportionment that had first been implemented in Fujian and Zhejiang in the early years of the Jiajing reign (1521–1567), changing from individual- and household-based apportionments of corvée services to taxes on individuals payable in silver or grain in an attempt to equalize taxation burden.[102] The reforms, as mentioned above, provided new historical opportunities for mitigating social conflicts, for improving the plight of farmers, and for the rise of the landlord system.

However, by the end of the Ming dynasty, land annexation reached an unprecedented level once again, farmers lost their land, and aristocrats and officers occupied huge fields. Against this background, the Donglin Faction members represented the power and interests of the local stratum of gentry and landlords, voicing "public opinion" and fighting against the central powers on issues such as mineral taxes and official farmland, and seeking the gentry-village community as the basis of rural order. If the equal-field (*juntian*) land policy from the Northern Wei dynasty to the Sui and Tang dynasties, which aimed to strike down the privilege of landlords and abolish the hierarchical system of land ownership, embodied the historical relationship whereby imperial power and landlords mutually supported and benefitted each other, then ideas about land reform in the late Ming dynasty opposed imperial power and the aristocratic and official annexation of land, trying to promote and reform rural landlord ownership in the context of the collapse of the Community Self-Monitoring system. Huang Zongxi, Gu Yanwu, and others inherited the Donglin Faction's agenda and put forward a systematic social reform plan. Among its provisions, the criticisms of imperial power, aristocracy, and the bureaucracy were particularly prominent.

In the process of implementing the early-Qing social reforms, the Qing rulers had already, to a large extent, transformed the rebellious ideas of Huang Zongxi and Gu Yanwu on the land system, patriarchal clan relationships, and the ritual system into a reasonable system and policy, thus breaking up antimonarchical sentiment that had originally been behind ideas about rural autonomy. In the eighth year of the Kangxi reign (1669), the Qing government ordered an end to the banner armies' practice of annexing land. It required all the land annexed in that year to be returned to the Han Chinese people, and compensated the banner groups with land from other places. During the Kangxi and Yongzheng eras, the imperial court prohibited Manchu nobles and Han landlords from "increasing rents and grabbing tenants." By the Qianlong era, some long-term workers and employers "sat and ate together" and were deemed "equally commensurate with each other"; "no contract was drawn," and "there was no difference between master and servant."[103] After the Qing dynasty conquered China, it announced it would continue the Ming dynasty's single-whip method to levy taxes; to eliminate the abuses in the single-whip method, in 1712, the imperial court declared the total level of taxation to be fixed at a level determined in a 1711 policy. "In the age of the Sage-King, taxation will never increase."[104] This policy, and the methods of combining land and household registration and of apportioning household and land taxation together in the Yongzheng era, were a continuation and development of the single-whip method from the Ming dynasty. A certain level of "autonomy" in rural areas was an organic part of the traditional imperial system, and especially in the social organization of the Qing dynasty. In this sense, on the one hand, the special role of gentry members in the Qing dynasty was indeed based on the disintegration of rural organizations, such as the Community Self-Monitoring system, and on the idea of rural autonomy in the late Ming dynasty. On the other hand, the role of gentry members became the local foundation of imperial power at the grassroots level of society (especially in the countryside) in the Qing dynasty, quite the opposite from their role as a force that deconstructed imperial power in the late Ming dynasty. Historian Li Wenzhi summarized the changes in land ownership in the early Qing dynasty under three aspects: First, changes in the distribution of land ownership, that is, the weakening of the enfeoffment system and the growth of peasant ownership; second, changes in the relationship between the peasant class and the landlord class—that is, the power of official and gentry landlords was weakened, and the majority of slaves, hired laborers, and tenant farmers were liberated, or their social status improved; third, the decline of aristocratic landlords and gentry landlords and the increase of plebeian landlords.[105] Through a policy of recognizing the property rights of the peasants who reclaimed land, the Qing dynasty reestablished the household registration system that had been disrupted by the peasant wars, organized farmers in definitive areas, and included them in village cooperatives to ensure tax collection. Economic historians believe that although these laws and the reclamation policy implemented in the early Qing dynasty aimed to reintegrate peasant labor and land so as to restore the collection of taxes and corvée labor, the objective result was that a considerable part of the peasants obtained land. As a result, the system of peasant land ownership developed further.[106]

The Kangxi, Yongzheng, and Qianlong emperors abolished the old taxation system based on the number of male household members and ushered in a new system of taxation, one based on the amount of land cultivated by each household. The new system reduced the peasants' personal attachment to the imperial system. It resulted from a precarious balance between imperial, clan, and gentry power, and between state, landlord, and peasant ownership of land. When we discuss the Qing dynasty's autocratic politics, we cannot avoid discussing the variety of its modes of rule. Even among Han Chinese, urban areas never achieved the same level of autonomy as rural areas. After the disintegration of rural organizations in the late Ming dynasty, new characteristics of governance arose in Qing society. Under a structure where the Manchu Qing minority monopolized the upper levels of power, gentry members, landlords, and clan lineages played an increasingly important role. Many Qing historians have addressed this interactive relationship between the gentry class, local clan power, and imperial power as precisely the Qing dynasty's political structure. In other words, while the Qing government strengthened minority rule through the Eight Banners system, it also absorbed structural changes from the late Ming dynasty and used them to maintain the new dynasty's control. In a nutshell, in addition to the Eight Banners system, Qing-dynasty rule had two related conditions: First, local power, especially of the gentry with the lineage / village as its base, became more assertive; and second, the legitimacy of the dynasty (and its vulnerability) was based not only on an ethnic hierarchy but also on the power of gentry members. If the development of land ownership and peasant ownership is a continuation of the social changes in the Song and Ming dynasties, then these new developments in the Qing dynasty's ruling structure were directly related to minority rule: the Manchu Qing nobility (as a minority who entered China) had to rely on Han Chinese landlords and gentry members to maintain rule at the grassroots level; and on the state level the Qing court had to strike a balance in the interest of political stability between the Han gentry and officials and the Manchu princes and nobles.[107]

In this sense, with the reform of the land system in the Qing dynasty, a system that was centered around gentry landlords and yeoman farmers gradually became the foundation for governance under the political and economic structure of the Qing dynasty, and the formation of an antimonarchical stance that was implied by the wealthy class's demands for power was gradually weakened. Gu Yanwu and Huang Zongxi's calls for rural autonomy had become institutionalized practice in the Qing dynasty.

This historical transformation removed antimonarchical inclinations from the rule and regulations implemented by the gentry at the grassroots level of society. On the contrary, the ritual and the institutional order they advocated had become the source of the Qing's political legitimacy. In this historical situation, the attitude of many scholar-officials (including Huang Zongxi himself) toward Kangxi's rule became increasingly complicated. Some of them not only recognized the legitimacy of the Qing dynasty but also entered officialdom and even became entangled in new factional struggles, as in the dispute between southerners and northerners in the Shunzhi era and the disputes among competing factions of southerners in the Kangxi court. Li Guangdi, Xu Qianxue (1631–1694), Xiong Cilu, and Gao Shiqi were renowned Neo-Confucian scholar-officials, and they became deeply involved in factional disputes for their fame and fortune. They advocated Neo-Confucianism and discussed Principle and human nature, but their actions did not live up to their words. During the late Ming and early Qing, scholar-officials were unreliable and easily changed their loyalties, inviting disdain.[108] Their shifting political positions weakened or even cancelled the critical significance of the new theory of institutions and the new theory of rites and music. The Qing court flaunted its unification of governance and the Way under the suggestion of famous and high-ranking officials like Li Guangdi. In such a political climate, the critical premises of the new theory of institutions and the new theory of rites and music gradually became vague and ambiguous vis-à-vis Qing politics.

However, can we think that the Qing dynasty's ethnic minority rule "had taken over the social foundation upon which the Donglin Faction had been based," and assert that Huang Zongxi's new theory of institutions "was a position taken within the institutions and systems of the Qing dynasty"? Such a characterization requires careful analysis. First, Gu Yanwu and Huang Zongxi's studies were broad social theories rather than particular policy discussions. Although they supported the land reform and rural landlord systems, their political and economic thinking was not limited to these questions. The idea of separation of powers, proposed using terms such as "enfeoffment" and "centralized administration," cannot be equated with the idea of gentry domination, nor can it be explained by the concept of "Community Compact." These discussions of enfeoffment and centralized administration continued arguments about the separation of powers that had been made since the Southern Song dynasty by Ye Shi (1150–1223). These discussions went beyond issues related to rural autonomy that centered on gentry landlords; their central concern was how to alleviate problems caused by imperial centralization through the separation of powers. For these reasons, discussions of enfeoffment and centralized administration did not generally discuss gentry members, landlords, and land systems but focused on the structure of taxation, official, military, judicial, and supervisory systems at the imperial level.[109] These questions were also crucial to Gu Yanwu and Huang Zongxi's scholarship.

Second, the Qing dynasty was a period of Manchu aristocratic rule and territorial expansion. The Manchu rulers implemented an aristocratic minority autocracy that favored centralized power in order to meet the conditions of minority rule over a multiethnic empire. In terms of political, economic, military, and judicial systems, the Qing dynasty paid particular attention to the centripetal forces of society toward the imperial center and to the concentration of power in imperial hands. Based on the Ming political system, the Qing government established the Grand Council, the secret memorials channel, and the practice of not disclosing the heir apparent in successions to the throne. It fully implemented governor-inspectors and governors as territorial managers. The degree of centralization was much higher than that of the Song and Ming dynasties. It is difficult, then, to understand Gu Yanwu and Huang Zongxi's scholarship, which valued the politics of separation of powers, from "within the system" (*tizhi nei*) of the Qing dynasty's institutional framework. In 1678, Zhu Yizun (1629–1709), Wang Wan (1624–1691), Mao Qiling (1623–1716), and Shi Runzhang (1619–1683), for example, all came to Beijing to take the civil service examination, but Gu Yanwu and Huang Zongxi refused to participate. Such an action was closely related to the particular political identity embedded in their thought.

The idea of centralization easily gives the impression that political centralization and separation of powers were diametrically opposite proposals. However, many centralized power systems have been built on different kinds of separation of powers, and it is challenging to discern an absolute form of centralized power. Karl August Wittfogel used the concept of "Oriental despotism" to describe China's traditional state structure: he equates a bureaucratic state with centralized authority, but, according to Anthony Giddens, "the small proportion living in cities in class-divided societies is indicative of the low level of administrative power which the traditional state was able to achieve over its subjects. . . . This presumption [that bureaucratic empires are highly centralized societies] is fundamentally mistaken if such societies are compared with modern states."[110] The diversity of the early modern empire's political structure does not only exist in the differences between towns and villages. S. N. Eisenstadt once distinguished city-states, feudalism, patrimonial empires, and nomadic empires from the "centralized historical bureaucratic empires," which began to evolve in the Han dynasty and took shape during the Tang dynasty. The primary features of the Chinese centralized bureaucratic state were as follows: "The autonomy of the political center and the dominance of the emperor-literati alliance took firm shape; the army played an important role, which tended to become a less important role in periods of stability. Confucianism and Legalist ideology occupied the dominant position in the center; and there were also accompanying secondary orientations, especially a powerful mixture of Daoist and Buddhist orientations."[111] Eisenstadt's research is a comparative typology of imperial systems in history, and he emphasized the integrity and stability of the Chinese monarchy. Within this framework, what he observed was a society of autonomous strata, in which the ability of autonomous organizations or of any social stratum to enter the central core would be relatively weak.

From a historical perspective, we can still find that attempts to use the category of "imperial China" to generalize about China's political culture will run into many problems, because many significant transformations took place in "imperial China." In the Qing dynasty, for example, first of all, the above classification of empires does not work because the Qing imperial system includes almost all types except for city-states. The Qing empire was a centralized bureaucratic polity that included elements of feudalism, centralized administration, hereditary monarchy, and a nomadic conquest empire. Second, Eisenstadt describes China's stratification system according to four aspects, namely (1) development of the imperial center as the core focus of the stratification system; (2) the establishment of political-literary standards that play a prominent role in defining status, as well as the limited status of the literati and officials within the official system; (3) the relative weakening of the nobility and the growth of the status of the gentry; and (4) the evolution of several subordinate modes of constructing social hierarchy. These descriptions reveal the general features of the Chinese imperial system as a whole. However, even if we accept this depiction, the following two points need to be considered: First, the defensive town (*fan zhen*) and enfeoffment systems were long-standing (rather than accidental) historical phenomena of the imperial system, and the aristocratic power of the Qing dynasty depended on these systems. Second, the gentry's growing status was an important historical phenomenon, and the relationship between the gentry-patriarchal clan system and the political authorities was not always a mutually reinforcing relationship.

The Qing's rule over the Han Chinese population continued the Ming-dynasty system of centralized administration (*junxian*) that was strongly criticized by Gu Yanwu and others. Several historians in China have conducted significant research on the relationship between the central and local governments. Here I will make a quick summary. First, the administrative system. The Qing dynasty built on the tripartite provincial government structure of the Ming to streamline territorial management in each province. The control of governors general and governors over one or several provinces through the provincial administration and surveillance commissions that they directed was completely regularized, thus forming a system of administrative subordination in which governors general and governors exercised direct authority from above over border areas, and through the provincial administration commissions held jurisdiction over administrative and criminal justice matters in the prefectures and counties. Apart from this, the Qing government also developed systems and measures on official appointments, official vacancies, selection of officials at various levels, avoidance of conflicts of interest, adequate procedures for an audience with the emperor, and so on. The Qing also focused on strengthening the imperial court, especially the emperor's strict control over local officials. "In the Qing dynasty, the central government's administrative subordination of local officials appeared under the emperor's personal control, so it had the dual nature of centralization of power and imperial autocracy."[112] For bureaucratic appointments, however, the central and the local official systems were in parallel. For example, the governors general, the governors, and the central government offices had equal status rather than subordinate relationships.

Second, the distribution of financial power. Centralization of power reached its zenith during the Qing dynasty. The distribution of financial resources between the central and local governments in the Ming dynasty had generally adopted a combination of centralization of power with regional management of funds. The imperial court took a fixed amount of tax from the provincial and local governments, while local governments in all regions retained the rest of the tax revenue for local expenditures. The tax surplus was all reserved to the local governments, and the court generally left them alone. The Qing dynasty, on the contrary, drastically reduced the tax surplus in the prefectures and counties. The "full disclosure and remission to the imperial treasury" (*xi shu jie si*) policy and the strict "accounting report of expenditure" (*zou xiao*) system of the Ministry of Revenue demolished the regional or local autonomy that had resulted from central finance systems in the Han and Tang dynasties, and also from regional tax surpluses in the Ming dynasty, until "every scrap [of any tax revenue from counties and prefectures] would eventually be sent under guard to the capital."[113]

Third, judicial power. In the Qing dynasty, the local judicial system's features were as follows: "[There was] a hierarchy of review from counties through prefectures to provincial governors and provincial judges, level by level. At the end all grace and punishment came from the top." And, "The overall effect of step-by-step judicial review and verification was that local judicial decisions were not final, and the system would ultimately benefit the central government and the emperor's centralization of judicial power."[114]

Fourth, the military system. The imperial court exercised direct control over the Eight Banners soldiers, and the provincial governors exercised separate control over the Green Standard army. The characteristics of rule by an ethnic minority were clearly apparent in the military system. After the Taiping Heavenly Kingdom, the military and financial systems of the Qing dynasty underwent significant changes, which eventually became the root cause of the growth of local power in the late Qing and facilitated the demise of the Qing dynasty. However, this fact proves from the opposite direction that there was a highly concentrated central power in the Qing dynasty. The provincial governors were critical in redistributing power between the central and local governments. Historian Li Zhi'an summarized the Qing centralization features as "power entrusted to the provincial governors." Based on the Confucian system of centralized administration, the imperial court would delegate responsibility for local administration, finance, military, and judicial systems to the provincial governors on behalf of the imperial court. Through the "delegation of power and responsibilities" to the provincial governors, the Qing further accomplished its goal of centralizing the entire bureaucracy and army.[115]

The development of the Qing empire was closely related to its territorial expansion. Before the Manchu forces entered China, the Manchu Qing polity had once called itself an "external border lord" and "guard of the frontier" for the Ming dynasty. It had accumulated unique historical experience of managing the border. As the Qing dynasty grew into a multiethnic empire, its management of frontiers was the most successful of any dynasty. Its governing model of the borders was very different from the establishment of the Chinese inland administrative system. At the end of the thirteenth century, the Mongolian empire—previously established by Genghis Khan—collapsed, and the competition among Mongolian lords resumed. In the early seventeenth century, during the rise of Manchuria, Hong Taiji defeated Ligdan Khutugtu Khan of Chahar Mongolia in the 1630s, occupied Inner Mongolia, and established the Mongolian Eight Banners system. After Qing soldiers entered China in 1644, the Qing dynasty successively put down the resistance of Khalkha Mongols and Xinjiang Dzungars. After the Qing suppressed Galdan's revolt in 1696, it established rule over Xinjiang. It disrupted the Mongolian aristocracy's historical connection with the Tibetan Dalai Lama that had been in place since the sixteenth century, and this decoupling provided conditions for the Qing to control Mongolia and Tibet soon thereafter. Across many battles and campaigns in Central Asia, this period's wars and conquests provided the historical basis for establishing the Kashag system or governing council in Tibet during the Qianlong Emperor's reign. The Qing used the Court of Frontier Affairs as the primary institution to coordinate and manage the northwestern frontiers. Its governing technique was not one-size-fits-all but to act according to each region's specific conditions. Depending on each region's situation, the Court of Frontier Affairs might send troops to the frontiers, set up a military government, or send generals, ministers, or governors to supervise local conditions. All methods revolved around strengthening the relationship between frontier ethnic groups and the central government. In the 1680s, the Qing dynasty put down the Revolt of the Three Feudatories (1673–1681) in the southwestern region, converted other peripheral territories into regular administrative regions (*gaitu guiliu*), and captured Taiwan controlled by the forces of Zheng Chenggong (also Koxinga, 1624–1662), a loyalist of the Ming dynasty. The Qing imperial regime began to take shape in this period.[116]

If we make a rough comparison of the Song and Ming dynasties with the Qing dynasty, we can conclude that the Song and Ming dynasties originated in the historical circumstances of ethnic conflicts, and that the empires based on centralized administration have the characteristics of a quasi-nation-state. The Qing dynasty, however, was a multiethnic empire built on the dictatorship of ethnic minority aristocrats. There was a tributary relationship between the Ming and Qing dynasties and Mongolia, Tibet, and other regions, but this relationship's nature under the two dynasties was very different. The tributary relationship between the Ming dynasty and Mongolia did not include supervising Mongolian leaders and formulating governance rules (including tax collection and criminal law). In terms of political systems, the centralized political model of the Qing empire had to adopt a form of enfeoffment or divided investiture to coordinate and manage the relationship between different ethnic groups. From an ideological perspective, the Qing took Confucian "culture" as the ethical foundation of its unified empire, while respecting Buddhism and other religions and rejecting "ethnicity" (*zuqun*) as a basis for political unity. Han Confucianism thus became the legal basis for rule by ethnic minorities.

Centralization and the separation of power in the Qing dynasty were institutionalized in a multilayered relationship between monarchical power, Manchu nobility, Mongolian and other ethnic minorities, Han Chinese bureaucrats, and local government organizations. Division of power at one level was likely to be centralization at another level, and centralization at one level could be division of power at another. For example, the state apparatus of the early Qing dynasty centered on the Manchu Eight Banners system. The method of eight families forming the state and their joint selection of a khan was a crucial feature of the Manchu confederacy in the Nurhaci era. Nurhaci's regime divided its political power among Manchu aristocrats, which can be traced back to banner armies' military alliance: "All sons of different branches of the [Aisin Gioro] clan now led a banner army with their people and property. They were equal politically. The confederacy would need a leader acceptable by all banner heads to coordinate all things among banners. It was the Eight Banners system's origin, and it gradually developed into eight confederate military states, which then developed into the Manchu Qing state of the Eight Banners."[117] Although the early Qing dynasty's bureaucracy was a continuation of the Ming system, outside the Grand Secretariat there was another body called the Deliberative Council (also known as the State Council), staffed exclusively by the Manchu nobility, and its power stood above that of the Grand Secretariat and the Six Ministries. Therefore, from the perspective of Qing dynastic rule, the Eight Banners system had the characteristic of a division of power, but this divided power was precisely the dictatorship of an aristocratic ethnic minority over the Han Chinese population.

The system of eight confederate military states eventually gave way to a more centralized administrative organization, namely the Six Ministries established in 1631. The centralization of power in the Hong Taiji era was mainly to restrict the political power of his brothers known as the Grand Beile.[118] The restriction was different from what we usually call the relationship between the central and local governments in the Qing dynasty. The Mongolian Eight Banners system extended the Manchu Eight Banners' unification of military and politics and the military-civilian organization to all Mongolian ministries. However, the Mongolian banners differed from the Manchurian Eight Banners in content and form. The Mongolian system's primary purpose was to limit them in a fixed political unit and to prevent them from becoming a unified Mongolian force. Under this division of power, the Eight Banners of Mongolia became an auxiliary force of the Eight Banners of Manchuria.[119] This policy of divided power was the same as the Qing dynasty's subsequent policies, such as promoting the Panchen Lama and establishing the four living Buddhas in Tibet, all aimed at maintaining stability and the unity of the empire. It is difficult, then, for us to discuss the significance of the division of power of the Qing dynasty solely according to the model of centralization and decentralization.

Because of the existence of ethnic privilege, the centralization and division of power in the Qing dynasty involved different layers of organizational meaning, which scholars often overlook. After the Manchu conquest of China, the centralization and division of power in the early Qing cannot be examined merely as a matter of relations between the central and local governments; power relationships among the Eight Banners, Three Border

Lords, and the ordinary Han Chinese officials must also be considered. The modern perspective, based upon modern nation-states' experience, focuses only on the relationship between the central and local governments. This perspective cannot reveal the complicated internal relations of multiethnic empires, nor can it explain the power relations of ethnic minorities in conquering dynasties. When Kangxi was in power, three regions in the North refused to submit to Qing authority. Mongolia, the Dzungar Khanate, and other aristocratic forces resisted the Qing dynasty's rule, while forces related to the Three Feudatories of Fujian, Guangdong, Yunnan, along with Guizhou, formed potential threats in the South. Within the imperial court, when Executive Minister Oboi controlled power as Regent, land enclosures and laws that called for brutal punishment of escaped drafted soldiers were all implemented. As a result, ordinary peasants suffered, the relationship between masters and bondservants was cruel, and the contradiction between Manchu and Han worsened. Frontier crises, bureaucratic abuses, and aristocratic influence, as mentioned above, provided the background conditions for Kangxi's autocratic centralization. He attacked and pacified the tribal forces in Mongolia, Tibet, and Xinjiang, enlisting Han officials for these tasks and easing the conflicts between Manchu and Han. Whether through the suppression of the Revolt of the Three Feudatories, the prohibition of land annexation, or the relaxation of the punishment of escaped drafted soldiers, Kangxi worked to limit the power of local feudalism and the Eight Banners aristocrats and eased the situation of the Han peasants and bondservants. In this sense, while the Qing dynasty strengthened its control over localities and frontiers, it reduced the contradiction between the minority aristocracy and the Han people, but it also contributed to future contradictions between the frontier minorities and the Han nationality in the late Qing dynasty (such as the conflict between Yunnan Muslims and Han Chinese).

The formation of centralized administrative power coincided with the struggle between imperial authority and the Manchu nobility, resulting in the weakening of the Eight Banners nobility. The Yongzheng Emperor redesigned the Grand Council to diminish the Eight Banners' power, a move that signaled the ultimate success of the Qing dynasty's centralization.[120] To weaken the Manchu nobility's control, the emperor had to rely on the Han bureaucracy, which led to the Han Chinese bureaucracy's rise in the political structure. In this sense, using centralization to weaken the Manchu nobility implied, to some extent, the formation of a division-of-power relationship between the ethnic Han and Manchu nobles, but this division of power did not shake the foundation of the Qing dynasty's minority aristocratic system. In the case of the civil service examinations, participation in the examinations was theoretically open to everyone, but the design of nominating and appointing officials based on the examination system still allowed for factors related to hereditary position and status.[121] In the mid-Qing dynasty, the Taiping Heavenly Kingdom started a brutal civil war that led to the development of regional militias, and the status of the Han Chinese bureaucrats also increased significantly. If we examine events from the perspective of the development of centralized power in the Qing, we see this trend can be traced back to the balance of power between the imperial power and the Eight Banners aristocracy in the early Qing dynasty. The imperial court rebuilt the relationship between the imperial power and the Han gentry-landlord class through institutional reform, and the resulting balance of power between the imperial power and landlords showed similarities to that between the imperial power in the Sui and Tang dynasties and the power of the aristocratic class.

Most scholars concede that the Qing dynasty achieved its success by governing "according to the social customs and adapting to what worked," following "practices that each was comfortable with," and "not changing social customs," using both carrot and stick to gain support from elites. The expansion of the Qing empire forced it to adopt a system closer to enfeoffment in frontiers such as Mongolia, Tibet, and Xinjiang. There are essential differences between the basic policies of multiethnic empires and those of nation-states; one difference was in military conquest, and another in political control. The Qing dynasty also appropriated the idea from the "Royal Regulations" (*Wang zhi*) chapter of the *Book of Rites* that "we should cultivate their teachings but not change their customs; we should put their politics in order but not change what worked there." The Qing then allowed local self-governing in the northwestern region as part of the Qing imperial framework. Unlike the province system in China proper, the relationship between local autonomy and imperial power in border areas or ethnic minority areas was not a relationship of direct subordination. After its military conquests, the Qing dynasty did not reform the Northwest's social structure by implementing the administrative system found in the interior. It divided or balanced local forces, allowing them to conduct autonomous management under the center's supervision. The hierarchical system of "league and banner" (*meng qi*) was a gradation of ruling Inner and Outer Mongolia. The league-and-banner system combined features of the Manchu Eight Banners system, the Mongolian grassland tribal and territorial system, and tribal confederations. According to the degree to which each tribe submitted to or opposed the Qing court, the Qing also applied different rules in Outer Mongolia and Inner Mongolia.[122]

Although the league-and-banner system came from the Manchu Eight Banners, its character was different from the Manchu Eight Banners. The Manchu dynasty ruled China with the Eight Banners according to what was called "controlling the soldiers with the banner," but the banners did not have a specific area to govern, and bannermen had only an affiliation to the banner and not to a specific locality. This banner system was based on military organization rules to regulate life across the entire society, with no distinction between military and civil affairs. The Mongolian league-and-banner system was different, however: First, Mongolian banners were made up of a tribe or part of a tribe, with jurisdiction over land and people. Second, although Mongolian tribes became banners, the original leaders of the tribes were enfeoffed with the title of prince, and each was supposed to rule a banner, but sometimes there was more than one prince in a banner. Through this new enfeoffment by the Qing, these idle princes, who had initially been members of the ruling class, became the aristocrats of Mongolian society. The Qing court conferred various preferential treatments on them, such as titles of nobility, salaries, marriages, positions, and so forth. Third, after Mongolian tribes became banners, the people in these banners lost any freedom that they might have once had to choose their masters, along with the freedom of movement they enjoyed when living nomadic lives. The mobility of Mongolian social organizations and economic activities also changed accordingly.[123] Whether it was the banner system's division or the league leaders' supervision, the Mongolian banner system followed the principle of maintaining security through divided rule. Under the league-and-banner system, the Qing dynasty sent a General, a Grand Minister of Border Affairs at Kulun, a Grand Minister Consultant, and other Manchu officials to regulate the trade between Outer Mongolia and Russia and to restrict the influence of Mongolian

Buddhism.[124] However, under the league-and-banner system, each banner's internal organizations, kinship, and regional rules maintained their original social structure as much as possible.

The basic principles of managing frontiers, as mentioned above, were expressed in different ways in Tibet, Xinjiang, and Southwest China. The Manchus had established alliances or subordinate relations with various tribes in Inner Mongolia well before the Manchu conquest of China, while Mongolia had a complicated historical relationship with Tibet and especially with Tibetan Buddhism. Before the Manchu conquest, the Manchu Qing state began to worry that Mongolia and Tibet's religious-political alliance constituted a threat to its authority and started to dabble in Tibetan affairs. The Qing dynasty's Tibet policy followed some of the practices held over from the Yuan and Ming dynasties: Let regional religious powers manage Tibet's affairs, while the imperial court acts as a patron. In 1652, after the Dalai Lama's visit, Emperor Shunzhi recognized the Mongolian ruler in Tibet and appointed Qing administrative officials. In 1717, the Dzungar invaded Tibet due to a problem in the succession of the Dalai Lama; and in 1720, Kangxi sent troops to Tibet to support the real Dalai Lama and to expel the Dzungar occupiers, and Tibet then formally became a vassal of the Qing dynasty. After Yongzheng recalled the army in 1723, there was a rebellion in Tibet, and Yongzheng established a permanent system of ministers stationed in Tibet in 1727. In the fifteenth year of the Qianlong reign (1750), the Qing court abolished the Tibetan monarchy, abolished the Diba system of Tibet's local chief executive, and replaced it with the Kashag governor. The Kashag was under the unified management of the Dalai Lama and the Qing Minister in Tibet. This policy reestablished the Dalai Lama's position as the supreme ruler.[125] In 1760, the Qing dynasty conquered Xinjiang. According to the conditions of Mongolian, Han, and Uyghur communities in different regions, the Qing imperial court implemented the Mongolian banner system, a system of centralized administration, and the Berke system (that is, Uyghur feudal lords appointed as various officials to manage the urban and village affairs in southern Xinjiang), the latter incorporating the Uyghur system into the Court of Frontier Affairs's regulation.[126] Urumqi, Turpan, Hami, and other places in the eastern part of Xinjiang were placed under Urumqi's jurisdiction, divided into prefectures and counties, and managed by the Court of Frontier Affairs. Local elites administered cities such as Turpan and Hami. A farming area was set up to the north of the Tianshan Mountains to provide economic support for the garrisoned troops. Most of the soldiers and troops came from within Xinjiang, but there were a few military colonies in the hinterland.[127]

In Sichuan, Yunnan, Guizhou, Xikang, Qinghai, and other Southwest and Northwest provinces, the Qing dynasty continued the Tusi system, offering local officials higher compensation than those with the same official ranks in other locations.[128] The central government required regular tribute and notifications when the chieftains and native officials alternated, and the imperial court did not interfere in their internal affairs.[129] During the Yongzheng period, when the court established regular administrative regions in non-Han areas in the Southeast (*gaitu guiliu*), the central administrative power continued to strengthen its control and infiltration of these regions. However, from a grassroots point of view, there were still significant differences between the Qing rule of the Southwest minority regions and inland China, because the suppression of ethnic minorities in Guizhou and Yunnan (primarily the suppression of Yunnan Muslims) was more severe than in other areas.[130] This was the political model of a multiethnic empire that combined the strategy of "following the local customs and what worked locally" (i.e., respecting the national culture and local customs) with the threat of military force, bringing together local autonomy and strong centralized power to form an imperial system that integrated centralized administration and enfeoffment. This large-scale imperial system combined ancient imperial ideals with the mature system of centralized administration of the Song and Ming dynasties to complete the Qing's conquest, expansion, and rule of inland China, the Northwest, and the Southwest.

The institutional configurations described above had formed and evolved over a long period of time, and some extended into the Qianlong era (1735–1796) and later. However, during the lifetimes of Gu Yanwu and Huang Zongxi in the mid- and late seventeenth century, the institutional changes in Qing-dynasty politics described above had already appeared in embryonic form when the long-extant Manchu and Mongolian banner systems began to see new developments. The Qing dynasty's reforms in the land system and in cultural and educational institutions were linked to its highly centralized politics, creating a complicated historical pattern. Since the Manchu Qing dynasty was an ethnic minority regime, Huang Zongxi and Gu Yanwu, who were loyalists of the Ming dynasty, could not have approved of the hierarchical ethnic policies and institutional settings implemented by this dynasty. Their new theory of institutions and new theory of rites and music combined the restoration of China's antiquity with contemporary political reform, revealing the inner connection between Confucian orthodoxy and anti-Manchu thought from two different directions. They could not have resolved the opposition between their academic thinking and the Manchu autocracy, and their overall political design and social theory would never become a political reality.

However, with the relatively successful institutional reforms of the Qing dynasty, some of Gu Yanwu's and Huang Zongxi's political, economic, and even cultural ideas were realized in these unique historical circumstances. Facing these new political conditions became a predicament for the next generation of scholar-officials. For instance, in addition to the "Foreign Customs" article mentioned earlier, there were also essays in *Record of Daily Knowledge* on "Migrant Rong" (*Xi Rong*), "Muslims in the Tubo Region" (*Tubo Huihe*), "Astronomy in the Western Regions" (*Xiyu tianwen*), "Three Koreas" (*San Han*), "The Great Qin [a Han-dynasty term for the Roman empire]" (*Da Qin*), and "Kantoli" (*Gantuoli*). On the one hand, these articles reminded their readers of the historical experience of neighboring nomadic polities' delegations to Beijing, gaining insight into China's internal conditions, and finally becoming a threat along China's borders. It summarized the experience of tributary relations among the Western Regions (Tibet, Nepal, India), the Three Koreas (the Northeast and the Korean Peninsula), and the island barbarians in Hainan (Southeast Asian countries).[131] These essays echoed the historical practice of the Qing dynasty since its founding.

The ambiguous attitude toward the Qing dynasty's political legitimacy was bound to permeate practices in everyday life. Huang Zongxi, Sun Qifeng, and others did not serve the Qing dynasty, but their disciples became important ministers in the Qing court. These changes in everyday life must have created a profound sense of identity crisis for their disciples, who had to find theoretically and psychologically appropriate explanations for their actions. Times had changed, and by the Qianlong-Jiaqing era, the situation faced by scholars then was different from that of loyalist scholars. For Qian Daxin (1728–1804), Dai Zhen, and others, the political situation of Huang Zongxi and Gu Yanwu as loyalists of the Ming dynasty and their overall opposition to the existing political system had disappeared. Professionalized investigations of classical learning had gradually lost the theoretical integrity and critical edge once found in the new theory of institutions and the new theory of rites and music. The specialization of Confucian classical studies, the imperial advocacy of Confucian learning, and especially the changes in the relationship between Confucian scholars and the Manchu Qing dynasty created a new environment: the academic practice of classical studies would either become a tool for the political legitimacy of the current political system under the illusion of the unity of governance and the *Dao* or become specialized research conducted only for the sake of research. In this respect, being able to adhere to the principle of seeking truth from facts and engaging in specific research work was already a rare quality for scholars. The "good quality" of unadorned learning or evidential scholarship could only be manifested in a passive or negative sense by refusing to "conduct evidential research to flatter [the wealthy and powerful], pretending to be benevolent and righteous in the house of grand officials" and instead adopting the posture of the "scholastic hermit" to conduct evidential research.[132]

Debates about the importance of the ritual system within classical studies could no longer play the sharp and profound critical role that they had done for Huang Zongxi and Gu Yanwu. Therefore, when Dai Zhen, Zhang Xuecheng, and later Wei Yuan and Gong Zizhen wanted to question and change the existing system and its ethical norms, they had to find a different way, or even reverse Gu and Huang's direction. To a certain extent, they had to break the links between the ritual system and moral evaluation and the unity of political legitimacy and the legitimacy of *Dao*. However, when Han learning enjoyed support from both government and private academies, even criticism of Han learning would have to take the form of Han learning into account. Dai Zhen, Zhang Xuecheng, and the up-and-coming New Text classical scholars would have to explore ways to attack and break the study of classics and history from the inside, and use this break to show their critical spirit. The form of classical learning and the conflict to break through this form would become a shared preoccupation of the most critical scholars of this era. The premises behind Qing-era scholarship were the result of a millennium of continuous struggle and reform within Confucian learning, and even the most rebellious figures would not abandon them lightly.

The following protest against Han learning, which was both official and private in the Qing dynasty, reveals the plight of a somewhat rebellious figure—Zhang Xuecheng—who confronted the reigning academic style and fashion:

> Prevailing customs are often biased, and what the knowing and the powerful uphold and the intelligent and talented pursue often have flaws that are not trivial. Those who use their brushes do not think about salvaging the current situation, and inaction is prized in their writings. If one wished to salvage the situation, one would have to go against the trend of the times. The trend of the times is terrifying, sometimes more so than the regulations of the criminal justice system. Dai Zhen once happened to criticize someone from the Zhu family of Xiushui during a banquet, and Chief Minister Tuoshi resented him for the rest of his life. Such things are chilling. Han Yu, in his "Letter in Reply to Director of Studies Zhang" (*Bao Zhang Siye shu*) said, since Buddhist and Daoist learning is revered by princes, dukes, and eminent persons, how can I be brave enough to speak out against it? Then I knew that his essays like "On the Origins of the Way" (*Yuan Dao*) had not been generally made known at the time.[133]

Under these conditions, the form of classical studies that integrated ritual systems and moral evaluation with political with moral legitimacy was no longer a liberating force, but had become a form that restrained people's intellectual capacities, suppressed people's critical edge, and propped up the existing political system. Both in politics and in the academic environment, theories of "the unity of governance and morality" and of "the unity of ritual and rationality" had gained unprecedented power. For those who wanted to be critical, should they return once more to a binary of Principle (*li*) / vessel (*qi*) to recover critical resources from the subjective side, or should they reinterpret the notion of unity itself, in order to separate their understanding of "unity" from the will to power of pursuing unity? In short, those restless minds had to face this pressing question: In a time when the form of classical learning had not yet lost its rationality and legitimacy, what form should critical thinking take?

CHAPTER 5

Classics and History (2)

Translated by JOHN EWELL

> The Six Classics are what can be seen of its vessels. Since later men cannot see the former kings, they must rely on what can be observed of its vessels, and think of the Way that is not seen.
>
> —ZHANG XUECHENG: "On the Way" *(Yuan dao)*

I. Critiques of Song and the Rise and Fall of Qing-Dynasty Zhu Xi Learning

Dai Zhen (courtesy name Dongyuan, from Xiuning Prefecture in Anhui, 1723–1777) is a representative figure of scholarship from the Qianlong (1735–1796) and Jiaqing (1796–1820) eras, who also embodies the inherent dilemmas and contradictions of evidential learning (*kaozhengxue*) and foreshadows the end of the Qianlong-Jiaqing school. Ever since the late Qing, when scientific methods and their worldview became the ideological symbols of a new era, Liang Qichao, Hu Shi, and others have traced them back to the achievements of Qing-dynasty textual research, which they considered to be the precursor of modern scientific methods and of modern intellectualism. Hu Shi's comments on Dai Zhen's philosophy are particularly striking. He believed that Dai inherited the Qing scholarly traditions of "focusing on practicality" (the school of Yan Yuan and Li Gong) and "focusing on classics" (Gu Yanwu) to create a "philosophy of the full flowering era of Qing scholarship" and become the successor of Gu Yanwu and Yan Ruoqu as another "anti-Neo-Confucian" or "anti-*lixue*" (*fan lixue*) thinker.[1] Hu Shi's philosophical concepts are rooted in the scientific methodology of pragmatism, and his concern is with the problem of how to rebuild a worldview based on a foundation of epistemology and scientific method.[2] In the perspective of "May Fourth" anti-Confucianism, Dai Zhen's intellectual orientation, his textual research methodology, and the critique of Confucian ethics as "killing with Principle" in his *Critical Exegesis of the Meanings of Words in Mencius* (*Mengzi ziyi shuzheng*) fit together perfectly, and were all serious protests against Song-Ming *lixue*. Therefore, Hu Shi's evaluation of Dai Zhen is made from the perspective of establishing an anti-*lixue* scientific worldview, and the empirical method and a scientific worldview are the two central pillars of this evaluation.

Qing Confucian evidential learning is premised on the unification of governance with the Way, on the unification of principle with ritual, and on using the essential ideas of the classics and histories to corroborate the talking points and texts of the learning of its Principle (*lixue*), and this is also exactly the premise of the Kangxi and Qianlong emperors personally advocating the study of sagely learning. The evidential (*kaozheng*) critique of Song-Ming *lixue* has a long history, but although it denies the dualism of principle (*li*) and material force (*qi*) in Song learning and its method of extending knowledge by seeking principle from within the heart, what it basically adheres to is still the Confucian orthodoxy of unifying governance, ritual order, and ritual performance, and in a linguistic context where the Qing rulers were also singing each other's praises for unifying governance and the Way, it was difficult for this (anti-Song) predisposition to constitute a significant ideological critique. In other words, once we leave the deep understanding and clear political orientation of Gu Yanwu and Huang Zongxi, the theoretical premise of *kaozheng* learning is not fundamentally different from that of Qing-dynasty Zhu Xi learning. Then, how should we understand the anti-*lixue* significance of its knowledge orientation and methodology? It is worth noting that in the Qianlong-Jiaqing era, those who censured Dai Zhen included two kinds of people. One kind were followers of Song learning, who bitterly hated his censure of the Cheng brothers and Zhu Xi.[3] But another kind were representatives of *kaozheng* learning, who held Dai Zhen's *kaozheng* learning in the highest esteem but showed indifference to his *On Goodness* (*Yuan shan*), *Threadwords* (*Xuyan*), and *Critical Exegesis of the Meanings of Words in Mencius*. Their criticism of Dai Zhen was not because in his writings he put forward the anti-*lixue* argument about "killing with Principle," and it was also not because he deviated from the classicism of unifying principle with ritual, unifying governance with the Way, and asserting a common origin for principle and *qi* or concrete things, or from the tenets of the Qing-dynasty Zhu Xi school; rather it was surely because in method and approach he deviated from the *kaozheng* tradition. In other words, it was not for opposing *lixue*, but in a certain degree for opposing Han learning or coming close to *lixue*, that Qianlong-Jiaqing scholars saw Dai Zhen as distinctive. In this sense, his approach itself contained a kind of ambiguity: he adopted a *lixue* way of satirizing Han learning as well as a Han learning way of criticizing *lixue*, and consequently the term "anti-*lixue*," couched in Hu Shi's argument, may be inadequate to reveal the characteristics of Dai Zhen's thought.

The relationship between classical studies and the learning of principle is by no means one of complete opposition. When Gu Yanwu said that "the study of Principle is the study of the classics" (*lixue, jingxue ye*), this was a criticism of *lixue*, but it was not a complete abandonment of *lixue*. When Zhu Xi's learning emphasized investigating things and extending knowledge, originally there was an aspect of using classical texts to gather in and rectify human hearts, so as to realize the tendencies of moral philosophy for oneself. He said: "The Confucian scholars of the Han and Wei dynasties had broad accomplishments in correcting pronunciations, understanding exegetics, examining institutions, and distinguishing names and things. If scholars do not first get involved in these specialties, then how would they be able to exert their strength in the task [of investigating things and extending knowledge]?"[4] From the beginning of the Qing onward, when many scholars who regarded themselves as leftover adherents of the fallen Ming took stock of the lessons of the Ming collapse and opposed empty talk of Mind and Nature, one can say that the revival of Zhu Xi learning and the rise of studies of classics and history were products of a single wave. Zhang Xuecheng (1738–1801) admonished the classical masters of unadorned learning (*puxue*), saying:

> Today there are those who belittle Zhu's learning, yet there are now many traditions passed down from Zhu that are again arising. . . . Theories of the nature[5] and of [Heaven's] decree enter easily into emptiness, yet Master Zhu sought a unifying thread amid the many modes of pursu-

> ing knowledge [*Analects* 15.3], lodging ritual restraint within broad learning [*Analects* 6.27]; his involvements were manifold and dense and his accomplishments solid and difficult, even though one cannot say that in all his undertakings he was without fault. But those who carried on his learning . . . all served antiquity by mastering the classics, studied to seek what was true, and were not of the kind who cling stubbornly to the past or discourse emptily on the nature and the decree.[6]

In the early Qing, Zhu Xi learning and classical learning both carried on Zhu Xi's tradition in criticizing the claim of Wang Yangming learning that "the Six Classics are my footnotes" (*liujing wei wo zhujiao*). But what must be pointed out is that ever since the late Ming, criticisms of Wang Yangming learning did not signify a complete departure from that tradition, but were rather mediations between Zhu Xi and Lu Jiuyuan, which, while emphasizing extending knowledge through the investigation of things, paid special attention to investigating things, immediate knowledge, moral practice, and statecraft. Zhang Xuecheng's discussion of Eastern Zhejiang learning provides evidence of this from another perspective. He holds that scholars of classics and history like Huang Zongxi, the Wan brothers, and Quan Zuwang "are mostly modeled on Lu Jiuyuan of Jiangxi, and yet in serving antiquity by mastering the classics and in not using empty words to discuss the moral nature, they do not contradict the teachings of Master Zhu," explaining that distinguishing between Zhu and Lu and between *lixue* and the study of classics and history also makes it hard to explain the actual characteristics of Qing thought and scholarship.[7] Qing-dynasty Zhu Xi scholars like Lu Shiyi, Lü Liuliang (1629–1683), and Zhang Luxiang regarded personal practice and statecraft as the lifeblood of *lixue*, and made profound inquiries into statecraft matters such as ritual and law, punishments and governance, schools and field systems.[8] For them, the systems of the Three Dynasties of Antiquity and the words of the early Confucians were exactly the resources for distinguishing inner from outer and for forming an identity during the transition from Ming to Qing. The early-Qing Zhu Xi scholars valued national integrity, and it was connected not only with classical learning, but also with criticizing Wang Yangming learning while at the same time drawing on the essence of Wang Yangming learning, and within the realm of personal practice adhering strictly to Cheng-Zhu distinctions between truth and falsity. Such were the tangled relations between classical studies and *lixue*.

The abovementioned characteristics of early Qing-era Zhu Xi learning both opposed and echoed the imperial court, which honored ritual and revered Zhu Xi. Just as in the scholarly community Zhu Xi learning and classical learning worked together without conflict, official Zhu Xi learning flaunted its opposition to Wang Yangming learning, and not only maintained connections with imperially sponsored classical learning but in certain respects developed orientations similar to those of men like Gu Yanwu and Lü Liuliang. This pattern stands in an ironic relationship with the thought and practice of Gu, Huang, and Lü: the political orientation on both sides is completely opposite, and yet some of their theoretical presuppositions are almost identical.[9] From the beginning of the Qing dynasty, opposition to Wang Yangming learning became a trend, and by the Qianlong-Jiaqing era scholars were upholding examination of texts and knowledge of correct pronunciations as the key to understanding the classics and illuminating the Way. Everywhere they invoked Gu Yanwu's maxim that "the study of Principle is the study of the classics," and yet in their textual criticism and glossing they strayed ever farther from his aim of practical statesmanship, discussing only how to verify the empty with the solid or the solid with the empty. In this sense, the distinction between Han and Song is definitely not sufficient to capture the internal divisions of Qing-dynasty thought. For example, Wang Fuzhi has always been regarded as part of a late wave of Song learning, but in works like his *Unofficial Notes on the Classic of Documents* (*Shujing baishu*) and his *Meanings Drawn from the Shang Shu* (*Shangshu yinyi*) there are many sections—for example, the analysis of the "Tribute of Yu" (*Yugong*) in the *Unofficial Notes*—whose research is well documented, prompting even official writings like the *Comprehensive Index of the Complete Writings of the Four Treasuries* (*Siku quanshu zongmu*) to acknowledge that "this volume interprets the text of the classic and also puts forth many new ideas. . . . It refutes the shortcomings of the commentaries of Su Shi and Cai Shen, and on the whole its remarks are well founded and rise above idle chitchat. Although strong points and faults both appear, the positive aspects are more numerous."[10] Although his academic style was different from Gu Yanwu's, his textual scholarship on the *Shang shu* was also similarly not just textual scholarship for its own sake. He cited the *Book of Documents* (*Shang shu*) in order to infer its great principles, "often drawing on the affairs of later ages to correct them," and repeatedly criticizing the failures of historical dynasties, especially the abuses of the Ming era.[11]

Once having left behind the specific atmosphere of early-Qing statecraft and the Ming loyalist spirit of Gu, Huang, and Wang, the tendency of evidential scholars to reject Song-Ming *lixue* inevitably became completely ensnared in investigations of method and knowledge, and no longer had the political concern or moral significance of statecraft thought or of the unity of knowledge and action.[12] Taking the critiques of "King Wu attacked Zhou"[13] in Gu Yanwu's *Record of Daily Knowledge* (*Rizhi lu*) and in Yan Ruoqu's *Hidden Grave Mound Reading Notes* (*Qianqiu zhaji*) as examples, "Gu Yanwu's focus on the righteousness of 'taking All-under-Heaven without destroying the state' was directed at the Qing's overturning of the Ming. But what the *Reading Notes* criticized was an exchange of titles between Song and Shang; one can say it was mired in trivialities."[14] Yan Ruoqu's *Critical Exegesis of the Ancient Text Book of Documents* (*Guwen shangshu shuzheng*) and Hu Wei's *Clarification of the Diagrams in the Book of Changes* (*Yitu mingbian*) can also be regarded as anti-*lixue* works: because of Yan's *Critical Exegesis,* the so-called "sixteen-character transmission of the heart" (*Shiliu zi xin chuan,* "the human heart is precarious, the heart of the Way is difficult, be discerning and single-minded, hold fast to the mean") was proved to have come from the forged *Da Yu mo* ("Declaration of Great Yu") chapter of the *Old Text Book of Documents;* the *Yitu* ("diagrams in the *Changes*") had been one of the starting points for the Song Confucian study of Nature and Principle, but Hu's *Clarification* traced them back by evidential methods to a forged text created by the Five Dynasties Daoist priest Chen Tuan. This research to get back to the root and trace the origin was not an original creation of Qing-dynasty evidential learning; rather, it was a preexisting undercurrent that developed within Song-Ming *lixue.* But when Lu Jiuyuan in the Song or Huang Zongxi in the Qing and their followers critically examined the Yellow River Chart and the Luo River Writings, it was to criticize the metaphysical cosmology of Zhu Xi learning in the interest of restoring the personal practice of statecraft, while here among the later Qing Confucians the above-described examples of "criticizing the Song" were nothing more than expressions of Han learning intellectualism.[15] This tendency is also reflected even in a person such as Dai

Zhen, who was deeply concerned with moral philosophy or expositions on meanings and principles (*yili*). He mainly relied on the methods of textual research to reject and defame the Song Confucians, yet he did not dare to rely openly on a moral philosophy of personal practice to oppose Song learning. Zhang Xuecheng's understanding of Dai Zhen may be biased, but we may take it as a critique of the general mood of the times: "Dai Zhen strongly criticizes the men of Song, yet, although in taking his own path he falls far short of them, he still defames their personal practice, regarding their similarities to Buddhists and Daoists as evidence of the Song Confucians falling into delusion. Perhaps there were hypocrites (*wei junzi*) among them, but in opposing them Dai Zhen was also truly a petty man (*zhen xiaoren*)."[16] Zhu Xi learning and classical learning were as one in rejecting and vilifying Lu and Wang, but because of this they lost the spirit of personal practice. In this sense the Qing Confucian critique of Song was continuous and uninterrupted, but whether using philology and textual criticism to belittle the Song actually amounts to a critique is open to serious question. Observing Dai Zhen's relationship with Song learning against this background, our conclusion is of course different from Hu Shi's. Dai Zhen was good at textual criticism, his learning was grounded in seeking truth from facts, and in his youth it flowed from Jiang Yong of Wuyuan. Jiang was deeply versed in the three ritual classics, and his ambition, continuing from Zhu Xi's, was to complete the transmission of writings on ritual and music. Under his influence, Dai Zhen's early scholarship did not in the least oppose the pathways marked out by Zhu Xi learning. In his own words: "The Way of the Sages is in the Six Classics. The Han Confucians understood its institutions and laws but missed its moral philosophy (*yili*); the Song Confucians understood its moral philosophy but missed its institutional systems." What he sought was the mutual completion of Han and Song.[17] His "Letter to Shi Zhongming" sums up the aims of his scholarship at the time, and the fact that in this letter he on the one hand reaffirms the existing aim of classical scholarship to understand sentences through words, classical texts through sentences, and the Way through classical texts, and on the other denounces the Lu-Wang school's emphasis on "honoring the moral nature" in the name of "pursuing inquiry and study" and yet directs not a single word against Cheng and Zhu, is enough to show that his evidential learning and Zhu Xi learning were two sides of the same coin:

> What the classics ultimately reach is the Way; that by which the Way is made clear is their expressions, and what expressions are composed of are written characters. It is from the written characters that the expressions are understood, and from the expressions that the Way is understood; this must be a gradual process. In seeking out the meaning of these written characters I examined ancient seal-script writings, and came upon [Xu Shen's] *Shuowen jiezi* (Explaining writing by interpreting words). In three years I knew its main divisions, and so gradually gained some insight into the beginnings and fundamentals of the ancient sages' formulations. Yet I doubted whether Mr. Xu's glosses were exhaustive, and so borrowed a copy of the *Annotations and Glosses on the Thirteen Classics* (*Shisanjing zhushu*) from a friend and read it. Then I knew that the meaning of a character must be threaded through all the classics and grounded in the six graphic principles before it can be regarded as definitively established. . . . Lu [Xiangshan] of Song and Chen [Bosha] and Wang [Yangming] of Ming abandoned the learning of mutual discussion and shared inquiry and borrowed what they called "honoring the moral nature" to embellish their reputations. But if they have abandoned "the path of inquiry and study," how can this be called "honoring the moral nature"?[18]

Differences do exist: the "things" of Zhu Xi's "investigation of things" extend universally to the myriad things under Heaven, whereas the objects of Dai Zhen's theory of investigating things are just the "names and things" in the Six Classics, even though he personally made a deep and detailed investigation of mathematics and other studies of the natural world. Qian Daxin summed up his achievements, saying of Dai Zhen that "in his expositions of systems, names and things, and even astronomical calculations in the ritual classics, he always penetrated right to the source, and in his detailed study of the Han Confucian commentaries and annotations, and of the *Fangyan* (regional dialects) and *Shuowen* dictionaries, he worked from the pronunciations and written forms of words to determine correct glosses, and from the glosses to seek out their moral significance (*yili*)."[19] This was the approach of evidential studies.

The form of classical learning was in itself a critique of *lixue*, but if Dai Zhen's "Letter to Shi Zhongming" and the viewpoints of Gu Yanwu and Duan Yucai are considered one by one, we can discover that the thread of classical studies that begins with Gu Yanwu, develops with Hui Shi and Dai Zhen, and is brought to completion by Duan Yucai and Wang Niansun, has a connection with *lixue* that in some respects makes them two sides of the same coin. Gu Yanwu, in his "Preface to a Punctuated Text of the *Classic of Ceremonies and Rites* with Zheng [Xuan's] Annotations" (*Yili Zheng zhu judu xu*), says:

> Latter-day gentlemen use punctuated readings to parse the text, follow the text to know its meaning, and follow its meaning to understand the source of the institutions. These are what Confucius called undertaking the Way of Heaven to govern human sentiments, and can be traced back to the heroes of the Three Dynasties, but their bitter sighs are not expressed in the legacy of Cheng Yichuan [i.e., in the legacy of Neo-Confucianism]. Heroes like Hou Ji [a legendary culture hero credited with introducing the cultivation of millet in the time of the Xia dynasty], were they not the first advocates of the peaceful tranquility of later generations?[20]

Does this not completely echo the "Letter to Shi Zhongming"? Duan Yucai's "Preface to *Dai Dongyuan's Collected Works*" takes Gu Yanwu and Dai Zhen's understanding of relying on the text to know the meaning to a deeper level, because he directly traces the foundations of philology and textual criticism to the high regard in which the Song Confucians held the *Doctrine of the Mean* (*Zhongyong*). In his view, the basis of classical learning lay in the fact that a sage cannot rely on emptiness to tread the void and grasp moral principles (*yili*) with his heart; if he cannot, as the *Doctrine of the Mean* says, "root it in his person, attest it among the common people, examine it against the Three Kings with no error, establish it in Heaven and Earth without opposition, present it before spiritual beings without question or fear, and wait a hundred generations for a sage without doubts,"[21] the sage would have no way to "exhaust the principles of Heaven and Earth and of the people and things." Therefore, he asked, since evidential research is "the way of the profound person" (*junzi zhi dao*), isn't moral philosophy what evidential research ultimately reaches? Duan Yucai said:

> Since the Way of the Sages is in the Six Classics, if one does not seek it in the Six Classics there is no way to attain the moral philosophy that the

> sages were seeking and to put them into practice in the family, in the state, and in All-under-Heaven; and if one's diction is not elegant, one again becomes lost in trivialities. [Dai Zhen's] study of the classics, with regard to glossing, phonology, mathematics, astronomy, geography, institutions, names and referents, the good and evil and truth and falsehood of human affairs, as well as yin and yang, transformations of *qi*, and the nature and [Heaven's] decree, was in each case to investigate them with regard to their actuality, and through textual research to reach an understanding of the nature and the way of Heaven. . . . He also once wrote to me saying, "Of all the books that I have written, the *Critical Exegesis of the Meanings of Words in Mencius* is the most important, because it gives the means of rectifying men's hearts." Ah! From this one may know the master.[22]

Duan Yucai criticized the sharp distinctions made at the time between expositions on meanings and principles or moral philosophy (*yili*), textual criticism (*kaoju*), and literary writing (*cizhang*), from the standpoint of the unity of the Confucian Way, and rejected their division by later Confucians into separate domains of activity; his critique not only precisely embodies Dai Zhen's own thought, but is also very close to the censure of Han learning and esteem for Song learning expressed by Fang Dongshu, who was biased toward *lixue*.[23] Working from opposite perspectives, Duan Yucai and Fang Dongshu jointly reveal that textual criticism and expositions on meanings and principles not only do not occupy opposing positions but rather mutually support each other, and that Song learning may be regarded as the mentor of Han learning.[24]

In Song-Ming *lixue* there was originally a dispute between the Cheng-Zhu and Lu-Wang schools, from which Confucian scholars of the late Ming and early Qing each took what they needed and gradually turned toward the study of classics and history. Historians of scholarship are accustomed to tracing the inner logic of scholarly developments, and to organizing the aspects of the thought of different times into a single uninterrupted thread. In discussing the characteristics of the Wu school's opposition to *lixue*, Qian Mu once said:

> When Tinglin [Gu Yanwu, 1613–1682] wrote his *Five Books on Phonology* (*Yinxue wushu*), his purpose was to rely on Tang to correct the Song and

> to rely on the ancient classics to correct the Tang, and thus by returning to the ancient to oppose the Song, and through classical philology to overthrow the Song-Ming recorded conversations (*yulu*). The trend spread through the lower Yangzi valley, and this was the origin of Wu learning. In the old town of Yaojiang in eastern Zhejiang the spirit of Yangming still persisted, and when scholars like Lizhou [Huang Zongxi, 1610–1695] and his brother [Zongyan, 1616–1686] refuted the *Yitu* (*Yi* diagrams), Chen Qianchu [Chen Que, 1604–1677] suspected the *Great Learning,* and Mao Xihe [Qiling, 1623–1716] energetically praised the *Old Text Great Learning* (*Daxue guben*) and strongly disputed Zhu [Xi]'s [view of the text], their motive was to take up the old case of Cheng-Zhu versus Lu-Wang, but the end result was coincidentally to reach the same goal as Tinglin by different routes, leading scholars to become conversant with classical texts without necessarily adopting a common stance. Similarly, when Yan Baishi [Ruoqu, 1636–1704] disputed the *Old Text Book of Documents* (*Guwen shangshu*), his intention was certainly to respect Zhu [Xi], but again the end result was also to lead men to know that understanding a classic begins with tracing it back to antiquity, that from Tang times on everything is doubtful, and even more so for Song and Ming.[25]

Ever since Kangxi began to revere Zhu Xi learning, the tension between Zhu Xi learning and classical learning had gradually subsided. The unity of governance and the Way and the unity of principle and ritual promoted by the *lixue* scholars and the "organic oneness of Way and vessels" (*daoqi yiti*) of the classicists shared a single origin, and as long as this fundamental presupposition did not waver, no diametrically opposed pattern could arise between them. Because of this, the classicism of Jiang Yong and Dai Zhen began by transmitting Zhu Xi, and Zhu Yun and other Qianlong-Jiaqing scholars continued to have high regard for Cheng and Zhu.

Hui Dong and Dai Zhen were respectively regarded as the leaders of the Wu (Suzhou) and Hui (Huizhou) schools of learning, and were also representative of Qianlong-Jiaqing-era critiques of Song. Wang Mingsheng held that "today's scholars decidedly esteem both masters, [saying that] in his study of the classics Mr. Hui seeks what is old, while Mr. Dai seeks what is true. But actually, if one abandons the old there is no way to determine what is true."[26] Qian Mu extended this analysis of their differences, saying:

> With the emergence of Mr. Hui Dong of Suzhou, the spirit of suspicion changed to sincere belief and the task of distinguishing falsehood turned toward a search for truth, but his return to the Han Confucians was grounded in his disdain for and rejection of Tang and Song. . . . Therefore, comparing Huizhou learning with Wu learning, Wu learning was more radical and progressive, and by advancing a step carried a revolutionary bearing, while Huizhou learning . . . on the whole continued the legacy of Donglin, and its first ambition was still to explain the Song and transmit Zhu. It was not as far-sighted as Wu learning, and its differentiation of Han from Song was like a matter of different pathways in the North and South.[27]

That both Hui Dong and Dai Zhen "disdained and rejected Tang and Song" and returned to Han Confucianism is a clear fact, but how to understand their relationship with Song learning still needs to be carefully analyzed. Since Huizhou learning's early ambition was still to explain the Song, and since critiques of Song began with Wu learning, we must look first at why Hui Dong criticized the Song and returned to Han.

In 1756, Hui Dong republished the Southern Song scholar Wang Yinglin's reconstruction of Zheng Xuan's (127–200 CE) *Commentary on the Book of Changes* (*Zhengshi Zhou Yi*), regarding it as the foundation of Han Confucian theories, and criticizing scholars since Wang Bi (226–249 CE) for having introduced Daoist theories into later *Yijing* commentaries. This scholarly orientation was fundamentally opposed to the Song Confucian theory of orthodox transmission of the Way (*daotong*), and implied resistance to Buddhist and Daoist elements in Song learning. In his "Preface" (*zixu*) to *Han Studies of the* Yijing (*Yi Han xue*), Hui Dong said: "The Six Classics were fixed by Confucius, destroyed in the Qin, and transmitted to the Han. Han learning was lost long ago, and only the three *Odes, Rituals,* and *Gongyang* classics still remained. . . . As soon as Wang Fusi [Wang Bi] used false images (*jia xiang*) to explain the *Yi* (*Book of Changes*), it became fundamentally a Huang-Lao [text], and nothing remained of the meanings of the Han classics masters."[28] According to Yang Xiangkui's account, Hui Dong's critique of Song had two aspects. One was to expose the groundlessness of the Yellow River Chart (*hetu*) and the Luo River Writings (*luoshu*), and the other was to offer a new explanation of the concept of "principle" (*li*). He used the critical methods of classical scholarship to offer a thoroughgoing critique of the Song

Confucians' "Prior to Heaven" (*xiantian*) and "Ultimate of Non-Being" (*wuji*) cosmologies, and exposed the "Prior to Heaven Chart" (*xiantiantu*) and "Ultimate of Non-Being Chart" (*wujitu*), as well as the "Yellow River Chart" and the "Luo River Writings," as forgeries.

Ever since the Song and Yuan, in order to overturn the foundations of Zhu Xi learning, Lu-Wang scholars had been using textual research methods to expose the groundlessness of Zhou Dunyi's "Explanation of the Diagram of the Supreme Ultimate" (*Taiji tu shuo*), and making important contributions to later developments in the study of classics and history.[29] Hui Dong's critique of the Yellow River Chart and Luo River Writings was actually just a continuation of this tradition. He also used textual research methods to explain "principle" (*li*), extending the implicit meaning of "related pairs" in the writings of Guanzi and others, and then maintaining that principle embraced yin and yang, the hard and the soft, humaneness and righteousness, and likes and dislikes. This way of using philological methods to deconstruct propositions that "treat Heaven and man, and principle and desire, as opposed" and hold that "Heaven is principle"[30] paved the way for Dai Zhen's analysis of the relation of principle and desire. Hui Dong's theory of principle was based on the writings of the Legalists, and Dai Zhen's theory was derived from Xunzi; both shared the tendency to explain principle in terms of human connections with rituals and laws. These are the traces of a new theory of institutions, as disclosed in their writings on moral philosophy and in their textual research.

But the relationship between Hui Dong's learning and Song learning is far from something that can be summarized as anti-*lixue*. When Pi Xirui (1850–1908) discussed the rejection of Song annotations by great masters of classical studies like Hui Dong and Dai Zhen, he went out of his way to comment on how they paraded the flag of Han learning:

> Hui's Red Bean Mountain Studio had a pillar couplet which read: "The lineage of the Six Classics begins with Confucius and Mencius; for daily conduct the models are Cheng and Zhu" (*liujing zong Kong Meng, baixing fa Cheng Zhu*), which shows that Hui never belittled Song Confucian learning. Dai Zhen . . . whose learning came from Jiang Yong, praised Yong's learning as unequalled since the Han classics master Kangcheng [Zheng Xuan]. Jiang Yong had written a commentary on Zhu Xi's *Re-*

> *flections on Things at Hand* (*Jinsi lu*), and his *Essentials of the Book of Rites* (*Lijing gangmu*) was based on Zhu's *Comprehensive Explanations of the Book of Rites and Ceremonies and its Commentaries* (*Yili jingzhuan tongjie*). Even though Dai Zhen's *On Goodness* and *Critical Exegesis of the Meanings of Words in Mencius* ran counter to Zhu Xi's explanations of the classics, this was only a matter of disputing the meaning of the single word "*li*" [variously understood as "principle," "pattern," or "coherence"]. Duan Yucai received his learning from Dai Zhen, and suggested that Dai Zhen should be honored along with Zhu Xi in his memorial temple and (his work) regarded as a later colophon to Zhu's philological studies (*xiaoxue*). . . . Duan Yucai and [other] Qing philologists did not use Han philology to belittle Zhu's philology. Truly the learning of Jiang Yong, Dai Zhen, and Duan Yucai never belittled the learning of the Song Confucians.[31]

Pi was trained in the New Text learning camp, and his critique of Hui Dong embodied the sensitivities of the New Text classical scholars.[32] Yang Xiangkui exactly confirmed Pi Xirui's viewpoint, arguing that "in his studies of the *Changes*, Hui Dong liked to substitute so-called ancient characters for their common forms and respected the Ancient Text classical system, and yet also adopted the theories of New Text scholars, relying greatly on the learning of *yin-yang* prognostications, and accordingly spoke of 'the Way of Heaven and man.' One can say that in his study of the classics, Hui Dong purely followed the 'Han Confucian' lineage."[33]

On the question of how to understand the comment that Hui Dong "purely followed the Han Confucian lineage" in this passage, we may further deliberate as follows: in his glossing of written characters, Hui Dong respected the system of the Old Text classics (substituting ancient characters for their common forms), but with regard to the moral philosophy (*yili*) behind his evidential research he was concerned with the Way of Heaven and man, and accepted New Text theories. From the age of fifty he concentrated his attention on classical scholarship, and was especially skilled in the *Book of Changes*. His discussions of the *Book of Changes* in his *Transmission of the Book of Changes* (*Zhouyi shu*), in his *Cases from the Book of Changes* (*Yi li*), in his *Han Studies on the Book of Changes* (*Yi Han xue*), and in his *Ancient Meanings of the Nine Classics* (*Jiujing guyi*) were important works in Qing-dynasty

Book of Changes studies, and have been highly praised by historians of scholarship.[34]

Song-dynasty *lixue* took repudiation of the two schools (of Laozi and the Buddha) as its banner, but its cosmology and psychology were closely related to Buddhism and Daoism. Hui Dong attacked the Yellow River Chart (*hetu*) and the Luo River Writings (*luoshu*), took restoring Han learning as his personal responsibility, and believed that Song theories of "before Heaven" (*xiantian*) and "after Heaven" (*houtian*) had originated with Wang Bi's misinterpretation of the *Book of Changes,* which had jumbled in many Lao-Zhuang elements; yet in using his pattern of opposing the Song and returning to the Han to reconstruct a "learning of Heaven and man" he was in secret accord with Buddhist and Daoist theories. Here, the bridge that linked classical studies with *lixue* was the Han-dynasty study of the New Text classics and prognostication texts and their Daoist elements within these texts. Hui Dong openly cited the *Kinship of the Three, According to the Book of Changes* (*Zhouyi Santong qi*), believing that in doing so he could continue a tradition of learning that had been cut off, and carry on its subtle remonstrances. In his *Transmission of the Book of Changes* he strongly attacked Zhu Xi, but when explaining the *Book of Changes* (*Yijing*) he often cited the *Yellow Emperor's Hidden Talisman Classic* (*Huangdi Yinfujing*), a work that Zhu Xi had greatly admired and repeatedly examined and corrected. Based on this, Yang Xiangkui said: "The development of Han learning was originally opposed to *lixue,* but in this one respect the two were united through the *Hidden Talisman Classic.*"[35] When Hui Dong viewed human affairs in terms of celestial abnormalities, confusion of divinatory symbols, disordered yin and yang, and the prevalence of natural calamities, he was completely following the old Han Confucian theories of the mutual linkages and similarities in kind of Heaven and man. His Han learning was focused on studies of the *Book of Changes,* and in his particular emphasis on theories of the yin and yang aspects of natural calamities he was also returning to Han learning's implicit complete accord with Daoism. This is the main reason why, at the same time when he was criticizing the Song, he was also able through his "Heaven and man" learning to remain in dialogue with Song learning.[36] Hui Dong's *Book of Changes* studies connected the *Book of Changes* with the *Spring and Autumn Annals,* with the former as the study of Heaven and the latter dealing with human affairs, and when he combined them as the Way of Heaven and man[37] there were many places in which this pattern echoed the treatment of Heaven and man in later *Gongyang* studies. Specifically, Yang says that "in the *Taiji shengci* (Great Ultimate's Stages of Life) section of his *Yi li shang* (*Book of Changes* examples, part 1) he held that the existence and development of Heaven and Earth and the ten thousand things were the same as the existence and development of the *Book of Changes.* The development of the ten thousand things was the substance of the universe, and the *Book of Changes* was the manifestation of the substance of the universe. The account of events in the *Spring and Autumn Annals* was modeled on the *Book of Changes,* and the fact that its account of successive dynasties begins with the era of *yuan* [origin] is modeled on the way that that the *Book of Changes* begins with the Great Ultimate [*taiji*]."[38] Hui Dong closely followed the Han Confucians in matching cosmic phenomena with the sixty-four hexagrams, and in discussing, one by one, concepts like the Way (*dao*), Origin (*yuan*), Genuineness (*cheng*), the nature (*xing*), and the Decree (*ming*), he was clearly echoing what Song learning spoke of as exhausting Principle to realize the nature, and their theories of the Way of Heaven and of *li* and *qi.* This kind of *Yijing* studies cosmology that united Heaven and man as one body was one of the important origins of *lixue.* When under the form of classical studies he returned to *Book of Changes* studies cosmology, this was not only a beginning of New Text classical studies from within Old Text classical studies, but also a way of providing a cosmological perspective from which to view human affairs.[39]

Dai Zhen and Qian Daxin both discussed academic matters with Hui Dong and also followed him in fiercely attacking the Song, and in the context of Qianlong-Jiaqing scholarship the Han / Song divide became like water and fire. But from the perspective of the mutual transmissions and interpenetrations of intellectual history, the problem becomes much more complicated. Dai Zhen's *On Goodness* was a work of *lixue* that was most unwelcome to the classical scholars of his day, but according to Qian Mu's theory, it came from the school methods (*jiafa*) of Hui Dong's Han learning.[40] In an essay on the Han-dynasty classical scholar Zheng Xuan, Zhang Taiyan (1869–1936) wrote: "The men of the Han dynasty were not good at logical reasoning (*mingli,* lit.: "names and patterns"), and so their classical scholars' accounts of the Way also did not measure up to the refined accomplishments of the late Zhou. But mixed in with their more ordinary discourses they had lucky glimpses of great value, and so became the teachers of Song-Ming School of Mind (*xinxue*)."[41] This view is also quite applicable to the relationship between Han learning and *lixue* in the Qing dynasty, but in reverse: Zhu Xi's learning and *yin-yang* learning, as well as *Book of Changes* studies and Daoist religion and prognostication theories, were also the teachers of Qing-dynasty Han learning. From within the confines of classical scholarship Hui Dong explored the meanings and principles of the learning of Heaven and man, and in his "On the Patterns of Celestial Symbols" (*Faxiang lun*), Dai Zhen used the patterns of the *Book of Changes* to observe human affairs.[42] Are not these both proofs of this? In this context, how Dai Zhen nevertheless came to criticize Song learning also becomes a problem.

There is also a more important question here: the Kangxi Emperor esteemed Zhu Xi, and high-ranking officials and eminent scholars of the time rushed to embrace him; but if Zhu Xi learning remained as the official learning of the Qing court, how could eminent Qianlong-Jiaqing scholars living in the capital have dared to take criticism of the Song as their banner? And how could Hui Dong's heated pronouncement, in his critique of the *Mao Annotations of the Odes* (*Mao Shi zhuan*), that "the harm [caused by] the Song Confucians was worse than the Qin [burning of the books]" have won the hearts of the commissioners of the Four Treasuries Project (Siku quanshu)? Before analyzing Dai Zhen's critique of Song and his relationship with Wu learning, we must speak of the fate and transformations of Zhu Xi learning in the Qing from the viewpoint of the connections between politics and scholarship. Liang Qichao once attributed the rise of *kaozheng* scholarship to the Qing literary inquisition. This viewpoint has been rebuked by many scholars. However, the connection between the literary inquisition and changes in the scholarly atmosphere of the Qing era is hard to ignore. The first to suffer the harm of the literary inquisition was Qing-dynasty *lixue*, especially Zhu Xi learning, and it indirectly influenced the relationship between classical learning and Zhu Xi learning, in that classical scholars were forced to reposition themselves in relation to Zhu Xi learning.[43] Coming down to the Yongzheng-Qianlong era (1722–1796), famous *lixue* scholars were dying off, and although sagely learning was still ranked as orthodox, its position began to undergo subtle changes. What plays a key role here is the relationship between official Zhu Xi learning and other factions, and also the intrinsic connection between folk Zhu Xi learning and national consciousness. Lu

Baoqian's "History of Qing Thought" has a brief but clear narrative about this. When the Yongzheng court launched its great literary inquisition, its first target was the so-called "examination factions," when Li Fu (1675–1750) was imprisoned for being involved in a case involving Tian Wenjing (1662–1732).[44] Li Fu was a famous official of that time, who in his studies followed Lu and yet gave equal weight to Zhu Xi and Lu Xiangshan, and so had become an important personage in the Kangxi reign that extolled the unification of governance and the Way. In 1728, when the examination faction case was not yet completely resolved, the Yongzheng Emperor, on account of the case of a letter sent by the Hunan licentiate Zeng Jing to Chuan-Shan Governor General Yue Zhongqi, became involved in the widely influential case of Lü Liuliang. Lü strictly upheld the fundamental distinction between Chinese and foreigners, and with verses like "Once having begun to understand the whole of things, how is it easy to discuss? One now knows that starving to death is the most trivial of matters," he had become a famous *lixue* scholar. He achieved *xiucai* status in the tenth year of Shunzhi (1652), but later cut his hair and became a monk, refusing to respond to the call to participate in the Erudite Literatus (*boxue hongci*) examination or to take office. The fact that Zeng Jing and his disciple Zhang Xi deeply respected Lü Liuliang, based their learning on the goal of unifying governance and the Way, strictly upheld the great distinction between Chinese and foreigners, and held that the emperor should "act from the learning of our Confucian scholars"—for example Confucius from the Spring and Autumn period, Mencius from the Warring States period, and Cheng and Zhu from post-Qin—and that the late-Ming emperors should have understood their responsibilities from the teachings of Lü Liuliang, should be sufficient to show that the difficulties encountered by Zhu Xi learning in the Qing were closely linked with issues of ethnicity.[45] When Lü Liuliang and his disciples esteemed Cheng and Zhu, it had the flavor of strictly discriminating the truth or falsehood of received Cheng-Zhu teachings, and the object of their critique was Kangxi's use of Cheng and Zhu to gather in and collect men's hearts, as well as Zhu Xi scholars like Lu Longqi (1630–1693) and Li Guangdi (1642–1718), who sang the praises of the Kangxi Emperor's "cultural governance" (*wenzhi*) that unified governance and the Way. This was to use a Confucian scholar's unification of governance with the Way to oppose the unification of governance and the Way by Qing imperial power. After the Zeng Jing case unfolded, Yongzheng not only ordered a search for Lü Liuliang and his disciple Yan Hongkui, but also commissioned commentaries on the writings of disciples like Zheng and Yan, and specifically ordered Grand Secretary Zhu Shi (1665–1736) and others to refute Lü Liuliang's lectures and recorded conversations on the Four Books. The corpses of Lü and his son were dug up and exposed, and his descendants and disciples over nine degrees of kinship were either killed or transported into penal servitude.

The aforementioned case of examination factions and the case of Lü Liuliang had a deep and far-reaching impact on the Qianlong-Jiaqing-era government and on the status of Zhu Xi learning.[46] From the perspective of the problem of factions, Qianlong carried on the viewpoint of Yongzheng. He was extremely alarmed by factions and sects, and apart from iron-handed rule he also endeavored through imperial editions and imperially sponsored compilations that relied equally on Han and Song to sweep away on a theoretical level the premises of sects and factions, as is clearly recorded in the *Veritable Records* of the Qianlong reign. For example, in 1758 (the twenty-third year of the Qianlong reign), when in an "Imperially Composed Preface" (*Yuzhi xu*) to the imperially compiled *Collected Explanations of the Spring and Autumn Annals* (*Chunqiu jijie*) he discussed the *Spring and Autumn Annals* and came to the phrases "narration through linked expressions" (*zhuci bishi*) or "subtle words with profound meanings" (*weiyan dayi*) that New Text scholars liked to speak of, he definitely did not hold fast to the explanations of Old Text scholars;[47] and in 1782 (the forty-seventh year of his reign), at the time of the "Classical Lectures of the Second Month of Spring," in response to Debao and Cao Xiuxian's discussion of the statement in the *Analects* that "the wise are joyful; the humane are long-lived," Qianlong criticized Zhu Xi's explanation that "humaneness is the substance of wisdom, and wisdom is the function of humaneness" for "not treating humaneness and wisdom equally," and held that Zhu had not understood Confucius's refined subtlety.[48] Thus, the Qianlong-Jiaqing period's trend of criticizing the Song echoed the decline of Song learning brought about in the Yongzheng period by opposition to sects and factions.

From the perspective of the problem of ethnicity, in the early Qing, Zhu Xi scholars outside the state apparatus used Confucius, Mencius, and the Six Classics to promote an ethnic ideal, and expressed the purpose of opposing the Qing within the framework of distinguishing between Chinese and foreigners. Wang Fuzhi and Lü Liuliang are important examples of this. Lü believed absolutely in Cheng and Zhu, and when he denounced Lu and Wang as "outwardly Confucian but secretly Buddhist,"[49] his purpose was to use Zhu Xi orthodoxy to repel the northeastern barbarians (i.e., the Manchus).[50] Starting from the perspective of Three Dynasties feudalism, he determined that the many varieties of systems of centralized administration since the Qin and Han were all based on selfishness and profit seeking, and had completely lost the spirit of the institutions of the Three Dynasties.[51] Lü followed the old path of *lixue,* criticizing the unification of commanderies and prefectures under centralized administration, admiring the systems of enfeoffment and well-fields of the Three Dynasties, and holding that "the abandonment of enfeoffment and well-fields was a matter of circumstance, not principle; it was chaos, not governance"; and he denounced later rulers as "heedlessly given over to cultivating their heart of selfishness and profit, and so unable to restore the Three Dynasties."[52] This was to regard the institutions of the Three Dynasties as the basis for evaluating governance and chaos, and implied a disparaging critique of the contemporary age. In his refutation of Zeng Jing, the Yongzheng Emperor also criticized Lü Liuliang's thought, and in addition to the issue of a distinction between Chinese and foreigners he also brought in the theories of Song-Ming *lixue* on the ethical bonds between ruler and minister, and the Three Dynasties enfeoffment system that they loved to dwell upon. In the Yongzheng era those who offended on account of *lixue* also included followers of Li Fu (1675–1750) and Cai Ting such as Xie Qishi and Lu Shengnan; the offense of the former was an annotated commentary on *The Great Learning* that slandered Cheng and Zhu, and the offense of the latter was to have written a "Discussion of the *Comprehensive Mirror* [of Sima Guang]" (*Tongjian lun*) that upheld separate enfeoffments and opposed centralized administration.

After the Lü Liuliang case, Yongzheng no longer respected Zhu Xi, and turned to engraving Buddhist scriptures and personally selecting quotations of the Buddha. He called himself the Retired Scholar of Perfect Enlightenment (*yuanming jushi*), and maintaining that there was no conflict with the respect due to a Son of Heaven, he opened a hall and taught students, and the learning of Cheng and Zhu gradually lost its former strength.[53] This formed a striking contrast with Kangxi's rejection of Buddhism and esteem for Confucianism.[54] If one consults Lei Mengchen's *Collected Studies of*

Qing-Dynasty Banned Books by Province (*Qingdai gesheng jinshu huikao*), books banned by request in each province during the Qianlong years still included many works of *lixue* that were connected with Lü Liuliang and Dai Mingshi. Examples include *Dai Tianyou's Writings on the Four Books* (*Dai Tianyou sishu wen*, written by Dai Mingshi), *Writings on the Four Books from the Covering Heaven Studio* (*Tiangailou sishu wen*, selected by Lü Liuliang), *Collected Lectures on the Four Books by Gao Panlong* (*Sishu jiangyi Panlong ji*, collected by Chen Meifa, with many references to Lü Liuliang's elucidations), and *Explanatory Notes on the Four Books* (*Sishu yizhu*, compiled by Wang Tan, with many references to Lü Liuliang's critical notes). From this we can imagine the situation of Zhu Xi learning among scholars of the Yongzheng-Qianlong era.

Against this background, how to evaluate the *kaozheng* scholars' rejection of Song learning is a question that needs to be reconsidered. In the absence of the Yongzheng-Qianlong-era attacks on factions and the change in the court's attitude toward Zhu Xi learning following the Lü Liuliang case, it would be hard for us to imagine that the classical scholars holding positions as Four Treasuries Project commissioners would have dared to openly repudiate the Song. From the standpoint of the Confucian concept of sincere belief in the unity of governance and the Way and in the unity of principle and ritual, there was originally no difference between classical scholars and Qing-era Zhu Xi scholars. But grand visions of classical and historical scholarship happened to arise during the same period as the court's subtle change of attitude toward *lixue*, and when exegesis and textual criticism became universally approved forms of knowledge and rejection of Song learning also became the trend of the times, we cannot say that these two developments were unrelated. In this sense, rather than saying that the rise of classical learning was a result of the literary inquisition, it would be better to say that the tendency of classical learning to oppose *lixue* was influenced by Zhu Xi learning's loss of favor, and because of this, whether or not it opposed *lixue* cannot be the standard for judging the critical nature of Qing Confucianism.[55] In this atmosphere, classical learning's premise of unifying governance and the Way and of unifying principle and ritual had not changed, but what had changed was the political consciousness of standing in opposition to alien rule that had been established earlier by men like Huang Zongxi, Gu Yanwu, and Lü Liuliang within these basic premises of classical learning. Critiques of Song Confucianism were mainly focused on methods of pursuing learning, and were definitely not directed at such universally recognized concepts and presuppositions of Qing Confucianism (including Zhu Xi learning) as the unity of governance and the Way, the unity of principle and ritual, and the unity of ritual and ceremonial implements. Evidential learning took the inner ideals of the unity of governance and the Way and of principle and ritual and established them as a method of learning, and Qing-dynasty Zhu Xi learning took these as proof of the reasonableness of what the emperor provided. From the standpoint of this "unity," both equally rejected the Cheng-Zhu dualisms of *li* and *qi,* of governance and the Way, and of principle and ritual, and through arguments about the connections between ritual and principle, governance and the Way, and the Way and its vessels, they rejected Lu-Wang explanations of principle as grounded in the heart and accordingly developed and overcame the tension within the Song learning tradition between inner and outer, *li* and *qi,* and the Way and its vessels. In these two respects, the difference between evidential learning and Qing-dynasty Zhu Xi learning was limited. Song Confucianism used Heavenly Principle to stand in opposition to the actual order of things, and thereby manifested a world in which ritual and music and institutions, status identity and moral condition were separated from each other; for them, the opposition between Heavenly Principle and the actual world was precisely the source of criticism. Gu Yanwu and Huang Zongxi relied on the unification of principle and ritual and of governance and the Way to negate dualisms of *li* and *qi* and of principle and desire, and on new theories of institutions and of ritual and music to reestablish early Confucian customs and institutions, to criticize the empty fabrications of the Ming Confucians, and while opposing Qing dynastic rule to provide at the same time intellectual resources and practical guidance for political and moral practice. When Dai Zhen and other Qianlong-Jiaqing scholars reaffirmed these propositions, they could not, like the Song Confucians, rely on Heavenly Principle to challenge institutions, nor did they, like Gu Yanwu or Huang Zongxi, find themselves opposed to current institutions in their entirety. So how much critical significance did these propositions actually have? What was the principal motivation and purpose of Dai Zhen's critique of the Song? This is the key to examining whether the trend of criticizing the Song and opposing Zhu Xi actually held the critical significance that Hu Shi had sought.

II. Classical Learning, *Lixue,* and Anti-*Lixue*

In 1757 Dai Zhen traveled south to Yangzhou and met with Hui Dong, and because of this his learning changed dramatically.[56] His "Colophon to a Drawing of Master Hui Dingyu Teaching the Classics" (*Hui Dingyu xiansheng shoujing tu*), written in 1765, and the preface he wrote four years later for Hui Dong's disciple Yu Xiaoke's *Research Notes for Explaining the Ancient Classics* (*Gu jingjie gouchen*), have always been seen as Dai Zhen's declaration of his repudiation of Song learning. The first said: "If [in pursuit of] so-called reason and rightness one could set aside the classics and rely only what is deep in one's heart, so that anyone could reach it by empty speculation, what then would be the use of what we call classical learning? The reason and rightness of the sages and worthies is nothing else than what is lodged in regulations and institutions."[57] The latter said: "What the classics reach is the Way, that by which the Way is illuminated is their words, and what completes the words can never be other than the philology of written characters (*xiaoxue wenzi*). From the written characters one may understand the spoken language, and from the spoken language one may understand the intent and aspirations of the ancient sages and worthies, as when in approaching a temple one must follow the entrance stairs and not skip steps."[58] This has the flavor of blotting out the Song Confucian study of moral philosophy at one stroke.

Dai Zhen's *Threadwords* and *Critical Exegesis of the Meanings of Words in Mencius* censure the Song Confucian concept of "Principle" (*li*) but in their theoretical shape they resemble his earlier *On Goodness* in striving to break through evidential classical studies and return again to *lixue*'s more abstract categories of the Way and its vessels, *li* and *qi,* principle and desire, Mind and Nature, spontaneity and necessity.[59] In this respect, Dai Zhen went farther than Hui Dong. The latter's *Transmission of the Book of Changes* and other works followed the school methods of New Text classicism to expound on the patterns of the *Book of Changes,* but he never put aside evidential methods to speak directly of the Way. Dai Zhen's *Critical Exegesis of the Meanings of Terms in Mencius* tries to use the form of "critical exegesis" to cover people's eyes and ears, but its form as a work on moral philosophy is already clearly revealed. If we compare *On Goodness* with its revised versions, such as *Reading Mencius on the Nature* (*Du Mengzi lun xing*) and *Critical Exegesis of the Meanings of Words in Mencius,* the connection of textual criticism with moral philosophy becomes completely clear. In a brief preface to his revised *On Goodness,* Dai Zhen frankly states:

> I first wrote *On Goodness* in three chapters. Later, apprehensive that scholars would be blinded by different tendencies, I adduced passages from the classics to explain and verify them. Taking each of the three chapters separately as a beginning, I then completed a first, second, and third *juan,* comparing and combining meanings according to category, so that all the complexities would be clearly set forth. The Way of Heaven and of man and the fundamental teachings of the classics are all complete in them. But since the present is already far removed from the ancient sages, and those who study the classics are unable to penetrate and synthesize them, habituated to what they see and hear and mistaking accumulated error for truth, I fear that my words may not be sufficient to arrest this decline. I have stored [this work] away in my family library, awaiting someone who may be able to develop it.[60]

Here he clearly says that the revised version was made from worry about the prejudices of scholars, and so he "adduced passages from the classics to explain and verify them." What then was behind these passages from the classics? If we look at the opening paragraph of the original version of *On Goodness,* the topics and their mode of presentation and the old Song Confucian way of speaking of Heaven (*tian*), pattern (*li*), and the nature (*xing*) are in perfect accord:

> "Goodness" (*shan*) consists in humaneness (*ren*), in propriety (*li*), and in rightness (*yi*). These three are the great root of All-under-Heaven. What manifests it as the clarity of Heaven is called the "decree" (*ming*). What substantiates it as the concordance of transformative process is called "the Way" (*dao*). What accords with it and is constant in its differentiations is called "pattern" (*li*). "Decree" refers to the clarity and reliability of Heaven and Earth's centrality. "The Way" refers to the unceasingness of the transformations. "Pattern" refers to the completeness of the details. "Goodness" refers to what is without confusion or blending.

> "The nature" refers to what is rooted in heaven and expressed as concerns and capabilities.[61]

The main theme of Dai Zhen's critique of Song is to substitute the methods of classical philology for the Song Confucian study of moral philosophy. But his sharpest critiques of Song learning come precisely from discussions in *On Goodness,* in *Threadwords,* and in his *Critical Exegesis* of the distinction between principle and desire (*li yu zhi bian*) and of the distinction between the spontaneous and what must be so (*ziran / biran zhi bian*). But are these works really in such sharp contradiction and conflict with his works of textual research?

Duan Yucai believed that Dai Zhen's critiques of Song learning accounts of terms like principle or pattern (*li*) and the nature (*xing*) were completely in accord with the standpoint of his classical scholarship. He said:

> As soon as the master had completed his *On Goodness* in three essays and his *Discussing the Nature* in two essays, he realized that the formulations of the Song Confucians on the nature (*xing*), on Principle (*li*), on the Way (*dao*), on capacity (*cai*), on genuineness (*cheng*), on understanding (*ming*), on assessment (*quan*), on humanity, righteousness, propriety, and wisdom (*ren, yi, li, zhi*), and on wisdom, righteousness, and courage (*zhi, ren, yong*), were not the formulations of Confucius, Mencius, and the Six Classics, and that [the Song Confucians] had blended [the Classical formulations] with the formulations of heretical learning. He therefore sought to show others, from a close study of the meanings of these words in *Mencius,* what was wrong with the [Song Confucian] maxim that "when human desires are completely stilled, the principle of Heaven flows forth" (*renyu jinjing jin, tianli liuxing*). What is known as "principle" must be sought in the ease that comes when human feelings are without regret, and one must not say that the nature is principle.[62]

What was Dai Zhen's own view of this? In the *Critical Exegesis,* Dai Zhen not only criticizes the theories of the Laozi and the Buddha, but also condemns Cheng and Zhu's understanding of learning that was based on a duality of *li* (principle) and *qi,* resulting in their being "detailed in discussing reverence but sketchy in discussing learning."[63] Thus, his method is definitely not to recapitulate the study of moral philosophy, but to use the methods of a textual critic to return each school to its proper place:

> From my seventeenth year I had my heart set on hearing the Way, and said that if I did not seek it in the Six Classics, Confucius, and Mencius I would not find it, and that if I did not devote myself to the meanings of characters, to instituted systems, and to names and things, I would have no way to understand their discourse. . . . After thirty years it is clear to me that the source of order and confusion in antiquity and in modern times is here. When the ancients spoke of "explaining patterns" (*lijie*) it was a matter of seeking out and analyzing internal textures, and when they spoke of "natural patterns" (*tianli*) it was like Zhuangzi's "going along with the natural makeup" (*yihu tianli*), and was what was meant by "there are spaces between the joints." The ancient worthies and Sages regarded embodying the people's feelings and following the people's desires as attaining principle, while men of today regard it as principle if their own opinions do not issue from selfishness, and thus even if their opinions kill people they still believe themselves in the right. This is like putting aside the meanings of characters, instituted systems, and the referents of names, rejecting the exegesis of spoken language, and yet wishing to get the way of the Sages from the remains of lost classics.[64]

But there are still some questions here. If the principles behind Han learning and the critique of Song are completely the same, why did Dai Zhen, instead of simply following the old pathway of philological exegesis, also return to the propositions and forms of Song learning? Why did Dai Zhen, while criticizing Song learning views of the distinction of principle and desire, have to return to the framework of Song learning ontology and to their theories of Mind and Nature? Dai Zhen's specific criticisms of Song learning's moral philosophy did not differ from the premises of Han learning, but they were expressed in an anti-Han learning form. This fact deserves our consideration.

We may wish to take Zhang Xuecheng's criticisms of Dai Zhen as a starting point for our analysis. In writings such as his "Postscript to the Essay on Zhu and Lu," his "Letter in Reply to Shao Eryun," and "Another Letter to Zhu Shaobo," Zhang held that "in his studies Mr. Dai has a deep understanding of philology, carefully investigates institutions and the referents of names, and gets to the reasons for them in order to illuminate the Way. . . . In his works such as *Discussing the Nature* and *On Goodness* he expounds aspects of Heaven and man and *li* and *qi* that have not previously been expounded."[65] This implies that Dai Zhen's learning carries on from Gu Yanwu and Yan Ruoqu, and originates in the school methods of Zhu Xi. Zhang Xuecheng greatly admired Dai Zhen's discussions of Heaven and man and of *li* and *qi*, but was very dissatisfied with the way he blended in his personal position with the current scholarly trend, speaking ambiguously with words that did not match his heart and lacking the courage of personal practice and sincere respect, to the point where in a climate in which "if one did not belittle Zhu Xi one could not be an accomplished scholar," he only feared that his critiques of the Song Confucians might not be strong enough.[66] The great majority of later Dai Zhen scholars have inherited Zhang Xuecheng's approach of combining academic scholarship with psychological analysis (positing impure intentions), but in putting more emphasis on the formal difference between his moral philosophy (*yili*) and his textual research (*kaozheng*), very few have addressed and traced the origins of the intellectual conflicts that underlay this formal difference.[67] Can a conflict between moral philosophy and textual research explain the characteristics of Dai Zhen's thought and his relationship with Zhang Xuecheng?

Before answering this question, I would like to point out a basic fact: the category of "moral philosophy" or "expositions on meanings and principles" (*yili zhi xue*) is more wide ranging than the "study of Principle" (*lixue*), but in combination with Zhang Xuecheng's judgment that Dai Zhen's contribution was not in exegetical studies and textual research but in the fact that he had "expounded aspects of Heaven and man and *li* and *qi* that had not previously been expounded," one can see that what drew the blame of Han learning scholars was his closeness to *lixue*.[68] However, from the viewpoint of scholarly methodology, Zhang's theory was not close to Song-Ming *lixue;* rather, it accepted the fundamental presuppositions of classical scholarship (such as embodying ritual in its implements, unifying governance and the Way, and unifying principle with ritual). His defense of Dai Zhen before the classical scholars was certainly not for the sake of explaining Dai's insights into "Heaven and man and *li* and *qi*." Shimada Kenji's explanation of Zhang's view in "The Theory that 'The Six Classics Are All History'" as "a philosophy that transcends textual criticism, and yet at the same time also is the philosophy of textual criticism" roughly indicates the characteristics of Zhang Xuecheng's scholarly thought.[69] Zhu Yun and Qian Daxin's criticism of Dai Zhen came from a tension within classical scholarship, since Dai Zhen was after all a pillar of evidential scholarship, and yet his works such as *On Goodness* and the *Critical Exegesis* were seen as the outer garments of a classical scholarship that proceeded from an understanding of written characters and words to an understanding of the Way. In other words, it was not Dai Zhen's opposition to *lixue,* but rather his formal return to *lixue,* that made the textual scholars feel uneasy. If they were really indifferent to books like Dai Zhen's *Critical Exegesis,* then why would Zhang Xuecheng and Hong Bang have needed to mount such a vigorous defense of them? And if Dai Zhen had really returned to the set patterns of Song learning, and if Zhang Xuecheng had wholeheartedly believed that the study of moral philosophy was the purpose of scholarship, then why would he have needed to defend him before classical scholars? The fundamental reason for defending him was to dispel misunderstandings, and was the meaning of dispelling misunderstanding not just to say that the two sides were actually not so different, or that both sides still shared some common premises? In Zhang Xuecheng's view, Dai Zhen had not completely returned to Song learning. It was rather that under the form of classical scholarship he was restoring Confucian scholarship's overall purpose of hearing the Way, and it was only for this reason that it was necessary to defend him. If it were not for this aspect, we would have no way of understanding why he would have defended Dai Zhen in front of Zhu Yun.[70]

Zhang Xuecheng emphasized "seeking the Way" and understanding change; he opposed blind adherence to the Six Classics, and his fundamental theory was that the "the Six Classics are all history." This theory was established on the premise that the Way and its vessels formed one body and that principle and ritual were unified, and in this respect, there was no fundamental difference between his viewpoint and that of the classical scholars. For most classical scholars, the question of "moral philosophy" (*yili*) was a methodological issue, but for Zhang Xuecheng and Dai Zhen it was a question of the fundamental orientation of Confucian learning. Zhang's interest in Dai Zhen's learning had a basic premise, which was that Dai Zhen's taste for *lixue* was a taste for *lixue* that was internal to classical learning, and that at its core his classicist thought had been influenced by the learning of moral philosophy. Therefore, Dai Zhen's entanglement with *lixue* had taken shape within the forms of classical learning, and these elements of *lixue* indicated that to a certain extent he hoped to break through the barriers of classical learning. Zhang Xuecheng's analysis of Dai Zhen makes use of the distinction between moral philosophy and textual research, but if we take a comprehensive view of his scholarly claims, we can discover that Zhang Xuecheng himself regards this distinction as the origin of the degradation of classical learning. He sought within the forms of classical and historical learning to restore discussions about *li* and *qi,* Mind and Nature, and problems of moral practice, in order to redress the triviality and fragmentation that classical studies had fallen into as a result of its insistence on a distinction between moral philosophy and textual research, but this did not mean that he identified with the forms of *lixue.* In this sense, Zhang Xuecheng's criticism of Dai Zhen was something that unfolded in a complex academic context between historical patterns and his own personal academic views, and if one relies on the opposition between moral philosophy and textual research to describe the difference between Dai and Zhang there is the possibility of falling into a formalism of strict distinctions between Han and Song. What we must continue to ask are: How did the entanglements of Dai Zhen's scholarship and thought actually come about? How should we explain his inner conflicts and the characteristics of his thought?

The multiple orientations of Dai Zhen's thought were formed in a complex intellectual atmosphere, and the object of his criticism was not just Song learning but also Buddhism and Daoism, especially Buddhism. Because of the special relationship between the Qing emperor and Buddhism (especially Tibetan Buddhism), the intellectual situation in which Dai Zhen found himself had some similarities with that of the Song Confucians; that is, he was situated in the midst of a subtle confrontation between Confucianism and Buddhism. The differences were, first, that the development of Qing-dynasty classical learning had fundamentally disintegrated the premises of *lixue,* and would not allow Dai Zhen, either under the premise of *li* / *qi* dualism or from within the categories of cosmology, to expound anew the concept of Heavenly Principle; and second, that in the pluralistic empire of the Qing, the supreme status of Confucian learning was premised on its inclusiveness, and it would have been difficult for an attempt like that of the Song Confucians to establish Confucian learning as orthodox by critiquing Buddhism to gain recognition. In this sense, Dai Zhen's intellectual situation was more complicated than that of the Song Confucians: the Buddhism and Daoism that he wanted to criticize was not just simple Buddhism and Daoism, but a Buddhism and Daoism that had permeated into the midst of *lixue;* and the tradition of Confucian learning that he seized upon to criticize was not the simple Han learning tradition, but a tradition of Confucian learning that maintained a critical stance toward Han learning. In the first *juan* of the *Critical Exegesis of the Meanings of Words in Mencius* there is a passage that says: "The interest of Master Cheng and Master Zhu in Daoism and Buddhism was all for the sake of seeking the Way. If they had come to see their way as true, they would have been unconcerned even if others regarded it as false. Their initial [intent] was not to turn against the Six Classics, Confucius, and Mencius and put their trust in [Daoism and Buddhism]." This was to point out and explain the relationship of *lixue* to Buddhism and Daoism; but in the same passage Dai also went on to say: "Master Cheng and Master Zhu saw that the explanations of order and rightness in the Six Classics, Confucius, and Mencius refer them to what is necessary and cannot change, and that this is something that Lao, Zhuang, and the Buddhists are unable to reach,"[71] to show that in the relation of Buddhism and Daoism to Cheng and Zhu there still were differences. Why is this so? On the one hand, what Dai Zhen was criticizing in the moral philosophy of Song learning was not the theories of Confucius and Mencius but the result of "doctrines of different learning that had been mixed in with them" (as Duan Yucai had suggested); and on the other hand, in his unmasking of Buddhism and Daoism he could not but rely on certain central themes of Song learning. His critique of Song was just a critique of different learning that presented itself under the form of Confucian learning, in order to restore the actual intent of Confucius, Mencius, and the Six Classics. What, then, did "doctrines of different learning" actually refer to? And what scholarly trend did these "doctrines of different learning" represent?

The Lü Liuliang case mentioned above is closely related to this. After the Lü case, Zhu Xi learning was thwarted, and classical studies greatly prospered; the trend of the times was for scholars to become trapped in trivial research, and for the study of moral philosophy, Mind, and principle among the elite to become gradually cold and insipid. Lü Liuliang distinguished strictly between Chinese and barbarian, and his critical studies of names and referents, institutions, and early Confucian moral philosophy were linked in tone to Huang Zongxi and Gu Yanwu, always seeking to express orthodox concepts through the pursuit of Confucian learning. But the cruel reality of the literary inquisition deeply inhibited these acolytes of *lixue,* and since they were unable to reaffirm the learning of the Cheng brothers, Zhu Xi, Lu Xiangshan, and Wang Yangming, and also had no taste for philological interpretation and textual criticism, in their feelings about the ways of the world they could not avoid becoming involved in inclinations to withdraw from the world. Men like Peng Shaosheng (1740–1796), Xue Qifeng (1734–1774), Wang Jin (1725–1792), and Luo Yougao (1733–1778) turned to Buddhist moral philosophy to interpret the purport of Confucius, Mencius, Cheng, Zhu, Lu, and Wang, and made evidential learning the target of their attacks. For example, Peng Shaosheng said:

> The shortcoming of current scholarly pursuits is that they are full of superficial verbiage, and do not know how to return to essentials. The vulgar are addicted to formalistic examination prose, elegant but without substance; their crude knowledge is engaged with the Six Classics, but they seldom seek solid attainment within themselves, and only seek approval from others and to be better than others. They compete to produce extraordinary literary works and engage in narrow partisanship, keep writing into old age, compose housefuls of books, yet all too often the pursuit of petty pleasures thwarts high aims, it is a great pity.[72]

They connected the moral philosophy of every school, and extinguished the difference between Confucianism and Buddhism; and, under cover of inherited customs, many famous Han learning scholars returned to Buddhism seeking comfort for their souls. Hui Dong's studies of the *Book of Changes* implicitly encompassed prognostication texts and Daoist religion, and he wrote an annotated commentary on the *Treatise of the Illustrious Sage on Response and Retribution* (*Taishang ganying pian*); Cheng Tingzuo (1691–1767), an informal student of Yan-Li learning, held that while in ancient times it was external teachings that harmed the Way, nowadays harm to the Way came from within Confucianism. Yet although he deeply criticized *lixue,* he also urged Yuan Mei to read the *Scripture of the Heroic Progress* (*Śūraṅgama*

Sūtra, Ch: *Lengyan jing*). Xiang Jinmen summed it up in a single sentence: "Among today's scholar officials there are none who do not esteem Buddhism,"[73] to point out the scholarly mood of that time. Thus, what were called "doctrines of a different learning" referred to Buddhism and Daoism, but they were a Buddhism and Daoism that had been mixed into the midst of Confucian moral philosophy. Peng Shaosheng and others used this to oppose evidential learning. He praised Dai Zhen for being different from the fragmented critical studies of contemporary vulgar Confucians and was inclined to cite him as having similar intentions with regard to the Way. Dai Zhen sympathized with Peng Shaosheng's critique of evidential learning as "losing its high aim in petty pursuits," but he definitely did not identify with Peng's Buddhist standpoint. Dai Zhen's *lixue* tendency was a *lixue* tendency within classical learning, in that it was a tendency of moral philosophy that was grounded in the unification of principle with ritual and in the organic unity of the Way and its vessels. He himself said that the purpose of his writings such as the *Critical Exegesis* was to distinguish the correct from the deviant, and that the target of his critiques was the common tendency of Peng and others to substitute the aims of Buddhism and Daoism for the aims of the early Confucians; he strove to link textual criticism with moral philosophy, and to explain how principle and ritual were unified and how the organic unity of the Way and its vessels was unchangeable. As to this "interpretive regime" within Confucian learning, not only did he point out the harm of it in many places in the *Threadwords* and in the *Critical Exegesis,* but Hong Bang and Duan Yucai touched on it as well.

In his *Chronological Biography of Master Dai,* Hong Bang said: "In his scholarship the master from his earliest years pursued comprehensive and penetrating investigations of antiquity, was broadly learned and strong in insight, and was especially good at analytical discussion. Late in life he delved increasingly into the transmitted teachings on the nature and the Way of Heaven (*xing yu tiandao*), and where the theories of Laozi, Zhuangzi, and the Buddhists enter most deeply into men's hearts he criticized and refuted them, so that they should by no means be mixed in with the Six Classics and the writings of Confucius and Mencius."[74] He not only believed that the whole purpose for the writing of *On Goodness* was to criticize Buddhism and Daoism, but pointed out that late in life Dai Zhen "delved increasingly into the transmitted teachings on the nature and the Way of Heaven," implying that the purpose of his later works was to clarify the difference between the Six Classics, Confucius, and Mencius, and Laozi and the Buddha, by recapitulating transmitted teachings on the nature and the Way of Heaven. In his "Letter to Zhu Yun," Hong Bang further discussed Dai Zhen's "Reply to Presented Scholar Peng Shaosheng," *On Goodness*, the *Critical Exegesis*, and other writings, and his exposition was detailed and to the point:

> Mr. Dai's letter to Presented Scholar Peng was not just to raise difficulties for Cheng and Zhu and to correct Lu and Wang, nor was it just to correct Lu and Wang and to criticize the false theories of Lao and the Buddha; rather than criticizing Lao and the Buddha, he was criticizing later scholars who, referring to books that are actually Daoist and Buddhist but present themselves as Confucian, draw the words of the Duke of Zhou and Confucius into the teachings of Lao and the Buddha, using their similarity to Lao and the Buddha to throw the truth of the Duke of Zhou and Confucius into disarray, and yet always adhere to the learning of Cheng and Zhu.[75]

Dai's critiques of Song and of Laozi and the Buddha were not really critiques of Song and of Laozi and the Buddha; they were critiques of bringing Laozi and the Buddha into Confucian books, and his theoretical boldness was of course not limited to refutations of men like Peng Shaosheng, but was directed against a larger intellectual and scholarly climate. In books like the *Critical Exegesis*, with regard to every kind of misunderstanding since the Song, Dai Zhen sought to clarify that:

> Masters Cheng and Zhu took what Laozi, Zhuangzi, and the Buddhists meant and transferred their theories to speak of Principle. It is not that they invoked the Confucian tradition to enter into Buddhism; it is just that they were misled by Buddhist doctrine and mixed it in with the Confucian tradition. But men like Lu Xiangshan and Wang Yangming took what the Buddhists meant and merely used Principle (*li*) to substantiate it, and in this they did invoke the Confucian tradition to enter into Buddhism.[76]

Hong Bang took Han Yu as an exemplar for Dai's critique of Song, because the purpose of the latter's scholarship, like that of Han Yu's "On the Way and its

Origins" (*Yuan Dao*), was to "make scholars clearly understand the falseness of Laozi and the Buddha." When we consider that after the case of Lü Liuliang, Zhu Xi learning was thwarted, Buddhism was gradually rising, and Confucianism and Buddhism were becoming interlocked to the point where even the Emperor Shizong himself regarded himself as a lay Buddhist, we can see that the purport of Dai Zhen's critique of Lao and the Buddha had a much deeper meaning than its surface appearance as a critique of Song learning.

In the first month of 1777, a few months before his death, Dai Zhen wrote a letter to Duan Yucai that said: "The single most important work in my lifetime of writings is the *Critical Exegesis of the Meanings of Words in Mencius,* for it contains the essentials for rectifying men's hearts. Men of today, no matter whether it concerns righteousness or evil, all wrongly identify their opinions as principle, and so bring disaster on the people. Therefore, my *Critical Exegesis* had to be written."[77] For Dai Zhen, "No matter whether it concerns righteousness or evil," the common characteristic is one of "wrongly identifying one's opinions as principle." If we interpret this statement in the light of Hong Bang's explanation of the general purport of *On Goodness,* then "wrongly identifying one's opinions as principle" refers not only to the doctrines of the *lixue* scholars but also to the treatment of "selfishness" (*si*) and "delusion" (*bi*) by Buddhists and Daoists.[78] If we look again at the "Reply to Presented Scholar Peng Shaosheng" that Dai Zhen wrote in the fourth month of the same year, it will also confirm this. Peng Shaosheng loved Buddhist learning. He held that Confucius, Mencius, Cheng, and Zhu provided critical explanations of Buddhist doctrines, and believed that Confucius and Mencius were not different from Buddhism and Daoism and that between Cheng and Zhu, Lu and Wang, and the Buddhists there was no essential difference.[79] And at the time there were others, such as Luo Yougao (1733–1778) and Wang Jin (1725–1792), who agreed with him.[80] In his "Reply to Shen Lifang" (*Da Shen Lifang*), Peng Shaosheng said: "The Way is one, that is all. Among Confucians it is Confucian, among Buddhists it is Buddhist, among Daoists it is Daoist, but although there are three teachings there cannot be three different Ways. Scholars enter into it through teachings, but nothing is prior to knowing the root. If one truly knows the root, then whether one approaches from the left or from the right there is nothing that will not be attained."[81] In another letter, he wrote: "The classics say: there is only this one reality, and other alternatives cannot be true. Between Buddhists and Confucians no differences can arise. Let us not discuss shortcomings or strengths, these are all foolish talk. What a man of character values is just knowing the root. If one truly attains the root, then the model for any disparities will all flow from this. How then can one bear to follow the twigs and gather leaves, and to dwell beneath the hedgerows of others?"[82]

In the midst of this current, Dai Zhen specially sent his *On Goodness* and *Critical Exegesis of the Meanings of Words in Mencius* to Peng Shaosheng, with the intent of distinguishing between Confucianism and Buddhism. After Peng Shaosheng had received and read these two works, and clearly had fully understood Dai Zhen's intention, he responded with a letter that began with polite formalities, and then continued: "I am muddled in scholarship, and with regard to paths of approach there are bound to be differences; but [when it comes to] principles which are common to all, [even] if I recklessly wished to engage in dispute, how would I be able to do it? Nevertheless, there are one or two major points on which I feel uneasy, and which I must ask you to explain more fully."[83] As to these "major points," one was the question of Heaven's decree, and the other was the question of emptiness and stillness. On the first, he criticized Dai Zhen for his viewpoint of externalizing Heaven in his account of the pattern of humanity and of explaining the decree (*ming*) as "division" (*fen*), and on the second, he forcefully affirmed the theory of no desires (*wu yu*). In the final analysis, what Peng could not agree with was Dai Zhen's critique of Cheng and Zhu and of Buddhism and Daoism. After receiving Peng Shaosheng's letter, Dai Zhen laid out the argument of *On Goodness* and the *Critical Exegesis* for Peng Shaosheng, and the gist of his reply was:

> To restore the purport of the Six Classics, Confucius, and Mencius to the Six Classics, Confucius, and Mencius; to restore the purport of Cheng and Zhu to Cheng and Zhu; and to restore the purport of Lu, Wang, and the Buddhists to Lu, Wang, and the Buddhists, so that Lu and Wang will no longer be able to falsely claim the legacy of Cheng and Zhu, and so that Buddhists will no longer be able to falsely claim the legacy of Confucius and Mencius.[84]

If this letter is read critically against *On Goodness* and the *Critical Exegesis*, Dai Zhen's purpose in criticizing the Buddhists becomes very clear. If his recapitulation of Song moral philosophy is very similar to Song learning's critique of Buddhism and Daoism, it is because in order to smash the ontology and theory of Mind and Nature of Buddhism and Daoism, he had to reconstruct the ontology and theory of Mind and Nature of Confucian learning.

Dai Zhen's strict adherence to the theoretical premises of textual research in his *Threadwords* and *Critical Exegesis* was for the sake of rejecting and devaluing Song learning, and his moral philosophy arose from his critique of Buddhism and Daoism, and of the Buddhism and Daoism that were mixed in with Song learning. From Peng Shaosheng's use of the Concealed Buddha-nature (*Rulaizang*) teachings of the *Scripture of the Heroic Progress* (*Śūraṅgama Sūtra*) to interpret the *Doctrine of the Mean's* so-called "great and small words" *(yu da yu xiao)*,[85] and from Luo Yougao's use of the *Book of Changes* to discuss *samsara*[86] and of the *Scripture of the Heroic Progress* to discuss "seeking the lost heart" (*qiu fang xin*) in the *Mencius*,[87] and so on, it is not difficult for us to understand why in his writings Dai Zhen wished to start from concepts like *li* (principle or pattern), *tiandao* (the Way of Heaven), *cai* (capacities), *dao* (the Way), *ren yi li zhi* (humaneness, righteousness, propriety, wisdom), and *quan* (assessment), and why he wanted to combine evidence-based explanations of the meanings of words with moral-philosophical interpretations. What he called returning Mencius to Mencius, Cheng and Zhu and Lu and Wang to Cheng and Zhu and Lu and Wang, and the Buddha to the Buddha required, from a methodological perspective, that he combine evidential and moral-philosophical modes of inquiry, and that he seek out the "original intent" of Confucian learning. If Dai Zhen had based his inquiries only on philology and textual criticism, he would have had no way to oppose the mysterious principles of Buddhism and Daoism; if he had only used moral philosophy to oppose them, then he would have been mixed together with Cheng and Zhu and Lu and Wang, and would have had no way to correct the root or clarify the source. The problems that Dai Zhen had to face were clearly more complicated than those of the Song Confucians: since Buddhism and Daoism were deeply hidden in the midst of *lixue*, then in criticizing Buddhism and Daoism he must also criticize *lixue*, and draw a sharp distinction between the Six Classics, Confucius, and Mencius and their Cheng-Zhu and Lu-Wang interpreters. This was also the basis for his classicist form of *lixue* that pursued "critical exegeses of words."

From the above discussion, we can appreciate the complexity of Dai Zhen's scholarly and intellectual situation: he was almost simultaneously at war with

Song learning, with classical learning, and with Buddhism and Daoism. In a nutshell, he used philology and evidential studies to criticize the Song, the cosmology of nature and principle and the Way of Heaven to criticize Buddhism and Daoism, and moral philosophy (*yili*) to oppose the classical learning of vulgar Confucian scholars. On each side there were aspects that he criticized, and also aspects that he affirmed and carried on. It is no wonder that people like Zhu Yun and Qian Daxin took exception to *On Goodness* and the *Critical Exegesis,* holding that they "need not be included [in Dai's corpus]; the nature and the Way of Heaven are matters one cannot hear of, why do we need additional theories beyond what Cheng and Zhu have already said? Dai's legacy is not in this." Nor is it surprising that Hong Bang then said, "Dai's discussion of the nature and the Way is nowhere more complete than in his book on Mencius, but the reason that he called this book a *Critical Exegesis of the Meanings of Words in Mencius* was to show that his purpose was not to discuss the nature and the decree, but just textual exegesis!"[88] In this complicated situation, Dai Zhen had to develop a set of forms of scholarship that would allow him to accept or reject aspects of every side. For example, when he used philology and textual research to criticize the Song, he had to rely on words and meanings, names and referents, and institutions; when he used the nature, principle, and the Way of Heaven to criticize the Two Gentlemen (Laozi and Shakyamuni), he had to elaborate on early Confucian theories of order and rightness and of the heart and the nature; and when he used moral philosophy to oppose the fragmented textual research of vulgar Confucians, he had to discuss topics of Song learning that lay outside the scope of textual research. To begin with Mencius, to rely on critical exegeses of the meanings of words as a form of expression, and in moral philosophy to combine Confucius and Mencius with Xunzi, this in my view is the fundamental characteristic of the *Critical Exegesis of the Meanings of Words in Mencius.* Apart from this multifaceted aspect of Dai Zhen's scholarship and thought, his views on the distinction of principle and desire and on the topic of spontaneity and necessity cannot be understood.

The theoretical form of Dai Zhen's scholarship is inclined toward a *lixue* form of argumentation, but the fundamental theory is based on Han learning premises, and does not deviate from the Classicist standpoint of opposition to a dualism of *li* and *qi,* or of the Way and its vessels. In the first *juan* of the *Threadwords,* which begins with the question, "What is the meaning of the word '*Dao*'?," he proceeds from a discussion of the Way and its vessels, of yin and yang, of what is before and after form, and of the Great Ultimate and its two primordial principles to infer conclusions about the relative priority of *li* and *qi,* and finally reaches his distinction of the spontaneous and the necessary: "The flowing forth of yin and yang is its spontaneity, and speaking precisely, when it is without regret, this is what is called 'pattern' (*li*). 'Pattern' is nothing other than its necessity. . . . Only a sage can fulfill pattern in the human realm, and when pattern is fulfilled in the human realm, this is just what it is for the activities of daily life to fulfill their necessity."[89] "The necessary is the ultimate norm of spontaneity, and it is in adhering to the necessary that spontaneity can be fulfilled."[90] It cannot be said that this is an entirely new viewpoint, for in Liu Zongzhou's and Huang Zongxi's "what fills Heaven and Earth is all mind" and "what fills Heaven and Earth is all *qi*" we have already encountered similar ideas. What distinguishes Dai Zhen is that he does not speak in general terms about the problem of *qi,* but rather, starting from the "patterns" (*tiaoli*) or "grain" (*fenli*) of things, holds that only by complying with the "spontaneity" (*ziran*) of things (which is to say their spontaneous patterning or fine structure) can one grasp their "pattern" or "coherence" (*li*). This provides a foundation for the taxonomy of a new kind of knowledge, and also provides us with an epistemological and cosmological basis for understanding the accomplishments of Dai Zhen's scholarship in the study of nature: "With regard to all matters in the domains of Heaven and Earth, humans and creatures and affairs and actions, it is only when their unchanging norms (*buyi zhi ze*) become clear that one can speak of pattern. These so-called norms are not something that I create, they must be sought in the things themselves." In interpreting lines from the *Odes* like "Heaven produced this teeming people, / And for each thing there is a norm," he extended the notion of "pattern" (*li*) from ordinary things to human affairs, as in "there is never a day when the world's people do not adhere to them as regular practices."[91] In this sense topics like negating private opinions and taking account of the intrinsic patterns of things have a close connection with experiencing and observing the people's feelings and emphasizing daily practice.

The spontaneity (*ziran*) / necessity (*biran*) distinction regards "ritual" and "pattern" not as something affected by personal opinions, but as something internal to an objective realm of human feeling and physical structure. This was a unique combination of Xunzi's theory of ritual norms and Zhuangzi's account of spontaneity. Speaking from the side of spontaneity, humaneness, rightness, ritual propriety, and wisdom all equally arise from the "spontaneity of the nature (*xing zhi ziran*)," and because of this the propriety and rightness that are known from learning cannot be separated from spontaneous patterning; and this is a critique of Laozi and Shakyamuni, who do discuss spontaneity apart from the realities of this life. And speaking from the side of necessity, Dai writes:

> Rites are the order of Heaven and Earth, and in speaking of the ultimate reach of order, if one does not know Heaven one will not be able to exhaust it. Ceremonial forms and degrees of rank are also something that the sages, in accordance with the order of Heaven and Earth, have fixed as models for All-under-Heaven over ten thousand generations. When rites are instituted as a means of regulating the sentiments of All-under-Heaven, curbing them where excessive or urging them where deficient, it is just so that the centrality of Heaven and Earth may be known.[92]

Ritual is order, and it is through "learning" that humans must understand and approach it: this is the meaning of necessity. This provides the theoretical premise for the critique of Song learning's dualism of principle and desire, and also provides the epistemological foundation for knowing ritual through "learning." "According with its spontaneity" (*yin qi ziran*) is to accord with and follow the "patterns of the people" or the order of things, and "adhering to its necessity" is to say that it must be through the work of learning that one grasps spontaneity. Clearly, the purpose of Dai Zhen's distinction of spontaneity / necessity was to oppose the "Two Gentlemen's" (Laozi's and Shakyamuni's) theory of spontaneity and the Song Confucian perspective of dividing *li* from *qi;* in his view the dualism of *li* and *qi* came originally from Lao-Zhuang and Buddhist theories of spontaneity, and was no part of the original meaning of the Six Classics, Confucius, and Mencius. If *li* (principle) is what "the world's people adhere to each day as regular practices" (*tianxia zhi min wu ri bu bingchi wei jingchang zhe*), then we cannot speak of *li* from the perspective of leaving the world (the spontaneity of Buddhists and Daoists), and we must see "*li*" (principle) and "*li*" (ritual) as internal features of everyday life, and as existing among desires and feelings.[93]

If we take the relationship of spontaneity and necessity as our starting point in discussing the relationship of *li* ("principle" or "pattern") and *li* ("ritual"), and also distinguish the category of ritual from unnecessary and overelaborate formalities, it becomes a concept that is closely related to the internal structure of things. It is the "ritual" of Gu Yanwu's "culture and ritual" (*wenli*), and it is also the object of "learning."[94] In this sense, the meaning of "learning" is not to mechanically reflect and copy dogma, but to investigate broadly and model oneself on the patterns of Nature or spontaneity. Dai Zhen's esteem for "ritual" has no direct relation to the patriarchal lineage system and ethical codes that flourished in the Qing era, because his "ritual" is a kind of spontaneous ordering, an ordering that can assist and harmonize people's emotions and desires and the requirements of everyday moral conduct. He combined the viewpoints of Mencius and Xunzi, explained "ritual principles" in terms of the categories of spontaneity and necessity, and accordingly on the question of achieving moral character he returned to the unified relation between ritual principles and the intrinsic patterns of human nature. Dai Zhen said:

> Xunzi knows that propriety and righteousness are the teaching of the sages, but does not know that propriety and righteousness also proceed from the nature (*xing*); he knows that propriety and righteousness [involve] understanding what is necessary, but does not know that the necessary is the ultimate norm of spontaneity, by which one's spontaneity may be perfected. From the standpoint of Mencius's writings, it is clear that order and rightness are [aspects of] what is meant by the nature. In adducing humanity, righteousness, propriety, and wisdom to articulate the nature, he holds that they also proceed from the nature's spontaneity: all men are capable of them without learning, and learning is only to extend and fulfill them. The importance of learning for Xunzi is that what is lacking within is obtained from without; the importance of learning for Mencius is that what exists within is nourished from without.[95]

He used the mutual evidence of Xunzi and Mencius to counter Song learning's dualism of *li* and *qi* and the Two Gentlemen's dualism of form and spirit,[96] and based on this, established that *li* and *qi*, form and spirit, and ritual principles are all intrinsically related to the nature. The common characteristic of Lao-Zhuang and the Buddhists is "to rely on spontaneity, and yet not to know that ritual principles are the highest standard of spontaneity,"[97] and when Zhang Zai, Shao Yong, Cheng, Zhu, Lu, and Wang "entered their house to seize the spear," the result was that they adopted Buddhist and Daoist concepts as their own premises.[98] This is very far from the "broad learning restrained by ritual" (*Analects* 6.27) that was the guiding ideal of classical learning, and it was a complete departure from "ordered at the beginning is the concern of the wise, ordered at the end is the concern of the sage" (*Mencius* 5B1), which was the bequeathed teaching of Confucius and Mencius. Dai Zhen regarded ritual as the ultimate norm of spontaneity, and so regarded the external nature of ritual as an expression of the intrinsic character of things. However, if there is no knowledge of spontaneity, then there is no way of understanding what the order of things actually is. In this sense, ritual is also a standard of measurement. Therefore, he held that one can use ritual to examine and test good faith, but that one may not rely on good faith to examine and test ritual.[99] This is how the spontaneity / necessity distinction is embodied in the context of ritual principles.

It is not correct, then, when Qian Mu argues that "the *Threadwords* is only concerned with the distinction of *li* and *qi,* and it is the *Evidential Commentary* that first takes up the distinction of pattern and desire (*yu*)."[100] In the third *juan* of the *Threadwords* we find statements like, "Abiding by pattern is nothing other than one thing, . . . when the eating and drinking and relations between the sexes that manifest as feelings and desires divide into two, the eating and drinking and relations between the sexes that are enacted truthfully are compliant with pattern (*li*), while those that are enacted falsely contravene pattern, that is all."[101] There is a close relationship between the spontaneity / necessity distinction and the distinction between pattern and desire, since they are two aspects of a single topic: if one says that the meaning of the spontaneity / necessity distinction is in the critique of Lao-Zhuang, Buddhist, and even Song Confucian theories of spontaneity, then Dai Zhen's account of the distinction of pattern and desire is a critique of the theory of "no desire" found in Daoism, Buddhism, and *lixue.*[102] In the first *juan* of the *Evidential Commentary,* Dai Zhen says:

> The sages accorded with the desires of their blood and spirits and so made the way of mutual nourishment: thus, to regard another as like oneself

> is loyalty; to rely on one's own [feelings] and extend them is reciprocity; to be concerned about and rejoice with others is humanity; what issues from the correct and not from the deviant is righteousness; to be respectful and reverent and not insulting and negligent is propriety; to be free from the flaws of mistake and error is wisdom. What else are they? . . . Desires are the spontaneity of blood and breath, and "liking this excellent virtue" [Ode 260] is the spontaneity of conscious knowing: this is the basis on which Mencius says that the nature is good. . . . Lao, Zhuang, and the Buddhists saw that it would not do for the ordinary man to give free rein to the spontaneity of his blood and breath, and [sought by] tranquility to nourish the spontaneity of their conscious knowing; the spontaneity of conscious knowing they called the nature, and the spontaneity of blood and breath they called desire. Although their theories are plausible and ingenious, essentially they have done no more than separate blood and breath from conscious knowing as two roots. Xunzi saw that the conscious knowing of the ordinary man [could] by means of propriety and righteousness become the heart of a sage; he saw that that it would not do for the ordinary man to give free rein to the spontaneity of his blood and breath and conscious knowing, but that [he could] advance by means of the necessity of propriety and righteousness. The spontaneity of blood and breath and conscious knowing he called the nature (*xing*), and the necessity of propriety and righteousness he called instruction (*jiao*). He united blood and breath and conscious knowing as one root, but did not get to the root of propriety and righteousness.[103]

Dai Zhen believed that desires were "the spontaneity of blood and breath," and that necessity (*biran*) or reason and rightness (*liyi*) were in the midst of this spontaneity, because necessity was nothing other than the ultimate norm of spontaneity. Laozi, Zhuangzi, the Buddhists, Cheng, Zhu, Lu, and Wang all used the method of "returning to spontaneity" to get rid of desires, and so made an absolute distinction between desires and knowledge and between spontaneity and necessity. In other words, if spontaneity and necessity are regarded as opposite poles, then desires are in conflict with reason and rightness, but if spontaneity and necessity are regarded as linked, or if necessity is what the knowledge of spontaneity reaches as its "ultimate norm," then one cannot and need not depart from desires (the "knowledge of blood and breath," or our actual existence) in order to speak of spontaneity or necessity (reason and rightness).

According to this logic, one has no way to leave behind the people's daily lives or the knowledge of blood and breath in order to speak of order and rightness. The Song Confucians believe that pattern and desire are divided as two, and what they call order and rightness is neither spontaneity nor necessity, but is only a matter of subjective opinion. Dai Zhen said: "It is only what hearts affirm alike that can be designated as order and as rightness; whatever does not reach what is 'affirmed alike' but remains lodged among one's personal opinions is not order and not rightness."[104] Here to say "what hearts affirm alike" is not to say that one need only return to the original heart in order to be able to seek out order and rightness. Rather it is to say that order and rightness must accord with the common feelings and needs of ordinary people, and that otherwise "order and rightness" will be nothing more than personal opinion. "With regard to Heaven and Earth, persons and things, and affairs and actions there is nothing that cannot be spoken of in terms of pattern. This is what it means for the *Odes* to say: 'For each thing there is a norm'" (*you wu you ze*).[105] Dai continues, "'Thing' refers to the concrete actuality, and 'norm' to its refined correctness. When the concrete actuality is entirely spontaneous and returns to the necessary, the patterns of Heaven and Earth, persons and things, and affairs and actions are attained." "What hearts affirm alike" is surely the "refined correctness" of the "norm."[106] In other words, order and rightness require a commonly recognized form to serve as a basis for judgment. This theory is close to the Legalist viewpoint of thinkers like Guanzi and Han Fei, and fits together with Xunzi's theory like the two halves of a tally. Guanzi and Han Fei hold that rulers and teachers need to manage or educate according to "patterns" (*li*) that are inherent in things and that transcend specific power relations, and Dai Zhen emphasizes that ritual relies heavily on the internal spontaneity of things and that it also supports the existence of standards with regard to things.

Dai Zhen and his disciple Ling Tingkan (1757–1809) and others all had the idea of substituting ritual for pattern or principle (*yi li dai li*), and this was because ritual can and indeed must be grasped from the practices of daily life, whereas the pure concept of "principle," because it had been bathed in Buddhism and Daoism, had become an unverifiable realm of "opinion." If there was no way to use a relatively objective standard or norm of spontaneity to weigh "opinion," then its use could only be subordinated to the operation of power. In comparison with the views of Guanzi and Han Fei, Dai Zhen saw the implications of principle or ritual more from the perspective of the lower strata of society, and his affirmation of the legitimacy of feeling and desire carried a strong critical import:

> Thus it is hardly surprising that nowadays those who govern others regard the people's feelings, which the ancient worthies and sages embodied, and the people's desires, which they fulfilled, as mostly base, trivial, and devious and pay them no heed; and when it comes to censuring with principle, they think nothing of picking out someone of unparalleled high integrity and manifest righteousness and condemning him. When the respected invoke principle to censure the lowly, or the old invoke principle to censure the young, or the noble invoke principle to censure the base, even if they are mistaken it is called compliance [with principle]; but when the lowly, the young, or the base invoke principle to contend with them, even if they are right it is called rebellion. On account of this, those below cannot rely on the common feelings and desires of All-under-Heaven and make them known to those above. When someone above invokes principle to censure someone below him, the faults of the one below are [regarded by] everyone as too numerous to count. When a man dies by law there are still some who pity him; but if he dies by principle, who will pity him? Alas! The harm of mixing in Daoist and Buddhist explanations when formulating doctrine is thus worse than [the harm from] Shen [Buhai] and Han [Feizi]! Where in the writings of the Six Classics, Confucius, and Mencius is principle taken to be as a kind of thing, external to the expressions of man's nature in feelings and desires and rigorously controlling them?[107]

It is worth noting that in the Qing Dynasty there was a great flourishing of ritual codes, and that patriarchal power was extremely strong. In addition to functioning in the operation of the official system, Cheng-Zhu *lixue* also played an important role at the grassroots level of society. The so-called "unity of governance and the Way" referred not only to government at the court, but also to the way that social relationships at the grassroots level were able to operate within the domain of morality. Here we need to make a necessary distinction between Dai Zhen's unification of pattern or principle with ritual and Qing society's unification of principle with ritual codes.

Modern scholars often combine Dai Zhen's protest against "killing with *li*" (Principle) with a critique of ritual codes, and the reason is that patriarchal lineages and ancestral halls often used the *Family Rituals* formulated by Zhu Xi as their own family codes and lineage regulations. The Huizhou merchant guildhall was named in honor of Zhu Xi, the guildhall and its lodgings were known as "Hall of Master Zhu" (*Zhuzi tang*) and "Shrine of the Duke of Letters" (*Wengong si*), and lineage patriarchs often used *lixue* doctrines to explain the reasonableness of the ritual codes. Then, why is Dai Zhen not reconstructing the transcendent nature of "principle" or the ontological character of "feeling" and "desire" to counter the proliferation of ritual codes, but instead reconnecting principle or pattern with ritual? Isn't the unity of principle and ritual the premise of ritual codes? This can be explained on several levels. First, Dai Zhen sees it as "*li*" (principle, pattern, coherence) when "feelings do not fail; there is never a case of not attaining the feeling and yet still attaining the principle." But when "Heavenly Principle" (*tianli*) is seen as "spontaneous patterning" (*ziran zhi fenli*), it does not transcend the domain of "feeling," but is a matter of "using my feelings to assess the feelings of others so that all reach their proper level."[108] He said critically that the difference between Cheng-Zhu and Lao, Zhuang, and the Buddhists was nothing other than using *li* (principle) as a substitute for the category of spontaneity, and that in their strictness on the distinction between principle and desire, they ended up banishing feeling and desire from the realm of principle.[109] Starting from this viewpoint of unifying feeling and principle and regarding principle and desire as an integral whole, Dai Zhen not only avoided Cheng and Zhu's dualism of principle and desire, but also ruled out the concept found in later Wang Yangming learning that treated feeling as an ontological principle. The concepts of feeling and desire are internal to principle, and the concept of principle is internal to ritual. This is the content of the unity of principle and ritual. Second, as mentioned above, Dai Zhen's ritual was the ritual of Gu Yanwu's so-called ritual and culture. It was not the moral doctrines of ritual codes but the spontaneity of the cosmos, and the order of ten thousand ages and of the ten thousand things. Thus, the connection between *li* (principle or pattern) and *li* (ritual) was the connection between *li* (principle or pattern) and the inherent regularity or unique characteristics of specific things, and it contains the meaning of respect for feelings and desires. "Ritual is where the norms of Heaven stop; when it is enacted in human relationships and among the manifold things, All-under-Heaven is at peace; it leaves no allotment unfulfilled, and it is therefore related to reciprocity." "Ritual" in this sense recognizes the legitimacy of "desires," and is unlike the Cheng-Zhu dualistic view of Principle and desire that holds that Principle must completely control desire.[110] Third, Dai Zhen's "*li*" (principle, pattern) includes an understanding of "Nature" (*ziran,* spontaneity), which uses an object-based standard (i.e., division, *fenli*) to establish a classification of things. This also provides an epistemological premise for his investigations into the study of spontaneity or Nature. He said: "The text [*Mencius* 6A7] says 'order' (*li*) to show that the heart can make distinctions, and 'rightness' (*yi*) to show that it can make judgments. When each element has its unvarying norm (*buyi zhi ze*), it is called 'order,' and when it is appropriately so, it is called 'rightness.' Thus to 'illuminate order' is to illuminate its distinctions, and to 'refine rightness' is to refine its judgments."[111] According to this, Dai Zhen's purpose was definitely not to deny order and rightness, but rather to seek out a new understanding of order and rightness, starting from the intrinsic connection between spontaneity and necessity. Where Lao, Zhuang, and the Buddhists, as well as the *lixue* scholars, understood seeking Principle or spontaneity as meaning a return to a void and empty realm of nonbeing, Dai Zhen required that the spirit of order and rightness be embodied in the midst of investigating and understanding affairs and things. In this sense, he not only linked order and rightness with ordinary life and ordinary human feelings, but also required deep insight into the inherent regular patterns of specific things through "intelligence" (*zhi*) and "learning" (*xue*). Thus, Dai Zhen's way of distinguishing principle and desires and his spontaneity/necessity distinction were a reconfirmation of the "broad learning restrained by ritual" mission of classical scholarship.

Dai Zhen contrasted law (*fa*) with principle (*li*), on the one hand opposing the use of principle to control desire, and on the other giving prominence to the problem of "law." These viewpoints had little connection with Mencius, and were closer to Lao, Zhuang, and the Legalists, especially to Xunzi.[112] Why did his critique of controlling desire with principle lead him to the problem of "law"? And how should we understand his comment that "when a man dies by law there are still some who pity him; but if he dies by principle, who will pity him? Alas! The harm of mixing in Daoist and Buddhist explanations when formulating doctrine is thus worse than [the harm from] Shen Buhai and Han Feizi"? Let us first examine the political aspect of the law (*fa*) / principle (*li*) distinction. Zhang Taiyan said:

> Dai Zhen was born at the end of the Yongzheng era, and saw men banished by imperial edict, not according to law but by selecting the words of Cheng and Zhu for mutual investigations; government offices were observed for hidden secrets, and criminal blame extended to social chatter. It was not that the Nine Regions were not spacious, and yet they were walled off with thistles and thorns, so that whatever the gentry and people did was always wrong, and their grief and sorrow were deep. From his early youth Dai Zhen engaged in trade, and in his extensive travels gained personal knowledge of the deep complexities of people's lives. Yet from those above there was no word of kindness, and so in indignation he wrote *On Goodness* and the *Critical Exegesis of the Meanings of Words in Mencius,* devoting his energies to fairness and forbearance, and calling out on behalf of the people to Heaven above. Clearly dying by the law is something one can be saved from, but from dying by principle there is no escape.[113]

Zhang Taiyan is discussing specific political behaviors, but when we consider that these kinds of actions occurred under a Qing court that congratulated itself on having unified governance with the Way, it is clear that substituting moral actions for legal actions can be more rigorous and cruel than legal actions alone. In the political sphere the so-called unity of governance and the Way amounted to abolishing the independence of law and making it operate in the name of morality. Accordingly, abolishing the law was definitely not a matter of abolishing punishments or the mandatory actions of criminal law, but of eliminating any moral standards that stood outside and transcended these punishments and mandatory actions. And if there was a need to restore once again the autonomy of the moral sphere, then it would first be necessary to restore the autonomy of the law itself. In other words, under the conditions of the unity of governance and the Way, the closer Dai Zhen came to the standpoint of the Legalists, the closer he also came to the attitude of *lixue,* which was the need for moral judgment outside the law.

We need to understand Dai Zhen's complex attitude toward ritual and law from a broader historical perspective, and in this context the fluctuating changes of the patriarchal clan system in the Qing dynasty constitute the key link in understanding Dai Zhen's viewpoint on these matters. The form of classical scholarship was that of a revolt against Song-Ming theories of the Way of Heaven and of the Mind in relation to the nature, and its core lay in reconnecting moral practice and moral evaluation with institutional practice, and especially with patriarchal lineage relationships. The central issue in early Qing scholarship was the ritual system. When Gu Yanwu, Huang Zongxi, and Wang Fuzhi (1619–1692) studied the governmental institutions and the written and spoken language of the former kings, it was all with the inner purpose of restoring the integrity of ritual and music, and they especially valued the patriarchal lineage and its ethical principles. This choice was not only a moral choice, but also a political choice, because it was the power of the patriarchal lineages that became the main support of a war of resistance after Qing soldiers had entered the passes, in an effort to sustain the political authority of the fallen Ming.[114] In the Shunzhi era, the Zhou lineage of Shuyang in Jiangsu, the Yang lineage of Yongfeng in Jiangxi, and the Yang lineage of Tingzhou in Fujian were all encircled and suppressed because they had raised troops to resist the Qing. These actions revealed the political implications of the ritual theory of early Qing. But the content of classicist ritual theory changed as the status of lineage power in Qing society changed. From the Kangxi reign onward, the Qing rulers gradually changed their attitude of exclusion and repression of the lineages, tried to reconstruct the authority of Confucian learning and the lineage system, and consciously adopted the lineage community as the grassroots organization that maintained social order. In 1770, Kangxi promulgated the "Sacred Edict in Sixteen Articles":

> Be honest, filial, and brotherly in order to give weight to human relationships; deeply esteem your lineage in order that harmony and peace may shine forth; harmonize village communities so that lawsuits may cease; emphasize farming and mulberry cultivation for sufficient clothing and food; value thrift in order to conserve wealth; promote schools to correct gentry practices; banish heterodox tendencies in order to venerate correct customs; explain the laws and statutes in order to instruct the

> ignorant and stubborn; cultivate courtesy and thoughtfulness in order to deepen customs and manners; devote yourself to your primary occupation in order to establish the people's aspirations; instruct sons and younger brothers to prohibit wrongdoing; desist from lawsuits in order to safeguard the good and honest; warn against harboring fugitives to avoid becoming implicated; pay your cash and in-kind land taxes in full in order to avoid penalties; participate in Community Self-Defense (*baojia*) to suppress robbers and thieves; abandon enmity and resentment in order to show respect for your body and life.[115]

Clearly, he is taking the lineage here as a structural pillar of political control. He not only paid soothing visits to the great houses of prominent lineages during the course of his six southern tours, but also provided legal protection to key elements of the lineage community (lineage property, lineage temples, lineage genealogical records, lineage structure, and lineage regulations, continuing into later generations).

This tendency underwent further development in the Yongzheng era. Its fundamental direction was toward a high degree of integration between government power and lineage power, using legal forms to clarify and regulate the role of the lineages as a first-level organization, acting in parallel with the *baojia* (Community Self-Defense) system, to support and supplement local political power and to maintain local order. After the Song dynasty the lineage community was generally established, but in Song, Yuan, and Ming times, or even in the Shunzhi and Kangxi reigns, this legal status for lineages in the political structure was unprecedented. In this sense, lineage law not only was the fundamental principle that regulated the conduct and bearing of lineage members and maintained the internal order of lineage society, but also received the legal protection of the state.[116] Against this background, the large-scale study and advocacy of ritual governance launched by Qing-dynasty Zhu Xi learning and classical learning had already lost the rebellious character of early Qing scholarship.

The growth of lineage power meant that its internal cohesiveness and external resilience increased together, creating a complicated situation. On the one hand, as the lineages of each locality bought property and established regulations, the scale of their land and production gradually expanded, and they infiltrated into the state machine by means such as entering officialdom through the examination system, creating a pattern in which government and business were closely related. In his early years Dai Zhen engaged in trade, and had close personal experience of the life of a Huizhou merchant. According to Tang Lixing's research, Huizhou families all attached great importance to their sons and brothers gaining office through reading books, and listed them at the head of family codes and lineage regulations. In the Qing dynasty Anhui ranked third among the provinces in the number of examination candidates achieving Principal Graduate (*zhuangyuan*) status in the civil service examinations, altogether nine men, four of whom were from Huizhou Prefecture.[117] On the other hand, as Tang shows, the combination of lineage power with commercial enterprise also created a new mechanism of social control. For example, when Huizhou people gathered in lineages to live they were extremely patriarchal, and the reason why merchants emphasized respecting kin and esteeming ancestors was that "in organizing lineages, they used kinship status distinctions to manage and bind lineage members, and used blood relationships, close and distant, superior and inferior, to maintain a strict status hierarchy in the management of organizational structures." Also, "The Huizhou merchants also used the patriarchal clan system to strengthen their control of the tenants who served them." According to Tang Lixing:

> Discriminating against and persecuting tenants became customary in Huizhou. In the "Customs" section of the Jiajing *Huizhou Prefectural Gazetteer* it was said that "the status distinction between masters and servants is very strictly enforced. People like slave girls and maidservants, even if they prosper and become wealthy, are never accepted in clan villages." In the same section in the Kangxi revision of the prefectural gazetteer, a note was appended: "This custom persists up to the present day. If there is any slight confusion in the distinction of master and servant, then a single person would fight against it, and a family, lineage, or indeed the whole country would unite in fighting against it, because it is deeply wrong."[118]

The rigor of the patriarchal lineage system and its ritual codes is also reflected in marriage relations and in the status of women. In Ming and Qing times Huizhou merchants traveled about to engage in commerce, and their tracks extended to all parts of the country. Often, they would set forth at about the age of sixteen to do business, and before leaving home many took the opportunity to become engaged or to marry. But because of the difficulties of commerce, the greater part of these enterprises failed and it was difficult to return home, to the point where "after the 'parting of newlyweds' to go out for business there were no children, and countless numbers died in other places. In general, the places visited by Huizhou merchants all have Huizhou graveyards."[119] Huizhou merchants had a characteristic pattern of early marriage and late childbearing, and with regard to the age difference between husbands and wives, on average the men were older than the women by more than 7.9 years.[120] The marital crises that arose on account of the men leaving for distant places can be imagined. But it was precisely the social fluidity caused by commerce that led the lineages to impose more stringent regulations on women's chastity. In the records of Huizhou customs in Ming and Qing times there are a great number of records of chaste widows and of their behavior. For example, the genealogy of the Huang family of Xiaoli, Tandun, records that in this merchant family, in the 270 years from the Ming Chenghua reign to the Qing Yongzheng reign, there were forty-two rigorously faithful widows.[121] Thus there is some foundation for the view that Dai Zhen's proposition about "killing with Principle" (*yi li sha ren*) has some reasonable connection with the development of commerce in Qing times.[122]

Because of the integration of lineages and commerce, conflicts caused by property disputes within or between lineages frequently occurred; and because the scale and power of the lineages was very great, their relationship with the power of local government was also tangled and complex. Frequent incidents of armed conflict between lineages affected social order, and the infiltration of lineage power into judicial processes also broke down judicial order. In the Yongzheng-Jiaqing era, a system of private punishments with lineage law at its core had taken shape that was to a certain extent independent of and outside the law of the state. Lineage institutions continued to strengthen the compulsory power of lineage law, to set up clandestine tribunals, to procure implements of punishment, and to exercise rights of trial, judgment, and punishment toward those who offended against lineage laws, to the point where in many places it frequently happened that lineages directly put their lineage members to death. The struggle between the lineages and the state over the right to try cases expanded day by day, and thus a serious conflict developed between lineage law and state judicial authority.[123] In 1727, based on the lineages' corrupt exercise of lineage law and encroachments on state judicial authority in many regions, Qianlong approved a memorial and clearly pointed out that "it is the [imperial] court that holds the great power of life and death, and which, if there is no applicable law, must directly clarify and correct the application of punishments, and not delegate this to lineage members to open up occasions for conflict."[124] He thus abrogated the regulations "permitting the exercise of domestic discipline" that had been established in the fifth year of Yongzheng (1727), and legally restricted the authority of lineage courts. In the Qianlong and Jiaqing reigns, local counties and prefectures repeatedly handled a great number of cases involving lineage patriarchs and other lineage leaders who had exceeded their authority in ordering executions or in severely harming lineage members. The struggle between Qing government authority and lineage power was manifested not only in restrictions on lineage law but also in areas like breaking up and dispersing the lineages' economic base and weakening the authority of lineage elders, but fundamentally speaking the Qing rulers did not want to destroy lineage power completely. Rather their purpose was to limit lineage power to the level of stabilizing social order and assisting local government administration, and thus to integrate the system of centralized power with lineage power.

It was under these background conditions that Dai Zhen and Zhang Xuecheng, each from his own different standpoint, saw moral practice and concepts of ritual, law, and history as a restoration of the teaching of the unity of knowledge and action, and that within the frameworks of their thinking, government statutes, penal codes, and cardinal human relationships were all various aspects of ritual and music. Dai Zhen openly criticized the power of the lineages, believed that it was more cruel to kill people with Principle than to kill people by law, and tried to link the interpretation of ritual with legal relationships. His critique of *lixue* was actually also a critique of the Qing dynasty's connection with patriarchal law, and when he turned to emphasize institutions and law, trying to restore the connection between moral evaluation and institutional practice, this was not only a theoretical effort to balance the internal contradiction between Three Dynasties ritual and music and a national state based on commanderies and prefectures, but also a practical effort to find a balance between patriarchal ritual codes and national laws. If there had been no effort by the Qing court to deal with a grassroots power struggle between patriarchal law and local government, the proximate meaning of Dai Zhen's above-described views would be hard to understand. However, this does not mean that Dai Zhen's position and that of the Qing court were the same. For Dai Zhen and for Zhang Xuecheng, the critical power of classical learning was rooted in a single core proposition: institutions and laws must be internal to (and are not external to) the existence of morality. This proposition, by emphasizing an integral connection between morality and institutions, constituted a critique both of *lixue* and of patriarchal relationships, and at the same time, by emphasizing the moral aspect of institutions, it constituted a critique of actual institutions.

This way of thinking is already somewhat different from the way early-Qing scholars used the unity of governance and the Way to resist historical conditions that also united governance with the Way. Early-Qing scholars refused to recognize the legitimacy of current institutions and laws, and saw investigation of ancient institutions, decrees, and cultural artifacts and reestablishment of a patriarchal lineage-based order as a pathway to establish a moral foundation and a Chinese identity. For them, the institutions of the former kings carried the vivid imprint of idealism: taking them as principles of virtuous rule that could be carried forward for later kings to discover and implement is not just something that cannot be understood as realistic institutional theory, for it existed as a form of resistance to actual institutions. In contrast with this, the critique of patriarchal ethics by the Qianlong-Jiaqing scholars did not constitute a critique of imperial power. On the contrary, this critique worked in concert with imperial power to restrain patriarchal lineage tendencies. In Dai Zhen's view, ritual that accords with human feelings was on the one hand a supplement to law and a critique of patriarchal law, and on the other hand it was both a supplement to and a restraint on the state's legal relationships, and a way of reestablishing an inner connection between ritual and law. In this regard, as between lineage law and state law, Dai Zhen preferred the latter. From this perspective, early-Qing classical learning was a moral theory that emerged in the form of an institutional theory or of a theory of ritual governance, whereas Qianlong-Jiaqing theories of institutions and ritual governance were a balance and integration between the power of lineage law and the national legal system.

Under these historical conditions, Dai Zhen's holding fast to the Han learning standpoint of uniting principle with ritual and upholding an organic unity of the Way and its vessels, his critique of the Song and of Buddhism and Daoism, and his return to the Six Classics, Confucius, and Mencius all arose from this "orthodoxy" of Confucian learning. Accordingly, he could not directly return to the standpoint of *lixue* and use a transcendental concept to criticize a political reality that combined governance and the Way as an organic unity. But in pointing out that censuring others with principle could constitute an even harsher situation than censuring them with law, he was suggesting that the abuses of current government were not the result of harsh laws and severe punishments, but were the product of substituting ritual for law. Starting from the distinctions of spontaneity versus necessity and principle versus desire, he sought to turn anew toward a new ritual order that would encompass both spontaneity and necessity and principle and desire, and where although there would be established norms, these would not be alien to the internal principles of things. From a political point of view, this would be to observe the people's feelings in implementing a kingly Way, and to accord with the "patterns of the people" (*min zhi li*) in establishing laws. From this viewpoint his relationship with Xunzi becomes complicated. Dai Zhen opposes Xunzi's argument that the nature of humans is evil, and is much closer to Mencius's theory that the nature is good.[125] But he emphasizes acquired knowledge (learning) and requires that spontaneity be sought through necessity, and these views incline him naturally toward Xunzi's viewpoint. On the one hand he distinguishes between Xunzi and Mencius:

> Xunzi knows that propriety and righteousness are the teaching of the sages, but does not know that propriety and righteousness also proceed from the nature; he knows that propriety and righteousness [involve] understanding what is necessary, but does not know that the necessary is the ultimate norm of spontaneity, by which one's spontaneity may be perfected. . . . The importance of learning for Xunzi is that what is lacking within is obtained from without; the importance of learning for Mencius is that what exists within is nourished from without.[126]

On the other hand, Dai openly acknowledges that Xunzi's argument that the nature is evil and Mencius's theory of the goodness of the nature "not only do not conflict, but seem to develop and clarify each other. . . . Xunzi's views place great emphasis on learning, but he does not know the whole substance of the nature. His articulations come from honoring the sages, from emphasizing learning, and from exalting propriety and righteousness."[127] According to Zhang Taiyan: "In the end what Dai Zhen discussed fit together with Xunzi like the halves of a tally. Understanding that Xunzi's explanation that the nature is evil was close to his own view, he wrote *On Goodness*. Of those who trust in spontaneity, there is none greater than Lao Dan [i.e., Laozi]. To rely on the name of Confucian scholar and yet entertain Lao Dan as one's guest, claiming descent from Meng Ke [i.e., Mengzi], this is indeed a fable!"[128] The spontaneity / necessity and principle / desire distinctions clearly came from Xunzi's argument on the nature and from his "Exhortation to Study." Qian Mu asserts categorically that among the various masters of late Zhou there was none more skilled than Xunzi in denouncing spontaneity, and that "Dai Zhen followed his ideas in rejecting Laozi and the Buddha, and then used Mencius's argument for the goodness of the nature to change and augment Xunzi."[129]

In the relationship between Dai Zhen and Xunzi, the relationship of ritual to "learning" is clearly a key link. The key to rebuilding the carpenter's line of ritual principles (*liyi*) is to banish selfishness, banish partiality, and banish delusion, but how can this be done? According to Dai, "Among the afflictions of men are selfishness and delusion. Selfishness arises from feelings and desires, and delusion arises from the heart's discernments." He continues:

> Thus, the way of the sages and worthies is to be without selfishness but not without desires, while that of Lao, Zhuang, and the Buddha is to be without desires but not without selfishness. It is by means of desirelessness that the latter complete their selfishness, whereas it is by means of unselfishness that the former communicate the feelings and fulfill the desires of All-under-Heaven. . . . The learning of the sages and worthies grounds earnest practice in broad learning, close inquiry, careful thought, and clear distinctions; one's practice is thus the undeluded practice of the daily functioning of human relationships, and not, like theirs, a discarding of the daily functioning of human relationships in the belief that absence of desire is a capacity for earnest practice.[130]

It is only when selfishness and delusion are removed through sagely wisdom and intelligence that ritual principles can be manifested in the daily practice of human relationships. Accordingly, although Dai Zhen opposed Xunzi and the Song Confucians on questions like whether the nature is good or evil or on the relation of principle to *qi*, yet still with regard to the relation of learning to ritual he developed and extended the viewpoints of Xunzi and Cheng-Zhu.[131] Here the key is that Dai Zhen regarded "learning"—an understanding of the patterns of things, which is bound to be reflected in the proper practice of knowledge—as the path that must be followed to understand and reach Mencius's order and rightness (*liyi*) or Xunzi's ritual principles (*liyi*).

Another reason for Dai Zhen's proximity to Xunzi and to Cheng and Zhu was determined by the object of his criticism, which was the reliance on spontaneity and the belittling of acquired learning by Lao, Zhuang, and the Buddhists. The Donglin learning of Peng Shaosheng and others that was described above emphasized the original heart (*ben xin*) and had little regard for learning as Dai Zhen understood it,[132] and men like Wang Jin, drawing inspiration from Zhu Xi learning, held that "Master Zhu's learning is just a matter of sincerity, and of subtle reverence for the arts of the mind. Sincerity, without action, without thought, and without concerns, is the single principle ordained by Heaven; reverence, without action, without thought, and without concerns, is the single principle that is lodged in my heart."[133] On this account Dai Zhen had to discuss "learning" (*xue*) and "sincerity" (*cheng*) in detail, and to accord primary importance to the question of acquired learning. He said:

> The ancient worthies and sages knew that humans differed in natural talent, and on this account emphasized learning and valued expansion and fulfillment; Lao, Zhuang, and the Buddhists say that all beings possessed of life are equal, and therefore emphasize getting rid of feelings and desires in order not to harm it, [holding that] it is not necessary to engage in learning to expand and fulfill it. . . . When Xunzi says that the nature of the ordinary man is [such that he can] know propriety and righteousness only after study, his theory can also be elaborated. Men like Lu Xiangshan and Wang Yangming are similar to Lao, Zhuang, and the Buddhists, but instead of reviling humanity and righteousness they hold that spontaneity is complete in humanity and righteousness, and are

> skilled in elaborating their theory. When Masters Cheng and Zhu honor Principle and regard it as something conferred on me by Heaven, it is like Xunzi honoring propriety and righteousness and regarding them as something conferred on me by the sages. When they say that Principle has been corrupted by physical form and materiality, so that for all who are not sages physical form and materiality are in all respects greatly deformed, this is Xunzi's theory that human nature is evil. They say that Principle is a separate thing that is anchored and attached [to physical form and materiality]. . . . If Principle is complete and self-sufficient it becomes difficult to say that one must study in order to illuminate Principle, and therefore they could not but distinguish "Principle" from "material force" as "two roots," and lay the blame [for the difficulty of apprehending Principle] on physical form and materiality. Their theory is put together from a variety of mixed elements.[134]

Dai Zhen is criticizing the dualism of *lixue* here, but clearly he treats Cheng and Zhu differently from Lu and Wang. Hu Shi greatly admired Dai Zhen's bold assertion that "[Neo-Confucian scholars had been] detailed in discussing reverence but sketchy in discussing learning," but he did not understand that the cutting edge of this critique was directed against contemporary efforts to accommodate Buddhism into Confucianism. Viewed from this aspect, Dai Zhen's viewpoint is nothing but a variant within the orthodox tradition, and what he wants to maintain is still the Han learning premise or Confucian orthodoxy of the unification of principle and ritual and the organic unity of the Way and its vessels. Qian Daxin said: "The Six Classics are the words of the sages, and to accord with their words in order to seek out their meaning one must begin with philology. To say that there can be moral philosophy (*yili*) outside of philology is like a priest saying that the highest vehicle is beyond words, and is not our Confucian learning."[135] One can say that Dai Zhen's theory is far from Qian's argument but also close to it.

Dai Zhen was an outstanding figure of the Qianlong-Jiaqing era. In the level of his scholarship and in the power of his thought he represents the highest accomplishments of that era, but he also manifests that era's profound intellectual and moral predicament. He lived in the capital, was universally recognized as a key scholarly figure, and was more sensitive and deeply aware than others of challenges and explorations from all sides. Dai Zhen circled round between Han and Song learning, raised difficult issues between Confucianism and Buddhism, and wavered between Daoism and Legalism, but although he wanted to restore Confucianism to Confucianism, Song to Song, Buddhism to Buddhism, and Daoism to Daoism, in the end he was still mediating between Xunzi and Mencius, and finally returned to the Confucian aims and Classicist doctrines of the unity of principle and ritual and the organic unity of the Way and its vessels. The critical power of Dai Zhen's analysis of principle and desire is based on this premise, and its limitation also comes from this premise. In Dai Zhen's cry that "when one dies from the law, there can be those who sympathize; but when one dies from principle, who can sympathize?" we can hear a faint suggestion that the unity of governance with the Way or of principle with law constitutes a form of severe repression. But the hint is only a hint, and the transcendental domain beyond the law from which sympathy can be expressed for the deceased turns out not to be separate, for if it were separate, then Dai Zhen would be a proponent of *lixue*. In his view, there was nothing wrong with the Confucian ideals of the organic unity of the Way and its vessels, of the unity of principle and ritual, and of the convergence of governance and the Way; the problem was how to interpret these fundamental principles. The seriousness of his protest and the orthodoxy of his arguments exactly express the intellectual predicament faced by the scholar-gentry of the Qing dynasty: as fundamental propositions internal to Confucian learning and as hard-won conclusions of Qing Confucian learning, the unity of principle and ritual and of governance and the Way constituted an intellectual premise that was hard to break through; yet it was just this very intellectual premise that was used by the system in which they found themselves and that they were trying to criticize.

Therefore, the more profound and thorough Dai Zhen's attainments in classical learning became, the greater the pressure he felt; the deeper his passion for moral philosophy, the greater his inner tension; the clearer his insight into intellectual predicaments, the more complicated his responses to these intellectual challenges; and the deeper and more exact his understanding of different schools and tendencies became, the more roundabout and complex the intensity of his critical tone inevitably grew. This intellectual complexity created a psychological and moral ambiguity, and it might be said that on account of the richness of his thought Dai Zhen showed a certain vulnerability. I suspect that Dai Zhen would not recognize any kind of one-sided censure, and he might hold that his own theory and scholarly method and style could absorb any contradiction. However this may be, Dai Zhen's nimble dodging and weaving, diplomatic maneuvering, and successive demolition of the power of various kinds of thought only goes to show that within the scope of classical learning there were implicit elements of self-doubt, and it betokens that from within classical learning new changes would develop.

III. "The Six Classics Are All History" and the Archaeology of Classical Learning

1. Spontaneity (*ziran*) and What Must Be So (*bu de bu ran*)

Zhang Xuecheng (courtesy name Shizhai, from Guiji Prefecture in Zhejiang, 1738–1801), attacked the shortcomings of philology and evidential scholarship with the argument that "the Six Classics are all history" and opened a long line of thinking that cast doubt on the classics. He scathingly denounced the scholarship of his contemporaries like a fishbone caught in his throat, and even when it came to Dai Zhen, when he set pen to paper he showed no mercy. This sharp style of writing and Zhang Xuecheng's investigations into the moral character and academic ethos of scholars have created the impression that his historical view was in complete opposition to classical learning. Zhang's scholarly approach was very clear-cut, and had none of the complications and fissures of Dai Zhen's psychology and scholarship, but if one considers carefully, one may also discover some contradictory elements. For example, he studied with Zhu Yun (1729–1781) and held that Cheng-Zhu *lixue* had opened the way to Qing scholarship, yet his fundamental outlook differed from that of Cheng and Zhu; he opposed empty talk of moral philosophy and had reservations about Wang Yangming's attacks on Zhu Xi, yet he also believed that Wang Yangming's learning had opened the way to the first beginnings of Qing historical scholarship, and solemnly placed himself in the rear guard of the Eastern Zhejiang school of learning; his critiques of the evidential style of learning were severe, and he had high regard for moral philosophy, yet in still strongly upholding the concepts of the organic unity of the Way and its vessels and of the unity of ritual and principle he was not far from the base premises of classical learning, to the point where we can say that the patterns he used in criticizing evidential learning provided some of the best examples of evidential reasoning. According to what logic, then, was this seemingly contradictory mode of thinking organized?

In an era when supporters of Han and Song learning traded insults and classical learning was becoming a major trend, Zhang Xuecheng's emphasis on returning from broad learning to ethical restraint, his high regard for Cheng and Zhu, his thorough mastery of moral philosophy, and his relinking of the purpose of learning with the goals of seeking the Way and governing the world made people feel that his scholarly standpoint was close to *lixue*.[136] But if while discussing the general purport of his arguments we also consider the views of classical scholars like Dai Zhen and Jiao Xun, we will realize that since these were not isolated critiques, we cannot say that he was on a completely different path from classical learning.[137] The fundamental difference between Zhang Xuecheng and the classical scholars was not over the connection between moral philosophy and evidential learning, but over the position of the Six Classics: according to practitioners of classical learning, the Way comes from the Six Classics, and if one does not start with glossing the meanings of words one will not find the key; for Zhang Xuecheng, the Six Classics are not enough to exhaust the Way, and he sought within the domain of history to find an alternative path for moral philosophy.[138] From the side of "moral philosophy" (*yili*) he praised Dai Zhen for not esteeming the "empty theories" of Song learning; he saw that Dai's learning was serious about philology and evidential scholarship, and did not get bogged down in the methods of particular schools. Zhang Xuecheng resonated with Dai Zhen's theory of spontaneity (*ziran*) / necessity (*biran*), whose abstract meaning was completely compatible with the guiding ideas of his historiography.[139]

Zhang Xuecheng valued moral philosophy or expositions on meanings and principles (*yili*), but his moral philosophy was not the moral philosophy of Song-Ming Confucian learning; it was a historical concept. Here, what history involves is not one among many academic disciplines in the humanities, but a way of understanding the tradition of Confucian learning, namely that the Confucian classics are a presentation of history itself, and that the moral practice of Confucian learning must thus be seen as a historical practice. In this sense, the proposition that "the Six Classics are all history" (*liujing jie shi*) and Wang Yangming's "unity of knowledge and action" (*zhixing heyi*) answer the same level of questions.[140] In an essay on "Eastern Zhejiang Scholarship" (*Zhedong xueshu*), Zhang holds that Qing-dynasty historical scholarship carried on the legacy of Lu Xiangshan–Wang Yangming scholarship, and he deeply accepts the teaching of the unity of knowledge and action. But within his historical view, the relation of knowledge and action has a historical connection with changes in institutional forms, and thus what is regarded as the knowledge and action of moral practice is knowledge and action within the scope of historically specific ritual protocols. Carefully reading his *Comprehensive Meaning of Literature and History* (*Wenshi tongyi*), his *Comprehensive Meaning of Bibliography* (*Jiaochou tongyi*), and other essays, we can see that in every kind of varied context, Zhang Xuecheng repeatedly discussed relationships and their changes between officials and teachers and between government and doctrinal instruction, and that his discussions of problems of classical scholarship, history, morality, and other fields of knowledge were nearly always connected with these issues. In his view, in ancient times government and instruction had not been divided, and officials and teachers were united in a single role: "The Minister of Education applied the Five Teachings, and the Manager of Music instructed the elder sons of the nobility; the schools of the Three Dynasties were all embedded in institutions, and those who in that time engaged in learning, on entering engaged in chanting, and on coming out relied on government instruction and decrees and regulations to handle matters. Because of this, scholars were all trusted and had proofs, and did not exchange empty words."[141] This was the age of the unity of knowledge and action. Zhang continues: "Officials and teachers separated, and the doctrines of the various masters and the Hundred Schools arose. Thereupon, learning began to be named according to the graded accomplishments of individual persons. . . . Learning became differentiated according to persons, and thus became subject to luxuriant and arbitrary growth. It was not on account of faults of action that it came to this; it came from faults of thinking."[142] Classical learning became a matter of studying without thought, the various masters engaged in thinking without study, the examination system encouraged Confucian arts through profit and emolument, and the goal of what Confucius called "learning below to get through to what is above" (*xia xue er shang da*, *Analects* 14.35) was completely lost. Thus, knowledge and action lost their unity and became divided. Zhang treats the problem of "knowledge" (*zhi*) as something to be examined under conditions of institutional change, and his field of vision is actually something that evolved from the view in Confucian learning on the "split between ritual and music and institutions" or between the "Three Dynasties of Antiquity and what came after them." He definitely does not think that talking about "the unity of knowledge and action" like Wang Yangming can restore the aim of "learning from below to get through to what is above," because "the unity of knowledge and action" is not a method of individual moral practice but a form of social operation; and it is also not simply a moral concept, but a historical concept, and a form of "learning" that may appear under particular institutional conditions.[143]

Zhang Xuecheng liberated concepts such as the unity of the Way and its vessels, the unity of governance and the Way, and the unity of principle and ritual from "classical learning," and transformed them into historical categories. To treat the classics from a "historical" perspective, or to take the classics as history, is to regard the classics as a record of the institutions and practices of the former kings. In this sense, "history" seeks to understand classical learning by placing it within the context of relationships of historical practice, and thus becomes a kind of reflective knowledge. The argument that "the Six Classics are all history" is not only a critique of evidential learning (*kaoju*), but also a negation of classical learning, in that it negates the attitude and method of treating the classics as classics. This feature draws a line of demarcation between him and Dai Zhen's and Jiao Xun's critiques of scholarly trends in textual research learning.[144] Then, by what pathway did he connect belief in classical learning with the tendency of historical learning to doubt the classics? Let us first take a look at a paragraph in the first *juan* of his treatise "On the Way" (*Yuan dao*):

> The Way has spontaneity, and the sage has that which cannot be otherwise. Are they the same? I say they are not the same. The Way is without action and so is spontaneous, whereas the sage has insight and so cannot be otherwise. Therefore, although one can say that the sage embodies the Way, one cannot say that the sage and the Way are one. The sage has insight, and therefore cannot be otherwise. The multitude have no insight, and so are as they are without knowing it. Who is closer to the Way? I say, those who are as they are without knowing it, are the Way. It is not that there is nothing for them to see, but they cannot see it. To be

unable to be otherwise is the means by which the sage is united with the Way, but he cannot immediately just be the Way. . . . The Duke of Zhou, in a time when it was possible to be steeped in and to transmit the perfected institutions of the Way, was thus able to govern by statecraft, and to sum up the great accomplishments of high antiquity; yet it was the particular circumstances of the times that made it so, and not that the sagely wisdom of the Duke of Zhou was able to make it so. From ancient times the sages all learned from what the multitude were without knowing it, and the Duke of Zhou likewise broadly surveyed what the sages from ancient times could not but have been, and understood how they were. . . . This was not something that the Duke of Zhou was able to accomplish by the strength of his wisdom, but was brought about by the particular circumstances of the times. . . . When [the roles of] ruler and teacher became separate, and accordingly governing and instruction could not be unified, this was fated by Heaven. When the Duke of Zhou summed up the accomplishments of governance, and Confucius illuminated the essentials of establishing instruction, from the patterns of circumstance this could not have been otherwise; it was not that the sages deliberately wished to seek in this way to be different from their predecessors, but that the patterns of the Way emerge from Heaven. . . . Later men . . . abundantly praised Confucius for having surpassed Yao and Shun, and because of this exalted the nature and the Decree and slighted practical accomplishments (*chong xingming er bo shigong*). As a result, the statesmanship of a thousand sages was considered by Confucian scholars as not worth discussing! . . . Respecting Confucius is not as valuable as being close to human sentiments, and focusing just on praising him without knowing the actuality [of these sentiments] is to fall into Daoist mysticism (*ze xuan zhi you xuan*). How does regarding the sage as a figure of divinity contribute to actual instruction?[145]

There are three facets from which we can analyze the above passage. First, Zhang explains "the Way" as "spontaneity," and opposes any dualism of the Way and its vessels (*li* and *qi*); he explains "learning" as "what must be so," and opposes any empty invocation of "the nature" and "principle." This is another expression of Dai Zhen's spontaneity / necessity distinction. There are differences among "affairs" (*shi*), and "the Way" also has disparities, and this is somewhat close to Dai Zhen's theory of "patterns of differentiation" (*fen li*). But there is a difference between them: Zhang emphasizes the aspect of "vessels," while Dai Zhen emphasizes intrinsic substance. Here, their different understanding of "affairs" is a key link. That "principles (or patterns) exist in the midst of affairs" (*li zai shi zhong*) is a concept common to both of them, but Dai Zhen's "affairs" prioritize the practices of daily life (the so-called "eating and drinking in daily life"), where the center of the discussion is personal moral practice. For Zhang, "affairs" were historical: he emphasized the way affairs change and the internal connection between institutions and discourse, and advocated observing the connection between ancient institutions and Confucian discourse through changes in affairs:[146]

> Affairs have actual proofs, but principles have no fixed form. Therefore Confucius, in his narration of the Six Classics, always drew on the institutions of the former kings, and never wrote of principles apart from affairs. Later Confucians took the words and actions of sages and teachers as patterns for the ages, and so designated their writings as classics. This was of course reasonable. But what one honors with ideas, one can also confuse and make doubtful with ideas. Ever since the time when officials became separate from teachers, when officials govern, the lowly cannot dare to act on their own, because there are proofs [of what is expected], but when teachers instruct, the unworthy often dare to put forth their own confused views, because there are no proofs. In the time of Mencius, Yang Zhu and Mozi were considered heterodox. Yang Zhu wrote no books, and the writings of Mozi were at first not called classics.[147]

In other words, there is a close relationship between the forms of moral philosophy and practice and the forms of particular institutions: when officials and teachers and government and instruction were not separated, the unity of knowledge and action was an institutionalized epistemology and theory of practice, but when officials and teachers and government and instruction were separated, moral philosophy had to find another mode of expression, of which the learning of the various pre-Qin masters and the *lixue* of Song and Ming are examples. It was only when knowledge and institutions had this kind of internal connection that the argument that the Six Classics are all history could become established.

Second, where Dai Zhen uses a distinction of "the spontaneous" from "the necessary" to draw out a distinction of principle and desire, Zhang subsumes the classics within the domain of history with his distinction of "the spontaneous" from "what cannot be otherwise." Within this domain, the formation of institutions, ritual, music, and moral philosophy is definitely not the achievement of sagely wisdom, but is rather something produced by "particular circumstances of the times" (*shi hui*). "From ancient times the sages all learned from what the multitude were without knowing it, and the Duke of Zhou likewise broadly surveyed what the sages from ancient times could not but have been and understood how they were." In this sense, the sages "also did not themselves understand how they were."[148] Zhang examined institutions, ritual, music, and actions from the perspective of change, and held that order itself was something that resulted "inevitably" from changes in "affairs." In other words, order is the result of people's free actions under certain conditions, and not a system that regulates all actions. To speak of "the Way" in the relationship between "the spontaneous" and "what cannot be otherwise," indicates that the institutions of ancient times were not in themselves the result of the actions of Sage-Kings as individuals, but were the product of changes in daily life, and that the moral philosophies that were produced from them were the sages' "inevitable" understanding of this spontaneous process. In this sense, the institutions of ancient times were not an intentional creation, but the spontaneous result of various combined forces. This is a typical evolutionary view of history, where human intentional action is just the internal aspect of spontaneous processes, and historical order is just the product of the movement of various combined forces. Humans exist within the relationships of groups, the cooperative division of labor within groups is a spontaneous tendency that allows them to manage their affairs, and the meanings and principles (*yili*) of "equitable and balanced order" are just a reflection of this spontaneous order itself. According to the same logic, the hierarchy of juniors and seniors, the order of ranks, and every kind of social institution are all the result of spontaneous evolution, and not regulations instituted by sages and worthies:

> If you fear that relationships will be characterized by strife, then you must promote elders to uphold fairness; this is an inevitable tendency, and thus distinctions of seniority and hierarchy are formed. When it comes to the

> myriad structures of social organization and their divisions, everyone of course values his own group, but when they multiply in their tens of thousands, then the multitude of men must rely on the capable and promote those of heroic talent to order their diversity, and untangle confused situations by promoting those of abundant virtue to manage their transformations, and this also is an inevitable tendency; the meanings of acting as ruler and as teacher, of defining boundaries and of demarcating territories, of well-fields, of enfeoffments, and of schools thereby become clear. Thus, the Way is not something that sages can create through their wisdom and strength, it is all the spontaneous tendency of affairs, gradually taking shape and gradually becoming clearer, arising inevitably and therefore spoken of as [the work of] Heaven.[149]

The regulations of the Three Dynasties accorded with spontaneous developments and cannot be otherwise; ancient laws and institutions are like this, and the changes of later generations must also accord with spontaneity, and need not rely on the personal opinions of individuals to represent "spontaneous tendencies." This view is in a direct line of descent from Liu Zongyuan's tendency to argue that institutions evolve spontaneously. Zhang holds that without relying on a "Way" that is separate from actual institutions and circumstances, and without relying on institutions and circumstances that are permanent and unchanging, institutions like the well-fields, enfeoffments, and schools of the Three Dynasties were produced by particular circumstances of the time. The integration of the Way with its vessels became a way of looking at knowledge, institutions, and historical change within the scope of history itself, and was no longer a moral ideal of Confucian learning.

Third, Zhang Xuecheng regards the changes of history, the differentiation of society, and the evolution of institutions as spontaneous processes, and this view changes the Classicist and *lixue* scholars' concept of the unity of governance and the Way. The order of ritual governance is produced by changes in "affairs," and the "affairs" themselves are products of spontaneity. In the saying that "the Duke of Zhou summed up the accomplishments of governing, and Confucius clearly established the ultimate principles of instruction," the difference between them was not that their moral philosophies were not the same, but that they were faced with different circumstances. When the sages established rituals and music and promulgated them in written texts, it was not that they embodied the Way as if they were divinities, but that they relied on spontaneity, and that from amid the "traces" of the world's transformations of yin and yang they intuitively understood the "Way." In this sense, to study the Duke of Zhou and Confucius is to understand "spontaneity," to the point where their understanding and actions themselves in response to spontaneity are also a part of the process of spontaneity. If you want to understand their thought as well as the differences between them, then you must understand the historical relationships that governed how their thought was produced. These are the "spontaneous tendencies" that they themselves did not understand.

The concept that the Six Classics are all history emerged from long-standing opposition within classical studies to speaking of principles apart from affairs, but conversely it also gave rise to doubts about the significance of classical studies: classical scholarship saw the classics as the subtle words and great meanings of the sages, and did not understand that "the ancients did not write books, and never spoke of principles apart from affairs. The Six Classics are all the governing systems and regulations of the former kings."[150] Even the *Book of Changes* (*Zhou Yi*) was also a book about governing, according to this argument. The concept that "the Way and its vessels form one body" (*daoqi yiti*) and the proposition that "the Six Classics are all history" are both aspects of the same idea, and they transformed the meaning of a "classic" (*jing*). This was a bit like the view of Guo Xiang (252–312 CE) and others in the Wei-Jin period: the Six Classics were not the Way of the sages, but the traces (or footprints) of the sages. Zhang Xuecheng said:

> The *Book of Changes* says: What is not yet formed is called the Way, and once it is formed it is called a vessel. The Way does not depart from vessels, just as a shadow does not depart from its form. Later generations, following the teachings of Confucius from the Six Classics, held that the Six Classics were books that conveyed the Way, but did not know that the Six Classics are all vessels. The *Book of Changes* as a book was used to thoroughly understand things and bring them to a successful conclusion; it was under the control of the Spring Official and the Grand Diviner, and thus was inherently under official supervision and regular direction. The *Documents* belonged to the External Secretary; the *Odes* were directed by the Imperial Tutor, the *Rituals* by the Minister of Rites,

> and the *Music* by the Director of Education; and the *Spring and Autumn Annals* each had their State Historiographer. Before the Three Dynasties, odes, documents, and the Six Arts were all used to instruct people, and were not, as in later ages, honored and upheld as Six Classics and separately made a school of Confucian learning, to be transmitted and raised up as writings that convey the Way. For as to what scholars practice, it does not depart from what officials managed and the institutions they preserved, and in their effect, governance of the state and education also do not depart from the constant daily practice of human relationships. Thus, one only sees affairs that must be as they are, and one never separately sees a Way that they transmit. When Confucius transmitted the Six Classics to instruct later generations, it also meant that the Way of the former kings could not be seen. The Six Classics are what can be seen of its vessels. Since later men do not see the former kings, they must rely on the vessels that can be preserved, and think of the Way that cannot be seen.[151]

If this passage is expounded with reference to Zhang's essays on "The Teaching of the *Change*" (Yi *jiao*), "The Teaching of the *Documents*" (Shu *jiao*), "The Teaching of the *Odes*" (Shi *jiao*), "The Teaching of the *Rituals*" (Li *jiao*), and "Explaining the Classics" (*Jing jie*), we can clearly see that the proposition that "the Six Classics are all history" is carried through as an explanation of every branch of classical learning. Zhang's view of classical writings is not just simply to explain that the Six Classics were all institutions of the royal court, but from a historical viewpoint to explain the connections among institutions, classical writings, and the writings of the pre-Qin masters, and from the classics, commentaries, masters, and histories and their organization and bibliographical formation to present a genealogical explanation.

From the perspective of genealogy, the theory that "the Six Classics are all history" conducts an inquiry with regard to the "classics" into the process of knowledge formation, and the questions that it raises are: How were the "classics" able to become separated from "history," and how could the "Way" gradually become a kind of verbal expression, and no longer something hidden within the existence of "vessels"? Zhang Xuecheng believed that the separation of classics from history arose from people's misunderstanding of the process of evolution, or in today's language, of the history of knowledge formation and of the process by which language was constructed. This can be seen from two different levels. The first is the relation of "classics" (*jing*) to "commentaries" (*zhuan*). The concept of a classic first appears in Warring States texts like the "Vigilance" (*Jie*) chapter of the *Guanzi*, the "Exhortation to Learning" (*Quan xue*) chapter of the *Xunzi*, and the "Way of Heaven" (*Tian dao*) chapter of the *Zhuangzi*, but in these contexts "classic" just has the meaning of ancient books and records.[152] The notion of "classic" as a knowledge or discourse did not arise from the Duke of Zhou's creation of rituals and music, or from the written records of court historians, or from the compilations and abridgements of Confucius, but at another historical juncture that had little direct connection with the content of the classical writings: classical scholarship came into being at a time when people were trying to make the early *Ru*[153] codes and records (and not the processes of actual life) into a source of moral philosophy. If one consults the "Biographies of Confucian Scholars" (*Rulin zhuan*) in the *Records of the Grand Historian*, or accounts of the establishment in the age of Han Wudi of Erudites in the Five Classics that are given in the "Biographical Evaluations of Confucian Scholars" (*Rulin zhuanzan*) of the *History of the Han* (*Han shu*), the statutory character of this time becomes very clear.

From the perspective of a taxonomy of knowledge, Zhang Xuecheng pointed out that the emblem of this time was the emergence of "commentaries" (*zhuan*) to explain the purpose of classics. What were commentaries? After the death of Confucius, when the time of subtle words and great meanings would soon be cut off, his disciples and followers each created writings, based on their recorded memories of what they had seen and heard, and in pursuit of their great meanings, works like *Zuo Commentary to the Spring and Autumn Annals* (*Zuo shi chunqiu*) and *Zixia's Mourning Apparel* (*Zixia sangfu*) became known as "commentaries": "Narrations of the lost writings of former times, which (originally) did not depart from the Six Arts, were all known as commentaries, as in what the *Mencius* said of the parks of Kings Tang, Wu, and Wen. And so, on account of the commentaries, there were works designated as classics, just as on account of sons there is a term for fathers."[154] In Gong Zizhen's *Rectifying Names in the Six Classics* (*Liu jing zheng ming*), a work that was deeply influenced by Zhang Xuecheng, Gong said:

> The Han worthy Liu Xin compiled the *Seven Genres* (*Qi lue*); Ban Gu continued this [in the *History of the Han* (*Han Shu*)], and made the "Bibliography of Arts and Letters" (*yiwen zhi*). He organized the Six Arts in nine categories, including classics, commentaries, records, and grouped writings. Commentaries were attached to classics, and the grouped writings which had some connection with the classics were also attached to them. What were the commentaries? For the *Documents* there were the greater and lesser Xiahou and Ouyang [writings], which were [treated as] commentaries; for the *Odes*, the Qi, Lu, Han, and Mao [writings] were commentaries; for the *Spring and Autumn Annals* there were the Gongyang, Guliang, Zuo, Zou, and Jia [writings], which were also [recognized as] commentaries.[155]

If "classics" did not have a corresponding relationship with "commentaries," then they would not exist, and if "commentaries" existed on their own, then there would be nothing to call "commentaries," and so Zhang Xuecheng said:

> If the Six Classics were not spoken of as classics, and the Three Commentaries [of the *Spring and Autumn Annals*, the Zuo, Gongyang, and Guliang] were not spoken of as commentaries, then this would be like everyone having a self, and yet not permitting the self to regard itself as a self (*you ren ge you wo, er burong wo qi wo ye*). Relying on classics and having commentaries is like having a self in relation to others. These [distinctions of] classic and commentary and self and other arise from the particular circumstances of the times but are not the fundamental substance.[156]

Later generations lack this archaeological field of vision, treat commentaries as classics, seek out the subtle words and profound meanings of the sages, and yet cannot understand that what in ancient times were called "classics" were something seen in the institutions and systems through which government and instruction were conducted. "Classics" were transformed from the recording and transmission of the institutions of the Sage-Kings into a kind of knowledge discourse.

Next is the relationship between "classics" (*jing*) and "masters" (*zi*). In Zhang Xuecheng's view, the so-called unity of governance and the Way was when the Duke of Zhou "as a sage of Heaven-endowed knowledge, well suited to transmit the accumulated accomplishments of antiquity, in a time when the methods of the Way were fully prepared, was thus able through acts of statecraft to sum up the accomplishments of a thousand ages, and yet it was the particular circumstances of the times that made it so."[157] Confucius was born in the Eastern Zhou, when the Three Dynasties were in decline and government and instruction had already been split apart. He had virtue but no position, and no means of attaining the power to create institutional structures, for the "enabling circumstance" (*shi hui*) of the unity of governance and the Way was missing. According to Zhang: "[Confucius] then drew upon the institutions of the Duke of Zhou, and alone with his disciples, in writings which embodied Heaven and man and preserved traces of transformative governance, expounded and clarified them, and this is why the Six Arts, despite having lost their official support, could come to depend on the instruction of teachers. But in the time of Confucius [these writings] were not called classics."[158] That Confucius transmitted but did not create, and definitely did not regard his writings as classics, was owing to the "logic of affairs that could not be otherwise." But after this the learning of the various masters took the form of private words (*si yan*), in contrast with the public words (*gong yan*) of the Six Arts, what Zhang referred to as "harsh critiques of reclusive scholars, when the various masters put forth a tangled profusion of writings and theories, so that in literary writings there began to be words of private scholars (*sijia zhi yan*), which did not all come from institutional government and instruction,"[159] and the public words of the Six Arts then came to be formed as classics. For this reason, if there had been no masters learning, there would also have been no classics, and classical learning and masters learning are related by a kind of common origin. One can summarize this common origin relation by saying: classical learning was a product of the formative process of masters learning.[160]

In a time of reticence, the Way was manifest and full, but in a time of words and speaking, the Way is hidden and empty. This was Zhang Xuecheng's summary of the inherent characteristics of classics and masters. That the Way is hidden in its vessels means that it is hidden in institutions and in daily practice itself, and is not to be found in discourse and in verbal formulations. Accordingly, "the Six Classics are all history" means that the Six Classics are all the institutions of the former kings, and their "historical meaning" is what can be gleaned from the Six Classics of the broad outlines of how emperors governed the world, and not the subtle words and great principles of the sages that proceed from interpretations of the meanings of classical texts. Just because of this, Zhang Xuecheng asked that scholarship approach the "ancient" and deal with the spirit and marrow of the Six Arts as contained in the learning of the masters, and not fall into squabbling between schools of textual research, moral philosophy, and rhetoric. But he certainly does not completely negate the significance of masters learning, because from the perspective of the "circumstances of the times," the birth of masters learning also had an aspect of "inevitability." This change, from ancestral transmission of royal institutions to confused discussions among the multitudes, was not something brought about by the subjective opinions of writers, but was an organic part of historical change. "When rulers and teachers were divided, governance and instruction could not be united as one, for it was an outcome fated by Heaven." That the Duke of Zhou was able to gather up the methods of the Way as practiced by Fu Xi and the Yellow Emperor and Yao and Shun and bring their gains and losses to perfection, while Confucius, who also needed to exhaust the methods of the Duke of Zhou's Way, "did not get to put them into practice but illuminated them as teachings," this was the expression of a spontaneous propensity (*ziran zhi shi*).[161] According to Zhang:

> [When it came to] the run of Confucian scholars, who venerated the Six Arts and upheld them as classics, this again was not just a way [for them] to gain fame from their commentaries. Xunzi said: "Learning begins with reciting the classics, and ends with the practice of ritual"; Zhuangzi said: "Confucius put words to (*yan*) the *Odes, Documents, Rituals, Music,* and *Spring and Autumn Annals* in the Six Classics, and he also said that . . . from the Twelve Classics one may see Laozi."[162]

This was also a spontaneous trend. The various masters used the institutions of governance and instruction of the former kings as the warp and weft of All-under-Heaven, but the general purport of the Six Arts did not appear, for the times required interpretations that were dispersed through the Six Classics.[163] Both Xunzi and Zhuangzi came from among the followers of Zixia, and their discourses prove that the name of Six Classics arose among the disciples of Confucius.

Zhang Xuecheng criticized the various masters for their extravagance in verbal expressions, but still believed that the various masters emerged from the Six Arts, and that their verbal expressions could not be seen purely as the language of private scholars. In the sense of "circumstances of the times" (*shi hui*), there was no absolute boundary between masters and classics. There was a close connection between the rise of the masters and the separation of government from instruction and of officials from teachers, and the Way of the former kings persisted amid the hubbub of the multitude. Therefore, from the archaeological standpoint of Zhang Xuecheng, if you want to explore the Way of the former kings you must clarify scholarship, inquire into its origins, and know that "Warring States writings originally emerged from the Six Arts." You must also understand that:

> When the various masters wrote books, they had reasons for what they upheld, and the logic of their discourse had to draw on an aspect of the body of the Way, for only then could they forcefully promote their theories and form a school of discourse. This so-called aspect, was nothing other than something included in the Six Arts, and so if one extended it in all aspects to reach its root, although one could not say that the various masters would thereby be able to restore the teaching of the Six Arts, their spoken words had to be grounded in this.[164]

For these reasons, Zhang had special regard for the "All-under-Heaven" chapter of the *Zhuangzi* (and for the "Against the Twelve Masters" [*Fei shi'er zi*] chapter of the *Xunzi*):

> The "Han Bibliography" ["Bibliography of Arts and Letters" chapter of the *History of the Han*] puts great emphasis on the origin and development of scholarship, and seems to draw on the meaning of the Grand Historian [Sima Qian's] "Biographical Prefaces," Zhuangzi's "All-under-Heaven" chapter, and Xunzi's "Against the Twelve Masters," for it sets forth the essentials of how these writings are connected with clarifying the Way, something which the bibliographic inventories of later ages do not attain.[165]
>
> For writings on the Six Arts and the doctrines of Confucian schools, one must consult the "Biographies of Confucian Scholars" (*Rulin liezhuan*).

> For the writings of the Daoist scholars, Logicians, and Mohist scholars, apart from their biographies, one should also consult Zhuangzi's "All-under-Heaven" chapter. Sima Qian's discussions of the general purport of the Six Arts in his biographical prefaces do not examine their branching genres, whereas Zhuangzi's "All-under-Heaven" chapter reliably gives balanced assessments of the learning of all the schools, and writers of all schools should model themselves on this. If one observes how the first chapter successively introduces old regulations and generationally transmitted histories, along with Six Arts versions of the *Odes* and *Documents,* [one can see that] these are the first origins of the classics and histories of later times; later it tells of the learning of Mozi and Qinhua Li, and [its account of] Mo Zhi [a disciple of Mozi], the "Mohists of different schools" [beginning with Qin and his fellow villagers], Mohist doctrines [from the time when Yu tamed the floods], and the Mohist Canon [meaning the followers of Ku Huo, Yi Zhi, and Deng Lingzi, who all chanted the Mohist Canon] is well ordered and complete. By comparison, what Liu Xiang and Ban Gu wrote was not as comprehensive, like Liu's "Biographies of Confucian Scholars" in relation to Ban's "Genre of the Six Arts." Song Xing, Yin Wen, Tian Bian, Shen Dao, Guan Yin, Lao Dan, up to Hui Shi and the adherents of Gongsun Long, are all found in the "Genre of the Various Masters," along with famous masters of the Daoist school. Thus, of all the ancients who wrote books, as long as they wished to illuminate the Great Way, there is none who is not discussed in relation to the origin and development of schools of learning.[166]

Through illuminating scholarship and clarifying its origins, even though the various masters have many opinions, we can still glean vestiges of the Six Arts, and see the historical processes of differentiation that are implicit in the differentiation of knowledge. The proposition of the unity of the Way and its vessels, or that the Six Classics are all history, is also applicable to understanding the rise of the learning of the various masters, and of other knowledge—such as astronomy, geography, calendars, and law.

In this sense, the unity of governance and the Way is not a description of political reality, but a way of observing forms of knowledge. It not only implies that forms of knowledge (systems of rules, interpretations of the language of classics and commentaries, doctrines of moral philosophy) are produced through particular historical relationships, but also clarifies some historical principles for treating ancient books and records, or what we might call an archaeology of knowledge. For example, Zhang said:

> What is above form is called the Way, what is below form is called a vessel. When good regulations are fully present, with roots and branches all included and parts that follow each other, complete in all respects and in good order, it becomes possible for those who write books to illuminate the Way from its vessels, and by assembling parts to reach the whole; Ren Hong's collation of military books and Li Zhuguo's collation of medical techniques come close to this. . . . Sun Wu's writings from the genre of military books, the inner and outer classics from the genre of medical writings, and those of the various masters who formed their own schools, are called the Way that is above form. The three sections in the genre of military writings on circumstances, on yin and yang, and on skilled techniques, and the three sections in the genre of medical techniques on prescriptions, on inner chamber arts, and on techniques of the immortals, all of which treat of arts and techniques, are called the vessels that are below form.[167]

Another example is Zhang's discussion of writings on law in his "Repairing and Collating the *History of the Han's* 'Treatise on Arts and Letters'" (*Bujiao Han yiwen zhi*): "In later ages books on law are very numerous, . . . Among the various masters one may pick out Shen [Buhai] and Han [Feizi] as discussing the doctrines of a School of Law; they are of the first rank, and are called the Way. Laws, edicts, and bureaucratic regulations that continue this tradition are of secondary rank and are called vessels."[168] Almost all realms of knowledge, including astronomy, geography, calendrical calculation, and so forth, embody this relationship between the Way and its vessels.[169]

2. The Unity of the Way and its Vessels and the Classification of Knowledge

After analyzing the theory that "the Six Classics are all history," we can further provide a summary and conclusion of Zhang Xuecheng's concept of what he called the unity of the Way and its vessels. The core content of this concept includes two aspects. First, knowledge, moral philosophy, and institutions are products of historical relations that "cannot be otherwise." People cannot understand moral philosophy or the Way from isolated personal experience of it, and also cannot reach an understanding of the "Way" through evidential analysis on the level of textual meaning. The "*Ru*" tradition is a part of history, and not the result of what Confucius as an individual wrote and transmitted, and the division and melding of relationships between governance and the Way are also historical products, and not something that individuals can accomplish.[170] If we ignore the changes in history and the evolution of institutional systems and just keep hold of glossing written characters, how could we understand the aims of the early Confucians? Second, the concept of the unity of the Way and its vessels is neither an ontological concept nor just a historical concept, but a theory about knowledge. On the one hand it provides specific principles for the treatment of ancient books and records, and on the other hand it also sets forth a new account of the taxonomy of knowledge. The core of the unity of the Way and its vessels lies in the differentiation between the Duke of Zhou and Confucius, and in the differentiated relationship between scholarship and government policies and institutions:

> Those who study Confucius should study what Confucius studied, and should not study what Confucius could not but have said. . . . To take what Confucius could not but have said and regard it, mistakenly, as his fundamental purport, is to accord empty praise to his moral expressions and to set them apart as a separate thing and to regard that which in its greatness is the warp and weft of the cosmos and in its refinement is the constancy of human relationships as no more than rough traces. Therefore, it is only in knowing that the Way and its vessels are one that one can speak of learning. For the fated course of the unity of the Way and its vessels, its beginnings must be sought in the differentiation between the Duke of Zhou and Confucius. This is the essential purport of ancient and modern learning.[171]

In Zhang's view, the books that later generations can see are just the remaining traces of the early *Ru* and the broken fragments of their history, except they have been recompiled by later authors into different categories. Because of this, if one cannot sort out their scholarship, rigorously test their origins, and clarify the basis of their sequence and structure, one will only be able to get lost among the subtle words and great meanings of these fragments. What is called illuminating the Way from the vessels is just to seek out threads from these books and records, and, through mutual authentication and classification, to restore the internal structure and integrity of the ancient systems and their historical relationships.

According to Zhang Xuecheng's view, since the time of the division between officials and teachers and between government and instruction, which was also the time when the various masters arose, the scholarship of later generations no longer formed a public transmission, but became the words of private scholars. So how can one find the "Way" implicit in these writings? The *Comprehensive Meaning of Bibliography* (*Jiaochou tongyi*) repeatedly uses the method of clarifying the Way from its vessels (*jiqi mingdao*) to explain the meaning of ancient books. In the field of vision of this methodology, ancient books and records are nothing other than the "traces" of the former kings and not the classical meanings themselves, and the classifications of knowledge result from dividing up the integral wholeness of history. Therefore, what he adhered to was a method of genealogy or archaeology, which was to regard the classification of written materials as a kind of discourse, and to engage in a genealogical analysis of its classifications and internal structure. In this there was a very important thread, which tracked changes in the taxonomy of knowledge: the pre-Qin "Six Arts" (*liu yi*) changed to become the "Seven Genres" (*qi lue*) of the Han, and the "Seven Genres" of the Han again changed to become the "Four Bibliographic Categories" (*Sibu*) of the Jin and later ages.

This classification not only regulated the way later generations understood knowledge, but also became a kind of imperially systematized knowledge. In 1772, the thirty-seventh year of the Qianlong reign, the Qing court ordered the collection of books and documents on a national scale, and the following year established the Four Treasuries Bureau, which undertook a critical compilation and classified index of every kind of book and record, an editorial effort that encompassed six billion characters, copied onto sixteen million pages over a period of fifteen years, and employed the services of more than 3,800 people. The editors of the "Complete Library in Four Treasuries"

(*Siku quanshu*) numbered more than 360, and apart from scholars like Ji Yun (1724–1805), it also included three imperial princes as well as imperial academicians and grand secretaries, and was truly a vast national project.[172] The flourishing of evidential learning and the status of the Four Treasuries officials were closely related to this. Zhang Xuecheng, in his exposition of the general purport of the unity of the Way and its vessels, regarded the classification of knowledge as a product of historical relationships and as an activity of knowledge, which not only shook the strict demarcation of classics (*jing*), histories (*shi*), masters (*zi*), and literary collections (*ji*), but also implied the overthrow of the Four Treasuries project, of the evidential learning that drove it, and of the theoretical premises of Song learning. In his historical studies he praised Liu Xin and Ban Gu, but he still upheld the viewpoint of the *Record of the Grand Historian's* "Biography of Confucius," holding that in the Three Dynasties official duties and scholarly occupations were unified, that the classics of *Change, Odes, Documents, Rites, Music,* and *Spring and Autumn Annals* were nothing other than the "Six Arts," and that the basis for this classification was the ancient system. Based on the metaphor of the Qin people "taking officials as their teachers," Zhang held that in the Three Dynasties, "rituals had the Minister of Sacrifices (*zong bo*) as their teacher, music had the Minister of Music (*si yue*) as its teacher, poetry had the Imperial Tutor (*tai shi*) as its teacher, documents had the Outer Scribe (*wai shi*) as their teacher, and the *Three Changes* and the *Spring and Autumn Annals* also just followed this pattern."[173] In using this archaeological approach to discuss classification systems like the Seven Genres (*qi lue*) and the Four Bibliographic Categories (*si bu*), these classifications are no longer a form of universal knowledge. Accordingly, what Zhang was concerned about was not the meaning of classification in bibliography, but whether classification itself could embody the structures of a society, whether classifications of knowledge could form a coherent relationship with institutional practices, and whether it was possible through classifications of knowledge to present the true meaning of the institutions of the former kings.

The "Seven Genres" (*Qi lue*) classification began with Liu Xin in the Han dynasty. His father, Liu Xiang, responding to an imperial summons, along with Ren Hong (responsible for military writings), Yin Xian (responsible for mathematical arts), and Li Zhuguo (responsible for mantic arts), took responsibility for separately compiling classics, commentaries, masters, and poetry, and for writing a general preface for each category.[174] Ruan Xiaoxu of Liang, in his "Preface to the Seven Records" (*Qilu xu*), says: "In former times Liu Xiang compiled writings and recorded them, discussed their intent and discerned their errors, then memorialized the emperor, and all of this is included in this book. At times he also collected other writings to record, and called them 'Differentiated Records' (*bie lu*), a designation that persists to this day."[175] Clearly, Liu Xiang's "Differentiated Records" category was meant to introduce and record compiled collections of many diverse types of writing. After Liu Xiang's death, Liu Xin ordered the collation of the Five Classics, collected a wide variety of writings on the Six Arts, and continued his father's work of collating and organizing a multitude of writings, dividing them into schools and distinguishing categories, and in the end completed the "Seven Genres" to sum up the threads of the hundred schools. The so-called "Seven Genres" were the compilation genre (*ji lue*), the Six Arts genre (*liu yi lue*), the Various Masters genre (*zhuzi lue*), the poetry genre (*shifu lue*), the military writings genre (*bingshu lue*), the mathematical arts genre (*shushu lue*), and the mantic arts (medicine and divination) genre (*fangji lue*). Among these "Seven Genres," apart from the "compilation genre," which served as a general summary of the other six, the remaining six broad classifications were no different from those of Liu Xiang's "Differentiated Records," except that Liu Xiang's "Classics and Commentaries" had become the "Six Arts."[176] In his "Liu Lineage" (*Zong Liu*), Zhang Xuecheng spoke highly of the contributions of the Lius, father and son, to bibliography, and held that they had provided a model of systematic classification for later generations of scholars of bibliography and the study of literary documents.[177] But more importantly, he believed that there must be a relationship of internal correspondence between classifications of knowledge and ancient systems, and that forms of writing themselves (such as private versus. public writings, writings versus compilations, elaboration versus transmitting without creating, etc.) must also express the distinguishing features of ancient systems. The advantage of the "Seven Genres" classifications was that they reflected a "deep understanding of the ancient Way of unifying officials and teachers, and enabled one to know the reasons why private teachers at first did not write or transmit anything."[178] In the "Seven Genres," the "Six Arts genre" (*Liu yi lue*) ranks first, and reflects the central thought of classical scholarship. Zhang Xuecheng's use of the viewpoint of knowledge classification to examine the Way of unification of officials and teachers, and the history of private teachers who did not write or transmit anything, gives a new account of the premises of classical learning from a different angle. Zhang says:

> In its narration of the Six Arts, followed in order by the various masters and the Hundred Schools, [Liu Xin's account] must be saying that the flow of any particular school would have emerged from the control in ancient times of some particular official, and then either flowed on to become some particular master's learning, or deviated to become some master's confusions. When it speaks of "the control . . . of some official," it means that the standard belongs entirely to the official, and that the official preserves the meaning of its writings. When it says that it "flows on to become the learning of some school," this means that the official has neglected his duty, so that there is transmission from master to disciple. When it speaks of "deviating to become some master's confusions," this is what Mencius analyzed and distinguished as [expressions that] "arising in the heart, harm the government," and "appearing in government, harm affairs" [*Mencius* 2A2]. For those who wish to approach the learning of "knowing words" [*zhi yan, Mencius* 2A2], it is clear that one should follow the Liu family's example in broadly seeking out the written records of ancient and modern times, taking note of their structure and sequence, and sorting out their branching development, in order to enfold the Six Arts and clearly reveal the great Way, and not just meet the needs of basic enumeration.[179]

The classificatory pedigree of knowledge itself is the result of historical evolution, and the relationship between knowledge and institutions is the central link in these changes.

Zhang admired the unity of knowledge and action in the institutions of the Three Dynasties of Antiquity, but whether in the realm of institutions or in the classification of knowledge, he had no intention of returning to ancient times. In his view, the evolution of knowledge and its classifications was entirely the result of changes in historical relationships, and the question was how to observe the true meaning of historical changes through changed knowledge classifications. He criticized the Four Categories (*sibu*) classification system not because the Four Categories classification had changed the

Six Arts or Seven Genres classifications, but because the Four Categories classification could not express the historical system or the tracks of its changes. The Four Categories classification arose during the turbulent time when Wei was overthrowing the Han, what the Four Categories classified was not accurate or precise, and "as to the intent of the authors, there was no discussion."[180] After this, Xie Lingyun in the Song dynasty implemented the *Four Categories Catalogue* (*Sibu mulu*), Wang Jian wrote a *Catalogue* (*Mulu*) and separately compiled the *Seven Treatises* (*Qizhi*), Wang Liang and Xie Fei of Qi re-created a *Four Categories Catalogue,* and Ren Fang and Yin Jun of Liang also made a *Four Categories Catalogue.* With the *History of the Sui's* "Treatise on Classical Documents" (*Jingji zhi,* actually a treatise in the *Five Dynasties History*), the four-part classification of classics, histories, masters, and literary collections (*jing, shi, zi, ji*), with the Daoist and Buddhist canons appended at the end, came to be definitively established, and from then on, the four-part classification system became the orthodox transmission and mainstream of ancient catalogues.[181]

Comparing the Seven Genres with the classifications of the Four Categories, the important differences are as follows: First, in antiquity there was no name for history. The Seven Genres did not list a history section, and it could not be distinguished as its own category; but according to the rigorous judgment of the Grand Scribe (*taishi gong,* i.e., Sima Qian), historical books could be classified alongside the *Spring and Autumn Annals.*[182] Second, the Seven Genres did not include a literary collections section (*jibu*), and the reason was that the ancients strictly adhered to specialized learning, forming either the Hundred Schools, or the Nine Streams, or Odes and Rhapsodies, unlike the collected writings of later men whose works are difficult to classify in distinct streams. Third, the Seven Genres included military writings, mantic techniques, and numerical arts as three sections that were ranked apart from the Various Masters, whereas in later ages these were all included in the masters category, for a more abbreviated treatment. From the "Seven Genres" to the "Four Categories," this change in the forms of knowledge classification was the result of changes in history and knowledge. Zhang Xuecheng's criticism of the "Four Categories" was not a criticism of this change, but a recognition that the classifications of the "Four Categories" were not as well able as those of the "Seven Genres" to fully reflect and embody the changes in institutions, knowledge, and society. He concluded that:

> The flow of the Seven Genres to become the Four Categories, like the flow of the [archaic] *zhuan* and *li* calligraphic styles to become the [more regularized] *xing* and *kai* scripts, was mandated by propensities of the times (*jie shi zhi suo burong yi zhe*) and not a matter of personal preference. That the history category (*shibu*) grew ever more crowded, and could not all be assigned to the *Spring and Autumn Annals* school, was the first reason why the Four Divisions could not return to the Seven Genres; that later generations no longer maintained a distinction between a School of Names and a Mohist School was a second reason; that literary collections flourished, and could not be defined within the nomenclature of the Hundred Schools and the Nine Streams, was a third reason; that the corpus of transcribed volumes was already neither traditional collectanea (*congshu*) nor classified reference books (*leishu*), was a fourth reason; that critical annotations on poetic writings both resembled and yet were not single-author collections (*bieji*), and resembled and yet were not multiauthor compilations (*zongji*), was a fifth reason. Whenever books existed only in ancient but not in modern times, or only in modern but not in ancient times, judging their characteristics was like comparing earth and sky. So how could one hold on to the completed methods of the Seven Genres to classify the writings of today? And yet when schools' methods are not clear, this is why the art of writing continuously declines; when classification methods are not precise, this is why scholarship becomes ever more scattered. By following the mature methods of the Four Categories one can discuss genres in order to come to full understanding of the reasons why in ancient times [the roles of] official and teacher were unified, and thus the ills of writing can to some extent be treated, and the main principles of the Seven Genres can also complement [the legacy of] the ancients.[183]

The Seven Genres emphasized rigorous examination of origins and clear differentiations in scholarship, and its classifications were based on the concept of specialized learning. The meaning of specialized learning, as reflected in the classifications of the Seven Genres or of the Four Categories, was also expressed in every specific instance of historical study. The meaning of "specialized" did not just refer to specialization of knowledge, but also referred to the history of the formation of knowledge, and specifically it referred to the historical meaning of the organization and form itself of books. In discussing his view that "private persons did not write or transmit," Zhang said:

> Since [the task of] ordering the great affairs [of All-under-Heaven] is broad and cannot be exhausted, the sages established government officials with differentiated responsibilities, and accordingly there were written characters to record this. Once there were officials, there were then normative standards (*fa*), and the standards were complete in the officials. Once there were normative standards, there were then writings (*shu*), and so the officials kept charge of these writings. Once there were writings there was then learning, and therefore teachers who specialized in this learning. Once there was learning there were professions, and therefore disciples who practiced these professions. Officials kept charge of the scholarly professions, all issued from one [source], and all the world was governed through the same writings; therefore, private persons did not write or transmit written texts (*wenzi*).[184]

The meaning and style of the Six Classics arose from the system of separate roles for scholars and officials, and this shows that the form itself of historical scholarship was the product of institutions. He further analyzed the relationship between the form of history and the political system:

> Distinguishing between the writings of different states originated with the *Discourses of the States* (*Guo yu*). In ancient times the states each had their own writings. Confucius wrote the *Spring and Autumn Annals,* and when the followers of Zixia sought out the precious books of a hundred states, I have not heard that anyone undertook to gather and unite them. Li Xunyan [1115–1184] said, "When Zuo was preparing his commentary on the *Spring and Autumn Annals,* he first collected writings from every state, and each state had its own way of speaking." Although this was an offhand remark, this was the first instance of attempting to unite [writings from] all the states in a single book. Unless there had been no separation between the "Discourses of Zhou" and the various states, what would it have meant for Confucius to have recorded the "Airs of the King" across many states? Or was it that when the *Odes* were lost he created

> the *Spring and Autumn Annals,* and when the *Documents* were lost he wrote the *Discourses of the States?*[185]

In this perspective, Zhang Xuecheng's questioning of the stylistic forms of historical writings was not an ordinary question of methodology, but an examination of the historical relations hidden within the forms of the living words of historical scholarship. For example, the struggle for hegemony among the various lords was an expression of the decline of the feudal order, while the establishment of local separatist domains arose within the order of administrative bureaucracy. But if one jumbles them together in a single discourse, and writes of them in a single history of hegemony (*ba shi*), this would clearly be to run counter to the fundamental historical relationships.[186] Here, the difference between enfeoffment (*fengjian*) and centralized administration (*junxian*) becomes an important support for understanding classifications in historical scholarship.

Zhang Xuecheng's historiography was a historical narrative of the development of the world and of knowledge, which explained how knowledge and institutions evolved into their current state by revealing the relationships between systemic historical change and the history of knowledge formation. Therefore, his concern was not only with the questions that occupied the *lixue* scholars on how to know (whether by investigating things or by investigating the heart, by reading books or by engaging in practice, by withdrawing in solitude or by entering the world, etc.), but even more to explain, from the internal interrelationships of institutions, knowledge, and morality, how they came to assume their present forms. These investigations into knowledge taxonomies gave rise to a series of methodological reflections. In Zhang Xuecheng's view, the essential point in classification and its methods lies in their suitability to the history of the institutions and their changes as expressed in historical writing, so as to achieve a "unity of knowledge and action" at this level. Accordingly, he did not believe in universally applicable methods. Methodology is a product of historical writing, and must change as the forms of historical writing evolve. For example, in ancient times there was no specialized study of literary norms (*yi li*), because when a book was complete the norm was already fully provided, just as in law when the writing is complete the law stands on its own. Another example is textual research (*kaoding zhi xue*), which in ancient times also did not exist. Zhang wrote:

> Specialized schools of learning honor knowing, acting, and hearing as all arising together. Where is there room for textual research? When officials lost control of teaching, the Hundred Schools arose in great numbers; in what was transmitted there was truth and falsehood, and among annotations some were right and some were wrong. When scholars arose to carry on their legacy, there had to be discriminations, in order to uphold a single truth. And since these discriminations could not be decided by empty words, evidence had to be adduced to support this and verify that, and so textual research emerged. This is what Sima Qian meant in saying "the scope of books is extremely broad, and not everything can be confirmed from the Six Arts." But where the ancients used textual research to complete their books, if later men rely on a single book to do textual research, this is to lose the transmission of solid learning.[187]

It is precisely because the classifications and methodologies of ancient knowledge were the product of historical relationships themselves, that if scholars of later ages wish to truly understand the meaning of classics and histories, it is necessary to link up every kind of stylistic norm and method, and thus arrive at an understanding of history, knowledge, and human cultural activities. This is the implication of "comprehensive meaning" (*tongyi*) in Zhang's histories of literature, culture, and bibliography.[188]

Zhang Xuecheng's examination of historical methods involves not only the "historical virtue" (*shi de*), "historical talent" (*shi cai*), and "historical knowledge" (*shi shi*) of historians as individuals, but also involves questions about history as an institution. No matter whether one chooses to write as an individual or under the control of official historians, historical writing is never a purely individual activity, because individualized writing styles themselves are determined by processes of social differentiation. Zhang Xuecheng crossed over genre-based standards of historiographical classification (such as annalistic versus biographical styles) to create a new distinction between "narrative composition" (*zhuanshu*) and "recording" (*jizhu*) (or "arranging," *bilei*) as two different kinds of history: the former referred to tracing historical events through the past and explaining their significance, while the latter referred to the collection, compilation, arrangement, and comparison of historical materials; the former were mostly the work of individual writers, whereas the latter were officially compiled. These two kinds of style each had their own structure and origin, and it was not that one was better or worse than the other. In "The Teaching of the *Book of Documents*" (*Shu jiao*), Zhang says, "In ancient and modern books, narrative composition wants to be round (*yuan*) and spiritual, while recording is square (*fang*) in order to be wise. For wisdom comes through storing away the past, but it is through the spiritual that the future is known."[189]

But Zhang Xuecheng's theory of "historical intentionality" (*shi yi*) clearly inclines toward a single historian's "narrative composition" and his historical knowledge, and seems to stray away from his viewpoint that "the Six Classics are all history" and that written books have emerged from the Six Arts.[190] Why is this so? We must look at this from two aspects: First, Zhang Xuecheng highly valued "historical meaning" (*shi yi*) in historical writing. What the so-called "historical meaning" issue marks out is an effort, in the context of the separation of officials from teachers and of government from instruction, and of the transformation of government institutions from enfeoffment to centralized administration, to seek out again the spirit of the unification of government and instruction and of officials and teachers, and to adapt it to the new historical conditions. Individual narrative composition and the style of expertise were formal expressions of the separation of officials from teachers and of government from instruction, but the significance of historical learning was that under the conditions of this fragmentation of the arts of the Way and branching divisions of literary form, it sought to get to the root and return to the source, and from amid the flow of historical change to search out the essential meaning of the Six Arts. Zhang Xuecheng's view of the form of narrative composition relied greatly on his understanding of the internal relationship between the formal structure of historical learning and the ceaselessly evolving social order. For example, the *Records of the Grand Historian* (*Shi ji*) and the *History of the Han* (*Han shu*) established the tradition of the biographical form (of historical writing), and set up the divisions of Basic Annals (*benji*), Tables (*biao*), Treatises (*zhi*), and Biographies (*liezhuan*). But in the thirteen official histories from the Eastern Han through the Sui there were only six treatises and not a single table. The nine dynastic histories completed since the Tang all included treatises, and seven of them had tables.[191] How to understand these relationships between the internal forms of historiography and history is an important question. Even if the historiographical forms of an earlier time were restored, they would not necessarily be able to express the essential meaning of these forms, because the implied meaning of a historiographical form takes shape from the interactions between historiography and the structure of society. Inheriting old-style structural forms in a changed social context does not guarantee the objectivity and significance of historical learning. Let us take a look at Zhang Xuecheng's discussion of historical methods:

> The reasons for the similarities and differences in historical writing before and after the Three Dynasties can be known. Before the Three Dynasties, recording (*jizhu*) had a defined method, and narrative composition (*zhuanshu*) had no fixed name. After the Three Dynasties, narrative composition did have a fixed name, and recording had no defined method.
>
> When the norms of the Zhou officials fell into decline, the *Documents* were lost; after the *Documents* were lost, the *Spring and Autumn Annals* were written, and there were no chapters for the words of the king. Thus, one may know the form of the *Spring and Autumn Annals*. What does it mean to say that when the norms of the Zhou officials fell into decline the *Documents* were lost? Since the ritual norms of the Zhou officials were detailed and dense, [the practice of] recording [court events] had a defined method, whereas composed narrations [of historical events] could have no fixed name. To express the detailed completeness [of the ritual order], there were those who oversaw the preparation of documents, so that when great and important matters were pointed out they were written down, in order to show the great essentials of the king's statecraft. . . . When the substance of officialdom was lost, and the [practice of] recording was no longer sufficient to fulfill the entirety [of its role], the *Spring and Autumn Annals* put words together to order events, and Zuo [Qiuming] could not but draw on anecdotes from the hundred officials, and precious books from the hundred states, to fill out the beginnings and ends of events, and it was circumstance that made it so. From Sima Qian and Ban Gu onwards, Zuo's legacy was extended and developed, so-called recording had no defined method, and narrative composition could not but have a fixed name. So it is said: when the traces of the kings ceased and the *Odes* were lost, one could see the *Spring and Autumn Annals*'s

> operations; when the norms of the Zhou officials fell into decline and the *Documents* were lost, one could see the *Spring and Autumn Annals*' substance.[192]

The difference between recording and narrative composition is not an ordinary methodological difference, but something created by the historical evolution of officials and teachers and of government and instruction; it is a historical difference. These two methods themselves do not differ in being greater or less important; the important matter is whether or not they can accommodate to historical change and clarify the great Way. Because of this, "change" (*bian*) is the key to this question. Zhang writes:

> By the Warring States era, the transformations of writing had been exhausted; in the Warring States there was specialized writing, and from the Warring States onward the forms of writing were complete, so that if one discusses writing in the Warring States, the causes of its rise and fall and prosperity and decline can all be known. People know that Warring States writing often gave rise to strange oddities that are split apart from the Way; but that their source comes from the Six Arts, people do not know. That the fundamentals of the writings of later generations were all prepared in the Warring States, people do not know; that their source mostly comes from instruction in the Odes [early works like those contained in the *Book of Odes*], still less do people know. Only after knowing that the fundamentals of writing were prepared in the Warring States, can one begin to discuss the writings of later ages; only after knowing that the various schools are grounded in the Six Arts, can one discuss the writings of the Warring States; only after knowing that Warring States writings came from instruction in the Odes, may one discuss the writings of the Six Arts; only if one can discuss the writings of the Six Arts can one leave writing and see the Way; only when one can leave writing and see the Way, can one participate in upholding the Way and break off the writings of the various schools.[193]

Zhang clearly believes that the selection of historiographical methods is not just related to individual interests and abilities, and that even more it is a kind of historical choice.

Second, the vast majority of the twenty-four standard histories were official compilations (the single exception was Ouyang Xiu's *New History of the Five Dynasties* [*Xin Wudai shi*]). Yang Liansheng summed up the last nine of the twenty-four histories, and extracted several major characteristics of these standard histories: First, the officially compiled standard histories were all the result of narrative composition or compilation by the following dynasty, or by an even later dynasty; second, the work of compiling the histories was undertaken by officially appointed specialized agencies composed of historians; third, these nine histories were all written in the biographical mode.[194] These three characteristics also had some methodological consequences for the officially compiled standard histories: official compilations of the previous dynasty's history at the same time displayed the orthodoxy of the current dynasty, and in their praise and blame were also subject to the influence of the current dynasty; officially compiled standard histories relied to a great extent on materials like the "Diaries of Activity and Repose" (*qiju zhu*) of the reigning emperors of the previous dynasty, and although the principle of traditional historians being responsible to later generations for strictly maintaining the factual accuracy of what they recorded was an important tradition in Chinese annalistic historiography, this did not prevent emperors and prime ministers from intervening in the process of their firsthand reporting, thus introducing taboo and concealment into the recording process. In the eighteenth century, Zhao Yi (1727–1814) once criticized the phenomenon of concealment in the official histories in his *Reading Notes on the Twenty-Two Histories* (*Ershi'er shi zha ji*), and in the Tang dynasty the famous historiographer Liu Zhiji (661–721) also set forth in a letter included in his *Comprehensive History* (*Shi tong*) a long list of faults and abuses in the officially compiled standard histories. Under this kind of contrast, the tradition of individual historical compilation as represented by Sima Qian stands out instead for its greater reliability. Zhang Xuecheng's emphasis on individually compiled history is intrinsically linked to the historiographical thinking described above.

Zhang Xuecheng's understanding of historical evolution left two seemingly opposite but actually complementary features in his historiography. On the one hand, he had high regard for specialized writing or "words of one school," opposed opening bureaus to write official histories, and had little interest in comparative compilations based on collecting multitudes of edited writings.[195] One the other hand, however, starting from the historical evolution from feudalism to centralized administration, he wanted to transform the public writings of the ancient historical scribes into the narrative composition of local gazetteers, and thus wanted local governments to establish specialized bureaus for the composition of local gazetteers ("Gazetteer Sections"). Scholars have always attached great importance to the differences between Zhang Xuecheng and people like Dai Zhen on the question of local gazetteers, that is, on whether local gazetteers should be considered as geography books or as an independent genre of historical study, but they have not paid much attention to what the connection might be between Zhang's emphasis on methods of individual narrative composition and his concern for publicly recorded local gazetteers.[196] In my view, these two different aspects are based on a single historical understanding: one takes account of the evolution in historiography that started from the separation of officials from teachers and of government from instruction in the Warring States period, the other is concerned with the evolution in the genre of historical recording that took place between the eras of the systems of enfeoffment and centralized administration, and both aspects are centered on the relationship between institutions and historical writing.

When Zhang Xuecheng emphasized that "local gazetteers are like national histories in ancient times, and at root are not strictly geographical,"[197] the crucial point was in the phrase "local gazetteers are like national histories in ancient times" (*fangzhi ru gu guoshi*). The transformation from national history to local gazetteer reflected the transformation from enfeoffment to centralized administration, but it is clear that, although they were compiled under the system of centralized administration, the content of the compilation of local gazetteers subtly brought in aspects and meanings of the system of enfeoffment. From the perspective of historiographical form, the narrative composition of local gazetteers can be traced back to collected biographies of local personages in the Wei-Jin period that Liu Zhiji referred to as "prefectural writings" (*junshu;* such as the *Biographies of Former Worthies of Runan* [*Runan xianxian zhuan*], *Biographies of Famous Elders of Xiangyang* [*Xiangyang qi jiu zhuan*], etc.), as well as to works like *Records of Luoyang* (*Luoyang ji*), *Records of Wu Commandery* (*Wujun ji*), *Han River Records* (*Hanshui ji*), *Records of Lushan* (*Lushan ji*), *Chronicles of Huayang* (*Huayang guozhi*), and *Buddhist Temples of Luoyang* (*Luoyang qielan ji*). The emergence of these prefectural books and writings about local people, scenery, and historic places was closely related to the feudal separatist situation and the practice of the Nine-Rank System in the Wei-Jin period. Local gazetteers were based on provinces and counties and were a product of the prefecture-and-county system, but the significance of the composition of local gazetteers was similar to the state histories of ancient times or to the Wei-Jin-period writings described above. Zhang's "Preface to the *Daming County Gazetteer*" (*Daming xianzhi* xu) says:

> The prefecture and county annals are the legacy of the historical officials of feudal times, yet today's gazetteer compilers mistakenly imitate the provincial and prefectural maps and charts of Tang and Song and lose [this legacy]. The outer histories of the *Officers of Zhou* "took the annals of the four directions," and the annotation says, "like the *Historical Records* (*Sheng*) of Jin, the *Taowu* of Chu, and the *Spring and Autumn Annals of Lu* [cf. *Mencius* 4b21—trans.]." Thus, in the history of a single state there was nothing omitted, and so it could be selected [for inclusion] in the history of a dynasty. When Confucius composed the *Spring and Autumn Annals,* he had to verify it with the precious books of a hundred states, in order to confirm its meaning. If it had just been a matter of books and charts, it would have been a specialized work of geography. . . . Comparing local gazetteers with maps and charts, their forms are completely different.[198]

Zhang Xuecheng compares the "history of a single state" (*yi guo zhi shi*) in the feudal era with local gazetteers in the era of prefectures and counties. Thus, he seeks to include biographies, institutions, and literary accounts within the scope of local gazetteers. This was to continue the intent of the *Spring and Autumn Annals,* and to restore the "history of the world" under the conditions of the system of centralized administration. If we try to summarize the methods, scope, and system of Zhang Xuecheng's historiography, we can say that in a historiographical dimension he reiterates Gu Yanwu's viewpoint, which is to imbue the spirit of enfeoffment within the system of centralized administration. Gu Yanwu's political outlook has a mixed character, and Zhang Xuecheng's historiography is also like this. He deeply believes that the Way resides in the propensities of spontaneity.

When we understand the true meaning of Zhang Xuecheng's "the Six Classics are all history" and "the Way and its vessels are one" on such a scale, the meaning of his critique and negation of the worldview of *lixue* and of the methodology of classical learning also becomes clear.[199] The concept that "the Way and its vessels are one" is a criticism of *lixue*'s dualism of *li* and *qi,* but seen from another angle it is also an affirmation of an implicit presupposition of *lixue,* which is that ever since the Three Dynasties, ritual and music have become separated from institutions, and that moral evaluations must therefore make use of new forms. Amid the complex changes of historical relationships, it is useless to adhere to the formalism of ritual systems, and it is also not enough to persist blindly in the critical examination of ancient institutions and of the ritual principles of classical texts. What is important is to penetrate the changes of ancient and modern times, to understand the world from the inside of living life practice, and from within "spontaneity" to understand "what cannot be otherwise." This is Zhang Xuecheng's view of history. "To speak immediately of the pattern from the affair" (*ji shi yan li*) and "to speak of the Way apart from affairs" (*li shi yan dao*): these two forms of knowledge are responses to the unity and to the separation of officials from teachers and of government from instruction, and cannot simply be seen as the choice of the sages or of later Confucians.

If ways of discussing the learning of the various masters and *lixue* were also the result of historical changes, then the principle of "speaking immediately of the pattern from the affair" is certainly not to discard the learning of the various masters and *lixue;* on the contrary, what it requires, starting from the basic belief that "the writings of later ages originated from the Six Arts," and casting off the views of particular schools, is from within the relationships of every kind of knowledge to have clear insight into institutions and their evolution.[200] "The Scholarship of Eastern Zhejiang," which discusses the relationship between Eastern Zhejiang studies of classics and history and the learning of Wang Yangming, definitely does not devalue and denounce the stream of Zhu Xi learning and the ideas of Western Zhejiang learning, but on the contrary puts aside the dispute between Zhu Xi and Lu Xiangshan to distinguish what was true or false in their respective historical relations and moral-philosophical logic.[201] In writings like "Zhu and Lu" and "After Writing the Essay on 'Zhu and Lu,'" he criticizes the attitudes of the evidential scholars toward Zhu and Lu for sectarian bias, but he also does not want to return to a *lixue* standpoint, and holds that the theoretical form of the views of Zhu and Lu was the product of specifically determined historical conditions. In Zhang Xuecheng's view, the philology of Fu Qian (206 BCE–8 CE) and Zheng Xuan, the rhetoric of Han Yu and Ouyang Xiu, and the moral philosophy of Zhou Dunyi and the Cheng brothers were all prone to sectarian prejudice and turbulent confusion. In reality they were all within the scope of the Way, but in taking up the role of worldly scholars they each flaunted their insights and defamed each other, in every case because they had lost their ability to know the future and preserve the past. This was a historical standpoint, and one that regarded scholarly evolution as a spontaneous propensity:

> Heaven is an integrated whole and has no name,. . . . but if it must be named, it could be defined as a tendency (*quxiang*). Later men, without examining its causes, have accepted the name, . . . and, rushing in, have lost their bearings [lit: entered confusedly as masters and left as slaves]. The mutual insults of Han and Song learning, the mutual defaming of philology and rhetoric, and incessant wrangling over the moral nature are all a matter of knowing how things are but not why they are so (*zhi qi ran er bu zhi qi suoyi ran ye*). The work of learning is for statecraft, for example in calendrical studies, where one exhausts human skill in seeking to accord with the operations of Heaven. When the Duke of Zhou inherited the legacy of kings Wen and Wu and himself became prime minister, he instituted ritual and music as the constitution of the age. Confucius was born in an age of decline, had virtue but not position, and therefore transmitted but did not create, in order to illuminate the Way of the former kings. Mencius lived in an age of unbridled criticism, and so distinguished Yang from Mo, in order to honor the legacy of Confucius. Han Yu lived in a time when Buddhism and Daoism flourished, and therefore expounded the Way of the sages, in order to correct the world's scholarship. Cheng and Zhu lived in a time of superficial learning and neglect of fundamentals, and so made clear distinctions concerning the nature and Principle, to save men's hearts from prevailing customs. Their work and merits were not the same, but all [were finding a way] to speak of statecraft. Thus, the work of learning is to open up and refute the prevailing mood. Where the prevailing mood is not open, the work of

> scholarship can open it; when the prevailing mood has become worn and corrupt, the work of scholarship can repair it. Human hearts and customs cannot last for a long time without corruption. . . . Unless one follows [these tendencies] out to their extremes to reflect on them, there would be no way to reach their appropriate correctness.[202]

From Zhang Xuecheng's analysis of scholarly evolution we see once again Dai Zhen's proposition on the distinction between "spontaneity" and "what must be so," and see that kind of connection between Zhuangzi's theory of spontaneity and Xunzi's discussions of ritual norms. The proposition that "the Six Classics are all history" returns classical learning to historical learning, and a return to historical learning also means a return to the practice of statecraft.

Zhang's concept of strictly preserving the unity of the Way and its vessels establishes an internal connection between Zhuangzi's theory of spontaneity and the theory of ritual norms. What these two have in common resides in the concept of "public" (*gong*), and an important connecting point is their answer to the following question: Is ritual an external standard or a spontaneous inner order? Zhang Xuecheng regards ritual as an internal order, but "internal" here does not refer to an a priori substance of humans or things, but rather means that ritual is intrinsically present in the midst of changes in historical relationships. The proposition of the "unity of the Way and its vessels" requires that scholars seek the Way from amid institutions and actual practice, and there is a close relationship between the concept of "vessels" and the institutions and ritual norms that were the focus of attention for Qing scholarship. These are all typical concerns of Confucian learning. From within the view that "the Six Classics are all history," institutional systems and prevailing trends in scholarship are not the meticulous product of the sagely wisdom of upright men, but are the result of spontaneous tendencies; the Way has spontaneity, learning has its inevitability, and different forms of knowledge all have their reasonableness.[203] Institutional systems and the practice of statecraft are not the accomplishments of private persons, but the propensity of spontaneous developments; for the Six Arts and the classics and commentaries, the authors' names are mostly unknown, and coming down to what later scholars have recorded of the seventy masters, there has been no way to sort out through evidential scholarship whose hand they are from.

This is a "public" state of affairs. "The reason why the words of the ancients are public is that they are never conceited about their diction, or privately seize upon it as something that belongs to them. Their aspiration is set upon the Way, their words are to clarify their aspiration, and their writings are to fulfill their words."[204] Under the concept that "words are public" (*yan gong*), the orthodox and the heterodox, the various masters, the Hundred Schools, and the popular multitudes of ordinary people all have the right to speak. Zhang writes:

> From the *Book of Changes* for singularity and the *Book of Odes* for correctness, the *Book of Rites* for integrity and the *Record of Music* for gentleness, to the *Zuo Commentary* for exaggeration and the *Zhuangzi* for recklessness, to Qu Yuan's rhapsodies for profundity and to the *Records of the Grand Historian* for succinct purity, there is nothing that is not encompassed; from the nature and destiny of Heaven and man, to the broad understanding of economic management, to Confucian prolixity and Mohist thrift, to the School of Names ability in analysis, or Legalist depth in scholarship, nothing is missing.[205]

Even including those unorthodox writings on astronomy, mantic arts, and military affairs, all can be called classics,[206] and from here the concept of a "classic" becomes a category that can be used at will.[207]

Zhang Xuecheng not only did not equate a historical view of the unity of the Way and its vessels with the political reality of the unity of governance and the Way, but he also did not use the concepts of the unity of principle and ritual and the unity of the Way and its vessels simply to negate the theories of the various masters and the Cheng-Zhu and Lu-Wang traditions. The key here is that his historiography firmly grasps the fundamental question that Confucian learning must answer, which is: What is the basis for morality, or how can a moral act be constituted? For Zhang Xuecheng, the concept of historical learning (*shixue*) was not what moderns call the study of history (*lishi xue*), but was a concept concerned with morality: that moral practice and moral meaning reside only in actual historical relationships and in the practice of statecraft, and that moral practice and historical change, moral evaluation and practical statecraft, are one and the same thing.[208] The arguments that the Six Classics are all history, that the Way and its vessels form one body, that the Way can be understood directly from its vessels, and that knowing and acting are one, can be seen as different expressions of the same proposition. From a local point of view, as the historical concept that the Way and its vessels are one, it is no longer equivalent to the concept of the unity of officials and teachers, of government and instruction, and of government and the Way, for what it actually establishes is a methodological vision for understanding the relationship between "classics and history." In this vision, relationships among officials and teachers, government and instruction, and governance and the Way are endlessly changing, but these changes themselves precisely explain why the correct meaning of the Way of the former kings can be understood only by adhering to the concept of the unity of the Way with its vessels: it does not exist in classical books, but in our own practice of statecraft. Accordingly, from a general perspective, the fundamental question to be resolved by these propositions is: What finally is the relationship between practice, knowledge, and institutions? Here I can use a few words to summarize the internal logic of the propositions that "the Six Classics are all history" and "the Way and its vessels are one body": knowledge must be integrated with practice, practice always exists within the context of institutional practices, and institutions also always exist within the realm of spontaneous processes; knowledge is the understanding of spontaneous process, and the process of understanding is also a part of the realm of spontaneous process. Why is it, then, that the form of knowledge must transcend the patterns of *lixue* and of classical learning, and adopt the form of historical learning? It is because the world is both a spontaneous process of integration and a result of the interplay of various people, forces, and rules. The spontaneous process encompasses divisions and combinations that "must be so" (like the split between officials and teachers, or government and instruction), and thus the form of understanding of this spontaneous process must encompass the concept of evolutionary development or change. It is just this concept that serves to open up a difference between history and *lixue* or classical learning, but the questions they answer are entirely the same. The core issue here is that Zhang Xuecheng values connections and expositions on meanings and principles (*yili*), but this historical concept that he puts forward is also a moral concept, which completely negates the possibility of forming moral evaluations through individual or other metaphysical concepts. From different aspects, Dai Zhen and Zhang Xuecheng both associate morality with a concept of spontaneity, but this concept of spontaneity is neither Zhuangzi's form of spontaneity, nor is it Xunzi's form of ritual governance, but something that transcends and synthesizes them, which is internal both to systems of ritual and music and to the spontaneity of historical evolution and change. Systems of ritual and music are the spontaneous result of historical evolution, and so are also internal to the fundamental circumstances and norms of human society.

Synthesizing the above account, what conclusions can we draw from Zhang Xuecheng's critique and summing-up of *lixue* and classical learning? First of all, *lixue,* classical learning, and history were all different forms of response to the same question, namely, What is the foundation or root of morality, and how can we reach the moral realm? *Lixue* scholars tried to answer this question within the framework of ontology or cosmology, while classicist scholars believed it was necessary to return to the teachings handed down by early Confucian scholars. Zhang Xuecheng held that these two approaches both had problems, because they forgot that moral behavior exists in a structure of practice, and that this structure of practice depends on continuously changing institutions. Accordingly, practice is a spontaneous process, and this spontaneous process is also expressed in the form of institutions and their evolution. In this sense, Zhang Xuecheng was closer than the classicist scholars to those who established the premises of classical learning. Secondly, for scholars from Gu Yanwu to Zhang Xuecheng, their understanding of moral behavior constituted a movement of criticizing *lixue;* they were all trying to rescue the moral practice of *lixue* (and of *xinxue,* the School of Mind) from metaphysical concepts, and to reintegrate it within the framework of institutional practice. But what was the meaning of this institutional framework? It was not simply understood according to the tenets of the early Confucians, nor was it implemented based on current actual institutions; because so-called institutions are the spontaneous result of human behavior, they are imbued with an elastic order that continually changes in pace with spontaneous processes. Therefore, institutions are part of the spontaneous process of history, and not the product of any intentional plan. Institutions are a kind of evolutionary, historical, spontaneous order. The moral view of Gu Yanwu, Huang Zongxi, Dai Zhen, and Zhang Xuecheng was a classicist moral view. They all rejected the moral concept of pure self-discipline, that is, a moral concept that constructed the self or Heavenly

Principle as the basis of morality. The object of their critique was of course not the modern moral view, but the *lixue* concept of Heavenly Principle. But from this critique, do we not see a more direct connection between the *lixue* worldview and the modern worldview? Modernists regard the formation of self-concepts as a breaking away from external authority (such as religious law, natural teleology, or hierarchical systems), but as far as these Confucians are concerned, institutions of ritual and music are not any kind of external authority, but an order that lies within our actions. This order is a spontaneous process, and our knowledge and actions with regard to this process, and even the form of our knowledge, are also a part of this spontaneous process, and through the form of "inevitability" at the level of knowledge they present the texture of spontaneous process

This is the unity of knowledge and action; this is the history of reflection becoming ethics and politics; and this is the theory of practice that emerges in the form of history.

CHAPTER 6

Inner and Outer (1)

The Concept of Ritual China and Empire

Translated by ANNE HENOCHOWICZ *and* JOHN EWELL

> The central states (*Zhongguo*) are also the new peripheral tribes (*Yi Di*).
>
> —LIU FENGLU, "Preface to *Tables of the Inclusion and Exclusion of Qin, Chu, and Wu*" (*Qin Chu Wu jinchu biao xu*)

I. Ritual, Law, and Classical Learning

1. The "Internal Horizon" of a Shifting World View

Gu Yanwu (1613–1682) "analyzed the characters and knew the sound" (*kaowen zhiyin*), interrogating the development of rites and music, customs, and institutions; Dai Zhen rejected Song Neo-Confucianism (*lixue*) and returned to the Han, thoroughly understood the institutional context of names and things, and became entangled between Mencius and Xunzi; Zhang Xuecheng made an innovative interpretation of the concept that "the *Dao* and its vessels and affairs are unitary" (*Dao qi yiti*) to prove that "the Six Classics are all histories" (*liu jing jie shi*). Their scholarly approaches were each different, but for all of them tensions arose between their restorationist discourses on rituals and institutions (*fugu de lizhilun*), their precise methods of textual research, and their concepts of "transformation" (*bian*), "expediency" (*quan*), and "spontaneous propensity" (*ziran zhi shi*). This is a paradoxical method, one that merges the orthodoxy of returning to antiquity (*fu gu*) with "statecraft and practical concerns" (*jingshi zhiyong*). What presuppositions did this aspect of thought provide to support the sudden rise of New Text classical studies (*jinwen jingxue*) in the late Qianlong period? (Zhuang Cunyu's turn to Gongyang scholarship occurred after 1780.)

The New Text classical studies of the late Qing began during the Qianlong-Jiaqing era in the Changzhou school of thought, led first by Zhuang Cunyu (1719–1788) and Kong Guangsen (1751–1786), then by Liu Fenglu (1776–1829) and Song Xiangfeng (1779–1860), and finally by Gong Zizhen (1792–1841) and Wei Yuan (1794–1857). Centered on the Gongyang commentary on the *Spring and Autumn Annals (Chunqiu Gongyang zhuan)*, they reinterpreted the classics from a New Text standpoint, and with this responded to real-world challenges. The Zhuang line of thought did not stand out at the time, and as a politician Zhuang Cunyu was not particularly interested in reform. Yet the Qing tradition of New Text studies that he forged was carried forward by Liu Fenglu, and in the hands of Gong Zizhen and Wei Yuan became the intellectual wellspring for political observation and analysis, and later the scholastic sensation of the late-Qing reform period. Inquiry into ritual, law, and history by Qing-era New Text scholars was closely linked to interethnic relations within the multiethnic empire, the basic principles and internal contradictions of social organization, the ever-shifting internal and external conflicts faced by the Qing empire, and so on. Beginning in the mid-Qing, figures such as Zhuang Cunyu, Liu Fenglu, Wei Yuan, and Gong Zizhen, within such categories as Yi-Xia (foreign and Chinese), inner-outer (*nei wai*, or within and without), the Three Sequences (*santong*), and the Three Ages (*sanshi*), ceaselessly investigated the issue of dynastic legitimacy, and rebuilt their understanding of "China" on the foundation of rites and law. From the horizon of classical learning, New Text scholars developed a series of ritual and legal concepts for managing the inner and outer relations of the imperial court, providing the theoretical prerequisites and horizon of thought for a new historical praxis—that of political reform under the conditions of the era of imperialism. In this sense, the New Text studies movement that began in the mid-Qing was a study of political legitimacy through classical learning, a theory of political practice, and the construction of a view of history and the world, suited to the dynastic system, that encompassed historical change and continuous improvement.

What enabled New Text classical studies to become a fundamental framework, embracing the whole range of intellectual and political theories, during the late Qing? It was its fiercely political nature, its constant interrogation of the historical basis and ethical conditions of the Qing system of Grand Unification, its sensitivity to historical change, and its nimble scholarship. There is a methodological problem inherent in studying the transformation of late-Qing thought from the perspective of New Text classical studies, namely that the meaning of late-Qing thought and the trajectory of its changes are fully visible only when observed within the horizon of classical learning. For example, Gongyang scholarship granted legitimacy to the modern scientific worldview, but could not itself have produced this new cosmology and worldview. This historical relationship facilitated change within New Text classical studies, but it had to overcome its own historical limitations in order to become an inclusive theory. In the end, the modern scientific worldview surmounted the framework of Gongyang scholarship to become the dominant system of knowledge and belief. To take another example, late-Qing Gongyang scholarship understood the expansion of the European capitalist state and its attendant concept of sovereignty within the framework of "inner-outer," but it dealt with inner-outer relations in a fundamentally different way from the European colonial practices of sovereignty and international law. New knowledge and institutions establish their dominance only through political, economic, and military hegemony. How, then, did this process alter and deconstruct the worldview of New Text classical studies, and how did it facilitate the transformation of its internal horizon? If we abstract the issues of sovereignty, ethnic relations, law, and rites away from the horizon of classical learning, we have no way of understanding those subtle historical and ethical pieces that comprised Qing-era political legitimacy, nor how the new conception of inner-outer relations supplanted and reconstituted its preceding form, yet was simultaneously constrained by the latter under the new historical conditions.

The "internal horizon" of New Text classical studies was not rigid. It encompassed the historical transformation of its own horizon, as well as the interactive relationship between this horizon and the political, economic, and military conflicts that facilitated its transformation. Wei Yuan, Gong Zizhen, Kang Youwei, and Liang Qichao put New Text classical studies to use in political praxis and social critique. Their contributions were not limited to the mere scholarly refinement of evidential learning. Through their efforts, Western knowledge—political, philosophical, economic, and especially scientific—was gradually absorbed into Gongyang scholarship. Thus, Gongyang historical theory melded with Western political thought and positivist scientific cosmology, forming an all-encompassing worldview. In this sense, the rise and development of New Text classical studies was a response to complex social and political problems, and cannot simply be observed from the perspective of the history of the discipline. We cannot avoid these questions: What is the relationship of Gongyang scholarship to the modern concepts of history, political theory, and law? And as a theory of history and as legal thought, why did Gongyang scholarship require a set of integrated, monistic worldviews as its foundation?

Neither applying classical learning to practical concerns nor determining the authenticity of classical texts through evidential learning was an independent invention of New Text classical studies. Since the beginning of the Qing, classical learning included an intrinsic drive to investigate institutions, rites and music, and historical change through exegesis and evidential learning. Even in the Qianlong-Jiaqing era, the likes of Dai Zhen and Zhang Xuecheng did not lose their sensitivity toward social issues, or their interest in applying classical learning to practical concerns. They clearly understood the predicament of Qianlong-Jiaqing evidential learning, and so forged a new path within Qianlong-Jiaqing scholarship. In this sense, the attitude of so-called evidential learning for the sake of evidential learning cannot describe all scholars of classical literature. The Zhuang Cunyu–Liu Fenglu and the Dai Zhen–Zhang Xuecheng schools of thought were born in the same era. If the Zhuang Cunyu–Liu Fenglu school had a response to the social crises of the Qianlong-Jiaqing period, wouldn't the Dai Zhen–Zhang Xuecheng school as well? New Text studies was not only a reaction to Qianlong-Jiaqing evidential scholarship, but also a response to the early-Qing scholars' principle of application of classical learning to practical concerns (and the elements of change incubated within Qianlong-Jiaqing scholarship); their relationship is extremely complex. If we demarcate Old and New Text studies merely as "ascertaining great principles from subtle words" (*weiyan dayi*) versus exegesis and evidential learning, and the application of classical learning to practical concerns versus learning for learning's sake, we will never find clarity.

2. New Text Studies and Qianlong-Jiaqing Scholarship

Accounts of the principal differences between the Old Text and New Text versions of the classics have always varied. Among these accounts, the earliest originates from the analysis of their textual differences in the *History of the Former Han's* "Bibliography of Arts and Letters" *(Han shu: Yiwen zhi),* and from the debate on whether the materials that, according to the *History of the Former Han* "Biography of Liu Xin" *(Hanshu: Liu Xin zhuan),* had been "obtained" by King Gong of Lu, who found them "in the ruined wall" of the former dwelling of Confucius (*de guwen yu huaibi zhi zhong*)—and that had later been amplified to become ancient-script versions of classics like the *Rites of Zhou (Zhou li),* the Zuo commentary on the *Spring and Autumn Annals (Zuo zhuan),* and the pre-Qin-script version of the *Book of Documents (Shang shu)*—had actually been forged in the Han period by Liu Xin.[1] Gong Zizhen's *Questions and Answers on the Great Declaration: Introduction to Names and Realities in the New Text and Old Text Writings of the Han Dynasty (Da shi dawen: zonglun Handai jinwen guwen mingshi),* widely influential during the Qing era, sets forth from this point. The modern script (*jinwen*) was the official script of the Han dynasty, while the ancient script (*guwen*) predated the Qin dynasty. The New Text school held that texts written in the ancient script were forged, while the Old Text school more or less took the opposing view. From this emerged the dispute as to whether scholarship of the classics should pursue "ascertaining great principles from subtle words" (New Text), or textual research (*kaogu*). Qianlong-Jiaqing evidential learning stressed the evidential learning (*kaozheng*) of texts, determining the age and authenticity of the Confucian classics from the perspective of the written word. In contrast, New Text studies emphasized oral transmission, holding that the implicit meaning of the *Spring and Autumn Annals* would be impossible to even glimpse without the knowledge that had been passed down orally from teacher to student. In this sense, New Text studies held that sound (oral transmission) embodies the intent of the sages more so than does writing (textual transmission).[2]

Yet even this distinction was not absolute. Early studies of the classics, in particular Gu Yanwu's *Five Books on Phonology* (*Yinxue wu shu*), were classic texts of Qing evidential learning. Gu attempted to find the true meaning of Zhou customs, laws, and institutions through the study of sound. Sound was extremely important to evidential learning. From the perspective of New Text studies, while their adherents emphasized the spoken word, they did not therefore abandon the evidential learning of the written word. Kang Youwei said, "Although the *Shuowen* [dictionary] contains forgeries and alterations, it remains the repository of ancient and modern writing, and scholars must read it to be truly literate," recommending that students take seriously Duan Yucai's (1735–1815) and Wang Mingsheng's (1722–1797) exegeses of written characters as complements to their study of the rhyming dictionaries *Erya* and *Guangyun*.[3] The central role of classical learning was to recover the laws and institutions of the Sage-Kings, the customs of the Three Dynasties of Antiquity, and the principles of righteousness of the sages, which had been concealed by time and history, superfluous rhetoric, and omission from the written record. The New and Old Text schools diverged widely on such questions as what constituted the orthodox Confucian lineage (paying allegiance either to the Duke of Zhou or to Confucius), but it was precisely these arguments that illuminate the shared Confucian orientation of "orthodoxy" of the two schools of thought. In the Qing linguistic context, disagreement about orthodoxy gets to the root of tradition: is it ethnic, geographic, or ritual?

The differences between New Text and Old Text studies during the Qing touch on complex questions of scholarly history, as well as broad political issues. These connections and divergences cannot be properly elucidated by simply examining the history of the disciplines and expounding on their political implications. We must therefore explain the relationship between New Text and Old Text studies within a broad historical and theoretical horizon. Evidential learning was the mainstream of Qianlong-Jiaqing scholarship, and its strict methodology and disciplinary standards forced New Text studies to turn frequently to textual criticism in its bid to challenge the dominance of the former. In this sense, the antagonistic relationship between New Text studies and Qianlong-Jiaqing evidential learning was shaped gradually through historical change. Dong Shixi (1782–1831) and Wei Yuan (1794–1857) arrived independently at the same conclusion in their respective prefaces to the work of Zhuang Cunyu, one emphasizing New Text studies as "the point of convergence of classical scholarship in the Qianlong period,"[4] and the other asserting that "much of what is true Han learning is to be found in Zhuang's work."[5] By insisting on the orthodox methodology of *Hanxue* (Han studies) to explain the confrontational approach of New Text studies, they in fact revealed the marginality of the New Text school. This situation would not truly change until the apogee of New Text studies during the late Qing.

The Qianlong-Jiaqing-era fields of Old Text and New Text were not the fierce rivals that later generations of scholars have portrayed them to be. In actuality, Qianlong-Jiaqing scholars drew from a variety of sources, and the intersection of Old Text and New Text disciplines is found throughout their work. From the perspective of New Text studies, the Zhuang Cunyu–Liu Fenglu school embodied many of the essential elements of evidential learning. In *Rectification of Terms in the Spring and Autumn Annals* (*Chunqiu zheng ci*), Zhuang Cunyu carries on the tradition of *Spring and Autumn* studies of the late-Yuan / early-Ming scholar Zhao Pang of Xiuning (1319–1369) to ascertain profound meanings from the subtle words of the *Spring and Autumn Annals* and also draws extensively from Dong Zhongshu's *Luxuriant Dew of the Spring and Autumn Annals* (*Chunqiu fanlu*). Yet Gongyang scholarship occupies just a fraction of his scholarship: *Posthumous Papers of Weijing Studio* (*Weijing zhai yishu*) draws from both Han- and Song-era studies, without distinguishing between Old and New or adhering to schools, touching in turn on the *Book of Changes*, the *Spring and Autumn*, the *Book of Documents*, the *Book of Odes*, the *Officers of Zhou* (*Zhou guan*, an early title for the *Rites of Zhou*), and the Four Books. Of these, *Records of the Officers of Zhou* (*Zhou guan ji*), *Zhou guan shuo (Discourse on the Officers of Zhou)*, and *Discourse on the Mao Commentaries to the Odes* (*Mao shi shuo*) fall chiefly within the domain of Old Text studies.[6] In *Principles of the Gongyang Commentary on the Spring and Autumn* (*Chunqiu Gongyang tongyi*), Kong Guangsen does not base his argument on He Xiu (129–182 CE), but rather draws on Gongyang thought through the Old Text unadorned learning (*puxue*) approach to textual analysis. Later scholars judged him fairly when they said, "He was adept at phonology and philology, but not so strong in classical scholarship." Zhuang Cunyu's use of the *Rites of Zhou* to supplement the insufficiencies of the Gongyang, and Kong Guangsen's use of Mencius to clarify the meaning of Gongyang, both prove that the doctrine was not rigid.[7] Liu Fenglu did bring into play He Xiu's "three branches and nine intentions" and open up the Gongyang emphasis on school methods, but this change in direction coincided exactly with the tradition of school methods in Qing-era classical learning. In *Collected New and Old Text Commentaries on the Book of Documents* (*Shang shu jinguwen jijie*), which he wrote "in order to fulfill the unfulfilled ambition of my maternal uncle," he lays out five guiding principles for reading his book, the first of which is to rectify characters, examine their sounds, demarcate sentences, and recognize similarities and differences. Every move comes from the Qianlong-Jiaqing evidential learning playbook.[8] Qing New Text studies stressed the application of classical learning to practical concerns, and were not as strict about school methods as the Qianlong-Jiaqing scholars. In "Assessment of the School Methods of New and Old Text Classics Masters of the Former and Later Han" (*Liang Han jingshi jinguwen jiafa kaoxu*), Wei Yuan attempted to find the roots of statecraft (*jingshi*) in historical change.

From exegesis and phonology to decrees and institutions, from decrees and institutions to subtle words and profound meanings (*weiyan dayi*), this path of "returning to antiquity" took Western Han New Text studies to be the final stage and goal of evidential learning and historical studies.[9] As the aforementioned examples illustrate, before Liao Ping differentiated Old and New Text studies by comparing the "Royal Regulations" (*Wang zhi*) and the *Rites of Zhou* in his 1886 (twelfth reign year of Guangxu) work, *A Study of the New Text and Old Text Schools,* the distinction was not so clear. (Liao took "Royal Regulations" to have been the regulations of the Four Dynasties of Yu, Xia, Yin, and Zhou, and the *Rites of Zhou* to be those of the Zhou dynasty.)[10] In the late Qing, before New Text scholars such as Kang Youwei and Liang Qichao and Old Text scholars like Zhang Taiyan started to attack each other, the New Text and Old Text schools did not form into neatly opposed camps of Qing classical learning. New and Old Text studies not only are distinguished by scholarly lineage, but are also the product of developments in Qing thought.

From the perspective of evidential learning, Dai Zhen and Zhang Xuecheng both took great interest in the study of moral philosophy or expositions on meanings and principles (*yili zhi xue*). Before them, Yan Ruoqu spent over thirty years on his eight-volume work *Inquiry into the Authenticity of the Ancient-Script Version of the Book of Documents* (*Shang shu guwen shuzheng*), asserting, based on numerous and complex evidential investigations of the *Book of Documents,* that its twenty-five ancient-script (*guwen*) chapters were forgeries. Afterward, Hui Dong quoted liberally from Yan in his two-volume *Investigation of Ancient-Script Book of Documents* (*Guwen Shang shu kao*), but concluded that although the twenty-four chapters handed down by Zheng Xuan (127–200 CE) were the genuine ancient texts found in the walls of Confucius's home, the twenty-five chapters unearthed later in the Eastern Jin did not conform with the *History of the Former Han*, and therefore could be classified as forgeries. This trend in Han studies of doubting the authenticity of classical texts provides a historical clue to the wave of skepticism that swept through New Text studies. Hui Dong's work emphasized the Confucian mysticism of the Han dynasty. His return to the Han may be seen as the forerunner to New Text studies.[11] The Zhuang Cunyu–Liu Fenglu school and Hui Dong's scholarship have a complicated historical relationship. In the fifth reign year of Jiaqing (1800), Liu Fenglu was selected to take the civil service examination in the Qing capital, where he consulted Zhang Huiyan (1761–1802) on Yu Fan's (164–233 CE) *Book of Changes* and Zheng Xuan's (127–200 CE) *Three Rites*. Liu's school method approach to the *Changes* in *Five Tellings of the Book of Changes by Yu Fan* (*Yi Yushi wu shuxu*) shows the clear influence of Zhang Huiyan. In turn, Zhang Huiyan's scholarship was the product of Hui's school methods. In "Introduction to *Explanatory Specimens from the Gongyang Commentary on the Spring and Autumn Annals*" (*Chunqiu Gongyang shili xu*), Liu links the rise of Gongyang scholarship to the shift in academic attitudes brought about by the herculean project of *The Emperor's Four Treasuries* (*Siku Quanshu*). He also considers New Text studies to be an organic part of Qianlong-Jiaqing scholarship:

> When the Qing had ruled the world for a hundred years they opened the road of submitting books, recruited literary scholars, and gave first importance to citations from the Six Classics. As a result, people were ashamed of unfounded interpolations (*xiangbi xuzao*) and competed in holding to the school methods of the Han masters. Outstanding examples were studies by Hui Dong of Yuanhe and Zhang Huiyan of Wujin on the *Book of Changes*, and by Cheng Yaotian of Huizhou [1725–1814] on the *Rites*. Salaried teaching of the classics that valued the writings of Dong Zhongshu and He Yan also fit this pattern.[12]

In this sense, New Text and Old Text studies were born of the same intellectual atmosphere. In fact, certain veins of thought in Hui Dong and Dai Zhen scholarship were harbingers of the Changzhou school.

3. The *Spring and Autumn Annals* in Qing Classical Learning

The relationship between New Text classical studies and early-Qing and Qianlong-Jiaqing evidential learning is intricate and complex, and cannot simply be explained by distinguishing similarities and differences between individual scholarly lineages and methodologies. Since study of the Gongyang tradition of the *Spring and Autumn Annals* was at the heart of New Text scholarship, it had to rank the *Spring and Autumn* at the top of the Six Classics. Kang Youwei said of the *Luxuriant Dew of the Spring and Autumn Annals*, "The *Odes, Documents, Rites,* and *Music* cannot be compared to the *Spring and Autumn,* as the *Odes, Documents, Rites,* and *Music* are brief and lacking in detail."[13] Among the Thirteen Classics that were recognized in the Qing, He Xiu's *Annotated Gongyang Spring and Autumn (Chunqiu Gongyang jiegu)* was the only New Text commentary. Thus, not only was the *Gongyang Spring and Autumn* the starting point of Qing New Text scholarship, but their different interpretations of the *Spring and Autumn* constituted the most important characteristic dividing Old and New Text studies.[14] Old Text studies treated the *Spring and Autumn* as history, emphasizing the role of the Zuo commentary; while New Text studies treated the *Spring and Autumn* as a book of governance, focusing on analysis of the Gongyang and Guliang commentaries. Kang Youwei firmly believed the *Spring and Autumn* to be Confucius's "subtle words and profound meanings" (*weiyan dayi*) for the purpose of institutional reform, and the Six Classics to be the laws and procedures as organized by Confucius.[15] In terms of content, there are extreme differences between the New Text explication of the intent of the *Spring and Autumn* and that of early Qing scholarship. For example, Gu Yanwu and Wang Fuzhi both had the highest regard for the ritual implications of the *Spring and Autumn* and Zuo commentary, with the latter's treatment of the Yi-Xia (foreign and Chinese) dichotomy coming into vogue in the late Qing, while New Text studies did the exact opposite, reinterpreting the intention of the *Spring and Autumn* through Gongyang thought (especially Dong Zhongshu's *Luxuriant Dew of the Spring and Autumn Annals*), attempting to relativize Yi-Xia and inner-outer relations. However, both early classical learning and the New Text school approached Yi-Xia relations as a question of ethics or of ritual, downplaying the absolute differences between ethnic groups. From the viewpoint of the history of classical learning, they shared no standard for appraising the classics, yet both placed *Spring and Autumn* above all other classics, and thus we cannot say they had nothing in common.

The *Spring and Autumn* begins with Yin (first year of Duke Yin of Zhou's reign, 722 BCE) and ends with Ai (fourteenth year of Duke Ai of Zhou's reign, 481 BCE). Tradition has it that Confucius revised the *Spring and Autumn* as it had been compiled by the historian of the State of Lu. The disagreement between the Old and New Text factions began with the Qianlong-Jiaqing reinterpretation of the *Spring and Autumn* and the Five Classics.[16] Those of the Han School of Unadorned Learning were fond of exegesis and evidential learning, gradually moving toward the pursuit of historical truth through a distinctly practical interpretation of the classics. They esteemed the Zuo commentary and dismissed the Gongyang and Guliang commentaries, pitting themselves against the New Text school on the question of the *Spring and Autumn*. Qian Daxin commented, "The *Spring and Autumn* describes things straightforwardly, leaving no good or evil hidden."[17] His inclination toward treating the classics as history is no different from that of Wang Mingsheng. This stance developed into Zhang Xuecheng's proposition that "the Six Classics are all histories," bringing to its zenith the argument that "there is no difference between the classics and history." Zhang gave weight to the Duke of Zhou and downplayed Confucius, emphasized the connection between the classics and the Six Arts, questioned the tendency to treat commentaries as classics, and devalued the pre-Qin masters and commentaries alike. Within the horizon of historical learning, the *Spring and Autumn* is only a book of history, and is no longer the "key to the Five Classics"; Confucius is but one of many thinkers of the Zhou period, and did not have the intrinsic quality of an "Uncrowned King." Stressing the Zuo commentary over Gongyang, esteeming the *History of the Former Han* over the *Records of the Grand Historian*, giving the *Rites of Zhou* prominence of place, emphasizing Liu Xiang and Liu Yin's "seven genres" (*qi lue*)—all of this coincidentally placed Zhang Xuecheng in opposition to the New Text school. But since there was no such pattern of opposition in Zhang's time, the opposition itself was the product of a split in classical learning.[18]

Zhang was little known to his contemporaries, and Liu Fenglu left behind no commentary on Zhang's assertion that "the Six Classics are all histories." He did, however, go line by line, disputing every last word of Qian Daxin's work. In fact, Liu was criticizing the intellectual tide of the Qianlong-Jiaqing era. In *Evidential Critique of the Zuo Spring and Autumn Annals (Zuo shi Chunqiu kaozheng)* he argues that Liu Xin forged the Zuo commentary, directly challenging the Old Text school's perspective on the classics, especially the argument that there is no difference between classics and history. His analysis provided the premise for later New Text scholars to break through the constraints of historical fact and bring into play the subtle words and profound meanings of Confucius as an institutional reformer. Following Liu Fenglu, Kang Youwei directly criticized Zhang Xuecheng's historical argument, believing that if one holds that the Duke of Zhou, not Confucius, epitomized Confucianism, the former would inevitably overshadow the latter's historical significance as philosophical creator and institutional reformer.[19] However, despite the differences of opinion among different schools and political contexts described above, there are still discernible traces of a connection between the argument that there is no difference between classics and history and New Text scholarship.

First of all, it was an important tradition in Confucian learning, and especially in classical learning, to regard the *Spring and Autumn* as "the key to the Five Classics." Countering the Neo-Confucians' emphasis on the Four Books, the reestablishment of the central role of the *Spring and Autumn* turned out to be a major step in Qing scholarship. One of the main disagreements between New Text and Old Text classical studies is whether the Six Classics were written by Confucius. The Old Text school adhered to the principle that Confucius "transmitted but did not create" (*shu er bu zuo*), and his praise for the images in the *Book of Changes,* his deletions from the *Odes* and the *Documents,* his revisions in the classics of *Rites* and *Music,* and his editing of the *Spring and Autumn* were the basis for this principle. The argument that "the Six Classics are all histories" or that "there is no difference between the classics and history" took the Six Classics to be records written by the Former Kings, thus highlighting the status of the Duke of Zhou as the one who synthesized them. The New Text school (led by Liao Ping and Kang Youwei) held that the Six Classics were written by Confucius; that the *Spring and Autumn* is not a record of events, but rather a text that Confucius wrote, based on the ancient past, that used subtle words and profound meanings to call for the reform of institutions; and that Confucius, and not the Duke of Zhou, represents the culmination of the Confucian tradition. Based on the statement in the Gongyang commentary that "the significance of the compilation of the *Spring and Autumn Annals* is to await the sages of later generations," Liao Ping further elaborated on Yu Yue's theory, in his *Survey of the Classics: The Three Rites: On the "Royal Regulations" as the New Text Source of the Uncrowned King's Philosophy in the Spring and Autumn Annals (Jingxue tonglun: san li: lun Wang zhi wei jinwen ji Chunqiu suwang zhi zhi)*, that the "Royal Regulations" (*Wang zhi*), esteemed by New Text scholars as the *Spring and Autumn's* commentary on ritual, was the work of Confucius. From this perspective, the Old and New Text schools are diametrically opposed to each other.

However, the New Text school's placement of *Spring and Autumn* above all other classics is in a direct line of descent from the Qing tradition of classical scholarship. Scholars in the early Qing used the study of classics and history to critique Zhu Xi and Wang Yangming, and their new theories of institutions and of rites and music to oppose Song-Ming discussions of topics like Heaven and Man, Mind and Nature. For all of them, the mission of scholarship was to investigate change and development in the laws, institutions, and regulations of the Former Kings, as well as the evolution of customs. Huang Zongxi's *Waiting for the Dawn: A Plan for the Prince (Ming Yi dai fang lu)* presents a theory of political and institutional reform that uses the laws and institutions of antiquity as its blueprint, and Gu Yanwu's theories of centralized administration, of decentralized enfeoffment, and of numerous other political systems explore the potential for reform from both historical and contemporary perspectives. New Text scholars substituted rites for principles, emphasizing rites as characteristic of institutions. The core issue here is political and institutional reform, and to integrate the concept of change with a theory of institutions was the intrinsic motivation of Qing classical scholarship. It was in the tide of reconstruction of the system of rites that the *Spring and Autumn* claimed its place at the heart of the Five Classics, and accordingly opened a trend in scholarship of using history to verify the classics. Gu Yanwu saw the *Spring and Autumn* as a book in which had been entrusted the political institutions of the Former Kings and the standards of ethical judgment, and not simply as a book of history; in response to the abstract theories of Song-Ming Confucianism, he regarded its discourses on "respect for the emperor, resistance to the barbarians, and punishment of rebellious subjects and undutiful sons" as fulfilling the categories of "the moral nature and the Way of Heaven" (*xing yu tian dao*).[20] This view highlights the ritual principles of inner versus outer and foreign versus Chinese, in contrast to the New Text school's relativization of the two. However, in regarding it as a book of criminal law, Gu's opinion of the *Spring and Autumn* was not so far off from the New Text school.

These characteristics of early-Qing classical scholarship presaged the revival of Gongyang scholarship, with its emphasis on institutions and its strong approval of the *Spring and Autumn*. From Liu Fenglu onward, Gongyang scholarship on the *Spring and Autumn* restored one of the main distinguishing features of Han-era Gongyang studies: its vigorous effort to unite rites and law as an integrated whole. In this enterprise, *Spring and Autumn* was the model for clarifying ritual and for deciding criminal cases. As Liu said:

> Some regard the *Spring and Autumn Annals* as the criminal code of the sages, while others say that among the Five Classics, the *Spring and Autumn Annals* are like the judgments of the law. And yet Master Dong of Wencheng [Dong Zhongshu (179–104 BCE)] takes it only as the great ancestor of propriety and righteousness. How can this be? Rites are the refined essence of punishments; if you lose the rites you will enter into punishment, and there is no neutral Way. Thus, punishments are the specifications of ritual.[21]

Liu Fenglu restored the pre-Qin concept of punishment and reward, clearly seeing ritual as the refined essence of legal punishment, and placing ritual punishment among laws and decrees. This tendency to synthesize ritual and law is especially clear in *Judicial Precedent in the Spring and Autumn Annals (Chunqiu jueshibi)*, written by Liu's disciple, Gong Zizhen. Gong states:

> In the Han dynasty, Sima Qian [145–86 BCE] said: "The *Spring and Autumn* is the great ancestor of propriety and righteousness." He also said: "The *Spring and Autumn*'s clarification of right and wrong is well suited to governing the people." The Jin official Xun Song [262–328] further stated: "The refined compassion of the Gongyang is excellent for making legal decisions." The contents of the Nine Schools of Thought [as listed by Liu Xiang (77–6 BCE) in what became the *History of the Former Han*] include 123 essays by Dong Zhongshu. Among these, the 16 that concern

> Gongyang decision-making on penal cases have mostly been lost. In those which remain, what begins as the words of Gongyang enters into the School of Names. He Xiu [129–182] often cited from the Han legal code, thus incorporating the Gongyang tradition into Legalism. And Han court officials, who frequently cited the *Spring and Autumn* when deciding rewards and punishments, brought it into the fold of the ritualists and again had interactions with the School of Names. One might ask: Which is more important to rely on, ritual or punishment? The reply is this: The penal code is that on which propriety and righteousness depend; when one departs from ritual one enters into punishment, and there is no middle ground. But it is also said that the *Spring and Autumn* is a hearing of cases, that it gives rise to law, that the offense rules over the person, that the emperor heeds the hundred kings, and that it is the penal code for all ages. Since it decides matters for all ages, how could it be invoked on behalf of a single person or a single matter? For this reason, there are cases where even when the facts (*shi*) are not given, the language (*wen*) remains.[22]

The esteem in which New Text classical scholarship held the *Spring and Autumn* for its centrality among the Five Classics, and its way of regarding the ritual system and law as mutually related, both continue the traditions of the early Qing.

Secondly, another side of "the Six Classics are all histories" is the supposition that the Six Classics are all accounts of dynastic systems. At its core, the theory understands the classics as traces of the political models of the Former Kings, while also viewing these models as the basis for practical governance. Starting from the connection between institutions and knowledge, Zhang Xuecheng stressed that subjective opinion must be overcome in the study of the works of the ancient philosophers, the classics, and their commentaries, so as to unearth the essence of the Six Arts buried within those texts. Consequently, the so-called devaluing of the *Spring and Autumn* does not mean devaluing the significance of the text itself, but rather treating it as a record of the political models and practices of the Former Kings. This point of view takes two directions of interpretation: one, it demands the discovery of the meaning of rites and music and political models through analysis of the historical record; and two, it requires that practical governance be based on these past political models and their development over time.

Zhang Xuecheng considered the Six Classics to be the "traces" of the Six Arts (*liushu*), and developed his archaeology of the classics from this premise. In this sense, his devaluation of the status of *Spring and Autumn* has the same origin as Gu Yanwu's emphasis on the *Spring and Autumn:* both regarded the classics as a theory of institutions or of rites and music, and as the basis for conduct within a horizon of development. This in fact paved the way for the rise of the New Text view of the *Spring and Autumn* and its attendant theory of political and institutional reform. For example, Wei Yuan argued in "Why Schools Should Pay Greater Homage to the Sage Duke of Zhou" *(Xuexiao ying zeng si xian sheng Zhou Gong yi)* that the original Five Classics came from the Duke of Zhou, that their transmission was fixed by Confucius, and that "in the institutions of the royal court, the Six Officials among whom responsibility for governance was apportioned were none other than the Grand Councilor (*zhongzai*), Minister of Education (*situ*), Minister of Rites (*zongbo*), Minister of War (*sima*), Ministry of Justice (*sikou*) and Ministry of Works (*sikong*) as described in the *Rites of Zhou.*" He thus traced all systems of rites and music back to the Duke of Zhou.[23] Wei Yuan interpreted all of the classics from the perspective of Gongyang thought, jumbling the Six Classics together. His difference from the Old Text scholars was not so much in whether or not he carried on the viewpoint of the Old Text classics as in his strained, blanket analysis.

Likewise, Gong Zizhen approached the classics with Confucius's attitude of "one single thread binding my way together." In the *Rectification of Names in the Six Classics (Liu Jing zhengming)* and *Explorations in Ancient History (Gushi gouchen lun),* Gong demands a strict approach to the rectification of names, "recovering the classics through the classics, the historical annals through the historical annals, the biographies through the biographies, the various genres (*qunshu*) through the various genres, and the pre-Qin masters through the masters" to arrive at a definitive version of all of the classics. This viewpoint is reminiscent of Dai Zhen's call for "recovering the Six Classics through the Six Classics, Confucius and Mencius through Confucius and Mencius, [the Neo-Confucian masters] Cheng, Zhu, Lu, and Wang through Cheng, Zhu, Lu, and Wang, and Lao Dan and the Buddha through

Lao Dan and the Buddha,"[24] and is also akin to Zhang Xuecheng's historical perspective of clearly distinguishing origins from later developments. The real difference between him and the Old Text scholars lies not in his understanding of the classics, but in how to utilize the classics. If we say that Zhang Xuecheng clearly distinguished origins from later developments in order to recover the Six Arts and to use them for contemporary purposes, then, contrarily, Gong Zizhen used the study of Heaven and Earth and the four directions to elucidate the Six Classics and the subtle words and profound meanings of the pre-Qin masters, thus intimately linking questions of classical learning to geographical studies, astronomy, and other social and political issues. He believed that the differences between Old Text and New Text learning lay in how the texts were read, and not in differences among the texts themselves. In *Explorations in Ancient History,* Gong elaborated on the theory that "the Six Classics are all histories":

> The great officials of the Zhou era were historians. Outside of history there was no spoken language, outside of history there was no writing, and outside of history there were no specifications of ethical human relationships. When history existed the Zhou survived, and when history was lost the Zhou was lost. . . . The Six Classics are the lineal descendants of Zhou history . . . and the works of the various masters are the collateral descendants of Zhou history.[25]

In his "Preface to *Writings of Lu Yanruo*" *(Lu Yanruo suo zhu shuxu),* Gong Zizhen further elaborated on the proposition that the Six Classics are all histories, saying that "the Five Classics are the source of wealth and the wellspring of virtue and longevity," holding that one cannot understand the classics if one is removed from economic activities such as commerce and farming. In this way, he developed the "classical" viewpoint into an argument about everyday practice.[26]

4. Mencius and Xunzi, Old and New Text Schools

The *Spring and Autumn* is but one example of the overlap of New and Old Text studies. We can prove the same point from their interpretations of other classical texts. New Text Studies attempted to link Mencius and Xunzi to

Gongyang scholarship. For instance, Kang Youwei wrote: "Among the later followers of Confucius there are two main branches. One is that of Mencius, whom no one reads without understanding that he was in the orthodox Gongyang tradition; the other is that of Xunzi, who was the great ancestor of the Guliang tradition. Nowhere does the meaning of the *Mencius* fail to conform with the Gongyang. The Guliang was made known and transmitted through Xunzi, and they also do not contradict each other."[27]

What is the relationship between the New Text interpretation of Mencius and Xunzi as described above, and that of such classical scholars as Dai Zhen? In his *Comparative Survey of the Principles of the Classics (Qunjing dayi xiang tonglun),* Liu Shipei (1884–1919), an Old Text scholar, compares the schools of thought of the ancient states of Qi and Lu. The chapter "Comparative Analysis of Gongyang and Mencius" (*Gongyang Mengzi xiang tongkao*) goes through seven examples, concluding that "the meaning of Xunzi is closer to Guliang, while Mencius is closer to Gongyang. Therefore, Xunzi is of the Lu school, and Mencius is of the Qi school."[28] Whether the *Mencius* and the Gongyang are of the same school remains to be determined, but there is no doubt that they share a similar orientation. For example, the theory of Confucius as "Uncrowned King and reformer," advocated by the New Text school, is based on the "Teng Wen Gong II" chapter of the *Mencius.*[29] As an Old Text scholar, Liu Shipei theorized a connection between Mencius and Gongyang, indicating that there was already a tendency within Qing classical scholarship to group the two together.

Beginning with Huang Zongxi and Gu Yanwu, the political orientation of Qing scholarship was closely linked to their rigorous application of evidential learning, exacting research, and historical explication of the laws and institutions of antiquity. For this reason, there is no direct connection between whether a classical scholar directly addresses politics in his writing and the presence or absence of political content in his research. Dai Zhen's discourse on Mencius is a case in point. He used his analytical distinctions of spontaneity versus necessity and of principle versus desire to attack the Song Confucian learning of Mind and Nature, and while developing the concept of rites simultaneously demanded that the subject be approached in accordance with the changing times. In the process of elevating the praxis of rites (a ritual praxis inherent in the laws of Nature and human emotion), he drew on Xunzi's conception of the ritual system and the law. Dai Zhen's understanding of changes in institutions, the law, and history subtly echoes several aspects of Gongyang scholarship, as both his and Gongyang scholars' interpretations of Mencius and Xunzi derive from their emphasis on the ritual system, laws, and institutions of antiquity. The focal point of this line of thought is starkly divided from Neo-Confucianism. The Qing theory of the ritual system is a critique of the Song-Ming theory of Heaven and Man, Mind and Nature (*tianren xinxing*). Huang Zongxi, Gu Yanwu, and Dai Zhen all tend to substitute rites for principles, and institutional theory for Mind and Nature. For Dai Zhen, this fascination with institutions is apparent in his contradictory attitude toward Xunzi: through a peculiar logic, his interpretation of Mencius's moral philosophy is oddly consistent with Xunzi's concepts of ritual, exaltation of law, and esteem for learning, to the point of creating a tense relationship between ritual and law, and between innate goodness and acquired learning. His *Critical Exegesis of the Meanings of Words in Mencius (Mengzi ziyi shuzheng)* uses the method of interpreting Mencius to counterattack the Song-era study of Heaven and Man, Mind and Nature, and to restore the centrality of rites, yet its compatibility with Xunzi's scholarship includes a certain flavor of making a Legalist out of Mencius. Looked at from this angle, the *Critical Exegesis* embodies tendencies that were later developed by the New Text Confucians.

Qing-era Gongyang scholars saw Mencius as a forerunner of Gongyang learning, and used him as the basis for their explanations of the subtle words and profound meanings of the *Spring and Autumn*. Liu Shipei's point of view is in fact built on the Qing Gongyang perspective. For example, in his *Study of the New Text and Old Text Schools,* Liao Ping argues that Mencius and Xunzi both relied on the theories of the "Royal Regulations" (*Wang zhi*); before him, in "Preface to the *General Meaning of the Gongyang Spring and Autumn*" *(Chunqiu Gongyang tongyi xu),* Kong Guangsen builds on Mencius's contention that the *Spring and Autumn* concerns "matters proper to the sovereign" (*tianzi zhi shi*) and argues for the interconnectedness of the Gongyang and *Mencius:*

> In the classics there are writings about transformations in the Zhou [dynasty], for in the substance of its succession from the Yin [dynasty], did the Son of Heaven not make changes? Among the lords of the royal domain there were three ranks, and among the regional guardians there

> were seven ranks. The outstanding Grand Masters (*da fu*), and the Grand Masters of small states whose position was not based on family name, were these not the ranks and stipends of the Son of Heaven? . . . If one takes the state as internal and the various feudatories as external, or the various feudatories as internal and the four borderlands as external, is this not almost the same as regarding All-under-Heaven (*Tianxia*) as rooted in the state, and the state as rooted in the family? I believe that the Gongyang scholars alone were aligned with Mencius. . . . Therefore Mencius was the most skilled in speaking of the *Spring and Autumn*, and it was no wonder that he saw the unexpected textual agreement of the treatise on the land tax (*shuimu*) and the biography of Bo Yuyang![30]

Here he equates the discussion of ritual order in *Mencius* (3B9) to the affairs of the emperor; that is to say, he turns Mencius into a Legalist in order to bring rites and law together as one. In this sense, there is still an intrinsic connection underlying the New and Old Text schools' disagreement on Mencius and Xunzi.

Through their interpretation of Mencius, New Text scholars equated the *Spring and Autumn* with Confucius's theory of institutions. Pi Xirui not only confused Mencius with Gongyang; he brazenly lumped them both together with Zhu Xi as a single school. In my view, this comes not from the perspective of school methods, but is instead a verdict reached from a perspective on history that grew in popularity from the mid-Qing on.[31] The inherent connection between ethical and institutional discourse is a defining feature of pre-Qin Confucianism, and the concept of "reward and punishment" (*de xing)* its concentrated expression. The division between Mencius and Xunzi portends the split of ethics from institutions in pre-Qin Confucianism. When Dai Zhen expounds on Mencius and brings in Xunzi, the Legalist elements hidden in Mencius are laid bare. According to Liu Shipei and Yang Xiangkui, Xunzi and Gongyang learning are of the same school of thought—a type of Confucianism that borders on Legalism. In his "Comparative Analysis of Gongyang and Mencius" (*Gongyang Xunzi xiang tongkao*), Liu Shipei writes: "In my view, Dong Zhongshu of Western Han was a practitioner of Gongyang *Spring and Autumn* learning, yet since his *Luxuriant Dew of the Spring and Autumn Annals* often praises Xunzi, he must have regarded Xunzi as the forebear of Gongyang learning. Moreover, He Xiu of Eastern Han was a specialist in Gongyang learning, and regularly used Xunzi's writings in his annotations."[32] Yang Xiangkui affirms Liu Shipei's point, taking it a step further: "Gongyang and Xunzi belong to the same school of thought: they are Legalist-leaning Confucians. In terms of political theory, they both advocate for reform, but the measures they propose are incomplete. Thus, they promote reform on the one hand and returning to antiquity on the other, leaving themselves no basis for advance or retreat and unable to justify their theories."[33] By "reform" he is referring to their respect for the changing tides of history, and to their emphasis on the need to establish a Grand Unification (*da yitong*) of centrally administered prefectures and counties (*junxian*); and by "returning to antiquity," he means that they view the decentralized enfeoffment of the Three Dynasties of Antiquity as the inherent ideal.

5. Rites, Laws, and Expediency

Without the capacity for historical and practical insight, it is easy to find oneself "without a basis for advance or retreat" when trying to think through the connections between the ritual system of the Sage-Kings and the changing tides of history, to understand the nexus between ethical praxis and the law, and to preserve a balance between the unity of centralized administration and the enfeoffment system of the Three Dynasties. In order to judge between right and wrong in the manner of deciding legal cases, we must talk about the significance of "expediency" or "raw practical assessment" (*quan*), in its dual sense as "authority" (*quanwei*) and "expedient accommodation" (*quanbian*). It is worth noting that the contradiction between classical standards and expedience is one of the most intrinsic to Gongyang thought, as clearly illustrated by its principle of "what is accepted in fact but not countenanced in language" (*shi yu er wen buyu*). "Not countenanced in language" refers to classical standards, while "acceptance in fact" refers to expedience.[34] The *Gongyang* gives a concrete example to explain the meaning of expedience in its entry for the eleventh year of Duke Huan of Qi (r. 685–643 BCE), which recounts that after the funeral rites for Duke Zhuang of Zheng, the Song arrested Ji Zhong, the prime minister of Zheng, and forced him to "exile Hu and enthrone Tu [the nephew of Song]." Ji Zhong thus faced a real dilemma: if he refused to obey, then he would die, and his state would be lost; if he did obey, he could live, and his country could be saved. Ji Zhong weighed each choice, finally deciding on the latter. Gongyang praises Ji Zhong for exercising expediency in this circumstance: "What does it mean to be expedient? One who is expedient acts against classical standards for the sake of a good outcome. Unless it is to prevent death or destruction, one does not act expediently. There is a proper way to wield expediency: one may belittle oneself, but must not harm others. To kill others to preserve one's own life, or to ruin others to establish oneself, are things that a noble person does not do."[35] The thought of New Text classical studies in the Qing on inner-outer relations and on political and institutional reform was permeated by the concept of expediency. A typical example comes from Liu Fenglu, who in his *Explanations of Special Cases* wrote that "an expedient act that is contrary to virtue yet facilitates virtue, is also a kind of assessment," setting forth important regulations for expediency between the realms of virtue and punishment.[36]

Still, the New Text school certainly did not have a monopoly on the thought of expediency. It was actually a fundamental topic in Confucian learning. As Mencius states in "Liang Hui Wang I": "By expediency [*quan:* "weighing"], we know what things are light, and what heavy. By measuring, we know what things are long, and what short. The relations of all things may be thus determined, and it is of the greatest importance to estimate the motions of the mind. I beg your Majesty to measure it."[37] Since people like Gu Yanwu and Dai Zhen stressed institutions and the law, in their discussions of ritual and law they inevitably returned time and again to the importance of expediency, highlighting the significance of subjective will and historical circumstance to ethics and politics. Dai Zhen gave prominence to the importance of expediency through his interpretation of Mencius, much to the shock of the Neo-Confucians:

> Expediency (or assessment) [*quan*] is that by which the light and the heavy are distinguished. Whenever this is heavy and that is light, and from earliest antiquity they do not change, this is constancy. Where there is constancy, these unchanging weights are clearly manifest to all. But when the heavy thereupon becomes light, and the light thereupon becomes heavy, this is transformation, and where there is transformation, unless one's wisdom is sufficient to discern and examine the circumstances with accuracy, one will not be able to understand

> it. . . . Understanding constancy but not transformation comes from not being deeply versed in subtle meanings, and from not fulfilling that by which the clarity of one's heart's discernments may be augmented and brought to the completeness of sagely wisdom.[38]

Expediency in this sense is a synthesized judgment and choice about a situation, law, or value arrived at through one's subjective will. Looking at the discussion in the *Critical Exegesis of the Meanings of Words in Mencius* of such fundamental themes as spontaneity versus necessity, emotion versus desire, and ritual versus law, it is not hard to see how expediency became an important concept in harmonizing these various categories.

Both Dai Zhen–Zhang Xuecheng learning and New Text classical learning contained a notion of "propensity" (*shi*), which gave legitimacy to the rise and fall of laws and rites. In my view, this is precisely the source of disenchantment with the classics as studied during the Qing: if everything is the result of historical evolution and the balancing of interests, then the moral connotations that scholars had invested in the rites and music and political models of the Former Kings must be relativized. The practice of political and institutional reform is legitimized by the relationship between institutions and historical change. This proof of legitimacy not only dissolves the absolute tie of institutions to ethics, but also leads to the demise of the classics as authoritative texts. The complexity of the issue lies in the fact that although political reform is a revolt against established legal regulations and ceremonial rites, its need for moral rightness is more urgent than in times of peaceful succession. Against this backdrop, New Text scholars assiduously differentiated "change" from "constancy," and institutional evolution from the unchanging Way. At the same time, they drew on Confucian mysticism and quietly borrowed from Song theories of Heaven and Man, until they reconstructed their cosmology and historical perspective through modern scientific thought. The scientific worldview lifted the veil from Confucian mysticism and superstition, but did not cover up this fact: they were born of the exigencies placed on their worldview by the process of reform; the concepts of change and of propensity of the times, and the requirements of cosmology, came concurrently. Therefore, the birth of modern thought was less a process of disenchantment or *Entzauberung* than one of creating new structures of enchantment.

6. Ritual, Reward and Punishment, and Dynastic Governance

From these somewhat frayed threads we can weave together some rudimentary conclusions.

First, Qing classical learning was a reaction against Song-Ming Neo-Confucianism (*lixue*), and it took as its central task research and analysis of the classics in order to revive the institutions of the Former Kings. In the vein of classical learning, Song-Ming moral philosophy (*yili*) had lost its legitimacy. As a result, when scholars chafed at the fetters of classical learning and sought a point from which to break free, they either resurrected the topics of Song learning in the form of "critical exegesis of the meanings of words," like Dai Zhen; or dismissed the absolute authority of evidential learning within the framework of history, like Zhang Xuecheng; or else repositioned Han-dynasty scholarship to provide support in the classical canon for their search, within the form of classical learning, for a motive force for transformational change. These changes did not go beyond classical learning's premise of unifying governance with the Way, and rites with Principle. In this sense, Qing classical learning provided a trajectory and an orientation for scholars of that time, and though even the most rebellious among them would have been hard pressed to develop new theories within the frameworks of cosmology, ontology, or learning of the Mind and the nature, it was through new interpretations and discoveries of essential meanings in the classics that they were able to tease out new theories of rituals and institutions as premises for change. It was just for this reason that although many New Text scholars had an abiding sympathy for and understanding of Song learning, they built their theories not in the Song style, but rather by forging new paths within classical learning, finding points of departure in obscure and forgotten New Text scholarship of the late-Han and post-Han period.

Second, Qing classical learning always embodied a tension between the pursuit of the laws and institutions of the Former Kings on the one hand, and respect for historical development on the other. We may also express this as a contradiction between institutions and rites and music, and between enfeoffment and centralized administration. In the context of classical learning, the contradictions of enfeoffment versus centralized administration and of rites and music versus institutions represent a dialectical relationship between the institutions of antiquity and the progress of history, which manifests on several different levels. One, on the institutional level, Qing classical scholarship attempted to synthesize the enfeoffment system of the Three Dynasties period with the system of centralized administration, finding an equilibrium between the ideal of Three Dynasties well-fields, schools, and enfeoffment, and the later politics of land taxes, civil service examinations, and Grand Unification. Gu Yanwu's view of All-under-Heaven (*Tianxia*), his theory of centralized administration, his theory of customs, and his method of "analyzing characters by first knowing their sounds" in the pursuit of the essential meaning of ancient institutions, all demonstrate the seemingly contradictory nature of this theoretical pursuit. Two, on the level of ethical practice, Qing classical learning integrated the ritual system of the former rulers with the desires of everyday life, in an effort to give shape to an internal coherence between necessity and spontaneity, principle and desire. Dai Zhen criticized "murder by Principle," integrating Mencius, Xunzi, and Zhuangzi and linking classical study with moral philosophy, all of which may be seen as a great effort at the level of moral theory to balance the ritual system (both the laws and institutions of the Former Kings and the ethics of the patriarchal clan system) and spontaneity (historical development of institutions and laws). Three, at the level of historical study, Qing classical learning used concepts of transformation and change to understand the propositions that "the Six Classics are all histories" and that "the *Dao* and its vessels are unitary," applying Gu Yanwu's theory of the ritual system and his political point of view with regard to centralized administration and enfeoffment to new methods of historical narration, according to which the system of centralized administration was indeed infused with the spirit of enfeoffment. In Zhang Xuecheng's treatment of the relationship between the Six Classics and the political institutions of the Former Kings, in his exacting demands on the moral character of scholars, and in his analysis of the relationship between his own writing on history (tracing back the spirit of enfeoffment) and the written history of the imperial family (relations of enfeoffment under centralized administration), we see his efforts to mediate between the laws and institutions of the Former Kings and historical change. These three levels, permeating one another, ultimately fused together the will for change and the understanding of antiquity as a single organic whole.

Within Qing classical scholarship lay intrinsic and abiding tensions between the institutions of the Former Kings and the developments of history, between enfeoffment and centralized administration, between All-under-Heaven and the nation-state, between the institutions of the Three Dynasties and the transmission of historical narrative via the classics, between individual yearning and ritual order. These were the roots of the discipline's creativity as well as its limitation. Qing-era classical learning's critique of the Neo-Confucianist view of the Way of Heaven and its theory of Mind and Nature aimed to restore the balance between these two aspects. However, these theoretical efforts quickly produced new crises, due to the following insurmountable contradiction: On the one hand, the purpose of classical learning was to find the essential meaning of the rites and music of the Three Dynasties and of the institutions of the Former Kings, yet its historical perspective of "change" (*bian*) was opposed to dogmatic imitation under the form of "restoring antiquity" to reform existing institutions; on the other hand, the concept of "change" provided legitimacy to the transformation of historical institutions, but also softened any moral critique of the existing system vis-à-vis the rites and music of the Three Dynasties. From Gu Yanwu and Huang Zongxi to Dai Zhen and Zhang Xuecheng, the forms of scholarship changed time and again, driven by the tensions and contradictions continuously generated between changing concepts of history and ritual norms. These tensions and contradictions ultimately formed into a historical impetus within classical studies, that is to say, the will to seek the roots of change and transformation through the practice of classical learning. Even so, the concept of "change" is a way of treating the patterns of institutions, morals, and rites and music in history; the concept is not itself capable of providing a basis for change. Scholars thus had to rely on the experiential process of "expediency." The concept of acting according to changing expedients provided the theoretical space for classical learning to consider political strategy, and laid the groundwork within classical learning to overcome its own barriers.

The contradictions and impulses of Qing classical learning described above provided the presuppositions and conditions for novel trends suddenly emerging in New Text studies: viewing the *Spring and Autumn* not only as a record of the political models of the Former Kings, but also as Confucius's theory of political reform; history not merely as a result of a "spontaneous propensity" (*ziran zhi shi*), but also as the product of subjective will for systemic reform; the historical elaboration of "change" not only as the suite of ancient histories described in the classics, but also as the bases of and precedents for institutional reform—from New Text scholars' "Royal Regulations" and Old Text scholars' *Rites of Zhou,* to Western politics and education, there was no ground it did not cover. In this, political institutions and laws became inextricably tied to the subjective will for reform: the laws of King Wen (father of the first King of Zhou) and his concept of Grand Unification were not the outcomes of spontaneous evolution, but instead were the patterns or subtle words and profound meanings inscribed by Confucius for the new king in response to the propensity of the times. The idea of political reform liberated these principles from the label of classical history, positioning them among models of transformation. In this sense, it was this shift in the focus of thought, and not a division between schools of thought, that constituted the fundamental change within classical learning. Rather than a choice of scholastic style, it was the result of this transformation that altered the reverence of Qing classical learning for the laws and institutions of the Former Kings and their view of the spontaneous orderliness of historical change, and conversely provided the basis for a subjectivist theory of political reform and a pragmatic conception of classical learning.

Third, the statecraft thought of New Text studies was based on rites, and at its center was the application of dynastic governance. While New Text studies returned to the concerns of the various Confucian schools of the early Qing, it did not share the oppositional tendencies of Confucian scholars of the early Qing, which were set against the backdrop of intense debates concerning the relations between Yi and Xia and saw many cases of subversive arguments made under the cloak of orthodoxy. Rather, it unfolded from the acknowledgment of dynastic legitimacy and the presupposition of historical progress. Undoubtedly, the most important motive for this shift in scholarly focus was the political reality of the Qing as a multiethnic empire ruled by a minority group. Viewed from classical learning itself, however, this shift is also closely connected to changes in scholarly identity. Compared to the representative scholars of Qianlong-Jiaqing evidential learning, those from various stages of the New Text movement were more tightly bound to dynastic governance, whether they were highly ranked court officials or central proponents of political reform. Zhuang Cunyu (1719–1788) was ranked second among the highest group of successful examination candidates, bringing him to the Hanlin Academy as an imperial compiler. By order of the Qianlong Emperor for "advancement in classical argumentation, great erudition and refined energy, and extraordinary scholarship of doctrine," Zhuang was connected to the Nanshufang reading room in the Forbidden City, serving successively as chief and vice imperial examiner of Hubei Province, educational commissioner of Hunan Province, vice supervisor of the Household Administration of the Heir Apparent, principal chief examiner of Zhejiang Province, educational commissioner of Shuntian (Beijing), and joint cabinet scholar and assistant minister of Rites. In 1819 (the nineteenth year of the Jiaqing reign), Liu Fenglu (1776–1829) passed the imperial examination, received the title of Hanlin *shujishi* (conferred for high marks on the civil service examination), and offered private tutelage as director of the Ministry of Rites. In the fourth reign year of Daoguang (1824), he supplemented this with the directorship of the Commission for Ceremony. His paternal grandfather, Liu Lunshi, was grand secretary of the Wenyuange Library, minister of defense, and imperial preceptor to the crown prince. Liu's pupils, Gong Zizhen and Wei Yuan, had less successful careers, but they both held lower-level positions in the capital for quite some time, and as private secretaries may have gotten involved in politics behind the scenes. As marginal actors, they were at the political center during times of crisis, bringing a more radical political perspective to the world of classical learning. Kang Youwei, Liang Qichao, and Tan Sitong were the central actors in the reform movement of the late Qing. They were able to enter into palace politics not only because of their political participation and consciousness, but also because in their hands Gongyang scholarship became a theory of political and legal reform, a theory that coalesced with Western knowledge into a model for practical change. If one wrote about New Text studies only with regard to their exposition of subtle words and profound meanings or discussed Qianlong-Jiaqing Han studies only in terms of evidential learning, one would miss the true significance of New Text studies, and would be at a loss to explain the continuous changes that took place within Qing scholarship.

Fourth, in the particular context of the Qing dynasty, affirmations of the evolution of history and of institutions necessarily touched on questions of ethnic relations. New Text studies' concern with historical development and reflection on "expedient practices" (*xing quan*) was focused on changing the early-Qing understanding of inner and outer, using examples from Gongyang studies to dispel the stark consciousness of nationality and the Yi-Xia distinction present in early classical studies and Neo-Confucianist thought.

When New Text scholars turned Gu Yanwu and Huang Zongxi's approach to the classics and history into political theory, they were not just changing the internal rules of classical learning, but also in doing so rebuilding their own identity: if they could not bridge Yi / Xia and inner / outer within the system, then they would not find the basis needed to put political reform into practice. For this reason, the strident national consciousness of Gu Yanwu, Huang Zongxi, and Wang Fuzhi was downplayed in New Text studies, and reoriented in the opposite direction, such that ritual and its culture formed the basis of political identity. Thus the boundaries between inner-outer and Yi-Xia were erased, reestablishing the legitimacy of the Qing empire.

For Gu Yanwu, Huang Zongxi, Wang Fuzhi, and Lü Liuliang, the institutions of the Three Dynasties of Antiquity constituted the intrinsic structure both of classical learning and of Neo-Confucianism, and were also regarded both as the source of moral (national / ethnic) identity and as the basis for the practice of governance. This orientation was aimed at the conquest policies, ethnic hierarchies, and aristocracy of the Manchu-Qing ethnic-minority empire, and accordingly brought with it an intense legitimist ideology and concept of a Yi-Xia divide. New Text classical studies considered these problems more from the perspective of dynastic change, viewing these institutions as the result of a mutual interaction between internal and external factors, and thus constructing a theory of dynastic legitimacy that was oriented toward erasing the strict internal-external dividing line and centered on governance, adaptability, and legal relationships. The historical perspective of New Text classicism and the value system of the imperial era both complemented and contradicted each other. We may summarize this contradictory relationship as follows: it recognized the legitimacy of the Qing dynasty and its laws, as well as the general direction of ritual reform; it attempted to base the political community on rites and culture, not on ethnicity; and under the banner of doing away with strict distinctions of Chinese versus barbarian and of inner versus outer or internal versus external, it offered a critique of hierarchical relationships within the Qing polity.

The leading characteristic of New Text classical studies is that it was the legitimizing theory of a "Grand Unifying" dynasty. Its concept of political reform was not a critique undertaken by scholars who self-identified as adherents of the previous dynasty; nor was it the equivocal scholarship of the editors of *The Emperor's Four Treasuries* (*Siku quanshu*), who were both officials and academicians; nor was it even similar to the allegorical critiques and "public opinion" of self-described uncontaminated political outsiders, like the Donglin Faction of the late Ming. It was a theory of political reform that emerged from the political system of the Qing dynasty, a theory created by ethnic Han officials who thought of themselves as reformers. It was therefore not oppositional national ideology, but rather utilitarian, institutional (ritual) relationships, that became the focus of concern in New Text classical studies. For these reasons, I summarize this shift in scholarly focus as follows: it moved from a theory of the ritual system or of rites and music, to a theory of institutions and laws, which was also precisely a shift from the critical traditions of Qing classical learning (including the evidential learning orientation of Qianlong-Jiaqing scholars) to the political theory and reform strategies of the New Text classical scholars. The centrality of ritual in New Text studies was born of the need for moral rightness vis-à-vis legal reform: the law had to include the moral significance of the rites. This was the prime reason for the resurgence of the concept of rites and punishment in New Text studies. The key link in this shift was a transformation in the basis of Chinese society's political identity: from an ethnic identity to a cultural one, from distinctions between Yi and Xia to arguments that there were no essential differences between inner (*nei*) and outer (*wai*), from ideas of an ethnic quasi-nation-state to an all-encompassing logic of "Grand Unification." Discussion of political and institutional reform thus became entangled with the redefinition of "China."

In short, the main features of New Text classical studies were its drive to abolish the internal-external divide, its emphasis on the historical progress of the institutions themselves, and its premising of multiethnic dynastic unity on ritual unity (and in reality also institutional and legal unity). This was the premise of New Text political praxis, as well as the historical basis for new ritual and ethical reappraisals. This political premise also presages the drowning of New Text classical studies in the turbulent waters of late-Qing nationalism: if we say that the legitimizing theory of "Grand Unification" is based on Confucian ritual, takes following custom and tradition as its principle, and gradually moves away from internal-external (i.e., from ethnic boundaries), then the expansion of the colonial, capitalist market set off a nationalist wave based on political sovereignty, with universalist law as its principle, and oriented toward strict division between internal and external (i.e., ethnic difference).

This is the conflict between the identity politics of a multiethnic empire and the identity politics of nationalism, where the political community of the former is based on culture (ritual and institutions), while the latter takes ethnicity as its premise. This historical conflict transformed the character of the "inner-outer" relationships that New Text classical studies had long been focused on, and the divergent tendencies of culture and ethnicity were precisely its concentrated expression.

II. New Text Studies and Legal / Institutional Pluralism of the Qing Dynasty

1. Palace Politics, or a Question of Legitimacy?

In *Classicism, Politics, and Kinship,* Benjamin Elman considers the political significance of New Text studies via the connection between classical learning and politics, opening a new horizon for the study of Qing New Text studies. In response to the tendency among historians to view Wei Yuan and Gong Zizhen as the central pillars of New Text studies, he asserts that Zhuang Cunyu occupied a central role on the imperial political stage; in contrast, while Gong Zizhen and Wei Yuan have been deemed important figures by twentieth-century historians, they were in fact politically marginal during their own lifetimes.[39] This shift in perspective naturally raises a question of intellectual history: If New Text studies did not grow out of the reform movement of the late Qing, then what was the impetus for its rise? Elman groups the patriarchal clan system, politics, and the study of the classics together in his scholarly horizon, then observes how they leveraged one another when pushed by the Heshen Incident.[40] From this critical juncture, Elman develops his study of the Changzhou school amid the intertwining of classical, clan, and imperial politics, thus bringing to light the social conditions for the rise of New Text studies in the Qianlong era. In Elman's view, Zhuang Cunyu's pivot to the Gongyang commentary is a political and strategic choice, because the "subtle words and profound meanings" of Gongyang learning provided a "a classical studies cover, and in particular the historical cover of the praise and blame (*baobian*) tradition of Confucius," allowing him to indirectly critique the current regime, particularly his dissatisfaction with Heshen and his accomplices. In this sense, the rise of New Text studies was not the result of a gradual shift in classical studies, but a political choice born of the confrontation between the literati and Heshen during the Qianlong era: it was "a harbinger of the 'voices of remonstrance' (*qingyi*) at the turn of the nineteenth century and an echo of [Zhuang's] Donglin [Faction] forebears, opposed to the tyranny of Wei Zhongxian [and the eunuchs]" and thus had no direct connection to the New Text studies of the late Qing that centered on responding to the challenges posed by the West and on undertaking political reform.[41]

The relationship between the Changzhou school and the dynastic government provided an important juncture for the rise of New Text classical studies. In this sense, it is not the school methods themselves through which classical scholars delighted in the Way, but rather the horizon of classical learning and politics, that can give us our fundamental methodology for understanding New Text classical studies. However, while there is no lack of evidence to attribute the rise of New Text classical studies to the political struggle between Zhuang Cunyu and Heshen, we still face some questions.[42] More importantly, this explanation limits the political horizon to palace politics, essentially eroding the link between New Text classical studies and broader sociopolitical concerns and making it difficult to explain why New Text classical studies emphasized imperial power, legal authority, and legal precedent. The political issues covered by New Text classical studies extended far beyond the Heshen Incident and palace politics. New Text classical studies centered on institutions, law, and imperial power. Its theory of ritual thus linked relevant laws and institutions to its thinking around dynastic legitimacy. This shift changed the inherent structure of Neo-Confucianism's theory of moral centrality, giving free rein to key topics from the early Qing, such as the unity of governance and morality, Principle and ritual, and ritual and punishment. If we view the rise of Gongyang studies merely as the echo of the Ming-era Donglin Faction, how would we explain the aforementioned theoretical peculiarities of New Text classical studies?

Here, I will attempt to expand the horizon of Elman's "classicism and politics" from a different angle. New Text classical studies took advantage of the trend away from Neo-Confucianism during the Qing in order to convert the idea of moral relations into a theory of dynastic legitimacy, the most important piece of which was its critique of the inner-outer relations and arrangements established during the reigns of Kangxi, Yongzheng, and Qianlong. The Zhuang Cunyu–Liu Fenglu school was born of the "flourishing age" of the Qianlong-Jiaqing era: the Han people's large-scale fight against the Manchu had ended; the Mongol, Tibetan, and Muslim-majority areas in the western regions had been incorporated into the empire; and the norm of bannermen and civilians living among one another had taken shape. The political implications of New Text classical studies must be considered in concert with the particular structure of the Qing empire: an empire built through unending conquest, expansion, and interethnic segregation and integration, whose imperial system and social hierarchy were rooted in diverse ethnic privileges and institutions and in the multivalent power centers that resembled decentralized enfeoffment.

The significance of New Text classical studies can only be fully comprehended in the political horizon, but the meaning of "politics" here goes beyond palace politics and clan relations. During the mid-Qing, New Text classical studies concerned itself with the legal authority of the Qing court vis-à-vis Manchu-Han relations and the political recognition and standing of Han officials, as well as the question of how to expand the concept of ritual within the country's inner-outer policies. In other words, mid-Qing New Text classical studies answered the following two questions: One, on which principles should the legal authority of the Qing empire be established? Two, on which principles could the legitimacy of Han officials be established within this legal authority? There is an intimate connection between the Heshen affair and Han clan genealogy, researched exhaustively by Elman, and the two questions asked above: the questions of Yi-Xia and inner-outer, debated again and again by the Zhuang Cunyu–Liu Fenglu school, all touch on the Manchu-Han issue. Zhuang Cunyu and Liu Fenglu both held key posts and were extremely sensitive to the relationship between the Manchu nobles and Han officials in the court power structure, but from the principles of Confucian ethics, it would be reductive to say the Manchu-Han issue was merely an issue of one's career. For them, the Manchu-Han issue was not a question of individual status and palace politics, because it was enmeshed with the political characteristics of the Qing imperial court, the court of an ethnic minority. This is exactly why the Zhuang Cunyu–Liu Fenglu school had a systematic theory, and why what they discussed was the question of the empire's political legitimacy. New Text studies took the empire's political structure and ethnic diversity as theoretical starting points, drawing critical conclusions from the Confucian horizon regarding the politics, laws, and institutions of the Kangxi-Yongzheng-Qianlong era. Accepting the legitimacy of the dynasty, New Text classical studies criticized the ethnic hierarchy within the imperial system, transcending the Yi-Xia dichotomy of Song-Ming Neo-Confucianism and early-Qing studies of the classics. Thus, while New Text classical studies had very little impact on legal praxis, making sense of Qing classical scholarship's abiding interest in the ritual system, laws, and imperial power is still an important historical question: New Text classical studies is a theory of the legitimacy of dynastic government.

2. Gongyang Studies and the Legitimacy of the Mongol Yuan Dynasty

One of the fundamental problems faced by the Qing government was that of legitimacy—that is, how to remake a Manchu dynasty as a Chinese dynasty. As a theory of political legitimacy, New Text classical studies—more specifically, Gongyang studies—provided an important channel through which the new dynasty could derive legitimacy from the Confucian system of ritual and laws. From a long-term historical point of view, the Gongyang discourse on legitimate succession, with its "Three Sequences discourse" (*santong shuo*), its concept of Grand Unification, and its viewpoint on law, had never been a purely Confucian theory, yet it had provided one of the main supports for legitimizing new dynastic foundings since the Qin and Han, to the point where it becomes difficult to give a historical account of it within the conceptual framework of Qing New Text classical studies.[43] Previous studies emphasize the sudden reemergence of New Text classical studies at the end of the eighteenth century, holding that the school had all but disappeared after the Eastern Han (25–220 CE). These discussions are based in the perspective of academic history, and rarely touch on the relationship between Gongyang thought and the political legitimacy of successive dynasties. Yet if we want to discuss the relationship between New Text classical studies and politics in the Qing, it will be impossible to understand the political implications and the development of New Text classical studies if we leave aside this context.

Let us begin our inquiry with the question of legitimate dynastic succession. In his "Discourse on Political Legitimacy" (*Zhengtong lun*), Wang Yi (1321–1372) of the Ming dynasty wrote:

> The discourse on political legitimacy (*zhengtong*) is based on the *Spring and Autumn*. When the Zhou moved eastward, the royal court declined. Barbarians entered the various states, and Chu, Wu, and Xu all laid claim to the title of king. The world's people came almost to the point of not knowing where legitimacy lay. When Confucius composed the *Spring and Autumn*, it was to ensure correctness when writing about the king, and to ensure that the king would call upon Heaven. And in usurped states, all descended and wrote as scholars, each in order to express the meaning [or righteousness] of respecting the king. Thus the commentator says: "The noble man greatly adheres to correctness." He also says: "The King greatly unifies the realm." Thus, the meaning [or righteousness] of political legitimacy was initiated. Ouyang Xiu [1007–1072] said: "Correctness is that by which all the world's incorrectness is rectified; unification is that by which the world's inconsistencies are reconciled. When there is incorrectness and inconsistency, truth and falsehood are hard to distinguish, and this is why the discourse on political legitimacy was instituted."[44]

In a response to this essay, Fang Xiaoru (1357–1402, courtesy name Xizhi, of Ninghai, Taizhou) also wrote, "Where does the term 'political legitimacy' come from? I say: it comes from the *Spring and Autumn*. How do I know this is so? Although the directives of the *Spring and Autumn* are subtle, its main purpose is just to distinguish the positions of ruler and minister, to emphasize the difference between Chinese and barbarian, to uphold Heavenly Principle, and to curb human desires."[45] Wang Yi believed that the *Spring and Autumn*'s discourse on political legitimacy (*zhengtong*) arose from the need to overcome the inconsistency of All-under-Heaven and the resulting difficulty of distinguishing right and wrong, whereas Fang Xiaoru emphasized that the discourse's perspective on inner-outer and on political hierarchy could be traced back to the intent of the *Spring and Autumn*. Each had a different point of focus. At points of dynastic regime change, scholars, strategists, and imperial power itself all attempted to appropriate the intent of Gongyang studies into a systematized relationship in order to establish the legitimacy of the new dynasty. It had nothing to do with whether they were of the New Text school. According to "Three Sequences discourse," the legitimacy of a new dynasty is built on inheritance, synthesis, and renewal of the rituals, laws, and institutions of the preceding two dynasties. The Qing dynasty had to fashion itself after the two dynasties of Yuan and Ming in order to establish its place in the dynastic lineage and its rule over the Han and other peoples. The same was true for the Yuan and Ming.

Even so, what exactly was the basis of their legitimacy? Every dynasty establishes its lineage according to its peculiarities, but they still must prove their legitimacy. For instance, both the Song and the Ming, facing threats from northern peoples, based their succession on explicit inner-outer / Yi-Xia relations. These relations, however, were not simple interethnic and regional relations. Regarding Song succession, Wang Yi said:

> When the Song took possession of the world, they adhered to correctness and united it as one, and in so doing they restored its continuity of rule. Accordingly, from the inaugural year of the Jianlong reign [960 CE], legitimate rule prevailed, until North and South split apart in the turmoil of the Jingkang reign [1125–1127]. Although the Jin occupied the Central Plain, it cannot be said that they adhered to the world's correctness, and as soon as the Song moved south, it cannot be said that they united the world as one. The situation was similar to the Wei, Shu, Eastern Jin, and Later Wei periods, when it was difficult to understand right and wrong, and legitimate rule was accordingly cut off. But once the Liao had been annexed into the Jin, the Jin had then been annexed into the Yuan, and the Yuan had then annexed the Southern Song, the resulting polity did adhere to correctness and unite the world as one, again restoring legitimate rule. The Yuan continuation of legitimate rule should be taken as beginning in the thirteenth year of the Zhiyuan reign period [1276, of Yuan Shizu, the Shengde founding emperor, better known outside of China as Kublai Khan]. From this point of view, from the time of Yao and Shun, what is called legitimate rule has been cut off four times and restored four times.[46]

The Jin occupied the Central Plains but could not be considered legitimate; the Song fled south, and so too could not be considered legitimate. The substantive premise of "legitimacy of rule" was territorial wholeness. The succession of the Yuan dynasty was founded on its inheritance of the Song lineage and the merger of the two dynasties' unification of All-under-Heaven. Fang Xiaoru was more attuned to the distinction between legitimate succession and the peripheral tribes, stressing the idea of those "not of our kind" (*fei wo zulei*) in the theory of dynastic succession. He wrote:

> If a barbarian ruler should enter the central state, how can this unwelcome intrusion be prevented? How can one be sure that this harm will not again be visited on the central state? . . . Whoever undertakes the responsibility of writing should never borrow the legitimacy of the central state to promote ill-omened aspirations, but rather should cause those who have the world to guard against this harm, exercising constant care and not daring to ignore it. Let the barbarians understand the strictness of the great principle that legitimate rule cannot be exercised by those who are not of our kind, and put an end to their greedy opportunism. In his way they may also more closely accord with the intentions of the sages.[47]

To state that "legitimate succession cannot be exercised by those who are not of our kind" is to strictly define the boundaries between Yi (foreign) and Xia (Chinese). There are clear discrepancies between Wang Yi's and Fang Xiaoru's points of view, but their arguments both originate in distinguishing between the legitimate succession of the Song and the conquest of the Central Plains by the Jin. The continuity or rupture of the standard line of succession is a historical narrative, a theory of succession that touches upon different eras and personages. The view of legitimacy espoused by Ming-era Confucian scholars, which strictly distinguished Yi-Xia and inner-outer, echoed the theory of legitimate succession held by Song scholars (such as Ouyang Xiu), and stood in sharp contrast with arguments for the legitimacy of the ethnic-minority dynasties of the Jin, Yuan, and Qing.

Before delving deeply into the relationship between Qing politics and Gongyang studies, we must first briefly analyze the question of the legitimacy of the Mongol Yuan dynasty and its connection to Gongyang studies. The legal authority of the Qing embodied not only its "legitimate" inheritance from the Ming, but also a synthesis of the rule of the Mongol Yuan khans. Just like the Qing, the Yuan was a multiethnic empire ruled by an ethnic minority. The Mongol rulers faced the problem of integrating themselves into the Chinese dynastic lineage—which was also exactly the problem of how to establish their own legitimacy while implementing their rule over Han people and other ethnic groups. This problem was taken into consideration long before the conquest of the Southern Song dynasty. In the "Biography of Liu Zheng" (*Liu Zheng zhuan*) in the *History of the Yuan* (*Yuan shi*) it is written:

> In the eleventh month of the fourth year of the Zhiyuan reign, [Liu] Zheng [1211–1275] had an audience with the Son of Heaven [Kublai Khan], where he advised him to fell the Song. Zheng said: "Since ancient times, there has never been an emperor or king who did not regard unifying all within the Four Seas as one family as the crux of legitimacy. Our Sagely dynasty possesses seven or eight parts out of ten of All-under-Heaven. How can we leave even one corner unattended, and abandon legitimate rule?" [The Emperor] Shizu replied, "My decision is made!"[48]

The advice to "fell the Song" stemmed not only from military and economic concerns, but was also closely linked to the establishment of the empire's political legitimacy. Jao Tsung-I has commented, "Therefore, when the Yuan possessed the Song, it was for the sake of securing legitimate political succession, and this legitimate political succession has the meaning of Grand Unification."[49] "Possesses" means that in conquering the Song, the Yuan inherited the Song legacy. This method of inheriting legitimate succession comes directly from the Three Sequences discourse of Han-dynasty Gongyang scholarship.

Why was it only through an inheritance of Song rule that the Grand Unification of the Yuan could be defined? This also must be explained from the horizon of views of legitimate succession from the Song onward. According to the divisions of inner versus outer and Yi versus Xia, the Song dynasty represented political legitimacy in this era, while the Liao and the Jin could not be brought into the lineage of legitimate succession. These divisions were entirely consistent with the implication of examples of inner versus outer in Gongyang studies. As Yang Weizhen (1296–1370) states in *Distinguishing Political Legitimacy* (*Zhengtong bian*): "[The Yuan emperor] Shizu held that legitimate rule of the seasons should be attributed to the Song, and that the present-day inheritance of Song legitimacy belonged to him." In response to the argument about whether "taking over from the Liao may be construed as legitimate succession," he further argues:

> The rule of China is correct and great. It does not reside in Liao or Jin, but in the brightness of Heaven-conferred lordship over living beings.

> That being the case, the Grand Unification of our Yuan resides in the pacification of the Song, and not in the days of pacifying the Liao and Jin. . . . For if we do not hold that the correctness of natural order and the greatness of civilizational rule belong to our Yuan by inheritance through possession of the Song, just as the Song inherited them from the Tang, and the Tang from the Sui by inheritance from the Jin and the Han, and absurdly rely on a substitute inheritance, wishing to attribute the counterfeit rule of rude tribes to our Yuan, then what sort of an age do today's gentlemen think we are living in, and what sort of ruler would a sage be in our times?[50]

He clearly rejects the possibility of establishing legitimate rule through an inferior succession from the Liao or Jin.

The Yuan dynasty, however, was built on the foundation of the Mongol Empire. Its ethnic relations, class system, and imperial scope, therefore, could not be straightforwardly absorbed into the Song order, nor simply contrasted with the Jin order. The strict division of foreign versus Chinese in the Song Confucian concept of ritual order provides no grounds to argue for the legitimate succession of the Yuan. In 1272, after conquering the Southern Song, Kublai Khan proclaimed the empire as the Yuan. This title was the suggestion of a Jurchen. On the fifteenth day of the eleventh month of that same year, Kublai Khan abrogated the Law of Taihe (*Taihe lü*), which had defined the Jin Taihe era. (The Tang legal code influenced all subsequent dynasties, either directly or indirectly. The Song, Jin, and Ming carried on Tang law, while the Qing followed Ming law.) The Law of Taihe was promulgated in 1201. According to the "Treatise on Criminal Law" in the *History of the Jin* (*Jin shi: Xingfa zhi*), this was the inherited Tang legal code, as practiced by the Jin dynasty (1115–1234). The Mongols conquered the Jurchens in 1234, but the Law of Taihe remained until Kublai abolished it in 1272, never to be reinstated. The Yuan did not reinstate the Song Penal Code when they abolished the Law of Taihe, nor did they ever put forth a formal legal code of their own. Thus, they are the only dynasty in Chinese history that did not promulgate new law.[51] In order to limit the legal autonomy of the nobility, patriarchal clans, religious groups, and ethnic groups, each dynasty would promulgate its own legal code in the early years of its rule. This was in fact meant to regulate legal and geographical space through regulation and unification. The promulgation of new laws and the continuous promotion of their codification and uniformity were therefore meant to draw legal practice as closely as possible into the political system of the bureaucratic empire, and to place the law under imperial authority. The lack of a unified set of decrees and regulations at once reflects the reality of legal autonomy in its various forms, while also signaling a loosening of the court's bureaucratization and of absolute imperial power.

Unlike other empires with more distinct legal traditions, the laws of the Chinese empire were regarded as the embodiment of rituals. However, this distinction should not be exaggerated, as the rulers of practically every early empire (Rome, Byzantium, the Sassanian Empire, and so on) "attempted to portray themselves and the political systems they established as the bearers of special cultural symbols and missions. . . . The rulers of these societies invariably tried to be perceived as the propagators and upholders of, and to present their polities as the bearers of, these cultural orientations and traditions."[52] If we say the law constitutes a fundamental element of the legitimacy of the Chinese empire, it is because proof of legitimacy of succession rests on a particular view of ritual order. From the perspective of Qu Tongzu's argument about the "Confucianization of Chinese law," the relationship between the law and ritual is an essential element of Chinese law and legitimacy of succession, and every edict, policy, and regulation is made to supplement this permanent legal framework.[53] The ruler may promulgate law, but he may not formulate laws arbitrarily; the historic nature of the legal code constitutes a type of authority, one that bounds the legitimacy of imperial power and the dynasty. Of course, the royal court may amend the law in accordance with historical changes, but if it fails to do so lawfully and rationally, these very revisions will jeopardize the legitimacy of the court and its policies. The legal code is the legal basis of Confucian values and institutions. Should this code become empty or ambiguous, Confucian values and institutions will be put in a precarious position. For this reason, from the Confucian point of view, the failure to promulgate law itself constitutes a crisis of legitimacy. In "A Request to Define the Auspicious Virtue of the Dynasty" (*Qing lunding deyun zhuang*), Wang Yun (1227–1304) explicitly uses discourse on the Fivefold Cycles (based on Five Elements cosmology) and Grand Unification to explain the ambiguity of the "legitimate succession" of the Yuan dynasty, and the need to determine its cosmologically grounded auspicious virtue:

> I have heard that since ancient times, no ruler has changed the mandate but in response to Heaven, inferring from the Fivefold Cycles to clarify the commencement of their founding reigns. Examples are Yao according with Fire, Shun with Earth, and Xia with Metal, the rulers of Yin and Zhou according with Water and Wood, and those of Han and Tang with Fire and Earth. At the beginning of the Taihe reign period [1200–1208] of the conquered Jin, its auspicious virtue had already been set, and the year-end sacrifice name and the style and color of its ceremonial garments had been renewed accordingly. Now our state has possessed the provinces of the Central Plain for more than sixty years, yet the matter of its auspicious virtue has never been discussed, amounting to an omission in the Way of Grand Unification. Why is this? With regard to the body of the state, this is truly a serious matter, which moreover touches on the ascendancy of current civil administration, the governance of court institutions, and the regulation of ceremonial insignia and bodyguards. If one does not first determine the auspicious virtue of a reign, how can the colors of carriage attire and flags be properly esteemed?[54]

In the model of dynastic change, the promulgation of new law is inseparable from the establishment of the legitimacy of succession. It is hard to establish the legal authority of a dynasty if the legal judgments of different times and places cannot be integrated into its own. Wang Yun's thoughts on the ambiguity of the Yuan dynasty's legitimate succession inevitably become a discussion of how to establish a new law or new king.

This way of linking discussion of Five Elements theory with Grand Unification thought continues from Dong Zhongshu's *Luxuriant Dew of the Spring and Autumn Annals.* In "General Preface to *Eight Cases of Legitimate Succession*" *(Zhengtong balie zongxu),* Yang Huan (1186–1255) refutes the theory of legitimate succession based on genealogy, changing the basis of legitimate succession to the new king's own governance, and citing "inner-outer" examples from the Gongyang as the root of legitimate succession. This clearly is because the Mongol Yuan were a foreign people who had entered into the

Central Plains, and thus had to reestablish inner-outer relations in order to claim legitimacy. He wrote:

> The Gongyang states: "Record the internal and omit the external." How is it that we reject the Liu Song [420–479 CE] and include the Northern Wei [386–535 CE]? It is from regret that China had no [legitimate] ruler. In the days of Daming [second reign period of the Liu Song emperor Xiaowu, r. 454–464 CE], the oppression of his cruel and dissolute rule was extreme. The central states practiced foreign ritual, and thus became foreign; and foreigners entered into the central states, and thus became of China. Moreover, when [the Tang emperor] Suzong [r. 756–762 CE] swept away the great robber [An Lushan (703–757 CE)] and returned to the imperial palace, one does not say that he recovered it, but only that he went to it. Why is this? It is because he ascended the throne by violence. . . . If the kingly Way is not clear, reward and punishment cannot last for long. And then, as between developing the sincerity of Heavenly Principle and conforming to the falsity of human feeling, without this which takes precedence? The Two Emperors and the Three Kings [Tang Yao, Yu Shun, Xia Yu, Shang Tang, and King Wen (or King Wu) of Zhou] extended governance and created law; [the tyrants] Jie and Zhou [of Shang] and You and Li [of Zhou] extended the chaos of past times. It is a general principle, and is the real story behind the rise and decline of Qin, Han, the Six Dynasties, Sui, Tang, and the Five Kingdoms.[55]

This is an argument, centered on ritual, that relativizes inner-outer and Yi-Xia relations, and describes legitimate succession from a standpoint of historical change. And it is also based on this understanding that Yang Huan, following Gongyang interpretations, takes up the claim that it was Confucius who wrote the subtle and profound words of the *Spring and Autumn*, transforming historical narrative into a legal code for governing the world. Xie Duan (1279–1340), Tao Zongyi (1329–1412), Bei Qiong (1314–1379), Ma Duanlin (1234–1322), Zhang Shen (fl. 1374), Chen Cheng (fl. late Yuan dynasty), Wu Cheng (1249–1333), and Wu Lai (1291–1340) were all among those who from different viewpoints and in different aspects expounded on the connection between writing history and establishing legitimate succession. Xie Duan talked about the problem of succession in the Liao, Song, and Jin dynasties, and opposed taking region or ethnicity as the basis for legitimate rule:

> Some also say: The Liao state occupied a secluded area, its laws and institutions were not unified, and so it is hard to compare it with the Yuan, the Wei, or the Northern Qi. I say: To put it in this way is even more superficial. If occupying the central land is what confers legitimacy, then the lands acquired by Liu Shi, Murong Fu, and Yao Helian are all the old capital of the Five Emperors and Three Kings. If having the Way is what confers legitimacy, then one who accords with Qin's measure and is possessed of bold talent and sagacity will surely be trusted; if one conducts affairs in the manner of Zhu Liang [the state of Later Liang (907–923), whose founder, Zhu Wen, forced the abdication of the last Tang emperor, Ai Di, and then had him murdered], with usurpation and civil strife, then even if one avoids death, comparing the two, who will gain succession? When there is the principle of passing on through granting and receiving there will be no censure on this account, and moreover from the inception of the Taihe reign [1200–1208] the [Jin] court already had this discourse. . . . Among the scholar-officials of the Central Region (*Zhongzhou*), there are those who do not understand that in their rise the Liao and the Jin were each completely different. If the *Liao History* had been completed earlier, the world would have a definitive judgment. What need would there be for further words?"[56]

By compiling the history of the Liao, he attempted to establish proper genealogy and legitimate succession.

By the same logic, the Yuan literati assiduously compiled prior laws, calling for the reinstatement of the legal system, but the Yuan court's work to revise the dynasty's laws and regulations was never fully realized. Ming Taizu believed that a major reason for the collapse of the Yuan was its failure to promulgate law, and therefore quickly set about restoring the legal system. From this perspective, not only do the efforts of the Yuan literati to reinstate the legal process dovetail with the Three Sequences discourse of Gongyang studies; the Ming dynasty's interpretation of the fall of the Yuan can also be channeled into "Three Sequences discourse." Why the Yuan did not promulgate its own legal code is a complicated question. In order to explore this latter issue, it is necessary to briefly mention two related arguments. One stresses that the Mongol Yuan dynasty has the characteristics of an empire—a multiethnic, multicultural court ruled directly by the Mongols, quite unlike the "quasi-nation-state" of the Song dynasty, which was ruled by the Han people. If we say that the Song criminal law and the Jin Law of Taihe are both laws of historically bureaucratic empires with the characteristics of quasi-nation-states, then they could have been adapted neither to the multifaceted ethnic relations of the Mongol Yuan empire, nor to the privileged position of the Mongol people in that empire.[57]

The other view emphasizes how shifts in Tang-Song social structure influenced Yuan society, and that the adoption of case law during the Yuan originates in the preceding social developments. Miyazaki Ichisada states: "The reason that the Yuan never made any laws had nothing to do with their being a foreign dynasty. On the contrary, the social changes that occurred during the Tang and Song in China left no time for such legislation as was made during the Medieval period." In the Yuan legal system, precedent was "characterized by Mongolian style, that is to say the Western style of that time, of the transition from medieval to modern."[58] Miyazaki is the major proponent of the argument that the Song dynasty was a "quasi-nation-state." This point is not limited to the Song political and economic systems, but extends to the affirmation of "modernity" in Chinese history, or even East Asian history, as a whole; the emphasis on the "Western characteristics" of Mongol case law is directly connected to this basic point about "modernity." Miyazaki refuses to accept that as an ethnic-minority dynasty, Yuan rule constituted a fundamental change to political and social structure. Demonstrating the break between the Song and the Yuan is a secondary objective; his main goal is to prove the continuity between the two. This is consistent with his argument that "China's Modern Age" began in the tenth century with the founding of the Song dynasty.

It is clear that the Yuan organized its political structure in accordance with Han law, but there are also significant differences and points of rupture as history progresses from the centralized administration of the Song dynasty to the Yuan imperial state. First, the Yuan was built on the foundation of the ever-expanding Mongol Empire, a unique pastoral empire whose sense of hierarchy was less defined than that of the Song. For example, the concept of property on the grasslands differs from that of agrarian society: the grasslands are ultimately collective property. Only with livestock does the issue of private property finally arise. This means that the legal system of the Central Plains, based on land ownership, is not totally compatible with the pastoral concept of property rights. While the developments during the Tang-Song that Miyazaki mentions had an important influence on the Yuan legal system, I am afraid that one cannot ignore the difficulty in assimilating the legal concerns of the Song Penal Code into the power system of a pastoral empire. (The coexistence of the Law of the Great Qing and the Law of the Mongols during the Qing dynasty presents the same problem.) Second, the Yuan also faced the problem of integrating the khanate with Chinese imperial power: on the one hand, the central government of the Yuan was formed from the "interior" of present-day Hebei, Shandong, and Shanxi provinces, with provincial administrations (branches of the Imperial Secretariat) set up in peripheral regions, a continuation of the bureaucratic state system that began to take shape under the Tang and Song. Within the political structure of this bureaucratic state system, a unified, nonindividualized legal system is essential; on the other hand, the Yuan "crossed the Yin Mountains in the north, the shifting sands of the remote west, the farthest reaches of the east, and the southern lands across the sea,"[59] a vast territory that cannot be compared to the Han or Tang dynasties. However, there was a consequence to this vastness: Even in its heyday, the Mongol Empire could not form a unified government. In order to control Helin, Yunnan, Huihui, Weiwu, Hexi, and Liaodong, Kublai Khan (Yuan Shizu) enfeoffed the kings of each region as garrison commanders. In this way, the pre-Song system of enfeoffment was somewhat restored. Prior to the Yuan, the trans-Eurasian empire built by Genghis Khan had already splintered into the independent khanates of the Golden Horde, Chagatai, Ögedei, and the Ilkhanate. While in name the Yuan emperor was the Great Khan in command of these khanates, in reality this could no longer be viewed as a unified political entity. From the perspective of the political structure of the Yuan, the four classes—the Mongols, the Semu (lit. "assorted groups" from West and Central Asia), the Han, and the Southerners—and the institutionalization of these classes in the political, economic, and military systems, differentiated Yuan society from that of the Song.

My question is this: How exactly did these particular imperial inner-outer relations and political-legal context affect the political perspective of the literati? What is the connection between this political-legal context and Yuan-era Gongyang studies? John D. Langlois, Jr. explains it thus: Among China's literati, the abrogation of the Law of Taihe produced two related movements, one calling for the reestablishment of lawmaking, the other looking for legal resources in the Confucian canon. In this historical relationship, Yuan literati in particular emphasized the Han-era take on the Gongyang, which regarded the *Spring and Autumn Annals* as a text of criminal law, thereby making it an applicable legal classic. According to their understanding, *Spring and Autumn* Gongyang studies was a repository not only of ethics, but also of legal and procedural tools. It could help rulers to implement their order of rule, as well as provide bureaucrat-scholars the basis to advise or dissent with the ruler; accordingly, it would allow regulations and supplementary adjudication to be seen as equivalent to law. (They compared these temporary regulations to Tang law, and thus brought Gongyang studies within the ambit of law, though the analogy itself is forced.)[60] Absent the specific political-legal context of the Yuan dynasty, we would not be able to understand why so many literati devoted so much effort to studying the *Spring and Autumn* as a "book of penal law." According to Li Zefen's evidential investigation, a total of 213 treatises on the *Book of Changes,* 149 on the Four Classics, and 127 on the *Spring and Autumn* were produced during the Yuan.[61] Langlois has already cited the following examples, so I will simply supplement his research here with findings from other sources.

One example comes from Hu Zhiyu (1227–1293). In *Reading the Spring and Autumn* (*Du Chunqiu*) and *On Methods of Governing* (*Lun zhifa*), he discusses the differences between Mongol and Chinese law, and argues for the necessity of combining the two into a unified legal system. In his view, due to the lack of a legal code, each level of local government had its own administrative system, laws, and legal precedents, while the six ministries of the central government each had their own "opinions" (*yi*) and the heads of each ministry had their own "theories" (*lun*). Therefore, whether looked at from the perspective of unifying legal institutions or of administering a multiethnic empire, it was of the utmost importance to strengthen central authority, maintain the balance of social relationships, and reestablish a unified legal system. From another aspect, this explains the multicentered structure of the Mongol Yuan empire and the connection between these multiple centers of power and the fracturing of judicial authority. The abrogation of the Law of

Taihe was likely due to Hu's advice. In the twenty-second *juan* of the *Complete Works of Zishan* (*Zishan daquan ji*), Hu suggests that the system of the conquered Jin dynasty and the Law of Taihe are unsuited to the Mongol and Han peoples: "In the present day, from the central government down to provincial administrators, all establish judicial officers, yet there is no law to examine; they dare not rely on the old Taihe Code. Han people cannot completely understand Mongol ancestral law, and with no explicit provisions promulgated they are unable to comply with it in their actions."[62] In reality, Yuan legal reform followed a different path of development, relying on regulations and legal precedent to fill in the gaps in the legal code. Hu's argument against the Law of Taihe did not simply support this development, however. On the contrary, what he called for was the establishment of a new legally constituted authority.

Wu Cheng (1249–1333) and Wu Lai (1297–1340) give us two other examples. According to the *Teachings of the Scholars of Song and Yuan* (*Song Yuan xue'an*), Wu Cheng studied under Cheng Ruoyong and followed Zhu Xi's focus on the Four Books. However, as *Overview of the Classics* (*Zhu jing xushuo*) and his other writings show, outside the pathway of Neo-Confucianism he was also committed to the study of the classics, and touched upon the problem of New and Old Texts. In his evaluation of the three commentaries on the *Spring and Autumn*, he held that "their explanations of the *Spring and Autumn* contain true sentiments and empty words. They do not ignore history in discussing affairs, do not depart from commentaries to seek the classics, and do not simply rely on praise and blame to doubt the Sages." He further argued for linking the *Book of Changes* with the *Spring and Autumn*, and proposed that "the classics definitely do not exceed the bounds of history."[63] This "middle ground" kind of view actually negated the tradition of giving weight only to the Zuo commentary, and promoted the Gongyang and Guliang commentaries as sound interpretations.[64] In "Succession of Learning" (*Xuetong*) and "Issues of Interpretation" (*Cewen*), Wu Cheng engaged in discussions of central authority and of legal issues. His *Compiled Explanations of the Spring and Autumn* (*Chunqiu zuanyan*) may be seen as a work of classical scholarship; and in its "general principles," according to his viewpoint of treating the *Spring and Autumn* as a book of penal law, Wu divides its meanings and objectives into seven categories: aside from the Five Rites of sacrificial ceremonies, funerals, receptions, military rites, and wedding ceremonies, he adds categories for the Way of Heaven and for human social order, so that the *Spring and Autumn* became a set of basic principles for dealing with every kind of human issue.[65] In Wu Lai's *Collected Works of Mr. Wu Yuanying* (*Yuanying Wu xiansheng wenji*) there are also similar discussions, touching on questions in the *Spring and Autumn* concerning Yi-Xia, "governing institutions," and "expedient measures." In his essay "On Changing Reign Titles" (*Gaiyuan lun*), he expresses his disapproval of the practice, and based on this, reinterprets the principles of the *Spring and Autumn*'s chronological records. At the very least, this proves that Yuan literati broadly considered some of the fundamental intentions of Gongyang studies in their arguments to confirm the legitimate succession of the Yuan.[66]

Ouyang Xuan (1283–1357), a descendant of Ouyang Xiu, was not a Gongyang scholar but a specialist in the *Book of Documents*. However, he broadly applied the *Rites of Zhou*, the *Book of Documents* (*Shang shu*), and the *Book of Changes* to expound on the importance of legal statutes and of ruling the people according to law, and in this he showed a strong tendency toward Gongyang studies. As Jao Tsung-I puts it, there was a difference of emphasis between north and south in Song-era scholarship on the *Spring and Autumn*:

> The Northern Song emphasized respect for the king (as can be seen in Sun Fu's *Twelve Essays on the Subtle Details of Venerating the King in the Spring and Autumn* [*Chunqiu zunwang fawei shi'er pian*]), while the Southern Song focused on repelling the barbarians (as in Hu Anguo's *Commentary on the Spring and Autumn* [*Chunqiu zhuan*] shows) . . . Respect for the king led to promotion of the Grand Unification theory, and what Master Ouyang's theory of legitimate succession gained from the *Spring and Autumn* lies in this. The Yuan era arose when peripheral tribes came in to rule the central states, and those who argued for its legitimacy could also only rely on the theory of Grand Unification to establish their discourse.[67]

Gongyang scholarship considered the *Spring and Autumn* as a book of penal law, as a renewal of kingship, and as orderly sequence itself, and thus provided a resource for Yuan literati in their discussions on the unification of imperial authority and on the unification of statutory law.[68] None of these works are Gongyang scholarship in the strict sense, but rather are writings on statecraft that bring questions of imperial law, institutions, authority, and historical legitimacy into the horizon of Gongyang studies. The *Spring and Autumn* and its doctrine of Grand Unification provided the theoretical basis for the centralization of power and the unification of the judicial system, and the emphasis put on this text and its legal content by the literati was a direct response to the Yuan empire's inherent institutional problems, that is, the political reality of its multiple centers of power and its lack of a unified judicial system.

3. The Manchu Qing and Chinese Dynastic Legal Authority

The fact that the "Three Sequences discourse" and the legal implications of Gongyang *Spring and Autumn* studies were used to prove the legitimacy of a new dynasty clearly indicates that dynastic legitimacy relied upon historical tradition. Legitimacy was not only founded on the strength of the dynastic ruler, but also relied on the recognition and judgment of the general public, as well as on their customs and practices and on their changing demands. In this sense, an "autocratic dynasty" (*zhuanzhi wangchao*) cannot be built solely on the power and will of the ruler. In Jao's judgment, "The Yuan era arose when peripheral tribes came in to rule the central states, and those who argued for its legitimacy could also only rely on the theory of Grand Unification to establish their discourse"; this situation was very much like that of the Qing. The Manchu were a Jurchen tribe, and believed themselves to be the descendants of the Jin. When he established the Great Jin State, Nurhaci was surely quite familiar with the battle for legitimate succession between the Jin and the Song.

Early on in their struggle with the Song dynasty, the Jin were already keenly concerned with the problem of the legitimacy of their own system. In their discussions of its auspicious virtue (*deyun*), recorded in *Explanations of the Auspicious Virtue Chart of Great Jin (Da Jin deyun tushuo),* Zhao Bingwen, Huang Chang, Wanyan Wuchu, Wang Zhongyuan, Shumu Lushiji, Lü Ziyu, Zhang Hangxin, Muyan Wudeng, and Tian Tingfang all provided arguments based on the Three Sequences theory and on the concepts of "greatly abiding in the correctness" (*da juzheng*) and "Grand Unification" (*da yitong*). The *Explanations* recorded views on legitimate succession that had been developed by Jin scholar-officials from theories of the Five Virtues. The "Opinion of Zhang Hangxin" *(Zhang Hangxin yi)* states:

> If we examine the natural portents from the time of the founding of our state, and rely on the narrative of the Han succeeding to the Zhou and of the Wei succeeding to the [Former] Jin, then they may be determined as the auspicious virtue of [our] Jin, confirming our inheritance from the Tang. Accordingly, we receive the unification of Heaven [the third of the "Three Sequences" (*santong*)], are united with ancestral intentions, do not depart from ancient standards, and also accord with human hearts.[69]

The "Opinion of Huang Chang" *(Huang Chang yi)* states:

> The [Gongyang] commentary says: "The noble man greatly adheres to correctness." It also says: "The King unifies the realm." Correctness (*zheng*) is that by which the incorrectness of All-under-Heaven is rectified; unity is that by which all inconsistencies under Heaven are unified. It is from incorrectness and inconsistency that the discourse on political legitimacy arises, and only when this discourse has arisen can discussions about a dynasty's auspicious virtue be settled. Speaking of this from the present time, the Tang ruled according to the virtue of Earth, and after the passage of three hundred years, Earth gave birth to Metal, so that for one who would follow the Tang and rule, his virtue must lie in Metal. . . . When Our Ancestral Emperor [Jin Taizu, r. 1115–1123] arose and first established the Shouguo reign period [i.e., in 1115, inaugurating the rule of the Jin dynasty], he said that of all things that do not change, there is nothing that compares with Metal [*jin,* which is also the character for gold, i.e., metal in its purest form]. Now all the ministries shall esteem the color white, which is the correct color of Metal [or Gold], and henceforth our state shall be known as Great Jin. How godlike was this pronouncement! It was almost as if Heaven had awakened it. He was succeeded by the Emperor Taizong [r. 1123–1135], who subsequently pacified the Liao and the Song. For where the Liao and the Song could not correct each other, We corrected them; and where they could not achieve unity, We united them. Legitimate succession [or "correct unification" (*zhengtong*)] certainly lies with us![70]

The "Opinion of Muyan Wudeng" *(Muyan Wudeng yi)* states:

> Since ancient times, there have been many rulers who have inferred their auspicious virtue. Some have designated it by sequence [i.e., according to the succession of the Five Elements], while others have selected it with the aid of omens. Thus, the Two Emperors and Three Kings have mutually relied upon the Five Elements, as related in the Han histories, and this has been a matter of designating the auspicious virtue they have succeeded to by sequence. Up to the Han era, if one were not persuaded by the discourses of Jia Yi or a Gongsun Chen [i.e., on the faults of the Qin dynasty], one could with one's banners exalt the color red, and this was to choose one's fortune by omens derived by cutting a snake [a reference to the story in the *Records of the Grand Historian* of how Liu Bang (251–195 BCE), the future Han Emperor Gaozu, decided to rise up in rebellion against the Qin after killing a white snake]. From this point of view, the sequence by which auspicious virtue is inherited when taking up the Heaven-conferred mandate is a matter determined through wise institutions. As to our Emperor Taizu, as soon as he put on the robe the matter was settled, and accordingly the state was called Great Jin, with winter sacrifices set for the second month. At this time, although the matter of auspicious virtue had not yet been thoroughly investigated, yet by a sagely stratagem he obtained its correctness, and was in brilliant accord with the portents of Heaven![71]

The preceding examples show that the Jin rulers carried on the Chinese discourse on legitimate succession, and that they definitely used the Three Sequences theory to provide a basis for Jin legitimacy. The *Explanations of the Auspicious Virtue Chart of Great Jin* included as an appendix a *Chart of the Auspicious Virtues of Past Dynasties* (*Lidai deyun tu*), which put in order the historical succession of auspicious virtues from Fuxi to the Song. Obviously, the Jin had already been situated within the Chinese dynastic system.

The Jurchen tribes were clearly no strangers to this particular theory of legitimacy from the Confucian tradition. Nurhaci's family name, Aisin Gioro, is composed of the Manchu words "Aisin," meaning "Jin," and "Gioro," meaning "surname"; the full name means Descendant of the Jurchen Clan. On the first month of the forty-fourth year of the Wanli reign (1616), after uniting the five Jurchen tribes and the four Haixi tribes, Nurhaci, a former general for the Ming, declared the founding of the Great Jin State (known historically as the Latter Jin), with Hetu Ala as the capital and the reign title of Tianming. In the third year of Tianming (1618), he roused his troops to right the injustices of the "Seven Great Hatreds" and attack the Ming. On November 22 (the thirteenth day of the tenth lunar month), 1635 (the eighth year of Ming Zongzhen, the ninth year of Jin Tiancong), Hong Taiji proclaimed that Taizu would be honored with the posthumous title of "Martial Emperor" (Wu Huangdi) and elaborated on Taizu's military victories, imitating the emperor's veritable records, and creating the name Manchu (thus changing "Zhushen" [Jurchen] to "Manchu"). Following the change to Manchu, the old names of the Jurchen clans and the ethnonym Zhushen were banned. The state of Jin became the Qing, and the reign title became "Chongde." Posthumous honors were bestowed on the four generations, and solemn preparations were made for the construction of the Imperial Ancestral Temple. All these measures implied that Hong Taiji was determined to become both a Chinese emperor and a great Mongol khan, with the obvious purpose of claiming All-under-Heaven. If we say that Nurhaci's "Seven Great Hatreds" proclaimed a determination to stand outside All-under-Heaven, then Hong Taiji's changing of names revealed the intention to reestablish legitimate succession, since abandoning the monikers Jurchen and Jin suggested the possibility of rejoining the category of "Chinese." From the perspective of imperial power, due to the unification of the dual roles of khan and emperor, when the Qing rulers inserted themselves into Chinese dynastic genealogy, the meaning of "China" differed significantly from that during the Song-Ming era.

According to scholars of Qing history, the title "Qing" is meant to outdo "Ming," and Taizong's change of reign title to "Chongde" (as compared with Chongzhen) serves as circumstantial evidence.[72] Soon after the Qing "entered the pass" (*ru guan*) they did away with their own legal tradition. The regulations they passed in 1646 were essentially copies of Ming law.[73] As for its political institutions, the Qing carried on many parts of the Ming system. Consequently, in order to expound on the legitimacy of the Manchu-Qing as "Chinese," late-Qing New Text scholars would argue that "the current dynasty is governed by Ming Taizu," that is, that the Qing continuation of the Ming system in Qing legal authority confirmed the propriety of Manchu rule.[74] In December 1634 (the seventh reign year of Ming Chongzhen, the eighth reign year of Jin Tiancong) the Mongolian Mergen Lama surrendered a statue of Mahākāla (a golden image of the Buddha cast by Drogön Chogyal Phagpa, the Imperial Preceptor under Kublai Khan, which successive Yuan emperors were required to consecrate prior to ascending the throne), which Hong Taiji enshrined in a temple he built in Shengjing (modern-day Shenyang); in May 1635, he ordered the selective translation of the Liao, Song, Jin, and Yuan histories, and he acquired the imperial seal from Ligdan Khan in Chahar, thus certifying his legal authority as Yuan emperor and Mongol khan. The Qing adopted Lamaism, accepted Phagpa's successor Changkya Khutukhtu (the Zhangjia Living Buddha) as Preceptor of State, and in keeping with Yuan precedent declared the Zhangjia lineage to be the religion of Inner Mongolia and the interior. It is worth mentioning that Hong Taiji only changed to the name Manchu four months after he ordered the translation of the Liao through Yuan histories and had acquired the imperial seal. His goal is clear: to first dissociate the Manchu from the Jurchen and the Jin, then confirm the Qing emperor as both Chinese emperor and Mongol khan, and the Qing dynasty as an imperial Chinese dynasty and as the Celestial Empire.[75]

These arrangements established the legitimate succession of the Qing according to Three Sequences discourse, quite possibly on the advice of a Han. Later, in the early eighteenth century, the Yongzheng Emperor refuted Lu Shengnan's "Discourse on Enfeoffment" (*Fengjian lun*), writing: "Unification of the central states began with the Qin, unification beyond the Great Wall began with the Yuan, and it has reached its zenith with our dynasty. This is all due to the spontaneity (*ziran*) of Heaven's seasons and of human affairs. How could it have been forced to occur by human effort?" This point of view is a direct continuation of the Hong Taiji era's conceptualization of the Qing empire.[76] This implies not only that the political theory of Gongyang studies contains institutionalized operation during the dynastic changeover, but that it had transformed into a system of rites and institutions. These legitimizing theories of rites and political institutions were not at the heart of Gongyang studies, but they did suggest an internal dialogue and symbiotic relationship between Gongyang studies and dynastic political institutions. If we fail to understand this point, we cannot fully grasp the historical root of New Text classical studies, nor its intrinsic connection to the legitimacy of the Qing empire.

The Qing dynasty was a multiethnic, multicultural empire that spanned a vast territory. As the dynasty of a northern people who came to the Central Plains, it was bound to face rebellion in the late Ming and early Qing periods, as well as challenges from the Yi-Xia distinction so deeply rooted within the Confucian tradition.[77] Thus readjustment of the Manchu-Han relationship was an important lever to establish the legitimate succession of the Qing dynasty, and the theories of "Manchu and Han are one" and relativization of Yi-Xia created for this purpose conflicted with its pluralistic imperial institutions and laws. From Kangxi onward, the Qing imperial court affirmed the traditional place of Confucianism, carrying on the institutions and laws inherited from the previous dynasty. While establishing a complete legal system (including criminal affairs, civil affairs, administration, litigation, and prison management), at the same time the Qing esteemed Confucianism as orthodoxy by loudly proclaiming the unity of rites and principles and of governance and the Dao. The crux of Qing institutional and legal reform was to revise the special privileges afforded the Manchu in the early years of the dynasty's rule, and to establish the principle of "Manchu and Han as one" advocated by Kangxi. Experts in Qing history have already made note of the following historical facts: In 1727, Yongzheng decreed that, excepting the grand secretary, no other posts would be divided between Manchu and Han, and would only be "ranked by sequence of appointment";[78] and furthermore exhorted the cabinet to "choose whom to employ solely according to ability, and not speak of them as Manchu or Han."[79] In order to ease the tension between the bannermen and the people, he also created a series of supervisory institutions and legal clauses, attempting to institutionally and legally narrow the gap between Manchu and Han.[80] When Qianlong ascended the throne, he became exceedingly concerned with the bias toward the Manchu in the employment system, saying:

> Both Manchu and Han are Our ministers and servants, and thus both are Our trusted assistants. They belong to one whole, and are bound together by their common cause. As for appointments, when measuring their ability and conferring rank, only their person and the suitability of the station are considered. We ought not to continue judging them as Manchu or Han. On the borderlands, military and garrison commanders report directly to me, regardless of whether they are Manchu or

> Han. . . . If in future there are requests like this that distinguish between Manchu and Han, or discriminate between bannermen and ordinary people, I will punish them severely.[81]

The passage above is addressed to vice military governor and bannerman Buyantu regarding his pushing for Manchus to fill the roles of provincial commander and governor in Fujian (Min), Canton (Yue), Guangxi (Gui), Guizhou (Qian), and Yunnan (Dian). Qing soldiers who crossed into China benefited from the help of Ming officers who surrendered and defected—in order to buy over these Han defectors, the Qing granted military and governing authority to the Han in the Southwest. After the pacification of the Three Feudatories, and particularly during the Qianlong period, Manchus occupied the positions of directors general, commissioners, provincial vice governors, and provincial judges. Thus, it became imperative for the Qing court to balance power relations in the Southwest and to redefine the status of Han soldiers and bannermen. According to historians of Qing law, Hongli's (Qianlong's) criticism of Buyantu was that although he protected Manchus from having to live and work together with the Miao people of these five provinces, in his personnel policies and conduct of government he held to an attitude of strict discrimination between Manchu and Han.[82] This proposition that "Manchu and Han are one" culminated in two legal formulations: first, the extension of banner criminal offenses to some "cases among the people";[83] second, the permission for Han who defected to the Manchu and held lower offices ("insignificant personnel" holding "civilian posts from the level of associate" and "military posts from the level of commandant" and below, as well as "those who have not yet taken an official post") to "leave the banners and become civilians."[84] "The imperial court's goal [in making these decrees and cases], while it did in part resolve the problem of supporting the growing population of bannermen and increase opportunities for the Han and Manchu to supplement each other's deficiencies, objectively functioned to remove the boundaries between the bannermen and ordinary people and to mitigate conflict between Manchu and Han."[85]

Given the multiple institutions, laws, cultures, and peoples of their empire, the Qing rulers sought in Confucianism a general principle that could encompass all differences, and used this as the basic premise for controlling the entire legislative process. To adapt to their new circumstances in China, the Manchu rulers based their own legitimacy on Confucian ritual, not only advocating for "Manchu and Han as one," but also restoring the legitimacy of the Confucian classics and literary Chinese in the imperial examinations. This process, however, was also fraught with danger, as the Confucian concept of ritual practice, and the distinction it makes between Yi and Xia, is an exclusionary concept. Thus, this utilization of ritual was by necessity one of reinterpretation and abstraction. Kangxi specifically emphasized "filial piety" as the basic principle governing the laws and institutions of the Qing. Filial piety is considered to be the core of Confucian ethics and ritual, but it is also a universally recognized moral principle. Although the Qing did not invent "ruling All-under-Heaven according to filial piety"—it was a tradition since the Han that tried to reconcile Confucianism and Legalism—in the multiethnic, multicultural environment of the Qing, filial piety was universalized and abstracted, thus providing different societies with a common moral base, including, clearly, the political sense.

Within Confucian ritual, "filial piety" (*xiao*) and "loyalty" (*zhong*) are two basic and tightly linked values, but Kangxi and Yongzheng rarely mentioned "loyalty," reiterating instead such Confucian terms as "righteousness" (*yi*), "bravery" (*yong*), "character" (*zhi*), and "culture" (*wen*). This did not change until the Qianlong era.[86] In the years following the fall of the Ming dynasty, "loyalty" came to refer to Han loyalty to the Ming and opposition to the threat of Manchu-Qing rule. It was thus imperative to pluck "loyalty" out of this historical context. From a political perspective, the tenet of "filial piety" is necessarily "abstract," since the Qing political structure was largely the bureaucracy that had been passed down and steadily developed since the Qin-Han era, and thus the polar opposite of the system of patriarchal clans and enfeoffment of the Western Zhou. The notion of "enfeoffment" cannot describe an imperial political structure or a national system of administration. We can only detect "feudal" elements at the upper levels of the aristocracy (the Eight Banners of the Manchu) along with similar systems among ethnic minorities (the Eight Banners of the Mongols), and among regional clan relations. In this sense, there is an abstract quality to the relationship between "filial piety" and institutional arrangements. Without this process of abstraction, the multiethnic, multicultural Qing empire would have been hard pressed to construct "Chinese identity" or to turn their history of conquest into a link in the chain of Chinese imperial history.

Filial piety in the abstract always complements institutional arrangements to a degree. If it did not, abstract principles of ritual—such as filial piety—could not be used as the basis for political legitimacy. How, then, can we observe the principle of "filial piety" in the law and in institutions? Along with the Qing's support for the patriarchal clan system as has already been discussed, the principle of filial piety seeped into the legal system itself. According to Qing law, when someone is sentenced to death or penal servitude, if the convicted is the only son of old and ailing parents, his sentence may be reduced; this is a norm carried over to the Qing from previous dynasties.[87] In 1805, this rule was entered into the Mongolian Statutes and Procedures: If one's parents are old and frail, the convict may care for his parents in lieu of serving a prison sentence. In addition, severe penalties were exacted on those who humiliated, assaulted, or murdered their elders or parents.[88] In this sense, the legislative process established an intrinsic relationship with the Confucian ethic of "filial piety." As the bannermen's customs became Sinicized, the Qing rulers rehabilitated relations between the former and civilians as they explored "Manchu and Han as one." An important aspect of this was that in theory the legitimacy of their rule was based on ritual, rather than on ethnicity. Legal historians divide banner decrees established in the Yongle-Qianlong era into general decrees and specialized decrees. General decrees include: bannerman homicides and cases of Manchu killing each other; regulations on mourning a parent's death for civilian and military bannermen; regulations for bannermen resigning from office in order to care for their parents at home; rules for garrisoned soldiers purchasing burial property; and private use of military equipment. Specialized decrees include: fugitive law, inheritance of official rank, and preserving the Manchu tradition of "domestic discipline."[89] All these particular laws and articles address filial piety in some way.

In order to adapt to the multiethnic empire's political order, under the premise of guaranteeing central control, the Qing dealt rather flexibly with matters of cultural and legal diversity and uniformity. Kangxi's call to "unite the hearts of inner and outer, fulfill the work of consolidation" articulates this effort. The Qing rulers combined military conquest with institutional reforms. In the Northwest, their policy was to "improve [local peoples'] education and leave their customs undisturbed; make uniform their governance and leave their customs unchanged." The Qing instituted laws to govern the ethnic-minority districts, such as the Mongolian Statutes and Procedures (*Menggu lüli*) and Huijiang Statutes and Procedures *(Huijiang zeli)*; and in the fifteenth to sixteenth year of Qianlong's reign established the Kashag system in Tibet and promulgated the Rules for Reconstruction in Tibet *(Xizang shanhou zhangcheng)*. The local chieftain system of the Southwest was changed by the suppression of the Revolt of the Three Feudatories (1673) and by the establishment of regular administrative regimes in non-Han areas (*gaitu guiliu*). By the Qianlong era, large-scale revolts against the Qing by the Miao (Hmong), Yi, and other peoples came to an end. In this historical period, when Qing rule was relatively stable and interethnic tensions had relaxed, the Qing government moved to weaken the "separation of Yi-Xia," making a series of decrees to reestablish legal and moral order. In the process of changing and integrating the ethnic and social groupings within the Qing empire, there was a trend toward legal and institutional convergence.

It is worth noting that in unifying either side of the Great Wall, the unity of law and territory became a critical factor in the enforcement of the law. Mongolian law, for example, was in constant flux under the Qing. The concept of property rights differs between nomadic and agricultural societies: the basic means of production in a nomadic society is livestock, not land, and "the herd constitutes the basic wealth of seasonal migration and herding life, and reflects the nature of its property system, so that nomadic societies often combine individual ownership of livestock with collective ownership of land."[90] Taking into consideration the different significance of livestock in the lives of nomads and of inland ethnic groups, the Court of Frontier Affairs recommended that a Han who steals animals from a Mongol should be sentenced according to the Mongolian Statutes and Procedures, while if they steal from another Han they should be sentenced according to the criminal law of the interior.[91] According to the principles of legal pluralism, most forms of compensation under the Mongolian Statutes do not apply to Han, meaning that a Mongolian victim of a crime may receive material compensation, while a Han victim would not enjoy the same treatment under the law. In 1761, a provision was added to the Mongolian Statutes stating that a Mongolian who commits a crime in the interior will be punished according to the criminal law of the interior, while a Han from the interior who commits a crime in Mongolia will be punished according to Mongolian statutes. Following this principle of geographic priority, the Mongolian Statutes and

Procedures would apply to territory beyond the Great Wall, and would no longer take into account the ethnicity of the victim. This provision reflected the growing interdependence of societies and intermixing of peoples on either side of the Great Wall. It was also the result of the Qing's reinforcement of the unification of imperial law. The language of the Mongolian Statutes and Procedures of the early Qianlong period was completely different from that of the documents and laws of the local judicature. It was divided into sections (twelve in all) and written in Mongolian, Manchu, and Chinese, expressions of the trend toward unification in the Qing legal system. By the nineteenth century, only certain provisions of Mongolian law differed from the law of the interior, and all Mongolian districts had to abide by the same statutes.

Still, some pluralism lingered in Qing social and legal institutions. As a pluralistic empire, the Qing did not impose the laws of the interior on the Mongols, nor did it nullify the Mongolian Statutes and Procedures. At the same time, several other factors influenced the unity of the Qing legal system. As Outer Mongolia submitted to the Qing, its laws and institutions became more and more like those of Inner Mongolia; but the law of the Dzungars, who had close ties to Mongolia, was vastly different. The Qing, which suffered heavy losses against the Dzungars, implemented strict local laws in order to exert their control. In addition to Mongolian law, there were also the "Muslim law" (*Huilü*) of the Uyghur regions and the "Foreign law" (*Fanlü*) of the Tibetan regions, as well as the Precedents of the Court of Frontier Affairs *(Lifan yuan zeli),* Ordinances on Criminal Punishment for the Xining Barbarians *(Xining fanzi zhizui tiaoli),* and Miao Cases *(Miao li),* which preserved the privileges of the Mongol and Tibetan aristocracy. The policy of "following local customs and conventions" was intimately tied with the submission of disparate people to Qing rule. The other side of "customs and conventions" is political control, military subjugation, and brute domination. These factors preserved internal differences between Qing institutions and Qing law. In view of this, several legal historians use the concept of "Qing legal pluralism" in discussions of the laws of the Mongols and other minority groups, and their relation to the laws of the interior of the empire. With "legal pluralism," the ruler implements different bodies of law according to the racial, religious, and ethnic groupings within the population.[92] If we transfer this concept elsewhere, we may say that an "institutional pluralism" existed during the Qing.

4. The Shifting Symbolism of the Great Wall

In the expanse of the Qing empire, legal and institutional pluralism entailed both the sense of equality and discriminatory policies. This is the intrinsic contradiction of the imperial system.[93] Important achievements were made in Manchu-Han relations under the reigns of Kangxi, Yongzheng, and Qianlong, but the essential elements of Manchu-Mongol aristocratic rule did not change as a result. The Eight Banner system included strict ethnic segregation through the distinction between bannermen and civilians: there was an inner-outer division between Han civilians on one end, and the Manchu and Mongol bannermen and eight Han military banners on the other. Han bannermen who resided long term "beyond the pass" or who won military merit in the Manchu conquest of the Central Plains had a certain privileged place in Qing politics, but they were never recognized as Manchu in terms of blood lineage (with several exceptions). Moreover, in Manchu parlance there was a distinction between the Internal Eight Banners and External Eight Banners (the former referring to the Affairs Office of the Internal Eight Banners). In this sense, there was an "inner" within the "inner." What political and legal pluralism reflect is precisely the multivalent political basis of Qing rule. Ethnicity and blood lineage were both of the utmost importance with regard to political, military, legal, and hierarchical relationships. As an ethnic-minority dynasty, the Qing rulers strove not only to uphold the unity and integrity of the dynasty through pluralism, but also to protect Manchu cultural identity. The Qing royal family adopted special protective measures, policies, and laws for the customs and regions of its Manchurian homeland. The policies and geographic planning for rites of ancestor worship and education in Manchuria differed from those of the mainland. In 1671, Kangxi established the "Eastern Tour" in which the emperor went to the Northeast at regular intervals to worship the ancestors and to make inspections. Qianlong, Jiaqing, and Daoguang all made several "Eastern Tours." Qianlong made visits to the Northeast in 1743, 1754, 1778, and 1783, and he attached great importance to the education and the preservation of Manchu culture among the children of bannermen in the region, as well as to Manchu-Han relations, successively promulgating policies and decrees to these ends.[94] These policies and decrees not only contradicted the principle of "Manchu and Han as one" which had persisted since Kangxi, but also directly conflicted with the long history of interethnic communities in the region.

As a border region, the inner and outer area on either side of the Great Wall had served as a center of trade and contact between nomadic and agricultural peoples over the long course of history. Mandatory policies of ethnic preservation were thus destined to have exclusionary or discriminatory consequences. In a certain sense, as Qing rule became more stable, its social institutions and laws grew more homogenous; and as its institutions and laws grew more homogenous, unresolved conflicts and contradictions that resulted from the heterogeneity within these same institutions and laws (including privileges and special protections) became more prominent. For example, in the process of lawmaking, the principle of integrated banner-civilian communities was not fulfilled. Ethnic inequality and segregation were encoded into Qing society through institutions and laws, conflicting with the Qing government's declaration that "Manchu and Han are one." From the legal perspective, the Qing retained ethnic privilege as stipulated by law. For example, Mongol and Manchu aristocrats were exempt from all types of physical punishment, but Han officials were not. The article "Exemption from Criminal Deportation" (*Fanzui mian faqian*) in the Qing Statutes and Procedures was designed to privilege bannermen. Institutionally, ethnic privilege was a hallmark of the Qing government. For instance, the power of the Court of Frontier Affairs was unprecedented in dynastic history. The ministry was run primarily by Manchu and Mongol officials, with the Manchu at the center; they never appointed Han as garrison generals of any border region, or as provincial commanders or cabinet ministers. Some members of the Han military banners held low-level office in the Chinese Archive (Handang fang), but never civilian Han.[95]

The Qing reinstated the imperial examination system, and made Chinese the main testing language. This policy, based on the principle of equality between Manchu and Han, was an attempt to lay the foundation for the new dynastic government. However, during one of his eastern inspection tours, Qianlong was shocked to discover that many Manchu children could not speak Manchu, nor were they versed in horsemanship or archery, the very skills which had enabled the Manchu to conquer All-under-Heaven. For this reason, on the second month of the twentieth reign year of Qianlong (1755), the court decreed that in the selection of talent from the three northeastern provinces and Ulaqi, "examinations in Chinese are permanently suspended," and that its master of ceremonies would thenceforth "clearly allow the Yi to enter the examinations along with all the others." This new policy lifted all restrictions on the selection of any minority person from the Northeast and expanded their opportunities for official careers,[96] though this obviously contradicted the requirement to use Chinese as the standard language of examination. According to the research of Zhang Jinfan and others, in the Qianlong period there was a specific agenda to decrees made regarding bannermen: to maintain the old customs of Manchuria, especially horsemanship, archery, and the spoken and written language. So that bannermen did not fall out of practice with the former two skills, Qianlong time and again made strict interdictions against any inner or outer official from the Eight Banners riding in sedan chairs, as well as severe criminal punishments for those who were not skilled in riding, shooting, or the Manchu language. He made the Manchu language, horsemanship, and archery requirements for official promotion. The following are several examples of such regulations: in the forty-first reign year of Qianlong (1776), it was decreed that all candidates who were inheritors of official rank would be tested first to "shoot three arrows," then "selected according to their examination scores."[97] In the fifty-ninth reign year of Qianlong (1794), the emperor saw that General De Ling of Taiyuan had submitted a memorial to the throne inscribed in Chinese. Qianlong not only rebuked him, but also decreed: "Notice is given directly to the Provincial Military Commander–cum–Regional Commander for the Protection of Imperial Mausolea in Manchuria that henceforth it is a civil offense to use only Chinese on inscribed memorials to the throne."[98]

The establishment of the Qing empire turned the conflict along the Great Wall from one among kingdoms or tribes into an internal conflict. In *Inner Asian Frontiers of China*, Owen Lattimore critiques the traditional historical narrative, which places southern society (or the Grand Canal) at the center, giving prominence instead to the role of the "border regions" in China's historical development. He reconstructs the central position of the Great Wall in "Inner Asia" against the backdrop of interaction between the nomadic and agricultural societies on either side. In his view, the history and internal boundaries of China are defined not by the clear "boundary" of the Great Wall, but by a series of "frontier regions" surrounding the Great Wall, constantly spreading and shifting from north to south. Grassland society is a product of history. Many "backward" nomadic tribes trace their origins to banishment from agricultural societies and share the same forebears as the Han. Grassland and agricultural societies are the products of historical interactions and entanglements, not of innately different tribes. From a Great Wall–centered point of view, the implications of the so-called frontier regions are defined not merely from the perspective of the interior or Central Plains, but also from the perspective of interrelations on either side of the Great Wall. The frontier regions connote mutually defined frontiers. There was never a clear demarcation between the peoples inside and outside the Great Wall, and the history of relations among the peoples along the Great Wall cannot be studied solely as a matter of political jurisdiction.[99]

According to the historical record, relations between the Western Regions and the dynasties of the Central Plains can be traced at least to 126 BCE, when Zhang Qian served as envoy to the Western Regions. Han (206 BCE–220 CE) and Tang (618–907) military control extended to the interior of the Western Regions, while the founding of the Mongol Yuan (1234–1368) set off an opposite historical wave of migration, trade, and culture moving from Central Asia to the Central Plains. The administrative map of the Ming was significantly reduced compared to that of the Yuan. Under the pall of military defeat, policies toward the Northwest and Northeast were fairly restricted during the latter Ming, with inner-outer difference and the separation of Yi and Xia coming to pervade scholarship and society.[100] In times of prosperity, however, the court always had expeditions to, and interest in, the Western Regions (*Xiyu*). (Fletcher particularly mentions the Ming interest in Mongolian horses.)[101] In the fourth reign year of Hongwu (1371), the provincial government of Yuan Liaoyang surrendered to the Ming, offering the administrative districts of Liaodong, troops and horses, and land taxes. Thereafter, the Ming set up the Liaodong Defense in Liaoyang, and the Nurgan Military Commission on the lower reaches of the Amur River. They also established self-sufficient station garrisons (*tuntian*), began construction of waterworks, and opened the market to trade in horses. After the reign of the Yongle Emperor (1402–1424), the inner palace official Yishiha, who had submitted to the Ming, traveled the East Sea nine times, attempting to reach every region that bordered China and the Pacific islands skirting the coast, as well as passage from Asia to America.[102]

As they established their legal authority, the Qing looked to the institutions and rituals of the Yuan and the Ming. Generally speaking, the diversity of institutions and laws had a historical basis. The Ming conducted trade and diplomacy with Central Asian commands through tributary trade, and forbade private merchants from direct trade with Central Asia. In actuality, though, illegal private trading never stopped. To control the Southwest, the Qing encouraged the Han to settle in the Yunnan-Guizhou region. Taiwan and most of the Southwest were already incorporated into China's administrative territory by the Ming, while the Northwest and Northeast were the original territory of the Manchu and Mongols. Against this backdrop, Qing policies in the Southwest and Taiwan differed from those in Mongolia, Tibet, and Xinjiang: The Northwest and Northeast had a complex of autonomous local governments and political structures, the Han were prohibited from mass migration to these regions, and Han were only permitted to do business there under certain conditions; whereas in the Southwest, after the local chiefs were supplanted by the direct control of the central government, the region was administered by centrally appointed, nonhereditary officials, and Han were encouraged to settle in the region. Under the influence of court policy, numerous conflicts arose between Han migrants and the local peoples (such as the Hui and the Miao).[103] From the perspective of New Text studies, such measures were in keeping with the principles of "linking the Three Sequences" (*tong santong*).

5. The Empire's Legal / Institutional Pluralism and Its Internal Contradictions

The establishment of the Qing dynasty symbolized the gradual dissolution of the Great Wall as a frontier region, providing the institutional prerequisite for New Text studies to apply the relativization of inner-outer and Yi-Xia to geographical studies of the Northwest. From the perspective of Qing imperial rule, the loss of the Great Wall as a meaningful frontier created a new problem: how to balance the application of different laws with inner-outer equality under the conditions of legal pluralism. In the case of interethnic integration, legal diversity and ethnic hierarchy were connected, and the growing migrant population exacerbated existing conflict. The Qing built *tuntian,* garrisons that produced their own food in the frontier regions, but prohibited the Han from reclaiming land in the Northeast. As early as the Kangxi era, farmers from Shandong, Shanxi, and Zhili fled land grabs and natural disaster, migrating north of Shanhaiguan. By the Qianlong era, the population of refugees from Shandong living beyond the Great Wall had grown even more. In the sixth reign year of Qianlong (1741), the newly recorded population of Fengtian was just over 13,800; by the forty-sixth reign year (1781), that number had grown to 390,000. In the month of February 1747 alone, there were between 2,000 and 3,000 migrants to the region.[104] In the thirty-sixth reign year of Qianlong (1771), the population of Jilin was tabulated at over 56,000; this grew to over 135,000 people by the forty-fifth reign year (1780). At first, the refugees were forced to work as seasonal laborers. Eventually, they became permanent residents, and Manchu-Han intermarriages increased.[105]

As droves of migrants came to Mongolian regions from the interior, legal conflicts between Mongols and Han also grew, bringing ethnic issues into the judicial process. The interethnic mixing that resulted from migration did not lead to centralization of the law. Quite the opposite, it undid some of the aforementioned unification. This was because the Manchu and Mongol aristocracies feared that the Han would assimilate, causing the region to lose its ethnic identity. In the fourteenth reign year of Qianlong (1749), the royal court sent its ministers to Josutu Aimag to investigate and prosecute claims of impoverishment of Mongolian land and a downturn in animal husbandry.[106] The ministers reclaimed land that the Mongols had leased to the Han by year of expiration, ordered Han to abandon their newly acquired properties and return to their ancestral homes, and strictly forbade the leasing of land in Josutu Aimag, Juuda Aimag, and Chahar Eighth Banner. They were not truly able to implement this program due to Han resistance, but the incident itself elucidates the interethnic conflict wrapped up in Qing-era migration and land reclamation policies. Ethnic minorities of the Northeast were still considered to be "of the same clan" during the Qianlong era, and were given preferential treatment by the law. The Regulations on Disbursement of Awards for the Red and White Incident (*Hong bai shijian xingshang zhangcheng*), promulgated in the fifth reign year of Qianlong (1740), expanded the range of awards afforded by Yongzheng-era imperial rules, guaranteeing reward not only for mid- and low-level banner officials for their work during the Red and White Incident, but also for ordinary clerks, and soldiers.[107] Such a particular ethnic law came in the wake of prohibitionary policies of the Yongle-Qianlong era: interdictions against Han reclaiming land in the Northwest, against Han and northwestern ethnic minorities secretly digging up ginseng or operating private mining operations, against Han traders doing business in the Northwest without a permit, and so on.[108]

In terms of policies for managing frontier peoples, Qing rule accomplished quite a lot. However, this does not mean it could ensure the continuity and integrity of its principles of rule simply by putting in place a generalized system; on the contrary, the Qing rulers had to constantly adjust frontier policy. Aside from armed suppression, they also had to create corresponding institutions to maintain balance among the abovementioned aspects. In the North, besides the early establishment of the Court of Frontier Affairs to handle Mongolian affairs, following Yongzheng's suppression of armed rebellion in Qinghai by the Khoshot nobleman Lobzang Danjin in 1723, the royal court issued one after the other the Thirteen Articles of Aid Following Troubles in Qinghai (*Qinghai shanhou shiyi shisan tiao*) and the Twelve Restrictions on Qinghai (*Jinyue Qinghai shi'er shi*), installed a minister of affairs in Xining, remapped part of Qinghai into Sichuan, and put another part of Qinghai under direct supervision of the Court of Frontier Affairs; during the punitive expedition against the Dzungars, the court created the Ministry of Defense, an important central organ. The Mongol Statutes and Procedures were amended under Qianlong to promote the banner system in Outer Mongolia. The process of creating these laws, regulations, and institutions entailed some segregationist policies. For example, "people from the interior were forbidden from marrying Mongolian women," Han were prohibited from learning written Mongolian or Uyghur, and Mongols were forbidden from learning classical Chinese.[109] In the South, once Yongzheng had taken the throne, aside from continuing to "install checkpoints," "build city walls," "set up massive military forces," and "[transfer] administration" in Miao (Hmong) regions, the court also instituted the Ordinance on the Tithing Security System (*Baojia tiaolie*), implemented "transfer of control from local chiefs to the central government" (i.e., abolishing the local chieftain system), reassigned general administrative officers, and undertook a large-scale survey of the peoples, population, customs, and economy (and taxable potential) of the Southwest, thus strengthening the centralization of control over the Southwest.

Many important gains were made under Qianlong in policies and legislation regarding Mongolians, Miao (Hmong), Hui, Uyghur, and other ethnic minorities, such as the considerations of ethnic characteristics in the legislative process and the allowance of certain legal exceptions, but it is not hard to find within them the trends toward centralization, coercive colonization, prohibition, and ethnic segregation. In the second reign year of Qianlong, the Reconstruction Aid Following Troubles in Taiwan (*Taiwan shanhou shiyi*) "forbids ordinary people from private purchase of foreign land," an exact carryover of the Yongzheng regulation: Han people living in Taiwan were strictly forbidden from entering "foreign land." Marriage with a native was a crime, punishable by divorce. Cases abound that contradict the principle of "Manchu and Han are one" touted by Yongzheng and Qianlong. If we place this state of legal affairs next to the "inner-outer" relations of Qing society, the historical picture we see is one of inherent contradiction and conflict. Qing rule was founded on Manchu privilege and the banner system, along with the subordination of the central / regional relationship. However, as a minority dynasty, its order would be unsettled if it could not systematically mitigate ethnic conflict and make legal and moral concessions to other peoples, especially to the Han. Easing Manchu-Han conflict, and placating and encouraging their Han subjects to actively contribute to the country's governance and production, were thus always key issues for Qing rulers.

All of the above goes to show that the Qing political structure embodied a composite of principles: equality and hierarchy, Chinese ritual and ethnic tradition, centralized administration and decentralized enfeoffment; this common legal and political order, composed of diverse legal systems and ritual principles, spurred thinking about political legitimacy. This composite approach was an important safeguard to protect the political structure of the multiethnic empire, and was once—or always—a bulwark of the plural legal principles and institutions of China's political, economic, and social life.

This is essentially the setting for the Qing revival of Gongyang studies. The Zhuang Cunyu–Liu Fenglu school used the Confucian concern of ritual to redefine the basic premise of "China" (*Zhongguo*), thereby attempting to supersede the ethnic meaning of "China" as defined by Yi-Xia relations, and to manage the relationship between plurality and unity within the ambit of "Grand Unification." Zhuang Cunyu and Liu Fenglu held important posts in the imperial court. They were well versed in the diverse and historic bases of Qing law, institutions, and policies, and even more sensitive to the essence of Manchu-Han relations in the royal court, especially the privileged position of Manchu nobility. Within the framework of *Spring and Autumn* Gongyang studies, Zhuang and Liu sought to use the "inner-outer" question to discuss both Manchu-Han relations in the court and the relationship between center frontier regions, thereby reconstructing the legitimacy of the multiethnic dynasty on the bases of Confucian ritual. The social setting of this "inner-outer" question was therefore the political framework of the multiethnic dynasty, and not merely palace politics.

It is worth noting that Gongyang studies was a theory of Han officials and Confucian scholars, not the Manchu rulers. By discussing political legitimacy through the themes of inner-outer and Yi-Xia, it at once echoed the official criticism, dating from Yongzheng onward, of the decentralized enfeoffment of the Three Dynasties and of the separation of Yi and Xia, while also attempting to turn the demand for equality of the peoples under Qing rule into a demand for legitimacy, and was thus inclined to oppose the ethnically based social hierarchy of the empire. In this sense, despite its conception within the imperial system, the Qing Gongyang studies' ideology of "Grand Unification"[110] and the concept of ritual China cannot be equated with imperial logic, given its notable criticism of ethnic rank, hereditary nobility, and the tendency of both toward violence. The problems dealt with by Qing Gongyang studies—as a theory of political legitimacy—included these intrinsic tensions, so that under certain conditions it could transform from a critical theory into a theory of reform, or even of revolution. This is a basic premise of our understanding of mid-Qing Gongyang studies.

III. New Text Classical Learning and the Problem of Qing Dynastic Legitimacy

1. "Grand Unification" and the Ruler Who Receives the Mandate of Heaven

As described above, New Text classical learning centered on inner-outer relations, used the methodology of reinterpreting the "subtle words and profound meanings" of the *Spring and Autumn Annals,* and rebuilt the legitimacy of the multiethnic dynasty on the two pillars of rites and law. One of the most distinguishing characteristics of the Qing legal system was the coexistence of and competition among multiple jurisdictions and systems of laws and institutions. This very pluralism of jurisdictions and legal / institutional systems forever wed the dynasty to the legitimacy and authority of "Grand Unification" (*da yitong*). As I see it, Qing New Text scholarship may be largely construed as a theory of political legitimacy, as it encompasses arguments for the legitimacy of the Qing dynasty as well as critiques of the internal conflicts within the Qing political system. New Text classical learning was Han scholars' answer to the social questions of the Qianlong era, and a critical summary of the management of inner-outer relations from the founding of the Qing state onward. This is the primary reason New Text studies centers on institutions, laws, and ritual.

From the perspective of classical learning vis-à-vis politics, what the work of Zhuang Cunyu and Liu Fenglu, the founders of Qing New Text studies, provided was reflection on the political legitimacy of the Qing dynasty. Zhuang and Liu dealt with issues of law, institutions, and ritual through the form of classical studies, attempting to provide basic principles for every matter political, economic, and cultural. Their studies carried normative significance. In this sense, Qing New Text studies is not only a revival of Han New Text studies, but also a reflection on contemporary issues. Liu Fenglu saw the *Spring and Autumn Annals* as a "Pattern and Doctrine for All Ages" (*wanshi fa*):

> When the *Spring and Autumn* set the patterns for all ages, it disdained to concern itself with single persons or with singular matters, and the various worthies also had no special or unique actions that could be established as teachings for the ages, or separately recorded in the accounts of their disciples: such was its discretion. Thus, with regard to Kingly government, [the *Analects*] says: "He carefully attended to the weights and measures, examined the body of the laws, and restored the discarded officers." And again: "He revived states that had been extinguished, restored families whose line of succession had been broken, and called to office those who had retired into obscurity." Kingly government was founded on these six actions. The *Spring and Autumn*'s inspection of the area-based land tax is "carefully attending to the weights and measures"; its interrogation of institutional reform is "examining the body of the laws"; its detailed explanation of the civil service system is "restor-

> ing the discarded officers"; its praise for moribund thrones is "reviving states that had been extinguished"; its clarification of lineages is "restoring families whose lines of succession had been broken"; and its praise of the able and virtuous is "calling into office those who had retired to obscurity." . . . Although [King] Zhuang of Chu [r. 631–519 BCE] and [Duke] Mu of Qin [r. 659–621 BCE] were worthy men, it treats them only as tribal chieftains, similar and close to China, who were gradually learning to be kings. Whether this polity of China is lost or functional, depends on distinguishing the inner from the outer.[111]

According to this inference, the *Spring and Autumn* speaks universal truths that transcend time; its methods proffer universal laws by which to guide systems of politics, agricultural land use, bureaucracy, and talent; its intention is to inquire into the fundamental path of this "polity of China" that "distinguishes inner and outer"; and New Text studies is the correct methodology to interpret this "pattern for all ages." New Text classical studies, which inserts itself directly into social and political patterns, gives us the classical texts and the methodology with which to shuttle between Gongyang studies and Qing politics.

Zhuang Cunyu's *Rectification of Terms in the Spring and Autumn Annals* (*Chunqiu zhengci*) is divided into nine "rectifications": receiving the Mandate of Heaven (*fengtian*), the emperor (*tianzi*), the inner (*nei*), the Two Elders (*Er Bo,* that is, the Duke of Zhou and the Duke of Shao), the various feudatories (*zhu Xia*), the outer (*wai*), prohibiting violence (*jin bao*), suppressing armed rebellion by punitive force (*zhuluan*), and leaving aside unsolved questions (*chuanyi*). If we compare these nine themes to He Xiu's three branches and nine intentions (*sanke jiuzhi*), we find that the Three Sequences, Three Ages, and other core issues of Gongyang studies are not at the center of the *Rectification.* They are merely sections four and nine of the ten-part treatise "Receiving the Mandate of Heaven" (*Fengtian ci*), and are of marginal concern. The expository structure of the *Rectification* may be summarized as follows: it takes establishing the five beginnings (*jian wu shi*) and modeling on King Wen (*zong Wenwang*) as the basis of law and rites, "Grand Unification" and its relationship with "inner-outer" as the center of its argument, "deriding hereditary postings" (*ji shiqing)* as its political orientation, and "filial piety" as the principle of ritual protocol. In terms of narrative structure, the treatises on "Receiving the Mandate" (*Fengtian ci*) and "Emperor" (*Tianzi ci*) emphasize the connection between dynasty and Heaven, and between an emperor and the Will of Heaven, and take these as the basis for the legitimacy of a new dynasty. The other seven sections—defining inner, the Two Elders, the various feudatories, the outer, prohibiting violence, suppressing rebellion, and leaving aside unsolved questions—touch on questions of ritual practice and inner-outer relations. This narrative structure centers on the issue of "inner-outer," clearly its point of investigative departure. In his discussion of these various topics, Zhuang erases the strict division between inner and outer. He reaffirms the value in Qing legal and ritual reform that "the peripheral tribes have entered China, and so are of China" and the presupposition that it is ritual, not ethnicity, that makes a dynasty.[112] Historically, scholars have not thought highly of Zhuang's New Text classical scholarship, as he does not strictly adhere to He Xiu's "three branches and nine intentions" method of organizing and interpreting the *Spring and Autumn*, as Liu Fenglu did. Even so, Zhuang's scholarship is far more influenced by Dong Zhongshu's *Luxuriant Dew of the Spring and Autumn Annals*, and more freely allows his political views to seep into the *Rectification*. It is for this reason that I interpret the *Rectification* as a work that seeks to understand the Qing political structure as well as its legitimacy.

Why did Zhuang Cunyu's perspective on the *Spring and Autumn* so closely knit together the theory of "Grand Unification" and the questions of inner-outer or Yi-Xia, but pay so little attention to discourse on the "Three Sequences" and the "Three Ages"? First of all, speaking from within the domain of classical studies, the issues of Grand Unification and inner-outer are closely related to the Three Sequences and the Three Ages. As long as one is not entrenched in the school methods of classical scholarship, the texts themselves can provide a basis for these crossovers. To take the Three Ages as an example, the *Spring and Autumn* divides the period from Duke Yin of Lu to Duke Ai of Lu into Three Ages: Zhao, Ding, and Ai are the "Age of What Is Seen" (*Suo jian shi*); Wen, Xuan, Cheng, and Xiang the "Age of What Is Heard" (*Suo wen shi*); and Yin, Huan, Zhuang, Min, and Xi the "Age of Rumors" (*Suo chuanwen shi*). He Xiu famously explained:

> In the Age of Rumors, governance is seen to arise in the midst of decay and chaos, and intentions are still broad and rough. Accordingly, the con-

> cerns of one's own state are regarded as internal, and those of the various feudatories as external (*nei qi guo er wai zhu Xia*); internal matters are given priority and close attention but matters of external governance are neglected (*xian xiang nei er hou zhi wai*); the great are given stipends and the small ignored; internal small failings are described in writing and external small failings overlooked; great states have senior officials, while in small states people are informally addressed; internally when meetings are held to resolve differences they are described in writing, while externally such meetings are not described in writing. In the Age of What Is Heard, governance reflects rising peace: the various feudatories are treated as internal and rude tribes as external (*nei zhu Xia er wai Yidi*), external meetings are described in writing, and small states have great officers; in the autumn of the eleventh year of Duke Xuan [598 BCE], the Marquis of Jin met with northern tribesmen at Zanhan, and in the twenty-third year of Duke Xiang [550 BCE], Biwo of Zhu came in flight. When it comes to the Age of What Is Seen, governance manifests great peace: rude tribes enter to become ennobled, and All-under-Heaven that are far and near and great and small are as one, and intentions are deep and detailed; accordingly, humaneness and righteousness are esteemed, the Two Names are mocked, Jin and Wei are at peace, and Zhongsun has no grounds for jealousy. In relation to the Three Generations, the "Ritual" is "three years for the parents, a similar period for grandparents, and three months for great-grandparents." Establishing care begins with those who are close, and therefore the *Spring and Autumn,* for hidden written expressions and proofs of grief, gave first importance to the management of ancestral temples.[113]

Taking the chronology of Lu as a reference point for wider developments in the Spring and Autumn era, He Xiu's Age of Rumors was an Age of Decline and Chaos (from Duke Yin to Duke Xi, ninety-six years: 722–627 BCE); the Age of What Is Heard was an Age of Ascendant Peace (Duke Wen to Duke Xiang, eighty-five years: 626–542 BCE); the Age of What Is Seen was an Age of Great Peace (Duke Zhao to Duke Ai, sixty-one years: 541–481 BCE). "Rude tribes enter to become ennobled, and All-under-Heaven that are far and near and great and small are as one" is the sign of the Age of Great Peace. The salience of this example of inner-outer harmony is significant, because it provides an implicit hint that the Qing dynasty was transitioning from Ascendant Peace to Great Peace. Accordingly, the prominence of inner-outer examples was in fact inseparable from the narrative framework of history as "extending through Three Ages." If we summarize the content of the "Three Ages" theory, then moving along the axes of both space and time it follows the principles of moving from near to far, and of giving greater weight to the near than to the far. Thus, ritual practice unfolds from "honoring kin" (the inherent spirit of this value is "filial piety"). This is why, in the logic of the "Three Ages," the closer the better to the point where Confucius, who lived during the collapse of Rites and the ruin of Music, could identify the order of Great Peace in his own time. From the perspective of evaluating the content of the "Three Ages," it is decline and chaos versus good government and peace, and the issues of inner versus outer and border tribes (Yi) versus Chinese (Xia), that constitute the criteria for judgment. Zhuang Cunyu and Liu Fenglu, living in the Qianlong-Jiaqing era, emphasized spatial relationships (inner / outer, Yi / Xia), whereas in the late Qing Kang Youwei and Liang Qichao brought the Darwinist concepts of evolution and progress to bear on their explanation of the "Three Ages," plotting the "Three Ages" along the axis of time as a straight line of evolutionary historical progress.

Secondly, emphasizing the problem of inner-outer is a political choice. If we say that the legitimation of the dynasty itself relied primarily on Three Sequences discourse and its correlating code of etiquette, then the main concern of ethnic Han scholars was not with establishing the dynasty's legally constituted authority, but with social relations within the dynasty, especially with regard to ethnicity. When the Zuo commentary says that the *Spring and Autumn Annals* "treats [affairs pertaining to] its own state as internal and those of the various feudatories as external" (*nei qi guo er wai zhu Xia*), and "treats [affairs of] the various feudatories as internal and [those of] the nomadic Yi and Di as external" (*nei zhu Xia er wai Yidi*), it certainly carries no implication of confusing the various feudatories with the Yi and Di. Yet the Qing New Text concept of Grand Unification, or Great Unity, is built on the dissolution of absolute divisions of Yi-Xia and inner-outer. The New Text standpoint on this issue is clearly their own elaboration. It is hard to understand this point without a specific political motivation and context. Until the mid-Qing, the dynasty was looked on by the Han literati as a foreign regime. The Qing politics of

Grand Unification completely reordered Yi-Xia relations. It fixed the legacy of the preceding dynasty, attempting to restore the authority of Confucianism. In the eyes of ethnic Han scholars, however, the Qing could not cast its legitimacy in the mold of dynastic continuity.[114]

The trouble was this: The Qing tried to legitimize its dynastic rule by means of Confucian orthodoxy, and therefore had to efface its historical genealogy in the regions beyond the Great Wall in order to insert itself into the line of dynastic succession. The *Rectification* has its reasons for tucking the essential themes of "Three Sequences" and "Three Ages" into the section "Receiving Heaven's Mandate," as the Qing ruled "by virtue of the Mandate of Heaven." Its legitimacy as a "new kingdom" came foremost from "Heaven," not from "ancestry." Qing literati confirmed the legitimacy of the dynasty on the premise that it be integrated into the historical line of dynastic succession, making it a segment or link in the dynastic chain, and thus jettisoning "non-Chinese" elements of its narrative. This narrative strategy is in perfect agreement with the aforementioned process and methodology of establishing the legal authority and title of the Qing. Zhuang Cunyu's "inner-outer" dialectic and esteem for the Two Elders may in part be seen as an acknowledgment of this direction in legitimization of Qing rule. The two elements described above provide the context and conditions for Zhuang Cunyu's development of Gongyang studies based on inner-outer precedent.

Let us first look at how the entry "Outer VI" (*Wai ci di liu: wai*) offers proof of the rise and fall of dynasties. Its discussion of the line from the *Spring and Autumn Annals* that recounts that "The Viscount of Chu and the Marquis of Cai encamped at Quhe" seems to be naked power worship:

> "He who steals a clothes hook is put to death, but he who steals a state becomes a feudal lord": later generations destroy the sages every day and doubt the Way of Heaven. How can such a situation be remedied? I say: one comes to understand the Way of Heaven by carrying out royal affairs [*wangshi:* "the business of a king"]. To be a king is to be a successor of Heaven. If a king does not punish criminals, even if Heaven punishes them but others do not know, it is as if there has been no punishment. Punishment by Heaven is not as clear as punishment by a king. The world cannot be without a king even for one day; this is how the Way of Heaven perfects people.[115]

"Royal affairs" are a manifestation of the Way of Heaven. Therefore the new king is legitimate, despite the discrepancies in convention and ritual. Here, the installment of a new king entails a change of surname, not inheritance. Gongyang scholars interpret such statements as "During a hunt to the west, a unicorn was captured" as signs that the sovereign has received the mandate, conceptually rooting the "new king" in the Mandate of Heaven. Three Sequences discourse establishes the legitimacy of the new king in the process of changing surnames. In this sense, the discourse on the Three Sequences and Three Ages fits perfectly into the rubric of "Receiving the Mandate of Heaven."

For a Han literatus during the Qing dynasty, it was impossible to ignore the fact that the Qing was a foreign regime: without the Will of Heaven, even direct invocation of "Three Sequences discourse" was not enough to convince people that the Manchu Qing was a Chinese dynasty; if the "new king" could not prove his own legitimacy, then "to be the new king" was the same as taking "the usurper as the noble" to be the Way of Heaven. Force alone could not legitimize the "new king." By starting with the terms "Receiving the Mandate of Heaven" and "Emperor," the *Rectification* clearly implies that imperial power is the highest authority.[116] "Royal affairs" are simply a substitute for Heaven. If the ruler were to violate the Will of Heaven and thus anger All-under-Heaven, he would have lost his legitimacy. In the chapter "Receiving the Mandate of Heaven," "Grand Unification" comes after "Establishing the Five Beginnings" and "Modeling on King Wen," indicating that compliance with the Way of Heaven and continuity with the ancestors are prerequisites of this principle. This narrative structure of classical learning is itself a manifestation of a basic principle, namely that the rationality of ritual is the foundation of political legitimacy, and that this rationality of ritual must be built on a cosmological premise. In this sense, the narrative structure of the *Rectification* brings the methods of classical learning back to the Song theory of the duality of Heaven and Man, which lines up precisely with Zhuang Cunyu's attempt to expound on the structure of classical learning in the context of cosmology. In "Observing the Heavens through the Eight Trigrams" (*Bagua guan xiangjie*), he writes:

> Heaven establishes positions, suspends the sun and moon, and distributes the stars and constellations.... Therefore, what delineates geograph-

ical boundaries, establishes rulers and ministers, sets up musical intervals and calendrical divisions, and lays out success and failure in order to instruct worthy persons, are called classics. The worthy person consults the classics and thus learns of devotion to the Way of Man. These are the *Book of Odes*, the *Book of Documents*, the *Book of Changes*, and the *Spring and Autumn Annals*. The *Changes* have yin and yang, the *History* has the Nine Patterns, the *Odes* have the Five Boundaries, and the *Spring and Autumn* has disasters caused by unusual phenomena. All are listed from beginning to end, the pros and cons are judged, and the heart of Heaven is examined, in order to speak of the safety and danger of the king's way, to speak of the world's deepest subtleties without dislike, and to speak of its most extreme changes without disorder. Thus, the threefold domains of Heaven, Earth, and Man are fully presented.[117]

When the classics are put in order within the cosmological horizon, the subject of "Grand Unification" is finally given weight. If we say that the cosmology of the Han era legitimizes the theory of political reform, then what exactly did Zhuang Cunyu mean here by placing "Grand Unification" within the horizon of cosmology (or the Law of Heaven)?

The patriarchal principle of inheriting from one's ancestors (which is the principle of filial piety) is a basic standard of imperial propriety, as well as a fundamental principle of Qing law. In Qing political parlance, however, this principle implied two inherent contradictions. Firstly, the Qing was widely regarded as a conquest dynasty. Even though the dynasty itself practiced sacrifice to the ancestors, if they applied this patriarchal principle in order to legitimize themselves, how would they then prove their rightful succession from the previous dynasty—that is, the Ming? When the Qing dynasty understood itself as the "new ruler," it could not rely on patriarchal sacrifice alone to justify itself. In this situation, it required the support of "establishing the five beginnings." Secondly, the Qing empire's erasure of the inner-outer divide, and its treatment of Manchu and Han as one, could not fit with the principle of patriarchal inheritance, as the privileges of the Manchu nobility were based precisely on blood lineage. Therefore, without also making known that they had "received the Mandate of Heaven" and "modeled [themselves] on King Wen" there would be no basis for "eschewing hereditary postings"—that is, they would have no grounds on which to critique the premise of dynastic legitimacy. "Hereditary postings" coexist with the system of patriarchal clans and decentralized enfeoffment. The entry "Emperor II" in the *Rectification of Terms in the Spring and Autumn Annals* states: "As to the decline of Zhou's virtue, [the late Shang sage] Jizi had already warned: 'Although your mother may have been fond of virtue, and although you enjoy rich emoluments, in your actions you are to blame and fecklessly run amok, giving rise to disasters. When officials hold the world, it is truly contrary to the discipline of Heaven.'"[118] "Inner III Part 1" reiterates: "In all the world, no one is born noble, and all are the sons of their parents. When King Wu was born, how could he have been different [by birth] from the rulers of his age?"[119] Zhuang Cunyu considered honoring the Son of Heaven to be an important principle. Why, then, did he also cast doubt on the inheritance of imperial authority? This was, first, because "Grand Unification" was a critical rejection of Zhou-era decentralized enfeoffment, and because the enfeoffment rituals that it demanded were based not on the patriarchal clan system, but on centralized administration; and second, because imperial authority was at heart of the Qing aristocracy. In the Qing, the Imperial and Gioro clans were all either direct or collateral descendants of the imperial family. Hereditary succession to noble rank was discontinued for twelve families, all of them imperial clan relatives. Therefore, the thrust of "rejection of hereditary postings" could not bypass the emperor: The emperor was nothing but a man, and if he could not comply with the Mandate of Heaven and act with imperial virtue, deviance and disaster would wrack All-under-Heaven. This was his fundamental understanding of imperial power: it is not unrestrained, absolute power. Imperial authority must be exercised according to the Mandate of Heaven, ritual, and ethics. In his *Rectifications* treatise, Zhuang Cunyu placed the topic of "Grand Unification" after those of "Establishing the Five Beginnings" in relation to the Way of Heaven and of "Modeling on King Wen" in relation to the ritual system, and the significance of this arrangement is manifest in his praxis of "eschewing hereditary postings." In other words, a legal system could not be established simply on the basis of continuity with clan and feudal relationships; rather, it must first reconstruct social relationships in keeping with the Will of Heaven, and then put forward the ethical principles of these relationships. Only then could its legitimacy be attained.

Zhuang Cunyu's explication of "Grand Unification" is at once proof of the legitimacy of the Manchu Qing and biting criticism of dynastic politics. His core argument, however, is that the Qing dynasty should base its political legitimacy on the ritual of the Former Kings. We may explain the significance of this problem to Qing society from three aspects: From the perspective of internal dynastic politics, if ritual could not heal the deep rift between Manchu-Han and the other minorities, and appointments could not be made based on merit and aptitude, then the dynasty's politics of Grand Unification would lack legitimacy; from the perspective of building imperial institutions, if the dynasty could not follow local customs and failed to respect the unique qualities and traditions of the various ethnic groups, the imperial court would be bound to protracted interethnic conflict; from the perspective of the Han people and their government officials, if the stress created by the domination of other peoples could not be alleviated by "inner-outer" precedent, then the identity and origins of the individual could not be settled. Thus in such works as the *Rectification, Examples Drawn from the Spring and Autumn Annals (Chunqiu juli),* and *Main Points of the Spring and Autumn Annals (Chunqiu yaozhi),* Zhuang Cunyu dealt with persistent questions in Qing politics and thought.

Why is this subject of inquiry so prominent in Zhuang and Liu Fenglu's New Text work? I believe there are three facets to the answer: First, unlike scholars who were loyal to the fallen Ming or even the Han learning scholars of the Qianlong-Jiaqing era, Zhuang and Liu were both Han officials who held important appointments and who were well versed in Confucian learning. Indeed, they approached the question of dynastic legitimacy from within Confucian moral philosophy; second, the Qianlong era was one of reconstructing and perfecting laws and regulations by building institutions, and they wanted these legal and institutional reforms to meet their ideals; third, as Han people holding high office in the imperial court, they at once disapproved of the inequality between the Manchu and the Han and of the inheritance of official positions, yet also could not completely deny the legitimacy of the dynasty. They attempted, through New Text studies, to reconstruct a theory of Grand Unification as the legitimizing theory of the dynasty, a theory that would eliminate Yi and Xia and erase inner and outer. "Grand Unification" therefore cannot be equated with the national policy of the empire, as it included a critique of the segregationist policies and ethnic hierarchy of the empire. I understand this problem as the ethnic Han Confucian scholar's consideration of relative equality in interethnic relations, premised on recognition of the legitimacy of the Manchu Qing.

2. The "Two Elders" and "Modeling on King Wen"

The Will of Heaven must specifically manifest in historical matters, or rather must be embodied in some historical force graced with the Mandate of Heaven. The proposition of "Grand Unification" is a response to social upheaval. By whom, then, is the heavenly will for "Grand Unification" specifically practiced, and how can it counter social chaos? Zhuang Cunyu reiterated the words of Dong Zhongshu:

> Today, masters have different ways, people have different discourses, the Hundred Schools have divergent methods, intentions and meanings differ, and thus those above have no way to maintain unity, legal institutions undergo many changes, and those below do not know what to hold to. In this minister's foolish opinion, it is from not adhering to the disciplines of the Six Arts, and from cutting off the Way transmitted by Confucius, not allowing them to advance together. When irregular and eccentric theories cease, only then can social order be unified and standards and measures be clarified, so that the people may know where to turn.[120]

The opening chapter of the Gongyang commentary on the *Spring and Autumn Annals,* "The First Year of Duke Yin's Reign," uses an exceptional style when expounding the concept of "Grand Unification," hinting that "Grand Unification" was not in fact the political reality of Duke Yin's era, but rather a demand or an ideal. Later generations of Gongyang scholars saw this as the particular style of Confucius, and took it as setting a pattern for a new king.[121]

Zhuang Cunyu's interpretation of Grand Unification suggests the necessity and historical inevitability of the emergence of a "new king." Closely following He Xiu's formulation that "these five, established together on the same day and taking form in mutual reliance, are the great root of Heaven and Man and the link that connects all things, and cannot but be closely observed," Zhuang designated the five topics of cosmic origination (*yuan*), spring (*chun*), king (*wang*), first month (*zheng yue*), and ascending the throne (*jiwei*), referred to in this passage as emerging at the same time, as "establishing the five beginnings" (*jian wushi*); also, citing Confucius's maxim (in *Analects* 3.14) of "following Zhou," he called for "kinship of the Six Directions" and for "coherence of the Nine Regions" on the basis of "rites." Thus, to find order amid the tumult as the royal house declined and society fell into chaos, it was necessary to rely on new political forces.[122]

The appeal of "Grand Unification" and the troubled reality of the time were the backdrop against which the "Two Elders," the Duke of Zhou (r. 1042–1035 BCE) and his younger brother, the Duke of Shao, took the stage. Zhuang Cunyu repeatedly touches on the significance of the Two Elders in the sections on the meanings of "Inner" (*Nei ci*), "Two Elders" (*Erbo ci*), and "Various Feudatories" (*Zhu Xia ci*), as providing legitimacy for the practice of feudal lords calling themselves kings. We might as well compare Zhuang's treatment with that of his predecessor, Zhao Fang (1319–1369), whom he clearly learned from. In his "Preface to *Collected Biographies in the Spring and Autumn Annals*" (*Chunqiu jizhuan zixu*), Zhao Fang says of the "Two Elders":

> When Heaven's Mandate had not yet changed, and yet above there was no Son of Heaven and below there were no Two Elders, the accomplishments of Huan and Wen [Duke Huan of Qi (r. 685–643 BCE), and Duke Wen of Jin (r. 636–628 BCE), two notable hegemons of the Spring and Autumn era] should not be defamed. For this reason, the Sage provides more detail about them, and thus says: "Examples of this are Duke Huan of Qi and Duke Wen of Jin."[123]

Expounding on the hegemons of the *Spring and Autumn*, Zhao goes one step further: "When the feudal lords did not exercise kingly rule the hegemons arose, when the central states were without a hegemon the Chu of Jing grew turbulent, and when great officers specialized in troops the feudal lords could not hold together. This was the reality of the Spring and Autumn [era]."[124]

Just for this reason, the *Spring and Autumn*, relying on the method of selective depiction, used the rhetoric of "accepted in fact but not countenanced in language" to express the intentions of the sages. The presentation of historical fact by *Spring and Autumn* Gongyang studies as "accepted in fact but not countenanced in language" primarily served to overcome the contradiction between ritual and practical demands. This approach to resolving the contradiction just so happened to suit Qing New Text classical studies' need to acknowledge the legitimacy of Qing rule on the premise of the veneration of ritual. Zhuang Cunyu elaborates: "The Duke of Zhou wanted All-under-Heaven to be at one with Zhou, and regarded dividing it as two with Jin as impermissible. When what he would not permit began, the gentleman strictly set his will on wanting All-under-Heaven to be at one with Zhou. . . . In the Spring and Autumn era there were some who were angered at this, and some who were pleased."[125] "At one with Zhou" was the ideal, but the conditions required to realize this ideal simply were not present. According to the Zhou system, rites and music and punitive expeditions all issued from the sovereign, and the feudal lords should not rule their own destinies. But since "at one with Zhou" could not be attained, they could only practice expedient strategies that were "accepted in fact but not countenanced in language." In the fifth chapter on "Various Feudatories," Zhuang says:

> The feudal lords had no Elder [i.e., no Regent, like the Duke of Zhou], and the *Spring and Autumn* deplores this. Was there then no way that Jin could be ruled? I say: When the feudal lords had no Elder, Duke Xiang of Jin [r. 627–621 BCE] began to enact the role. Zhou having no [formal] control over Jin began with this, and yet the Kingly Way was enacted. When [Dukes] Huan [of Qi, r. 685–643 BCE] and Wen [of Jin, r. 636–628 BCE] acted [as hegemons], the *Spring and Autumn* used the term "Elder" [to describe them], accepting [their roles] in fact yet not countenancing them formally in language.[126]

Gu Donggao (1679–1757) maps the pattern of territorial annexation in "Tables of Major Events in the Spring and Autumn Period" (*Chunqiu dashi biao*) number four, "Table of Territories Claimed by the Various States" (*Lieguo jiangyu biao*): Lu claimed the land of nine states, Qi claimed the land of ten; Jin annihilated eighteen, Chu swallowed up forty-two. . . . Each state was constantly at war: Qin and Jin attacked each other eighteen times, Jin and Chu fought each other in three wars, Wu and Chu sent twenty-three punitive expeditions against each other, Wu and Yue attacked each other eight times, Qi and Lu went to war thirty-four times, the wars of Song and Zheng number thirty-nine.

Historians thus lamented the terrible misfortune wrought by the system of decentralized enfeoffment, "and knew that All-under-Heaven could not for one day be without an Elder."[127] So-called Grand Unification arises just when the emperor is weak and feudal lords lay claim to the throne. The emergence of the Two Elders presages the need for a hegemonic ruler and foreshadows the replacement of bickering lords with the uniting of All-under-Heaven. Looked at from the decentralized enfeoffment of the Western Zhou, this process is in fact that of the downward transfer of power, which Zhuang Cunyu affirms through "acceptance in fact without being countenanced in language."

"Acceptance in fact without being countenanced in language" implies an internal contradiction, namely, a conflict between political legitimacy and moral rightness. Zhuang Cunyu endorsed Grand Unification and also regarded King Wen as the great ancestor of propriety and righteousness, attempting to integrate the moral rationality of patriarchal clan ethics with the politics of unification under a centralized administration. Thus the focus of his argument was not on institutional reform, but on correcting ritual and ceremony, meaning emphasis on the moral rightness of the new king. Zhuang's exposition regarding the claim that "the Grand Unification of the *Spring and Autumn* is the constant warp of Heaven and Earth, and the common rightness of ancient and modern" originates with Dong Zhongshu, yet the most cursory comparison between Dong's and Zhuang's interpretations of Grand Unification will reveal clear differences. With legal and institutional reform as his guiding principle, Dong writes in the "King Zhuang of Chu" chapter of the *Luxuriant Dew:*

> The Way of the *Spring and Autumn* is to serve Heaven and to take antiquity as one's pattern. Therefore, although you may have skilled hands, if you do not master the compass and measuring square you will not be able to rectify the square and the round, and although your ear may be trained, if you do not hear the six tones, you will not be able to set the five notes. . . . With regard to the affairs of the world, the *Spring and Autumn* values restoring antiquity, derides changing constant principles, and wishes to take the Former Kings as its pattern. Yet let us interpose one word to say: "The king must change institutions and keep himself secluded." . . . If one simply follows previous institutions, cultivating the old patrimony without any change, this is no different from continuing

> the reign of the previous king. A king who receives the mandate is Heaven's great manifestation. . . . Today those who greatly manifest their own concerns, inheriting from what they replace and following in similarity, are neither manifest nor clear, and are not what Heaven intends. Therefore, he must move his place of residence, replace honorary titles, change the first month, and shift the style and color of clothing. There is no other way: he dare not fail to comply with what Heaven intends or to clarify its manifestation.[128]

This is his creative elaboration on the profound meaning of the *Spring and Autumn,* clearly placing institutional change above "restoring antiquity." Looking back at Dong's "Three Strategies on Heaven and Man" (*Tianren sance*), the question pursued by Emperor Wu was why rites and music had lost their efficacy, not why rites and music should be scrupulously followed to the last detail. He said that the Way of the Five Emperors and Three Kings was to change institutions in accord with music so that All-under-Heaven would be in harmony, and the hundred kings followed suit. Those so-called literalist power-holders who scrupulously followed the institutions of the Three Dynasties of Antiquity, however, had no way to reform either small deficiencies in the Great Way or the rampaging tyranny of a Jie or a Zhou. Emperor Wu could not help but ask: How is all this to be understood, and what can we rely on to resolve it? Dong Zhongshu's argument is as boundless as the sea and sky, but in the end his response to Emperor Wu's question about "changing institutions in accord with music" was just that "through institutional change, governance may be improved, and when governance is improved, calamities diminish and prosperity increases day by day."[129] Zhuang Cunyu builds on Dong's argument in "Three Strategies on Heaven and Man," interpreting such matters as the King receiving Heaven's Mandate, rectifying his officials, and receiving the obedience of the people and the support of the feudal lords as "establishing the five beginnings," but clearly taking restoration of ritual and music and not institutional change as the heart of the argument. Zhuang quotes from He Xiu:

> In government there is nothing more important than correct beginnings. Therefore, the *Spring and Autumn* relies on primal *qi,* to rectify Heaven's uprightness [*tian zhi duan:* also, "sprouts of Heaven," "springtime,"

> or "spontaneous impulses"]; on Heaven's uprightness, to rectify Kingly government; on Kingly government, to rectify the accessions of the feudal lords; and on the accessions of the feudal lords, to rectify governance within the realm. If the feudal lords do not accept the government of the King, they are not allowed to accede to their positions.[130]

This is a demand for strict ritual.

Although the social disorder that is "the collapse of the rites and the ruin of music" grants legitimacy to the emergence of the "Two Elders," the "Two Elders" or the "new king" must act in strict adherence to ritual to win their legitimacy. Recalling the political practices from Kangxi's reign onward, including the veneration of Zhu Xi, the reinstatement of the civil service examinations, the revival of the patriarchal clan system, the reaffirmation of ritual, and the proclamation of "unity of governance and the Way," it is not hard to see why the Qing imperial court had to cement its legitimacy in proper ritual, rather than in political reform. It is worth noting that Zhuang's treatment of the "Two Elders" clearly illustrates how he expounded on Qing legal authority from the position of a Han official. In Zhuang's time the Manchu-Han question still loomed large, recognizing that the "new king" and strict ritual had become an inherently tense problem area. Here I will bring up just one example. According to the record for "The First Reign Year of Duke Yin" in the *Spring and Autumn Annals,* Duke Yin abdicated in favor of Duke Huan, only for Duke Huan to murder his elder brother, Duke Yin, later on. Gongyang scholars thought that the *Spring and Autumn* contained censure of Duke Yin's abdication. Accordingly, Zhuang Cunyu points out:

> The intent of the *Spring and Autumn* is that heavenly bonds [i.e., between family members] should be given due weight, and that the life [or "mandate" (*ming*)] of one's father should be respected. If yielding the state is sincere, then according to Heaven's principle, inheriting the mandate from one's father is not sincere, and although there was the event of ascending the throne, it was as if there had been no event, and thus it is not written that he ascended the throne. The throne is the foundation of the state. Those to the south do not have the heart for a monarchy, and those to the north have the will of two kings, so what throne is there? For ten years this was not rectified, and if Duke Yin did not rectify it

> himself, the state would have no means by which it could be rectified. In the first year of his reign there was rectification; it was the correct role of Yin to carry out rectification, yet he did not himself carry it out. There cannot be a single day without rectification![131]

Zhuang Cunyu's interpretation of "Grand Unification" departs from Dong Zhongshu's proposals to Han Wudi regarding "further changes," as Zhuang would rather that the emperor keep strict social order in governing the state, taking ritual and ceremony as the premise of governance. Here, then, "Grand Unification" is not the unconditional approval of imperial authority, nor is it advice for the emperor on political reform; rather, it is the norm and conceptualization of a political ideal. If we situate this interpretation in the language of the Qing, we may infer that it implies the ethical demands put on the Qing rulers by Han officials, and the critical perspective of the latter regarding political realities.

The narrative logic of "Receiving the Mandate of Heaven, I" *(Fengtian ci di yi)* moves from "establishing the five beginnings" to "modeling on King Wen," thereafter discussing "Grand Unification" and "linking the Three Sequences." What Zhuang Cunyu truly valued here was the legitimacy of receiving the Heavenly Mandate and the basic principles of "modeling on King Wen," demonstrated by "establishing the five beginnings," thereby connecting the concepts of "change" (starting afresh) and "constancy" (imitating the first sovereigns). "Grand Unification" demands to be premised on this dialectic of change and constancy.[132] "Establishing the five beginnings" provides legitimacy to the emergence of the new king—this is what Dong Zhongshu means by "receiving the Mandate of Heaven." But why is it "modeling on King Wen," and not establishing an alternative institution of ritual protocol when "becoming the new king"? In Zhuang's use of the terms, the topics of "establishing the five beginnings" and "modeling on King Wen" have a complicated relationship. Let us first read the entry on "modeling on King Wen":

> Master Gongyang said: "What is it to be a King? It is to be like King Wen." Hearing this, I say: A king who receives the mandate is called the Great Ancestor, and the king who succeeds him is called the Successor. The Successor is the one who succeeds to the Great Ancestor. If one does not dare to say that the mandate is received from Heaven, one says that it is

> received from the Ancestor, and from ancient times it has been so. King Wen [1152–1050 BCE] was the Ancestor who received the mandate, and Cheng [r. 1042–1021 BCE] and Kang [r. 1020–996 BCE) succeeded to King Wen's embodiment of it. King Wu [r. 1046–1043 BCE, who established Zhou rule by militarily defeating the Shang] had clear virtue, and when in receiving the mandate he attributed it to [his father] King Wen, this was called the "Way of Heaven." King Wu did not dare to transmit the mandate, but his son and grandson [i.e., kings Cheng and Kang] did dare to endorse this. The mandate is the Mandate of King Wen, the throne is the Throne of King Wen, and the law [or pattern] is the Law of King Wen. Thus is the Ancestor respected, and so also is Heaven respected.[133]

If all that Zhuang Cunyu wanted were to carry on the enfeoffed patriarchal ways of the Zhou dynasty, then his concept of "Grand Unification" would be limited to mere "worship of the royal family," nothing more. However, Zhuang's learning clearly took the principle of "inner versus outer" and "derision of hereditary postings" as its guiding aims, and was filled with resentment at the system of hereditary aristocracy. The narrative structure of *Rectification of Terms in the Spring and Autumn Annals* harbors implications of changing the principles of patriarchal enfeoffment; "worship of the royal family" in fact reflects a contradiction between imperial authority and the nobility, and the need for absolute imperial authority. The appeal of absolute imperial authority constitutes a lingering thread in Qing New Text classical studies: from Zhuang Cunyu's demand for imperial unity to Kang Youwei's attack on the late-Qing "regency" and reaffirmation of absolute imperial power, all express a political outlook of establishing unified authority.

The "modeling on King Wen" principle is identical to the "unity with Zhou" concept of Gongyang studies, but "unity with Zhou" is establishing a pattern for the new sovereign, not simply a reinforcement of the patriarchal clan system and decentralized enfeoffment. This is one and the same with the basic principles of "Grand Unification." As previously explained, the key to understanding "unity with Zhou" is its situation in a time when feudal lords were battling each other for power, a time quite bereft of "unity with Zhou." In this context, the patriarchal principle of complying with Heaven and following the ancestors is a standard for imperial power and political order, and there is no requirement that it be carried out among the various lords in the form of enfeoffment. In other words, "unity with Zhou" is another term for "Grand Unification," but it is difficult to equate this directly to decentralized enfeoffment. In this sense, the legal authority of the Zhou became the moral imperative and proof of legitimacy for the unification of imperial power, but was no longer that principle from the Yin-Zhou system of the patriarchal clans and decentralized enfeoffment. "Grand Unification" and "unity with Zhou" imply another layer of meaning and purpose: to rehabilitate ritual protocol, and to curtail the monopolization of power by hereditary officials and the division of power among the nobility. Zhuang Cunyu builds on this sense of "Grand Unification" when he states, "Heaven does not have two suns, earth does not have two kings, the state does not have two sovereigns, the family does not have two heads. Each is governed by one." He upholds the royal prerogative on the one hand, while on the other he alludes to a firm denunciation of the monopolization of power by hereditary officials and division of power among the nobility, both of which are violations of "Grand Unification" and betrayals of "unity with Zhou." "Modeling on King Wen" and "unity with Zhou" are abstract principles of ritual, and do not adhere to a given discriminatory policy or point of view of the ruling people. Zhuang Cunyu attempts to make this a premise of dynastic legitimacy.[134]

3. "Eschewing Hereditary Postings" and the Inherent Contradiction of Dynastic Politics

One result of the decay of rites and music during the Spring and Autumn period was the downward transfer of power, that is, from the Zhou emperor to the Two Elders, from the monarch to the hereditary official. But the position of the hereditary official was built on the system of patriarchal clans and decentralized enfeoffment, and thus the officials could not avoid losing their position if they were degenerate or cruel. According to Gu Donggao's "Major Events in the Spring and Autumn Period," the *Spring and Autumn Annals* records forty-seven feudal lords who murdered a senior official, fourteen senior officials who did work for other states, two feudal lords who freed senior officials, and fifty-seven ministers, senior officials, and princes who fled their country—as well as countless murders and attacks between ministers and officials.[135] "Eschewing hereditary postings" has an important place in the *Rectification of Terms in the Spring and Autumn Annals,* not only as a key element of *Spring and Autumn* studies, but also because this theme is tightly linked to the age in which Zhuang Cunyu lived, and to Zhuang's own political views. The Zhuang school's criticism of "hereditary postings" conforms with the Qing political principle of legitimacy, and echoes the attack, criticism, and suppression of factions, cliques, and the nobility by the Kangxi, Yongzheng, and Qianlong emperors. Here we have more explicitly political material. The entry "The King's Servants Assemble the Vassals" (*Wangchen hui peichen*) in "Emperor II" *(Tianzi ci di er)* warns the reader: "When the Son of Heaven is weak, the feudal lords form cliques, the small are made to serve the great, and the weak are made to serve the strong. . . . When there are small evils within, the gentleman must first examine and rectify himself, respecting himself and expecting little of others."[136]

"Eschewing hereditary postings" and "Grand Unification" fit together, both being based on the principles of Qing rule and on its internal doctrines of classical learning. In this sense, Zhuang Cunyu's condemnation of the phenomena of corruption, monopolization of power, and the like is an affirmation, not a denial, of Qing political principles. This is because the eras of Kangxi, Yongzheng, and Qianlong all went through struggles to unify imperial power and weaken the influence of the nobility. "Grand Unification," "modeling on King Wen," and "eschewing hereditary postings" are all interconnected. The entry "Death of a Senior Official" (*Dafu zu*) states: "Since the reigns of King Cheng [1042–1021 BCE] and King Xiang [651–619 BCE], the sons of dukes no longer became dukes, the Way of treating family members with affection was lacking, and the harm of hereditary officials to family and state was something that the king's law had to forbid. How widespread this was! How many of the *Spring and Autumn's* words were directed entirely to this!"[137]

According to Wei Yuan's suggestion and Elman's research, the goal of Zhuang's New Text work is intimately connected to the Heshen disaster. Heshen (1750–1799) came from an upper-mid-level Manchu military family. In the twenty-fourth reign year of Qianlong (1769), he inherited his father's rank of Third-Class Commandant of Light Chariots, and was made a Third-Class Imperial Guard three years later. In the fortieth reign year of Qianlong (1775) Heshen rose to the positions of Palace Guard and Vice Commander in Chief of the Manchu Plain Blue Banner. From there he steadily climbed the ranks, holding office as Vice Minister of Revenue, Minister of Revenue, Minister of Defense, Grand Minister-Supervisor of the Imperial Household Department, Commander General of Infantry, Chongwenmen Superintendent of Tax Administration, Minister in Attendance, Vice Commander in Chief of the Plain Blue and Bordered Yellow Banners, Director General of *The Emperor's Four Treasuries,* Minister of Minority Affairs, Lecturer Officer of the Classics Colloquium, Director General of the Historiography Institute, Administrative Supervisor of Wenyuange, Director General of the Office of Buddhist Scriptures in Manchu, Minister of Personnel, Joint Grand Secretary, Grand Secretary of Wenhuadian, Palace Examination Grader, and Grand Guardian of the Crown Prince. He was also conferred with the titles of First-Class Baron, Third-Class Loyal Beneficent Duke, and First-Class Distinguished and Courageous Duke. Heshen long dominated the ministries of Personnel, Revenue, and Justice and the Imperial Household Department, the Court of Frontier Affairs, and the Scouting Brigade, amassing ever more political, economic, and cultural power, and marrying his children into the imperial household. Over two decades in politics, Heshen undermined the administrations under his command and openly practiced bribery, creating a highly corrupt state-within-a-state.[138] Elman provides a thorough, in-depth analysis of Heshen's power grab and the Zhuang Cunyu–Liu Fenglu school of political thought. However, as previously stated, the significance of the *Rectification* does not stop here. From the reign of Hong Taiji (r. 1644–1661) onward, succession was anything but smooth. In the Kangxi era, the question of designating a crown prince sparked a fierce struggle among the princes, high officials, and the emperor himself, a tale told in both official and unofficial historical materials, and gossiped about during the Yongzheng-Qianlong era. The fighting among the emperor and members of the royal family during the Yongzheng era reverberated through Qianlong's reign. One need not look far to discover that Zhuang Cunyu's "derision of hereditary postings" is a reflection of and argument for the political legitimacy of the Qing, as well as a summation of his lived historical experience.

The political legitimacy of the Qing was based on a delicate, fragile balance, and its political principles embodied inherent contradictions. The establishment of the Eight Banners system, multiple rounds of government restructuring, the granting of power to government officials, and the formation of the internal hierarchy of the court each institutionalized divisions of inner-outer, Manchu-Han, and social classes, conflicting with New Text scholars' assumptions about ritual. This state of affairs also had its high and low points for the Qing rulers' claims about the principles on which they had established the state. In order to maintain the balance of power among the Manchu, Mongols, and Han and the legal authority for autocratic rule among ethnic minorities, the Qing rulers based their own legitimacy on the dissolution of the Yi-Xia divide. For example, they carried on the civil service examination system of their predecessors, striving to ensure that men of all nationalities had the opportunity to serve in the government. However, as a dynasty built on the aristocratic hierarchy of an ethnic minority, the Qing institutionalized the prioritization of the Manchu. These are the institutional conditions under which hereditary assignments and the politics thereof came into being. This contradiction is especially visible in the civil service examinations and the system of appointment: On the one hand, Chinese was the principal language of the exams, and the Qing opposed preferential treatment or privilege for Manchu exam-takers; on the other hand, in order to protect the right of the Manchu to participate in the government and to mitigate against imbalance among the Manchu, Mongol, and Han in the exams, they conversely set up two vacancies or "lacks" (*que*) in every government agency in the capital (designating the lack of an adequate number of Manchu, Mongols, or Han), while also dividing each "lack" among these three ethnic groups and setting a quota for each, thus checking the expansion of the number of Han officials. This preferential policy defeats the purpose of the civil service examinations, as it obviously brings the enfeoffed, aristocratic standards of ethnicity and pedigree into the candidate selection process. The Qing bureaucracy itself embodied this contradiction between so-called equality and policies based on status.[139]

Zhuang Cunyu served successively as Inspector of Schools in Shuntian (Beijing) and Hunan and then as Chief Examiner and Vice-Examiner of Hubei, and was well acquainted with the inconsistencies in the examination system. He took it upon himself to advise Qianlong to cap the number of successful candidates by locality. In 1758, his rigorous correction of bannermen's examinations soured the general mood, sending bannermen up in arms. Zhuang himself was impeached by his colleagues. Ultimately, the Qianlong Emperor protected him: Zhuang was made a cabinet scholar, giving him two secure postings. How was Zhuang able to avoid impeachment and receive yet another important post? His special relationship with Qianlong was no doubt a factor, but I believe that more important was that Zhuang's own standpoint basically aligned with the policy of the Qing government. The internal crisis of the Qing political system resided here: it based its legitimacy simultaneously on mutually contradictory principles, such as ethnic equality versus ethnic hierarchy, examination versus nominations in the appointment of official posts, and the common people versus the nobility. The stability of the dynasty hung in this balance, and Zhuang Cunyu saw straight through to the most sensitive and important part of this political balancing act: "eschewing hereditary postings" was no violation of imperial principle. On the contrary, it was a fundamental condition of staying in power.

Thus, Zhuang Cunyu's revelations regarding the above-mentioned conflict cast no doubt on the legitimacy of Qing rule. Rather, he was elucidating the internal conflicts of the Qing government via the very principles on which the Qing based its rule. "Emperor II" states:

> Master Gongyang said: Eschew hereditary postings. Hereditary postings do not conform to ritual, so how could they be the intent of the Sage? He created the *Spring and Autumn* in expectation of a later Sage. If the changes of later ages, harmful to families and inauspicious for the states, had not all been due to hereditary postings, then how would the Sage, who understands the causes of misery and suffering, not have known this, and why would he have eschewed them? Those who report above on behalf of the people [must] know the root of Heaven and Man, and faithfully uphold the righteousness of ruler and minister. He informed Duke Ai [of Lu (r. 494–468 BCE)]: Righteousness is what is fitting, and what is most fitting is to honor the worthy. . . . For this reason, one who is not worthy may not serve as an official, and a sovereign who does not honor the worthy loses that by which he is a sovereign. Those hereditary officials, when they lose the path of worthiness, are moths who obscure the worthy. . . . Hereditary emoluments [i.e., ranks and salaries enjoyed by noble families over many generations] accord with the regulations of King Wen; but hereditary postings [i.e., ranks and offices held by right of inheritance] are contrary to the regulations of King Wen. Without regard to tradition or novelty, there should only be kindness among relatives, and domestic regulations that honor and nurture those who are

> worthy. . . . If one says that officials may not enjoy hereditary emoluments, or that a state may be without multigenerational officials, this is not the meaning of eschewing hereditary postings.[140]

"Hereditary postings do not conform to ritual"—they violate the basic principles of the *Spring and Autumn.* "Not conforming to ritual" is not the outcome of one individual's misconduct, but a systemic imbalance. The principle of "modeling on King Wen" is the criterion against which the propriety and correctness of institutions is measured. In the passage quoted above, Zhuang Cunyu distinguishes carefully between hereditary emoluments (*shilu*) and multigenerational officials (*shichen*, i.e., "ministers sprung from families which have been noted for generations") on the one hand, and hereditary postings (*shiqing*) on the other, with the goal of separating the system of patriarchal enfeoffment from the monopolization of power by hereditary officials. His concerns were, politically, how to forge a path for the virtuous and, ethically, how to spread filial piety. In a note on the entry "The Heavenly King Frequently Sends his Uncle's Son as an Envoy: Fifth Year of Duke Huan" (*Tianwang shi reng shu zhi zi lai pin: Huan Gong wu nian*), Zhuang Cunyu says: "Master Gongyang said: 'Elders are mocked, and sons pursue political careers. The path of the worthy is blocked! The deeds of the filial sons are despised!'"[141]

4. "Distinguishing Between Inner and Outer": The Internalization of Foreign Relations and the Redefinition of "China"

Following the logic of "eschewing hereditary postings," Zhuang Cunyu's take on Gongyang studies has the potential for radicalization, revealing this in his exposition on the status of imperial authority and the emperor. However, the intention of the *Rectification of Terms in the Spring and Autumn Annals* is not to undermine the legitimacy of the dynasty, but rather to consider how the distinctions between inner-outer and Yi-Xia may be erased, and how the internal conflicts within the Qing political structure may be rooted out, thereby establishing the legitimacy of the multiethnic empire based on ritual. This constitutes a rejection of the ethnonationalism of the imperial order, and a renunciation of the ethnic consciousness of the Confucian tradition: "Grand Unification" is a correction of earlier policies of subjugation, an attempt to create a politics that neither protects nor compares the divides of inner/outer and Yi/Xia. We must therefore differentiate the demands of "Grand Unification" from imperial policy. The *Rectification* leaves behind the traditional focus on the "Three Sequences" of Han-Tang Gongyang studies, turning instead to the problem of "inner-outer," the purpose of which is to transform definitions of ethnicity and social status in the imperial order through the meaning and goals of "Grand Unification": the inner-outer problem is at the root of Qing political legitimacy, as well as the dynasty's most intractable conflict. If this dilemma could not be clarified through theory, then the Han literati would never achieve political equality, nor would they have the basis on which to locate themselves in dynastic politics. In this sense, the "inner-outer" problem is not a question of political legitimacy, but rather a question of individual background or recognition. "Inner-outer" is at the heart of the epoch's moral dilemma; in terms of political domination in a multiethnic dynasty, if interethnic conflict could not be ameliorated, and responsive arrangements and safeguards could not be created institutionally, then the dynasty would be unable to overcome its crisis of legitimacy. This is the grim reality faced by Qing Confucian scholars.

The above analysis of "eschewing hereditary postings" lays the ground for us to comprehend the significance of "inner-outer" cases in Zhuang's school of thought. The meaning of "inner-outer" changed completely under the originally foreign dynastic rule of the Manchu Qing: from a matter of internal and external as relations between Yi and Xia under the imperial system, to an internal matter of relations among "inner and outer" ethnic groups within the dynasty, thereby changing the meaning of the inner-outer precedent in He Xiu's "three branches." This is the change from imperial politics to the politics of "Grand Unification." Xu Yan, citing from He Xiu's "Standards for Civil Posthumous Titles" (*Wenshi li*), writes:

> [When He Xiu says that] "The Three Branches and Nine Intentions are to renew the Zhou, based on the principles of [the ancient state of] Song, and to take the *Spring and Autumn* as [regulations for] a new King," these are the three intentions of the first branch. When he again speaks of "the strange expressions that one sees, that one hears, and that one hears of [i.e., as rumor]," these are the intentions [four through six] of the second branch. And [when he again speaks of] "treating the affairs of one's

> own state as internal, and those of the various feudatories as external, or of treating the affairs of the various feudatories as internal and those of the peripheral tribes as external," these are the intentions [seven through nine] of the third branch.[142]

The examples of "inner and outer" are thus the concern of the third branch of the nine intentions, and Zhuang Cunyu understood this very well. When using Gongyang analysis to explain the *Book of Changes,* he clearly points out that "eschewing hereditary postings" in the Gongyang commentary follows the principle that "those who treat the affairs of their own state as internal and of the various feudatories as external, and yet neglect the internal to serve the external, are eschewed":

> In the *Spring and Autumn,* those who regard the affairs of their own state as internal and the affairs of the various feudatories as external, and yet neglect internal matters to serve what is external, are eschewed. The feudal lords are the guardian officials of the Son of Heaven, are corrected with gentleness, and do not despise themselves if they are not employed. It is by winning over the people for the Son of Heaven that they gain favor with the Son of Heaven, and those who gladly serve all respond to and emulate him. To care from within oneself only for being loved by the king, is the core of gentleness. Protecting the sovereign to make sure that he does not lose the people, is to avoid losing oneself.[143]

However, the derision of hereditary postings in the *Rectification of Terms in the Spring and Autumn* implicitly contains criticism of the hereditary officials who monopolized power within the imperial court, and the focus of its derision also shifts accordingly: The "inner-outer" problem becomes a question of internal dynastic political structure. According to the principle of "Grand Unification," "inner and outer" does not refer to relationships between the central royal court and the external world, but rather to internal relationships between ranks within the dynasty. In this sense, "Grand Unification" is a great and all-encompassing order, as its "inner-outer" relations are internal to the dynasty.

Zhuang's elaboration on the problems of inner-outer and Yi-Xia presages a fundamental verdict: that an institutional form of multiethnic coexistence must be formed on the basis of Chinese ritual and ceremony, and that absolute distinctions between inner-outer and Yi-Xia must therefore be erased. Consequently, "China" is not a clear political territory, not a homogeneous ethnic entity, and not a notion of sovereignty in foreign affairs; instead, it is a matter of ritual. This is a concept of "ritual China" (*liyi Zhongguo*), and it constituted the basis for a new identity for its imperial subjects. It was a product of the interaction between an ethnic-minority ruler and its multiethnic subjects, and it was the outcome of internal Qing politics and social relations. This concept was at the core of Zhuang's idea of "Grand Unification," and it was the embodiment of the concept of All-under-Heaven. The key issue here is that the concept of "ritual China" is a transcendence of the ethnic hierarchy of the imperial era, and that it also stands as a rebuke to a social order based on ethnicity. The substance of "inner-outer" precedent is not about the management of relations between inner and outer, but rather the management of relations among China's social strata. Hierarchical relationships are labeled "inner and outer" because ethnic relations lay at the center of the Qing political and social hierarchy. Let us look at how "Outer VI" (*Wai ci di liu*) connects the "peripheral tribes" to "China":

> In Chu there was no one whose qualities, from beginning to end, surpassed those of [Xiong] Zi [i.e., King Wen of Chu (r. 690–677 BCE)]. He launched attacks far into the central states (*Zhongguo*), annexing several of them, to the point where those below adhered to him, though hating his presumption. There were men who at Xi allied with [Duke] Huan of Qi [r. 685–643 BCE], sending tribute to the [Zhou] King. Zi pursued his own career, and when conditions in Jin were not correct, Chu attacked Chen. When Xiang Zhao went to meet him, what was the use of treating him as an outsider? And when Zi complied, what could the various feudatories say? It is said that although the peripheral tribes (*Yidi*) have rulers, they are not worth letting the various feudatories be destroyed, and Zi of Chu at last knew the Great Way.[144]

While Qi, Jin, and Qin each had their unique characteristics, they were all geographically close to the Zhou court, and could easily be categorized as "Chinese." The state of Chu, located midway along the Yangtze River, occupied a civilizational space between Yi and Xia. The achievements of Qi, Jin, and Qin could be described within the categories of King and Hegemon, whereas Chu touched on the divide between Yi and Xia. How, then, could this division be overcome? Through ritual. The heart of the passage quoted above is this: the *Spring and Autumn* respects rites and emphasizes trust. Trust is more important than locality, and rites are revered above status. Therefore, any adjudication based on locality or status violates the principles of ritual. That being said, if ritual is the most important criterion for differentiating Yi and Xia, it implies the potential for transformation—that is, so long as a peripheral tribe acknowledges ritual, it may become "Chinese" or one of the "various feudatories." This is the basic premise behind the statement "the peripheral tribes have entered China, and so are of China." In this sense, any (legal) judgment or provision based on region or status is in violation of ritual principle. In discussing the entry from the thirtieth reign year of Duke Xiang for "Crown Prince Cai Wildly Killed His Lord in the Fourth Month of Summer," in "Suppressing Rebellion VIII" (*Zhuluan ci di ba*), Zhuang asks why this entry does not record the day, and answers: "It does not complete the words. Completing them would signify respect for the assassin as one who is close. Why does it matter if the day is omitted? Peripheral tribes would complete the record, but when in the central states we act as peripheral tribes we become as peripheral tribes, changing sameness into difference." "When in the central states we act as peripheral tribes we become as peripheral tribes" is the inverse of "when peripheral tribes have entered the central states, they become central states," and together they reveal that the "central states" and "peripheral tribes" are not ethnic concepts, but ritual and cultural concepts. If the "central states" lost ritual, they would therefore be "peripheral tribes." Consequently, through the cases of "inner and outer" described above, the relationship between Yi and Xia may be determined according to people's attitudes toward ritual.[145]

Now, what is the precise ritual basis for the assertions that "if you are of the central states but act as peripheral tribes, then you are a peripheral tribe" and "if you are a peripheral tribe and enter the central states, you are a central state"? It is Zhuang's principle of "modeling on King Wen." I would sum it up as: it is by the actions of a filial son, that one carries out the "business of a king" or "royal affairs." The distinguishing feature of this maxim is that it first differentiates such rituals as filial piety and fraternal duty from the rituals of the sovereign (distinguishing ethics from politics), and then broadens the principles of filial piety and fraternal duty into the ambit of royal affairs: "As a grandfather or father, one wants his son or grandson to be benevolent and filial, and wanting him to be benevolent and filial, one must take the law of China as one's family law."[146] This is a flexible application of the principle of "modeling on King Wen," but it is precisely this flexible application that exposes the inherent fissures in "ritual and ceremony": Zhuang Cunyu had no choice but to separate the principle of filial piety from that of loyalty, for how could "peripheral tribes who had invaded China" accord with the ritual of "loyalty"?

Zhuang Cunyu was well aware of this contradiction. In his entries on "The People of Chu Attack Zheng" (*Chu ren fa Zheng*) from the first reign year of Duke Xi, "The People of Chu Invade Zheng" (*Chu ren qin Zheng*) from the second reign year of Duke Xi, and "The People of Chu Attack Zheng" (*Chu ren fa Zheng*) from the third year of Duke Xi's reign, he offers a broad interpretation starting from the question, "How did the Chu come to be called 'people' (*ren*)?" Zhuang writes: The four peripheral tribes did not acknowledge the rule of China, and were closest to Chu. However, after Duke Huan forged the Alliance of Zhaoling, Chu began to refer to itself as a vassal, and therefore in all of his documents Duke Qi began to call the Chu "people." Zhuang inversely uses "accepted in language but not countenanced in fact," distinguishing between the attitude of the four peripheral tribes toward China and their attitude toward the rituals of sovereign and vassal: even if they in fact violated the ritual, so long as they nominally deferred to it, then the ritual order still existed. Although Chu invaded the central states, it scrupulously preserved the name of "vassal" (*chen*) and continued to be called "people" (*ren*) by the Gongyang commentary. Zhuang Cunyu elaborates: "From then on, even if [Chu] invaded the central states, it did not dare to offend against the Son of Heaven, and so the Chu were permanently addressed as "people." . . . The *Spring and Autumn* deeply addressed the ills of the central states, but it was also strict in distinguishing its ranks, and so its kingly institutions remained intact."[147] The key rhetorical framing here separates China from the emperor: the Son of Heaven represents ritual, whereas China is a political and geographical entity. If the peripheral tribes who come to China are faithful to the ritual of the sovereign, then China must refer to them as "people." If we put this side by side with "men from the state of Chu defeated the state of Xu at Loulin" in the fifteenth reign year of Duke Xi, the two complement each other perfectly. The entry on "men from the state of Chu" states: "Why record the mutual defeat of peripheral tribes? China saved them, so they were of China." In short, the relationship of "China" to "peripheral tribe" is not absolute. Only the form of ritual is permanent. This ritual form, however, is not necessarily substantive, but is rather a perpetually abstract principle, and thus can accommodate a multitude of cultures, customs, institutions, and laws while recognizing several basic principles, such as filial piety.[148]

Here Zhuang Cunyu shifts again from law to ritual, making this the foundation of dynastic political legitimacy: it is a proof of "Grand Unification" and a call for "modeling on King Wen." Absent this differentiation of Yi and Xia centered on ritual, we could hardly imagine how the dynasty and literati of the late Qing could conceive of themselves as "Xia" and the West as "Yi," and it would be nearly impossible to understand the true meaning of "Chinese in essence and Western in application" (*Zhong ti Xi yong*).

All of this, however, was beyond what Zhuang could have imagined.

5. The Ritual Practice of "Grand Unification" and the Relativization of Yi and Xia

Liu Fenglu, the grandson of Zhuang Cunyu by Zhuang's daughter, was active in the Jiaqing-Daoguang years (1796–1850). A tumultuous time was on the horizon. Liu's systematic studies not only pushed ahead the New Text studies that his grandfather had initiated, but also created the conditions for his pupils Gong Zizhen and Wei Yuan to use elements of New Text learning to articulate statecraft learning in the imperial era. Liu's contributions to Qing Gongyang studies may be expressed in the following points: One, his rigorous application of evidential learning to Gongyang doctrine and New Text approach to analysis of the classics broadened the scope of New Text studies from the *Spring and Autumn* to the Five Classics. Two, on the aforementioned premise, from the platform of New Text studies he unequivocally responds to and interposes himself into debates within classical learning (such as his blunt rebuttal of Qian Daxin in "Discourse on the Spring and Autumn Annals I" [*Chunqiu lun shang*]), garnering the attention of the mainstream school of evidential learning and orienting New Text analysis of the meanings and principles (*yili*) of the *Spring and Autumn*

Annals.[149] Three, in the internal context of Qing Gongyang studies, he criticized Kong Guangsen's three branches and nine intentions for "not using the old Han Confucian commentaries, and for separately establishing calendrical astronomy as the branch for the Way of Heaven; for ridiculing, devaluing, and failing to practice the branch of kingly law; and for honoring 'holding worthies close' as a branch of 'human feelings.'" In this mode, Liu asks, "How are Gongyang studies different from the Guliang, and how do they give access to profound meanings?"[150] He reestablished the school methods of Gongyang learning, and took the three branches and nine intentions of the Eastern Han scholar He Xiu as the basis for understanding the profound meanings of the *Spring and Autumn Annals.*[151] The importance of this last point is that it again defines preserving the Three Sequences, magnifying the Three Ages, differentiating inner and outer, and the theory of reforming Lu to achieve kingship as the fundamental theories and themes of New Text studies. In the internal context of classical learning it argues for the universal significance of Gongyang studies and its various elucidating cases, and accordingly provides an intellectual resource for the reform thought of the mid- and late Qing.[152]

Explanatory Specimens from the Gongyang Commentary on the Spring and Autumn Annals (Chunqiu Gongyang shili) (also known as *Mr. He's Explanatory Specimens from the Gongyang Classic* [*Chunqiu Gongyang jing He shi shili*]), Liu's representative contribution to Gongyang studies, is a comprehensive review of the basic principles of He Xiu's explanatory notes. Working in the format of a transcription and compilation to reaffirm He Xiu's conception of the three branches and nine intentions, Liu Fenglu puts into practice Mencius's comment on Confucius's authorship of the *Spring and Autumn* as "enacting matters proper to the sovereign" (*xing Tianzi zhi shi*) (*Mencius* 3B9) and "continuing the traces of sovereign rule" (*ji wangzhe zhi ji*) (*Mencius* 4B21), situating Gongyang doctrinal exposition as a universally applicable political theory.[153] This was clearly to take Gongyang studies as the basis for political praxis. With this premise, Liu's *Explanatory Specimens* is no longer a collection of isolated studies, but rather ideas plotted on "matters proper to the sovereign," with their own internal interconnection and logic.[154] Liu believed that He Xiu "cultivated learning and sagacious judgment, judged between black and white and decisively seized on the thread of Dong Zhongshu and Humu Sheng, repaired the omissions of Zhuang and Yan, decided the cases of Chen Yuan and Fan Sheng, and cured the faults of Zhen Mingchi." Therefore, he wrote,

> seeking out its proper arrangement and correcting its main threads, I completed the *Explanatory Specimens* in thirteen sections; also, cutting through its sluggish [passages] and strengthening its defenses, I wrote "Responding to Difficult Issues" (*Da nan*) in two *juan;* also, examining widely what was incorrect in the histories and books of criminal punishment and ritual, I wrote "Resolving Criminal Cases through Ritual" (*Li yijue yu*) in two *juan;* also, examining from first principles the defects in the commentaries of Zuo and Guliang, I wrote a treatise in two *juan* explaining He's critique of Zheng [Xuan], expressing his resolve to uphold [the order of] the world.[155]

Liu thus announces unequivocally that his evidential learning of the classics constitutes a revival of Gongyang studies, and that consequently there exists an inherent theoretical structure and direction. The *Explanatory Specimens* is quite inclusive, examining not only He Xiu's three branches and nine intentions, but also Kong Guangsen's nine intentions. Yet Liu's thirty entries have a clear focus, not merely moving item by item. In comparison with Zhuang Cunyu's *Rectification of Terms in the Spring and Autumn Annals,* the *Explanatory Specimens* restores the centrality of the Han Gongyang themes of magnifying the Three Ages and linking the Three Sequences and distinguishing inner and outer, while relegating "establishing the five beginnings" and "modeling on King Wen" to secondary status.[156]

In the second part of his "Discourse on the *Spring and Autumn Annals* II" (*Chunqiu lun xia*), Liu Fenglu examines the differences between the Gongyang commentarial tradition and those of Zuo and Guliang from the perspective of the history of scholarship. Liu argues that if the commentaries are not "threaded together by the significance of displaying the Three Ages and understanding the Three Sequences," then their interpretive principles would be "clear on this point but blocked on another, straight on the left but confused on the right."[157] Liu thereby returns the question of "inner and outer" to the framework of "Three Sequences" and "Three Ages" discourse. Because he relied on He Xiu's three branches and nine intentions in interpreting *Spring and Autumn* Gongyang studies, and because He Xiu's three branches include ideas about clearly distinguishing inner from outer and Yi from Xia, Liu Fenglu's thinking also included related ideas. However, this did not fundamentally alter the basic principle of relativizing inner and outer that began with Zhuang Cunyu. For Liu here the Three Sequences and Three Ages may also be seen as a kind of special rhetoric, through the management of which the Qing court could gain confirmation of its position in the genealogy of dynastic succession. The idea of "Spring and Autumn Grand Unification" organizes All-under-Heaven according to ritual practice, and so its inner and outer are not absolute, but instead are internal matters of inner and outer that fall within ritual. Not only does this suggest that the legitimacy of the new dynasty is rooted in the genealogy of dynastic succession, but it also makes clear that "Grand Unification" is exactly the outcome of Three Ages evolution. In *Discourse on Ritual in the Gongyang Commentary (Chunqiu Gongyang yili)* he says:

> The Grand Unification of the *Spring and Autumn* respects transformation through closeness (*qin*), and extending this to all who have blood and breath is that by which Heaven and Earth become great. But it must be by the various feudatories that the capital is assisted, and by the peripheral tribes that the various feudatories are assisted. The capital occupies an area of a thousand *li*, the various feudatories eight areas of a thousand *li* [surrounding it], and the peripheral tribes sixteen areas of a thousand *li* [surrounding these]. Therefore, the reason why there must be three grades, with distinctions regarding court employment, mourning protocols, and funeral ceremonies, is just a matter of phased closeness or distance, and not a matter of adherence to different teachings. The feudatories of the central regions regard renewal of court appointments after five years as correct. The various feudatories serve for five-year terms, but in the peripheral tribes, kings rule for life. If their sons and younger brothers wish to enter state schools, receive them; but if they are unable, do not force them. Thus He [Xiu] says: "The king does not govern the Yi and Di. It is recorded of his meetings with the Rong that when they came, he did not refuse them, and when they left, he did not pursue them."[158]

Let us now look at how Liu's "Preface to *Tables of the Inclusion and Exclusion of Qin, Chu, and Wu*" (*Qin Chu Wu jinchu biao* xu) formulates the themes of inner-outer and Yi-Xia:

> With regard to the *Spring and Autumn's* treatment of the late period of [alternating] rise and fall between Chu and Wu, I often sigh in praise of the Sage's deep and subtle insights into the conduct of external affairs. . . . Consequently, in his judgment that the replacement of Zhou and the alteration of Zhou laws began with Qin, how broad, profound, and penetrating are his words. Qin at first was a small state, obscure and out of the way, which was excluded by the Xia feudatories (*zhu Xia*), and ranked with the peripheral tribes of Rong and Di. Yet its territory was that of the early Zhou, it had honest and upright civil and military teachings and no wayward or extravagant ambitions, and was also without lewd or indolent customs, so that in its poems one could hear the tones of Xia, and in the Spring and Autumn [period] it did not presumptuously attempt to claim kingship or craftily manipulate the Xia, nor did it undergo the misfortunes of regicide or usurpation. Therefore, in the *Spring and Autumn* it is treated as a small state and as "inner." Wu was the last to join the upper states, and as its rise was most sudden, its fall was also the most abrupt. Qin's strength was in internal governance, but after defeat and confusion, it did not exhaustively focus on long-term strategies, though its rise was also vigorous. Chu's long-distance control was stronger than Qin's, and its internal control was stronger than Wu's, and therefore it was Chu that in the end overturned Qin after Qin had extinguished six states. The Sage took the alternating rule of inner and outer that had occurred in response to Heaven's fortune and attributed it conversely to ritual and rightness, and was thus able to fashion a Way to assist Heaven and Earth, without exceeding [the bounds of] things. Therefore, in attributing the status of worthies to King Zhuang of Chu [r. 613–591 BCE] and to Duke Mu of Qin [r. 659–621 BCE], in the end he held that even if China [*Zhongguo:* the central states] had no Duke Huan of Qi [r. 685–643 BCE] or Duke Wen of Jin [r. 636–628 BCE], in the long term it could revert to them, for why wait until the end of mourning, when Chu would become the capital? As to the defeat of [Prince] Guang of Wu [Helü, r. 514–496 BCE] by Chen Xu, which was known throughout the central

> states, reflecting deeply on its causes he said: "The central states are also the new peripheral tribes" (*Zhongguo yi xin Yi Di ye*). . . . Therefore, from observing the books of *Odes* and *Documents* one may know that it was by Qin that Zhou was replaced, and that the laws of Zhou had fallen into such ruin that even the Sage could not restore them. But from observing the *Spring and Autumn,* one may know that it was through the alternation of Wu and Chu that Heaven ruled the central states, and that the significance of their enthronements and dethronements will persist through the ages and cannot be changed. Expanding on [what may be learned from] these three states in order that succeeding ages might be governed was the heart of the burden that the Sage assumed, and he also took pleasure in this.[159]

Liu takes He Xiu's study of the *Spring and Autumn* as his model, differentiating himself from Zhuang Cunyu; Liu persists in the goal of *Spring and Autumn* studies to "separate inner from outer." However, as the above passage shows, Liu turned the inclusion or exclusion from the central states into a reaffirmation of the absolute nature of ritual: those who follow ritual are of China, those who violate ritual are barbarians. "China" becomes ritual China, a political entity based on neither ethnicity, nor territory, nor the power of the hegemon.

Liu Fenglu recentered the concept of China on ritual. This laid the groundwork for observing political reality through the lens of the ritual of the Three Dynasties of Antiquity, all the while recognizing the political legitimacy of the Qing dynasty (that is, recognizing that the Qing dynasty was also "China"). Reaffirming the discourse of the Three Sequences and of "form and substance," he championed the spirit of decentralized enfeoffment within the system of centralized administration, all based on his interpretation of ritual in the *Spring and Autumn.* For Liu, rites were not abstract morals, but an order from inner to outer, from the Way of husband and wife to the political and legal order of the state.[160] He understood the *Spring and Autumn* from this point of view, implying that he considered the system of patriarchal clans and decentralized enfeoffment, and its arrangement of inner and outer, to be the essence of "Grand Unification." The relativization of Yi-Xia relations does not alter the relationships of ritual order among the capital, the kingdoms, and the barbarian tribes, but instead allows these relationships to be seen as internal relationships and as relationships based on ritual.[161] In this sense, Liu's interpretation of "Lu Kingship" (*wang Lu*) or of "becoming the new king" (*zuo xin wang*) is both a reaffirmation of enfeoffed ritual and a rebuke of centralized administration. Looked at from the Gongyang commentary's and He Xiu's idealization of Grand Unification and a bureaucracy under centralized administration that shared power with local authorities, Liu was attempting to unite Grand Unification with the ideal of early-Zhou enfeoffment.[162] His "Explanations of Examples of Inner Affairs I: Public Affairs from Beginning to End" (*Shi neishi li: Gong zhongshi*) begins by discussing how with regard to the institutions of the Three Dynasties, "the age was in decline and the Way had become faint and obscure, to the point where there was no oath-supported teaching of propriety, but instead competition to establish favoritism, and even ministers who committed regicides . . . so that the intent of enfeoffment had become effaced," and then provides arguments for the legitimacy of Lu Kingship and reform: "Since the Way of Zhou had already been harmed, how could it be right to abandon Lu, the undertakings of whose twelve Dukes had been fraught with sorrows. . . . Thus, the *Spring and Autumn* stands up against what is yet to come, and is the great ancestor of propriety and rightness." And yet, from the perspective of propriety and rightness, Lu lacked the title of king, and consequently Lu Kingship must invoke the righteous pattern of "acceptance in fact without being countenanced in language." "Therefore, the *Spring and Autumn* begins with the primal origin and ends with the sighting of a unicorn, and Lu thus has no end or beginning. To have no end or beginning is to lack correctness, and how can there be such a state?"[163] Yet it is precisely because Lu Kingship has no beginning and no end, that the pattern of Confucius is not the pattern of the singular Zhou dynasty, but a pattern and doctrine for all ages (*wanshi zhi fa*).[164]

It is also in this sense that "Case Studies of Military Affairs: Attacking, Encircling, Entering to Destroy, and Capturing Towns" (*Shi bingshi li: Qinfa zhanwei rumie quyi*) associates images of universal chaos with the faults of centralized administration, and from there takes the system of decentralized enfeoffment of the Three Dynasties of Antiquity to be the basic strategy for putting an end to soldiers and prohibiting violence. This close linking of "Grand Unification" and "decentralized enfeoffment" is characteristic of Liu Fenglu. The following passage may be compared with the aforementioned "Preface to *Tables of the Inclusion and Exclusion of Qin, Chu, and Wu*":

> As to the pattern of centralized administration, spontaneous propensity (*shi*) cannot restore its power nor prolong its tenure, as [was seen] in the time of the feudal lords of old. As soon as wicked people flow about and robbers and bandits arise and swarm, the disaster of their harm to the people extends throughout the realm. . . . This being so, what can the *Spring and Autumn* do to rescue Zhou from its decline? I say: control the state as in early Zhou, so that the domains of dukes and marquises do not exceed areas of a hundred *li*, and those of earls do not exceed seventy *li*, or fifty *li*. For military taxation, great states are those with a thousand chariots and fifty thousand resident farmers, and after them those with five hundred or two hundred fifty chariots, and populations of fifty or twenty-five thousand. . . . Thus, everything commends people to obey their local officials, and the eldest sons of the feudal lords are taught with learning, and pledge loyalty to the Son of Heaven. If sagely and worthy talents do not emerge in due season, there is no better response than to cultivate the institutions of enfeoffment, in order to obtain local officials of the caliber of Duke Huan of Qi or of Duke Wen of Jin, so that the disasters of extinguished states may be brought to an end and forceful seizures rectified. To reign over a state by treating its people as sons, seeking out men of worth and ability to examine as officials to assist the royal house, in order to save the central states (*Zhongguo*) and support the important business of the age, is the correct governance of Great Peace, and the meaning of the concluding *Ode* [in the *Book of Odes*], "King Wu of Yin."[165]

The system of centralized administration has a clear legal form, but as a political entity is bloated and lacks the flexibility to implement expedient measures, and so can easily lead to disastrous consequences for state and people alike. The question here is: Why does Liu admit the function of the Two Elders, yet also believe that it is necessary to "govern the state as did the early Zhou," denying the legitimacy of the centrally administered state? One important reason is that the partition of inner and outer and the rigid institutions of the centrally administered state are in fact the cause of the decline of ritual practice and the rise of military provocation. Liu's criticism of centralized administration seems to contradict Zhuang Cunyu's derision of hereditary postings, but they are not simply calling for a return to antiquity, but rather calling for a politics of "Grand Unification" premised on ritual as the foundation of China, and on expedient measures (that is, a flexible system that adapts to the particulars of a given situation) as its method, and the rejection of absolute divisions between Yi-Xia and inner-outer. This is a transcendence of earlier imperial politics.

IV. Grand Unification and the Empire: From the Horizon of Ritual to the Horizon of Geographical Studies

1. Grand Unification, Ritual China, and the Empire

The Qing dynasty merged the traditions of enfeoffment and centralized administration in their administration of the Northwest and Southwest, while in the Central Plains they allowed bannermen and ordinary citizens to live among one another. This was the heart of the new imperial system. In this respect, the Qing dynasty differed from the centrally administered systems of the Song and Ming, and took on certain characteristics of enfeoffment. In a nutshell, the Qing was a territorially vast, ethnically complex, multicultural political community. Built on the imperial system of its early conquests, it grew into a new system, one that brought together local systems of enfeoffment (such as the Eight Banners, local chieftain, and Kashag systems), administrative systems (central authority, provincial administration, and the bureaucracy), military occupation, and vassal state policies, in an attempt to establish a community of multiple legal and institutional systems on the basis of an acknowledgment of a continuity of ritual, culture, and history—and also to take this as the basis of its external relations. *Spring and Autumn* Gongyang studies are intimately linked to the systems of "Grand Unification" of the Han and Qing. If we say that such figures as Gu Yanwu and Zhang Xuecheng tried to integrate enfeoffment and centralized administration at various levels, then New Text classical scholars, through an elimination of boundaries between inner and outer, Yi and Xia, and under the aegis of concepts like enfeoffment and centralized administration, created a theory of "Grand Unification" as multiethnic dynasty.

Zhuang Cunyu and Liu Fenglu's "views on inner and outer" furnished New Text studies with the basis for its theory of "Grand Unification." There is no notion of "empire" in the technical language of New Text classical studies. The term they more frequently used was the familiar one of "Grand Unification" (*di yitong*). However, these two concepts are easily confused, because of the latter concept's historical connection to the Qin empire and its centralized administration. The term "unification" (*yitong*) is first seen in the "Biography of Li Si" in the *Records of the Grand Historian* (*Shiji: Li Si zhuan*), and in the "Basic Annals of Qin Shihuang" *(Shiji: Qing Shihuang benji):*

> Commandant of Justice [Li] Si and others all said: "In ancient times when the Five Emperors [reigned over] their territory of five thousand *li*, their outer nobles wore the apparel of peripheral tribes, and whether vassals appeared at court or not was a matter that the Son of Heaven could not control. Today your Majesty raises righteous armies, slays injurious bandits, pacifies the world, and treats all within the seas as prefectures and counties; your laws and decrees are grounded in unification (*faling you yitong*). This has never happened since ancient times, and is something that the Five Emperors never achieved." . . . "Today all within the seas rely on your Majesty's divinely efficacious unification (*shenling yitong*), all [domains] have become prefectures and counties, the various sons and meritorious officials are amply rewarded from the public treasury, and their feet [i.e., their comings and goings] are easy to control. Under Heaven there are no differing opinions, and the arts of peace and tranquility [prevail]. There is no need to establish feudal lords." . . . The world was divided into thirty-six commanderies, and within each commandery were established governors, defenders, and supervisors; the people were renamed as *Qianshou* ("common people").[166]

In the language of Qin Shihuang, the "grand unification" that Li Si speaks of entails subduing the feudal lords and establishing an imperial system centered on absolute imperial power. Even so, in the hands of Han-era scholars this concept gradually became linked with the ideal of the Three Dynasties of Antiquity. For example, in the chapter on "The Substance and Form of Institutional Change in the Three Dynasties" (*Sandai gaizhi zhiwen pian*) in his *Luxuriant Dew of the Spring and Autumn Annals,* Dong Zhongshu connects "unifying All-under-Heaven" (*tong tianxia*) to "incorporating the feudal lords" (*zhao zhuhou*) when he adduces the Three Sequences to prove that "the Three Dynasties must occupy the central states, model on Heaven in attending to fundamental matters, and grasp the essentials in order to unify All-under-Heaven and incorporate the feudal lords."

In the language of Zhuang and Liu, the theory of "Grand Unification" acknowledges the legitimacy of the dynasty and of its system of unification but questions the empire's military conquests, its segregation of the various ethnic groups, and the inheritance of official postings by the nobility; and therefore it cannot be equated with the concept of empire. Their idea of "Grand Unification" is closer to that of ritual China: both are idealized, abstract outlines evidenced by history. For ease of analysis, one must first succinctly define the concept of "Grand Unification" with regard to the relationship among enfeoffment, centralized administration, empire, and "Grand Unification." In the Qing political context, "Grand Unification" is a political theory and discourse of an oppressed yet distinguished group of Han scholars that is intensely concerned with court politics. By acknowledging the legitimacy of the dynasty, it expands the demands for interethnic equality, social equality, and ritual into a proposal for a political community. The reason we compare this discussion (or discourse) with the institutional forms of enfeoffment, centralized administration, and empire, is because over the long course of history these forms have often existed because they constituted a set of discussions (or discourses). The logic behind separating "Grand Unification" as a unique concept of community from enfeoffment, centralized administration, and empire, is as follows:

First, unlike the Qin, who conceived of unification as the replacement of decentralized enfeoffment by centralized administration, Zhuang and Liu's usage of the term "Grand Unification" and its attendant concept of ritual China admitted the historical rationale behind imperial authority and centralization, but still esteemed the rituals of enfeoffment. In particular, they accepted and continued the pre-Qin ritual geography of *dian* and *fu*, conceived of as a central "capital region" (*dian*) five hundred *li* in width, surrounded by nine concentric "vassal regions" (*fu*) each also five hundred *li* in width. (For instance, by this principle Liu calculated the distance separating the *yifu* [seventh concentric vassal region] from the *fanfu* [ninth or outermost region], thereby persuading the Vietnamese diplomatic mission to accept the edicts of the Chinese emperor.) They also esteemed the ritual order of the *Rites of Zhou*, endorsing its policy of "customs and traditions." As a political proposition, "Grand Unification" disavows centralized administration: it seeks, in the centralized era, to establish a political structure that separates / limits powers, supports meritocratic appointments, reaches near and far, and respects the cultural and institutional characteristics of every nationality on the basis of ethnic equality. As a result, although Grand Unification or ritual China takes something like the system of the Three Dynasties of Antiquity, and in particular the system of enfeoffment of the Zhou, as its foundation, it does not orient itself toward the reinstatement of a hereditary nobility or of an enfeoffed patriarchal clan system, but rather acknowledges the historical rationale for centralization.

There is a historical link between this concept of "decentralized enfeoffment" and the realities of court politics: the vast territory of the Qing, composed of various ethnic groups and regions, synthesized tributary relationships, administrative management, and regional autonomy according to particular circumstances, taking a ritual practice of inner-outer—and not the model of co-extant patriarchal enfeoffment and feudal lords that prevailed under the Western Zhou—as its political / organizing principle. The interior was under centralized administration, while the ethnic minorities in the Northwest and Southwest worked according to different conditions. Different systems were constructed within the framework of the empire, and different types of administrative bodies were established. The Mongolian banners, the Kashag of Tibet, and the local chieftains of the Southwest were each created to accommodate local characteristics and history. They did not operate among each other like the feudal states under the patriarchal clan system, nor did their relationship to the central court resemble that of the feudal states to the King of Zhou. Here I must point out that "Grand Unification" and "ritual China" are idealized ritual relationships, and are not one and the same as the Qing political reality. The Qing professed its respect for "customs and traditions," but in practice built an ethnic hierarchy, all the while drawing the authority of the Northwest and Southwest back to central supervision. In this respect, the rituals of enfeoffment that were venerated by "Grand Unification" and "ritual China" were ones that could accommodate cultural difference while maintaining imperial unity, and were in tension with the reality of the empire.

Second, "Grand Unification" and its attendant concept of ritual China acknowledged historical change, and therefore accepted the political framework of centralized administration as a matter of practicality. At the same time, however, it offered sharp criticism of the centralized system as it was implemented by the empire, putting special emphasis on the concurrence of enfeoffment under centralized administration. There are two main characteristics of the centralized system: one is its strict division of inner-outer and Yi-Xia, the other is its unified administration and management of different regions. These facets turned traditional enfeoffment into relationships defined clearly as central / local and center / periphery. Looked at from the viewpoint of differences between enfeoffment and centralized administration, the protectors (*shou*) and magistrates (*ling*) of prefectures and counties in the centralized system differed from enfeoffed nobles in the following respects: One, the royal court had the authority to appoint and dismiss protectors and magistrates, but not ennobled officials; two, the imperial government taxed prefectures and counties directly, and was responsible for disbursing funds, whereas feudal states could not be taxed directly, nor was a central body directly financially responsible for them; three, the bureaucracy was the basic institutional framework of the centralized administration, whereas in a system of enfeoffment relations between the center and regions are maintained through ennoblement;[167] finally, the centralized system embodied the absoluteness of imperial authority, while a system of enfeoffment allows for power in multiple centers. In fact, however, the concept of "Grand Unification" may be correlated not only with centralized administration but also with decentralized enfeoffment, as the latter does not exclude the notion of unification. When Confucius said, "When good government prevails in the empire, ceremonies, music, and punitive military expeditions proceed from the Son of Heaven" (*Analects* 16.2), was he not describing "unification" under the conditions of enfeoffment?

During the Qing, "Grand Unification" demanded an end to the boundaries of inner / outer and Yi / Xia ("China and the Western Tribes are on the same track" [*Hua Rong tonggui*] and "unification of China and the peripheral tribes" [*Yi Xia heyi*]), and also respected the authority of local gentry and the customs and traditions of ethnic minorities, making its political structure distinctly pluralistic. The Qing was a multiethnic dynasty that carried on the legacy of the Mongol Yuan, an ethnic-minority dynasty that unified the country. It drew on the achievements of the Song and Ming, yet inevitably challenged the strict national consciousness and clear sense of borders inculcated by these two predecessors. Kangxi revered the Cheng-Zhu school of Confucianism, but in his use of it, which completely removed any premise of ethnic consciousness that it might contain, he took it as an essential technique of governance, without which "one cannot know the profound interrelationship of Heaven and Man, or govern the ten thousand states from one's sleeping mat, or extend one's benevolent heart and benevolent governance to All-under-Heaven, or treat the inner and the outer as one family."[168] Following the Treaty of Nerchinsk (signed in 1689), in May of 1691, the Kangxi Emperor issued an edict forbidding repair of the Great Wall. Economic considerations aside, the more crucial reasoning behind this decree was that the Qing empire had penetrated deep into the regions north and south of the Taklamakan Desert and north and south of the Tianshan Mountains, and into Qinghai and Tibet (not to mention its own origins in the Northeast), and was planning to define a new scope of domination, as well as to delineate its borders in certain regions (such as the border with Russia).

Kangxi's understanding of the frontier differed from that of the Song and Ming rulers: externally, some of the borders in the Northwest had been made clear; domestically, formerly frontier regions had become part of the interior. This border policy, which diverged completely from that in the past, suggested a fundamental change to the meaning of the "interior." Against this backdrop, the Qing carried on the centralized administration inherited from the Song-Ming era, while simultaneously constructing the Manchu-Mongolian banner system, the Kashag in Tibet, the local chieftain system in the Southwest, and so on, along the principles of enfeoffment—uniting centralized authority with indigenous social and political structures to form a dynastic system in which "near and far, large and small are as one." This political praxis worked in concert with "Grand Unification": New Text studies criticized the Yi-Xia distinction so often drawn by Song-Ming Confucian scholars, attacking the Song-Ming system of centralized administration in order to escape the enfeoffed tendencies of inner-outer, in essence downplaying Han nationalist tendencies toward ethnic revanchism (which eventually reached their height in the late Qing) and creating an inclusive, pluralistic dynastic system by accepting the Qing's legitimacy.

Third, "Grand Unification," its concept of ritual China, and empire all tended to deemphasize the "outer," lacking the explicit ideas about excluding foreign peoples that had prevailed under the Song and Ming. (New Text scholarship's "detailed attention to inner and limited attention to outer" [*xiang nei er lue wai*] fit perfectly with "Grand Unification" and the empire.) Yet there was a subtle tension between "Grand Unification" and the empire: "empire" generally points to a political system consisting of highly centralized control over a vast territory, as well as complex relations among multiple ethnic groups and cultures. This system, built on the emperor and the central political structure, relied on violence (tribute and taxes) and trade monopolies to ensure economic flows from the periphery to the center. The early Qing empire can be seen as an expansive political, military, and economic community, dominating through armed subjugation, military occupation, and tributary trade, built on the might of the nobility, and preserved by ethnic hierarchy and segregation. "Grand Unification" is characterized by the merger of ritual relationships with political order, demanding the abolition of imperial policies of segregation, the enfeoffed nobility, and brazenly violent conquest. The ambiguous relationship between "Grand Unification" and empire in part arises from this fact: the Confucian scholars who advocated for "Grand Unification" recognized the legitimacy of Qing rule and the vast, diverse dynasty created by the Manchu Qing's subjugation of the Central Plains, the Northwest, and the Southwest, thus overlapping historically with imperial politics.

New Text scholars demanded that their rulers respect the diversity of peoples, religions, languages, and cultures within the imperial or tributary system, arguing that the dynasty's ritual foundation and its ethical implications should not be used as grounds to exclude other cultural values and political traditions. In this sense, "Grand Unification" cannot be equated with the reality of court politics; rather, it is a Confucian cultural ideal, waiting to be realized. However, this ideal is a sense of order incubated by imperial politics, as the Qing imperial system did in fact include several types of autonomous fiefs or fiefdoms, embodying the plurality of religious beliefs. For example, in order to maintain the balance of power after putting down the rebellion in the Tibetan area of Sichuan, the Qing did not return jurisdiction to the Dalai Lama, instead allowing other religious forces (such as the Red Sect) to retain their dominance, with the ultimate goal of balancing power with the Dalai Lama's Yellow Sect.[169] Thus "Grand Unification" differs from centralized administration, decentralized enfeoffment, and empire, yet includes many elements of each. Its view of ritual China is a critique of imperial politics, and also articulates the cultural—rather than ethnic—premise of China's form as a "sovereign state" in the age of colonialism. This particular Confucian form does not, however, validate imperial history, as if the empire had truly been built purely on ritual foundations; as a theory of political legitimacy, New Text studies has a mutually overlapping, contradictory relationship to the empire.

In order to contend with Old Text classical studies, Liu Fenglu had to adhere strictly to school methods, and his descriptions of the "Three Sequences," "Three Ages," and "inner-outer" are thus unable to give full expression to New Text classical studies as a political theory and as a guide for practice. It would take the work of Gong Zizhen and Wei Yuan to fully develop New Text studies as a field of statecraft. In a time of crisis, their wide-ranging, sharply worded studies observed a wide range of social issues from the horizon of New Text studies. Their work changed the very course of the New Text horizon, and had a profound impact on reformist thinking during the late Qing. Yet when we home in on their critique of internal politics, from the perspective of inner-outer, we see that their horizon of "China" gradually folded itself into the horizon of empire. This is especially evident in their views on geography.

2. Empty Titles of Nobility: The System of Centralized Administration and Empire with and without an "Outside"

Gong Zizhen had deep roots in scholarship, but did not adhere as strictly to school methods as did Liu Fenglu. On the contrary, he devoted himself to the "study of Heaven, Earth, and the four directions," developing his own intellectual practice around a study of imperial geography and customs. He was a Metropolitan Graduate (*jinshi*)—a rank earned by passing the highest imperial examination—in the Daoguang period (1820–1850), and served successively as Secretary of the Court of the Imperial Clan and Secretary of the Ministry of Rites. After initially failing the Metropolitan Examination of 1819, he studied Gongyang learning with Liu Fenglu, and began to use ideas from the Gongyang *Spring and Autumn* to conduct a comprehensive interpretation of the Five Classics. He published two representative works in this vein, *Profound Meanings of the Five Classics from Beginning to End (Wujing dayi zhongshi lun)* and *Questions and Answers on the Profound Meanings of the Five Classics from Beginning to End (Wujing dayi zhongshi dawen)*, in 1823.

But his other writings on the classics, including *Rectification of Names in the Six Classics (Liujing zhengming)* and *Questions and Answers on the Great Oath (Da shi wenda),* are hard to categorize as Gongyang studies, and many of the viewpoints expressed in these works are more closely aligned with Old Text studies. In a "Preface to the *Written Records of Ding'an*" (*Ding'an wenlu xu*), Wei Yuan says of Gong: "In classics he thoroughly understood the Gongyang *Spring and Autumn,* and in history he was adept in the geography of the Northwest. His writings were grounded in the fundamentals of philology and in the etymology of written characters. They included the various masters of Zhou and Qin within their scope, as well as sacrificial vessels and musical stones, and took the institutions of antiquity, the ways of the world, and the people's sorrows as their subject matter. In his later years he was particularly drawn to Western books, and remarked on their subtle profundity."[170] Geographical studies was originally an integral part of classical and historical studies, and of historical studies in particular.

Gong Zizhen's scholarly outlook was deeply influenced by Zhang Xuecheng's theory that "the Six Classics are all history," and the horizon of his historical studies, and especially of his geographical studies, was intertwined with his studies of the classics. Synthesizing classical scholarship with geographical studies was one of the major facets of Gong's work, and his other knowledge and statecraft views were woven into the warp and weft of the classics (Gongyang studies) and history (geographical studies). As to his understanding of Grand Unification, his main difference from Liu Fenglu was that Liu attached great importance to the values of enfeoffment and was sharply critical of the system of centralized administration; whereas Gong, though he nominally respected the system of decentralized enfeoffment, fundamentally conceived of "Grand Unification" as founded on the idea of centralized administration. In his "Answer to Questions on the Marquis of China within the Passes" (*Da ren wen guannei hou*), Gong states:

> One of the excellent institutions of the Han, which became a model for all [subsequent] ages, was the [office of] Marquis of China within the Passes (*guannei hou*) [the second highest in a system of twenty empire-wide honorary ranks of nobility]. The Han not only adopted the prefecture and county system of the Qin, but also admired the enfeoffment system of the Zhou. Feudal kingdoms had given way to

> centrally administered prefectures and counties in the Nine Regions of Yu [i.e., in the ancient territories of China], resulting in great upheavals on every hand. Feudalism resembles a formal system of family discipline, while prefectures and counties represent a more substantive system, and both could not exist together. If both could not exist together, which would be abandoned and which would stand? Heaven must have its tendencies, and Heaven's abandonment of enfeoffment and its tendency toward central administration is clear and obvious. Yet they were locked in stalemate for more than two thousand years, before reaching a definitive resolution. How was this resolved? Only in our dynasty was it finally settled.

The Marquis of China within the Passes was a titular rank of nobility from the Han dynasty. It fit the form of the system of decentralized enfeoffment in name, but had "no sacrifices of earth and grain, no military power, and no power to appoint subordinates."[171] The creation of a "Marquis of China within the Passes" typified the hollowing out of ritual enfeoffment, opposition to actual enfeoffment and its ritual values, and erosion of the system of hereditary nobility and of enfeoffment's tradition of loyalty. Such titles also granted these classes of nobility the opportunity to gain advancement within the framework of the system of centralized administration, the key to which was the complete separation of aristocratic ennoblement from territorial authority. Thus, the various factions were incorporated into the centralized bureaucracy, under the condition of accepting the absolute dominance of the central authority. Using the form of "Marquis of China within the Passes" to accommodate the power of enfeoffment, while nonetheless weakening the influence of the hereditary salary system in court politics, was a way of maintaining unified political governance in the centralized empire.

Gong Zizhen's suggestion touched on a key issue in the construction of dynastic legitimacy: the central imperial authority was trying to limit the power of the nobility and to create more flexible identity groups, but the process of centralization still relied on the status symbols of the landed aristocracy or the religious elite, as the latter formed the basis for expressing and maintaining the integrity of the ritual system. This is the same reason why the aristocracy consistently called upon ancestral rules and rituals in their struggle with imperial power. In the context of Qing politics, using the installation of a Marquis of China within the Passes as a metaphor for mocking censure of the banners, the local chieftains, and the system of hereditary nobility was a tradition that continued unbroken from Gong Zizhen to Kang Youwei.[172] Gong Zizhen used Gongyang *Spring and Autumn* scholarship's ideas of form versus substance to describe enfeoffment in relation to centralized administration, arguing that the distinguishing features of "Grand Unification" lay in its synthesis of form and substance, in its abrogation of enfeoffment, and in its taking of the Han-dynasty installation of a Marquis of China within the Passes as a "pattern for all ages," and in so doing he started to unravel the tightly knit, intrinsic link between "Grand Unification" and "enfeoffment" as described by Liu Fenglu. This inclination is even more evident in Kang Youwei's discourse on Grand Unification during the late Qing.

Based on what has been described so far, one can see that Gong Zizhen's favorable view toward the system of centralized administration divided ritual from institutions yet again: Marquis of China within the Passes was a ritual position, while centralized administration was the real substance of the empire. This was a rather nimble use of the New Text motif of "deriding hereditary postings." In order to heal the rift between ritual enfeoffment and political institutions, Gong used the Three Dynasties' concept of form (*wen*) versus substance (*zhi*), categorizing the idea of centralized administration as "substance," thereby imparting ritual orthodoxy to this system. After the Qing put down the Revolt of the Three Feudatories, all of the meritorious princes stayed in the capital, while "members of the imperial clan, from princes down to favored generals, nine ranks in all, were granted lands in Zhili and in the Northeast, to support them in the manner of ancient benefices. By the standard of Han institutions, these were Marquises of China within the Passes. Meritorious officials from the first rank down were granted salaries, and these were also all Marquises of China within the Passes."[173] "Grand Unification" preserved the empty titles of enfeoffed nobility, and inherited and continued the substance of centralized administration. Form and substance were merged under the unification of imperial authority, with "substance" (centralized administration) given primacy. This better defines "Grand Unification" and further elaborates on "deriding hereditary postings" at the institutional level. At its core, ritual enfeoffment must be abstract if it is to become the premise of Grand Unification. Precisely for this reason, if we interpret Gong Zizhen according to New Text classical school methods, we will have no way to understand the significance of Gongyang learning in the development of his thought. Most important here is to observe what type of horizon the topics of Gongyang learning provided for Gong's thought and scholarly activities, and what kind of relationship his study of Northwest geography, his political commentary and policy advice, and his classical scholarship formed with Gongyang studies.

From the perspective of classical scholarship, early New Text classical studies emphasized inner-outer and Three Sequences discourse, while Gong Zizhen emphasized the significance of the Three Ages of Antiquity. He developed "Three Ages" (*san shi*) discourse into a fundamental theory of historical perspective, and used the "Age of Great Peace" (*taiping shi*) concept to criticize the "China-peripheral states (*Yi-Xia*) dichotomy," clearly contrasting the Gongyang concept of Grand Unification with the nationalist ideology of Song-Ming Confucianism. This idea shows up not only in his New Text classical scholarship, but also in his political commentary. In the treaty negotiations following the first pacification of the Dzungars, Gong wrote a "Memorial for the Imperial Examinations about Subduing the Frontier and Pacifying Faraway Lands" (*Yushi anbian suiyuan shu*), which describes in detail the Qing empire's internal relations and methods of rule. His outlook extends far beyond "separation of Yi and Xia," and draws a clear distinction between the Qing structure of "inner and outer as one family" and "previous dynasties":

> The border situation of our era is different from that of previous history. The land opens up for twenty thousand li, and this must not be considered far fetched; watchtowers face each other, yet there are no designated nine borderlands. By treating its land as territory and its people as sons, we can successfully transform land which has been unmeasured and effectively abandoned for ten million years into something not seen before in history, because Yi and Xia are [now] one family.[174]

It was by looking at "China" from this perspective on "Yi and Xia as one family" that Gong could finally turn to the distant frontiers. Within the horizon of empire, these regions were no longer "outer": his many studies of the ethnic minorities of the Northwest and their historical geography included the thoughtful analysis of the origins and course of Yellow Sect Lamaism and its relationship to the Qing in "Introduction to *Mongolian Buddhist Symbolism*" *(Menggu xiangjiao zhi xu);* the investigation into each Mongolian banner and its geographic situation in "Preface to the *Gazetteer of Mongolia*" *(Menggu shuidi dizhi);* the study of the topolects of the Mongolian, Tibetan, and Hui Muslim regions in "Preface to *Table of Sound Types in Mongolian*" *(Menggu sheng lei biao xu),* including phonetic comparison to the northern topolect of Chinese, and with additional discussion of the classic books of the regions and their translations; the tracing of the origins of written Mongolian to the "grandfather of the Qing writing system," and comparison with written Manchu, in "Preface to *Table of Mongolian Letters*" *(Menggu zi lei biao xu);* the accounting for the origin of each Mongolian clan, supplementing deficiencies in the *Yuan History,* in "General Preface to *Tables of Mongolian Clans and Summary Table of Clans in the Capital*" *(Menggu shizu biao ji zai Jing shizu biao zong xu);* and the recording of "suitable vassal states for princesses of our dynasty" in "Introduction to *Mongolian Documents of Surrender*" *(Menggu ce xiangbiao xu),* as well as "Preface to *Noble Envoys of Mongolia (Menggu ji jue biao xu),* "Preface to *Qinghai Gazetteer*" *(Qinghai zhi xu),* and "Preface to *Ulanghai Table*" *(Wulianghai biao xu).* Each of these documents demonstrates the cultural and political perspective of a multiethnic empire, using ritual order to remove the simplistic distinction between Yi-Xia and inner-outer, then substantiating these abstract ritual relationships, and turning to concrete studies of geography, customs, population, culture, and language. The expansion of this knowledge is closely connected to the political structure of the Qing, reflecting a keen awareness of the size of the empire, its cultural diversity, and changes to its ethnic makeup and customs. These works are characterized by investigative, empirical, objective statements. Yet apart from the above-discussed particular characteristics of the Qing dynastic polity, we would have no way of understanding why so many scholars turned their attention to geographical studies during this period.

If we say that the "Marquis of China within the Passes" is a title that makes ritual enfeoffment (the system of the hereditary nobility) into empty symbolism, then the geographical studies and provincial administration of the Northwest concretely extend the conception of a unified system of prefectural and county administration. Gong Zizhen's geographical studies inherently resonate with such New Text works as his *Profound Meaning of the Five Classics from Beginning to End* and his *Explorations in Ancient History,* the latter written between 1825 and 1832: the New Text classical studies theories linking the Three Sequences, amplifying the Three Ages, distinguishing inner and outer, and Grand Unification provided a theoretical perspective for the multiethnic and multicultural landscape of empire, while the imperial landscape itself provided substantive content for these classical theories. Like Zhuang Cunyu and Liu Fenglu, Gong Zizhen was concerned with problems in Manchu-Han relations and with the literati who were "adherents of the former dynasty" (*yimin*) under the current regime, but these issues became increasingly tied to his historical narrative of dynastic Grand Unification. In *Explorations in Ancient History,* he discusses ritual respect for officialdom using Three Ages discourse, and uses the *yimin* status of the semilegendary late Shang-era sage advisor Ji Zi (a royal relative imprisoned for remonstrating with King Zhou of Shang [r. 1075–1046 BCE] before his overthrow by King Wu of Zhou, and who later gave political advice to King Wu) to hint at the basis of the position, words, and deeds of the Han literati. But his discussion is also no longer limited to the question of individuals taking and leaving office, and is instead linked with the ideals of "Grand Unification." When we have taken this in, we must take note of two things: First, that the concept of Grand Unification constitutes a criticism of Han ethnic nationalism from the Song-Ming period onward; and second, that Gong's emphasis on the Northwest is related to the Qing origins in the Northeast and Mongolia. We therefore must not look at his thought on these matters as "Han-centrism." Gong writes:

> Question: What is the meaning of Great Peace and Grand Unification? Answer: Song and Ming scholars in their remote mountains and forests spoke much about separation of China from the foreign (*Yi Xia zhi fang*), and drew far-fetched comparisons with the Spring and Autumn, but they did not understand the Spring and Autumn. Between the Spring and Autumn and the present age, Wu and Chu [i.e., kingdoms once seen as foreign] have joined, and I dare not speak contemptuously of them or treat them as outsiders. The *Ode* says: "And without distinction of territory or boundary, The rules of social duty are diffused throughout these great regions." There is nothing external to the Sage, and also nothing

> external to Heaven. But in that case, how is it that in the text of the *Three Branches* there are differences drawn between inner and outer? Answer: For the Age of Chaos it is so, for the Age of Rising Peace it is so, but for the Age of Great Peace it is not so.[175]

Here, "Great Peace and Grand Unification" or the "Age of Great Peace" is a rejection of the "separation of the Yi from the Xia" or the distinction between inner-outer made by the Song-Ming Neo-Confucians. Gong expressed this rejection in his comment that "for the Age of Chaos, it [i.e., division and separation] is so, for the Age of Rising Peace, it is so, but for the Age of Great Peace, it is not so." From Gong's perspective, the great principle of the *Spring and Autumn,* which everywhere does away with inner versus outer and weakens the distinction of foreign versus Chinese, is a notion that overturns and corrects the ethnic segregation, armed suppression, and hereditary hierarchy of the empire. The Manchu Qing claimed to have made "inner-outer" and "separation of the Chinese from the foreign" disappear, but under its principles of ethnic equality and cultural pluralism, it nonetheless operated through military control, cultural discipline, and ethnic privilege. As illustrated by his explanation of the Qing era's "Profound and Subtle Teachings of the Lofty Yellow Sect" and his inquiry into the mutual relationships among the Manchu, Mongols, and Tibetans in Qinghai in "Letters to People" *(Yu ren jian;* i.e., "Letters to People on the Affairs of Qinghai"), what Gong proffered was a method of rule to maintain political stability.[176] Because of this, and despite using the *Spring and Autumn* as a mirror, he was still taking the reality of the relationships between imperial government and military affairs as his point of reference, and his cancelling of absolute boundaries between inner-outer and Yi-Xia was not so much a permanent fulfillment of the principles of Great Peace as a critical proposal for the political relationships of the dynasty.

In the above context, the questions of Yi-Xia and inner-outer are situated within the horizon of geographical studies, thus overlapping with imperial knowledge. Gong Zizhen and Wei Yuan considered themselves to be among the idealists in the empire, having put into intellectual practice the Qing government's principle of "Manchu and Han are as one" (*Man Han yiti*). As far as they were concerned, since there was no need to prove the legitimacy of the Qing empire, it followed that there was also no need to justify the legitimacy of their own activities within the empire. In *The Silent Goblet,* Wei Yuan took up the Confucian moral principle that held that "before the Three Dynasties, ruler and teacher were at one with the Way, and ritual and music were methods of governing; after the Three Dynasties, ruler and teacher were distinct from the Way, and ritual and music were empty forms." Wei asked: "How could it be that the ancients brought together only ruler and teacher? At that time, from the Minister of State (*zhongzai*), Minister of Education (*situ*), and Minister of Rites (*zongbo*) down to Palace Master (*shishi*), Palace Protector (*baoshi*), Minister (*qing*), and Grand Master (*dafu*), who was not an exemplary teacher to the elite class?" Wei furthermore put forward the proposition of "practicing the art of the classics as the art of governance" (*yi jingshu wei zhishu*).[177] The Dao cannot only be effected in rites and music, but must also be fulfilled in military punishment and food and commodities. The *Dao* is thus no longer antagonistic toward real institutions, but a moral guide within the ambit of the system. From the perspective of statecraft, this is a return to the spirit of Gu Yanwu and Huang Zongxi. Yet this return also implies an enormous shift: Wei Yuan's work does not show the tension with the Qing dynasty seen in Gu and Huang's work, as the center of Wei's focus was the "state" itself. If morals must be built on achievement, and classical learning must be converted into direct governance, then the legitimacy of rule is the basic premise for all of the above. This theory of statecraft had a significant impact on the reform movement of the late Qing: The movement to reform or establish a modern state was not aimed at deconstructing the empire, nor was it meant to divide the empire into multiple nation-states based on ethnic or regional identity. Rather, the empire in its entirety was the object of reform, with the goal of adapting it to the new terrain of the age of nation-states. This is the context in which Gong Zizhen, Wei Yuan, and the like were drawn to geographical studies.

3. The Horizon of Geographical Studies and the Transformation of Inner-Outer Relations

The rise of geographical studies (*yudi xue*) as a field is intimately linked with the tradition of statecraft of the early-Qing literati, but there are major differences between the scholarship of that period and what followed.[178] In *Advantages and Disadvantages of the Administrative Regions of All-under-*

Heaven (Tianxia junguo libing shu), Gu Yanwu compiled twenty-one histories and the gazetteers of every administrative region, the collected writings of a generation of illustrious officials and nobles, memorials written to the emperor, and other such material, "in part as a record of geographical studies, in part as an account of the good and the bad." This book pioneered geographical studies within the tradition of classical scholarship. As a work of statecraft, Gu's work sought to harmonize the political frameworks of decentralized enfeoffment and centralized administration, in opposition to the hereditary bureaucracy of imperial Grand Unification. Qing Confucianists held fast to the classical texts of the Han dynasty, and had some knowledge of the section on geography in the *History of the Former Han (Han shu: Dili zhi).* The origin of their scholarship was closely connected to traditional Confucian history. The flourishing of geographical studies under the Qing, however, was motivated more by affairs in the Northwest; Confucian scholars who were concerned with border issues were particularly keen to understand the geography of the Northwest and Southwest frontier regions. The techniques of surveying and mapping brought by missionaries in the late Ming and early Qing were put to practical use in border surveys and mapmaking of the Northwest and Southwest frontiers.[179] For example, all three editions of the *Complete Map of Routes for the Emperor's Chariot (Huangyu quan lan tu,* 1717–1721) that were produced during the Kangxi era were drawn up with the assistance of the Jesuits, from whom Kangxi himself studied geometry, and were used to define the terrain during the conquest of the Northwest.[180] It is worth noting that the Russians and Europeans were engaged in surveying the territory of Russia, including its borders with the Qing empire and Mongolia, at the same time. After Russia defeated Sweden in 1721, its hunger to expand its borders grew sharper. According to Peter Perdue, in 1723 Swedish prisoner of war Philipp Johann Strahlenberg, who was being held in Moscow, drafted a map including all of Russia, Central Asia, Mongolia, and parts of China. Strahlenberg's map was published in German in 1730, and in English in 1736. This English edition was widely influential in Europe. Its full title is rather long: *An Historico-Geographical Description of the North and Eastern Part of Europe and Asia; but more particularly of Russia, Siberia, and Great Tartary; both in their Ancient and Modern State: Together with An entire New Polyglot-Table of the Dialects of 32 Tartarian Nations; and a Vocabulary of the Kalmuck-Mungalian Tongue, as also a large and accurate*

Map of those countries, and variety of cuts, representing Asiatick Scythian Antiquities. Clearly, this map is an anthropological description of Russia and the Far East. Strahlenberg considered the Ural Mountains to define the boundary between Europe and Asia, a definition later taken up by the Russian historian and geographer Vasilii Tatishchev.[181] If we make a side-by-side comparison of these to the work of missionaries in Europe during the same period, such as Jean-Baptiste du Halde's 1735 *Description of the Geography, Chronology, Politics of the Chinese Empire and Chinese Tartary (Description geographique, chronologique, politique de L'empire de La Chine et de Tartarie Chinoise),* we see that their appearance is not at all accidental. The requirements of boundary surveys and the imperial perspective furnished Qing-era geographical studies with the tools for its development.

Looking at the development of geographical studies, during the Qing the discipline was closely linked to tracing the history of the Mongol Yuan conquests, with particular interest in the Yuan's expansion into Europe (a point to which I will return in my later discussion of Wei Yuan). In the process of compiling *The Emperor's Four Treasuries,* Qing scholars learned of *The Secret History of the Mongols* (*Yuan mishi*) and the *Record of Imperially Conducted Yuan Military Campaigns* (*Huangyuan shengwu qinzheng lu*) from the *Yongle Dictionary (Yongle dadian).* Thus, Yuan history and corresponding historical and geographical studies came to grow in importance, accelerating Qing research on the terrain and history of the Northwest.[182] This horizon of knowledge has echoes of the knowledge-gathering projects created by Qing rulers for the sake of imperial control.[183] Geographical studies during the Qing therefore cannot be seen simply as the product of the literati turning their attention to statecraft; in a certain sense, it was an organic component of the imperial knowledge-building project. Starting in the Kangxi period, the Qing began surveying the country as a whole, producing *Complete Map of Routes for the Chariot of the Emperor (Huang yu quan lan tu)* and improving upon it with the *Copper-plate Map of the Treasury of the Palace of Qianlong (Qianlong neifu Tongban yutu),* as well as compiling the *Gazetteer of the Unified Qing Empire (Da Qing yitong zhi)* and the *Gazetteer of the Western Regions (Xiyu tongzhi)* (along with revisions to the latter in late-Qing publications such as the *Xinjiang Gazetteer [Xinjiang tongzhi]*). The imperial court undertook such studies, and the work of individuals in this vein was not rare. It took over seventy years to pacify Xinjiang, an enterprise of the reigns of Kangxi, Yongzheng, and Qianlong. Following Qianlong and the recovery of all territory in the Western Regions, westward traffic and migration increased, and scholarly interest in Xinjiang, the Muslim-majority areas, and Mongolia grew enormously. However, geographic study of the Northwest was not well developed prior to the Jiaqing and Daoguang periods, and there was little writing on the subject by individuals.[184] Beginning in the seventeenth century, as the Russian empire began its own expansion, the frontiers of Xinjiang, Mongolia, and Russia became entangled in incessant conflict. After the signing of the Treaty of Nerchinsk, Zhang Penghui's *Diary of a Diplomat in Russia (Fengshi Eluosi riji),* Qian Liangyi's *Chronicles across the Frontier (Chusai jilüe),* and Xu Yuanwen's *Inscriptions of Events at the Russian Border (Eluosi jiangjie beiji)* were published in succession. The Sino-Russian frontier is also described in *Chronicles of Longsha (Longsha jilüe),* written in the form of a garrison dispatch; Yang Bin's *Willow Margin Chronicles (Liu bian jilüe);* and Wu Zhenchen's *Ningguta Chronicle (Ningguta jilüe).* In the middle years of the Jiaqing reign (1796–1820), trade disputes in the border town of Kyakhta frequently erupted, and troubles in the Northwest became an important factor in the literati philosophy of statecraft. A keen awareness of problems at the frontier (including borders, frontier territory, populations, customs and geography, and the extent of governance) pushed research into the geography of the Northwest.[185] In 1806, Yu Zhengxie, who had studied the region, published *Preliminary Manuscript on Russia (Eluosi changpian gaoba),* and in the following year came out with *Compilation of Russian Affairs (Eluosi shiji),* describing in detail the boundaries and historical development of Russia and of Sino-Russian conflict, noting that outside of the Yongzheng-Qianlong period "Russia stations its troops in the west, and thus has no intention of invading the south,"[186] thereby placing Sino-Russian relations within a broader strategic perspective. Following this, Zhang Mu filled in the gaps left in Yu's work with information from Song Yun's (1732–1835) *Campaign Summaries with Illustrations and Poems (Suifu jilue tushi,* 1805), creating a *Supplementary Compilation of Russian Affairs (Eluosi shi buji).* These works, along with Gong Zizhen and Cheng Tongwen's edited edition of *Strategies for Russian Pacification (Pingding Luosha fanglue)* written in the late Jiaqing period, all constitute studies of Sino-Russian border geography and relations between the two empires. Strictly speaking, these works do not fit neatly into the ambit of geographical studies, as they included broad descriptions of the peoples, folkways, languages, religions, and cultures of these regions, greatly expanding the horizon of discourse on geographical studies and customs pioneered by Gu Yanwu.

The Qing literati were prodigious in their scholarship on the Western Regions, and their work on the subject comprises an important part of the empire's base of knowledge. Some examples include: Liang Fen's (1641–1729) *Three Accounts of the Western Borderlands* (*Xichui san lue;* a three-volume work including the titles "Hikes Through the Western Borderlands" [*Xichui haibu*], "Maps of the Western Borderlands Explained" [*Xichui tushuo*], and "Brief Accounts of the Western Borderlands in Modern Times [*Xichui jin lüe*]); Qi Yunshi's (1751–1815) *Table of Nobility in the Muslim-Majority Regions and the Mongolian Feudatories* (*Waifan Menggu Huibu wanggong biao*), *An Outline of the Feudatories* (*Fanbu yao lüe*), *Explaining the Territory of the Western Regions* (*Xiyu shidi*), *An Outline of the Western Borderlands* (*Xichui yao lue*), and *An Outline of the New Territories* (*Xinjiang lue*); Xu Song's (1781–1848) *Waterways of the Western Regions* (*Xiyu shuidao ji*), *A Primer of the New Territories* (*Xinjiang shi lüe*), and *Supplementary Annotations to the New Territories Biographies in the History of the Former Han* (*Han shu xiyu zhuan buzhu*); Hong Liangji's (1746–1809) *Record of Things Heard beyond the Great Wall* (*Saiwai jiwen*), *Tianshan Guest Talks* (*Tianshan kehua*), *Ili Diary* (*Yili riji*), *Record from beyond the Wall* (*Saiwai ji*), *Tianshan Chronicle* (*Tianshan jicheng*), and *Bearing Arms Afar Collection* (*Wanli hege ji*); Fu Heng's (1720–1770) *Illustrated Gazetteer of the Imperial Western Regions* (*Huangyu xiyu tuzhi*) and *Annals of Translation in the Western Regions* (*Xiyu tongwen zhi*); seventy-one more works with titles like *Things Heard and Seen in the Western Regions* (*Xiyu wenjian lu*), *Natural Conditions and Social Customs of the Muslim Territories* (*Huijiang fengtu ji*), *Brief Account of Xinjiang* (*Xinjiang jilue*), *Examination of Customs and Conditions in the Imperial Territories of Xinjiang* (*Xinjiang yudi fengtu kao*), *Folklore of the Western Regions* (*Xiyu jiuwen*), and *Table of Military Outposts and Roadways* (*juntai daoli biao*); Ji Yun's (1724–1805) *Summary Account of River Sources* (*He yuan jilue*), *Urumqi Miscellaneous Notes* (*Wulumuqi za ji*), and *Urumqi Miscellaneous Poems* (*Wulumuqi za shi*); Lin Zexu's (1785–1850) *Account of Bearing Arms* (*He ge ji cheng*); and Wei Yuan's (1794–1856) *Answering Questions about the Northwest Frontier Regions.* In 1807, Qi Yunshi, a military official and former Provincial Coinage Service supervisor under the command of Ili General Song Yun, was ordered to compile a geographical treatise, and under Song Yun's direction maps of the Western Ningxia region were added, resulting in a *Comprehensive Summary Account of the Affairs of the Western Borderlands* (*Xi chui zongtong shilue*) in twelve volumes: volumes 1–4 contained a summary discussion of the topographical features of Xinjiang, volumes 5–7 dealt with affairs within Ili, volumes 8–10 separately discussed affairs in individual cities outside Ili, volume 11 dealt with distant lands, and volume 12 contained miscellaneous essays. In 1814, Song Yun once again served as a general in Ili, and again ordered Xu Song (1781–1848), a former Hunan Provincial Education Commissioner who was serving on his staff in atonement for an offense, to revise it under the title *Comprehensive Summary Account of the Affairs of Ili* (*Yili zongtong shilue*). This work, after extensive critical review, was completed in 1820, and was presented to the newly acceded Emperor Daoguang by Song Yun. Daoguang wrote a preface, and conferred a new title: *Knowledge and Strategies for Xinjiang* (*Xinjiang zhilue*). In this book, there are a "General Account of Xinjiang Waterways" (*Xinjiang shuidao zong xu*) and a "Xinjiang Waterways Table" (*Xinjiang shuidao biao*), which describe the twelve rivers and lakes in Xinjiang. The geographical studies produced by Qi Yunshi and Xu Song were completed in the service of the military general of Ili, and cannot be considered as purely the work of private persons. Yet their works were broadly influential among the Qing literati, and confirm that ethnic Han literati already regarded the imperial state and the internal crises of its border regions as important matters of statecraft.

The year 1820 was an extraordinary year for Qing geographical studies: It was the year Xu Song was recalled from exile in Xinjiang. The thinkers surrounding him (including Zhang Mu [1805–1849], Shen Yao [1798–1840], Cheng Tongwen, Wei Yuan, Gong Zizhen, Yang Liang, Yu Zhengxie [1775–1840], Dong Youcheng [1791–1823], and Chen Chao [1801–1835]) were all low-ranking officials, who nevertheless cared about court administration and the fate of the country.[187] Together they created a certain ambiance around the field of study; even Li Zhaoluo (1769–1841), Yao Ying (1785–1853), and Wang Liu (1786–1843) in the outer provinces were in close contact with them. It was also in this year that Jahangir Khoja (Ch. Zhang Ge'er, 1788–1828), in the Muslim-majority area of Xinjiang, joined forces with the English and Kokand to resist the Qing, attacking the city limits of Kashgar. Jahangir Khoja was the grandson of Burhan ad-Din (Ch. Dahe Zhuomu, ?–1759), the tribal leader of the Muslim regions who in 1756, at the instigation of Xiaohe Zhuomu, set his troops against the Qing and declared the Batur Khanate. When they were defeated in 1759, soldiers fleeing west were slaughtered by Badakhshan tribesmen. The rebellion of 1820 failed, but a series of insurrections followed, culminating in 1826 when the troops of the Kokand state captured Kashgar, Yingjisar, Yarkand, and Khotan, controlling half of the territory of Xinjiang until they were finally routed by the Qing army in 1827. This is the essential background against which Qing geographers of the nineteenth and twentieth centuries paid such keen attention to the Northwest.

From the perspective of inner and outer, such studies of geography or customs were already interwoven with the imperial perspective. The sense of inner-outer and Yi-Xia molded by Ming-dynasty-era knowledge, and the image of "China" founded on this sensibility, were completely rewritten: the opposite sides of the Great Wall, not Jiangnan and the region around the Grand Canal, were the frames of reference for observing and understanding China. The Qing rulers spoke of Manchu and Han as one whole, and of Yi and Xia as one family, a concept based on the boundaries of the empire and the scope of governance. The emperors and cabinet ministers spoke Manchu, Mongolian, Chinese, and even Uyghur and Tibetan, an important hallmark of the minority dynasty. In 1750, Prince Zhuang Yunlu (1695–1767) and others oversaw the compilation of a *Compendium of Matching Written Words and Sounds* (*Tongwen yuntong*) in six volumes, which "compared similarities and differences between the letters of the Sanskrit and Tibetan alphabets, and matched Chinese written words with their pronunciations in Manchu." And in 1763, Grand Secretary Fu Heng (1720–1770) and others compiled a *Treatise on Translating the Languages of the Western Regions* (*Xiyu tongwen zhi*) in twenty-four volumes. Each entry "was divided into four main segments: first a Manchu text is listed, followed by Chinese characters, followed by Chinese phonetic (*qieyin*) representations, followed by Mongol, Western Sichuan (*Xifan*), Clear Script Oirat, and Hui [Perso-Arabic] characters, so that [words of] similar meaning could be looked up."[188] Other such examples may also be enumerated. These cultural productions of the empire resonated with Gong Zizhen, as both pushed back against "strict separation of Yi and Xia" and the idea that "the inner is China (*Zhonghua*) and the outer is barbarian." If we consult Gong Zizhen's other memorials to the emperor, such as

"Draft Memorial Forwarding a Treatise on the Geography of Mongolia with Maps" (*Ni jin shang Menggu tu zhiwen*), "Memorial Submitted to the Grand Defender of Turpan, [and to its] Group Leaders, Grand Ministers, and Notables" (*Shang zhenshou tulufan lingdui dachen bao gong shu*), "Memorial Submitted to the Director General of the Historiography Institute Supervising Summary Compilations" (*Shang Guoshiguan zhongzai tidiao zong zuan shu*), "Draft Table of Regional Dialects" (*Ni shang jin fangyan biao*), "Interposing a Suggestion on the Northern Regions [of Xinjiang]" (*Bei lu ancha yi*), and "Memorial for the Imperial Examinations about Subduing the Frontier and Pacifying Faraway Lands" (*Yushi anbian Suiyuan shu*), we can clearly see the political blueprint for a Chinese empire that is vast and multilayered, that does not distinguish between inner and outer but is nonetheless culturally diverse. This is a complete departure from the distinction between inner and outer made by Neo-Confucianism, as well as from that of the centrally administered state; neither is it the European political horizon of internal homogeneity of the nation-state. In this perspective, "China" must be organized according to the ritual relationship of near to distant in order to form a political order where inner and outer work in concert with each other. It is the product of gradual historical change, and is itself an ever-changing historical entity. From Zhuang Cunyu and Liu Fenglu to Gong Zizhen, the concept of "China" is mutually exclusive of the category "Han."

Unlike Zhuang Cunyu and Liu Fenglu, Gong Zizhen and the abovementioned works on statecraft no longer approached the empire's questions of inner-outer and Yi-Xia from the perspective of equality between Manchu and Han. On the contrary, through his studies of the geography, customs, military affairs, and economics of these regions they were brought within the horizon of the empire. Gong's inquiries into the historical geography, religions, and cultures of the Northwest were closely connected to the study of the geography and history of the region that sprang from the work of Xu Song (1781–1848) and his peers. Gong wrote extensively about Mongolia, Tibet, Qinghai, and the Muslim-majority areas. His perspective transcended border walls, in concert with Kangxi, Yongzheng, and Qianlong's unification of the northern frontier through military conquest and political praxis. Perhaps best known among Gong's writings on the subject are his "Opinion on Establishing Provincial Administration in the Western Regions" *(Xiyu zhi xingsheng yi;* hereafter the "Opinion"), "Memorial on Examinations and Border Pacification in Suiyuan," "Memorial Submitted to the Grand Defender of Turpan, and to its Group Leaders, Grand Ministers, and Notables," his incomplete manuscript of the *Illustrated Gazetteer of Mongolia (Menggu tuzhi),* and "Memorial Submitted to the Director General of the Historiography Institute Supervising Summary Compilations." The "Heaven, Earth, and the four directions" he studied were not metaphorical, but rather grounded in rigorous geographical and ethnocultural study. According to Wu Changshou's *Chronological Biography of Gong Zizhen,* Gong's "study of Heaven, Earth, and the four directions" began when he became a proofreader at the Historiography Institute in the first reign year of Daoguang (1820), where he worked on revisions to the *Gazetteer of Unification (Yitong zhi):*

> The master [i.e., Gong] sent a memorial to the Director General, discussing the evolution of the various tribes outside the wall and repairing the omissions of older gazetteers, eighteen items in all. Earlier, Cheng Tongwen . . . [who held the title of] Chamberlain for Law Enforcement (*dali*), had revised the *Collected Statutes,* and when its materials related to the Court of Frontier Affairs (*Lifan yuan*), along with various maps of Qinghai and Tibet, all obtained by geometric projection (*jie kai xiefang er de zhi*), fell to him for collation, this was the beginning of the master's study of Heaven and Earth and the four directions. Devoting his energies to the study of tribal lineages and customs, landforms and river flows in two areas outside the wall in the Northwest, he gained a deep understanding of borderland affairs and became known as an expert. He personally composed the *Illustrated Gazetteer of Mongolia,* and, to give some precise examples, it included twenty-eight maps, eighteen tables, and twelve biographies, altogether thirty chapters. There were also two tables of the Kazakh and Bulute tribes that had previously been drawn up by Xu Song of Daxing, a Drafter (*sheren*) [in the Central Secretariat] who was proficient in the geography of the Northwest. The master sighed that they were a masterpiece of the contemporary age, and so included them in his gazetteer.[189]

From the perspective of classical learning, Gong Zizhen used the methodology of geographical studies to scrutinize the features of China within the horizon of a multiethnic dynasty, broadening the textual research on writing systems, phonology, and customs that had been undertaken by early-Qing Confucian scholars, extending their work to the study of the frontier and its cultures and demonstrating its truly expansive historical horizon.

Mid-Qing frontier studies were quite similar to their early-Qing counterpart in their emphasis on military conquest and political reform of subduing the Three Feudatories and the shift from the local chieftain system to direct central control. Starting in the middle of the Jiaqing period, however, frontier studies became fused with a new crisis mentality, as their depictions of the Western Regions came to include maritime coastal concerns. In his preface to Li Huiyuan's *Study of Han Maps of the Western Regions* (*Han xiyu tu kao*), Chen Li wrote:

> According to the *Histories of the Western Regions of the Two Han Dynasties* (*Liang Han xiyu zhuan*), the farthest [of these regions] were the Roman Empire (*Da Qin*) and Parthia (*Anxi*). Today, apart from the Roman Empire, people of the northwestern coastal areas [i.e., the British] have occupied India (*Tianzhu*), which is only a little more than a thousand li from Yunnan. They have ceased hostilities with China, engaged in peace negotiations, established increased frontier trade, marched through the world, and lodged in the capital. And apart from Parthia, people of the southwestern coastal areas [i.e., Arabs and Persians] have entered China for more than a thousand years, have grown numerous, and are dispersed through all the provinces. Recently moreover there have been disturbances in the Guanlong region, and military engagements do not cease. Alas! They stir up trouble for China like this, and the people of China are frustrated, not knowing the source of it. Is it not a great sorrow?[190]

There are two points worth noting here: First, the author approaches the problems the Qing was facing in the West from the perspective of the Western Regions, suggesting that the interest of Qing scholars in the knowledge of the Han dynasty included an interest in the Han empire's historical horizon (such as the Han's first conquest of Xinjiang in the first century CE); second, the author mentions that "people of the northwestern coastal areas [of the Eurasian continent] have occupied India," indicating that the reconstruction of the map of the Western Regions from the Former and Latter Han was done partly in response to the occupation of India and other western areas (Xinjiang, Tibet) and to the expansion east and north by the British and other European countries. The author's reference to the early presence of "people from the southwestern coastal regions" (mostly Muslims from Arabia and Persia) in China and to recent conflict in the Southwest of the Qing state also shows that the mid-Qing sense of crisis was not directed solely at powerful northern neighbors such as Russia, but in fact extended to other regions as well.[191] We are hard pressed to confirm a direct connection between the study of the Northwest and research into the geography of Southeast Asia, but the former was certainly sensitive to issues along the coast. Indeed, Li Zhaoluo, who was in contact with Xu Song's circle, further organized some of the materials in Xie Qinggao's *Record of the Oceans* (*Hailu*) and added maps to this work, titling it *Record of Things Heard from Maritime Countries* (*Haiguo jiwen*), and compiling more information in an attached postscript, *Compiled Views of Maritime Countries* (*Haiguo jilan*).

Gong Zizhen's scholarship continued the historical and geographic traditions of classical learning, but his geographical studies included some entirely new elements. First, Gu Yanwu and other early-Qing scholars, via their research of institutions, material culture, language, customs, and institutions, were providing a basis for ethnic identity and moral judgment; Gong and his peers, by tracing the historical roots of the "reigning dynasty" (the Manchu Qing) through the histories of Mongolia, Tibet, and the Muslim-majority areas, were constructing a new prospect of "Grand Unification," for which they were tracing the historical veins and arteries. Within the perspective of the former, all of the above falls under "foreign customs," whereas there is already an organic "Chinese" part within the perspective of the latter. Second, scholars in the early Qing were keen to learn from the demise of the Ming dynasty, and their evidential learning regarding geography and customs was intimately connected to their effort to reconstruct their identity in the wake of foreign invasion; whereas Gong Zizhen and Wei Yuan's study of the Northwest and the empire's perspective were one and the same, and their studies of the northwestern borderlands were already permeated by the crisis along the southeastern coast.

There is a resonance between the concept of "Grand Unification" and the imperial order, as they share the common feature of doing away with the inner-outer distinction, forever engaged in incorporating outer areas into the empire's political and cultural affairs. In this sense, "Grand Unification" accepts the history of imperial conquest as history. In fact, in the context of the geographical studies, the argument for decentralized enfeoffment and the ritual perspective found in the early notion of Grand Unification were being replaced by a more pragmatic statecraft, thus dissolving the tension between Grand Unification and empire. This is not to say that the New Text classical studies idea of "Grand Unification" condoned imperial ethnonationalism or violence. The saying "It is so large that nothing is outside it" (*zhi da wu wai*) is an acknowledgment that China was a complex and diverse "China" of many ethnicities, customs, languages, religions, cultures, and geographies, and that its ritual foundations should not hinder the pluralism of its cultures, languages, religions, and political structures. This is clearly different from the nation-state's tendency toward homogeneity. Within the horizon of tributary ritual, "China" was a type of political order, as well as a ritual order: since it was not premised on ethnicity, it had no clear demarcation between inner and outer. The imperial state's respect for foundational ritual did not signify that one particular cultural or religious value system ought to govern the cultures and cultural values of all other peoples; on the contrary, ritual was a form of political order, and its ethical character was simply a formal element in the political relationships of a pluralistic empire. However, the tributary network of the Qing empire coexisted with boundaries defined by treaties, and "no outside" or "no outer" within the empire did not mean that there were no clear boundaries. In this sense, we cannot know for certain whether Gong Zizhen's "China and foreign as one family" did not presuppose an "outer part."

A close reading of Gong Zizhen's writing on statecraft shows us that the "Grand Unification" concept was in the process of a subtle transformation: If we say that the original concept of "Grand Unification" and its overlap with imperial politics were expressed by its preservation of cultural diversity, then Gong provided the basis for a tendency toward homogenization. This presages the shift of "Grand Unification" from a concept that was critical of empire into one that legitimized the unification of the state. Of course, as far as Gong was concerned, this shift was not at all apparent. In his view, whether it was the New Text theory of Grand Unification, or knowledge of statecraft under the guidance of this theory (such as description and research into the geography and customs of the multiethnic empire), it was not meant as something to flaunt to the masses, but was fundamentally for the purpose of applied statecraft. We must read Wei Yuan's *Gazetteer of the Maritime States* (*Haiguo tuzhi*) and *Records of Imperial Military Affairs (Shengwu ji)* together with Gong's writings, as each approaches the problems of its time from a different angle. In the spring of 1819, Gong sat for a special Palace Examination, but did not pass. He stayed in the capital, and began to receive instruction in the Gongyang *Spring and Autumn* from Liu Fenglu, studying Han learning and becoming familiar with methods alleged to have been transmitted from before the Zhou dynasty. The next year he once again failed the palace examination, and then immersed himself in the study of contemporary laws and institutions. This was the year in which he wrote his "Opinion on Establishing Provincial Administration in the Western Regions," and "Preface to Lineage Charts in the *Huizhou Prefectural Gazetteer*" (*Huizhou fuzhi shizu biao xu*), as well as his now-lost "Opinion on Stopping Foreign Merchant Ships in the Southeast" (*Dongnan ba fangbo yi*), demonstrating his understanding of the Western interior, the coastal Southeast, and the Yangtze region. The "Opinion on Establishing Provincial Administration in the Western Regions" begins: "What surrounds the great things of this world is the boundless sea. As seen from the Four Borderlands it is known as the Four Seas, and of the countless lands encompassed by the Four Seas, none is greater than our Great Qing. The great kingdom of Qing has from the time of Yao been called the Central Kingdom (*Zhongguo*) [i.e., China]."[192] Here, although Great Qing is the largest, it has already been placed among a countless number of "states of the Four Seas." According to Wu Changshou, the "Opinion" was completed in the first year of the reign of the Daoguang Emperor (1821). In that year, in which Duke Wenzhuang of Jueluo (Baoxing) was appointed as minister in charge of Turfan, Gong Zizhen submitted a memorial in which he "analyzed in detail matters concerning the Tianshan Southern Circuit and policies for the governance of the Hui people, and also wrote and submitted an 'Opinion on Establishing Provincial Administration in the Western Regions,' a comprehensive discussion of what should be changed and what should be set up, including elimination of military encampments and registration of civilian households to make use of the fertile soil for the benefit of the people of China. It was truly an excellent plan for managing the borderlands."[193] In this work of statecraft writing, Gong was responding not only to the inner-outer question in the Western Regions (which involved conflict with Muslim peoples or border issues with Russia), but to the same question for all of China. He systematically described the economic and population changes of every region of the Great Qing Empire, pointing out that "today China's population is becoming increasingly numerous, meteorological conditions are becoming increasingly severe, and the Yellow River is increasingly prone to disasters." If the policy response still followed old patterns, such as soliciting increased donations and land taxes and raising the salt levies, it would clearly be to no avail in resolving these issues. He therefore recommended establishing provinces in the West, encouraging mass migration from the interior, and developing western lands.[194]

This was a response to internal population pressures, but it was also a strategic concept to counter the new crisis of the "Maritime Age" (*Haiyang shidai*). At its core was the central administration of the Western Regions: that is, the direct penetration of imperial authority into the frontier, promoting economic integration of the empire by changing its internal political structure. In turn, this altered the original pluralistic institutional structure characterized by following local traditions and customs, as well as by the assumption that "the Western Regions should govern the Western Regions." Gong's recommendation was set aside because its calligraphy was considered unacceptable, but in the late-Qing period it was greatly admired by Li Hongzhang, who praised it as "a crucial contribution to the study of statecraft" and specifically recommended that the Guangxu court put it into practice.[195]

The political structure formed by the tribute system embodied institutional pluralism, but at the same time it also weakened the ability of the central authority to directly allocate finances and resources. China's state organization was a compound system of central administration and multiethnic empire, brought together in the form of the dynastic state. Despite this high degree of centralization, if we consider the institutional diversity of the Northwest and Southwest and their differences from the interior, we can see clearly that China's political unity was built on the continuation of the "dynastic" political form. This is why "Three Sequences discourse" was so important to the process of dynastic succession. In such a form of political unification, there will always be complex relationships—and the institutional forms of these relationships—between the center and a frontier, majority and minority ethnic groups, a ruling ethnic group, and other groups. The form of the dynasty provided a basic social unity that made its disparate parts compatible, creating a unique type of hybrid state. Despite the tendency toward the concentration of power, never once could the Qing state condense the diversity of its territory, peoples, and modes of productions into a singular political framework, shaping itself into the closely knit state structure of the absolutist states of Western Europe or of its neighbors, Japan and Russia. Revolutionaries of the late Qing saw the autocratic state as having a perhaps overly relaxed relationship with the structures of society: Sun Yat-sen lamented that China and its concentrated political power structure amounted to "a sheet of loose sand," while Zhang Taiyan maintained that autocratic China was a genuinely "anarchic society." The central task of modern nationalism was under various forms to organize this multifaceted society into a singular internal political framework.

A comparison of post-1800 inner-outer relations in China and Britain gives us a clear picture of their differences: while the Qing maintained tributary relationships in name or in the ritual sense, these relationships lacked substantial economic significance; whereas Britain's foreign diplomacy, military conquest, and trade formed a closed system, and its internal economy relied heavily on "tribute" from India. Under internal and external pressures, the Qing government tended toward centralization and homogenization of its political institutions in order to increase tax revenue to the central government, allocate more resources, directly negotiate and manage regional migration, strengthen combat readiness at the frontier, and exercise control over all centers of power, in an attempt to channel multiple elements of the dynastic state into a unitary political structure. Precisely for this reason, the formation of a unitary state structure could not divorce itself from relations between China and the outside world and the changes those relationships were undergoing.

Gong Zizhen's "Opinion" reflects this demand, and thus may be seen as a harbinger of the Qing empire's transformation into a modern centralized state. We generally regard centralized authority or absolute monarchy as traditional state forms, and the concept of absolute monarchy is valid in the sense that the imperial authority has final say on policy decisions. Throughout Chinese history, including Qing history, the form of centralization included the government's dominance over financial administration, tax revenue, and the military, which I have discussed before with regard to early-Qing classical scholarship. In reality, however, imperial or central authority was limited in several aspects within the scope of the Qing empire: in addition to the restrictions of the ritual system, the border areas, the tribute system, and the institutional forms inflected by decentralized enfeoffment (such as the Kashag system in Tibet, the local chieftain system in the Southwest, the banner system in Inner and Outer Mongolia, and the autonomous forms of Muslim parts of the Western Regions) prevented the central government from direct intervention into regional affairs. From this perspective, the modern state is much better equipped to organize and intervene in society than was the imperial system, although from the perspective of power checks and balances, the process of exercising its power must be constrained by legalized systems, procedures, and morality.

As internal social crises and external pressure mounted prior to the Opium Wars, the imperial system faced pressures for reform from within, primarily through establishing a stronger and more organic centralized state, and through strengthening military mobilization and the capacity for tax collection. Concentration of power and the rise of military industry were the most important factors in this process, and the proposal to govern the Western Regions as provinces, and its implementation after several decades, were manifestations of this trend toward centralization and institutional homogenization. It was precisely this trend toward centralization of state power that laid the path for the empire to become a "nation-state." China's form as a republic emerged directly from the imperial model. Nationalist activists quickly switched to the language of "Five Nations under One Republic" (*wuzu gonghe*), illustrating how the "republic" could only be considered a nation-state in the sense that it was a member of a system of nation-states. "National self-determination" in this context was classic "political self-determination," not identity politics centered on ethnicity. Hereafter, I will refer to this as the "self-transformation of the empire into a sovereign state."

Gong Zizhen's proposition presaged an organizational direction of social change, namely that, in order to guarantee China's state interests and resolve the problems created by inner-outer crises, the administrative system and tax revenue had to be further integrated, thus pulling closer together the issues of the border regions and of governance. This was a prerequisite for the transition from an imperial system to a modern centralized state. As an ethnic-minority dynasty, and furthermore as an empire with so vast a territory, so large a population, such complex interethnic relations, such a pluralistic political culture, and such swift and violent expansion, the Qing had not only to manage the affairs of its ever-expanding frontier, but also to resolve tensions among the Manchu, Han, and other ethnic groups. Any external threat could set off centrifugal tendencies within its borders. The empire's most natural response to external threat was therefore to start by strengthening internal unity. Gong Zizhen's ideas were not accepted in his time. Gong's proposal preceded that of Zuo Zongtang's "Coordinating the Overall Situation of Xinjiang" (*Tongchou Xinjiang quanju shu*, 1878) by more than fifty years. The series of policies and reforms that appeared in the late Qing are distant echoes of Gong Zizhen: Xinjiang came under provincial administration in 1884; the Court of Frontier Affairs was renamed to the Ministry of Frontier Affairs (*Lifan bu*) in 1906, and in 1907 a special office of Mongolian migration was established; 1907 was also the year when the provinces of Fengtian, Jilin, and Heilongjiang were created, bringing the Northeast and the interior under the same provincial system; in 1909 the School of Border Relief (*Jibian xuetang*) was created to manage border affairs; and so on. More importantly, the Xinhai Revolution and the dissolution of the Qing empire did not change what has been described above. The revolution did not halt the progress of national self-determination that had begun within the empire. On the contrary, against the backdrop of colonialism, the revolutionaries built their state according to the ideas of Kang Youwei and their other avowed opponents in debate, undertaking the transition from traditional empire to sovereign state. As a sovereign state that had evolved from a traditional empire within a global system of nation-states, China could not completely cast off the troubles wrought by its imperial legacy.

One of the key tasks of New Text classical studies was to resolve the above-mentioned conflicts at a theoretical level: to interpret, from a particular "inner-outer" perspective, the relations among the Manchu, Han, and other ethnic minorities within the political framework of the Qing empire, mitigating the ethnocentrism that was brought about by the distinction of foreign (Yi) from Chinese (Xia). Through a series of complex examples, Qing Gongyang theory explained the legal, ritual, and cultural institutions of the dynasty, and by constructing a tension between respect for historical change and seeking profound principles from subtle words, provided a relatively complete theory for political praxis in a multiethnic dynastic age. From early-Qing Confucianism to New Text classical studies, the concern was always how to infuse the system of centralized administration with the spirit of decentralized enfeoffment and institutional pluralism; thus, the inner-outer issue was closely tied to creating a resilient system. At the same time, the opium crisis had already erupted by Gong Zizhen and Wei Yuan's time, and the meaning of "inner-outer" was changing: turning from both sides of the Great Wall to the sea, and from Manchu and Han as one to a newly defined distinction between Yi and Xia. The New Text classical studies theory of reform was organized around these new meanings of inner-outer and Yi-Xia. As he sought a political structure that would solve the challenges of inner-outer faced by the Qing empire by allowing the centralized state to directly control finance, taxation, and the military, Gong Zizhen changed the dialectical relationship between "decentralized enfeoffment" and "Grand Unification" in the tradition of New Text studies. After the Opium War(s), geographical studies shifted from the Northwest to the "maritime nations," while inner-outer shifted from "foreign (*Yi*) and Chinese (*Xia*) as one" (*Yi-Xia yiti*) within the dynasty to a dialectical relationship of Yi and Xia in the age of European colonialism. We must further inquire: was the Qing distinction between Yi and Xia a remnant of the Confucian tradition, or a product of the political conditions of the age of European colonialism, or was it the result of an interweaving of inner and outer?

4. The Northwest Plan and the Maritime Age

Gong Zizhen's imperial plan centered on administration of the Northwest; he produced penetrating analyses of the history, geography, institutions, customs, languages, and cultures of Mongolia, Qinghai, and the Muslim-majority areas. This vision of "China" erases the symbolic meaning of the Great Wall as a border between inner and outer, and dilutes, or annuls, the Yi-Xia distinction that prevailed during the Song-Ming and early-Qing periods, thus touching on the New Text conception of inner-outer; the differences between them, however, are obvious: "creating provinces for the administration of the Western Regions" is a proposition of centralized administration, a departure from the early-Qing border policy of following local customs and traditions, as well as from Liu Fenglu's orientation toward the system of decentralized enfeoffment. This presaged the new connection to be formed between the concepts of Grand Unification and centralized administration. The blueprint it outlined for the empire is quite similar to the notion of Inner Asia that Western historians would describe a century later, but its strategic intent was quite the opposite. Gong Zizhen's borderland theory focused on the Northwest and was silent on the Southeast, but this does not mean that he regarded the southeastern coast as unimportant. On the contrary, his theory of the Northwest was a model of Qing statecraft studies, but it was also a response to the Maritime Age, or to the age of European colonialism. This is an important point of distinction between his theory of the Northwest and the geographical studies of his contemporaries.

From the perspective of geographical studies, concerns about maritime affairs in the mid-Qing were not directly expressed as an acknowledgment of the relationship between maritime trade and hegemony. Quite the opposite: the literati concerned themselves primarily with the northwestern regions, evincing that they and the dynastic rulers saw the relationships between the Northwest and the empires of China and Russia as more important, while maritime issues would later take precedence of others. Gong Zizhen's "Opinion on Establishing Provincial Administration in the Western Lands" is a thoughtful discussion of frontier defense, migration policies, stationing troops to develop land, creating administrative provinces, and so on. However, as previously stated, Gong was sensitive to maritime threats. For him as for other sensitive scholars of the era, this kind of awareness was like lingering smoke that curled through their understanding of the world.

Wei Yuan, a good friend of Gong Zizhen, made a pointed criticism of the debate over "relinquishing the West and protecting the East" in "Answers to Questions about the Northwestern Frontier," referencing Han and Tang history and realities faced during the Qing:

> Some people say that the [northwestern] lands are vast and of no use, that the cost of official salaries and of military pay and supplies will come to hundreds of thousands a year, and that, in exhausting the center to serve the borderland, there is only loss and no benefit. Yet one should also consider that in the times when armies in the West had not been recalled, during the reign of three successive emperors [Kangxi, Yongzheng, and Qianlong, i.e., the Dzungar-Qing Wars], affairs in the western regions

> were a matter of diligent concern. Moreover, . . . if the great armies of Gansu and Shaanxi were simply dismissed and returned to civilian life, can we say the cost [of inaction in the Northwest] would have been only five times greater?[196]

His concerns about the ever-growing population in the interior and the urgent need for migration beyond the Great Wall, and his advocacy for developing the Northwest, were all in lockstep with Gong Zizhen. As early as the Kangxi and Yongzheng eras, the Qing rulers were aware of the strategic relationship between east / west and north / south. The Revolt of the Three Feudatories across the southwestern provinces from 1673 to 1681 was crucial to this strategic awareness. Wei Yuan was so troubled by the signing of the Treaty of Nanjing in 1842 that he was spurred to finally complete his decade-long project, the *Records of Imperial Military Affairs* (*Shengwu ji*), where he explained his intention thus: "In my later years, living in the region between the Yangtze and Huai Rivers, there were sudden and violent warnings [about threats from] the sea, and inquiries about the military piled up. Sadly turning to these accumulated dispatches, extracting and organizing their content, I first drew on the military matters they touched on and discussed them in several essays, making up fourteen *juan* and altogether some four hundred thousand words, and completed it in the month that the maritime barbarians were received in Jiangning [Nanjing]."[197] The *Records* were a direct response to the Opium War, yet they barely mentioned the problems along the southeastern coast, and focused instead on the founding of the Qing dynasty, the suppression of the Three Feudatories, the wars of consolidation and unification under Kangxi, and the pacification of revolts by the Miao people, the White Lotus religion, the Tianli Sect, and so on. The book is thus centered on the wars in and unification of the Northwest and Southwest.

There was, however, a kinship between the *Records of Imperial Military Affairs* and the *Gazetteer of the Maritime States*, as both were sensitive to the ever-encroaching maritime threat. The first direct record of the Opium War, found in the first section of the *An Account of Sea Battles in the Reign of Daoguang* (*Daoguang yangsou zhengfu ji*), printed in 1878 by the Shanghai Customs Declaration Office, has some overlap with Wei Yuan's "Strategies of Maritime Affairs" *(Chou hai pian)*.[198] In addition, the reprinted edition of the *Gazetteer of the Maritime States* draws on the description of Vietnam's position vis-à-vis the Tang, Ming, and Qing dynasties in Wei Yuan's *Records.* Wei Yuan's summation of the failures of the Opium War unfolds from the empire's internal horizon (which includes the horizon of the tribute system): England and the other Western states, even former vassal states such as Vietnam, had all used disbanded Chinese soldiers or Chinese pirates as guides; therefore, one method of defense against outside enemies was to strengthen the unity of the empire itself through some form of paramilitary nationalism. Eliminating maritime threats and promoting internal unity were interconnected:

> Therefore, in the past, when the emperor lived in a world of long-running prosperity, on days when he handed down an edict he would issue military orders to represent the hearts of All-under-Heaven, augustly relying on the military to nourish and augment all human talents. When human talents come forward, military and political affairs are repaired and strengthened, and when the hearts of the people are solemn, the country is majestic. . . . When the five senses are strong, the five armaments prosper, prohibitions and decrees are obeyed, and peripheral tribes from the four quarters attend the royal court, this is what it means to achieve victory in the imperial ancestral temple.[199]

Here it is clear that military orders ought to be deployed to win hearts and minds, command All-under-Heaven, and recruit talent. In this strategic perspective, the Manchu-Han, Yi-Xia, and internal-external relations within the empire handled by Zhuang Cunyu and Liu Fenglu were not simply replaced by maritime relations. Rather, Gong Zizhen and Wei Yuan, and men like Kang Youwei and Liang Qichao later on, developed and utilized this achievement, applying it to political reform under new historical conditions.[200]

In this sense, the interaction between maritime and mainland plays an undeniable role here. Theorizing about the Northwest from the mid-Qing onward was not merely a continuation of the traditional theory of statecraft; its emergence was intimately bound to new historical changes, and especially to maritime pressures. When Gong Zizhen said that "the Northwest does not overlook the sea," he revealed a defining characteristic of Northwest geography. The dawn of the Maritime Age filled him with dread. This is made particularly clear if one compares his theory of the Northwest with that of Wei

Yuan from the same period. In his "Preface to *Records of Ming-Dynasty Food and Military Policies*" (*Mingdai shibing erzheng lu xu*), Wei Yuan says:

> In a year without incidents, annual maintenance on the Yellow River costs millions, and when incidents happen, tens of millions are needed for repairs; yet now there is never a year when no disaster is encountered or when no repairs are needed, and in earlier ages it was never so. Foreign smoke wafts through the interior, currency leaks away overseas, and on this account salt transport daily diminishes, and governing the people grows ever more difficult. It is far worse than the disasters caused by the Japanese pirates.[201]

Wei Yuan revealed the inner link between the decline of grain transport on internal waterways, the decline of the national treasury and of the people's strength, and the opium trade. Against this background of linkage between China's internal economic crisis and widespread international conditions, using traditional methods to resolve the crisis would clearly be of little benefit. It was in this sense that mid-Qing theorizing about the Northwest differed from traditional theories of statecraft: facing the coastal areas and backed up against the Northwest, it responded to new conditions of "foreign smoke wafting through the country and currency leaking abroad" that were "worse than the disasters caused by Japanese pirates." We have lost Gong Zizhen's "Opinion on Stopping Foreign Ships in the Southeast" (*Dongnan ba fanbo yi*), and so have no way of knowing what he actually meant by "stopping foreign ships"; but his trepidation about the opium trade and silver flowing overseas is evidenced in a "Preface to Send Off Imperial Commissioner Lin Zexu of Houguan" (*Song qinchai dachen Houguan Lin gong xu,* 1838). Gong wrote in great detail about trade, tariffs, public sentiment, local administration, and arms in the Southeast, adding honest advice on the differences between naval and land warfare and on the strategies corresponding to each. Gong made a keen, sober assessment of naval defense and trade, and of the effect they had on "the price of silver, actual material resources, and the sense of ease among the people in the eighteen provinces of China."[202] As Lin Zexu said himself, "The value of critical policy assessments [lies in the fact that] only with astute insight and far-reaching knowledge can one make them, and that only with close attention and deep interest is one willing to make them."[203]

Yet even in the Maritime Age, continental land power was still of the utmost importance to the fate of the country. With this presupposition in mind, when we again return to Gong Zizhen's 1821 exposition on the complicated relationship between his theory of the Northwest and his ideas about maritime affairs, we cannot help but feel his sensitivity toward historical circumstances:

> The Northwest does not overlook the sea. . . . Now, to the west, the frontier reaches as far as Aiwugan [Afghanistan]; and to the north it reaches the area governed by Wulianghai [Tannu Tuva]. Whether dry roads or water routes, great mountains or small mountains, great rivers, small rivers or flat lands, they all differ from the domains of Liaoning, Shandong, Fujian, and Guangzhou, which end at the sea. The Western Regions are regarded in Buddhist scriptures as the center of the world, but both in ancient and in modern times they have been designated as the Western Regions. . . . When the Shunzhi Emperor entered the passes [in 1644], he completely possessed an area that since the time of Tang Yao [the second of the Five Legendary Emperors of antiquity, ca. 2200 BCE] had comprised East, South, West, and North [above the] Southern Sea, where the Eighteen Provinces had been established, and expanded an area of some twenty thousand li to two million li. Those who in antiquity held the world called it "All-under-Heaven," but still did not hold [even] one sea, . . . today our Sagely Dynasty possesses the entire Southeast and its two [adjacent] seas, and also controls the Mongolian Khalka tribe, [so that] in the North it cannot be described as overextended. The Qianlong Emperor was born in response to Heaven's destiny and used military force in response to Heaven's destiny, and so was able to inherit the military strength of his ancestors, and use troops from the Southeast and North to open up and develop the West. At its farthest extent it is seventeen thousand li from the capital, and although the vassal states of the West have not anticipated it, will Heaven then open the way to the Western Sea? We cannot conjecture.[204]
>
> The domain [of the Great Qing] begins at the Liaohai Sea. From the coastal region westward, [one first traverses] the eighteen established provinces, but to complete one's journey across the entire territory, it is a distance of as much as thirteen thousand *li*.[205]

One may infer that the direct motive of the "Opinion on Establishing Provincial Administration in the Western Regions" was through the establishment of provincial administration to encourage migration into Xinjiang, to lessen ethnic resistance within Xinjiang, to counter the threat posed by Czarist Russia, and to search for a passage to the Western Sea. Qianlong had conquered Xinjiang in 1758–1759, after which sixty years of peace in the region had followed. This situation had been brought about first of all by strong military control of Xinjiang and by the dissolution of various local government bureaus, and also by the fact that the Qing had sought out local elites as partners, and had permitted the local authorities to govern according to Islamic law. But big changes occurred around 1820: The White Lotus Uprising posed a serious threat to the dynasty, and the Miao revolt was reignited; the Tianli Sect directly attacked the Forbidden City in 1813; and as the Russian Empire began once again to expand eastward, the China-Russia border was thrown back into crisis. Against this backdrop, the Xinjiang region experienced grave unrest.[206] Gong Zizhen, tracing back the history of migration and territorial expansion from the Southeast to the Northwest from the process through which the Qing dynasty had been founded, was primarily concerned with the rebellion of local peoples in the Northwest and with the menace of Russia, and the measures he proposed in response included establishing provinces, promoting migration, and strengthening the Northwest's capacity for paying taxes.

Yet in Gong's description, the distant "sea" was always a key element of his picture of the Northwest, and the coastline is clearly presented against the backdrop of the vast Asian hinterland along the coast. The basic thread of Chinese historical narrative had always been centered on the Yellow River, Yangtze River, and Grand Canal basins, while the Northwest was forever an amorphous, far-off frontier; and while maritime trade and association had always been a part of that history, it had never been dominant, particularly for the Qing. Now, the features of this frontier region and its historical geography appear on the horizon of a history formed by the interconnectedness of continents and oceans. The sharpening of the contours of the Northwest was a product of the military and economic expansion of the Maritime Age. When Gong suggested the possibility of finding a passage to the "Western Sea," he likely meant the Indus River estuary that traverses Central Asia to the Indian Ocean. We perhaps ought to mention here that 1820–1821 marked a turning point in the import of opium into China, reaching upwards of five thousand cases (each case weighed sixty-five kilograms); and the rate of import continued to grow dramatically. We can therefore still say that Gong's Northwest theory shared a historical connection with Columbus's discovery of America. In Lattimore's words, "The Age of Columbus was not inherently 'maritime' in its characteristics, but from the beginning it took on a maritime appearance, partly because it was a reaction against vested interests that were based on a 'continental' distribution and structure of power."[207] In contrast, Gong Zizhen's theory of the Northwest was a response to the social crisis of the Qing, and a reaction to the so-called Maritime Age—an era whose actual content was defined by the expansion of military, industrial, and political systems.

If the Maritime Age was marked by the expansion of the nation-state system and by efforts to dissolve the system of tributary relations and pluralistic ritual in the ethnic-minority regions of Northern China by attributing nation-state-like characteristics to them, then, because of internal developments and the need to avoid splitting apart, the Qing empire had no choice but to change its internal political structure. By strengthening internal unity, the Qing transformed itself from a pluralistic empire "without an 'outer' or 'outside'" (*wu wai*) into a "nation-state" that drew a clear line between inner and outer. The tension between unity and division in the era of the nation-state was different from tendencies toward separation or integration in the imperial era. The former involved changing global norms, premised on unitary sovereign authorities that were formally equal and internationally recognized. If the transition from an imperial framework to a framework of unitary sovereign states was the historical prerequisite for the formation of modern China, then the gradual development and deepening of centralized imperial authority in the course of empire-building is interwoven with the trend toward consolidation of power in the process of state-building. This is why, as a theory of dynastic legitimacy, New Text studies played such an important role in state-building during the late Qing.

CHAPTER 7

Inner and Outer (2)

Empire and Nation-State

Translated by DAYTON LEKNER *and* WILLIAM SIMA

> By what means is the Dao implemented? It is through rites and music.
>
> By what means is the Dao adjudicated? It is through military force and punishment.
>
> By what means is the Dao sustained? It is through finance and the economy.
>
> —WEI YUAN

I. The "Maritime Age" and a Reordering of Continental Relationships

In terms of the relationship between North and South found in Chinese history, Gong Zizhen's (1792–1841) and Wei Yuan's (1794–1857) treatises on the Northwest appear as a historical about-turn: the traditional flow from North to South of migration, expansion, subjugation, and trade is now inverted in a movement from South to North. How should we understand this change? In analyzing historical interaction along the Great Wall, Owen Lattimore very clearly differentiated between "pre-Western" and "post-Western" factors and viewed the mutual influence between these two kinds of factors as the fundamental force that formed new frontier relationships. In this view, the continuous transformation of the old Chinese society—the transformation of elements such as ethnic relations, systems of state and economy, social customs and culture, and structures of immigration—was not propelled in the main by trade or suppression from across the seas, but was rather a kind of "intra-Asian" movement, a movement that flowed within the continent from North to South. Quite opposite to this, the "Maritime Age" (*Haiyang shidai*) is a synonym for European capitalism and its overseas expansion: Under the invasion, occupation, and expansion of the West and Japan, new elements from across the seas, including railroads, industry, and finance, expanded the scope of old frontier relationships to the extent that without the deployment of new categories it would be impossible to describe this historical relationship that was at once new, and old.[1]

If we say that the movement from North to South is defined by the reconstruction of war, tribute, trade, migration, law, and rites, then the route of expansion from littoral to hinterland is, on the other hand, accompanied by the frequent emergence of the following concepts: trade, treaty, borders, sovereignty, colony, industry, finance, urbanization, and nation-state. In Lattimore's view, the seventeenth-century Manchu invasion was the last wave of the inward impact of frontier forces along the Great Wall. After this, he believed that movement within the mainland must be defined by the new era, the so-called Maritime Age.

Lattimore's depiction of "inner Asia" is an embryonic form of the "littoral-hinterland" model found in American research on China; it is also an elaboration of "maritime history." In Qing history, the flow from South to North did not begin with the European invasion or the development of long-distance maritime trade; it should be seen rather as an inevitable outcome of the invasion of the Qing troops and the establishment of a united dynasty. The complicated back-and-forth of China's North-South relationship is driven by factors even more complex, more diverse, and more endogenous than what is found in Lattimore's description. In sum, the basic conditions that brought about this shift in the direction of historical movement include three aspects: First, the Qing dynasty entered the Central Plains from the North. After uniting the realm, settling the capital in Beijing, and pacifying the "Three Norths" (Northeast, Northwest, and North China—Dongbei, Xibei, Huabei), it was of no surprise that they would recenter domestic economic and cultural relations around their places of origin in the Northeast and Northwest regions. Following the loss of importance of the border regions along the Great

Wall and the increase in domestic population, what had been frontiers on both sides of the Great Wall became instead the interior. The development of the movement from "within the pass" (*guan nei*) to "outside the pass" (*guan wai*) in the early Qing—of migration, intermarriage, mutual assimilation, and corresponding legal revision—shows that the movement from South to North has its origin in the power of the unification of the Qing dynasty. As the border regions drifted further north, Qing scholar-officials were bound to view the Northwest as a part of domestic affairs. Gong Zizhen's treatise on the Northwest was thus an organic part of traditional Qing statecraft.

Second, the expansion and construction of the Qing empire occurred at the same time as the expansion of the Russian Empire; thus the stability of the Sino-Russian border region in the Northeast and Northwest became central to Qing politics and economy. The demarcation and trade treaties that emerged out of this relationship were at the same time linked to war and conquest in Xinjiang, and particularly in the Dzungar region. Following the fixing of external borders and the development of transnational trade and military conflict, not only did the Northwest borderlands become the focus of ever-increasing attention and research by Qing scholar-officials, but both the effective control of, and demands on, this region by the center increased with equal intensity. The Qing suppression of the so-called Hui upheaval (*Hui luan*) in the Northwest and Xinjiang (such as the 1862–1863 Islamic uprising) was tightly bound up with the internal and external pressures and relations active across the imperial borders.

Third, proposals for the opening up of the Northwest came under a situation of increased tensions between land and population, military pressure and the opium trade exerting pressure along the Southeast, the outflow of silver from the country, and the Qing government's inability to balance its budget. This period was both the continuation of the historical movement of the early Qing, and a reaction to pressure from "the sea." In this way, the view that the shift in turn of events during the Qing dynasty was merely the result of maritime pressure combined with industrialization—that is to say, Western influence—requires revision.

The Maritime Age used the modes of trade and treaty to establish its own legal foundation, and disparaged preexisting trade and political systems—such as the tribute system—as traditional or antimodern. The Maritime Age encapsulates so much, but under the dominance of expansionism, the central theme of this age has become oceanic hegemony. Because of this, people tend to view the dominance of naval power over the world's politics and economy as the main characteristic of the age. The American naval strategist Alfred Thayer Mahan's 1890 work *The Influence of Sea Power upon History, 1660–1783*, offers an historical example. Since ancient times, whether in war or peace, maritime relations have retained a deep influence on international conflict (contested via navies) and national prosperity (via maritime trade).[2] However, while many nation-states strive for maritime hegemony, few achieve this goal. Why is this so? In the case of the Qing, while its ports and coastline were suitable, and tension between the domestic population and land created pressure for overseas colonization (civilian migration never ceased), these conditions were still insufficient to bring about any policy of foreign colonization. There were four key reasons for this. First, the Qing domain was vast, and colonization took place largely within imperial territory (such as the migration to the Northwest and Southwest). Second, as military pressure had, over a long period, come from the North, the military focus of the Qing had always been on the defense of, and expansion into, the Northwest, thus creating a clear inward tilt in dynastic policy. Third, assaults by Koxinga (Zheng Chenggong, 1624–1662) and smuggling along the coast prompted the Qing to implement a policy of prohibition toward oceanic endeavors; this interrupted the Ming's previously advanced development of navigational capabilities and interest in the oceans and meant that the overseas expansion of trade and population was largely of a private or clandestine nature. Fourth, although the rise of the Ottoman Empire blocked traditional trade routes between East Asia and Europe, this disruption in fact had a much smaller impact on China's trade with Central Asia, Western Asia, and South Asia than it had for Europe. Due to the vast territory of the Qing dynasty and the strong complementarity of its internal economies, this also limited its motivation for overseas expansion.

It was not until after the Opium Wars that the conflict and military relations of the Maritime Age gradually became the foundation for treatises by Han scholar-officials. Such conditions also prompted these scholar-officials to reexamine Qing history, cultural identity, national reform, and China's geopolitical relations. From this perspective, we can find that there are three fundamental aspects of nationalism in effect from the late Qing to the Republican period. First, in the era of "maritime states" (*haiguo*), in which dichotomies between the inner (*nei*) and the outer (*wai*) and between Yi and Xia were eroded, and under new international competition, China's "internal identity" was reconstructed.[3] That is, a multiethnic empire became the basis for the political, economic, and military affairs of a sovereign nation-state. This is a further development of Gong Zizhen's thought, in which the political practice of empire, the sense of the inner and outer of New Text Confucianism (*Jin wen jingxue*), and the pressures of the nation-state coalesce. Second, the state policy of valuing mainland over maritime development was inverted. The push to develop a maritime military industry prompted the development of civilian and other industries, which created an integrated military-civilian social structure. Third, there was a drive to, through a reconstruction of naval power, propel the nation's industrialization and commercial mechanisms and restore control of *Nanyang*[4] (even though this control eventually ended with the failure of the First Sino-Japanese War).

New distinctions between Yi and Xia, and between the inner and outer, were developed in accordance with understandings of the inner and outer and the sovereignty of the nation-state. In this new nomenclature, the empire's perspective was rendered as the "interior" of the dichotomous pair, thus fundamentally refactoring the empire's knowledge of itself and the world. It is precisely here that we see again the historical bond between the nationalism of the late Qing and the New Text Confucian perspective. This also explains why anti-Manchu revolutionaries in the late Qing—such as Zhang Taiyan (1869–1936)—were bound to deploy Old Text Confucianism against the New Text school. These revolutionaries transformed Western nationalism into Yi-Xia divisionism (*Yi Xia zhi fang*), Han-centrism, and Chinese orthodoxy, which in turn were taken as the basis to mobilize the Han to counter imperial politics and Confucianism, which considered Manchu and Han as united and Yi and Xia as indistinct. Kang Youwei, Liang Qichao, and others, on the other hand, upheld the political legitimacy of the Qing and emphasized a united Manchu and Han, taking this unity as a precondition for the new nationalism. Liang Qichao called these two nationalisms "large nationalism" (Chinese nationalism) and "small nationalism" (anti-Manchu Han nationalism). Notably, after the founding of the Republic of China, "small nationalism" gave way again to "large nationalism." Sun Yat-sen's modification of his nationalism is a stark example: he turned an anti-Manchu nationalism into a nationalism of Five Nations under One Republic (*Wuzu gonghe*)—a nonethnocentric nationalism. From a historical perspective, this nonethnocentric nationalism overlaps with the notion of abolishing divisions between Yi and Xia and the inner and outer, as advocated by Qing New Text Confucians. Thus, this is further testimony of the inherent bond between imperial tradition and modern Chinese identity.

It was precisely because of this that Gong Zizhen, like Owen Lattimore, understood the new historical movement as a relationship of tension between the continental and the oceanic, even if Gong's expression of this relationship was far less clear than Lattimore's. In his 1940 work, *Inner Asian Frontiers of China,* Lattimore described an "Asian continent," with the Great Wall at its center, against a maritime background. He repeatedly used the concept of "periphery" to suggest that "Inner Asia" had already become a borderland between China and the "maritime." The implications of this terminology will gradually become clear in what follows.[5] Such a description of Inner Asia as centered about the Great Wall softens the distinction between "interior" and "exterior" and thus bears some resemblance to the New Text Confucian approach to these labels. But this similarity obscures a profound discrepancy: For Lattimore, "Inner Asia" has already been located in the marginal zone, or borderlands, between China and the "maritime."

The above historical geography views the Qing dynasty's defense of sovereignty as a competition of strength between the mainland and the "maritime." It transforms the new power relationships of trade, colonization, politics, and industry, and so forth, into universally applicable global relationships. It relegates other laws and moral norms of domestic and foreign relations to the status of tradition and outdated knowledge, and lays the foundation for the emergence of a new kind of historical perspective. This perspective includes two aspects that appear in opposition, but in practice are aligned.

The first aspect is the construction of "regional" horizons. The concepts of "Inner Asia" and "Far East" render imperial China and its perimeter as a region; they overlook or downplay the internal complexity of the frontier areas along the Great Wall, as well as their history of interaction with the empire. In addition, the continent, so replete with its own "inner-outer" relations, is rendered, in line with strategic goals, as a unified whole and thus differentiated from "China" (*Zhongguo*). "China," in this definition, refers predominantly to the Central Plain, the domain of the Han people. This unified whole is thus seen not as the product of long-term historical interaction, nor as a historical product of the daily interaction of diverse ethnicities and peoples. Rather, it is the "Far Eastern region" of a strategic studies perspective; at its essence lies the concept of the frontier region and the geopolitics of Western colonialism. By rendering "Inner Asia" as an independent region, the long-standing connections between China, Central Asia, Southwest Asia, and Eurasia are lost.

The second aspect is the construction of the "ethno-nation-state." The concept of the "nation-state," in taking nationality as the fundamental category, cleaves the internal composition of society (the traditional connections of culture, religion, ethnicity, and politics), rendering such historical relationships and political forms as secondary and outdated, and through this process asserts itself as the universal political imperative. The concept of the nation-state is based upon a clear and explicit distinction between inner and outer and between subject and object, while the concepts of borders and sovereignty become the major expressions of this new outlook on the internal and external. According to such a schema, the Three Norths, including the place of origin of the Qing dynasty, were divided into a number of nation-states outside China, foreclosing on three hundred years of complex relationships between various ethnic groups. The concepts of "region" and "nation-state" worked in tandem to draw tangled and complicated traditional relationships into the colonial world-system. Unlike the military conquest, political conflict, and equilibrium of the traditional imperial age, conflicts of unity and division faced by modern China were effects of a new kind of global schema. Modes of conflict and conflict resolution lay pre-embedded within the nation-state and its principles. In this sense, questions of unification or division come about precisely due to the belittling and toppling of traditional political relationships and norms.

But this was not a one-way process. Facing pressure along the Southeast coast, Qing empire-building began to take on the forms of state-building. That is, the empire's internal structure of plural centers of power was transformed in a trend toward unification. The Qing was an expansionist empire, but due to time, region, and the areas it colonized, the mode and details of expansion were extremely varied. To take Mongolia as an example, before the Qing invasion, relations between the Manchu and Mongols were already extremely close. Most Mongol tribes had already voluntarily attached themselves to the rapidly rising Manchu power. In 1636, Southern Mongolia (approximately coterminous with today's Inner Mongolia) had already pledged loyalty to Manchuria, and by 1691 Khalkha Mongolia was also under the Qing court. The direct reason for this allegiance was not military subjugation, but rather a desire to deploy Qing power to eliminate the threat of the Dzungar Khanate. Among all the regions of North China, it was the Dzungars who presented the most protracted resistance to the Qing, and in turn the Qing suppression of the Dzungars was particularly harsh. A series of treaties concluded between Manchuria and Mongolia in the 1620s provided new strength for Manchuria's invasion of the Ming dynasty, and also provided for Mongolia's privileged status within the Qing dynasty. That Mongolia retained unique and relatively autonomous political and legal systems under the Qing was due to this historical antecedent.

However, once its position was secure, the Qing court adopted a series of measures to promote homogeneity among domestic relations in a trend toward the concentration of power. The motivations for this centralization of power under the Qing included the following aspects. First, after the Manchu invasion, and adapting to the stability of Manchu rule, the special status of Manchu-Mongol relations tended away from relative parity and toward one that favored the Manchu. According to studies of Mongolian law, this process in fact started before the Manchu invasion. After 1631 or 1632, there exists no record of bilateral Manchu-Mongol legal consultations.[6] Second, key events such as Kangxi's pacification of the Three Feudatories (*san fan*), Yongzheng's replacement of local leaders (*tusi*) with state-appointed officials, the suppression of the Miao uprising, and the Jinchuan campaigns against Tibetan leaders in Sichuan all strengthened the Qing control of the Southwest and greatly reduced the disparity between the administrative systems of the Southwest and the interior. But this concentration of power had not yet reached the point of homogeneity: the Northwest region had not yet installed the domestic administrative system, and areas under ethnic minorities in the Southwest—such as the Tibetan ethnic areas of Sichuan and the Liangshan Yi region—retained a level of autonomy. Third, in the era from Kangxi to Yongzheng, the imperial power constantly faced the challenge of counterbalancing the influence of Manchu nobility. To this end, the Qing court raised the status of Han officials and put into practice new policies, including economic measures such as the combining of poll and land tax (*tanding rumu*), in an attempt to overturn the special status held by the Manchu elite. Fourth, the Qing centralization of power was driven by external as well as internal factors. Chinese rural land tenure and municipal economics did not alone necessitate a high level of centralization of power under the nation-state. The expanding power of both clan and rural gentry since Kangxi and Yongzheng is one example in which the nation's power at the grassroots level was partially diluted, and to a great degree counterbalanced the Manchu elite's control of society. If not for the wars against the Northwest and Southwest during the reigns of Kangxi and Yongzheng, the Manchu elite would not have been organized so closely around the emperor, a process that further strengthened the central regime's domination of local power. The main pressure during the first half of the Qing dynasty came from China's border with Russia and its interconnected regions, such as the ongoing war in Dzungar and the resistance of the Hui.

Qing imperial expansion, subjugation, and stabilization occurred throughout in tandem with the Russian imperial expansion, subjugation, and stabilization. From the fifteenth to the sixteenth centuries, the Grand Duchy of Moscow annexed Novgorod, Kazan, and Astrakhan and expanded its territory by a factor of eleven. In the seventeenth century, the empire annexed western Ukraine and parts of Belarus. By the eighteenth century it had captured the Baltic coast, the rest of Ukraine, and Crimea. In the later eighteenth century, Sino-British opium trade continued to increase, and pressure on the Chinese Southeast coast increased sharply. As Russia expanded east once more, the Sino-Russian border fell into crisis, bringing about the resistance movement in Northwest China. Thus the multiple pressures of trade, war, and internal crises compelled the Qing to strengthen central rule, foreshadowing the transformation from empire to nation-state: On the one hand, the preparation for war demanded higher taxes, which in turn relied upon a fixed institutional framework; on the other hand, an increase in tax yield required a relatively centralized power structure, and thus could easily lead to a rebellious mood among local elites, and military resistance in ethnic-minority areas (predominantly those in which original structures of governance had been replaced with the establishment of unified administrative systems).

Under the pressure described above, the Qing dynasty attempted to establish an even more unified administrative system and singular source of sovereignty. The action called for by Gong Zizhen to establish a province in the Northwest, though not yet put into practice, was a clear omen. In this sense, we can see an interactive relationship between the expansion of European colonialism and the imperial concentration of power. Not only did trade and war, through military, industrial, and market activity, directly transform preexisting mainland relationships; historical circumstance also compelled the dynasty to carry out institutional reform—to either transform itself, or be transformed—from an empire of diversity into a "nation-state." If we see colonialism as a replanning of the continent through the application of a comprehensive system of knowledge (pairing military conquest with commercial penetration), then Gong Zizhen and his followers in turn reconstructed their understandings of the Northwest through the combined perspectives of New Text Confucianism, statecraft, and dynastic unity. Taking into account the continuous migration of population from the Central Plains outward since the early Qing dynasty, Gong Zizhen's proposal for a "Province of the Western Regions" (*Xiyu zhixing sheng*) at once offered a plan for migration, and expanded the centralized administration system to the Western Regions. This constituted a major revision of the Qing dynasty's frontier policy. It was bound to strengthen the central government's administration of the Western Regions, and it afforded the Qing empire a more united, more homogenous, system. If we consider Gong's suggestion in the context of discussions of the Russian border by those such as Yu Zhengxie (1775–1840), we can arrive at a more comprehensive understanding of the challenges China faced from both the Orient (inland) and the Occident (maritime).

Gong Zizhen's recommendation and the arrival of European colonialism occurred at the same time. Together these events effected a fundamental transformation of the significance of the Northwest, but their vision and standpoint were sharply opposed. The Europeans saw the ambiguous peripheral areas of traditional empire as distinct borders of sovereignty, and the mainland (constituted by trade, migration, conflict, and governance) as made up of mutually independent nation-states. They redefined the inner and outer according to notions of ethnicity, sovereignty, and borders, thus providing a new premise for distinguishing Yi from Xia. Gong Zizhen's treatise on the Northwest does precisely the opposite. His recommendation for the establishment of a province attempted to unite the Northwest with the administrative system of the interior, thus providing a foundation for the transformation of the Qing empire into a unified "nation-state" (in reality, the Qing was never a country founded on ethnicity), or an absolute state (*juedui guojia*). These two views, while sharply at odds, both pointed toward the establishment of an internally homogenous national structure. The only difference lay in the fact that the former saw ethnicity as the starting point for the construction of this homogenous state, while the latter presupposed a pluralistic empire as the foundation for a new kind of state. This vision constituted a bidirectional challenge to ideas of the inner and outer held by both the New Text Confucians and the dynastic order.

In this sense, even though Gong Zizhen's treatise on the Northwest was a direct response to a social crisis of the interior, this conclusion should not eclipse another aspect of the problem: It was the crisis presented by the Western maritime capitalist force along the Southeast coast that most profoundly motivated the production of Gong's treatise on the Northwest, and prompted the further homogenization of the empire's internal administrative system. Under this fundamental motivation, the "great unity" of New Text Confucianism encountered an extremely serious challenge; its calls for ethnic equality, its conception of a diverse political system, and its critique of the distinction between Yi and Xia were bound to be transformed into a new historical relationship. To the New Text Confucians, to actively confront this situation and conceive of a new approach was to act out the principle of "expedient action" (*xingquan*). To install provinces in the Western regions implied the basic logic of a modern process of development. In such a logic, if China wanted to play an independent role in a global network of economics and trade, it absolutely must not become a mutually splintered, nor excessively loose economic unit. Rather, it must preserve the integrity of this economic unit. At the same time, it must undergo administrative reform and implement a quasi-nation-state organizational structure under the imperial sovereign. We could view the Hundred Days' Reform movement, along with Kang Youwei and Liang Qichao's political practice, as natural extensions of such a line of reasoning.

Now let us return to the relationship between the interior and exterior and between Yi and Xia to ask the following questions: How was the transformation outlined above perceived, and according to what mode was it understood? At what time, and in what manner, did the relationships between Yi and Xia, and inner and outer, shed the relationships of imperial ritual order to become "foreign affairs"? At what time, and how, was this Confucian theme reorganized within the framework of the late-Qing reforms?

II. *Gazetteer of the Maritime States* (*Haiguo tuzhi*) as Military Treatise and the Structural Crisis

1. A Return from Eastern Han to Western Han

After the Opium War and the Unequal Treaties, the new forms of international relations did not immediately replace the principles and laws deployed by the empire to deal with "inner and outer" relationships. Instead, the imperial government and its scholar-officials sought to adapt the old principles and laws of such "inner and outer relations" (*neiwai guanxi*) to these new international relations. Such an approach attempted to provide a basis in ritual propriety for a Western-oriented political reform and reorganization of knowledge. Sovereignty obtained through mutual recognition takes on an appearance of equality, but this equality of sovereignty had to be established via unequal treaties. Therefore, Chinese scholars were forced to search for sources of legitimacy beyond this form of sovereignty in order to establish their own secure and prosperous place in the world.

Wei Yuan's intellectual practice is an expression of such a search. On the one hand, he advocated learning Western craftsmanship, strengthening the empire's defensive capability, and "learning the advanced techniques of the Yi in order to resist them." On the other hand, he reshaped the empire's historical traditions and worldview, further marking out China's position within this global perspective. The signing of the Unequal Treaties resulted from a contrast between military strengths. Therefore, any demonstration of the sovereign status of a country must be a product of intensive military relations. The layered complexity of the inner and outer depicted in the worldview of *Records of Imperial Military Affairs* (*Sheng wu ji*), and especially in his *Gazetteer of the Maritime States* (*Haiguo tuzhi*), represents Wei Yuan's struggle well. The former paves the way for the historical terrain after the Opium War through a narrative of the history of the conquest of the empire, and the latter provides a blueprint for China's military, economic, and cultural policies from a global geographic perspective. These two aspects together constituted the most profound understanding of legitimacy and sovereignty among Qing-dynasty scholar-officials during the period of the Opium Wars. The concept of inner and outer from New Text Confucianism played an important role in reconstructing this image of the world and its power relations.

Before analyzing Wei Yuan's views on the inner-outer and Yi-Xia dyads, let me first clarify a few basic points. First, the New Text relativization of the concepts of inner and outer provided New Text scholars such as Gong Zizhen, Wei Yuan, Kang Youwei, and Liang Qichao with the basis for a rather open attitude to the West. In such a process, their concepts of the inner and outer underwent a fundamental change, in which relationships of ritual order *within* the empire were transformed into inner-outer relationships *between* sovereign states. Second, this new vision of inner-outer relations was not a simple transplant of the European nation-state model, but rather a reorganization of the traditional structure of tributary relations. Such a reorganization extended the empire's political, military, and economic practices from the Northwest inland to the coast and *Nanyang,* thereby formulating an entirely new model of inner-outer relations. Third, the relative nature of inner-outer relationships was expressed not only in the reorganization of the empire's internal relationships between center and periphery, but also as areas under the traditional tribute system themselves came to apprehend the relationship between China and Western nations. However, this relativization of inner-outer relationships and the resurrection of its representative Confucian ideal—"the peripheral tribes fall under the noble rank; All-under-heaven, be they far or close, great or small, are like one"[7]—might better be described as reflecting a major disturbance of relations between the internal and the external, one that led New Text scholars to recognize that China had slipped from ascendency to troubled times. On the one hand, a traditional understanding of the inner and outer and of the horizons of imperial politics played an important bridging role while a new worldview was being established. Through these paradigms a relationship of stark opposition between Yi and Xia came to be understood as a complex and layered relationship between the inner and outer. On the other hand, the disorder of this relationship laid the foundation for a revision of the entire inner-outer nexus.

Such an evolution in how the inner-outer relationship was understood does not, however, mean that the New Text Confucian stance on this relationship was completely abandoned. On the contrary, in the process of institutional reform and the creation of a new national identity, their conception of the inner and outer provided, in a circuitous manner, the historical precedent for a multiethnic sovereign state. Recalibrated understandings of Yi and Xia encapsulated a deep anxiety about the colonial era. However, this anxiety was not directly expressed as a radical gesture of resistance against the external, but rather transformed into efforts to strengthen internal identity. Propelled by such a nationalist logic, a domestically focused softening of the Yi-Xia polarity corresponded closely with a crystallization of divisions between the inner and outer. The problems of Manchu and Han conflict and ethnic equality thus gave way to a new kind of distinction between Yi and Xia. Han intellectuals adopted the fate of the empire as their responsibility, so much so that the previous tension between New Text Confucianism and the empire's perspective disappeared nearly completely. From this perspective, whether consciously or not, in the process of interpreting the crisis of the new era, Han intellectuals found a path to the mainstream from their previously sidelined position.

Wei Yuan was a vital link in this evolution. An important advocate of the study of statecraft in the Qing dynasty, the sources of Wei Yuan's scholarship were spread throughout the Han and Song dynasties, and it is difficult to simply label his thought as New Text Confucian. He passed the provincial civil service examination at the age of twenty-nine but failed after numerous attempts to pass the Metropolitan Examination. He later donated funds to become a secretary of the Grand Secretariat (*neige zhongshu*). At fifty-two, Wei Yuan passed the highest imperial examinations. He was then dispatched to Jiangsu, served as the magistrate of Dongtai and Xinghua counties, the Transport Assistant of the Haizhou branch of the Lianghuai (Huainan and Huaibei) salt distribution commission, and head Prefect of the state of Gaoyou. Before arriving in Beijing in 1814 and studying Gongyang theory from Liu Fenglu (1776–1829), he had learned Han studies from Hu Chengyi (1776–1832) and Song studies (*Song xue*) from Yao Xueshuang (1766–1826). From the perspective of a history of Confucian classical studies, Wei Yuan was pivotal in shifting the study of New Text Confucianism in the Qing dynasty from an emphasis on He Xiu (129–182) to a focus on Dong Zhongshu (179 BCE–104 BCE). Wei Yuan wrote the seven *juan* of *Explaining the Esoteric Meaning of Dong Zhongshu's Commentary on the Spring and Autumn Annals* (*Dongzi Chunqiu fa wei*) around 1829. From the surviving prefaces, we can see that he was dissatisfied with Kong Guangsen (1751–1786) and Liu Fenglu's approach that "all a scholar can do is correct minor errors" (*zhi weihe shi shiyi buque*), and thought that Dong Zhongshu's work should be expounded upon: "His works on the three branches (*sanke*) and nine intentions (*jiuzhi*) are clear and comprehensive. They betray deep understanding that is both refined and vast, a sage within and a king without."[8] This to some extent restored Zhuang Cunyu's (1719–1788) interest in Dong Zhongshu's thought. Such a change meant that the reformist view of Western Han–dynasty Confucian classics gradually became the central concern of New Text Confucianism in the Qing. Wei Yuan's study also involved elements of Neo-Confucianism or learning of Principle (*lixue*). He had a strong interest in cosmology and moral philosophy or expositions on meanings and principles (*yili*). The revival of Western Han Confucianism and Wei Yuan's attitude toward Song studies are likely to have some connection, but this connection should not obscure the following differences: Since the middle of the Qing, Song learning tended toward strict divisions between Yi and Xia, which is, obviously, in contradiction with Wei Yuan's thought of "learning from the Yi (*shi Yi*)."[9] Further, a relativization of the Yi-Xia dyad was certainly not the main thrust of either the *Spring and Autumn Annals* (*Chunqiu*) or the Gongyang commentary but was rather an innovation of Dong Zhongshu's *Luxuriant Dew of the Spring and Autumn Annals* (*Chunqiu fanlu*).

Following this exegetic realignment, Wei Yuan reinterpreted the theories of the Three Sequences (*san tong*) and the Three Ages (*san shi shuo*), affording a central role to the concept of "Three Ages" (*san shi*). This is the sign of a shift in Qing New Text Confucianism, from a paradigm centered on inner-outer divisions, to one that centered on the theory of the Three Ages. Let us look at how he interprets the Three Dynasties of Antiquity from an evolutionary point of view:

> There are three principal ways in which the later ages were superior to the Three Dynasties: The Emperor Wen of Han abolished punishments that involved mutilation of the flesh [for example, cutting off arms and legs]. In this regard the Three Dynasties were cruel and the later ages humane. [The Tang scholar-official] Liu Zongyuan was outspoken against the enfeoffment system; indeed, the institutions of the Three Dynasties were particularistic (*si*) and the later ages universalistic (*gong*). The

> change from selection of officials from aristocratic families (*shizu*) to the rise of the examination system paralleled the transition from the enfeoffment system to the system of centralized administration. The weakness of the Three Dynasties' employment of men was that with aristocratic familism, high and low statuses were hereditary; this system had arisen along with enfeoffment in high antiquity and both systems were unfair. It is true that the ancient people educated their youths properly, and among the eldest sons of dukes and ministers, most were versed in the Six Arts [ritual, music, archery, charioteering, calligraphy, arithmetic]. But how could they have always been more worthy than men from the countryside, generation after generation? Since the Tang Dynasty, there seem to have been no specific rules to select sages, and it was not until the Song and Ming dynasties that this began to change completely. Although the system changed, the teachings remained the same. However, it was indeed that the system proposed in the Three Dynasties favored private parties, and that of the later era became universal.[10]

The idea that "the Three Dynasties were particularistic and the later ages universalistic" marks an about-face in the Confucian conception of history and provided a novel element in Wei Yuan's understanding of the theories of the Three Sequences and the Three Ages. Wei Yuan's discussion of the Three Sequences was not exceptional, but his theory of the Three Ages was imbued with ideas born of the above historical shift, and foreshadowed Kang Youwei's evolutionary theory of the Three Ages. Its vision of progress and decline—together with Gong Zizhen's theory of the Three Ages—provided a rationale for political transformation.

In contrast to Gong Zizhen's rather free interpretation, Wei Yuan's study of the classics was more rigorous. His *Ancient Esoteric Meaning of the Book of Documents* (*Shu gu wei*) and *Ancient Esoteric Meaning of the Book of Odes* (*Shi gu wei*) delineated the Mao commentary (*Mao zhuan*), the *Order of Great and Small* (*Daxiao shu*), the *Old-Text Documents* (*Guwen shangshu*), and the Kong commentary (*Kong zhuan*) as examples of apocryphal texts. These works by Wei introduced an orientation toward the classics that was later adopted by Liao Ping (1852–1932) and Kang Youwei and ushered in a pattern of confrontation between the schools of New and Old Text Confucianism.

However, we should not understand Wei Yuan solely through his orientation toward the classics, nor leave behind the intellectually progressive characteristics that he shared with his age when discussing his study of the classics. Gong Zizhen, in works such as *Seventh Treatise on the Twentieth and Twenty-First years of the Reign of Jiaqing* (*Yi bing zhi ji zhe yi*), *Incipient Views of the Transition from 1822 to 1823* (*Rengui zhi ji taiguan*), *Explorations in Ancient History* (*Gushi gouchen lun*), and *Honoring the Recluse* (*Zun yin*), described a turbulent picture of the late age (*mo shi*). Gong argued that "the laws of a single ruler are never perfect; the opinions of the multitudes never go unheard. Rather than furnish other people with reasons to conduct reforms, would not self-reform be better?"[11] Wei Yuan, on the other hand, drew out from within the classics a forceful response to this. His treatises on topics such as canal transport, salt administration, and river conservation were closely related to his reflection on the classics. However, his exposition of the concepts of the inner and outer found in the classics was connected to complex and shifting global relations, and both in scale and content transcended the traditional limits of the classical canon.

2. From the Northwest to the Coast

The inner-outer relationship remained at the core of Wei Yuan's thought, but what this relationship implied began to undergo a transformation. *Silent Goblet* (*Mo gu*), published twenty-one years after Wei Yuan's death and not at all a study of the classics, very likely represents his early thought. Several propositions set out in this work clearly continue the Gongyang learning inherited from Liu Fenglu, retaining the orientation of the early New Text school that was formed through critiques of the empire's colonial policy of subjugation and system of ethnic rank. Wei Yuan critiqued the parochial quality of the centralized administration (*junxian*) system of the Song and Ming, and praised the advantages of the decentralized system of enfeoffment (*fengjian*), attributing these advantages to its focus on rites and music and its interpretation of "the peripheral tribes and China as one" (*Yidi yu Zhongguo wei yi*). Such a perspective is replete with an imagined lack of differentiation between the inner and outer in the era before the Spring and Autumn period. As a development of Confucianism, the critique of the system of centralized administration was not novel, but a refusal to divide the internal from the external was a standpoint unique to the New Text school. In the second volume of *Silent Goblet,* Wei writes:

> Before the Three Dynasties, the world was regulated by rites and music; after the Three Dynasties, the world was controlled by taxation and corvée. . . . Prior to the Spring and Autumn period, the feudal princes were controlled by endowing them with status; after the Spring and Autumn period, they were conquered by military force. Prior to the Spring and Autumn period, in society there were no roving bandits, only refugees; after the Spring and Autumn period, roving bandits had sprung from among these refugees. . . . In the *Book of Odes* (*Shi jing*), the poem "Master Rat" (*Shuo shu*) said, "leave for that happy place"; "Yellow Bird" (*Huang niao*) in "Minor Odes of the Kingdom" (*Xiao ya*) said, "Back to my hometown"; "Swan-Goose" (*Hong yan*) used the metaphor of the swan-goose to illustrate the masses' toil, but nowhere was there heard a concern about civil rebellion. In these essential ways the system of enfeoffment is superior to the system of centralized administration. Following the Spring and Autumn period, the peripheral tribes were distinct from China whereas before the Spring and Autumn period, they were as one. From the *Book of Odes* and the *Spring and Autumn Annals,* we can learn that in ancient times, the mountains and swamps were not enfeoffed to the vassals, and the vassal states would not set up guards in dangerous places in the wild. Thus the tribes of Western Rong (*xi rong*), Xu Rong (*xu rong*), Rong of Luhun (*Luhun zhi rong*), Red Di (*chi di*), White Di (*bai di*), Jiang Rong (*jiang rong*), and Rong of Taiyuan (*Taiyuan zhi rong*) were able to exploit these unmanaged gaps. In later periods, fortresses were set up in these areas under the control of the dynasty. With the Great Wall as boundary, the Chinese (*Hua*) and Yi tribes were separated, and the Rong and Di peoples were stopped at these fortresses. This is how the centralized administration system is superior to the enfeoffment system. From the first three points mentioned above, although the Five Hegemons (*Wu ba*) betrayed the tradition of the Three Kings, they were the heroes of the Chinese Central Plains (*Zhongxia*). Judging from the last point mentioned above, although the Seven Kingdoms (*Qi Xiong*) and the Qin state (*Ying qin*) were guilty of crimes in their own time, their contributions are eternal.[12]

To regard the Five Hegemons as the saviors of the Central Plains, and the Seven Kingdoms and the Qin state as paragons of all ages, was clearly to take the implied meaning of Zhuang Cunyu's *Rectification of Terms in the Spring and Autumn Annals* (*Chun qiu zheng ci*) as a political declaration. From the perspective of the political system, Wei Yuan's admiration for the system of enfeoffment does not mean that he wanted literally to restore that system; otherwise he would not have afforded such respect to the Five Hegemons, the Seven Kingdoms, and the Qin state. Both the Three Sequences and the theory of the Three Ages contain a consciousness of historical change. Thus even "talking about the system of enfeoffment in an era of centralized administration" cannot be seen as equivalent to an intention of returning to the ritual relations of enfeoffment. It is impossible to restore enfeoffment. What future generations can do is weave the ritual elements of enfeoffment into the flow of history. This means while moving with or even upholding the times, restoring ritual propriety (*fu li*). Wei Yuan therefore asserted that "a monarch that rules the country without the heart-mind of the Three Dynasties is doomed to be vulgar. However, if he has no sense of the situation after the Three Dynasties, his rule will become pedantic and inflexible." The change from enfeoffment to centralized administration encapsulated a raft of transformations—from the well-field system (*jing tian*) to the raised-path (*qian mo*) division of fields; from the *zu-yong-diao* system (in which peasants supplemented their corvée labor with cloth or silk) to the Two-Tax law (*liang shui*); from the Two-Tax law to the Single-Whip law (*tiao bian*); from the methods of raising an army of *Bing-jia* (enlistment from among the general population) to the *Fu-bing* system (in which troops fell under the governance of the military); and from the *Fu-bing* system to divisions of mounted (*ji*) and barracked (*ying*) units (*wu*). Such transformations followed universal and global patterns. A relativization of the Yi-Xia dyad is a product of historical development. Who today can differentiate whether "the people of Huaizhou and Xuzhou are the descendants of Rong or Yi?" Similarly, the saying popular in coastal areas that "trade of tea and rhubarb, is an important method by which to control the Yi"[13] must not be refuted once again simply on principles of the separation of Yi and Xia.

The conception of enfeoffment outlined above does not represent a restoration of the Three Dynasties. Rather, it should be seen as a struggle, while taking historical change as its premise and ritual order as its foundation, to inject a spirit of decentralized enfeoffment into the system of centralized administration, thereby achieving a unified political order with inherent diversity. To view "the peripheral tribes and China as one" (*Yidi yu Zhongguo wei yi*) is an ideal of the Three Dynasties. Without undergoing a certain process of transformation or taking changes in history itself into account, such an ideal could not be put into practice. Elemental to New Text Confucianism is an inclination to oppose a strict distinction between the peripheral tribes (*Yidi*) and the Chinese; to respect the cultures, religions, and systems of different ethnicities; and, on the foundation of ritual, to strive to construct an order of rites and music in which near and far are brought into harmony. In such a new context, there is one basic precondition for viewing "the Yi and Di and China as one." That is, both "China" and "Yi and Di" must fall within the political structure of the empire. In this way, a relativization of the Yi-Xia relationship becomes a demand for equality within the empire. That political restructuring eventually became a central concern has its own logical premise within New Text Confucianism: Regardless of whether Yi-Xia polarities were drawn together, or whether "China was within and the Yi and Di without" (*nei zhu xia er wai yidi*), all such views demanded the taking of the empire's territory, population, tributary relations, and multiethnic conditions as preconditions for the discussion. This is a refactoring of the empire's internal political order, characterized by the homogenization of internal ruling relations in the name of equality. Judging from its final outcome, such an orientation is exactly opposite to New Text Confucianism's ideas about decentralized enfeoffment, but it is one that is well suited to the self-transformation of an empire that finds itself within the "nation-state" system.

We can observe these developments both inside and outside of classical learning. Wei Yuan's "On the Gongyang *Spring and Autumn Annals*" (*Gongyang Chunqiu lun*) may serve as an example from within classical learning. In this treatise, Wei Yuan, following Mencius, regards Confucius's views on kingship of the Lu state and reforming the present (*wang Lu gai zhi*) as the "Third Rule," following, as it did, King Yu's taming of the flood (*Yu yi hong shui*), and the Duke of Zhou's annexation of the peripheral tribes (*Zhou gong jian Yidi*). Thus Wei wrote, "Although Confucius's book *Spring and Autumn* avoids talking about Lu as the new suzerain, such an idea was not ruled out." If "the *Spring and Autumn Annals* established the rule of a hundred kings (*bai wang zhi fa*)," then the basic content of political restructuring can be explained with the example of the *Spring and Autumn Annals.* Wei Yuan wrote:

> It has been said that "the *Spring and Autumn Annals* changed the words used in the Zhou Dynasty, while following the system of Shang Dynasty." Is this not at once a revolution and an upholding on the part of the emperor (*tian zi*)? People living five hundred miles from the kingdom are divided into three classes, feudal princes are divided into seven classes. The senior official (*dafu*) is without a clan. Senior officials of smaller feudal states had neither name nor clan. Is this not a system in which the emperor endows status and salary? He deposed the Qi state, regarded the Song state as his ancestral past, praised the ritual fathers (*yifu*) of the states of Teng, Xue, and Zhulou. He despised the states of Gu and Deng, while honoring the states of Sheng and Gao. Are these appraisals not made from the perspective of an emperor? Within lay his own state, without lay the other states of the central domains (*zhu xia*); within lay the central domains, without lay the peripheral tribes. Is this not exactly the behavior of an emperor, respecting the interior, valuing the origin? Although he avoided the terminology "emperor of Lu," he nevertheless wrote the *Spring and Autumn Annals* depicting this reality. I am not convinced that he did not intend to end his allegiance to the Zhou emperor.[14]

Confucius redrafted the ritual order, differentiated right from wrong, and afforded, within his new system, a prominent place for the tenet, "Within lay his state, without lay China; within lay China, without lay the peripheral tribes" that at essence "respected the interior and valued the origin." The question of order between the inner and outer is here once again at the fore.

An example from outside of classical learning can be found in *An Account of Sea Battles in the Reign of Daoguang* (*Daoguang yangsou zhengfu ji*). According to his work *The Diary of Yue Mantang* (*Yuemantang riji*), Li Ciming (1830–1895), on June 2 in the sixth year of the Guangxu reign, questioned the authorship of the *Account.* In one paragraph, he deployed a Gongyang studies approach to argue that the account may in fact be Wei Yuan's work.[15] His account detailed the Opium War and reasons for defeat through analysis of the situation and praising or criticizing the figures involved. In the process, however, Wei Yuan interpreted these historical experiences according to the meanings of the *Spring and Autumn,* and particularly its conceptions of the inner and outer:

> According to the principle of the *Spring and Autumn,* inner governance should be comprehensive, while external security could be more expansive. The pernicious presence of the foreigner (*wai yang*) has grown more severe over the years. In confronting this malady, about to burst like a dam under great strain, Lin Zexu [1785–1850] strived to eliminate such long-accumulated trouble in China. However, such an approach led only to disaster in the coastal areas. Those of narrow vision scrambled to place blame on the forced seizure of the enemy's opium, while those who better understood the matter knew that failure came not from this, but from the cessation of all business with foreigners. The reasons for stopping trade with foreigners were, first of all, that the [British] refused to guarantee [that opium will no longer be sold], and secondly, that they were unwilling to surrender foreign criminals. However, [foreign] cargo ships were willing to abide by the Qing government's regulations [and promised not to carry illegal goods], and also openly offered rewards for the capture of foreign criminals [who had committed crimes in China]. They sought, and waited for, their own king's orders. This clearly indicates that they held no rebellious intentions. Moreover, if those external to the Culture (*Hua wai*), such as Mongolians, violated the law, according to previous cases they were allowed to be fined with cattle as a substitute for [more severe] punishment. Insisting on punishing the foreign criminals with internal laws might be excessive. Even the chief commander of the navy, who was stripped of his duties and interrogated, was still exempt from such punishment. Should not the foreign criminal be punished by their own laws of confiscation of property? . . . Adopting Western advanced techniques as China's own . . . this is what is known as governing the external by governing the inner. Why be impetuous and rash when dealing with the foreign?[16]

The principle contained in the *Spring and Autumn Annals* not only shows that internal governance should be more detailed than external governance, but also shows that responsibilities imposed on the talented

> should be more comprehensive than those imposed on the mediocre. . . . In the beginning, Chinese statutes were applied to foreigners; later, heroic achievements were expected of ordinary people. Is such a prescription not overly ambitious?[17]

On the one hand, Wei Yuan revealed the domestic factors for the failures of the Opium Wars, advocating reform of internal affairs and the appropriate use of human talents, thus meeting the *Spring and Autumn's* principle of "detailed attention to inner and limited attention to outer" (*xiang nei lue wai*). On the other hand, he advocated the use of foreign laws and technology to curb opium imports while at the same time opening up trade to take advantage of conflicts of interest between Western countries to tackle British hegemony.[18] This we can see as a nimble application of the principles of "once within China, the peripheral tribes become China" (*Yidi ru Zhongguo ze Zhongguo zhi*), and the relativization of the Yi and Xia.

The Opium Wars forced China to establish its own sovereignty and defend its own interests and territories through military relations. This meant that a remobilizing of the experience of military conquest in the imperial era became one of the basic approaches for Wei Yuan and others to confront the new historical situation. If at the core of Zhuang Cunyu and Liu Fenglu's conception of the inner and outer lay rites (*li*), it was conflict (*bing*) that served as the cornerstone to Wei Yuan's understanding of the internal-external dyad. However, the two foci are not mutually exclusive: *li* presumes military force (imperial hegemony), while military force is directed by *li* (reconstituting the ritual order with military strength). In the revolutionary thoughts of Gong Zizhen and Wei Yuan's generation lay the origins of modern Chinese nationalist discourse, and this nationalist discourse happened to be directly expressed as a narrative of imperial history and culture. Regarding its primary feature, this overlapping relationship between empire and "nation-state" determined that Chinese nationalist discourse would be founded not on racial difference, but on the erasure of absolute differences between the inner and outer and between the Yi and the Xia. This is significantly different from European nationalism, with its frequent appeals to the particularity and uniqueness of race, language, and culture in opposition to the multiethnic, multilingual, and even multireligious empire. Wei Yuan's conception of the inner and outer, and of the Yi and the Xia, was a response to new external threats. It inherits the early New Text Confucian conception of "Middle Kingdom" (*Zhong guo*), of which the key characteristic was an elimination of dichotomous relations between the inner and outer and between the Yi and the Xia. But the key purpose was not a deployment of this conception of "Middle Kingdom" (and its implied appeal to ethnic equality) in resistance against the military conquest and ethnic hierarchy of empire (adopting *li* to temper military force). Rather, by observing relations between the internal and external, between Yi and Xia from the perspective of an external military strategy, it attempted to restore the vision and spirit of the era of imperial military expansionism. This is the historical premise of adopting military force as ritual order.

Not only did military affairs and war shape relations between European states; they also had a major influence on the domestic systems of these countries. For non-European countries, military construction and its institutions have had an even more decisive influence on nation-building, institutional reform, and the demarcation of borders.[19] Confucianism has always been concerned with specific political structures and power relations; it is by no means merely a "learning of the Mind (*xin*) and the nature (*xing*)" (*xin-xing zhi xue*). With Wei Yuan, the Confucian (especially New Text Confucian) narrative of ritual surrounding the inner and outer, the Yi and the Xia, has already become transformed into a narrative of military strategy and tactics. Thus the tension between early New Text Confucianism and empire has almost entirely dissipated. The military nature of the modern world determined the intimate link between ritual and military relations. Among Wei Yuan's writings, of course we can regard as military treatises historical works such as *Records of Imperial Military Affairs* (including *An Account of Sea Battles in the Reign of Daoguang*), the *Yuan History of Dali Biography* (*Yuan Shi Dali chuan xu*), *Treatise on the Situation of the Central Shaanxi Plain* (*Guan zhong xing shi lun*), *Treatise on Wang Jian and Fu Jian* (*Wang Jian Fu Jian lun*), and the *Jin History of Wan Yan Yuan Yi* (*Shu jin shi wan yan yuan yi chuan hou*). However, as will be seen below, the *Gazetteer of the Maritime States* is itself a study of the art of war. This work was the first to apply more detailed and accurate geographical knowledge (as well as knowledge of politics, economy, customs, and property in various regions and countries around the world) to determine China's position in the era of colonialism, relocating the inland empire *within* the complex network of the Maritime Age. It thus provided the intellectual basis for the transformation from a continental empire to a sovereign state of the Maritime Age. Therefore, this is not a work of pure geography, but rather—and first of all—a military treatise.[20]

The importance of "geography" (*dilixue*) in the modern epistemic system is determined by the military nature of the modern world-system, or we could say by the dependence of modern trade on the military and its technology. The trade of British colonialism is not a natural, spontaneous, private commerce. It is a trade that is placed under the protection of the national military—particularly a navy with the capacity for long-range navigation—and it has the effect of integrating the world economy under British dominance. Here is how Wei Yuan observed the role of the East India Company: "As it [Britain] commenced trade with other countries, it first had to build ships and cannons, construct canals, occupy ports, and construct living quarters. The cost was extremely high, and could not be met by just one or two merchants alone. Thus, it had to be carried out collectively, and even draw on the capital borrowed from the crown. Therefore, it was impossible to achieve without incorporation of a public company."[21] This is an accurate summary of British colonial trade. The British opium trade with China was not only a smuggling operation under military protection, but also a coercive operation that drew British-Sino trade into the structures of capitalist commerce.[22] If long-distance maritime trade was not placed under military protection, and if there was no interrelationship between reciprocal trade, military occupation, and state protection, it would not have been possible for Britain to establish its own economic hegemony. It was this hegemony that in return strengthened Britain's maritime military ability to permeate into other regions.

3. Attacking through Defense

The *Gazetteer of the Maritime States* grew from fifty *juan* (1842) to sixty *juan* (1847) and then one hundred *juan* (1852). Opinions vary over when exactly the book was finally completed. According to Wu Ze and Huang Liyong, Wei Yuan began his composition in the twenty-first year of the reign of Daoguang (1841), after being enjoined while in Jingkou (Zhenjiang, Jiangsu) by Lin Zexu to compose *Gazetteer of the Maritime States,* and had completed it by the twenty-second year of Daoguang's reign (1842). This inference is entirely consistent with examples in the first two *juan,* "Strategies of Maritime Affairs" (*Chou hai pian*).[23] "Strategies of Maritime Affairs" itself consists of four sections: "A Discussion of Defense" (*Yi shou*) (two sections), "A Discussion of War" (*Yi zhan*), and "A Discussion of Negotiation" (*Yi kuan*), which together examine the military experience and lessons of the Opium Wars, and lay out detailed strategies, tactics, and long-term plans for resisting external enemies in the Maritime Age. Taking the concept of "defense" (*shou*) as its core, it lays out various strategies and tactics for defense, war, and negotiation. Within the framework of modernization theory, the "art of war" nature of *Gazetteer of the Maritime States* has been almost completely obscured by narratives of "reform and opening up" (*gaige kaifang*) and "learning from the West." This has occurred to the extent that what was in fact a military stance of "learning the advanced techniques of the Yi in order to resist them" has become simply an archetypal expression of learning from the West. In his *Records of Imperial Military Affairs,* Wei Yuan reveals that this was in fact a method for controlling the enemy deployed by the ancestors.[24] In *An Account of Sea Battles in the Reign of Daoguang,* Wei Yuan cites Lin Zexu's memorial to the court: "Let the enemy attack the enemy, and China's expenses for building ships and casting cannons will not exceed three million, learning the advanced techniques of the enemy in order to resist them."[25] This very clearly shows that Wei Yuan's stance was an elaboration of Lin Zexu's "military strategy" of vanquishing the enemy (*ke di zhi sheng*). In the original preface to the sixtieth *juan* of the work, Wei Yuan states very clearly: "Why is this book written? I reply: It is written to pit Yi against Yi; to negotiate with the Yi by their own means; to subdue the Yi by learning from their advanced technologies. . . . However, can we rule those Yi from without by relying on this book? My answer is this: Yes and no. This is a work on the strategies, not the origins, of conflict. It is about actual, not intangible conflict."[26] This division between the strategies and the origins of conflict, between real and intangible conflict, evolved from a conscious understanding on Wei Yuan's part. That is, in the Maritime Era, confrontation between China and the West was not a simple military issue.

Public opinion and strategy following the Opium Wars could be summed up by the axiom "To avoid war, negotiate; if you avoid negotiation there will be war" (*fei zhan ji kuan, fei kuan ji zhan*). In response to this, Wei Yuan offered a strategy of "attack through defense" (*yi shou wei zhan*) and the tactic of "negotiation through defense" (*yi shou wei kuan*). From a tactical point of view, the key to such "defense" was: "First, defense at sea is inferior to defense at the port, defense at the port is inferior to defense upriver; second, dispatching troops from afar is inferior to training local troops, dispatching the navy is inferior to training a local naval force."[27] Such a strategy hinged upon the acceptance of two circumstances: First, that the European nations (and particularly Britain) possessed superior battleship power, and that the disparity in quality of weapons, equipment, and military personnel between the two sides was great. Second, that continental empires were adept at inland battles, while maritime empires were adept at ocean battles. Sino-British conflict therefore necessarily revolved around "defense." From a geostrategic perspective, an emphasis on defense was also the fundamental method of land-to-sea warfare. At the end of the first part of "A Discussion of Defense" (*Yi shou*) in *Gazetteer of the Maritime States,* Wei Yuan put this strategy to a historical test, uncovering many examples of wars that had been fought through defense. In 1616, the ambassador of the British East India Company, stationed at the court of the Mughal Emperor, advised the British sovereigns: "Keep to this rule if you look for profit: seek it out on the seas and in peaceful trading; for there is no doubt that it would be an error to maintain garrisons and to fight in India on land."[28] Viewing Wei Yuan's strategy of deploying land battles in a maritime war alongside the views of a Western strategist, we can immediately see that Wei Yuan had grasped the crux of the military struggle between East and West.

4. Land Power vs. Maritime Power

The method of responding to a maritime war with land war determined Wei Yuan's strategy for the deployment of troops. This was the in-situ military training laid out in the second volume of "A Discussion of Defense": to counterattack the invading enemy through a military-civilian alliance. He opposed the waste of resources and fruitless toil of transferring troops to and fro, and instead emphasized local recruitment. Land wars required "acclimatization," "familiarity with roads and routes," and ability to "look after one's self and one's family" found in local soldiers. The recruitment of locals familiar with water conditions was also the best solution for river or coastal battles. During the Opium Wars, the British forces employed many such "water warriors" (*shuiyong*) that had been disbanded by the Qing. They were familiar with local conditions and military installations and were a source of important intelligence for the British. Because of this, Wei Yuan recommended raising local military forces; that is, the complete incorporation of local gangs, tobacco and salt profiteers, and pirates and smugglers into the ranks of local militia. On the one hand this conserved military resources; on the other it removed the opportunity for these people to be bought by the British forces and resolved problems of local law and order.[29]

Wei Yuan's strategy was a response to the historical experience of Southeast Asia and India, and to the practical circumstances of the Opium Wars. Among the armies raised by the East India Company in each nation, the vast majority of personnel were constituted by local recruits. In Batavia around 1763, every 1,000 to 1,200 European troops of "various nations" were joined by 9,000 to 10,000 auxiliary Malay personnel and 2,000 Chinese troops.[30] The recruitment of Indians (so-called native soldiers, or sepoys) toward the subjugation of India was a pivotal invention of the European colonials. This fundamental approach was also employed by the British toward the Chinese during the Opium Wars (and later by the Japanese during the War of Resistance against Japan). Without the cooperation of local merchants and officials, the opium trade could not have advanced so swiftly—this was the greatest problem that Lin Zexu encountered when he outlawed opium. Dichotomous conceptions of Yi and Xia, interior and the exterior, fundamentally cannot describe such tangled and complicated relationships as these. Without reform that began from within, there was no way to resist the enemy without.

It was precisely because of this understanding that Wei Yuan's theories of "conflict" (*bing*) were concerned with concrete strategy and tactics, and also with long-term plans for peace and stability. In Wei Yuan's vision, the meaning of "conflict" extended far beyond techniques for attack and defense. He saw the deployment of military force as an important aspect of ritual, or as he put it, "Conflict is one of the five rituals, and must be studied as one."[31] One series of Wei Yuan's works expresses the military relationship undergirding the ritual order. In it, he not only interpreted Principle (*li*) and *Dao* as ceremonial, but also implemented the practice of ritual into military strategy and economic planning. In his *Notes on Sunzi* (*Sunzi ji zhu xu*), Wei

Yuan very precisely summarized the military theories and strategies of works such as the *Book of Changes* (*Zhou yi*) and the *Laozi:*

> The *Book of Changes* is a book of conflict! "The force of that phrase—'exceeding the proper limits'—indicates the knowing to advance but not to retreat; how to survive but not how to perish, how to gain but not how to lose." This kind of action will lead to regret. In this I see the situation of conflict. The *Laozi* (*Dao de jing*) is a book of conflict! "There is nothing in the world more soft and weak than water, and yet for attacking things that are firm and strong there is nothing that surpasses it." In this I see the pattern of war. The *Art of War* (*Sun wu*) is a book about the Way (*Dao*)! "To fight and conquer in all your battles is not supreme excellence; supreme excellence consists in breaking the enemy's resistance without fighting. . . . Therefore, the skillful military leader achieves neither reputation for wisdom, nor credit for courage." In this I see the essence of conflict. Therefore, regarding the *Book of Changes* of the Confucian classics, *Laozi* of the Hundred Schools, and the *Art of War* and of the Hundred Schools of War, their truths cover all things; their thoughts reflect the universe; and their arts accord with the principle of nature and human, integrating the eternal changes of all things.[32]

Thus, for Wei Yuan the *Book of Changes* and *Laozi* are books of conflict (*bing*) and the *Art of War* is a book about the Way. Such a conclusion reveals the dialectical relationship between *Dao* and conflict. In comparison with the narrative in the original preface of *Gazetteer of the Maritime States,* we can clearly see how a book about conflict becomes inseparable from books on the Mind (*xin*), the Way, and governance.[33]

The major motivation for the composition of *Gazetteer of the Maritime States* was to provide concrete countermeasures and plans, and at the same time to redraw, geographically, the world's inner and outer relations. The work also sought to transform the ceremonial worldview in which "within lay the central domains, without lay the peripheral tribes" into an impetus for self-transformation, and attempted to apply modern military relations to the internal social system. Here, military victory still relied on diplomatic methods and tributary relations, differentiation from the enemy, uniting with allied forces, and the construction of an elaborate network by which to resist enemy forces. "A Discussion of War" and "A Discussion of Negotiation" both tightly connected the back-and-forth of diplomatic relations, tributary ritual, and trade, with techniques for repelling the enemy, thus leaving the concrete tactics of the two volumes of "A Discussion of Defense" to a discussion of extensive strategic relationships. This is perhaps the best illustration of the tangled relationship between ritual and war.

"A Discussion of War," taking "controlling Yi with Yi" (*yi Yi zhi Yi*) as fundamental strategy, and land-based response to maritime attack as military method, presented a treatise within the context of a vast historical-geographical perspective and the complicated and intertwined relations between strategy and benefit. England's interests were at odds with those of Russia, France, and America, and at the same time the nation was in conflict with the traditional Chinese tributaries of the Gorkha Kingdom (Nepal), Siam (Thailand), and Annam (Vietnam). Observing this, Wei Yuan suggested that land-based operations should be carried out in alliance with Russia and the Gorkha Kingdom, with the struggle centered on India. Kangxi had previously made use of Holland in negotiations with Russia, and united with Russia to pressure the Dzungar. To Wei Yuan, such historical examples showed that one could use the contradictions between England and Russia to resist the British invasion. In 1691, England had troops stationed in ports in eastern, southern, and central India; Russia had taken the nomadic areas between the Black Sea and the Caspian Sea and was bordering on western and central India. Therefore, a confrontational situation between Britain and Russia took shape around opium production in southeast India. The Gorkha Kingdom (located in the west of what would become Tibet) and the east of India were in conflict with British India. In 1815, British India invaded the Gorkha Kingdom, leading to the Treaty of Sugauli, and the British possession of much Gorkha territory. In 1841, in response to the British merchants' strike, the Gorkha expressed their willingness to send troops into India to the Qing councilor (*da chen*) in Tibet. In light of this, the best approach to continental war was to let the Gorkha attack eastern India and Russia storm western India in a form of pincer attack, causing the potential collapse of British India.[34] Maritime battles, on the other hand, would need to rely on French and American disputes with Britain. The American colonies had previously launched an independence movement to resist British rule; England had vied with Holland and France for control over India.[35] As England's interests conflicted with those of other Western nations when it came to China's foreign trade, the strategy of uniting with these other Western nations to jointly resist England was not without grounding in reality.[36] Such a conceptualization embodied a kind of pragmatic understanding of Yi and Xia. In the long military history of Chinese empire, many similar examples can be found, including the Han's use of the Western Regions (*xiyu*) to attack the Xiongnu; the Tang's deployment of the Tibetan Empire to attack India, and then the Hui He (early nomenclature for the modern Uyghur) to attack the Tibetan Empire; and Kangxi's use of Dutch sailing ships against Taiwan, his alliance with Russia to threaten the Dzungar, his use of cannons designed by Flemish missionary Ferdinand Verbiest (1623–1688) to eliminate the Three Feudatories (*san fan*), and admitting foreigners into the Imperial Observatory (*Qin tian jian*) to serve in the role of officer in charge of the calendar (*li guan*).

5. Knowledge, Military Affairs, and Trade

Extensive trade relationships have long existed between China and England. If we look simply from the perspective of the market, it is possible that both market freedoms and development of other certain aspects were more extensive in the Chinese case. What constituted the substantive difference between the two was the relationship between trade and the state's military defense: Because of the raids of Koxinga, the Qing court implemented a policy of prohibition along the coast. This meant that the great majority of trade that developed along tributary routes was carried out by non-state actors or smugglers and thus not under the organized military protection of the state. British maritime trade was precisely the opposite, installed completely under the protection of the Royal Navy. One of the primary conclusions of *Strategies of Maritime Affairs* was that problems of trade must be solved as if they were also military problems. Wei Yuan's military strategy took "defense" and land battles as central, but he understood very clearly that naval battles were unavoidable. The high profits of long-distance trade; the rapid developments of navigational techniques; the expansionist policies of Western nations; the reliance of the British taxation and financial system on the opium trade; the intimate relationship between Western trade and military affairs; China's position as a land of great natural resources—all of these factors combined to usher in an age of maritime contention, and thus "to avoid sea battles altogether is not an option." This view of Wei Yuan's would go on to have a great influence on the naval construction of the Self-Strengthening Movement. The 1910 establishment of a naval department by the Qing court could also be seen as a political manifestation of this view. Europe's Asiatic trade was founded on the basis of two strengths: the first was the great quantity of silver produced in the Americas; the second was highly maneuverable warships, fitted with a variety of sails that enabled upwind navigation. Once the former exhibited a shortage, the latter immediately protected opium smuggling through military force, creating a new equilibrium between import and export. Because of this, Wei Yuan believed that a resolution of the opium trade dispute must be found through a policy of "strengthening the military" (*qiang bing*), a substantial enhancement of military force, and a systematic rationalization of the relationship between trade and military defense. All of these fell under the rubric of "learning the advanced techniques of the Yi in order to resist them."[37]

The primary condition for "learning from the Yi" was an understanding of the "affairs of the Yi" (*Yi qing*). Whether one could learn of the opposing side's internal affairs while protecting the secrets of one's own military and commercial operations was a key differential between East and West when dealing with trade and other issues. The clearly set price for Chinese tea and other products lies in contrast to the strict prohibition against employees of Western traders divulging business secrets.[38] It was due to such an understanding that Wei Yuan held: "If we want to counter the Yi, we must start by familiarizing ourselves with the affairs of the Yi. Those who want to understand the affairs of the Yi, must begin through the establishment of a translation bureau and the translation of Yi books. Those who want to cultivate diplomatic talents, must start by using governors who pay attention to foreign affairs."[39] According to the results of his investigation, "The advantages held by the Yi are threefold: first warships, second firearms, third the methods of maintaining and training an army."[40] The former two related to military technology, while the last touched upon institutions and their methods. In light of this, Wei Yuan offered three recommendations. First: the establishment of shipyards and armories in Shajiao and Dajiao, outside of Humen in Guandong; the hiring of French and American technicians and craftsmen to carry out production; and the engagement of Western skippers to teach navigation and cannonry. This, Wei Yuan believed, would simultaneously transform the means of trade and eliminate Western technological dominance. Second: the formation of a dual-function military-civilian and military-merchant network. On the one hand, this would allow Western nations to offset the trade imbalance through ships and arms, that is, by transferring the benefits of import and export, to purchase ship equipment and weaponry. On the other hand, it would allow coastal merchants to copy factories to build ship equipment, either for their own use or for sale, thus forming an alliance in foreign trade and military affairs between civilians (*min jian*) and the state. Civilian vessels, normally used only for trade, could thus in wartime be converted into a naval fleet.[41] Military technology could also be applied for commercial use. Shipyards, for example, did not have to be limited only to the production of warships; they could also produce merchant vessels, thus advancing Chinese coastal merchants' connections within *Nanyang* and expanding trade in the open ocean. Third: transformation of the status quo political, economic, and education systems toward the goal of militarization centered around the navy, thus providing systematic safeguards for effective military mobilization. This meant using water and land transport, the imperial examination system, and the establishment of an army toward an increase in capabilities of both naval power and waterborne transport.[42]

If he was only investigating military strategy and tactics and summarizing the lessons learnt in defeat in the Opium Wars, why did Wei Yuan lay out his strategic thought against such a vast geographical and global-historical background? Why would a book on the "art of war" need to employ this kind of historio-geographical methodology? Wei Yuan's deployment of global history and geography in the exposition of military strategy reflects his understanding of the crisis. This understanding was that the opium trade was not simply a dispute between China and Britain: China was facing a structural crisis, and thus specific military strategy and tactics must be placed within an equally structural perspective. Opium, silver, taxation, and the conflict among Western nations surrounding trade with China were all products of a new form of global relations. As Wei Yuan further believed that the land on which Indian opium was grown was the government's (*guan di*), and that the growth and smuggling of opium was the greatest source of British profit, he saw no possibility whatsoever of putting an end to the opium trade simply through a policy of isolation.

This meant that apart from domestic administration and restriction, the only option was to use the methods of trade to allow Britain and other Western nations sufficient profit, letting them achieve "sufficient tax revenue above, and sufficient wealth below." Wei Yuan recommended reducing the import tax on foreign rice, and increasing the export tax on Chinese goods such as Huzhou silk and tea leaves, in order to offer a legal devolution of power in exchange for a removal of the illicit nature of the opium trade on the part of the Western nations. This was the adoption of a policy of "negotiating with the Yi" (*kuan Yi*) in accordance with both the new international trade relations, and China's handling of tributary relations.[43] The opium trade had an important influence on Sino-foreign trade relationships, as well as the internal financial balance of each nation. It reflected a transformation of the relations of exchange of silver and other goods (cotton, cotton goods, raw silk, tea, ceramics) between Britain, India, and China.

Wei Yuan asked: The export of tea and the import of opium both began in the Kangxi era; why was there a great change during the reign of Daoguang? Taking trade between Britain and Guangdong in the seventeenth year of Daoguang's reign (1837) as an example, Britain purchased goods including Huzhou silk, tea, alum, pearl clusters, camphor, cassia bark, porcelain, rhubarb, musk, scarlet cloth, white sugar, crystal sugar, and umbrellas from Guangdong to a grand total of 21,816,000 silver dollars. The same year they exported to China products including cotton, foreign rice, broadcloth, camlets (fabric of camel or goat's hair), serge, camlet silk, longcloth, cotton yarn, mercury, tin, lead, iron, saltpeter, sandalwood, ebony, ivory, pearl, pepper, rattan, betel nuts, shark fins, fish maws, printed kerchiefs, and madras kerchiefs, at the total price of 14,470,000 silver dollars, more than 7,000,000 less than they imported.[44] This situation basically continued the patterns of import-export trade since Kangxi. Opium entered China in Kangxi's reign, first coming on the market as a medicinal ingredient, and up to the thirtieth year of Qianlong's rule (1765) annual imports of the drug did not exceed two hundred cases. However, the British East India Company obtained its first territorial rights in Bengal in 1757, and expanded its territory to Bihar in 1765. In 1773, the company achieved a monopoly over the smuggling of opium to China. By the end of the reign of Jiaqing (1796–1820), annual illicit imports had reached three thousand cases. In the seventeenth year of Daoguang's rule (1837), Britain was selling forty thousand cases each year for the total sum of 22,000,000 silver dollars, thus leading to the reversal of the Sino-British trade balance. In the same year, America imported goods from China for the total sum of 13,277,000 silver dollars, and exported 3,670,000 silver dollars' worth of goods to China for a trade imbalance of 9,600,000 silver dollars. No supplement in silver was made, though, because America's trade deficit from the export of Turkish opium from China was first deducted. Because of this Wei Yuan held: "We have learned that the source of foreign currency flowing into the mainland was foreign cargo ships that supplemented trade with their own currency prior to the opium trade. After opium prevailed in China, there was no need for such a supplement by foreign traders, and instead it became China that had to pour out money for opium. Foreign money and silver become more expensive every day, while transport along canals, the salt monopoly, and foreign affairs all become increasingly difficult."[45] This is an extremely accurate estimation. Once there is no way to adjust such an economic imbalance, it must rather be transformed into a struggle between military powers; thus discussion of political, economic, and other problems must finally all return to a comparison of military force.

From the late eighteenth to the early nineteenth century the British Industrial Revolution, with cotton at its center, boosted demand for raw cotton and cotton products, thus bringing about a transformation of the entire global market. British industrial capitalists expressed strong dissatisfaction with the long-held monopolization over Indian trade by the East Indian Company, and in 1814 this monopoly was abolished. Facing ever-expanding exports of Chinese tea, in the later part of the eighteenth century (from 1780 onwards) Britain began the large-scale export of opium to China, thus putting an end to the outflow of silver toward the purchase of Chinese goods. Takeshi Hamashita sums up this transformation as:

> the construction of a triangular system of trade toward Asia that exports cotton products to India, Indian opium to China, and imports tea from China. Such a structure combined the three key conditions that Britain saw necessary in Asia—revenue from the cotton market, tea, and the

> control of India; the forcing into opium cultivation of Indian farmers; and the forcing into opium consumption of the Chinese people—as one cohesive structure. Indio-Chinese trade that developed through the exchange of opium and silver played an important role in Britain's own domestic economy: The East Indian Company first loaned funds to merchants in India and Guangdong, and on repayment of these loans in silver taels to London, repayment took the form of the purchase of company vouchers; this was then channeled into the company's repayments and dividend payments to its own country (Home Charge), as per standard practice in the plundering of colonies, and finally absorbed into the London financial markets. Thus the Chinese remittance for trade (the company's monopoly on Chinese trade ended in 1834) formed a link in the chain of the colonial remittance system.

In 1784, America's *Empress of China* freighter reached Guangdong, Chinese tea exports to America grew sharply, and with this silver flowed into the country.[46] After the Opium War, for the purposes of the raw silk and cotton trades, Europe and the United States made innovations in shipping speed. In 1848, the American Committee on Naval Affairs member T. Butler King submitted a report to Congress in which he recommended the establishment of a shipping route to China from the Pacific coast. The goal was a monopoly over the Chinese cotton market, and competition with Britain over sales to China of textile products. This recommendation was passed in 1865.[47] From the Song dynasty on, in addition to the Two-Tax (*liang shui*) system on land, a tax on goods (among which the tax on salt was primary) was charged. Tax collected from merchants formed an ever-greater share of the national tax revenue. But beginning in the late Qing, because of the development of foreign trade, new customs tax revenue rose sharply. According to estimates at the time, among the annual income for the central Ministry of Revenue (*Zhongyang hu bu*) the customs tax made up 72 percent of the total, with the salt tax at only 13 percent.[48]

Therefore, the structural crisis was as follows: the opium trade unequally and forcibly (with smugglers operating under military protection) drew China into a global system of trade with London at its center. What was forced upon China was not trade itself, but rather the unequal, or even illegal, relationships of trade. Its primary characteristic was to relegate China, as a major subject of import and export, to the role of peripheral region in a system of colonial trade. Immanuel Wallerstein has described this "modern world-system" as a system "unlike empires, city-states, and nation states," because "it is an economic but not a political entity. . . . It is a 'world' system, not because it encompasses the whole world, but because it is larger than any juridically-defined political unit. And it is a 'world-*economy*' because the basic linkage between the parts of the system is economic, although this was reinforced to some extent by cultural links and eventually, as we shall see, by political arrangements and even confederal structures."[49] In European history, central states were strong nations of absolute sovereignty, defined by a developed bureaucracy around centralized power and a large standing army, while peripheral states were those that lacked such strength. While relegating other economies and societies to the status of peripheral regions, Western states used the means of smuggling, colonization, forced trade, and military subjugation to expand into other regions. However, this trend also pushed extant traditional empires toward their own transformation to the form of the sovereign state.

As this economic system relied upon military violence and a highly homogenous political structure, it would of course encourage other regions and states to harmonize themselves with the system by addressing problems of trade, strengthening military capabilities, and reinforcing the political infrastructure and operational capacity of the state. Wei Yuan wrote: "The fact that armaments and military provisions must be revitalized shall not depend on the willingness of the Yi to negotiate with China."[50] Trade, treaties, and other international relationships all relied entirely upon the balance of military force—this was a structural, not local, condition. The problem of trade created by the above historical conditions was converted into impetus for a military strategy of "learning the advanced techniques of the Yi in order to resist them," and then this military strategy in turn transformed into motivation for the political reform and restructuring of nation-building. As a treatise on war, *Gazetteer of the Maritime States,* and its novel use of geography and even global history, constructed a complicated and interactive network through trade, war, political structures, and regional relationships. Wei Yuan was clearly convinced that the challenge faced by China was structural and systemic, and thus that there was no way to respond to and resolve this challenge through specific measures of war and trade alone. His description of the democratic system of the United States and other Western nations was adapted to a basic goal, which was to strengthen the nation's organizational power and capabilities of mobilization, to establish a coherent nation, strict allegiance, and a unified system able to effectively compete internationally.[51] Beginning with Wei Yuan, the introduction, advocation, and construction of democratic political and education systems (e.g., universities) by scholar-officials of the late Qing was not founded upon the concepts of reason, liberty, or democracy, but on a concern with military mobilization, industry, and capability. The earliest motivation for the so-called rationalization or modernization of the social system was the militarization of this social system. The formation of the modern nation and its institutions has an intrinsic historical connection with militarization.

III. The Tribute System, Sino-Western Relations, and New Yi-Xia Distinctions

1. The Center according to Whom: The West, *Nanyang*, or China's Tribute System?

In the original preface to *Gazetteer of the Maritime States,* Wei Yuan summarized the novel characteristic of his work that "differentiated it from maritime works that came before" as that "rather than discussing foreigners from the perspective of the Chinese, this discusses the West from the perspective of the Westerner." In the epilogue to *Gazetteer of the Maritime States,* composed in 1853, to illustrate the extreme importance of Western works, Wei Yuan cited Matteo Ricci's *Illustrated Explanation of the Entire World* (*Kun yu tu shuo*) and Giulio Alenio's *Records of Places Beyond the Tribute States* (*Zhi fang wai ji*), composed during the Ming emperor Wanli's reign, and Ferdinand Verbiest and Michel Benoist's *The Complete Map of the Globe* (*Diqiu quan tu*), composed while the two were serving at the Imperial Observatory during the Qing. Constituting the major reference works for *Gazetteer of the Maritime States* were foreign studies of geography such as *A Geographic Reference* (*Dili beikao*) by the Portuguese Jose Martinho Marques; *A Short Account of the United Provinces of America* (*Meilige he sheng guozhi lue*) by the American Elijah Coleman Bridgman; *A Short History of Foreign Countries* (*Waiguo shi lue*) by the Englishman Robert Morrison; *A General Account of*

Trade (*Maoyi tong zhi*) by the German missionary Karl Gützlaff—as well as his *Universal Geography* (*Wanguo dili quan tu ji*);[52] *Illustrated Geography* (*Diqiu tu shuo*) by the American missionary (Wei Yuan mistakenly thought him British) Richard Quarterman Way; and *The Peace Almanac* (*Ping'an tongshu*) by the American missionary Divie Bethune McCartee. These books were cited with great frequency and provided much more accurate information than was found in previous Chinese geographical works. For a long period, most Chinese scholars have developed their expositions on *Gazetteer of the Maritime States* along the two lines suggested by Wei Yuan himself—that is, "discussing the West from the perspective of the Westerner" (*yi Xiyang ren tan Xiyang*) and "learning the advanced techniques of the Yi in order to resist them." Such scholars thus on the one hand have shown how, in terms of methodology, *Gazetteer of the Maritime States* combined direct investigation with textual exegesis, and was the product of consultation of modern Western geography—taking Chinese study of Western geography to new heights. On the other hand, they present the work as the beginning of modern Chinese learning from the West, and an end to Chinese self-centeredness. *Gazetteer of the Maritime States* had an important influence on both the Self-Strengthening and the Hundred Days' Reform movements, and people's understanding of the meaning of these two movements is largely from the perspective of "learning from the Yi" (from craftsmanship and technology to institutions and culture).

But as the contemporary scholar Xiong Yuezhi (1949–) has already calculated, of the more than a hundred foreign and domestic works cited in the *Gazetteer of the Maritime States,* more than twenty were official imperial histories, approximately seventy were Chinese classical works concerned with extraterritorial geography and related topics, and only twenty were Western works. "Discussing the West from the perspective of the Westerner" and "learning from Yi" were indeed characteristics that set *Gazetteer of the Maritime States* apart from earlier studies, but these aphorisms cannot sum up the overall worldview and strategic thinking of the work. The inclusion of a great number of Chinese documents shows that the traditional perspective played an extremely important role in Wei Yuan's construction of his new worldview. The geography and geographic relations of the "Maritime Age" laid out in *Gazetteer of the Maritime States* contained also an understanding of China and its border regions. The author did not adopt the traditional

"Nine Domains" (*jiu fu*) of "monitored" (*hou*), "cultivated" (*dian*), "managed" (*nan*), "governed" (*cai*), "guarded" (*wei*), "near-barbarian" (*man*), "Yi," "garrisoned" (*zhen*), and "border" (*fan*).[53] Nor did he, like the later Xue Fucheng (1838–1894) and Liao Ping (1852–1932), adopt the classification system of "Nine Great Provinces" (*jiu da zhou*). Instead, Wei Yuan used the European concept of five continents to explain the underlying structure of the various regions (despite his clear critique of the five-continent theory). But this worldview still complied with a narrative strategy that moved from the near to the distant—we can still feel the implicit structure of such a worldview. The relatively central status of *Nanyang* within the account could only be established through such a perspective. Looking at the stylistic choices and layout of the hundred *juan* of *Gazetteer of the Maritime States,* the first two *juan* are made up of "Strategies of Maritime Affairs" (four sections in total), while the third and fourth *juan* consist of various maps. The third *juan* includes maritime maps as they developed through history, maps of the globe from different angles, and various maps of Asia. The fourth *juan* contained maps of Africa, Europe, and the Americas. The placement of maps of Asia in the third *juan,* rather than among the maps of various regions in the fourth *juan,* gave a prominent place to Asia within the global system of the Maritime Age. *Juan* 5–18 covered the histories and evolutions of various states within eastern *Nanyang,* and *juan* 19–32 discussed the states of western *Nanyang* (South and West Asia). *Juan* 33–36 did the same for smaller Western countries, and *juan* 37–53 addressed nations of the Atlantic. Russia and northern Europe were discussed in *juan* 54–58 (placed within the category of *Bei-yang*).[54] *Juan* 59–70 covered the Americas of the outer Atlantic. The remaining *juan* discussed religion (*jiaomen*), calendar systems, and various other strategies and information. This arrangement was in alignment with the traditional conception of the interior and exterior that moved from the center to the periphery. But the investigation of the complex interweaving of the Yi-Xia relationship within *Nanyang* also complies with another basic purpose, which was to effectively reinstate the traditional status of the imperial tribute system.

Gazetteer of the Maritime States offered a reconstructed view of the world: it was not simply a work that discussed Western geographical learning, nor did it locate the Maritime Age as a sharp divergence from the Continental Age. This was a work of anthropology that drew in discussion of global geography, social evolution, and the customs of diverse peoples as well as culture and institutions. As a geographical study, in both motive and method the work shared many similarities with Qing geographical research on northwest China. The impulse for its creation, and the method by which it was compiled, are in line with earlier research on the northern frontiers such as Yu Zhengxie's (1775–1840) *A Brief Account of Russia* (*Eluosi shi lue*); the only difference lay in the elevation (in Wei Yuan's work) of the status of the oceans as the emphasis shifted to the global relations of the colonial age. That Qing geographical research on the southeast coast fell far short of that on the northwest regions is a basic fact. In the early Qing, Zhao Yi's (1727–1814) *An Outline for the Pacification of Taiwan* (*Pingding Taiwan shulue*), Lin Qianguang's (birth / death dates unclear) *An Account of Taiwan* (*Taiwan jilue*) and *An Account of Penghu* (*Penghu jilue*), Zhang Rulin's (birth / death dates unclear) *Notes on the Situation in Macau* (*Aumen xingshi pian*) and *Notes on the Foreigners in Macau* (*Ao fan pian*), as well as Liu Shiqi's (birth / death dates unclear) *Collected Materials of Indigenous Society* (*Fanshe caifeng tukao*), were all extremely brief and simple. What we might call real research only appeared after the reign of Jiaqing (1796–1820).[55] *Gazetteer of the Maritime States* is without a doubt the most complete account and catalog of the southeast coast and Maritime Age of this era. If we look at the data drawn from the Ming dynasty cited in the work, we can see a close connection between Wei Yuan's understanding of the oceans, and the maritime outlook of the Ming.

Jane Kate Leonard's *Wei Yuan and China's Rediscovery of the Maritime World* analyzes the *Gazetteer of the Maritime States* against the background of traditional tributary relationships between China and Southeast Asian countries, adopting a *Nanyang* perspective on the entire maritime world. Leonard believes that such a perspective corrects the traditional approach that takes Japan and the Indian Ocean as poles of East and West, and critiques the Qing neglect of policy toward *Nanyang* states, stressing the importance of the strengthening of naval forces in order to protect the strategic relationship between China and *Nanyang*.[56] Leonard argues that *Gazetteer of the Maritime States* represents a resurrection of the maritime outlook of the Ming dynasty, thus drawing the questions of *Nanyang* and tributary relations into an exposition of the work. This is an important contribution, but Leonard's work ends immediately after her analysis of the question of *Nanyang*, thus leading to the conclusion that *Gazetteer of the Maritime States* is at heart merely a work on relations with *Nanyang*. The maritime-centrism of

Modern Chinese history, and especially economic history, is not an isolated phenomenon; this is because discussion of the modern world-system is based upon networks of oceanic trade. In this regard, Fernand Braudel is perhaps the most influential. He argues that China is an immense entity, the center of an earlier economic system. Surrounding China are a number of primitive economies (Tibet, Japan up until the sixteenth century, the Malay Archipelago, Indo-China), with which it has tight connections. He mentions Tibet, but his account is centered around *Nanyang*. Rather than saying that *Nanyang* is a peripheral area to China, it would be better to say that it created an exception to a China-centered economic system: Malacca was a transport hub between India and China, to which currency flowed freely; Western Sumatra produced an abundance of spices, and a number of cities had sprung up surrounding gold-mining operations; Java was very populous, and was already the site of the early stages of monetary activity.[57] To Europeans, this was the region of greatest interest, and was also the principal access route to the Chinese economic region. Miyazaki Ichisada and Takeshi Hamashita each, from different approaches, adopt "maritime theory" to study relations between China and its periphery, in the process shifting the center of their discussion to Japan, Korea, and Southeast Asia and their relationships with mainland China. As an overall trend, maritime-centered discourse focuses on the long-distance trade and trade networks of European capitalism, thereby downplaying, in different regards, the role of inland relations within the modern world-system.

Affirming the "art of war" nature of *Gazetteer of the Maritime States* is extremely important if we are to understand the intellectual goal of the work. Beginning from a kind of military thinking, Wei Yuan resolutely opposed "abandoning the Western [frontier] to protect the Eastern [coast] (*juan xi shou dong*)," advocating instead land-based battles to parry maritime war, emphasizing to a high degree the significance of the continent in the Maritime Age and attempting to discover, within the parallel relationships of the maritime and the continental, the intrinsic networks of, and challenges faced by, the Chinese tributary system. Thus, while he placed great emphasis on the question of *Nanyang*, what *Gazetteer of the Maritime States* provided was a worldview that took as its nexus China and its land- and seaborne tributary network. Unlike *Records of Imperial Military Affairs* and former geographical works on the Northwest, *Gazetteer of the Maritime States* discussed inland relationships within the broader context of maritime relationships. Maritime-centrism, and especially Maritime Age discourse that took the nation-state as central, is a product of the colonial era; it downplays the critical role in modern history played by other areas—particularly the mainland. According to Wei Yuan, this is a challenge that must be confronted. His fundamental strategy of attack through defense led to his inclination to view the Chinese mainland as the bastion of resistance against maritime pressure.

The formation and transformation of the Chinese tributary system is a result of the expansion of the imperial network from the interior to the coast. If we look at *Gazetteer of the Maritime States, Records of Imperial Military Affairs,* and Wei Yuan's later works on Yuan imperial history (particularly the ninety-five *juan* of *New Edition of the Official History of the Yuan Dynasty* (*Yuanshi xin bian*) as one body of work, we can see that he looked at China as a hybrid of inland and oceanic empire. *Records of Imperial Military Affairs* is woven together from the political and military achievements of the Great Qing. *Gazetteer of the Maritime States* attempted to resurrect the historical networks of the Ming's maritime empire, and Wei Yuan's writing on Yuan history even more directly connected relations between Eurasia and the Pacific coast. The scope of these writings varies in each case, but the fundamental thrust remained the same: that is, to combine the horizons of traditional empire with the geographical knowledge of the West to establish a comprehensive understanding of the inner and outer relationships of the "Maritime Age." At the heart of such a comprehensive understanding lay the reconstruction of military protection for the tributary networks and trade relations of the empire. In reality, the West was not some delimited geographical area, but rather a latticework of colonial and trade relations that stretched around the globe. It was upon this understanding that Wei Yuan's strategy of seeing the Chinese mainland as a bastion of resistance against maritime power was founded. Therefore, the conception of such a strategy was itself a product of the dual relationships between actual conditions and the imperial perspective. To illustrate the importance of the western *Nanyang,* Wei Yuan raised as examples three military conflicts from antiquity. In each example, the military lines touched upon were related to the military lines or conditions of the Opium War era. First, during the reign of Tang emperor Taizong (r. 626–649), Wang Yuan pitted the armies of the Tibetan Empire against India—these were the same lines along which the Gorkha attacked Bengal. Second, the invasion into, and return from northern and central India by the armies of Genghis Khan, and Möngke Khan's (1209–1259) ordering of the feudal prince Hulagu Khan (1218–1265) to attack and seize western India (Wei Yuan mistakenly believed that Iran, Arabia, and Turkey were all in western India), and then turn back to conquer all of India—this was the route taken by Russia in its attack on Hindustan. Third, the Ming admiral Zheng He (1371–1433) and his navy's defeat of Sri Lanka (then the Kingdom of Kotte), and the taking of its king (Alakeshvara) as a prisoner to present to the Ming court—this was the route taken to South India by Cantonese warships. Wei Yuan wrote, "If the goal is western *Nanyang*, then in reality the goal is the West (*Xiyang*)."[58] Without understanding the above military thought, it is very difficult to precisely grasp the meaning of these words.

Wei Yuan repeatedly mentioned the important role that landlocked countries such as the Gorkha Kingdom and Russia could play in resisting Britain, and saw the tributary relations of northwest China and *Nanyang* as key factors that in tandem sustained China's stability and security. In *Gazetteer of the Maritime States*, "western *Nanyang*" refers to the Indian continent, which shares land borders with western China, while "the North" (*bei-yang*) refers to Russia, to which northern China is connected by land. Wei Yuan afforded detailed discussion to these two continents and China's strategic relationships with them. Similar to Gong Zizhen's discussion on the Northwest, in Wei Yuan's perspective Southwest Asia, India, and Russia (connected to China's Southwest and Northwest) are continental areas that lead in turn to vast oceans. Thus, continental relations (such as Sino-Russian relations) are closely related to the sea. It is worth pointing out, however, that while *Gazetteer of the Maritime States* adopted the modern Western categorization of five continents as its foundational framework, in his "Introduction to National Territories: An Explanation of the Five Continents" (*Guo di zonglun: shi wu dazhou*) Wei Yuan critiqued the five-continent theory of "Western illustrations and descriptions" (*Xiyang tushuo*) through the deployment of Buddhist scripture's discussion of the "four great continents" (*si da zhou*).[59] Taking the *Shuowen*'s explanation, "A place one can live between waters is called a continent (*zhou*)," as foundational, Wei Yuan objected to the artificial cleaving apart of contiguous landmasses.[60] According to this standard, Europe, Africa, and Asia should be seen as one great continent (equivalent to the Buddhist

Jambudvīpa), and North and South America should be seen as one continent (equivalent to the Buddhist *Aparagodānīya*). Wei Yuan went so far as to position the remaining two Buddhist continents (*Uttarakuru* and *Pūrvavideha*) in the Arctic and Antarctic Oceans. During the reign of Guangxu (1871–1908), Jin Xifu (birth / death dates unclear), Xue Fucheng, and others refuted such a view.[61] On the basis of the achievements of Western modern geographical science, they criticized Wei Yuan's "four-continent" theory as excessively "bold and imaginative" (*hong da bu jing*), but none examined this theory of Wei Yuan's in connection with his thoughts on the strategic relationships of land and sea. For Wei Yuan, the continent was both a hinterland to resist maritime pressure, and a channel through which to encircle and outflank seaborne forces.

Wei Yuan's concern with the question of maritime and continental relationships can be observed through his efforts to reconstruct imperial history. Historical research on the Yuan dynasty underwent something of a renaissance among Qing scholars. Early on were works such as Shao Yuanping's (birth / death dates unclear) *Topical Studies of Yuan History* (*Yuanshi leibian*) and Qian Daxin's (1728–1804) *Supplement to the History of the Yuan: A Bibliographic Treatise* (*Bu Yuanshi: yi wen zhi*), *Supplement to the History of the Yuan: A Table of Clans* (*Bu Yuanshi: shizubiao*), and *Critical Notes on the Twenty-Two Histories* (*Ershi er shi kao yi*). In Wei Yuan's time there were Wang Huizu's (1731–1807) *Textual Studies on the Yuan History* (*Yuanshi ben zheng*), and Xu Song's (1781–1848) *Notes on the Geography of the Northwest in the Yuan History* (*Yuanshi xibei dili fu zhu*). Such revisions of Yuan history and the rise of geographical studies of the Northwest belonged to the same trend, and also have a historical connection with the Qing empire's development of the northwest frontier and turbulence in the Sino-Russian border region. Wei Yuan was himself part of this trend. The ninety-five *juan* of his *New Edition of the Official History of the Yuan Dynasty* were completed after his dismissal from the position of head Prefect of the state of Gaoyou, but he had begun collecting materials for the work even as he was composing *Gazetteer of the Maritime States*. Because the Yuan dynasty spanned Eurasia, and the Roman Empire penetrated into Africa and Asia, Wei Yuan held a deep-rooted view of the scale, territory, and patterns of rule of empire. He said of the Roman Empire: "At that time, the continents of both Europe and Africa, as well as western Asia, tens of thousands of *li*, were in the territory of the Roman Empire. Rome alone administered All-under-Heaven (*Tianxia*). Envoys from all countries in the world converged upon Rome, all paying tribute and tax to the Roman Empire."[62] He also wrote of the Asian expansion into Europe: "Suddenly the Xiongnu nomads of China's Northeast raised an army to head west, massacring men and women, old and young; the Germanic people crossed the river, seized their territory and divided up others, splitting the lands and grasping power. During the reign of the Tang emperor Xuanzong (713–756), the Hui [i.e., Central Asian and Arab Muslims] invaded, and the Buddhist lands combined forces to repel them."[63] From an imperial perspective, there are historical connections between Europe, Asia, and Africa formed through links of war, trade, occupation, and cultural transmission. Thus envoys, Jesuits, merchants, armies, and migrants became conduits of movement between empires. Even the great sea voyages of Columbus began as extensions of the traditional routes of empire; their first goal was not the Americas but rather the Far East. Wei Yuan's clear vision of the historical connections between Europe, Asia, and Africa was arrived at through a reconstruction of imperial history. His goal was the establishment of global strategic relationships in the form of vertical and horizontal alliances.

In Wei Yuan's view, western *Nanyang* is not an isolated continent. Its importance stems from its historical and practical relationship with *Nanyang*. *Nanyang* was an important channel for India's trade with China and Japan, and occupies an important position in world trade relations, but it was the Dutch and British East India companies that were the main apparatuses to seize and control this intersection. In analyzing the Dutch entry into India, Braudel commented, "It was impossible to maintain any presence in the East Indies without some contact with India, which dominated the whole Asiatic world-economy, from the Cape of Good Hope to Malacca and the Moluccas."[64] Conversely, as long as the pivotal position of *Nanyang* in the world economy is understood, it is impossible to ignore the extreme importance of India. The following passage illustrates that "western *Nanyang*" holds an important role in Wei Yuan's strategic vision:

> East India is a major center for British garrison defense. Regardless of which country it sends troops to, Britain dispatches troops from Bangladesh. Each soldier's salary is about twenty yuan a month. Bangladesh

> is adjacent to, and feuding with, China's tribute states Myanmar and Gorkha. Therefore, if Britain wants to threaten China, or if China wants to figure out how to resist Britain, the key lies in east India. . . . If we do not know the situation in south India, then we cannot cooperate with France and America. Neither can the plan of purchasing and building warships be carried out. If we do not know the situation in central India and north India, an alliance with Russia cannot be forged. We ponder the distance between the capitals of Russia and Britain, not realizing that the point that they meet is at the border of India, not in their capitals.[65]

Wei Yuan clearly understands India's position in world economy and trade, but he is more concerned about how to use the geographical and historical connections within Eurasia to build a strategic situation and military alliance against the British Raj.

The most important details of the narrative of western *Nanyang* include two aspects. The first is the interrelationship of Western countries in this region and their military and trade networks, which is the root of the opium trade. In the later reprint version of the "Overview of the Five Indias" (*Wu Yindu zongshu*), he traced the process of Dutch merchant ships entering India and setting up a company (*compagnie*) during Ming emperor Wanli's reign, as well as a series of conflicts between Holland, France, and the Britain in competition for trade interests in *Nanyang* and India. As a commercial venture collectively funded by a group of merchants for trade, there was a close relationship between the British "Company" (that is, the East India Company) and the British government. It was monopolistic by nature: purchasing land, opening ports, picking fights, and instituting colonial rule. It was not purely a commercial organization.[66] The second aspect is India's geographical relationship with China's northwest and southwest borders, especially Tibet and Xinjiang. To the east of east India is Myanmar, and to the east of north India were countries such as the Gorkha (today Nepal) and Sikh kingdoms. These countries were close to Tibet and maintained tributary relations with the Qing dynasty. By the time Wei Yuan was compiling the *Gazetteer of the Maritime States,* the Sikhs, Gorkhas, and others had been conquered by the British. Bangladesh in east India had already begun trading with Tibet. North India bordered Russia, and the two had fought ceaselessly over the benefits of the opium trade. Strategically, Wei Yuan believed that China should unite with the Gorkha, which had invaded Tibet, in order to resist Britain, stabilize Tibet internally, and restore a stable tributary relationship.[67] At the same time, Russia "trades with us over land, but not sea" while the United Kingdom "trades with us over sea, but not land." If Russian sea vessels were allowed into Guangdong for trade, it would be possible to make use of the conflict between the United Kingdom and countries like the United States and France, to further implement the so-called pitting Yi against Yi strategy. The background of this proposal was that the ban on intercourse with foreign countries was abolished during Qianlong's reign, with only Russian merchant ships prohibited to carry cargo. This situation stemmed from the fact that the Qing had already been trading with Russia on the Mongolian border, and it was worried that lifting the ban on Russian entry to southeast seaports would affect Mongolia's economy.

The "Annals of Five Indian Nations" (*Wu Yindu guo zhi*) mentions the struggle over Indian spoils between Russia and Britain, which shows that there was an inherent relationship between western *Nanyang* and Russia, which Wei Yuan called the "the North" (*bei-yang*). In "The Chronicle of Russia," Wei Yuan quoted the materials from *The Strategy of Kangxi Pacifying Russia* (*Kangxi ping ding Luosha fang lue*) and asked the following question: At that time, the numbers of troops Russia stationed in the cities of Albazino and Nerchinsk were only a few hundred each, while the Qing army in Heilongjiang numbered many thousands. It was very easy to break through these two cities, so why did Kangxi, instead of conquering the cities with military force, write to Chaghan twice, and also write to the Netherlands (inviting missionaries to help demarcate the border), before establishing a border? The crux here is that the motive for reaching out to Russia was to contain the Dzungar and Gorkha, which bordered Russia, in order to maintain stability in northwestern China. This historical event of defending the borders and yielding to the distant contains great significance; it embodied the belief that "to discuss the North (*bei-yang*), it is necessary to discuss the West (*Xiyang*)."[68]

Russia's territory spans Eurasia and a web of ethnic groups. It conquered the Polish tribes, Turkey, Sweden, and multitudes from France. Its importance stemmed even more from the fact that as an empire it bordered China's frontiers such as Manchuria and Mongolia. Russia had long before signed a treaty of demarcation with the Qing, and it also had a bureau set up in

Beijing. The relationship with Russia played an important part of foreign relations in the Qing dynasty. From Wei Yuan's point of view, how to unite with Russia to stabilize the domestic frontiers and jointly combat British penetration into the Far East would become an important strategic choice for China. Judging from Wei Yuan's analysis and attitude toward Kangxi's pacification of Russia, he obviously hoped to form a line of defense against the British and other maritime forces in the hinterland of Eurasia based on common interests and in the form of mutually beneficial treaties.

2. Sino-Western Relations within *Nanyang*

With the help of the achievements of modern Western geography, Wei Yuan corrected many errors of traditional geography and expanded China's understanding and views of the oceans in the Ming dynasty and earlier times. But as suggested by the idea of "learning the advanced techniques of the Yi in order to resist them," the real motivation of *Gazetteer of the Maritime States* remained an examination of the relationship between China and the West. The work is unique in its treatment of the relationship between China and West as a deepening of the Chinese tributary system, narrating this relationship through the existing narrative of eastern *Nanyang*, western *Nanyang*, and other regions of that system. China's maritime expansion during the Song and Ming dynasties and the later European conquest of Asia formed the distant historical background of this narrative. The Ming expelled the Mongols in 1368. Chinese sailboats sailed to Ceylon, the Strait of Hormuz, and even to the Zanj Empire of the African east coast. This drove out or disrupted the Muslim trade. The Far East then became a "super world-economy," of which Islam, India, and China constituted the three major economic spheres.[69] But this world was not simply an Asian world. Since the arrival of Vasco da Gama in Calicut on May 27, 1498, the Portuguese, the Dutch, the British, the French, and other European players had entered the Asian region. By then, "Three world-economies in the Far East might already be thought a lot. But the arrival of the Europeans brought into being a fourth."[70]

Wei Yuan, in the middle of the nineteenth century, grasped with great accuracy the above-mentioned characteristics of *Nanyang*, and used them as a foundation on which to develop a treatise on Sino-Western relations. He summed up the aim of *Gazetteer of the Maritime States* by offering that "discussion of *Nanyang* is in order to discuss *Xiyang* (the West)," explaining that Sino-Western relations can be understood to a certain extent as relationships within the empire's tributary network.

In *Gazetteer of the Maritime States*, the defining characteristic of the *Nanyang* region is not the relationship between Asia and Europe as two separate geographical units, but an intricate and interlocking inner-and-outer relationship that exists within *Nanyang* itself. Thus *Nanyang* is simultaneously a region as well as a hub that connects in all directions. Western countries as well as their economic and military forces entered into the tributary system of *Nanyang*, resulting in complex historical relations that could not be expressed through traditional understandings of the inner and outer.

Therefore, on the one hand, Wei Yuan redefined the categories of Yi and Xia through the dialectics of "learning from the Yi and "resisting the Yi" (that is, regarding the central area of the tributary relationship as a unified and holistic "Xia," and all other regions as "Yi"). However, on the other hand, he also described the formidable presence of India, Islamic culture, and "*Xiyang*" (the West) within the tributary area of *Nanyang*. This was an omen of emerging disorder in the inner-outer and Yi-Xia relationships.

The opening of "A Narrative of Eastern Nanyang" (*Xu dong Nanyang)* came straight to the point that "no record about the maritime states is presented in more detail than the *Ming History: Account of Foreign Countries* (*Mingshi: Waiguo zhuan*)," but that the account "does not differentiate between *Xiyang* and *Nanyang*," "does not differentiate between island state and coastal state," and at times "divides states that share an island or coast and that should not have been separated." Wei Yuan went on to ask:

> Did the situation in the world suddenly change in the Ming dynasty? Did the great oceans that encircle the lands flow from west to east? In the past dynasties, let alone the time of grand unification, even in dynasties of the Eastern Jin, the Southern Tang, the Southern Song, the Qi, and the Liang, these regimes, which only partially occupied the Central Plains, all had island nations offer treasures to them in tribute. They accepted gorgeous costumes, fur clothing and other precious items. There are endless examples in the histories. Now there is no foreign government seeking an audience with the empire. Why? The Europeans [lit. "the Red Yi"]

> sailed eastward: when they found a coast, they seized it, when they found land they occupied it. They established ports and set up military camps. The key ports of *Nanyang* have all become Western cities. The status quo has changed, and along with it must change our historical models. To discuss *Nanyang* today is to discuss *Xiyang* (the West). Therefore, I now use the five countries of Spain, the Netherlands, France, the United Kingdom, and Portugal to frame the history of *Nanyang*. The four countries of Vietnam, Thailand, Myanmar, and Japan, although not invaded by Western nations, have much to do with countering Western nations, so I have also recorded these. As to Korea, Ryukyu, and other places, I mention only those aspects involved in resisting these countries.[71]

Here, Wei Yuan took five European countries to "structure the history of" *Nanyang:* the Netherlands, the United Kingdom, Spain, France, and Portugal.

It is precisely in this process of tracing the loss of an imperial outlook that the worldview of the "Maritime Era" gradually revealed its true face. The "Maritime Era" was an era in which the "West" penetrated into the Asian tributary network. Relations between China and the West; between North and South; and even between Western nations, all became internal relations within the network of empire. During the Ming emperor Wanli's reign, the Dutch entered Java despite its having a large Chinese population. Then France conquered the Dutch during the Jiaqing era of the Qing (1796–1820), and replaced the Dutch as rulers of Java. Britain then fought against France and aided another Dutch attack on Java. The Dutch thus regained control. How could the nature of such conflicts and struggles be accurately described through the inner-outer, Yi-Xia relations of the tributary system? It was not simply the British invasion or the opium trade, but rather the disorder of the tributary network itself that constituted a real threat to China's security. In this sense, dealing with a symptom of the problem instead of its cause was of no avail. The most important steps were to assess the situation, integrate vertical and horizontal alliances, and rebuild the inner-outer, Yi-Xia networks of the tributary system, thus creating an effective zone of protection for China's security. This is why *Gazetteer of the Maritime States,* as a military treatise, must also serve as a global geopolitical encyclopedia of race, customs, religion, culture, trade, and politics.

According to the description of eastern *Nanyang* in *Gazetteer of the Maritime States,* the countries and regions of Vietnam, Siam, Philippines, Myanmar, Japan, and Java each occupied important positions, but it was Vietnam that was most exposed. First, Vietnam was a tributary adjacent to China, but was riddled with internal strife. It therefore threatened China's position in the region. Second, Vietnam, while a small country, had defeated countries larger than itself. In addition to the military victories against Western colonists mentioned before, Vietnam had also "achieved great victory over the Chinese warships," such as when, in the fifty-fourth year of Qianlong's rule (1789), Ruan Hui (Nguyễn Huệ, 1753–1792) defeated the army of Sun Shiyi (1720–1796), Viceroy of Guangdong and Guangxi, and took back the country with his armies. He recruited Chinese pirates, and invaded Fujian (*Min*), Guangdong (*Yue*), Jiangsu (*Jiang*), Zhejiang (*Zhe*), and other places. Third, due to internal conflicts, Vietnam had later allowed the introduction of external forces. This led to Western penetration of the region.

Of the hundred *juan* of *Gazetteer of the Maritime States, juan* 7 and 8 present an historical overview of the evolution of Siam. Wei Yuan regards the relationship between China and Siam as a model of the Chinese tributary system. French control of Annam and British control of Burma threatened China's security, and Siam happened to be connected to both regions. Therefore, during the Qianlong and Jiaqing reigns, the Qing court invested Siam with rank, which resulted in a Burma controlled from the west, and a Vietnam controlled from the east. From a geopolitical point of view, Siam is an important channel between China and the *Nanyang* archipelago, which itself served as a hub for European access to Asia. Stabilizing relations with Siam thus also secured a barrier against the West. Wei Yuan explained China's relations with these areas through the aspects of tributary trade and civil migration along the coasts of Fujian and Guangdong. *Juan* 9, "The Course of Development of Siam and Southeastern Countries to Present-Day British Singapore" (*Xianluo dongnan shuguo jin wei Yingjili Xinjiapo yange*), extensively described Southeast Asian regions, including Malacca, Pattani, Kelantan, Terengganu, Pahang, and Johor. Its central issue is the Sino-Western relations within eastern *Nanyang.* Wei Yuan cited materials such as the *Ming History* to explain the vassal relations between places like Malacca and China, and Portugal's penetration into the region in earlier times. During Emperor Zhengde's rule of the Ming (1505–1521), when migrants from the coastal areas of China had just begun their journey to eastern *Nanyang*, the Portuguese had already launched an offensive against Malacca in search of trade advantages, gaining many benefits in the process. This area thus became a site of complex interaction and coexistence between the Chinese and the foreign.[72]

The success of Western countries in Southeast Asia depended not only on armaments, trade, and guile, but also on internal conflicts in the region and a series of Chinese missteps in policy toward Southeast Asia. Without both this disorder and cooperation from within, the West could never have found success so quickly. While European countries were using military and political forces to protect their business interests in *Nanyang*, the Qing was focusing on affairs in the Northwest, neglecting the responsibility to protect Chinese merchants and residents in the *Nanyang* region. Similarly, a large number of Chinese and merchants living in Luzon (Philippines), Java, and other areas endured mistreatment, to which the central government responded only slowly and ineffectively. The Dutch used opium to seduce the Javanese, weakening their resistance, to which China also turned a deaf ear. This was the beginning of a process that, many years later, would lead to the pernicious influence of opium in China, and to the great predicament that followed. The disorder of China's tributary system was the result of multiple factors such as intraregional trade imbalances, Western invasion, and faults in the policy of the Qing court, as well as the voluntary abandonment of responsibilities. Hence, to restore the maritime outlook of the Tang, Song, and especially Ming was also to resurrect the dynasty's foundational responsibility for the tributary system.

Civilian overseas commercial activities were completely separated from the political and military protection of the Qing empire. European countries, especially Britain, on the other hand, established a trade system that integrated force and commerce. Back in the Jiajing reign of the Ming, the Portuguese had controlled Malacca, while the Dutch later defeated Portugal and entered this area during the Tianqi and Chongzhen reigns. During the Qing Jiaqing reign (1796–1820), Britain first traded control of Malacca for that of other regions, and then went on to attack and retake Malacca in 1818. The British built a citadel, armed it with troops, reclaimed land, and recruited businessmen to turn Malacca into a new state capital and city of trade. In 1834, during the Daoguang reign (1820–1850), the goods traded in Singapore by Western countries, China, Vietnam, Siam, and others reached in total a value of ten million silver dollars. Wei Yuan's attention to trade is always closely linked to strategic military considerations. He noted not only the link between Singapore's opening of the port and the decline of Malacca, but also the strategic importance of Singapore, which stood as a halfway mark between India and China. Countries such as Britain and the United States, but especially Britain, set up academies in this region, hired Chinese teachers to teach Chinese, and published a collection of Chinese classics, as well as illustrated histories and geographies. From this they had great insight into China's national condition, whereas China remained in the dark as to whom it was dealing with. Wei Yuan believed that such a situation presented enormous risk. It illustrated the importance, from yet another perspective, of "learning from the Yi," as well as the dialectical relationship between "learning from the Yi" and "resisting the Yi."

3. Yi-Xia on a Global Scale

Gazetteer of the Maritime States presents a global, rather than imperial, outlook. In order to grasp this new reality, Wei Yuan had to develop new conceptions of the interior and exterior. It was because of this need that his understanding toward the interior-exterior and Yi-Xia paradigm differed in important ways from those of the early Confucian scholars:

> As for those lands that have, through the ages, never communicated with China, I must lay out their landscapes and characteristics in such a way that readers could see them as if they were looking at a picture in the *Unified Gazetteer* (*Yi tongzhi*). I must also reveal their natural conditions and folk customs, so that readers can observe them as if they were reading a geography of the seventeen provinces of China. How the flow of the world has changed; from the Northwest it swung to the Southeast, rendering the center and the exterior (*Zhong-wai*) as one![73]

We could perhaps compare the above excerpt with Gong Zizhen's conception of the "inner and the outer as one" following the Qing empire's reclaiming of the borderland, found in his "Memorial on Imperial Efforts to Pacify Inner Mongolia" (*Yushi anbian suiyuan shu*) discussed in Chapter 6. While both discuss "the inner and outer as one," Gong Zizhen viewed the empire's domain as one, whereas Wei Yuan's discussion already focused on global historical relationships. The Kangxi Emperor's goal for producing the *Atlas of the Imperial Territories* (*Huang yu quan lan tu*) was to bring the vast territories of the empire within his view, and Gong Zizhen's exposition was in concert with this goal. Wei Yuan, however, attempted to use the cartographical method to bring the world into view, as if read from a *Unified Gazetteer.* Theories of the empire's interior and exterior as integrated, and of the Yi and Xia as without distinction, took as foundational the concept of "no outside" found in imperial politics and culture. The new global perspective made it very difficult for such a Sino-centric approach to justify this lack of "outside" or "exterior." Such a novel historical perspective would offer the intellectual basis for Kang Youwei's world of great unity (*Datong shijie*) formulated forty years later—"the day will come when everything on earth, great or small, far or near, will be as one."

To this end, Wei Yuan had no choice but to redefine the concepts of Yi and Xia along the following lines: First, following expositions on this division by Zhuang Cunyu and Liu Fenglu, the geographical and ethnic connotations of the contrasted pair were erased; second, while Zhuang, Liu, and other New Text Confucians developed their expositions of the Yi-Xia relationship within the scope of the empire, Wei Yuan expanded this discourse to a greater scale, thus recognizing that there existed "nations of rites and ritual" (*li yi zhi bang*) that existed external to "Chinese rites and ritual" (*Zhongguo li yi*). A new theory of the "center and the exterior as one" took an acknowledgment of that exterior, or we could say of a multicivilizational world (rather than a world divided into the civilized and its boundaries) as its premise. In his "Discussion of the Westerner Jose Martinho Marques's 'Geographic Reference,'" (*Xiyang ren "Majishi dili beikao" xu*), Wei Yuan wrote:

> The appellations Man, Di, Qiang, and Yi refer to those cruel-tempered ethnic groups who know nothing of the moral beneficence of the sovereign . . . only in truly coming to know those who came from afar do we find that there are people who understand etiquette and behave in benevolence and righteousness. They are versed in astronomy and geography, have a comprehensive understanding of the situation and truth of things, and connect ancient and modern history coherently. They are geniuses from across the seas and friends from abroad, how can we still call them Yi-di?[74]

In order to obtain internal equality and recognize the legitimacy of the empire, early New Text Confucians adopted a strategy of redefining China through the removal of absolute divisions between the inner and outer and between Yi and Xia. Wei Yuan then in turn expanded this strategy to a global scale: labels such as Yi-di came to mean not only peoples or regions at China's periphery, nor were they used to differentiate China from other states. The concept of "Yi-di" initially referred to whether or not a person or area was considered civilized, and was established on the basis of relations between the empire and its periphery. Such an outlook in reality was very close to the historical perspective of the Europeans: the geographical division of ancient Europe was bounded not by Europe itself, but by the Mediterranean basin civilized by the Greeks and Romans. To a great degree, Europe itself belonged to what the Greeks and Romans called the "barbarian world," which was to say the external world. It was only in the Middle Ages that Europe as an entity was established through the forms of Christianity. Wei Yuan, in describing the Roman Empire and its periphery, wrote: "Early on after Rome had conquered many countries, outside its borders remained Yi-di who had not been subdued. Later descendants squandered armies on far-off missions, deep into the desert and as far as the North in pursuit. Only after a trail of destruction and massacre were they subdued."[75] In this iteration, these paired concepts of Yi-Xia and inner-outer began to separate from one another, so that the outer could no longer be simply defined as the peripheral tribes (*Yi-di*), and such tribes (*Yi-di*) were not necessarily in the exterior. "All-under-Heaven as one" (*Tianxia yi jia*), in acknowledging the real boundaries between the inner and outer, at the same time acknowledged that outside the empire there existed states with their own rites, ritual, and civilizations. This was a harbinger of the transformation from empire to nation-state, and it was a precursor to Kang Youwei's declaration that each of the nine continents had its own revered figures (*jiao zhu*), and in the Occident existed something akin to Xia (with its own "unity").

However, the cultural significance of Yi-Xia and interior-exterior relationships was not rendered entirely relative. Ideas of what it meant to be either Yi or Xia still revolved about the civilizing project of Confucianism. *Gazetteer of the Maritime States*' description of "West India" (Wei Yuan mistakenly located western Asia as part of west India) is a useful example for this point. When introducing various countries of western Asia, apart from discussing the geographical importance of these states (such as "to the east, the west, the south, each borders the sea, to the north is Turkey . . . the situation and location are pivotal," and the presence of both European and American trade and military operations in the region), Wei Yuan dedicated specific *juan* of the work to a discussion of the origins and characteristics of, and mutual relations between, Islam and Catholicism. He clearly exhibited his concern with the function of religion in both western Asian society and global relations. In the coda of the twenty-fourth *juan,* "The State of Aden" (*Adan guo*), Wei Yuan connects the question of religion in western Asia with that of Buddhism:

> Buddhism emerged in India. Its ultimate pursuit is the end of suffering. Literati and officials on the continent promoted and developed such ideas, and founded an intellectual school that practiced meditations for joy. The gist of the Ten Commandments of Moses is very simple, and the text contains nothing extraneous. The miracles performed by Jesus [recorded in the scriptures] were intended to persuade people to do good deeds, and thus were also in line with Moses's remarks. Confucian teachings, such as those by The Duke of Zhou or Confucius himself, were unable to be translated and propagated. Foreign wise men of moral character who educated the people and persuaded them to do good had no intention of harming the world. However, if they wanted to preach in China (*Zhonghua*), then they might have overestimated their capabilities. Muhammad used to be just a merchant. From this life he emerged and founded Islam. The Islamic ritual is the same as that of Catholicism. . . . After the Tang dynasty, Islam gradually prevailed in the Western Regions (*Xiyu*). Nowadays, from the west of Yumen Pass (*Yumen*) to the west side of Asia, within tens of thousands of miles, there is no one who is not a Muslim![76]

At the opening of the twenty-fifth *juan,* "Collected Notes on Islam across Various Lands" (*Geguo Huijiao zongkao*), Wei Yuan even more clearly explained his motivation for researching the origins and transformations of Islam:

> Today, from the south of Tianshan Mountain, west of Yumen Pass, and around the Pamirs Plateau, all the way to the regions of the Aral and Caspian Seas, this half of Asia, to every prefecture (*fu*), province (*ting*),

> state (*zhou*), and county (*xian*) in mainland China, there are mosques and temples of worship for Muslims. Scholar-officials in the central basin who do not know the situation might easily follow the faith. . . . If the world is peaceful, Muslims will not bring any disasters, but their character is fierce and radical; it therefore will be difficult to educate them. Such are the results of research into Islam.[77]

If we carefully consider Wei Yuan's discussion of Islam, Judaism, and Catholicism, we can draw out a few fundamental characteristics.

First, when confronted with issues of race, Wei Yuan's conception of Yi and Xia was relatively open minded, but as soon as questions of culture and religion arose, so too did notions of "a people not of our kind" (*fei wo zulei*). Why was this? Both the Yi-Xia conception of Qing-era New Text Confucianism and the so-called unity of Manchu and Han (*Man Han yi ti*) of the Qing empire were concerned with the ethnic relations of the interior; at their core lay deference to the enlightened sovereign, not the differentiation of peoples. The Yi-Xia conception of such an antiethnocentrism dissolved absolute Yi-Xia and inner-outer dichotomies, but undergirding this dissolution was the assumption of the unified cultural universalism of Confucian rite and ritual. Therefore, compared to differences of ethnicity, differences of culture remained more fundamental. In questions of faith and custom, Wei Yuan consistently exhibits a prejudice fundamentally opposed to his open-minded approach to questions of ethnicity. While Wei Yuan's research on Catholicism relied to a great degree on the work of Ming-dynasty missionaries such as Matteo Ricci (1552–1610), Diego de Pantoja (1571–1618), Giulio Alenio (1582–1649), Francesco Sambiasi (1582–1649), Alfonso Vagnoni (1566–1640), and Francisco Furtado (1589–1653), his attitude toward the religion was no more positive than his views toward Islam:

> Beginning with Matteo Ricci, Westerners began entering China. The introduction of Western religions to China also started from the thirty-five articles. . . . The tenet within [the thirty-five articles] was mostly plagiarized from Buddhism, and the language is inferior. Western religions, in fact, are just Buddhism adopted and converted by Europeans, and they have yet to break away from the essence of Buddhist thought. After these religions were introduced to China, the missionaries studied the Con-

> fucian classics, and drew on Confucian ideas to perfect their discourse. In the end, the arguments became diffuse and scattered, and the logic unable to be drawn out through research. Despite this, they thought themselves to have surpassed the three schools of Confucianism, Buddhism, and Taoism.
>
> Among the three major religions in the Western Regions, both Catholicism and Islam exclude Buddhism and worship God, which is the *devakula* of Brahmanism in Buddhist scriptures. These religions all originated from ancient times. When Shakyamuni was alive, their power declined, but they flourished again after Buddha's Nirvana. However, while I was studying the texts of the gospel, there was no mention of the methods of awakening the mind nor of the matters of spiritual practice. . . . In the ancient times of India, there was Brahmanism that worshipped God. Both Islam and Catholicism were in fact later developments of this school, and are even more bizarre.
>
> God is regarded as the Most High, idolatry and ancestor worship are forbidden. So why are the statutes of Jesus and the Virgin, as well as a crucifix hung in each and every household, placing God on High in second place?[78]

Not only does Wei Yuan trace the origins of Catholicism to Asia; he traces it back to the Indian Brahmin tradition and to Buddhism. There are two reasons for this: One, if Catholicism and Islam are traceable back to Buddhism, then Confucianism's relationship with these religions may be regarded as one internal to China (from the Ming onward, the question of Catholicism did indeed evince an "interior nature"). Two, extrapolating from this, the manner in which Confucianism dealt with internal differences could be applied to such "exterior" relationships. In Confucian studies of the Qing dynasty, there remained an exegetical tradition in which the three schools were viewed as separate, with Confucianism belonging to Confucianism, Buddhism belonging to Buddhism, and Daoism belonging to Daoism. In this sense, the strict divisions drawn between Confucianism and the religions of western Asia and Europe can be seen as inherited from those drawn in the Confucian tradition between Confucianism and Buddhism. Thus, Wei Yuan's investigation into the religion and culture of the West rehabilitated the exegetical practice of Qing-dynasty Confucian studies—and particularly Old Text

Confucianism—which sought to strictly separate the schools of Confucianism, Buddhism, and Daoism.

Second, despite the above situation, an opposition to strict divisions between the interior and exterior and between Yi and Xia still left its mark on Wei Yuan's view of religion. He held a relatively liberal attitude toward foreign religions, searching within various religions for beliefs that may be universally identified. To Wei Yuan, there were practical conditions that explained the fact that Confucianism had not found followers in other regions, such as the absence of transport links making it hard to expect those in other regions to follow Confucian teachings. But still, Wei Yuan believed that there must exist the possibility of communication between various faiths and religions. For example, Islam's foundational goal of encouraging virtue and punishing wrongdoing was not, according to Wei Yuan, in itself wrong. All religions have their own systems of faith; it is extremely difficult to judge from a single standard as to "which is the authentic" (*shu wei zheng wei*). This is not a fundamentalist attitude. However, whether in his tolerance toward other religions, or in his discussions of connections between various religions, the yardstick remained a Confucian one.[79]

We can best describe the concern with religion present in *Gazetteer of the Maritime States* as secular, rather than religious. Wei Yuan's interest in western Asia, Africa, and religion, similar to his concern with *Nanyang*, derived from his understanding of the West and China's relationship with that West. "A General Discussion of Africa" (*Liweiya zhou zongshuo*) offered an explanation for the hubs of transport and cultural connections between Asia, Europe, and Africa. The route by which British steamships delivered documents was from the Indian Ocean to Aden, into the Red Sea to Suez, then overland to the southeast edge of the Mediterranean Sea, then west by steamship again to the Port of Gibraltar, reaching the British capital in about fifty days. From before the Ming, Europe's path to China was always via this route.[80] Wei Yuan's descriptions of areas and states such as Morocco, Algeria, Libya, and Tunisia were intended to illustrate the historical relationships between Africa and Europe (Rome in particular). "Reference Works on Catholicism" (*Tianzhujiao kao*) made special reference to Christianity's origins in Asia, and its migration to Europe and then, following colonial routes, to America. According to Wei Yuan, the Old Testament was constituted "half by the records of the Israelites of Western Asia, half by the records of Greeks of eastern Europe."[81] In this sense, can we draw a clear line between Europe and Asia? In Wei Yuan's eyes, the center of power in Europe was in Italy, which was not only the origin of China's relations with Europe, but also the foundation of modern European civilization. Wei Yuan offered the following parallel: Sovereigns of Western states when ascending the throne all required investment by the Pope. Thus the status of the Pope was similar to that of the Dalai Lama in theocratic Tibet, and the archbishops from various states holding appointments in the Vatican were similar to the Jebtsundamba Khutuktu administering various monasteries in Mongolia.[82] In this light, despite the fact that the conflict between East and West was in essence one of interest, behind this relationship of interest lay hidden a deeper cultural division. Such an understanding provided a rational and legitimate foundation for a new differentiation between Yi and Xia and between the inner and outer. In Wei Yuan's exposition on the origins of various religions, cultural divergences were afforded only a very limited importance. But once distinctions between Yi and Xia, the inner and outer, were defined along axes of religion, ethics, and degree of civilization, even under the approach of emulation and learning from the institutions and technology of Western nations, the binaries of these labels remained clear. Indeed, such distinctions were a fundamental precondition for the proposition of "learning the advanced techniques of the Yi in order to resist them," as they were for Wei Yuan's own extensive and affirmative appraisal of European and American institutions and technology. From the technology of naval warfare and methods of trade to political and legal systems, from democratic experiment to colonial experience, all fell into the category of "means" (*yong*) and were thus unrelated to essential Yi-Xia or inner-outer distinctions.[83] In his view, the fundamental difference between nation-states such as Britain and France and the Roman Empire was this: Empires are concerned with religion and cultural values, while the nation-state is not concerned with these issues but rather with activities of trade and commerce, in particular military safeguards for the smooth exchange between mutual markets. "Mutual aid between merchants and the military" (*bing jia xiang zi*) constituted the fundamental secret of British world hegemony. Wei Yuan warned: "Those who excel in learning from the four Yi nations, may subdue those nations; those who do not excel in learning from the Yi, will be subdued by them."[84]

4. The Secret of the Rise of the British Economy and European Capitalism

The Opium Wars made very clear that the primary threat faced by China came from Europe, and especially from Britain. The "Yi" of "learning from the Yi" referred in practice to Britain and other Western colonial powers. These nations constituted the true "exterior" of the empire. In October of the fiftieth year of his reign (1711), Kangxi wrote in a decree that, "After some hundreds of years, China will suffer from the growth of foreign nations such as those from the West. This I predict." Wei Yuan then developed this prophecy of Kangxi's into a historical and geographical treatise. His discussion of Europe was distinctive in two ways: First, Wei Yuan described a Europe replete with conflicts of interest, cultural differences (of language, religion, and political system), and changing power relations. He thus corrected a view prevalent in pre-Ming China that equated Europe with either Italy (*Da Qin*—the Roman Empire) or Portugal (*Fo lang ji*). In comparison to the rather general descriptions of "the West" in the "East-West culture" popular in the late-Qing and May Fourth eras, Wei Yuan held a far richer view of Europe. He described the fall of the Roman Empire and its division into nation-states;[85] he described the wars between the Roman and Ottoman empires; he described conflict between Catholics and Protestants; he described, among other aspects, Europe's geographical environment, national institutions, schools and learning, taxation, and political administrations. Most importantly, Wei Yuan described the ebbs and flows of power of European states such as Portugal, Spain, Holland, Russia, and Britain, thus providing an important perspective to help Chinese people both understand the rise of Europe and conceive strategies in response to this rise. Second, Wei Yuan situated intra-European conflict and its military and trade expansion within the wider domain of various regions of the globe, thus putting an end to the view of European industrialization and outward expansion as unidirectional developments. Rather, the transformation of European society, politics, and military relations was tightly related to transformations underway in other regions. Thus, Wei Yuan established clear historical relationships between the rise of Europe (and particularly Britain), and geographical relations, natural environments, internal pressures, and overseas trade, as well as the outcome of foreign and trade policies toward areas such as China.

Britain lay at the center of Wei Yuan's concerns. In "A Summary of Various States of Atlantic Europe" (*Da Xiyang Ouluoba zhou geguo zong xu*), he wrote: "Today I write about the English Yi with particular detail, because if we want to know of the West, we must learn of England. To guard against its ills and learn its strengths, both are for our own strength."[86] During the Opium Wars, Wei Yuan travelled to the front lines in Zhejiang, and compiled his "A Short Record of England" (*Yingjili xiao ji*) from the oral testimony of a British prisoner. Of the hundred *juan* of *Gazetteer of the Maritime States*, *juan* 37–53 are concerned with European countries, among which *juan* 50–53 are devoted to a detailed discussion of Britain. "General Notes on England" (*Yingjili zong ji*) offered a brief introduction to topics such as British courts, Parliament, the cabinet, the Privy Council, the military, political life, taxation and state finance, and banks.[87] Here Wei Yuan makes clear his view that the reform of British internal institutions was the effective pillar of its status as hegemon. However, there were areas of similarity between the internal political structure of Britain and China's highly developed bureaucratic system, so this could not be pinpointed as a decisive factor.[88] More importantly, Britain was an empire that "widely colonized other countries' vassal states," and was characterized by massive colonization into geographically distant regions that were connected via trade networks established through the shipbuilding industry and commercial ports.[89] Therefore, the internal institutions of England's three islands alone were insufficient to describe Britain's unique situation. What was foremost among Wei Yuan's concerns was this: Why had other countries not developed empires in the English mold? Or rather, what factors had led to England's transformation from an island nation to the global hegemon that controlled global trade and ruled over so many vassal states? From Wei Yuan's narrative we can glean the following interrelated conclusions.

First, tension between Britain's large population and small land area prompted technical innovation, bringing about a situation in which more people were involved in industry and commerce than in agriculture, and in which long-distance trade was more profitable than its domestic counterpart. The rapid increase in population, limited land resources, and long-distance trade coalesced to cause new divisions of labor, and a complete transformation of the fundamental structure of the former agricultural society. According to Wei Yuan's data, 30 percent of Britain's population was engaged in agriculture, 10 percent in mining, 10 percent in manufacturing, and 20 percent in trade and commerce, with the remaining population working as teachers, lawyers, doctors, in the military, as sailors, or in other professions.[90]

Second, Britain's industry was largely centered around spinning and weaving, taking wool and cotton as raw materials, and requiring the support of industry and energy: that is, machines and their driving force—coal.[91] As luck would have it, the domestic resources of Britain, and the resources of the Americas and India, provided exactly the conditions required for textile production. Scotland was covered in pasture, plentiful for pastoral nomadism and providing wool; the Americas were the source of an unending supply of cotton. England's Northeast was home to abundant coal, and tin and iron ore deposits; each year more than 20,000,000 silver taels' worth of iron, 340,000 silver taels' worth of tin, and 830,000 silver taels' worth of lead were extracted. Coal production was even more lucrative, netting up to 24,000 silver *dan* per year.[92] In other words, Britain's own natural resources, in tandem with its connections with the Americas, meant that it obtained excellent conditions for industrial development. Britain's development was thus the contingent result of a serendipitous match between domestic and foreign conditions, particularly its colonies in the Americas and India.

Third, British economic reliance on long-distance trade, and its expanse of overseas colonies, prompted rapid advances in British shipbuilding and military technology. Military and commercial affairs also coalesced, which in turn strengthened Britain's capacity for overseas colonization. The most important way that the British model for commerce differed from its traditional counterparts was not in the freedom of markets or trade, but in military protection, and the close connection between military and commercial activities.[93] After calculating the numbers of British naval ships and cannons, Wei Yuan noticed a fundamental fact: It was during the reign of the Ming emperor Wanli (1573–1619) that British maritime activities began to spread beyond Europe, at which time Spain enjoyed dominance over maritime trade. Britain first defeated Spain, then Holland and France, to finally attain preeminence in trade relations. Thus, in practice, power over trade sprang from military power over the seas. It was precisely because of the above observation that Wei Yuan recommended strengthening the connection between civilian commercial activity and national military protection, with the shipbuilding industry at the center of this relationship. The development of the

Self-Strengthening Movement from military industry to civilian industry would follow precisely this path.

Fourth, related to the intrinsic connection between trade and military affairs is this: British trade was not spontaneous popular trade, but rather a kind of monopolistic and entrepôt-based trade in the organizational form of the East India Company. This was a systemic precondition for the enormous profits returned. Very different from China's sailboat-based and spontaneous trade, British merchants "did not bring their own domestic product to market, but purchased from other domains, particularly from Madras and the East Indies. They then exchanged these purchases for commodities such as tea and silk and returned home with these. All European states and those along the western border of Russia took advantage of this system of exchange." Here, market dominance was an effective organizational mode for long-distance trade activity driven by the pursuit of higher profit. The division of companies into stocks in no way diminishes such a monopoly. This monopoly not only resulted in the development of wide-scale smuggling operations; it could also mobilize state policy and the allocation of military strength toward the protection of such organized smuggling operations (in the name of free trade). It was precisely because of this that Wei Yuan believed in the necessity of dissolving such companies, and thus collapsing the opponent's power. Failing this, it would be impossible to resist the British invasion and infiltration of China, as well as its concomitant opium trade.

Fifth, the risks of such long-distance trade and reliance on currency exchange brought about the rise of the British insurance industry, the formation of the gold-standard system, and a comprehensive taxation system. Such systems that were directly related to foreign trade followed the development of British domestic and foreign taxation systems, creating unprecedented levels of state power. Increased taxation allowed Britain to assemble armed forces. It not only held a standing army in its own country, but had garrisons stationed throughout its colonies, and enlisted local militias (*tubing*).[94] Wei Yuan did not offer a precise explanation of the process by which the world economy was rebuilt around the British financial system, but he did briefly summarize the establishment of the gold standard: Britain used gold as a hard currency; three taels of gold were fixed at a price of twenty-two silver dollars, with the silver again divided into copper cash. This overlapped with the use of banknotes in silver value and other forms of currency, all price-matched to gold and silver values. Due to highly developed trade, robust institutions, and the establishment of the gold standard, British banks enjoyed unparalleled trust, and established Britain's position at the center of the global financial system. Consulting Wei Yuan's discussion on the relationship between the opium trade and the silver crisis in his *An Account of Sea Battles in the Reign of Daoguang* and *Strategies of Maritime Affairs,* as well as the sections of *Gazetteer of the Maritime States* that describe the abundance of gold in the Americas, we can see that discussion here of British finance, insurance, and the gold standard is clearly established against a vast background of global history. Wei Yuan held a clear understanding of the problems of the opium trade and of the outflow of silver, but it seemed he did not fully apprehend the connection between the decline in the silver standard, gold production in the Americas, and their effects on the financial system centered about London. The fundamental point that Wei Yuan was concerned with was this: British colonialism had created a kind of global market tied together through the military, monopoly, occupation, entrepôt trade, industry, and financial credit, and its internal division of labor and systematic development were tightly interrelated with the global market. This was the true foundation of Britain's hegemony, and of its wealth and power.

5. The Political Structure of the "United Provinces" and the Image of Grand Unification

Wei Yuan introduced the British political system, but it is clear he harbored no particular enthusiasm for it compared with his extensive emphasis on America's democracy and the historical experience of American independence. In the opening chapter of his "General Outline of North America," Wei evoked six terms of praise from the Confucian tradition to describe the spirit and politics of the country: martial virtue (*wu*), in veneration of American revolt and resistance; wisdom (*zhi*), of its tact in conducting intercourse with faraway countries and attacking those nearby; acting in the public interest (*gong*), of America's federal politics; universality (*zhou*), in praise of its electoral system; wealth (*fu*), of its fair trade; and, amity (*yi*), of its not taking advantage of the weak. Yet while Wei described America's discovery by Columbus, Magellan, and da Gama, he barely mentioned the genocide of the Indians by European colonists; the independence movement and American resistance to Britain, and the uniqueness of the American political system, are at the center of his narrative. From an Yi-Xia perspective we might ask: considering the US population mainly comprised English, Scottish, Dutch, Spanish, German, French, Swedish, and other European migrants (but most especially those from the British Isles), and thus bore no substantive ethnic difference from Europeans ("In their physique and countenance, the people of the new country are no different from the people of England," Wei wrote),[95] why then was his attitude toward America so starkly different from his attitude toward European countries? First, during the Opium Wars the US government, along with most American consulates and merchants, was opposed to British ambitions in China, creating an atmosphere of closeness between China and the United States. Second, Wei Yuan was mainly concerned about politics, that is, the inner workings and outward dispositions of various countries—questions of race were not central in his reckoning. Regarding the former, the Americans resisted British colonial rule and established a burgeoning, independent country, which in terms of trade and diplomacy was not as aggressive as the traditional colonial powers. On the latter, America had abandoned slavery and the status of African Americans had improved, and its adoption of a federal system reflected a trend toward racial equality. These are the reasons Wei Yuan showed greater enthusiasm for the United States.

America was also attractive for Wei Yuan not only because it was different from Europe but also because of its similarities with China. He never simply compared China and America; on the contrary, he scorned the categorization of people based on ethnic groups. When discussing the relationship between Yi and the center of the empire, he hinted that the relationship between the Roman Empire and its periphery was analogous to that between China and its tributary system. In Wei Yuan's view, the United States was a culturally and ethnically diverse, yet unified empire, in stark contrast to the European nation-state model (although, he noted, somewhat similar to that of Switzerland). Its multiethnic character did not affect national unity—an important point for those intellectuals in the late Qing who stressed preserving the empire's internal cohesion. When discussing the rich mining resources and highly developed transportation in the United States, Wei Yuan highlighted another similarity between America and China, namely, the importance of having a unifying language among diverse ethnic groups—another important difference from the complex linguistic situation of Europe. Therefore, the European model of nationalism based on language, ethnicity, and religion was as unsuitable for China as it was for the United States. Wei cited material from *A Short Account of the United Provinces of America* (*Meiligeguo zhilue*) as proof that America and China were "identical in the east, south, and north"[96] (a reference to what he perceived to be similarities in their geographical situation), and that there were similarities between the two countries in terms of their size, culture, and language.

That America's democratic presidential system was vastly different from China's political order was another reason for Wei Yuan's attraction to the country. Britain, Germany, and other European states were still monarchies, bearing little difference from China's imperial system; the states of the United States (what Wei Yuan called its "tribes" [*buluo*]), on the other hand, each had governors, and there was no king. The commander in chief was "chosen from among all of them by public nomination to take overall control," which was why America was known as the "United States"—which Wei translated as "jointly administered states" (*jianshe bangguo*).[97] Wei Yuan repeatedly noted that the president was elected by various ministries and by the people to a term of four years, with no possibility of reelection after two terms. He was enamored with America's having eradicated hereditary rule, praising its democratic system as one in which "the right to elect and the right to hold office derives not from the top, but rises up from below."[98] It should be noted that hereditary rule was seen as problematic among many other thinkers during the Qing period as well, and indeed this was one of the main themes in the New Text studies tradition, from Zhuang Cunyu (1719–1788) down to Gong Zizhen (1792–1841). In Wei Yuan's view, in contrast to China's hereditary imperial system, the US presidential and electoral systems were a means to avoid the unchecked power inherent in hereditary postings (*shiqing*), and for the promotion of talent in an ideal meritocratic system.

The aforementioned two aspects are closely related to the federal system of the United States. From the perspective of New Text learning, federalism shares similarities with the vision of a great unification of the systems of enfeoffment (*fengjian*) and centralized administration (*junxian*). Both are political systems that can preserve the ideals of an empire within a balanced political structure. The meaning of the "Great Unification" (*Da yitong*) is to restore the spirit of feudalism within the framework of centralized administration, and to form an institutional structure combining decentralization and centralization.[99] Therefore, the federal political system is a political order whose internal and external properties are distinct and interconnected. Of this multilayered order, Wei Yuan wrote:

> The new state system has five legislative layers: first, national-level laws, which apply to all twenty-six states; second, state (*buluo*) laws, which are different in each of the states; the third layer is the laws of prefectures (*fu*), which apply only to those born in (*shengyu*) the prefecture; fourth are county (*xian*) laws, set up by various counties individually and binding only to local county residents; finally there are laws for offices of local bureaucracies (*si*), established by the bureaucracy and applicable only to those serving in official positions. Among these five legislative layers, lower-level laws may not overrule those of the highest—for instance, laws of local bureaucracies may not contradict those of counties.[100]

This emphasizes the decentralized enfeoffment (*fengjian*) or separation of power inherent in federal politics. Regarding the actual administrative practices of this unified national system, Wei Yuan commented that

> the head of state is called the president [*tongling*], with authority similar to that of a king; in each of the states there is a governor, with powers analogous to provincial governors in China (*dufu*); each state is then divided into various middle-sized parts, such as prefectures (*zhifu*), which are then subdivided into still smaller units such as district magistrates (*zhixian*). In the national capital there are six branches of government, which are comparable to [China's] Six Ministries (*liubu shangshu*). The only difference [from China's system] is that there is no Ministry of Works (*gongbu*), but there is what is known as a postal ministry (*yibu*).[101]

Here, Wei Yuan is emphasizing areas of similarity between federal politics and the system of centralized administration (*junxian*) in China. In his translation of various articles of the American Declaration of Independence into Confucian language, Wei allows us to hear the charm of *Spring and Autumn* Gongyang studies: "Because there is no King, and governance is undertaken by a number of people, affairs of state are ordered in accordance with public opinion. What is announced is always implemented and harmful things are made known; governance is efficient and effective, orders are enacted and injunctions carried out effectively. This is no different from the governance by a sagacious ruler (*xianpi*); it is an administrative system at variance with the decentralized enfeoffment (*fengjian*) and centralized administration (*junxian*) systems [in China], and defines itself on its own terms."[102] Wei found the real presence of a kind of Grand Unification (*Da yitong*) in American federalist politics, and adopted the Grand Unification principle in making sense of American federalism. His attitude of conceiving a political system on the premise of political unity would be inherited by later New Text scholars, but the federalist system was clearly rejected by Kang Youwei, who attempted to combine local autonomy—dissolving provincial administration (*xingsheng*) while retaining self-autonomous units from the prefecture (*fu*) level and below—with centralized power, in order to avoid the national separatism and warlord politics that could potentially arise under the banner of decentralization.[103]

In his understanding of the political structure of the separation of powers, Wei Yuan did not show the same enthusiasm for the presidential election or federal systems. He emphasized the discursive function of Congress—calling it a "discussion chamber" (*yishi ge*) or "deliberation office" (*xuanyi chu*) covering "any matter of state pertaining to agriculture, labor, the military, trade, rewards and punishments, criminal law, international exchange (*laiwang*), foreign envoys, and construction"—but he barely even mentioned that Congress is also a legislative body with the power to remove the president.[104] When Wei discussed the function of the judiciary he spoke of a "conference system" (*huiyi zhili*), clearly lumping questions of legislation and the administration of justice together. In terms of executive power, he believed that the American and Chinese systems were not substantially different from one another. For instance, he referred to the executive power and ministries of the US government as the "Personnel Government" (*li zhengfu*), "Revenue Government" (*hu zhengfu*), "War Government" (*bing zhengfu*), "Department of Navy" (*shuishibing bu*), the "Rites Government" (*li zhengfu*), and "Postal Government" (*yi zhengfu*), totally mirroring the Six Ministries (*liu bu*) of the Chinese state, with the only difference being a "government" for the postal service in place of the "Ministry of Works" (*gong bu*). Wei Yuan described judicial questions in terms of China's Censorate (*ducha yuan*), emphasizing the principle that judges cannot serve concurrently as legislators.[105]

6. Historical Foresight and the Logic of Modernity

Wei Yuan's strategy for allying with Russia, the United States, and other countries failed at the time, although this was not so much due to his own strategic error as a result of the comparative strengths of these powers. "Pitting Yi against Yi" (*yi Yi zhi Yi*), "learning the advanced techniques of the Yi in order to resist them" (*shi Yi changji yi zhi Yi*), and other such principles required corresponding state capacity and political strategy. The late-Qing period saw numerous disputes within the imperial court and among intellectuals about whether to ally with Russia or with the United Kingdom and Japan, but not once was the loss or lease of territory, or compensation or transfer of rights to the powers, seen to be a reasonable price. Zheng Guanying stated: "It can be said that if [the parties to an agreement] are alike in their position and strength, then their agreement is reliable; only when the agreement has been signed can law be said to be present." In the absence of actual power, even if right was on one's side, Zheng reasoned, "Laws cannot be relied upon. Intelligence and strategic cunning are vital in the world today; mere clever words cannot be relied upon."[106] In the decades since the publication of the *Gazetteer of the Maritime States,* the contest between Europe and North American countries had reached an unprecedented level. In Asia alone, in 1878–1880 British forces launched a second war in Afghanistan, reducing the country to a British protectorate; in 1884–1885 Russia gave military support to west Asia and clashed with Afghanistan; between 1874 and 1887 Britain invaded the Malay region and formally subjugated it as a colony; in 1885–1886 France and Britain invaded Vietnam and Burma respectively, reducing them to French and British colonies; and Siam was also divided between Britain and France. These processes of partitioning in turn intensified conflict among the imperialist powers. The 1898 Spanish-American War marked the beginning of yet another wave of drastic redistribution of the globe, but the conflict did not involve any alliance with China on the part of either side. On the contrary, Western countries had reached a tacit understanding about their spheres of influence, with numerous wars breaking out on Chinese soil due to competition between them. A series of unequal treaties were signed following the Franco-British invasion of China in 1857, the Sino-French War of 1884, the Sino-Japanese War of 1894–1895, and the invasion of the Eight-Power Alliance in 1890. In 1897–1898 Germany occupied Jiaozhou Bay, bringing Shandong into its sphere of influence; Britain occupied Weihaiwei, thus extending its power to the Yangtze River basin; France occupied Guangzhou Bay, and agreed with Britain to include Guangdong, Guangxi, and Sichuan as part of the two countries' sphere of influence; and Fujian became part of Japan's sphere of influence. Under the name of its apparent "Open Door Policy," in 1899 the United States demanded "equal opportunity" in dividing China's interests for itself.

However, these events did not so much prove the failure of Wei Yuan's strategic vision as validate his historical foresight about the terminally declining strength of the Qing. An examination of Japan's experience of modernization shows that Wei Yuan's strategic conception of the latter half of the nineteenth century had already partially come to pass. Between 1850 and 1853 four copies of *Gazetteer of the Maritime States* were introduced to Japan, but as its government was pursuing an isolationist policy at this time, including orders to suppress Western learning, the work was banned from publishing. In March 1854 Japan was forced to sign the Kanagawa peace treaty with the United States, which allowed American ships to purchase food and coal at the ports of Shimoda and Hakodate, and soon thereafter concluded treaties with Britain, Russia, and the Netherlands. Fifteen copes of the *Gazetteer* were introduced to Japan at this time: seven for use in the imperial court and eight distributed on the market. More than twenty reprint editions appeared in the following two years, along with numerous translations, commentaries, and serializations, exerting a profound influence on Japan's modernization in the opening of ports, methods of dealing with foreign powers, reforms, and militarization.[107] In 1854, the Japanese scholar Yoshida Shōin commented critically of the *Gazetteer* that "those who should be concerned about the Qing dynasty are its own citizens, not foreign barbarians. Why is there not a word about this [in the book]?"[108] Yoshida also contended that Wei Yuan's strategy of "pitting the Yi against the Yi" (that is, aligning with Russia, the United States, and France to contain the United Kingdom) "knows the first but does not know the second. Barbarians (*Yi*) do not comprehend righteousness, only what is beneficial to them. If it is beneficial for one's enemies to unite together, those who harm such an alliance will become its enemies, and this is only to be expected."[109] From the longue-durée perspective, however, Wei Yuan's foresight is more clear. First, he appreciated the interdependence between commerce, the economy, politics, and military affairs in the modern world, and tried to use military strategy and industry to spur the development of national construction and civil industry, while also promoting military and economic development through internal systemic reform. Between 1860 and 1890 the Qing government established more than twenty military industrial enterprises, which in turn expanded into transportation, shipping, mining, smelting, textiles, and other civilian industries. In these early stages of China's industrialization private capitalist industry was struggling to make progress and even to survive, and government offices, or government-supervised commercial offices, became the monopoly form of China's early capitalist industrial development. (This is not to say that Wei Yuan advocated government monopoly of commerce; in his proposal to encourage private participation in the manufacture of ship guns, for instance, he advocated the involvement of private enterprise in modern industry, including defense.) The Self-Strengthening Movement's promotion of new learning, machinery, manufacturing, and commerce was in line with Wei Yuan's ideas. Its mercantilist policies such as "using commerce to control commerce" (*yi shang di shang*), government support for private enterprise, and joint stock companies to promote trade also echoed Wei Yuan's proposals. Second, Wei Yuan understood the internal working of the modern world-system, opposed fighting foreign armies in isolation, and advocated a strategy of "learning from the Yi" and cooperating vertically and horizontally to change China's overall situation. More importantly, the relationship between China's national strength in light of the global situation, and military strategy, provided the basic logic for the late Qing's external understanding to eventually turn to internal reforms. European colonialism spurred China's turn toward a nation-state, but this process was premised on the historical legacy of imperialism; at the same time it was demonstrated by restoring the historical heritage and outlook of the empire. International relationships in the Maritime Age provided the historical conditions for the emergence of a new view of Yi-Xia, but it was precisely during the course of constructing this new view—"learning the advanced techniques of the Yi in order to resist them"—that Wei Yuan rediscovered the relationship between China and Southeast Asia during the Ming period and earlier, reconstructed China's tributary network, and developed his geographical description of Europe, America, and other regions based upon it. In this sense, he saw restoring ritual and legal norms of the Ming and pre-Ming as an important task for China. Canvassing a new vision of the world from the perspective of tributary relations means that national sovereignty can be traced back to the *Rites of Zhou* and the kind of historical relationships described in *Spring and Autumn* Gongyang studies, wherein the relationship between the tributary and treaty systems is not entirely opposing. When state-building is situated in the context of the world nation-state system, the absolutization of internal and external relations transforms concurrently into relativization and homogenization of the internal and domestic relations. China's Self-Strengthening Movement, reformists, and the Japanese modernization movement were all based on the premise that only with a unified internal political authority could international recognition be effectively secured. The connection between nationalism, militarism, statism, imperialism, and the concept of institutional reform was established within a new global relationship. In *Gazetteer of the Maritime States*' narrative on global relations, the criticism of Qing imperial violence and hierarchical relations found in earlier New Text studies gradually disappeared, such that we can barely distinguish between its critical vision and imperial vision.

IV. The Question of Sovereignty: Ritual Relations in the Tributary System and International Law

1. Tribute, Treaties, and External Relations

Nationalism arose in China, Japan, and other parts of East Asia in response to encroaching European hegemony. The first wave of nationalism developed within the traditional framework of both Yi-Xia and internal-external divisions, and may be understood in terms of what Benedict Anderson calls "official nationalism." In European discourse "official nationalism" arose from around 1820 in reaction against popular nationalism; in the great dynastic empires (such as Britain and Russia) it entailed the establishment of compulsory education for the elevation of the language of predominant ethnic groups to the status of national languages.[110] In Asia, however, and especially in

Chinese discourse, separatist nationalism played only a partial role in melding nation and empire. Two other roots of nationalism can also be identified.

First, there had always existed in China a comingling between empire-building and state-building, such that the process of consolidating the modern nation, when it began to develop, was premised in imperial state traditions. In terms of its political form, although the popular and revolutionary nationalism that developed from within the Qing court was anti-Manchu in character, the polity that eventually developed from it was a union of Five Nations under One Republic (*Wuzu gonghe*) in an imperial mold. In terms of cultural form, modern linguistic nationalism was never based on any particular dialect, with popular nationalism coming instead to entail a reinvigoration of a kind of elite semivernacular style that was already part of the imperial tradition. This linguistic nationalism integrated multiple cultural traditions under the rubric of "national language," with popular, common, and modern values replacing the hitherto orthodox status of classical language. As a system of writing, however, this vernacular writing (*baihua wen*) was in no way a model for a nationalism derived from any dialect.

Second, this dynastic-imperial nationalism was a reaction to the normative European concept of statehood; it cannot simply be reduced to the response of the singular empire to the international system of nation-states. Qing-European conflicts were not ordinary state-against-state conflicts, but rather conflicts between two visions of international order. Citing Maruyama Masao's example of the Japanese concept *sonnō jōi* (revere the sovereign, expel the barbarians), Anderson situates Japanese nationalism in between the Confucian "civilized / domestic, barbarian / external view," and the mutually recognized sovereignty that underpins European international law. He concludes that while "European" national consciousness was premised in a consciousness of international society, the East Asian states, being steeped in the "civilized / barbarian dichotomy," did not grasp the implications of the "international." In addition to Anderson's reflection of these ideas, Maruyama makes the following comments on Fukuzawa Yukichi's *Comings and Goings of the Foreigners* (*Tōjin Ōrai*) and *Encouragement of Learning* (*Gakumon no Susume*):

> Here [in a passage in *Encouragement of Learning* dealing with the "comprehensive rights" (*quanli tongyi*) that should prevail between states—*the*

> *author*] the arrogance of the "China-barbarian" (*Zhonghua-Yidi*) dichotomy is challenged and replaced by an new attitude of national self-esteem, one "based on reason, as it implies acknowledging one's guilt even before the black slaves of Africa; but it also means standing on principle without fear of the warships of England and America."[111]

Here, the "China-barbarian" dichotomy is construed as a kind of self-centeredness, rooted in Confucian and imperial systems and bereft of the concept of equality between nations; Benedict Anderson describes this self-centeredness as an important reason for the persistent cohesion between nationalism and imperialism in Japan.[112] Researchers of China have made similar findings. John K. Fairbank was unequivocal in his contention that the Yi-Xia dichotomy and the tributary system that ensued from it lacked concepts of equality and respect, and even stifled the development of political nationalism and an international trade system in China.

Whether the formation of nationalism in modern China entailed an "internationalist orientation" is worth considering further. It is first useful to note that, in a Qing imperium administered by a minority ethnic group, the dichotomous notions of Yi-Xia and internal-external realms were not mainstream concepts; their resurgence during the late Qing was an intellectual response to European invasion. Two points are worth mentioning here. First, when New Text classical studies advocated moving beyond Yi-Xia and "inner-outer" dichotomies in the eighteenth century, and in the process sought to reaffirm the legitimacy of Manchu rule, their ideas contained concepts of equality between nationalities. Second, the normative incompatibility between the tributary and treaty systems is unable to explain the internal and external relations of Qing society, because the system itself encompasses numerous relationship models, with treaty-based international relations foremost among these. The New Text school's probing into the inner-outer and Yi-Xia dichotomies, and questions of the Grand Unification, was a learned articulation of the Qing dynasty's political legitimacy. Their efforts produced fruitful treatises on relationships within the imperium, and also broached the standards of the dynasty's relationship with the outside world. Therefore, understanding the New Text school and their political praxis is helpful to understanding how the dynasty's internal and external relationships changed.

Before addressing how New Text classical studies became the *locus classicus* for political reform thought in the late Qing, it is essential to first understand how scholar-officials appropriated the classics to advance their own worldviews and consciousness of national sovereignty, so as to accord with Wei Yuan's treatise on shifts in international relations. Secondly, we must take note of how Western missionaries and jurists, as well as Chinese intellectuals, variously appropriated the classics to bolster arguments about the legitimacy of international law and national sovereignty. The basic characteristic of the era of the nation-state is the demarcation of internal and external boundaries on the basis of strict recognition of sovereignty and, in principle, of noninterference in the internal affairs of other states. This concept of sovereignty, characterized by the conscious recognition of sovereignty as such, underpinned the reaffirmation of internal-external, Yi-Xia distinctions in the late Qing. But while earlier Gongyang studies had mainly dealt with relationships between nationalities within the empire—and, in making ritual distinctions, encouraged some flexibility as to what constituted Yi versus Xia, internal and external, and the implications for the hierarchies between these groups—it was now essential to consider the reality of political, economic, military, and diplomatic relations among nation-states. The discourse of "China-centrism" (*Huaxia zhongxin zhuyi*) in the late Qing was precisely contrary to the New Text tradition of eliminating strict internal-external and Yi-Xia distinctions; indeed, China-centrism was premised on the strict separation of Yi and Xia. The concept of the Yi-Xia dichotomy was a response to the glaring discrepancy between the Unequal Treaties and the system on which they were ostensibly based (that is, the system of sovereign relations). It challenged the long-held view in New Text thought that internal-external, Yi-Xia polarities should be abolished, even while echoing the conservative expression of the Neo-Confucian Yi-Xia distinction. In this context, Westernized nationalist thought developed alongside Neo-Confucianism and its strong antiforeign sentiments, giving rise to sharp ideological conflicts. We must ask, therefore: where did "China-centrism" come from? In terms of late-Qing discourse, was this novel manifestation of the "Yi-Xia distinction" an inevitable corollary of China's historical tradition, or rather the result of changed historical conditions?

Secondly, by the late-Qing period there was continuous debate among government ministers and scholar-officials about closing the country to resist foreign encroachment. The year 1900 saw the Boxer Rebellion, antireligious movements, and other instances of rising xenophobia, along with harsh, historically grounded criticism of the "celestial mentality" of traditional Chinese society from among reformist intellectuals who had had dealings with the West. However, it should not be inferred from this that Qing society in general was ignorant of the outside world, let alone that it rejected foreign culture wholesale. In addition to the interethnic relations within the Qing empire discussed above, the Qing court had had ample experience in dealing with Western missionaries and other phenomena of imperialism. For instance, in the 1660s Yang Guanxian's (1597–1669) two treatises *On Exposing Heterodoxy* (*Biexie lun*) and *I Cannot Do Otherwise* (*Budeyi*) had expressed concern about Catholic missionary activity (which as well as proselyting had included introducing novel methods of cartography and social surveyance); subsequently Emperor Kangxi dismissed the German astronomer Johann Adam Schall von Bell (1591–1666) from the Qing Directorate of Astronomy, on the grounds that Schall von Bell's advice on the adoption of the Islamic calendar to replace the European calendar was based on erroneous calculations. Kangxi then arranged for the Belgian Ferdinand Verbiest (1623–1688) to take over as Director of Astronomy, and under Verbiest's supervision a sizeable Jesuit community was established in Beijing and within the Forbidden City. Secondly, during this same period the Qing resettled ethnic Russians captured during Sino-Russian border conflicts at Nerchinsk (Albazin). Some of them settled in Shengjing (present-day Shenyang) and Beijing, and as their community grew, a Russian company of the Bordered Yellow Banner was established in Dongzhimen. The Qing government even bequeathed temple land to the Russian community for the construction of a church, known as St. Nicholas Church—and colloquially among the locals as "Rakshasa Temple"—which was administered by the Orthodox priest Maxim Leontev (d. 1698) and permitted to appoint its own priests at the direction of the Russian government. A third instance of sophisticated early intercourse between China and foreign powers is found in the third volume of *Zhong-Xi jishi* (*Accounts of China and the West*), which recorded that after Taiwan was pacified in the twenty-second year of the Kangxi reign (1683), the southeastern coastal provinces requested a lifting of the ban on maritime trade. After some deliberation on the trade question, in 1685 Macao, Zhangzhou in Fujian Province, Ningbo in Zhejiang, and Yuntaishan in Jiangnan implemented tax exemptions or reductions for trade with the Netherlands, Siam, and other powers in Southeast Asia. Finally, to take a fourth example, in June of the fifth year of the Yongzheng reign (1727) the Qing government signed the Treaty of Kyakhta with the Russian government, establishing Kyakhta, a Russian city straddling what is today the Russo-Mongolian border, as a hub for bilateral trade, and reaffirming Russia's right to continue sending priests to Beijing. Such missionary communities often also engaged in gathering and stealing intelligence. The Orthodox Church in Beijing oversaw the production of the *Huangyu quanlan tu* (*Overview Maps of the Imperial Territories,* 1717), a copy of which subsequently appeared in Paris. Located in the so-called South Pavilion (St. Mary's Church) in the Beijing legation quarter, the Orthodox Evangelical Mission fell under the direct jurisdiction of the Russian Ministry of Foreign Affairs, and in effect operated as a kind of spy agency for the Russian government.[113] Of course, similar espionage practices were carried out by the Chinese side, which procured Russian maps and intelligence reports with the help of its European Jesuit conspirators based in the Qing court. Within the imperial system, the dynasty determined the nature of its various tributary relations based on their degree of closeness, and dealt with internal and external relations based on long-established principles of ritual procedure and dynastic politics. It is therefore not fitting to understand tributary relations and ritual procedure as a model of governance that was purely self-centered and closed off from the outside world.

Thirdly, the manner in which the Qing dynasty handled internal and external, Yi-Xia relations was varied and complicated, with Manchu-Han and Manchu-Mongolian relations, and indeed the relations between the dynasty and other ethnic groups on its periphery all displaying different manifestations of what may be understood as "tributary relationships." While tributary relations cannot be understood according to current sensibilities about international relations, aspects of this system nonetheless coexisted alongside, and overlapped with, the international relations frameworks that were evolving at the time. The uniqueness and ambiguity of tributary relations has led to misunderstanding among many scholars, due to a tendency among many to conceive of one or another aspect of it in the context of the system of treaty relations between nation-states. For instance, John K. Fairbank regarded the tributary system as an obstacle to China's entry into the international treaty system;[114] Takeshi Hamashita and others have contended the opposite, emphasizing aspects of historical inheritance and continuity in the tributary system all throughout the process of its integration into the treaty system.[115] However, distinguishing too starkly between the tributary and treaty systems makes it impossible to interpret the meaning of the Treaty of Nerchinsk, and the Treaty of Kyakhta mentioned above; clearly, such accords evince an overlap between elements of the two systems. Other scholars still have described a dichotomy between Rites and Law in explaining the difference between tribute and treaties. However, from a historical perspective such a distinction is still ambiguous for the reasons alluded to above: China's tributary networks were active across various treaty systems and encompassed a broad array of trade regulations. Beginning in the Kangxi period (1661–1722) the Qing court formulated a set of theories, rites, and laws for carrying out Yi-Xia and internal-external relations. It established numerous political institutions, such as the Lifan Yuan (Court of Frontier Affairs) in 1663 for the management of Mongolian affairs, which inherited part of the portfolio of the earlier Libu (Ministry of Rites), and a series of special military councils for the management of internal and external relations. Established in the Xianfeng era (1850–1861), the Zongli Yamen was tasked with adapting the Qing state to Western diplomatic practices and presiding over the treaty relationships between China and Western countries. Such multifarious institutions as these reflect the diverse and complex nature of the empire's internal and external relations, as well as the institutional coexistence of tributary ritual relations alongside a treaty system encompassing different empires.

The Qing court had evoked both rites and the law to conclude treaties and adjust its relationships variously with Russia, Britain, France, the Netherlands, Japan, Siam, Korea, Vietnam, and other powers from as early as the Shunzhi and Kangxi eras (1644–1722). Yet when the "tributary" (*chaogong*) concept is applied to this type of interstate relations, it is difficult to use later international relations categories to distinguish between what constituted rites as opposed to what is normatively considered "diplomacy"—so-called modern international relations as defined in European international law. But although the concept of tributary relations does not presuppose notions of equality and sovereignty among nations in the same way as international law does, this is not to say that it was entirely bereft of legal and ritual systems that could be adjusted over time. While China was the epicenter of the tributary system, other tributary countries exercised their own agency in the expression of rites. As a vassal state of the Ming dynasty, Korea contributed forces to aid in the Ming's wars against the Jin and Qing; the Qing later invaded Korea and forced its emperor to cease using Ming reign dates and titles and to replace them with those of the Qing, to declare himself a vassal, and to pay tribute, thereby establishing a tributary relationship on the basis of conquest. In 1875, the queen of Korea sought investiture from the Qing for her son as the legitimate successor to the throne.[116] But even so, until the threat from Europe and Japan increased in the nineteenth century, the Qing did not interfere in Korean internal affairs and Korea did not have a permanent envoy in Beijing (Vietnam and Ryukyu, whose emperors were also conferred their titles by the Qing, also did not have permanent envoys in Beijing). Formal relations between the Qing and Japan began in the twelfth year of the Kangxi era (1673) and centered mainly on trade, but as the Tokugawa Shogunate adopted a closed-door policy—which included restrictions on Japanese merchants traveling to China, on the outflow of gold and silver, on bilateral trade, and on the control of goods by Chinese merchants, the absence of a fixed trade law, and a wide variety of import taxes—relations between the two countries were not close.[117] Yet tributary relations were never homogenous, with significant variation among tributary vassals such as Korea, Vietnam, Ryukyu, and Laos. While the tributary relationship may be understood as hierarchical and ritualistic in nature, this did not mean that the central dynasty had the right to interfere in the internal affairs of the tributary state; there are vast gaps between the understanding of various relationships as recorded in the Qing court documents, and those of other parties to the relationships.[118] In this sense, the tribute system was not a unilateral hierarchy, but rather a set of historical relationships formed through the involvement of multiple relationships over time.

The Qing was by no means an empire without external relations, and its bilateral relations with tributary states often assumed the character of interstate relations. Max Weber defines three features of the state, according to the characteristics of modern society: first, the presence of fixed administrative officials; second, the ability of these officials to maintain a legitimate monopoly on the means of violence; and finally, their ability to maintain this monopoly within a given territorial area. In other words, Weber takes executive power, the tools of violence, and territorial sovereignty as the main characteristics of the modern state.[119] Considering that the above three characteristics can all be said to have been present in both the Qing empire and the modern Chinese state, however, Weber's formula does not get us very far in differentiating the form of nation-state from its imperial predecessor. Other scholars argue that Qing governance in the Northwest displayed modern characteristics of territorial sovereignty: effective administrative divisions and management; a periodic, fixed-rate taxation system; and the building up of border defenses, including stationed armies, military-administered agricultural colonies (known as *Tunken*), courier stations, military forts (*Kalun*), boundary demarcation markers, and regular border patrols.[120] All these phenomena are characteristic of a close relationship between territorial expansion and bureaucratic administration, according to commonly accepted standards of what constitutes nation-states, when frontiers became "national" boundaries (that is, mutually recognized borders) in the eighteenth century. Earlier, however, between the 1670s and 1690s there was a long-running crisis in relations between the Qing dynasty and the Russian Empire, centering mainly on the jurisdiction of ethnic minorities in Siberia. On September 7, 1689, the Qing and Russia concluded the Treaty of Nerchinsk, which primarily dealt with controlling the movements of ethnic minorities along the shared border; both parties were concerned that minority groups would migrate into the other's territory and harm the interests of their empires. These issues of border demarcation were also closely related to trade. The treaty was written in Latin and appended with text in both Manchu and Russian. After it was concluded, a border demarcation stele engraved with Manchu, Chinese, Russian, and Latin text was erected on the Qing-Russian border. Its specific contents—pertaining to the delineation of an eastern Sino-Russian border along the Xing'an ranges and Ergun River, the sacking of Yaksa (Albazin) by the Qing and the ejection of the Russian population from the city, the prevention of cross-border aggression, and provisions for the exchange of fugitives between the two sides, along with the development of stronger bilateral trade—are ample evidence that concepts of national borders, mutually recognized sovereignty, and access to trade were not products of a "Maritime Age," nor the exclusive preserve of nation-states. The demarcation of the eastern border region involved both sides exercising authoritative power within distinct boundaries: the fugitive laws broached questions of nationality and the administrative rights of the respective powers to enact exclusionary policies toward those of their nationality, and residents of the border regions were legal subjects of a region defined by a faraway central administration. The aspects of the treaty pertaining to bilateral trade, even though the language of tributary relations was used in framing it, entailed a clear understanding of the state as the defining unit of the market exchange. It also clearly stipulated that those crossing the border needed to bear "identity certificates" (*wenpiao*) and "pass documents" (*lupiao*), official papers of a kind not dissimilar from modern "passports."[121]

Nonetheless, the Treaty of Nerchinsk did not guarantee peaceful relations between the two powers forever; ongoing Qing-Russian disputes over territory and the citizenship jurisdiction of border communities continued to be addressed in a series of subsequent treaties. Soon after subduing the Dzungar Khanate and the Altishar Khojas Revolt, in 1762 the Qianlong court dispatched more military generals to Ili (in what is today the far north of Xinjiang Province), and set up regular border patrols; during the Jiaqing reign (1796–1820) there were eighty-three military posts in Ili and the surrounding region. However, by the time of the Taiping Rebellion (1850–1864) and Second Opium War (1856–1860) Russia again called the parameters of the border into question, and on June 13, 1858, compelled the Qing to sign a Sino-Russian addendum to the Treaty of Tianjin, subsequently ratified as part of the Treaty of Beijing in 1860, which set in motion a series of new efforts to redefine the border.[122] A subsequent series of unequal treaties saw further Russian encroachment on Qing-controlled territory: the Treaty of Livadia of 1879 (signed by the Qing diplomat Chonghou [1826–1893], also known as the "Eighteen Articles Treaty"); the 1880 Sino-Russian Revised Treaty, also known as the Treaty of St. Petersburg; along with five additional treaties pertaining to specific border issues, namely the October 1882 China-Ili Border Treaty, the December 1882 Kashgar Border Treaty, the August 1883 Kota Border Treaty, the Southwest Tarbagatay Border Treaty of October 1883, and a further amendment to the Kashgar Border Treaty in June 1884. It is worth noting that negotiations for these treaties broached questions of citizenship jurisdiction in the border regions—for example the question of Kazakh identity during the negotiations for the Kota Border Treaty—and on account of China's insistence it was agreed that local people's sense of self-identity should be respected. Among the Kazakh Chagatai-language documents unearthed by Hu Xingliang in 1983 was a document titled "Letter on the Sixth Day of the Seventh Month of the Ninth Guangxu Year," Article C of which stipulated the conditions of Sino-Russian border division, with Articles E through H outlining in great detail "special ritual edicts for the Kazakh residents of these regions." Article E expressed "willingness for those Kazakh people who wish to reside in the lands of the Great Qing to do so; and for those who wish to return to Russian lands to do so. Kazakh peoples may make their own choice on this matter, without let or hindrance from the Great Qing or from Russia." Article F clarified that "the time frame for this freedom of movement is limited to one winter, and before the winter pastures." Article G elaborated that "thereafter, those who wish to return to their original jurisdiction of residence, or who have not yet but still wish to enter the other jurisdiction, in addition to escapees, will not be permitted any further movement. If captured, they will be dispatched to their respective jurisdictions and decapitated." In summary, Article H stipulated that "those crossing the border without identification will receive due punishment upon capture."[123] It is evident, then, that the Qing and Russian empires pursued cross-border relations with a clear awareness of the areas under each other's jurisdiction, the concept of differing allegiances among the peoples under their jurisdiction, and the importance of a mutually acceptable relationship in solving territorial and population questions. Mutual recognition of processes used to define borders and the inherent complications in applying them, along with the requirement that treaties be drafted in multiple languages, all evince a certain standard of objectivity that could be recognized by the two parties themselves, or a third party. Such standards are no different from those regarded as acceptable in treaties between nation-states.

The Qing empire's foreign relations were endowed with a ritual element, a central aspect of the so-called tributary relationship. What constitutes ritual protocol in this case refers to both moral / political and legal / economic aspects of the relationship; its inherent complexity depends on the historical complexity of the relationship in question. Owen Lattimore took the Great Wall as the center of his broader narrative of conditions in China's border regions; Western theorists have frequently evoked it as a basis for distinguishing ancient walled borders and frontiers, and modern national borders. However, if the demarcation between China and Russia during the seventeenth century is taken into account, the scale for comparison is not necessarily that of an empire with a nation-state but rather on the level of that between empires. The Sino-Russian demarcation treaties and the borders they established are different from perceptions of borders based on the Great Wall, and the concept of sovereignty underpinning them was scarcely different from that associated with modern states. Far from pursuing its foreign relations in an arbitrary manner, in terms of both tributary relations and interimperial contact, the Qing developed rich and complex ritual protocols and laws, along with techniques and procedures for negotiating with foreign powers. In order to adapt to constantly changing dynamics in internal and external relations, by enriching and developing ritual and legal standards, in the period before the Opium Wars, the Qing successfully managed both its regional tributary relationships and its treaty-based relationships with other empires. Questions of ritual protocol taken up in classical learning—especially where the classics stipulated appropriate standards for different kinds of internal and external relationships—included much thinking related to these questions. The *Spring and Autumn Annals* and *Rites of Zhou* were not just objects of research interest, but the basis for ritual guidance, dealing as they do with issues such as solving disputes over rights of inheritance, funerary procedures, and ritual conduct between monarchs and ministers, through to tributary relations, foreign affairs, and numerous other issues. Qing rulers consciously evoked the *Rites* and Confucian theory in dealing with border issues, forming a flexible institutional structure and normative theory.

Which factors, then, constituted the difference between interempire relations, or metropole-tributary state relations, and the emerging system of relations between nation-states? Firstly, early treaties between empires and ceremonial agreements in tributary relations were not based in any kind of "international law"; they were instead the product of mutual considerations of relative power and cultural exchange, or they were a corollary of domestic considerations. In interempire relations, treaties and accords between empires are themselves the product of the recognition of relative power and mutual norms. The treaty itself is not based in any normative legal system that somehow transcends domestic legal or ritual systems. Secondly, some political entities within the tributary system have certain characteristics of countries, such as Korea, Vietnam, and Ryukyu; others, such as the Qing-appointed tribal headsmen (*tusi*) in the Southwest, and the areas they administered, are perhaps not describable as countries. Whatever their situation, however, the national entities at this time differed in an important respect from the nation-states that arose out of the disintegration of empire, or through national self-determination. Treaties or accords within the tributary system were not documents based on formal equality between countries, but rather the products of specific ritual relations. From China's perspective, this system of rites takes China as its center and so is often regarded as a Sinocentric tributary system; from the perspective of other participants the tributary system, while hierarchical in nature, also included two-way interactions stemming from the interests of the other party, in spaces apart from China's own interpretations. Joseph Fletcher evokes the relationship between the Ming emperor and the Tibetan Dalai Lama to illustrate the possibility of reciprocal relations in the forms of expression and rhetorical strategies of tributary parties, showing that reciprocity was present not only in tributary relations along the maritime boundary, but also throughout tributary networks on the mainland.[124]

The tributary system was based on the premise that the countries party to it share a certain understanding of the world and an adherence to common ritual standards, with the traditional dynastic or imperial system providing support for this. As treaties between two empires, the Sino-Russian treaties of Nerchinsk and Kyakhta also illustrate another model of reciprocity in the tributary relationship. Covering the definition of borders, the management of fugitives crossing borders, and trade, these treaties were drafted in Latin with copies made in Russian and Manchu, and from the perspective of the Qing administration showed that equal treaty relations could in fact complement the hierarchical tributary system. In this sense, although the tribute system itself did not clearly distinguish between the international and the domestic, it nonetheless evinced clear differences in terms of specific practice; if this were not the case it would be difficult for us to explain the delimitation treaty between China and Russia. Takeshi Hamashita evokes the Sino-Japanese Xinwei Treaty (also known as the Treaty of Reconciliation) to show that even when China was in a dominant position, the treaty reflected the equal relationship between the two countries, and

> it can be said that the treaty already possessed aspects of equality found in modern international relations, such as the mutual recognition of consular jurisdiction. . . . However, it remains doubtful whether the aspects of equality in this treaty would be seen in the same way from both the

> Japanese and Chinese sides . . . because, according to China's understanding of the foreign or outside, the order for dealing with the foreign or outer (as with the domestic or inner) was based on a hierarchical order established in ritual (*li*), and the emperor occupied a fixed position in this order.[125]

Under the conditions of the nation-state becoming the dominant framework, if this ritual relationship is not understood as the basis for separatism, then it is shown to be the basis for indivisible sovereignty. However, the real problem is: compared to the multifarious aspects of the tributary system outlined above, the nation-state system was completely novel. Between the hierarchical nature of ritual protocol and an autonomy in the manner in which different parties interpret these relationships lies the real possibility of genuine equality, and this equality is rooted in historical circumstances that are decidedly different from those that gave rise to nation-states. It is therefore necessary to consider further: What are the political, economic, and cultural conditions under which tributary hierarchy and reciprocity find a balance, and how is this balance broken?

2. International Law and Sovereignty

One of the great global phenomena of the nineteenth century was Europe's signing of bilateral and multilateral treaties with political entities in Asia and Africa; by means of these treaties the latter's territory, sovereignty, and interests were transferred to European countries in a "legal" form. For a long time after a prevalent view among European scholars was that this process, being based on bilateral and multilateral treaties that assumed a legal form, was therefore "equal." But there are four questions that need to be asked here. First, considering that throughout the nineteenth century European jurists defined international law as that among civilized countries, and never recognized political entities in Asia and Africa as sovereign units of international law, how then should we reconcile this view with their practice of "legally transferring" the sovereignty, territory, and wealth of Asian and African countries? Second, as many countries and societies in Asia and Africa had their own laws and standards of ritual practice, what function did such indigenous laws and mores play during the period of "transferal"? Third, if the Asian, African, and European countries involved in this process do not share the same appreciation of a system and its normative functions, how is it that a "bilateral" or "multilateral" agreement or treaty can be "lawfully" produced? Fourth, regarding the process of concluding treaties between European powers and Asian countries such as China, as originally European laws were extended outside of Europe to create an historical premise for universalism in international law, how should we understand the "universalness" of the international order thus created? Is the nation-state and its sovereignty a product of universalism in European international law, or a product of war, exchange, and interaction between European countries and the rest of the world? As Onuma Yasuaki put it, to answer these kinds of questions it is essential to first consider a fundamental question: What is international law?[126]

European international law established sovereignty on the basis of mutual recognition between independent countries, thus posing a challenge to traditional concepts of sovereignty. In the sixteenth and seventeenth centuries, in the face of religious wars, Jean Bodin (1530–1596) and Thomas Hobbes (1588–1679) believed that unitary authority (that is, a political monism with national sovereignty at its center) was the best way to establish a political order. In this sense sovereignty implies first and foremost authoritative organization within a country and the scope of what it effectively controls; sovereignty is the power to create new laws to which subjects must adhere unconditionally. However, as sovereignty includes the exclusive authority to handle domestic affairs, it is bound to have relations with the outside. Under the influence of the Peace of Westphalia (1648), the concept of internal sovereignty was gradually supplanted by that of mutual recognition of sovereignty, shifting the concept of sovereign legitimacy from internal rule to external recognition, and demarcating imperial rule and decentralized fiefdoms in legal theory. From an historical perspective, international law emerged from a process of transition from the European absolutist state to the nation-state system. The emergence of European international law is often traced to the Dutch theologian Hugo Grotius's (1583–1645) seminal work *On the Law of War and Peace*, in which Grotius argued that international law first emerged in the Amphictyonic League (the "league of neighbors") and Rhodian Sea Law in ancient Greece; the notion of a Greek antecedent for international law gained currency among European legal scholars after

Grotius's text was consulted in the Treaty of Westphalia. The Peace of Westphalia is therefore regarded as the dividing line between a medieval world of overlapping authorities, and the emergence of nation-states. In the form of a treaty system, the sovereign state system transformed the traditional concept of sovereignty.

Before colonial national liberation movements redefined the parameters of European international law, the sovereign state was a concept mainly confined to European countries. When European countries signed treaties with countries in other regions, they also presupposed the existence of some notion of the sovereign state, but at this time the concept of sovereignty was still merely formalistic and ill fitting to describe actual relations between states. How then was this European archetype transformed into "international law"—a normative system also recognized outside of Europe? Firstly, the historical vision of the Enlightenment and the Enlightenment concept of natural law provided a universalist basis for the formalist concept of sovereignty, regarding international law as the result of humanitarianism in international relations—a realization of the apparent principles of humanity and mutual respect. In this regard it was a purely modern phenomenon.[127] This narrative archetype replaced substantively unequal relationships with formalistically reciprocal relationships, evoking reciprocal relations in opposition to the normative systems of other regions, such as the tributary system, thus providing an excuse for imperialist behavior. Secondly, since the nineteenth century, many invaded and colonized countries have adopted the aforementioned Enlightenment slogans of universal rights, and through anticolonial struggles and liberation movements realized national self-determination, lending substantive weight to the concept of sovereignty. In the latter sense the idea of "sovereignty" in the contemporary world can no longer be seen as simply the preserve of European international law; it has come to represent the historical experiences and achievements of anticolonialism and self-determination for repressed nations.

In nineteenth-century discourse, the treaties between European, Asian, and African countries were the product of European imperialist policy, with the international law purportedly giving a normative authority to these treaties being in fact nothing more than European international law. This becomes more clear when we turn our attention away from the universalist view of Enlightenment, and toward the then-mainstream narrative of Eurocentrism.

According to this more prevalent narrative, "international law" certainly does not include dialogue and deliberation with different cultures and societies on questions pertaining to international relations; it is a thoroughly "Western" or "European" conception of international law. As the British legal scholar T. J. Lawrence (1849–1919) put it in his study *The Principles of International Law:* "It [international law] grew up in Christian Europe, though some of its roots may be traced back to ancient Greece and ancient Rome. It has been adopted in modern times by all the civilized states of the earth."[128] This sentence makes two assumptions: first, that international law is not only the unique preserve of Europeans, but something that could be "adopted . . . by all the civilized states of the earth"; second, that international law is not the product of the nation-state, but was in fact part of the prevalent legal order in European classical antiquity. Lawrence also mentioned why, and how, countries outside of European territory adopted Western civilization. Other Western scholars have explicitly stated that international law is a product of modern Christianity, and that it was impossible for international law to have appeared in other civilizations such as China.[129] In his 1905 study *International Law,* Lassa Oppenheim (1858–1919) wrote: "International Law as a law between Sovereign and Equal States based on the common consent of these States is a product of modern Christian civilization, and may be said to be hardly four hundred years old."[130] In Oppenheim's view, then, international law emerged from the real circumstances of independent states and communities in seventeenth-century Europe. Medieval Europe was a patchwork of different political systems, its political territory staggered across various kinds of vassal relationships, asymmetrical sovereignty, and irregular enclaves. Formal diplomatic relations cannot arise from such circumstances because there is no consistent peer relationship between partners. The process by which the independent states emerged from the disintegration of empire is generally seen as a "modern" European development; so too is the evolution of intra-European political relations regarded as a modern process. The positivist concept of an international law marked by mutual recognition therefore has an inherent historical relationship with the Enlightenment concept of international law; together, the two formed a framework for international law based upon Christian civilization or the European Enlightenment.

Yet precisely for these reasons, this universalist international legal system was still only a regional one in the nineteenth century, with the vast majority of humanity living in regions outside of its purview. In fact, right up until 1844 Americans recognized the autonomy of Chinese judicial authority, albeit in a somewhat negative way; in that year Caleb Cushing, the American negotiator for the Sino-American Treaty of Wangxia, when dealing with an altercation between an American and a Chinese, refused to hand over the American and instead tried him according to US law. This case became a precedent for the legal trial of Americans accused by the Chinese. In the US Senate Documents for the year 1844–1845 (document number 58 of the 28th Congress), Cushing stated that:

> The United States ought not to concede to any foreign State, under any circumstances, jurisdiction over the life and liberty of any citizen of the United States, unless that foreign State be of our own family of nations; in a word, a Christian State.
>
> The States of Christendom are bound together by treaties, which confer mutual rights and prescribe reciprocal obligations. They acknowledge the authority of certain maxims and usages received among them by common consent, and called the law of nations, but which, not being acknowledged and observed by any of the Mohammedan or Pagan States, which occupy the greater part of the globe, is *in fact* only the international law of Christendom.[131]

Cushing acknowledged that China and other regions did not recognize the international law and regulations of Christian countries, but noted also that these non-Christian countries occupied most of the earth's land surface. Therefore, treaties and regulations between Christian countries were based on a distinct internal and external global relationship, that is, the distinction between the Christian world and the non-Christian (or pagan) world. The concept of extraterritoriality was based on this premise, and entailed an understanding of the boundaries of the legal norms of European Christian countries.

It was only during the long twentieth century that European international law gradually expanded from being a "European," or "Christian," international law to a fully global world-system. Two political conditions were central to this change. The first was the establishment of extensive treaty relationships between European nations and sovereign entities in other regions, which provided the historical conditions for the transformation of what were essentially unequal state relations into formally equal state relations. Second, following the expansion of colonialism and capitalism around the globe, anticolonial movements in Asia, Africa, and the Americas began to transform into national self-determination and nation-building movements, giving rise to a concept of mutually equal sovereign states as determined by European international law. Here it is worth mentioning the role of national liberation movements in the reconstructions of the concept of European sovereignty: it connects this concept with the traditional forms of sovereignty in various regions, so that we cannot completely equate the concept of sovereignty in the contemporary world with colonialism. Nor can the concept of sovereignty in the contemporary world be completely traced back to Westphalian sovereignty. The concept of sovereignty in the contemporary world may be viewed as the result of the kind of dual movement mentioned above.

Like the Sinocentric tributary system, Islamic law, and other normative legal systems, European international law from the sixteenth to eighteenth centuries was also a regionally realized universalist system. From this horizon, the new world order formed in the nineteenth and twentieth centuries is a special exception. This is especially clear if we compare the world maps included in Wei Yuan's *Gazetteer of the Maritime States,* which displayed latitude and longitude, with other traditional maps: the difference between these maps is the difference not between China and the world, but rather between *Tianxia* and the world as understood today. Without this particular image of the globe it would not have been possible for Kang Youwei to devise a longitude- and latitude-based Great Unity and a Confucian universalism. The conception of the world outlined in *The Great Unity* (*Datong shu*) demonstrates a vivid interconnectedness between transformations in knowledge and transformations in the blueprint of idealism. For Asian countries the implementation of European international law was not so much an agreement reached between states as it was the result of coercion by colonialist policies.

We may summarize European colonialism in the following two points: first, it required the establishment of a hegemonic international relationship structure based on international law, and on that basis promoted trade, colonization, and international relations that were beneficial to the colonizer; second, to achieve this goal it was essential to construct the target of exploitation as a formally equal subject, according to that subject's own criteria. The so-called Unequal Treaties encompassed both of these contradictory aspects: on the one hand both parties to the treaty were regarded as subjects, meaning that the dynasties, city-states, and various political entities were all sovereign states; on the other, the only purpose of regarding such political entities as sovereign states is to give them a legal prerequisite for the transfer of domestic interests. Recognized sovereignty in a relationship is by no means an indication that the relationship is one of equality between subjects; it is rather a legal condition for depriving peripheral regions of resources and labor by way of contractual agreement. Without the European colonial expansion that began at the end of the fifteenth century, and without the worldwide resistance to colonialism, and conflict and bloodshed among new European states, then there would never have been a transition from "European international law" to a more universalist concept of international law.

The treaties between China and the European powers after the Opium War violated China's sovereignty and dealt a ruthless blow to the Sinocentric tributary system and its norms. British aggression and manipulation in Thailand, Burma, and Tibet, France's control of Vietnam and Cambodia, and Russia's infiltration into Xinjiang and northeast China spelled the destruction of traditional tributary networks and encouraged separatism among the countries and regions formerly party to these networks. In the expansion of the European treaty system, the equality of state relations contained in the treaty system provided a theoretical premise for nationalism within the tributary area. It is worth noting that in terms of their psychological impact on scholar-officials during the late-Qing period, the 1884 Sino-French War and 1894–1895 Sino-Japanese War surpassed even the Opium War. This is because the latter two wars not only involved China, France, and Japan, but also engendered the total disintegration of the Chinese tributary system and its norms. The former involved China's relationship with the nearest tributary country, Vietnam, and the latter involved the status of Korea, the closest tributary country, and Japan with its special status within the tributary system. In 1882 the Korean Joseon dynasty concluded a trade treaty with Great Britain and the United States that caused anxiety for the Qing government. In the records of his assignment as an envoy to Korea, the Qing official Ma Jianzhong (1845–1900) wrote with fury about Korea concluding treaties with Britain, the United States, and other countries independently of Chinese involvement. Ma demanded that the Koreans clarify in their treaties that they are "a vassal state of China and as such adopt the title of vassal, and that they will not interfere with or hinder other states of vassal status."[132] During the Sino-French War the Chinese envoy Zheng Guanying chastised Siam for failing to pay tribute to China for a period of many years, while at the same time imposing head taxes (*rentou shui*) on Chinese traders in Siam; he hoped that Siam would come to the aid of Vietnam in the Sino-French War and undertake its proper responsibilities in the tributary system. It is therefore clear that European colonialist wars and infiltration in Asia were not isolated questions of victory and defeat, but rather questions of the collapse of the existing tributary system and its normative order.

The First Sino-Japanese War and the resulting Treaty of Shimonoseki were truly pivotal events in late-Qing intellectual history. First of all, the Sino-Japanese conflict began with Japanese aggression in Korea, and involved China as the protector of Korea. The loss of this war was a severe blow to China and spelled the end of the tributary system. Second, although Japan had a special position in the tributary relationship and enjoyed full sovereign state status, from the perspective of China's ritual order the Sino-Japanese War raised the question of whether the very symbolic integrity of the tributary system could be maintained. The conflict engendered a sense of impending crisis and systematic collapse. Following failures in the Sino-French War, the First Sino-Japanese War, and a series of other conflicts, China's position in the tributary system was shaken and the system itself collapsed. The concept of sovereignty based on the formal quality assumed in European international law provided new nationalist norms for the tributary countries in the region, as well as a means for Japan to conclude unequal treaties with tributary countries on the basis of formal equality, and a basis for its colonial wars and aggression against Asian countries. "European International Law" established itself as a universal law by directly concluding unequal treaties, and by goading tributary countries to break away from the tributary system, such that the universal norms inherent in the original tributary system could no longer be recognized as "universal norms." The collapse of the tributary system was therefore a product of interactions between internal and external pressures.

Between 1884 and 1895, although the Qing dynasty itself had not yet collapsed, China's imperial system was in a state of rapid disintegration. This collapse spelled the end of a system of long-standing, widely recognized norms for law and ritual protocol, and made evident a dire need to reconstruct Confucian universalism and its views of global order. European expansion, far from being confined to military and commercial affairs, saw the expansion of a new kind of system of states, of the regulatory norms governing this new system, and in legal knowledge about its workings. The Qing government therefore faced a crisis in terms of military and economic strength in comparison to other countries, while the very legitimacy of the moral and political system within which it had operated was fundamentally undermined. While the concept of equal sovereignty between nations in European international law gave legitimacy to European colonization and domination in Asia and elsewhere, there was also no new universalist vision that might transcend old tributary hierarchies. It was therefore impossible for China to resist and reject such hegemonic European law and its normative protocols. For these reasons, the problem of how to transcend a tributary model that had been proven unable to adapt to the age of imperialism became entwined with the problem of how to transcend a universalism rooted in European exceptionalism. The Qing government required a two-tiered system to deal with such a twofold problem: it needed on the one hand to create a model of statehood based on the inherent imperialist principles of nation-states; and, on the other hand, to recognize the identity and equal status of the sovereign tributary states with which it had traditionally dealt. The former required rationalizing and homogenizing the imperial center, while the latter called for modifying traditional tributary norms and China's hitherto self-centered outlook.

3. The *Spring and Autumn Annals*, *Rites of Zhou*, and International Law

For China, the Westphalian concept of sovereignty was intimately related to the realities of foreign interference and invasion, yet it was precisely due to this that China took noninterference in domestic affairs as the premise of recognition of sovereignty. Because treaty negotiations most often involved imperial states and political units that had not yet achieved recognition, the basic premise of treaties was to recognize substantive concepts of sovereignty based on internal political authority and enduring historical tradition.

Westphalian sovereignty was unable to completely explain the meaning of sovereignty in China (and also in other regions). Partly to allow China to abide by the protocols of international law, and partly to criticize racial prejudices in Western society, some missionaries assisting Western governments strived to build a bridge between sovereignty as recognized in international law, and the sources of rites and law in Chinese tradition. By incorporating Chinese sovereignty into the colonial world-system, their hope was to foster a new kind of international relationship. From the late nineteenth century, some missionaries and legal historians begun to evoke a novel concept of "international law in ancient China."

European missionaries had made great strides in introducing Chinese legal knowledge to the West since the eighteenth and nineteenth centuries. A prominent example is George Thomas Staunton (1781–1859), who, after accompanying his father on the Macartney Mission to China in 1792, at the age of just twelve, translated the *Da Qing Lüli* under the title *The Great Qing Legal Code.* Upon its publication in 1810 the *Edinburgh Review* gave Staunton's translation a glowing review, one that spoke to the influence of missionary culture and the Enlightenment tradition in spreading understanding of China's legal traditions in Europe. In his foreword to the 1894 work *Hanlin Papers: Essays on the History, Philosophy, and Religion of the Chinese,* W. A. P. Martin explained the aims of his research in terms of a connection between ancient China and the West, especially Rome and Greece. In addition to demonstrating the history of long-term interaction between ancient Europe and China, he evoked Max Müller's comparative philology, in which Müller had demonstrated an ethnic connection between Indians and Europeans, in an attempt to explain even earlier, and more fundamental, connections between the Chinese and Indo-European language families.[133] This was another kind of Yi-Xia relativism. In addition to essays on topics like "Plato and Confucius—a Coincidence," and "The Cartesian Philosophy before Descartes," Martin's work included essays on international law and diplomacy in ancient China.[134]

Ideas about the existence of international law in ancient China certainly had a degree of influence on European jurisprudence. This is illustrated in the University of Paris professor of law Louis Le Fur's (1870–1943) comments on international law as deriving from natural law; as such, international law could arise in any region, with China as no exception:

> [Ancient] China possessed many theories [of international law], of a kind that only arose in Europe some fifteen centuries later; for instance, the negation of absolute sovereignty, . . . the notion of the equality of States, . . . of solidarity between States, and attendant questions concerning the creation of special taxes, with a view of enabling States to come to the aid of neighboring states in times of famine, flood, earthquakes *et cetera.*
>
> Therefore, it may be necessary to make reservations regarding the inexistence of international law among some ancient people, and this is especially true for China, which from the point of view of international law was indeed highly advanced.[135]

The above views take advantage of the internal relationship between Confucian ritual protocol, moral and legal systems, and regulations. From various angles they all recognized principles for handling relations between states and the tributary system in the *Rites of Zhou, Spring and Autumn Annals,* and other classical texts.

The concept of an "international law in ancient China" is inconsistent with the prevalent logic among Western colonists in the decades after the Opium Wars. In 1864, twenty-four years after the first of those wars, William Alexander Parsons Martin (nom de plume Ding Weiliang, 1827–1916), a former student of the American jurist and diplomat Henry Wheaton then serving as head instructor at the School of Languages (*Tongwen guan*) in Beijing, translated *Elements of International Law* into Chinese under the title *Wanguo gongfa.* In 1858 Martin had served as interpreter for the American minister William B. Reed (1806–1876) during negotiations for the Treaty of Tianjin, and thereafter at discussions between Franco-British forces and the Manchu government after the Battle of Dagu Forts.[136] Because the United States did not directly take part in British military operations and supported Chinese sovereignty at this time, it was largely inevitable that Americans acted as translators and introducers of international law between China and the Western powers. Martin's time at the Imperial College coincided with Anson Burlingame's tenure as US minister to China (1861–1867), with the latter maintaining close rapport with the Qing imperial court. The Qing government and the broader Chinese literati did not understand that anti-Chinese sentiment was already on the rise in the United States—and that American missionaries' prejudice against Chinese culture was the cause of this sentiment. Coming after Lin Zexu's translation of the Swiss jurist Emmerich de Vattel's (1714–1767) *The Law of Nations* (*Le Droit des Gens*), Martin's translation of *Elements of International Law* was another major attempt at rendering international law into Chinese, even if the motivations behind each of these translations were markedly different. One of Martin's self-declared motives was a "notable paucity of such works in China"[137]—yet there were certainly deeper motives still. The first was practical: to establish norms for exchange between China and the West based on European international law. The second was conceptual, an attempt to generalize the principles of European natural law so that the Chinese might accept the legality of European "international law" as a universal principle.

4. W. A. P. Martin's *International Law in Ancient China*

However, seventeen years after translating *Elements of International Law*, W. A. P. Martin proposed the concept of international law in ancient China—completely changing his earlier assertions that there was a lack of legal texts in ancient China. Addressing the International Congress of Orientalists in Berlin in 1881, Martin gave a lengthy address titled "International Law in Ancient China," with reference to the work of Henry Wheaton, T. D. Woolsey, Johann Bluntschli, and other leading Western legal theorists. In 1883 the text of Martin's speech appeared in the journal *International Review*, and was later collected in the second series of the *Hanlin Papers*, along with his "Diplomacy in Ancient China." His address started with comments about the Sino-Western treaties:

> The recent treaties, by which China has been brought into closer relations with the nations of the West, and especially the establishment of intercourse by means of permanent embassies, have led Chinese statesmen to turn their attention to the subject of international law.
>
> For them, it is a new study, involving conceptions which it would hardly have been possible for their predecessors to form at any time in the course of the last two thousand years; though, as we shall endeavor to show, they possessed something answering to it in their earlier history.[138]

In his other address in this collection, "Foreign Relations in Ancient China," read before the Oriental Society of Peking, Martin opened in a very similar vein:

> International diplomacy is an art new to the Chinese, but one for which they evince marvelous aptitude. From the inquiry on which we are about to enter, it will, we think, be made apparent that with them it is rather the revival of a lost art,—an art in the creation of which they can claim the distinction of precedence over all existing nations.
>
> Under that famous dynasty of Chow, when sages were born, and when those books were produced which rule the thought of the empire, diplomacy took its rise. . . . Diplomacy may be defined as the art of conducting the intercourse of nations. It supposes the existence of states who carry on their intercourse on a footing of equality. This makes it evident why it flourished in the period referred to, and why it disappeared for two thousand years, to re-appear in our own day, like a river that, after flowing for a time underground, rises to the surface with an increase of volume. As etiquette is the outgrowth of a society of individuals, so diplomacy springs from a society of states. . . . The triumph of Ch'in, by which these numerous States, "discordant and belligerent," were swept from the arena, was the death-blow of diplomacy. The empire was thenceforth one and indivisible, from the desert of Tartary to the borders of Burmah, and from the foot of the Himalayas to the shores of the eastern sea. No rival, no equal was known to exist on the face of the globe. Envoys no longer sped on secret missions from court to court.[139]

The question was clear: as an empire uniting *Tianxia*, China had no diplomacy and no international law; like Robinson Crusoe on his deserted island, it was a lone monarch. It was only with the advent of the Opium Wars, after China signed a succession of treaties with Western countries, that it came "under the aegis of what may fairly be called the public law of the civilized world." "Such are the steps by which China has been led to accept intercourse on a footing of equality with nations which, for three centuries, she had been accustomed to class with her own tributaries."[140]

But by what means could the Chinese be led to enter such a system of mutually recognized international law among the "civilized countries," and by what rationale might the Chinese happily sign, affirm, and implement treaties between themselves, the United States, and the European countries? Addressing this point, Martin first outlined an historical narrative in which Chinese history could be incorporated into European history:

> Their [China's] modern history commences two centuries before the Christian era; and, for our purpose, it may be divided into three periods. The first, extending from the epoch of the Punic wars down to the discovery of the route to the Indies by the Cape of Good Hope; the second, comprehending three centuries and a half of restricted commercial intercourse; and the third, commencing with the so-called "opium war," in 1839, and covering the forty years of treaty relations.[141]

This was the process by which China had stepped into a system of nations of the same equal footing. In such an historical situation, then, how should Europeans treat China, and how ought the Chinese adapt to this new era? Martin pointed the way in two speeches delivered in Berlin and in Beijing. International law and diplomacy, he reasoned, were not so much forcibly imposed on China as part of a Chinese tradition that was being resurrected in a new time. In these speeches not only did Confucius become the foreign affairs minister for the state of Lu; a slew of political strategists from other ancient kingdoms assumed the roles of career diplomats. "Post-feudal Europe" and "pre-imperial China," despite being two thousand years and thousands of miles apart in time and space, take shape in Martin's narrative as if part of the self-same system of nations. As in almost all historical discourses in the late Qing, the era of unified empire under the Qin and Han dynasties is understood as an historical phenomenon in opposition to the "modern."

In Martin's view China had been a unified power for the past two thousand years, one lacking the two conditions necessary for the formation of international law and diplomacy between nations: the existence of independent countries, and exchange between them on an equal basis. This was to view China not as a country, but as a self-contained global system with nothing outside of it. Judging from unique and varied diplomatic practices during the Han, Tang, Song, Yuan, Ming, and Qing periods, however, Martin's argument lacked historical grounding. Yet Martin's argument may be used to illustrate another point, namely that China had a rich "state culture" prior to the Qin and Han, especially during the Eastern Zhou period. First, like the European states that emerged during the collapse of the Roman Empire, the enfeoffed states of the Zhou were the product of the division of empire and independent states. Second, these states were different from the barbarian tribes of the periphery of ancient Greece in that they inherited the civilization and laws of the former empire, thus emerging as civilized, equal states.[142] Third, although Martin did not explicitly state it as such, it runs throughout his thinking that the conflict and division during the Warring States period gave rise to an ideal system of states that possessed formal equality. Confucius regarded a situation in which rites and music were not directly anointed by the sovereign as a sign that "the rites are sure to be in ruins, . . . [and the] music is sure to collapse,"[143] while in the eyes of European and American writers this situation was precisely what nurtured a "rationalized" order.

In this sense Martin's interpretation of Chinese legal history was at once tactical and theoretical, and deeply rooted in the presuppositions of modern European rationalism. Max Weber placed the accounts of various missionaries whose works about China he had read in an even more complete rationalist perspective, such that in his *Religion of China* we can easily find political rationalism in Weber's descriptions of the warring states of the Zhou dynasty. Weber argued that, identical to the relationship between war and reason in Christian countries, political rationality during the Zhou was also attributed to competition, war, negotiation, alliances, and other phenomena of power relations between countries; he viewed the unity of the Zhou empire as primarily a "cultural unity," rather than in occasional gatherings of princes. The emperor as supreme priest had ritual privilege, but this did not prevent the occurrence of military mutiny. "Just as the Bishop in the Roman Empire claimed the chair in church councils, so the Chinese emperor or his legate claimed the chair in the princely assemblies; this is repeatedly mentioned in the [historical] Annals. At the time when great individual vassals were powerful *major-domos* (lord protectors) this claim was disregarded—in literary theory, a ritual offence. Such princely councils met repeatedly."[144] In this sense, the composition of the relationship between vassal states is similar to that between the Christian states, and is based on the special distinction between civilization and barbarism. Conflict between these civilized states became the root of political rationalism. As Weber explains:

> In practice, princely politics appeared instead to be a relentless struggle between great and small vassals. The sub-vassals sought every opportunity to gain independence. With single-mindedness the great princes awaited the opportunity to fall upon their neighbors so that the whole epoch, to judge from the *Annals,* was an age of unspeakably bloody wars. Yet the theory was not without significance *and was a rather important expression of cultural unity.* The representatives of this unity were the literati, i.e., the scriptural scholars whose services the princes utilized in *rationalizing* their administrations for power purposes just as the Indian princes used the Brahmans and occidental princes the Christian clerics. . . .
>
> Competition of the Warring States for political power caused the princes to initiate rational economic policies. The literati executed them. Shang Yang, a representative of the literati, is regarded as the creator of rational internal administration; another, Wei Yang, founded the rational state army system which was later to surpass all others.[145]

W. A. P. Martin's view can be understood in relation to Weber's: both were in fact looking at Chinese history from the perspective of nineteenth-century European rationalism, and within the framework of an empire / nation-state binary that is the product of rationalist concepts.

If European international law presupposes the concept of law "between civilized countries," then the law of the Zhou dynasty cannot apply to the category of "barbarians," and law between princely states is based on Yi-Xia and internal-external distinctions. Clearly Martin was successful in finding ties between the Zhou dynasty and the Roman Empire, principalities and European nation-states, providing a premise for applying the characteristics of "between civilized states" and "equality" to the nations of the Warring States period:

> Accordingly, if we turn to the history of the period, in quest of such an indigenous system, we shall find, if not the system itself, at least the evidence of its existence. We find, as we have said, a family of States, many of them as extensive as the great States of Western Europe, united by the ties of race, literature, and religion, carrying on an active intercourse, commercial and political, which, without some recognized *Jus gentium,*

> would have been impracticable. We find the interchange of embassies, with forms of courtesy, indicative of an elaborate civilization. We find treaties solemnly drawn up and deposited for safe keeping in a sacred place called *meng-fu.* We find a balance of power studied and practiced, leading to combinations to check the aggressions of the strong and to protect the rights of the weak. We find the rights of neutrals to a certain extent recognized and respected. Finally, we find a class of men devoted to diplomacy as a profession, though, to say the truth, their diplomacy was not unlike that which was practiced by the States of Italy in the days of Machiavelli.[146]

Through a careful reading of the *Analects, Mencius,* and numerous works from the main schools of thought as well as anecdotal histories—and most especially of the *Rites of Zhou*—Martin found traces of international law in references to the exchange of envoys, the signing and material preservation of treaties, laws of war and peace, the status of neutrality and its associated rights, the emergence of diplomacy as a profession, and other related phenomena. In light of his further discussion of this topic in other passages, we might include the following:

1. Territorial rights and borders: the land belonging to the twelve feudal lords of the Zhou empire is divided according to sacred heavenly protocol, which, being based on special astronomical and geographical principles, is sacrosanct;
2. The twelve fiefdoms and lesser principalities dependent on them: as multifarious and complex a political organization as that which existed in Germany under the "Holy Roman Empire," the chiefs of the twelve fiefdoms are ranked with respect to nobility in five orders, but all pay homage to the Son of Heaven;
3. Forming alliances: the coalitions of nations described in the *Spring and Autumn Annals* and Zuo commentary have the function of promoting friendly international relations, and constitute the basis of international law in this era;
4. International law as law between civilized nations: barbarous savages are not within the scope of governance defined by the *Rites of Zhou,* and are regarded as "our natural enemies";

5. Envoy system: there existed large numbers of diplomats who passed information between, and negotiated treaties among, the feudal lords.[147]

Martin also made a point of summarizing a series of "rules of war" found within classical texts:

1. The persons and property of noncombatants were required to be respected;
2. For war to be legitimate it must be declared, giving the enemy time to prepare his defense;
3. A war was not to be undertaken without a decent pretext (*shi chu you ming*);
4. The preservation of the balance of power was always recognized as a just cause for war;
5. All states have a right to their existence, and;
6. The right to maintain neutrality.

Having thus outlined his argument, Martin anticipated that the time had already arrived "when some Chinese Grotius will gather up these desultory hints as carefully as the illustrious Hollander did the traces of international usages in Greece and Italy."[148] Yet his analysis concedes that such a "Chinese Grotius" figure was none other than he himself: "enough remains, as we have shown, to prove that *the States of ancient China had a Law, written or unwritten, and more or less developed, which they recognized in peace and war.* The *Book of Rites* and the histories of the period attest this."[149]

But before excitedly concluding that ancient China had international law, we should first consider the circumstances and motivations that might lead one to assert its presence in the *Rites of Zhou, Spring and Autumn Annals,* and other ancient texts. In the first place, W. A. P. Martin's recognition of international law in Chinese history came after the Opium War, after the British and other European states evoked the rules of "international law" to force China to accept numerous unequal treaties. The question is: Why didn't Martin directly quote the *Rites,* the *Annals,* the *Comprehensive Rites of the Great Qing* (*Da Qing tongli*), or *Laws and Precedents of the Great Qing* (*Da Qing lüli*) when he agreed to undertake the translation of Lawrence's *Princi-*

ples of International Law? Furthermore, Martin was attentive to the works of Jesuit missionaries active in China during the Ming dynasty, praising in particular Matteo Ricci's translation style as one that "complemented, supplemented and transcended Confucian study"; that is, wrapping Western thought in Chinese garb and spreading universal truths to the Chinese people. In this sense, construing the *Rites* and other Chinese texts as "international law" is simply to recognize international law as itself a universal knowledge rooted in natural law, and to expand its scope to Asia and China. The purpose of discovering international law in ancient China, Martin wrote, was for the Chinese to find "[i]n their own records . . . usages, words, and ideas, corresponding to the terms of our modern international law; and they are by that fact the more disposed to accept the international code of Christendom, which it is no utopian vision to believe will one day become a bond of peace and justice between all the nations of the earth."[150] In this way the laws of ancient China could be drawn upon to repudiate contemporary Chinese law, and the logic of the Zhou dynasty and even the Warring States could be used to refute the logic behind two thousand years of imperial unity. In recognizing the presence of international law in China's history, Martin was by no means advocating that China's affairs should be handled according to Chinese methods, or that the general principles of international law should be amended to account for China's legal heritage. His aim was rather undoubtedly, having incorporated China into the European "law of nations" system, to naturalize and legitimize the coercive processes that had been imposed on China by theorizing certain "coincidences" between European and Chinese legal heritage.

The legitimacy of international law is based on two premises: the worldwide transformation of political entities into equal sovereign units, so as to realize the *inter*-national implications of law; and, universal recognition of the norms governing international relations by peoples all over the world. Understanding Martin's concept of so-called ancient Chinese international law from this perspective, we can clearly see the following substantive implications.

First of all, within the parameters of the feudal system of the Zhou dynasty, the relationships between vassal states / principalities may not be equated with relationships between sovereign states. According to feudal clan rules, these vassals all belong to the Zhou kings, who occupy the paramount position in accordance with patriarchal feudal principles, and thus are not sovereigns that are formally equal. That is to say, there is no implication that the subjects of treaties of allegiance are equal and sovereign units / countries according to the presumptions of "international law." Taking the concept of "diplomacy" as an example, during the first year of his reign (722 BCE) Duke Yin of Lu received a visit from the Earl of Cai. Of this visit, the Guliang commentary on the *Spring and Autumn Annals* (*Chunqiu Guliang zhuan*) recorded: "Princes within the imperial domains, unless by order from the Son of Heaven, do not go out and meet with other princes. Being not justified in his external intercourse, he is therefore not permitted to court."[151] As the Earl of Cai sent this envoy personally and without securing the order of the emperor, the text derisively emphasized that he merely "came" (*lai*)—rather than formally "attended the court" (*laichao*)—in contravention of ritual protocol. In the Guliang commentary, the term *waijiao* is used pejoratively to indicate an unsanctioned "external intercourse"—rather than the complimentary notion of "diplomacy" implied by the term in other contexts.[152]

Martin regarded the unified empire after the Qin and Han period as an interregnum in China's "diplomatic" tradition. This view needs to be questioned with regard to both the qualities of diplomacy in the Zhou dynasty, and whether or not diplomacy even existed after the Qing and Han. The historian Li Hu contends that it was precisely during the Han and Tang that China for the first time opened its doors to the outside world and pursued diplomatic relations, fostering diplomatic practices of true international significance. He divides the Han-Tang diplomatic system into three layers: One, diplomacy between the Central Plains empire of China proper and the Kushan, Dayuan, Kangju, and Parthian empires, in what would later be known as central and western Asia; the Roman Empire in what would later be Europe; the Sindhu, Hindu, Kanchipuram, and Shan empires in south Asia; and, the Korean, Japanese, and Indochinese empires of the eastern seas. Two, diplomacy between the Central Plains empire and surrounding ethnic-minority regimes, such as the Xiongnu during the Han dynasty, the Rongru and Göktürks during the Northern and Southern dynasties (420–589 CE), and the Uyghurs, Tibetans, Nanzhao, and Bohai during the Tang dynasty. Three, diplomatic relations between independent regimes within Chinese borders, such as those between countries during the Three Kingdoms period, the sixteen kingdoms of the Eastern Jin, and the Northern and Southern dynasties. According to Li's classification the pre-Qin period saw only the embryonic stirrings of ancient diplomacy, with more substantive establishment taking place during the Han and Tang, and the Song, Yuan, Ming, and Qing witnessing a continuous development and transformation of the ancient diplomatic system.[153]

Second, in the various legal responsibilities and obligations signed between the Qing and its neighboring countries, the two parties interpreted various provisions on trade, tributary protocols, and mutual trust under specific conditions, and in accordance with mutually recognized (traditional) ritual protocols. These relationships were understood in accordance with a definite regard to ritual hierarchy, but it did not follow that the parties involved had no expectation of reciprocity. The *Spring and Autumn Annals* and *Rites of Zhou,* and classical scholars' interpretations of them, both serve as a record of ancient decrees and regulations and offer clues about how they may be interpreted anew.

Third, in the context of Confucianism and Chinese history, actual historical relations are so critically important to these principles that once they become abstracted, the possibility of understanding them is lost. The "states" (*guo*) or "countries" (*bangguo*) mentioned in the *Spring and Autumn Annals, Rites of Zhou,* and other classics, and states as understood in European international law (that is, sovereign countries or nation-states), are two vastly different concepts that belong to different relational models. When W. A. P. Martin listed the apparent "principles of international law" in ancient Chinese classics he did so from a European international legal perspective, thereby drawing these principles out of their discursive historical context. The most important part of his interpretation of "international law in ancient China" is the universal application of the concepts of "state" (*guo*) and "international" (*guoji*); by Martin's reckoning, sovereign, formally equal states were apparently ubiquitous all throughout ancient and modern China and elsewhere, while the legal norms used to regulate the behavior of these normatively equal states are regarded as constant, universal laws permeating past and present Chinese and foreign contexts. Yet overseas colonization by European countries saw the proliferation of a new type of state system and its rules; without consciousness of this background Martin did not find it necessary to construe the "states" mentioned in the *Annals* and *Rites* as sovereign countries, and the relationships between ancient fiefdoms as international relations.

Martin regarded conflict and peace in the relations between the vassal states (*zhuhou guo*) of the Zhou period as characteristic of formally equal relations, and equated the "rites, music, and punitive expeditions" (*liyue zhengfa*) under the system of decentralized enfeoffment with nation-state relationships. This approach inevitably confused the protocols of ritual and music within the Zhou enfeoffment system with European international law, which are of course substantially different. A number of scholars researching the relationship between international legal terminology and Chinese terms have pointed out that the correlation of these words is the product of the translation process, rather than of any normative connections or correlations. For instance, W. A. P. Martin was hesitant to render the English word "right" into the Chinese *quanli,* as *quan* and *quanli* have pejorative associations with terms like "power" (*quanli*), "privilege" (*tequan*), and "influence" (*quanshi*), terms that have no inherent connection with international relations.[154] Martin's translations used a modified *quan* that encompassed a number of meanings, such as "rights of civil and criminal legislation," "rights of equality," "rights of property," "national rights," and "private rights." The legal historian Wang Jian writes: "*Quan* (and *quanli*) [as used in Martin's translation] does not always infer the 'rights' in the original text; indeed, Anglophone terms like 'authority,' 'sovereignty,' 'power,' and 'privileges' are rendered [throughout the text] as *quan* and *quanli.*"[155]

Here I would add that the terminology in the Gongyang exegeses of the *Spring and Autumn Annals* does in fact include a concept of "expedients" (as *quan*) in relations between "states" (*guo*), one that encompasses the idea of contingencies and trade-offs being made by subjects in specific situations. Such an adaptability and weighing of options indicates a reciprocal balancing between ritual principles, and the specific situations to which they are applied. In Confucian rites and law, the distinction between internal and external is a distinction of ritual; or, put another way, the internal and external are themselves constituted on the basis of ritual. Qing-dynasty Gongyang studies attempted to eliminate the strict distinction between internal-external and Yi-Xia, instead construing ritual relations as emanating from the internal out toward the external, questioning the absoluteness of ritual relations and paying attention to specific conditions and motives. Therefore, to apply international law is also to strike a balance between rites and expediency. Liu Fenglu (1776–1829) regarded the *Spring and Autumn Annals* as a Doctrine for All (*wanshi fa*), yet at its core was an emphasis on the relationship between right and wrong in specific situations—thus precluding the possibility for any certain principle from being seen as eternal. This is why New Text studies emphasized the dialectical relationship between classical standards (*jing*) and expedience (*quan*). In this sense, the concept of "expedience" is crucially different from that of rights in statutory law, and has none of natural law's connotations of natural rights. "Expedience" instead refers to a coordinated, flexible mode of action between the subject's will, the specific context in which he finds himself, and rites (*li*); it is impossible to "exercise expedience" outside of that specific context. The key difference between the *Spring and Autumn* exegeses of New Text studies and international law is that the latter regards certain principles and rules to be universal, while the former emphasizes judging right and wrong and settling cases in accordance with specific and changing historical relationships. In this way it rejects taking any one principle as a permanent and unchangeable statutory code.

5. "Power among Nations" (*Lieguo zhi shi*), the Nation-State, and Reconstructing the Confucian Worldview

While it is clear from the preceding discussion that the *Rites of Zhou* and *Spring and Autumn Annals* both deal with conflict and peaceful relations between rival feudal lords, these texts cannot be said to have a common grounding in legal principles with so-called international law. Why, then, did W. A. P. Martin conclude that there was such a similarity? In this section I will leave aside questions of what his own personal motivations may have been, and instead focus on the possible interpretations of Martin's writings. In a certain sense the *Rites of Zhou, Spring and Autumn Annals,* and international law all stipulate principles and rules that are malleable in accordance with a given situation; all contain the possibility for flexibility in their interpretation. When concluding treaties, the Qing adopted a practical approach to international law, making choices based on a considered balance between ritual principles and the situation at hand. It is worth noting that while W. A. P. Martin explicitly cited the *Spring and Autumn* as the international law code of ancient China, he nonetheless quoted primarily from the *Rites of*

Zhou as the source of early international law in explicating his argument. Why, then, did he choose to "evoke the *Rites* to make up for the deficiencies in the Gongyang commentary" in his exegesis on international law?[156] If his argumentation concerning specific clauses in the *Rites of Zhou* is characteristic of Gongyang studies, why did he mainly use the *Rites* to draw comparisons with European international law? And even more interestingly: as a foreign missionary Martin would not have been beholden to the traditional methodologies of classical studies—so why did similar interpretations appear in the discourses of other Qing classical scholars?

There are two basic facets to these questions. A central text in European international legal discourse, Grotius's *On the Law of War and Peace* distinguished between natural law and *jus gentium* (the law of nations); as distinct from the rational principles with which national law scholarship deals, it construed international law as the commonly observed principles by which nations abide in their interactions. This distinction between natural law and the law of nations has been widely recognized in international legal scholarship ever since Grotius's time, and clearly implied a corollary distinction between domestic and international law, whereby international relations became based on statutes. By contrast, among Chinese classics the *Spring and Autumn Annals* passes judgment on numerous matters in concise language, whereas the *Rites of Zhou* describes the official system of the Zhou imperial household and those of various other states during the Warring States period, reflecting Confucian political ideals. The Gongyang studies exegeses of the *Annals* necessarily related to a specific discursive context, resulting in highly convoluted interpretations, while the system of rules recorded in the *Rites* bore the characteristics of a statutory code. Commenting on Zhuang Cunyu's use of the *Rites* in his study *On the Rites of Zhou (Zhouguan ji)*, the historian Yang Xiangkui writes: "Using the *Rites* to make up the deficiencies of *Gongyang* can be said to be in the intellectual tradition of Liu Xin. . . . In politics Gongyang studies is only effectual in the area of theory; it is a philosophy of history rather than a political program and does not present a practical system of rules and regulations. It is simply empty theorizing. It is therefore necessary to borrow from the *Rites of Zhou*."[157] In real political practice the *Rites* presents a system of rites constantly open to interpretation (it is certainly not a statutory law), but it does resemble statutory law in form. Wang Mang's reforms during the Han dynasty and the Wang Anshi reforms of the Song dynasty were both based on the *Rites.* In the interpretations of Dong Zhongshu and other Gongyang scholars of the Qing period, the relations between countries described in the *Spring and Autumn* are understood to have included differentiation between China, Yi, and Di, but no international and external difference between them was perceived; the *Rites,* on the other hand, differentiated quite clearly between peoples, such as the Dian, Fu, Yi, and Fan. Therefore, it is more logical that Ding Weiliang would have misappropriated the *Rites* in discussion of modern international law.

Within classical studies more broadly, New Text studies can be divided into two different traditions: in the interpretation of the scholar Meng Wentong, the Lu studies (*Lu xue*) originating in the Han-dynasty Guliang commentary (of which Liao Ping was a notable exponent); and Qi studies (*Qi xue*), originating with the Gongyang commentary and drawing on the apocryphal texts (*weishu*) interpretations (Kang Youwei was a notable exponent of this tradition). The former tradition relied mainly on the *Rites of Zhou* in interpreting the classics.[158] The *Rites of Zhou* deals with a much larger area of territory than the "Royal Regulations" (*Wang zhi*) in the *Book of Rites,* and discusses territorial administration in much further detail; Liao Ping, therefore, following the Lu studies tradition, considered this grounds for regarding the *Rites of Zhou* as a global legal code.[159]

Empire-building and state-building overlapped during the Qing, which despite being an imperial dynasty had some characteristics of a sovereign state. In fact, ever since the Han and Tang dynasties the imperial system had embodied a relatively mature state form, with a sophisticated corpus of laws, rites, and institutions of diplomacy. In this case, evoking the Zhou system of enfeoffment to disparage Chinese traditions since the Qin and Han dynasties was a product of the historical perspective of modern European states. The self-perception of European nation-states was based on a dichotomous characterization of the Christian and Ottoman empires, and in this binary comparison between nation-states and empires, the notion of competitive relationships between countries is always privileged over the model of a unified empire. Yet in practice European international law was constantly violated in legal treaties, and is better thought of as a discourse of pragmatism in the realities of power relations rather than as a body of universally recognized principles. This is why European countries in the seventeenth and eighteenth centuries were able to find a suitable space between their own legal norms, and the ritual norms of the Qing dynasty, in concluding bilateral treaties.

Just as the ritual protocols dealing with internal affairs, tributary relationships, and external relationships in the *Rites of Zhou* and *Spring and Autumn Annals* may be used in the practice of international relations, international law is also often applied in domestic relations. When international law emerged in Germany its main purpose was not to establish a sovereign autonomy within the boundaries of the Holy Roman Empire, but to explicate principles of religious tolerance to resolve religious conflict within Germany. In the nineteenth century the Balkan states were concerned about the rights of ethnic minorities, which had been clearly stipulated in peace agreements following the Napoleonic Wars. In 1999 NATO intervened in the internal affairs of these sovereign states in accordance with international law, applying the Westphalian concept of sovereignty to resolve questions of national self-determination within nation-states. In this sense the history of international law is one of constant misappropriation, just as the *Rites of Zhou* and *Spring and Autumn Annals* have often been misappropriated. Therefore, the link between what W. A. P. Martin called "international law in ancient China" and "Chinese diplomacy," European "international law," and "modern diplomacy" warrants a more nuanced historical investigation.

The hegemony of European international law was a product of interactions between external and internal forces. Establishing connections between international law, the *Spring and Autumn Annals*, the *Rites of Zhou*, and Qing-dynasty rites and laws was an important strategy, in that it furnished the legitimization of international law in Chinese discourse with a traditional premise. However, the proliferation of a universalist view of law was just as much the result of conscious effort on the part of Chinese scholar-officials as it was the work of W. A. P. Martin and other missionary writers. Martin's misappropriation of the *Annals* and *Rites* in fact shared many similarities with the reinterpretation of the Confucian classics by New Text scholars in the late-Qing period, for instance: referring to Yi-Xia relativization in dealing with relationships between countries, and regarding countries hitherto regarded as Yi as civilized nations; making a connection between the stature of nations during the Spring and Autumn or Warring States period, and the European nation-state system, in such a way as to deny the imperial system of Grand Unification and its tributary relations; establishing diplomacy based on formal equality in place of hierarchical ritual relations; and evoking what was actually "ancient" to refute claims of the "ancientness" of the Qin and Han dynasties and even later, so as to subvert their authority and relevance.

It is therefore also problematic to regard the use of the *Spring and Autumn, Rites of Zhou,* or the *Comprehensive Rites of the Great Qing* in international relations as a direct projection of Western hegemony; Western hegemony was the product of multifarious interactions. On the one hand, in Qing history since the seventeenth century, these Confucian classics and legal systems were already being used to handle foreign affairs, so the tributary system itself had already adapted in response to more recent treaty relationships. On the other hand, restoring the meaning of the *Rites of Zhou* and the Gongyang commentary was an abiding preoccupation in a range of late-Qing thought, not an invention of missionaries like W. A. P. Martin. For instance, in his "Dong Zhongshu's Studies of the *Spring and Autumn Annals*" (*Chunqiu Dong shi xue*), Kang Youwei wrote:

> The *Spring and Autumn* loves the people, and warfare kills them. What pleasure does a noble man derive from killing what he loves? Thus in the case of prearranged battles, the *Spring and Autumn* [takes a] similar view, as it does in the case of the [Sinitic] states. When describing the state of Lu, it refers to [the other states as] external; when describing the Yi and Di peoples, it refers to [the other states] as internal. Compared with a deceitful assault, a prearranged battle is considered righteous. Compared with [the alternative of] not fighting, a prearranged battle is not righteous. Therefore no alliance is better than an alliance, and yet there are references to praiseworthy alliances. No battles are better than engaging in battle, and yet there are references to praiseworthy battles. Within an unrighteous act, righteousness may dwell. Within a righteous act, unrighteousness may dwell. When the terminology cannot be explicit, in every case [the explanation] rests with the guiding principles [of the *Spring and Autumn*]. How could one who lacks a refined mind and penetrating thoughts understand this![160]

Ever since the Han dynasty, the *Spring and Autumn Annals* had often been regarded as a book for prescribing punishments, dealing with conflicts between countries, and judging the nature of wars. Comparing the preceding quotation with the final paragraph of W. A. P. Martin's "International Law in Ancient China," the internal logic of Martin's definition of the *Annals* as "international law" is clear to see. Martin wrote:

> Of these histories, one was acknowledged as constituting in itself a kind of international code. I allude to the *Spring and Autumn Annals,* edited by Confucius, . . . Native authors affirm that the awards of praise and blame in that work, often in a single word, were accepted as judgements from which there was no appeal, and exercised a restraining influence more potent than that of armies and navies. Chinese statesmen have pointed out the analogy of their own country at that epoch with the political divisions of modern Europe. In their own records they find usages, words, and ideas, corresponding to the terms of our modern international law; and they are by that fact the more disposed to accept the international code of Christendom, which it is no utopian vision to believe will one day become a bond of peace and justice between all the nations of the earth.[161]

This is the general essence and motivation of Martin's misappropriating the *Rites of Zhou* and *Spring and Autumn Annals* in the context of European international law, and also of the movement in New Text studies toward attempting to relativize the traditional Yi-Xia category for the purposes of creating a reciprocal relationship structure. After the first Opium War, the Sino-British Treaty of Nanjing, and a series of subsequent wars and treaties, the "internal-external" categories as they had been understood in late-Qing society underwent fundamental change. No longer did they refer to internal and external relationships within the empire or in the tributary system, but rather to those between nation-states. China had to regard itself as a sovereign state in an era of competition between states, and Qing scholar-officials could not but ask themselves: did China's ritual and legal heritages in handling internal and external affairs still have significance and purpose?

Because China's worldview was based on relationships between center and periphery, inner and outer realms, it faced both a national and a broader "systemic" crisis. If the Opium Wars could be regarded as a conflict between two countries, the Sino-French War of 1884 and Sino-Japanese War of 1894–

1895 were evidence that center-periphery, internal-external categories had been shaken to their foundations, and that the tributary system and its ritual norms were declining toward collapse. The former inspired the Self-Strengthening Movement, centering on military and industrial development, while the latter provoked Qing scholar-officials to reconstruct a new worldview and recreate Confucian universalism. Kang Youwei's *Lectures from the Thatched Hut among Ten Thousand Trees* (*Wanmu caotang jiangyi*) has sections on "Amended Table on the Laws of Nations in the *Spring and Autumn*," "An Examination of Legal Precedents in the *Spring and Autumn*," and "An Examination of Legal and Political Precedents in the *Spring and Autumn*."[162] Thereafter Chinese concepts of international law were closely related to this line of thinking on international relations.[163] Kang Youwei clearly saw that traditional global networks were being supplanted in a new era of globalization, and attempted to synthesize and integrate diverse fields of knowledge on top of Confucianist foundations, in order to furnish this new era with norms and reference points for explanation. Late-Qing scholar-officials saw clearly that if Confucian thought could only establish a Doctrine for All (*wanshi fa*) within China, then China's only option in an era of competition among states would be to close off its borders and, even then, eventually lose the doctrinal and practical basis for gaining a foothold in this competition.[164] The most urgent task therefore was not to emphasize the uniqueness of Chinese tradition, but to establish anew a perception of the world that could take the fundamentals of Confucianism as the basis for a universalist worldview and international law. Without such an ideological atmosphere Confucianism would not be able to achieve its true transformation; in the absence of a universalism China would be compelled to submit to foreign rule.

Among the New Text scholars it was Liao Ping (1852–1932) who most strongly regarded the *Rites of Zhou* as a global "Doctrine for All" (*wanshi fa*). His approach to studying the classics underwent its third shift at around the time of the Hundred Days' Reform. In giving Confucius a new place in global relations Liao did not hesitate to change his position on classical learning, as he went from "revering the present and deriding the past" (*zunjin yigu*) to regarding Old Text learning as the orthodox school of Confucian theory. Emblematic of this turn are works including *New Meaning of the World (Diqiu xinyi), New Meaning of the Rites of Zhou (Zhouli xinyi), Geographic*

Charts of the Imperial Territories (Huangdi jiangyu tu), and *Treatise on Knowing the Sage (Zhisheng pian),* in which Liao developed a broad, geographically informed perspective in which land and territory formed the basis of Great Unity theory. "The distinguishing characteristic of the emperor from his earls is the size of the territory they control," Liao wrote, and therefore "to elucidate the learning on the Great Unity among the Three Kings and Five Emperors of Antiquity [*san huang wu di*], it is imperative to begin by discussing land. All natural conditions and social customs stem from the land; to learn how to rule, it is essential to first take stock of one's territories."[165] Liao Ping separated out the main branches of Confucian learning into a Minor Branch (*xiaotong*) covering China, and a Greater Branch (*datong*) encompassing the whole world, and characterized these two branches on the basis of geographical relationships. Classical works with a "small" (*xiao*) designation in the text, Liao reasoned, could be considered part of the Minor Branch—for instance the "Minor Odes of the Kingdom" ("Xiaoya"), and references to "small tributes from states" (*xiaogong*) in the *Book of Odes*; the hexagrams "slight restraint" (*xiaoxu*) and "slight excess" (*xiaoguo*) in the *Book of Changes*; "Rites by Dai the Younger" ("Xiao Dai li") in the *Book of Rites*; "Small Tranquility" (*xiaokang*) in the *Conveyance of Rites* (*Li yun*); and Zou Yan's (305–240 BCE) concept of the "Lesser Nine Provinces" (*xiao jiuzhou*). Classics and classical concepts containing the word "big" (*da*) could be considered part of the Greater Branch—including the discussions of "senior messengers" (*da xingren*) in the *Rites of Zhou*; the "Greater Odes of the Kingdom" ("Daya") in the *Book of Odes*; the hexagram "Great Restraint" (*daxu*) in the *Book of Changes*; the concept of "Great Union" (*datong*) in the *Conveyance of Rites*; and the "Great Nine Provinces" (*da jiuzhou*) in the work of Zou Yan.[166] The key indicators that distinguish the Minor and Greater Branches are, firstly, the relative size of the territory.[167] Liao Ping cited the lines about "small and large rank-tokens [of the States]" (*xiaoqiu daqiu*) from the *Book of Odes'* "Sacrificial Odes of the Shang" to compare the Lesser Nine Provinces and the Great Nine Provinces, using them as references for China and the world respectively. He also contended that some phrases in the *Book of Odes,* and the "Ministry of Education" section of the *Rites of Zhou,* were early examples of references to the theory of the Five Great Provinces (*wudazhou*),[168] and that theories of five continents in Western geography were derivations from and developments of Confucian classics. The second key indicator is the distinction between empty words (that is, the Confucian ideals in the Six Classics that had not yet been realized) and action (things in Chinese history that had already been put into practice). Liao Ping's classification held that the *Spring and Autumn* was the locus classicus for the Minor Branch of Confucian learning, and that the *Book of Rites's* "Royal Regulations" was the text that popularized the Minor Branch; while it was highly respected in New Text studies, the "Royal Regulations" was therefore a text only applicable within China itself. What Liao called the Greater Branch took the *Book of Documents* as its classical basis, was popularized by the *Rites of Zhou,* and included all the subgenres of classical and historical works; respected in Old Text but derided in New Text scholarship, the *Rites of Zhou* became an important text for the Greater Branch, and applicable to a much greater area encompassing the Great Nine Provinces (*dajiuzhou*) and linking the Chinese and Western worlds. In his *New Meaning of the Rites of Zhou,* Liao used Zheng Xuan's (127–200 CE) commentary to the *Rites of Zhou* to contend that the work was "a book of the Greater Branch [of learning] about the emperor [and a book for] and understanding All-under-Heaven."[169]

Why did Liao Ping suddenly reverse the strict demarcation of New Text and Old Text (*jingu*) that had characterized earlier phases of his classical studies, only now to define the *Rites of Zhou* as a classic of the Greater Branch of Confucian learning? In the postscript to his "Diagram of Imperial Territories in the *Rites of Zhou*" (*Shujing Zhouli Huangdi jiangyu tubiao*), Liao's disciple Huang Rong commented: "The Erudites (*boshi*) of the Western Han believed [the *Annals of Zhou*] was applicable on a small scale, but that on any larger scale it was as useless as saying nothing at all. At the end of the Western Han, when the *Annals of Zhou* was published, nobody in fact knew the significance of *biyong* [Imperial Academies during the Zhou dynasty] or *xunshou* [royal inspections]; their lackluster techniques were no match for a strong enemy. It may be concluded that [one] must be cultivated if they are to govern All-under-Heaven [*Tianxia*]."[170] Liao Ping believed that the Han-dynasty Erudites evoked the *Spring and Autumn* and "Royal Regulations" in their classical commentaries because Han borders suited the smaller scope of the Minor Branch, and that as this method was passed down over a long period of time, imperial practices were eventually forgotten. Learned scholars over the two thousand years since the Han dynasty were limited in their adherence to the "Tribute of Yu" ("Yugong") chapter of the *Book of Documents,* in turn reducing the Six Classics—formerly regarded as being global in their scope—to works applicable only to a Chinese context. What therefore can the *Rites of Zhou* amount to if not a law of nations of global application?[171] Liao Ping believed that Western intrusion provided precisely the conditions for the advent of the Great Unity, because it connected together the five continents: "The growing reach of the Bible in the world portends the foreign powers getting stronger by the day."[172] The preceding discussion has reorganized the traditional view of empire, one stemming from the interior outwards and reaching from close proximity to faraway lands, according to a new geographical and political framework. In his 1897 treatises *On the Five Levels of Vassal States* (*Wudeng fengguo shuo*), the *Examination of the Three, Five, and Nine Outer Territories, and the Nine Capitals* (*Sanfu wufu jiufu jiuji kao*), and other writings on ancient geographical and ethical categories, Liao Ping set out a new worldview integrating classical learning and Western geography. "The Nine Provinces of distant lands overseas are an extension of those [described in] the 'Tribute of Yu'; while formerly small territories have become larger their basic principles remain unchanged," Liao wrote. "Therefore the laws for overseas territories may all still be found in the 'Royal Regulations,' and there is no need to search elsewhere for any novel laws. What is different is similar, what is similar is different; what has been taken from or added to [the original laws found in the 'Royal Regulations'] over time is something that can be understood, the right path is close at hand."[173] When the geographical scope expanded from "China" to "the world," and "the benign guidance of the emperor extended from near to far and expanded in size,"[174] as Liao put it, the meanings of inner and outer, near, far, great and small were also transformed. As nonsensical as they may seem from the perspective of modern geography and European political theory, in the historical discursive context of a drastic reordering of global relations, Liao's views did have a certain cohesion and point to them.

As New Text classical scholars' understanding of history changed within the context of relations between the system of enfeoffment (*fengjian*) and the system of centralized administration (*junxian*), they came to regard conflict between sovereign states in the colonial era as analogous to competition between vassal states during the Spring and Autumn and Warring States periods. Liao Ping's contemporary Kang Youwei conceived of a new schema of global relations, principles, and management, based on the Confucian concept of Great Unity. From the perspective of classical studies, if the world cannot be explained in a framework of Confucianism, then Confucianism cannot serve as a "Universal Principle" or "law." How then did Kang Youwei incorporate global relations into the Three Sequences (*san tong*), and from there discuss world relations in light of the Three Ages (*san shi*), the internal-external, and other principles? Kang wrote that

> Confucius applied universal rules to the heavens, and this is no different from the thirty-six worlds of Heaven in Buddhism. There are three seasons in India, spring, summer and winter, each lasting four months, in Myanmar there are two seasons of six months each; in Russia the twelfth month is taken as the beginning of the year, while in England, France and elsewhere in Europe it is the eleventh month—all of [these differences] fall within the scope of Confucius's Three Sequences [*Santong*]. . . . The [relationship] between the states of Lu and Zhou during the Spring and Autumn times is analogous to that between Korea and our Qing today. From the dark robes of the Han period and the sky-blue official dress of the present dynasty, [all reflect] the influence of Confucius. European people all appreciate the color black, and also start each new day from the first ring of the bell. In many foreign countries white is used on festive occasions, while red is the color used in Russia.[175]

From the perspective of New Text classical studies, the question of a Great Union, or global order, could only be legitimate if global relations were to be incorporated into the Three Traditions. Kang Youwei's conception of the Great Union was accompanied by an approach on world relations that took the modern nation-state as the basic political form.[176] He evoked the states of the Spring and Autumn period as a metaphor for the pattern of nation-states in the modern world, and the Warring States to illustrate discord in the ritual order. "With the way the various nations of the world are today in conflict, it will be several hundreds of years before [the world] may enter the realm of Great Union," Kang wrote—and China was still very clearly in the "Age of Disorder" (*juluan shi*).[177] It was therefore imperative for China to assume a form other than an empire of the Grand Unification in its entry into this global structure:

> For the past two thousand years in China, laws have governed All-under-Heaven [*Tianxia*], but today the country has fallen into poverty and weakness and in fact faces imminent collapse. Considering the insufficiencies of our laws, this is only to be expected. Our ancestors have been governing the country for hundreds of years—who then would dare state that [their] laws are not viable? The laws of our empire derive from the Ming. . . . To govern the country today, [we must] be open and innovative in our governance of All-under-Heaven, not be conservative and inflexible; [we must] adopt a position of recognizing ourselves among the other countries, rather than unwaveringly following only our own doctrines on All-under-Heaven.[178]

This description revises the methodology of Zhuang Cunyu, Liu Fenglu, and others who relativized Yi-Xia to imply that China was in a state of transcendence from the Age of Approaching Peace to the Great Peace. The so-called competition among nations (*lieguo zhi zheng*) implied that the world was presently in a state of chaos, and that it was imperative to make law on the basis of a strict demarcation between the inner and outer, and to undertake militarized social mobilization. The strengthening (or homogenization) of internal relations was accompanied by an opposite trend, namely, a strict insistence on difference in external relations, yet the aim of such insistence on difference with regard to external groups was not to isolate China from the world. It was rather to establish China's sovereign status in the new world-system and to recognize the legitimacy of a formally equal and sovereign state system. Yet the concept of "competition among nations" illustrated the essence of enfeoffment relationships in ancient China, and also implied the characteristics of the nation-state system, as Kang stated: "The fiefs of the Warring States are analogous to [our] vassal states today; when [our country] is strong, they obey us, when we are in weakness they rebel."[179]

Under international law, sovereign states are the unit upon which international relations are based, presupposing strict internal and external relations and clearly demarcated borders as the basis of this order. Military affairs occupy a central position in this schema and are closely related to the clarification of sovereignty and borders. The unified Manchu-Han character of the Qing polity and the relativization of Yi-Xia in New Text scholarship legitimized the trend toward internal homogeneity, which in its turn gave a historical and theoretical basis for transforming empire into a unified sovereign state under new international conditions. The practice of banning the opium trade during the mid-Qing, the subsequent flurry of unequal treaties, and various movements aimed at resisting foreign aggression brought China into a treaty system characterized by mutual recognition of sovereignty. In an international relations system based on the power of the law, the only way for China to obtain equal status would have been to place itself in an environment of international disputes, and amend the original "methods of unification" to effect reform and become stronger. It was at this moment that the relationship between the *Spring and Autumn Annals* and international law was established.

Under the conditions described above, the internal-external view of traditional New Text studies would inevitably change. There were two aspects to this change: First, through the revitalization of internal-external relations within the empire, to shift the political structure of the internal regions to the original frontier regions, thereby transforming tributary relations into a political form of direct management, with a single source of political authority for the empire. Second, to place China as a whole within a new system of global maritime relations, thereby strictly distinguishing what constitutes internal and external in international relations, and transforming China from a diverse, multiethnic, and multicultural empire with no distinction between internal and external into a sovereign state. It is clear from these points that shifting perceptions of what constituted internal and external by no means meant that the traditional tributary system and its ritual systems lost their meaning. Rather, in the course of searching for the source of their own sovereignty, it was precisely with recourse to restoring the vision of the tributary system that Qing scholar-officials reconstructed the historical foundation of "China." This foundation was not located in "China" itself, but rather broadly in global relations. In order to maintain the internal cohesion of the empire and to resist external threats, the Qing government incorporated tribute, trade, and treaty relations into ritual relations. Thus, on the one hand, an erstwhile strict demarcation between the internal and external was replaced by subtle differences in etiquette, while on the other, more sophisticated institutional arrangements were needed for dealing with specific conflicts of interest, providing the conditions for establishing a more unified internal governmental order.

The title of Grotius's *Law of War and Peace* implies that international law deals with the laws of war and peace; it follows that military relations are an important component of relations between states. For Kang Youwei and Liao Ping, if Grotius's writings can be regarded as law to be used in governing competition between states, why couldn't the *Spring and Autumn Annals* be conceived as the basic law of the era of competition among nations, and the concepts of *liyun* (conveyance of rituals) and *datong* (the Great Union) in Confucius's thought as a Doctrine for All, transcending competition between states? Militarization had been a centerpiece of reform proposals from the Self-Strengthening Movement up until the 1898 Hundred Days' Reform, and ritual relations between the internal and external, Yi and Xia were first and foremost military relations. Kang Youwei stated: "Under the benevolent governance of the Three Dynasties [Xia, Shang, and Zhou] militias were established among the peasantry, and the Tang dynasty's prosperity and strength lay in the power of their civilian militias. In recent times the country has faced difficulties with the [Taiping] rebellion, yet the armies of all the provinces united and were able to defend their homelands and dedicate themselves to their country. As many countries around the world draw their armed forces from among the population, it would be right for our country to restore its ancient practices."[180] This attention to the Three Dynasties' "benevolence in establishing militias from among the peasantry," and the idea of recruiting soldiers from among the people, represents a rediscovery of the Confucian tradition. The ancient well-field system was an aspect of both ritual and military systems, as the historian Xu Zhongshu notes: "The original meaning of the term 'field' [*tian*] referred to military-led hunting expeditions [*tianlang*] and forming battle arrays [*zhanzhen*], yet after more than two thousand years most scholars are unaware of these connotations."[181] The Zhou-dynasty system of decentralized enfeoffment was in certain ways militarized in its basic structure.

Kang Youwei's effort to restore the military connotations of Three Dynasties decentralized enfeoffment, albeit under a new rubric of the nation-state, is crucial to understanding the mobilization mechanisms of nation-states. "When there is no Emperor, All-under-Heaven relies on an Uncrowned King [*suwang*],"[182] as Kang's description of the Uncrowned King put it. The tasks for which the Uncrowned King was responsible were those of All-under-Heaven, not just China, and in this sense Confucius's commentary on the Zhou institutions in the *Spring and Autumn Annals* is broadened to encompass global truths and laws, with Confucius the man serving as an unanointed "Law-Giving King." But while the works of both Confucius and Grotius may be considered as legal principles for the whole world, for Confucius's legislating, righteousness (*yi*) was the central concern, whereas Grotius's focus was on "precedents" (*li*); where Confucius deals with incontrovertible "Universal Principle" (*gongli*), Grotius emphases a "public law" (*gongfa*) arrived at via a process of contest. New Text scholars during the Qing period by turns both imbibed and criticized the *Rites of Zhou* and were flexible in their reinterpretations of the *Spring and Autumn Annals,* in part because they felt no need for a set of ready-made rules; what they sought was to deal with various public affairs in a changing historical environment, and to implement unprecedented reforms inspired by the classics.

The main conclusion to be drawn from the preceding analysis is that the conflict beginning in the mid-Qing period was one not only between states, but between world-systems and their attendant rules. The European contradistinction between empires and states, the historical imaginary of unity and conflict between states in the minds of Chinese scholar-officials, and the dualistic view of tributary and treaty systems in subsequent academic research were all intellectual expressions of this global conflict of rules. The intellectual reaction to this conflict was not limited to deliberations about military strategy but entailed wide-ranging self-reflection and reform: in the confrontation, interaction, and intermingling of two worldviews, taking the other and its norms as a reference point for rearranging oneself anew in a new global landscape; determining the relationship between oneself and other countries, and the internal reforms required to meet these changes. In this sense, modern Chinese nationalism had a clear international orientation from its very beginning. Once popular and revolutionary nationalism had replaced dynastic imperial nationalism and became mainstream, a transitioning imperial tradition merged with cosmopolitan orientations (in the thought of Kang Youwei and Liang Qichao) and internationalist orientations (in the thought of Sun Yat-sen and Mao Zedong), which make up the most important currents of nation-building in modern China. The cosmopolitan nature of this nationalism was totally different from Maruyama Masao's theory of "Revering the Sovereign and Expelling the Barbarians" discussed earlier in this chapter, which lack an international orientation. It is from here that we can now turn to discuss the intellectual orientation and problematic of which Kang Youwei was a representative figure: how to integrate the reform of an imperial system centered on monarchy with the future direction envisioned by Great Unity (*datong*) thought?

CHAPTER 8

Confucian Universalism and the Self-Transformation of Empire

Translated by CRAIG A. SMITH

> Confucius established a righteous design for All-under-Heaven (*Tianxia*) and for all the clans, and this is now a true design for the citizens. Therefore, there must be small differences in the rites and the laws. This is in keeping with the changing times.
>
> —KANG YOUWEI

I. Exegetical Classical Studies and Confucianism as "Doctrine for All"

Each generation of Confucian scholars developed an elaborate exegetical approach to the classics to align the major concerns of Confucian moral philosophy or expositions on meanings and principles (*yili*) with the specific fluctuations of their societies. They were thus able to organize new social relations within the framework offered by the classics and preserve Confucianism's position as a timeless "Doctrine for All" (*wanshi fa*). This effort to preserve the universal applicability of Confucianism was the very thing that led to the incessant changes to the defining characteristics of Confucianism. The standpoints of the Confucian scholars, the recurrent interaction between societal circumstances and the Confucian classics, random change, and elastic interpretation produced Confucian universalism. New Text learning developed an exceedingly complicated method for interpreting the classics in order to align with the establishment of the empire's system and the permutations of customs and rites, as well as the new interethnic relations that were a result of regional expansion. In the mid-Qing dynasty, but particularly coming to the fore in the late Qing, New Text learning operated as a means of exegesis of the classics. Through topics such as reform, the internal versus the external, the Three Ages (*san shi*), and the Three Sequences (*san tong*), New Text learning interpreted and harmonized the internal contradictions between the historical situation and the Confucian classics, thereby reconstructing Confucianism's universalism.

It is a common belief that filial piety on a familial level led to the innate cohesion of Confucian society. Max Weber believed that the solid connection between Confucianism and family ethics placed a form of barrier to "impersonal rationalization" for Confucianism.[1] That is, "It tended to tie the individual ever anew to his sib members and to bind him to the manner of the sib," thereby lacking the kind of intermediate link situated between ethics and the lives of a citizenry. This kind of family ethics is difficult to develop into a rationalization of the state and its correlating ethics.[2] However, Weber's argument was not intended as an accurate description of Confucian ethics, but rather as an internal understanding of the modernity of the Christian world. Throughout the ever-changing history of the imperial dynasties, Confucianism dealt with political, economic, and various social issues by means of its versatility, and it implemented its ethics into a series of social constructions that cannot be generalized as "the family." Confucianism's ethics and perspective on history have always been in flux, as it was entirely possible that the ideological factors that transcended blood lines and regional difference could be integrated into Confucianism. Therefore, an argument that limits Confucian ethics to familial ethics or within the parameters of blood-related communities is excessively narrow minded. Yet why did the European understanding of modernity that Weber generalized become the exact problem of the late-Qing reform movement?

With the tide of nationalism, both reformers and revolutionaries interpreted the predicaments they faced as limits to the relationships of blood and region, and they therefore connected their efforts to create a new form of social community with the process of breaking free from regional and blood connections. There are two points that need to be raised here: First, the universalism of European nationalism also transcended localized factors of region and blood, forming the "imagined community" that is the nation-state. Therefore, the difference in ethics described by Weber cannot be interpreted as a clash between Confucianism or Chinese tradition and Christianity or Western tradition but rather as an ethical clash that has emerged through the processes of nationalism, industrialization, and urbanization. Second, Confucianism was not at all lacking calls to construct an ethics that transcended the filial piety of the family. For example, within the broader context of Confucianism, Kang Youwei reconstructed the classical concept of All-under-Heaven, creating a kind of universalist Confucian ethics for the new structures of state politics. His Confucian universalism was not only characterized by its rising above familial ethics; it also included a refutation of the institution of the family. Kang did not at all see these two characteristics as constituting a deconstruction of the Confucian thought and religion that he believed in.

Since the Opium War, China's relationship with the outside world experienced profound change. Confucians were faced with the unavoidable challenge of redefining the position of the "Middle Kingdom" and the applicability of Confucian thought. Wei Yuan had a profound understanding of the "external" (*waibu*), yet he still attempted to characterize the "four continents" (*si zhou*) based upon their descriptions in the Buddhist classics. Liao Ping (1852–1932) inherited Wei's thought, and continued to maintain Confucian "universalism" through a geography of the traditional Nine Continents. Their efforts marked an orientation in sharp contrast to that of the exceedingly conservative officials and literati, yet they were almost identical to these conservatives in their maintaining of Confucian universalism: Reformists tried to incorporate new transformations and knowledge into the purview of Confucianism, and reconstructed Confucian universalism through the expansion of this purview; and conservatives, whether they disregarded new learning as no different from classical knowledge or condemned it as heresy, attempted to deal with the "external" by bringing it into the horizon of traditional knowledge, thereby maintaining the illusion of Confucian universalism. Even if universal knowledge was not "without external" (*wuwaide*), it had to affirm orthodoxy or legitimate succession (*zhengtong*). The development of New Text classical learning's perspective on the internal and external was inextricably linked with the transformation of interethnic relations, the extent of territories, and the construction of institutions. The breadth of Qing territory, including its inland areas and territorial waters, comprised a pluralistic empire with extremely complicated interethnic relations. It broke from the system of centralized administration (*junxian zhi*) that had characterized the Song and Ming dynasties, and, with extensive momentum, constructed a set of epistemic systems suitable for its changing territorial and interethnic relations. It built an epistemic view and imperial vision that was entirely unlike that of the Song-Ming period through such feats as the compilation of the *Emperor's Four Treasuries* (*Siku quanshu*), the flourishing of Qing New Text learning, the unprecedented development of geographical studies (*yudi xue*), and the diversity of its rites and laws. The interpretative strategies of New Text learning concerning the relativizing of the relationships of internal-external and Yi-Xia (foreigners and Chinese), as well as their manifestation in Qing geographical studies, clearly explained the influence that the imperial territory and interethnic relations exerted upon Confucianism. Without this interpretation of the Qing empire's relationship with the outside world it would have been impossible to maintain Confucianism's position as a "Doctrine for All."

However, in the seafaring age, the purview of empire that "is so great there is nothing external to it" (*zhida wuwai*) was no longer extant. The collapse of the so-called Celestial Empire was first and foremost a collapse of a worldview. No matter how vast the empire's purview, no matter how powerful the empire's hold over culture and ethnicity, the understanding of empire composed of a center and borderlands could not offer an episteme that regarded the entire world. How could it interpret those unique values found in the various religions that originated in west Asia and spread across the world? How could it interpret the magnificence of the Roman Empire, the warships of the British Empire, the advancements and prosperity of American society? Traditional Confucianism was entirely at odds to explain such things as the astonishing development of modern Europe, the internal and external complications of the tribute system, the unequivocal challenge of the British warships, the constant advances of science and technology, and the increasingly accurate knowledge of the outside world that accompanied these. The clear existence of this outside world provided a violent disturbance to the universality of the "Doctrine for All": "From this point on, China entered the world of competing nations and left behind the period of unification and isolation. These competing nations are connected and competitive on politics, technology, culture, and knowledge. Therefore, they may coexist. And on the occasion that one is unworthy, it will be defeated and destroyed through competition."[3] China was no longer All-under-Heaven, but was one country among many. This was Kang Youwei's summary of the age of nation-states.

The greatest issue for late-Qing Confucianism was that the Doctrine for All could not help but be reduced to outmoded local knowledge alongside the empire's new position as a marginal region in global capitalism. The Doctrine for All had been established through the intrinsic historical relations between Confucian rites and the "Middle Kingdom." Once the Middle Kingdom and its rites could no longer be abstracted as universal, once such concepts as customs, ethnic groups, and regions exceeded the extent of the Middle Kingdom and could no longer be brought within it, once the existence of the Middle Kingdom could no longer be self-demarcated but needed the external to demarcate and define it, then the universality and applicability of this Doctrine for All was inevitably faced with a crisis. When Liu Fenglu (1776–1829) said, "The central states (*Zhongguo*) are the new peripheral tribes (*Yi Di*)," he was returning the "Middle Kingdom" to the domain of rites through a confirmation of Qing legitimacy. However, for Kang Youwei, the issue was not whether or not the Confucian rites could be adjusted to fit a China that was defined by region or ethnicity, but that even if these could be made to fit, there was no way to establish the universal value of the Confucian rites.

Recognition of the "external," as well as the corresponding need for this recognition, comprised the intellectual content of this crisis. In 1864, the first Chinese translation of international or general law[4] was presented to Chinese readers through the work of missionaries. The title *Wanguo gongfa* (International Law of the Myriad States) clearly informed these readers: Firstly, international law transcends the universal standard of Chinese rites, laws, and principles; secondly, those Confucian classics and their rites, which had long been seen as the standard Doctrine for All, were now merely local knowledge, outdated, inapplicable, and nonuniversal; thirdly, in order to find a place in "the world," the "Middle Kingdom" should adhere to this universal international law and not the Doctrine for All of Confucianism. In the preceding series of humiliating treaties, both the Qing government and the scholar-officials had already come to understand the practical implications of this international law. Therefore, there existed fundamental differences of language in the traditional Confucian Doctrine for All and the efforts to reestablish Confucian universalism in the late Qing. Could Confucianism remain tenable if it was no longer a universal law?

The historical transformation mentioned above cannot simply be attributed to external forces but was intrinsically correlated with crises engendered by Qing society. The Taiping Rebellion (1850–1864), the Nian Rebellion (1851–1868), and the Dungan Revolt (1862–1877) operated in concert with foreign attacks, bringing change to the politics, territory, and interethnic relations of Qing society from different directions. Among these, the geographic breadth, long duration, and military scale of the Taiping Rebellion were on a scale rarely seen in the history of Chinese peasant wars. In order to suppress the rebellion, the Qing government was forced to elevate the positions of ethnic Han officials, giving them true military power. As the Taiping Heavenly Kingdom continued to develop, in the process of resisting the Taiping military attacks, what Philip A. Kuhn has called "local militarization" began to occur through the middle-Qing period. According to his explanation, this was not only a source of the decline of the Qing dynasty, but was also a source of transformation of the structures of traditional society, as this process led to the gentry losing their intermediary roles between state administration and local communities.[5]

The Taiping Rebellion had two major consequences for culture: Firstly, the rebellion created or disseminated a new form of universal episteme, one in opposition to that offered by Confucianism. Under the name of a religion that worshipped God, this movement syncretized various Western values, concepts of church and state, and China's traditional egalitarianism. Not only did it fiercely attack traditional knowledge and institutions at the level of ideology; it also raised such issues as land reform, gender equality, and racial oppression in both political theory and practice. Secondly, it called into question the legitimacy of Manchu rule through an enormous mobilization, once again raising the necessity of the divisions between internal-external and Yi-Xia. Actually, the opposition to the political system of empire came from the trend toward a quasi nationalism within the paradigm of the universalism of a God-worshipping religion. While New Text learning attempted to relativize both internal-external and Yi-Xia under the premise of recognition of the political system of empire, the Taiping Heavenly Kingdom utilized strong language that referred to the Manchus as such as "Qing Demons" (*Qing yao*) to reconstruct clear contrasts in these same binaries of internal-external and Yi-Xia, combining with the ideas on the Chinese-foreign distinction (*Yi-Xia zhi bian*) that were popular in the late Ming and early Qing. This was also the first hint of a rising tide of nationalism that also foreshadowed the appearance of unprecedented ideas about equality. The Taiping Heavenly Kingdom's questioning of the legitimacy of Manchu rule developed within the frameworks of clear-cut interethnic relations, which led to Han nationalism, and of a God-worshipping religion, which led to the concept of equality for all. The failure of this movement did not bring about the end of anti-Manchu nationalism. Not long after the rebellion, the late-Qing nationalist movement once again brought forth waves of anti-Manchu sentiments, integrating them with much more complicated and diversified forms of universal knowledge, including understandings of nation-state, science and technology, industrialization, and knowledge of the future to come. While the Taiping Heavenly Kingdom turned to understandings of God, values of universal equality, new land policies, and new perspectives on ethnicity, late-Qing nationalism turned to the model of nation-state politics, including the values of freedom, equality, and republicanism. Both movements shook the foundations of Confucianism's "Doctrine for All" with an unprecedented fury.

The transformational stages of Qing Gongyang studies were closely connected to the process described above: The thinkers Zhuang Cunyu (1719–1788) and Liu Fenglu represented stages in which New Text learning emphasized the dynasty's legitimacy and its relations with the outside world. It was through this that the "internal-external paradigm" (*nei-wai li*) and "deriding hereditary postings" (*ji shiqing*) became important subjects for classical studies. In the periods of expansion, represented by Gong Zizhen (1792–1841) and Wei Yuan, along with the internal-external paradigm expanding from an issue of ethnicities within the empire to an issue of the management of the empire's border regions, geographic studies (*yudi xue*) and other studies on public affairs were organized into the scope of classical studies. This was a tremendous break from the original framework of classical studies. In the ascendant period of Gongyang studies, personified by Kang Youwei and Liao Ping, Eurocentric "global knowledge" was just becoming the dominant form of knowledge. Should Confucianism lack the framework necessary to incorporate this "global knowledge," and should the reformers be unable to design blueprints for the reforms based on this new Confucian universalism, then Confucianism would be unable to escape from its fate of decline.

Each of the above-mentioned periods both permeated the others and can be differentiated from the others, clearly indicating the interactions between the internal changes of classical studies and the historical context. Scholars generally see the beginnings of late-Qing New Text learning around 1884, but they are not consistent in their periodization.[6] Looking at classical studies, Liao Ping's 1886 book *A Study of New Text and Old Text Learning* (*Jin gu xuekao*) was evenly divided between New and Old Text learning in his study of the "Royal Regulations" (*wang zhi*) and the *Rites of Zhou* (*Zhou li*). Within the context of Qing classical studies, this was an important demarcation. Liao Ping was developing this line of thought around 1884. Looking at this from a broader perspective, the following phenomena mark the changes in late-Qing classical studies: Following the ascension of such topics as "reform" (*gai zhi*), the Three Ages (*san shi*), and *datong* (Great Unity),[7] such topics as internal-external and deriding hereditary postings became respectively less popular. As this happened, dynastic reform and a global vision became topics for reflection. This process propelled Qing New Text learning to transform from a legitimizing theory for the dynasty toward a theory of political change for the dynasty, from a perspective on the Chinese Doctrine for All to one of universal truths for the entire world, and finally into a critical rethinking of the nation-state, the colonial system, and the process of industrialization as fundamental keys in global relations. Therefore, late-Qing Confucian universalism was not merely focused upon issues for China but concerned issues of global governance.

II. *Datong*'s Triumph Over the State and the State's Progression to *Datong*

The significance of late-Qing Confucianism, especially New Text learning, can only be truly understood within the context of the reconstruction of Confucian universalism. Kang Youwei appeared at the end of the Qing dynasty's period of New Text learning, and he is the most important figure to consider in this reconstruction. His works were prominent in two separate intellectual developments: the effort for political reform to strengthen the country, and the utopianism of *datong*. The former permeated his political practice, while the latter permeated all aspects of his thinking on this practice and its discourse. Kang had a clear understanding of the political structures that lay behind the expansion of the strength of the West's maritime trade and military power. Therefore, just like Wei Yuan, he attempted to copy the logic of the West's perspective on wealth and power in response to the historical challenges that accompanied the Maritime Age. This led to his efforts to reconstruct the greatness of "China" by calling for the centralization of monarchical power, setting Confucius and Confucianism as foundations for the nation, reforming the political system, and pushing for industrialization and militarization.

Kang Youwei's recognition of China and its crisis was formulated in accordance with the paradigm of the Great Qing Empire and its tribute system. At the end of 1888, in "First Memorial to the Qing Emperor" (*shang Qingdi diyi shu*), Kang lamented that state affairs were beleaguered and crisis ridden, imploring the emperor to issue edicts identifying those accountable and immediately enact measures for governance. The anxiety of his register should be understood in the context of the regional political setting:

> The Ryukyu Kingdom has been destroyed; Annam lost; Burma ruined. Our wings have been stripped away, and our belly and heart might be next. Japan has plans for Korea and has sights on Jilin from the east. The British are opening up Tibet, and eyeing Sichuan and Yunnan from the west. The Russians are constructing a railway from the north as they approach Mukden [Shenyang]. In the south, the French incite rebellions in order to take territory in Yunnan, Guangxi, and Guangdong. And the missionaries and secret societies cause chaos among the interior areas from Gansu to the mouth of the Yangtze River.[8]

These events were accompanied by other disasters—floods, windstorms, and earthquakes—as one calamity gave way to another. Kang found the soldiers in the capital to be weak, the merchants poor. Traditional customs were in decline, while law and stability had given way to disorder and chaos.[9] The events narrated a centripetal movement: The first portents of crisis manifested at the outer edge of the tributary system: Ryukyu, Annam, Burma, Korea, and Tibet, before continuing into Sichuan, Yunnan, Guangxi, and Guangdong. To reverse the decline of the Middle Kingdom, Kang Youwei requested that reforms be implemented in all areas of governance, including the military, justice, taxation, duty, religion, education, and the civil service. Kang believed that ending Cixi's regency was of paramount importance in the quest to bring about political transformation. Imitating the West to maintain the legal authority of China and the stability of its interior, he wanted to make the Guangxu Emperor (r. 1875–1908) the political center; reconstruct the political, economic, and military systems; and launch a movement to bring about real political reform and national strengthening. To push forward such a movement, he needed to first disprove the legitimacy of the existing system. Works such as *Forged Classics of the Wang Mang Period* (*Xin xue wei jing kao*) and *Explorations of the Reforms Advocated by Confucius* (*Kongzi gai zhi kao*) developed this "revolutionary movement" from within Confucianism in accordance with this need. Their publication indicated the transformation of New Text learning from theory on the legitimacy of the empire to theory on political reform. And the central issue of political reform was the state system. Therefore, discourse on political reform was actually a kind of theorizing of the state.

While implementing the above-mentioned political practices, Kang Youwei was always concerned with a more distant issue: the question of how to transcend the state and its borders in order to create the world of *datong.* With his vision set on *datong,* Kang regarded the sovereign state as a source of disorder, rejecting capitalism—as well as its political structure of the nation-state and its historical foundations of naval and military strength—through a worldview centered upon *datong.* This is an approach to the world that is closely related to what Weber discussed as the "pacifist character of Confucianism."[10] Why did Kang Youwei actively devote himself to the practice of state-building on the one hand while focusing on the issue of overthrowing the very idea of the country and pontificating on the world that would follow on the other hand? There are a number of reasons to consider:

Firstly, the West's creation and dissemination of "universalism" was intimately connected to the expansion of European trade and its system of colonialism. This "universal knowledge" reduced knowledge found in any other locale to local knowledge, thereby encapsulating the particular nature of the self within this expression. Therefore, resistance against invasion or infiltration by such countries as Britain, France, Japan, or Russia was inevitably resistance against this "universalist knowledge." Kang Youwei attempted to create a universal ethics based in global relations, and this ethics relegated

Eurocentric universalism to European particularism. In *The Book of Great Unity* (*Datong shu*), Kang did not discuss the issue of specific political structures by focusing on the nation-state or empire. Rather, he discussed the issue of "world governance" by making the global his unit of analysis. The essence of his argument was a rethinking of the global political framework through a negation of the nation-state and its systems. He renarrativized global history through the Three Ages of Gongyang studies, thus allowing the applicable scope of New Text learning to break free from the category of "China."

Secondly, Kang Youwei turned to the Confucian "Doctrine for All" belief of the previous era, refusing to see Confucianism, especially New Text learning, as a form of knowledge restricted to a specific locale or specific society, and instead attempting to extend it to a form of adaptable universal knowledge. He attributed the new situation that arose in the nineteenth century to the transition from the age of the Grand Unification (*da yitong*) to an age of war between the various states, and the specialty of Confucian universalism was none other than overcoming this age to rebuild the system of the Grand Unification. Just like the early New Text learning, this new Confucian universalism was a theoretical argument for overcoming the logic of one type of state (of enfeoffed lords) and providing justification for another type of state (the unified empire). European colonialism expanded power through the conceptualization of both the nation-state and industrialization; more importantly it established the rules of interaction for the universal knowledge trinity of individualism-rationalism-nationalism with the social community. For Kang, the logic of *datong* and the logic of "strengthening the country" were in conflict because the reasoning behind the movement toward strengthening China was a resistance against colonialism, yet the fundamental logic that it adhered to acquiesced to the above-described reiteration and affirmation of universalism. This entailed a reproduction of the European path of colonialism and industrialization, confronting the invasion and challenges posed by a foreign enemy through the self-construction of a "sovereign state." As the final goal of Confucian universalism was not the simple replication of the logic of wealth and power, but rather entailed a critique of this process, it was necessary to offer a vision and theoretical logic for the transcendence of this. In this respect, efforts to reconstruct Confucian universalism inevitably led to deliberations on and critique of the relationship between capitalism and the system of nation-states and colonies.

Thirdly, this vision of *datong* was essentially established upon a negation of the state and its authoritarian tendencies. The critique levelled by this *datong* logic against the state was established upon the conceptualization of a kind of historical evolution—the transformation from traditional society to the state and from the state to *datong*. The existence of the state was a necessary antecedent for the overthrow of the state. In this respect, the logic of *datong* not only endorsed the antecedent of the worldview of "strengthening the country"; it also accommodated the knowledge systems of individualism, rationalism, and nationalism. Therefore, within *datong* there resided both tension and contradiction: Its adversarial relationships with both the real world and its episteme formed an intrinsic tension. We can rudimentarily summarize this as a conflict between a logic of the transcendence of modernity (displayed as the ideal of *datong* and its vision of putting the world to order) and a logic of modernity (as a theory of political reform with the goal of strengthening the country). The intrinsic thesis of Kang Youwei's thought lay in neither the logic of *datong* nor the logic of wealth and power, but in the lasting entanglement, contradiction, and disjunction between the transcendence of the nation-state found in the logic of *datong* and the desire for wealth and power found in the logic of strengthening the country. To a certain degree, the rise of the discourse on the "Three Ages" and Confucius as the "Uncrowned King" (*suwang*), and their replacement of other themes as the main topics for this period's New Text learning, were closely connected to the efforts to bridge the above-mentioned contradiction. The importance of the early relativization of internal and external by New Text learning was still prominent at this time, but the focus had somewhat drifted. It had moved from a discussion of the relationships between internal-external and Yi-Xia to discussions on how such things as the age of Great Peace (*taiping*) in the *Spring and Autumn Annals,* "far and near, great or small, all are one," as well as on "the unity of the Earth." The Great Peace or a unified Earth was an example of internal-external in a new historical context, in which the relationships of internal-external and Yi-Xia had been thoroughly relativized.

Kang's Confucian universalism was built upon a background of scientific cosmology, differentiating it from earlier manifestations of Confucianism. It was a scientific theory on "Heaven and humanity" (*Tian ren*). The question he raised was clear: Should it not be possible to reaffirm the universal value of Confucianism, then how could one grasp the contemporary changes in the world or offer a basis for political reform? In other words, if we cannot explain contemporary changes, then how can we maintain the universalism of Confucianism? On this level, the logic of political reform was reliant upon the universal nature of Confucian knowledge. And Confucian universalism was established on the universal nature of connections with the relations of ritual propriety. Therefore, if one views the rites-centric Confucian knowledge system as a kind of universal knowledge, then one must establish universal connections between rites and the world, thereby also subverting the intrinsic or historical connection between the Confucian rites and China. In this respect, the universal nature of the rites indicates the following: Firstly, the rites are a kind of universal world relation (thereby relaxing the absolute relationship between China and the rites); secondly, the rites must change and take in new elements. (Venerating the rites does not mean adhering to the old ways. This therefore relaxed the relationship between the universal nature of the rites and specific codes of rites, such as the *Rites of Zhou* [*Zhou li*].) The two factors mentioned above lead us to a basic conclusion: The "rites" defined by the phrase "rites are established by the ruler and serve as a model for all" are the rites of the current ruler, and therefore particular. And what the sage saw as human nature or "change in accord with the people" were the rites of the "Uncrowned King" and therefore universal.[11]

The universal nature of knowledge or rites did not originate from authoritative practice but from an a priori and abstract essence. Kang Youwei applied an abstract method, separating the historical relationship between Confucian rites and the practice of the sage ruler, thereby endowing rites or humaneness (*ren*) with a natural quality. He explained:

> Confucius said, "For setting the rulers at peace and making the people orderly, nothing compares to the rites." Rites are the natural human way and a necessity in the laws of nature. From time immortal, the various and foolish barbarian and primitive tribes all remained unable to dispose of the rites. . . . Although ancient times are different from the present, China and the external tribes are different, and the rites cultivate good and eliminate evil. Their principles are the same.[12]

The rites were not a system decreed by orders or the practice of past monarchs but were "the natural human way, and a necessity in the laws of nature," indicating that they were the highest of principles, similar to the universal natural laws. I call this conceptualization of rites the idea of "natural rite" (*ziran li*). And on this idea of "natural rite" Kang also formulated the idea of "natural humaneness" (*ziran ren*). The rites were predicated upon a universal and natural human nature (*benxing*), and this universal nature was an idea of "humaneness" that transcended China, or even humanity itself. Humaneness is not merely the essence of human morality, but the essence of the entire world and universe. The difference between humans and animals is not a difference of humaneness but a difference of intelligence.

In this respect, Kang Youwei returned to the logic of a universal Heavenly Principle (*tianli*) found in Song-dynasty Neo-Confucianism: Humaneness and rites were a priori and objective knowledge that transcended cultural difference and historical experience. In the 1886 *Kang's Essays on the Internal and External* (*Kangzi neiwai pian*), he explained:

> Not only humans but all beings have humaneness, righteousness (*yi*), and rites. Crows[13] repaying their parents, or goats kneeling for their mother's milk, is humaneness. Oxen and horses may be large, but they never bite humans. This too is humaneness. Deer call to each other and ants walk in file. This is rites. Dogs' guarding of their masters is righteousness. Only intelligence (*zhi*) is missing. And thus they are content to be beasts. Only humans have intelligence. They can make food and drink, architecture, and clothing. They can learn the rites and music, politics, writings, the trappings of life. They can put order to human ethics (*lunchang*) and refine them through moral philosophy (*yili*). All of these stem from intelligence. . . . Therefore, only with intelligence can we create the myriad principles by which we live. . . . Humaneness is common to all of humanity in Heaven and on Earth.[14]

Humaneness is a common quality for all in the universe, but intelligence is a unique product of human culture. In other works that he wrote during the same period, such as *The Complete Book of Practical Principles and International Law* (*Shili gongfa quanshu*), this differentiation of Confucian humaneness and intelligence transformed into a differentiation between Universal Principle (*gongli*) and international law (*gongfa*).

Within the discourse of political reform, Confucian universalism had to be accommodated with Confucian pragmatism. The notion of "natural humaneness" or "natural rites" provided Confucian universalism with the framework of a theory but was unable to resolve the historical challenges faced by Confucianism. As a system of universal knowledge, Confucianism had to adapt to changes developed through history and offer an explanation of the real issues and clear changes that were evident in people's lives. For example, with the entire globe coming together and with China "learning superior foreign techniques," how should one learn from the past? To achieve this, Kang Youwei brought the wearing of Western clothes, the adoption of Western institutions, and the study of Western learning into discourse on the Three Sequences, thereby maintaining the universal meaning of the Three Sequences by nullifying their historicity. Also, the relativizing of the Yi and Xia was used for interethnic relations across the empire, but in the age of the nation-state, if the internal and external could not be strictly demarcated, how could the independence of the nation be maintained and how could China gain wealth and power? The relativization of internal and external did not apply to the principle of sovereignty in international relations, and making the internal-external rule absolute had potential to lead to internal divisions within the empire. In response to these questions, Kang integrated the relativization of internal and external with maintaining the unity and entirety of the empire: The external was no longer defined by its distance within the order of rites, but was rather a new center of the world now defined by its mutual differentiation from the internal. A further example: Following the elevation of position for Han officials, the need for political will to be expressed by "deriding hereditary postings" diminished significantly. Therefore, it was not the derisions of these hereditary official postings but universal laws (that adjusted according to changing times) that brought about transformations of these institutions and constituted the central themes of Kang's theory. Following this logic, the position of topics such as the "internal-external paradigm" and "deriding hereditary postings" declined in importance in New Text learning while topics such as the Three Ages, *datong,* and the Grand Unification were elevated to become fundamental narrative frameworks and principles. In Kang Youwei's thought, the position of discourse on the Three Ages was particularly important. It provided a narrative framework for the entirety of world history while also providing a historical basis and future direction for reform.

Late-Qing Confucian universalism, as well as the arguments for it, originated from the expansion of empire. More precisely, it originated from a feeling of despair, an anxiety over the inability to ascertain the "external" (*waibu*) and "internal" (*neibu*). That which was normally formulated as the "external" had permeated into the "internal," and there existed a rising dread that the Doctrine for All was being diminished into a local knowledge. Had there been no understanding of the limitations on aspects of the "Middle Kingdom" such as geography, institutions, economy, and culture, had there been no recognition of non-Confucian writings, knowledge, and beliefs—that is to say, had there not been a clear appreciation of the "external"—then there would not have existed any impetus toward a reconstruction of Confucian universalism. I will only raise one example of this. In his *Catalogue of Japanese Books* (*Riben shumu zhi*), Kang Youwei stated:

> In the field of politics, nothing can surpass our Six Classics. Investigating the reasons behind the strength of the West, I found concord with the truths of our doctrines. The origins of the West's self-strengthening are to be found in educating the people (*jiaomin*), nurturing the people (*yangmin*), protecting the people (*baomin*), according with the feelings of the people (*tong minqi*), and sharing in the pleasures of the people. On this, both the appreciation of the people in the *Spring and Autumn Annals* (*Chunqiu*) and the *Mencius* have stated that [to be a ruler] "one should be one with the people, taking pleasures in their pleasures and suffering in their suffering. One should protect the people to be a king." How could we know that after suffering through the hegemons of the Qin and the Yuan, China no longer follows the true meanings of the sages of old? The rites have been lost and must be recovered in the wild areas. Foreign countries have captured the spirit of our classical teachings. When Confucius composed the *Spring and Autumn Annals*, [he showed that] when the foreign Yi entered into China, they followed the ways of China. When the Rong-Di took China, the Chinese themselves became the Yi. The meaning and principles of the *Spring and Autumn Annals* favor virtue above all. The Japanese did not emphasize this enough. However, by translating the books of the West, they were able to take care

> of their people and self-strengthen. Japan's political path is worthy of emulation.[15]

Kang Youwei interpreted the strength and prosperity of the West as a result of political knowledge, and this knowledge happened to be exactly the same as the theories contained in the Six Classics. In accordance with the principle that "when the Yi enter into China, they become Chinese," emulating the political practice of the West and Japan was entirely in line with the teachings passed down from the sages. Therefore, to concede that China had limitations, or to acknowledge the knowledge of the external, was in no way equivalent to conceding that Confucianism was nothing more than a form of local or particular knowledge. Quite the opposite, through an elastic—or perhaps even forced—interpretation, knowledge from the external was taken into the "internal" of classical learning. This entirely concurs with the aim of New Text learning to see differences between external tribes and China as differences of virtue (*de*) rather than geography (or the relativization of the Yi-Xia).[16] For the Confucian, the universal meaning found in the Six Classics was not at all affected by the overlapping of the internal and external or the problem that "the rites are lost and must be recovered from those in the wild areas." The issue at stake was how to interpret its meaning, and Confucianism had already incorporated the principle and exegetical strategy of adaptation.

In this age of competition between states, the position of the Doctrine for All was dependent upon the incorporation of Western knowledge into Confucianism. Were the doctrines of Confucius not specifically designed to interpret the historical relations of the Age of Disorder? In Kang's writing, "linking the Three Sequences" (*tong santong*), the philosophical traditions of the Xia, Shang, and Zhou dynasties, became the basis from the classics for learning from state and religious knowledge from the West; "Unfolding the Three Ages" (*zhang sanshi*) became a Universal Principle (*gongli*) in line with the evolution of the entire human race. The division of internal and external was resituated as the division between China and the West, and this required the original concept of no division between the internal and external to become the basis for discourse on "pan-nationalism" (*daminzuzhuyi*) or the "multi-nation-state" (*duoyuande minzu-guojia*). Kang published his *Catalogue of Japanese Books* in 1898, and it is likely that he composed the book before November 15, 1897.[17] His intellectual practice of reconstructing Confucian universalism started very early on and cannot be limited to one work. We can see Kang summarizing historical developments and bringing together the traces of all sorts of knowledge under the frameworks of theories such as *datong* and the Three Ages in books such as *The Book of Great Unity, Forged Classics of the Wang Mang Period,* and *Explorations of the Reforms Advocated by Confucius,* although they were produced at different times in his life.

Kang Youwei's representative contributions to New Text learning are *Forged Classics of the Wang Mang Period* (1891), *Explorations of the Reforms Advocated by Confucius* (1892–1898), and *Dong Zhongshu's Annotations of the Spring and Autumn Annals* (1893–1897). The first two were seminal books that burst onto the scene during the reform movement. Without a new Confucian universalism to serve as a base, how could Kang Youwei have launched such an intellectual storm?[18] A unique element of late-Qing New Text learning was this reconstruction of Confucian universalism against a global backdrop, which led to the creation of a classical learning contextualized in the changes of the modern world. It was this classical learning that provided the bases for the theories of reform. *The Book of Great Unity* appeared much later and is seldom seen as a work on the classics, but it was this book that synthesized various natural sciences and social sciences. It developed several basic teachings of Confucianism and the Three Ages development theory of New Text learning into a criterion by which Kang described the framework of the world and judged the world, thereby reviving Confucian universalism to the highest degree. With both the world and the universe as a backdrop, Kang's Confucian universalism sought to find a place for China in the world and the universe, as well as the path that it could take. Within the horizon of this Confucian universalism, the Middle Kingdom was no longer synonymous with universal rites, nor was it a vast and limitless empire. Rather it was a country stuck in the past among a world of innumerable states, a decrepit wooden boat sailing along on a vast sea of iron warships competing for power. Even if Confucianism was a Doctrine for All, in this boundless world, its effectiveness was questionable. Kang Youwei asked: If the Six Classics were the Doctrine for All, why were all the seamen aboard this vast vessel of China all blind as bats? If the only way for China to escape from this predicament was to submit to the logic of war espoused by these competing states, then, in addition to proposing rationalization through the theory of reform in order to submit to the logic of the changing world, was Confucianism capable of becoming a universal knowledge that could rethink the entire process?

Therefore, in order to restore its universalism, it was necessary to break Confucianism free from its unitary connection to the Middle Kingdom while simultaneously resituating the Middle Kingdom in the world, thereby reconstructing the relationship between China and the world. On the one hand, as Confucianism gradually lost its hold over the world, it became more and more necessary to construct or revive the universalist scope by which it could incorporate the elusive external or exceptional into familiar realms of experience; on the other hand, the more Confucians became familiar with the realities of the world, the more they needed to reconstruct the internal into a united and efficacious whole through reform, which would inevitably make the Middle Kingdom regress—"with no division between the internal and external"—to a sovereign unit with a clearly demarcated external. It was from within this paradox that Kang Youwei launched his sweeping vision of *datong.* Unlike Zhuang Cunyu and Liu Fenglu, Kang did not persist in a redefinition of the Middle Kingdom but was rather fixated upon a reordering of the world. Confucianism's universal nature would no longer purely rest upon the concept of the Middle Kingdom but would instead be a universal rule for the world and the universe, just like the science and political science of the West. This was a softening of the intrinsic relationship between Confucianism and the Middle Kingdom.

III. Writing *The Book of Great Unity* and Kang Youwei's Early Understanding of Universal Principle

Identifying the publication period of *The Book of Great Unity,* as well as its relationship with Kang Youwei's other writings, is an important issue. Sections 1 and 2 appeared in 1913 editions of the journal *Unbearable* (*Bu ren*), while a more complete version of the manuscript was not published until 1935, eight years after the author's death. In "Preface to *The Book of Great Unity,*" written in 1919, Kang clearly indicates that he wrote the book in 1884.[19] In the first section of the book, "Entering the World and Seeing Universal Suffering: Introduction," there is a record of Kang hiding in his Tranquility Pavilion (Danru Lou) to write *The Book of Great Unity* and escape from the Sino-French War of 1884.[20] However, the most extant explanation of the writing can be found under "Guangxu Year 10" (1884) in *An Autochronology of the Life of Mr. Kang of Nanhai* (*Kang Nanhai zibian nianpu*):

> Through spring and summer, I stayed in Banxiang Alley, in the south of the city. With the encroachment of the French troops, Canton was under military lockdown, so I returned to Danru Lou in the countryside. In those early days, I read the writings of the Song, the Yuan, the Ming, and the *Topically Arranged Conversations of Master Zhu* (*Zhuzi yulei*). At Haizhuang and Hualin temples, I read many of the Buddhist classics, originating from the works of the Brahman. I devoured the four studies. I took up mathematics and drifted through books on Western learning. Through autumn and winter, I passed my days alone in Danru Lou. Cut off from all, I only bent my head to my books and only raised it in contemplation. Through to the twelfth month, my understanding deepened day after day. I understood that large and small have the same principle by witnessing the power of a microscope, which, through magnification in the thousands and tens of thousands, makes a flea unto the wheel of a cart, or an ant unto an elephant. I understood that the principle of fast and slow are the same, as an electric light can send a ray hundreds of thousands of *li* in one second. Knowing that beyond large there is still larger and beneath small there is still smaller, that one can whittle the small down by degrees but never fully exhaust it, and that each thing is different, I saw that we must start from the disorder of the original *qi* (*yuanqi*) to advance to the Age of the Great Peace. . . . The way takes original *qi* as essence (*ti*) and yin-yang as function (*yong*). Hence, we have the eight systems: *Qi* can be both hot and cold; power can be an attractive or repulsive force; matter can be solid or liquid; shape can be square or round; light can be bright or dark; sound can be clear or muddled; bodies can be male or female; spirits can be ethereal (*hun*) or corporeal (*po*). It is so in the realm of all the heavens, all the celestial bodies, the realm of Earth, the corporeal realm, the ethereal realm, the realm of our blood cells, and the unified world. All the universe is understood through courage (*yong*), rites (*li*), righteousness (*yi*), wisdom (*zhi*), humaneness (*ren*), and the five stages (*wu yun*). The sages are expounded upon through the Three Sequences, the future is advanced through the Three Ages. But we must give primacy to

> humaneness, we must revere Heaven and accord with Earth, in order to unify the planet by uniting the countries, races, and religions.[21]

According to evidence presented by Kang Youwei, he wrote *The Book of Great Unity* in 1884.

However, many scholars remain unconvinced by this evidence: The preface was written for a 1919 reprint of the first and second sections of the book. Kang finished the *Autochronology* in 1899 (although he wrote the sections before "Guangxu Year 21" in 1895. Also, *The Book of Great Unity* was one of Kang's most important works. Why did the texts quoted above never mention *The Book of Great Unity* by name? And even more damning counterevidence: The *Book* mentions numerous events that occurred after 1884, including the Hague Convention of 1899, Chen Qiangqiu's death in 1895, and the establishment of the Anti-Footbinding Society by Kang Guangren in 1897. Kang Youwei concealed Liao Ping's influence on *Forged Classics of the Wang Mang Period* and *Explorations of the Reforms Advocated by Confucius*. He also rewrote the 1898 memorials to the emperor based on changing political needs. These facts have added to people's doubts about whether Kang actually wrote the book when he said he did. For example, Tang Zhijun has cited the above evidence to argue that Kang provided this information on writing the book because he had falsified the time that he wrote it. Not only does Tang refute the notion that Kang wrote *The Book of Great Unity* in 1884; on the basis of his argument that Liang Qichao made edits to the preface, he goes on to argue that the book was written in 1902.[22]

It is simply a fact that many events found in *The Book of Great Unity* occurred after 1884, but this does not indicate that Kang did not write some of the book in an 1884 draft. There are a few points in need of clarification. Firstly, it is common for authors to make repeated revisions and amendments to their drafts. One cannot conclude that Kang Youwei did not begin writing *The Book of Great Unity* in 1884 simply because events in the final edition occurred after this date. Nor can one prove that the 1902 draft was the earliest. The first talk of 1902 came from Liang Qichao, but Liang himself has provided entirely contradictory and much more conclusive evidence. In *Autobiography at Thirty*, he stated: "In 1891, when I was nineteen, Mr. Kang began giving lectures at the Wanmu Caotang ('The Thatched Hut Among Ten Thousand Trees') in the Changxing area of Guangzhou. . . . Our teacher would also write books such as *Universal Principle* (*Gongli tong*) and *Study of the Great Unity* (*Datong xue*), engaging the students in deep deliberations and disputations. At such times, I would sit at the back, listening but never debating, understanding much of the greatness of his words but remaining unable to apply them."[23] Liang Qichao began studying with Kang Youwei in 1890. In Kang's *Autochronology*, the heading "Guangxu Year 16, Gengyin (1890), thirty-three years of age" contains text matching the above description by Liang Qichao. In the 1901 *Biography of Kang Youwei*, Liang Qichao wrote: "Our teacher expounded upon Confucius's true meanings in *The Meaning of the Three Ages in the Spring and Autumn* (*Chunqiu sanshi yi*) and *The Theory of Great Unity* (*Datong xueshuo*). This will be the second phase in the restoration of the Confucian religion." Liang also provided a systematic introduction to the *Theory of Great Unity.* At the very least, this indicates that Kang wrote the earliest draft of *The Book of Great Unity* before 1901. The argument that *The Book of Great Unity* was written in 1902 is untenable.[24] In *An Introduction to Qing-Dynasty Learning* (*Qingdai xueshu gailun*), Liang Qichao reaffirmed that a draft of *The Book of Great Unity* was extant during the period of the Wanmu Caotang, explaining,

> Although [Kang] Youwei wrote this book, it was a secret, not shown to others, and never used for teaching. He referred to our time as the Age of Disorder, in which we can only work toward lesser tranquility (*xiaokang*) and not even hope for the Great Unity (*datong*). To do so would drive All-under-Heaven into scourges equal to the floods and great beasts. Among his students, only Chen Qianqiu and Liang Qichao were given the pleasure of reading this book, and they were eager to reveal some of its content to others. Youwei would not agree to this, but he was not capable of disallowing it. Soon all the students of the Wanmu Caotang were discussing the Great Unity.[25]

From this we can infer that at least a partial draft of *The Book of Great Unity* was already in existence before 1890.

Another reason that has been cited to reject the proposal that Kang wrote *The Book of Great Unity* in 1884 is that "Kang Youwei began citing from the New Text school in 1889–1890, after he discovered Liao Ping. In order to express that his work was 'in no way plagiarism, in no way an imitation,' Kang had to say that he wrote it before 1889."[26] Furthermore, in *Autochronology,* Guangxu Year 6 (1880), he wrote: "Throughout this year, I studied the classics and Gongyang studies. I wrote a book on He Shaogong [Xiu], which I called *A Rectification of Mr. He (He-shi jiuzheng).* Soon after, I realized it was folly and burned it."[27] This indicates that Kang was critical of New Text learning early on. However, one cannot assume that Kang Youwei would reject Gongyang thought around 1884 because he had come into contact with New Text learning in 1880 and "realized it was folly." Liang Qichao had said: "Early on, Youwei was enthralled by the *Rites of Zhou* and endeavored to channel it when composing *The Comprehensive Meaning of Education* (*Jiaoxue tongyi*). Later, he read all of Liao Ping's books and forgot everything that he had learned before." It is true that Kang was enthralled with the *Rites of Zhou* in his early years. According to recordings in the *Autochronology,* in Guangxu Year 4 (1878) Kang attacked Old Text classics such as the *Rites of Zhou, Yili, Erya,* and *Shuowen,* two years before his attack on He Xiu when he "realized it was folly." The books mentioned by Liang, *The Comprehensive Meaning of Politics* (*Zhengxue tong yi*) and *The Comprehensive Meaning of Education,* were written in 1886. In Kang's *Bibliography of Books from the Wanmu Caotang* (*Wanmu Caotang congshu mulu*), he notes them as "early works, no longer extant." These manuscripts have been rediscovered and were published in volume 1 of the *Kang Youwei Complete Works* (*Kang Youwei Quanji*). These works include clear traces of New Text learning, but Liang Qichao's account was inaccurate. I will try to explain this below.

Firstly, while *The Comprehensive Meaning of Education* extolled the Duke of Zhou's statecraft, it also levelled unequivocal criticism of the tradition of Old Text learning through the theory of Three Ages and an orientation that overlapped with New Text learning. Kang hoped to maintain the universal value of Confucius's theories through comprehensive reform (*tong bian*). Liao Ping was the first to critique and divide New and Old Text through the "Royal Regulations" and the *Rites of Zhou,* but such studies have been common since Zhuang Cunyu and Liu Fenglu utilized the *Rites of Zhou* under the name of New Text scholars. Considering this, even if, as Liang Qichao has stated, Kang Youwei's *The Comprehensive Meaning of Education* was permeated with the *Rites of Zhou,* this in no way indicates that Kang did not have a New Text perspective at that time. In the chapter titled "From Today: 13" (*Congjin dishisan*), Kang remarked: "Frivolous writing on Confucius or

Mencius is not acceptable, so how is it that today scholars engage in such frivolous discussions of Xu and Zheng?" He expressed exasperation with Old Text scholars' veneration of Xu Shen and Zheng Xuan. Then in "Respecting Zhuzi: 14" (*Cun Zhu dishisi*) Kang clearly expressed that the disorder in Confucianism began with Liu Xin (50 BCE–23 CE) and instead voiced his respect for Zhu Xi, who had mastered all the classics. This shows that in 1886 Kang Youwei already had a defined opinion on Liu Xin's forgery of the classics.[28] In "Spring and Autumn: 11" (*Chunqiu dishiyi*), his respect for the ways of Gongyang studies is evident: Belittling the Zuo commentary and favoring the Gongyang commentary and Guliang commentary, he believed, "Those who now wish to read Confucius's new works while ignoring the Gongyang and Guliang cannot grasp his thought." Kang wrote:

> In the *Spring and Autumn Annals,* Confucius, feeling frustrated with those who contributed to the disorder, consulted the *Rites of Zhou* and historical texts to expound upon regulations, to establish the Kingly Way (*wang dao*). He recorded what should be recorded and deleted what should be deleted. This is what is known as his "subtle words and profound meanings" (*weiyan dayi*). These were passed down to Zixia.... The Gongyang commentary and Guliang commentary, which were transmitted through the work of Zixia, actually contain the subtle words (*weiyan*) of Confucius. They are all in alignment with the classics and commentaries. The Zuo commentary, however, was a work of the history of the State of Lu and does not transmit the meaning of the classics.... Disparaging hereditary postings, explaining laws on farming lands, disparaging marriage during mourning periods, limiting feudal regimes to an expanse of one hundred *li,* limiting nobility to three ranks, and preserving the righteousness of the Three Sequences were all results of the subtle words of Confucius and had nothing to do with the Duke of Zhou.... Confucius's *Spring and Autumn Annals* continued the work of Yao, Yu, and the Duke of Zhou in guiding the emperor's affairs.... Therefore, from the Zhou to Han dynasties, everyone saw the *Spring and Autumn Annals* as Confucius's writing on reform."[29]

In the above quote, Kang used the tone of a New Text scholar in both classifying the position of classical texts and interpreting the *Spring and Autumn*

Annals. This evidence indicates that Kang Youwei was already in the process of converting to Gongyang studies three years before he met Liao in 1890.

Borrowing a feature of New Text learning, the basic narrative structure of Kang's *The Book of Great Unity* followed the division of the Three Ages from the *Spring and Autumn Annals.* Does *The Comprehensive Meaning of Education* contain related traces? Let us examine the following passage:

> The *Spring and Autumn Annals* transmit moral duties that divide those above from those below and give the people purpose. This is the grand meaning of the *Spring and Autumn Annals.* From the Han dynasty on, as the *Annals* became more and more respected, the monarchs became more honorable and the ministers became ever base. This historical change has passed through three ages:
>
> One age stretches from the Jin dynasty to the Six Dynasties. In this period, the ministers controlled the power and inherited their positions. These included the Six Minister-Commanders of the Jin and the Three [Huan] Families of Lu. Some of the most extreme of these included Tian Chang [Tian Chengzi], Zhao Wuxu, and Wei Ying [King Hui of Wei].
>
> Another age stretches from the Tang to the Song dynasty. Striving to implement the *Spring and Autumn Annals'* rejection of inherited positions, the court allowed few hereditary postings. The monarch was clearly distinguished from the ministers. The children of wives were distinguished from the children of concubines. And the position of the monarch was fixed. Usurping the throne or killing one's ruler seldom occurred in this period, yet some high ministers still clung to power.
>
> From the Ming to this current dynasty, the emperor has ruled above all others and the ministers have loyally carried out orders from above. Across all the lands, every single life and every single coin is determined by the emperor. . . . The illustrious achievements of Confucius in the *Spring and Autumn Annals* are not only followed in China. Japan too is greatly influenced by these. . . . These later generations that learned governance from the *Spring and Autumn Annals* were all sincere when they referred to them as an inheritance from the Zhou dynasty.[30]

The division of the Three Ages into the Jin dynasty to the Six Dynasties, Tang to Song, and Ming to Qing found in *The Comprehensive Meaning of*

Education differed from the division explained in *The Book of Great Unity*, but both books clearly demarked enfeoffment (*fengjian*) and hereditary nobility as the origin of chaos, indicating an orientation toward the unifying system of centralized administration.

Kang Youwei's theory of Three Ages was not an objective narrative of history but a device that could be flexibly applied to the world. The division of the Three Ages was dependent upon one's specific needs and difficult to generalize. More importantly, *The Comprehensive Meaning of Education* and *The Book of Great Unity* applied the *Spring and Autumn*'s Three Ages not only to Chinese history but to the history of everywhere in the world. The former connected the Japanese restoration of the emperor with the Three Ages, expressing Kang's support for unity (*yitong*) and opposition to enfeoffment, as well as his vision to serve the emperor and reform the political system. The latter volume employed the Three Ages to expound upon the Middle Ages in India and Europe, as well as American modern history. Kang denounced the corruption of systems of nobility, slavery, and class, explaining the connection between equality and the Great Peace. In this respect, these two books saw New Text learning as a universal rule by which one could understand both Chinese history and world history.[31]

The discussion above shows that (1) Kang Youwei's turn to New Text learning was not entirely under Liao Ping's influence; (2) one cannot argue that *The Book of Great Unity* was written in 1902; and (3) throughout the period from 1884 until sections of *The Book of Great Unity* were published in 1913, and even later than this, Kang Youwei was continuously expanding, editing, supplementing, and even rewriting sections. In 1902, Kang Youwei engaged in a year of fairly systematic revision and large-scale supplementation of his existing draft. Traces of Kang's post-1902 revisions and supplementation still exist in the current *Book of Great Unity*, including impressions from his trips to Italy in 1904 and 1906, Canada in 1905, and Spain in 1906. According to Liang Qichao, Kang Youwei refused to publish the *Book* while at the Wanmu Caotang, so the complete text was not released until after his death. However, if Kang Youwei wanted to express his prophetic vision on this issue, then why did he not publish the book while he was alive? My basic understanding is that as Kang had persisted in the rethinking, writing, editing, and supplementing of *The Book of Great Unity* for twenty or thirty years, this book represents the starting point of his philosophy as well as his final goal. The period in which a complete draft of *The Book of Great Unity* was first written does not affect this basic understanding.

In the later years of his life (1926), Kang published *Lectures on the Heavens* (*Zhu tian jiang*), which can be regarded as a sequel to *The Book of Great Unity*. Around 1884, Kang had plotted out the theme of *Great Unity* as a discussion of Universal Principle and international law based in geometry and astronomy. The framework that he imagined not only transcended the Middle Kingdom related in territorial studies; it transcended Earth. He evidently hoped to discover a much more objective horizon that could transcend the cultural differences found on Earth and establish a new universalism based on this. This was an outcome that synthesized the worldview of scientism and traditional cosmology, a result that would revise traditional cosmology under the influence of the conceptualization of European natural law. It is particularly interesting to note that Kang found this cosmological universalism in no way contradictory with his veneration of Confucius. Kang Youwei once expressed his understanding of *datong* to Chen Qianqiu and Liang Qichao thus:

> I explained to them that the way of humaneness (*ren*) is the source to unite all of humanity and they can discard the useless old learning of evidential scholarship. . . . I taught them on the civilization of the Three Dynasties under Yao and Shun and how Confucius turned to this time. This is truth and can be proven. I taught them that humans are born of horses and horses are born of humans. Humans evolved from apes. This is truth and can be proven. I taught them about the realms in the many heavens, the realms in the many planets, the realm of the Earth, the realm of the body and of the blood. Each of these has a national territory, a people, a species, a state and a religion, rites, and refined writings. This is truth and can be proven. And I taught them about the Three Ages, the final age being that of *datong*, and of the repetition of the Three Sequences. This is truth and can be proven.[32]

In *Explorations of the Reforms Advocated by Confucius*, he also stated: "Therefore, Confucius was the original unifier for all. The heavens also fall within the bounds of his governance. This planet is just one among countless more. And a king rules just one country among the countless on the planet. How can any king be compared to Confucius?!"[33] Above the "realm of Earth" are the myriad heavens and the celestial bodies, but all of these fall within the scope of Confucius as "the original unifier." If *The Book of Great Unity* is the "outer tract" on Confucian universalism, indicating that it concerns the Earth's world order, then the *Heavens* was the "inner tract" on Confucian universalism, indicating that it concerned principles that applied to the entire universe. In this respect, Kang's ideas on *datong* were related to some of his thinking on "Universal Principle" (*gongli*) and "international law" (*gongfa*).

The key elements in *The Book of Great Unity* are extremely complex. Aside from the theories of Three Ages and *datong*, Kang included many ideas from Buddhism, Daoism, Neo-Confucianism, Wang Yangming thought, Western political science, geography, and science. Among these, many sections were clearly taken from *A Review of the Times* (*Wanguo gongbao*) and other popular publications. Before embarking on a deep analysis of the main content of *The Book of Great Unity*, we should first consider Kang's reading and writing around 1884, as this will illustrate the conditions of knowledge and the intellectual contexts from which the main themes of *The Book of Great Unity* were formed. From 1876 to 1878, Kang Youwei studied under Zhu Ciqi. In Kang's words, Zhu "promulgated the essence of the great way of the Sage, promoting the significance of self-cultivation and love for others, dispensing with the factions from the Han and Song dynasties and returning to the real Confucius."[34] This teaching provided an important influence for Kang Youwei's basic understanding of and attitude toward Confucianism. *The Book of Great Unity* begins from "entering the world and seeing universal suffering," which clearly bears traces of Buddhist thought. In the first lunar month of the fifth year of the Guangxu reign (1879), Kang Youwei began to diligently study Buddhist writings, abandoning his study of texts for the imperial examinations in favor of cultivating the mind. However, the Buddhist classics did not cultivate a desire to step back from the world; rather they aroused an impulse to "guide the age" (*jingshi*) through statecraft: to eliminate suffering and bring happiness to all the people under Heaven, the entire world, and all of humanity. Kang Youwei's motivation of a statecraft based in morality was clearly related to his studies of Wang Yangming thought and his research into Buddhism. He did not limit this moral impulse to self-cultivation. In his understanding, it was necessary to holistically understand the changes of the world by consulting a variety of works together, including the *Rites of Zhou*, the "Royal Regulations," *The Book of Administering the Country toward the Great Peace* (*Taiping jingguo zhi shu*), *Compendium of Documents* (*Wenxian tongkao*), *Documents on Statecraft* (*Jingshi wen bian*), *The Complete Texts on the Advantages and Disadvantages of a World of Divided States* (*Tianxia junguo libing quanshu*), *Essentials of Geography for Reading History* (*Du shi fangyu jiyao*), and books on the West, such as *Compendium of Recent Western Affairs* (*Xiguo jinshi huibian*) and Li Gui's *New Record of Travel around the World* (*Huanyou diqiu xinlu*). In this same year, Kang Youwei happened to have an opportunity to visit Hong Kong and recorded the deep impressions left on him by the magnificent palaces, clean roadways, and order under the care of the police: "From that point I understood that Westerners had moral standards in their governance. Their efforts were not resultant of the ancient systems of the Yidi." It was due to this that on his return he "read books such as *Gazetteer of the Maritime States* (*Haiguo tuzhi*) and *Concise Records of the World* (*Yinghuan zhilue*), bought a map of the world, and began collecting books about the West in order that I might know the basics of Western learning."[35]

The most significant element of the above-mentioned texts is Kang's integration of various ideas on statecraft and Western knowledge with Buddhist and Daoist theories on the cosmos and the relationship between the heavens and humanity. He was not researching the West simply to research the West. He was not even "learning the advanced techniques of the Yi in order to resist them" as Wei Yuan had done. Rather, he was providing theoretical and intellectual preparations to "manage All-under-Heaven." Another intense period of Kang Youwei's focus on reading studies on the West occurred in the year before his early draft of *The Book of Great Unity*. In 1883, Kang moved the focus of his study from such fields as geography and the relationship between state and religion to a much broader examination of science and history:

> I read *Records Compiled at the Eastern Gate* (*Dong hua lu*), *The Great Qing Canon of Governance* (*Da Qing huidian zeli*), *Imperial Edicts from Ten Reigns* (*Shi chao sheng xun*), and other stories of the current dynasty. I would purchase *A Review of the Times* (*Wanguo gongbao*), set upon the Western studies of sound, light, chemistry, and electricity,

> the historical records of all countries, and all the travel writings. I waded into all of these works. Thus, I hoped to collect texts from the myriad countries for my study, as well as studies of music, phonology, and cartography. At the time I rejected official work to concentrate upon the pursuit of knowledge and to contemplate this new knowledge, marveling with comprehension of profound reasoning. I bent my head to my books and only raised it in contemplation, advancing with each new day.[36]

Through their discussions of the West, technology, and the future, periodicals and books, such as *Compendium of Recent Western Affairs, Gazetteer of the Maritime States,* and *Concise Records of the World,* offered new intellectual backgrounds and sources of imagination for Kang's writing of *The Book of Great Unity.*

Within this new intellectual horizon, the Middle Kingdom transformed from an internal world surrounded by its external to one state among many. The *All-under-Heaven* that Kang Youwei hoped to manage was no longer restricted to the Middle Kingdom but expanded to the entire world. Although the problem of the Middle Kingdom remained the focus of his concern, this problem was no longer simply about the Middle Kingdom alone. Therefore, it could not be solved through an analysis that was limited to the Middle Kingdom. From 1883 until 1888, when Kang went to Beijing to take the civil service exam and wrote the "First Memorial" to the Qing emperor on December 10, 1888, it is evident that an even more abstract and far-reaching issue lingered in Kang's mind: How to find an international law that could be applied to the entire world, and a Universal Principle that could be applied throughout the cosmos to resolve the predicament that China and all of humanity found itself in. In order to achieve this, on the one hand he had to invent a worldview that was more objective and could transcend the differences of particular cultures. On the other hand, he also needed to reconstruct the relationship between Confucian universalism and the world of this Universal Principle. Had Confucianism's position as a Doctrine for All not suffered a disturbance, then there would have been no need for Kang Youwei to trouble himself with the synthesis of different knowledge systems to reconstruct the universal nature of Universal Principles and international law. Continuing on from 1884, in which Kang Youwei "understood that large and small (or fast and slow) have the same principle" and promoted "the age of Great Peace," in 1885, he "drew on concepts of mathematics and geometry in writing *A Universal Principle for Humankind* (*Renlei gongli*). . . . Examining manuscripts that still remain of this book . . . it was only then that I mapped out the system of *datong*." The following year, in *Kang's Essays on the Internal and External* (*Kangzi neiwai pian*), he explained: "The essays on the internal discuss principles concerning Heaven, Earth, humans, and living beings. The essays on the external discuss matters related to the state, religion, art, and music. Also referred to as *The Book of Universal Principle* (*Gongli shu*), it was based upon geometry" and also investigated issues of astronomy and the phases of celestial bodies, attempting to offer a new interpretation of the planet and the distribution of its civilizations.[37]

It is worth pointing out here that, as New Text learning included research on legal studies and astronomy, it was therefore relatively easy for New Text scholars to incorporate new knowledge on the natural world. In 1887, Kang Youwei traveled to the capital and entered into the world of political activity. Kang was thirty years of age. He recorded the events:

> In the year that I compiled *A Universal Principle for Humankind*. I pontificated on all the heavens, so there were no limits to the book. In *Essays on the Internal and External*, I engaged with Western learning, the classics, and the various schools to expound upon the controlling of the great floods in antiquity and China's beginnings with Yu's governance in the Xia dynasty. I considered the feudal lords that resembled local chieftains (*tusi*), the emperors and hegemons wielding power and ruling All-under-Heaven, and the old institutions of the Three Dynasties. All had not yet experienced civilization (*wenming*). I examined the reasoning found in Confucius's theory of the Age of Disorder, Age of Ascending Peace, and Age of Great Peace. I believe that raising armies and learning languages is too taxing for human minds and bodies. We should establish a global Institute of Languages (*diqiu wan yin yuan*) to study languages and scripts. We should establish a world parliament (*gong yiyuan*) to bring together representatives to discuss the universal principle of uniting countries. And we should build a world army to dispose of countries that will not ally with us. This is my plan for uniting the world.[38]

There are two important points to consider from the texts above: Firstly, Kang Youwei separated the principles (*li*) of "Heaven, Earth, humans, and living beings" from things and affairs (*shi*) of "the state, religion, art, and music" based upon a distinction of internal and external. Therefore, he situated his thinking on reform as an "outer" essay in the system of Universal Principles. Secondly, the Three Ages was not a Universal Principle in the old system but was a manifestation of the system of rites and music in specific circumstances and, therefore, not at all an invariable principle that could be applied universally. Kang Youwei saw transportation and language as the basic conditions for the advancement of human knowledge. Once transportation and language provided new parameters for human interaction, the rites, institutions, and other knowledge would inevitably experience change, and a sage is the kind of person that can adapt to these changes to create new rules. Due to this, as the late-Qing period experienced accelerating scientific development and human interaction, parameters limited to the Middle Kingdom were unable to ensure Confucian universalism. The Three Ages theory of Confucius had to be narrated on a global or even cosmological level.

We will never know whether *A Universal Principle for Humankind* was an early draft of *The Book of Great Unity* or another book altogether, but Kang's own account can be confirmed through a comparison with his other works from the period, including *Essays on the People's Work* (*Min gong pian*), *The Comprehensive Meaning of Education, Kang's Essays on the Internal and External, A Catalogue and Summary of the Myriad Bodies of International Law* (*Wan shen gongfa shuji mulu tiyao*), *The Complete Book of True Principles and International Law,* and *International Law* (*Gongfa hui tong*). These books were comprehensively inclusive, from the Three Dynasties of the sage emperors Yao, Yu, and Shun, when the code of rites first began, through the successive developments of institutions of governance, religion, and learning. From scientific principles on the natural universe to the basic laws and tenets of human society, Kang Youwei tried to construct a comprehensive worldview that included historical change and Universal Principles. On the one hand, in *Essays on the People's Work, Kang's Essays on the Internal and External,* and *The Comprehensive Meaning of Education,* he employed historical investigation to show that the way of the Former Kings "changes to accord with the people," and that the system of rites and regulations of the Sage-Kings was consistently amended to suit the needs of the people in a particular time. This argument opposed those who posited Confucianism as eternal and unchanging. On the other hand, in each of the essays concerning Universal Principle and international law, he explored the systems and ethics of human life based on fields of universal applicability, including geometry and observational studies, thus reorganizing the Sage-Kings' moral philosophy (*yili*) into a system with a universal and scientific nature. *The Complete Book of True Principles and International Law* was predicated upon the important theoretical division of "true principle" and "international law." A true principle is one that is universal, and an international law is a man-made law or rule that is aligned with a principle of universal applicability. For example, humans' physical characteristics and nature all belong to the category of "true principle," but legal statutes that are established through sovereignty and revolve around humans are "international laws." In this respect, the basis of humanity's international laws does not reside in the statutes of former monarchs or in historical change but rather in abstract, transcendent, and objective principles. These principles must be reached through scientific methods such as geometry and observational studies (empirical or experiment-based). Here science is employed as an objective standard that can transcend particular historical relations and particular power relations.

"True Principle and International Law" (*shili gongfa*) was a set of Universal Principles and international laws intended for the entire world. Kang listed the books needed to understand these principles in "A Summary of Books on International Law for Everyone" (*Wanshen gongfa shuji mulu tiyao*), as well as "Organizing the World's Catalogue of Books" (*Zhengqi diqiu shuji mulu gong lun*), the final section of *The Complete Book of True Principles and International Law* (*Shili gongfa quanshu*), These lists included *Correct History of the World* (*Diqiu zheng shi*), *Global Scholarship* (*Diqiu xue'an*), penal codes of all countries, dictionaries from all countries, and writings on international law. "International law is a collation composed by the efforts and materials of people from antiquity to today," and it is of great benefit to humanity. Kang did not hope to suddenly replace the laws, codes, and customs that had been formulated through history with this universalist international law. On the contrary, he suggested that international law be gradually introduced by adapting it to local customs and concentrating upon overlaps between the established rites and Universal Principles or international laws.[39]

His evolutionary theory of the Three Ages used a teleological historical narrative to draw a connection between real issues of the present and the future world of *datong.* His exploration of Universal Principle and international law abided by the ethics categorization scheme established in Confucianism. This included husband and wife, parents and children, teacher and student, monarch and minister, old and young, friends, rites and protocol (this category included titles for the emperor, calendrical systems, comportment [*weiyi*], and rest days), punishment and penal codes, issues of education, and issues of governance (this included bureaucracy, the rites for the body, the home, utensils, food, and drink), funerals, and sacrifices. But to Kang, this categorization system was not unique to Confucianism. Rather, it was a system of international law based in Universal Principle. Within the discursive framework of Universal Principle and international law, this was a moral genealogy based on the Universal Principles of geometry. Its universality as international law depended on a more objective and universal set of knowledge. The universal value of the institutions of the Former Kings was relativized and historicized for this purpose. Without a more universal and objective episteme, the sacred nature of the institutions of the Former Kings could not be dispensed with. The design and writing of *The Book of Great Unity* took decades and inevitably involved much revision and modification of the content, but this effort to integrate Universal Principle, international law, and history to form a universalist knowledge of historical change was concerted and focused throughout.

IV. *Datong* as a Means for Global Order

As Kang Youwei read Wei Yuan's *Gazetteer of the Maritime States* (*Haiguo tuzhi*) multiple times while he was imagining and drafting *The Book of Great Unity,* it is reasonable to consider these volumes together: Firstly, both of these works examined matters on a global scale; secondly, both expanded from an issue facing the Middle Kingdom to a study concerning the entire world; thirdly, both volumes regarded the world under the influence of New Text learning.[40] Considering the world as described in *Gazetteer of the Maritime States* as a backdrop, one can more clearly demonstrate the intellectual features of *The Book of Great Unity.*

Gazetteer of the Maritime States offers a historical-geographical description of relations in the world. Wei Yuan employed a great amount of Western geographic knowledge, but his volume also quoted from many historical accounts. It suffered from the influence of the empire's perspective when discussing global frameworks. In imagining relations around the world, *The Book of Great Unity* constructed a narrative in the style of historical fiction. Kang Youwei used religious, philosophical, and scientific knowledge to establish an even more holistic perspective for understanding the world. However, although this perspective employed Confucian knowledge, the knowledge stemming from both empire and Confucianism was merely "localized knowledge." Confucianism only possessed universal significance once it coincided with Universal Principle. Kang Youwei was trying to find a perspective that could transcend the problems of the Middle Kingdom and to understand both the Middle Kingdom and the world. His methodology was to integrate the approach of geometry with geographic knowledge and a Buddhist worldview and categorize the "suffering of all living things." For example, he divided "suffering" into life, nature, and society. This classification ignored the relationship with historical origins and viewed natural disasters and societal suffering as basic characteristics of humanity and the world. Under the category of "suffering from natural disasters," not only did Kang Youwei list fires, floods, and epidemics; he also included "suffering from shipwrecks" and "suffering from train accidents." Under the category of "the suffering of human life," in addition to his list of being widowed, being alone, or being sick, he also included poverty and lowliness, which included slavery. He did not view these societal issues as historical issues but as ontological issues of being alive. In this regard, abstract concepts such as happiness and suffering replaced real-world historical relations, constituting the central themes of the narrative that Kang employed to understand the world.

Kang integrated the idea that "all living things suffer" (*zhongsheng ku*) with the contemporary drive to eliminate suffering and pursue happiness, and he constructed a system of thought that was Buddhist on the outside but Confucian on the inside. The inner Confucianism was fundamental to this vision, but the outer Buddhism was also extremely important as Confucian moral philosophy could only achieve a universal applicability that could transcend particular historical relations with the framework offered by this

Buddhist worldview.[41] Kang Youwei clearly needed an ontology to express a new universalism and Confucianism could not supply this framework. Kang equated religious Confucianism with the Huayan School of Buddhism: "Therefore, [the nature of] human life depends upon what men consider to be the Way . . . and the mutual intimacy, mutual love, mutual hospitality, and mutual succoring of fathers and sons, husbands and wives, elder and younger brothers—which is not altered by considerations of profit or loss, or of difficulties—are what give pleasure to man."[42] The nations, tribes, rulers and subjects, and the laws of governance were nothing more than the sages according with the nature of human affairs and formulating plans to allow humans to avoid suffering. Once the institutions, rites, and morality become the sources of suffering themselves, then, no matter be they national laws, military laws, familial laws, or even divine laws, all are in violation of the human way. In Kang Youwei's narrative of the suffering of all living things, we can realize a few fundamental principles of Confucianism, particularly New Text learning, but the universality of Confucian moral philosophy was already relativized. Kang Youwei explained:

> China has one great accomplishment in that it has few hierarchies of class! . . . Confucius was the first to drive away the system of class, deriding hereditary postings, establishing the idea that the literati should not inherit titles of nobility and that scholars should not inherit their posts. After the fall of the Qin and Han dynasties, the nobility was wiped out, all were equal and all were the common people. . . . That there is no remnant of class throughout all of China, and seeing the misery caused by divisions of ethnicity and class in India and Europe, the joy of our equality and freedom is akin to residing in Heaven and looking at Hell. This is truly Confucius's great accomplishment![43]

According to this understanding, the greatest achievement of Confucius's theory is the elimination of class boundaries, and the elimination of class is intimately connected with some of the foci of New Text learning, including "ending the system of enfeoffment" (*qu fengjian*), "the Grand Unification" (*da yitong*), and "deriding hereditary postings," indicating the historical connection between class issues and the system of the state:

> Confucius originated the idea of equality. He made clear the idea of unification (*yitong*) so as to do away with enfeoffment (*fengjian*), and he derided the institution of hereditary nobility so as to do away with hereditary office. He transmitted the ancient system of assigning fields so as to do away with slavery, and wrote the constitution of the *Spring and Autumn Annals* so as to put a limit to the monarch's powers. He did not exalt himself to his followers, and he rejected the authority of great priests. Hereby class was completely swept out from Chinese institutions. Everyone became a commoner; anyone could rise from common status to be ennobled, to be a minister of state, to be a teacher or scholar; anyone could aspire to official advancement, could "show his stuff." The evils of class did not exist. Verily this was the remarkable accomplishment of Confucius, and he did it two thousand years before it was done in Europe.[44]

Kang Youwei's persistence with the theories of Confucius was premised upon this conforming to a more fundamental Universal Principle. Therefore, he inevitably distanced the theories of Confucius from particular historical relations.

The "scientific" knowledge, particularly the geographic knowledge, found in *Gazetteer of the Maritime States,* was an approach that more truly and realistically described the world. The book described science and technology as a force that could be utilized, but science was not a framework by which the entire world could be regarded. The narrative on the relationships between regions found in the *Gazetteer* indicated the perspective of an exceedingly vast imperial strategy, while science and technology were nothing more than technical skill. In *The Book of Great Unity,* "scientific" knowledge is presented as objective knowledge, a framework by which to understand the world, a principle by which global relations can be reprogrammed, and a natural law. It was therefore integrated with ontological or cosmological perspectives. The description of the world in *Gazetteer of the Maritime States* also included an exploration of historical relations, while the reconstruction of global relations in *The Book of Great Unity* was actually a refutation of the idea of historical relationships. The principal issue in Kang Youwei's conceptualization of *datong* was "the destruction of national boundaries and the uniting of the Earth." He divided the world into two halves of North and South, each composed of fifty degrees, based upon geographic knowledge. West and East also added up to one hundred degrees. Each degree was further divided into ten minutes, whereby a square degree would have one hundred square minutes. And each minute was divided into ten *li*, whereby a square minute would have one hundred square *li*. One's citizenship would be defined by the square minute in which one lived, and an autonomous government would have sovereignty over that minute. The entire planet would record years from the establishment of *datong*. All forms of measurement would be standardized, and a universal language and calendar would be used. Kang used the Three Sequences (*san tong*) and Three Ages (*san shi*) of New Text learning to describe the above-mentioned program, attempting to develop the theories of Confucius to a global scale. This presents an ahistorical categorization, one that denies traditional historical connections. Any historical theory must comply with this scientific classification in order to achieve rationality.

Some of the traditions of New Text learning were in line with this kind of scientism. Early New Text learning had a tradition of establishing calendrical systems based on lunar sequences, as seen in all the precedents from Dong Zhongshu to Kong Guangsen. New Text learning's internal-external paradigm also had a similar application in *The Book of Great Unity*. The first chapter of Section 2, "The Harm Caused by States," offers a thorough relativizing of relations between China and its peripheral tribes (*si Yi*) and the relations between Earth and the universe, arguing for the negation of internal-external, Yi-Xia, and enfeoffment (*fengjian*)–centralized administration (*junxian*), as well as borders and demarcations.[45] In this respect, the idea that "according to Confucius, the Grand Unity is a theory through which we unite under one (*ding yu yi*)" became the basis for eliminating states to end war.[46] Through this he reaffirmed the positive nature of replacing enfeoffment with a centralized system as historical evolution. "End the system of enfeoffment (*fengjian*) and establish a centralized government (*junxian*). . . . In truth this is the meaning of Confucius's Grand Unity. It is an effective means to protect the people and put an end to war." According to the logic of the "Grand Unity," centralization was superior to decentralization (*fengjian*); unity was superior to division; a united empire was superior to various kingdoms waging war; and the ultimate solution was to disband armies, eliminate national borders, and realize *datong*. The principle of "relativizing the internal and external" was an expression of weariness toward national borders and the wars that arise from them. "[T]he state is the highest form of human organization. Outside of God (*tiandi*) there is no superior law to govern it."[47] Then on what grounds can one eliminate states to end war? None other than "Universal Principle" (*gongli*) or "the natural path of propensity" (*shi zhi ziran*). "The progression of national borders from division to union is the natural path of propensity."[48] While "the natural path" was in accordance with Universal Principle, it was no different from the law that the strong devour the weak. In this respect, this process is a realization of Universal Principle or a precursor to *datong*: "That the great power attacks and swallows up the small country, that the weak is the meat and the strong eats it, are matters of the natural path of propensity to which [ideal] Universal Principles cannot apply."[49] Through an approach that is antihistorical and converts this process to Universal Principle, Kang Youwei examined the world in which the strong devour the weak and actually transformed the historical changes under the logic governed by the powerful into a specific undertaking of Universal Principle.[50]

Within this framework of striving for Universal Principle, the Grand Unity logic that rendered internal-external and Yi-Xia as relative was already constructed upon scientific classification. Thereby, Kang fell into the scientific prejudice that divided races based upon skin color and bloodlines. In "Part 3: Abolishing Class Boundaries and Equalizing All People" and "Part 4: Abolishing Racial Boundaries and Amalgamating the Races," he described the doctrines of Confucius through the egalitarianism of Grand Unity as "doing away with enfeoffment"; "deriding hereditary nobility so as to away with hereditary office"; and "granting arable lands to do away with slavery," unequivocally assessing the hierarchical differences of classes, nations, states, and races as the enemies of *datong*. Early on, New Text learning used rites or culture as the basis for the "relativizing of internal-external and Yi-Xia." This not only involved a negation of the system of hierarchical policy found in Qing-dynasty social relations; it also involved a negation of the idea of social ranks divided by nation or ethnicity. The idea of the Middle Kingdom based on rites was established upon these two negations. In *The Book of Great Unity*, although Kang continued with his goal of relativizing internal-external and Yi-Xia, against the background of scientific Universal Principle, he was once again drawn into the idea of "objective knowledge" on race. Therefore, his criticism of racialization became an affirmation of the very premise of racialization. The concept of "race," as well as the measures by which races could be divided—skin color and bloodlines—had already become a premise of this work, fundamentally changing the understandings of Yi-Xia and internal-external as being based in rites and culture. Kang Youwei considered the following problem: The European races of the Romans, Teutons, and Slavs are all similar and can easily be united. Likewise, the Asian peoples, including the Chinese, Mongolians, and Japanese, all became civilized and are similar in appearance, so will have little difficulty in assimilation. However, how can the white, yellow, brown, and black races be assimilated? There is no way to precisely ascertain when the arguments on race were written into *The Book of Great Unity,* but the knowledge and perspective of this racialization played an important role in late-Qing politics. For example, after the first Sino-Japanese War, Japan won over reformer literati through racialization in order to counterbalance Russia's influence in China. Reformers including Zheng Guanying (1842–1922), Tan Sitong (1865–1898), Xu Qin (1873–?), and Tang Caichang (1867–1900) were all influenced by Japan. While running a school in Japan, Xu Qin stated: "The scholars of Japan are so benevolent, so chivalrous! Day by day their fears for China's demise grow. Should China be destroyed then the yellow race will be weakened and Japan will be endangered! Therefore, there are those among the government above and the common people below who hope to save this world. They have established the Raise Asia Association (Kōakai) hoping to support the yellow race and protect East Asia, and to prevent Russia and Germany from running rampant."[51] Kang's understanding of equality was based upon the premise of a hierarchy of races. On the path to realize *datong,* he saw it as necessary to transform or even eliminate the lesser races:

> If we wish to join mankind in equality and unity we must begin by [making] the appearance and bodily characteristics of mankind alike. If appearance and bodily characteristics are not alike, then manners and occupations and love cannot of course be the same. Now, if we wish to amalgamate appearances and bodily characteristics which are completely dissimilar, and change them and make them the same, [and if we] set aside the method of intercourse between man and women, there is no way by which to change them.[52]

> That mankind should be equal, that mankind should be completely unified in the Great Peace of *datong;* this is of course a Universal Principle. But the inequality of creatures is a fact. . . . If not, then even though it be enforced by state laws, constrained by a ruler's power, and led by Universal Principles, it still cannot be effected.[53]

Within the scope of the Universal Principle of evolution, accepting difference does not lead to an egalitarianism that recognizes difference but to an egalitarianism that posits the white race as the standard and eliminates racial difference. Scientific knowledge only played a delimited role in racialization, while historical factors were foundational. Kang Youwei admired American political culture, believing that historical and scientific rationality within this culture justified racial discrimination toward black people and the system of slavery.[54] "Science" was a model form of legitimizing knowledge.

Gazetteer of the Maritime States explained the historical basis and complicated network of power relations in the maritime period. Its purpose was not to reconstruct the entire world but to protect the self from foreign invasion. Characteristic of a war manual, it favored discussion of strategy, military tactics, and specific historical relations. Never did it enter into a comprehensive plan for other civilizations, nations, and states based upon an abstract universal principle. Wei Yuan's critique was like an acupuncture needle painfully pressing through the skin of Qing society, but his conceptualization of reform was largely based on inspiration from history, experiences of the empire, and his insight into the essential forces that brought about change to global patterns. *The Book of Great Unity* was quite the opposite. It focused upon the idea of ending war by eliminating states, aiming to nullify historical spatiotemporal relationships on the basis of Universal Principle, providing a comprehensive plan for the world and designing a universalist system of international law. The fundamental differences between *datong* and the system of traditional society were not only due to the former being a form of global administration but also because *datong* divided the world on the basis of scientific knowledge, completely eliminating all kinds of regional, racial, cultural, and historical factors. In this regard, *The Book of Great Unity* is an antimodern text on modernity and a non-Western genealogy of Western knowledge.

Considered from the perspective of the development of New Text learning, Kang's conceptualization of *datong* was an extreme expansion of Gong Zizhen's refutation of enfeoffment (*fengjian*), expanding the concept of unification (*yitong*) to a global scale. *Datong* was no longer historically premised on the world of rites as Zhuang Cunyu and Liu Fenglu had imagined, but was rather a thorough eradication of enfeoffment. Kang not only scorned the Three Dynasties of Antiquity (*sandai*), decried the Spring and Autumn period, and highly praised the Qin unification; he also offered a similar analysis to the areas of India, west Asia, south Asia, and Europe, saying: "With regard to Europe, during the thousand years of enfeoffment, there were three hundred thousand German lords, one hundred and ten thousand French lords, and more than ten thousand Austrian and English lords. Today they have all been subordinated to the rule of the kings."[55] He even went as far as to view the Russian annexation of north Asia, the French annexation of Annam and Tunisia, the British annexation of Burma, and the Japanese occupation of Korea and Ryukyu, as well as the European colonialist partition of Africa, as a sign of the progression from enfeoffment to unification. Therefore, Kang's theory of *datong* and conceptualization of a world government was a rejection of war and annexation while simultaneously positing war and annexation as routes toward *datong*. If we are to place Kang's thought that is discussed above into the context of the late-Qing reform movement for examination, its substantive implications cannot be ignored. After the first Sino-Japanese War, there was an evident acceleration in the powers' partitioning of China. The literati promoting the reform movement tried to temporarily alleviate this partition through means such as alliances (*hebang*), selling off territory (*mai di*), and signing treaties. Yang Shenxiu (1849–1898) sent a memorial to the Guangxu Emperor about the intentions of countries such as Russia, Germany, and France to divide China. He proposed: "In this current crisis, the only policy that will offer survival is alliance with Britain, the United States, and Japan. . . . I hope that our Emperor soon establishes a state policy to unite with the three countries of Britain, the United States, and Japan. Do not distrust the word alliance (*hebang*) as distasteful, as it can truly bring about the fortune of all the common people under Heaven."[56] In order to realize the goals of the Hundred Days' Reform, Kang Youwei also promoted the idea of "selling off territory to raise funds." If even the annexation of states was seen as a way forward to *datong*, then it is understandable that the shocking proposals above gained some sort of legitimacy.

As he was operating within the framework of Gongyang studies' Three Ages theory, Kang Youwei's imagining of the relationship between federation (*lianbang*) and *datong* was somewhat similar to classical studies theorists' understanding of the relationship between enfeoffment (*fengjian*) and centralized administration (*junxian*) or unification (*yitong*). In discussing his conceptualization of international unions, Kang differentiated between three possible systems: The first was a system in which each country would join together in an equal alliance (*lianmeng*); the second was a system in which each state would govern its own domestic issues, but the individual governments would unite to form a federal government to replace the state governments; in the third form, each would establish autonomous administrative units united under a universal government. Following the divisions in Three Ages theory, the political systems mentioned above can be classified as "unity of the Age of Disorder" (*lianhe zhi juluanshi*), "unity of the Age of Approaching Peace" (*lianhe zhi shengpingshi*), and "unity of the Age of Great Peace" (*lianhe zhi taipingshi*), interconnected through a progression from one stage to the next. And of Kang's three models, the united federal government, which corresponded to the unity of the Age of Approaching Peace, was closest to the system of enfeoffment (*fengjian*) described in the *Spring and Autumn Annals* as the political system of the Three Dynasties of Antiquity.[57] Kang Youwei expanded Gong Zizhen's argument against enfeoffment or for the extirpation of the rites of enfeoffment to a global scale. In his examples, the federations of Germany and the United States were examples of states that had extirpated enfeoffment. Although the political formation in the final stage of *datong* that Kang Youwei had envisioned included no competition between political parties, no arguing in parliament, and no corrupt officials, it maintained vestiges of the Three Dynasties as imagined by Confucian scholars:

> In the Age of Great Peace (*taiping shi*), the people will be of excellent virtue and their education will be profound, while the representatives in the legislature will be people of great ability and wisdom, having none of this uncivilized behavior. In the Age of Great Peace, there will only be three levels of government: the local autonomous body, the government of the degree, and the world government. The local autonomous bodies shall reside in rural areas, while governments of degrees shall operate in cities. Humanity cannot do without these.[58]

In this flexible division of labor, "The age of *datong* will have no civilians." All will be responsible for managing the world: "There will be no officials." Although there will be posts both high and lowly, the carrying out of these duties will be extremely flexible. Aside from performing their responsibilities, "All the people of the world will be equal. There will be no privilege of rank or title, nor distinction by carriage and clothing, nor difference of company and entourage."[59]

The world of *datong* will be a global village established upon highly developed technologies of transportation and communication, and the former autonomous units of state and nation will no longer be efficacious. Kang Youwei divided the political units in the world of *datong* based upon "degrees" and discarded all traditional political concepts, such as family, clan (*zu*), townships (*xiang*), states (*guo*), and provinces (*zhou*). In this political framework, not only do the elements of *fengjian* autonomy completely disappear; even the autonomous forms of political federations disintegrate. "Then, we shall unify the entirety of the Earth and divide longitude and latitude into one hundred degrees, whereby each square degree shall have one government. The thousands of small governments shall then establish one world government for all. No less, no more; none added, none removed. None can be left out and no more can be brought in. None can be added and none can be removed."[60] Why did Kang choose to use "degrees" as administrative units? And why was this degree of such an appropriate size that none can be left out and no more can be brought in? Firstly, determining administration by degrees rather than states, races, or geography resulted in units that could no longer be big enough to subsume other administrative units, nor would they be so small that they would be unable to engage in global management. Therefore, dividing the world into autonomous units based on degrees could result in the greatest efficiency. Secondly, degrees were autonomous units. They were unique for breaking free from factors such as geography, culture, and race, thereby eradicating the basis of differentiation in political structures and implementing autonomy at the most basic level of society. "In the world of *datong*, autonomy will be enjoyed across the globe. Officials will be the local people and there will be no divisions of great and lowly."[61] The above perspective had a parallel relationship with Kang Youwei's perspective on autonomy in the actual political environment. He advocated for a dual system with an efficient central government (a structure with the people at the center of its functionality) and smaller local administrative structures. He opposed the practice of provincial administration, and its form of autonomy that had been in place since the Yuan dynasty, because it was inefficient and could lead to divisions in society. Considering the above, he combined the necessity for the centralization of authority (especially praising the political systems of the Three Dynasties) with social or civic autonomy, advocating for the self-management of the basic levels of society.[62]

Much like Wei Yuan, Kang was interested in the federal systems of the United States and Switzerland as working systems but firmly opposed to federalism like China's system of political administration.[63] Kang Youwei and Liang Qichao's understanding of local autonomy and their discourse on statism essentially revolved around and expanded out of this. The narrative of historical geography in *Gazetteer of the Maritime States* outlined a world in which internal and external were in a state of disorder, but its essential goals were to formulate a system of order for both internal and external and establish the sovereignty of China in this world of competition between nations. The book saw China as a competitive nation entering a world-system dominated by the hegemony of commerce and military might. Therefore, it focused its efforts on duplicating the logic of European modernization through the development of a capitalist economy, by strengthening the state and its military power, and by rebuilding the tributary networks with the empire as center, ultimately protecting China's traditions. Gong Zizhen and Wei Yuan both utilized the understanding of internal and external found in New Text learning to attempt a relativization of differences within the inner empire while clearly demarcating the boundaries and relationships between the internal and external, the empire and its outside. This was an important link in the transformation from empire to nation-state. In this respect, the global perspective raised by Wei Yuan also underwrote the concept of modern statism. *The Book of Great Unity* was just the opposite. It tried to outline a global law that was entirely in contrast with real conditions, to not only eliminate competition, militaries, and wanton killing, but eliminate the bases of these factors, including the state, sovereignty, class, private property, and even gender difference. In this respect, the *Treatise* was an affirmation of the logic of capitalism and its historical basis, while *Great Unity* was a negation.

The Book of Great Unity not only engaged in a rethink of issues such as state, nation, and race, but also offered a critique of capitalism's intrinsic logics of class, gender, and property rights. This critique was couched within the framework of Gongyang learning's theory of the Three Ages and universalist egalitarianism, and therefore an understanding of this critique that examines its form poses it as a criticism not of the particular historic logic of capitalism but of the universal phenomena found in human life. In previous research on *The Book of Great Unity,* there existed a controversy over whether the book was a work of utopian socialism that criticized capitalism or a work about the enlightenment of the capitalist class.[64] *Great Unity* focused upon revising global relations. It was premised upon uniting the Earth and humanity and the dissolution of states, technological development, and a transformation in the mode of production through this unity. In this respect, then, the logic of *datong* was directly opposed to modern capitalism, and the meanings in the doctrines of Confucius could only be universal through overcoming the internal logic of capitalism. According to the logic of the Three Ages of Disorder (*juluan*), Approaching Peace (*shengping*), and Great Peace (*taiping*), each phase represented a transition toward *datong.* Confucius established the doctrines of equality, did away with enfeoffment (*fengjian*), derided hereditary postings (*ji shiqing*), granted arable lands (*shou jingtian*), eliminated slavery, and limited the monarch's powers. Due to these efforts, China became a society free of class, in which "class was completely swept out from Chinese institutions. Everyone became a commoner; anyone could rise from common status to be ennobled, to be a minister of state, to be a teacher or scholar."[65] The state of decline in Chinese society was due to the abandonment of the teachings of Confucius and the rebuilding of systems of hierarchy.

Part 5 of *The Book of Great Unity,* "Abolishing Sex Boundaries and Preserving Independence," extended the egalitarianism of Approaching Peace and Great Peace to the issue of the emancipation of women, denouncing the sexual discrimination throughout human history as "the most appalling, unjust, and unequal matters and affairs, the most inexplicable theory under heaven. . . . Therefore, speaking of it according to universal principles, women should be considered exactly the same as men. As proved by results, women should be considered as exactly the same as men. This is the most universal aspect of natural principles, the most equal aspect of humaneness, and the whole universe does not divert from it."[66] Although Kang's conceptualization of equality between the sexes was a kind of ethics based in *datong,* his criticism was directed at the traditions of both China and the West. Kang listed eight points in his analysis of the societal inequality between men and women in history: Women have been not been allowed to serve as officials; not allowed to take the civil service examinations; not allowed to serve as legislators; not allowed to be full citizens; not allowed to become involved in public affairs; not allowed to become scholars; not allowed independence; and not allowed freedom. He went further in his demonstration of the suffering of women in four passages that said women had been treated as "prisoners," "criminals," "slaves," and "property."[67] His discussion of women's liberation was primarily directed at traditional customs, institutions, and culture, and his methods for resolving these issues were more aligned with the Age of Approaching Peace, rather than the Great Peace. *The Book of Great Unity*'s criticism of the institution of family also contained a double meaning and can be regarded as an early sign of the May Fourth New Culture Movement's criticism of the family. Part 6, "Abolishing Family Boundaries and Becoming a Natural People," contrasted natural relationships (*tian lun*) with human relationships (*ren lun*). This section explained that the way (*dao*) of fathers and sons is natural, yet this relationship is not necessarily a product of a biological relationship between the parent and child or the relationship of marriage.[68] By classifying the way of fathers and sons as natural or "universally understood and universally practiced," Kang demarcated a boundary between the way of fathers and sons and the institution of marriage or family, marking the latter as a man-made construction. Under the logic of the Three Ages, Confucius had formulated the institution of marriage for the Age of Disorder, and this institution had to be discarded in the ages of Approaching Peace and Great Peace.

However, eliminating the family did not mean discarding the world or leaving one's family to become a monk or nun, as is the case in Buddhism. Instead the logic of *datong* was based upon "seeking happiness" (*qiu le*) or a "happy life" (*le sheng*). If the existing institutions of marriage and family were eliminated, then how could the freedom of relations between the two sexes and the results of this freedom be managed? Kang Youwei's response was to socialize the reproduction of humanity. He formulated a detailed conceptualization of the system of this socialization, summarized as follows:

1: INSTITUTIONS FOR PUBLIC NURTURING: Human Roots Institutions (*renti yuan*) shall be established to take care of pregnant women and implement prenatal education, relieving fathers from responsibility. Infant-Rearing Institutions (*yuying yuan*) shall be established to take care of the infant babies, relieving mothers from this work. Nurseries shall be established to educate children beyond three years of age.

II: INSTITUTIONS OF PUBLIC EDUCATION: Public primary schools shall be established to educate children older than six years of age. Elementary schools shall be established for the education of children aged ten to fourteen; Middle schools shall be established for the education of teenagers aged fifteen to seventeen; Universities shall be established to educate young adults aged eighteen to twenty.

III: INSTITUTIONS OF PUBLIC SUCCOR: Hospitals shall be established to heal people's illnesses; Aged centers shall be established to take care of the elderly beyond sixty years of age who are unable to take care of themselves; Institutions for the poor shall be established to help those impoverished who have no one else to rely on; Disability centers shall be established for all those with impediments; Crematoriums shall be established to deal with the affairs of the deceased. This is a socialist conceptualization based on the Three Dynasties.

In addition to the socialization of human reproduction, *The Book of Great Unity* also provided a detailed elaboration on the socialization of production and distribution. What Liang Qichao referred to as "socialist philosophy" received a focused expression in this book.[69] Kang Youwei believed that the law of competition stemmed from the system of private property: "If we have the selfishness of the family, and private enterprise, then certainly individuals will manage their enterprises themselves. There is actually no help for this in the Age of Disorder."[70] Therefore, agricultural production cannot be equalized, and people are bound to starve; in industry, struggles between labor and capital will develop into national disorder; commerce will produce swindlers and goods will be produced to extravagant wastefulness. The corresponding measures proposed by Kang were premised on the implementation of a system of public ownership, which included public agriculture, public labor, and public commerce. Public ownership would eliminate private property rights, thus eliminating the traditional conceptualization of rights.

However, Kang found that this system was constructed upon human rights, an even more extensive form of rights, one that was premised upon the self-reliance of the individual. According to the logic of *The Book of Great Unity,* the system of private ownership was produced by the institution of the family, and the family was established upon the condition of inequality between men and women. Kang Youwei then inferred:

> Therefore, do the people of the whole world wish to abolish the burdens of the boundary of family? The solution lies in making clear the equality of men and women; it begins in each having the right of independence. This is a right which heaven has bestowed on humanity. Do the people of the whole world wish to abolish the evils of private property? The solution lies in making clear the equality of men and women; it begins with the independence of each. This is a right which heaven has bestowed on humanity. Do the people of the whole world wish to abolish the fighting between national states? The solution lies in making clear the equality of men and women; it begins with the independence of each. This is a right which heaven has bestowed on humanity. Do the people of the whole world wish to abolish the struggles caused by the boundary of race? The solution lies in making clear the equality of men and women; it begins with the independence of each. This is a right which heaven has bestowed on humanity. Do the people of the whole world wish to attain the age of *datong,* the bounds of the Great Peace? The solution lies in making clear the equality of men and women; it begins with the independence of each. This is a right which heaven has bestowed on humanity.[71]

In this sense, the comprehensive realization of public ownership was based on the human right of equality between men and women.

V. Classical Scholarship, Religious Confucianism, and the State

1. *Datong* and the State, Imperial Power, and Civil Liberties

If the writing of *The Book of Great Unity* ran through Kang Youwei's political thought from beginning to end, then there are three questions that cannot be avoided. First: Kang used a form of relativism to observe phenomena in the universe, thereby downplaying issues of the Middle Kingdom to small issues for the world: "The world is small, and China is even smaller."[72] But then why did Kang persist with the goal of saving the Middle Kingdom? Second: While Kang was writing *The Book of Great Unity,* which raised a fierce criticism of the state, why did he maintain such a positive affirmation of the authority of the emperor? Third: Was the criticism mounted against the political formation of the state in *The Book of Great Unity* not contradictory to Kang's efforts toward reform? Before embarking on a reading of his classical learning studies, including *Forged Classics of the Wang Mang Period, Explorations of the Reforms Advocated by Confucius,* and *Dong Zhongshu's Annotations of the Spring and Autumn Annals,* I first offer a brief response to these three questions.

From the perspective of political theory, these questions can all be interpreted within the context of New Text learning. The first question can be understood by placing it inside the framework of the Three Ages: Firstly, the Age of Great Peace, which does not differentiate between internal and external, is preceded by the Age of Approaching Peace, which followed a strict ritual order. Therefore, the rejection of the concept of the Middle Kingdom is a necessary condition of saving the Middle Kingdom. When Kang visited Guilin to give a lecture in 1895, a student asked about *The Book of Great Unity.* Kang replied: "In this current Age of Disorder, we can only speak of the lesser tranquility (*xiaokang*) and not of the Great Unity (*datong*). To speak of this too early would invite harm and offer no profit."[73] In this theory of evolution proposed by Kang there could be no skipping of steps in historical evolution. Secondly, the concept of the Middle Kingdom included the idea of *datong,* as the Middle Kingdom was neither a nation-state nor an empire but was rather a symbol of and vehicle for culture.

According to Kang's understanding, the conflict between China and the Western powers not only was a normal conflict between states but was also a conflict of cultural norms. This understanding of saving China then also included a cultural commitment to Confucian universalism. And Confucian universalism—viewing the theories of Confucius as a Doctrine for All (*wanshi fa*)—was required not only for China's rites and laws but for the rites and laws of the world. He adhered to the theories of Confucius, using "the rectification of names" (*zheng ming*) to define the parameters of Confucianism and the implications of the Middle Kingdom.

> The Hakka are similar to the Miao, in that neither are of the ethnicity (*zhong*) of the emperor. Before the Ming dynasty, Guizhou was part of the Luoshi Ghost Kingdom (*Luoshi gui guo*).[74] Yunnan was reformed by the Yuan dynasty, while Guizhou was reformed by the Ming. The logician (*ming xue*) Gongsun Long (325–250 BCE) discussed the *Hard and White* (*jianbai*), and those who follow the European schools of thought are similar to Gongsun Long.[75] Names of foreign countries come from India, while Japan, Annam, and Korea are all under the influence of Confucius.[76]

Here, Kang sees the Middle Kingdom as transcending ethnicity (such as the Miao people), region (such as Yunnan and Guizhou), and even culture (such as types of logic [*ming xue*]), positing the theories of Confucius as doctrine that transcends the category of the state: "Japan, Annam, and Korea are all under the influence of Confucius." If saving China corresponds with restoring the teachings, rites, and music of Confucius, then this process has no essential conflict with *datong*. Seen from the perspective of New Text learning, scholars such as Kang Youwei and Liao Ping had already expanded their thinking outwards from the inward focus of the Three Sequences (*santong*) to an argument that encompassed the relations between China and foreign countries.[77]

The second question can be responded to by considering the "internal-external paradigm" (*nei-wai li*). The legal authority of the Qing dynasty was closely related to the formation of imperial power. The most important issue for the legitimacy of the Manchu Qing dynasty was transforming the khan-king (*hanwang*), who ruled as commander in chief over his own tribe, into an emperor with universal authority over all ethnic groups, including both the internal and the external. Kang Youwei had a clear understanding of the empire's relationships with its internal and external, as well as the historical developments of these relationships. On the one hand, he employed the "internal-external paradigm" of New Text learning to reiterate the principle that "the difference between the *Yidi* (external tribes) and the Middle Kingdom was a difference of virtue (*de*) not geography (*di*)," thereby strengthening the unity of the empire's internal relations. On the other hand, he reinterpreted the Three Sequences (*santong*) to position the Manchu dynasty within the succession of Chinese dynasties, thereby subtly confirming its recognition as China.[78] A possibility was raised through the Qing rulers' announcement that "both Manchu and Han shall serve equally as my officials," as well as that "there is no division between internal and external" and "China and its external are one family." This possibility was for imperial authority to become a symbol for the Middle Kingdom's unity through the abstraction of various cultures amid the expansion of the Qing empire. Without such a symbol, the various ethnic groups, including the Manchu, Mongolians, Han, Hui, and Tibetans, could not have come together as a united people, and there would have been no way to establish the substantive and symbolic tributary system with China as its center. It was in this context that Kang reconstructed the historical relations between imperial power and China's unity through an interpretation of Confucius's writings on the imperial sacrifices.[79] In the reform movement of the late Qing, efforts to promote the centrality of the emperor were in part related to the political goal of opposing those who sided with the empress dowager, and in part these efforts were a social movement to strengthen the recognition of the Chinese nation (*Zhonghua minzu rentong*)—imperial sovereignty acted as a symbol for maintaining the political system while also bearing responsibility for maintaining the rites and social customs. Therefore, the position of the emperor was not only a position of political power but also a symbol for the unity of rites and culture.[80]

Centralizing power upon the emperor did not mean investing the emperor with absolute power over his subjects, and this is of the utmost importance in understanding Kang's theory on imperial power. Firstly, in the discursive environment that followed the Taiping Heavenly Kingdom, the movement to centralize power upon the emperor, as well as the idea of combining this movement with Confucian universalism, held very specific implications. From the Xinyou Coup of 1861 until 1873, the two empress dowagers "held court from behind a screen" (*chui lian ting zheng*) as regents of the Tongzhi Emperor (r. 1861–1875). A series of incidents and controversies dominated internal court matters, including regencies, succession, and the transfer of power. In addition to the political struggles for power, this change also influenced rites issues that governed the basis and regulations for the emperor's authority. The most important of these included the separation of the emperor from the throne, leading to issues with the legitimacy of this "regency." The Xianfeng Emperor (r. 1850–1861) suddenly died on August 22, 1861, one year after the invasion of the Anglo-French armies. On August 24, the emperor's oldest son was announced as his successor to the throne. As the new emperor was still young, and the empress dowager's regency was plagued by problems, conflict emerged between Sushun (1816–1861) and the other seven ministers of the imperial court who had been close to the emperor. After the coup in November, Sushun and the others were stripped of their titles, tried, and executed. The empress dowagers proclaimed their policy of "holding court from behind a screen" in the name of the emperor. According to Marianne Bastid's research, Dong Yuanchun (birth / death dates unknown), the Qing censor who first advocated for the dowagers to be made regents, emphasized three points in his memorial: "the importance of a physical embodiment of imperial authority, the ties of affection that bound subjects to the ruler, and the adaptation of political practice to changing circumstances. For Dong, imperial authority could not be an abstract notion." If the emperor was too young to rule, the empress dowagers must be made regents to maintain the status of the emperor.[81]

Controversy plagued the legitimacy of the regency. The Qing court was divided into two camps over the nature of imperial authority. Those who supported the dowagers' regency understood the throne as a practical necessity for the authority to rule. This indicated the throne was produced out of the need for national unity and the regency was therefore a necessity. Those who opposed the dowagers' regency saw the monarchy as an institution. The throne and the position of the emperor acted as a guarantee for the continued existence of the state. The regency had no precedent and was not required. The Tongzhi Emperor passed away on January 12, 1875, leaving no sons to succeed him. Under the title of a tutelage (*xun yu*), the dowagers designated the emperor's three-year-old first cousin Zaitian as successor and adopted son of the Xianfeng Emperor.[82] Two days later, the regency of the dowagers as "holding court from behind a screen" was announced by decree on January 12, 1875. Nearly twelve years later, in December 1886, "Guangxu began to endorse memorials to the throne with his own hand." On March 4, 1889, his formal rule began, but Empress Dowager Cixi maintained the authority to make final decisions on all memorials, reports, and policy decisions, including the approval of the appointment of high officials.[83] The status of imperial power had become divisive. According to Bastid:

> Just as it was accepted that the powers of the emperor could be shared out in the same way as those of any government post, so it was that the monarchy was defended purely as a rational political institution, with no consideration for its sacred nature or religious function, when it appeared endangered from 1898 onwards. This marked a continuation of the trend to equate the role of the imperial institution with that of any other high office of government. Hence the doctrinal rebuttal of reformist ideas in 1898 came from the pens of scholars and lower-ranking provincial officials, and not from officials at court.[84]

This historical context provides us important directions for reinterpreting Kang Youwei's writings on the classics. On the one hand, Kang reaffirmed the centrality of imperial power, endorsed the sacred status of the throne, and, through a refutation of Old Text studies of the Duke of Zhou, entirely eliminated the legitimacy of the regency in the exercise of imperial power. On the other hand, he posited Confucius as the model reformer, and placed upon him, rather than the emperor, various sacred titles, including the Former King (*xian wang*), the Latter King (*hou wang*), the Uncrowned King (*su wang*), the Sage-King (*sheng wang*), and the King Who Created the Laws (*zhifa zhi wang*). He placed the sacred nature of the throne above the sanctity of the system. Through this, Kang offered an intrinsic Confucian base for the formulation of a social system that followed a Western-style separation of state and religion. China's traditions of imperial power and a massive bureaucracy were so closely related that one could never characterize the practice of imperial power in China as the absolute power of the emperor. Both the imperial authority and aristocracy were subject to the balance of the rites, institutions, and bureaucracy, and, therefore, the contradictions between the imperial authority and the aristocracy were not absolute. Kang's argument for the centralization of imperial power included a rejection of the legitimacy of the regency, but the method that he adopted was a reaffirmation of the teachings of Confucius with the clear presupposition that ritual authority was superior to imperial power. Actually, even in the time when Cixi was "holding court behind a screen," she was compelled to abide by the rituals of the imperial family and the restrictions found in the Statutes of Ruling behind a Screen (*chuilian zhangcheng*). For example, after the Hundred Days' Reforms of 1898, Cixi had planned to do away with the Guangxu

Emperor's position, but she "ruled from behind the screen" and required the consent of the governors of the southern provinces before she would dare to implement such a move. She also secretly consulted such figures as the Governor General of Liangjiang, Liu Kunyi (1830–1902), and the Governor General of Lianghu, Zhang Zhidong (1837–1909).[85] However, Liu Kunyi resolutely opposed the removal of the Guangxu Emperor in a memorial: "The distinction between the monarch and his ministers is firm. Those inside and outside of the court should hold their tongues."[86] And Zhang Zhidong expressed that he "dare not dissent."[87] Even after the coup, Cixi was still unable to dethrone the Guangxu Emperor because of Qing traditions of imperial power and Confucian perspectives on rituals regarding the throne, as well as the balance of power relations between the central government and regional actors in the late Qing.[88]

Secondly, Kang Youwei's argument for the centrality of imperial power included two contradictory features. On the one hand, it established the emperor as the absolute central position. On the other hand, it limited the scope of imperial power through the symbolic position of Confucius and the values, rituals, and institutions he represented. The emperor was the center of power, but his power was never absolute, because executive, judicial, and moral authority had to adhere to a set of regulations. The idea of centralized authority contained a distinction between legal authority and decree: Confucius was the king who created the laws, embodying supreme justice, and the emperor had to exercise power in accordance with this fundamental law, and his decrees were limited to the extent allowed by legal authority. It was in this regard that Kang constructed a theory with imperial power at its center but limited the scope of its use. His theory posited the emperor as the center but also loudly heralded Confucius as reformer, the Sage-King, and the sole source of authority. This was to be a Confucian constitutional monarchy. Therefore, aside from his interest in the issue of the emperor's relationship to the regent, Kang's proposal for centralizing imperial authority was closely related to the following considerations: In China, only the implementation of a constitutional monarchy was feasible, certainly not a revolution; in China, only the integration of the central authority with the lowest levels of administrative autonomy was feasible, not provincial autonomy. This fundamental perspective was expressed much more clearly after the failure of the Hundred Days' Reform. In his 1902 "On Why China Must Implement a

Constitutional Monarchy Not Revolution: A Letter to Overseas Chinese in South and North America," Kang expressed indignation that the emperor could not be restored, and that Empress Dowager Cixi and Ronglu (1836–1903) still wielded power. He also expressed his doubts toward the French Revolution and the autocracy that followed it, proposing that China learn from the countries of Europe and the Americas "by implementing a constitution to define the rights of the monarchy and the people." Based on the Three Ages theory from the *Spring and Autumn Annals,* he opposed revolution as a means by which China could "leap directly into the world of democracy":

> Confucius compiled the *Book of Documents* (*Shangshu*) to state that Yao and Shun established democracy. He compiled the *Book of Odes* (*Shijing*), showing that King Wen established the monarchy. He supplemented the *Book of Rites,* stating that only when there are no leaders will All-under-Heaven be brought into order, and we can be equal with no masters. With the *Spring and Autumn Annals,* he divided the three ages into the Age of Disorder, the Age of Approaching Peace, and the Age of Great Peace. . . . Now is the Age of Disorder, and so the state cannot transcend directly to global *datong;* those in the old ways of an absolute monarch can likewise not transcend directly to the age of democracy. . . . In China, I was the first to speak of Universal Principle (*gongli*), the first to speak of the people's rights (*minquan*). The essence of people's rights must be carried out, but Universal Principle cannot be carried out to the fullest at this time. . . . The three methods of absolute monarchy, constitutionalism, and democracy must be undertaken successively.[89]

Kang saw constitutional monarchy as an intermediate stage coming after the form of state based upon the imperial court (*chaoting guojia*) and leading to a form of state based in the people's rights (*minquan guojia*).

Why could China not eliminate the Manchu emperor and create a country with democracy for the masses through revolution? Firstly, the abolishment of imperial power signified the loss of state control and the advent of the division of the state. "China's territory is vast, its people many, and languages differ in each province and prefecture. . . . Inevitably, each county will rise up, each province will establish a government. None will give way and all will attack each other. Each will hope to lead and each will swallow up the other. Each will slaughter the other, and the rivers will run red with blood. . . . Within the land, violence will inevitably work to the advantage of those in the external (*wairen*)."[90] In a letter to Liang Qichao and others in the spring of that same year, he opposed a simple imitation of the European model with national self-determination and provincial autonomy. He cited India as an example, arguing that there was a causal relationship between the independence of the provinces and Indians becoming a conquered people. Kang Youwei strongly rebuked Liang Qichao and others' advocation for the autonomy (*zili*) of the eighteen provinces: "If one can unite dozens of small enfeoffments (*fengjian*) and reform them, then small states like those in Japan can unite and also become powerful and wealthy. If the united are to break into dozens of small states, then even countries as large as India will be defeated."[91] Kang's critique of the concept of revolution was not levelled at the measures needed to achieve revolution but at the demand for revolution and the conception of the Middle Kingdom behind it, which was an idea of a future China reconstructed through national self-determination and the autonomy of the provinces.

Secondly, aside from his hopes for the Guangxu Emperor himself, Kang Youwei's motives for preserving imperial authority also included a redefinition of the Middle Kingdom that transcended the divisions between Manchu and Han, internal and external. In his own words:

> The revolutionaries are attacking the Manchus with every word, and this criticism cannot be countenanced. Great China opened up Mongolia, Xinjiang, Tibet, and the Northeast (*dong san sheng*) and has been at peace under the same government for two hundred years, yet these revolutionaries unceasingly and arrogantly invite the French and Americans to cause internal strife, bringing great turmoil through their clamor to expel the foreign and divide the races (*zhong*). Will this never end?! . . . Yet the Manchu and Mongolians are all of the same race as us. By what reasoning should we separate them from ourselves or treat them as different. . . . They point out the problems of political autocracy, but this has been so from the old dynasties of Han, Tang, Song, and Ming. The Manchus are not special in this regard. . . . Manchus and Han are equal in the institutions of the dynasty. The Han have many of great talent and any man may now become prime minister. . . . Today's revolutionaries speak

> of civilization (*wenming*), yet how can they also implicate themselves in these crimes and abandon the country? The revolutionaries speak of Universal Principle (*gongli*), yet try to divide this country that is now one people based on race. Is this not absurd?! . . . When I was in Beijing in 1898, inquiring into the system of government, I was wont to say, "Manchu and Han cannot be divided. The monarch and the people are one." We only spoke of China as there is no Manchuria. The ruling emperor and his clan, be it the Liu of the Han, the Li of the Tang, the Zhao of the Song, or the Zhu of the Ming, are simply one family.[92]

This understanding can only be based in a particular conceptualization of the Middle Kingdom and the Chinese: China and the Chinese people do not stem from one single race or ethnic group but are a nation that was formed through historical developments and the mixing of ethnic groups. Any understanding of internal division or racialization was in conflict with this unique concept of the Middle Kingdom. We must understand Kang Youwei's thinking on the classics in relation to this broad conceptualization of the Middle Kingdom that premised his political vision. Kang praised Confucius at the sole patriarch of the religion, as the Sage-King, and the king who created the laws in such works as *Forged Classics of the Wang Mang Period, Explorations of the Reforms Advocated by Confucius,* and *Dong Zhongshu's Annotations of the Spring and Autumn Annals.* Not only did he thoroughly negate the legitimacy of the Duke of Zhou's regency; he rejected the idea that anyone would share the title of "king" (*wang*) with Confucius. This narrative expressed a historical understanding and political implication that the king's authority could not be divided, the monarch must be placed at the center, and China must be united.

And finally, Kang's efforts to preserve both the country and imperial authority were inherently connected with his belief in *datong.* In *Forged Classics of the Wang Mang Period* and *Explorations of the Reforms Advocated by Confucius,* Kang's insistence on the sanctity of imperial power and its sole origin included a very conspicuous characteristic. The absolute authority of the king that he esteemed was not that of the emperors from history but was that of Confucius. The sanctity of the king's position that he advocated came from the sanctity of the rituals and institutions created by Confucius. The Six Classics came from Confucius, but they were also outlined in the institutions.[93]

Therefore, the sanctity of the institutions was above the sanctity of any real authority because the former were created by the hand of Confucius the Sage-King. In other words, Kang restored the sanctity of the king's authority, but this restoration was premised upon the priority of the rites, music, and institutions.

And it is in this respect that our answer to the third question closely correlates to the two preceding questions. This understanding should be interpreted within the context of the *Spring and Autumn Annals's* concept of "creating new kings" (*zuo xin wang*) or Confucius's maxim "External tribes (*Yidi*) with rulers are inferior to Chinese states without rulers,"[94] indicating that the importance of the ritual systems was of greater significance than the importance of any specific monarchy. The moment a centralized state is formed, the state begins its separation from the monarchy. Firstly, if the Middle Kingdom's existence was based upon the existence of the system of rites, then the refutation of imperial power did not indicate the demise of the Middle Kingdom after the reforms supported by the emperor shifted in the direction of statism. The separation of state and empire, monarch and state, is the main process that occurs as a centralized monarchy changes into a nation-state. Secondly, while the universal authority of the absolute monarch was constructed upon the concept of "the people" (*renmin*) as universally existing or possessing an innate continuity, the homogeneity of "the people" derives from the national homogeneity as represented by the monarch. Therefore, once the state and monarch begin to diverge, the idea that sovereignty resides with the people becomes the dominant political conceptualization of the nation-state. The goal of the reforms was the divergence of monarchical power and the state, thereby achieving the unity of the Middle Kingdom and China's own civilization, religious Confucianism. In this respect, political transformation focused upon constitutional monarchy contained a negation of monarchical authority. The following passage describes Kang Youwei's logic in connection to the classics: "Of all the great masters under Heaven, Confucius is the greatest. Our moral philosophy (*yili*) and institutions all come from Confucius. Therefore, scholars only emulate Confucius. As it has been three thousand years since Confucius left this world, where can we find his learning? The answer is in the Six Classics. . . . The reason that we call Confucius a sage is that, through his reforms, he righted all, and his influence is universal."[95] Positing Confucius as the Sage-King and turning to the *Spring and Autumn Annals* for laws and institutions indicated that the rites and institutions were above the emperor. Unity under religious Confucianism provided the premise for a separation of church and state centered around traditional Confucianism while also providing the internal logic for the transformation of the political system toward the future world of *datong* that would transcend imperial authority and the state. In this context, revering Confucius and his teachings became synonymous with political reform. Because the laws and rites of the Three Dynasties were created by Confucius, it followed that the way to return to the order of this age was not through "the king following the ways of the ancestors" (*zushu wang zhi*), as stressed by the Old Text scholars, but was through the very practice and process of "creating the institutions" (*chuang zhi*). At the political level, the centralization of imperial authority was a link in the transition between empire and nation-state. And for the rites, this centralization was simply the historical condition for the implementation of the kingly rule as set out by Confucius and a bridge for the transition to *datong*. This was the internal logic of the self-transformation of imperial authority and its systems of power.

2. *Forged Classics of the Wang Mang Period*

In the fifth month of the fourteenth year of Guangxu's reign, 1888, Kang Youwei traveled to Beijing to take the civil service examination. He was thirty-one. In the ninth and tenth months of that year, he became aware of the pressing national situation and determined to write a memorial calling for swift reform. However, his language was too critical for him to submit the memorial and he was instead content to "declare the falsity of Old Text learning and realize that New Text learning was correct."[96] In the ninth month of the following year, he left Beijing, traveling through such places as Hangzhou, Suzhou, Jiujiang, and Wuchang before returning to Guangdong at the end of the year. In early 1890 he met Liao Ping, who had traveled south to Guangzhou to work on the editing of the *Qing-Dynasty Commentaries on the Thirteen Classics* (*Guochao shisanjing shu*).[97] In 1888, Liao Ping finished writing *Treatise on Liu Xin (Bi Liu pian)* and *Treatise on Knowing the Sage* (*Zhi Sheng pian*). He had begun the second of his so-called *Six Changes in the Classics* (*Jingxue liu bian*), but he had not yet sent it off for publication. The *Treatise on Liu Xin* is no longer extant, but one can find *A Review of Old Text Studies* (*Gu xue kao*), which was a later revision based on the earlier text. It was published in 1897, while *Treatise on Knowing the Sage* was published in 1902. Neither of these books was the first of Liao Ping's manuscripts that included his ideas on "three changes in the classics." In 1896, Liao Ping wrote *First Text on the Classics* (*Jing hua jia bian*). In sections 107 and 108, he stated that Kang's *Forged Classics of the Wang Mang Period* was taken from *Treatise on Knowing the Sage*.[98] The relationship between Liao and Kang thus became a popular case in the history of scholarship. Earlier studies, such as Qian Mu's *The Last Three Hundred Years of the History of China's Scholars* (*Jin sanbai nian Zhongguo xueshushi*), as well as recent scholarship, such as Huang Kaiguo's *Biography of Liao Ping* (*Liao Ping pingzhuan*), have already combed through the similarities and differences between *Treatise on Knowing the Sage* and *Explorations of the Reforms Advocated by Confucius*, as well as *A Review of Old Text Studies* and *Forged Classics of the Wang Mang Period*. It is now thoroughly accepted that Kang was influenced and inspired by Liao.

However, Kang did not simply follow in Liao Ping's footsteps. In the two works discussed above, he posed arguments on matters such as the sages' reforms, the importance of the people, and the Three Ages theory, all of which Liao Ping seldom discussed. It can also be shown that Kang had already begun to doubt the veracity of Liu Xin's compilations before his encounter with Liao Ping's work. More importantly, although Liao Ping's writings included some political implications, he lacked Kang Youwei's political insight and immediate political motivations. Kang's specific plans for reform, including the establishment of a legislature, opening schools, and women's equality, can only be understood in the context of his political vision. After the Hundred Days' Reform, Liao Ping encouraged his son, Liao Shishen, to write *Family Lessons from the Wooded Studio* (*Jiaxue shu fang*), which included "Reading the *Treatise on Knowing the Sage*" (*Zhi sheng pian* dufa) to clarify the differences between Liao Ping's thinking and that of Kang Youwei.[99] Although this was an attempt to absolve Liao's Gongyang learning from any relation to Kang's political thought in the aftermath of the failed reforms, to a certain degree it did define fundamental differences between Liao's and Kang's interpretations of Gongyang studies. In terms of the development of New Text learning, the discourse on reform and the Uncrowned King was all found in Dong Zhongshu's *Luxuriant Dew of the Spring and Autumn Annals* (*Chunqiu fanlu*). As Wei Yuan and other New Text scholars had moved the focus of the school from He Xiu to Dong Zhongshu, the theme of transformative reform had become increasingly evident. Qing-dynasty Gongyang scholars expanded their horizon from the "directive to reform" (*shouming gaizhi*) in the Gongyang commentary on the *Spring and Autumn Annals* to the idea of institutional reform, making the "Royal Regulations" (*wang zhi*) a central issue.[100] In this respect, both Liao Ping's discussion of "Royal Regulations" and Kang's specific conceptualization of reform came from historical debates. Within the contexts of a changing New Text learning and the trajectory of Kang's own thinking, the formulation of both *Forged Classics of the Wang Mang Period* and *Explorations of the Reforms Advocated by Confucius* contained threads that can be traced from these debates. Without such preparation, it is difficult to imagine that Kang would have been able to publish a book on the scale of *Forged Classics of the Wang Mang Period* in such a short period of time. For these reasons, the following discussion will not dwell on similarities and differences between Liao and Kang or the question of who influenced whom. Rather it will center upon the basic themes of Kang's classical studies and their political implications.

We begin with the *Forged Classics of the Wang Mang Period* (*Xin xue weijing kao*). If Old Text learning focuses on old texts and old classics, why then does Kang refer to them as "Xin" or "New Studies" in his title? Kang explains that the name "Old Learning" (*guxue*) is derived from the discovery of classic texts in the wall of Confucius's home centuries after his death. These texts were all written in the old pre-Qin scripts. If the story of these books in the wall proved to be false, then the Old Texts were also false; in that case, "Old Texts" should be "New Texts" and should not be called "Old." Liu Xin, the figure behind Old Text learning, was a minister in Wang Meng's Xin dynasty (new dynasty). Therefore, his "Old classics" were merely "Xin classics," "Xin" meaning new. In this respect, according to Kang, what later generations referred to as "Han learning" (*Han xue*), including the work of Jia Kui, Ma Rong, Xu Shen, and Zheng Xuan, was "actually 'Xin learning' and not 'Han learning.' The classics that those in the Song adhered to were likewise false classics. They were not the classics of Confucius. Using the appellation 'Xin learning,' scholars can be brought closer to Confucius, while those in the Han and Song stepped further away to their reproval. When rebuking the myopia of past times, the critic is not false."[101] Clearly, Kang's condemnation of "Xin studies" was in the same vein as his condemnation of the "*Xin zheng*," the new policies that followed his 1898 exile.

Kang's purpose in attacking "Xin learning" was not to prove something in a historical debate. His ambitions were far grander. The goal of *Forged Classics of the Wang Mang Period* was clear from the outset: the assertion that two thousand years of classical studies were false studies, that two thousand years of rites and music were false standards.

> The falsification and disorder of the systems set in motion by the Sage began with Liu Xin, and then Zheng Xuan (127–200 CE) employed the false classics to usurp Confucius's domination. Two thousand long years of months, days, and hours passed, amassing erudite inquiries by hundreds, thousands, and millions of learned scholars. The rites, music, and institutions across the rule of monarchs from twenty dynasties have all been led by false classics posing as the laws of the Sage. They have been solemnly chanted and trusted, held aloft and brought to implementation. This vilifies the sages and contravenes the law, yet none dared to dissent, and none dared to question. They pillaged the classics of Confucius and those of the Duke of Zhou, suppressing the transmission of Confucius's ideas. Thereby, they swept away the sagely laws (*sheng fa*) of Confucius's reforms, treating them as rotten old papers. . . . They began as pillaging usurpers but were then seen to be truth. They were first seen as pretenders but then seen as orthodox tradition.[102]

The destructive force found in the above passage was one reason that Kang's book fomented such a strong ideological response. However, without a clearer political meaning, this work would not have been considered a cornerstone of the theories of reform, and the 1894 and 1898 editions would not have been destroyed. Liang Qichao offered a summary of the essential points in *Forged Classics of the Wang Mang Period:*

> (1) In Western Han classical learning there were no so-called Old Text scholars. The Old Texts were all fabricated by Liu Xin. (2) The calamity of the Qin burning of the books did not befall the Six Classics. The books passed down by the fourteen *boshi* (erudite masters) were all the complete editions from Confucius's disciples. Nothing was missing from them. (3) In the time of Confucius, the Seal Script (*zhuanshu*) of the Qin-Han period was in use. Considering the script, there was no Old or New.

> (4) Liu Xin wished to hide the evidence of his falsifications, so he altered all the Old Texts when he worked as curator in the imperial library. (5) Liu Xin falsified the classics in order to assist Wang Mang in usurping the Han. The first task was to eradicate Confucius's subtle words and profound meanings (*wei yan da yi*).[103]

However, was there a more specific intention underlying the above discussions of classical studies?

To answer this, we must begin with Kang's particular interpretation. Firstly, his initial reason for exposing the false classics was to prove that the Qin burning of the books did not wipe out the Six Classics. Kang Youwei reinterpreted Qin Shi Huang's burning of the books and burying of Confucian scholars (*fenshu kengru*) to revisit the political, ritual, and linguistic levels of the intense conflict between enfeoffment (*fengjian*) and unification (*yitong*) at that historical juncture. He used this as an entry point through which to determine which classics were authentic and how this authenticity related to their being passed down. As the New Text / Old Text debate emerged due to the Qin book burning, there was no avoiding a reinterpretation of the burning of the books and burying of the Confucian scholars. On the surface, the issue concerned whether or not the books of the Six Kingdoms that had been conquered by the Qin were all burned. However, on a deeper level, the issue concerned whether the political system should be premised on centralization (*junxian*) or enfeoffment (*fengjian*). Therefore, the debate on the burning of the books was closely related to the issue of unification. The "Biography of Li Si" in the *Records of the Grand Historian* states: "Today the feudal lords have submitted to Qin as if they were its commanderies and counties (*junxian*). Qin's might and your talent, Great King . . . are sufficient to destroy the feudal lords, to accomplish the imperial enterprise, and to bring unity to the world. This is the chance of ten-thousand generations!"[104] In the section "The First Emperor of Qin," it is also said: "Now your Majesty has raised a righteous army to punish the savage and the villainous and has pacified the world. The land within the seas has been made into commanderies and counties (*junxian*), the laws and ordinances are ruled by one. Since antiquity it has never been so. This is what [even] the Five Emperors could not reach." "No, thanks to Your Majesty's divine sagacity, the lands within the seas are united under one and have become commanderies and counties."[105] It is entirely possible that key phrases from the Gongyang commentary, "the gentleman follows the correct path" (*junzi da juzheng*) and "the king creates the Grand Unification" (*wangzhe da yitong*), can be traced to this emphasis on centralization.[106]

Embedded in Kang Youwei's refutation of the false classics was a clear argument for unification (*yitong*). *Forged Classics of the Wang Mang Period* included the following discussion of the Six Classics that were not wiped out by the Qin book burnings: Firstly, there was an order to burn books, but it was the common books of the people that were burned, and the books that the Erudites specialized in did not suffer the Qin's flames, including the *Book of Odes*, the *Book of Documents*, the Six Arts, and the Hundred Schools (*baijia*).[107] The Qin "made legal officials teachers" (*yi li wei shi*), establishing official education systems and abolishing the private schools to unify the laws, institutions, and rites of the empire. Even were the Confucians not laid to waste during this period of unity, the legitimacy of the period could still have been established. Secondly, on the level of script, Kang saw the heterogeneity of script as an expression of the heterogeneity of the feudal lords' styles of rule, and his attack on Liu Xin's falsification of the "Old Texts" was an assertion that the Great Seal Script (*zhou*) and Seal Script (*meng*) were not considerably different despite admitted variations.[108] He said:

> Confucius's handwritten classics were passed down through Kong Fu, Kong Xiang, and Kong Guang, across more than ten generations without fail. In addition to these, there were volumes passed down to the *boshi* (erudite scholars) of the Qin and Wei, including Gu Shan, Fu Sheng, and the scholars of Lu. Books were passed from master to disciple, from father to son. How could they be corrupted? Thus, the records that the Han Confucians read were the records from Confucius. There were no other versions. Zi Si (483–402 BCE) said: "Now the scripts of All-under-Heaven are all one." Xu Shen (58–148 CE) stated: "The feudal lords ruled with might and did not fall under the rule of the king. They were divided into seven states, and the scripts were written in different forms." Jiang Shi expressed: "After that, the seven states all followed their own direction and their scripts remained diverse. When the Qin emperor commanded All-under-Heaven, Prime Minister Li Si petitioned the throne to abolish those scripts that differed from the Qin script." In his "Four Styles of

> Calligraphy" (*Si tishu shi*), Wei Heng expressed: "In the Qin dynasty, people used the Lesser Seal Script (*zhuan shu*). During the burning of the books, all of the ancient scripts were destroyed." All of these writers relied upon the false words of Liu Xin, continuing his lying and cheating.[109]

According to this explanation, the New Texts were directly from Confucius without any deviation and no other versions. Critiques by Old Text studies scholars such as Xu Shen were not confined to the study of the scripts but were also related to political philosophy and historical understanding, because these scholars conceded that irregularities in script were a result of "feudal lords" holding political power and not being united "under the rule of the king" or because "the Seven Kingdoms all followed their own direction."[110] If there had been no heterogeneity of scripts in the time of Confucius, then would unity not have been a standard tradition for the early Confucians? And would the enfeoffment of the feudal lords not have been the false politics trying to usurp and supplant?

There is no question that this discussion of the Qin burnings was directly concerned with a political judgment on centralized administration (*junxian*) and enfeoffment (*fengjian*), unity (*yitong*) and divided rule (*fenfeng*). If the burning arose from the conflict of centralization and enfeoffment, then did the Qin implement centralization in order to adhere to the Six Classics? Before Kang, Liao Ping had already answered this question: "The Qin implemented centralization in compliance with the truth of the classics and as a step toward the Grand Unification (*da yitong*). In accordance with the rites, the king's territory (*wang ji*) cannot be divided by enfeoffment, and only the eight states (*ba zhou*) could be divided among the feudal lords. China is the king's territory in this unification (*da tong*), so its territory cannot be divided among the feudal lords."[111] However, Liao's discussion was focused on the level of classical textual studies, and he had no interest in the political implications of centralization and enfeoffment. On this point, *Forged Classics of the Wang Mang Period* examines the various levels of the relationship between unity under the emperor and enfeoffment with equality between the states. Firstly, Kang offered elaborate examples to support his argument for the centralization of imperial power and the worship of Confucius, thus providing a foundation in moral philosophy for the system of Grand Unification (*da yitong*) or the centralized state (*junxian guojia*). Within the historical contexts of Cixi's regency and a decentralization of power, Kang clearly displayed his political inclinations through his advocacy of Grand Unification and centralization while fiercely attacking the "regency" (*jushe*), "usurpation of the throne" (*cuanwei*), and enfeoffment.

Secondly, following almost the same logic, Kang argued that the Six Classics came from a single source and that the position of Confucianism should be venerated. The *Records of the Grand Historian* listed Confucius under the noble families as a "Hereditary House" (*shi jia*). Because of this, Kang asserted: "Those that spoke of the Six Arts all came from the master, or one could say the Sage. . . . Confucius amended the Six Classics. Confucius created the rites and the music. All-under-Heaven was within the purview of Confucius's learning and teaching."[112] The venerable position of the Six Classics and the unparalleled position of Confucius were mutually sustaining, resulting in: (1) A review of the content and order of the classics, ordering the Six Classics as: the *Book of Odes*, the *Book of Documents*, the *Book of Rites*, the *Book of Music*, the *Book of Changes*, and the *Spring and Autumn Annals*.[113] This was in opposition to the Old Text order of the classics as the *Book of Changes*, the *Book of Documents*, the *Book of Odes*, and the *Book of Rites*. While ensuring the sacred status of the Six Classics, he diminished the importance of a number of texts seen as "classics" by more recent generations, relegating them to the status of "commentaries" (*zhuanzhu*). They included the *Analects*, the *Classic of Filial Piety*, the "Royal Regulations," the *Commentaries* (*Jingjie*), and the *Records on Education* (*Xueji*), including those concerning the *Book of Changes*, the *Book of Documents*, the *Book of Odes*, the *Rites of Zhou*, as well as elementary learning (*xiaoxue*). (2) As the Qin burning had not wiped out the Six Classics, Western Han classical studies held a canonical position, but revisions and additions by later generations had to be purged. This established the "authentic texts" for exegetical studies of the classics. (3) Diminishing the position of King Wen and the Duke of Zhou so as to establish the absolute primacy of Confucius as the Sage-King. Liu Xin's forgeries "assert that the beginning and the end of the *Book of Changes* were written by King Wen and that the *Rites of Zhou* and the *Erya* were written by the Duke of Zhou. . . . These efforts see King Wen and the Duke of Zhou as the original authors of these works, just as Xu Xing [372–289 BCE] modelled his work on Shennong, and Mozi modelled his work on Yu. The goal was to steal Confucius's throne. This vilifies the sages and contravenes the law."[114]

(4) Diminishing the position of the various philosophical schools (*zhuzi*) was an assertion that the feudal lords venerated the teachings of Confucius, placing the power of all the states under Confucius's unity of All-under-Heaven (*yitong tianxia*). "The seventy-two disciples of Confucius dispersed throughout the lands of the feudal lords. The greater among them became advisors to the lords, while the lesser engaged with the scribes and the literati. Therefore, although the Seven Kingdoms did not truly follow the way, all learned from the teachings of Confucius." The claims of Daoists, Mohists, the Logicians, the Legalists, and the Agriculturalists that their teachings were on equal footing with those of Confucius only served to prove the supreme position of Confucius. The concurrent existence of the various schools and their overlapping teachings showed that the time of the Grant Unification was not yet approaching. This competition between the nine schools would only come to its final end in the period of Han Wudi, when Dong Zhongshu asserted that "the teachings of the various schools are not found within the laws of the Six Arts and the skill of Confucius. Please do not bring them in."[115] From the above, we can see that the sole motivation for Kang Youwei's writings on the Six Classics, and the reason behind his veneration of the position of Confucianism, was centered upon Grand Unification (*da yitong*) and his desire to eliminate enfeoffment (*fengjian*).

Thirdly, we shall revisit Kang's understanding of historical text compilation (*lishi bianzhuanxue*) and intellectual categorization (*zhishi fenleixue*). Defining Confucius as the Sage-King indicated that it was also necessary to view the Six Arts as law. Similar to people like Zhang Xuecheng (1738–1801), Kang had built his understanding of historical text compilation and intellectual categorization upon the interaction between systems of compilation and history, but his perspective on Liu Xin's *Seven Epitomes* (*Qi lue*) was in sharp contrast with these others. Complicated political implications are evident in Kang's criticism of the systems of historical compilation and intellectual categorization. In his account, the confrontation of scholarly thought between the collective Nine Schools and the leading position of Confucian unity corresponded to a political reality: both the confrontation between the enfeoffment (*fengjian*) of the feudal lords and the unity (*yitong*) of centralized administration and the conflict between the Yi on the periphery and the Xia of the empire. Only a historiographical system and intellectual categorization that accurately expressed the historical changes in the above relationships could serve as a correct system and classification. On the one hand, historical change is the basic object for historiographical systems and intellectual classifications. On the other hand, validating a historiographical and intellectual classification system is the only way by which one can clarify historical relations. In this context, there was no difference between the bases upon which Kang approved of the *Records of the Grand Historian* while rejecting *History of the Former Han* and upon which Zhang Xuecheng approved of *History of the Former Han* and criticized the *Records of the Grand Historian.* For example, the "Biographies of Confucian Scholars" (*Rulin liezhuan*) in the *Records of the Grand Historian* includes thinkers from non-Confucian schools, revealing a historical moment in which "the heterodox teachings had not yet been distinguished." The *Records* "place Confucianism alongside Daoism and Mohism. This is the same as placing the Liao . . . alongside the Song."[116] From Han dynasty on, Confucianism reigned supreme, but from the Han to the Ming, official histories followed the old format of the "Biographies of Confucian Scholars," which both obscured and even misrepresented changes in historical relationships.

Historical text compilation and intellectual categorization were a manifestation of historical and political relationships. Therefore, revealing these inherent contradictions in intellectual categorizations, such as Liu Xin's *Seven Epitomes,* and in historical compilations, such as Ban Gu's *History of the Former Han* (*Han shu*), had to involve an understanding of and reorganization of the historical and political relationships. Historiographical systems and intellectual categorizations were in no way independent issues for the history of scholarship but in fact contained specific political implications. I have already thoroughly examined this point in my discussion of Zhang Xuecheng's view on history. The main reason behind the divergence between Kang's and Zhang's views on historiography rests in their different political outlooks, particularly their different attitudes toward enfeoffment (*fengjian*) and unity (*yitong*). Kang saw unity as the true path for Chinese civilization, while Zhang saw enfeoffment as fundamental for China's system of rites. In the context of the Hundred Days' Reform, it was imperative that Kang formulate the centralization of imperial power and instigate reforms based upon the institution of the emperor. He was therefore critical of the regency and any division of power. This political stance was also visible in his perspectives on the classics and history. For example, he criticized Liu Xin for fabricating stories about the Three Sovereigns and the Five Emperors. Kang argued that "Chi You was one of the ancient feudal lords. Shao Hao was also a feudal lord, just like Chi You. It is clear that they were not the Five Legendary Emperors, and they were certainly not the children of the Yellow Emperor."[117] This was a reaffirmation of the position of the emperor. For another example, consider Kang's interpretation of the following quote, found in the biography of Wang Mang in *The History of the Former Han:* "The *Book of Documents* (*Shang shu*), in the chapter, 'The Announcement to the King's Uncle of K'ang,' says, 'The King speaks in the following fashion, "The chief of the nobles (*menghou*), Our younger brother, my little one, Feng . . ."'"[118] Kang Youwei pointed out that the Duke of Zhou was referred to as "king" here while serving as regent for King Wen. He argued: "In the *Spring and Autumn*, 'Duke Yin was not discussed as a king but as a regent.' These two classics [the *Book of Documents* and the *Spring and Autumn Annals*] were edited by the Duke of Zhou and Confucius to create the laws (*fa*) for later generations. Knowing this, it is clear that Liu Xin's falsification of the *Zuozhuan* was intended to support Wang Mang's regency and usurpation. I have not seen a similar meaning in the Gongyang commentary or the Guliang commentary."[119] The above example clearly presented the political meaning behind Kang Youwei's affirmation of the Gongyang commentary and the Guliang commentary, and his rejection of the *Zuozhuan*. It was actually a rejection of "regencies" and "usurpers," and a call to maintain the correct position of the monarch (*zhengwei*).

In summarizing the points discussed above, we come to a fundamental conclusion: in Kang's view, the learning of Confucius was the only force that reflected unification in the divisive world of the Age of Disorder. This was what was meant by "the creation of a new king" (*zuo xin wang*) in the *Spring and Autumn Annals*. Confucius lived in a time in which "the rites, music, and military expeditions came from the feudal lords." Therefore, "he was compelled to accept a posting with the feudal lords, providing answers on the rites, conduct, and virtue." However, the doctrine supplied by Confucius in no way represented the interests of the feudal lords. In fact, it did quite the opposite in its reflection of the teachings of the Former Kings (*xian wang*). Confucius claimed: "I transmit but do not innovate; I am truthful in what I say and devoted to antiquity."[120] This was a firm critique of the situation in which "the rites, music and military expeditions came from the feudal lords." Kang Youwei said:

> "Confucius edited the *Book of Documents* beginning with the "Canon of Yao" (*Yao Dian*). He extolled the *Classic of Music* (*Yue Jing*) and praised the virtue of the "Court Music and Dance" (*Shao Wu*). He placed the "Odes of Zhou and the South" (*Zhou Nan*) as the paramount section of the *Book of Odes*. He compiled the *Rites of Zhou*. He recorded the achievements of the Twelve Dukes in the *Spring and Autumn Annals* in keeping with King Wen and King Wu, creating a moral kingship for all of time. His edits ended with the Dukes' hunt for the *qilin*. In his later years, he enjoyed the *Book of Changes*, reading it voraciously to prepare a commentary. This was to employ the learning of the Former Kings to assist in matters for contemporary sages."[121]

By the same reasoning, no matter whether the seventy-two disciples were dispersed among the feudal lords or whether they had disappeared not to be seen again, they remained an intrinsic unifying force in a situation where All-under-Heaven was in competition. Kang strived to prove that Confucius's learning was not destroyed in the Qin burning of the books, repeatedly asserting that Confucianism had continued unbroken in the states of Qi and Lu, and that scholarship during the Han dynasty followed the traditions of Confucianism. This was not a defense of the Qin emperor but an assertion that saw the study of Confucius as a force for overcoming the competition that raged across All-under-Heaven.

It is worth noting that, aside from expressing the political conceptualization of the Grand Unification (*da yitong*)—or an opposition to enfeoffment (*fengjian*)—through the worship of Confucian unity (*yitong*), the accord between the classics and the narrative concerning contemporary politics contained an argument for the legitimacy of the process of the development of imperial power. As for his exposing of the false classics and their related false governance, it was through this direct connection between Wang Mang's usurpation of the Han dynasty and Liu Xin's usurpation of Confucius that Kang touched on the crisis of imperial power in the Guangxu era caused by the regency of the empress dowager. Kang wrote: "Wang Mang usurped rule over the Han through his false deeds. Liu Xin usurped Confucianism through his false classics. Both were false and both were usurpers. A false monarch (*jun*) and a false scholar. A usurper monarch and a usurper scholar. In their time, their falsities deceived All-under-Heaven. The monarch and his minister are the same!"[122] Within the contexts of Cixi's regency, such a reformulation of orthodox legitimacy and rectification of the imperial throne included a strong critique of Qing politics. It would be difficult to interpret the motivation behind Kang's exposing of the false classics without this overlap between politics and scholarship. To Kang, Wang Mang's usurpation of the Han was based on Liu Xin's usurpation of Confucius. The monarch and the scholar were walking hand in hand.[123]

In terms of classical learning, Kang held that the *Seven Epitomes* praised the Six Arts as the first epitome, venerating Confucius before all the books, reflecting the historical reality that Confucius had already been established in the orthodoxy. Placing the Six Arts at the beginning was part of a narrative system, the implications of which were exactly the same as the veneration of the dynastic founder Emperor Han Gaozu in the first "Imperial Biographies" (*benji*) chapter in the *History of the Former Han* and the veneration of Song Yizu in the "Imperial Biographies" of the *History of the Song* (*Song shu*). If the position of Confucius was the same as that of Han Gaozu and Song Yizu, then from the perspective of historical compilation, the seventy-two disciples of Confucius should be listed in the "Imperial Biographies," just like emperors Wen, Jing, Wu, and Zhao of the Han, and Zhen, Ren, Ying, and Shen of the Song. Or taking a step back, their positions should at least be recognized as part of a royal family. And in relation, the position of the Logicians, Legalists, Daoists, and Mohists should be recognized in much the same way as the Xiongnu and the Western Lands (*Xiyu*) were for the Han, or the Liao, Xia, Jin, and Yuan for the Song, listing them under "Biographies" and clearly classifying and demarcating them from the centrality of the Confucians. It was from this point that Kang's criticism of the *Seven Epitomes* began, pointing out that it did not include a "heterodox learnings epitome" (*yixue lue*) to list the various schools; instead it included the Confucians alongside the Logicians, Legalists, Daoists, and Mohists "as the various schools, unrelated to the Six Arts, and called them the Nine Schools of Thought (*jiu liu*)." This equated the historical conditions of the Grand Unification (*da yitong*) to tales of competing states described in such books as Chen Shou's *The Three Kingdoms*, Cui Hong's *History of the Sixteen Kingdoms* (*Shiliu guo chunqiu*), and Xiao Fang's *History of the Ten States of South China* (*Shi guo chunqiu*). This was as absurd "as if Guangwu had revised the record of Gaozu, first emperor of the Han, but instead listed the records of the Han, the Xiongnu, Xiyu, and the Southwestern Yi as equal factions."[124] Kang's central point was: Intellectual categorization and historical collation after the Han dynasty reversed the hierarchy of rites and conflated unity (*yitong*) with the enfeoffment (*fengjian*) of the feudal lords. In this sense, the rejection of Liu Xin's *Seven Epitomes* was closely and inseparably related to the reconstruction of Confucius's status as the Sage-King. However, this reconstruction also derided usurpation and regency on the level of politics.

3. Explorations of the Reforms Advocated by Confucius

Kang's thinking in *Forged Classics of the Wang Mang Period* was more abundantly developed in *Explorations of the Reforms Advocated by Confucius.* He explained: "As the rites developed by Confucius differed from the old ways of the Three Dynasties, and were even more in opposition with the false rites presented by Liu Xin, there was much disorder related to the Old and New Texts as it was not possible to follow a path between them and it was difficult to study them. Therefore, I investigated the discourse on rites from the Old and New Texts and completed a guide to summarize them."[125] Kang integrated his theory on the centralization of imperial power with his plans for the veneration of Confucius's teachings, showcasing Confucius's practice of reform as the Sage-King. The political implications of *Explorations of the Reforms Advocated by Confucius* included the following:

3.1 Enfeoffment and Unity

In *Explorations of the Reforms Advocated by Confucius,* competition among feudal lords (*zhuhou*) had a historical correlation and metaphorical relationship with the rise of different schools of thought: Clashes between the lords and the concurrent rise of the different schools were a reflection of a time of incessant divisions and war; Confucius's efforts to establish his teachings and reform were entirely in keeping with the political practice of King Wen, including his creation of rites and music, and his unification of All-under-Heaven. In this respect, Confucius was no different from King Wen. In other words, Confucius established his teachings on reform, and the other schools' establishment and attacks on Confucianism were the historical manifestation of the relationship between the discourse on unity (*yitong*) and enfeoffment (*fengjian*). Books 2–6 of *Explorations of the Reforms Advocated by Confucius* were titled "On the Various Schools that Rose in Parallel during the Late Zhou" (*Zhou mo zhuzi bingqi chuangjiao kao*), "The Various Schools Establish Their Teachings on Reform" (*zhuzi chuang jiao gaizhi kao*), "The Various Schools Turned to the Past for Their Reforms" (*zhuzi gaizhi tuo gu kao*), "The Various Schools Competed and Attacked Each Other" (*zhuzi zheng jiao hu gong kao*), and "Mozi and His Disciples" (*Mozi dizi hoxue kao*). Books 7–13 set out the specific content of Confucius's reforms, while books 14–20 returned to the struggle between Confucianism and the other schools: "The Various Schools Attack Confucianism" (*zhuzi gong Ru kao*), "The Daoists and Mohists' Many Attacks on Confucianism" (*Mo Lao gong Ru you sheng kao*), "Confucianism and Mohism in Conflict" (*Ru Mo zheng jiao jiao gong kao*), "Confucianism's Attacks on the Various Schools" (*Ru gong zhuzi kao*), "Confucianism and Mohism Rise in Parallel" (*Ru Mo zui sheng bing cheng kao*), "The Entire State of Lu Adopts Confucianism" (*Luguo quan cong Rujiao kao*), and "Confucianism's Ascendancy throughout All-under-Heaven during the Warring States, Qin, and Han Periods" (*Rujiao biao chuan tianxia Zhanguo Qin Han shi you cheng kao*). The work concluded with book 21: "The Unity of Confucianism that Followed the Reign of Han Wudi" (*Han Wudi hou Rujiao yitong kao*). The Confucian unity (*yitong*) was a product of the concurrent rise of the various teachings and only came to be defined after a long period of conflict. The Grand Unification (*da yitong*) of the Han dynasty defined the position of Confucianism's unity, indicating that Confucius provided meaning and guidance to the dynasty's establishment of institutions and laws.

> Of the Ten Schools, there are only nine to be considered. They arose when the Kingly Way (*wang dao*) was diminished and the feudal lords (*zhuhou*) were ruling through might. Different rulers of different generations had their preferred schools. The nine schools rose and operated in parallel, each with their own standards and each revering what it believed to be good, thus persuading the feudal lords to adopt it. . . . Then one school [Confucianism] engaged with a more enlightened ruler and he deigned to cooperate, then [Confucius] was finally able to serve as a great talent and right-hand man for the ruler. . . . As the country could cultivate the techniques of the Six Arts and listen to the words of the nine schools, it could dispense with shortcomings and build on strengths, thereby it was able to flow across the borders of many lands.[126]

The motivation behind the various schools' establishment of their teachings was intricately connected to the feudal lords' rule of might, in which "different rulers of different generations had their preferred schools." In addition to Confucius, other schools that founded teachings and reform based on the ancients included Mozi, Guanzi, Yanzi, Jin Zicheng, Song Xing, Yin Wen, Yangzi, Huizi, Xuzi, Baigui, Gongsun Longzi, Deng Xi, Daoism, Legalism, the Logicians, the Yin-Yang School, the School of Diplomacy (*Zongheng jia*), and the strategists (*bing jia*). This was a world of divided feudalist rule (*fengjian geju*) in which the feudal lords vied in competition. In this context, the establishment of a "New King" (*xin wang*) was a historic choice and proof of the superiority of the teachings of Confucius. Kang Youwei strongly argued for the teachings of Confucius but did not deny the insight and significance of the various schools. Confucius was operating at a time in which "the rites have been lost and must be recovered in the wild areas." His significance rested in his ability to find a middle path from the various schools, to dispense with shortcomings and build on strengths, establishing a holistic set of teachings.

Kang's discussion of the establishment of the various schools and Confucius's reforms was really a discussion of the relationship between enfeoffment and unity in Chinese history, with Confucian unity as China's final destination. Firstly, within Kang's narrative these teachings are part of the political order, and the political order is part of these teachings. The separation of church (or teachings) and state was the result of chaotic governance and political usurpation, and, conversely, the relationship between the teachings and the state in earlier times can be represented by the expression "All rivers flow from the different sources and all flow to the sea, just as all the schools of thought have their specific work but all serve to create order."[127] This perspective corresponded with the political angle to Kang's later discussion on local autonomy:

> The ancients governed the people through the system of enfeoffment. If such rule could not be actualized, then conditions would deteriorate into an impractical and unenlightened system. . . . The ancients' system of enfeoffment was a form of local autonomy (*difang zizhi*). However, the ancients' time was the Age of Disorder, with each feudal land ruled by one person, and so the calamities of selfishness and war continued from one generation to the next in an intolerable way that could not continue. For

> the people of today living in an Age of Ascending Peace, each enfeoffment is ruled by the people, allowing autonomy for the people and giving a voice to everyone. Thereby, each of us is able to engage in planning for the individual's benefit and the greater good. Then natural resources can be opened up and human labor can progress, our habits and lifestyles will be perfected, and talent will be put to good use. The states in America are given autonomy in the fashion of the enfeoffment practiced by ancient lords in the great states, and just like those found in the federation of German states.[128]

He still favored centralization (*junxian*) and unity (*yitong*), hoping that unified, centralized administration could bring together the autonomous localities. The establishment of the various schools' teachings and Confucian unity placed this political vision on the level of classical learning. According to his interpretation, the teachings of the various schools all belonged to "political order" (*zhi*). Therefore, there was not a sharp distinction between the teachings of the various schools and the competition of the feudal lords, or between the teachings and the states. Consequently, the struggle between unity and enfeoffment was not only a political struggle but a conflict among doctrines and beliefs.

Secondly, the pre-Qin conflicts between feudal lords and competing schools served as a metaphor for the rise of competing states and clash of civilizations in the colonial era. Although the various schools had inherited the knowledge and wisdom that had been building since Yu's founding of the Xia dynasty, they pursued different paths as they built their theories and gathered disciples, reforming established systems and planning to change All-under-Heaven. However, as the talents and abilities of each varied, each expounded upon one theory. They all had shortcomings and biases and were unable to communicate, finally leading to a situation in which they attacked each other. Kang continued with and gave free rein to this train of thought:

> The many schools of thought and religion in foreign lands were not exempt from this. In the past, Buddhism, Brahmanism, and ninety-six other schools created doctrines and learnings in India, while Zoroastrians attracted disciples to their teachings in Persia. In the West, when the culture and learning of Greece reached a zenith, those known as the

> Seven Sages taught at the same time, and Socrates gathered together their accomplishments. The emergence of teachings around the world was particularly vibrant during the Spring and Autumn and Warring States periods! Gathering the greatness of various schools, one was so outstandingly sacred that all people followed it, culminating in the Grand Unification (*da yitong*) succeeding as a model for countless generations. . . . When All-under-Heaven followed Confucius, the great Way of virtue (*dadao*) found unity, so there have been no new schools since the Han dynasty.[129]

The relationship between unity and enfeoffment not only describes the situation of the various competing schools; it can also be utilized to explain the religions and philosophies of foreign countries. Therefore, the statement "All-under-Heaven followed Confucius" described the post-Han age in which the people venerated only Confucian learning and excluded all other factions, yet it also alluded to Kang's belief that all competing schools of thought around the world would all inevitably turn toward unity (*yitong*). In this way, the historical phenomena of the system of enfeoffment of the feudal lords and the clash of the various schools find a connection to the conflict between nation-states, all centered around the contingency of "rivalry" (*bing zheng*). This constituted an allegorical link between the Grant Unification (*da yitong*), "venerating only Confucian learning" (*du zun Ru shu*), and *datong*. The following passage is taken from Kang's *Lectures from the Thatched Hut among Ten Thousand Trees* (*Wanmu caotang jiangyi*), but can be understood within the context of the clash of the various schools described in *Explorations of the Reforms Advocated by Confucius:*

> Histories of the world begin with the time of Yu the Great, when the world was found to have its beginning in Kunlun. Confucius differentiated between the three classes of emperor (*tianzi*), feudal lords (*zhuhou*), and ministers (*daifu*). The *Spring and Autumn Annals* was specific in curtailing the authority of these ministers. In the Age of Disorder, one should curtail the ministers. In the Age of Ascending Peace, curtail the feudal lords. In the Age of Great Peace, curtail the emperor. . . . Civilization (*wenming*) reigned after Confucius established his institutions. The Han dynasty was much like the Roman Empire. . . . When states are

> many, so too will conflict be frequent. Such is the case in Guizhou and Yunnan, where local chieftains abound. . . . The West had three great ages: the Babylonian, the Greek, and the Egyptian. . . . In India, monarchs appropriated power from the people, just as shamans appropriated power from the gods. Races and language spread out from India. . . . Those in the time of Confucius followed a fire religion that worshipped the sun.[130]

Kang Youwei clearly did not confine his discussion of "rivalry" to the Middle Kingdom. The common denominator for various schools of the Spring and Autumn period, religions around the world, and the feudal lords, was the limits to their understandings and judgments on the world they saw. Unable to "determine the good in Heaven and Earth, appraise the reasoning of the myriad of living things, or observe the plenitude of the ancient, few [of these scholars] could grasp the greatness of Heaven and Earth which can match the face of the gods (*shenming zhi rong*). . . . Unfortunately, the scholars [of the Spring and Autumn period] could not see the purity of Heaven and Earth or the designs of the ancients, and the way was broken for All-under-Heaven."[131] The Grand Unification (*da yitong*), Confucianism, and *datong* all arose in response to this need for a holistic, unified perspective, allowing both an overcoming of and integration of the conflict between the various schools, religions, and states.

Why did Kang Youwei need to discuss the various schools, the conflicts between various teachings, the attacks on Confucianism, and Confucian unity (*yitong*) to express his argument on Confucius's reforms? Why did he go as far as to use the conflicts between nation-states as a metaphor for the conflicts between various philosophies, rather than discussing them as direct political conflicts? Aside from countering the prevalent perspective maintained by the Old Text learning through extensive use of evidence and employing academic rhetoric to express political will, the most important reasons are: (1) Kang saw the Middle Kingdom as a civilization rather than merely a state. Also, he understood the conflict between states in the nineteenth century as a clash of civilizations. In this respect, political conflict could be expressed as civilizational or religious conflict. (2) Kang saw Confucianism as the synthesis and balance of the various doctrines, rather than as one among many schools. The above two points focused upon an interpretation of Confucianism and its power: Confucianism embodied a synthesis of historical relations and a civilization and not a theory restricted to a singular vision. It was a result of Confucius's teachings but also a product of historical relations and conflicts. Kang never avoided the fact that Confucius was one of the many who established doctrines. Only amid these complicated historical relations could opposing forces, such as Confucius and Yang Zhu, and subtle differences—such as those between Confucius and Mozi—distinctly emerge between Confucianism and the other teachings. At the same time, only through the mutual attacks between different philosophies could a syncretic form be created, as these conditions provided a possibility for divergence and synthesis, finally resulting in the Confucian unity as the natural result of historical forces, the realization of the Mandate of Heaven.

The examples shown here are all taken from book 18 of *Explorations of the Reforms Advocated by Confucius*, "The Rivalry Between Confucianism and Mohism during Their Height" (*Ru Mo zuisheng bing cheng kao*), to examine the implications of Kang Youwei's argument about Confucius's teachings. After this book, there are three that narrate the history of Confucianism's comprehensive triumph: book 19, "The Entire State of Lu Adopts Confucianism" (*Luguo quan cong Rujiao kao*); book 20, "Confucianism Spreads throughout All-under-Heaven and Flourishes during the Warring States, Qin Dynasty, and Han Dynasty" (*Rujiao bian chuan tianxia Zhanguo Qin Han shi you sheng kao*); and book 21, "The Unity of Confucianism that Followed the Reign of Han Wudi" (*Han Wudi hou Rujiao yitong kao*). Clearly, it was Confucian unity that triumphed in the final battle of the conflict between the Confucians and the Mohists. Both Confucians and Mohists based their teachings on humaneness (*ren*). They both narrated the lives of Yao and Shun, and both used learning and institutions to pacify the people. Both Confucianism and Mohism became "monarchs with no land, and they became leaders without being officials." Although they were divided, they were similar in many ways. The Confucians then divided into eight schools and the Mohists three. During the Warring States period, All-under-Heaven was divided between the disciples of Confucianism and Mohism. The great emperor could not engage in the dispute. Mohism became the adversary of the Confucian unity of All-under-Heaven. Here, the similarities between the two include: Both were called the "Former King," and evidence of this can be found in the ancient works; both had "universal love for All-under-Heaven," and therefore enjoyed the support of the people; and both were different from the various schools, and so were popular across All-under-Heaven. Their differences included lavish versus frugal funeral ceremonies, the use of *gong* (universal) versus *jian* (all-inclusive), the idea that fate played a role or played no role in one's life and death, and that "[t]he Confucians with their learning bring confusion to the law; the knights with their military prowess violate the prohibitions."[132] However, the final reason that determined their fate was the idea that, "When the Zhou house declined, the Kingly Way was abandoned."[133] The widespread popularity of Confucianism was simply due to its capacity for enlightenment (*dahua*). Therefore, Kang Youwei adopted the perspective of New Text learning that saw Confucius as "the king ordained by Heaven" (*shouming zhi wang*).[134] Without the practice of Confucianism in the State of Lu and the widespread travels of the seventy-two disciples, without the tendency toward warfare between the kingdoms to show the value of Confucian civilized administration, and especially without the political conditions of the unity that occurred under the Han, "it would have been difficult to forge ahead and make the achievements" of the Confucian unity across All-under-Heaven. In this respect, we can understand why Kang related the unity of monarchical rule with the unity of Confucianism in such a peculiar fashion. He stated: "The Qin took All-under-Heaven through force but was able to establish the Erudites to revere the classics of Confucius. The more than seventy of them were able to ensure that the learning of Confucius continued to flourish."[135]

Han Wudi venerated only Confucian learning and excluded all other factions (*bachu baijia, duzun Rushu*). Under him, Dong Zhongshu promoted Confucian learning and appointed education ministers. In the counties, Han Wudi appointed those of talent, of virtue, those filial, and those upright. The unity of monarchical authority and the unity of Confucianism were integrated as one. Confucius's institutions continued to be of great importance during the time of Han Wudi. It was known as the "Great Way" (*da xing*) or "Unity" (*yitong*). Han Wudi was to Confucianism as Ashoka was to Buddhism. From his time to now, Confucius remained a venerated figure.[136] This was a unique system that integrated church and state, taking recognition of the secular power of imperial authority as a base to venerate Confucianism as the state religion and Confucius as the Sage-King. And what would Confucius be if not the Sage-King who created the institutions? After Confucius established his doctrines, his clothes were referred to as Confucian (*Ru*) clothes, his books as Confucian books, his words as Confucian words, his students as Confucian students. In addition to the teachings created by Confucius, what was Confucianism? In "A Record of Being Kang Youwei's Student" (*Nanhai shicheng ji*), it is noted that Kang Youwei set Han Wudi's veneration of Confucius on a par with "Ashoka's veneration of the Buddha" and the Romans' veneration of Jesus Christ. Mentioning this, he lamented that all of these "phenomena happened at the same time during the Han dynasty."[137] The implications of this integration of church and state were to establish schools, select officials, and exalt the rites, all centered around Confucius and turning to the ancients to reform the present. The Grand Unification (*da yitong*) was not based in the institutions inherited from the Former Kings but was set in the new institutions made by Confucius, so Confucianism itself included the doctrine of the New King. Within the contexts of the late-Qing reforms, identifying Confucius as a religious patriarch and Confucianism as a shared creed became the basis for the political reforms required to progress to the institutions of *yitong*. In this respect, the discussion of the New King (*xin wang*) in the *Spring and Autumn* Gongyang studies indirectly expressed an attack on traditional systems while directly pointing at the basic direction for late-Qing political reform.

3.2 *The Three Sequences and the "Royal Regulations"* (wang zhi) *of Confucius*

If the conflict and unity of the various philosophies simultaneously represent the political concepts of enfeoffment and unity, then, as the patriarch, Confucius is none other than the Sage-King to unify All-under-Heaven. It was due to this that Kang identified Confucius as "King Wen" (Wen Wang), and argued he was the New King (*xin wang*) identified in the *Spring and Autumn Annals*. To Kang, King Wen was the Sage-King of the Middle Kingdom. Therefore, Confucius's incarnation as the Sage-King and the form and content of his formulation of the rites could provide an argument for China's centralization of imperial power (the New King). This argument included two aspects: Confucius as the universal patriarch and Confucius as China's Sage-King. This double identity offered the argument a dialectical relationship for Gongyang studies' Three Sequences, the Yi-Xia distinction, and the enfeoffment-unity binary. Kang quoted Dong Zhongshu's "Reform in the

Three Dynasties" (*sandai gaizhi*) in the *Luxuriant Dew of the Spring and Autumn Annals* (*Chunqiu fanlu*):

> In ancient times, those who were kings received the Mandate and then reigned. They altered the regulations, titles and designations, and the first month [of the calendar year]. Once the color of clothes [worn at court] had been determined, [the king] performed the Suburban Sacrifice to announce [the accession of the new dynasty] to Heaven, Earth, and the numerous spirits. He offered sacrifices to his distant and nearer ancestors and then proclaimed [the accession of their dynasty] throughout the empire. The Lords of the Land received [the proclamation of the new statutory color and beginning of the civil year] in their ancestral temples. They then announced it to their spirits of the land and grain, to the ancestors, and to the spirits of mountains and streams in their respective territories. Only then were the movements and responses of the various officials united. As for the alternations of the Three Sequences, neither the Yi and Di tribes who lived near [the Central States] nor the more distant states promulgated them. It was a matter for the Central States alone. That being so, the Three Dynasties inevitably used the Three [Sequences] to administer the world. It is said: "The Three Sequences and the Five Inceptions are the basis for transforming the Four Quarters [of the world]." When Heaven begins to withdraw [the Mandate from the old dynasty] and begins to bring forth [the new dynasty], Earth necessarily waits [passively] at the center. For this reason, the Three Dynasties necessarily occupied the Central States.[138]

Dong Zhongshu's "Reform in the Three Dynasties" (*sandai gaizhi*), a chapter in the *Luxuriant Dew of the Spring and Autumn Annals* (*Chunqiu fanlu*), lists three main points on the unity of *All-under-Heaven:* (1) The imperial court must start in the first month and value control over the calculation of the calendar; (2) One must be in the central states (*Zhongguo*) of the central plains and not in the lands of the Yi and Di; (3) Attire must be of defined style and color. These changes to clothing must be expressed. Carrying out these three would lead to the unification of All-under-Heaven. For this reason, Kang Youwei elevated the position of the Three Sequences to a hitherto unprecedented level in late-Qing New Text learning, positing reform as a requisite path for the construction of the new unity. Originally, the concept "royal first month" (*wang zhengyue*) indicated that the monarch should instigate changes and reforms in compliance with Heaven, yet here it does not refer to issues of the monarchy but to true revolution. From the perspective of Gongyang studies, "linking the Three Sequences" (*tong santong*) was an important step in connecting the rites to political legitimacy, indicating the order and basis upon which the New King could establish his own legitimacy through reform. The Three Sequences referred to the three ancient dynasties of Xia, Shang, and Zhou, which provided this model for political succession and rule, creating a sequence of kings each respectful of and learning from those before them. In the chapter "King Zhuang of Chu" (*Chu Zhuang wang*), Dong stated: "The king must instigate reforms." According to Kang's interpretation: Confucius, the New King who created the laws and institutions, was ordained by Heaven and a king with a different surname (*yi xing geng wang*). He was therefore different from those emperors who inherited their titles. In his efforts to posit Confucius as the New King, Kang liberally cited Dong Zhongshu's arguments on the New King and "linking the Three Sequences" in *Luxuriant Dew* because it was within the framework of linking the Three Sequences that the king signified reform.[139]

For Kang, Confucius's status as king was best reflected in the category of the King Who Created the Laws (*zhifa zhi wang*). This was not a king who saved a generation, but one who saved countless generations, one who was not interested in ruling people but was here to create moral laws. From Liu Xin's decimation of the Gongyang with the *Zuozhuan,* he used the Old Texts to falsify records and attack the New Texts. He altered the legacy of Confucius through the Duke of Zhou, altering deeds through words. He transformed the identity of Confucius's brilliance from the first king to a man of high erudition. Kang not only distinguished between the concepts of patriarch (*jiaozhu*), Uncrowned King (*su wang*), and Sage-King (*sheng wang*); he also distinguished between the Sage-King that all All-under-Heaven will follow and the emperor, monarchs, or other kinds of secular power. For Kang, the concept of "king" referred to Confucius as the patriarch, the King who Created the Laws, and the original unifier.[140] This "king" was absolute and singular, and the title could not be applied to the kings of countless nations or even the rulers of the countless planets. Confucius represented an absolute form of king's power, a universal monarch, and a sovereign for the Grand

Unification. There are two crucial points related to this: (1) Kang's examination of Confucius's reforms included an affirmation of unity under monarchical authority and an adulation of the king's power. (2) His emphasis on unity under monarchical authority presupposed a redefining of this unity or the power of the king: The "king" was "the King Who Created the Laws" to which all All-under-Heaven would submit, the original unifier and the king for the entire universe. Therefore, the concept was unrelated to the emperor or appointed nobles who governed the country through law or force. The "laws" (*fa*) created by the "king" do not refer to legal or penal codes but the basic rules created by the Sage-King, including moral philosophy (*yili*), institutions, and rites. According to Kang's definition, "The patriarch for all the lands created all the institutions and laws. . . . The moral philosophy and institutions of China were all established by Confucius. His disciples learned his ways and transmitted his teachings, bringing them across All-under-Heaven and changing the old ways. Some of the greatest and most remarkable of these include official attire and its insignia, three years of mourning, marriage customs, land divisions, schools, and means of choosing officials."[141]

There existed a clear distinction between "the King Who Created the Laws" and the emperor, but when Kang Youwei designated Confucius with titles that everyone was familiar with, including King Wen, the Former King (*xian wang*), and the Latter King (*hou wang*), the distinction between "the King Who Created the Laws" and the more political power of the king was obscured. The discourse on the Three Sequences infers that Confucius was the Uncrowned King in substance but King Wen in form. The *Xunzi* explained, "Confucius was humane, was wise, and was not fixated, and so through his study of various methods, he was worthy of being one of the former kings."[142] In the *Zhuangzi:* "The *Spring and Autumn Annals* are the records of Former Kings." In the *Mengzi:* "The Former Kings had hearts that were not unfeeling toward others, so they had governments that were not unfeeling toward others." Kang said: "Those who followed Confucius and guided in the rites were all using the rites of Confucius. Only Confucius should be praised as the 'Former King,' not those of the Three Dynasties."[143] He also said, "No evidence of the Xia and Yin dynasties remains. All remnants had already disappeared in the Zhou dynasty. We do not know about the ages before 841 BCE (*gonghe*), and it is only after the Qin and Han dynasties that our knowledge of events is detailed."[144] Because of this, none of the archaeological finds related to ancient texts are to be trusted. "Our understanding of the flourishing culture of the Three Dynasties is due to Confucius promulgating it."[145] Here, the replacement of Yao, Shun, and the Duke of Zhou with Confucius not only provided the basis for reform centered on the ancients; it also confirmed Confucius's status as king. There is a close relationship between the *Xunzi*'s "modelling oneself on the Latter Kings" (*fa houwang*) and the political power of a king. Kang changed this topic to view Confucius as the "Latter King," arguing:

> In the time of Xunzi, although the virtue of the Zhou dynasty was in decline, the Mandate of Heaven had not yet passed, and the Qin emperor had not taken the throne. Yet the Qin emperor followed the Zhou in establishing noble titles, and the Zhou followed the Shang. Therefore, the title of "Latter King" (*houwang*) is an earlier title and not related to the Zhou king. Nor is it a later title of the Qin emperor. If Confucius is not the Uncrowned King (*suwang*), then who else could be? Mencius called Confucius the "Former King" (*xianwang*). Xunzi called him the "Latter King" (*houwang*). In fact, they are the same. Xunzi stated that "the noble titles are from the Zhou," but penal and ceremonial names are not from the Zhou. Then if the true name of the Latter King is not Confucius, who could it be? Therefore, I believe that ritual, penal, and ceremonial names predate the Zhou. It would be a mistake beyond discussion to not indicate Confucius as the originator of the institutions.[146]

If we say that before Xunzi, the rulers Yu, Tang, Wen, and Wu were called the Former Kings, and their ways were known as the "laws of the hundred kings" (*bai wang zhi fa*), then the way of the Latter King came about due to the collapse of the rites and the destruction of the music. Xunzi said: "The rites make trust weak and are the beginning of disorder."[147] Kang asserted: "When Xunzi mentioned the 'Latter King' [i.e., the king who should be followed], he was always referring to Confucius." According to what he wrote in another section, however, Confucius's role as the creator and enforcer of the laws and institutions was even more distinctly portrayed.

> The many debates on Confucianism are not about its nature but about its system of rites. . . . In administering the affairs of an office, a minor official will take care of the affairs for a limited period of time in a given dynasty. Confucians must administer All-under-Heaven from antiquity to the present. Their task is great. In the matters of All-under-Heaven from antiquity to the present, we venerate Confucius for his laws and statutes. Should one fail to understand Confucius's laws and patterns, how can one administer? Should one understand, then one can understand the various schools (*zhuzi*), the *Twenty-Four Histories,* all books, and all situations. Should one not study the laws and statutes, not investigate affairs, then one cannot serve as an official. Should one not understand Confucius's laws and pattens, not investigate the great and small affairs of All-under-Heaven from antiquity to the present, then how could one hope to be a Confucian?[148]

The distinction between the rites and laws and the classics and legal judgments was exceedingly ambiguous.

Were his argument only about the reforms, then the Three Sequences, the meanings and guidance found in the Lu, Zhou, and Shang (Yin) dynasties would have been enough. There would have been no need to designate Confucius as the historical emperor-king (*diwang*), Sage-King, Former King, and Latter King. Clearly, the crux of Kang's argument was to place Confucius in a position with the absolute power of the king. This is evident in the following passage:

> The others—Shun, Yu, the Five Legendary Emperors, the Nine Great Emperors, and the Sixty-Four Emperors of old (*liushisi min*)—all were championed by Confucius. Those surnamed Yao, Si, Zi, and Ji [i.e., the surnames of the first rulers] all were employed as examples set by Confucius. White and black, square and round, different and same, generation to generation, all are in alignment with Confucius's institutions. Although we call them the Three Dynasties, in truth they are all of the same house.[149]

As Confucius's reforms would alter the world for all living things for all of time, his position was higher than that of all of the emperors. However, if the ancient emperors provided Confucius with his champions, models, and systems, the distinction between the Sage-King and the power of the king would also inevitably be ambiguous.[150] As the *Spring and Autumn Annals* was focused upon the state and the monarch, New Text learning was a theorizing of the state. In *Dong Zhongshu's Annotations of the Spring and Autumn Annals,* Kang stated:

> According to Wei Zixia: "Those who have a state must study the *Spring and Autumn Annals.* Neglecting this, one will not be able to see the dangers all around. One will be unaware of the larger patterns for states or the responsibilities of the monarch." Humaneness is Heaven's Will. Confucius detested the inhumaneness of his time, so he wrote the *Spring and Autumn Annals,* illuminating the Way of the King (*wang dao*), emphasizing humaneness (*ren*) and love of the people. He gave thought to disasters and prepared for them, moving back and forth between humaneness and inhumaneness. This was his intention for the entire volume of the *Spring and Autumn Annals.*[151]

"States" and "those who have a state" are of central importance here. Late-Qing nation-building and conceptualizations of a republic involved a reconsideration of the identity of members of society: The sovereign state was a specific kind of political order that required its members to assume a range of obligations, from paying tax to providing military service, in accordance with the needs of the state.[152]

3.3 *The Three Sequences and the Transcendence of the Centralization of Imperial Authority*

Confucius based his reforms on Yao and Shun, both symbols of the Age of Great Peace that existed before the Middle Kingdom. Therefore, the discourse on reform within Kang's centralization of imperial power included a logic of self-negation, a shift from the Grand Unification of the Middle Kingdom toward a global or universal Great Peace of *datong.*[153] From the perspective of New Text learning, concepts used to argue for the absolute central position of Confucius, including the Uncrowned King, the Sage-King, the Former King, the Latter King, and the King Who Created the Laws, implied the negation of secular monarchical authority. Moreover, the "Three Ages" theory from New Text learning also provided the theoretical basis for the self-negation of the centralization of imperial power (or statism). The Sage-King determined his historical duty based on the era,[154] and in the Age of Disorder this duty was to establish the absolute power of the king and prevent the ministers (*daifu*) from seizing power. In the Age of Ascending Peace, the main task was to establish unity (*yitong*) under the king and cease the enfeoffment (*fengjian*) of the feudal lords. In the Age of Great Peace, the very existence of monarchical authority is denigrated, and a rulerless world of rites and music will be established. This theory of the Three Ages constructed an intrinsic logic of self-transformation that adjusted according to the era, changing between the absolute monarch, the absolute state, and the world of *datong*. This theory thereby established an intrinsic and integrated logic between *Explorations of the Reforms Advocated by Confucius* and *The Book of Great Unity.*

The evolutionary elements of the theory of Three Ages were mutually compatible with the idea that "Confucius established institutions to remove the system of enfeoffment and establish the Grand Unification." The Grand Unification was a rejection of both the enfeoffment of the feudal lords and competition between states, yet it was through the establishment of the state's authority that Kang hoped to realize the Grand Unification. As Kang stated, "'The Royal Regulations' mention eighteen hundred feudal states. As it is unreasonable that these institutions could have existed in the Zhou dynasty, they were clearly devised by Confucius. The rule limiting feudal states to one hundred *li* was also made by Confucius as his principle for establishing states."[155] Establishing a system of centralized governance was thus a negation of the establishing of feudal states or competing states.[156]

Kang Youwei's reconstruction of the relationship between the Three Ages created a unique logic that saw the establishment of the Middle Kingdom as a state as the beginning of the struggle between unity and enfeoffment that had been waged since Yu the Great and his Xia dynasty. At the same time, a self-negation of this process is found through Confucius's reverence for the ancients of Yao and Shun. If the time of Yao and Shun was a time of the Great Peace, then this era was a time in which states, including China, did not exist. Therefore, while Confucius wrote the *Spring and Autumn Annals* to create a king for All-under-Heaven, the logic of the Three Ages in the *Spring and*

Autumn also indicated that the New King was nothing more than a transition, a procedure. This was the case in the Xia dynasty, and things were no different in the Qin, Han, or Tang. Kang explained:

> In the time of Yao and Shun, the people were their own masters. It was a time of the Great Peace when humanness reached its full extent. Therefore, the Confucians held them as the ultimate example. . . . The time of Yao and Shun was before the taming of the great floods, before China was created, so the *Book of Zhou* (*Zhou shu*) makes no reference to it. . . . We can continue with this reasoning. From when Yao and Shun passed on the title of ruler to those most virtuous, the Great Peace was magnificent. Confucius came later, much like the Seventh Buddha. . . . Confucius tamed the disorder to enter the age of Ascending Peace. Through his words about King Wen, he sought to enact humane governance, focusing on achieving the Great Peace. Through his words about Yao and Shun, he sought to enact the rule of the people and the Great Peace that ended disorder.[157]

From the relationship between China and the Age of Great Peace in the time of Yao and Shun, we can explain why the internal-external paradigm is not brought to the fore as a central theme in *Forged Classics of the Wang Mang Period, Explorations of the Reforms Advocated by Confucius,* and *Dong Zhongshu's Annotations of the Spring and Autumn Annals.* Compared to Zhuang Cunyu and Liu Fenglu, Kang had a somewhat different interpretation of this, from emphasizing the relativization of the Yi and Xia to highlighting the principle of "transformation" (*bianhua*). Kang returned to Dong Zhongshu and quoted him:

> The usual terminology of the *Spring and Autumn* grants that the Central States participate in proper ritual, but not the Yi and Di peoples. Why, on the contrary, is this [principle] contravened when it comes to the battle of Bi? The answer is: The *Spring and Autumn* does not employ consistent terminology but rather follows alterations [in circumstances] by shifting [its phrasing]. Now if Jin changes and acts like the Yi and Di peoples, or conversely, if Chu changes and acts like a noble man (*junzi*), then it shifts its terminology [to refer to them] to reflect these facts.[158]

The question of internal and external was an issue particular to the feudal period, and Kang's central concern was to use a system of unity or centralized state to overcome the political structure that allowed for the internal division of power. This central concern created the premise for the self-negation of the state, the self-negation of the differentiation of internal and external. However, this did not indicate that the internal-external issue had simply disappeared. On the contrary, the internal-external issue had been delicately bundled into the narrative of Confucius's creation of the unifying institutions.

The real question is: When trying to instigate national reforms through the centralization of imperial power, why did he argue for the legitimacy of these reforms based on Confucianism rather than imperial authority? Why single out Confucius and his conflict with the various schools (or feudal lords) and the Yi and Di, taking Confucianism as the historical basis for the concepts of "king," All-under-Heaven, and unity (*yitong*)? In one respect, the difference between the "New King" and the emperor was based in moral philosophy: Confucius's concept of humaneness (*ren*) and the idea of *datong* that derived from it contained a transcendence of the "Royal Regulations," so the purport of acting as the "New King" included the meaning or logic of *datong*. At the same time, universalist Confucianism includes an overcoming of ethnic relations internal to the dynasty, or the internal-external differentiation. It incorporates all social relations into the idea of ritual order, finally offering the basic logic to overcome divisions of internal-external and Yi-Xia. In this respect, Confucius's position as the Sage-King was a basic strategy for overcoming the issue of internal-external or inner-outer.

More importantly, the systems devised by Confucius were universal systems and the Era of Great Peace was a concept that transcended the categories of China and Yi-Xia. If the learning of Confucius was universal, then the system it advocated could not be considered that of any Chinese dynasty. Echoing his inclusion of Western institutions such as parliamentary systems, republics, and gender equality into Confucius's systems in *Explorations of the Reforms Advocated by Confucius*, Kang was much more direct and explicit in *Lectures from the Thatched Hut among Ten Thousand Trees* (*Wanmu caotang jiangyi*): "All the foreign nations use Confucius's institutions. . . . The 'Royal Regulations' were the systems proposed by Confucius and not at all those proposed by the Zhou. There were but a hundred states during the Spring and Autumn period. . . . The Xia, Shang, and Zhou were all Confucius's systems."[159] This included not only parliamentary systems and schools but also attire and measurements of time: "Those in the Three Dynasties all wore Western attire, favoring the fashion of short robes. The way of Confucius is the natural path. As the origin, he unifies all."[160] The reforms had to follow the Western systems, but these Western systems were not actually from the West. The Western systems were universal and because of this they could not be called Western. These were Confucius's systems, and this was the reasoning by which Kang Youwei could accept European universalism.

On June 19, 1898, Kang stayed up all through the night writing to the emperor. He offered the emperor "The Meiji Reforms in Japan" (*Riben Mingzhi bianfa kao*), "The Reforms of Peter the Great" (*E da Pide bianzheng zhiqiang kao*), "A Record of the Turks' Refusal to Reform and Their Subsequent Fall" (*Tujue shoujiu xuerou ji*), "A Record of Poland's Division and Annihilation" (*Bolan fen mie ji*), and "The French Revolution" (*Faguo geming ji*), all volumes that he had compiled himself. He also presented printed editions of the *Explorations of the Reforms Advocated by Confucius, Forged Classics of the Wang Mang Period,* and *Dong Zhongshu's Annotations of the Spring and Autumn Annals.* At the same time, he memorialized the throne to "Honor the Sage Confucius with a National Religion; Establish a Ministry of Religion and Churches; Record Years from Confucius; and Stop the Worship of Heterodox Beliefs" (*Qing zun Kong sheng wei guojiao li jiaobu jiaohui yi Kongzi jinian er fei yinci zhe*). There were three important points to note in this memorial: Firstly, he criticized China for maintaining polytheistic customs: "Heterodox temples abound, the influence of this custom is felt everywhere. Even abroad Chinese people establish temples to demons, to the sneering merriment of Westerners. How could this not be a source of shame for our countless citizens?"[161] He asked for Confucius to be enshrined as patriarch, reflecting the conflict between unity and enfeoffment on a religious level through the exclusion of all other denominations. Secondly, modeling his ideas on the Western understanding of a separation of church and state against the backdrop of competition between nation-states, he proposed establishing Confucius as a global and absolute patriarch. At the same time, Kang changed the old custom of integrated governance and religion through this separation of church and state, thereby leaving space for a secular imperial power. Kang Youwei explained:

> The Way of Confucius is universal. It is applicable to both humans and deities and covers both governance and religion. There is none higher. . . . Therefore, when governance and religion are integrated, those who follow its teachings are not Buddhist monks or Daoist masters; they are simply the people. In the past, the unified [state] (*yitong*) was a closed world. Standards of righteousness were set high, and conduct was strict, leading to perfection. However, in today's world, the powerful states can roam widely. Ancient times are very different from the present, so some of Confucius's ways need not be implemented. From their many details, we must uphold what is most important. For example, Confucius established righteousness to benefit All-under-Heaven and established righteousness to benefit clan groups. Today, however, this righteousness is purely for the benefit of the national citizen (*guomin*), and, because of this, the laws and rules [of today] cannot but show minor differences [to those established by Confucius]. This [state of affairs] is what is called adapting to the era.[162]

On the grounds that the times were changing, Kang quietly removed references to Confucius as Sage-King while honoring Confucius as patriarch, as this provided a space for the systematic reform that would support the separation of church and state and the centralization of imperial authority. However, if Confucius's time was the Age of Disorder and the contemporary time was the Age of Ascending Peace, then it follows that their political difference was that between a unified or divided governance and religion. Then, the relationship between governance and religion must once again turn to unity during the transition from the Age of Ascending Peace to the Age of Great Peace when Confucius is finally installed in a supreme position. For Kang, this was the dialectic between imperial power and Confucian religion, between state and *datong*. In this age with competing state powers, this was also the theoretical basis for the implementation of reform centered upon constitutional monarchy. The monarch, or imperial authority, represented a transition or a method, while Confucianism and its systems were the most fundamental universal laws.

The final notable feature of this memorial was its open call to adopt a calendar with a system of years based on Confucius, further emphasizing the necessity to reform and reconstruct the idea of legitimate succession (*zhengtong*) during the transformation from an empire into a sovereign state. Ouyang Xiu explained: "The theory of legitimate succession began with the writing of the *Spring and Autumn Annals*." Jao Tsung-I said: "The defining of legitimate succession is the first task completed in the compilation of the annals (*bian nian*), so the meaning of legitimate succession is intricately related to these compilations." Jao also stated: "The concept of succession (*tong*) is most closely related to the calendar system, so the *Book of Changes*' phrase 'govern the calendar to elucidate the time' (*zhili mingshi*) is profound. And the 'Treatise on the Royal Offerings to Heaven and Earth' (*Fengshan shu*) in the *Records of the Grand Historian* states: 'The ordering of the calendar should be based on succession [of the throne].'"[163] Defining a calendar system was of the utmost importance in the Gongyang learning of the Spring and Autumn period. As the *Spring and Autumn Annals* recorded events based on a chronological system of years, differentiating subjects and objects, those interpreting the *Annals* throughout history have studied the question of legitimate succession over and over again. Calendars were closely related to the establishment of new rulers. The symbolic importance of establishing a calendar was implied in the terms "rule the age" (*tongji*) and the "royal first month," which denoted the eleventh month of the lunar calendar. Kang compared changes to the calendrical systems of China, the West, and India. Adopting the ways of the New Text school, he favored Confucius as marking the beginning of the era due to his position as the Sage-King who initiated reforms. Although Kang never openly called for people to respect Confucius as "king" (instead of a patriarch), when we consider the importance placed on the calendar in establishing Grand Unification, as well as the position given to Gongyang learning's Three Sequences theory, which drew a close connection between changing the surname of the ruling house and a new political order, then it is clear that Kang's statements implied radical reform and the creation of a new order. For the dynasty, this was a call to reconstruct the entire system while preserving the continuity of imperial authority. For China's reforms, this was a fundamental strategy to use Confucius as a means to maintain internal cultural unity and to contend with Western universalism.

VI. From Empire to Sovereign State: The Self-Transformation of the Middle Kingdom

Kang Youwei's classical scholarship and political practice not only represented the final stage in Qing-dynasty New Text learning; they also reflected the theoretical and practical directions of the Hundred Days' Reform. However, these two aspects are not enough to explain the significance of his academic and political writings for intellectual history. Through the aspects outlined below, I will summarize the historical implications of Kang's thought.

I. Kang redefined the unique nature of the contemporary world and China's place in it through classical studies, thereby establishing a basic direction for the reforms: "The current world is similar to the climate of rivalry that existed during the Spring and Autumn and Warring States periods. It is unlike the unified rule found in the Han, Tang, Song, and Ming dynasties, about which people say China did not change for thousands of years. . . . Now is the time to begin a new governance across all of All-under-Heaven, not to maintain the governance of All-under-Heaven that past rulers created. It is the time of many competing states governing All-under-Heaven, and not the time of a unified and passive governance of All-under-Heaven."[164] Using the concept of "competing states" to describe the world situation connected the meanings found in the *Spring and Autumn Annals* with the system of nation-states. This identified within classical learning the basic foundation and logic of development for a reform program centered upon state-building. Regardless of whether one uses "competing" or "united," these terms could not describe the situation of the Middle Kingdom and instead described the world situation. The difference between these two conditions was defined by the position of the Middle Kingdom: "Competing" indicated that the Middle Kingdom was in a weak or marginalized position, while "united" indicated that it was in a strong or central position. The corresponding understanding for "united" was a boundless empire, while "competing" indicated a clear distinction between the internal and external with the system of nation-states. Kang made comprehensive proposals regarding the political system, the military, the education system, science and technology, the economy, domestic transportation, the bureaucracy, the news media, and diplomacy, and he tried to put these proposals into practice through reforms. This was the most comprehensive of the reform programs in the late Qing dynasty, one that also had global significance.

II: While promoting the process of China's nation-building, Kang brought together the achievements of Qing-dynasty New Text learning, reinterpreting the meaning of the Middle Kingdom. While eliminating internal factors of race, he also rejected arguments to divide authority through systems of provincial administration or federalism. In doing so, he sought a basis for the identity of the Middle Kingdom on a cultural level and, on a political level, discovered a state-building theory that opposed ethnic nationalism, self-determination, and ethnocentrism. The central themes in Kang's political conceptualization were: opposition to traditions of hereditary nobility and localized autonomy; opposition to the empire being divided into numerous nation-states or into a federal system like those found in Europe; and opposition to the nationalist traditions that began with the French Revolution. Instead he hoped to directly transform the empire into a sovereign state through administrative reform led by imperial authority, which would allow a united Middle Kingdom to keep its place in the world-system of competing states. While Dong Zhongshu's *Luxuriant Dew of the Spring and Autumn Annals* focused on the necessity of transforming the empire, Kang Youwei's classical scholarship, including his *Dong Zhongshu's Annotations of the Spring and Autumn Annals,*[165] focused on the necessity for China to transform directly from an empire into a sovereign state in the age of nation-states. Therefore, the crux of Kang's political program was a united state and the cultural and institutional means for this unification. The different levels of this program for reform can be described as follows:

1. Establish a basis for China's identity that relied on neither political structure nor racial or bloodline connections. This would be accomplished by promoting state reform through the centralization of imperial power, establishing national identity focused on the doctrines of Confucius, and establishing the concept of China on the foundations of a civilizational discourse. There was an important difference between traditional understandings of imperial authority and this new understanding, which represented the spirit and enthusiasm of this new age, the spirit and enthusiasm of statism. The centralization of imperial power represented the replacement of the old state system of aristocratic power and clan enfeoffment with a new system that

aimed to reconstruct local power and social structures into a more formalized and uniform political system. Within this statist framework, bureaucratic ranking and legal systems were institutions with universal applicability as these held much in common with the approaches favored by other states. This universal system was not an extension of the European formation but a return to the political culture of the Middle Kingdom. Kang believed that the identity of China was based in a Confucian universalism that transcended dynastic changes, race relations, and political orientations. As his understanding of China was born out of imperial history and his Confucian environment, he opposed revolution and promoted reform. For Kang, "revolution" indicated the toppling of old orders in the fashion of the nationalism of the French Revolution. It would involve a transformation of the internal ethnic relations of the imperial period and then a remaking of the state's political relations. "Reform," however, indicated the direct transformation from empire to sovereign state based on a cultural identity formed in the imperial period. It involved transforming the political and economic structures of the state through a preservation of the unity maintained by the central authority and encouraging the self-management of local societies.[166] Revolution was a strategy for founding a new state, while reform was the path for the self-transformation of empire.

2. To directly transform the empire into a state, it was necessary to remove the ethnic contradictions that existed inside the empire, to make the Middle Kingdom into a political and cultural symbol that transcended ethnic relations. A defining feature of the nation-state system was internal homogeneity, indicating a high level of ethnic, linguistic, cultural, and political uniformity. Empire, however, included a mélange of ethnic, linguistic, cultural, and political factors. As an empire, China was characterized by loose internal relations and diverse cultural relations. "The people have no involvement in affairs of the state, only being familiar with their own families and clans. We see all others as external. In many cases, the people remain divided by their surnames, village, counties, and provinces. The dynasty first ascended in the eastern lands before prevailing over central China, subduing the Mongolians, the Muslim-majority areas, and the Tibetans, thereby creating a Grand Unification. However, this was all done through governing by the old customs of these peoples."[167] While in this process of transforming

into a sovereign state under threat from powerful neighboring states, the utmost care was needed in managing the empire's different ethnic groups, their political boundaries, and their unique customs. By directly transforming from an empire into a sovereign state, the Qing could meet both internal and external challenges.

3. To overcome the threat of division due to the empire's diverse ethnicities and political systems, Kang Youwei redefined the concept of "Chinese" by negating the essentialist categories of Yi and Xia and the idea of a unitary Han ethnicity. The decision of Emperor Xiaowen of the Northern Wei dynasty (r. 461–499) to adopt Han surnames to Sinicize his own people may be Kang's best example of a negation of the myth of a unitary ethnicity. For Kang, it would not be difficult to imitate political institutions common throughout other countries, including a constitutionally defined parliament, a balance of powers, an independent judiciary, responsible government, and elections. However, it would be much more difficult and take much longer to form a unified nation. It was based on this that Kang differentiated the Middle Kingdom from the title of the dynasty (Qing), trying to make *Zhongguo* (the Middle Kingdom) or *Zhonghua* (China) the name and the basis of the identity of a unified sovereign state:

> China has always used dynastic titles. A change in the name of the ruling family was a change to the entire system. For those past generations, in any foreign relations, the country has been called China since antiquity. Now, those in countries both East and West refer to our country as China (*Zhina*), yet these characters were not found in our classics. I understand this to be based on phonetics. "China" may be based upon the sound of the old name of "*Zhuxia*" or "*Zhonghua*." The ancients used the term "*Zhuxia*" or "*Zhuhua*," both of which are often found in the records. The phonetics of "*Huaxia*" changed in the central states. The Mongolians, Muslim peoples, and Tibetans established schools to study the language through the classics, and came to know and integrate with the central lands, bringing them closer together. The current name for the country is a foreign name based in documents and recordings from the past. It would be better if they used the name "*Zhonghua*." The emperor's reforms bring unity and progress toward *datong*.[168]

The reforms were not a negation but a reinterpretation of "legitimate succession" (*zhengtong*). Within the context of late-Qing politics, a reliance on "legitimate succession" was the inevitable response to the model for the transformation from empire to sovereign state. Reform could not change into the complete collapse of the imperial system.

4. Against a theoretical backdrop of eliminating the system of enfeoffment and establishing unity, Kang opposed systems of federation and confederation that had the potential to divide authority into large political bodies, but he also supported the ideas of a constitutional monarchy and local autonomy. This involved organizing local units and the centralized authority into a unique political system in which the state administrative systems permeated all of society through a form of shared authority. Kang's vision was designed to prevent the dissolution of the empire. This political conceptualization was premised on the international conditions of competing states and powerful countries on all sides. It also compared Chinese and Western historical contexts and trajectories from a republican perspective. Contrasting these narratives with Kang's opposition to the state in *The Book of Great Unity,* we can see that his opposition to the state and his criticism of federation were both due to their connection to the model of the nation-state. In *The Book of Great Unity,* Kang opposed the nation-state and promoted global *datong,* but in *Explorations of the Reforms Advocated by Confucius* and other works, he opposed provincial autonomy through federation and endorsed the power of a unified empire as a means to contend with the powers in the global system of competing states. This offered an opposition to the implementation of national self-determination from the perspective of the empire. Kang had touched upon fundamental characteristics of China's political reforms: implementing political transformation while preserving the empire's territory, demography, and cultural identity. How to maintain the unity of the state during this transformation was a central question that would test the entire process of the reforms. To a certain extent, this could be seen as a uniquely Chinese issue.

There was an intrinsic connection between the democratic reforms and nationalism found in the modern West: As self-determining nation-states broke off from empires, the national community became a vehicle for the state, and the rights and equality of members of the nation became the fundamental feature of the legal and political systems in those nation-states.

> The political and social philosophies that sprang from the Enlightenment were religions because they ascribed ultimate meaning and sanctity to the individual mind—and also, it must be added immediately, to the nation. The age of individualism and rationalism was also the age of nationalism: the individual was a citizen, and public opinion turned out not to be the opinion of mankind but the opinion of Frenchmen, the opinion of Germans, the opinion of Americans. Individualism, rationalism, nationalism—the Triune Deity of Democracy—found legal expression in the exaltation of the role of the legislature and consequent reduction (except in the United States) of the law-creating role of the judiciary; in the freeing of the individual actions from public controls, especially in the economic sphere; in the demand for codification of criminal and civil law; in the effort to make predictable the legal consequences of individual actions, again especially in the economic sphere.[169]

However, China's state-building was a process of self-transformation from empire to sovereign state. Therefore, the fundamental issues for China's political system, legal system, regional relations, and civil rights were: How to preserve centralized authority in order to maintain the unity of the state; how to liberate social members from regional relationships to organize them into the subjects of the sovereign state; and, amid different regional and cultural identities, how to form a political structure that allows for equality and diversity. Because of the intrinsic continuity between sovereign state and empire, it was impossible for the internal political relations of the state to reach the level of cohesion found in the nation-states of Europe. The tension between dissolution and unity was dependent on the fluctuations of the relationship between the internal and the external. Even though later political actors and intellectuals may not have agreed with the political decisions made by Kang, his ideas and the issues that he faced remain pivotal questions for Chinese society today and the most crucial tasks in Chinese societal transformation and state identity.

III: Kang integrated the outlook of Confucian universalism with various Western sciences and understandings of the state and religion to conceptualize a utopic vision of *datong.* This prophecy of *datong,* heavily colored by socialism, corresponded with his oft-repeated discussion of a universalist Confucian world and offered a conceptual means to transcend hierarchies of relationships between states, races, classes, and genders. Comparing Kang's vision of *datong* with the theorizing of the state formulated in his classical scholarship, there is an overlap between the understanding of the state in *datong* and the Grand Unity (*da yitong*). Both include a negation of the model of the nation-state. The central political point of *The Book of Great Unity* was the transcendence of the state. While reconstructing the centrality of imperial authority, Kang clearly saw the inevitable autocratic nature of the modern state and the authoritarianism of state theory. This was an appeal to transcend the very capitalist modernity that modern China was striving for, an antimodernist modernist program, and a religionist revolt against organizing China into the secularizing program of capitalism. This conceptualization followed the temporal logic of linear evolution and a forward-looking optimism, and it remained in line with basic nineteenth-century assumptions about the nation-state, territory, sovereignty, race, and the division of labor but employed these to imagine the paradoxical world of *datong*. If the reconstruction of Confucian universalism and the logic of the Grand Unification (*da yitong*) that is argued alongside this reconstruction are an effort to reconstruct the past for the sake of "modernity," then the construction of the world of *datong* and its governing rules is an effort to construct the future for the sake of modernity. Although this world invariably assumes its form from a kind of Confucian universalism, its bold distant vision is rooted in the context of the vicissitudes and intrinsic contradictions of modern history, to the extent that this conceptualization became a symptom of the problem of Chinese modernity, an intellectual source that is constantly revisited, constantly reviewed, constantly reinvigorated, and critiqued.

In this respect, it was not the feasibility of this conceptualization but the modern contradictions that prompted it that constitute the source that compelled modern Chinese thought to look both backward and forward. Although Kang's theory included a tendency toward the centralization of state power similar to that of the European nation-state, his reformist plan and theoretical framework of *datong* had a socialist orientation against the secular tendency toward authoritarianism. If European socialism was a historical movement that developed from the Christian tradition in response to the secular religion of the nation-state, then Kang's concept of *datong* was an intellectual challenge that developed from the Confucian tradition in response to the independence of the nation-state, but the goal of this challenge was to transform China into a sovereign state. As Kang Youwei predicted, this utopian vision could not resolve the real problems facing China at that time, yet through the construction of this utopian vision, the deep contradictions facing the modern world were revealed. For China and the rest of the world in the midst of modernization, this vision not only revealed the contradictions inherent in this process; it also offered a moral orientation outside of this modernization project, thus raising the possibility of self-criticism and imagination for modern society.

IV: This utopic vision was intertwined with a statism that stemmed from the historical antecedent of empire and a religious bearing with Confucius as patriarch, providing a religious dimension to the reform movement. In 1856, Alexis de Tocqueville argued that "[t]he French Revolution, though political, assumed the guise and tactics of a religious revolution." It was "[a] political revolution . . . which inspired proselytism."[170] According to his understanding, religions are concerned with humankind in the abstract and pay no attention to the "laws, customs or national traditions" that make up particular components in communities. Tocqueville's concept of religious revolution was built upon the differentiation of two understandings of religion, that is, the differentiation between Christianity and the paganism of ancient Rome and Greece:

> The old forms of paganism, which were all more or less interwoven with political and social systems, and whose dogmas wore a national and sometimes a sort of municipal aspect, rarely traveled beyond the frontiers of a single country. They gave rise to occasional outbursts of intolerance and persecution, but never to proselytism. Hence, the first religious revolution felt in Western Europe was caused by the establishment of Christianity. That faith easily overstepped the boundaries which had checked the outgrowth of pagan systems, and rapidly conquered a large portion of the human race.[171]

With this differentiation, Tocqueville saw the secular French Revolution as a religious revolution because:

> The French Revolution acted, with regard to things of this world, precisely as religious revolutions have acted with regard to things of the other. It dealt with the citizen in the abstract, independent of particular

> social organizations, just as religions deal with mankind in general, independent of time and place. It inquired, not what were the particular rights of French citizens, but what were the general rights and duties of mankind in reference to political concerns.[172]

We see the same aspect of universalism in Kang Youwei's theories for reform: He was investigating the social and political formations found not only in China but also for all of humanity. Both his Confucianism and the scientific knowledge he employed to reclassify the world shared this universalist feature. Tocqueville saw the universalism of the French Revolution as transcending states, as well as regional and particular political and legal formations. It resisted the regional nature of institutions and the particular nature of culture through the universalism of the concept of humankind. However, he also unwittingly alluded to the differences between paganism and Christianity in the context of empire, indicating that Christianity was an imperialist religion. Kang's concept of *datong* was a description of the human condition, but it was born of and developed in the universality of the Middle Kingdom. The use of the concept of the Middle Kingdom assumes the concept of All-under-Heaven, and universalist Confucianism transcended the legal and political systems of any region, any ethnicity, or any particular dynasty. It reconstructed the politics, laws, and customs of a particular period with the universal concepts of the Middle Kingdom, All-under-Heaven, and *datong.* Kang's strong statist inclinations also reflected a political anarchism that transcended the state and a universalism that, through culture, transcended any particularism.

In this respect, modern statism manifested out of a quasi-religious revolutionary formation and was destined to be closely linked to a universalism that transcended the state. However, just as the final analysis of the French Revolution found it to be a sociopolitical revolution, statist reforms and all later revolutions all carried similar inclinations to destroy the feudal institutions or aristocratic hierarchies that remained in the empire and replace them with a sociopolitical order that was more unitary, less complicated, and demanded comprehensive egalitarianism. This order was the source for imagining all the ideology, emotions, habits, and ethics of the reform.

To what extent was this institution and its order a new innovation? And to what extent was it a renewal of the past? Kang's efforts to map out the future world through natural sciences and Western ideas of politics, education, and law were new innovations. Yet, given the history of how this new knowledge had spread, Kang's efforts, much like the form of his New Text learning, were but a continuation of a long historical process. The following elements were constantly regenerating within the historical evolution of the empire: The centralization of imperial power; the concentration of power on the emperor that was hidden behind this centralization; the centralized state's negation of pluralist politics and legal systems; and the traditions of classical learning that served empire-building. For these reasons, we can view modern China's state-building as empire's self-transformation.

The Hundred Days' Reforms, which Kang played a significant role in organizing, ended in failure, but the basic direction of political changes that he planned was not buried with the Reforms. If the centralization of authority was integral to the traditional system of empire, then Kang's thought and practice of reform indicated that the new society's reliance on centralized authority would far exceed that of the imperial period, to the extent that the state system would be much more hostile to diversity and pluralities of authority or culture than the early imperial period was. This is the primary reason for the continued expansion of the traditional system of centralized administration (*junxian tizhi*) and the progressive decline of forms of local autonomy. Centralized authority and its corresponding administration systems were not innovations initiated by reformers or revolutionaries but the remnants of the old institutions. These remnants are able to continue to develop in this new society because they are the only parts that could adapt to the needs of the new society. The roots of the modern state's hostility to certain traditional political formations are not to be found only within the traditions of authoritarian states themselves; we must also search for the bases of this hostility in the broader global relations that take the nation-state as their basic form. This is the fundamental conclusion gained from our reading of Kang Youwei's classical scholarship and *The Book of Great Unity.*

I conclude this discussion of Kang's Confucian universalism with his own explanation of the Three Ages and *datong:*

> The Three Ages was a grand design made by Confucius and articulated in the *Spring and Autumn Annals.* The era that information was passed down about was known as the Age of Disorder. The era that Confucius

heard about directly from others was known as the Age of Ascending Peace. And the era that Confucius witnessed was known as the Age of Great Peace. In the Age of Disorder, culture and learning were not yet enlightened. In the Age of Ascending Peace, culture and learning gradually developed, and the time was known as "lesser tranquility" (*xiaokang*). In the Age of Great Peace, it was a time of *datong* in which the distant and the near, great or small, all were one. Culture and learning were perfectly accomplished. The profound meanings (*da yi*) concern the time of lesser tranquility, while the subtle words (*wei yan*) are about the Age of Great Peace. In the study of Confucius, these should be separated into two categories. This is the primary grand design of the *Spring and Autumn Annals*.[173]

NOTES

TRANSLATORS

INDEX

Notes

Preface to the English Edition

This text has some slight overlap with the text of chapter 2 of my 2011 Harvard University Press book, *The Politics of Imagining Asia,* first published in an English translation prepared by Wang Yang in *Modern China,* 34, no. 1 (January 2008): 114–140.

1. Fei Xiaotong first put forward his well-known discussion on the plurality and unity of the Chinese people at the Tanner Lectures at Chinese University of Hong Kong in 1988 and published them the following year. See "Zhonghua minzude duoyuan-yiti geju," *Beijing Daxue xuebao,* 1989, no. 3: 3–21.

2. Fei Xiaotong, *Zhonghua minzu duoyuan-yiti geju* (Beijing: Zhongyang Minzu Daxue chubanshe, 2018), 17. [English is from Fei Xiaotong, "Plurality and Unity in the Configuration of the Chinese People," *The Tanner Lectures on Human Values, XI* (Salt Lake City: University of Utah Press, 1990) 167–168.—Trans.]

3. Per Ernest Gellner, "Nationalism is primarily a political principle, which holds that the political and national unit should be conrguent. Nationalism as a sentiment, or as a movement, can be best defined in terms of this principle." Gellner, *Minzu yu minzuzhuyi,* trans Han Hong (Beijing: Zhongyang bianyi chubanshe, 2002), 1. [English translation from Gellner, *Nations and Nationalism* (Oxford: Blackwell, 1983), 1.—Trans.]

4. Immanuel Kant, "Yongjiu heping lun" [Perpetual peace], in *Lishi lixing pipan wenji* [Critiques of historical reason], trans. He Zhaowu (Shanghai: Shangwu yinshuguan, 1991), 99. [Translation borrowed from *Perpetual Peace: A Philosophical Essay,* trans. M. Campbell Smith (London: Allen and Unwin, 1903), 109.—Trans.]

5. See Wang Hui, *Dong Xi zhijiande "Xizang wenti"* [The "Tibet question" between East and West] (Beijing: Sanlian shudian, 2014), 269–277. [A portion of Wang Hui's work on Tibet is published as "The 'Tibetan Question' East and West: Orientalism, Regional Ethnic Autonomy, and the Politics of Dignity," trans. Theodore Huters, in *The Politics of Imagining Asia,* ed. Theodore Huters (Cambridge, MA: Harvard University Press, 2011), 136–227.—Trans.]

6. Chen Yinke, "Tangdai zhengzhishi lunshu gao" [Manuscript on the political history of the Tang Dynasty], in *Chen Yinke shixue lunwen xuanji* [Selected essays on history and historiography by Chen Yinke] (Shanghai: Shanghai renmin chubanshe, 1992), 567.

7. Luo Youzhi [Evelyn Rawski], "Zaiguan Qingdai: lun Qingdai zai Zhongguo lishi shangde yiyi" [Reexamining the Qing dynasty: On the significance of the Qing in Chinese history] in *Qingchaode guojia rentong* [The state identity of the Qing dynasty], ed. Liu Fengyun and Liu Wenpeng (Beijing: Zhongguo Renmin Daxue chubanshe, 2010), 1–18. [For the English, see Rawski, "Presidential Address: Reenvisioning the Qing: the Significance of the Qing Period in Chinese History, *Journal of Asian Studies* 55, no. 4 (1996): 829–850.—Trans.]

8. He Bingdi, "Niewei Hanhua" [In defense of Sinicization], in *Qingchaode guojia rentong,* 19–52. [For the English version, see Ping-ti Ho, "In Defense of Sinicization: A Rebuttal of Evelyn Rawski's 'Reenvisioning the Qing,'" *Journal of Asian Studies* 57, no. 1 (1998): 123–155.—Trans.]

9. In their research on the history of the Liao dynasty, Karl Wittfogel (1896–1988) and Feng Chia-sheng (1904–1970) sparked controversy by including both the Yuan dynasty and the Khitan into one category of "dynasties of conquest," which they contrasted with "dynasties of infiltration" such as the Northern Wei dynasty. Wittfogel and Feng, *History of Chinese Society: Liao* (Lancaster: Lancaster Press, 1970).

10. Ping-ti Ho, "Niewei Hanhua," 52. [For the English, see Ho, "In Defense of Sinicization," 152.]

11. Chen Yuan, *Yuan Xiyu Huahua kao* [The *huahua* of the peoples of the Western Regions in the Yuan dynasty], in *Zhongguo xiandai xueshu jingdian: Chen Yuan juan* [Classics of modern Chinese scholarship: Works by Chen Yuan], ed. Liu Mengxi (Shijiazhuang: Hebei jiaoyu chubanshe, 1996), 54.

12. Zhang Taiyan, "Zhonghua Minguo jie" [Explaining "The Republic of China"], *Min bao* 15 (1907): 2. See Wang Hui, *Shijide dansheng* [The birth of the century] (Beijing: Sanlian, 2020), 136. [Translation modified from Zhang Taiyan, "Explaining 'The Republic of China,'" trans. Pär Cassel, *The Stockholm Journal of East Asian Studies* 8 (1997): 17–18. The phrase "central domains" is used to translate *Zhu Xia* in Year 21 of Lord Xi in *Zuo Tradition: Commentary on the Spring and Autumn Annals,* trans. Stephen Durrant, Wai-yee Li, and David Schaberg (Seattle: University of Washington Press, 2016), 351.—Trans.]

13. Mao Zedong, "Lun xin jieduan" [On the new stage], *Jiefang* (Yan'an), no. 57 (November 25, 1938). See also "Zhongguo gongchandang zai minzu douzhengde diwei,"

Mao Zedong xuanji [Selected works of Mao Zedong] (Beijing: Renmin chubanshe, 1966), 522–523. [Translation modified from "On the New Stage," in *Mao's Road to Power: Revolutionary Writings, 1912–1949,* vol. 6, *The New Stage,* ed. Stuart Schram (London: Routledge, 2004), 539.—Trans.]

14. Huang Xingtao, "Qingchao Manrende 'Zhongguo rentong'" [The "Chinese identity" of Qing-dynasty Manchus], in *Qingdai zhengzhi yu guojia rentong* [Qing-dynasty politics and national identity], ed. Liu Fengyun, Dong Jianzhong, and Liu Wenpeng (Beijing: Shehui kexue chubanshe, 2012), 1: 19, 21.

15. R. Bin Wong [Wang Guobin], "Liangzhong leixingde minzu, shenme leixingde zhengti?" [Two types of nation, what type of polity?], in *Minzude goujian: Yazhou jingying jiqi minzu shenfen rentong* [Creating nations: Asian elites and national identities], ed. Timothy Brook [Pu Zhengmin] and Andre Schmid [Shi Ende], trans. Chen Cheng et al. (Changchun: Jilin chuban jituan, 2008), 134–135. [English from Wong, "Two Kinds of Nation, What Kind of State," in *Nation Work: Asian Elites and National Identities,* ed. Brook and Schmidt (Ann Arbor: University of Michigan Press, 2000), 113.—Trans.]

16. Marshall Sahlins, "The Stranger King," *Indonesia and the Malay World* 36, issue 105 (2008): 177–199.

Editor's Introduction

1. For reviews that also substantial summaries of *The Rise of Modern Chinese Thought,* see Zhang Yongle, "The Future of the Past: On Wang Hui's *Rise of Modern Chinese Thought,*" *New Left Review* 62, (March–April 2010): 47–83; Philip C. C. Huang, "In Search of Chinese Modernity: Wang Hui's *The Rise of Modern Chinese Thought,*" *Modern China* 34, no. 3 (2008): 396–404; Wang Ban, "Discovering Enlightenment in Chinese History: *The Rise of Modern Chinese Thought,*" *boundary 2* 34 (2007): 217–238; and Viren Murthy, "Modernity Against Modernity: Wang Hui's Critical History of Chinese Thought," *Modern Intellectual History* 3, no. 1 (2006): 137–165. Other discussions and reviews include Claudia Pozzana and Alessandro Russo, "Circumstances, Politics, and History: Reading Notes on Wang Hui's 'General Introduction' to *The Rise of Modern Chinese Thought,*" trans. Michaela Duranti, *positions: east asia cultures critique,* 20, no. 1 (2012): 307–327; and Kai Marchal, "Die Wiederkehr der Moral? Wang Hui und das Ethos der Chinesischen Moderne," *Deutsche Zeitschrift für Philosophie* 65, no. 3 (2017): 535–553. For essays and interviews in English by Wang Hui that speak directly to *The Rise of Modern Chinese Thought,* see "A Dialogue on *The Rise of Modern Chinese Thought,*" trans. Tani Barlow, *positions: east asia cultures critique,* 20, no. 1 (2012): 287–306; Wang Hui, "How to Explain 'China' and its 'Modernity': Rethinking the *Rise of Modern Chinese Thought,*" trans. Wang Yang, in *The Politics of Imagining Asia,* 63–94; Wang Hui, "Rethinking *The Rise of Modern Chinese Thought,*" trans. Audrea Lim, in *The End of the Revolution,* 105–138; and "The Liberation of the Object and the Interrogation of

Modernity," *Modern China* 34, no. 1 (2008): 114–140. For a useful overview of the so-called New Left, with reference to Wang Hui's work: Shi Anshu, François Lachapelle, and Matthew Galway, "The Recasting of Chinese Socialism: the Chinese New Left since 2000," *China Information* 32, no. 1 (2018): 139–159.

2. The four volumes are *Li yu wu* [Principles and things], *Diguo yu guojia* [Empire and state], *Gongli yu fangongli* [Universal Principle and anti-Universal Principle], and *Kexue huayu gongtongti* [The community of scientific discourse.] The fourth volume also included two long essays that were included as appendices. Translations of condensed versions of these essays were published as "The Politics of Imagining Asia," trans. Matthew Hale, and "Local Forms, Vernacular Dialects, and the War of Resistance against Japan: The 'National Forms' Debate," both in Wang Hui, *The Politics of Imagining Asia*, 10–62, 95–135.

3. See, for example, Wang Hui, "The Fate of 'Mr. Science' in China: The Concept of Science and Its Application in Modern Chinese Thought," trans. Howard Y. F. Choy, *positions: east asia cultures critique* 3, no. 1 (Spring 1995): 1–68; and Wang Hui, "On Scientism and Social Theory in Modern Chinese Thought," trans. Gloria Davies, in *Voicing Concerns: Contemporary Chinese Critical Inquiry*, ed. Gloria Davies (Lanham, MD: Rowman and Littlefield, 2001), 135–156. The four-volume *Rise of Modern Chinese Thought* published in Chinese in 2004 has many shared concerns and points of overlap and dialogue with these pieces.

4. Wang, "A Dialogue on *The Rise of Modern Chinese Thought*," 295; Zhang, "The Future of the Past," 52–53.

5. See Wang Hui, *China's New Order: Society, Politics, and Economy in Transition*, ed. Theodore Huters and Rebecca Karl (Cambridge, MA: Harvard University Press, 2006); *The End of the Revolution: China and the Limits of Modernity* (London: Verso, 2009); *The Politics of Imagining Asia*, ed. Theodore Huters (Cambridge, MA: Harvard University Press, 2011); and *China's Twentieth Century: Revolution, Retreat, and the Road to Equality*, ed. Saul Thomas (London: Verso, 2016).

6. This term has also been translated as "conditions," "historical circumstances," and "conditions of the times." For a detailed discussion of this term in Chinese thought, see François Jullien, *The Propensity of Things: Toward a History of Efficacy in China*, trans. Janet Lloyd (New York: Zone Books, 1999). Wang Hui also provides a discussion in *China from Empire to Nation-State*, trans. Michael Gibbs Hill (Cambridge, MA: Harvard University Press, 2014), 61–86.

7. *The Gonyang Commentary on the Spring and Autumn Annals: A Full Translation*, trans. Harry Miller (New York: Palgrave Macmillan, 2015); *A Forgotten Book: Chun Qiu Guliang Zhuan*, trans. Liang Gen (Singapore: World Scientific, 2011); and *Zuo Tradition: Commentary on the "Spring and Autumn Annals,"* trans. Stephen Durrant, Wai-yee Li, and David Schaberg (Seattle: University of Washington Press, 2016). Work on new scholarly translations of the Gongyang and Guliang Commentaries was also recently funded by the National Endowment for the Humanities.

1. Heavenly Principle and the Propensity of the Times

1. Naitō Konan, "Gaikuo de Tang Song shidai guan" [Overview of the Tang and Song eras], in *Riben xuezhe yanjiu Zhongguoshi lunzhu xuanyi* [Selected works by Japanese scholars on Chinese history], ed. Liu Junwen (Beijing: Zhonghua shuju, 1992), 1: 10.

2. Miyazaki Ichisada, "Dongyang de jinshi" [Early modernity in the Orient], in *Riben xuezhe yanjiu Zhongguoshi lunzhu xuanyi,* ed. Liu Junwen, 1: 159.

3. Ibid., 1: 168

4. Ibid., 1: 159–160.

5. Ibid., 1: 217.

6. Joseph Needham, *Zhongguo kexue jishu shi* [Science and civilization in China] (Beijing: Kexue chubanshe, 1990), 2: 444. [For the English edition, see Joseph Needham, *Science and Civilization in China,* vol. 2: *History of Scientific Thought* (Cambridge: Cambridge University Press, 1956), 417.—Trans.]

7. Xu Fuguan has expressed this view most accurately: "The Western work, in early modern times, of finding liberation of Reason, *lixing,* from the authority of religion was first fully completed before by us during the age of Laozi and Confucius, and second, in the hands of the Cheng brothers, Zhu Xi, Lu Jiuyuan, and Wang Yangming. The main trunk of Chinese traditional culture was originally an ideology of reason, *lixing;* it developed, however, in the moral and artistic fields." See Xu Fuguan, "Fan chuantong yu fan renxing" [Against tradition and against human nature], in *Xu Fuguan zawen bu bian, liang an san di juan, shang* [Essays of Xu Fuguan, I], ed. Li Minghui and Li Hanji, *Zhongguo wenzhe zhuankan* 21 (2001): 201.

8. See Tu Weiming, *Rujia sixiang xin lun—chuangzaoxing zhuanhuan de ziwo* (Nanjing: Jiangsu renmin chubanshe, 1991), 8–9. [The reference is to the Chinese translation of Tu's *Confucian Thought: Selfhood as Creative Transformation* (Albany: State University of New York Press, 1985).—Trans.]

9. Mou Zongsan, *Xinti yu xingti* [Substance of mind and substance of human nature] (Shanghai, Shanghai guji chubanshe, 1999), 1: 4–5.

10. Ge Ruihan [A. C. Graham], *Zhongguode liangwei zhexuejia: Er Cheng xiongdide xin ruxue* [Two Chinese philosophers: The metaphysics of the Brothers Ch'eng], trans. Cheng Dexiang (Zhengzhou: Daxiang chubanshe, 2000), 46. A. Forke has written, with another idea in mind, "*Li* is the rational as opposed to the material principle, in fact Reason, which creates and masters Matter." See *Geschichte der Neueren Chinesischen Philosophie* (i.e., from the beginning of Sung to modern times), (Hamburg: De Gruyter, 1938), 171; the reference here is from Needham, *Science and Civilization in China,* 2: 505 (of the Chinese edition). [The relevant quote can be found in Joseph Needham, *Science and Civilization in China,* vol. 2, *History of Scientific Thought* (Cambridge: Cambridge University Press, 1956), 473. Note (d) gives the

German as, "*Li* ist das rationale Prinzip im Gegensatz zum materiellen; die Vernunft, welche den Stoff schafft und beherrscht."—Trans.]

11. James T. C. Liu (Liu Zijian), *Zhongguo zhuanxiang neizi—liang Song zhi ji de wenhua neixiang* [China turning inward: Intellectual Chinese in the early twelfth century], trans. Zhao Dongmei (Nanjing: Jiangsu renmin chubanshe, 2002).

12. See Tu Weiming, *Lun Ruxue de zongjiaoxing* [Centrality and commonality: An essay on Confucian religiousness] (Wuhan: Wuhan daxue chubanshe, 1999).

13. Seen from European intellectual fields, the binary discourse of world and religion also includes the overlooking of the modern evolution of European Christianity. Tu Weiming particularly mentions Schleiermacher and Kierkegaard as examples illustrating how the process of secularization and the evolution of modern religion show signs of internal relation. See ibid., 4–5.

14. Chen Lai, *Song Ming lixue* [Song and Ming Schools of Principle] (Shenyang: Liaoning jiaoyu chubanshe, 1991), 10.

15. See *Ming ru xue an* [Major schools of Ming Confucianism], *Huang Zongxi quanji* (Hangzhou: Zhejiang guji chubanshe, 1992), 8: 387–388.

16. Regarding the earliest uses and interpretations of the terms of *lixue* and *xinxue,* see Lao Siguang, *Xin bian Zhongguo zhexue shi* [A new history of Chinese philosophy] (Taipei: Sanmin shuju, 1983), 3a: 41.

17. Peter K. Bol criticizes this, saying, "The problem goes back to Chu Hsi himself, but it has entered into modern scholarship most directly through Ch'üan Tsu-wang's (1705–1755) enlargement of Huang Tsung-hsi's (1610–1695) *Case Studies of Sung and Yuan Learning* (*Sung Yuan hsüeh-an*), the most comprehensive study of Sung thought yet written." See Bol, *Si wen: Tang-Song sixiangde zhuanxing,* trans. Liu Ningyi (Nanjing: Jiangsu renmin chubanshe, 2001), 31. [For the original English, Peter K. Bol, *"This Culture of Ours": Intellectual Transitions in T'ang and Sung China* (Stanford, CA: Stanford University Press, 1992), 28.—Trans.].

18. Ibid., 31–32.

19. Feng Youlan, *Zhongguo zhexue shi* [History of Chinese philosophy] (Beijing: Zhonghua shuju, 1992), 1: 55. [This English version is lightly modified from Fung Yulan, *History of Chinese Philosophy,* vol. 1, *The Period of the Philosophers (From the Beginning to Circa 100 BC),* trans. Derk Bodde (London: George Allen and Unwin, 1952), 31.—Trans.]

20. *Shi ji,* "Tian guan shu di wu," see *Shiji* [Records of the grand historian] (Beijing: Zhonghua shuju, 1982), 1342–1343.

21. Yang Bojun, ed., *Chunqiu Zuozhuan zhu* [Commentaries on the Zuo commentary to the Spring and Autumn Annals] (Beijing: Zhonghua shuju, 1981), 1459. [Translation modified from *The Ch'un Ts'ew, with the Tso Chuen,* trans. James Legge, in *The Sacred Books of the East* (rpt., Delhi: Motilal Banarsidass, 1966), 3: 708.—Trans.]

22. Zhang Zai, "Da Fan Xuan zhi shu" [Letter in reply to Fan Xuan], in *Zhang Zai ji* [Zhang Zai collection] (Beijing: Zhonghua shuju, 1978), 349.

23. Mou Zongsan, *Xinti yu Xingti,* 1: 42–43.

24. Li Zehou, "Shou wu shi chuantong," in *Bozhai xin shuo* [New interpretations from Boulder Studio] (Hong Kong: Tiandi tushu gongsi, 1999), 50.

25. Fu Sinian, "Lun Kongzi xue shuo suoyi shiying yu Qin Han yi lai de shehu de yuangu" [On how Confucius's thought and words were adapted to society since Qin and Han times], in *Fu Sinian xuan ji* (Tianjin: Tianjin renmin chubanshe, 1996), 300–301.

26. Ibid., 299.

27. Li Zehou, *Zhongguo gudai sixiang shi lun* [On the intellectual history of ancient China] (Beijing: Renmin chubanshe, 1985), 20–21.

28. See *Li ji jijie* [Collected commentaries on the *Book of Rites*], ed. by Sun Xidan (Beijing: Zhonghua shuju, 1989), 2: 585. [Translation modified from *The Lî Kî,* trans. James Legge, in *The Sacred Books of the East* (rpt., Delhi: Motilal Banarsidass, 1966), 27: 367.—Trans.]

29. Ibid., 3: 1411. [Translation modified from *The Lî Kî,* trans. James Legge, in *The Sacred Books of the East* 28: 425–426.—Trans.]

30. Ibid., 3: 1414. [Translation modified from *The Lî Kî,* trans. James Legge, in *The Sacred Books of the East,* 28: 427.—Trans.]

31. Ibid. [Translation modified from *The Lî Kî,* trans. James Legge, in *The Sacred Books of the East,* 28: 427.—Trans.]

32. Mou Zongsan, *Xinti yu Xingti,* 1: 42–43.

33. "Chuyu, xia" [Discourses of Chu, II], *Guoyu* [Discourses of the states] (Shanghai: Shanghai guji chubanshe, 1978), 559.

34. Xu Xusheng, *Zhongguo gushi de chuanshuo shidai* [The age of mythology in ancient Chinese history], revised and enlarged edition (Beijing: Kexue chubanshe, 1960); Yang Xiangkui, *Zhongguo gudai shehui yu gudai sixiang yanjiu* [Studies on ancient Chinese society and thought] (Shanghai: Shanghai renmin chubanshe, 1964); Zhang Guangzhi, *Zhongguo kaoguxue lunwen ji* [Collected papers on Chinese archaeology] (Beijing: Sanlian shudian, 1999), 393.

35. *Lunyu zhengyi* [Collected commentaries on the *Analects*], ed. Liu Baonan (Beijing: Zhonghua shuju, 1990), 2: 691.

36. Ibid., 1: 115.

37. Ibid., 1: 81.

38. Ibid., 2: 691.

39. See "Gao tao mo" [The great declaration of Gao], *Shangshu jinguwen zhushu* [Notes and commentaries on the Old and New Text *Shangshu*], ed. Sun Xingyan (Beijing: Zhonghua shuju, 2004), 3: 87. [Translation modified from *The Shû King,* trans. James Legge, in *The Sacred Books of the East,* 3: 56.—Trans.]

40. *Li ji,* "Ji tong," in *Li ji jijie,* 2: 1238–1239. [Translation borrowed from *The Lî Kî,* trans. James Legge, in *The Sacred Books of the East* 28: 239.—Trans.]

41. The phrase "fragmenting, formalization, and rationalization" is from Li Zehou: "'Reverence' (*jing*) refers to all sorts of emotions that include fear, worship, and

reverence. Proclamations of the early Zhou dynasty use the character *jing* a lot. It originates in prehistoric "shamanic rituals" (*wushu liyi*), or ancient shamanic activities, completed in a crazed or possessed psychological state and which had undergone processes of fragmentation, formalization, and rationalization. See Li Zehou, "Shuo wu shi chuantong" [On the tradition of shamans and historians], *Bozhai xin shuo,* 51.—Trans.

42. Confucius, "Xiangdangpian," in *Lunyu zhengyi,* 1: 368–436.

43. Wang Guowei, Guo Moruo, Dong Zuobin, Chen Mengjia, Hu Hou-hsüan, Xu Fuguan, K. C. Chang, Ho Ping-ti, Li Xueqin, David N. Keightley, H. G. Creel, Benjamin Schwartz, and other Chinese and international scholars have all presented varying interpretations of the constitution of early Chinese society, along with worship of deities. But they agree in affirming that the Yin-Shang civilization worshipped *Di,* or *Shangdi,* as well as nature deities and ancestral clans. As Ho Ping-ti asserted, "Clan organization was the most important systemic element in the formation of Hua and Xia humanism; ancestor worship was most important element of religious belief." See Ho Ping-ti, "Hua-Xia renbenzhuyi wenhua: Yuanyuan, tezheng, ji yiyi" [The humanist culture of China (Huaxia): origins, characteristics, and significance], *Ershiyi shiji* 33 (1996): 93.

44. On the origins of the concept of *tian,* "Heaven," there are two views in academia: one holds that *tian* evolved out of the clan spirits of the Zhou, while another maintains that *tian* already existed before the establishment of the Zhou dynasty. For a discussion on the issues, see Fu Pei-jong, *Rudao tian lun fa wei* [Detailed study of *tian* in Confucian and Daoist discourse] (Taipei: Xuesheng shuju, 1985), 11–14.

45. Ibid., 2.

46. Translation modified from *The Lî Kî,* trans. James Legge, in *The Sacred Books of the East,* 28: 212.—Trans.

47. Translation modified from *Confucian Analects, The Great Learning and the Doctrine of the Mean,* trans. James Legge, in *The Sacred Books of the East,* 1: 135–136. —Trans.

48. Zhang Guangzhi [K. C. Chang], "Zhongguo gudai wang de xingqi yu chengbang de xingcheng" [The rise of ancient kingdoms and formation of city-states in China], in *Zhongguo kaoguxue lunwenji* [Collected papers on Chinese archaeology] (Beijing: Sanlian shudian, 1999), 389, 388.

49. Two major sources on the patriarchal clan systems of the Zhou dynasty are the *Dazhuan* "Great Treatise" and *Sangfu xiaoji* "Record of Small Matters in the Dress of Mourning" chapters of the *Book of Rites.* Key points include, "When a son other than (the eldest) became the ancestor (of a branch of the same line), his successor was its Honoured Head, and he who followed him (in the line) was its smaller Honoured Head." And also, "Thus he regulated the services to be rendered to his father and grandfather before him—giving honour to the most honourable. He regulated the places to be given to his sons and grandsons below him—showing his affection to his kindred. He regulated (also) the observances for the collateral branches of his cousins—

associating all their members in the feasting. He defined their places according to their order of descent; and his every distinction was in harmony with what was proper and right." *Liji jijie,* 2: 867–878; 2: 902–905; 2: 914–918. [Translation modified from *The Lî Kî,* trans. James Legge, in *The Sacred Books of the East,* 28: 43, 61.—Trans.]

50. *Xunzi jijie* [Collected commentaries on the *Xunzi*] (Beijing: Zhonghua shuju, 1988), 1:134. [See John Knoblock, *Xunzi: A Translation and Study of the Complete Works* (Stanford, CA: Stanford University Press, 1990), 2: 68.—Trans.]

51. *Zuozhuan* [Zuo commentary on the *Spring and Autumn Annals*], Duke Xi, 24th year, in Yang Bojun, *Chunqiu zuozhuan zhu* [Annotated Zuo commentary on the *Spring and Autumn Annals*] (Beijing: Zhonghua shuju, 1981), 420. [Translation modified from *The Ch'un ts'ew,* trans. James Legge, in *The Sacred Books of the East,* 5: 192.—Trans.]

52. Regarding the relation between the systems of *tian* (fields) and *bing* (the military), the most detailed account is by Xu Zhongshu, "Jing tian zhidu tan yuan" [An inquiry into the *jingtian* system], in *Xu Zhongshu lishi lunwen xuanji* [Selected historical papers of Xu Zhongshu] (Beijing: Zhonghua shuju, 1998), 2: 713–760.

53. Ibid., 2: 724.

54. *Zuozhuan,* Duke Ding, 4th year, in *Chunqiu zuozhuan zhu,* 1538–1539.

55. See Chapter 5 of this book.

56. See chapter 48, "Jingjie," number 26, in *Liji jijie,* 1: 1254–1255. [Translation modified from *The Lî Kî,* trans. James Legge, in *The Sacred Books of the East,* 28: 255.]

57. See *Liji jijie,* 2: 956–957.

58. Zhu Xi's commentary on the "Record of Studies" (*Xue ji*) chapter of the *Book of Rites* says, "It tells the order of instruction by which the presiding instructor at the school transmits the Dao, regarding the reasons for success and failure, rise and fall, covering these in lessons great and small." Ibid., 2: 956.

59. Ibid., 2: 958.

60. Ibid., 2: 959.

61. Regarding the various meanings of the character *de* in the *Yishu* [Old Text *Book of Documents*], see Jao Tsung-I (Rao Zongyi), *Zhongguo shixue shang zhi zhengtonglun* [The theory of legitimate succession in Chinese historiography] (Shanghai edition), 10–12. This text is also a source for information about "the Ancient Lost Text That Comes after Copy A of the Laozi." The text comes in four parts, now titled "Five Phases" (*Wu xing*), "Nine Rulers" (*Jiu zhu*), "Enlightened Lord" (*Ming jun*), and "Virtue and Sageliness" (*De sheng*).

62. Ibid., 12.

63. Yang Xiangkui, "Guanyu Xi Zhou de shehui xingzhi wenti" [On the problem of the nature of Western Zhou society], in *Yishizhai xueshu wenji* [Collected academic writings from Yishizhai Studio] (Shanghai: Shanghai renmin chubanshe), 43.

64. Wang Guowei, Yin Zhou zhidu lun ["On the regulations of the Yin and Zhou], *Guan tang jilin* [Collected essays of the grove of Guan Hall], in *Wang Guowei yishu* [Extant works of Wang Guowei], (Shanghai: Shanghai guji shudian, 1983), 2: 14. Also,

when Guo Moruo discusses the Zhou-dynasty concept of *de,* virtue, he writes: "From the appearance of *yi* wine vessels of the Zhou, the character *de* included not only cultivation, in the subjective sense, but also norms, in an objective sense—what later people would call 'propriety,' *li. Li* is a character that arose later, for it is not seen on the bronze *yi* vessels of the early Zhou. *Li* comes to us as a metamorphosis of the written ritual codes, *jiewen,* regarding *de* in its objective sense. All ancient forms of conduct taken to typify the possessor of *de* virtue were collected and categorized to form the *li* propriety of later ages. Objective written codes of *de* virtue are very rare among the documents of the *Zhou shu,* but promulgation of the spirit of *de* virtue is clear from the emphasis on the character *jing,* 'reverence.'" See Guo Moruo, "Qingtong shidai: Xian Qin Tiandaoguan zhi jinzhan" [Development of views on Tian and Dao, a chapter from the Bronze Age], in *Guo Moruo quanji* [Collected works of Guo Moruo], history section (Beijing: Renmin chubanshe, 1982), 1: 336. Yang Xiangkui has expressed a different interpretation of this same topic. He believes neither that propriety is a derivation of virtue, nor that "all ancient forms of conduct taken to typify the possessor of *de* virtue were collected and categorized," but that circumstances were rather the reverse, because the origin of *li* propriety was very early. "In the ideological system in which *de* virtue is derived from normalized conduct of *li* propriety, *de* virtue is a cultivation and a supplement to *li* propriety." See Yang Xiangkui, *Zong Zhou shehui yu liyue wenming* [Western Zhou society and its civilization of rites and music], revised and updated edition (Beijing: Renmin chubanshe, 1997), 337.

65. Xu Fuguan, *Liang Han sixiang shi* [Intellectual history of the Western and Eastern Han dynasties] (Shanghai: Donghua Shifan Daxue Chubanshe, 2001), 1: 12.

66. See the "Liu de" documents in Jingmen Municipal Museum, *Guodian Chumu zhujian* [Bamboo slips from a Chu tomb at Guodian] (Beijing: Wenwu chubanshe, 1998), as well as Liao Mingchun, "Jingmen Guodian Chu jian yu xian Qin Ruxue" [The Jingmen Guodian Chu slips and Pre-Qin Confucian thought], and "Guodian Chu jian yanjiu" [A study of the Chu slips of Guodian], in *Zhongguo zhexue,* issue 20, 62–63.

67. Zhang Xuecheng, *Wenshi tongyi* [Comprehensive integration of literature and history]: "Yuandao zhong" [General Principles, II] in *Zhang Xuecheng yishu* [Extant works of Zhang Xuecheng] (Beijing: Wenwu chubanshe, 1985; references below also refer to this edition), 11.

68. *Mencius,* Book 5a, in *Mengzi zheng yi* [Collected commentaries of the *Mengzi*] (Beijing: Zhonghua shuju, 1987; references below also refer to this edition, proofread by Jiao Xun), 2: 643.

69. Gu Jiegang in a letter to Fu Sinian, October 18, 1926 (Year 15 of the Republic of China); see Fu Sinian, "Lun Kongzi xue shuo suoyi shiying yu Qin Han yi lai de shehu de yuangu," in *Fu Sinian xuan ji,* 297.

70. See "Zhongyong" [*The Great Learning*], in *Shisan jing zhushu* [Commentaries on the Thirteen Classics] (Beijing: Zhonghua shuju, 1980), 406.

71. Confucius, Book 13 of the *Analects,* in *Lunyu zhengyi,* 2: 538. [Translation modified from *Confucian Analects, The Great Learning and the Doctrine of the Mean,* trans.

James Legge, in *The Sacred Books of the East* (rpt., Delhi: Motilal Banarsidass, 1966), 1: 135–136.—Trans]

72. Confucius, Book 1 of the *Analects*, in *Lunyu zhengyi*, 1: 7. [Translation modified from *Confucian Analects, The Great Learning and the Doctrine of the Mean*, trans. James Legge, in *The Sacred Books of the East*, 1: 3.—Trans.]

73. Zhang Taiyan, "Shuo wu" [On things], *Zhang Taiyan quanji* [Complete works of Zhang Taiyan], 4: 41.

74. Confucius, Book 12 of the *Analects*, in *Lunyu zhengyi*, 2: 483–484. [Translation modified from *Confucian Analects, The Great Learning and the Doctrine of the Mean*, trans. James Legge, in *The Sacred Books of the East*, 1: 114.—Trans.]

75. Confucius, the "Yanghuo" chapter of the *Analects*, in *Lunyu zhengyi*, 2: 683. [Translation modified from *Confucian Analects, The Great Learning and the Doctrine of the Mean*, trans. James Legge, in *The Sacred Books of the East*, 1: 184.—Trans.]

76. Whether a Zisi-Mencius school actually existed remains a major controversy in the field. In the chapter "Eminence in Learning" (*Xian xue*), Han Feizi writes that after the death of Confucius, "the Confucian school split into eight factions," one being the Zisi-Mencius school. But these two figures are by no means members of the same school. In Xunzi's "Contra Twelve Philosophers" chapter, both Zisi and Mencius are said to be advocates of "five-phases" (*wu xing*) theory, the one inheriting the precepts of the other, meaning they are part of one intellectual network. But the notion that Zisi and Mencius form a single school emerged and spread alongside the discourse of Confucian orthodoxy during the Tang and Song dynasties. Under the influence of these views, the Si-Meng school was seen as the orthodox tradition of Confucianism. Han Yu believed that Yao, Shun, Yu, Tang, Wen, Wu, the Duke of Zhou, and Kongzi all formed one orthodox line, as we see in his essay "The Origins of the Way" (Yuan Dao). "Mencius," writes Han Yu, "took Zisi as his teacher, and Zisi's learning was accrued from Zengzi" ("Preface for Xiucai Scholar Wang" *Song Wang Xiucai xu*). The Cheng brothers and Zhu Xi accepted this view. As they certified the systems of Zengzi, Zi Si, and Mencius, they redacted *The Great Learning* (*Da xue*) and the *Doctrine of the Mean* (*Zhong yong*) from the *Book of Rites* (*Li ji*) to form, along with the *Analects* of Confucius and the *Mencius*, the Four Books. They understood *The Great Learning* as an exposition by Zengzi on the thought of Confucius. For all these reasons, elucidating the Zisi-Mencius school became one of the concerns of Song and Ming Confucianism. When the Mawangdui silk manuscripts were unearthed in 1973, among them were four lost books appended to an edition of the *Laozi* text. Pang Pu called one of these texts the "Five-Phases Chapter" (*Wu xing pian*), saying that the five phases in this text correspond to the term in the Zisi-Mencius theory. Bamboo slips unearthed in October 1993 at the Chu excavation in Guodian town, Jingmen, Hubei Province, and presented to the public in May 1998, give further evidence. Li Xueqin finds these to contain a chapter called "The Black Robe" (*Zi yi*), which records the five-phases theory in a manner related to that of the Mawangdui text. He also cites the text "Duke Mu of Lu Asked Zisi" (*Lu Mu Gong Wen Zisi*) as evidence that the *Doctrine of the Mean* text, so

beloved of Song Confucians, was indeed by Zisi. *The Great Learning,* then, could very well bear relation to Zengzi. On the contemporary academic controversies surrounding this topic, see Pang Pu, *Bo shu wu xing pian yanjiu* [Studies on the silk manuscript of the *Wuxing pian*] (Jinan: Qilu shushe, 1980); Li Xueqin, "Jingmen Guodian Chu jian zhong de Zisizi" [The Zisizi in the Jingmen Guodian Chu slips], *Wenwu tiandi,* 1998, no. 2; and *Sixiang, wenxian, lishi: Si-Meng xuepai yanjiu* [Thinking, texts, history—A new investigation of the Si-Meng school of thought], ed. Tu Wei-Ming (Beijing: Beijing daxue chubanshe, 2008).

77. Li Gou, "Chang yu" [Discourses on norms] excerpted in the *Song Yuan xue'an,* in *Huang Zongxi quanji* [Collected works of Huang Zongxi] (Hangzhou: Zhejiang guji chubanshe, 1992), 3: 222–223.

78. Mencius, Book 3a, in *Mengzi zheng yi,* 1: 315. [Translation modified from *The Life and Works of Mencius,* trans. James Legge (Philadelphia: J. B. Lippincott and Co., 1875), 27.—Trans.]

79. Mencius, Book 7b, ibid., 2: 991. [Translation modified from *The Life and Works of Mencius,* trans. James Legge, 375.—Trans.]

80. Mencius, Book 4a, ibid., 2: 315. [Translation modified from *The Life and Works of Mencius,* trans. James Legge, 236.—Trans.]

81. *Mencius,* Book 6a, ibid., 2: 906. [Translation modified from *The Life and Works of Mencius,* trans. James Legge, 236.—Trans.]

82. *Mencius,* Book 6a, ibid., 2: 878. [Translation modified from *The Life and Works of Mencius,* trans. James Legge, 313.—Trans.]

83. *Mencius,* Book 6a, ibid., 2: 757. [Translation modified from *The Life and Works of Mencius,* trans. James Legge, 312.—Trans.]

84. Xu Fuguan, "'Zhongyong' de diwei wenti" [On the problem of the status of the *Doctrine of the Mean*], in *Zhongguo sixiangshi jilun* [Collected papers on Chinese intellectual history] (Taizhong: Zhongyang shuju, 1959), 78.

85. Tu Wei-Ming, *Lun Ruxue de zongjiaoxing,* 21.

86. Li Xueqin writes, "The discovery of these Confucian documents not only proves that the Doctrine of the Mean is by Zisi, but also allows the conjecture that the Great Learning may indeed be connected to Zengzi. Many of the categories used in the Great Learning, including cultivation, individual prudence (*shendu*), and renewal of the people (*xinmin*), show up multiple times in the bamboo slips. The Great Learning has the structure of a *jing* followed by *zhuan,* text and transmission [commentary], just with the *jing* and *zhuan* of the *Wu xing,* or Five Elements. From this, we now know that it was not without some basis that the Song scholars especially admired the Great Learning and the Doctrine of the Mean, believing both texts to best exemplify the theories of the Confucius school." See Li Xueqin, "Xian Qin Rujia zhuzuo de zhongda faxian" [An important discovery in pre-Qin Confucian writings], *Renmin zhengxiebao,* June 8, 1998, 3.

87. See *Doctrine of the Mean,* chapter 20 and chapter 25, excerpted in Zhu Xi, *Si Shu zhangju jizhu* [Commentary on the Four Books] (Beijing: Zhonghua shuju, 1989), 31,

33–34. [Translation borrowed from *Confucian Analects, The Great Learning and the Doctrine of the Mean,* trans. James Legge, in *The Sacred Books of the East,* 1: 411–412.]

88. *Doctrine of the Mean,* chapter 26, ibid. 34–35. [Translation modified from *Confucian Analects, The Great Learning and the Doctrine of the Mean,* trans. James Legge, in *The Sacred Books of the East,* 1: 283–284.—Trans.]

89. Zhou Dunyi, "Cheng shang" [Sincerity, pt. 1], *Tong Shu* [Penetrating the text of the *Book of Changes*], in *Zhou yuan gong ji* [Collected works of Zhou Dunyi], Wenyuange siku quanshu edition, juan 1: 10a.

90. Zhou Dunyi, "Sheng di si" [The sage, pt. 4], *Tong Shu,* in *Zhou yuan gong ji,* juan 1: 14b.

91. *Zhuzi quanshu* [Collected works of Zhu Xi], ed. Zhu Jieren, Yan Zuozhi, and Liu Yongxiang (Shanghai: Shanghai guji chubanshe and Hefei: Anhui jiaoyu chubanshe, 2002), 23: 3279. [Translation modified from *A Sourcebook in Chinese Philosophy,* trans. Wing-tsit Chan (Princeton, NJ: Princeton University Press, 1963), 1: 593–594. The opening sentence is by one of the Cheng brothers, notes Wing-tsit Chan.—Trans.]

92. See Dai Zhen, *Mengzi ziyi shuzheng* [Critical exegesis of the meanings of words in *Mencius*], in *Dai Zhen quanji* (Beijing: Qinghua daxue chuanshe, 1991), 1: 207.

93. *Chuanxi lu* [Instructions for practical living], *Wang Yangming quanji* [Complete works of Wang Yangming] (Shanghai: Shanghai guji chubanshe, 1992), 1: 26. [Translation modified from *A Sourcebook in Chinese Philosophy,* trans. Wing-tsit Chan, 675–676.—Trans.]

94. *Er Cheng ji* [Collected works of the two Chengs] (Beijing: Zhonghua shuju, 1981), 274.

95. Cheng Yi, *Yichuan yi zhuan* [Yichuan's Commentary on the *Book of Changes*], *Er Cheng ji,* 1025–1026.

96. *Zhuzi yulei* [Conversations of Master Zhu, categorized] vol. 1, juan 6 (Beijing: Zhonghua shuju, 1986), 112.

97. David Hall and Roger Ames emphasize that "Confucius attends more to a particular person's behavior in particular context, and not the abstract nature of good and bad in morality." See *Kongzi zhexue siwei* [Thinking through Confucius], trans. Jiang Yiwei (Shanghai: Jiangsu People's Publishing House, 1996), 7.

98. Wang Yangming, *Chuan xi lu,* in *Wang Yangming quanji,* 1: 6–7. [Translation modified from "A Record for Practice," translated by Philip J. Ivanhoe, in *Readings in Later Chinese Philosophy,* ed. Justin Tiwald and Bryan W. Van Norden (Indianapolis: Hackett Publishing Company, 2014), 272.—Trans.]

99. Throughout history, people believed that the discourse of the five elements originated with Zou Yan, but Jao Tsung-I, using various sources new and old, concluded that the discourse of the five elements actually originated with Zisi (the grandson of Confucius and purported author of the *Doctrine of the Mean*). For a detailed account, see *Zhongguo shixue shang zhi zhengtonglun* [The theory of legitimate succession in Chinese historiography] (Shanghai: Shanghai yuandong chubanshe, 1996), 10–16.

100. Gu Jiegang, *Qin Han de fangshi yu rusheng* [Masters of technique and Confucians during the Qin and Han dynasties] (Shanghai: Shanghai guji chubanshe, 1998), 2–4.

101. See Chen Mengjia, "Shang dai de shenhua yu wushu" [Myth and Shamanist technique in the Shang dynasty], *Yanjing xuebao* 20 (1936): 535; K. C. Chang, *Art, Myth and Ritual* (Cambridge, MA: Harvard University Press, 1983), 73.

102. Joseph Needham, *Zhongguo kexue jishu shi*, 2: 148–159. [For the English edition, see Joseph Needham, *Science and Civilization in China*, vol. 2: *History of Scientific Thought* (Cambridge: Cambridge University Press, 1956), 132, 134.—Trans.]

103. Li Zehou, "Shuo wu shi chuantong," in *Bozhai xin shuo*, 43. [Wang Hui refers to the character *shi* 史, an ancient pictograph that first referred to recorders of religious ceremonies of prognostication, but gradually came to refer to court historiographers.—Trans.]

104. *Li ji*, "Quli," in *Li ji jijie*, 1: 94. [Translation modified from *The Lî Kî*, trans. James Legge, in *The Sacred Books of the East*, 28: 43, 94.—Trans.]

105. *Li ji*, "Jiaotesheng." See *Li ji jijie*, 2: 706–707. [Translation modified from *The Lî Kî*, trans. James Legge, in *The Sacred Books of the East*, 27: 494.—Trans.]

106. *Li ji jijie*, 2: 706–707.

107. Ibid., 707. [Translation modified from *The Lî Kî*, trans. James Legge, in *The Sacred Books of the East*, 28: 275.—Trans.]

108. *Li ji*, "Zhongni yanju." *Li Ji jijie*, 3:1272. [Translation modified from *The Lî Kî*, trans. James Legge, in *The Sacred Books of the East*, 28: 275.—Trans.]

109. Zhang Xuecheng, "*Yi* jiao shang" [Teachings of the *Book of Changes*], *Wenshi tongyi* [Comprehensive integration of literature and history], in *Zhang Xuecheng yishu* [Extant works of Zhang Xuecheng] (Beijing: Wenwu chubanshe, 1985), 1.

110. Gong Zizhen, "Gu shi gouchen lun" [Tracking ancient history], in *Gong Ding'an quanji leibian* [Complete works of Gong Ding'an, categorized] (Beijing: Zhongguo shudian, 1991), 99.

111. There is much research on the *Luxuriant Dew of the Spring and Autumn Annals*. For a clear, brief overview of the structure and nature of the work, consult the relevant entry by Steve Davidson and Michael Loewe in *Early Chinese Texts: A Bibliographical Guide*, 81–91. [Wang Hui likely refers to the Chinese translation of *Early Chinese Texts*, published as *Zhongguo gudai dianji daodu*, trans. Li Xueqin (Liaoning Jiaoyu chubanshe, 1997). For the English edition see *Early Chinese Texts: A Bibliographical Guide*, ed. Michael Loewe (New Haven, CT: The Society for the Study of Early China, 1993), 77–87.—Trans.]

112. J. G. Frazer, *Jin zhi* [The Golden Bough] (Shanghai: Zhongguo renmin wenyi chubanshe, 1987), 1: 19–20. [For the English, see Sir James George Frazer, *The Golden Bough: A Study in Magic and Religion* (London: Macmillan and Co., 1925), 11.—Trans.]

113. Needham, *Zhongguo kexue jishu shi*, 2: 307. [For the English edition, Needham, *Science and Civilization in China*, vol. 2: *History of Scientific Thought*, 282–283.—Trans.]

114. Translation modified from *Luxuriant Gems of the Spring and Autumn,* ed. Sarah A. Queen and John S. Major (New York: Columbia University Press, 2016), 440.—Trans.

115. The "Feng chan shu" and the "Basic Annals of the Qin Shihuang" in the *Records of the Grand Historian,* as well as the *Jiao ji zhi shang* [Records of the suburban sacrifice] chapter of the *Qian Han shu* [History of the former Han dynasty] all mention Zou Yan's follower Xianmen Gao and his arts. Needham infers from these that the term *Xianmen* could be a predecessor to the term "shaman," which is equivalent to *wu* 巫. See Needham, *Zhongguo kexue jishu shi,* 2: 149.

116. Frazer, *Jin zhi,* 1:19–20. [For the English, see Frazer, *The Golden Bough,* 11–12.—Trans.]

117. Henri Hubert and Marcel Mauss, "Esquisse d'une théorie générale de la magie," *L'Année sociologique,* 1904: 7, 56, cited and excerpted in Needham, *Zhongguo kexue jishu shi,* 2: 281. [For the English, see Needham, *Science and Civilization in China,* vol. 2: *History of Scientific Thought,* 280.—Trans.]

118. "Lü li zhi" [Record on patterns and calendars] in *Han shu* (Beijing: Zhonghua shuju, 1962), 974.

119. Xu Fuguan writes, "Many scholar-officials of the two Han dynasties understood the study of the classics through the heavy influence of the *Lü Commentary on the Spring and Autumn Annals,* taking the great influence of the political events on the *Lü Commentary on the Spring and Autumn Annals* as an influence on the study of the classics in general. One cannot understand the nature of Han-dynasty academia without the *Lü Commentary on the Spring and Autumn Annals.*" See *Liang Han sixiang shi* 2: 1.

120. For a clear and concise overview of the *Master Lü's Spring and Autumn Annals,* and how many characters were in each scroll, with evaluations of the text, see *Zhongguo gudai dianji daodu: Lü shi chun qiu* [Reading guides to the ancient Chinese classics: *Master Lü's Spring and Autumn Annals*], ed. Lu Weiyi (Shenyang: Liaoning jiaoyu chubanshe, 1997), 344–451.

121. See Xu Fuguan, *Liang Han sixiang shi,* 2: 11–12. Xu has also argued that the five elements were originally the five types of materials used for planning the people's livelihood, and only later evolved into the basic elements of the universe and became attached to the dual *qi* elements of yin-yang theory. This process could be traced back only as far as Zou Yan. See ibid., 182. This view is also on display in corresponding passages from Joseph Needham's *Science and Civilization in China.*

122. "The Way of the *Spring and Autumn Annals,* certainly has constancy and has flexibility (changes, *bian*). Flexibility is employed in transformative circumstances; constancy is employed in normal circumstances. Each has its category; they do not interfere each other." Dong Zhongshu, "Zhulin, section three" in *Luxuriant Dew of the Spring and Autumn Annals.* See Su Xing, ed., *Chunqiu fanlu yizheng* [Collected commentaries on the *Luxuriant Dew of the Spring and Autumn*] (Beijing: Zhonghua

shuju, 1992), 53. [Translation modified from *Luxuriant Gems of the Spring and Autumn,* ed. Queen and Major, 97.—Trans.]

123. Zhao Yi, *Nian'er shi zhaji jiaozheng* [Annotated and corrected notes on the *Twenty-Two Histories*] (Beijing: Zhonghua shuju, 2013), 37.

124. "Bai guan wu" [Treatise on the Hundred Officials], treatise 82, in *Hou han shu* [History of the later Han] (Beijing: Zhonghua shuju, 1965).

125. Dong Zhongshu, *Chunqiu fanlu, Meng hui yao di shi* [*Luxuriant Dew of the Spring and Autumn Annals,* "The Essentials of Covenants and Meetings," chapter 10], *Chunqiu fanlu yizheng,* 141–142. [Translation modified from *Luxuriant Gems of the Spring and Autumn,* ed. Queen and Major, 164.—Trans.]

126. Dong Zhongshu, *Chunqiu fanlu,* "Er duan di shi wu" ["Two Beginnings," chapter 15], *Chunqiu fanlu yizheng,* 155–156.

127. Feng Youlan writes: "Although he [the first Han emperor] like his predecessors, gave fiefs to his relatives and meritorious ministers, these fiefs from this time on had only political and not economic significance. By the middle of the Han, the new political and social order had already gradually become stabilized, and in the sphere of economics the people had become accustomed to the changed conditions arising from the natural economic tendencies of the time. The *History of the Former Han* says: 'Among the common people, though they were (theoretically) of equal rank, some by power of their wealth could become the masters of others, while even should they become slaves, they were without resentment.' In the eyes of the former aristocracy, it would have hardly seemed credible that equal ranks and attaining power through wealth should be possible!" Feng Youlan, *Zhongguo zhexue shi* (Beijing: Zhonghua shuju, 1992), 1: 41–42. [Translation modified from Fung Yu-lan, *History of Chinese Philosophy,* vol. 1: *The Period of the Philosophers (From the Beginning to Circa 100 BC),* trans. Derk Bodde (London: George Allen and Unwin, 1952), 18–19.—Trans.]

128. Fu Sinian, "Lun Kongzi xue shuo suoyi shiying yu Qin Han yi lai de shehu de yuangu," in *Fu Sinian xuan ji,* 301.

129. Dong Zhongshu, "Zhulin disan" [Bamboo Grove, section three], *Chunqiu fanlu yizheng,* 46–7. [Translation modified from *Luxuriant Gems of the Spring and Autumn,* ed. Queen and Major, 91–92. The historical context of this account is more fully narrated in the *Gongyang Commentary;* Queen and Major helpfully give footnotes to the translations in Göran Malmqvist, "Studies on the Gongyang and Guliang Commentaries," *Bulletin of the Museum of Far Eastern Antiquities* 43 (1971): 184.—Trans.]

130. Sima Qian, "Mengzi Xun Qing liezhuan" "Biographies of Mengzi and Xun Qing," in *Shi ji* [Records of the grand historian], Zhonghua shuju edition, 7: 2344.

131. Zou Yan's theory of the big and small nine continents was revived in the late Qing by Liao Ping and other classical studies (*jingxue*) specialists, with a goal of explaining the relationship between China and other parts of the world. See Chapter 6 of this book, on Liao Ping.

132. Charles Sanft describes the document as "a collection of legal decisions and commentary attributed to Dong Zhongshu." The commentary describes how "to ob-

tain verdicts by drawing on the classics" (*yin jing jue yu*), considered foundational in Chinese legal history, though Sanft argues that new archeological evidence makes the work not so much an originating influence as itself influenced by earlier practice. See Charles Sanft, "Dong Zhongshu's 'Chunqiu jueyu' Reconsidered: On the Legal Interest in Subjective States and the Privilege of Hiding Family Members' Crimes as Developments from Earlier Practice." *Early China* 33 / 34 (2010): 141–169.—Trans.

133. Dong Zhongshu, *Chunqiu fanlu yizheng,* 214–218. [Translation modified from *Luxuriant Gems of the Spring and Autumn,* ed. Queen and Major, 257, 258, 263.]

134. *Chunqiu fanlu yizheng,* 238. Regarding the relationship between the system of officials and numbers and symbols, Xu Fuguan's analysis is the most penetrating. See "Zhou guan chengli zhi shidai ji qi sixiang xingge" [The age of establishing Zhou official positions and the nature of their political doctrines], in *Xu Fuguan jingxue shi er zhong* [Two works by Xu Fuguang on the history of classical studies] (Shanghai: Shanghai shudian chubanshe, 2002), 224–226. [Translation modified from *Luxuriant Gems of the Spring and Autumn,* Queen and Major, 278.—Trans.]

135. Dong Zhongshu, "Xianliang duice" [On elevating the worthy and good] in the *Han shu,* 2503–2504.

136. "Shi huo zhi" [Treatise on food and goods], *Han shu,* 1137. [Translation borrowed from *Sources of Chinese Tradition,* ed. Wm. Theodore de Bary and Irene Bloom (New York: Columbia University Press, 1999), 1: 357–358.—Trans.]

137. Dong Zhongshu, "Renyi fa" [Standards of humaneness and righteousness], *Chunqiu fanlu yizheng,* 250–254. [Translation modified from *Luxuriant Gems of the Spring and Autumn,* ed. Queen and Major, 313–316. Dong Zhongshu alternates between prosaic language and rhyming verse, which Queen and Major reflect in this lineation.—Trans.]

138. See *Zhongguo zhengzhi zhidu shi* [History of the Chinese political regulations], ed. Bai Gang (Tianjin: Tianjin renmin chubanshe, 1991), 246.

139. "Li ji zhuyuan shu" [Commentaries on the *Rites of Zhou*] in the *Siku quanshu zongmu tiyao,* juan 19, reads, "The Rites of Zhou was written in the early Zhou . . . more than three hundred years before it moved east, reform of the officialdom, breaking of political precedent, and generally getting rid of the old and laying out the new, were too common to count . . . and then, later, laws and policies were altered and disordered, leaving records much in disarray." Further, regarding the author of this work and the age in which the text was completed, writers of the Northern Song including Sima Huang (1019–1086), Hu Anguo (1074–1138), Hong Mai (1123–1202), and Su Zhe (1039–1112) were all most interesting in how they spoke of this text, all of them determining that the "Zhou guan" was a forgery by Liu Yin. These could be seen as a forerunner to the views of Kang Youwei in the late Qing. Such statements were produced under the conditions of Wang Anshi's reforms in accordance with the *Rites of Zhou,* and are completely lacking in a firm academic basis.

140. Xun Yue (148–209) believed that the change of title from *Zhou guan* to *Rites of Zhou* was the doing of Liu Xin.

141. See *Zhou li zheng yi* [Collected commentaries of the *Rites of Zhou*], ed. Sun Yirang (Beijing: Zhonghua shuju, 1987), 1: 1.

142. In "Zhou guan chengli zhi shidai jiqi sixiang xingge" [On the age in which Zhou officialdom was established, and the nature of its political thought], Xu Fuguan has made the most marvelous analysis. He writes, "The ranks of officials express the ideals of government. They are a special form of what develops in the history of political thought. . . . From the *Book of Odes* to the *Book of Documents* to the Zuo commentary to the *Narratives of the States* and the *Documents of Zhou,* and when we examine all the books and documents by the vying masters of philosophy from Confucius onward, we engage issues only at the level of 'wise men are best used,' and 'stick to superior men, keep distant from small men.' Rarely is it thought how the ideals of political offices per se might help achieve the ideals of political thought. That political offices should express political ideals did not develop until the middle of the Warring States period; I suspect it first emerged in the term *san gong,* the three top posts [of the state of Chu, including the posts of *mo'ao, lingyin,* and *sima*]." He further inferred, "Wang Mang and Liu Xin followed the system in which ranks of officials express the ideals of government. When Wang Mang ruled in a tyrannical government by *da sima,* he set up common ideals for government, utilizing the group of Confucian masters that could be utilized, the great formation that collects here in one system serving to realize a blueprint for political ideals." *Xu Fuguan lun jingxue shi er zhong,* 213, 245.

143. On these units, see Y. Edmund Lian, "Reconstructing the Postal Relay System of the Han Period," in *A History of Chinese Letters and Epistolary Culture,* ed. Antje Richter (Leiden: Brill, 2015), 31–32.—Trans.

144. Ibid., 228–232.

145. "Zhong Zhangtong zhuan" [Biography of Zhong Zhangtong], in the *Hou Han shu* [History of the later Han dynasty] (Beijing: Zhonghua shuju, 1965), 1657.

146. Liu Zongyuan, "Shi ling lun" [On seasonal observances], part one, in *Liu Zongyuan ji* [The collected Liu Zongyuan] (Beijing: Zhonghua shuju, 1979], 85–86. [On this essay, see Ro-shui Chen, *Liu Tsung-yuan and Intellectual Change in T'ang China, 773–819* (Cambridge: Cambridge University Press, 1989), 106–107, parts of which appear in this translation.—Trans.]

147. Liu Zongyuan, "Fengjian lun" [On enfeoffments], *Liu Zongyuan ji,* 70. [Translation modified from William H. Nienhauser et al., *Liu Tsung-yüan* (New York: Twayne, 1973), 54–55. Here Nienhauser translates *shi* as "historical situation." —Trans.]

148. The essay "On the Origins of the Way" (*Yuan Dao*) derives "the Way of mutual living and mutual cultivating" from the sages, and not from the Mandate of Heaven. The patterns of living, as with clothing, food, and residences, and the social division of labor, as with artisans, merchants, doctors, funeral specialists, and specialists in ritual propriety, music, government, and punishment, are all the products of sagely guidance into progress in the struggle for existence. In his "Letter to Wei Zhongxing," Han Yu also says, "The worthy official cares nothing for his own existence.

Noble or mean, disaster and great fortune all accrue from Heaven, while reputation, good or ill, accrues from humans. He who lives for himself, I abhor. Those who live for Heaven and who live for humanity I employ in that and do not use my power for it." See *Han Changli wen ji jiao zhu* [Collected works of Han Changli, with commentary], ed. Ma Qichang (Shanghai: Shanghai guji chubanshe, 1986), 194.

149. Han Yu, "Da Liu Xiucai lun shi shu" [Letter in reply to the Xiucai scholar Liu on history], *Han Changli wen ji jiao zhu,* 667.

150. Han Yu, "Song Meng Dongye xu" [Preface to poem sent to Meng Dongye], *Han Changli wen ji jiao zhu,* 235.

151. Han Yu, "Yuan xing" [On original nature], *Han Changli wen ji jiao zhu,* 21.

152. Han Yu, "Ben zheng" [The root of government], *Han Changli wen ji jiao zhu,* 50–51.

153. Feng Youlan, *Zhongguo zhexue shi,* vol. 2, presents the relations of continuity here in great detail.

154. Zhou Dunyi, "Shunhua di shi yi" [Compliance and transformation, pt. 11], in *Zhou Lianxi ji* [The collected works of Zhou Lianxi] (Shanghai: Shangwu yinshuguan, 1936), vol. 2, juan 5: 97–98.

155. Shao Yong, "Guan wu wai pian" [Outer chapters on the observation of things] in *Huang ji jing shi shu* [Book of the supreme principles governing the world] (Shanghai: Shanghai guji chubanshe, 1992), 33.

156. *Zhuzi yulei,* ed. Li Qingde (Song dynasty), section 65, punctuated and collated by Wang Xingxian (Beijing: Zhonghua shuju, 1986), 1611

157. For the former statement, see *Zhu Wengong yi shuo* [Uncollected statements of Zhu Xi]; for the latter, see the note in Hu Wei, *Yi tu ming bian* [Charts of the changes, illuminating distinctions]. Regarding the interpretation of the numerical diagrams in *hetuluoshuo,* see Jin Chunfeng, *Han dai sixiang shi* [Intellectual history of the Han dynasty] (Beijing: Zhongguo shehui kexue chubanshe, 1997), 380–385.

158. Shao Yong, "Guan wu nei pian," in *Huang ji jing shi,* 4.

159. Ibid., 17.

160. Ibid., 41.

161. Ibid., 57.

162. Ibid., 49.

163. Cheng Hao, *Henan Cheng shi yi shu,* section 2a, in *Er Cheng ji* [Collected works of the two Chengs], 45. [This translation is by Bryan Van Norden, in an email message to the translator, March 30, 2022. Prof. Van Norden appends the following notes to his translation: "Wang Hui follows the punctuation of this line as found in the Er cheng ji, so I have translated according to that text. However, because yi (意), yan (言), xiang (象), and shu (数) are four technical terms in Shao Yong's thought, it is likely that the original meaning of the preceding sentence is 'The learning of Shao Yong derives Thought, Doctrines, Images, and Numbers from Principle.' Further down, phrase 'the four' probably refers to the terms yi, yan, xiang, and shu again, but Wang Hui seems to understand this sentence differently. Wang probably regards the phrase as a reference to 'the four

Images' mentioned in the 'Great Appendix' to the Classic of Changes: greater yin, lesser yin, greater yang, and lesser yang. Below, 'the Great' presumably refers to the 'Great Ultimate.' Finally, while Wang Hui takes Cheng Hao to be quoting Shao Yong, I cannot find the quoted passage in Shao Yong's works, and it is likely that Cheng Hao is writing with his own voice, interpolating Shao Yong."—Trans.]

164. Shao Yong, *Huang ji jing shi: guan wu wai pian,* 49.

165. Section 427, "Dao xue zhuan" [Memoir of Daoxue] in the *Song shi* (Beijing: Zhonghua shuju, 1977), 12724; *Zhang Zai ji* [Collected works of Zhang Zai] (Beijing: Zhonghua shuju, 1978), 259.

166. Zhang Zai, *Zheng meng* [Correcting youthful ignorance], "Qian cheng" [Divine evolution], in *Zhang Zai ji,* 63.

167. Zhang Zai, *Zheng meng:* "Tai he pian" [Supreme harmony], in *Zhang Zai ji,* 7.

168. Chen Junmin, "Guan xue sixiang liu bian" [Evolution of the thought of the Guan learning], in *Lun Song Ming lixue* [On the Schools of Principle in the Song and Ming], 109.

169. These are the words with which Zhang Shi evaluated his student, Sun Zhaoyuan. See "Ba Sun Zhongmin tie" in *Zhang Nanxuan xiansheng wenji,* 109. Congshu jicheng chubian edition (1936).

170. Li Ye, "Xu" [Preface] to *Ce yuanhai jing xi cao* [The sea mirror for measuring the circle] (Shanghai: Shangwu yinshuguan, Zongshu jichengben, 1936), 3; Li Fu, "You da Cao Yue xiucai" in *Jue shui ji,* 5, 6. Wenyuange sikuquanshu edition.

171. Zhu Xi accepts Zhang Zai's views on *qi,* critically. In both the *Explanation of the Supreme Ultimate* and *Conversations of Zhu Xi, Categorized* (parts one and two), he exposits a discourse of stars and clouds with the earth at its center, thus giving specific expression of natural phenomena as manifestations of the Supreme Ultimate Principle.

172. Wang Fuzhi, *Zhang Zi Zheng meng zhu, Juan 8* [Annotated *Correcting Youthful Ignorance* of Master Zhang, 8], in *Chuanshan quanshu* [Complete books of Wang Fuzhi] (Changsha: Yuelu shushe, 1992), 12: 335.

173. Zhang Zai writes, "Out of the Great Void we have the name of Heaven; out of the changes of Breath (*qi*) we have the name of the Dao. Combining the Void and the Breath we have the name of Nature (xing). Combining Nature with knowledge and sensation, we have the name of the heart-mind." "Zheng meng: Tai he pian," in *Zhang Zai ji,* 9.

174. Zhang Zai's "discourse on Nature" still placed extra emphasis on the discourse of the cosmos, and so was included among the "Cheng ming pian," and without a monograph; this point seems unquestioned. On the controversies over the academic work of Zhang Zai, see Chen Junmin, *Zhang Zai zhexue yu Guan xue xuepai* [The philosophy of Zhang Zai and the Guan Learning School] (Taipei: Taiwan xuesheng shuju, 1990), 7–14. On Zhang Zai's views on the relationship between heart-mind, Nature, and the cosmos, see Lao Siguang, *Xin bian Zhongguo zhexue shi* (Taipei: Sanmin shuju, 1981), 3a: 179–183.

175. Cheng Yi, *Er Cheng ji*, 247.

176. Yichuan [Cheng Yi] criticizes Shao Yong's theory of signs and symbols in Nature, writing, "The theory of Yaofu [Shao Yong] first conjectures intention from Principle. It speaks of the signs and symbols and says Principle of All-under-Heaven, must come from the four. . . . In brief, difficult indeed is it to order the states under Heaven. As a person, he all along lacked propriety and had no reverence, but only trifled and teased." Cheng Yi, *Er Cheng ji*, 54.

177. Cheng Hao, *Er Cheng ji*, 132.

178. As when he writes, "The Mandate of Heaven is called Nature, which refers to the Principle of Nature. . . . This Principle of Nature, is in every respect Good. What speaks of Heaven is the Principle of the Natural World." Cheng Yi, *Er Cheng ji*, 312.

179. "Human nature is *li*. This is what is meant by the term *li xing*, the rational nature. The *li* of All-under-Heaven, originates in and of itself, traced to its source, will be found always to have been good." Cheng Yi, *Er Cheng ji*, 292. [Translation adapted from Yung-ch'un Ts'ai, *The Philosophy of Ch'eng I* (Singapore: Springer, 2018 [1950]), 94.—Trans.]

180. Ibid., 312.

2. Heavenly Principle and the Centralized State

1. As Zhi Daolin (Zhi Dun) puts it in his "Da xiao pin dui biyao chao xu" [Preface to a synoptic extract of the larger and smaller versions (of the Prajnaparamita)]: "Knowledge is associated with definite things, whereas the Reality remains unmanifested; 'names' are born from objects, whereas the Principle is beyond words. When Principle is dark and empty, it is reduced to a nameless state. When Enlightenment is forgotten, then Wisdom is complete." *Zhongguo fojiao sixiang ziliao xuanbian* [Selected materials from Chinese Buddhist thought] (Beijing: Zhonghua shuju, 1981), 1: 60. [Translation modified from Erik Zürcher, *The Buddhist Conquest of China* (Leiden: Brill, 1959), 124–125.—Trans.]

2. Xuanjue, *Chanzong Yongjia ji* [Collected works of Yongjia of the Chan school], in *Zhongguo fojiao sixiang ziliao xuanbian*, 131.

3. Gu Fang, "Li de zaoqi xingtai jiqi yanbian" [Early forms of *Li* principles and their transformation], in *Lun Song-Ming Lixue: Song-Ming Lixue taolunhui lunwen ji* (Hangzhou: Zhejiang renmin chubanshe, 1983), 57–75.

4. Xu Shen, "Yu bu" [The *Yu* radical], in *Shuowen jiezi* [Discussing writing and explicating characters] (Beijing: Zhonghua shuju, 1963), 12, 1.

5. See: Guo Qingfan, *Zhuangzi ji shi* [Collected commentaries on the *Zhuangzi*] (Beijing: Zhonghua shuju, 1961), 1: 539. [Translation modified from: *The Complete Works of Zhuangzi*, trans. Burton Watson (New York: Columbia University Press, 2013), 120.—Trans.]

6. Ibid., 735. [Trans. Watson, 178.]

7. Ibid., 4: 1066–1067. [Trans. Watson, 287–288.]

8. *Han Feizi jijie* [Collected commentaries on the *Han Feizi*], ed. Wang Xianqian, *Zhuzi jicheng* edition (Shanghai: Shanghai shudian, 1986), juan 6: 107. [Translation modified from Sarah A. Queen, "*Han Feizi* and the Old Master: A Comparative Analysis and Translation of *Han Feizi* Chapter 20, 'Jie Lao,' and Chapter 21, 'Yu Lao,'" in *Dao Companion to the Philosophy of Han Fei,* ed. Paul R. Goldin (Dordrecht: Springer, 2013), 239.]

9. Xiong Shili, *Du jing shi yao* [Essentials for reading the classics] (Taipei: Guangwen shuju, 1960), 145.

10. "Junchen xia" [The sovereign and his ministers, Part II], in *Guanzi jiaozheng* [The *Guanzi* revised], ed. Dai Wang, Zhuzi jicheng edition (Shanghai: Shanghai shudian, 1986), juan 11: 177. [Translation modified from *Guanzi: Political, Economic, and Philosophical Essays from Early China,* trans. W. Allyn Rickett (Princeton, NJ: Princeton University Press, 1985), 1: 419.]

11. "Xingshi jie" [Explanation of "Conditions and Circumstances"] in *Guanzi jiaozheng,* juan 20: 325. [Translation modified from Rickett, 66.]

12. *Guanzi jiaozheng,* juan 5: 77–78. [Translation modified from Rickett, 235–236.]

13. "Xingshi jie," in *Guanzi jiaozheng,* juan 20: 324.

14. "Quanxue," in *Lüshi Chunqiu,* juan 4: 37.

15. *Guanzi jiaozheng,* juan 1: 14. [Translation modified from Rickett, 117.] Also: "Accordingly, it is in the nature of things for ordinary men to serve the sovereign, for physical strength to serve intelligence, and for the body to serve the mind" ("Guanzi: Junchen xia," *Guanzi jiaozheng,* juan 11: 77) [Rickett, 418]. And again: "Thus, to differentiate relationships and correctly maintain social distinctions is called establishing order" ("Guanzi: Junchen shang," *Guanzi jiaozheng,* juan 10: 165) [Rickett, 406].

16. *Laozi,* Part II, Chapter 38: "As for ritual propriety, it is the thinnest veneer of doing one's best and making good on one's word, and it is the first sign of trouble." See *Laozi jiao shi* [The *Laozi* collated and annotated], ed. Zhu Qianzhi (Beijing: Zhonghua shuju, 1984), 152. [Translation from *Dao De Jing: A Philosophical Translation,* trans. David L. Hall and Roger T. Ames (New York: Random House, 2003), 93.—Trans.]

17. According to "Lilun" [Discourse on ritual] in the *Xunzi:* "Deep indeed is the principle of ritual! Investigations into the hard and the white, the same and the different drown when they try to enter into it. Vast indeed is the principle of ritual! Those expert in creating institutions and the purveyors of perverse, vulgar doctrines are lost when they try to enter it. High indeed is the principle of ritual! Those who take violent arrogance, haughty indulgence, and contempt of custom for loftiness fall when they try to enter it." *Xunzi jijie,* juan 12: 237. [Translation modified from *Xunzi: The Complete Text,* trans. Eric L. Hutton (Princeton, NJ: Princeton University Press, 2014), 205.—Trans.]

18. Jia Yi, *Xinshu jiaozhu,* collated and annotated by Yan Zhenyi and Zhong Xia (Beijing: Zhonghua shuju, 2000), 325.

19. Zheng Xuan, "Yueji" [The *Record of Music*], in *Liji zhushu,* juan 37: 9b. Wenyuange siku quanshu edition.

20. Ban Gu, *Baihu tongyi* [Virtuous discussions from the White Tiger Pavillion], juan 2: 34a. Wenyuange siku quanshu edition.

21. See Liu Shipei, "Lixue ziyi tongshi" [Commentaries on the meaning of terms in the School of Principle], *Beijing Daxue bainian guoxue wencui* (Beijing: Beijing Daxue chubanshe, 1999), 90.

22. Dong Zhongshu, "Meng hui yao" [The essentials of covenants and meetings], *Chunqiu fanlu yizheng* [Verification of meanings in the *Luxuriant Dew of the Spring and Autumn Annals*], 142. [Translation modified from *Luxuriant Gems of the Spring and Autumn,* trans. Sarah A. Queen and John S. Major (New York: Columbia University Press, 2016), 164.—Trans.]

23. Dong Zhongshu, "Yinyang churu shangxia" [Yin and Yang emerge, withdraw, ascend, and descend], *Chunqiu fanlu yizheng,* 342. [Trans. Queen and Major, 416.]

24. Liu Shao, "Jiu Zheng" [Nine proofs], *Renwuzhi,* 848: 762. Wenyuange siku quanshu edition.

25. Liu Shao, "Cai Li" [Principle of human talent], *Renwuzhi,* 848: 767. Wenyuange siku quanshu edition.

26. Noritoshi Aramaki, "Zhongguo dui Fojiao de jieshou: 'li" de yi da zhuanbian" [Chinese reception of Buddhism: A major transformation of the *Li* principles], Section 2, in *Ribenyu Riben wenhua yanjiu lunji* (Daban daxue wenxuebu, 1988); cited in Yuzo Mizoguchi, "Zhongguo liqilun de xingcheng," in *Zai Yazhou sikao,* vol. 7: *Shijiexiang de xingcheng,* 77–130.

27. Wang Bi, "Ming yuan" [Clarifying the judgments], *Zhouyi lueli* [General remarks on the *Zhouyi*], in *Wang Bi ji jiaoshi,* collated and annotated by Lou Yulie (Beijing: Zhonghua shuju, 1980), 591. [Translation from *The Classic of Changes: A New Translation of the I Ching as Interpreted by Wang Bi,* trans. Richard J. Lynn (New York: Columbia University Press, 1994), 25.]

28. Wang Bi, "Laozi zhilue" [The structure of the *Laozi*'s subtle pointers] in *Wang Bi ji jiaoshi,* 199. [Translation from *A Chinese Reading of the Daodejing: Wang Bi's Commentary on the Laozi with Critical Text and Translation,* trans. Rudolf G. Wagner (Albany: State University of New York Press, 2012), 102–103.—Trans.]

29. Wang Bi, quoted in *Lunyu Huang shu* [Huang Kan's commentary on the *Analects*], in *Wang Bi ji jiaoshi,* 622.

30. Pei Wei's *Chongyoulun* (Disquisition on esteeming the existent) regards *li* as the concrete laws and internal necessity of things. In contrast with the "nothingness-based" (*yi wu wei ben*) position of Wang Bi and He Yan, not only does Pei's *li* leave traces that can be discerned or fathomed, but the essence upon which it is based actually exists: "The complex operation of natural transformation and mutual influences is the source of the discernible principles (*li*)." Also, "existence can be fathomed, and this is what is meant by the term 'principle." Where principle comes to be embodied, this is what is meant by 'being.'" On the concept of *li* in the work of Wang Bi, He Yan, and so on, see: "Wei-Jin-Nan-Bei chao shiqi li de sixiang" [The Idea of *Li* in the Wei, Jin, and Northern and Southern dynasties], in *Li,* ed. Zhang Liwen (Beijing:

Zhongguo renmin daxue chubanshe, 1991), 69–96. [Translation of Pei quotations from Alan K. L. Chan, "Pei Wei's 'Critical Discussion on the Pride of Place of Being,'" in *Dao Companion to Xuanxue (Neo-Daoism),* ed. David Chai (Cham: Springer, 2020), 327, 329.—Trans.]

31. Guo Xiang, "Qiwu lun zhu" [Annotations to "Making All Things Equal"], in *Zhuangzi Guo Xiang zhu* [Guo Xiang's commentary on the *Zhuangzi*] (Shanghai: Shanghai guji chubanshe, Yingyin Zhejiang shuju edition, 1989), 10. [Translation from Yuet Keung Lo, "Lone-Transformation and intergrowth: Philosophy and self-justification in Guo Xiang's commentary on the *Zhuangzi,*" in *Dao Companion to Xuanxue (Neo-Daoism),* ed. Chai, 374.—Trans.]

32. Ibid., 10. [Translation from Chris Fraser, "Metaphysics and Agency in Guo Xiang's Commentary on the Zhuangzi," in *Dao Companion to Xuanxue (Neo-Daoism),* ed. Chai, 345. The translations of *zisheng* as "autogeneration" and *ziran* as "self-so-ness" are borrowed from Fraser as well.—Trans.]

33. Guo Xiang, "'Zhi bei you' zhu" [Comments on "Knowledge Wandered North"], in *Zhuangzi Guo Xiang zhu,* 114. [What Guo wrote was, "As the maker of things has no master (*zaowuzhe wuzhu*), each thing makes itself." "The maker of things" or "the Creator" was a term Zhuangzi had used for the Way as "the transformative process of life." So Guo's idea here was not necessarily that there was no Creator, but that beyond the creation process itself there is no "all-embracing original reality that would create, control and guide them." See Jana S. Rošker, "The Metaphysical Style and Structural Coherence of Names in *Xuanxue,*" in *Dao Companion to Xuanxue (Neo-Daoism),* ed. Chai, 43.—Trans.]

34. Ibid., 131–132.

35. Ibid., 4–5.

36. Guo Xiang, "'Qi wu lun' zhu," ibid., 19.

37. Ibid., 82.

38. Ibid., 140.

39. Guo Xiang, "Dazongshi zhu" [Comments on "The Great and Venerable Teacher"], ibid., 38.

40. Tian Yuqing, *Dongjin menfa zhengzhi* [Aristocratic clan politics of the Eastern Jin dynasty] (Beijing: Beijing daxue chubanshe, 1991), 349, 359, and 362.

41. Scholars such as Zhang Liwen came to this conclusion: Whereas Wang Bi and Guo Xiang had interpreted the *li* as "necessary" or "resulting from causes," Buddhism regarded it as more deeply based in Dharma-nature or Buddha-nature, linking the idea of "becoming a sage by embodying the Principles" (*ti li cheng sheng*) to that of "becoming a Buddha through monastic practice," thus exhibiting features of Buddhist philosophical categories. After Wang Bi's formulation of the *li* as "rooted in nothingness," *li* began to be regarded as an illusory essence, emerging in the history of philosophical categories to play a germinal role in Song-Ming Neo-Confucianism's treatment of the *li* as foundational. Se *Li,* ed. Zhang Liwen, 89–90.

42. Ibid., 95 and 91.

43. Liu Zongyuan, "Wei Pei Zhongcheng he po Dongping biao" [A memorial congratulating Prefect Pei on the defeat of Dongping], in *Liu Hedong Quanji* [Complete works of Liu Zongyuan] (Beijing: Zhongguo shudian, 1991), 543.

44. Liu Zongyuan, "Da Yuan Raozhou lun zheng li shu" [A response to Governor Yuan of Rao Prefecture's letter on governmental principles], in *Liu Zongyuan ji* [Collected works of Liu Zongyuan] (Beijing: Zhonghua shuju, 1979), 833.

45. Liu Zongyuan, "Duan xing lun xia" [On ending punishments (part two)], in *Liu Zongyuan ji,* 91.

46. A. C. Graham, *Zhongguo de liang wei zhexuexia: Er Cheng xiongdi de xin ruxue* [Two Chinese philosophers: Cheng Ming-tao and Cheng Yi-chuan], trans. Cheng Dexiang (Zhengzhou: Daxiang chubanshe, 2000), 45–46.

47. *Henan Cheng shi yishu* [Surviving works of the Cheng Brothers from Henan], *Er Cheng ji* [Collected works of the Cheng Brothers] (Beijing: Zhonghua shuju, 1981), 1: 30.

48. For example, "Among the *li* of the myriad things of Heaven and Earth, all come in pairs, with none in isolation; all come of their own accord, with none of them arranged. Each night we are in thought, and then our hands move without our knowing, and our feet stamp without our knowing." See: *Henan Cheng shi yishu, Er Cheng ji,* 1: 121.

49. In the Cheng brothers' surviving writings, there is a passage whose author is not indicated, but which Zhu Xi believes to have been written by Cheng Hao. It says, "That which generates is called Nature (*xing*); Nature is energy (*qi*); energy is Nature, which is called that which generates." This can be taken as evidence. *Henan Cheng shi yishu, Er Cheng ji,* 1: 10.

50. Lao Siguang, *Xinbian Zhongguo zhexue shi* [A new history of Chinese philosophy], 3a: 54–55.

51. Graham, *Zhongguo de liang wei zhexuexia,* 32.

52. *Henan Cheng shi yishu, Er Cheng ji,* 1: 43.

53. Ibid., 247.

54. Ibid., 193.

55. Feng Youlan, *Zhongguo zhexue shi* [The history of Chinese philosophy], 2: 875–876.

56. Ibid., 2: 875–876.

57. Lu Xiangshan [Lu Jiuyuan], *Xiangshan quanji* [The complete works of Xiangshan] (Four-volume edition), juan 34: 38.

58. Lu Xiangshan, *Xiangshan quanji,* juan 15: 55.

59. Han Yu, "Yuan dao" [The original way], in *Han Changli ji* [Collected works of Han Yu], juan 11. [Translation by Charles Hartman from *Sources of Chinese Tradition,* Vol. 1: *From Earliest Times to 1600,* compiled by William Theodore de Bary and Irene Bloom (New York: Columbia University Press, 1999), 568–573.—Trans.]

60. Zhang Liwen, *Zou xiang xinxue zhi lu* [The path to *Xinxue*] (Beijing: Zhonghua shuju, 1992), 5.

61. Liu Zongyuan, "Shou dao lun" [On protecting the Way], in *Liu Zongyuan ji*, 82.

62. According to Zhu Xi, "The Supreme Ultimate is the formless (*xing er shang*) Way; yin and yang are the formed (*xing er xia*) instruments. According to what is evident, although activity and stillness do not occur at the same time, and yin and yang are not the same, there is nowhere that the Supreme Ultimate does not exist therein. Seeing from what is subtle, the principles of activity and stillness, and of yin and yang, are entirely contained within." See Zhu Xi, "'Taijitu shuo' zhu" [Commentary on "Explanation of the Diagram of the Supreme Ultimate"], in Zhou Dunyi, *Zhou Lianxi ji* [Collection of works by Zhou Dunyi] (Shanghai: Shangwu yinshuguan, 1936), juan 1: 7.

63. Zhu Xi, "Da Chen Tongfu" [Reply to Chen Tongfu] in *Zhuzi quanshu* [Complete works of Master Zhu], 21: 1590.

64. Yang Jian, *Cihu yishu*, juan 7: 1–10. Dayoushan Fangkan edition.

65. Jacques Gernet explains the development of these institutions as a result of military factors strengthening the independence of local rulers (*zhuhou*) within a society defined by religious and sacrificial categories. See: Jacques Gernet, *Zhongguo shehui shi* [A history of Chinese civilization], trans. Geng Sheng (Nanjing: Jiangsu renmin chubanshe, 1995), 55.

66. "Li yue zhi" [Record of rites and music], in *Xin Tang shu* [The new history of the Tang] (Beijing: Zhonghua shuju, 1975), 307–308.

67. Sima Guang (Song-dynasty editor and author) and Hu Sanxing (Yuan-dynasty commentator), "Zhou Ji, Part I," in *Zizhi tongjian* [Comprehensive mirror for aid in government] (Beijing: Zhonghua shuju, 1987), 1: 2–3.

68. Ibid., 1: 6.

69. Ibid., 1: 14–15.

70. Qian Mu, "Lue lun Wei-Jin-Nan-Bei chao xueshu wenhua yu dangshi men-di zhi guanxi" [On academic culture and contemporary clan relations in the Wei, Jin, and Northern, and Southern dynasties], in *Zhongguo xueshu sixiangshi luncong* [Collected essays on the history of Chinese academic thought] (Taipei: Dongda tushu gongsi, 1977), 3: 141.

71. Chen Yinke, "Sui-Tang zhidu yuanyuan luelungao" [On the origins of the institutions of the Sui and Tang dynasties], in *Chen Yinke shixue lunwen xuanji* [Selected works of Chen Yinke on historical scholarship] (Shanghai: Shanghai guji chubanshe, 1992), 534.

72. Chen Yinke, "Lun Tangdai zhi fanjiang yu fubing" [On the Tang-dynasty institutions of *Fanjiang* (foreign rulers given the title of protector general) and *Fubing* (local militia)], in *Chen Yinke shixue lunwen xuanji*, 383.

73. In Kang Youwei's "Fubing shuo" [On the *Fubing* militia system] (written before 1891), the focus is different from that of Chen Yinke. Kang argues that the *fubing* benefitted from the Three Dynasties, and that the martial spirit of the Three Dynasties

only began its decline after the abandonment of the *fubing.* See *Kang Youwei quanji* [Complete works of Kang Youwei] (Shanghai: Shanghai guji chubanshe, 1987), 1: 527–528.

74. Chen Yinke, "Sui-Tang zhidu yuanyuan luelungao," 100.

75. See: Fu Sinian, "Yi Xia dong xi shuo" [Theory of the Yi in the East and the Xia in the West], in *Fu Sinian quanji* [The complete works of Fu Sinian] (Tianjin: Tianjin renmin chubanshe, 1996), 247. Perhaps Fu's theory could be revised in some respects on the basis of more recent archaeological findings about the Three Dynasties, but the idea that "North-South Chinese history" emerged from social transformations at the end of the Eastern Han is completely reasonable.

76. Li Shuji, *Beichao lizhi faxi yanjiu* [Research on systems of ritual and law in the Northern dynasties] (Beijing: Renmin chubanshe, 2002), 2.

77. Though the southward migrations of the Jin and Song courts were separated by eight hundred years, they shared important features. Both spurred the development of southern Confucianism and culture, to the point that Jitsuzō Kuwabara argued it was necessary to renarrate Chinese history from the vantage point of North-South relations. Jitsuzō Kuwabara, "Lishi shang suo jian de Nanbei Zhongguo" [Northern and Southern China as seen in history], in *Riben xuezhe yanjiu Zhongguo shi lunzhu xuan yi* [Selected translations of Japanese scholarship on Chinese history], 1: 19–68.

78. Quoted in Qian Mu, "Xiangshan Longchuan Shuixin" [Xiangshan, Longchuan, and Shuixin], in *Zhongguo xueshu sixiangshi luncong* [Collected essays on the history of Chinese academic thought], 5: 269–70.

79. See: Hoyt Cleveland Tillman, *Gonglizhuyi rujia: Chen Liang dui Zhu Xi de tiaozhan* [Utilitarian Confucianism: Ch'en Liang's challenge to Chu Hsi], trans. Jiang Changsu (Nanjing: Jiangsu renmin chubanshe, 1997), 35–36.

80. Peter K. Bol, *Si wen: Tang-Song sixiang zhuanxing* [This culture of ours: Intellectual transitions in T'ang and Sung China], trans. Liu Ning (Nanjing: Jiangsu renmin chubanshe, 2001), 37.

81. Xu Yangjie, *Song-Ming jiazu zhidu shi lun* [On the history of the clan system in the Song and Ming dynasties] (Beijing: Zhonghua shuju, 1995), 84.

82. Li Tao, *Xu zizhi tongjian changbian* [Extended and expanded *Zizhi tongjian*] (Beijing: Zhonghua shuju, 1985), 8: 2380.

83. Qian Daxin, *Qianyantang ji* [Collected works of Qianyantang], ed. Lü Youren (Shanghai: Shanghai guji chubanshe, 1989), 451.

84. Zheng Qiao, "Shizu lue" [Treatise on clans], *Tongzhi ershi lue* [The twenty treatises of the *Tongzhi* encyclopedia] (Beijing: Zhonghua shuju, 1995), 1.

85. The "Da zhuan" in the *Liji* [Book of Rites] states: "Thus the course of humanity (in this matter of mourning) was all comprehended in the love for kindred. From the affection for parents came the honouring of ancestors; from the honouring of the ancestor came the respect and attention shown to the Heads (of the family branches). By that respect and attention to those Heads all the members of the kindred were kept together." *Liji jijie*, 916–917. [Trans. James Legge.]

86. Zhang Zai, "Zongfa" [Clan law], *Jingxue liku* [Principles for the study of the classics], in *Zhang Zai ji* [Collected works of Zhang Zai], 259.

87. Cheng Yi, "Ruguan yulu" [Recorded discourses on crossing the threshold], in *Er Cheng ji,* 150.

88. Cheng Yi, "Yichuan Xiansheng yu" [Discourses of Master Yichuan], in *Er Cheng ji,* 242.

89. Zhu Xi, "Jia li" [Rites of the family], in *Zhuzi quanshu* [Collected works of Zhu Xi], eds. Zhu Jieren, Yan Zuozhi, and Liu Yongxiang (Shanghai: Shanghai guji chubanshe and Hefei: Anhui jiaoyu chubanshe, 2002)], 7: 875.

90. Zhu Xi, "Ba san jia li fan" [Epilogue to rites and regulations of three masters], in *Zhuzi quanshu,* 24: 3920. On Zhu Xi's theory of the clan law and familial rites, see Xu Yangjie, *Song-Ming jiazu zhidu shi lun,* 94–95.

91. Zhu Xi, "Du da ji" [Reading the great law], in *Zhuzi quanshu,* 23: 3376.

92. Zhu Xi, "Zengsun Lü shi xiangyue" [The Lü Family community compact, with additions and deletions] in *Zhuzi quanshu,* 24: 3594.

93. Hiroaki Terada, "Ming-Qing shiqi fa zhixu zhong 'yue' de xingzhi" [The nature of "yue" (compacts) in the legal order of the Ming and Qing], in *Ming-Qing shiqi de minshi shenpan yu minjian qiyue* [Civil trials and contracts in the Ming and Qing], eds. Shūzō Shiga et al. (Beijing: Falü chubanshe, 1998), 153.

94. Ibid.

95. Setsuko Yanagida, "Songdai xiangcun de hudengzhi" [The rural household classification system in the Song dynasty], in *Riben xuezhe yanjiu Zhongguo shi lunzhu xuanyi* [Selected translations of Japanese scholarship on Chinese history] (Beijing: Zhonghua shuju, 1993), 5: 189.

96. Yoshiyuki Sudō, "Songdai de guanliao zhi he da tudi zhanyou" [Bureaucracy and large estates in the Song dynasty], in *Riben xuezhe yanjiu Zhongguo shi lunzhu xuanyi,* 5: 166.

97. The vehement criticism on the part of Ming and Qing thinkers such as Li Zhi on the teachings of rites and Community Compacts (especially prohibitive ones), and Dai Zhen on the notions of Heavenly Principles and Nature, reveal the devastation that these institutions and theories of clan law had wrought upon ordinary people, especially women. From the perspective of May Fourth–era thought, the rural landlord system and imperial power were completely interdependent.

98. Zhang Zai, "Jisi" [Sacrificial rites], *Jingxue liku* [Principles for the study of the classics], in *Zhang Zai ji* [Collected works of Zhang Zai], 295.

99. Xu Yangjie, *Song-Ming jiazu zhidu shi lun,* 468.

100. Cheng Yi, "Huan" [Dispersion], *Yijing Cheng shi zhuan* [The Cheng brothers' commentary on the *Book of Changes*], in *Er Cheng ji,* 1002.

101. Cheng Yi, *Er Cheng ji,* 352.

102. Zhu Xi, "Jia li" [Family rituals], juan 1 in "Tong li: ci tang" [General rites: The offering hall], in *Zhuzi quanshu,* 7: 875.

103. Xu Yangjie, *Song Ming jiazu zhidu shi lun* [On the history of clan institutions in the Song and Ming dynasties] (Beijing: Zhonghua shuju, 1995), 475.

104. See Ellen Neskar, *The Cult of Worthies: A Study of Shrines Honoring Local Confucian Worthies in the Sung Dynasty (960–1279),* Columbia University Ph.D. dissertation, 1993. According to her research, although temples for worshipping local worthies appeared no later than the Han dynasty, during the periods 1163–1190 and 1210–1241, there were waves of revival involving building and renovating such temples. Also see Hoyt Cleveland Tillman, "80 niandai zhongye yilai Meiguo de Song dai sixiang shi yanjiu" [Study of American intellectual histories of the Song dynasty since the mid-1980s], *Zhongguo wenzhe yanjiu tongxun* (Taipei) 3: 4, 65.

105. Yuzo Mizoguchi, "Zhongguo gong si gainian de fazhan" [Development of Chinese concepts of public and private], *Guowai shehui kexue,* 1: 1998, 64.

106. Hiroaki Terada, "Ming Qing shiqi fa shixu zhong 'yue' de xingzhi" [On the qualities of yue agreements in Ming and Qing legal order], in *Ming Qing shiqi de minshi shenpan yu minjian qiyue* [Civil courts and people's contracts during the Ming and Qing dynasties], 142.

107. Hiroaki Terada, "Ming Qing shiqi fa shixu zhong 'yue' de xingzhi" [On the qualities of compacts in Ming and Qing legal order], in *Ming Qing shiqi de minshi shenpan yu minjian qiyue* 154.

108. The relation between the *zu-yong-diao* and the equal-field tax system was a subject of debate during the 1950s in the journal *Historical Research,* with Deng Guangming believing that there was no relationship between the *zu-yong-diao* and the equal-field system, while Cen Zhongmian, Han Guopan, and Hu Rulei all supported the opposite view. See *Lishi yanjiu* 1954, no. 4 and 1955, no. 5.

109. Fu Yiling, *Ming-Qing tudi suoyouzhi lungang* [Overview of land tenure in the Ming and Qing dynasties] (Shanghai: Shanghai renmin chubanshe, 1992), 10–11.

110. On the contents of the Two-Tax Policy, see the biographies of Yang Yan in the *Xin Tang shu* and the *Jiu Tang shu;* the *Tang huiyao,* juan 83, "Zu shui" [Rents and taxes], part 1; and *Lu Xuangong hanyuan ji* [Collected memorials of Lu Zhi], juan 22, "Junjie fu shui xu bai xing" [Adjusting tributes and taxes for the relief of the common people], entry 3. Much work has been done on Yang Yan and his Two-Tax Policy; see, recently, Li Zhixian, *Yang Yan ji qi liangshuifa yanjiu* [A study of Yang Yan and the Two-Tax Policy] (Beijing: Zhongguo shehui kexue chubanshe, 2002), which is a most detailed exposition.

111. See Jian Bozan, *Zhongguo shi gangyao* [Outline of Chinese history], 2: 199.

112. See Chen Jiyu, "Zhongguo fengjian shehui tudi ji qi fu yi zhidu bianqian de tantao" [An investigation into the transformations of the land and taxation and tribute systems of Chinese feudal society], in *Yangzhou daxue xuebao,* 1998, no. 3: 70–71.

113. Li Ao, *Li Wengong ji* [Collected works of Li Ao], juan 3: 6b.

114. *Lu Xuangong hanyuan ji,* juan 22, "Junjie fu shui xu bai xing" [Adjusting tributes and taxes for the relief of the common people].

115. On the "substitution of taxes in kind for monetary taxation" (*shena*), see T. Funakoshi, "Tang dai liangshuifa de hudou zhengke ji liangshuiqian de shena wenti" [Grain tribute and the substitution of taxes in kind in the Tang dynasty's Two-Tax Policy], in *Riben zhong qingnian xuezhe lun Zhongguo shi: Liu Chao Sui Tang juan*" [Young Japanese scholars discuss Chinese history: The Six Dynasties and the Sui and Tang dynasties] (Shanghai: Shanghai guiji chubanshe, 1995), 485–508.

116. On the state of circulation of copper and iron money during the Song dynasty, also see Gao Congming, *Song dai huobi yu huobi liutong yanjiu* [Money and monetary circulation in the Song dynasty] (Baoding: Hebei daxue chubanshe, 2000), 35–49.

117. Ichisada Miyazaki, "Dongyang de jinshi" [Early modernity in East Asia], in *Riben xuezhe yanjiu Zhongguoshi lunzhu xuanyi,* 1: 172.

118. On the state of Song-dynasty commercial and urban development, see Laurence J. C. Ma, *Commercial Development and Urban Change in Sung China (960–1279)* (Ann Arbor: University of Michigan Press, 1971).

119. Naitō Torajirō, "Gaikuo de Tang Song shidai guan" [Overview of the Tang and Song eras], in *Riben xuezhe yanjiu Zhongguoshi lunzhu xuanyi,* 1: 17–18.

120. *Lu Xuangong hanyuan ji,* juan 22, "Junjie fu shui xu bai xing" [Adjusting tributes and taxes for the relief of the common people]; *Li Wengong ji,* juan 9, "Shu gai liangfa"; *Tang huiyao,* juan 84, Yuanhe Year 15; Jian Bozan, *Zhongguo shi gangyao* [Outline of Chinese history], 2: 199–200.

121. *Song shi* [History of the Song], juan 173, "Shi huo zhi" [Record on food and goods] (Beijing: Zhonghua shuju, 1977), 4164.

122. *Song huiyao ji gao: shi huo: yi er* (Taibei: Xinwenfeng chuban gongsi, 1976), 4994.

123. Li Gou, "Pingtu shu" [On the equalization of land], in *Li Gou ji* [Collected works of Li Gou] (Beijing: Zhonghua shuju, 1981), 183.

124. Li Gou, "Qianshu shiwu pian bing xu" [Deep thoughts in ten sections with an introduction], in *Li Gou ji* [Collected works of Li Gou], 214–15.

125. Zhang Zai, *Jingxue liku: Zhou li* [Assembled principles in the study of the classics: The *Rites of Zhou*], in *Zhang Zai ji* [Collected works of Zhang Zai], 248–49.

126. In reality, the well-field system of the Zhou dynasty was characterized by serfdom (*nongnuzhi*), with peasants subject to the most stringent controls on movement. Yang Xiangkui, "Cong *Zhou li* tuilun Zhongguo gudai shehui fazhan de bupinghengxing" [Deductions on the unbalanced nature of social development in ancient China based on the *Rites of Zhou*], *Yishi Zhai xueshu wenji* [Collected academic works of Yishi Studio] (Shanghai: Shanghai renmin chubanshe, 1983), 25. [Translation from *Mencius,* trans. Irene Bloom (New York: Columbia University Press, 2009), 54.—Trans.]

127. Zhang Zai, *Jingxue liku: Zhou li,* in *Zhang Zai ji,* 248–249.

128. Zhang Zai, *Jingxue liku: Zong fa* [Assembled principles in the study of the classics: Clan law] in *Zhang Zai ji* [Collected works of Zhang Zai] (Beijing: Zhonghua shuju, 1978), 260. [Translation of the opening line of this passage is modified from Ira E. Kasoff, *The Thought of Chang Tsai (1020–1077)* (Cambridge: Cambridge University Press, 1984), 13.—Trans.]

129. Hui Shiqi, a Qing scholar of the Suzhou school, made a detailed study of the *Rites of Zhou*, and had this to say about the *zong*, or "clans": "When the *zu* [small lineage groups or clans] are too numerous, it leads to dissolution; when the clans flourish, they become strong. For this reason the great clans (*dazong*) were established, to bring the lineage groups (*zu*) together, and to maintain and make use of them. They made the lineage groups love each other like kin, and treat each other with respect, for which reason the poor and elderly were never left behind, and the dastardly and unscrupulous among them never dared to commit offenses. And so all took their clans (*zong*) as their patriarchy, and All-under-Heaven was put in order. This is what is meant by the saying, the lineage groups employ the clans and the clans settle the people by means of the lineage groups. And so it was, down to the Spring and Autumn era, when the lineage groups no longer employed the clan, and the clan patriarch did not serve the lineage group . . . and so the patriarchal clan law (*zongfa*) was broken." Yang Xiangkui supplements this with the following: "The clans settle the people by means of the lineage groups, or *zu*, which meant that the patriarchal law system was the foundation of feudal society. From the Spring and Autumn period onward, patriarchal clan law (*zongfa*) deteriorated, following which the Zhou dynasty's 'Son of Heaven' was no king; great and small clans were not distinguished, and the lineage groups could not be used to settle the people, leading to uprisings throughout the seven states, and scholar-gentry (*shi*) and commoner were not distinguished." See Yang Xiangkui, *Qing ruxue an xin bian, san* [Scholarly records of Qing Confucians, revised] (Jinan: Jilu shushe, 1994), 3: 111.

130. Hu Hong, *Zhi yan* [Knowing words], juan 3: 2b. Wenyuange siku quanshu edition.

131. Ibid., juan 1: 11a.

132. Ibid., juan 6: 6b.

133. Ibid., juan 6: 4b.

134. Ibid., juan 5: 14b–15a.

135. Xiao Gongquan, *Zhongguo zhengzhi sixiang shi* [History of Chinese political thought] (Shenyang: Liaoning jiaoyu chubanshe, 1998), 2: 471–72.

136. Zhu Xi, *Kai qian mo bian*, in *Zhu Wengong ji* [Collected works of Zhu Xi], Shangwu yinshuguan bianyin mingkan edition, 311.

137. Zhu Xi, *Zhuzi yulei* [Classified Sayings of Master Zhu], 2680.

138. Ibid., 2495.

139. Ibid., 207, 224.

140. Wang Anshi, "Yu Ding Yuanzhen shu" [Letter to Ding Yuanzhen], *Linchuan Xiansheng wenji* [The collected master Linchuan] (Shanghai: Shangwu yinshuguan, 1929), 8: 32.

141. See Kang Youwei, "Jiao xue tong yi: li xue di shi er" [General discussion on education: 12. establishing schools] in *Kang Youwei ji* (Shanghai: Shanghai guji chubanshe, 1987), 1: 132.

142. Ma Duanlin, *Wenxian tongkao* [Critical history of institutions], juan 42, teaching materials, set 3, put into order by the graduate institutes of ancient texts at

Shanghai Normal University and Huadong Normal University, in *Chuanshi zangshu, shiku* [Heritage and rare books, history category] (Haikou: Hainan guoji xinwen chuban zhongxin, 1995), 545–546.

143. Zhang Xiqing, "Lun Song dai keju qu shi zhi duo yu rongguan wenti" [On Song-dynasty examination-based uptake of scholar-officials and the problem of redundant officials] in *Beijing daxue xuebao,* 1987, no. 5.

144. Miao Shumei, *Song dai guanyuan xuanren he guanli zhidu* [The system for selecting and managing officials during the Song dynasty] (Kaifeng: Henan daxue chubanshe, 1996), 3.

145. Cai Xiang, "Guo lun yao mu, ze guan" [Essential topics of the state: Selecting officials] *Duan Ming ji,* juan 22: 2a–b. Wenyuange sikuquanshu edition.

146. *Jiu Tang shu, ru xue shang* [Old history of the Tang, Confucianism, 1] (Beijing: Zhonghua shuju, 1975), 4941.

147. *Xin Tang shu, xuan ju zhi* [New Tang history, record of examinations and selections] (Beijing, 1975), 1160. An exposition to accompany this source is in Zhang Quancai, *Song Ming jingxue shi* [History of classical studies in the Song and Ming] (Guangzhou: Guangdong renmin chubanshe, 1999), 16–17.

148. Chen Zhongmian records in his *Sui Tang shi* [History of the Sui and Tang dynasties], that the first test in illuminating the classics was to "copy in good calligraphy one great classic, like the *Book of Rites* or the *Zuo Zhuan,* as well as the *Classic of Filial Piety,* the *Analects* of Confucius, and the *Erya* dictionary. Ten passages should be completed of each; those who could complete five or more could be selected." The second test was "to ask for oral expositions on the meaning of ten passages; those who mastered six or more could be selected." A third test was "to answer on three topics in current political affairs, on which the students would be ranked in order of the style and coherence of their answers." See his *Sui Tang shi* (Shijiazhuang: Hebei jiaoyu chubanshe, 2000), 182.

149. See Xie Shanyuan, *Li Gou zhi shengping ji sixiang* [Life and thought of Li Gou], chapters 5, 6, and 7 (Beijing: Zhonghua shuju, 1988).

150. *Song shi, liezhuan di bashi liu* [History of the Song, biographies, 86] (Beijing: Zhonghua shuju, 1977), 10550.

151. Wang Anshi, *Zhou li yi, xu* [Preface to "*On the Meaning of the Rites of Zhou*"], *Wang Wengong wenji* [Collected works of Wang Anshi] (Shanghai: Shanghai renmin chubanshe, 1974), 426. [Translation from Peter Bol, "Wang Anshi and the Zhou Li," in *Statecraft and Classical Learning: The Rituals of Zhou in East Asian History,* eds. Benjamin Elman and Martin Kern (Leiden: E. J. Brill, 2010), 235.—Trans.]

152. According to Charles O. Hucker, "Worthy and Upright" and "Extraordinary Talents" refer to classes of government officials outside of the standard civil service examination, whether through recommendation or specially arranged exams. See *Dictionary of Official Titles in Imperial China* (Stanford, CA: Stanford University Press, 1985), 242, 328.—Trans.

153. Wang Anshi, "Yan shi shu" [A letter on affairs] in *Wang Wengong wenji,* 3–6.

154. Cheng Hao, "Qing xiu xuexiao shiru qushi zhazi," in *Er cheng ji*, 448.

155. Lü Gongzhu, *Song ming chen zouyi*, juan 78, "Shang shen zong dazhao lun xuexiao gongju zhi fa," 10. Wenyuange sikuquanshu edition.

156. Wang Anshi, "Qi gai ketiao zhi" [Plea for changes to the examinations], in *Wang Wengong wenji*, 363. Wang Anshi's suggested reforms fall into three main areas of content: first, that the *jinshi* examinations be changed to center on the meanings of the classics, *jingyi;* second, to abolish, in phases, the *zhuke*, or all non-*jinshi* examinations; third, to reconcile the policies of northwestern candidates [with those in the Southeast]. His ultimate concept was to nullify the imperial examinations, institute a school system, and take officials from among the graduates of higher education, *taixue*. As Kazunari Kondo puts it, [Wang Anshi] "wanted to bring to pass what many commentators had talked about since Qingli times, which was the unification of the selection and the cultivation of scholar-officials. And this was something that could be confirmed." See "Wang Anshi keju gaige" [The examination reforms of Wang Anshi], in *Riben zhong qingnian xuezhe lun Zhongguo shi: Liu Chao Sui Tang juan*" [Young Japanese scholars discuss Chinese history, volume on Song, Yuan, Ming and Qing dynasties] (Beijing: Zhonghua shuju, 1995), 137.

157. On Wang Anshi's editing of the *San jing xinyi*, see Zhang Quancai, *Song Ming jing xue shi*, 109–113.

158. For related materials see *Xu zizhi tongjian changbian*, juan 227, 243, 266, and the related discussion in Deng Guangming, "Song chao de jiafa he Bei Song de zhengzhi gaige yundong" [Song-dynasty family law and political reform movement in the Northern Song], in his *Bei Song zhengzhi gaigejia Wang Anshi* [Wang Anshi, reformer of the Northern Song] (Shijiazhuang: Hebei jiaoyu chubanshe, 2000), 364.

159. Pi Xirui, *Jing xue tong lun* [Collected commentaries on classical studies] (Beijing: Zhonghua shuju, 1954), 58.

160. According to Li Tao in the *Xu zizhi tongjian changbian* in the record of the third month of the sixth year of Xining, and the corresponding account in Chen Zhensun's *Zhizhai shulu jieti*, the composition of the *San jing xinyi* not only entailed a large assemblage of scholars, but also realized the intentions of the highest rulers.

161. See Deng Guangming, *Bei Song zhengzhi gaigejia Wang Anshi*, 51–52.

162. *Er Cheng ji*, 562–576.

163. Lu Xiangshan, *Lu Xiangshan quanji* [Complete works of Lu Xiangshan] (Beijing: Zhongguo shudian, 1992), 231–232, 233–235.

164. Yichuan [Cheng Yi] wrote in his biographical obituary notice for Ming Dao (Cheng Hao), "The master studied from the age of fifteen or sixteen, and when he heard Zhou Maoshu speak on the Dao, he then spurned the enterprise of examinations, turning with passion his sights toward seeking the Dao. . . . He fully explained things, and observed the order of human relations. He understood the depth of 'knowing the mandate by fully understanding inner nature,' which must be based on the practice of filial piety. He fully comprehended spiritual principle and knew of all the changes, from which he gained full comprehension of the rites and music." *Er Cheng ji*, 638.

165. Zhu Xi, *Zhuzi yulei,* 3101, 3097.

166. Ibid., 3098.

167. Zhu Xi, "Da Chen Shide" [Reply to Chen Shide], *Zhuzi quanshu,* 23: 2671.

168. Zhu Xi, *Zhuzi yulei,* 2801.

169. On the topic of school lands and rents, the most detailed study is from Li Wenzhi, *Qing Ming shidai fengjian tudi guanxi de songjie* [The loosening of feudal land relations in the Ming and Qing], chapter 4, "Qing Ming shidai de xuetian dizu" (Beijing: Zhongguo shehui kexue chubanshe, 1993), 402–442.

170. Li Hongqi, *Song dai guanxue jiaoyu yu keju* [Education and examinations for officialdom during the Song dynasty] (Taibei: Lianjing chuban gongsi, 1994), 24–25.

171. The meanings of the classics had one Way, with agents each putting in order one classic. The *Shi,* or *Book of Odes,* was mainly ordered by Zhu Xi; the *Shangshu,* or *Book of Documents,* by Cai Shen; the *Zhou yi,* or *Book of Changes,* by Cheng Yi and Zhu Xi; the *Chunqiu,* or *Spring and Autumn Annals,* made use of the three commentaries and the tradition of Hu Anguo; the *Li ji,* or *Book of Rites,* used the ancient annotations.

172. Regarding the contents of the subjects, school administration, and schools, see *Ming shi* [History of the Ming], juan 70, "Record of Selections and Examinations," part 2; juan 69, "Record of Selections and Examinations"; and juan 62, "Record of Schools."

173. Benjamin Elman, "Wan Ming ruxue keju dawen zhong de 'ziran zhi xue'" ["'Natural studies' in examination answers among late-Ming Confucians"], translated by Lei Yi in *Zhongguo wenhua,* 13: 133.

174. Ibid., 137.

175. Song Lian, "Luoshan za yan" [Luoshan miscellanies], in *Song Lian quanji,* ed. Luo Yuexia (Hangzhou: Zhejiang guji chubanshe, 1999), 1: 52.

176. Rong Zhaozu, *Ming dai sixiang shi* [History of Ming thought] (Jinan: Jilu shushe, 1992), 8–9.

177. Yuzo Mizoguchi believes that the diametric opposition of School of Principle and School of Mind risks cutting off the observation of a larger evolution from Song learning to the school of Wang Yangming. See Mizoguchi, *Zhongguo qian jindai sixiang de yanbian* [Evolution of Chinese thought before early modern times] (Beijing: Zhonghua shuju, 1997), 62. Since the 1980s, Wing-tsit Chan and William Theodore de Bary have begun to expand the scope of research into Song thought. In De Bary's *Neo-Confucian Orthodoxy and the Learning of the Mind-and-Heart* (New York: Columbia University Press, 1981) and *The Message of the Mind in Neo-Confucianism* (New York: Columbia University Press, 1989) no longer is it said that the School of Mind originated in Lu Jiuyuan, or Wang Yangming, but rather in Zhu Xi and his system.

178. For example, recently discovered among the Guodian bamboo slips are chapters from *Cheng zhi wen zhi* that used the Way of Heaven concept to logically approach the problem of seeking the self. See Liao Chunming, "Jingmen Guodian yu xian Qin ruxue" and "Guodian Chu jian yanjiu" in *Zhongguo zhexue,* 20 (1999): 52.

179. Wang Fuzhi, *Zhangzi zheng meng zhu* [Commentary on Zhangzi's *Correction of Youthful Ignorance*], *Chuanshan quan shu* [Complete works of Chuanshan] (Changsha: Yuelu shushe, 1992), 12: 362.

180. Li Ao, "Qu fo zhai lun" [Against Buddhist fasting rituals], *Quan Tang shu* (Shanghai: Shanghai guji chubanshe, 1990), 2846.

181. See Patricia Ebrey, "Women, Marriage, and the Family in Chinese History," in *Heritage of China: Contemporary Perspectives on Chinese Civilization,* ed. Paul S. Ropp (Berkeley: University of California Press, 1990), 214–215.

182. *Jin shu* [History of the Jin], "Cai Mo zhuan" [Biography of Cai Mo], juan 77:16b. Wenyuange sikuquanshu edition.

183. *Nan Qi shu* [History of the Southern Qi], "Gu Huan zhuan" [Biography of Gu Huan], juan 54: 10a. Wenyuange sikuquanshu edition.

184. Han Yu, "Lun Fo gu biao" [Memorial on the bone of the Buddha], in *Han Changli wenji jiao zhu,* 613–16.

185. Han Yu, "Yuan dao" [Origin of the Way], in *Han Changli wenji jiao zhu,* 17–18.

186. Feng Youlan, *Zhongguo zhexue jianshi* [A brief history of Chinese philosophy] (Beijing: Peking University Press, 1985), 298.

187. Li Fangzi, "Zizhi tongjian gangmu houxu" [Afterword to the *Summary of the Comprehensive Mirror For Aid in Government*], in *Yupi zizhi tongjian gangmu,* juan 1b: 7, afterword. Wenyuange sikuquanshu edition.

188. Zhu Xi, *Yupi zizhi tongjian gangmu,* juan 1b: 38. Wenyuange sikuquanshu edition.

189. Zhu Xi, "Renwu zhao ying feng shi" [Sealed document requested by the Emperor in the year of Renwu], in *Zhuzi wenji* (Taibei: Caiyuan faren defu wenjiao jijinhui, 2000), 348.

190. On discussions of *Spring and Autumn Annals* scholarship during the Song dynasty, and Hu Anguo's commentary, see Zhang Quancai, *Song Ming jing xue shi,* 151–181 and 203–208.

191. Chen Liang, *Longquan wenji* [Collected writings of Chen Liang], juan 1: 1a. Sibu beiyao edition.

192. Chen Yinke, *Sui Tang zhidu yuanyuan luelungao* [Preliminary study of the origins of Sui-Tang institutions] (Shanghai: Shanghai guji chubanshe, 1982), 515.

193. Chen Yinke, *Tang zhengzhi shi lunshugao* [Manuscript on Tang political history] (Shanghai: Shanghai guji chubanshe, 1982), 515.

194. See Jennifer Holmgren, "Widow Chastity in the Northern Dynasties," in *Papers on Far Eastern History* 23 (1981): 165–186; "Observations on Marriage and Inheritance Practices in Early Mongol and Yuan Society: With Particular Reference to the Levirate," *Journal of Asian History* 20 (1986): 127–192.

195. Ebrey, "Women, Marriage, and the Family in Chinese History," in *Heritage of China,* 220–221.

196. Yang Xiangkui, "Shi lun Dong Han Bei Wei zhi ji Zhongguo fengjian shehui de tezheng" [Preliminary discussion of features of Chinese feudal society in the Eastern Han and Northern Wei], in *Yishi zhai xueshu wenji,* 58–61.

197. Ibid., 58–61.

198. See Tillman, *Gongli zhuyi rujia,* 96–97.

199. Zhu Xi, "Da Huang Zhiweng" [Reply to Huang Zhiweng], in *Zhuzi wenji,* juan 44: 1986.

200. Zhu Xi, "Gu shi yu lun" [Remnant remarks on ancient history], in *Zhuzi wenji,* juan 72: 1297.

201. Zhu Xi, *Zhuzi yulei,* 3303.

202. Faced with the tension between enfeoffment and centralized administration, Zhu Xi pointedly evaluated them as follows: "After the Zhou dynasty moved east, the kingly court became weaker and weaker . . . until Qin times, when this propensity of affairs exhausted itself. It was not possible to do away with [centralized government], it was necessary for it to be done so."

203. Zhu Xi, *Zhuzi yulei,* 599.

204. Ibid., 599. Tang Fuqin has made a detailed analysis of how the categories of "Principle" and *shi* ("propensity" or "influence"), are used in the historical views of Zhu Xi. See Tang, *Zhu Xi de shixue sixiang* [The historical thought of Zhu Xi], 23–31.

205. Zhu Xi, *Zhuzi yulei,* juan 1, 2, and 4.

206. Alasdair MacIntyre, *Dexing zhi hou* [After virtue], trans. Gong Qun et al. (Beijing: Zhongguo shehui kexue chubanshe, 1995), 56. [For the original, see Alisdair MacIntyre, *After Virtue: A Study in Moral Theory* (London: Bloomsbury Editions, 2013), 69–70.—Trans.]

207. Ibid., 58–59.

3. The Transformation of "Things"

1. *Han Shu* [History of the Former Han] (Beijing: Zhonghua Shuju, 1962), 1775.

2. *Shiji* [Records of the Grand Historian], 1342.

3. Jao Tsung-I, "Yingyang wuxing sixiang you 'xing,' 'qi,' eryuan yu 'deli' guanlian shuo" [Regarding the concept of form and qi within yin/yang and Five Elements thought, and their relations to the concept of Moral Rites], *Zhongguo shixue zhi zhengtonglun* [A theory of orthodoxy grounded in Chinese historiography] (Shanghai: Shanghai yuandong chubanshe, 1996), 285–288. Regarding the relationship between *wen* and *li,* see the discussion of Gu Yanwu in the fourth chapter in this book.

4. Zhu Xueqin, ed., *Shisan jing zhushu: Zhouli zhushu* [Commentary and explanations on the Thirteen Classics: The *Rites of Zhou*] (Beijing: Beijing daxue chubanshe, 1999), 859. Also see *Zhou Li ju jie* [Interpreting the *Rites of Zhou*], in [Complete books of the four storehouses from Wenyuan Hall], Zhu Shen (Song dynasty) annotation: "One thing is said to conform to one category," juan 8. Wenyuange Sikuquanshu edition.

5. *Zuozhuan Dulin hezhu* [The integrated Du-Lin commentaries to the Zuozhuan], juan 19: 11a. Wenyuange Sikuquanshu edition.

6. *Chunqiu Zuozhuan zhushi* [Commentary and explanations on the *Chunqiu* and *Zuozhuan*], juan 23: 8b. Wenyuange Sikuquanshu edition.

7. When it comes to the integrated relationship between rites and music and the myriad things, there are many other illustrations to choose from. Qiu Xigui compiled the many examples found in the *Rites of Zhou,* the *Book of Documents,* the *Spring and Autumn Annals of Master Lü,* and the *Huai Nanzi* of music being used as a means of engaging with things. For example, in the "Grand Officer of Music" portion of the "Office of Spring" section of the *Rites of Zhou,* we find: "The six singular-pitch tubes, the six dual-pitch tubes, five sounds, eight musical instruments, six dances all integrate into a great musical [performance] which reaches the ghosts and gestures to the spirits . . . in all there are six musical performances, in performing once they reach the plumed animals and gesture to the rivers and ponds, in performing twice they reach the tigers and leopards and gesture to mountain forests, three times they reach the animals with scales and gesture to the highest peaks, four times they reach the animals with fur and gesture to the graves, five times they reach the animals with shells and gesture to the earth, six times and they reach the phoenix and dragons and gesture to the heavenly spirits." See Qiu Xigui, "Shuo gewu" [Speaking of investigating things], *Wenshi conggao: shanggu sixiang, minsu, yu guwenzi xueshi* [Writings in literature and history: Ancient thought, folk customs, and the historiography of ancient philology] (Shanghai: Shanghai yuandong chubanshe, 1996), 8–9.

8. Zhu Xueqin, ed., *Shisan jing zhushu: Liji zhengyi* [Commentary and explanations on the Thirteen Classics: A rectified interpretation of the *Liji*], 1450.

9. Ibid., 1076.

10. I have chosen to render *Xin* as "heart-mind" throughout this chapter, following the convention set out by noted scholars of Neo-Confucianism Stephen C. Angle and Justin Tiwald. As Angle and Tiwald note, Neo-Confucians "take a great deal of interest in the seat of mental and emotional phenomena which is called, in Chinese, *xin* 心, a term that is variously translated as 'mind,' 'heart,' or some combination of the two. In the most basic sense of the term, *xin* refers to the organ that we today call the heart but, like virtually all Chinese thinkers, Neo-Confucians take this organ to be the locus of both conation (emotions, inclinations) and cognition (understanding, beliefs). 'Heart-mind' expresses this unity well." Stephen C. Angle and Justin Tiwald, "Neo-Confucianism: A Philosophical Introduction," *Polity* (2017): 71. The eminent sinologist Victor Mair has discussed the complexities around translating *Xin* in detail, with wide input from a variety of colleagues in the field (including the aforementioned Angle and Barnwell). The question of how to translate it is, of course, comple and far from settled. See Victor Mair, "Heart-mind," Language Log, https://languagelog.ldc.upenn.edu/nll/?p=14807, accessed November 16, 2022.

11. Zhu Xueqin, ed., *Shisan jing zhushu: Zhouli zhushu,* 266.

12. For example, in the "Second Xici" commentary on the *Book of Changes* it is stated: "One looks upward to see the images in Heaven, one looks downward to see laws on Earth. . . . One engages closely with various bodies, across distance with various things, and as such in the beginning the eight hexagrams were made." See Zhu Xueqin, ed., *Shisan jing zhushu: Zhouli zhushu,* 298. Here, things and the body correspond, but this correspondence is organized in terms of such abstract concepts as images and law. Regarding the notion of "things" in pre-Qin thought, Zhang Taiyan has an article on "Shuo wu" [Speaking of things], *Zhang Taiyan quanji* [Complete works of Zhang Taiyan] (Shanghai: Shanghai renmin chubanshe, 1985), 4: 40.

13. "Zhi bei you" [Knowledge rambling in the North], in Guo Qingfan, ed., *Zhuangzi Ji Shi* [The collected and annotated Zhuangzi] (Beijing: Zhonghua shuju, 1961), 731.

14. Cheng Hao, "Da Hengqu Zhang Zihou xiansheng shu" [In reply to Mr. Zhang Zihou of Hengqu], *Er Cheng wenji* [Selected writings of the Cheng Brothers], juan 2: 460.

15. These lines are from Ode 260 in the *Book of Odes.* See Bernard Karlgren, *The Book of Odes: Chinese Text, Transcription, and Translation* (Stockholm: Museum of Far Eastern Antiquities, 1950), 228–230.—Ed.

16. Cheng Hao, *Henan Chengshi yishu* [The remnant writings of the Cheng Brothers from Henan], *Er Cheng ji* [Selected writings of the Cheng Brothers], 123.

17. See "Xing li yi" [On Nature and Principle as one], "Xing Ming tiao" [Entry on Nature and fate], *Yu Zhuan Zhuzi quanshu* [Imperial compilation of the complete works of Zhu Xi], juan 42: 31a–32a. Wenyuange Sikuquanshu edition. Some of this passage can also be found in "Zhongyong huowen" [Questions and answers on the doctrine of the mean], *Zhuzi quanshu* [The complete works of Zhu Xi] (Shanghai: Shanghai guji chubanshe and Hefei: Anhui jiaoyu chubanshe, 2002), 6: 551.

18. Precisely because of this, Qian Mu summarized Shao Yong's learning as "the ontology of the new person." As he put it: "It is not said that humans are separated from things, but that humans are connected to things. This is to understand humans from within the category of things, and from within this very category discover people's position, meaning and value." He also believed that it was precisely the importance of the category of things that led "Kangjie [Shao Yong] to insights beyond [traditional notions] of divination, he expended efforts in observing things. In China, when it came to the scholarship of this particular school, there were very few outstanding scholars to emerge from it." See Qian Mu's "Liangxi, Baiyuan, Hengqu zhi lixue" [The Neo-Confucianism of Lianxi, Baiyuan, and Heng Qu], *Zhongguo xueshu sixiang shi luncong wu* [Chinese intellectual history series five] (Taibei: Dongda tushu gongsi, 1978), 60–61.

19. Ibid., 62.

20. Mou Zongsan, *Xinti yu xingti* [The structure of heart-mind and the structure of Nature], (Shanghai: Shanghai guji chubanshe, 1999), 14–15.

21. Regarding the amended version of the *Great Learning's* role within the interrelated fields of the School of Principle, evidentiary studies, and politics, see Huang Jinxing, "Lixue, kaojuxue, yu zhengzhi: yi *Daxue* gaiben de fazhan wei lizheng" [The School of Principle, evidentiary studies, and politics: Taking the developmental trajectory of the amended *Great Learning* as a case study], *Youru shengyu: quanli, xinyang, yu zhengdangxing* [Entering sacred space: power, belief, and legitimacy] (Taipei: Yunchen wenhua shiye gufen youxian gongsi, 1994), 352–391.

22. Zhu Xi, *Sishu zhangju jizhu* [Interlinear analysis of and collected commentaries on the Four Books] (Beijing: Zhonghua shuju, 1983), 3.

23. Ibid., 1.

24. Regarding the relationship between the *Great Learning* and the School of Principle, particularly the way that Zhu Xi in the *Interlinear Analysis of and Collected Commentaries on the Four Books* recuperated and amplified the notion of investigating things and extending knowledge, Chen Lai's *Zhu Xi zhexue yanjiu* [Research on Zhu Xi's philosophy] (Beijing: Zhongguo Shehui Kexue Chubanshe, 1993) presents detailed evidentiary research. I will not elaborate here.

25. See Zhu Xi, *Sishu zhangju jizhu,* juan 1: 54.—Trans.

26. Qian Mu, "Cheng Zhu yu Kong Meng" [The Cheng Brothers, Zhu Xi and Mencius and Confucius], *Zhongguo xueshu sixiang luncong (wu)* [Chinese intellectual history series five], 206.

27. Zhu Xi, *Sishu zhangju jizhu,* 1.

28. Zhu Xi, *Sishu zhangju jizhu,* 6–7.

29. The clause "the comprehensive structure and grand purpose of one's mind-heart will no longer be unclear" comes from Zhu Xi, *Daxue zhangju* [Interlinear commentary on *The Great Learning*], *Zhuzi quanshu* [Complete works of Zhu Xi], ed. Zhu Jieren, Yan Zuozhi, and Liu Yongxiang (Hefei: Anhui jiaoyu chubanshe, 2010), 6: 20. The clause "the benevolence of illustrious virtue" is Wang Hui's own paraphrase of Zhu Xi's words from the tenth chapter of the Interlinear Commentary.—Trans.

30. Zhu Xi, "Da Zhao Minbiao" [Replying to Zhao Minbiao], *Zhuzi wenji* [The writings of Master Zhu], juan 64: 3220–3221.

31. Zhu Xi, "Da Chen Qizhong" [In reply to Chen Qizhong], *Zhuzi wenji,* juan 39: 1649.

32. Qian Mu has stated: "The practice of investigating things expounded on by Zhu Xi is still a practice of the heart-mind, one that takes the principle that is already known by the human heart-mind and extends it to unknown realms" (See *Zhuzi xin xue'an,* 93). Qian Mu's article "Zhuzi xinxue lüe" [Master Zhu's strategy of the study of the heart-mind] contains a detailed discussion of the various topics involved with Zhu Xi's study of the heart-mind as well as its relationship to the study of the heart-mind proposed by the Lu-Wang school. See *Zhongguo xueshu sixiang shi luncong wu,* 131–158.

33. Akatsuka Kiyoshi et al., eds., *Zhongguo sixiang shi* [Chinese intellectual history], trans. Zhang Zhaoze (Taibei: Rulin tushu gongsi, 1981), 247.

34. Cheng Hao, "Henan Chengshi yishu," *Er Cheng ji*, juan 18: 188.

35. Zhu Xi, "Da Chen Qizhong," *Zhuzi wenji*, juan 39: 1649.

36. Zhu Xi, *Zhuzi yulei* [Thematic discourses of Master Zhu] (Beijing: Zhonghua shuju, 1986), 102.

37. However, in the end what the particularistic practice of the investigation of things ultimately concerns itself with is not the individual character of things and affairs, but rather how one can gain an understanding of the whole through the extension of knowledge. In responding to the notion that "the investigation of things is the observation of natural principle," Zhu Xi said: "The investigation of things illuminates this heart" (*Zhuzi yulei*, 2856–2857). This of course indicates that the goal of the investigation of things is not the pursuit of an objective understanding of the experiential world. Yet regardless of whether it is the process of the investigation of things, or the goal of illuminating the heart and seeing Nature, they all conflict with the notion of a domineering, mysterious Heaven.

38. Zhu Xi, *Zhuzi yulei*, 2436. Zhu Xi also said: "Today those who speak of affairs believe that there is first Principle and then there are affairs. Likewise, those who speak of Principle emphasize only Principle, not affairs. But these formulations are all incomplete, and as such engendered the critique of later scholarship. It is better to speak of affairs directly, and in doing so come to illustrate fulsomely the principle within them." "Si shu huo wen. Zhong yong huo wen juanshang" [Question and answers regarding the Four Books: Questions and answers regarding the *Doctrine of the Mean*], *Zhuzi quanshu*, 6: 560.

39. Cheng Hao, "Henan Chengshi yishu," *Er Cheng ji*, 1: 143, 316, 323.

40. Zhu Xi, *Zhuzi yulei*, juan 15: 284; juan 18: 400.

41. Zhu Xi said: "So we say 'to restrain at a precise point.' To restrain at a precise point is similar [to what is expressed in the formulation] 'the ruler restrains himself with humaneness, the minister restrains himself with respect,' this is in complete conformity with Heavenly Principle; in terms of interiority one does not see oneself, in terms of exteriority one does not see the other; one sees only Principle, not human desires." *Zhuzi yulei*, juan 49: 2413.

42. Ji Wenfu, *Wanming sixiang shi lun* [On the history of late-Ming thought] (Beijing: Dongfang chubanshe, 1996), 175.

43. The Four Books comprise the *Doctrine of the Mean*, *The Great Learning*, the *Mencius*, and the *Analects*, and became after the Song dynasty the major texts tested in the civil service examinations of the imperial state bureaucracy, whose successful passing was a necessary step for any male to obtain public office.—Trans.

44. Zhu Xi, *Zhuzi yulei*, juan 6: 104.

45. For more on the intellectual and institutional history of the "Community Compact" as a mode of local popular self-government understood within a Confucian framework, which can be traced back to the Lü family's Lantian Village Covenant es-

tablished in 1076, see Guy S. Alitto and Stella Xing Tan, "Liang Shuming's Theory of Rural Reconstruction and the Lü-Family Village Convenant," *Asia Major* 3d series, 34, no. 1 (2021): 95–110.—Trans.

46. Cheng Yi, "Henan Chengshi yishu," *Er Cheng ji*, 108.

47. Ibid., 204.

48. Ibid., 204.

49. Ibid., 461.

50. Zhu Xi, *Zhuzi Yulei*, juan 62: 1496.

51. Cheng Hao, "Henan Chengshi yishu," *Er Cheng ji*, 1, 10, 29–30.

52. As an example [of such discourse]: "When people typically discuss nature, they only say it is the inheritance of benevolence. Mencius spoke of human nature in terms of benevolence. The inheritance of benevolence is like water that flows downward. All water flows into the sea, and in the end there are no impurities to speak of; how could this be produced by the power of common people? When water flows without moving far it steadily becomes turbid; when it flows farther onward, at points it can become turbid; there are points when it is more turbid, points when it is less so; while there are differences between clarity and turbidity, it never becomes so turbid that it is not water." Cheng Hao, "Henan Chengshi yishu," *Er Cheng ji*, 10–11.

53. Ibid., 121.

54. Ibid., 142.

55. Ibid., 193.

56. Zhu Xi, "*Zhongyong* zhangju" [Interlinear commentary on the *Doctrine of the Mean*], *Si shu zhangju jizhu*, 17.

57. Zhu Xi, "Hui An xiansheng Zhu Wengong wenji" [Collected writings of Mr. Hui An (Master Zhu)], *Zhuzi Quanshu*, 23: 2960.

58. Zhu Xi, "Da Chen Weidao" [Reply to Chen Weidao], *Zhuzi wenji*, 2899.

59. Qian Mu, "Cheng Zhu yu Kong Meng," 207.

60. *Lu Xiangshan quanji* [The complete works of Lu Xiangshan] (Beijing: Zhongguo shudian, 1991), 95–96.

61. Ibid., 152.

62. The Moment of Enlightenment at Longchang refers to an event that occurred in 1508. While serving as a junior official in the Ming dynasty's Ministry of War in 1506, Wang Yangming wrote a petition to the Emperor Zhengde critiquing the powerful eunuch Liu Jin, whose close relationship with the emperor had allowed him to consolidate power at court in an authoritarian manner. Outraged that a minor official would publicly challenge him when so many senior civil and military officials at court had been effectively silenced, Liu Jin released a falsified imperial edict calling for Wang's arrest. Wang was subsequently subject to *tingzhang*, a form of corporal punishment widely used in the Ming court that subjected victims to repeated lashes with a bamboo switch or rod. Having barely survived the beating, Wang was banished to a remote outpost in Longchang, Guizhou, where he meditated and reflected on the meaning of the teachings of Zhu Xi. Wang had previously tried and failed to put the notion

of "investigating things and extending knowledge" into practice, thus leading him to have doubts about the concept. However, one night at Longchang he came upon a realization, summarized by the phrase: "My own internal nature is sufficient for realizing the way of the sage, it is an error to seek Principle in things," emphasizing the internal heart-mind as the central conduit to understanding the myriad things of the universe, rather than Zhu Xi's emphasis on investigating things. After this realization, Wang began teaching his philosophy to disciples and local people in Longchang. For more, see Wei-Ming Tu, *Neo-Confucian Thought in Action: Wang Yang-Ming's Youth* (Berkeley: University of California Press, 1976), 63–72; Ping Dong, *Historical Background of Wang Yang-Ming's Philosophy of Mind: From the Perspective of his Life Story* (Singapore: Springer, 2020), 19–61.—Trans.

63. Wang Yangming, "Da Gu Dongqiao shu" [Reply to Gu Dongqiao], *Chuan xi lu* [Instructions for practical living], *Wang Yangming quanji* [Complete works of Wang Yangming] (Shanghai guji chubanshe, 1992), 1: 45.

64. Ibid., 43.

65. Wang Yangming, "Daxue wen" [Inquiry on *The Great Learning*], *Wang Yangming quanji,* 3: 972.

66. Wang Yangming, "Da Gu Dongqiao shu," *Wang Yangming quanji,* 1: 47.

67. Mou Zongsan, *Cong Lu Xiangshan dao Liu Jishan* [From Lu Xiangshan to Liu Jishan] (Shanghai: Shanghai guji chubanshe, 2001), 163–172.

68. Wang Yangming, "Chuanxi Lu," *Wang Yangming quanji,* 1: 90–91.

69. Wang Yangming's assertion that the notion of "knowledge" (知) or the concept of "knowing Heaven" (知天) was the same as the concept of knowledge entailed in the concepts of "knowing prefectures" (知州) and "knowing counties" (知縣) was an attempt at suggesting that Heavenly Principle was found in the immanent realm of bureaucratic service to the state. For *Zhizhou* (知州) and *Zhixian* (知縣) were the official titles of the administrative heads of prefectures and counties during the Song, Ming, and Qing periods. The terms are generally translated in English as "prefect," though it is important to note that there were prefects of different ranks corresponding to different territorial and military units during the Ming and Qing.—Trans.

70. Dan Zhu is a reference to the son of the legendary sage emperor Yao, who is described in the "Chronicle of Yao" chapter of the "Book of Yu" section of the *Book of Documents* as being intelligent but quarrelsome. See *The Most Venerable Book (Shang Shu),* trans. Martin Palmer with Jay Ramsay and Victoria Finlay (New York: Penguin Books, 2014), 6.—Trans.

71. Wang Yangming, "Da Gu Dongqiao shu," *Chuanxi Lu, Wang Yangming quanji,* 1: 54.

72. Ibid., 1: 45.

73. Ibid., 1: 54–55.

74. Wang Yangming, "Nangan xiangyue" [Nangan Village Compact], *Wang Yangming quanji,* 1: 599–600.

75. This comment is taken from a dialogue between Nie Bao and Wang Ji. See "Zhi zhi yi bian" [A discussion on extending knowledge], *Wang Longxi quanji* [Complete works of Wang Ji] (1822, rpt. Taipei: Huawen shuju, 1970), juan 6: 12b–13a.

76. Ibid.

77. Wang Ji, "Xinan Doushan shuyuan heyu" [Conversations at Doushan Academy at Xinan], *Wang Longxi quanji,* juan 7. For a slightly different rendering see juan 12 of *Mingru xue'an* [Teachings in Ming Confucianism], in *Huang Zongxi quanji* [The complete works of Huang Zongxi] (Hangzhou: Zhejiang daxue chubanshe, 1985), 7: 283.

78. The term "statecraft" comes from Ge Hong (284–364). In the "Examining Promotions" chapter of the *Baopuzi,* it is stated: "Thus by reading the 'The Great Plan' one knows that Jizi had the tools of statecraft, while from looking at the 'Nine Methods' one knows that Fansheng considered strategies for the governance of the country." ["The Great Plan" is a chapter in the *Book of Documents,* while the "Nine Methods" is a chapter in the work *The End of the Kingdom of Yue,* compiled by the Han-dynasty writer Yuang Kang, providing a history of the Yue kingdom in Southeast China during the Eastern Zhou Period.—Trans].

79. The term "Donglin Faction" refers to a complex and interlocking series of intellectual and social phenomena in seventeenth-century China. To borrow the words of historian John W. Darness, "In seventeenth-century China, the name 'Donglin' meant three different but partly overlapping things. It stood for an ethical revitalization movement; it referred to a national Confucian moral fellowship; and it also labeled a Beijing political faction. The name comes from the Donglin ("East Forest") academy of Wuxi county, located about fifty miles west of Shanghai, in what is now Jiangsu province. . . . The Donglin academy, from its refounding in 1604, disseminated through its widely attended lecture sessions, open to officials and students from all over China, an ethically intense and militant Confucianism. . . . Donglin leaders also labored to place their adherents in key offices of the central government and, through them, to achieve nothing less than the remaking of a troubled Ming China starved, they believed, of morally right-guided leadership." See Darness, *Blood and History in China: The Donglin Faction and Its Repression, 1620–1627* (Honolulu: University of Hawai'i Press, 2002), 1.—Trans.

80. Regarding Zhu Xi's teachings on statecraft and practical studies, see Tang Fuqin, *Zhu Xi de shixue sixiang* [The historical thought of Zhu Xi], 35–43.

81. Lu Xiangshan, "Yu Wang Shunbo shu" [Letter to Wang Shunbo], *Xiangshan quanji* [The complete works of Lu Xiangshan], juan 2: 1–2.

82. Wang Ji, "San shan lize lu" [Lustrous records on three mountains], *Wang Longxi quanji,* juan 1: 11b, 12a–13b.

83. Zhou Changlong, "Liangzhi yu jingshi: cong Wang Longxi liangzhi jingshi sixiang xiang kan wan Ming Wang xue de zhenmao" [Conscience and statecraft—Glimpsing the true face of late-Ming learning regarding Wang Yangming's thought

from the perspective of Wang Longxi's teachings regarding conscience and statecraft], *Zhang Yiren xiansheng qishi shouqing lunwen ji* [Essays in honor of the seventieth birthday of Zhang Yiren], 967–969.

84. Wang Gen, "Ming zhe baoshen lun" [On the illuminating wisdom of preserving the self], in juan 32 of *Mingru xue'an,* in *Huang Zongxi quanji,* 7: 833. The characters in juan 3 of the Japanese woodblock print edition of this work and the one cited above have some difference; here the citation comes from *Mingru xue'an.*

85. Wang Gen, "Yulu xia" [Sayings (part II)], *Wang Xinzhai quanji* [The complete works of Wang Gen] (1846 Japanese woodblock, rpt. Taipei: Guangwen shuju, 1975), juan 3: 3a–b. Regarding the Japanese woodcut edition of this work, it is the same situation as above.

86. Huang Zongxi, *Mingru xue'an,* in *Huang Zongxi quanji,* 7: 829–830.

87. Liang Qichao believed that the movement to revise Wang Yangming's teachings had two phases: "During the Wanli and Tianqi reigns, the teaching of Wang Yangming become one with Chanzong Buddhism. Leaders of the Donglin Clique such as Gu Jingyang (Xiancheng) and Gao Jingyi (Panlong) advocated the "investigation of things," in order to rectify the malady [in intellectual discourse] of engaging in empty and abstract talk; this can be considered the first revision of Wang Yangming's teachings. Liu Jishan (Zong Zhou) emerged later, and he advocated being "blameless and circumspect," doing so in order to rectify the malady [in intellectual discourse] of ostentatious and self-indulgent talk; this can be considered the second revision of Wang Yangming's teachings." See *Liang Qichao lun Qing xueshi erzhong* [Liang Qichao's two discourses on Qing intellectual history] (Shanghai: Fudan daxue chubanshe, 1985), 138.

88. Gu Xiancheng wrote: "Cheng Hao said: 'benevolence and things are unified'; if we extend this one phrase to its completion, how can one then also say: 'righteousness, rites, wisdom, sincerity are all humaneness'? In the beginning I suspected [such sayings] were superfluous, and I examined those in the world who claim knowledge about benevolence; they were always ever so crafty and lively in their affairs, [in their attitude toward] the outside world toadying toward the latest vulgar customs, and [in their] inner life filled with selfishness; they had no sense of shame, breaking restraints of all kinds, evasive in their scheming, deceiving themselves and others; never did they consider just what kind of things are righteousness, rites, wisdom, and sincerity, but still regarded themselves as benevolent: later did I know of the depth of meaning associated with Cheng Hao." See Gu Xiancheng, *Xiaoxin zhai zhaji* [Jottings on the minute heart-mind], collated by Feng Congwu and Gao Panlong (Taipei: Guangwen shuju, 1975), juan 1: 4b–5a.

89. Gao Panlong, "Chongwen huiyu xu" [Introduction to Chongwen dialogues], *Gaozi yishu* [Remnant books of Gaozi], ed. Chen Longzheng, 1292: 550–551. Wenyuange Siku Quanshu edition.

90. Gao Panlong, "Da Wang Yihuan er shou" [Two replies to Wang Yihuan], *Gao Zi yishu,* juan 8: 68b.

91. Li Zhi, "Da Geng Zhongzheng" [In reply to Geng Zhongzheng], *Fen Shu; Xu Fen Shu* [A book for burning and a book for burning, continued] (Beijing: Zhonghua shuju, 1975), 17.

92. Luo Zheng'an said: "To study but not to seek confirmation in the classics, to approach everything through the study of one's heart-mind and its application, is a self-inflicted mistake." See *Zheng'an Xiansheng kun zhi ji* [Records of the constrained knowledge of Mr. Zheng'an], juan 2: 13. Congshu jicheng edition.

93. Liu Zongzhou, "Zi Liuzi xueyan" [Master Liu's teachings], *Huang Zongxi quanji,* 1: 304.

94. Liu Zongzhou, "*Zhong yong* shouzhang shuo" [On the first section of the *Doctrine of the Mean*], *Liu Jishan Ji* [Collected writings of Liu Jishan], 1294: 510: Wenyuange Siku Quanshu edition.

95. Liu Zongzhou, "Zi Liuzi xueyan," *Huang Zongxi quanji,* 1: 263.

96. Wang Yangming, *Wang Yangming quanji,* 1: 254.

97. Huang Zongxi, "Jishan Xue'an" [Jishan's teachings], *Mingru Xue'an,* in *Huang Zongxi quanji,* 8: 899.

98. Huang Zongxi, "Zixu" [Introduction], *Mingru Xue'an,* in *Huang Zongxi quanji,* 7: 3.

99. Huang Zongxi, "Yuanjun" [On the prince], *Mingyi daifang lu* [Waiting for the dawn: A plan for the prince], in *Huang Zongxi quanji,* 1: 2.

100. Huang Zongxi, "Yuan Chen" [On ministership], *Mingyi daifang lu,* in *Huang Zongxi quanji,* 1: 4.

101. Huang Zongxi, "Yuanfa" [On law], in *Huang Zongxi quanji,* 1: 6–7 [Translation modified from Huang Tsung-Hsi, *Waiting for the Dawn: A Place for the Prince,* trans. by Wm. Theodore de Bary (New York: Columbia University Press, 1993), 97–99.—Trans.]

102. Huang Zongxi, "Xuexiao" [Schools], *Mingyi daifang lu,* in *Huang Zongxi quanji,* 1: 110.

103. Huang Zongxi, "Tianzhi er" [The field system (two)], *Mingyi daifang lu,* in *Huang Zongxi quanji,* 1: 25.

104. Kang Youwei, "Nanhai shicheng si" [Records of Nanhai's teachings], *Kang Youwei quanji* [Complete works of Kang Youwei] (Shanghai: Shanghai guji chubanshe), 2: 515.

105. Huang Zongxi, "Tianzhi yi" [The field system (one)], *Mingyi daifang lu,* in *Huang Zongxi quanji,* 1: 23.

106. Yan Yuan, along with his disciple Li Gong (1659–1733), inherited the critique of Neo-Confucian metaphysical speculation that was launched by the Southern Song Yongjia school, emphasizing discussion of practical actions, policies, and directives instead of extended elaborations regarding metaphysical concepts such as the nature of Heavenly Principle, heart-mind, and internal nature. Yan Yuan also integrated a positive assessment of the pursuit of individual interest and benefit into his moral and social philosophy, which touched on issues such as techniques of warfare, agriculture, monetary matters, and hydrology.—Trans.

107. This work of Yan Yuan's is one part of a larger overall text known as *Si cun bian* [The four treatises on preservation], which encompasses four books: "Cun xing bian" [On the preservation of character], "Cun xue bian" [On the preservation of teachings], "Cun zhi bian" [On the preservation of governance], and "Cun ren bian" [On the preservation of humaneness]. The third of these works, "On the Preservation of Governance," had an original title of "On the Kingly Way" (*Wang dao lun*).—Trans.

108. The scholarship on Yan Yuan in general presents his teachings as finding their origins in the works of Hu Yuan and Zhang Zai. In the "Understanding Familial Relations" section of Yan's "On the Preservation of Teachings," it is stated: "Regarding Song Confucianism, it was only Huzi [Hu Yuan] who executed the affairs of government in a manner grounded in the classics. Though there exist issues with his analysis [of the classics], the manner in which he conducted his affairs was most true; Zhang Zi [Zhang Zai] instructed people to use rites as the basis for well-field agriculture: though he was never able to implement his designs, his aspirations were lofty indeed." *Yan Yuan ji* [Collected writings of Yan Yuan] (Beijing: Zhonghua shuju, 1987), 43. He also stated: "Regarding Song Confucanism, aside from Huzi, there is only Heng Qu [Zhang Zai], with his regard for the well-field system, as well as his teaching people in the conduct of rites, that can be considered the orthodox inheritor of Confucius and Mencius. See "Xing li ping" [Critique of Nature and Principle], "Cun xue bian" [On the preservation of teachings], *Yan Yuan ji*, 60.

109. The six elements and three affairs come from the *Book of Documents* (the section on the Counsels of Great Yu) and the *Zuo Commentary to the Spring and Autumn Annals*. The former refers to the elements of water, fire, gold, wood, earth, and millet. The latter refers to the principles of Upright Morality, Utility, and Honesty. The notion of three things comes from the *Rites of Zhou*, and its meaning has already been described above. The four teachings include "culture" (*wen*), "action" (*xing*), "faithfulness" (*zhong*), and "sincerity" (*xin*); they come from the *Analects*' "Shu Er" section. Yan Yuan understands the six elements, three affairs, three things, and four teachings as the substance of what the ancients taught, linking the notion of personal praxis to questions of technique and technical ability. He thoroughly repudiated various popular writings.

110. Yan Yuan, "Ji Tongxiang Qian Sheng Xiaocheng shu" [A letter to Qian Xiaocheng of Tongxiang], from juan 3 of *Yan Zhai ji yu* [Records of Yan Zhai], *Yan Yuan ji*, 440–441.

111. Yan Yuan, "Song Wang Yunde jiaoyu Qingyuan xu" [To Wang Yunde on his departure to take up the position of Jiaoyu in Qingyuan], *Yan Yuan ji*, 403.

112. Yan Yuan, "Yu Gaoyang Sun Zhongyuan shu" [Letter to Sun Zhongyuan of Gaoyang], *Yan Yuan ji*, 456.

113. The Southern Yongjia school was a school of Confucian thought dedicated to matters of statecraft, organized in and around the city of Yongjia (today's Wenzhou) in the Zhedong region of Zhejiang (from whence the intellectual group derives its name). The Yongjia school is often discussed in conjunction with another school that

emerged in the Zhedong region at the same time, the Yongkang school (*Yongkang xuepai*). Linked to the thinkers Ye Shi and Chen Liang, Yongjia and Yongkang scholars set themselves up in opposition to both Zhu Xi's Study of Principle and Lu Jiuyuan's Study of Heart-Mind, emphasizing questions of human interests, merits, and benefit, understood in material and transactional terms, over valuing such metaphysical concepts as Principle, the heart-mind, and internal nature. Their contention that moral righteousness (*yi*) and material profit (*li*) went hand in hand was provocative, for Confucians had traditionally critiqued the maximization of individual self-interest as selfish. Ye Shi in particular integrated a positive assessment of mercantilism, banking, and entrepreneurship into his understanding of moral action. Ye Shi and Chen Liang opposed the Neo-Confucian emphasis on the moral cultivation of the heart-mind as self-righteous and disconnected from social policy, emphasizing instead practical action in political governance as the measure of moral accomplishment.—Trans.

114. Yan Yuan, "Si shu zheng wu" [Rectifying mistakes in the Four Books], *Yan Yuan ji*, 159.

4. Classics and History (1)

1. Gu Yanwu, "Yu Yang Xuechen" [To Yang Xuechen], in *Gu Tinglin shiwen ji* [Collected poetry and prose by Gu Yanwu] (Beijing: Zhonghua shuju, 1983), 139.

2. Jiang Fan and Fang Dongshu, *Hanxue shicheng ji (wai erzhong)* [Interpretative comments on the *Records of the Genealogy of Han Learning* (and two other texts)], ed. Qian Zhongshu, Zhu Weizheng, and Xu Hongxing (Beijing: Sanlian, 1998), 158.

3. Zhang Taiyan, "Da Tiezheng" [Reply to Tiezheng], in *Zhang Taiyan quanji* [Complete works of Zhang Taiyan] (Shanghai: Shanghai renmin chubanshe, 1982), 4: 371.

4. In order not to confuse or frustrate readers, I have kept the number of untranslated phrases to a minimum. The exception is the particular phrase *Tianxia*. As I stated earlier, *Tianxia* refers to "all under Heaven." The English translation of Zhao Tingyang's book, *All under Heaven: The Tianxia System for a Possible World Order*, provides a good starting point for discussion in the Anglophone world. Wang Hui and Zhao Tingyang use the term *Tianxia* as a critical intervention based upon their new interpretative strategy in Chinese political philosophy. Wang Hui's contemporary interpretation of *Tianxia* invokes Gu Yanwu, a seventeenth-century thinker, as its foundation. Wang and Zhao are familiar with each other, so I believe they discussed this usage and chose to use the term deliberately. Therefore, I want to leave it untranslated to maintain its original meaning. See Zhao Tingyang, *All under Heaven: The Tianxia System for a Possible World Order*, trans. Joseph E. Harroff (Berkeley: University of California Press, 2021).—Trans.

5. Gu Yanwu, "Zheng shi" [Correct beginning], in *Ri zhi lu jishi (wai qizhong)* [Collected commentaries on *Record of Daily Knowledge* (and seven other texts)], ed. Huang Rucheng (Shanghai: Shanghai guji chubanshe, 1985), 1015.

6. Duan Yucai, "*Dai Dongyuan ji* xu" [Preface to Dai Dongyuan collection], in *Dai Zhen quanji* [Complete works of Dai Zhen], 6: 3458–3459.

7. Gu Yanwu, "Bo xue yu wen" [Scholarly erudition is revealed in cultural scope], in *Ri zhi lu jishi,* 539–540.

8. Gu Yanwu, "Yu Shi Yushan shu" [Letter to Shi Yushan], *Gu Tinglin shiwen ji,* 58.

9. Dai Zhen, "Xu yan" [Overview], in *Dai Zhen quanji,* 1: 94.

10. Gu Yanwu, "Waiguo fengsu," *Ri zhi lu jishi,* 2: 2175.

11. Gu Yanwu, "Da youren lun xue shu" [Letter to a friend on learning], *Gu Tinglin shiwen ji,* 135.

12. Wang Yangming, *Chuan xi lu* [Instructions for practical living], in *Wang Yangming quanji* [Complete works of Wang Yangming] (Shanghai: Shanghai guji chubanshe, 1992), 1: 6–7. [Translation modified from Wing-Tsit Chan, *Instructions for Practical Living and Other Neo-Confucian Writings by Wang Yang-ming* (New York: Columbia University Press, 1963), 16.—Trans.]

13. Gu Yanwu, "Yu ren shu" [Letter to a friend], *Gu Tinglin shiwen ji,* 93.

14. Gu Yanwu, "Yu youren lun xue shu," *Gu Tinglin shiwen ji,* 40.

15. See Gu Yanwu, *Ri zhi lu jishi,* 1: 538.

16. Gu Yanwu, "Xin xue" [Learning of the mind], in *Ri zhi lu jishi,* 2: 1397–1398.

17. Gu Yanwu, "Yu Shi Yushan shu," *Gu Tinglin shiwen ji,* 58.

18. Gu Yanwu, "Fuzi zhi yan xin yu tiandao" [The master's discussion on human nature and the Way], *Ri zhi lu jishi,* 2: 536. [Translation modified from *Record of Daily Knowledge and Collected Poems and Essays,* trans. Ian Johnston (New York: Columbia University Press,) 65.—Trans.]

19. Hou Wailu, ed., *Zhongguo sixiang tongshi* [General history of Chinese thought] (Beijing: Renmin chubanshe, 1956), 5: 206.

20. "There are those who discussed the learning of principles by disregarding classical studies. As a result, heretical theories began to emerge in their doctrines. [Some scholars] don't know that the learning of principles without classical studies is the equivalent to the Chan Buddhism." Quan Zuwang, "Tinglin xiansheng shendaobiao" [Obituary to Mr. Tinglin] in Quan Zuwang, *Jieqi ting wenji xuanzhu* [Selected commentaries on writings from the Jieqi Studio], ed. Huang Yunmei (Jinan: Qilu shushe, 1982), 114.

21. Gu Yanwu, "Yu Youren lun xue shu," *Gu Tinglin shiwen ji,* 41.

22. It was Ling Tingkan (1757–1809) who clearly put forward the proposition that ritual studies should replace the study of principles. As a new orientation in intellectual history, this proposition reflected the basic aspects of how Qing intellectual orientation differed from Song and Ming Neo-Confucianism. Regarding Ling Tingkan and his theory that "ritual studies should replace the study of principles," see Zhang Shou'an, *Yi li dai li: Qing zhongye ruxue sixiang zhi zhuanbian* [Ritual studies should replace the study of principles: The transformation of Confucianism in the Mid-Qing dynasty] (Shijiazhuang: Hebei jiaoyu chubanshe, 2001).

23. Gu Yanwu criticized the declining phase of Wang Yangming learning as follows: "If you don't learn, you can use the rhetoric of one big thing [explaining everything] to camouflage your vulgarity; if you don't behave, you can hide in the [discursive] land of human nature and Heavenly Mandate so that people cannot question your scholarship." "Zhuzi wannian dinglun" [The final conclusions of Zhu Xi in his later years], in *Ri zhi lu jishi,* 2: 1421.

24. Gu Yanwu, "Xia xue zhinan xu" [Preface to the Guide to Lower Learning], *Gu Tinglin shiwen ji,* 131.

25. Jiang Fan and Fang Dongshu, *Hanxue shicheng ji,* 158. [Here the author refers to but does not quote from Wang Yangming's "Master Zhu's Conclusions of His Later Years" (*Zhuzi wannian dinglun*). For a discussion of this text and Wang Yangming's revision of Zhu Xi, see Thomas A. Wilson, "Genealogy and History in Neo-Confucian Sectarian Uses of the Past," *Modern China* 20, no. 1 (1994): 15–26.—Ed.]

26. Zhang Xuecheng, "Zhedong xueshu" [Eastern Zhejiang scholarship], in *Zhang Xuecheng yi shu* [Posthumous collection of works by Zhang Xuecheng] (Beijing: Wenwu chubanshe, 1985), 15.

27. *Kaozheng* research began in the Tang dynasty and developed further in the Song dynasty. Zhang Xuecheng traced it accordingly and included Gu Yanwu and Dai Zhen in the genealogy of Zhu Xi's paradigm. See *Wenshi tongyi* [Comprehensive meaning of literature and history], in *Zhang Xuecheng yi shu,* 15.

28. Liang Qichao said: "On the one hand, Gu Yanwu criticized the purely subjective approach of Wang Yangming's paradigm for not being scholarly enough, and on the other hand pointed out many objective approaches to learned inquiry. So the climate of the academic world drastically changed and many followed the path he led for two to three hundred years. Gu Yanwu was therefore a unique contributor to the intellectual history of the Qing dynasty." Liang Qichao, *Zhongguo jin sanbainian xueshu shi* [Three hundred years of intellectual history in modern China], in *Liang Qichao lun Qing xue shi'erzhong* [Two works by Liang Qichao on Qing-era scholarship] (Shanghai: Fudan daxue chubanshe, 1985), 153, 157.

29. Gu Yanwu, *Ri zhi lu jishi,* 1: 511–512. [For an alternate translation, see *Record of Daily Knowledge,* trans. Johnston, 60–61.—Ed.]

30. "Three *wu*" refers to the "three things of the village" (*xiang san wu*) taught by the Duke of Zhou. They include the "Six Virtues" (*liu de*), the "Six Practices" (*liu xing*), and the "Six Arts" (*liu yi*).—Ed.

31. Chen Xunci and Fang Zuyou, *Wan Sitong nianpu* [Chronological biography of Wan Sitong] (Hong Kong: Zhongwen daxue chubanshe, 1991), 211.

32. Gu Yanwu, *Ri zhi lu jishi,* 1: 511–512.

33. Ibid., 1: 549–550.

34. Gu Yanwu, "Da Li Zide shu" [Responses to Li Zide], *Gu Tinglin shiwen ji,* 73.

35. *Li Ji jijie* [Collected commentaries on the *Book of Rites*], ed. Sun Xidan (Beijing: Zhonghua shuju, 1989), 978.

36. Ibid., 982–983.

37. Sima Qian, *Shi ji* [Records of the Grand Historian] (Beijing: Zhonghua Book Company, 1982), 1935–1937.

38. "Yue ji," *Li Ji jijie,* 2: 985–986. [Translations modified from Scott Cook, "'Yue Ji'—Record of Music: Introduction, Translation, Notes, and Commentary," *Asian Music* 26, no. 2 (Spring–Summer 1995): 24–25.—Trans.]

39. Ibid., 986–987.

40. Ibid., 987.

41. Ibid., 976.

42. Ibid., 977.

43. Gu Yanwu, "Yu ren shu," in *Tinglin wenji,* 98. In his "Da Li Zide shu" [Response to Li Zide], he clearly pointed out that the purpose of phonology is to clarify ancient meanings and verify ancient systems, rather than *kaozheng* research for *kaozheng*'s sake. *Gu Tinglin shiwen ji,* 69–73.

44. Gu Yanwu, "*Yinxue wu shu* xu" [Preface to the *Five Books on Phonology*], see *Yinxue wu shu* [Five books on phonology] (Beijing: Zhonghua shuju, 1982), 2. [Translation reprinted with permission from University of Hawai'i Press from Gu Yanwu, "Preface to Five Treatises on Phonology," trans. Thomas Bartlett, *The Hawaii Reader in Traditional Chinese Culture,* ed. Victor Mair, Nancy Steinhardt, and Paul Goldin (Honolulu: University of Hawai'i Press, 2005), 546.—Trans.]

45. In this section of the chapter, Wang Hui's use of *yin* 音 encompasses covers concepts related to music, performance, language, and dialect, and is translated variously as "sound," "rhyme," "voice," "pronunciation," and "sound and voice."—Ed.

46. Ibid., 2–3. [Translation reprinted with permission from University of Hawai'i Press from "Preface to Five Treatises on Phonology," trans. Thomas Bartlett, *The Hawaii Reader in Traditional Chinese Culture,* 546–547.—Trans.]

47. Gu Yanwu also said: "It started when Emperor Ming of the Tang dynasty revised the *Book of Documents,* and later generations often followed his example. The revision pattern went like this: 'the old version says such and such, and now I change it to such and such.' . . . But nowadays, . . . ancient writings are all revised arbitrarily, and the old versions are no longer given. As a result, the ancient sounds are lost, and the culture [or textual context] is also lost." "Da Li Zide shu," *Gu Tinglin shiwen ji,* 69.

48. Wei Yuan, "*Shi gu wei* xu" [Preface to the *Ancient Subtlety of the Book of Songs*], *Wei Yuan ji* [Collection of works by Wei Yuan] (Beijing: Zhonghua shuju, 1976), 120.

49. Dai Zhen said: "We should use the *Er Ya* dictionary to explain the *Book of Songs* and the *Book of Documents,* and then use the *Book of Songs* and the *Book of Documents* to verify the *Er Ya* dictionary. From there we should extend our verification to all ancient texts before the Qin dynasty. For all ancient texts that have survived to our time, we should examine them one by one and synthesize them. We should use the six principles of character formation and the ancient sound of each word as the basis of our examination, and the etymological origins of the ancient texts could be affirmed, and

we can say with confidence we can master the learning [of the *Er Ya*]." "*Er Ya* wenzi kao xu" [Preface to the investigation of *Er Ya* dictionary], *Dai Zhen quanji* [Complete works of Dai Zhen] (Beijing: Qinghua daxue chubanshe, 1997) 5: 2181.

50. See D. C. Lau, *Analects,* 135; the quotations from the *Zuo Commentary* are from Years 25 and 31 of Lord Xiang, translations borrowed from *Zuo Tradition: Commentary on the Spring and Autumn Annals,* trans. Stephen Durrant, Wai-yee Li, and David Schaberg (Seattle: University of Washington Press, 2016), 1153, 1281.—Ed.

51. Kang Youwei, "Jiaoxue tongyi: yanyu" [General discussion on education: Language], *Kang Youwei quanji* [Complete works of Kang Youwei] (Shanghai: Shanghai guji chubanshe, 1987), 1: 155.

52. Wang Hui suggests that, in the above example, these classical passages provide some prototype that he calls a "fixed substance" that has more or less maintained its basic shape throughout history.—Trans.

53. *Kang Youwei quanji,* 1: 157.

54. Gu Yanwu, "*Yinxue wu shu xu,*" 2. [Translation reprinted with permission from University of Hawai'i Press, Gu Yanwu, "Preface to Five Treatises on Phonology," trans. Thomas Bartlett, *The Hawaii Reader in Traditional Chinese Culture,* ed. Victor Mair, Nancy Steinhardt, and Paul Goldin (Honolulu: University of Hawai'i Press, 2005), 546.—Trans.]

55. Here the text references the "Correct Naming" (*zheng ming*) chapter of the *Xunzi*. Translation modified from *Xunzi: The Complete Text,* trans. Eric L. Hutton (Princeton, NJ: Princeton University Press, 2014), 236.—Ed.

56. Kang Youwei, "Jiaoxue tongyi: yanyu," *Kang Youwei quanji,* 1:156.

57. Pan Lei, "*Ri zhi lu* xu" [Preface to *Record of Daily Knowledge*], *Ri zhi lu jishi,* 1: 23.

58. Huang Rucheng, "*Ri zhi lu* xu lu" [Introduction to *Record of Daily Knowledge*]," *Ri zhi lu jishi,* 1: 7–8.

59. Hou Wailu, *Zhongguo sixiang tongshi,* 5: 243, 245.

60. Gu Yanwu explained that he was committed to the exploration of the "the intentions of the ancient sages' Six Classics, the origins of order and disorder under the state, and the fundamental plan for the people's livelihood." Gu's purpose is the same as Huang Zongxi's "recovering the problems of a hundred kings" and "slowly returning to the prosperity of the Three Dynasties." Quoted in Huang Zongxi, "Si jiu lu" [Remembrances], *Huang Zongxi quanji* [Complete works of Huang Zongxi] (Hangzhou: Zhejiang daxue chubanshe, 1985), 1: 390–391.

61. The well-field system of land ownership in ancient Chinese society divided one large square into nine small ones (like the Chinese character 井). The eight outer squares were allocated to serfs who had to cultivate the central one for the landowner.—Trans.

62. Gu Yanwu, "Junxian lun" [On the system of centralized administration], *Gu Tinglin shiwen ji,* 17.

63. Gu Yanwu, "Baoju" [Recommendation of candidates], *Ri zhi lu jishi,* 1: 692

64. Gu Yanwu, "Shengyuan lun" [On examination candidates] *Gu Tinglin shiwen ji*, 22.

65. Gu Yanwu, "Wenren qiu gu zhi bing" [The literati's faulty search for answers from antiquity], *Ri zhi lu jishi*, 1469–1470.

66. For the establishment of official positions in the Qing dynasty, see Charles Hucker, *A Dictionary of Official Titles in Imperial China* (Stanford, CA: Stanford University Press, 1985).

67. Gu Yanwu, "Shengyuan lun," *Gu Tinglin shiwen ji*, 24.

68. Gu Yanwu, "Liang Han fengsu" [The customs of the Former and Later Han dynasties], *Ri zhi lu jishi*, 1009.

69. Gu Yanwu, "Yu ren shu," *Gu Tinglin shiwen ji*, 91.

70. Gu Yanwu, "Junzhi lun" [On military system], *Gu Tinglin shiwen ji*, 122.

71. Gu Yanwu, "Waiguo fengsu" [Foreign customs], *Ri zhi lu jishi*, 2175.

72. Gu Yanwu, "Junxian lun," *Gu Tinglin shiwen ji*, 12.

73. Ibid.

74. Gu Yanwu, "Zi Zhang wen shi shi" [Zi Zhang asks about the tenth generation], *Ri zhi lu jishi*, 528.

75. Gu Yanwu, "Junxian lun," *Gu Tinglin shiwen ji*, 14.

76. Gu Yanwu, "Shouling" [On commandery administrators and magistrates], *Ri zhi lu jishi*, 718.

77. In Hou Wailu's words, "The system of county magistrates he advocates is related to the patriarchal organization he supports. This is quite similar to Quesnay's 'economic table' (the economic theory of the Physiocrat school), which brought the circulation of capital into play in the framework of the feudal rural village, although its true meaning was related to the requirements of urban citizens. Gu Yanwu put the ideal of local autonomy into the frame of the outdated patriarchal organization." Hou Wailu, *Zhongguo sixiang tongshi*, 5: 243.

78. Dai Zhen, "Ti Hui Dingyu xiansheng shou jing tu" [Colophon for an illustration of Hui Dingyu teaching the classics], *Dai Zhen quanji*, 5: 2614–2615. It is generally believed that this piece was written in the second period of Dai Zhen's intellectual development, after his first meeting with Hui Dong during a visit to Yangzhou in 1757, and was one of his clearest expressions of the aims of textual research scholarship.

79. Liang Qichao, *Zhongguo jin sanbai nian xueshu shi*, in *Liang Qichao lun Qing xue shi er zhong*, 162.

80. For further discussion, see Minghui Hu, *China's Transition to Modernity: The New Classical Vision of Dai Zhen* (Seattle: University of Washington Press, 2015), 10–12.—Trans.

81. Quoted from Qian Daxin, "Wan Xiansheng Sitong zhuan" [Biography of Wan Sitong], *Qian yan tang wenji* [Collection from the studio of submersion and deliberation] (Shanghai: Shanghai guji chubanshe, 1989), 682.

82. Zhang Xuecheng, "Wenshi tongyi: Zhedong xueshu" [Comprehensive meaning of literature and history: Eastern Zhejiang scholarship], *Zheng Xuesheng yi shu*, 15.

83. This statement, which approves of the Qin dynasty's burning of the books of the Hundred Schools, is attributed to the statesman Li Si (280–208 BCE) in Sima Qian's *Records of the Grand Historian*. For an English version, see Sima Qian, *The Grand Scribe's Records: The Basic Annals of Pre-Han China*, ed. William H. Nienhauser (Bloomington: Indiana University Press, 1994), 147.—Ed.

84. Zhang Taiyan, "Yu ren lun puxue baoshu," *Zhang Taiyan quanji*, 4: 153–154.

85. *Shi'er chao Donghua lu* (Taipei: Wenhai chubanshe, 1963), section on Kangxi Emperor, juan 4: 9.

86. This comment is recorded in *Huangchao wenxian tongkao* [Comprehensive history based on imperial literary and documentary sources], juan 217. Wenyuange sikuquanshu edition.—Ed.

87. Lu Baoqian, *Qing dai sixiang shi* [Intellectual history of the Qing] (Taipei: Guangwen shuju, 1983), 119–158.

88. Huang Zongxi, "Yu Xu Qianxue shu" [Letter to Xu Qianxue], *Huang Zongxi Nanlei za zhu gao zhenji* [Miscellaneous manuscripts of Huang Zongxi from Nanlei] (Hangzhou: Zhejiang guji chubanshe, 1987), 278. For related discussion, see Huang Jinxing, *Youru shengyu: quanli, xinyang, yu zhengdangxing* [Entering the realm of sanctity: Power, belief, and political legitimacy] (Taipei: Yunchen wenhua, 1994), 91–96.

89. Dai Zhen, "Jiang Shenxiu xiansheng shilue Zhuang" [A brief sketch of the life and accomplishments of Mr. Jiang Shenxiu], *Dai Zhen quanji*, 5: 2608.

90. Kangxi, *Yuzhi wenji* [Collection of imperial writings], vol. 1 (Taipei: Shijie shuju, 1986), juan 19: 3b.

91. Li Guangdi, "Jin dushu bilu ji lun shuo xu ji zawen xu" [Preface to the Essays and Notes on Prefaces and Argumentation," *Rongcun quanshu* [Collected works of Li Guangdi], (n.p., n.d., 1829), juan 10: 3a–3b.

92. Kangxi himself said, "The Way of Governing has prospered since the ancient times of Tang Yao and Yu Shun, and its ability to serve as a Way of governing is grounded in accomplishments of learning." He also said, "I was brought forth by Heaven as a sage and am worthy to rule and to teach. The transmitted coherence of the Way over ten thousand generations is precisely what has held together the coherence of governing for ten thousand generations. After (the Sage Emperors) Yao and Shun and (the Sage-Kings) Tang, Wen, and Wu, there were Confucius, Zengzi, Zisi, and Mencius. . . . It was on account of these four masters that the Way of the Two Emperors and the Three Kings was transmitted, and on account of their accomplishments that the Way of the Five Classics was completed." Kangxi, *Yuzhi wenji*, vol. 1, juan 19: 3b–4a, 1a–2b.

93. Wang Zhonghan, "Li Guangdi shengping yanjiu zhongde wenti" [Some issues in the historical research on Li Guangdi's life], *Yanjing xuebao*, no. 1 (1995): 111–126.

94. See Ruan Yuan, "Xing ming guxun" [Ancient glossing of "human nature" and "mandate"], "Fu xing bian" [Discussion on recovering human nature], and "Ta xing bian" [Explanation of towering nature], in *Yan jing shi ji* [Collection of the studio of studying classics] (Beijing: Zhonghua shuju, 1993), 211–236, 1061, 1059–1060.

95. Ruan Yuan, "Shu Dongyuan Chen shi 'Xuebu tongbian' hou" [Postscript to *The General Discussion of Scholarly Divisions* by Mr. Chen of Dongguan]," *Yan jing shi ji,* 1062.

96. Translation borrowed from Stephen Durrant, Wai-yee Li, and David Schaberg, *Zuo Tradition* (Seattle: University of Washington Press, 2016), 712–713. The full quotation attributed to Confucius reads: "It is precisely ritual objects [*qi*] and names that cannot be granted to others, for these are things by which a ruler governs. The right names are for bringing forth trust; trust is for guarding ritual objects; ritual objects are for embodying ritual propriety; ritual propriety is for carrying out justice; justice is for bringing benefit; benefit is for governing the people" (713).—Trans.

97. Ruan Yuan, "Shang Zhou qingtong shuo" [Shang and Zhou bronze ware], *Yan jing shi ji,* 632–633.

98. Kangxi: "With the rise of the Song Confucians came the name of Neo-Confucianism (*lixue*), and once Zhu Xi was able to expand and fulfill it, Principle was illuminated and the Way was complete. Although future generations may bring forth forth mixed arguments, they can never break the correct principles of a thousand ages." ["Expand and fulfill" here is a Mencian rhetorical trope.—Trans.] Kangxi, *Yuzhi wenji,* vol. 4, juan 21: 1b–2a.

99. Yuzo Mizoguchi, *Zhongguo qian jindai sixiang de yanbian* [Evolution of Chinese thought before early modern times] (Beijing: Zhonghua shuju, 1997), 248.

100. In the *lijia* ("communities and tithings") system, 110 households form one *li,* and one *li* is divided into ten *jia.* There is a *li* head for each *li,* and a *jia* head for each *jia.* People within the *li* and *jia* serve as each other's guarantors, to prevent concealed domiciles and random migrations. In the *Guanjin* system, inspection divisions are set up at various gates to check pedestrians.

101. *Zhongguo shi gangyao* [An outline of Chinese history], ed. Jian Bozan (Beijing: Renmin chubanshe, 1979). According to this work, the amount of cropland is somewhat exaggerated due to the use of "small bow" units by local officials, but, after all, a large amount of land was cleared out methodically. See 186, 196.

102. According to the "Record of Food and Goods" (*Shi huo zhi)* chapter of the official *History of the Ming Dynasty:* "The single-whip tax is a method of taxation that collects taxes by measuring size of landholdings and assigns corvée labor based on the number of male laborers. After the officials finish calculating, they will collect taxes and allocate corvée labor for each year. If corvée labor is insufficient, then the officials could compute the difference and decide the number of goods equivalent to the cost of food for corvée labor. If the tax is insufficient, the official could compute the difference and decide the total fees to make up the difference. All other quotas, assignments, annual demand, retention, and supply costs of the court are converted into a single currency—silver. All silver payments will then be computed and converted by the same official standard. We call this method of taxation the single-whip system." And also, "From the [Ming] Jiajing and Longqing reigns onward, a whip method was implemented which counts one province's grain and assigns one province's corvée so that

officials could combine the corvée labor and monetary taxes into one. It is easy to collect [taxes] without disturbing people." *Ming shi* [History of the Ming dynasty] (Beijing: Zhonghua shuju, 1974), 186, 196.

103. See "Xingbu dang chao" [Documents of the criminal department], in *Zhongguo jindai nongye shi ziliao* [Materials on the history of modern Chinese agriculture], ed. Li Wenzhi (Beijing: Sanlian shuju, 1957), 113.

104. *Qing Shengzu shilu* [Veritable records of the Kangxi reign], juan 249, the second month of the fifty-first year of the Kangxi reign. See Jian Bozan, ed., *Zhongguo shi gangyao,* 3: 264–265.

105. Li Wenzhi, *Ming-Qing shidai fengjian tudi guanxide songxie* [The weakening of feudal land relations in the Ming and Qing dynasties] (Beijing: Zhongguo shehui kexue chubanshe, 1993) 513–540.

106. Ibid., 542. The changes in the land system in the Qing dynasty not only were manifested in the formation of the landlord system, but also included the emergence of peasant ownership. Therefore, the contradiction in economic relations was shifting from the tension between the gentry and landlord class and the imperial power to the contradiction between landlord ownership and the peasant class. On this point, please see Shi Zhihong, *Qingdai qianqide xiaonong jingji* [The small peasant economy in the early Qing dynasty] (Beijing: Zhongguo shehui kexue chubanshe, 1994).

107. During the Shunzhi and Kangxi reigns, not only were Han people employed, but a dual system (of Han and Manchu bureaucracy) gradually formed. During the Shunzhi period, Fan Wencheng, Jin Zhijun, and Hong Chengchou all joined the Grand Secretariat. After the nineteenth year of Kangxi, the Three Palace Academies were combined into a Grand Secretariat. Both the Manchu and Han ministers were allowed to join the Grand Secretariat as Grand Secretaries. See Xie Guozhen, *Ming-Qing zhiji dangshe yundong kao* [An investigation on factional alliances in the Ming and Qing dynasties] (Beijing: Zhonghua shuju, 1982), 98.

108. Ibid., 96–118.

109. The idea of the division of power is not necessarily antimonarchy. For example, on the one hand Guo Xiang's view contains a concept of "cogovernance." On the other hand, centralization and imperial autocracy are also two related but different political concepts. The former refers to the relationship between the central and local governments. The latter refers to the relationship between the emperor and his officials, but these two aspects are often entangled. Ye Shi of the Southern Song dynasty said: "The worries of a hundred years and the troubles of a dynasty are all borne by the emperor alone, and the officials are not sharing the responsibility. When from a distance of ten thousand *li,* all are submitting draft regulations, then the ruler above is truly benefitted; but when the worries of a hundred years and the troubles of one dynasty are borne by him alone, the harm is immeasurable!" Ye Shi, *Ye Shi ji* [Collection of works by Ye Shi] (Beijing: Zhonghua Shuju, 1983), 768. Regarding centralization and the imperial autocracy, see *Tang-Song-Yuan-Ming-Qing Zhongyang yu difang guanxi yanjiu* [Researches on the relationship between the central and local

governments in the Tang, Song, Yuan, Ming, and Qing dynasties], ed. Li Zhi'an (Tianjin: Nankai University Press, 1996), 442.

110. Anthony Giddens, *Minzu-guojia yu baoli* [The nation-state and violence], trans. Hu Zongze et al. (Beijing: Sanlian, 1998), 47. [The English is from Giddens, *The Nation-State and Violence* (Berkeley: University of California Press, 1985), 38.—Ed.]

111. S. N. Eisenstadt, preface to *Diguode zhengzhi tizhi* [The political systems of empires], trans. Shen Yuan and Zhang Lüping (Nanchang: Jiangxi renmin chubanshe, 1992), 9–11.

112. *Tang-Song-Yuan-Ming-Qing Zhongyang yu difang guanxi yanjiu,* ed. Li Zhi'an, 368–369.

113. *Qing shilu* [Veritable records of the Qing], juan 240, eleventh month of the forty-eighth year of the Kangxi reign. Quoted in *Tag-Song-Yuan-Ming-Qing Zhongyang yu difang guanxi yanjiu,* ed. Li Zhi'an, 383. Local government financial expenditure income was all subject to the command and order of the Ministry of Revenue. The local government expenditures below the provincial level must be reported to and ordered by the Ministry of Revenue. They cannot have any independent action or arbitrary arrangements. See Li Sanmou, *Ming-Qing caijing shi xintan* [A new exploration into the history of finance and economics in the Ming and Qing Dynasties] (Taiyuan: Shanxi jingji chubnshe, 1990), 280, 296. See also *Tang-Song-Yuan-Ming-Qing Zhongyang yu difang guanxi yanjiu,* ed. Li Zhi'an, 376–383.

114. *Tang-Song-Yuan-Ming-Qing Zhongyang yu difang guanxi yanjiu,* ed. Li Zhi'an, 406.

115. Ibid., 428.

116. On the issue of the Southwest chieftain system, see John E. Herman, "Empire in the Southwest: Early Qing Reforms to the Native Chieftain System," *Journal of Asian Studies* 56 (1997): 47–74.

117. Chen Wenshi, "Qing Taizong shidaide zhongyao zhengzhi cuoshi" [Important political measures in the era of Emperor Taizong in the Qing dynasty], *Lishi yuyan yanjiusuo jikan* 40 (1968): 299–300.

118. Li Zongtong, "Qingdai Zhongyang zhengquan xingtaide yanbian [The evolution of the central political power in the Qing dynasty], *Lishi yuyan yanjiusuo jikan* 37 (1967): 101.

119. Regarding the establishment of the Mongolian banner system and its internal rules, see Yuan Senpo, *Kang-Yong-Qian jingying yu kaifa beijiang* [Management and development of northern frontiers in the Kangxi, Yongzhen, and Qianlong reigns] (Beijing: Zhongguo shehui kexue chubanshe, 1991), 260–286.

120. Li Zongdong, "Banli junchu beikao" [A brief study on the Grand Council], in *You shi xuebao* 1, no. 2 (April 1959). Regarding the functions of the Grand Council, there are also different opinions. For example, Zhuang Jifa said, "The reason why the Yongzhen Emperor set up the Grand Council was to use the army to manage the military supplies secretly, not to implement centralization and reduce the powers of the ministers. In terms of the establishment of the Grand Council, the background and

development of dictatorship should not be overemphasized." Zhuang Jifa, "Qing shizong yu banli junjichude sheli" [The Qing dynasty and the establishment of the Grand Council], in *Shihuo yuekan* 6, no. 12 (March 1977): 23.

121. Yan Ziyou, "Qingchao zongshi fengjue zhijdu chutan" [A preliminary study of the Qing dynasty's royal clan system], *Hebei xuekan* 1991, no. 5: 67–74; Lai Huimin, "Qingdai huangzude fengjue yu renguan yanjiu" [Researches on the royal family's nomination and appointment in the Qing dynasty], in *Di er jie Ming-Qing zhi ji Zhongguo wenhuade zhuanbian yu yanxu xueshu yantaohui lunwenji* [Second symposium on the transformation and continuation of Chinese culture during the Ming and Qing dynasties] (Taipei: Wenshizhe chubanshe, 1993), 427–460.

122. Zhao Yuntian, *Qingdai Menggu zhengjiao zhidu* [The Mongolian political and religious system in the Qing dynasty] (Beijing: Zhonghua shuju, 1989), 74; *Tang-Song-Yuan-Ming-Qing Zhongyang yu difang guanxi yanjiu,* ed. Li Zhi'an, 421–422.

123. Tao Daonan, *Bianjiang zhengzhi zhidu shi* [History of the frontier political system] (Taipei: Zhonghua congshu bianshen weiyuanhui, 1966), 7–40.

124. For the Qing dynasty's administrative system in Mongolia and its formation, see Nicola Di Cosmo, "Qing Colonial Administration in Inner Asia," *The International History Review* 20, no. 2 (June 1998): 287–309.

125. See entry for forty-eighth year of the Kangxi reign, *Qing shilu* (Beijing: Zhonghua shuju, 1985), 6: 362; Yuan Senpo, *Kang-Yong-Qian jingying yu kaifa beijiang,* 131.

126. Yuan Senpo, *Kang-Yong-Qian jingying yu kaifa beijiang,* 207–208.

127. See Di Cosmo, "Qing Colonial Administration in Inner Asia," 298; Joanna Waley-Cohen, *Exile in Mid-Qing China: Banishment to Xinjiang, 1758–1820* (New Haven, CT: Yale University Press, 1991), 24–32; Dorothy V. Borei, "Economic Implications of Empire-Building: The Case of Xinjiang," *Central and Inner Asian Studies* 5 (1991): 22–37.

128. *Tusi,* often translated as "headmen" or "chieftains," were hereditary tribal leaders recognized as imperial officials by the Yuan, Ming, and Qing dynasties of China.—Trans.

129. She Yize, *Zhongguo tusi zhidu* [China's chieftain system] (n.p.: Zhongguo bianjiang xuehui, 1947).

130. Laura Hostetler studied the ethnography and cartography of Guizhou Miao areas in the eighteenth century. She consulted local archives in Guizhou and argued that the description of the Miao areas in these documents showed the Qing's administrative control over the non-Han ethnic minority had expanded, and she called it "Qing colonialism." (See Laura Hostetler, "Qing Connections to the Early Modern World: Ethnography and Cartography in Eighteenth-Century China," *Modern Asian Studies* 34, no. 3 (2000): 623–662.) The Qing dynasty strengthened its control in the southwestern region after the Rebellion of the Three Feudatories. The most obvious example of the administrative control over the Southwest is the establishment of regular administrative regimes in non-Han areas (*gaitu guiliu*). With the establishment of this new administrative regime and the increase of immigration, the institutional

difference between the Southwest and the Mainland was been significantly reduced. However, it is necessary to mention two points here: following similar research on the Northwest of the Qing dynasty, the author applied the concept of "colonialism" to the Southwest, but ignored two basic facts: First, From the vantage point of the Manchu conquest of China, we can not discuss the Southwest of the Chinese subcontinent as independent from other issues in the interior (*neidi*). Second, Southwest China belonged to the territory of the Ming dynasty, and the Qing inherited the Ming territory but had noticeable differences between its policies in the Southwest and the Northwest. Moreover, in the Southwest region, the Qing dynasty exercised greater control over the Miao people than over other ethnic groups, whereas both the Sichuan-Tibet area and the area inhabited by Yi peoples in the Daliang Mountains maintained aspects of self-governance, and local customs were respected and preserved.

131. Gu Yanwu, *Ri zhi lu jishi,* 2: 2175–2201. ["Gantuoli" refers to Kantoli or Kuntala, a fifth-century CE state in present-day Indonesia that had extensive tributary and trade relations with the Liu Song state in China.—Trans.]

132. Zhang Taiyan, "Jianlun," in *Zhang Taiyan quanji,* 3: 481.

133. Zhang Xuecheng, "Shang Xingmei gongzhan shu" [Letter to Qian Daxin], *Zhang Xuecheng yi shu,* 332.

5. Classics and History (2)

1. In this chapter, *lixue,* previously translated as School of Principle, Learning of Principle, and, more broadly, as Neo-Confucianism, often remains untranslated, in part because of the scrutiny Dai placed on the idea of *li* (principle) itself.—Ed.

2. "Dai Zhen's philosophy, from a historical perspective, can be said to be a fundamental revolution in the Song-Ming learning of Principle, and it can also be said that it was the construction of a new learning of Principle—a philosophical renaissance." Hu Shi, *Dai Dongyuan de zhexue* [The philosophy of Dai Zhen] (Shanghai: Shangwu yinshuguan, 1927), 80–82.

3. For example, Weng Fanggang (1733–1818) said: "In recent days Dai Zhen of Xiuning has devoted lifelong effort, with erudition and diligence, to the study of names and their referents and of mathematical astronomy, which are aspects of textual scholarship. But, not content to be just a textual scholar, he wants to discuss the nature and the Way, to try to be different from Cheng and Zhu." And Yao Nai (1732–1815) wrote: "Dai Dongyuan's evidential studies are of course excellent, but his wish to explain moral principles (*yili*) in order to unseat [the masters of] Luo and Min can be described as ignorantly conceited and self-deluded." See Weng Fanggang in his *Fuchuzhai wenji* [Collected writings from the Studio of Restoring the Original Condition], in *Qingdai shiwenji huibian* [Qing-dynasty literary collections reprint series] (Shanghai: Shanghai guji chubanshe, 2010), 382: 80; Yao Nai, *Xibaoxuan chidu* [Cherishing lofty models] (Hefei: Anhui daxue chubanshe, 2014), 104.

4. Shao Jun, ed., *Zhuzi xuedi* [Concise compendium of the learning of Master Zhu], 15. Congshu jicheng edition.

5. In the discourse of the School of Principle (*lixue*), the word *xing*, translated in this chapter as "the nature," is a technical term, whose meaning is quite different from *ziran*, a term often translated simply as "nature," but usually rendered in this chapter as "spontaneity." *Xing* is a core term in the Chinese philosophical lexicon, attested from earliest times. It has been rendered by many English-language translators as "human nature," as in "human nature is good" (*xing shan*) or "human nature is evil" (*xing e*) in the famous fourth-century BCE debate between Mencius and Xunzi. But in the context of intellectual debates in the Song, Ming, and Qing periods as well as in earlier times its meaning is both broader than this, since it also extends to the natures of animals and things in the nonhuman realm, and also more specific, because of its systematic connection with other terms such as *ming* ("fate," "life," "destiny," "decree") and *li* ("principle" or "pattern"), where it is often taken as the ontological source of specifically moral proclivities in human nature.—Trans.

6. Zhang Xuecheng, *Zhu Lu* [Zhu Xi and Lu Xiangshan], *Wenshi tongyi* [Comprehensive meaning of literature and history], in *Zhang Xuecheng yishu* [Posthumous works of Zhang Xuecheng] (Beijing: Wenwu chubanshe, 1985), 15–16. Zhang Shunhui plays up Zhang Xuecheng's view, holding that there is nothing in all of Qing learning that does not rely on Song precedents. For all of philology, classical learning, and historical criticism, there is nothing that does not originate in the Northern and Southern Song. See his *Shixue sanshu pingyi* [Critical appraisal of three works of history] (Beijing: Zhonghua, 1983), 190–191.

7. Zhang Xuecheng, "Zhedong xueshu" [Eastern Zhejiang scholarship], *Wenshi tongyi*, in *Zhang Xuecheng yishu*, 14–15.

8. For example, sections on matters like the civil service system, military affairs, judicial administration, enfeoffment, the well-field system, and schools in Lu Shiyi's *Sibianlu jiyao* [Summary record of analytical thought] (*Congshu jicheng* edition), and Lü Liuliang's *Tiangailou sishu yulu* [Conversations on the *Four Books* from the Heavenly Canopy Tower] (compiled by Zhou Zaiyan and published in 1683), and *Ershi kecheng moguanlue* [Twenty brief regulations and guidelines] (occasional critiques from Tiangailou, also published in the Kangxi reign). See Lu Baoqian, *Qingdai sixiangshi* [A history of Qing thought], chapter 3, "Kangxi shidai zhi Zhuxue" [Zhu Xi learning in the Kangxi era] (Taibei: Guangwen, 1983), 147–158.

9. Zhang Lie's *Wangxue zhiyi* [Raising doubts about Wang learning] (published by the Fuzhou Zhengyi Book Bureau in 1865) is an example of official Zhu Xi learning. It launches its attack around the three themes of "the identity of Mind and Principle," "extending knowledge through the investigation of things," and "the unity of knowledge and action." It calls for extending knowledge and exhausting Principle and for a return to the Six Classics, and although from a theoretical perspective it is extremely crude, one can see from it the general orientation of Zhu Xi learning in the Qing Dynasty.

10. *Siku quanshu zongmu* [Catalog of the complete imperial library], juan 12, *jingbu* [classics], *shulei* [categorized writings] (Beijing: Zhonghua, 1965), 2.1: 101.

11. Ibid., 114.

12. On questions related to Qing-dynasty debates on the authenticity of the *Shang Shu,* one may consult Liu Qiding, *Shangshu xueshi* [History of *Shangshu* studies] (Beijing: Zhonghua, 1989), 334–421.

13. A reference to the overthrow of the last king of Shang, remembered as "Tyrant Zhou," by King Wu, the founder of the new Zhou dynasty. Mengzi, when asked about this by King Xuan of Qi (*Mengzi* 2A8), explains that because Tyrant Zhou had outraged the benevolence and righteousness proper to his nature, he had become a robber and a ruffian, and a "mere fellow" who no longer merited the title of sovereign. This story becomes the locus classicus for discussions of regicide and legitimate succession in later Chinese history.—Trans.

14. Lu Baoqian, *Qingdai sixiangshi,* 182–183.

15. These legendary auspicious charts, with symbols resembling the eight trigrams of the *Yijing,* were thought to have appeared in ancient times on the backs of mythical animals emerging from the waters of the Yellow or Luo River, and became the basis for cosmological speculations of various kinds in the Han and Tang. These speculations caught the interest of Shao Yong and Zhu Xi in the Song, whose reflections on them, not uncontroversial at the time, became incorporated into the Neo-Confucian canonical literature.—Trans.

16. Zhang Xuecheng, "Yu Shi Yucun" [Letter to Shi Yucun], *Zhang Xuecheng yishu,* 644.

17. Dai Zhen, "Yu Fang Xiyuan shu" [Letter to Fang Xiyuan], in *Dai Zhen quanji* [Complete collected writings of Dai Zhen], ed. Dai Zhen Yanjiuhui et al. (Beijing: Qinghua daxue chubanshe, 1991), 5: 2590.

18. Dai Zhen, "Yu Shi Zhongming shu" [Letter to Shi Zhongming], Dai *Zhen quanji,* 5: 2587–2588.

19. Qian Daxin, *Dai xiansheng Zhen zhuan* [Biography of Master Dai Zhen], *Dai Zhen quanji,* 6: 2429.

20. Gu Yanwu, "*Yili Zheng zhu judu* xu" [Preface to the *Punctuated Classic of Ceremonies and Rites,* with Zheng Xuan's annotations], in *Qingdai shiwenji huibian,* 43: 23.

21. *Zhongyong* [Doctrine of the Mean], 30.

22. Duan Yucai, "*Dai Dongyuan ji* xu" [Preface to Dai Dongyuan's collected writings], *Dai Zhen quanji,* 6: 3458–3459.

23. In his "Letter to Fang Xiyuan" (1755) Dai Zhen said: "From antiquity to the present there have in general been three pathways in the pursuit of learning. One may take moral philosophy (*yili*) as one's task, or philology (*zhishu*), or literary expression (*wenzhang*)—and to work at literary expression is generally ranked as least essential. . . . Loving the Way and exerting your strength in ancient prose, you must seek its root (*qiu qi ben*); but in seeking its root there is also what may be called the Great Root (*daben*). Only when the Great Root is reached can one then say: 'This is the Way,

and not art.'" This suggests that the study of moral principle ranks first. *Dai Zhen quanji*, 5: 2589–2590.

24. Fang Dongshu censured Qianlong-Jiaqing-era Han learning for an overly refined division of labor, which was unconnected with "the life of body and mind, with national policy and the people's livelihood, or with the great aims of scholarship." Fang Dongshu, *Hanxue shangdui* [Deliberations on Han learning], juan 2; see Qian Zhongshu, editor, and Zhu Weizheng, executive editor, *Hanxue shichengji (wai er zhong)* [Record of the transmission of Han learning (and two supplemental texts)] (Beijing, Sanlian, 1998), 405.

25. Qian Mu, *Zhongguo jin sanbainian xueshushi* [A history of the last three hundred years of scholarship in China] (Beijing: Zhonghua, 1986), 1: 320.

26. See Hong Bang, *Dai xiansheng xingzhuang* [Chronological biography of Master Dai], *Dai Zhen quanji*, 6: 3383.

27. Qian Mu, *Zhongguo jin sanbainian xueshushi*, 324, 321.

28. Hui Dong, *Yi Han xue* [Han studies of the *Classic of Change*], Congshu jicheng chubian [first series] edition (Shanghai: Shangwu yinshuguan, 1937), 1. The Wenyuange siku quanshu edition of this preface differs slightly, saying that "only the *Odes* and *Rites* classics still remained, and not mentioning the *Gongyang* [commentary on the *Spring and Autumn Annals*]. ["Image" is a standard rendering for *xiang* in the lexicon of *Yijing* interpretation. It refers to the images ("mountain," "swamp," etc.) that are associated with each of the trigrams, as explained in the early *Xiangzhuan* commentary. Wang Bi generalized these images, as part of his conversion of the *Yi* into a more "philosophical" text, and it is this kind of reinterpretation that Hui Dong is objecting to. For a convenient brief discussion, see the glossary entry for "*Hsiang*" in Kidder Smith Jr., et al., *Sung Dynasty Uses of the I Ching* (Princeton, NJ: Princeton University Press, 1990), 255.—Trans.]

29. For a translation of the *Taiji tushuo*, see "Explanation of the Diagram of Supreme Polarity," in *Sources of Chinese Tradition*, ed. William Theodore de Bary and Irene Bloom, 2nd ed. (New York: Columbia University Press, 1999), 673–676.—Trans.

30. Hui Dong, *Zhouyi shu, yi weiyan xia, li* [Transmitting the *Zhou Yi*, subtle words in the *Yi*, part 2, "Principle"]; see *Qingru xue'an xin bian* [Case studies of Qing Confucian scholarship, new compilation], 3: 121.

31. Pi Xirui, *Jingxue lishi* [History of classical learning] (Beijing: Zhonghua shuju, 1989), 313.

32. Jiang Fan's *Hanxue shicheng ji* strictly distinguishes Han from Song, but his *Songxue yuanyuan ji* [Record of the origins of Song learning] also cites, as does Pi Xirui's *Jingxue lishi*, Hui Dong's pillar couplet to illustrate the internal entanglement of Han and Song in Qing learning. See Jiang's *Guochao Songxue yuanyuanlu* [Record of the origins of Song learning in our dynasty], and Qian Zhongshu and Zhu Weizheng, eds., *Hanxue shichengji (wai er zhong)*, 187.

33. Yang Xiangkui: *Yishizhai xueshu wenji* [Collected scholarly essays from the Studio of Continuous History] (Shanghai: Shanghai renmin chubanshe, 1983), 514–515.

34. Jiang Fan, *Hanxue shichengji (wai er zhong)*, 30.

35. Yang Xiangkui, *Qingru xue'an xinbian*, 3: 120.

36. Ibid., 3: 116.

37. Hui Dong, *Zhouyi shu, Yi weiyan xia*, section on *xingming* [the nature and the decree]. See Yang Xiangkui, *Qingru xue'an xinbian*, 3: 176.

38. Yang Xiangkui, *Qingru xue'an xinbian*, 3: 118.

39. Why in *Yijing* studies were the views of Old Text classical scholars so close to those of the New Text classical scholars? This is because among all the classics, the distinction between Old Text and New Text views of the *Yijing* was different. "One reason was that the *Yijing* never encountered the Qin fire, so that both the original text and the commentaries of its teachers survived and were transmitted, and there are no obvious discrepancies between philological reconstructions and paragraph- and sentence-level commentaries. Another comes from the fact that the *Yijing* was a prognostication text, with emphasis on yin and yang and natural calamities, and these were things that that the New Text masters of Western Han were skilled in, so that in this sense all schools of *Yijing* learning belonged to the New Text camp." Yang Xiangkui, *Qingru xue'an xinbian*, 3: 116.

40. Qian Mu, *Zhongguo jinsanbainian xueshushi*, 1: 327. [Qian Daxin said that in writing this abstract treatise on the nature of goodness, Dai Zhen was "wasting his talents in a field of futility." Zhang Xuecheng, who is our source for this remark, disagreed, but was unable to persuade Qian to change his view. Yu Ying-shih builds his interpretation of Dai Zhen as "a hedgehog in a world of foxes" on what he sees as this mainstream classicist rejection of Dai Zhen's interest in *yili* as an unexpected and unwelcome survival of Song learning tendencies in an otherwise admired Han learning scholar, and Wang Hui is agreeing with Yu's interpretation here. Wang has much more to say about Dai's "On Goodness" later in this chapter.—Trans.]

41. Zhang Taiyan, "Kangchengzi yongwei Song Ming xinxue daoshi shuo" [How Zheng Xuan became a teacher of Song-Ming *Xinxue*], *Zhang Taiyan quanji* [Complete works of Zhang Taiyan], 5: 63.

42. Dai Zhen, *Faxiang lun* [On the patterns of celestial phenomena], *Dai Zhen quanji*, 1: 1–2.

43. Lei Mengchen, *Qingdai gesheng jinshu huikao* [Collected studies of Qing-dynasty banned books by province] (Beijing: Beijing tushuguan chubanshe, 1989), 4.

44. For short biographies of Li and Tian, see *Eminent Chinese of the Ch'ing Period*, ed. Arthur Hummel (rpt. Taipei: SMC Publishing, 2002), 455–457, 719–721.—Trans.

45. Chinese Academy of Social Sciences Qing History Unit, *Qingshi ziliao* [Qing historical materials], vol. 4, *Dayi juemi lu* [(Zeng Jing's) righteous confession of error] (Beijing: Zhonghua Shuju, 1983), juan 2: 48.

46. On the connection between Qing-dynasty Zhu Xi learning and the factions case, consult Lu Baoqian's *Qingdai xueshushi* [History of scholarship in the Qing dynasty] (Taibei: Guangwen shuju, 1983).

47. *Qing shilu* [Veritable records of Qing] (Beijing: Zhonghua shuju), 16: 211–212.

48. Ibid., 23: 409–410.

49. Lü Liuliang, *Lü Wancun xiansheng sishu jiangyi* [Master Lü Liuliang's lectures on the *Four Books*], juan 35, "*Mengzi* [*Mencius*] 6, Teng Wengong II," 9a.

50. Ibid., juan 17, "*Lunyu* 14, *Xian wen* [*Analects* 14, Xian asked]," 9a.

51. Ibid., juan 19, "*Zhongyong* [*Doctrine of the Mean*] 6," 10a.

52. Ibid., juan 35, "*Mengzi* 5, Teng Wengong I," 10a.

53. Lu Baoqian, *Qingdai xueshushi,* 158. Lu's writings focus on the Lü Liuliang case and Qing-era changes in Zhu Xi learning, and have given us valuable clues for understanding critiques of Zhu Xi learning by Qian Jia scholars in this period.

54. The Manchu Qing rejection of Buddhism is connected with their evaluation of the decline of Mongol national fortunes under the influence of the (Tibetan) Yellow Sect. The Emperor Taiji said: "The Mongolian *beizi* abandoned the Mongol language and all took names from lamas, and as a result the national fortunes declined" (*Qing Taizong shilu* [Veritable records of Qing Taizong], juan 18, *Tiancong* 8 [1634], fourth month, *xinyou*). Kangxi practiced Confucian learning from childhood, and in 1673 he said to Xiong Cilü and others: "When I was ten years old a lama came to the court and brought up the Western Buddhist dharma. Speaking to him directly I brushed aside his absurdities, and he was stunned and at a loss for words. From birth I have been disgusted to hear this kind of thing" (*Kangxi qiju zhu* [Kangxi Emperor's diary of activity and repose], 12th year [1671], 8th month, 26th day).

55. In the nineteenth century, Wei Yuan in his role as a New Text scholar attacked Han learning works of textual criticism, including Dai Zhen's, and also mocked their attitude as Four Treasuries commissioners of attacking Song learning. Wei Yuan made his judgments under the requirements of the age of reform, and yet in following the New Text path he came close to the general meaning of Gu Yanwu. He himself had many criticisms of Song learning, but he was quite dissatisfied with the attitude of the Four Treasuries commissioners. In his "Shu *Song mingchen yanxinglu* hou" (Letter written after reading the *Words and Deeds of Famous Song Officials*), he criticized Ji Yun, saying: "Ji Yun thus did not like the Song Confucians, [a sentiment] which his *General Catalogue* often expresses, but he lacks the depth of Zhu Xi's *Words and Deeds of Famous Song Officials*. . . . His words are full of criticism and definitive judgments, clear enough to hang at the kingdom's gates and unchangeable as the Southern Mountains! And yet I do not know what his views are based on" (Wei Yuan, *Wei Yuan ji* [Wei Yuan's collected writings] (Beijing: Zhonghua shuju, 1976), 1: 217). These examples are enough to make clear that to discuss the meaning of Dai Dongyuan's thought as simply a matter of opposing *lixue* does not get to the heart of the matter.

56. Qian Mu, *Zhongguo jinsanbainian xueshushi,* 1: 321–322.

57. Dai Zhen, "Hui Dingyu xiansheng shoujing tu," *Dai Zhen quanji,* 5: 2614.

58. Dai Zhen, "*Gu jingjie gouchen* xu" [Preface to (Yu Xiaoke's) *Research Notes for Explaining the Ancient Classics*], *Dai Zhen quanji,* 5: 2631.

59. Weng Fanggang criticized Dai Zhen as follows: "In recent days, Dai Zhen of Xiuning has devoted his life's energies to philology and calendrical astronomy. His

learning is broad and diligent, and this is definitely an aspect of *kaozheng*. But not content with making philology his profession, he wants to talk of the nature and the Way, in order to be different from Cheng and Zhu." Weng Fanggang, "Li shuo bo Dai Zhen zuo" [Explaining principle to refute the writings of Dai Zhen], *Fuchuzhai wenji* (Taibei: Wenhai chubanshe, 1966), 1: 321.

60. Dai Zhen, "Yuan shan shang" [On goodness, pt. 1], *Dai Zhen quanji*, 1: 9.

61. Ibid., 1: 3.

62. Duan Yucai, *Dai Dongyuan xiansheng nianpu* [Chronological biography of Master Dai Dongyuan], in *Dai Zhen quanji*, 6: 3403. According to Qian Mu's research, what Duan Yucai heard of in the *bingxu* (thirty-first) year of Qianlong (1766) was actually not the *Critical Exegesis of the Meanings of Words in Mencius* but the expanded version of *On Goodness* in three sections. See Qian Mu, *Zhongguo jin sanbai nian xueshushi*, 1: 326–327.

63. Dai Zhen, *Mengzi ziyi shuzheng*, juan 1.14, *Dai Zhen quanji*, 1: 166.

64. Dai Zhen, "Yu Duan Yucai shu" [Letter to Duan Yucai], see Duan Yucai, *Dai Dongyuan xiansheng nianpu*, in *Dai Zhen quanji*, 6: 3417. [The quoted phrases are from Burton Watson's translation of the story in the "Secret of Caring for Life" chapter of the *Zhuangzi*, in which Cook Ding explains to Lord Wenhui how he is able to butcher an ox so effortlessly, by passing his "knife which has no thickness" through the "spaces between the joints," and so "going along with the natural makeup" of the ox. Dai Zhen also explicitly cites this passage in his explanation of the meaning of *tianli* in section 2 of his *Critical Exegesis*.—Trans.]

65. Zhang Xuecheng, "Shu Zhu Lu pian hou" [Postscript to the essay on Zhu and Lu], in *Wenshi tongyi, Zhang Xuecheng yishu*, 16.

66. Zhang Xuecheng, "Da Shao Eryun shu" [Letter in reply to Shao Eryun], *Zhang Xuecheng yishu*, 645; "You yu Zhu Shaobo shu" [Another letter to Zhu Shaobo]: see *Zhang shi yishu* [Posthumous writings of Mr. Zhang], *buyi* [addendum], section 8: 25–26.

67. Yu Ying-shih, *Dai Zhen yu Zhang Xuecheng* [Dai Zhen and Zhang Xuecheng] (Taibei: Huashi chubanshe, 1977), 86–87.

68. Zhang Xuecheng, "Shu Zhu Lu pian hou," *Zhang Xuecheng yishu*, 16.

69. Shimada Kenji, "Liujing jie shi shuo" [The theory that "The Six Classics are all history"], in *Riben xuezhe yanjiu Zhongguo shi lunzhu xuanyi* [Selected translations from Japanese scholarship on Chinese history] (Beijing: Zhonghua shuju, 1993), 7: 185.

70. In his "Letter in Reply to Shao Eryun," Zhang Xuecheng said: "At that time among the aspirants for high court office, Mr. Zhu of Daxing and Mr. Qian of Jiading were truly outstanding. They praised Mr. Dai, but only by saying that in textual exegesis and the study of names and their referents, and in the Six Classics and the nine mathematical arts, he was diligent and deeply precise. But when it came to his writings like *On Goodness*, they all regretted that he was wasting his spirit in a field of futility. At that time, I strongly disputed this before Master Zhu, saying that this was like

buying the glittering case but returning the pearl. But my standing was slight and my words carried no weight, and I was unable to change their opinion." *Zhang Xuecheng yishu*, 645.

71. Dai Zhen, *Mengzi ziyi shuzheng*, juan 1.15, in *Dai Zhen quanji*, 1: 168–169.

72. Peng Shaosheng, "Yu Wang Dashen" [Letter to Wang Dashen], *Er linju ji* [Twice retired collection] (Guangxu xinsi [1881] edition), juan 3: 15.

73. Yuan Mei, "Da Xiang Jinmen" [Reply to Xiang Jinmen] in *Xiao Cangshan fang chidu* [Model correspondence from Cangshan Cottage], *Suiyuan 30 Genres* edition, juan 7: 8. For the condition of Buddhism in this period, see Lu Baoqian's *Qingdai sixiang shi*, 197–219.

74. Hong Bang, *Dai xiansheng xingzhuang*, in *Dai Zhen quanji*, 6: 3382.

75. Hong Bang, "Yu Zhu Yun shu" [Letter to Zhu Yun], see Jiang Fan, *Hanxue shicheng ji (wai er zhong)*, 117.

76. Dai Zhen, *Mengzi ziyi shuzheng*, in *Dai Zhen quanji*, 1: 166.

77. Dai Zhen, "Yu Duan Yucai shu" [Letter to Duan Yucai], see Duan Yucai, *Dai Dongyuan xiansheng nianpu*, *Dai Zhen quanji*, 6: 3417–3418.

78. Hong Bang, *Dai xiansheng xingzhuang*, in *Dai Zhen quanji*, 6: 3386–3387.

79. Hong Bang described it saying, "Today's scholars are eager to accept learning, and when they speak of Principle and of the Way and of the heart and of the nature, the terms 'Principle,' 'Way,' 'heart' and 'Nature' are all words of the Six Classics, Confucius, and Mencius; and yet in their explanations of what it means to be 'Principle,' 'Way,' 'heart,' and 'Nature,' they often mix in Daoist and Buddhist meanings. Supposing that the fruit of their explanations were true, then one should follow and expound them; but if the fruits are false, then those who study the classics simply cannot remain silent. If one supposes that Jia (Yi), Ma (Rong), Fu (Sheng), and Zheng (Xuan) had been born in the present age, then they also would be unable to keep silent." "Yu Zhu Yun shu"; see Jiang Fan, *Hanxue shicheng ji (wai er zhong)*, 119.

80. For example, Wang Jin said, "When I travel among Confucians and Buddhists, truly I see that the Ways of our Confucius and of Shakyamuni fit together almost like the two halves of a tally. For example, where Confucius says no thought and no action (*wusi wuwei*), the Buddhists say fundamentally there is no birth (*ben wusheng*); and where Confucius says without direction and without embodiment (*wufang wuti*), the Buddhists say that what one regards as born is not born (*dangsheng wusheng*)." Wang Jin, "Yu Luo Taishan shu" [Letter to Luo Yougao], in *Wangzi wenlu* [Writings of Master Wang], *Wangzi yiji ben* [Master Wang's posthumous collection], printed in the eighth year of Guangxu (1882), juan 5: 11.

81. Peng Shaosheng, *Yixingju ji* [Unity of action and repose collection] (Nanjing: Jinling kejing chu, *minguo* 10 [1921]), juan 4: 15.

82. Peng Shaosheng, "Da Wang Fengyie" [Reply to Wang Mingsheng], *Yixingju ji*, juan 4: 12.

83. Peng Shaosheng, "Yu Dai Dongyuan shu" [Letter to Dai Zhen], in *Dai Zhen quanshu 7*, *fulu zhi er* [Appended materials, 2] (Hefei: Huangshan shushe, 1997), 134.

84. Dai Zhen, "Da Peng jinshi Shaosheng shu" [Reply to Presented Scholar Peng Shaosheng] as summarized by Duan Yucai in his *Dai Dongyuan xiansheng nianpu;* see *Dai Zhen quanji,* 6: 3417.

85. Peng Shaosheng, "Du *Zhongyong* bie" [Reading the distinctions in the *Great Learning*], *Yixingju ji,* juan 2: 20.

86. Luo Taishan, "*Zui liuxuan ji* xu" [Preface to the *Tipsy Pomegranate Studio Collection*], *Zunwen jushi ji* [Collection of the retired scholar who respects what he has heard] (n.p. Guangxu 7 [1880] edition), juan 2: 8.

87. Luo Taishan, "Yu Dashen lun *Jushizhuan* pingyu, diliu ping" [Comments to Wang Dashen on *Biographies of Retired Scholars,* 6th comment], *Zunwen jushi ji,* juan 2: 21–22.

88. He even said, "Dai's learning has rendered great service to the teachings of the Six Classics, Confucius, and Mencius, and causing later scholars not to rush after lofty subtleties but to examine clearly into human relationships and the myriad things must begin with Dai." Hong Bang, "Yu Zhu Yun shu"; see Jiang Fan, *Hanxue shicheng ji (wai er zhong),* 117–119.

89. Dai Zhen, *Xuyan,* in *Dai Zhen quanji,* 1: 67.

90. Ibid., 1: 83.

91. Ibid., 1: 69. How to judge the difference between opinion and pattern? The *Critical Exegesis of the Meanings of Words in Mencius* says: "It is only what hearts affirm alike that can be designated as order and as rightness; whatever does not reach what is 'affirmed alike' but remains lodged among one's personal opinions is not order and not rightness. When any man would affirm it and the whole world through every generation would say "this cannot be changed," this is what is meant by 'affirming alike'" [1.4]. *Dai Zhen quanji* 1: 153.

92. Dai Zhen says, "For the difference between humans and creatures is that humans can understand what is necessary, whereas in the life of the hundred creatures each [merely] fulfills its spontaneity" [1.15]. His concern is, that when Lao, Zhuang, the Buddhists, and the Song Confucians are all equally convinced that "the Way is modeled on the spontaneous" [*Laozi Daodejing,* 25—Trans.], they eliminate the need for learning. See his *Mengzi ziyi shuzheng,* juan *xia* (3.9), in *Dai Zhen quanji,* 1: 200.

93. Dai Zhen said, "In the Six Classics, Confucius, and Mencius one never hears of a distinction between *li* and *qi;* it was the Song Confucians who started speaking in this way, and when they associated *Dao* (the Way) with *li,* truly they lost the meaning of the word. See *Xuyan* in *Dai Zhen quanji,* 1: 65. Also, as Qian Mu explains, "The emphasis in *Threadwords* is on the priority of *li* and *qi,* whereas in the *Critical Exegesis* the emphasis is on distinguishing the similarities and differences of Principle and desire."

94. This is one of the reasons why Dai Zhen attached importance to Xunzi. He said: "Xunzi's views place great emphasis on learning, but he does not know the whole substance of the nature. His words come from honoring the sages, from emphasizing learning, and from exalting propriety and righteousness. His introductory chapter is

an 'Exhortation to Learning' . . . Such is the excellence of Xunzi's articulation of learning! Moreover, when he says, 'penetrate to godlike understanding and be a third with Heaven and Earth,' he also knows that the farthest reach of propriety and righteousness, where the sage and Heaven and Earth unite their virtues, is here. Were a sage to arise again, wherein could he change his words?" *Mengzi ziyi shuzheng,* juan 2.10, in *Dai Zhen quanji,* 1: 183

95. Dai Zhen, *Xuyan,* in *Dai Zhen quanji,* 1: 86–87. [See also Dai's *Shuzheng,* section 26, juan 2.11, where the identical text is reproduced.—Trans.]

96. Dai Zhen said, "When Xunzi esteemed ritual principles, and the Song Confucians esteemed *li,* there was no harm in this to the teachings of the sages, it was just that they did not know the nature. But when Lao Dan, Zhuang Zhou, and the Buddhists preserve themselves as self-sufficient, this is not just a matter of not knowing the nature, but is indeed a teaching that harms others." Dai Zhen, *Xuyan,* in *Dai Zhen quanji,* 1: 111.

97. "The theories of Lao Dan, Zhuang Zhou, Gaozi, and the Buddhists all arise from selfishness, and all take spontaneity as their model . . . they rely only on themselves." Dai Zhen, *Xuyan* [Threadwords], in *Dai Zhen quanji,* 1: 99–101.

98. Dai Zhen, *Xuyan,* in *Dai Zhen quanji,* 1: 102–103.

99. Dai Zhen, *Xuyan,* in *Dai Zhen quanji,* 1: 95.

100. Qian Mu, *Zhongguo jin sanbainian xueshushi,* 1: 350–351.

101. Dai Zhen, *Xuyan,* in *Dai Zhen quanji,* 1: 110.

102. Dai Zhen said, "Ever since the Song, explanations of [the relation of] Principle and desire have simply taken it as the distinction of the correct from the deviant, so that whatever 'does not issue from the deviant and issues from the correct' is spoken of as 'responding to affairs with Principle.' Principle and affairs are divided as two [things], and [Principle is] united with opinion as one [thing], and thus affairs are harmed. . . . People knew that Lao, Zhuang, and the Buddhists differed from the sages, and when they heard their theories of desirelessness were not inclined to believe them. But among the Song Confucians [these theories] were believed and regarded as similar to [the teachings of] the sages, [and now] everyone can explain the 'distinction of Principle and desire.'" Dai Zhen, *Mengzi ziyi shuzheng,* juan 1.10, in *Dai Zhen quanji,* 1: 160–161.

103. Dai Zhen, *Mengzi ziyi shuzheng,* juan 1.15, in *Dai Zhen quanji,* 1: 170–171. [For a translation of Ode 260, see Bernard Karlgren, *The Book of Odes: Chinese Text, Transcription, and Translation* (Stockholm: Museum of Far Eastern Antiquities, 1950), 228–230.—Trans.]

104. Dai Zhen, *Mengzi ziyi shuzheng,* juan 1.4, in *Dai Zhen quanji,* 1: 153.

105. This quotation refers to the opening lines of *Ode* 260. See Karlgren, *The Book of Odes,* 228–230.—Trans.

106. Dai Zhen, *Mengzi ziyi shuzheng,* juan 1.13, in *Dai Zhen quanji,*1: 163.

107. Dai Zhen, *Mengzi ziyi shuzheng,* juan 1.10, in *Dai Zhen quanji,* 1: 161. [Shen Buhai and Han Feizi are Legalist thinkers from the Warring States period, traditionally

denounced by Confucian thinkers for their statist disregard for human feelings. —Trans.]

108. Dai Zhen, *Mengzi ziyi shuzheng,* juan 1.2, in *Dai Zhen quanji,* 1: 152.

109. Dai Zhen, *Mengzi ziyi shuzheng, Dai Zhen quanji,* 1: 204.

110. Dai Zhen, *Yuan shan,* in *Dai Zhen quanji,* 3: 21.

111. Dai Zhen, *Mengzi ziyi shuzheng,* juan 1.4, in *Dai Zhen quanji,* 1: 153–154.

112. In fact, Dai Zhen's spontaneity / necessity distinction and his discussions of the relationship between ritual and feeling both have connections with Xunzi; his concept of *fenli* as "fine structure" may also have been influenced by Xunzi's definition of ritual as "the great differentiations of law" (*li ye, fa zhi dafen*) in his *Quan xue* [Exhortation to study], but "fine structure" puts more emphasis on the internal ordering of things, while Xunzi is closer to the concepts of Legalism.

113. Zhang Taiyan, "Shi Dai" [Understanding Dai Zhen] *Zhang Taiyan quanji,* 4: 122.

114. For example, the late-Ming high official Yu Yang said in his *Pu bian jishi* [Chronicle of changes in Puzhou], "After the national change and the chaos of *dinghai* and *wuzi* [1647–1648], mountains and seas conspired together, every village planted a banner, every household raised a traveler, there was enmity between countryside and city, and south and north became enemies." See *Qingshi ziliao* [Qing history materials], vol. 1 (Beijing: Zhonghua shuju, 1980).

115. "Xiangli bu" [Fellow townsmen division], in *Youyi dian* [Documents of friendship], juan 27, in Chen Menglei, comp., *Dingwenban gujin tushu jicheng* [Dingwen edition of the *Gujin tushu jicheng*] (Taipei: Dingwen Book Company, 1977).

116. See Zhang Jinfan, ed., *Qingdai fazhi shi* [History of the legal system of the Qing dynasty] (Beijing: Falü chubanshe, 1994), 498–505.

117. In Xiuning there is a *Mingzhou Wu shi jiadian* [Family code of the Wu family of Mingzhou], which in juan 1 says: "The sons and brothers of the lineage have extraordinary poise and are well endowed with intelligence, but lack the strength to follow a teacher; they must be taken in hand and instructed, either by enrolling them in a family school or by providing tuition fees, so as to train up one or two good men to serve as future examples. This will be the hope of the lineage and the glory of the ancestral lineage, and the resulting connections will not be small." Tang Lixing, *Ming Qing yilai Huizhou qucheng shehui jingji yanjiu* [Research on the regional social economy of Huizhou since the Ming and Qing dynasties] (Hefei: Anhui University Press, 1999), 19.

118. Ibid., 17, 25–26. In the book's chapter on "The Fangs of Huizhou and Social Change," the author also records cruel massacres of the Fang family lineage during the suppression of tenant servant revolts. Ibid., 56.

119. Ibid., 39.

120. Ibid., 37–38.

121. Ibid., 45–46.

122. Yoshida Jun also points out in his "*Yuewei caotang biji* xiaolun" [Brief discussions of (Ji Yun's) *Notes on a Minutely Observed Thatched Hut*], in *Zhongguo—*

shehui yu wenhua, 1989 (4): 182–186: "Dai Zhen's argument developed unexpectedly from the merchant households of Huizhou. Because their husbands went out to engage in trade, women became subject to more serious social and moral pressures. There were many merchant wives who, on account of suspicions of having lost their virtue, followed the path of suicide. This view has many similarities with Chinese scholars' discussions of Li Zhi's view of women." See also Benjamin Elman, *Jingxue, zhengzhi yu zongzu: Zhonghua diguo wanqi Changzhou jinwen xuepai yanjiu* [*Classicism, Politics, and Kinship: The Chang-chou School of New Text Confucianism in Late Imperial China*], Chinese translation by Zhao Gang (Nanjing: Jiangsu renmin chubanshe, 1998), 7.

123. Zhang Jinfan, ed., *Qingdai fazhi shi,* 507.

124. *Qinding daqing huidian shili* [Imperially ordered collected statutes of Great Qing], juan 82, *Xing bu: xing lü* [Board of Punishments: Criminal statutes], 507.

125. "[Whereas] Xunzi adduced its lesser [aspects] and left out its greater [aspects], Mencius illuminated its greater [aspects] and did not neglect its lesser [aspects]." Dai Zhen, *Xuyan,* in *Dai Zhen quanji,* 1: 87. [See also Dai's *Mengzi ziyi shuzheng,* juan 2.11.—Trans.]

126. Dai Zhen, *Mengzi ziyi shuzheng,* juan 2.11, in *Dai Zhen quanji,* 1: 183–184.

127. Dai Zhen, *Mengzi ziyi shuzheng,* juan 2.10, in *Dai Zhen quanji,* 1: 182–183.

128. Zhang Taiyan, "Shi Dai," in *Zhang Taiyan quanji,* 4: 123–124. [Here Zhang Taiyan is referring to Laozi and Mencius by their personal names.—Trans.]

129. Qian Mu, *Zhongguo jin sanbainian xueshushi,* 357–358, 359.

130. Dai Zhen, *Mengzi ziyi shuzheng,* juan 3.12, in *Dai Zhen quanji,* 1: 204–205.

131. In Dai Zhen's view, on the question of "learning" Cheng and Zhu were much closer to Xunzi, and because of this there was a difference in his attitude toward Cheng and Zhu and toward Lao and the Buddha. For example, he said: "Masters Cheng and Zhu did indeed 'enter the house and grasp the spear' of Lao-Zhuang and the Buddhists, and changed their words, thinking that Confucius, Mencius, and the Six Classics were like this; but although (what they said) happened to have come quite close to Xunzi, it was not the Six Classics, Confucius, and Mencius." *Mengzi ziyi shuzheng,* juan 2.12, in *Dai Zhen quanji,* 1: 187.

132. After reading the writings of Yang Jian [1141–1226], Peng said: "The learning of the original heart is direct and penetrating. The Master said, 'Am I someone possessed of knowledge? I have no knowledge' [*Analects* 9.7]. To have no knowledge and yet leave nothing unknown, this is what it means to be 'entirely free of the four' [impediments, viz: foregone conclusions, arbitrary predeterminations, obstinacy, egoism: *Analects* 9.4—Trans.]; this is what is meant by the 'original heart.'" "Du Yangzi shu" [Letter on reading Master Yang], see *Erlinju ji,* juan 2: 3.

133. Wang Jin, "Ming zun Zhu Zhizhi" [Understanding and respecting what Zhu has pointed out], *Er lu* [Second collection], *Wangzi yishu* [Posthumous writings of Master Wang], 5.

134. Dai Zhen, *Mengzi ziyi shuzheng,* juan 1.14, in *Dai Zhen quanji,* 1: 167.

135. Qian Daxin, "*Zangyulin jingyi za shuo* xu" [Preface to "Miscellaneous Explanations of the Meanings of the *Classic of Hidden Jade*"] in *Qianyantang wenji* [Collection from the Hall of Intensive Study], juan 24: 218. Sibu congkan edition.

136. When Zhang, following Confucius's directive to "learn below and get through to what is above" [*Analects* 14.35], holds that through studying the "vessels which are subsequent to form" one may reach the "Way that is antecedent to form" [*Yijing, Appended Words,* 1.12], this way of discussing moral practice makes him seem like a follower of Wang Yangming, but if we examine closely there are still great differences. The most important of these is that he gave a historical explanation for the evolution of "learning." Zhang Xuecheng, "Yuan xue" [On learning], *Wen shi tong yi,* in *Zhang Xuecheng yishu,* 12–13.

137. In his "Yu Liu Duanlin jiaoyu shu" [Letter to Instructor Liu Duanlin (Liu Taigong, 1751–1805)] Jiao Xun said: "When Ancient Learning had not yet arisen, the Way was in preserving its learning. When Ancient Learning greatly flourished, the Way was in seeking to penetrate it. The fault of the first was in the risk of not studying; the fault of the second was in the risk of not thinking. Verifying it with facts and yet able to put it to use in the void is close to the Way of studying the classics. In recent times scholars who engage in learning have suddenly set up a plethora of topics to be investigated, (and) I . . . have repeatedly discussed the falseness of these topics." Jiao Xun, *Diaogu ji* [Rice carver's collection], *Yu Liu Duanlin jiaoyu shu,* juan 13: 25a-b. Wenxue shanfang edition.

138. Ling Tingkan summed up the methodology of Qian-Jia scholarship, which can be compared and contrasted with Zhang's view: "In ancient times Hejian advised the king to seek truth from facts. For when, with the facts before us, we call it truth, others cannot with sophistry make it false; and what we call false, others cannot with sophistry make it true. The six graphic principles, the nine methods of calculation, and the study of institutions and systems are examples of this. But with empty principles before us, when I say something is true, another may uphold a theory that makes it false; and when I say something is false, another may also uphold a theory that makes it true. The study of moral philosophy is an example of this." Ling Tingkan, *Dai Dongyuan xiansheng shiluezhuang* [A brief biographical sketch of Dai Dongyuan], in *Xiaolitang wenji, Anhui congshu* 4 (1935), juan 35: 8a.

139. He said, "In explaining the classics, Mr. Dai did not completely follow the theories of Zheng Xuan, and in writing books for young students, he avoided lightly citing [Zheng's commentaries]. Everyone was suspicious, and could not tell whether what he said was true." *Wenshi tongyi,* outer chapter 2, "*Zhengxue zhaiji* shuhou" [Postface to "A Record of the Studio of Zheng's Learning"], in *Zhang Xuecheng yishu,* 74.

140. The perspective of regarding the classics as history had been a continuous thread in the Wang Yangming (1472–1529) tradition. In Wang's own *Chuanxi lu* [Instructions for practical living], there was already the formulation, "the Five Classics are all history" (*wujing jie shi*), and in the *Yiyuan zhiyan* [Remarks on the arts] section

of his *Yanzhou shanren sibu gao* [Writings in the four categories from Yanshou], Wang Shizhen (1526–1590) said: "Between Heaven and Earth there is nothing but history. The Six Classics are history's articulation of principle." In the "Jing shi xiang wei biaoli" [Classics and history are two sides of the same coin] section of his *Fenshu* [Book to be burned], Li Zhi (1527–1602) said: "The *Spring and Autumn* classic is the history of the Spring and Autumn period; the *Odes* and *Documents* classics are the history of the time since the Two Emperors and Three Kings. The *Classic of Change* shows people whence the classics arise and where history comes from, how the Way is endlessly changing, that its transformations are not constant, and that it cannot be definitively grasped. Therefore, it is said that the Six Classics are all history." Zhang Shunhui inferred from this that "it is clear that the theory that the Six Classics are all history had already been developed in the Ming, and did not begin with Zhang Xuecheng. Extending this through the words of many scholars, when observing ancient writings and teachings, which of them cannot be integrated into history? Gong Zizhen frequently remarked, 'Outside of history there is no writing' (*Gushi gouchen lun* [Explorations in ancient history]), and this was no exaggeration. Whatever is articulated in the Six Genres can serve as material for archaeology, even if it cannot be put into practice. Classics and commentaries on the Six Arts number in the tens of thousands, and nowadays they must all be regarded as historical materials" (Preceding passages quoted in Zhang Shunhui, *Shixue sanshu pingyi* [An appraisal of three works of history] (Beijing: Zhonghua shuju, 1983, 180). But here Zhang Shunhui takes the word "history" in the proposition that "the Six Classics are all history" as equivalent to "historical materials," and does not explain the meaning that the concept of "history" had in Confucian learning. The meaning of "history" as a basis for moral practice cannot be revealed in the framework of this empirical historiography.

141. Zhang Xuecheng, "Yuan xue" [On learning] *Wenshi tongyi, Zhang Xuecheng yishu,* 13.

142. Ibid.

143. See all three chapters of Zhang Xuecheng's "Shi jing" [Interpreting the classics], *Wenshi tongyi, Zhang Xuecheng yishu,* 8–9.

144. For example, Jiao Xun said: "From Zhou and Qin to the Han, everyone called it learning, . . . there was no such thing as textual criticism. . . . Classical learning takes the classical texts as primary, and takes things like the masters and chroniclers of the Hundred Schools, techniques of astronomical calculation, yin and yang and the Five Agencies, the six graphic principles and the seven phonological elements as supports, and by combining and penetrating them, analyzing and debating them, seeking (correct) interpretations and examining institutional (contexts), and clarifying their ethical import, . . . (seeks to) unite one's own temperament with the temperaments of the ancient sages, and to link them up with the temperaments of the tens of thousands of authors who have written books to establish their words. . . . Without this temperament one cannot speak of classical learning." Jiao Xun, "Yu Sun Yuanru guancha lun

kaoju zhuzuo shu" [Letter to Sun Yuanru surveying writings on textual criticism], *Diaogu ji,* juan 13: 21b–31a.

145. Zhang Xuecheng, "Yuan dao," [On the Way], in *Wenshi tongyi, Zhang Xuecheng yishu,* 10.

146. "Shu jiao" [The teaching of the *Documents*] says: "The affairs of the ancients are seen in their words, words were taken as affairs, and there was never any distinction made between words and affairs." Zhang Xuecheng, *Wenshi tongyi,* in *Zhang Xuecheng yishu,* 3.

147. Zhang Xuecheng, "Jing jie" [Explaining the classics], *Wenshi tongyi, Zhang Xuecheng yishu,* 8.

148. Ibid., 10.

149. Ibid.

150. Zhang Xuecheng, "*Yi* jiao" [The teachings of the *Book of Changes*], in *Wenshi tongyi, Zhang Xuecheng yishu,* 1.

151. Zhang Xuecheng, "Yuan dao" [On the Way], in *Wenshi tongyi, Zhang Xuecheng yishu,* 11.

152. For example, in the "Vigilance" (*Jie*) chapter of the *Guanzi,* in the phrase "steeped in the Four Classics" (*zeyu sijing*), the "Four Classics" are just the "Four Arts" (poetry, documents, rituals, and music); in the "Exhortation to Learning" (*Quan xue*) chapter of the *Xunzi,* in the passage "Where does learning begin? And where does it end? Its accomplishments begin with chanting the classics (*song jing*) and end with reading the rituals; its righteousness begins with acting as a gentleman, and ends with acting as a sage," the reference to "the classics" means just "books and records." The "Way of Heaven" chapter of the *Zhuangzi* does have the passage "Confucius . . . [gave an abstract of] the Twelve Classics," but the "Way of Heaven" is one of the "outer chapters" and was written by a later author, and so one cannot take this as a Warring States viewpoint. Because of this, historians of scholarship often hold that "the interpretation of 'classics' as books written by Chinese *ru* scholars must come after the Warring States period," especially during the period when the Han Wu Emperor dismissed the Hundred Schools and only respected Confucian arts. See Tang Zhijun, *Jindai jingxue yu zhengzhi* [Modern classical scholarship and politics] (Beijing: Zhonghua shuju, 1989), 2–3.

153. This term is often translated as "Confucian," but it refers to a mode of scholarship traditionally held to have predated the historical Kong Qiu (551–479 BCE) (now Latinized as "Confucius" and known in later historical texts as Kongzi) and in which Kong is held to have participated as perhaps its highest exemplar.—Trans.

154. Zhang Xuecheng, "Jing jie," *Zhang Xuecheng yishu,* 8.

155. Gong Zizhen: *Liujing zheng ming* [Rectifying names in the Six Classics], in Zhang Shunhui, ed., *Wenxian xue lun zhu jiyao* (Xi'an: Shaanxi renmin chubanshe, 1985), 99. Pi Xirui said: "What Confucius defined we call classics (*jing*); the explanations of his disciples we call commentaries (*zhuan*) or records (*ji*); what they passed along and discussed with each other we call teachings (*shuo*)." Pi Xirui, *Jingxue lishi,* 67.

156. Zhang Xuecheng, "Jing jie," *Zhang Xuecheng yishu*, 8.

157. Zhang Xuecheng, "Yuan dao," *Zhang Xuecheng yishu*, 10.

158. Zhang Xuecheng, "Jing jie," *Zhang Xuecheng yishu*, 8.

159. Ibid.

160. On the writings of the various masters, see Song Lian, *Zhu zi bian* [Discriminating the various masters], in Zhang Shunhui's compilation, *Wenxianxue lunzhu jiyao* [Synopsis of treatises on historical philology], 196–217.

161. Zhang Xuecheng, "Yuan dao," *Zhang Xuecheng yishu* 11.

162. Zhang Xuecheng, "Jing jie," *Zhang Xuecheng yishu*, 8.

163. Zhang Xuecheng said in "Yan gong" [When words are public]: "The various masters seek to win over the world with their learning, and contend that there is nothing that can be added to what they call the Way, and their language and writings are never private in what they express. . . . That the various masters arise, is owing to the fact that the arts of the Way have already been split apart, and that each according to the inclination of his intelligence and talent, and from what he has understood from his corner of the Great Way, then wishes to win over the world with it. From the reasons for what he upholds and from the logic of his words, he will elaborate a school of learning and transmit it to his disciples." *Wenshi tongyi, Zhang Xuecheng yishu*, 29.

164. Zhang Xuecheng, "*Shi* jiao" [The teachings of the *Odes*], *Wenshi tongyi, Zhang Xuecheng yishu*, 5.

165. Zhang Xuecheng, "Bujiao Han yiwenzhi di shi" [Repairing and collating the Treatise on Arts and Letters in the *History of the Han*, chapter 10], second of ten essays, in *Jiaochou tongyi*, in *Zhang Xuecheng yishu*, 99. Zhang Xuecheng refers to the "Against the Twelve Masters" chapter as "Against the Ten Masters," based on an inference from the fact that "when the biography of Han Yingshi cites this chapter from Xunzi (it observes that) it contains no mockery of Zisi or of Mencius."

166. Zhang Xuecheng, "Han zhi zhuzi di shisi" [Han (dynastic history) treatises, Various Masters, section 14], 22nd item, in *Jiaochou tongyi, Zhang Xuecheng yishu*, 105.

167. Zhang Xuecheng, "Bujiao *Han yiwenzhi* di shi," *Zhang Xuecheng yishu*, 99.

168. Ibid., 100.

169. Ibid., 99.

170. Analyzing the relationship between Confucius and the former kings, Zhang said: "It is not that Confucius praised and esteemed the former kings, his intent rested in modestly shepherding (their legacy) and not in doing anything himself. Fundamentally there was nothing that Confucius could do. He had virtue but no position, and thus had no power to create (institutions), and with empty words he could not teach others, because without proofs there is no belief. . . . The run of *ru* scholars venerated Confucius, as if he had privately made himself the founding teacher of a *ru* lineage, and so they also did not know Confucius." Zhang Xuecheng, "Yuan dao," *Zhang Xuecheng yishu*, 11.

171. Zhang Xuecheng, "Yu Chen Jianting lun xue" [Letter to Chen Jianting discussing learning], *Wenshi tongyi,* in *Zhang Xuecheng yishu,* 86.

172. See Dai Yi, "Siku quanshu he faguo baike quanshu" [The *Siku Quanshu* and the *French Encyclopedia*], in *Qianlong di ji qi shidai* [The Qianlong Emperor and his times] (Beijing: Zhongguo renmin daxue chubanshe, 1992), 369–387.

173. Zhang Xuecheng: "Yuan dao diyi, you yi zhi yi" [On the Way, 1: 1], *Jiaochou tongyi, Zhang Xuecheng yishu,* 95. [The *Lianshan* ("Linked Mountain"), *Guicang* ("Return to Concealment"), and *Zhou yi* ("Classic of Change") were divination manuals of the Xia, Shang, and Zhou dynasties.—Trans.]

174. See "*Han shu yiwenzhi* zongxu" [General preface to the Treatise on Bibliography in the *History of the Han*], also anthologized in Zhang Shunhui, ed., *Wenxianxue lunzhu jiyao* (Xi'an: Shaanxi renmin chubanshe, 1985), 23.

175. Ruan Xiaoxu, "*Qilu* xu" [Preface to the Seven Records] in Zhang Shunhui, ed., *Wenxianxue lunzhu jiyao,* 26.

176. Ibid., 26.

177. Zhang Xuecheng, "*Jiaochou tongyi* xu" [Preface], in *Zhang Xuecheng yishu,* 95.

178. Zhang Xuecheng, "Yuan dao," *Jiaochou tongyi,* in *Zhang Xuecheng yishu,* 95.

179. Ibid.

180. Zhangsun Wuji: "*Sui shu, jingji zhi,* zongxu" [General preface to the *Sui History*'s Treatise on Classical Documents], in Zhang Shunhui, ed., *Wenxianxue lunzhu jiyao,* 30–31.

181. For the establishment of the Four Categories, please also refer to works like Zhang Shourong's "*Bashi jingji zhi* xu" [Preface to *A Treatise on Classical Divination Texts*], Ji Yun's "*Siku quanshu zongmu tiyao* xu" [Preface to the *Summary of the Comprehensive Catalogue of the Four Treasuries*], Qian Daxin's "Lun jing shi zi ji sibu zhi fen" [Discussion of the Four Categories of classics, history, masters, and literary collections], and Jin Xiling's "Qilue yu sibu fenhe lun" [Discussion of similarities and differences between the Seven Genres and the Four Categories]. For all of these see Zhang Shunhui, ed., *Wenxianxue lunzhu jiyao,* 34–81.

182. Zhang Xuecheng, "Shikao zhailu" [Excerpts from historical investigations], in *Zhang Xuecheng yishu,* 655.

183. Zhang Xuecheng, *Zong Liu di er* [The Liu lineage, second essay], in *Jiaochou tongyi, Zhang Xuecheng yishu,* 95–96.

184. Zhang Xuecheng, "Yuan dao di yi," *Zhang Xuecheng yishu* 95.

185. Zhang Xuecheng, "Shikao zhailu," *Zhang Xuecheng yishu,* 654.

186. Ibid., 655.

187. Ibid.

188. Zhang Xuecheng said: "Comprehensiveness or generality (*tong*) is what permits what [otherwise] does not communicate in the world to communicate (*tong*). . . . A general history (*tongshi*) may cover a thousand years of human cultural activity, but where stylistic intents can communicate, then separate ages will not fear to take up common tasks" ("Shi tong" [Explaining "generality"]), in *Wenshi tongyi, Zhang*

Xuecheng yishu, 37). He also said: "Today you have asked if writers have 'intents, . . . that cannot help but turn away from the teachings of Confucius?' . . . I say: Of all the words under Heaven, each has its appropriateness, and the words of the classics and commentaries are also like this. When we read the words of the ancients, and cannot thoroughly understand their intent, [we sometimes] vainly hold to a dubious reading, thus trying to settle the matter on the basis of one corner. But [a reading from] one corner cannot settle it." "Da ke wen" [Reply to the questions of a guest], in *Wenshi tongyi, Zhang Xuecheng yishu,* 38.

189. Zhang Xuecheng, "*Shu* jiao xia," in *Wenshi tongyi, Zhang Xuecheng yishu,* 4.

190. Zhang Xuecheng said: "If in one's way one wishes to make a profession of being well versed in its methods, one must concentrate on one thing; in learning one must seek out what is to be gained from study, and in one's profession one must value detailed concentration." ("Bo yue xia" [Breadth and concentration, part 2], in *Wenshi tongyi, Zhang Xuecheng yishu,* 14.) He also said: "What a historian values is meaning (*yi*); what completes it are affairs (*shi*), and what it depends on is literary accomplishment (*wen*). . . . Without knowledge one will be unable to judge the meaning, without talent one will be unable to improve one's writing, and without learning one will be unable to become versed in the affairs." Zhang Xuecheng, "Shi de" [The virtues of a historian], in *Wenshi tongyi, Zhang Xuecheng yishu,* 40.

191. See *Zhang Xuecheng yishu,* 369–370.

192. Zhang Xuecheng, "*Shu* jiao shang," in *Wenshi tongyi, Zhang Xuecheng yishu,* 2–3.

193. Ibid.

194. Yang Liansheng, *Guoshi tanwei* [A detailed exploration of national histories] (Taibei: Lianjing, 1983), 351–353.

195. This does not mean that he turned toward the single schools of the various masters or of Song-Ming *lixue,* but that he carried on the great principles of the *Spring and Autumn Annals* and the comprehensive knowledge of Sima Qian, and that in his historical writings he drew on his personal insight to understand the changes of ancient and modern times. Zhang Xuecheng: "Da ke wen shang" [Reply to the questions of a guest, first part], in *Wenshi tongyi, Zhang Xuecheng yishu,* 38.

196. See essays like "Shi tong" [Explaining "generality"] in *Jiaochou tongyi* and "Fangzhi lueli yi" [Rules for the genre of local gazetteers, part 1] in "Ji yu Dai Dongyuan lun xiuzhi" [Records of discussions with Dai Zhen on the compilation of gazetteers], *Zhang Xuecheng yishu,* 35–37, 128.

197. Ibid., 128.

198. Zhang Xuecheng, "*Daming xianzhi* xu" [Preface to the *Daming County Gazetteer*], *Zhang Xuecheng yishu,* 129.

199. For example, he said: "The run of Confucian scholars preserve their Six Classics, and hold them to be writings which specially carry the Way. Yet how in the world could one speak of the Way apart from its vessels, leaving the form to preserve the shadow? That would be to cast off the affairs of the world and the daily practice of

human relationships, holding fast to the Six Classics to speak of the Way; but with such people one definitely cannot speak of the Way." "Yuan dao zhong," in *Wenshi tongyi, Zhang Xuecheng yishu,* 11.

200. In fact, this was not just the view of Zhang Xuecheng alone, for in a time of mutual recrimination between the Han and Song schools, when the evidential [trend in scholarship] was strongly rising, an opposite current inevitably appeared. For example, Jiao Xun's view in this respect was almost exactly the same as Zhang's: "Those who create are sages, and those who transmit understand and clarify. There is no difference between creating and transmitting, it is just that each is appropriate for its time. . . . It is not that Confucius was unable to create, but that the times did not require him to create. . . . Ever since the Song and Yuan, . . . everyone considered themselves transmitters of Confucius, but A defamed B as heterodox, and B denounced A as Yang and Mo, . . . so could they be transmitting what Confucius transmitted?" Jiao Xun, *Diaogu ji,* juan 7, *Shu nan* [Difficulties of transmission], section 2, *Baibu congshu jicheng* [Compilation of a hundred categories of collectanea], 1st ed. (Shanghai: Shangwu yinshuguan, 1937), 103.

201. Zhang Xuecheng, "Zhedong xueshu," in *Wenshi tongyi, Zhang Xuecheng yishu,* 15.

202. Zhang Xuecheng, "Tian yu" [Understanding Heaven], in *Wenshi tongyi, Zhang Xuecheng yishu,* 51.

203. Zhang Xuecheng, "Yuan dao zhong," in *Wenshi tongyi, Zhang Xuecheng yishu,* 11.

204. Zhang Xuecheng, "Yan gong shang," in *Wenshi tongyi, Zhang Xuecheng yishu,* 29.

205. Zhang Xuecheng, "Yan gong xia," in *Wenshi tongyi, Zhang Xuecheng yishu,* 32.

206. Zhang Xuecheng, "*Shu* jiao zhong," in *Wenshi tongyi, Zhang Xuecheng yishu,* 3.

207. "When it came to the Warring States period, the writings of Fu Xi, Shen Nong, and the Yellow Emperor all confusedly emerged at once, and their writings were all praised as [the work of] ancient sages. Examples are the *Ganshi xingjing* [Sidereal classic of Gan (Gong) and Shi (Shen)] in astronomy, and the *Ling (shu)* [Numinous pivot], *Su (wen)* [Basic questions], and *Nanjing* [Classic of difficult cases] in medicine. Their kinds were very numerous, and since craftsmen revered Lu Ban and soldiers revered Chi You, it was not necessary to write books to be regarded as a sage; for those who practiced these arts raised them up as guides, and inevitably they were revered for their classical sayings." "The learning of the hundred schools all contended to claim support from the writings of the Three August Ones and the Five Lords; skilled cultivators entrusted themselves to Shen Nong, military strategists and medical classics relied on the Yellow Emperor, and busybodies transmitted them as lost writings of the Three August Ones." Zhang Xuecheng, "Jing jie zhong," *Zhang Xuecheng yishu,* 9.

208. "The study of the life and nature of Heaven and of human beings (*tian ren xingming zhi xue*) cannot be discussed in empty words. Therefore, Sima Qian took

Dong Zhongshu's explanations of the life and nature of Heaven and of human beings as the basis of his writings on statecraft. . . . Knowing that the study of history is based on the *Spring and Autumn Annals,* is to know how through the *Spring and Autumn Annals* one may practice statecraft. . . . Those who discourse on learning must be involved with practical affairs, and not simply avoid involvement with factions." Zhang Xuecheng, "Zhedong xueshu," in *Wenshi tongyi, Zhang Xuecheng yishu,* 15.

6. Inner and Outer (1)

1. The "books hidden in the wall" of Confucius's residence include the *Book of Rites, Book of Documents,* the *Spring and Autumn Annals,* the *Analects,* and the *Classic of Filial Piety.* With the addition of the *Zuo Zhuan* [Zuo commentary on the *Spring and Autumn Annals*], contributed by Zhang Cang, Marquis of Beiping, this is the basis of the "Old Text" tradition. See Kang Youwei, *Xin xue weijing kao* [A new study on forgeries of the classics], *Kang Youwei quanji* [Complete works of Kang Youwei] (Shanghai: Shanghai guji chubanshe, 1987) 1: 747.

2. Kang Youwei said, "Taking the *Spring and Autumn* as a means of beseeching the king, its words are subtle and its intention rich, as it relies entirely on the spoken word." *Nanhai shicheng ji* [Records of the Nanhai disciple], *Kang Youwei quanji,* 2: 498. [Here, "the spoken word" is related to the "ascertaining of profound meanings from subtle words" (*weiyan dayi*) mentioned above.—Trans.]

3. Kang Youwei, *Nanhai shicheng ji, Kang Youwei quanji,* 2: 445.

4. Dong Shixi, "*Yi* shuoxu" [Ramblings on the *Book of Changes*], see *Weijing zhai yishu* [Posthumous papers of Weijing Studio], juan 1.

5. Wei Yuan, "*Wu Jinzhuang shao Zong Bo yishu* xu" [Preface to the posthumous papers of Wu Jinzhuang and Zong Bo the Younger]: see *Weijing zhai yishu,* juan 1, and *Wei Yuan ji* [Wei Yuan reader] (Beijing: Zhonghua shuju, 1976), 1: 238.

6. Ruan Yuan, "Zhuang Fanggeng Zong Bo shuo jing xu" [Preface to Zhuang Fanggeng and Zong Bo's discourse on the classics]: see *Weijing zhai yishu,* juan 1.

7. As Yang Xiangkui wrote, "This may also be thought of as Liu Xin's tradition: using the luminaries of the New Text school to advocate for the Old Text classics. Perhaps this was their last resort. Gongyang studies could only contribute to political theory. It is a philosophy of history, not a political guide. It does not provide a workable system of rules and laws. It is nothing but empty debate, which is why it had to borrow 'carrying on the lessons of the Ming' from the *Rites of Zhou.*" Yang Xiangkui, "Qingdai de jinwen jingxue" [New Text studies in the Qing era], *Yi Shizhai xueshu wenji* [Collected scholarly works of Yi Shizhai] (Shanghai: Shanghai renmin chubanshe, 1983), 328.

8. Liu Fenglu, *Shangshu jin guwen jijie xu* [New and Old Text commentaries on the *Book of Documents*], in *Liu Libu ji* [Liu's classification of rites], juan 9, Yan Huicheng woodblock edition from the Renchen reign year of Guangxu (1892), the same hereafter.

9. Wei Yuan, "Liang Han jingshi jin gu wen jiafa kaoxu" [Assessment of the New and Old Text doctrines of the Former and Latter Han dynasties], *Wei Yuan ji,* 1: 152.

10. There is no consistent claim regarding the timeline dividing Liao Ping's New and Old Text affinities. The collected materials and evidence place the line around 1885–1886. See Liao Ping, *Jin gu xuekao* [A study of the New Text and Old Text schools], *Liao Ping xueshu lunzhu xuanji* [Selected scholarly works by Liao Ping] (Chengdu: Bashu shushe, 1989), 1: 35–110.

11. Qian Mu, *Zhongguo jin sanbai nian xueshu shi* [Chinese intellectual history of the past three hundred years] (Beijing: Shangwu yinshuguan, 1997), 2: 582–583.

12. Liu Fenglu, "*Chunqiu Gongyang shili* xu" [Preface to *Explanatory Specimens from the Gongyang Commentary on the Spring and Autumn Annals*], *Liu Libu ji,* juan 3: 22–23.

13. Kang Youwei, entry on *Luxuriant Dew of the Spring and Autumn Annals,* in *Wanmu caotang koushuo* [Instructions from the thatched hut among ten thousand trees], *Kang Youwei quanji,* 2: 383.

14. The five classics in general use during the Western Han were the *Odes, Documents, Rites, Changes,* and *Spring and Autumn Annals.* The *Classic of Filial Piety* and the *Analects* were added during the Eastern Han, making seven classics. Nine classics were acknowledged during the Tang dynasty: *Changes, Odes, Documents,* the *Book of Etiquette and Ceremonial (Yili),* the *Rites of Zhou (Zhouli),* the *Book of Rites,* the Zuo commentary, the Gongyang commentary *(Gongyang zhuan),* and *Guliang zhuan*—excepting during the period of Great Harmony under the reign of Tang Wenzong, when the *Analects, Classic of Filial Piety,* and *Erya* were added, making twelve classics in total. Following the rise of Old Text studies in the waning years of the Eastern Han, New Text studies gradually declined. All that survives of pre-Tang New Text writing is He Xiu's *Explanatory Notes for the Spring and Autumn Gongyang (Chunqiu Gongyang jiegu). Mencius* was added in the Song, making thirteen classics.

15. Kang Youwei, *Nanhai shicheng ji, Kang Youwei quanji,* 2: 444.

16. Pi Xirui wrote, "The *Spring and Autumn Annals* are the particular work of Confucius, and there has been not a word of dissent from this since Mencius and the various scholars of the Former and Latter Han dynasties. Using Confucius's *Spring and Autumn,* Mencius compared Yu's restraint of the floodwaters and the Duke of Zhou's simultaneous expulsion of the peripheral tribes and the ferocious beasts; he also drew on Confucius's righteousness and adopted his words, succeeding Shun, Yu, Tang, Wen, Wu, and the Duke of Zhou; this is enough to show that Confucius's achievements continued the work of the sages, all of which are in the *Spring and Autumn.*" See Pi Xirui, *Jingxue lishi* [History of the classics] (Beijing: Zhonghua shuju, 1959), 67.

17. See Liu Fenglu's rebuttal to Qian Daxin in both parts of *Chunqiu lun* [Discourse on the *Spring and Autumn Annals*], quoted in *Liu Libu ji,* juan 3: 16–21.

18. Kang Youwei later said, "During the Tang, the Duke of Zhou was thought of as the first sage, and Confucius as the first master. Now it is up for debate. Zhang Xuecheng

also thinks the Duke of Zhou is the be-all and end-all, not Confucius. All who admire this [view] are pernicious." *Xin xue weijing kao, Kang Youwei quanji,* 1: 696.

19. Kang Youwei, *Kongzi gaizhi kao* [An investigation of Confucius as a reformer], *Kang Youwei quanji,* 3: 191.

20. Gu Yanwu, "Fuzi zhi yan xing yu tiandao" [The nature of Confucius's words and the Way of Heaven], *Ri zhi lu jishi (wai qi zhong)* [Collected commentaries on *Record of Daily Knowledge* (and seven other texts)], ed. Huang Rucheng (Shanghai: Shanghai guji chubanshe, 1985), 1: 536.

21. Liu Fenglu, *Shi tebi lie zhong* [Explanations of special cases], *Liu Libu ji,* juan 4: 21–22.

22. Gong Zizhen, "*Chunqiu jueshibi* zishu" [Author's preface to *Judicial Precedent in the Spring and Autumn Annals*], *Gong Ding'an quanji leibian* [Selections from the complete works of Gong Ding'an] (Beijing: Zhongguo shudian, 1991), 56–57.

23. Wei Yuan, "Xuexiao ying zeng si xiansheng Zhou gong yi" [Why schools should pay greater homage to the sage Duke of Zhou], *Wei Yuan ji,* 1: 155.

24. Dai Zhen, "Da Peng jinshi Shaosheng shu" [Reply to Presented Scholar Peng Shaosheng] as summarized by Duan Yucai in his *Dai Dongyuan xiansheng nianpu* [Chronological biography of Dai Zhen]; see *Dai Zhen quanji* [Complete collected writings of Dai Zhen], ed. Dai Zhen Yanjiuhui et al. (Beijing: Qinghua daxue chubanshe, 1991), 6: 3417.—Ed.

25. Gong Zizhen, *Gushi gouchen lun er* [Explorations in ancient history, part two], *Gong Ding'an quanji leibian,* 99–100.

26. Gong Zizhen, "*Lu Yanruo suozhu Shu* xu" [Preface to the writings of Lu Yanruo], *Gong Ding'an quanji leibian,* 34–35.

27. Kang Youwei, *Nanhai shicheng ji, Kang Youwei quanji,* 2: 442.

28. Liu Shipei, "Gongyang Mengzi xiang tongkao" [Comparative analysis of Gongyang and Mencius], *Qunjing dayi xiang tonglun* [Comparative survey of the principles of the classics], *Zhongguo xiandai xueshu jingdian: Huang Kan, Liu Shipei juan* [Classics of modern Chinese scholarship: Liu Shipei and Huang Kan] (Shijiazhuang: Hebei jiaoyu chubanshe, 1996), 575–577.

29. See Yu Yue, *Gujing jingshe ke yi wen* [Lessons in arts and letters from the Refined Lodge of the Exegesis of the Classics], collection (*ji*) no. 3 (Wuchen shang [Before the Wuchen year of 1868]) (Shanghai Library copy), 3–4.

30. Kong Guangsen, "*Chunqiu Gongyang jingzhuan tongyi* xu" [Supplement to *Principles of the Spring and Autumn Gongyang*], *Huang Qing jing jie* [Imperial Qing commentaries on the classics, hereafter abbreviated as *HQJJ*], ed. Ruan Yuan (rpt. Shanghai: Shanghai shudian, 1988), juan 691: 1–2.

31. Pi Xirui, *Jingxue tonglun* [Survey of classical scholarship] (Beijing: Zhonghua shuju, 1954), 1.

32. Liu Shipei, *Qunjing dayi xiang tonglun,* in *Zhongguo xiandai xueshu jingdian: Huang Kan, Liu Shipei juan,* 596–601.

33. Yang Xiangkui, "Gongyang zhuan zhong de lishi xueshuo" [Historical theory in the Gongyang commentary], *Yishizhai xueshu wenji,* 87.

34. For example, in "Xi gong yuan nian" [The first year of Duke Xi's reign], the Gongyang commentary provides the following explanation for the statement "The armies of the states of Qi, Song, and Cao encamped at Niebei, in order to rescue the state of Xing":

> Rescue expeditions aren't usually said to involve encampments. Why is the encampment mentioned here? *Because the rescue was too late.* How was the rescue too late? *The state of Xing was already lost.* To whom was it lost? *Probably it was the Di who destroyed it.* Why does the record not say it was the Di who destroyed it? *Because saying so would reflect poorly on Duke Huan.* How would it reflect poorly on Duke Huan? *With no son of heaven above or leader of the feudal lords below, all the feudal lords in the empire were destroying one another. Duke Huan's inability to help one of them counts as a mark of shame upon him.* Why does the record mention first the encampment and then the attempt at rescue? *Because the rulers of the various states were commanding their armies.* If the rulers were in command, then why does the record specify only "armies"? *In order to express disapproval of the notion of feudal lords themselves wielding the power of enfeoffment.* Why the disapproval? *Because, although the wielding of the power of enfeoffment by feudal lords is accepted in fact, it cannot be countenanced in language.* Why can't it be countenanced in language? *Because the term "feudal lord" means one who is enfeoffed, not one who enfeoffs.* If the term "feudal lord" means one who is enfeoffed, not one who enfeoffs, then why is the wielding of the power of enfeoffment by feudal lords "accepted in fact"? *Because, with no son of heaven above or leader of the feudal lords below, and all the feudal lords in the empire destroying one another, it is only on the basis of sheer power that such rescues may be effected; thus the rescuing of a state should be deemed permissible.* See *Chunqiu Gongyang zhuan jin zhu jin yi* [Modern annotation and translation of the *Gongyang Commentary on the Spring and Autumn Annals*], ed. Li Zongdong (Taipei: Taiwan shangwu yinshuguan, 1973), 1: 167–168. [Translation borrowed from *The Gongyang Commentary on the Spring and Autumn Annals: A Full Translation,* trans. Harry Miller (New York: Palgrave MacMillan, 2015), 81–82.—Trans.]

This states that the troops of Qi, Song, and Cao saved Xing, but that what they did cannot be spoken of, and further asks why the text mentions that the troops of Qi were first encamped there, but does not mention the successful defense. The answer is that Duke Huan of Qi is a sovereign. But why first state that they were encamped, then mention the rescue? Because in principle feudal lords were not allowed to rule frontier territory, but in fact were permitted to do so. This simply cannot be openly stated in the text. This is what is meant by "accepted in fact but not countenanced in language."

35. *Chunqiu Gongyang zhuan jin zhu jin yi,* 1: 65.

36. Liu Fenglu, "Shi tebi lie zhong," in *Liu Libu ji,* juan 4: 21–22.

37. Mencius, "Liang Hui Wang Shang" [King Hui of Liang I]. See Jiao Xunzhuan, *Mengzi zhengyi* [Interpretation of Mencius] (Beijing: Zhonghua shuju, 1987), 1: 87. [English translation borrowed from *Mencius* IA7, translated by James Legge.—Trans.]

38. Dai Zhen, *Mengzi ziyi shuzheng* [Critical exegesis of the meanings of words in *Mencius*], in *Dai Zhen quanji* , 1: 203.

39. Benjamin Elman, *Jingxue, zongzu, yu zhengzhi: Zhonghua diguo wanqi Changzhou jinwen xuepai yanjiu* [Classicism, politics, and kinship: The Changzhou New Text school and late imperial China], trans. Zhao Gang (Nanjing: Jiangsu renmin chubanshe, 1998), 2. [For the English, see Elman, *Classicism, Politics, and Kinship: The Ch'ang-chou School of New Text Confucianism in Late Imperial China* (Berkeley: University of California Press, 1990), xxi–xxiii.—Trans.]

40. Wei Yuan's "Introduction" to the *Posthumous Writings of Vice Minister Zhuang of Wujin* (Zhuang Cunyu, 1719–1788), written in the first reign year of Daoguang (1820), provides a basis for this: "The gentleman served together with Grand Secretary He Shen in the late Qianlong era, but felt deeply depressed and out of place, and thus, applying himself to the *Book of Odes* and the *Book of Changes* at a time when small men were bustling in pursuit of their careers, the gentleman was often filled with vehement indignation, sighing with deep regret, as in his readings he mourned his clouded ambition." This passage disappeared from handwritten copies, replaced with wording like "the gentleman's learning was abundantly attuned, having no need of instruction from teachers, transmitting spiritual brilliance, harnessing both the Way and its vessels, and there was no one who could fully grasp his meaning," proof enough that the Heshen Incident was still quite sensitive in the Daoguang years. Wei Yuan, "*Wujin Zhuang Shaozong bo yishu* xu" [Introduction to the posthumous writings of Vice Minister Zhuang of Wujin], *Wei Yuan ji*, 1: 238.

41. Elman, *Jingxue, zongzu, yu zhengzhi*, 15, 77, 79. [For relevant passages in the English, see Elman, *Classicism, Politics, and Kinship*, 21–22, 111–116.—Ed.]

42. Liu Danian gives two examples as counterevidence: First, Zhuang Cunyu and Kong Guangsen both wrote about Gongyang, but who did it first is hard to say. Kong wrote a treatise on *Principles of the Spring and Autumn Gongyang Classic and Commentaries (Chunqiu Gongyang jingzhuan tongyi)* while serving as a compiler at the Hanlin Academy, and died in 1786; Zhuang Cunyu's *Rectification of Terms in the Spring and Autumn Annals (Chunqiu zhengci)* must have been written after he resigned from office and returned to Changzhou in 1786. Thus it cannot be proven that New Text studies was the product of political struggle. Second, Gongyang studies had always argued that "the *Spring and Autumn* deplores hereditary postings," that "the *Spring and Autumn* avoids certain topics for the sake of the virtuous," and that its nine decrees in three sections were "completely opposed to capital punishment," and so on. The politics illustrated by these examples from Gongyang studies thus do not bring much clarity. I believe it is worth considering Liu Danian vis-à-vis Elman's aforementioned analysis, but it cannot be used to negate the political nature of New Text studies, as "political nature" has broad implications and cannot be boiled down to palace politics. See Liu Danian, *Ping jindai jingxue* [Critique of modern classical learning], in Zhu Chengru, ed., *Ming Qing lun cong* [Studies of the Ming-Qing], no. 1 (Beijing: Zijincheng chubanshe, 1999), 2.

43. For tracing the origins of the study of law and discipline and the concept of Unification in evidential learning, Jao Tsung-I (Rao Zongyi) offers the most detailed, economical account in *Zhongguo shixue shang zhi zhengtong lun* [Theories of legitimate succession in Chinese historiography] (Shanghai: Shanghai yuandong chubanshe, 1996). (The first edition was published in 1977 in Hong Kong by Longmen shudian.)

44. Wang Yi, "Zhengtong lun" [On political legitimacy], in *Wang Zhongwen gong ji* [Collected writings of Wang Yi], (Shanghai: Shangwu yinshuguan, 1936), juan 1: 7–8. Wanyou wenku edition.

45. Fang Xiaoru, "Hou zhengtong lun" [Response to Wang Yi's "On political legitimacy"], *Xun zhi zhai ji* [Anthology of works from the Xunzhi Studio], juan 2: 55. Sibu congkan edition.

46. Wang Yi, in *Wang Zhongwen gong ji,* juan 1: 9.

47. Fang Xiaoru, "Hou zhengtong lun," in *Xun zhi zhai ji,* juan 2: 56–57.

48. This quotation can be found in the "Liu Zheng zhuan" [Biography of Liu Zheng] in juan 161 of the *Yuan shi* [History of the Yuan]. For an online version, see https://ctext.org/wiki.pl?if=gb&chapter=603276. Last accessed November 29, 2022.—Ed.

49. Jao Tsung-I, *Zhongguo shixue shang zhi zhengtong lun,* 57. Jao's study, an extremely important historiographical work, undertakes systematic analysis, categorization, and selection of quotations regarding the concept of legitimate rule in Chinese historiography.

50. See Tao Zongyi, *Chuogeng lu* [Record of giving up the farming life], Congshu jicheng chubian edition (Shanghai: Shangwu yinshuguan, 1937), juan 3: 55. (The first juan of Yang Weizhen's *Dongweizi ji* [Dongweizi collection], titled "Zhengtong bian" [Discerning orthodoxy], is based on the *Chuogeng lu* edition; I therefore cite *Chuogeng lu* directly.) See also Bei Qiong, "Tie Ya xiansheng zhuan" [Biography of Mr. Tie Ya], in *Qingjiang Bei xiansheng wenji* [Collected works of Mr. Bei of Qingjiang], juan 2: 19. Sibu congkan edition.

51. Ichisada Miyazaki states: "There was the Yuan dynasty, yet there were no new laws. The statutes compiled into the Great Yuan were supplementary decisions written in the style of Song rescripts, and may be thought of as a compendium of the Six Laws." "Song Yuan shidai de fazhi he shenpan jigou" [Laws and courts in the Song-Yuan era], in *Riben xuezhe yanjiu Zhongguo shi lun zhu xuan yi* [Selected translations of Japanese scholarship on Chinese historiography] (Beijing: Zhonghua shuju, 1992), 8: 271.

52. S. N. Eisenstadt, *Diguo de zhengzhi tizhi* [The political systems of empires], trans. Shen Yuandeng (Nanchang: Jiangxi renmin chubanshe, 1992), 145–146. [The English here is from Eisenstadt, *The Political Systems of Empires* (London and New York: The Free Press of Glencoe, 1963), 141.—Trans.]

53. Qu Tongzu, "Zhongguo falü zhi Rujiahua" [The Confucianization of Chinese law], *Qu Tongzu faxue lun zhu ji* [Works on legal theory by Qu Tongzu] (Beijing: Zhongguo zhengfa daxue chubanshe, 1998), 361–381.

54. Wang Yun, "Qing lunding deyun zhuang" [A request to define the auspicious virtue of the dynasty], in *Qiu Jian ji* [Collected works of Qiu Jian], juan 85: 5a. Wenyuange siku quanshu edition.

55. Yang Huan, "Zhengtong balie zongxu" [Summary of eight cases of legitimate succession], from *Huan Shan yi gao* [Posthumous writings of Huan Shan], cited in *Yuan wen lei* [Yuan writings by category], ed. Su Tianjue (Shanghai: Shangwu yinshuguan, 1936), juan 32: 418–419.

56. Xie Duan, "Bian Liao Jin Song zhengtong" [Debating the legitimate succession of the Liao, Song, and Jin], in *Yuan wen lei,* juan 45: 653. This quotation is also found in *Qiu Jian ji,* juan 100: 6a–7a, with slight discrepancies of language.

57. See Masaru Uematsu, "Yuan chu fazhi lunkao—zhongdian kaocha yu Jin zhi de guanxi" [Study of the legal system of the early Yuan—focusing on its relationship to the Jin-dynasty system], in *Riben zhongqingnian xuezhe lun Zhongguo shi* [Young and mid-career Japanese scholars on Chinese history], ed. Liu Junwen (Shanghai: Shanghai guji chubanshe, 1995), 3: 298–328; and John D. Langlois Jr., "Law, Statecraft, and the *Spring and Autumn Annals* in Yuan Political Thought," in *Yuan Thought, Chinese Thought and Religion Under the Mongols,* ed. Chan Hok-lam and Wm. Theodore de Bary (New York: Columbia University Press, 1982), 95.

58. Miyazaki, "Song Yuan shidai de fazhi he shenpan jigou," 252.

59. "Dili zhi" [Treatise on geography], *Yuan shi* [History of the Yuan] (Beijing: Zhonghua shuju, 1976), 1345.

60. Langlois, "Law, Statecraft, and the *Spring and Autumn Annals,*" 89–152.

61. Li Zefen, *Yuan shi xin jiang* [New lectures on Yuan history] (Taipei: Zhonghua shuju, 1978) 1: 6.

62. Hu Zihe, "Lun ding fa" [On establishing the law], in *Zishan daquan ji* [Complete works of Zishan], juan 22: 35b. Wenyuange siku quanshu edition.

63. Wu Cheng, "*Yi* xiang *Chunqiu* shuo" [Explaining the images in the of *Book of Changes* in relation to the *Spring and Autumn*]; see *Song Yuan xue'an* [Teachings of the scholars of the Song-Yuan], in *Huang Zongxi quanji* [Complete works of Huang Zongxi] (Hangzhou: Zhejiang guji chubanshe, 1992), 6: 606.

64. Wu Cheng, "*Chunqiu* xulu" [Collated notes on the *Spring and Autumn Annals*], in *Huang Zongxi quanji,* 6: 593–594.

65. Wu Cheng inherited Song Learning and rejected the strained textual analyses of Han scholars. He leaned more toward Zhu Zi and Shao Yong's opinion that the *Spring and Autumn* offers a straightforward narration of events, which in themselves manifest good and evil. At the same time, however, he also quotes Shao Yong on the unifying principles (*tongji*) of history, offering a legitimizing argument for the Yuan. See Wu Cheng, "Chunqiu zhuguo tongji xu" [Introduction to the unifying principles of the various states during the Spring and Autumn period] in *Wu Wenzheng gong ji,* juan 20, and "*Huangji jingshi xushu* xu" [Preface to *A Sequel to Imperial Governance of the World*], in *Wu Wenzheng gong ji,* juan 16.

66. Wu Lai, "Gai yuan lun" [On changing reign titles], in *Yuan Yingwu xiansheng wenji* [Collected works of Mr. Yuan Yingwu], juan 5: 10a–14a. Wenyuange siku quanshu edition.

67. Jao Tsung-I, *Zhongguo shixue shang zhi zhengtong lun,* 56.

68. For all all of the preceding discussion, see Langlois, 90–152.

69. "You jianyi dafu Libu shilang Zhang Hangxin yi" [Opinion of Grand Master of Remonstrance and Vice Director of Civil Appointments Zhang Hangxin], in *Da Jin deyun tushuo* [Explanations of the auspicious virtue chart of Great Jin], 16a. Wenyuange siku quanshu edition. All subsequent references to *Da Jin deyun tushuo* are to this edition.

70. "Yingfeng Hanlin wenzi Huang Chang yi" [Opinion of Huang Chang, provisioner of letters at the Hanlin Academy], in *Da Jin deyun tushuo,* 9b.

71. "Chaoqing dafu yingfeng jian bianxu Muyan Wudeng yi" [Opinion of Muyan Wudeng, joint grand master for court audiences, provisioner, and compiler], in *Da Jin deyun tushuo,* 16a-b.

72. Jin Qicong, "Cong Manzhou zuming kan Qing Taizong wenzhi" [Understanding Qing Taizong's civil administration from Manchurian clan names], in *Manzu lishi yu wenhua* [Manchu history and culture], ed. Wang Zonghan (Beijing: Zhongyang minzu daxue chubanshe, 1996), 13.

73. Derk Bodde and Clarence Morris, *Law in Imperial China: Exemplified by 190 Ch'ing Dynasty Cases with Historical, Social, and Judicial Commentaries* (Cambridge, MA: Harvard University Press, 1967), 60.

74. Kang Youwei, "Chunqiu fanlu" [Entry on *Luxuriant Dew of the Spring and Autumn Annals*], *Wanmu caotang koushuo,* in *Kang Youwei quanji,* 2: 388.

75. For more on Hong Taiji's change of title, see Meng Sen, "Manzhou mingyi kao" [Study of Manchurian names], *Ming Qing shi lunzhu jikan xubian* [Continuation of collected treatises on Ming-Qing history] (Beijing: Zhonghua shuju, 1986) 1–3; Jin Qicong, "Cong Manzhou zuming kan Qing Taizong wenzhi" and Zhao Zhan, "Dui Huang Taiji suowei Zhushen de bianzheng" [Identification and correction of Hong Taiji's so-called Jurchen], both in *Manzu lishi yu wenhua,* ed. Wang Zonghan, 12–17 and 18–31.

76. Yongzheng, "Denunciation of enfeoffment" [Bo fengjian lun], *Qing Shizong shilu* [Veritable Records of Qing Shizong], juan 83, seventh month of the seventh year of the Yongzheng reign.

77. Starting with the Yuan's reliance on the discourse of unification to justify its own legal authority, discussions of the relationship of peripheral tribes to legitimacy of succession gradually unfolded among the Han literati. For example, the Ming scholar Fang Xiaoru described the rule of peripheral tribes as "aberrant" (*biantong*), implying that resisting the barbarians is righteous. This echoes Huangfu Ti's argument that the Yuan and Wei emperors did not obtain the righteousness of the *Spring and Autumn.* Fang's focus on the peripheral tribes was influenced by Hu Han, who in the early Ming proposed the distinctions between Yi-Xia and inner-outer, and who in

Rectification of Records (Zheng ji) criticized Tang Taizong for placing himself among the peripheral tribes. See Jao Tsung-I, *Zhongguo shixue shang zhi zhengtong lun*, 57.

78. *Yongzheng chao qijuzhu* [Record of the daily activities of the Yongzheng court], twenty-second day of the ninth month of the fifth reign year of Yongzheng.

79. *Shangyu neige* [Imperial edicts of the cabinet], sixth day of the tenth month of the sixth reign year of Yongzheng.

80. See *Qingchao fazhi shi* [History of the Qing legal system], ed. Zhang Jinfan (Beijing: Zhonghua shuju, 1998), 484–485.

81. *Qing Gaozong shilu*, juan 8.

82. *Qingchao fazhi shi*, ed. Zhang Jinfan, 486. The following descriptions and data regarding Qianlong's criminal law reform may all be found on pages 486–487.

83. For example, if a bannerman committed a capital crime and extraordinary amnesty was not granted, but his execution would leave a "household without a proper male head" or a "single elderly head of household," he would be sent home to care for his parents "in accordance with civil precedent." See *Qing Gaozong shilu*, juan 437, fourth month of the eighteenth reign year of Qianlong.

84. Ibid., juan 189, fourth month of eighth reign year of Qianlong. In the seventh year of his reign, Qianlong decreed that the Han army would no longer be part of the banner system; in the eighth, nineteenth, and twenty-eighth years of his reign, he made more specific rules, chiefly: One, "incorporation into the Community Self-Defense (*baojia*) system"; two, "permission for men and women to marry civilians"; three, permission to "benefit [from the privileges of] the Green Banners" for those who wish to do so; four, permission for inherited rank to be "brought out of the banner" "in accordance with the Han practice of inheritance of rank"; five, "inclusion in the Hanban exam for supplementary use" by [those holding] hereditary rank, candidates who pass the imperial examination, and scholars recommended for [supervisory roles] by local governments, as well as alternates for vacant positions, candidates for positions, and those who are demoted. See ibid., juan 164, fourth month of seventh (*Renyin*) year; for items two, three, and four, see juan 469, seventh month of ninth (*Jiawu*) year; for item five, see juan 681, second month of twenty-eighth (*Guichou*) year.

85. *Qingchao fazhi shi*, ed. Zhang Jinfan, 487.

86. For the relationship of Qianlong's emphasis on loyalty to the social and political changes of this period, see Pamela Kyle Crossley, *A Translucent Mirror: History and Identity in Qing Imperial Ideology* (Berkeley: University of California Press, 1999), 89–128. Her work references Abe Takeo, "Shicho to Ka I shisho," *Jimbun Kagaku* 1, no. 3 (December 1946): 150–154.

87. This article is carried over from *Ming lüli* [Ming laws and statutes]. See *Da Qing lüli huiji bianlan* [Manual of collected laws and statutes of the Great Qing], juan 4, articles "Ming li xia" [Article one clause two] and "Fanzui cunliu yangqin" [Caring for parents at home after committing a crime].

88. See *Da Qing lüli huiji bianlan*, juan 29, "Xinglü: mali" [Criminal law: Verbal abuse and defamation], "Ma zunzhang" [Speaking ill of one's elders], and "Ma zufu

zumu" [Speaking ill of one's paternal grandfather or parents]; juan 26, "Xinglü: renming" [Criminal law: Human life]; "Mousha zufu fumu" [Murdering one's paternal grandfather or parents]; juan 28, "Xinglü: dou'ou" [Criminal law: Fights and beatings] and "Ou zufu fumu" [Beating one's paternal grandfather or parents]; and so on.

89. See *Qingchao fazhi shi,* ed. Zhang Jinfan, 487–496.

90. Perry Anderson, *Cong gudai dao fengjian zhuyide guodu* [Passages from antiquity to feudalism], trans. Guo Fang et al. (Shanghai: Shanghai renmin chubanshe, 2001), 234. [This quotation is back-translated from the Chinese translation of Anderson's *Passages from Antiquity to Feudalism.*—Ed.]

91. *Qing Gaozong shilu,* juan 342, sixth month of fourteenth year of Qianlong reign.

92. Dorothea Heuschert, "Legal Pluralism in the Qing Empire: Manchu Legislation for the Mongols," *International History Review* 20, no. 2 (June 1998): 310–324. My use of the term "legal pluralism" comes from John Griffiths, "What Is Legal Pluralism?" *Journal of Legal Pluralism* 24, no. 5 (1986): 39.

93. Discussion of Qing law and ethnic relations has always been an important aspect of Qing historical studies, and the results of this discussion have provided important clues to many scholarly questions in the reinterpretation of Qing intellectual history. Regarding Qing legislation and ethnic relations, I primarily draw from the *Qingchao fazhi shi,* edited by Zhang Jinfan, and Yuan Senpo's *Kang-Yong-Qian jingying yu kaifa beijiang* [Management and exploitation of the northern frontier under the Kangxi, Yongzheng, and Qianlong emperors] (Beijing: Zhongguo shehui kexue chubanshe, 1991). The collation and narration of this information by these authors have provided my discussion of the historical significance of New Text studies with historical materials, supporting evidence, and background. I also refer to several English-language authors, such as Joseph F. Fletcher, *Studies on Chinese and Islamic Inner Asia* (Aldershot, UK: Variorum, 1995); Crossley, *A Translucent Mirror;* and Mark C. Elliott, "The Limits of Tartary: Manchuria in Imperial and National Geographies," *The Journal of Asian Studies* 59, no. 3 (August 2000): 603–646.

94. Mark C. Elliott, who has made deep inquiry into Manchu identity during the Qing, stresses that they formed this particular identity from ritual, geography, and the worship of a singular ancestor, and furthermore links this identity formation to Japanese-controlled Manchukuo. It is a historical fact that the Manchu Qing consciously maintained their identity, but the more fundamental question is how to reconcile this imperial identity, and its internal conflicts, with the legal or institutional pluralism of the Qing empire. Elliott's argument is premised on Manchuria as an independent state or region. Judging from Qing history, the imperial system is itself a pluralistic system, thus including the common recognition of regional and ethnic identities, but this pluralistic system and its admission of these multiple identities were premised on preserving the unity of the empire. Within a multiethnic dynasty, the Qing rulers, in order to defend their dynastic rule, implemented a series of measures to advance equality of the Manchu and Han as well as other peoples, thus creating internal

conflict within its pluralistic, hierarchical imperial system. This is especially true of the issue of Manchuria, as it touches on questions of the Qing empire's origins and the special status of the Manchu in the Qing court. In this sense, it is still worthwhile to investigate the relationship of the "Manchu narrative" to the "Great Qing narrative." In reality, the Qing was plagued by this conflict from beginning to end, and the two sides of late-Qing nationalism—Zhang Taiyan's anti-Manchu nationalism, and Kang Youwei and Liang Qichao's pan-nationalism (which saw "China" as unitary)—both arose from this historical precedent. For this reason, it is difficult to fully explain the question of Qing identity solely as one of Qing imperial identity. See Elliott, "Limits of Tartary."

95. See Yuan Senpo, *Kang-Yong-Qian jingying yu kaifa beijiang*, 293.

96. *Qing Gaozong shilu*, juan 482.

97. Ibid., juan 1015.

98. Ibid., juan 1451, fifty-ninth year (Yihai year) of the Qianlong reign. Every point above references *Qingchao fazhi shi*, ed. Zhang Jinfan, 469–471.

99. See Owen Lattimore, *Inner Asian Frontiers of China* (New York: America Geographical Society, 1940).

100. Pamela Kyle Crossley gives an excellent description of Manchu-Han relations in Liaodong during the late Ming, based on the case of the Tong family and the Eight Han Banners in *A Translucent Mirror*. The intersection of Manchu and Han relations was not merely a Qing phenomenon, but one that predated the Manchu entrance into China. See "Part I: The Great Wall," 53–128.

101. Fletcher, "China and Central Asia, 1368–1884," in *Studies on Chinese and Islamic Inner Asia*, 207.

102. For more on Yishiha, see *Ming Yingzong shilu* [Veritable records of Ming Yingzong], juan 186, fourteenth year, twelfth month, *renzi* day of the Zhengtong reign (1449), in *Ming shilu* [Veritable records of the Ming] (rpt. Beijing: Zhonghua shuju, 2016), vol. 30.; and *Liaodong zhi* [Annals of Liaodong], juan 5, in *Liaohai congshu* (Shenyang: Shenliao shushe, 1985), series two. For information on the Northeast region during the Ming, see Yang Yang, ed., *Zhongguo de dongbei shehui (shisi-shiqi shiji)* [The society of China's Northeast (fourteenth to seventeenth centuries)] (Shenyang: Liaoning renmin chubanshe, 1991).

103. This crested with the cruel suppression of the Muslims in Yunnan in 1873, and with Qing policies that created conflict between the Han and the Muslims. The Muslim population in Yunnan shrank dramatically after this suppression. Although this occurred in the second half of the nineteenth century, it allows us to see some of the ultimate results of official Qing policy in the Southwest. See Jacqueline Armijo-Hussein, "Narratives Engendering Survival: How the Muslims of Southwest China Remember the Massacres of 1873," *Traces*, no. 2 (Hong Kong: Chinese University of Hong Kong Press, 2001), 293–322.

104. *Qing Gaozong shilu,* juan 284 (second month of twelfth reign year of Qianlong).

105. Scholars have calculated this figure according to statistics found in juan 24 ("Tianfu" [Land tax]), juan 36 ("Hukou" [Household registration]), and the Qianlong-era *Shengjing tongzhi* [Shengjing gazetteer], juan 37–38 ("Tianfu" [Land Tax]). See Jian Bozan, *Zhongguo shi gangyao* [Compendium of Chinese history] (Beijing: Renmin chubanshe, 1979), 3: 268.

106. For more about migration beyond the Great Wall, see Yuan Senpo, *Kang-Yong-Qian jingying yu kaifa Beijiang,* 410–411.

107. *Qing Gaozong shilu,* juan 133.

108. See *Qingchao fazhi shi,* ed. Zhang Jinfan, 498–501.

109. *Da Qing hui dian* [Laws and institutions of the Great Qing], juan 64, "Lifan yuan" [Court of Frontier Affairs].

110. In response to the doctrine of returning to the ancients (*fuguzhuyi*) and the ethnic mentality of the Han people and Confucian scholars, Yongzheng saw the distinction between Chinese and barbarian as a tired relic: "The Three Dynasties of Antiquity [and their predecessors] had Miao, Jingchu, and Xianyun, known today as Hunan, Hubei, and Shanxi. Do we now consider them to be [the territory] of the peripheral tribes?" He argued for the doctrine of Manchu and Han as one, providing as evidence the examples of Shun (as ruler of the eastern barbarians) and King Wen (as ruler of the western barbarians): "Our dynasty is Manchurian, yet its birthplace is in China." What he opposed was "disloyalty in the name of China." *Dayi juemi lu* [Resolving confusion with a discourse on righteousness], juan 1, in *Qing shi ziliao* [Materials on Qing history], ed. Zhongguo shehui kexueyuan lishisuo Qingshi yanjiushi (Beijing: Zhonghua shuju, 1983), 4: 5.

111. Liu Fenglu, "Bao li" [Examples of praise], *Shi jiu zhi li xia* [Explaining examples of the nine indications II], in *Liu li buji,* juan 4: 11. [Quoted passages on Kingly government are from *Analects* 20.1, as translated here by James Legge.—Trans.]

112. At the outset of *Qingmode Gongyang sixiang* [Gongyang thought in the late Qing], Sun Chun notes that the *Rectification of Terms in the Spring and Autumn* focuses on inner-outer precedents. Through succinct, this book combs through late-Qing Gongyang thought systematically and with precision. See Sun Chun, *Qingmode Gongyang sixiang* (Taipei: Taiwan shangwu yinshuguan, 1985), 27

113. He Xiu, "First year of Duke Yin's reign" [Yin Gong yuan nian], *Chunqiu Gongyang jiegu* [Explanatory notes for the Spring and Autumn Gongyang], in *Chunqiu Gongyang zhuan zhushu* [Annotations of the Gongyang commentary on the *Spring and Autumn Annals*], Shisan jing zhushu edition (Beijing: Beijing daxue chubanshe, 1999), 24.

114. The discourse of "Three Sequences" (*santong*) is based in the historical perspective of "change" and "cycles." It holds that every dynasty has its own sequence, and that the cycle of the "black sequence," "white sequence," and "red sequence" proceeds in accordance with the Mandate of Heaven. When a dynasty complies with the Mandate of Heaven and returns to such a sequence, it must follow the order of this sequence for "dynastic and sartorial change" and embark on a "punitive expedition."

The institutions of the Xia (black sequence or sequence of man), Shang (white sequence or sequence of earth), and Zhou (red sequence or sequence of Heaven) dynasties each "moved through gain and loss" according to this cycle. This is a conception of history that connects the system itself to the course of its change. Both Dong Zhongshu in "Substance and Refinement of Institutional Change in the Three Dynasties of Antiquity" (*Sandai gaizhi zhiwen*), in *Luxuriant Dew of the Spring and Autumn Annals (Chunqiu fanlu),* and the Eastern Han book *Principles of White Tiger Hall (Bai hu tong):* "Righteousness of the Three Dynasties" (*San zheng zhi yi*) in the section "Three Dynasties" (*San zheng*), expound on this concept, based on the theory that "Heaven has Three Sequences." Three Sequences discourse is also associated with music theory. For example, the "Treatise on Pitchpipes and the Calendar" (*Lüli zhi*) of the *History of the Former Han (Han shu)* states: "The Three Sequences [follow] the outline of heavenly plan, earthly change, and human affairs. Therefore the note *huangzhong* is the heavenly sequence, *linzhong* is the earthly sequence, and *taicou* is the human sequence."

115. Zhuang Cunyu, "Wai ci di liu" [Outer VI], *Chunqiu zhengci* [Rectification of terms in the *Spring and Autumn Annals*], in *HQJJ,* juan 382: 6.

116. Following the passage on "royal affairs" quoted above, Zhuang Cunyu reminds us that higher still than "royal affairs" is the existence of Heaven, thus echoing the general ideological structure of *Rectification of Terms in the Spring and Autumn Annals.* Zhuang Cunyu, "Wai ci di liu," *Chunqiu zhengci, HQJJ,* juan 382: 10.

117. Zhuang Cunyu, "Bagua guan xiangjie" [Observing the heavens through the eight trigrams], Part 1, in the *Weijing zhai yishu* yearbook of the eighth reign year of Guangxu, 27–28.

118. Zhuang Cunyu, "Tianzi ci di er" [The Emperor, II], *Chunqiu zhengci, HQJJ,* juan 375: 7.

119. Zhuang Cunyu, "Nei ci di san shang" [Inner III part 1], *Chunqiu zhengci, HQJJ,* juan 377: 11.

120. Zhuang Cunyu, "Fengtian ci di yi" [Receiving the Mandate of Heaven, I], *Chunqiu zhengci, HQJJ,* juan 35: 3.

121. Original text: "In the spring of the original year, the King rectified the month." Why does the text say "original year"? It was the ruler's first year. Why does it say "spring"? Because it was the beginning of the year. Who does "the King" refer to? It refers to King Wen. Why does it first say "King" and then "rectified the month"? Because it is the King who rectifies the month. What does "the King rectified the month" speak of? It speaks of Grand Unification. Why does the Duke not speak of "ascending the throne"? It is to complete the Duke's intention." *Chunqiu Gongyang zhuan jin zhu jin yi,* ed. Li Zongdong, 1.

122. Zhuang Cunyu, "Fengtian ci di yi," *Chunqiu zhengci, HQJJ,* juan 35: 3.

123. Zhao Fang, "*Chunqiu jizhuan* zixu" [Preface to the collected biographies in the *Spring and Autumn Annals*], in *Song-Yuan xue'an* [Scholarly lives of the Song and Yuan], in *Huang Zongxi quanji,* 6: 627.

124. Specifically, he explains: "Accordingly, for those who reject names and adhere to facts, if the various lords have no king, they do not write of kings; if the central states have no hegemon, they do not delineate a sequence of rulers. The great officers do not adhere to their formal titles, and are spoken of as men." Ibid., 6: 629.

125. Zhuang Cunyu, "Tianzi ci" [Emperor], *Chunqiu zhengci, HQJJ,* juan 376: 15.

126. Zhuang Cunyu, "Zhu Xia di wu" [Chinese kingdoms V], *Chunqiu zhengci,* in *HQJJ,* juan 381: 12b–13a.

127. Gu Donggao, "Song-Zheng jiaobin biaoxu" [List and description of battles between Song and Zheng], *Chunqiu dashi biao* [Major events in the Spring and Autumn period], juan 37: 1a. Wenyuange siku quanshu edition.

128. Dong Zhongshu, "Chu Zhuang wang di yi" [King Zhuang of Chu I], *Chunqiu fanlu* [Luxuriant dew of the *Spring and Autumn Annals*] (Beijing: Zhonghua shuju, 1991), 7–8.

129. "Dong Zhongshu zhuan" [Biography of Dong Zhongshu], *Han shu* [History of the Former Han] (Beijing: Zhonghua shuju, 1962), 2495–2505.

130. Zhuang Cunyu, "Fengtian ci di yi," *Chunqiu zhengci, HQJJ,* juan 375: 2.

131. Zhuang Cunyu, "Nei ci di san shang," *Chunqiu zhengci, HQJJ,* juan 377: 11.

132. Regarding the five beginnings and new political order, Wang Bao of the Han dynasty writes in "In Praise of the Sage Ruler Obtaining Worthy Officials" *(Shengzhu de xianchen song):* "The record says: Respect for the *Spring and Autumn*'s emphasis on taking the five beginnings as a model, is for the sake of judging one's own legitimacy." Yan Shigu adds regarding the five beginnings: "The Primal is the beginning of qi; Spring is the beginning of the four seasons; the King is the beginning of receiving the mandate; the First Month is the beginning of government instruction; Enthronement of a Duke is the beginning of a state. These are the five beginnings." Tang Lüxiang adds: "When the throne is correct one may legitimately rule All-under-Heaven." See Jao Tsung-I, *Zhongguo shixue shang zhi zhengtong lun,* 3.

133. Zhuang Cunyu, "Fengtian ci di yi," *Chunqiu zhengci, HQJJ,* juan 375: 3.

134. Regarding the collapse of the Chamber of the Generations, "The Thirteenth Year of Duke Wen's Reign" of the Gongyang commentary states: "What was the Chamber of the Generations? *It was the ancestral temple of the dukes of Lu. What for the Duke of Zhou was called the Great Temple was, for the dukes of Lu, called the Chamber of the Generations.* . . . But why would only the Duke of Zhou's temple be called the Great Temple, even in the usage of our state of Lu? *Because it was on account of the Duke of Zhou that the dukes of Lu were enfeoffed.* . . . If such was the arrangement, then why would the Duke of Zhou not simply have moved to the state of Lu? *The answer is that it was not necessary for the Duke of Zhou to move to the state of Lu, precisely because the Duke of Lu had been enfeoffed for the express purpose of directing the sacrifices for the Duke of Zhou.* Even so, why didn't the Duke of Zhou go to the state of Lu anyway? *Because he wanted the empire to be unified under the house of Zhou.*" *Chunqiu Gongyang zhuan zhushu,* 302. [Translation borrowed from *The Gongyang Commentary on the Spring and Autumn Annals,* trans. Harry Miller, 136.—Trans.]

135. See Xu Fuguan, "Fengjian zhengzhi shehuide bengkui ji dianxing zhuanzhi zhengzhide chengli" [The collapse of decentralized enfeoffment and the success of classic autocracy], *Liang Han sixiang shi* [Intellectual history of the Former and Latter Han] (Shanghai: Huadong shifan daxue chubanshe, 2001), 1: 43.

136. Zhuang Cunyu, "Tianzi ci," *Chunqiu zhengci, HQJJ,* juan 376: 10.

137. Zhuang Cunyu, "Nei ci di san shang," *Chunqiu zhengci, HQJJ,* juan 379: 5.

138. See Feng Zuozhe, "Heshen lüe lun" [A brief discussion of Heshen], "Lüe tan Heshen chushen, qiji wenti" [Summary of Heshen's background and banner status], "You guan Heshen jiazu yu huangshi lianyin de jige wenti" [On several questions regarding Heshen's clan and marriages into the imperial family], and "Heshen fanzui zui'an" [Criminal case against Heshen], *Qingdai zhengzhi yu Zhong-wai guanxi* [Qing politics and Sino-foreign relations] (Beijing: Zhongguo shehui kexue chubanshe, 1998), 1–53.

139. See Chen Wenshi, "Qingdai Manren zhengzhi canyu" [Manchu political life during the Qing], *Lishi yuyan yanjiu suo jikan* No. 48 (1977): 551–552.

140. Zhuang Cunyu, "Tianzi ci" [Emperor], *Chunqiu zhengci,* in *HQJJ,* juan 376: 11.

141. Ibid., juan 376: 8.

142. Xu Yan, "Yin Gong yuan nian," *Chunqiu Gongyang zhuan zhushu,* 5.

143. Zhuang Cunyu, "Tuanxiang lun" [Discussing the judgments on the images in the *Book of Changes*], *Weijing zhai yishu,* 3.

144. Zhuang Cunyu, "Wai ci di liu," *Chunqiu zhengci, HQJJ,* juan 382: 1.

145. Zhuang Cunyu, "Zhuluan ci di ba" [Suppressing rebellion VIII], *Chunqiu zhengci, HQJJ,* juan 384: 12.

146. Zhuang Cunyu, "Wai ci di liu," *Chunqiu zhengci, HQJJ,* juan 382: 7.

147. Ibid., juan 382: 3.

148. Ibid.

149. For example, Wei Yuan's "*Gongyang Chunqiu* lun" [Discourse on the Gongyang *Spring and Autumn Annals*] refutes Qian Daxin's point that "the way of the *Spring and Autumn* is to truthfully record events, so that neither good nor evil is hidden," then sets off to interpret the *Spring and Autumn* based on its method of presenting the facts and its standard of judgment. See *Wei Yuan ji,* 1: 130.

150. Liu Fenglu, "*Chunqiu* lun xia" [Discouse on the *Spring and Autumn Annals* II], in *Liu Libu ji,* juan 3: 19. Later generations of New Text scholars, such as Wei Yuan, drew on Liu's aforementioned standpoint. For example, in "Discourse on the Gongyang commentary on the *Spring and Autumn Annals* II" *(Gongyang Chunqiu lun xia),* Wei Yuan lambastes Kong Guangsen's notion of the three branches and nine intentions, saying, "He does not use the old Han commentaries, and separately establishes calendrical astronomy as the branch for the Way of Heaven; he mocks, devalues, and fails to practice the branch of kingly law, and honors holding worthies close as a branch of 'human feeling.' Approaching it like this, how is the Gongyang different from the Guliang! And how does one participate in its profound meanings?" See *Wei Yuan ji,* 1: 133.

151. Liu Fenglu states, "Without the three branches and nine intentions there is no Gongyang, and without Gongyang there is no *Spring and Autumn.* And how would one appreciate its subtle words!" "*Chunqiu* lun xia," *Liu Libu ji,* juan 3: 20.

152. Liu Fenglu writes, "The *Spring and Autumn* establishes laws for a hundred kings, how could it establish them for a single matter or person!" Ibid., juan 3: 20–21.

153. Ibid., juan 3: 22.

154. The learning of the Former Han was devoted to general principles, and thus what the scholar Dong transmitted was not the scholarship of chapter and sentence exegesis." Liu Fenglu, "*Chunqiu Gongyang jiegu* xu" [Introductory notes on explaining the Gongyang commentary on the *Spring and Autumn Annals*], *Liu Libu ji,* juan 3: 28.

155. Liu Fenglu, "*Chunqiu Gongyang shili* xu," *Liu Libu ji,* juan 3: 22–23.

156. For example, the subject of "establishing the five beginnings" is only briefly mentioned in the entry on "establishing beginnings" in "Explanations of Exemplary Writing II" (*Shi tebi xia*), then in the entry on "marriage and return" in "Shi lizhi li xia" [Explanations of examples from the ritual code II]. The role of Zhuang Cunyu's *Rectification* is completely absent. See *Liu Libu ji,* juan 4: 23, 31.

157. Liu Fenglu says, "In its possession of the Gongyang tradition, how does the *Spring and Autumn* differ only from the Zuo commentary? It differs also from the Guliang." "*Chunqiu* lun xia," *Liu Libu ji,* juan 3: 19.

158. Liu Fenglu, "Zhi guo yi di wu" [Entry 5: Administration of the state and the city], *Chunqiu Gongyang yili* [Discourse on ritual in the Gongyang commentary], *Liu Libu ji,* juan 5: 13.

159. Liu Fenglu, "*Qin Chu Wu jinchu biao* xu" [Preface to *Tables of the Inclusion and Exclusion of Qin, Chu, and Wu*], *Liu Libu ji,* juan 5: 45.

160. Liu Fenglu, "Shi lizhi li xia: Qu gui zhongshi" [Explanations of examples from the ritual code: Marriage and divorce from beginning to end], *Liu Libu ji,* juan 4: 31–32.

161. "The teachings of the sage, broadening with writing and restraining with rites [*Analects* 6.27], the images of the *Book of Changes,* the *Odes* and the *Documents,* all are grounded in ritual. The *Spring and Autumn* does not record constant matters, and certainly does not speak exclusively of ritual, but when there are alterations in ritual it mocks them, and in distinguishing right from wrong and in illuminating governance and chaos, without ritual there would be nothing by which to correct people. . . . When future kings examine ritual and ceremony according to this measure, when they accord with it there will be governance, and when they do not there will be chaos." Liu Fenglu, "*Chunqiu Gongyang yili* xu" [Preface to *Discourse on Ritual in the Gongyang Commentary*], *Liu Libu ji,* juan 5: 1.

162. Liu Fenglu greatly valued the stringency of institutions, withholding any discussion of Gongyang and He Xiu's "worship of giving way" and maintaining the precedence of rules over emotions. This also seems to prove that Liu granted some form

of approval to centralized administration. This insistence that imperial power not be transferred become an important theme of Kang Youwei's New Text studies. Zhong Caijun's "Liu Fenglu Gongyang xue gaishu" [Overview of Liu Fenglu's Gongyang scholarship] offers a fairly detailed discussion of the question of "yielding the throne." See *Di yi jie Qing dai xueshu yanjiu yantaohui: Sixiang yu wenxue—lunwen ji* [First symposium on Qing studies: Thought and literature—collected essays] (Kaohsiung: Guoli Zhongshan daxue Zhongguo wenxue xi, 1989), 164–169.

163. Liu Fenglu, *Shi nei shili shang: Gong zhongshi* [Explanations of examples of inner affairs I: Public affairs from beginning to end], *Liu Libu ji,* juan 4: 33–34.

164. "The Master said: If there is any use for me, would it be for the sake of Eastern Zhou? When a sage is put to use, it is the work of Heaven; it is not that Heaven wishes Master Kong to save the chaos of Eastern Zhou, but rather that it orders him through the *Spring and Autumn* to save the chaos of ten thousand generations. How could a sage dare to rely on the taboo of respecting kin, and decline to render the judgments of Heaven!" Ibid., juan 4: 35.

165. Liu Fenglu, "Shi bingshi li: Qinfa zhanwei rumie quyi" [Case studies of military affairs: Attacking, encircling, entering to destroy, and capturing towns], *Liu Libu ji,* juan 4: 38–39.

166. Sima Qian, *Shiji* [Records of the Grand Historian] (Beijing: Zhonghua shuju, 1985), 1: 236, 239.

167. In his discussion of the Qin centralized administration, Xu Fuguan makes special mention of two points: that "within the Qin system of centralized administration commandants were put in charge of the armed forces, but it seems that in actuality they did not [have military power], let alone the ability to mobilize troops"; and that "the royal court dispatched investigating censors charged with supervising local officials who were in arrears." See Xu, *Liang Han sixiang shi,* 1: 78.

168. Kangxi, "Yuzhi xu" [Imperial preface], *Yuzuan Zhuzi quanshu* [Imperially compiled complete writings of Zhu Xi], 3a.

169. Aside from large districts such as Xinjiang, Tibet, Mongolia, and Xi'nan, there were smaller autonomous regions in other areas, such as the region inhabited by Tibetan and other minorities in western Sichuan Province. For more on Qing subjugation and administration of this region, see Joanna Waley-Cohen, "Religion, War, and Empire-Building in Eighteenth-Century China," *The International History Review* 20, no. 2 (June 1998): 336–352.

170. Wei Yuan, "*Ding'an wenlu* xu" [Preface to the Written Records of Ding'an], *Wei Yuan ji,* 1: 239.

171. Gong Zizhen, "Da ren wen guannei hou" [Answer to questions about the Marquis of China within the Passes], *Gong Ding'an quanji leibian,* 208.

172. Kang Youwei wrote: "The feudal lords of antiquity, who are today's Territorial Chiefs (*tusi*), each ruled their own states, and each subordinated their own people. Since the Han's institution of [the office of] Marquis of China within the Passes, there

first began to be internal officials, who were different from feudal lords. In our dynasty's Koryo, Miandian, and Annam, those who each year ceremonially greet the New Year are called officials, but these are not quite the same. And those who are called officials when they submit memorials, but who in their own states are called kings and even inaugurate reign periods, need not be counted. Today's Governors and Inspectors General directly serve as officials. The passage [in the *Spring and Autumn* and its commentaries] that describes the Prince of Teng as "coming to the court" (*Teng zi lai chao*) is very strange. If you don't know that Confucius entrusted the king to reform the system, and used praise and criticism to advance and retreat the feudal lords, it would be impossible to understand." *Nanhai shicheng ji*, in *Kang Youwei quanji*, 2: 483.

173. Gong Zizhen, "Da ren wen guannei hou," in *Gong Ding'an quanji leibian*, 209.

174. Gong Zizhen, "Yushi anbian Suiyuan shu" [Memorial for the imperial examinations about subduing the frontier and pacifying faraway lands], *Gong Ding'an quanji leibian*, 187. Because it does not meet the standard, this sparse frontier area is not ranked as first-class.

175. Gong Zizhen, *Wu Jing dayi zhongshi dawen qi* [Questions and answers on the principles of the Five Classics from beginning to end VII], *Gong Ding'an quanji leibian*, 82–83. [For a translation of Ode 275, see Bernard Karlgren, *The Book of Odes: Chinese Text, Transcription, and Translation* (Stockholm: Museum of Far Eastern Antiquities, 1950), 243–244.—Trans.]

176. Gong Zizhen, "Yu ren jian" [Letters to (various) people], *Gong Ding'an quanji leibian*, 206–207.

177. Wei Yuan, "Xue pian jiu" [Scholarship IX], *Mo gu shang* [The silent goblet, part I], *Wei Yuan ji*, 1: 23–24.

178. The translation "geographical studies" for *yudi xue* is used here to make clear Wang Hui's distinction between this scholarship and the contemporary discipline of geography or *dili xue*.—Ed.

179. Joseph Needham believed that the traditional Chinese surveying and cartographic techniques laid the ground for the development of Western surveys and cartography, brought to China during the Ming and Qing by the Jesuits (see the section on Geography and Cartography in Needham, *Science and Civilization in China* [Cambridge, 1954], 3: 497–590), whereas the latest research shows that the influence of Western methods was fairly limited. A case in point is *Tushu jicheng (Illustrated compendium)*, whose maps lack a great deal of detail, including lines of longitude and latitude (Cordell D. K. Yee, "Traditional Chinese Cartography and the Myth of Westernization," in *Cartography in the Traditional East and Southeast Asian Societies*, vol. 2, book 2 of *The History of Cartography*, ed. J. B. Harley and David Woodward [Chicago: University of Chicago Press, 1994], 170–202). Peter C. Perdue notes that the Jesuits published two versions of each map they produced in China: one was precise, broad in scope, and including markers of longitude and latitude; while the other type, produced for the general public, lacked these markings. The former version was offered to the royal court

for military planning, while the latter was mass produced. However, the secret court maps were in fact widely distributed in Europe. D'Anville published a great number of these maps in du Halde's *Description de la Chine.* For more information on surveys of the empire's frontiers in the seventeenth and eighteenth centuries, see Perdue, "Boundaries, Maps, and Movement: Chinese, Russian, and Mongolian Empires in Early Modern Central Eurasia," *The International History Review* 20, no. 2 (June 1998): 263–286.

180. Walter Fuchs, *Der Jesuiten-Atlas der Kanghsi-Zeit* (Beijing, 1943); see Perdue, "Boundaries, Maps, and Movement," 274.

181. Philipp Johann Strahlenberg, *An Historico-Geographical Description of the North and Eastern Part of Europe and Asia* (London, 1736). For related treatment, see Perdue, "Boundaries, Maps, and Movement," 281–282.

182. Xiang Bo, *Jin erbai nian guoren duiyu Zhongya dili shang zhi gongxian* [Two centuries of contributions by our compatriots to Central Asian geography], *Zhongyang Yaxiya jikan* 2, no. 4 (1943): 9–11; Wang Yujun, "Xu Song de jingshi sixiang" (Xu Song on the philosophy of statecraft), in *Jinshi Zhongguo jingshi sixiang yantaohui lunwen ji* [Proceedings of the Academia Sinica symposium on modern Chinese statecraft thought] (Taipei: Academia Sinica Institute of Modern History, 1984), 181–197.

183. See Joseph Fletcher, "Ch'ing Inner Asia c. 1800," in *The Cambridge History of China,* vol. 10, ed. D. Twitchett and J. K. Fairbank (London: Cambridge University Press, 1978); Kent Guy, *The Emperor's Four Treasuries: Scholars and the State in the Late Ch'ien-lung Era* (Cambridge, MA: Harvard Council on East Asian Studies, 1987).

184. For example, *Xinjiang Huibu zhi* [Gazetteer of Xinjiang and the Muslim-Majority Areas] by Yong Gui, *Menggu yange zhi* [Gazetteer of Mongol development] by Shen Zongyan, *Saibei jixing* [Travel notes from north of the wall] by Ma Siha, *Xizheng jilue* [Western expedition chronicle] by Yin Huaxing, *Congjun zaji* [Jottings of a soldier] by Fang Guancheng, and seventy-one other volumes with titles like *Xiyu wenjian lu* [Notes on things heard and seen in the Western Regions], and so on. Among these, Yong Gui's *Gazetteer of Xinjiang and the Muslim-Majority Areas* and *Things Heard and Seen in the Western Regions* make the greatest contributions. For related discussion, see Guo Shuanglin, *Xichao jidang xia de wan Qing dilixue* [Late-Qing geography amid the tide of Western knowledge] (Beijing: Beijing daxue chubanshe, 2000), 78.

185. For instance, *juan* five of Xu Song's *Xiyu shuidao ji* [Record of waterways in the Western Regions] gives a detailed account of the terrain at the border between Russia and the Great Qing Empire, as well as an introduction to Russia's current situation. See Xu Song, *Xiyu shuidao ji* (rpt. Yangzhou: Yangzhou guji shudian, 1991).

186. Yu Zhengxie, *Guisi leigao* [Manuscripts on the Guisi year] (Shangwu yinshuguan, 1957), juan 49. For a related discussion, see Guo Shuanglin, *Xichao jidang xia de wan Qing dilixue,* 87.

187. Guo Shuanglin, *Xichao jidang xia de wan Qing dilixue,* 80–83.

188. See Yuan Senpo, *Kang-Yong-Qian jingying yu kaifa Beijiang,* 565.

189. Wu Changshou, *Ding'an xiansheng nianpu* [Chronological biography of Mr. Ding'an], in *Gong Zizhen quanji* [Complete works of Gong Zizhen] (Shanghai: Shanghai renmin chubanshe, 1975), 604.

190. Chen Li, *Dongshu ji* [Eastern school collection]. For more on Gong Zizhen and Qing history and geography, as well as the above-mentioned quotation, please refer to Zhu Jieqin, *Gong Ding'an yanjiu* [Studies on Gong Ding'an] (Shanghai: Shangwu yinshuguan, 1930), 109–162.

191. In the Jiaqing era, Christian missionaries all along the southeastern coast were introducing Western geographic knowledge to the Chinese interior. In addition to recruiting overseas Chinese from Southeast Asia to Ying Wa College (founded 1818 in Malacca) and other schools, they also published *Cha shisu meiyue tongji zhuan* [Monthly statistical review of popular customs] (Malacca, 1815–1821), *Tianxia xinwen* [News of the world] (Malacca, 1828–1829), and *Dong xi haiyang meiyue zhuan* [East-West maritime monthly statistical studies] (in Canton at first, later Singapore, 1833–1837), including a good number of geographic treatises. In 1806, Wang Dahai's *Haidao yizhi* [Island aspirations] was published, covering the geography, natural resources, terrain, life of overseas Chinese communities, and prevailing customs of Java and the surrounding islands, as well as the location, peoples, dress, products, trade, temperament, and customs of Holland, England, and France. In 1820, Yang Bingnan wrote down and organized Xie Qinggao's accounts of the South Seas in ninety-five issues of *Hai lu* [Record of the seas], touching on the geography, customs, sentiments, religions, and national government of the Malay archipelago. See Guo Shuanglin, *Xichao jidang xia de wan Qing dilixue,* 88–89.

192. Gong Zizhen, "Xiyu zhi xingsheng yi" [Opinion on the provincial administration installed in the western frontier], *Gong Ding'an quanji leibian,* 164.

193. Wu Changshou, *Ding'an xiansheng nianpu,* in *Gong Zizhen quanji,* 604.

194. Gong Zizhen, "Xiyu zhi xingsheng yi," in *Gong Ding'an quanji leibian,* 165.

195. This text was added later by others to "Xiyu zhi xingsheng yi": see ibid., 164.

196. Wei Yuan, "Da ren wen Xibei bianyu shu" [Answers to questions about the Northwest frontier]. See He Changling, ed., *Huangchao jingshi wenbian* [Compiled documents on statecraft from the present dynasty], juan 80.

197. Wei Yuan, *Shengwu ji* [Records of imperial military affairs] (Shanghai: Shijie shuju, 1926), 1.

198. For information on past disputes regarding the original version and authorship of this document, see Yao Weiyuan, "Zai lun *Daoguang yangsou zhengfu ji* de zuben he zuozhe" [Reopening the discussion of editions and authorship of *An Account of Sea Battles in the Reign of Daoguang*], in *Wei Yuan sixiang yanjiu* [Studies of Wei Yuan's thought], ed. Yang Shenzhi and Huang Liyong, (Changsha: Hunan renmin chubanshe, 1987), 278–291.

199. Wei Yuan, "*Shengwu jing* xu" [Preface to "Records of the wise and valiant ruler"], *Wei Yuan ji,* 1: 167.

200. Their debate with Zhang Taiyan and other anti-Manchu nationalists is based on the New Text perspective on inner-outer, as well as on the historical practice of the empire's management of interethnic affairs. Following the Xinhai Revolution, Sun Wen's proposed Republic of the Five Nationalities constituted a complete departure from his earlier anti-Manchu nationalist stance, and indeed is more closely aligned with Kang Youwei and Liang Qichao's vision of inner and outer.

201. Wei Yuan, "*Mingdai shibing erzheng lu* xu,"[Preface to *Records of Ming-Dynasty Food and Military Policies*], *Wei Yuan ji,* 1:165.

202. Gong Zizhen, "Song qinchai dachen Houguan Lin Gong xu" [Preface to send off Imperial Commissioner Lin Zexu of Houguan], *Gong Ding'an quanji leibian,* 224.

203. This quotes from Lin Zexu's letter in reply to Gong Zizhen. Lin's letter is appended to Gong Zizhen, "Song qinchai dachen Houguan Lin'gong xu," in *Gong Ding'an quanji leibian,* 224–225.

204. Gong Zizhen, "Xiyu zhi xingsheng yi," *Gong Ding'an quanji leibian,* 164.

205. Gong Zizhen, "Song Guangxi xunfu Liang Gong xu" [Preface to farewell address for Liang Gong, governor of Guangxi], *Gong Ding'an quanji leibian,* 227.

206. For more on local political and military rule in this region under the Qing and resistance thereto, see Fletcher, *Studies on Chinese and Islamic Inner Asia,* 220–221.

207. Owen Lattimore, *Inner Asian Frontiers of China; Asia in a New World Order* (New York: Foreign Policy Association, 1942), 8.

7. Inner and Outer (2)

1. Owen Lattimore, *Inner Asian Frontiers of China* (New York: American Geographical Society, 1940); *Asia in a New World Order* (New York: Foreign Policy Association, Incorporated, 1942), 15.

2. This book represents the first part of Mahan's treatise on maritime supremacy. Two more followed, with the three works collectively known as the "Sea Power Trilogy": *The Influence of Sea Power upon History, 1660–1783* (1st ed., Boston, 1890, repr. London: Methuen, 1965); *The Influence of Sea Power upon the French Revolution and Empire* (London: Sampson Low, 1892); *Sea Power in its Relations to the War of 1812* (London: Sampson Low, 1905).

3. The two terms Yi (夷) and Xia (夏) have been translated elsewhere as "barbarian" (or sometimes "foreign") and "Chinese," respectively. However, in this chapter, as Wang Hui discusses the evolution of the terms away from such a dichotomous relationship, we elected to render them in Pinyin so that the reader may better follow this evolution.—Trans.

4. In this chapter we elected to retain the Pinyin for *Nanyang.* Wang Hui uses the term to refer to a specific imagining of cultural and geographical space that is not well represented by translations such as "Southeast Asia," "the South Seas," or "the

Southern Ocean." Further, as with Yi and Xia, Wang Hui discusses at length Wei Yuan's understanding of this term. We thus felt that the reader would be better served by retention of the original term.—Trans.

5. Lattimore, *Inner Asian Frontiers of China*, 3.

6. Dorothea Heuschert, "Legal Pluralism in the Qing Empire: Manchu Legislation for the Mongols," *The International History Review* 20, no. 2 (June 1998): 313.

7. For this English rendering, see Julia C. Schneider, *Nation and Ethnicity: Chinese Discourses on History, Historiography, and Nationalism (1900s–1920s)* (Leiden; Boston: Brill, 2017), 138.—Trans.

8. Wei Yuan, *Dongzi chunqiu fa wei* [Explaining the esoteric meaning of Dong Zhongshu's commentary on the *Spring and Autumn Annals*], *Wei Yuan ji* [Collection of Wei Yuan's works] (Beijing: Zhonghua shuju, 1976), 1: 135.

9. Wei Yuan offered a stern attack against this view: "In the Three Dynasties and before, Heaven was completely different from the Heaven of today. The Earth was completely different from the Earth of today. People were all different from the people of today. All things were different from all things of today. . . . Song Confucians only talked about the Three Dynasties. The well-field system, the system of decentralized enfeoffment, or the civil service examination procedures of the Three Dynasties cannot be revived by any means. Such talk only allows those who are practically orientated to criticize Confucian methods for their ineffectiveness." See Wei Yuan, "Mo Gu" [Silent goblet], *Wei Yuan ji,* 1: 47–49.

10. Wei Yuan, "Mo Gu," *Wei Yuan ji,* 1: 60–61. [The English translation is here adapted from *Sources of Chinese Tradition,* ed. William Theodore de Bary, 2nd ed. (New York: Columbia University Press, 2000), 2: 194.—Trans.]

11. Gong Zizhen, "Yi bing zhi ji zhe yi di qi" [Seventh treatise on the twentieth and twenty-first years of the reign of Jiaqing], *Gong Zizhen quanji* [Complete works of Gong Zizhen] (Beijing: Zhonghua shuju, 1959), 1: 6.

12. Wei Yuan, "Mo Gu," *Wei Yuan ji,* 1: 42.

13. Ibid., 1: 47–49.

14. Wei Yuan, "Gongyang *Chunqiu* lun" [Treatise on Gongyang and Chunqiu], *Wei Yuan ji,* 1: 133–134.

15. Li Ciming, *Yue man tang riji* [Yue man tang diary] (rpt. Shanghai: Shangwu yinshuguan, 1936), 36: 8.

16. Wei Yuan, "Daoguang yangsou zhengfu" [An account of sea battles in the reign of Daoguang], *Wei Yuan ji,* 1: 185–186.

17. Ibid., 1: 186.

18. Ibid., 1: 206.

19. See Morris Janowitz, *Military Conflict: Essays in the Institutional Analysis of War and Peace* (Beverly Hills, CA: Sage, 1975).

20. The military nature of *Gazetteer of the Maritime States* was, on the other hand, seen more clearly by the Japanese, who at just that time were striving to establish their

own nation-state. In his translation to the introduction of *Gazetteer of Maritime States,* Shionoya Tōin wrote: "This text is compiled from original European works, both verified and hearsay. The essence of the book lies in chapters on strategies of maritime affairs, strategies of foreign affairs, warships, and military confrontation. Once the military knows the details of the geography, is familiar with the affairs of the *Yi,* and has sufficient weapons, it can defend or negotiate as it wishes and further influence the situation. All depends on capital. In name it is a gazetteer, but in reality, it is a great encyclopedia of armaments and military provisions." (Shionoya Tōin, *Tōin sonkō,* juan 4). Nan'yō Teiken, in his preface to *Gazetteer of Maritime States,* held that the work was "one that all warriors of the world must read," and that it should be published widely for state use. Yoshida Shoin wrote that "the articles 'Strategies of Maritime Affairs,' 'A Discussion of Defense,' 'A Discussion of War,' and 'A Discussion of Negotiation,' by Wei Yuan are deeply accurate and incisive; if the Qing government had applied the concepts found within his writing, this alone would have been enough to resist England and win victory over Russia and France" (Yoshida Shoin, "Diary of a Journey West," in *Yeshanyu wengao* [Wild mountain prison notes], 23). All from Xiao Zhizhi, "Ping Wei Yuan de *Haiguo tuzhi* ji qi dui Zhong Ri de yingxiang" [An assessment of *Gazetteer of the Maritime States* and its impact on Sino-Japan relations], in *Wei Yuan sixiang yanjiu* [Research on the thought of Wei Yuan] (Changsha: Hunan renmin chubanshe, 1987), 344.

21. Wei Yuan, "Chou hai pian—yi kuan" [Strategies of maritime affairs—A discussion of negotiation], in Chen Hua et al., eds., *Haiguo tuzhi* [Gazetteer of maritime states] (Changsha: Yuelu Shushe, 1998), 38.

22. In his *An Account of Sea Battles in the Reign of Daoguang,* Wei Yuan makes clear that he is already fully aware of this. He had a deep understanding of the nonprivate nature and military consequences of the British opium trade. This is the foundational premise of his strategy.

23. Wu Ze and Huang Liyong, "Wei Yuan *Haiguo tuzhi* yanjiu" [Research on Wei Yuan's *Gazetteer of the Maritime States*], in Huang Shenzhi and Huang Liyong, eds., *Wei Yuan sixiang yanjiu,* 292–333.

24. The first to draw attention to this point was Xu Guangren, in "Shilun Wei Yuan xiang xifang xuexi de xisiang" [A discussion of Wei Yuan's thinking concerning learning from the West], in *Nanhua shifan xueyuan xuebao* 1981, no. 2; see also Huang Shenzhi and Huang Liyong, eds., *Wei Yuan sixiang yanjiu,* 125.

25. Wei Yuan, "Daoguang yangsou zhengfu," *Wei Yuan ji,* 1: 177.

26. Wei Yuan, "*Haiguo tuzhi*—yuan xu" [Gazetteer of maritime states—Original preface], *Haiguo tuzhi,* 1.

27. "Attack through defense, so that the foreign Yi must adhere to our schedule, this is called pitting Yi against Yi; negotiation through defense, so that the foreign Yi will follow our lead, this is called negotiating Yi with Yi." Wei Yuan, "Chou hai pian: yi shou," *Haiguo Tuzhi,* 1.

28. *The Embassy of Sir Thomas Roe to the Court of the Great Moghol* (London: Printed for the Hakluyt Society,1899), cited from Fernand Braudel, *Civilization and Capitalism, 15th–18th Century* (Berkeley: University of California Press, 1992), 3: 493.

29. Wei Yuan, "Chou hai pian—yi shou," *Haiguo Tuzhi*, 16–22.

30. Braudel, *Civilization and Capitalism, 15th–18th Century,* 3: 489.

31. Wei Yuan raised the following example: "'Cultural activity relies on military defense,' 'Be fond of adjusting plans and putting them into action,' 'If I fight, I will overcome,' 'The master studies the spear, eliminates the enemy, and wins three hundred suits of armor.' Dispatching troops is a very dangerous thing, but Zhao Kuo described it as something very simple, which is contrary to record in military works." See Wei Yuan, "Sunzi ji zhu xu" [Notes on Sunzi], in *Wei Yuan ji,* 1: 227.

32. Wei Yuan, "Sunzi ji zhu xu," in *Wei Yuan ji,* 1: 226–227. [Translations adapted from James Legge's version of the *Zhou Yi,* paragraph 24 (https://ctext.org/book-of-changes/qian), from Legge's version of the *Dao De Jing,* paragraph 78 (https://ctext.org/dao-de-jing), and from Lionel Giles's version of *Sunzi Bingfa—Mou gong,* paragraph 1 (https://ctext.org/art-of-war/attack-by-stratagem).—Trans.]

33. Wei Yuan, "*Haiguo tuzhi*—yuan xu," *Haiguo tuzhi,* 1–2.

34. Wei Yuan, "Chou hai pian—yi zhan," *Haiguo tuzhi,* 24–25.

35. In his study of the *Mingshi* [Ming histories] Wei Yuan mistakenly read *Folangji* (Portugal) as *Falanxi* (France), and thus some errors exist in his historical narrative.

36. Wei Yuan, "Chou hai pian—yi zhan," *Haiguo tuzhi,* 25–26.

37. Ibid., 26–29.

38. "Thus it is that when a Western merchant meets a local official who enquires about the affairs of the *Yi,* he pretends to know nothing. However, of China's employees, administration, and officials, there is nothing that he does not know. Wei Yuan, "Yingjili guoguang shu zhong" [A description of the expansion of the English state—pt. 2], *Haiguo tuzhi,* 1437.

39. Wei Yuan, "Chou hai pian—yi zhan," *Haiguo tuzhi,* 26.

40. Ibid.

41. Self-built and self-purchased ships and cannons and trained soldiers were distributed about the coastal regions, and finally the goals were attained of self-made ships and weapons; the raising of a navy; reduction of excess personnel; economization of military salaries; and that "China's navy can send ships over the seas, and can do battle with Western powers on these seas." Ibid., 27.

42. Wei Yuan's specific recommendations were as follows: (1) River and canal transport must be changed to seaborne transport accompanied by warship escorts; (2) Naval leaders and high officials must travel by sea when visiting the capital; (3) Merchants may apply for official warship escorts when transporting goods; (4) The national examinations for military students and candidates for the military provincial and imperial exams (*wusheng, wuju ren, wujinshi,* etc.) must be changed from an emphasis on land-borne divisions (e.g., archery and equestrian skills), naval academies must be es-

tablished in Fujian and Guangdong, and those with naval artillery skills must be recognized as of the same class as graduates of the imperial examination system; (5) naval generals must come from a background of shipbuilding, the bureau of arms, or helmsmanship, sailing, or artillery, a significant shift from the traditional evaluation criteria. Wei Yuan was deeply impressed by the strict discipline and courage of the British and Portuguese troops, and knew that the skill of the West lay not only in technology, but also in training methods. Therefore, he suggested that the Qing army follow the Western method of raising and training soldiers by eliminating redundancies, increasing the number of elite soldiers, guaranteeing sufficient salaries, and training sailors and the Green Standard Army (the standing infantry of the Qing) through the opportunities for ocean-borne activities presented by the pursuit and arrest of pirates and tobacco smugglers, and the escorting of commercial shipping.

43. Wei Yuan, "Chou hai pian—yi kuan" [Strategies of Maritime Affairs—A discussion of negotiation], *Haiguo tuzhi*, 40–41.

44. Ibid., 36.

45. Ibid., 37.

46. Takeshi Hamashita, "Ziben zhuyi zhimindi tizhi de xingcheng yu yazhou—shijiu shiji wushi niandai yingguo yinhang ziben dui hua shenru de guocheng" [Asia and the formation of the capitalist colonial system—The penetration of British bank capital into Asia in the 1850s], in *Riben zhong qingnian xuezhe lun Zhongguo shi* [Young Japanese scholars on Chinese history] (Shanghai: Shanghai guji chubanshe, 1995), 614–616.

47. For a discussion of these debates, see Mary Gertrude Mason, *Western Concepts of China and the Chinese* (New York: 1939), 120–121.

48. Miyazaki Ichisada, "Dongyang de jinshi" [East Asian early modernity], in *Riben xuezhe yanjiu Zhongguo shi lunzhu xuan yi* [A selection and interpretation of Japanese scholars' research on treatises of Chinese history] (Beijing: Zhonghua shuju, 1992), 1: 178.

49. Immanuel Maurice Wallerstein, *The Modern World-System* (Berkeley: University of California Press, 2011), 1: 15.

50. Wei Yuan, "Chou hai pian—yi zhan," *Haiguo tuzhi*, 26.

51. Ōtani Toshio's "*Haiguo tuzhi* dui 'mumo' riben de yinxiang" [The influence of *Gazetteer of the Maritime States* on Bakumatsu Japan] discusses the fact that court officials of the Abe Masahiro government, such as Kawaji Toshiakira, Shōzan Sakuma, and others, were all influenced by *Gazetteer of the Maritime States*. This regime sought to establish a leadership coalition after the Shogunate had renounced its authoritarian status and the Imperial court had united with various forces, including the clans. Its slogan was "*Kōbu gattai*" (Union of the Imperial Court and the Shogunate), but in form it sought to bring about the system that unified the whole nation in order to respond to national calamities. In external relations, the Abe Masahiro regime and the Great Powers agreed upon and signed trade treaties, initiating the opening of the

country; internally, the regime steadfastly carried out reform of the Shogunate. Following this, the emperor's absolute monarchy would follow the direction set by Abe Masahiro. *Wei Yuan sixiang yanjiu,* 361–362.

52. Wei Yuan did not make clear the source of this book. However, according to research by Xiong Yuezhi, it is very likely to have been a variant edition of Karl Gützlaff's *Universal Geography: Its Discovery and Significance.* See Xiong Yuezhi, *Xixue dongjian yu wan qing shehui* [Western knowledge, Eastern learning, and late-Qing society] (Shanghai: Shanghai renmin chubanshe, 1994), 260.

53. These were the areas that lay outside the capital with diminishing reliance on the court. See Victor Cunrui Xiong, *Historical Dictionary of Medieval China* (Lanham, MD: Rowman & Littlefield, 2017), 460.—Trans.

54. *Bei-yang* here, as discussed below, was used by Wei Yuan to refer to Russia as a region, and in relation to Nanyang.—Trans.

55. Such as the 1806 *Haidao yizhi* [Records and anecdotes of the island world] by Wang Dahai, which recorded in great detail the geography, natural resources, and lives of Chinese migrants in Java and the surrounding islands, and went as far as to offer an outline of the geographic position, racial characteristics, dress, language, manufacturing, trade, temperament, and customs of European nations such as Holland, England, and France. Also representative is the 1820 *Hailu* [Oceanic records], based on oral testimony by Xie Qinggao (1765–1821), and recorded by Yang Bingnan (birth/death dates unclear), composed of ninety-five entries, in which the geography, customs, natural resources, government, clan system, and water and land transport routes of *Nanyang,* India, and several European countries (in particular England and Portugal) were discussed. See Guo Shuanglin, *Xichao jidang xia de wan Qing dili xue* [Geography of the late Qing under the surging tide of the West] (Beijing: Beijing daxue chubanshe, 2000), 88–89.

56. Jane Kate Leonard, *Wei Yuan and China's Rediscovery of the Maritime World* (Cambridge, MA: Council on East Asian Studies, Harvard University: Distributed by Harvard University Press, 1984), 3.

57. Braudel, *Civilization and Capitalism, 15th–18th Century,* 1: 452.

58. Wei Yuan, "Wu Yindu guo zhi" [Annals of five Indian nations], *Haiguo tuzhi,* 666–667.

59. Wei Yuan had studied the Buddhist scriptures under Qian Yian (birth/death dates unclear) in Hangzhou, Zhejiang, in order to "seek the essentials of being out of the world, concentrate on Zen, and explore the scriptures. Following Xi-Run and Ci-Feng, two Masters to talk about the Mahayana of Shurangama and Dharma." Wei Yuan, "Shaoyang Wei fujun shilue" [A biographical outline of the late and honorable Wei of Shaoyang], *Wei Yuan ji,* 2: 848.

60. Wang Hui here refers to the *Shuowen Jiezi,* presented to the court in 121 CE and held by some to mark the beginning of the philological tradition in China. —Trans.

61. Regarding the ubiquity of the "five continent" theory, the "rediscovery" of the "nine great provinces," and debate over the "four continents" within Qing geographical studies, see Guo Shuanglin, *Xichao jidang xia de wan Qing dili xue*, 258–267.

62. Wei Yuan, "Da xiyang geguo zong yange" [The development of various Atlantic states], *Haiguo tuzhi*, 1112

63. Wei Yuan, "Folanxi guo zongji" [Collected notes on the French nation], *Haiguo tuzhi*, 1221.

64. Braudel, *Civilization and Capitalism, 15th–18th Century*, 3: 215.

65. Wei Yuan, "Wu Yindu guo zhi" [Annals of five Indian nations], *Haiguo tuzhi*, 666.

66. "Wu Yindu zongshu shang" [Overview of the five Indias, pt. 1], *Haiguo tuzhi*, 671–672.

67. Wei Yuan, "Dong Yindu geguo" [Various states of East India], *Haiguo tuzhi*, 727.

68. Wei Yuan, "Eluosi guo zhi" [The chronicle of Russia], *Haiguo tuzhi*, 1479.

69. Braudel, *Civilization and Capitalism, 15th–18th Century*, 3: 486.

70. Ibid., 3: 488.

71. Wei Yuan, "Xu Dong Nanyang" [A narrative of East Nanyang], *Haiguo tuzhi*, 347–348.

72. Wei Yuan, "Xianluo dongnan shuguo jin wei Yingjili Xinjiapo yange" [The course of development of Siam and Southeastern countries to present-day British Singapore], *Haiguo Tuzhi*, 439

73. Wei Yuan, "Haiguo tuzhi—hou xu" [Gazetteer of maritime states—Later preface], *Haiguo tuzhi*, 70–71.

74. Wei Yuan, "Xiyang ren 'Majishi dili beikao' xu" [A discussion of the Westerner "Jose Martinho Marques's" geographic reference], *Haiguo tuzhi*, 1888–1889.

75. Wei Yuan, "Da xiyang geguo zong yange," *Haiguo tuzhi*, 1112.

76. Wei Yuan, "Xi Yindu xi adan guo yange" [The development of the state of West Aden in West India], *Haiguo tuzhi*, 785.

77. Wei Yuan, "Geguo Huijiao zongkao" [Collected notes on Islam across various lands], *Haiguo tuzhi*, 791.

78. Wei Yuan, "Tianzhujiao kao" [Reference works on Catholicism], *Haiguo tuzhi*, 835, 838–839.

79. Wei Yuan, "Tianfangjiao kao" [Reference works on Islam], *Haiguo tuzhi*, 802.

80. Wei Yuan, "Liweiya zhou zongshuo" [A general discussion of Africa], *Haiguo tuzhi*, 989.

81. Wei Yuan, "Tianzhujiao kao," *Haiguo tuzhi*, 833.

82. Wei Yuan, "Daxiyang Ouluoba zhou geguo zong xu" [A summary of various states of Atlantic Europe], *Haiguo tuzhi*, 1092.

83. Wang Hui's "means" here refers to the axiom "Chinese learning as essence, Western learning as means" (*Zhongxue wei ti, Xixue wei yong*), a formulation by which Zhang Zhidong, at the end of the nineteenth century, called for a balance between cultural conservatism and institutional and technological reform.—Trans.

84. Wei Yuan, "Daxiyang Ouluoba zhou geguo zong xu," *Haiguo tuzhi,* 1093.

85. Wei Yuan drew on *A Brief Description of the Ocean Circuit* (*Yinghuan zhi lue*), by Xu Jiyu (1795–1873), which claimed: "Before the end of the Five Dynasties, Rome had descended into chaos, and Europe broke into warring states." Wei Yuan, "Da xiyang geguo zong yange," *Haiguo tuzhi,* 1104.

86. Wei Yuan, "Daxiyang Ouluoba zhou geguo zong xu," *Haiguo tuzhi,* 1093.

87. Wei Yuan, "Yingjili zongji" [General notes on England], *Haiguo tuzhi,* 1380–1383.

88. Wei Yuan, "Yingjili guo guang shu" [A description of the expansion of the English state], *Haiguo tuzhi,* 1422.

89. Ibid., 1405.

90. Ibid., 1407.

91. Wei Yuan wrote: "In their production process, craftsmen use only fire-powered machines, they are all set in motion by one thing—coal." "Yingjili guo guang shu," *Haiguo tuzhi,* 1420.

92. Ibid., 1420.

93. Ibid., 1408.

94. Wei Yuan, "Yingjili guo guang shu," *Haiguo tuzhi,* 1447–1448.

95. Wei Yuan, "Milijian ji Meiligeguo zongji shang" [Collected notes on America, first volume], *Haiguo tuzhi,* 1627.

96. Wei Yuan, "Milijian ji Meiligeguo zongji" [Collected notes on America], *Haiguo tuzhi,* 1622.

97. Wei Yuan, "Milijian ji Yunaishidie guo zongji" [Collected notes on America and the United States] *Haiguo tuzhi,* 1676.

98. Wei Yuan, "Milijian ji Meiligeguo zongji," *Haiguo tuzhi,* 1635.

99. Ibid., 1632.

100. Ibid., 1633.

101. Ibid., 1635.

102. Wei Yuan, "Milijian ji Yunaishidie guo zongji," *Haiguo tuzhi,* 1662.

103. Kang Youwei, "Feisheng lun" [On the abolition of provinces], *Buren* 1: 5–11; "Feisheng yi" [Discussion of the abolition of provinces], *Buren* 2: 21–29; and "Cunfu yi" [Discussion of retaining prefectures], *Buren* 2: 43–47.

104. Wei Yuan, "Milijian ji Meiligeguo zongji," *Haiguo tuzhi,* 1633.

105. Ibid., 1633.

106. See *Zheng Guanying ji* [Collected works of Zheng Guanying], 1: 801–802.

107. Xiao Zhizhi, "Ping Wei Yuan de *Haiguo tuzhi* ji qi dui zhong ri de yingxiang" [*Gazetteer of the Maritime States* and its impact on Sino-Japan relations], in *Wei Yuan sixiang yanjiu,* 350–351.

108. Yoshida Shōin, "*Yeshanyu wengao,* du 'Chouhai pian'" [*Wild Mountain Prison Notes,* On reading the "Maritime Strategies"], as cited in Ōtani Toshio, "*Haiguo tuzhi* dui 'mumo' riben de yinxiang," in *Wei Yuan sixiang yanjiu,* 364.

109. Yoshida Shōin, "*Yeshanyu wengao,* du Jiayin Lundun pingpanji" [*Wild Mountain Prison Notes,* On reading London judicial cases of the Jiayin year (1854)], in *Wei Yuan sixiang yanjiu,* 364.

110. Benedict Anderson, *Imagined Communities* (London: Verso, 1983), 100–111.

111. Maruyama Masao, *Fuze Yuji yu Riben jindaihua* [Fukuzawa Yukichi and the modernization of Japan], trans. Ou Jianying (Shanghai: Xuelin chubanshe, 1992), 150. [For the Fukuzawa quotation, see Fukuzawa Yukichi, *An Encouragement of Learning,* trans. David A. Dilworth (New York: Columbia University Press, 2012), 6.—Trans.]

112. Ibid., 113–114.

113. For detailed discussion see Dai Yi, *Jianming Qingshi* [A concise history of the Qing] (Beijing: Renmin chubanshe, 2004), 2: 119–122.

114. See John K. Fairbank, ed., *The Chinese World Order: Traditional China's Foreign Relations* (Cambridge, MA: Harvard University Press, 1968).

115. See Takeshi Hamashita, *Jindai Zhongguo de guoji qiji—chaogong maoyi tixi yu jindai yazhou jingji quan* [The international emergence of modern China: Tributary trade and the economy of modern Asia], trans. Zhu Yingui and Ouyang Fei (Beijing: Zhongguo shehui kexue chubanshe, 1999).

116. Key-hiuk Kim, *Korea, Japan, and the Chinese Empire, 1860–1882* (Berkeley: University of California Press, 1980), 249.

117. *Qingshi gao* [Draft history of the Qing] (Beijing: Zhonghua shuju, 1976), juan 158, zhi 133, "Bangjiao" [Foreign relations] 6, "Riben" [Japan], 4617–4644.

118. See Joseph F. Fletcher, "China and Central Asia, 1368–1884," in *Studies on Chinese and Islamic Inner Asia* (Aldershot, UK: Variorum, 1995), 206–224, 337–368.

119. See the discussion in Anthony Giddens, *The Nation-State and Violence* (Oxford: Polity Press, 1985), 18.

120. Yuan Senpo, *Kang-Yong-Qian jingyi yu kaifa Xinjiang* [Control and development of Xinjiang in the High Qing] (Beijing: Zhongguo shehui kexue chubanshe, 1991), 558.

121. Hu Xingliang has shown that "identity certificates" and "pass documents" had been replaced by "licenses" (*paizhao*) by the 1940s; by the 1950s, the term *paizhao* had generally been replaced by *zhizhao.* After 1885 the term "passport" (*huzhao*) had mostly replaced *zhizhao* and had become a fixed term still in use today. See Hu Xingliang, *Bianjie yu minzu* [Borders and nationalities] (Beijing: Zhongguo shehui kexue chubanshi, 1998), 6.

122. Ibid., 12–13. The author shows that one reason the Qing lost territory as a result of these treaties was due to a discrepancy between the Russian and Chinese versions, relating to what constituted "Chinese-owned *Kalun* [military forts]" and "*Kalun* intermittently occupied by Chinese forces." In general, the wording of the treaty was ambiguous. See Ibid., 13–16.

123. Ibid., 69. This is the author Hu's Chinese translation from the original Kazakh Chagatai documents.

124. Fletcher, "China and Central Asia, 1368–1884," 206–224, 337–368.

125. Hamashita, *Jindai Zhongguo de guoji qiji,* 49.

126. Onuma Yasuaki, "When was the Law of International Society Born?—An Inquiry of the History of International Law from an Intercivilizational Perspective," *Journal of the History of International Law* 2 (2000): 1–66.

127. F. de Martens, *Traité de Droit International,* trans. Alfred Leo (Paris, 1883–1887), 34.

128. T. J. Lawrence, *The Principles of International Law* (Boston: Macmillan, 1923), 26.

129. See W. E. Hall, *International Law* (Oxford: Clarendon Press, 1880), and T. D. Woolsey, *Introduction to the Study of International Law* (London: Sampson Law, Marston, Searle & Rivington, 1879).

130. Lassa Oppenheim, *International Law* (London: Longmans, Green, and Co., 1905), 46.

131. "Senate Documents, 28th Congress, 2nd Session (1844–45), Doc. 58," as cited in Mary Gertrude Mason, *Western Concepts of China and the Chinese, 1840–1875* (New York, 1939), 129.

132. Ma Jianzhong, *Shikezhai jiyan jixing* [Conversations and travel notes from the Just-Right Studio], in Takeshi Hamashita, *Jindai Zhongguo de guoji qiji,* 284.

133. Martin had great personal fondness and respect for Chinese culture, especially philosophy and literature. See Esson MacDowell Gale, *Salt for the Dragon: A Personal History of China, 1908–1945* (Ann Arbor and East Lansing: Michigan State College Press, 1953). See also Xiao Gongquan, *Jindai Zhongguo yu shijie: Kang Youwei bianfa yu datong sixiang yanjiu* [Modern China and the world: Yang Youwei's thought on reform and the Great Union], trans. Wang Rongzu (Nanjing: Jiangsu renmin chubanshe, 1997), 340.

134. W. A. P. Martin, *Hanlin Papers, Second Series, Essays on the History, Philosophy, and Religion of the Chinese* (Shanghai: Kelly & Walsh. The Tientsin Press, 1894), x, 199–206, 207–234.

135. Louis le Fur, *Précis de Droit International Public* (Paris: Dalloz, 1939), 23, and as translated in Hong Junpei, *Chunqiu guoji gongfa,* 6.

136. For more on the politics and translation of international law in the late Qing, and Martin's participation in the negotiations between Anglo-French and Qing forces, see Wang Jian, *Goutong liangge shijiede falü yiyi—wan Qing Xifang fa de shuru yu falü xinci chutan* [Bridging two legal worlds—A preliminary survey of the introduction of Western law and legal neologisms in the late Qing] (Beijing: Zhongguo zhengfa daxue chubanshe, 2001), 138–186; see also Lydia H. Liu, "Legislating the Universal: The Circulation of International Law in the Nineteenth Century," in *Tokens of Exchange,* ed. Lydia H. Liu (Durham, NC: Duke University Press, 1999), 127–164.

137. Henry Wheaton, "Yizhe xu" [Translator's introduction], in *Wanguo gongfa* [Principles of international law] trans. W. A. P. Martin (Beijing: Jingshi tongwenguan, 1864), 1.

138. Martin, *Hanlin Papers, Second Series,* 111.

139. Ibid., 142–144.

140. Ibid., 112–113.

141. Ibid., 112.

142. Ibid., 113–115.

143. *The Analects,* trans. D. C. Lau (London: Penguin, 1979), 147.—Trans.

144. Max Weber, *The Religion of China: Confucianism and Taoism,* trans. Hans H. Gerth (Glencoe, IL: The Free Press, 1951), 39.

145. Ibid., 40–41. Emphases added.

146. Martin, *Hanlin Papers, Second Series,* 116–117.

147. Ibid., 118–123.

148. Ibid., 118.

149. Ibid., 141. Emphases in the original text.

150. Ibid., 141.

151. Translation borrowed from Gen Liang, ed. and trans., *A Forgotten Book: Chun Qiu Guliang Zhuan* (Singapore: World Scientific, 2011), 6.—Trans.

152. See Li Hu, *Han-Tang waijiao zhidu shi* [The diplomatic system of the Han and Tang] (Lanzhou: Lanzhou daxue chubanshe, 1998), 1.

153. Ibid., 10.

154. See Liu, "Legislating the Universal."

155. Wang Jian, *Goutong liangge shijiede falü yiyi,* 168, 221–229.

156. This comment is from Yang Xiangkui, "Qingdai de jinwen jingxue" [New text classical studies in the Qing], *Yishizhai xueshu wenji* [Collected essays from the studio of unravelling history], 328.

157. Ibid., 328.

158. Meng Wentong, "Jingyan Liao Jiping shi yu jindai jinwei xue" [Master Liao Jiping of Jingyan and modern New Text classical studies], as cited in Xiao Gongquan, *Jindai Zhongguo yu shijie,* 340.

159. See Huang Kaiguo, *Liao Ping pingzhuan* [A critical biography of Liao Ping] (Nanchang: Baihuazhou wenyi chubanshe, 1993), 64.

160. Kang Youwei, "Chunqiu Dong shi xue" [Dong Zhongshu's studies of the *Spring and Autumn Annals*], juan 1, in *Kang Youwei quanji,* 2: 647. [Translation borrowed from Dong Zhongshu, *Luxuriant Gems of the Spring and Autumn,* trans. Sarah A. Queen and John S. Major (New York: Columbia University Press, 2016), 95.—Trans.]

161. Martin, *Hanlin Papers, Second Series,* 141.

162. Kang Youwei, *Wanmu caotang jiangyi* [Lectures from the thatched hut among ten thousand trees], *Kang Youwei quanji,* 2: 574–575.

163. See, for example, Chen Guyuan, *Zhongguo guoji fa suyuan* [The origins of international law in China] (Shanghai: Shangwu yinshuguan, n.d.), and *Xian Qin guoji fa zhi yiji* [Vestiges of pre-Qin international law], ed. Xu Chuanbao (Zhongguo kexue

gongsi, 1931). These works arrange the subject of international law and its disciplines, and the essential elements of nations, in categories of "Chinese international law" or "pre-Qin international law," and on that basis examine topics such as "the number of pre-Qin nations" and "the characteristics of pre-Qin nations."

164. Liao Ping, "Jingyan xian zhi, wenyi zhi, diqiu xinyi tiyao" [Jingyan county gazetteer, treatise on literature, précis on the new meaning of the world], in *Zhongguo difangzhi jicheng, Sichuan fuxian zhi ji* [Collected Chinese local gazetteers, prefectures, and counties of Sichuan] 40, *Guanxu Jingyan zhi* [Guangxu Jingyan gazetteer] (Chengdu: Bashu shushe, 1992), juan 13: 22a–b.

165. See Liao Ping, "Yuanyuan men" [Bureau of learned tradition] (and the sections "Shijie men" [World bureau], "Zhengxue men" [Governance bureau], "Yanyu men" [Discussion bureau], "Wenxue men" [Bureau of letters], "Zixue men" [Bureau of filial study]), in "Zhixue dagang" [Research outline], in *Liuyiguan congshu* 42 (Chengdu: Sichuan cungu shuju, 1923).

166. See Liao Ping, "Daojia rujia fen daxiao tong lun" [On the division of Daoist and Confucian learning in greater and minor branches], *Diqiu xinyi,* juan 1: 45, 1935 (Publisher unclear).

167. Liao Ping, "Shujing Zhouli Huangdi jiangyu tubiao" [Diagram of imperial territories in the *Rites of Zhou*], in "Shujing Zhouli xiaoda fentong biao" [Diagram of the greater and minor branches in the *Rites of Zhou*] juan 42, in *Liuyiguan congshu* 33 (Chengdu: Sichuan cungu shuju, 1921), 109.

168. Liao Ping, "Ciqiu" [Elucidation of the world] (Drafted by Ren Feng of Ziyang), in *Diqiu xinyi* (n.p., 1898), 58. See also Liao Ping's "Yishuo, bagu fen zhongwai jiuyou tu" [Diagram of the demarcations of great nine provinces of China and the world in the *Explanation of the Book of Changes* and the eight trigrams] in the same volume.

169. Liao Ping, "'Zhou' zi mingyi" [The naming of the character 'Zhou'], "Zhouli xinyi fanli sishiqi tiao" [Forty-seven instructions for *New Meaning of the Rites of Zhou*], in *Liuyiguan congshu* (Chengdu: Sichuan cungu shuju, 1917), 34: 1.

170. Liao Ping, "Shujing Zhouli Huangdi jiangyu tubiao" [Diagram of imperial territories in the *Rites of Zhou*], in "Shujing Zhouli xiaoda fentong biao" [Diagram of the greater and minor branches in the *Rites of Zhou*], juan 42, in *Liuyiguan congshu* 33: 109.

171. On Liao Ping's concepts of the Greater and Lesser Branches, and the imperial territories associated with each of the branches, see Huang Kaiguo, *Liao Ping pingzhuan,* 168–178.

172. Liao Ping, "Shuchu shi siguo riji lun dajiuzhou hou" [After the publication of the commentaries on the Great Nine Provinces in *A diary of a diplomatic mission to foreign countries*] (Drafted by Hu Yi of Weiyuan), (n.p., 1898), 58.

173. Liao Ping, "Diqiu xinyi xu" [Introduction to *New Meaning of the World*], in *Diqiu xinyi* (n.p. 1935), juan 1: 1.

174. Liao Ping, "Fanli" [Instructions], in *Chongding Guliang Chunqiu jingzhuan guyi shu* [Revisiting the original meanings in the Guliang *Spring and Autumn* commentaries] (Rixin shuju keben, 1900), 4.

175. Kang Youwei, "Chunqiu fanlu" tiao [On the *Luxuriant Gems of the Spring and Autumn Annals*], *Wanmu caotang koushuo* [Instructions from the thatched hut among ten thousand trees], in *Kang Youwei quanji,* 2: 426–427.

176. In discussions of *junxian* (centralized administration), *fengjian* (decentralized enfeoffment), and *da yitong* (Great Unity) in early New Text classical studies, the most commonly occurring concept was that of *lieguo* ("various nations" or "among the various nations"). This term suggested the situation of conflict during the Spring and Autumn and Warring States periods as a metaphor for the modern system of nation-states. In 1895 Kang Youwei evoked the expression when he presented translations of political treatises by the Welsh missionary Timothy Richard (1845–1919) to the Guangxu Emperor, under the titles *Lieguo biantong xingsheng ji* [Notes on prosperity after reform in various nations] and *Lieguo suiji zhengyao* [Annual budgets and governance of various nations].

177. Kang Youwei, *Datong shu* (Beijing: Guji chubanshe, 1956), 117. After the failure of the 1898 Reform Movement Kang Youwei traveled to Europe and America, and modified his earlier views that these countries had already reached the Age of Approaching Peace (*shengming*); Kang concluded that a key reason for this was that even the latest European thinking was still centered on the notion of competition between nations. He wrote: "Beholding the Three Ages (*san shi*) of Confucius today, it is clear that the Age of Approaching Peace is far from being realised in this world—to say nothing of the Age of Great Peace (*taiping*)! The novel theories of Europe all adopt the premise of competition between nations, in a manner that could not be further from the Way of Confucius, . . . I used to regard the Europeans and Americans too highly, believing that they were gradually approaching the Great Peace. But based on what I see there today, it is clear that [they] are not yet even in the Age of Approaching Peace."

178. Kang Youwei, "Shang Qingdi disan shu" [Third memorandum to the Qing Emperor], *Kang Youwei zhenglun ji* [Collected political writings of Kang Youwei] (Beijing: Zhonghua shuju, 1981), 1: 140.

179. Kang Youwei, "Nanhai shicheng ji" [Records of Master Nanhai's lessons], *Kang Youwei quanji,* 2: 498.

180. Kang Youwei, "Shang Qingdi disan shu," in *Kang Youwei zhenglun ji,* 1: 142–143.

181. Xu Zhongshu, "Jingtian zhidu tanyuan" [On the origins of the well-field system], *Xu Zhongshu lishi lunwen xuanji* [Selected historical essays of Xu Zhongshu] (Beijing: Zhonghua shuju, 1998), 2: 713.

182. Kang Youwei, "Mengzi shiwang ranhou *Chunqiu* zuojie" [Exegesis on "when the odes ceased to be made, the *Spring and Autumn* was produced" in the *Mencius*], in *Wanmu caotang yigao* [Posthumous manuscripts from the thatched hut among ten thousand trees] (Taipei: Chengwen chubanshe, 1978), juan 1: 7.

8. Confucian Universalism and the Self-Transformation of Empire

1. Max Weber, *The Religion of China: Confucianism and Taoism*, trans. Hans H. Gerth (Glencoe, IL: The Free Press, 1951), 236.

2. Ibid., 265–266.

3. Kang Youwei, "Qing guang yi Riben shu, pai youxue zhe" [A recommendation to extensively translate Japanese books and send students there to study], *Kang Youwei zhenglun ji* [Kang Youwei's political writings] (Beijing: Zhonghua shuju, 1981), 1: 301.

4. *Gongfa* (general law) could also be translated as "universal law."—Trans.

5. Philip A. Kuhn, *Rebellion and Its Enemies in Late Imperial China, Militarization and Social Structure, 1796–1864* (Cambridge, MA: Harvard University Press, 1970), 1–36.

6. According to Liao Ping's own explanation and corroborated by academics' studies, he developed the main ideas of *A Study of the New Text and Old Text Schools* (*Jin gu xuekao*) from 1883 to 1885. There are differing views on when the transition occurred in Liao Ping's thought, but generally scholars mark it as occurring in 1883, 1884, or 1885.

7. The concept of *datong* (Great Unity) is ubiquitous in late-Qing Chinese writing and remains an important part of Communist Party discourse today. For this reason, and also to avoid any confusion with *da yitong* (translated here as Grand Unification—but also sometimes translated by others as Great Unity), I leave it untranslated in the English text.—Trans.

8. Kang Youwei, "Shang Qingdi diyi shu" [First memorial to the Qing Emperor], *Kang Youwei quanji* [The complete works of Kang Youwei] (Beijing: Zhongguo Renmin raxue chubanshe, 2007), 1: 353.

9. Ibid., 353–362.

10. Weber, *The Religion of China*, 169.

11. Kang Youwei, "Jiaoxue tong yi" [The comprehensive meaning of education], *Kang Youwei quanji*, 1: 143 and 149.

12. Ibid., 142.

13. Wang Hui writes "*niao*" (bird) here, but Kang used the very similar character "*wu*" (crow), which is in keeping with the traditional story.—Trans.

14. Kang Youwei, "Kangzi Neiwai pian" [Kang's essays on the internal and external], *Kang Youwei quanji*, 1: 190–2.

15. Kang Youwei, "Riben shumu zhi" [Catalogue of Japanese books], *Kang Youwei quanji*, 3: 743–744.

16. Kang Youwei, "Wanmu caotang koushuo" [Instructions from the Thatched Hut among Ten Thousand Trees], *Kang Youwei quanji*, 2: 422.

17. On this day, Liang Qichao published an article in the *Shiwu Bao* (*Chinese Progress*) with the title "Du Riben shumu zhi hou" [After reading the catalogue of Japanese books].

18. *Explorations of the Reforms Advocated by Confucius* was a theoretical work on the reforms. The seventh juan states: "The great Confucians united All-under-Heaven, made changes according to the time, and adapted to the needs of the age. Though they made countless changes, their *dao* was singular. This was the governance of the great Confucians." This shows that the reforms themselves had to be premised on Confucian universalism, and making Confucianism adapt to historical conditions was a central issue for discourse on the reforms. *Kang Youwei quanji,* 3: 196.

19. In "*Datong shu* tici" [Preface to *The Book of Great Unity*], Kang wrote: "I was twenty-seven years of age in the Jiashen year of Guangxu's reign [1884]. The Qing army was striking Guangzhou, and I hid from the war in the Danru Lou of the Seven Juniper Garden (*Qi gui yuan*) in the north of Yintang County by Xiqiao Mountain. Upset by the national crisis and sorrowed by the struggle of the people, I wrote *The Book of Great Unity.*" See the front matter to the 1935 edition of *Datong shu* [The book of Great Unity] (Beijing: Zhonghua shuju, 1935).

20. Kang Youwei, *Datong shu,* 1.

21. Kang Youwei, *Kang Nanhai Zibian Nianpu: wai er zhong* [An autochronology of the life of Mr. Kang of Nanhai] (Beijing: Zhonghua shuju, 1992), 12–13.

22. Liang Qichao explained: "My mentor developed the idea of *datong* found in the "Li Yun." Throughout, his reason finds a compromise between the masses and the Sage and is established as doctrine to save the mortal world. Twenty years ago, he offered his lectures to the students. Then in 1901 and 1902, he compiled them into a book while in exile in India. Humbly, I begged him to publish them, but he believed that the national situation was not yet ready to receive them." See Tang Zhijun's articles "Lun *Datong shu* de chengshu niandai" (On *The Book of Great Unity* and the era in which it was written) and "*Datong shu* shougao ji qi chengshu niandai" (On drafts of *The Book of Great Unity* and the era in which it was written). Both are found in Tang Zhijun, *Kang Youwei yu wuxu bianfa* [Kang Youwei and the Hundred Days' Reform] (Beijing: Zhonghua shuju, 1984), 108–133.

23. Liang Qichao, "Sanshi zishu" [Autobiography at thirty], *Yinbingshi heji: wenji shiyi* [The collected works of Liang Qichao: Vol. 11] (Beijing: Jingwenshe, 1944), 16.

24. Liang Qichao, "Kang Youwei zhuan" [A biography of Kang Youwei], in Kang Youwei, *Kang Nanhai Zibian Nianpu: wai er zhong,* 249.

25. Liang Qichao, "Qingdai xueshu gailun" [An introduction to Qing-dynasty learning] *Liang Qichao lun Qingxueshi erzhong* [Two studies by Liang Qichao on the history of Qing learning], ed. Zhu Weizheng (Shanghai: Fudan daxue chubanshe, 1985), 67.

26. Tang Zhijun, *Kang Youwei yu wuxu bianfa,* 123.

27. Kang Youwei, *Kang Nanhai zibian nianpu,* 10.

28. Kang Youwei, "Jiaoxue tongyi," 137–138. Kang also stated: "Confucius said: 'I adhere to the Zhou.' Therefore, New Text learning must be considered."

29. Ibid., 124–125.

30. Ibid., 125–126.

31. Kang also engaged with the Three Sequences in a way similar to his engagement with the discourse on Three Ages. He explained: "Currently, Europe remains mostly in the White, implementing what Confucius called the White Sequence (*bai tong*) of the Three Sequences." He also explained: "In Europe, positive things are related to the color white, while negative things are related to the color black. In India, punishments are abolished in the first, fifth, and ninth months. "Confucius's State of Lu was akin to the Western Paradise of Buddhism. Japan's Meiji period and Annam . . . followed the doctrines of Confucius." Kang Youwei, "Wanmu caotang koushuo," 384–385.

32. Kang Youwei, "Kang Nanhai zibian nianpu: wai er zhong," 19.

33. Kang Youwei, *Kongzi gaizhi kao* [Explorations of the reforms advocated by Confucius], *Kang Youwei quanji*, 3: 226.

34. Kang Youwei, *Kang Nanhai zibian nianpu: wai er zhong*, 7.

35. Ibid., 9–10.

36. Ibid., 11.

37. Ibid., 13–14.

38. Ibid., 14–15.

39. Kang Youwei, "Gongfa huitong" [A comprehensive study of international law], *Kang Youwei quanji*, 1: 308–309.

40. Kang studied the *Gazetteer of the Maritime States* (*Haiguo tuzhi*) when he was still young, but the developments in geographical knowledge had been significant by that time and he thoroughly criticized the misconceptions found in the book. Still, this did not deter him from his interest in territorial studies (*yudixue*). Kang Youwei, "Nanhai shi chengji," *Kang Youwei quanji*, 2: 451.

41. "Happiness" (*le*) is even more fundamental than "suffering" (*ku*), and it constitutes life's meaning and purpose. Liang Qichao provided an excellent summary of the meaning in his teacher's "ideal for the phenomenal world" (*fajie de lixiang*). Liang Qichao, "Kang Youwei zhuan," 264.

42. Kang Youwei, *Datong shu* [The book of Great Unity] (Shenyang: Liaoning renmin chubanshe, 1994), 5–6. [Translation modified from Kang Youwei (K'ang Yu-wei), *Ta-T'ung Shu: The One-World Philosophy of K'ang Yu-wei*, trans. Laurence G. Thompson (London: Allen and Unwin, 1958), 69.—Trans.]

43. Ibid., 45–46.

44. Ibid., 109–110. [Translation modified from: Kang Youwei, *Ta T'ung Shu* (Thompson translation), 135.—Trans.]

45. Ibid., 55–56.

46. Ibid., 58

47. Kang Youwei, *Ta T'ung Shu* (Thompson translation), 84.

48. Kang Youwei, *Datong shu*, 69.

49. Ibid., 69. [Translation modified from Kang Youwei, *Ta T'ung Shu* (Thompson translation), 84.—Trans.]

50. Ibid., 69–70.

51. Quoted in: Tang Caichang, *Tang Caichang ji* [The collected works of Tang Caichang] (Beijing: Zhonghua shuju, 1980), 178.

52. Kang Youwei, *Datong shu*, 118. [Translation borrowed from Kang Youwei, *Ta T'ung Shu* (Thompson translation), 144.—Trans.]

53. Ibid., 118. [Translation modified from *Ta T'ung Shu* (Thompson translation), 143.—Trans.]

54. Kang explained: "The Americans talk of equality yet refuse to admit black people to office. Despite bureaucratic studies that condemn such actions, Americans do not allow black people into hotels, nor do they allow them to sit in first class or even at the same table. Even were they to have a virtuous president support them, it would be to no avail. Truly, they are of a different color." Ibid., 115–116.

55. Ibid., 70. [Translation modified from Kang Youwei, *Ta T'ung Shu* (Thompson translation), 85.—Trans.]

56. *Wuxu bianfa dangan shiliao* [Historical documents on the Hundred Days' Reforms] (Beijing: Zhonghua shuju, 1959), 170. For a related discussion, see Luo Yaojiu, "Wuxu weixinpai dui diguozhuyi de renshi yu fandi douzheng de zhanlue celue sixang" [The 1898 reformers' understanding of imperialism and their strategies and tactics for the anti-imperialist struggle] in *Lun wuxu weixin yundong ji Kang Youwei, Liang Qichao* [On the 1898 reform movement and Kang Youwei and Liang Qichao] (Guangzhou: Guangdong renmin chubanshe, 1985), 58–59.

57. Kang Youwei, *Datong shu*, 70–71.

58. Ibid., 260–261.

59. Ibid.

60. Ibid., 257.

61. Ibid., 256.

62. See "Guanzhi yi" [A discussion of bureaucracy], an article that he wrote while living in India. Kang Youwei, "Guangzhi yi," *Xinmin congbao*, vol. 35–50. For a related discussion, see Xiao Gongquan, *Jindai Zhongguo yu xin shijie: Kang Youwei bianfa yu datong sixiang yanjiu* [Modern China and the new world: Kang Youwei's reforms and research into the idea of *datong*] (Beijing: Jiangsu renmin chubanshe, 1997), 246–261.

63. See: Kang Youwei, "Haiwai Ya Mei Ou Fei Ao wuzhou erbai bu Zhonghua xianzhenghui qiaomin gongshang qingyuan shu" [A request to the Court from the Chinese Constitutional Association located in Two Hundred Ports across the five continents of Asia, the Americas, Europe, Africa, and Australasia] (1907), *Kang Nanhai xiansheng wenchao*, vol. 5, "memorials," 17–19; "Cai xingsheng yi" [Removing the provincial assemblies] (1910), *Kang Nanhai xiansheng wenchao*, 4: 28–46; "Fei sheng lun" [On abolishing provinces] (1911), *Bu Ren*, 1: 5–11; "Zhonghua jiuguo lun" [On saving China] (1913), *Kang Nanhai xiansheng wenchao*, 1: 1–22; "Lun gonghe lixian" [On the republic and a constitution], *Wanmu caotang yigao*, 1: 69–71. For a related discussion, see Xiao Gongquan, *Jindai Zhongguo yu xin shijie*, 254–261.

64. Engels's differentiation between "utopian socialism" and "scientific socialism" is very important here. Chinese intellectuals have often accused Kang of utopian socialism, which is *kongxiang shehuizhuyi* or fantastical socialism in Chinese. Here, Wang Hui is pointing out Kang's contributions in combining the scientific elements of socialism with classical Confucian concepts.—Trans.

65. Kang Youwei, *Datong shu,* 109–110. [Translation based on Kang Youwei, *Ta T'ung Shu* (Thompson translation), 135.—Trans.]

66. Ibid., 126–127. [Translation based on Kang Youwei, *Ta T'ung Shu* (Thompson translation), 150–151.—Trans.]

67. Kang Youwei, *Datong shu,* 127–146.

68. Ibid., 169.

69. Liang Qichao, "Kang Youwei zhuan," 253.

70. Kang Youwei, *Datong shu,* 237. [Translation modified from: Kang Youwei, *Ta T'ung Shu,* (Thompson translation), 216.—Trans.]

71. Ibid., 252–253. [Translation based on Kang Youwei, *Ta T'ung Shu,* (Thompson translation), 227.—Trans.]

72. Kang Youwei, "Zhi Shen Zipei shu" [A letter to Shen Zipei] (1891), *Kang Youwei quanji,* 1: 544–545.

73. Liao Zhongyi, "Kang Youwei diyici lai Guilin jiang xue gaikuang" [Kang Youwei's first visit to Guilin to deliver a lecture], *Guilin wenshi ziliao* [Documents from the cultural history of Guilin] (Lijiang: Lijiang chubanshe, 1991), 2: 52.

74. The Luoshi Ghost Kingdom was a kingdom of the Yi ethnicity. The Luo family ruled the kingdom from 1042 to 1279, when the Yuan dynasty finally conquered the South and divided the kingdom into Yi Chiefdoms.—Trans.

75. A member of the Logicians, or the School of Names, Gongsun Long was known for his philosophical discussions, which often concerned an object's characteristics and how those characteristics did or did not define the object. In this regard, Kang Youwei may be thinking of René Descartes.—Trans.

76. Kang Youwei, "Wanmu caotang koushuo," 422–423.

77. Liao Ping, "Zhi sheng pian" [Treatise on knowing the sage], *Liao Ping xueshu lunzhu xuanji* [Liao Ping's selected scholarly writings] (Chengdu: Bashu shushe, 1989), 1: 180–181.

78. Kang Youwei, "Wanmu caotang koushuo," 388.

79. Kang Youwei, "Kangzi Neiwai pian," 165–166.

80. Kang Youwei, "Wanmu caotang koushuo," 425–427.

81. Marianne Bastid, "Official Conceptions of Imperial Authority at the End of the Qing Dynasty," in *Foundations and Limits of State Power in China,* ed. S. R. Schram (London: School of Oriental and African Studies, 1987), 152.

82. Ibid., 160–161.

83. Ibid., 170–171.

84. Ibid., 173.

85. Song Yuqing, "Wu ren lu" and "Lichu shimo," in *Qingdai yeshi* [The unofficial histories of the Qing] (Beijing: Beijing guji chubanshe, 1999), juan 1: 352.

86. Wang Wusheng, "Shu an mi lu" and "Guangxudi zhi ji fei," *Qingdai yeshi,* 3: 352.

87. Tian Xia, "Qingdai waishi," di 7 pian, di 11 zhang, "Huangsi zhi biangeng," *Qingdai yeshi,* 1: 151.

88. See Yang Zhen, *Qingchao huangwei jicheng zhidu* [Rules for the imperial lineage of the Qing dynasty] (Beijing: Xueyuan chubanshe, 2001), 539–581.

89. Kang Youwei, "Da Nan Bei Meizhou zhu Huashang lun Zhongguo zhi kexing lixian bukexing geming shu" [On why China must implement a constitutional monarchy not revolution: A letter to overseas Chinese in South and North America], *Kang Youwei zhenglun ji,* 1: 475–476.

90. Ibid., 479–481.

91. Afterwards, he continued this discussion on "federation" (*lianbang*), stating: "Since my ignorant and naive disciples, including Liang Qichao, Ou Jujia, and others, rashly proposed division into eighteen provinces, each of the provinces has engaged in disputes for their succession. This is because of Liang Qichao. . . ." Kang Youwei, "Yu tongxue zhuzi Liang Qichao deng lun Yindu wangguo youyu gesheng zili shu" [A letter to Liang Qichao and the other students on the fall of India being due to the independence of the provinces], *Kang Youwei zhenglun ji,* 1: 502–503, 500, 497, 504.

92. Ibid., 487–489.

93. Liao Ping, "Zhi sheng pian," 185, 182.

94. See Confucius, *The Analects,* trans. D. C. Lau (London: Penguin Books, 1979), 67.—Trans.

95. Kang Youwei, "Guixue dawen," *Kang Youwei quanji,* 2: 52–54.

96. Kang Youwei, *Kang Nanhai zibian nianpu,* 15–16.

97. See Huang Kaiguo, *Liao Ping pingzhuan* [A critical biography of Liao Ping] (Beijing: Baihuazhou wenyi chubanshe, 2010), 237–279.

98. Liao Ping, "Jing hua jia bian juan yi," *Liao Ping xueshu lunzhu xuanji* [A selection of Liao Ping's scholarly writing] (Chengdu: Baoshu shushe, 1989), 447–448.

99. Huang Kaiguo, *Liao Ping pingzhuan,* 156–157.

100. Song Xiangfeng's 1840 *Lunyu fawei* (Ruminations on the *Analects*) (originally titled *Lunyu shuoyi* [*Interpretations of the Analects*]) was the first to distinguish New and Old Text learning based on the issue of institutions (*zhidu*): "The New Text scholars continued the traditions of the erudite masters (*boshi*), accepting the teachings from the seventy-two disciples in an unbroken line to the Han dynasty. The institutions (*zhidu*) described by Mencius and the "Royal Regulations" are all the same as these. As the Old Text scholars found the *Rites of Zhou* (*Zhou guan jing*) in the wall, the end of the Western Han was recorded in the archives, and the Duke of Zhou was considered to be the writer." He also wrote: "Confucius's writings denoted the rites through the Three Dynasties, establishing the institutions of the *Spring and Autumn* that would remain unchanged for not ten but a hundred generations. . . . Confucius's

writing of the *Spring and Autumn* was to be the New King and link the Three Sequences." In *Huang Qing jingjie xubian* [The royal Qing commentaries on the classics], juan 389: 3, 13.

101. Kang Youwei, *Xinxue wei jing kao*, *Kang Youwei quanji*, 1: 572–573.

102. Ibid., 572.

103. Liang Qichao, "Qingdai xueshu gailun," 63–64.

104. Sima Qian, *Shi ji* [Records of the Grand Historian] (Beijing: Zhonghua shuju, 1959), 2540. [Translation borrowed from Ssu-ma Ch'ien, *The Grand Scribe's Records*, ed. William H. Nienhauser (Bloomington: Indiana University Press, 1994), 7: 336.—Trans.]

105. Ibid., 236, 239. [Translation borrowed from *The Grand Scribe's Records*, ed. Nienhauser, 1: 136–137.—Trans.]

106. See Jao Tsung-I, *Zhongguo shixue shang zhi zhengtong lun: Zhongguo shixue guannian tantao zhi yi* [Discourse on legitimate succession in Chinese historiography: A discussion in Chinese historiography] (Hong Kong: Longmen shudian, 1977), 3.

107. For related evidence of this, see works such as Cui Shi, *Shiji tanyuan* [Investigating the sources of the *Records of the Grand Historian*] (rpt. Beijing: Zhonghua shuju, 1986), juan 3; Zheng Qiao, "Jiaochou lue" [Treatise on bibliography], included in his *Tong zhi* [General history] (rpt. Beijing: Zhonghua shuju, 1987); and Wang Guowei, "Han Wei boshi kao" [Investigation of the Erudites of the Han and Wei dynasties], in *Guan tang ji lin* [Collected papers of Wang Guowei] (rpt. Beijing: Zhonghua shuju, 1954), juan 4.

108. Kang Youwei, *Xinxue wei jing kao*, 784.

109. Ibid., 687

110. Ibid., 784.

111. Liao Ping, "Zhi Sheng pian," 188.

112. Kang Youwei, *Xinxue wei jing kao*, 692.

113. Ibid., 792.

114. Ibid., 694.

115. Ibid., 693–694.

116. Ibid., 694.

117. Ibid., 612.

118. Translation based on *The History of the Former Han Dynasty*, chapter 49, "The Memoire of Wang Mang" (online version: http://www2.iath.virginia.edu/saxon/servlet/SaxonServlet?source=xwomen/texts/hanshu.xml&style=xwomen/xsl/dynaxml.xsl&chunk.id=d2.56&toc.depth=1&toc.id=0&doc.lang=bilingual).—Trans.

119. Kang Youwei, *Xinxue wei jing kao*, 613.

120. Translation borrowed from Confucius, *The Analects*, trans. D. C. Lau, 86.—Trans.

121. Kang Youwei, *Xinxue wei jing kao*, 703.

122. Ibid., 723.

123. Ibid., 743–744.

124. Ibid., 695.

125. Kang Youwei, *Kang Nanhai zibian nianpu,* 20.

126. Kang Youwei, *Kongzi gaizhi kao* [Explorations of the reforms advocated by Confucius], *Kang Youwei quanji,* 3: 38–39.

127. Ibid., 23.

128. Kang Youwei (pen name: Ming Yi), "Gongmin zizhi pian" [Autonomy for the citizens], *Xinmin congbao* 7: 28.

129. Kang Youwei, *Kongzi gaizhi kao,* 11–12.

130. Kang Youwei, "Wanmu caotang jiangyi," 561–563.

131. Kang Youwei, *Kongzi gaizhi kao,* 16.

132. Han Feizi, *Han Feizi: Basic Writings,* trans. Burton Watson (New York: Columbia University Press, 2003), 106.—Trans.

133. See Liu An, "Two: Activating the Genuine," trans. Harold D. Roth and Andrew Meyer, in *The Huainanzi,* ed. John S. Major et al. (New York: Columbia University Press, 2010), 99.—Trans.

134. Kang Youwei, *Kongzi gaizhi kao,* 480–490.

135. Ibid., 514.

136. Ibid., 525.

137. Kang Youwei, "Nanhai shi chengji" [Knowledge passed down by Kang Youwei], *Kang Youwei quanji,* 2: 499.

138. Ibid., 2: 499. [Translation borrowed from Dong Zhongshu, *Luxuriant Gems of the Spring and Autumn,* ed. and trans. Sarah A. Queen and John S. Major (New York: Columbia University Press, 2016), 246.—Trans.]

139. Kang Youwei, *Kongzi gaizhi kao,* 229.

140. Ibid., 225–226.

141. Ibid., 249.

142. Eric L. Hutton, *Xunzi: The Complete Text* (Princeton, NJ; Oxford: Princeton University Press, 2014), 227.—Trans.

143. Kang Youwei, *Kongzi gaizhi kao,* 235–236.

144. The *Gonghe* Regency refers to the fourteen years from 841–828 BCE: 841 BCE marks a turning point, as the historical record of events before this date is unclear. The grand historian Sima Qian found older sources to be unreliable, and his chronology is only detailed from 841 BCE.—Trans.

145. Kang Youwei, *Kongzi gaizhi kao,* 2.

146. Ibid., 238.

147. Ibid., 239. [Although Kang indicates this quote is taken from the Xunzi, it appears to be from the *Daode jing.*—Trans.]

148. Kang Youwei, "Nanhaishi chengji," 443–444.

149. Kang Youwei, *Kongzi gaizhi kao,* 255.

150. Kang Youwei, "Nanhaishi chengji," 441–442.

151. Kang Youwei, "Chunqiu Dongshi xue," 636.

152. Kang Youwei, *Datong shu,* 7.

153. Kang Youwei, "Nanhaishi chengji," 553.

154. Ibid., 246.

155. Ibid., 275–276.

156. Ibid., 276.

157. Ibid., 333.

158. Kang Youwei, "Chunqiu Dongshi xue," *Kang Youwei quanji,* 2: 646. [Translation modified from Dong Zhongshu, *Luxuriant Gems,* 91–92.—Trans.]

159. Kang Youwei, "Wanmu caotang jiangyi," 599–600.

160. Ibid., 565.

161. Kang Youwei, "Qing zun Kong sheng wei guojiao li jiaobu jiaohui yi Kongzi jinian er fei yinci zhe" [Honor the Sage Confucius with a national religion; Establish a Ministry of Religion and Churches; Record years from Confucius; and stop the worship of heterodox beliefs], *Kang Youwei zhenglun ji,* 1: 280.

162. Ibid., 282.

163. Jao Tsung-I, *Zhongguo shixue shang zhi zhengtong lun,* 1, 6.

164. Kang Youwei, "Shang Qingdi disishu" [Fourth memorial to the Qing emperor], *Kang Youwei zhenglunji,* 1: 151–152.

165. Michael Loewe, "Imperial Sovereignty: Dong Zhongshu's Contribution and His Predecessors," in *Foundations and Limits of State Power in China,* ed. S. R. Schram (Hong Kong: Chinese University Press, 1987), 33–58.

166. Kang stated, "The political form which I have theorized is based on this: 'The Manchu and Han cannot be divided. The monarch and people shall rule together!' There should be no talk of Manchu and Han when we are in fact one family." In "Da Nan Bei Meizhou shu," 487, 489, 475, 495–505.

167. Kang Youwei, "Qing jun min hezhi Man Han bufen zhe" [A memorial requesting shared rule by monarch and people, and that the Manchu and Han are indivisible], *Kang Youwei zhenglun ji,* 1: 340–341.

168. Ibid., 341–342.

169. Harold J. Berman, *Law and Revolution: The Formation of the Western Legal Tradition* (Cambridge, MA: Harvard University Press, 1983), 32.

170. Alexis de Tocqueville, *The Old Regime and the Revolution,* trans. John Bonner (Petersfield, UK: Harriman House, 2013), 25.

171. Ibid., 25–26.

172. Ibid., 26.

173. Kang Youwei, "Chunqiu Dongshi xue," 671.

Translators

John Ewell is an independent scholar living in Berkeley, California.

Jesse Field has translated work by Ge Zhaoguang, as well as Yang Jiang, Qian Zhongshu, and other modern Chinese writers. After living in China for ten years, he recently relocated to New York City, where he teaches at Avenues: the World School.

Matthew A. Hale has researched rural cooperatives, social movements, and industrial relations in China and the United States. His translation work has focused on anthropology, labor, and Buddhist studies.

Anne Henochowicz translates and writes in the Washington, DC, area.

Michael Gibbs Hill teaches in the Department of Modern Languages and Literatures at William and Mary.

Minghui Hu earned his PhD in History at The University of California, Los Angeles in 2004 and joined the faculty of History at The University of California, Santa Cruz in 2005.

Dayton Lekner researches, translates, and writes histories of the Chinese twentieth century.

Mark McConaghy is Assistant Professor in the Department of Chinese Literature at National Sun Yat-sen University in Kaohsiung, Taiwan.

William Sima is a doctoral candidate and tutor at the College of Asia and the Pacific, Australian National University.

Craig A. Smith is Senior Lecturer of Translation Studies at the University of Melbourne's Asia Institute.

Index